THE CAMBRIDGE HISTORY OF
MUSIC

The Cambridge History of Music comprises a group of reference works concerned with significant strands of musical scholarship. The individual volumes are self-contained and include histories of music examined by century as well as the history of opera, music theory and American music. Each volume is written by a team of experts under a specialist editor and represents the latest musicological research.

The Cambridge History of American Music
Edited by David Nicholls

The Cambridge History of Western Music Theory
Edited by Thomas Christensen

The Cambridge History of Nineteenth-Century Music
Edited by Jim Samson

The Cambridge History of Twentieth-Century Music
Edited by Nicholas Cook and Anthony Pople

THE CAMBRIDGE HISTORY OF TWENTIETH-CENTURY MUSIC

*

EDITED BY
NICHOLAS COOK AND ANTHONY POPLE

CAMBRIDGE
UNIVERSITY PRESS

PUBLISHED BY THE PRESS SYNDICATE OF THE UNIVERSITY OF CAMBRIDGE
The Pitt Building, Trumpington Street, Cambridge, United Kingdom

CAMBRIDGE UNIVERSITY PRESS
The Edinburgh Building, Cambridge, CB2 2RU, UK
40 West 20th Street, New York, NY 10011-4211, USA
477 Williamstown Road, Port Melbourne, VIC 3207, Australia
Ruiz de Alarcón 13, 28014 Madrid, Spain
Dock House, The Waterfront, Cape Town 8001, South Africa

http://www.cambridge.org

First published 2004

Printed in the United Kingdom at the University Press, Cambridge

Typeface Renard 2 9.5/13 pt. *System* LaTeX 2ε [TB]

A catalogue record for this book is available from the British Library

Library of Congress Cataloguing in Publication data
The Cambridge history of twentieth-century music / edited by Nicholas Cook
and Anthony Pople.
p. cm. – (The Cambridge history of music)
Includes bibliographical references and index.
ISBN 0-521-66256-7
1. Music – 20th century – History and criticism. I. Cook, Nicholas, 1950–
II. Pople, Anthony. III. Series.
ML197.C26 2004
780′.9′04 – dc21 2003055131

ISBN 0 521 66256 7 hardback

Contents

Notes on the contributors

JOSEPH AUNER is Professor of Music at SUNY Stony Brook. His main areas of research are the Second Viennese School, music in the Weimar Republic, and music and technology. He is Editor-in-Chief of the *Journal of the American Musicological Society*, and the recipient of awards from the Alexander von Humboldt-Stiftung and The Getty Center for the History of Art and the Humanities.

STEPHEN BANFIELD is Stanley Hugh Badock Professor of Music at the University of Bristol, and the author of *Sensibility and English Song* (1985), the award-winning *Sondheim's Broadway Musicals* (1993), and *Gerald Finzi* (1997). He edited *Music in Britain: The Twentieth Century* for the Blackwell series and has worked further on the American musical.

ANDREW BLAKE is Professor of Cultural Studies at King Alfred's College, Winchester. He taught cultural studies at the University of East London during the 1990s, and played wind instruments for various post-minimalist and world-music bands during the 1980s. He is the author or editor of *The Music Business* (Batsford, 1992), *The Land Without Music: Music, Culture and Society in Twentieth-Century Britain* (Manchester University Press, 1997), and *Living Through Pop* (Routledge, 1999).

LEON BOTSTEIN is President and Leon Levy Professor in the Arts and Humanities at Bard College, NY. He is music director of the American Symphony Orchestra, and has made many recordings both with them and with overseas orchestras. He is Editor of the *Musical Quarterly*, and his books include *Judentum und Modernität: Essays zur Rolle der Juden in der Deutschen und Österreichischen Kultur 1848–1938* (1991, English translation forthcoming), *Jefferson's Children: Education and the Promise of American Culture* (1997), and the edited volume *The Compleat Brahms* (1999).

CHRISTOPHER BUTLER is Professor of English Language and Literature and Student of Christ Church, Oxford. His books include *Early Modernism:*

Literature, Painting, and Music in Europe 1900–1916 (Oxford University Press, 1994) and *Postmodernism: A Very Short Introduction* (Oxford University Press, 2002).

JAMES LINCOLN COLLIER is the author of many books on jazz, including *The Making of Jazz* (a finalist for the National Book Award). His fiction for children has won many awards, and he is also the author of books on American history widely used in American schools. He has been a Fellow of the National Endowment for the Humanities, and a Research Fellow of the Institute for Studies in American music. He plays jazz regularly in New York City and elsewhere.

NICHOLAS COOK is Professor of Music at Royal Holloway, University of London, and Director of the AHRB Research Centre for the History and Analysis of Recorded Music. His books include *A Guide to Musical Analysis* (1987), *Music, Imagination, and Culture* (1990), *Beethoven: Symphony no. 9* (1993), *Analysis through Composition* (1996), *Analysing Musical Multimedia* (1998), and *Music: A Very Short Introduction* (1998). Current projects include a contextual study of Schenker and a book on the analysis of performance. He was Editor of the *Journal of the Royal Musical Association* from 1999 to 2004, and was elected a Fellow of the British Academy in 2001.

SUSAN C. COOK is Professor of Music at the University of Wisconsin-Madison, where she also teaches in the Women's Studies programme. Her teaching and research focus on twentieth-century, contemporary, and American musics of all kinds and demonstrate her abiding interest in feminist methodologies and cultural criticism. She is currently completing a book on the gendered and racialized meanings of ragtime social dance, entitled *Watching Your Step: Ragtime Dance and American Culture*.

MERVYN COOKE is Professor of Music at the University of Nottingham. He is the author of *Jazz* and *The Chronicle of Jazz*, and co-editor of *The Cambridge Companion to Jazz*. His other books include studies of Britten's *Billy Budd* and *War Requiem*, a monograph *Britten and the Far East*, and *The Cambridge Companion to Benjamin Britten*. He is currently editing *The Cambridge Companion to Twentieth-Century Opera* and writing a history of film music, also for Cambridge.

HERMANN DANUSER is Professor of Historical Musicology at the Humboldt University, Berlin; he also directs research at the Paul Sacher Foundation in Basel. He holds higher degrees from the University of Zurich and the Technical

University of Berlin. He has taught in Hanover, Freiburg, and (as a visiting professor) at Cornell and Stanford. His research interests include the history of modern music, theory, and the study of musical interpretation. He is author of *Die Musik des 20. Jahrhunderts* (Laaber, 1984).

PETER ELSDON studied composition at Queen's University, Belfast, before completing a doctorate on the pianist Keith Jarrett at the University of Southampton. He now lectures in Creative Music Technology at the University of Hull, and researches the techniques and aesthetics of free improvisation in jazz.

ROBERT FINK is Associate Professor of Musicology at the University of California, Los Angeles. He focuses on music and society after 1965, with a special interest in minimalism, postmodernism, and the intersection of cultural and music-analytical theory. *Repeating Ourselves*, a study of American minimal music as a cultural practice, is currently in press at the University of California. Other interests include historical recordings and performance practice in the twentieth century, the music of Stravinsky, and electronic dance music from funk to trance. His next major project looks like an optimistic book on the death (and transfiguration) of classical music.

PETER FRANKLIN is Reader in Music, and currently Head of Department, at the University of Oxford, where he is also a Fellow of St Catherine's College. His published work includes *Mahler: Symphony no. 3* (1991) and *The Life of Mahler* (1997). He also writes on early-twentieth-century opera and classical Hollywood film music.

DAI GRIFFITHS is Principal Lecturer in Music at Oxford Brookes University. He has published papers on songwriters including John Cale, Michelle Shocked, and Anton Webern, on cover versions, words in songs, and 'the high analysis of low music'.

BJÖRN HEILE is Lecturer in Music at the University of Sussex. He has published on a variety of topics in twentieth-century music, and is currently writing a book on the music of Mauricio Kagel.

PETER JONES recently completed his Ph.D. in Modern History at the University of Southampton, and works at the Hampshire Record Office.

DAVID NICHOLLS is Professor of Music at the University of Southampton. He is author of *American Experimental Music, 1890–1940* (CUP, 1990) and a forthcoming musical biography of John Cage (UIP, 2004); contributing editor of *The Whole World of Music: A Henry Cowell Symposium* (Harwood, 1997), *The Cambridge History of American Music* (CUP, 1998), and the *Cambridge Companion to John Cage* (CUP, 2002); and editor of the journal *American Music*.

DAVID OSMOND-SMITH is Professor of Music at the University of Sussex. He has written extensively on the music of Luciano Berio, but has also prepared entries on a wide range of post-war Italian composers for the *New Grove Dictionary of Music*, the *New Grove Opera Dictionary*, and the *New Penguin Opera Guide*. He has chaired the British Section of the ISCM and acted as Music Commissioner for the Venice Biennale. He lectures regularly for Glyndebourne Festival Opera, and also in France, Scandinavia, and Italy.

ANTHONY POPLE was Professor of Music at the University of Nottingham, having previously held chairs at Lancaster and Southampton. A former editor of *Music Analysis*, he specialized in the theory and analysis of twentieth-century music. His edited or authored books include *Berg: Violin Concerto* (1991), *Theory, Analysis and Meaning in Music* (1994), *The Cambridge Companion to Berg* (1998), and *Messiaen: Quatuor pour la fin du temps* (1998). His 'Tonalities' software (designed primarily for the analysis of twentieth-century pitch structures) attracted wide attention. He died in 2003.

MARTIN SCHERZINGER teaches at Eastman School of Music. His research spans the fields of music theory, historical musicology, ethnomusicology, cultural studies, and philosophy as they intersect with European and African music in the nineteenth and twentieth centuries. Recent awards include the Emerging Scholar Award (2002–3) from the Society for Music Theory, and the Mellon Fellowship for Junior Faculty from the American Council of Learned Societies, 2002–3.

DEREK B. SCOTT is Chair of Music at the University of Salford. He has published numerous articles concerning music and ideology, and is author of *The Singing Bourgeois* (Ashgate, 2nd edn 2001) and editor of *Music, Culture, and Society* (Oxford, 2000). His latest book is *From the Erotic to the Demonic: On Critical Musicology* (Oxford, 2003). He is also a composer whose works include two symphonies for brass band.

ROBYNN STILWELL is Assistant Professor at Georgetown University, Washington. Her research interests primarily centre on the meaning of music as cultural work, whether it is the way that 'abstract' musical forms articulate identities and narratives, or the iconic workings of artists, pieces, and styles. Her publications have ranged from film and television music, Beethoven and masculinity, rock music and femininity, and French/American musical and dance culture interactions, to classical ballet, science fiction, and figure skating.

JONATHAN STOCK is Reader in Music at the University of Sheffield, where he founded the ethnomusicology programme. Current co-editor of *The World of Music* journal, he is a recent recipient of the Westrup Prize for his 2002 article on place and music in 1930s Shanghai (*Music and Letters* 83). His third book, *Huju: Traditional Opera in Modern Shanghai*, was published by Oxford University Press earlier this year.

RICHARD TOOP was born in England in 1945. He studied at Hull University, where his teachers included Denis Arnold. In 1973 he became Karlheinz Stockhausen's teaching assistant at the Staatliche Hochschule für Musik in Cologne; in 1975 he moved to Sydney, Australia, and is currently Reader in Musicology at the Sydney Conservatorium (University of Sydney). Publications include a monograph on Ligeti, and the *New Grove* entries on Stockhausen and Ferneyhough.

MICHAEL WALTER is Professor of Musicology at the University of Graz, and his work focuses on social and cultural history. Particular areas of specialism include the intellectual history of medieval music, opera, and the music of the Weimar Republic and Third Reich. His most recent book is *Richard Strauss und seine Zeit* (2000).

ARNOLD WHITTALL is Professor Emeritus of Music Theory and Analysis at King's College London, and the author of two comprehensive studies of music since 1900: *Musical Composition in the Twentieth Century* (Oxford, 1999) and *Exploring Twentieth-Century Music* (Cambridge, 2003), the latter based on lectures delivered when he was Distinguished Visiting Lecturer at Royal Holloway, University of London, in 2000–1. He has also written many detailed technical studies of twentieth-century composers, from Debussy and Britten to Birtwistle and Adès.

ALASTAIR WILLIAMS is Senior Lecturer in Music at Keele University, UK, and in 2002 was an Alexander von Humboldt Fellow at the Humboldt University, Berlin. He is author of *New Music and the Claims of Modernity*, *Constructing Musicology*, and several book chapters. He has also published articles in *Cambridge Opera Journal*, *Music Analysis*, and *Perspectives of New Music*.

Preface

Sadly, Anthony Pople became ill soon after work on this book had started, and died while it was in press. The book is dedicated to his memory.

I would like to thank Han-earl Park for his indefatigable work in preparing the index, and Jim Samson, Robert Morgan, and Arnold Whittall for their advice at various stages in the project. I would also like to acknowledge the financial assistance of the British Academy and the University of Southampton. Permission to reproduce copyright materials has been granted by the Mills Music Library, University of Wisconsin-Madison, Americana Collection (Figures 6.2 and 6.4).

Nicholas Cook

· Introduction ·

Trajectories of twentieth-century music

NICHOLAS COOK WITH ANTHONY POPLE

We have not even begun to tell the history of twentieth-century music.

Susan McClary[1]

The Cambridge History of Twentieth-Century Music? What sort of a history of twentieth-century music might that be? The word 'Cambridge' is something more than a publisher's imprint, for it locates this volume in a century-long tradition of *Cambridge Histories* and so emphasizes that this first large-scale, retrospective view of the twentieth century in music is a view *from somewhere*. As the title would lead you to expect, it is history written from a distinct and relatively homogeneous geographical, social, and cultural perspective: predominantly Anglo-American (though there are two authors from Germany and one each from South Africa and Australia), more male than female (gender representation in musicology, at least in the UK, remains far from equal), and white. That does not, of course, mean that our authors simply accept the traditional geographical, ethnic, and gender hierarchies of music history, for there is a strong revisionist strain in the book, one that attempts to contextualize and critique familiar narratives by juxtaposing them with alternative constructions of twentieth-century music. Like all historical writing, this *Cambridge History* is best understood as in essence a status report, a series of position statements in an ongoing dialogue, for no history can be more than a temporary stopping-point in a never-ending process of interpretation – which means that history is less a reflection of the facts than a construction of historians. What follows, then, is one particular set of constructions, the record of what a particular group of authors thought at a particular point in time.

If there is a problem with the title, it lies in 'The . . . History', that is to say 'History-with-a-capital-H'. Georg Knepler and Carl Dahlhaus, the respective grand old men of East and West German music historiography in the decades before reunion, represented almost diametrically opposed views of the past: for Knepler music was to be understood in terms of its social embeddedness and function, whereas for Dahlhaus it was to be understood in terms of its

1 Susan McClary, *Conventional Wisdom: The Content of Musical Form*, Berkeley, 2000, p. 196.

autonomy, its ability to transcend time and place (so that whereas for Knepler the basic category of music history was the musical event, for Dahlhaus it was the work). But their disagreement took place within a shared understanding of 'History', in other words history as an interpretive process that involves making joined-up sense of the facts – or to be more accurate, as Dahlhaus himself explained,[2] of the mass of data transmitted from the past, for even a fact is an interpretive construct. The historian literally *makes* the sense, that is to say, because it lies not in the data but in the interpretation, and there may be different ways of making it – but according to the Knepler/Dahlhaus viewpoint what turns the enterprise into history is the narrative construction, the building and judging of interpretive frameworks expressed in (and at the same time giving meaning to) chronologies, canonic repertories, and aesthetic values. One might call this 'critical' history, in the sense that it is predicated on an intimate relationship between historical interpretation and value judgement.

It would take an unusually stable historiographical juncture, or a hand-picked and unusually compliant set of authors, to make a collaborative history into anything more than a compromise when viewed in such a light. Certainly this volume, considered as a whole, does not exemplify that kind of history. The problem isn't simply one of aesthetic disagreement between the contributors, though there is certainly that (as will be clear from a comparison between, say, Alastair Williams's chapter on modernism at the century's end and Dai Griffiths's account of contemporary pop); some of our authors celebrate the breakdown of aesthetic categories in the later part of the century, while others are more inclined to deplore it – and some contrive to do both at once. The problem is more basic than that. It is that different authors work from different assumptions regarding the relationship between history and value judgement.

For Arnold Whittall, writing about the 'moderate modernisms' of the mid-century, critical selection lies at the heart of historical interpretation, and one might perhaps say that for him the most important role of history is to underpin aesthetic judgement; his approach is in this respect consistent with Dahlhaus's work-oriented approach to music history, direct echoes of which may be found in Hermann Danuser's account of what he calls 'modernist classicism'. At the opposite extreme, Jonathan Stock and Peter Franklin (writing respectively on the 'world music' context and music between the wars) explicitly argue the need to disengage historical interpretation from critical judgement, so that history can become something more than an attempt to legitimize and naturalize certain aesthetic values. And other contributors implicitly endorse the same position through refraining from overt value judgements – a position, however,

2 Carl Dahlhaus, *Foundations of Music History* (tr. J. B. Robinson), Cambridge, 1983, chapter 3.

which 'critical' historians might attack as not just an evasion of responsibility, but simply incoherent: after all, they might say, writing any history (let alone a one-volume history of a century's music) implies selection, for the simple reason that you can't fit everything in, and if this is not done by means of explicit criteria of value then it will be done silently, by sleight of hand, resulting in a history that purports simply to say how things were rather than engaging the reader in the process of interpretation. There is a kind of historiographical Catch-22 here: in trying to avoid the embrace of aesthetic ideology you merely fall deeper into it. The irresolvable tension between these two opposed positions gives rise, in this book, to a diversity of historiographical strategies. These range from critical interpretations that forge a close link between history and criticism, though the underlying aesthetic values may be quite different (Whittall, Williams, Griffiths), to explorations of specific musical or historical ideas (Danuser, Christopher Butler, and Leon Botstein on classicism, innovation, and the musical 'museum'); from comparisons of alternative historical interpretations (Franklin, Griffiths, and Robynn Stilwell) to chronologically organized narratives (Jim Collier and David Nicholls); from case studies (Stock) to chapters organized around a particular individual (Franklin), event (Joseph Auner) or technology (Andrew Blake).

One might say, then, that this book presents not so much 'The . . . History' of twentieth-century music, or even 'a history' of it, as a series of complementary, sometimes overlapping, and often competing histories that reflect the contested nature of interpretation. Different approaches and different selections reveal both individual priorities and effects of chance: it would probably be hard to read anything very significant into Franklin's focus on Tauber rather than Thill. And Williams's discussion of Gubaidulina and Saunders at the expense of, say, Lindberg and Adès may reflect little more than personal taste (perhaps coupled with the desire to resist a continuing bias towards males in both composition and composer-oriented histories of music – a bias that is sometimes challenged in this book, notably by Stilwell and by Susan Cook, but at other times simply reflected). Griffiths's self-proclaimed passing over of Abba and Lloyd Webber, on the other hand, exemplifies a critical resistance to the equation of cultural significance with commercial success; a similar resistance perhaps explains the absence of any reference to Ireland's extraordinary success in the Eurovision Song Contest during the 1990s, and the way in which our authors tended to swerve away from the references to light music in the editors' original plan (there was a stage at which it looked as if even Sinatra was going to slip through the net, and Derek Scott's chapter acts as a kind of long-stop for a number of historically under-represented individuals and trends). But what about the perhaps surprisingly limited attention given to progressive rock? Or the way in which Bartók has been reduced to a series of cameo parts rather than the leading role he occupies in most histories written in the latter part of the twentieth century? It is hard to know whether this is to be seen as an accidental shortcoming that the editors should have remedied, or as symptomatic of a revaluation of twentieth-century classicism that makes Bartók's particular synthesis appear less important than it once did. Time will tell; pending that, our authors' priorities stand.

But if this volume takes the form of a series of competing histories, this is not merely a reflection of the authors' priorities: it reflects the competing attempts of twentieth-century musicians to inscribe themselves in history. This is most evident in the concept of the musical 'mainstream', which weaves confusingly in and out of the book. Historical surveys of twentieth-century music written in the last decades of the century are generally organized around what may be termed a progressive, modernist mainstream. According to this account, an energetic but diffuse avant-garde in the years before the First World War was consolidated and focused through Schoenberg's development of the serial technique, leading after the hiatus of the Second World War to the increasingly systematic approaches associated with the 'Darmstadt' composers; but total serialism was so to speak corroded from within by the influence of Cage's indeterminacy, resulting in an increasingly chaotic situation in the last part of the century as successive reactions (the 'New Romanticism' associated with Rihm, the 'New Complexity' associated with Ferneyhough) followed one another within increasing speed, ultimately coming to coexist in a kind of pluralistic steady state. This orthodoxy, offering a headline story around which a range of more conservative or simply different traditions can be clustered, not only construes history as a quasi-evolutionary process but also locates that process in compositional technique: it is the same kind of approach that you might use in writing the history of, say, the internal combustion engine, and for this reason Christopher Williams has dubbed it 'techno-essentialism'.[3] And this approach to history has been exported to other areas of twentieth-century music: Gunther Schuller has interpreted the history of jazz as an 'extraordinarily condensed', high-speed recapitulation of the technical development of 'art' music – an interpretation that not only assimilates jazz to modernist values, but contributes to deciding what jazz *is*, what is central to its story and what is peripheral or even not part of the story at all.[4] (Scott DeVeaux has emphasized the degree to which the very idea of 'jazz' represents an aesthetically or ideologically motivated construction: 'even a glance at jazz historiography makes it

3 Christopher Williams, 'Of Canons and Context: Toward a Historiography of Twentieth-Century Music', *Repercussions* 2/1 (1993), pp. 31–74.

4 Gunther Schuller, *Musings: The Musical Worlds of Gunther Schuller*, New York, 1986, p. 97.

clear that the idea of the "jazz tradition" is a construction of relatively recent vintage, an overarching narrative that has crowded out other possible interpretations of the complicated and variegated cultural phenomena that we cluster under the umbrella *jazz*'.[5])

Maybe this modernist orthodoxy should be called 'The Vienna History' of twentieth-century music; at all events, as Auner documents, its origins lie in Schoenberg's highly successful positioning of himself as the successor to Beethoven and Brahms – and the predecessor of the great German composers who would follow, for Schoenberg famously told his pupil Josef Rufer that 'Today I have discovered something which will assure the supremacy of German music for the next hundred years', the something in question being serialism.[6] In short, the significantly named 'Second Viennese School' took possession of the historical mainstream (though it is sobering to reflect just how marginal, in simply quantitative terms, the entire phenomenon of Viennese modernism probably seemed to the average Viennese culture consumer of the time, by comparison with the conservative traditions that history has largely left behind). But there were other, less successful contenders: Pfitzner, Schoenberg's reactionary contemporary, saw himself as defending the tradition of German music against the modernists, and had the Nazis won the Second World War it is possible that we would now see the musical mainstream of the first part of the century as stemming from Pfitzner (or at least Richard Strauss) instead of Schoenberg.

And that, of course, would still be a specifically (Austro-)German construction of the mainstream. A more dispersed Northern European mainstream might be imagined round – say – Ravel and Milhaud in France, Elgar and Holst in Britain, Nielsen and Sibelius in Scandinavia, Rachmaninov and Stravinsky in and out of Russia. (This kind of history might provide an adequate context for composers like Geirr Tveitt, who stand here as representative of the huge numbers of composers of astonishingly high-quality music who simply haven't made it into the history of twentieth-century music, whether for reasons of nationality, politics, or pure contingency: as a Norwegian composer who came dangerously close to collaborating with the Nazis, Tveitt never had a chance.) Then again, the picture would look different when seen from the other side of the Pyrenees (Barcelona was the centre of a modernism in many ways unlike any other), and even more so the Alps, for – as Stephen Banfield remarks in his

5 Quoted (from Scott DeVeaux, 'Constructing the Jazz Tradition: Jazz Historiography', *Black American Literature Forum* 25 (1991), pp. 525–60) in Robert Walser (ed.), *Keeping Time: Readings in Jazz History*, New York, 1999, p. 422.

6 Josef Rufer, *The Works of Arnold Schoenberg: A Catalogue of his Compositions, Writings and Paintings* (tr. Dika Newlin), London, 1962, p. 45. The authenticity of Rufer's account has been questioned, but other writers record similar statements.

chapter – modernism was a fundamentally northern phenomenon. Nor is it just in the history of European 'art' music in the first part of the century that such issues arise: Stilwell points out that a major problem in rock historiography is that the music mainly developed in the southern states – the states that lost the American Civil War – whereas its historians have generally come from the dominant north. (History, it is often said, is written by the victors.) Indeed the relatively short history of rock offers particularly clear examples of how the idea of the mainstream is contested, and of how such contests are an integral part of musical culture rather than simply *post facto* constructions on the part of historians.

The principle of historicism, particularly associated with nineteenth-century historiography, sees the historian's central task as to articulate and explain the terms in which past ages saw themselves and the values that informed them. (So, for example, Jim Samson defends a focus on 'great music' in *The Cambridge History of Nineteenth-Century Music* on the grounds that 'this was an age which thought of itself in precisely those terms'.[7]) There is a historicist element in much contemporary historiography – as illustrated for instance by Auner's chapter, which attempts to reconstruct the values underlying Schoenberg's claim to the mainstream, as well as to establish and assess the connections between such values and those of the present day. But there is also a quite different conception of the historian's task, which is embodied in Walter Benjamin's maxim that history should be written from the standpoint of the vanquished rather than the victors.[8] There is a literal sense in which that is just what Stilwell attempts. But so, in a more general way, do other contributors. Banfield reconstructs the world of 'bourgeois tonality' in the first half of the century, a world of conventional music supporting conventional social values – and one which has been sidelined by 'techno-essentialist' historiography, with its identification of the bourgeois and the boring (as David Osmond-Smith, citing Baudelaire, puts it in his chapter on the post-war European avant-garde): thus Whittall's account of the 'moderate mainstream' in the years after the Second World War is consciously opposed to the orthodox interpretation according to which the mainstream of the post-war period flowed through Darmstadt. These, then, are examples of what might be termed oppositional mainstreams, like Michael Nyman's 'alternative history' of twentieth-century music that runs from Satie through Ives and the Futurists to Cage, and in this way 'studiously – or perhaps, rather, deliberately unstudiously – avoids all composers with claims to historical significance as part of Western formal

7 Jim Samson, 'Editor's Preface', in Jim Samson (ed.), *The Cambridge History of Nineteenth-Century Music*, Cambridge, 2002, pp. xiii–xv; p. xiv.

8 Walter Benjamin, *Illuminations* (ed. Hannah Arendt, tr. Harry Zohn), London, 1973, pp. 258–9.

music's main narrative, or "mainstream"'.[9] (Even that, however, appears conventional by comparison with Wadada Leo Smith's genealogy of free jazz: Henry Cowell, William Grant Still, Harry Partch, Thomas J. Anderson, Henry Brant, John Cage, Milton Babbitt, Edgard Varèse, and Ollie Wilson.[10])

Mainstreams in twentieth-century music, then, have been multiple and contested – which is really a way of saying, as does Michael Walter, that there was no mainstream after the 1930s, or even (as Susan McClary has written) that 'there never was such a thing'.[11] But how do you write history without a mainstream to provide the central narrative thread, to locate different developments in relation to one another, and to create a sense of continuity? It is a remarkable fact that modernist music history – Christopher Williams's techno-essentialism – survived the heyday of modernist music by the best part of a generation: purism gave way to pluralism (as Richard Toop puts it in his chapter) around 1970, but the 'far more diversified way of telling the history of music than we have previously permitted ourselves to entertain' that McClary has called for remained a largely unrealized project at the century's end. Some of the central issues, however, are clear, and once again we can focus matters round this book's title, this time passing over 'The', 'Cambridge', and 'History' to alight on 'Music'. To speak of a 'history of music' is to posit a stable object of investigation – an effect that is even more pronounced in German, where one speaks not of 'music' or even 'Music-with-a-capital-M', but of *die Musik*. (As Philip Bohlman puts it, the definite article ascribes a 'hegemonic universality' to the concept.[12]) But if this book is a series of complementary or competing histories, its subject matter is a series of complementary and competing constructions of what music is and might be: to define a mainstream is not only to invoke a particular kind of 'History-with-a-capital-H', but to say what music *is*. This book, then, is about different ideas of what music is. In a word, it is about different musics.

The Cambridge History of Twentieth-Century Musics, then? Yes, but this still begs the question: *whose* musics? The issue revolves around the word that should really have been in the title, but couldn't be, owing to the series in which the book appears: 'Western'. The reader will look in vain for an account of Beijing opera between the wars, even though this genre has as much right as any to representation in a genuinely comprehensive, which is to say infinitely extensive, history of twentieth-century music(s). There are, however,

9 Keith Potter, 'Cornelius Cardew: Some Postmodern (?) Reflections on Experimental Music and Political Music', in Mark Dalaere (ed.), *New Music, Aesthetics and Ideology*, Wilhemshaven, 1995, pp. 152–69; p. 155, referring to Michael Nyman, *Experimental Music: Cage and Beyond* (2nd edn), Cambridge, 1999.

10 Eric Porter, *What is this Thing called Jazz? African American Musicians as Artists, Critics, and Activists*, Berkeley, 2002, p. 263.

11 McClary, *Conventional Wisdom*, p. 169.

12 Philip Bohlman, 'Ontologies of Music', in Nicholas Cook and Mark Everist (eds.), *Rethinking Music*, Oxford, 1999, pp. 17–34; p. 25.

references to many encounters (to borrow Stock's word) between Western and non-Western musics. These include, of course, such familiar examples as the influence of traditional Japanese musics – not always as traditional as they might appear[13] – on Messiaen and Sculthorpe, as well as on the internationally minded composers of the post-war Japanese avant-garde; more radically, Martin Scherzinger emphasizes the 'systematically under-narrated' contribution of African music to Western 'art' composition in the final decades of the century, while any number of contributors provide support for McClary's related claim that 'the musical innovations that have most shaped people in the course of this century have principally come from African Americans'.[14] (As might be expected, such issues have been fought out most explicitly in the history of jazz: claims that the music embodies a distinctively African or African-American sensibility have been countered by those who see this as marginalizing the contribution of white jazz musicians, and who accordingly claim that 'the music may at one time have been African-American, but it is no longer exclusively so'.[15]) The encounters documented in this book also include the reverse influence: the impact of Western musical practices, commodities, and institutions upon non-Western cultures, as evidenced in particular by Stock's case studies (which, coming at the beginning of the book, provide a larger context for the understanding of Western traditions, and are matched at the end of the book by Scherzinger's account of 'art' composition in contemporary Africa). The rationale, in short, is that non-Western musics fall within the book's scope to the extent that they can be seen as integral to the historical development of Western music, 'our' music. That can't to any great extent be said of Beijing opera between the wars, but it becomes more generally the case as the century progresses, with globalization replacing a pattern of sporadic encounters by one of sustained interaction. Indeed there is a sense in which, by the time you get to the end of the century, it is in principle impossible to justify leaving *any* music, anywhere, out of the book. (At which point, of course, you have to give up on principles.)

And it is here that, for all its attempts to eschew taken-for-granted mainstreams, totalizing narratives, and 'History-with-a-capital-H', the book arguably ends up constructing a grand narrative of its own. It charts a transition between two quite different conceptions of 'our' music: on the one hand,

13 A consensus has recently emerged that *gagaku*, long seen as the traditional Japanese music par excellence, is a primarily nineteenth-century construction (papers presented by Allan Marett, Endō Tōru, Tsukahara Yasuko, and Terauchi Naoko at the round table '*Gagaku* and Studies on *Gagaku* in the Twentieth Century', International Congress of the Japanese Musicological Society, Shizuoka, November 2002).

14 McClary, *Conventional Wisdom*, p. 60.

15 Travis A. Jackson, 'Jazz as Musical Practice', in Mervyn Cooke and David Horn (eds.), *The Cambridge Companion to Jazz*, Cambridge, 2002, pp. 83–113; p. 93.

the Western 'art' tradition that was accorded hegemonic status within an overly, or at least overtly, confident imperial culture centred on Europe at the turn of the twentieth century (a culture perhaps now distant enough to have become 'their' music rather than 'ours'), and on the other hand, a global, post-colonial culture at the turn of the twenty-first, in which 'world' music from Africa, Asia, or South America is as much 'our' music as Beethoven, and in which Beethoven occupies as prominent a place in Japanese culture as in German, British, or American. To put it another way, the book charts a kind of diaspora: 'Western' music, clearly located around 1900 in the urban centres of Europe and North America, has become a global currency in the same way as the hamburger, and one sometimes has the impression that the 'art' tradition flourishes more in East Asia, Israel, and parts of South America than in its former heartlands. It is not so much that there has been a relocation from the centre to the periphery as that the distinction between centre and periphery has become increasingly fuzzy (except economically, since the transnational capital generated by 'world' music flows from the Third to the First World). And so it is appropriate that the accumulating emphasis, as the book proceeds, on increasingly globalized and hybridized popular musics leads, in Scherzinger's chapter, to a kind of reverse discourse: issues of musical modernism and autonomy, increasingly sidelined in the First World, ironically take on a new cultural significance when relocated to the Third. (This chapter might be described as a sustained case study in the relocation of musical values, and the local perspective that it offers upon twentieth-century music history could have been replicated from any number of other places: Norway, Barcelona, Argentina, or East Asia, for example. In fact our first idea was to offer in its place a study of the musics of the Pacific Rim at the century's end.)

Western and non-Western is not, of course, the only way the 'Whose musics?' cookie crumbles. Another obvious way is the high-middle-lowbrow distinction, a kind of social categorization of music that was often made in the first half of the century – and particularly in the class-obsessed culture of the United Kingdom. (The programming policy of the British Broadcasting Corporation, which weaves in and out of the book, can hardly be understood without reference to such categories.) Whittall quotes the composer Robin Holloway, who characterized the Western 'art' tradition around 1970 in terms of a 'flight to the extremes that leaves the centre empty'; Scott, in his chapter, concurs, even as he traces a continuing, though increasingly marginalized, 'middle ground' from light music to easy listening to chill-out. Overall, then, and while recognizing the internal stratification of both the 'art' and popular traditions, one may speak of a three-way division (with light music combining the immediate appeal of popular music with the technical resources of classical music, and so encouraging crossover) being supplanted by a two-way one. Fundamental to this development was the rise in 1960s America and Britain of youth culture, charted in Stilwell's chapter, which embodied a division between 'ours' and 'theirs' that cut across social classes, and so reduced music to two broad categories: 'art' (combining classical and modern) and 'popular'. Any division based on a generational gap, however, is necessarily time-limited, and the category of 'popular' music grew steadily less well defined as the 1960s generation grew up, without however giving up on the music of their teenage years: on the contrary, it was this generation who replaced their ageing vinyl collections in the 1980s and 90s with CD reissues of rock classics from the 1960s and 70s – and the term 'rock classics', of course, illustrates the blurring of hitherto more or less clearly defined boundaries (a blurring anticipated by the 'classic jazz' of Collier's chapter title).

All this provides the context for another, and perhaps even grander, narrative that emerged (rather to the editors' surprise) from this book. The story begins with the connection drawn by Whittall between his 'moderate mainstream' and minimalism, on the grounds of their shared 'embrace of comprehensibility and positive thinking' (Toop similarly refers to minimalism's 'affirmative' qualities). In saying this Whittall seeks to locate minimalism between Holloway's extremes, but the contributors to the final section of the book take the story in a different direction: Fink sees minimalism and its direct successors (what he calls 'post-minimalism') as representing 'a new mainstream', and he goes further – much further – when he claims, near the end of his chapter, that 'The future belongs to minimalism's stepchildren: ambient and electronic dance music.' That in turn links up with Griffiths's refreshingly old-fashioned characterization of pop music as 'arguably, the supreme art form of the late twentieth century' (no qualms about value judgements here!), suggesting a history of music in the twenty-first century that is remote indeed from how most present-day music historians, at least in academia, see that of the twentieth. (It has to be said that if Griffiths and Fink are right – and frankly who can tell? – then today's music students are for the most part poorly prepared for the world that lies ahead of them.) And in case Griffiths's and Fink's diagnosis seems too drastic, Walter takes an even more direct route to the same conclusion when he speaks of the fragmentation and decline of 'serious' music in the face of a newly global popular culture; as early as the 1940s, he says, 'the dominance of serious music . . . had obviously reached its end'. Maybe as much is implied by Nicholls's comparison between pre-war experimentalism and 1990s club culture. It is also striking that historical patterns previously characteristic of the 'art' tradition, such as the tension between modernism and conservatism, have been relocated to popular music (through the tension between a self-styled 'progressive' rock and a pop culture increasingly seen as commercially rather than artistically motivated). Of course, any narrative as broad-brush as this must have its limitations (how exactly does Zorn fit into this story?), and once again, there is irony in the fact that it is left to Scherzinger, discussing 'art' music in a context where it is easily suspected of being a colonial imposition, to resist this flight from modernism by arguing for its cultural importance as a site of resistance to global commercialization, in terms which almost precisely match Williams's account of a modernism now widely seen – at least in the English-speaking world – as in possibly terminal decline.

Yet another way the cookie crumbles is in the relationship between production and consumption. Until quite late in the twentieth century there hardly seemed to be an alternative to seeing musical culture – that is, 'art' musical culture – as organized round composers' works, themselves defined as (or at least underwritten by) notation. That of course created problems if non-notated or improvised traditions were to be brought within the historian's purview, though there were some fairly determined attempts to apply traditional musicological approaches to rock (for instance by seeing bands as collectively equivalent to a single author, and by seeing studio recordings as equivalent to a classical composer's autograph or authorized first edition[16]). Several circumstances combined to undermine the 'Life and Works' approach to music history to which this work-oriented approach had given rise. One, undoubtedly, was the impact of popular music studies, which (as Stilwell records) began in sociology rather than musicology: music historians realized that, if they were to engage at all with the music most people actually listened to, they had to broaden their approaches to include the patterns and circumstances of consumption from which popular music evidently derived much of its meaning. There is also no doubt that music historians were influenced by broader historiographical trends that tended in the same direction, in particular reception history. Less provable – but hardly less plausible – influences include a significant change in compositional culture: the transition from purism to pluralism to which we have already referred, which tended to place less emphasis on the score and more on the circumstances of its realization, as well as putting issues of music's social or personal meaning back onto an agenda from which they had long been absent (Williams calls this 'a shift from means to meaning').

At all events, music historians today are less likely than their predecessors to see musical meaning as embedded in 'works' conceived as tangible repositories

16 See Nicholas Cook, 'Music Minus One: Rock, Theory, and Performance', *New Formations* 27 (1995–6), pp. 23–41.

of human achievement, and more likely to see it as arising from the social contexts within which music is produced, reproduced, interpreted, evaluated, contemplated, consumed. In other words music history is seen less as a matter of repertories and styles, and more as a species of cultural history (with the term 'culture' being generously defined). Hence the emphasis that some – though not all – of our contributors place on the economic, institutional, industrial, technological, or legal contexts of the creation and consumption of music, and the extent to which these contexts mould musical practices, experiences, and values; as Williams says, 'music flows through a number of channels and cannot be understood in only one dimension'. Seen in such a manner, music history proliferates endlessly and historical understanding is always incomplete. The contexts you put in only accentuate the contexts you leave out, and among the more important areas arguably under-represented in this book are amateur music-making (whether 'art' or vernacular, including folk traditions) and music education. There has however been a distinct effort to do justice to music as a component of everyday life in the twentieth century, for instance through Franklin's discussion of the 'little people' from the suburbs and Banfield's of the 'little traditions', or in terms of the technologically mediated relocation of the experience of 'great' music from the concert hall to domestic or even (with the Walkman) more personal spaces. Several authors, Banfield and Blake among them, attempt to trace the changes in listening practices that represent the inner dynamic of music history.

And with listening we pass through a further boundary, from consumption to interpretation. Related to new patterns of listening are the new constructions of authenticity with which several authors are concerned, including Susan Cook, Walter, Blake, and Stilwell (whose observation that many of The Band's original compositions were heard as authentic folksongs exactly replicates Walter's comment about Copland): what matters here is not simply what people heard, but what they heard it *as*. And whereas only Toop and Stilwell treat critical interpretation as a significant music-historical topic, several contributors at least flirt with the idea of a history of music in which performance interpretation plays a more central role than it has in traditional composer- or work-centred approaches. This can take several forms. For writers on popular music, of course, composition and performance are frequently inseparable. But Auner, Toop, and Williams emphasize the role of performers in the generation of new 'art' musical styles; recognition of the historical impact of figures such as Steuermann, Tudor, and Arditti is arguably long overdue. As already mentioned, Franklin (who comments that progressive ideologies of music have prevented adequate consideration of performance) structures his chapter round Tauber, depicting him as both agent and exemplar of a variety of historical forces, and emphasizing the way in which Tauber's activities cut across the perhaps over-confidently drawn boundary between modernism and conservatism. Other contributors present performance as simply an essential element in the circulation of the musical economy, whether the performance in question is of old music, new music, or music that is at the same time old *and* new – most obviously in the case of the 'early music' movement of the 1970s and 80s, in which (at least if you accept Richard Taruskin's account[17]) music too ancient to have any surviving performance tradition was treated in a thoroughly modern style, resulting in new music for listeners who didn't like new music. Whittall explains the slightly earlier Mahler revival in very similar terms, except that here the music was not ancient but simply unknown to most listeners, and the same might be said of Ives, Korngold, or Schreker.

The point to be made is really quite a dramatic one. The twentieth century is the first whose history we are in a position to write on the basis of recordings – in other words, on the basis of actual sounds rather than silent documents. That also means it is the first century of which we can (or perhaps need to) write a history in which the performance of old music is as central as the composition of new music. In other words, when we think about 'twentieth-century music' we should think as much of Toscanini or Tauber as of Webern or Weill. And we should see the availability, at the pressing of a CD button, of Machaut's, Monteverdi's, or Mozart's music as contributing as much as that of Tuku beat or Korean court music to the 'all-world, all-time cultural bazaar' as which Robert Morgan characterized musical life in the closing years of the twentieth century.[18] But getting away from a model of history which takes its bearings from composers and their works – from a conception of music that makes it more like a document than an event, and from a conception of authorship that sees it as driving the historical process – is easier said than done, and in none of the following chapters is the idea of a history of music in which performance plays a central role fully consummated. As editors, then, shouldn't we have made good this deficit by commissioning a chapter on the history of twentieth-century performance, perhaps a potted version (and continuation) of Robert Philip's ground-breaking book on the development of performance style?[19] Perhaps so, and yet there are some powerful counter-arguments.

One concerns the danger of premature or simply inappropriate generalization. Philip advances two general principles to distinguish between

17 Richard Taruskin, 'The Pastness of the Present and the Presence of the Past', in Nicholas Kenyon (ed.), *Authenticity and Early Music: A Symposium*, Oxford, 1988, pp. 137–207.

18 Robert Morgan, 'Tradition, Anxiety, and the Current Musical Scene', in Kenyon (ed.), *Authenticity and Early Music*, pp. 57–82; p. 67.

19 Robert Philip, *Early Recordings and Musical Style: Changing Tastes in Instrumental Performance, 1900–1950*, Cambridge, 1992.

performance style before and after the Second World War. One is that there was a greater degree of variation in tempo and nuance in the first half of the century than in the second; the other is that, after the Second World War, tempo was increasingly regulated by the ability to cleanly articulate the shortest notes of the music in question. Putting these two factors together, one would expect to find a lower average tempo in post-war performances, and a higher degree of tempo convergence. If complete statistics were available, that might well be what we would find. But in any given case we may find something completely different; Stravinsky's successive interpretations of *Le sacre du printemps*, for example, do not conform to this pattern at all.[20] The suspicion, then, is that what we see as global tendencies in the history of performance style may represent no more than statistical aggregations of quite distinct individual cases; perhaps, in other words, different works have their own distinct historical trajectories, in which case valid generalization will not be possible until we know what the relevant factors underlying individual cases may be (assuming that such a thing is possible at all).

A second, and related, argument concerns the vantage point from which such a history of twentieth-century performance style could be written. In this book we offer no one-chapter overview of the development of twentieth-century compositional style for precisely the reasons which this Introduction has set out: it would be like doing arithmetic with apples and oranges, to the extent that each music needs to be understood in its own terms, in its own context, in terms of its own values. (There is, in other words, a strong historicist current in this book that aims to recover the plurality of practices and concepts – the ways of the hand and the head – that gave rise to the diversity of twentieth-century musics, for this was an age which increasingly lost the ability to think of itself in terms of 'great music'.) And precisely the same applies to performance: the problems about generalization to which we have referred are a practical demonstration of the problem. But there is also a third argument, one which applies equally, for instance, to issues of gender representation: if performance is to be fully integrated into the history of music, then the last thing we want to do is to ghettoize it by treating it separately, as a topic in its own right. (That would be like devoting one chapter to women's music and leaving the remaining twenty-one to the men.) Integrating performance into the history of music should not mean gesture politics, but rather telling the story of performance through all aspects of music, and telling the story of all aspects of music through performance. Such a history may be possible, but it has to be admitted that, if so, we have hardly even begun to tell it.

20 See Nicholas Cook, 'Stravinsky Conducts Stravinsky', in Jonathan Cross (ed.), *The Cambridge Companion to Stravinsky*, Cambridge, 2003, pp. 176–91.

This book, then, is framed by two chapters (1 and 22) that locate the history of Western music in the twentieth century within the context of music outside the West – or rather, as it is necessary to say with particular reference to the later part of the century, outside the westernized world (for cultural and geographical boundaries by no means coincide). Chapter 2 sets out a kind of agenda for the history of Western music in the twentieth century, in the form of an inventory of central issues and problems; it ranges across the entire period and offers a sober – some will say downright pessimistic – assessment of the state of and prospects for 'art' music at the century's end. Otherwise the structure of the book is essentially chronological, though many of the chapters run in parallel. Chapters 3–6 all start around 1900, though their approximate terminus dates range from 1920 to 1945. Of course, 1900 is an essentially arbitrary starting point (the entire period up to 1914 could reasonably be considered part of a 'long' nineteenth century), and so these chapters are largely concerned with identifying and following through the most salient developments of the later nineteenth century (as is evident from their relationship to Anthony Pople's chapter in *The Cambridge History of Nineteenth-Century Music*,[21] which straddles the centuries and could just as well have been placed in the present volume). In short, they provide a historical introduction to classical and light music, the avant-garde, and jazz on both sides of the Atlantic during the first decades of the century. Chapters 7–12 all focus on the period from the end of the First World War to the end of the Second, though the last of these continues well beyond this date; given that chapters 5–6 go up to 1945, this means that there are no fewer than eight parallel accounts of music in this period, the most at any one time in the book – and not surprisingly, for it was a period marked by an unprecedented degree of fragmentation both within and between the 'art' and popular traditions. By comparison there are five chapters covering each of the third and fourth quarters of the century (chapters 13–17 and 18–22 respectively); in this way the book as a whole falls into roughly quarter-century sections, with chapter 12 (which covers the many facets of 'light' music from Coates to Sinatra) spanning the second and third quarters. Only time will tell whether the end of the century turns out to be any more meaningful in musical terms than its beginning, and for now it is hardly possible to improve on Banfield's suggestion that the twentieth century ended abruptly on 11 September 2001.

The book may be read as a whole, read as a series of more or less separate chronological sections, read thematically, or browsed. Each chapter is a

21 Anthony Pople, 'Styles and Languages around the Turn of the Century', in Samson (ed.), *The Cambridge History of Nineteenth-Century Music*, pp. 601–20.

self-sufficient essay, but some chapters fall into distinct pathways: chapters 5 and 15, for instance, give a more or less continuous history of jazz, and chapters 16 and 21 do the same for rock and pop, while a consecutive reading of chapters 9, 13, 17, and 19 will provide a narrative of the modernist tradition (this is the nearest the book comes to 'techno-essentialism'). There is also a variety of finding aids, ranging from the detailed contents list to a comprehensive index that links sometimes dispersed discussions of individuals, works, and topics; the effort of following the weaving of different subjects through different chapters will hopefully be compensated by the multiple perspectives afforded through complementary treatments in different contexts. Additional orientation is provided by two extensive appendices that partly reflect and partly complement the emphases of the main text: one is a set of brief biographies collecting information on individual musicians, while the other is a chronology that not only sets musical events in the context of other cultural and political developments, but also – when used in conjunction with the index – provides a further means of access to the book's contents. And so this book is offered less as a pre-packaged historical solution than as a set of resources and commentaries designed to help the reader to make his or her own sense of the music of a century which it is hard, even now, to think of as consigned to a rapidly receding past.

Bibliography

Benjamin, Walter. *Illuminations* (ed. Hannah Arendt, tr. Harry Zohn), London, 1973.
Bohlman, Philip. 'Ontologies of Music', in Nicholas Cook and Mark Everist (eds.), *Rethinking Music*, Oxford, 1999, pp. 17–34.
Cook, Nicholas. 'Music Minus One: Rock, Theory, and Performance', *New Formations* 27 (1995–6), pp. 23–41.
'Stravinsky Conducts Stravinsky', in Jonathan Cross (ed.), *The Cambridge Companion to Stravinsky*, Cambridge, 2003, pp. 176–91.
Dahlhaus, Carl. *Foundations of Music History* (tr. J. B. Robinson), Cambridge, 1983.
Jackson, Travis A. 'Jazz as Musical Practice', in Mervyn Cooke and David Horn (eds.), *The Cambridge Companion to Jazz*, Cambridge, 2002, pp. 83–113.
McClary, Susan. *Conventional Wisdom: The Content of Musical Form*, Berkeley, 2000.
Morgan, Robert. 'Tradition, Anxiety, and the Current Musical Scene', in Nicholas Kenyon (ed.), *Authenticity and Early Music: A Symposium*, Oxford, 1988, pp. 57–82.
Nyman, Michael. *Experimental Music: Cage and Beyond* (2nd edn), Cambridge, 1999.
Philip, Robert. *Early Recordings and Musical Style: Changing Tastes in Instrumental Performance, 1900–1950*, Cambridge, 1992.
Pople, Anthony. 'Styles and Languages around the Turn of the Century', in Jim Samson (ed.), *The Cambridge History of Nineteenth-Century Music*, Cambridge, 2002, pp. 601–20.
Porter, Eric. *What is this Thing called Jazz? African American Musicians as Artists, Critics, and Activists*, Berkeley, 2002.

Potter, Keith. 'Cornelius Cardew: Some Postmodern (?) Reflections on Experimental Music and Political Music', in Mark Dalaere (ed.), *New Music, Aesthetics and Ideology*, Wilhemshaven, 1995, pp. 152–69.
Rufer, Josef. *The Works of Arnold Schoenberg: A Catalogue of his Compositions, Writings and Paintings* (tr. Dika Newlin), London, 1962.
Schuller, Gunther. *Musings: The Musical Worlds of Gunther Schuller*, New York, 1986.
Taruskin, Richard. 'The Pastness of the Present and the Presence of the Past', in Nicholas Kenyon (ed.), *Authenticity and Early Music: A Symposium*, Oxford, 1988, pp. 137–207.
Walser, Robert (ed.). *Keeping Time: Readings in Jazz History*, New York, 1999.
Williams, Christopher. 'Of Canons and Context: Toward a Historiography of Twentieth-Century Music', *Repercussions* 2/1 (1993), pp. 31–74.

· 1 ·

Peripheries and interfaces: the Western impact on other music

JONATHAN STOCK

Introduction

The theme of this chapter is the encounter with Western musics of other peoples during the past one hundred years. Often only occasional and sporadic at the start of the twentieth century, contact with the music of elsewhere was by the end of that century part of the everyday lives of huge numbers of people worldwide (as much within as outside the Western world). The history of this shift might be written in several ways. From a technological perspective we would discuss the invention of sound recording and broadcasting, for instance, and the dissemination of music notation and certain instruments, including the piano, guitar, accordion, and microphone. As historians of intercultural politics, we might instead emphasize the widespread creation through cross-cultural interaction of new genres and ensembles based in some form or other on the emulation of people seen as privileged. An ethnographic approach would look at the changing role of music in the lives of certain individuals, drawing on their own accounts of music-related events as well as on observation of and participation in some of that music-making. Meanwhile, taking the study of social institutions as a starting point, our review of the century would find common ground in the creation in many nations of music-making bodies, including orchestras of revised folk instruments, ministries of culture, competitions and festivals, bodies that regulate copyright, and colleges where music theory and performance are imparted to generations of would-be professionals; from this perspective, a key characteristic of music history in the twentieth century has been the application of similar processes to the organization of music around much of the world, providing, in some cases, pressures that result in the transformation of the musics themselves. A more postmodernist account might stress instead the ironies, discontinuities, misunderstandings, and co-options just as characteristic of the last hundred years: Allied use of a distinctly German motto (the opening tattoo of Beethoven's Fifth Symphony) to represent victory in the Second World War, say, or the numerous newly invented and transformed traditions that claim far greater historical or national precedent than the evidence might support; here it is as if music has come to signify more and more during the last hundred years but has also come to mean, in absolute terms, less and less.

Each of these histories has its attractions and its points of irony. In the case of the technological history, for example, we might trace the dissemination of the piano and its music outside Europe. This not only allowed Americans, Asians, and others to enjoy at first hand the music of Bach, Chopin, and Liszt; it also led some of them to compose their own pieces in quite different styles. Moreover, the very success of the export of the piano and all it symbolized provided the impetus for American and then Asian factories to drive European piano-making firms out of business. Instrument and gramophone salesmen once stood alongside military bandsmen and missionaries at the forefront of the West's attempts to export its ways of music-making. Their position has now been taken by an equally diverse array of recording salesmen (now selling the recording as an end in itself, not simply as a means to sell the technology to play it back on), composers of film music, examiners for the various British boards that offer graded performance exams, and jet-setting superstar performers, all based on a musical product that is instantiated directly in the homes of numerous peoples through the intervention of the broadcast media.

The approach taken below is that of a short series of case studies, each of which illustrates a contrasting instance of the encounters between peoples and musics in the twentieth century (though the emphasis is on the influence of the West on other musics, complementing the reverse influences documented at various points in this volume[1]). Taken together, these instances chart some of the main themes of the history of Western-impacted musics in the twentieth century, though necessarily in an incomplete fashion. First, however, it is necessary to address the issue of westernization versus modernization or change. Change can be quickly dealt with: almost all musical traditions are in a constant state of change, and therefore the historian's job is to explain paths of change, not to contrast change to putative stability. As for westernization against modernization, the basic problem (as several of the cases that follow will show) is that what appears a clear case of westernization to one observer seems to another a straightforward instance of modernization. Musical nationalists in Turkey, Egypt, and China, for instance, adopted staff or cipher notation in the early decades of the twentieth century to reform local traditions into a national style able to withstand incoming Western music: they explained such notations as forms of modernization which might be deployed against westernization. It

1 See, for instance, James Collier (chapter 5) on the origins of jazz; Hermann Danuser (chapter 10) on Villa-Lobos; Michael Walter (chapter 11) on Chávez; Robynn Stilwell (chapter 16) on the origins of rock and roll; Richard Toop (chapter 17) on Messiaen, Sculthorpe, and Meale; Alastair Williams (chapter 19) on Ligeti; and Martin Scherzinger (chapter 22), *passim*.

follows that writing the history of the Western impact on other music requires an understanding of the motives of those involved in cross-cultural interaction: there is often no substitute for detailed, first-hand field study among the community in question.

Case studies

Instrument design in a global context

If, in 1900, we had assembled a small ensemble of instrumentalists from different societies – a *charango* lutenist from the Bolivian Andes, perhaps, a *gaida* bagpiper from Bulgaria or a player of the Sardinian *launeddas* double-clarinet, an executant of the *mbira* lamellaphone (thumb piano) from Zimbabwe, a Turkish *bağlama* lutenist, and a Chinese *erhu* two-stringed fiddler – there would have been a good chance that they would not sound very well together. By 2000, matters had changed: there was now a much greater chance that these musicians would share a tuning system, and some explicit music theory too. Of these instruments, only the *charango* (famed for its sometime use of an armadillo-shell soundbox) is commonly described as a hybrid, one acknowledged as resulting from contact between European and native Andean groups in or before the eighteenth century. Yet each of the others has come into sustained encounter with Western music and music theory over the past century. Even where an older instrumental form has been retained, redesign in accordance with Western principles has often occurred, and playing techniques are at least as malleable as the physical forms of these instruments themselves.

The Chinese *erhu* offers an instance of an instrument thoroughly overhauled as a result of Western influence. Lü Wencheng (1898–1981), one of the originators of the urban entertainment style of Cantonese music, began the process in the 1920s by replacing the higher-pitched of the two silk strings on his own, small-sized instrument with a violin E string. Other *erhu* players gradually followed, finding the steel string both more durable and smoother in sound across the whole register. At first, and since *erhu* strings are longer than those of the violin, violin strings were extended by use of a silk cord; by the late 1950s purpose-built steel *erhu* strings had been adopted by many players in place of both of the original silk strings, and standardized instruments were mass-produced in large factories for sale across the nation. Variable tuning was largely superseded by the selection of d′ and a′ as standard pitches for the open strings, and larger-sized instruments were invented to act as viola, cello, and bass in the bowed string section of the modern Chinese orchestra.[2]

2 Jonathan Stock, 'A Historical Account of the Chinese Two-Stringed Fiddle *Erhu*', *Galpin Society Journal* 46 (1993), pp. 83–113; p. 103.

New music, such as the ten influential solos by the nationalist music reformer Liu Tianhua (1895–1932), took advantage of the new ease with which shifts of register could occur. These solos, which were set down in uncharacteristically detailed notation, demanded the use of new techniques (fingering with the tips of the fingers, for example, or violin-style vibrato), many of which were subsequently applied in the performance of existing traditional pieces. Reform of the *erhu*, then, led to the rise of new instruments and repertory, and also to the transformation of the instrument's performance technique.

These transformations are not restricted to the continents outside Europe. Timothy Rice has described the transformation of the bagpipe *gaida* when it became part of the Bulgarian folk orchestra in the 1950s. Again, the reshaping of the *gaida* that allowed it to play in the same keys as other redesigned instruments led to alteration of musicians' attitudes and technique, as well as to changes in the sound of the instrument itself. Pipers had to learn to play without the drone, which clashed with the constantly changing harmonies of the folk orchestra. On lower-pitched, equal-tempered bagpipes, with a less shrill sound than the original instrument, they also learnt new ornamentational styles and acquired notation-based ways of imagining musical form.[3]

Nor are such musical revisions restricted to (former) communist nations. Turkish musicians reformed the *bağlama* extensively in the twentieth century, aiming to systematize its construction and technique, and an electronic version, named the *elektrosaz*, is now widely used in the entertainment music market, where an amplified sound is more audible. Of course, the electronic version favours some techniques less effective on the acoustic *bağlama*, leading to further adaptations in the instrument's performance technique.[4] Meanwhile, Bernard Lortat-Jacob's research in southern Sardinia led him to Attilio Cannargiu, a maker of the *launeddas*, a cane double-clarinet with two melody pipes and one drone. Conventionally, each of the melody pipes of the *launeddas* covers a different set of pitches, but there is some flexibility in the exact combination of melody pipes – or, to put it another way, there are differently pitched forms of the instrument. Having learnt something of formal Western music theory, Cannargiu's aim at the time of Lortat-Jacob's arrival was to systematize the design of the instrument until he could produce a *launeddas* in every single key.[5] Cannargiu is more interested in the acoustics of the instrument than its public performance, but the potential for transformation of a tradition through the agency of an externally influenced instrument designer is clear.

Performing musicians and instrument designers are not the only sources of potential influence on instrumental style. UK-based *mbira* performer Chartwell

3 Timothy Rice, *May It Fill Your Soul: Experiencing Bulgarian Music*, Chicago, 1994, pp. 188–95.
4 Martin Stokes, *The Arabesk Debate: Music and Musicians in Modern Turkey*, Oxford, 1992, pp. 70–88.
5 Bernard Lortat-Jacob, *Sardinian Chronicles* (tr. Teresa Lavender Fagan), Chicago, 1995, pp. 39–49.

Dutiro recalls being instructed by a record producer in a London studio to tape down the buzzers on his instrument as they were making too much sound, an instruction that assumes timbre to be an aspect of sound secondary to and quite separable from pitch.[6] This sudden demand for the instrument's sound to be repackaged closer to conventional, 'purer-toned' Western norms runs exactly opposite to the experience of another UK-based musician from overseas, Yoshikazu Iwamoto: a Japanese *shakuhachi* (end-blown flute) expert who has carried out numerous collaborations with European 'art' music composers, Iwamoto comments that some of them become so fascinated by what he considers the special effects of his instrument that they write using only those breathing techniques not found in Western flute music. As a result, newly written *shakuhachi* music sometimes sounds much more exotic to the typical Western listener than that written in the past.[7]

As these several instances show, the topic of Western influence groups together quite distinct transformations. Some push directly towards the norms of particular kinds of Western music; others seem to push diametrically away from them (although the exoticization of music for *shakuhachi* might also be seen as an instance of a Western tendency to concentrate on difference in its coming to terms with the products of other peoples); some lead directly to the creation of new repertories; and yet more again open out technological possibilities that themselves lead to the revision and renewal of playing technique and performance practice.[8]

Radios Shanghai and Cairo: disembodied voices, embodied stars

New technology introduced from the West is central to the second case study. An American entrepreneur who hoped to sell wireless receivers in the city established Shanghai's (and China's) first radio station in 1923. Expansion was rapid: by the mid-1930s, approximately half of China's eighty-nine radio stations were competing for listeners in Shanghai. Programming was heterogeneous. Other than traffic and city government stations, there were two religious channels; all the rest were commercial channels combining news, entertainment and advertising. Other than Chinese music of numerous kinds, stations broadcast Japanese music and much Western dance music.[9] Most popular of

6 Chartwell Dutiro, personal communication, Sheffield, March 2000.

7 Yoshikazu Iwamoto, workshop, Sheffield, November 1999.

8 See further Max Peter Baumann, 'The Local and the Global: Traditional Musical Instruments and Modernization', *World of Music* 42/3 (2000), pp. 121–44.

9 Liu Guangqing (ed.), *Jiu Zhongguo de Shanghai guangbo shiye* [The Shanghai Broadcast Industry of Old China], Beijing, 1985, pp. 807, 809. See further Carlton Benson, 'The Manipulation of *Tanci* in Radio Shanghai During the 1930s', *Republican China* 20/2 (1995), pp. 117–46.

all these musics was *tanci*, balladry from the nearby city of Suzhou; its sparse textures – voice and either *pipa* or *sanxian* (respectively four- and three-stringed lute) – lent themselves well to the early broadcast microphones, not to mention the small budgets and studios of most channels. Second in popularity to *tanci* were pared-down versions of *shenqu*, local Shanghai opera. *Shenqu* singer Kong Jiabing (who lived from the 1910s until 1998) reminisced on the contrast between acting in the theatre and on the radio in this period:

> On the stage not only do you have to sing and act, but you must do so above the hubbub of the background noise in the theatre. Using your voice and acting, which are influenced by your technique and physical condition, you have to put across your movements, gestures, songs, and speech for an audience to see and understand. Radio didn't have these same limitations. You could freely and comfortably elaborate. But there were still certain basic constraints: you had to know many old dramas; you had to have a bright voice; your singing style had to be rich with colour and lively; you had to pay attention to the breath so that the audience didn't notice you breathing in or out; enunciation had to be clear; and since there was no audience in front of you, you had to think of the thousands of listeners sitting in their own places.[10]

Kong contends that radio both made demands and offered opportunities. Zhu Jiesheng and Xu Yinping propose this explanation in a historical outline of *shenqu*: the competitive role of singers, who also acted as commercial radio advertisers, they write, led them to increase the expressivity of their singing as compared with the plainer style characteristic of ballad-style performance in public teashops. The slowing down of tempo was one such change, allowing the building up of melodic expressivity through the insertion of ornaments; other singers used the slower tempo to develop a weeping style the better to move their listeners. At the other end of the spectrum, some singers pushed tempo forward, finding a means thereby to depict more heroic or anxious situations.[11]

Shenqu performers are just one class of musicians whose work was transformed by the impact of new technologies during the twentieth century. Indian classical singers found the microphone lent carrying power to their lower registers; this allowed them to exploit that vocal range far more than previously. American crooners employed the radio microphone to sigh directly into the ear of the individual listener. (Amplification, in this latter case, had the interesting

10 Kong Jiabing, 'Wo zai diantai shang chang tanhuang' [How I Sang Tanhuang on Radio], *Shanghai xiqu shi liao huicui* 2 (1986), pp. 103–6; p. 104. *Tanhuang* is an alternative term for *shenqu*; the tradition is today named *huju*. For further on this genre, see Jonathan Stock, *Huju: Traditional Opera in Modern Shanghai*, Oxford, 2003.

11 Zhu Jiesheng and Xu Yinping (eds.), *Huju yinyue jian shu* [An Introduction to Huju Music], Shanghai, 1988, pp. 2–3.

effect of making the music softer, not louder.) Even as it stimulated change in musical style, broadcasting changed the way people heard music and thought of its star performers: *shenqu* singers, Indian vocalists, and crooners alike reached through the broadcast airwaves into the homes of listeners, and into public spaces such as dance halls, hotel lobbies, restaurants, and shops. As such, they came to stand, temporarily at least, in front of a far wider range of listeners than they could ever have reached personally. There is a curious irony in that just as radio disembodies musical performance by attenuating direct contact between performer and listener (one and the same person in many traditional settings), so too its expansion of the reach of performance and its reliance on the professional specialist created in many places a whole new system of musicians as public figures whose achievements were followed by mass, non-participatory audiences.[12]

Few individuals exemplify this better than the prime Egyptian vocalist of the twentieth century, Umm Kulthūm (?1904–75).[13] Beginning in 1937, Umm Kulthūm's monthly first-Thursday live broadcasts became a musical institution across the Arabic-speaking world that endured almost four decades. Through these concerts and other activities, she became a kind of cultural ambassador for her nation and an inescapable part of the fabric of Egyptian cultural life; in her selection and development of music for these broadcasts, she explored processes of modernization and westernization. And while her pathway was personal and specific to mid-century Egypt, the pressures she faced were experienced by many elsewhere. Too much reliance on traditional materials left her exposed to the charge of not moving with the times, and fans might desert to more progressive singers; too much input of European style, on the other hand, alienated existing fans and jarred with her own nationalist sentiment. As a result, the singer regularly had to renegotiate her own image by finding new means of combining her established strengths with incipient new fashions. Her success in doing exactly this over such a long period, in being not just a fine singer but Umm Kulthūm, explains why she became such a striking persona in twentieth-century Egyptian public life, a role unthinkable for a female musician in previous centuries.

The increased access to certain kinds of music permitted by Western-derived broadcasting technology, with all that implies, is then a key change which has transformed both musics and ways of conceiving them in many parts of the world. It may be that this particular shift, which presents music as disembodied

12 Specialists and professional musicians have long been found in many folk and traditional cultures; the difference is that radio sees some of them taken up as stars observed by a mass public, not functionaries to be hired by a specific group for a specific role or occasion.

13 See Virginia Danielson, *The Voice of Egypt: Umm Kulthūm, Arabic Song, and Egyptian Society in the Twentieth Century*, Chicago, 1997.

product (what in nineteenth-century Europe was termed 'pure music') and star performers as outstanding public figures, represents the greatest instance of Western impact on other traditions in the twentieth century.

New soundscapes 1: diaspora and culture-contact

Radio offers just one instance of the rise of new soundscapes. Music's function in creating, informing, and transforming space relates in a host of ways to a history of Western-impacted musics in the twentieth century. Numerous music-related research themes and concepts interconnect here, including: utopia, heterotopia, and distopia; technoscape, soundscape, and ethnoscape; home, migrancy, diaspora, colonialism, and transculturalism; centres, thresholds, and peripheries; places of work, study, and leisure; ritual sites; architecture; antiphony; locality; belonging, displacement, and identity; the seen versus the heard; music as a venue for memory and imagination; public and private domains; male and female space; the body as a special space; and bodily movement across, between, and through spaces.[14] This and the following two case studies each select one instance from this list. First, we look at musical outcomes of the movement of peoples characteristic of the twentieth century; then we examine the impact of Western means of organizing musical performance, both as they affect touring groups from other parts of the world, and the associated rise of performances at home for incoming tourists. Finally, we consider the special space of the music conservatory as a place of work and study that generates particular kinds of music.

The twentieth century was a period of continued human mobility, the displacements and migrations of earlier centuries often accelerated by mechanized transport. Culture-contact intensified as colonial officers, travelling salesmen, missionaries, troops, migrants, tourists, and refugees crossed paths and as populations increased. One strand among many, or more properly a set of multiple strands in itself, is the Jewish movement to the New World. Typically, a community's identity is marked out through their becoming minority residents in another place. It is also multiplied: American Jews are exactly that, both American and Jewish, and they are members of particular subcommunities along each vector as well. Music is a primary means of expressing and experiencing group identity, and becomes a highly significant tool in forming the character of a subcommunity. Ethnomusicologist-cum-Rabbi Jeffrey Summit has made a comparative study of religious music among five American

14 A key reference in this area is Martin Stokes (ed.), *Ethnicity, Identity and Music: The Musical Construction of Place*, Oxford, 1994. See also Michel de Lannoy, 'De l'universelle intimité des espaces musicaux', in *La musique et le monde*, Paris, 1995, pp. 59–74; Andrew Leyshon, David Matless, and George Revill (eds.), *The Place of Music*, New York, 1998.

Jewish communities in Boston, and argues that the challenges for the uninitiated offered by the richly multilevelled Hebrew-language prayers lead to an emphasis being placed on music as a key factor in defining a style of worship: 'Style makes people either feel at home or uncomfortable and alienated from communal prayer: Ultimately, it can affect whether or not they attend and affiliate with synagogues.'[15] We return to multilevel Hebrew texts in a moment. First, let us note that in situations of this sort music is subject to two pressures, each of which reflects a contrasting form of authenticity. The first propels it towards difference, to the maintenance (or retrospective establishment[16]) of that group's distinct heritage; the second thrusts it towards similarity, towards assimilation of traits that signal not the past but the heterogeneous realities of the here and now.

Two contrasting Jewish musical practices illustrate the transformation of musics under these forces. One is the *pizmon*, a paraliturgical hymn sung by a group of men outside the context of the formal religious service, a practice particularly associated with Syrian Jews in New York and other major North American cities.[17] Songs in this form set new Hebrew texts to existing (or adapted) melodies. In the early decades of the twentieth century, *pizmon* composers in Aleppo drew melodies from popular Arabic song, including the tunes of Egyptian singer Umm Kulthūm. These songs are now sustained as memories of a time and place now long departed, and of the people who lived there, and references to individuals are layered within the song text. Their performance brings this society temporarily back to life for those who were there, and, through its emotional qualities, teaches those not there of the experience and value of this body of memories. Subsequent to the move to America, songmakers adopted other tunes from the society in which they now live, including popular songs, classical themes and, occasionally, melodies such as 'O Tannenbaum' that carry a non-Jewish religious symbolism. The change in musical language these recent adoptions reveal is a direct consequence of the Syrian Jews' migration to a new home in the New World. But, alongside this

15 Jeffrey A. Summit, *The Lord's Song in a Strange Land: Music and Identity in Contemporary Jewish Worship*, New York, 2000, p. 20. Communal prayer is a central aspect of the Jewish practice of belief.

16 There are now numerous studies of invented musical traditions, and American folklorists have made effective use of the notions of reformed and transformed traditions; see, for instance, Burt Feintuch, 'Musical Revival as Musical Transformation', in Neil Rosenberg (ed.), *Transforming Tradition: Folk Music Revivals Examined*, Urbana, 1993, pp. 203–19. An African instance of the creation of a pan-Yoruba identity in Nigeria by means of music is investigated in Christopher A. Waterman, *Jùjú: A Social History and Ethnography of an African Popular Music*, Chicago, 1990. Several East European transformations are considered in Mark Slobin (ed.), *Retuning Culture: Musical Changes in Central and Eastern Europe*, Durham NC, 1996.

17 See Kay Kaufman Shelemay, *Let Jasmine Rain Down: Song and Remembrance among Syrian Jews*, Chicago, 1998.

shift, the use of music in this community as a means of encoding personal and collective memories has endured unchanged.[18]

The second musical instance to be examined here is that of the klezmer revival. Primarily a secular, professional, and instrumental form, klezmer provides an immediate contrast with the sung *pizmon*. Moreover, its late-nineteenth-century repertory was not entirely shared by the 'co-territorial' communities in East Europe, where the music arose: once-distinct genres merged together as the repertory was renewed in New York from the 1880s onward. The music, however, retained an air of notoriety. In the Jewish community in Eastern Europe, many characterised the hereditary *klezmorim* as disreputable men: violent, low-class seducers. Many of their American-born offspring took the opportunity their parents' migration offered to find other professions, even if remaining within music, and by 1950 klezmer was performed by only a few.[19]

By the late 1970s, however, a klezmer revival had begun. The revival was multifaceted from the beginning, as Mark Slobin points out, combining the transformation of the tradition into a Jewish heritage music and its reinvention as an innovative and exciting American concert music by performers, many of them not of Jewish descent.[20] Slobin (citing Kirschenblatt-Gimblett) defines a heritage music as one that looks old, and has recourse to the past, but is actually new. It is a music that has been 'singled out for preservation, protection, enshrinement, and revival'.[21] In emphasising its Americanness, Slobin meanwhile draws attention to the constructedness of the revival, both as largely rediscovered from early American-made recordings (themselves tailored to the American market) and as a part of a larger American musical superculture. As well as attitudes, sometimes mixed, to the music as a whole and a body of recorded materials, this superculture provided many ingredients to contemporary klezmer. Two contrasting instances illustrate the impact of the superculture: on the one hand, the klezmer revival occurred within a particular economic system with pre-existing structures, opportunities, demands; on the other, klezmer violinists could draw from a heterogeneous repertory of violin techniques from styles as diverse as European folk, classical, and bluegrass.

18 John Blacking makes a useful distinction between surface-level alteration in musical resources and deeper-seated changes of heart among those who represent the tradition itself; see his 'Some Problems of Theory and Method in the Study of Musical Change', *Yearbook of the International Folk Music Council* 9 (1977), pp. 1–26.

19 Walter Z. Feldman, '*Bulgăreascǎ/Bulgarish/Bulgar*: The Transformation of a Klezmer Dance Genre', *Ethnomusicology* 38 (1994), pp. 1–35; pp. 1–5.

20 Mark Slobin, *Fiddler on the Move: Exploring the Klezmer World*, New York, 2000, p. 4.

21 Barbara Kirschenblatt-Gimblett, 'Sounds of Sensibility', *Judaism* 47 (1998), pp. 49–79; p. 52; cited in Slobin, *Fiddler*, pp. 12–13.

The histories of *pizmon* and klezmer in New York suggest several ways in which music changes as it is maintained or revived in new locations. In each case, remembrance of an earlier home provides some musical materials, values, and means. The new host culture offers others, and a setting that generally leads to new understandings of the original cultural materials, a process to which secondary revival adds further layers. Those involved have to choose between sometimes perplexing and loaded options as they revisit their musical performances not simply as music but as one style among many. It is little wonder that the soundscapes their music calls up often reflect a transnational stamp.

New soundscapes 2: tourist shows and touring musicians

By the last three decades of the twentieth century it had become commonplace for those from the wealthier parts of the world to travel overseas for leisure, and for musicians from all over the world to journey to Western cities in search of new audiences. Performances for tourists and those by touring musicians are not entirely the same thing, of course, although they intersect at international music festivals and competitions,[22] but each can have an impact on musical practice in societies far from the West. All instances of intercultural musical contact can set change in train, and so it is not the quality or otherwise of the event that is at issue in this case study.

At a tourist show in Malaysia which I attended in the mid-1980s, ten-minute extracts represented each of the major ethnic groups of peninsular Malaysia. (Somewhat unaccountably, the pre-Malay indigenous population was not represented.) Music was pre-recorded and piped into the auditorium while a troupe of young performers took their turns: first a Malay theatre item glorifying village life; then an Indian performance of the snake-charming type; and finally a Chinese lion dance. While performance standards were high, village life was cloyingly over-romanticized in the first piece, and the Indian item felt a poor choice as the sole representative of Malaysia's Indian community (most of whom weren't snake charmers). Moreover, the announcer's claims that the performance demonstrated Malaysia's happy present as a united, multi-racial nation jarred not just with the reality of day-to-day life, but specifically with the fact that public performances of lion dances, like many non-Malay cultural genres, were actually banned or tightly restricted outside the special environment of the tourist show. In short, the experience was tokenistic.

22 On festivals, see, for instance, Karl Neuenfeldt, 'Good Vibrations? The "Curious" Case of the Didjeridu in Spectacle and Therapy in Australia', *World of Music* 40/2 (1998), pp. 29–51. On competitions, see Amy Ku'uleialoha Stillman, 'Hawaiian Hula Competitions: Event, Repertoire, Performance, Tradition', *Journal of American Folklore* 109 (1996), pp. 357–80.

In a relatively wealthy, large-scale urban society little harm is done by an unconvincing show. Elsewhere, however, effort placed into tourist shows replaces effort put into other cultural activity; here the tourist show may bring in much-needed cash but also leads to an impoverishment of musical life, as full-scale indigenous forms are gradually replaced by simplified versions. Further changes encouraged by staged tourist shows (at their worst) include the secularization of religious forms, with rituals, sacrifices, and possession simulated; the revision of classical styles such that longer pieces are abridged, improvisatory forms replaced by memorized compositions in fixed form, and older forms modernized, for instance through the addition of harmonized accompaniments or Western-style vocal techniques; the attribution of a false antiquity to newly created styles; the presentation of short excerpts from multiple genres one after another in a superficial and incongruous manner; the exoticizing of costumes; the exaggerated dramatizing of dance movements for the better amusement of the first-time viewer; and the overlaying by the organizing authority of a bogus social symbolism quite foreign to the music and people on show.

At their best, by contrast, tourist shows can lend new life to genres that might otherwise disappear under the impact of imported or westernized forms, allowing performers to find new confidence in indigenous forms of expression perhaps now disregarded by many in the host community itself. The establishment of a sense of cultural authority in an effective tourist show invokes in visitors the impression that they temporarily share in a genuinely foreign soundscape, that they really have journeyed elsewhere. Nonetheless, and even when all participants feel that effective intercultural communication has been achieved, it will be clear that the concert-style performance format typical of these shows will tend to favour the selection of some local genres over others; for instance, those that are display-oriented may prove more effective than those that involve much verbal exchange in a language the tourists may not understand. Moreover, the assumptions tourists bring to the event can still have a gradual impact on the performers, as can the assumptions performers make about the needs and preferences of their audiences.[23]

These same issues come into play when musicians perform overseas. Black Sea Turkish musicians touring in Ireland in the early 1990s found audience attention drawn not to the singer or *bağlama* lute player but to the accompanying *kemençe* box fiddle, perhaps because of its perceived affinity with the violin, a leading instrument in the Irish context; in Istanbul, on the other hand, the

23 See further, Timothy J. Cooley, 'Folk Festival as Modern Ritual in the Polish Tatra Mountains', *World of Music* 41/3 (1999), pp. 31–55; Helen Rees, *Echoes of History: Naxi Music in Modern China*, New York, 2000, pp. 147–57.

kemençe had been treated as the least significant part of the trio. By the end of the tour of Ireland, the *kemençe* player was taking a more authoritative role in the performances, providing prominent polyphonic lines in place of the simple background accompaniments with which he had begun.[24] A second case in point is offered by a group of Peruvian musicians who visited Britain and the Netherlands in 1984. The group, Ayllu Sulca, were initially surprised to find that their European audiences preferred to hear them perform old items and Quechua songs rather than the more contemporaneous, Spanish-oriented music then in vogue among urban audiences in Peru. (Indeed, at home the singing of Quechua songs was sometimes interpreted as an expression of support for the Shining Path guerrillas, and performance was a risky matter.) Moreover, the musicians gradually learnt to declare authorship and claim copyright on items that were actually well-established traditional tunes in their homeplace; impetus for this came from their growing understanding of the Western music industry, which would otherwise not pay them authorship fees for any such tracks.[25]

A single tour will not be enough to reshape a whole tradition, but a series of these may have an appreciable impact, particularly when performance overseas is seen as a high-status opportunity. Nusrat Fateh Ali Khan, for instance, took the esoteric Sufi devotional style *qawwālī* from the shrines of saints in Pakistan to the concert stages and recording studios of several continents. During this transformation, he introduced a number of innovations, including the practice of virtuosic singing to solmisation symbols (*sargam*). Solmisation is a well-established part of the art music traditions in Pakistan, but was formerly rejected by many performers of *qawwālī* because its display-oriented character ran contrary to the generation of an air of spirituality. Now, however, younger singers who wish to tour overseas have to do so in an environment where Nusrat Fateh Ali Khan's innovations, themselves partly tailored to his new audiences, have become part of the norm and speak to the secularization that follows the transformation of traditional ritual into concert music for overseas audiences.[26]

Professionalization, of several kinds, is one of the regularly encountered results of culture contact in the new soundscapes of tourist and touring performances, and groups together a number of assumptions about musical performance, including virtuosity, individual authorship, and music's commercial

24 Martin Stokes, 'Place, Exchange and Meaning: Black Sea Musicians in the West of Ireland', in Stokes (ed.), *Ethnicity, Identity and Music*, pp. 97–115.

25 Jan Fairley, '"The Blind Leading the Blind": Changing Perceptions of Traditional Music. The Case of the Peruvian Ayllu Sulca', in Max Peter Baumann (ed.), *Music in the Dialogue of Cultures: Traditional Music and Cultural Policy*, Wilhelmshaven, 1991, pp. 272–89; pp. 279, 281.

26 Laurent Aubert, *La musique de l'autre: les nouveaux défis de l'ethnomusicologie*, Geneva, 2001, pp. 52–4.

role. Westernization, here as elsewhere, takes several forms: some of these involve the direct adoption of Western musical ingredients, while others reveal a reconsideration of the tenets of the tradition itself. From this point of view, Nusrat Fateh Ali Khan's use of *sargam* syllables, or the Black Sea fiddle-player's gradual departure from Istanbuli accompanimental norms, is as Western-impacted as would be their respective adoption of *bel canto* vocal technique or the electronic keyboard.

New soundscapes 3: conservatories

If many twentieth-century musics have been transformed through their recreation in new places, one privileged set of sites in this process are the specialist institutions of music conservatories. Specialist institutions are an ancient phenomenon, and musical specialization far predates the twentieth century. Nonetheless, in many parts of the world the previous century saw the establishment of new institutions that have had a major influence on the official music culture of those nations. Radio and television stations are one obvious instance, and national ensembles of reformed instruments playing scored folk arrangements have at times become ubiquitous on the airwaves of much of the world.

Often associated with each of these is the special place for music represented by the conservatory, another Western export to other parts of the world that favours particular kinds of change. In Bali, among other places,[27] the establishment of government-sponsored conservatories had several results, including, first, the growth of a sense of unique, individual creativity as signalled by the separation of composing from other musical skills and the marking out for special attention of composers as the primary figures of music history. Second, conservatories encouraged the rise of a group of musicians interested in the preservation or reconstruction of historical genres; in combination with the first observation, this further separates the increasingly one-off act of creating new repertory from the day-to-day continuance of the old. Third, the conservatories produced musicians trained across a range of genres, often through an explicit attention to formalized music theory. These musicians were often able to use notation, for instance, and familiar with the abstraction of fragments for dedicated practice; as such they began to think of their music and their techniques in ways distinct from those of preceding generations. Fourth, musicians

27 See further, Michael B. Bakan, *Music of Death and New Creation: Experiences in the World of Balinese Gamelan Beleganjur*, Chicago, 1999, pp. 200–3. On Java, see Benjamin Brinner, *Knowing Music, Making Music: Javanese Gamelan and the Theory of Musical Competence and Interaction*, Chicago, 1995, pp. 157–9. On China, see Jonathan Stock, *Musical Creativity in Twentieth-Century China: Abing, His Music, and Its Changing Meanings*, Rochester, 1996, pp. 142–67.

in the conservatories created a body of music intended for Western-style concert performance. While much of this music and its performance style was based on that of traditions outside the conservatory, the original models were often seen as inferior (out of tune, irrational, crude, parochial) as compared to the modern new repertory, or as raw material at best. Nonetheless, and despite these pejorative views, the new repertory may standardize certain elements such that its musical language is actually more limited in certain aspects than the folk original. Finally, the establishment of music conservatories was accompanied by the growth of elite audiences who favour this reformed repertory and its performers, for instance through political patronage, and graduates of the conservatories often become a musical elite who come to dominate educational and sometimes media institutions in the nation as a whole.

The kinds of musical spaces created in these conservatories overlap with those of the national and international supercultures in several ways, as may be inferred from the above list. Here, let us note two characteristics of the privileged space of the music conservatory: preservation and cultural hegemony. Preservation in the conservatory and the shift to an art-music performance tradition abstracts even very faithfully rendered local musics from their former cultural emplacements, offering new ways of hearing and recreating those sounds; there is something of a parallel here with the prominence of 'world beat' in Western record shops as against older styles of world music (see below). In each case, music is lifted out from other, older traditions, whether by the globalized music industry or by the staff of Western-inspired educational institutions. In each case, the reformed music is performed by a new class of highly trained urban musicians familiar with other westernized musical forms.

Conservatory-mediated performance traditions can come, despite their minority status in demographic terms, to dominate the official culture of a nation. One might view this hegemony as a sign of civilization. According to this view it is appropriate that society as a whole, through its appointed experts, channels funding and prominence to those who sustain the higher art forms. (Funding popular traditions would be absurd – if they are genuinely popular, they hardly require subsidy, and can be delivered by the music industry without governmental interference.) Or one might see it as cause for concern, as fascinating, diverse indigenous traditions are obscured by the media dominance and smoother access to cultural funding of a more uniform, official culture on the one hand and the commercial power of the mainstream music industry on the other; despite a licence subsidy, educational mission, diversity statement, and numerous channels, for instance, BBC Radio attempts no coherent or sustained coverage of the many folk-music traditions currently found in Britain, concentrating its resources almost exclusively on the classical and popular styles. Whatever one's preferences for or against change in particular cases, there is little denying the impact of these official styles in their respective homes across much of the world today, including, as mention of the BBC suggests, the Western continents. Musical preservation and hegemony sound like forces for continuity, as repertories born in one here-and-now are refashioned and validated in another. In historical terms, of course, the selection and development of such musics for careful preservation often represents a significant change.

Out of Africa: Tuku beat and world music

At first glance, the designers of Oliver 'Tuku' Mtukudzi's initial CD with German company Shava were unsure what they were selling: 'Modern Traditional African Soulmusic', states one line around the liner's border; 'The Grand Master of Zimbabwe Traditional Pop', proclaims another; 'African Township-Jive Trance Dance Music', offers a third. Further large text tells us that this is 'Rhythm for Life' and 'Roots World Music', while an equation points out that 'Mbira + Mbaqanga = Tuku Beat'.[28] As it turns out, the designers have precisely identified the disc's content, for Mtukudzi's recording thrives on the interwoven musical interchanges of the late twentieth century. Recorded in Copenhagen in June 1993 for issue primarily to Mtukudzi's (potential) European fans, but featuring songs composed since the 1970s for his home audiences, the songs alternate in Shona and English. Lyrics range from appeals for heavenly support to words of farewell to a beloved grandmother and veiled calls for Zimbabwean independence, all of these apposite subjects for a traditional singer from this nation, if not stock themes of the international pop star. Tuku (b. 1952), however, was never a traditional singer. His early vocal training was in a township school choir. Like many a teenager, he bought a teach-yourself tutor book and made himself a guitar on which to learn rock music from the radio. His subsequent adoption of traditional elements, then, is exactly an adoption, a deployment of an additional musicality.

Looking at the musical mix itself in a little more detail, we find further traditional content in the intricate, multi-layered, melodic idioms, as played at all-night spirit festivals on *mbira* lamellaphones and *hosho* rattle. Yet these are rendered on a conventional international pop-band instrumentation of three electric guitars, keyboard, drum kit, percussion, and two backing voices.[29] And the mix is not only one of Shona and Western musical traditions. Mtukudzi

28 Oliver Tuku Mutukudzi, *Ziwere MuKøbenhavn* (Shava, 1994). Mtukudzi's name appears in several variants on his discs and in the literature.

29 In this Mtukudzi follows the internationally better-known Zimbabwean musician Thomas Mapfumo. For further on music for *mbira*, see Paul F. Berliner, *The Soul of Mbira: Music and Traditions of the Shona People of Zimbabwe*, Berkeley, 1978. Zimbabwean popular music is the subject of study in Thomas Turino,

draws in the *mbaqanga* township jive style of neighbouring Ndebele South Africa as well as Zimbabwe's own *jit* style, a fusion that allows him to propose at once two diverging trajectories for his listeners: one, marked by Shona lyrics and *mbira* style, signals national, even native, tradition, rural roots, the wisdom of the singer as ritual interlocutor with the ancestral spirits; the other, made manifest by use of English, electric instruments, and the *mbaqanga* rhythmic drive of the Ndebele people, points at modern life, urbanization, Pan-African cosmopolitanism, world beat. And the songs activate other dualisms too: thus, even as the music primes the listener for dance, it is also heavily laden with stimulus for thought – there is the moral message of the lyrics, the temporary emergence of melodic lines from the kaleidoscopic cycle of *mbira*-style sound, and the deliberate juxtaposition of so many symbols of modernity and tradition.

The twentieth century saw in many places a decline in musical performance as an inextricable part of some broader traditional way of life – singing a rice-husking song, for instance, was part of the daily task of preparing food among the Li people in Hainan Island, southern China, before the introduction of electric husking mills.[30] The disappearance of such forms, and the rise of new, commercialized genres, led some in the middle years of the twentieth century to despair. Fearing the impending 'cultural grey-out' of global Westernization, American folklorist Alan Lomax grimly forecasted: 'Soon there will be nowhere to go and nothing worth staying home for.'[31] Mtukudzi's output, at once pointing at the new and richly indexing tradition, shows exactly how the twentieth century's new genres generate and disseminate new layers of meaning. Syncretism, here, is not an uneasy jumble of irreconcilable stylistic traits, but a compositional-cum-production strategy reflecting the point that one can be both African and modern, rooted in tradition and forward-looking.

World beat is not normally painted as a kind of champion instance of positive musical semantics. There are hard questions too little asked about the economic structures that underpin the international music industry.[32] It is increasingly evident that the copyright system brings benefit and profit to the owner of certain kinds of musical product while placing legal restriction in the way of others (though the music industry is hardly alone in this). The same recording technology that brings attention to Tuku beat outside Zimbabwe also brings all manner of external competitors into the Zimbabwean market. The weight of distributive muscle behind these external competitors means that it is easier,

Nationalists, Cosmopolitans, and Popular Music in Zimbabwe, Chicago, 1999; see particularly pp. 294–300. Analysis of the broader genre of world music is provided by Timothy Taylor, *Global Pop: World Music, World Markets*, London, 1997 and Aubert, *La musique de l'autre*.

30 Yang Mu, 'Music Loss Among Ethnic Minorities in China: A Comparison of the Li and Hui Peoples', *Asian Music* 27/1 (1995–6), pp. 103–31; pp. 108–9.

31 Alan Lomax, *Folk Song Style and Culture*, Washington, 1968, p. 4.

32 See also Martin Scherzinger's chapter in this book (pp. 587–90 below).

as Timothy Taylor notes, 'to buy, say, Madonna in China than Cui Jian, the leading Chinese rock musician, in the US.'[33] It is certainly easier to buy Madonna in Britain than Mtukudzi, or even Mapfumo. Moreover, it is currently true that top Zimbabwean musicians can make more money in a single Western concert than in a year of performing at home.[34] As a result, many now live and perform primarily overseas (Mtukudzi remains a rare exception to this), a tendency that some interpret as a further expression of colonial exploitation: where we once deployed military might to gain preferential markets and natural resources, now we use economic power and international legislation to do the same, enticing away the best musicians to provide for our own entertainment in a framework that encourages their voices to be contrasting from our own (which we like to take as culturally and spiritually 'authentic') but not entirely distinct (Mtukudzi's discs sell better than what are sometimes called ethnographic CDs). Whatever the accuracy of these criticisms in particular instances, a striking feature of the last several decades of the twentieth century is that insofar as Western-based music industries and institutions have co-opted non-Western musicians as exotic others for display, this co-option has also given them a platform from which to project their own voices. The global commercialization of world music has not reduced the ability of musicians to wed together potent and affective social symbols that demand decoding by the listener. The eloquent syncretism of the most effective world beat tracks, then, suggests one of the key characteristics of twentieth-century musical change: music's widespread uncoupling from traditional social roles worldwide has hardly divested it of social meaning. Rather, the syncretism itself points at the ongoing search for new meanings, new roles in a world increasingly joined up but resolutely not averaged out.[35]

Change, continuities and conclusions

The changes brought by Western music to the traditions of elsewhere during the twentieth century have been profound and numerous. Western instruments and music have been widely adopted around the world. Where indigenous instruments and repertories have been retained, these instruments and their performance techniques have been subjected to major revision in many locations; while standardization towards Western norms is most usual there has

33 Taylor, *Global Pop*, p. 201. Not incidentally, my own observations during several trips to China suggest that it has for some time also been easier to buy Madonna there than Cui Jian. Cui's dubious reputation among political circles contributes to this.

34 Judy Kendall and Banning Eyre, 'Zimbabwe', in Simon Broughton, Mark Ellingham, and Richard Trillo (eds.), *World Music: The Rough Guide*, London, 1999, Vol. I, pp. 706–16; p. 706.

35 See also Philip V. Bohlman, *The Study of Folk Music in the Modern World*, Bloomington, 1988, pp. 121–40.

also been a less commonly encountered trend towards exoticization. The new technology of sound recording and broadcasting, centred throughout much of the century on the radio, brought new musical experiences to listeners in many parts of the world; it also led many of them to key transformations of musical concepts, as music became a disembodied product and its top performers larger-than-life media stars. Meanwhile, while accelerated human movement during the last one hundred years underlined the continuing contribution of musical performance to migrants' collective experiencing of identity, new transnational complexities appear in the soundscapes summoned up in song and instrumental performance as musicians adapt to the realities of a new cultural system. Intercultural musical contact occurs at other venues also, and can feed back from these to musicians' home communities. Tourist and touring performances, for instance, are contexts susceptible to several kinds of musical change, including the secularization and the professionalization of folk traditions. These same changes are typically reinforced with the rise of Western-derived music conservatories, and the rethinking of traditions that conservatories, state ensembles, or the multinational music industry set in train runs parallel to several of the other shifts already mentioned.

Yet, and despite a widespread decline under Western impact of musical performance as an inherent part of a traditional way of life in many locations, music's social role can hardly be said to have diminished in the twentieth century. Instead, new meanings have been pushed forward by the many new contexts within which music is seen, heard, or discussed. Neither has pervasive change and the rise of so many new and transformed musics necessarily led to a breakdown in musical continuity. On the contrary, several of the case studies above suggest that many of the changes in twentieth-century music-making can be explained as tending towards the ensuring of musical continuity. Technological means, such as broadcasting and the cassette recorder, play a crucial role: learners worldwide not only get to hear the music of another time and place but, potentially, to hear it repeatedly until they can imitate it minutely, and the stars of the past live on through their recorded backlist. Those who have moved elsewhere permanently often retain a deep attachment to the music of their former homes, while many journey temporarily (if only to the nearest concert hall or CD shop) in order specifically to hear the music of elsewhere. Specialist institutions further act to preserve musics, even if this preservation itself equates to a transformation of a kind.

Not all is change, then. A few yards from a street stall selling pirated CDs of Taiwanese aboriginal pop star A-Mei, with their westernized instrumentation and song structures, Mr Chen Shiwen takes up his *suona* (shawm) and, like his father before him (whose ensemble place he now fills), adds its strident sound to the swirling melange of rhythm and virile melody that fills the upper courtyard of the Chenghuang Miao Temple, Jilong, Northern Taiwan; dedicated to Xiqin Wangye, in front of whose image wavers a stream of incense, the performance is a commemoration of ancestors distant and close. Again, every year since 1848, celebrants in Glen Rock, Pennsylvania, have stepped out from midnight until dawn on Christmas Day to make the rounds of the community, singing carols originally imported from northern England. And it is not only religious traditions that exhibit continuity: as English music researcher and violinist Paul Davenport commented, 'You know, we came to this music with ideas of preserving the national tradition, and there is that, but really we keep doing it because we like it, because we like playing music together.'[36]

The Western impact on other musics is clearly a major strand of a history of music in the twentieth century. This impact has been felt in terms of musical language (equal-tempered tuning, for instance, and fixed song forms in popular music), and in technology (the many musical roles of the saxophone, for example). Many genres have been lifted out of previous contexts and roles by the forces of musical globalization, generating new patterns of power, value, and emotion in the process. Perhaps most notable of all, however, has been the widespread westernization of ideas about music, and about the kinds of institutions set up to mediate it. But, in the end, a history of music in the twentieth century is not only a story of change, Western-induced or otherwise. It may be that the key musical occurrence in the twentieth century was not a high-profile, one-off event or stream like the invention of the synthesizer, the development of serialism, the rise of music video, or the excavation of the Bronze Age ritual bells of Marquis Yi.[37] Instead, it may be the much-repeated, often unassuming, realization that each of us makes in some form: that music is something we take recourse to for rewards including personal and collective expression, intellectual and emotional stimulation, and interpersonal fellowship. In that, at least, music at the end of the twentieth century is exactly what it was at the end of the nineteenth, Western impact or no.

Bibliography

Aubert, Laurent. *La musique de l'autre: les nouveaux défis de l'ethnomusicologie*, Geneva, 2001.

Bakan, Michael B. *Music of Death and New Creation: Experiences in the World of Balinese Gamelan Beleganjur*, Chicago, 1999.

36 These observations were made during the author's fieldwork on 2 August 2000. Little is published in English on the Taiwanese genre of *beiguan*. Information on the Glen Rock carollers may be found at <http://www.glenrockcarolers.org>. Paul Davenport, personal communication, Sheffield, 5 July 2000.

37 Jenny F. So (ed.), *Music in the Age of Confucius*, Washington, 2000.

Baumann, Max Peter. 'The Local and the Global: Traditional Musical Instruments and Modernization', *World of Music* 42/3 (2000), pp. 121–44.

Benson, Carlton. 'The Manipulation of *Tanci* in Radio Shanghai During the 1930s', *Republican China* 20/2 (1995), pp. 117–46.

Berliner, Paul F. *The Soul of Mbira: Music and Traditions of the Shona People of Zimbabwe*, Berkeley, 1978 [repr. Chicago, 1993].

Blacking, John. 'Some Problems of Theory and Method in the Study of Musical Change', *Yearbook of the International Folk Music Council* 9 (1977), pp. 1–26.

Bohlman, Philip V. *The Study of Folk Music in the Modern World*, Bloomington, 1988.

Brinner, Benjamin. *Knowing Music, Making Music: Javanese Gamelan and the Theory of Musical Competence and Interaction*, Chicago, 1995.

Cooley, Timothy J. 'Folk Festival as Modern Ritual in the Polish Tatra Mountains', *World of Music* 41/3 (1999), pp. 31–55.

Danielson, Virginia. *The Voice of Egypt: Umm Kulthūm, Arabic Song, and Egyptian Society in the Twentieth Century*, Chicago, 1997.

Fairley, Jan. '"The Blind Leading the Blind": Changing Perceptions of Traditional Music. The Case of the Peruvian Ayllu Sulca', in Max Peter Baumann (ed.), *Music in the Dialogue of Cultures: Traditional Music and Cultural Policy*, Wilhelmshaven, 1991, pp. 272–89.

Feintuch, Burt. 'Musical Revival as Musical Transformation', in Neil Rosenberg (ed.), *Transforming Tradition: Folk Music Revivals Examined*, Urbana, 1993, pp. 203–19.

Feldman, Walter Z. '*Bulgărească/Bulgarish/Bulgar*: The Transformation of a Klezmer Dance Genre', *Ethnomusicology* 38 (1994), pp. 1–35.

Kendall, Judy and Banning Eyre. 'Zimbabwe', in Simon Broughton, Mark Ellingham, and Richard Trillo (eds.), *World Music: The Rough Guide*, London, 1999, Vol. I, pp. 706–16.

Kirschenblatt-Gimblett, Barbara. 'Sounds of Sensibility', *Judaism* 47 (1998), pp. 49–79.

Kong Jiabing. 'Wo zai diantai shang chang tanhuang' [How I Sang Tanhuang on Radio], *Shanghai xiqu shi liao huicui* 2 (1986), pp. 103–6.

Lannoy, Michel de. 'De l'universelle intimité des espaces musicaux', in *La musique et le monde*, Paris, 1995, pp. 59–74.

Leyshon, Andrew, David Matless, and George Revill (eds.). *The Place of Music*, New York, 1998.

Liu Guangqing (ed.). *Jiu Zhongguo de Shanghai guangbo shiye* [The Shanghai Broadcast Industry of Old China], Beijing, 1985.

Lomax, Alan. *Folk Song Style and Culture*, Washington, 1968.

Lortat-Jacob, Bernard. *Sardinian Chronicles* (tr. Teresa Lavender Fagan), Chicago, 1995.

Neuenfeldt, Karl. 'Good Vibrations? The "Curious" Case of the Didjeridu in Spectacle and Therapy in Australia', *World of Music* 40/2 (1998), pp. 29–51.

Rees, Helen. *Echoes of History: Naxi Music in Modern China*, New York, 2000.

Rice, Timothy. *May It Fill Your Soul: Experiencing Bulgarian Music*, Chicago, 1994.

Slobin, Mark. *Fiddler on the Move: Exploring the Klezmer World*, New York, 2000.

(ed.). *Retuning Culture: Musical Changes in Central and Eastern Europe*, Durham NC, 1996.

Shelemay, Kay Kaufman. *Let Jasmine Rain Down: Song and Remembrance among Syrian Jews*, Chicago, 1998.

So, Jenny F. (ed.). *Music in the Age of Confucius*, Washington, 2000.
Stillman, Amy Ku'uleialoha. 'Hawaiian Hula Competitions: Event, Repertoire, Performance, Tradition', *Journal of American Folklore* 109 (1996), pp. 357–80.
Stock, Jonathan P. J. 'A Historical Account of the Chinese Two-Stringed Fiddle *Erhu*', *Galpin Society Journal* 46 (1993), pp. 83–113.
Huju: Traditional Opera in Modern Shanghai, Oxford, 2003.
Musical Creativity in Twentieth-Century China: Abing, His Music, and Its Changing Meanings, Rochester, 1996.
Stokes, Martin. *The Arabesk Debate: Music and Musicians in Modern Turkey*, Oxford, 1992.
(ed.). *Ethnicity, Identity and Music: The Musical Construction of Place*, Oxford, 1994.
'Place, Exchange and Meaning: Black Sea Musicians in the West of Ireland', in Martin Stokes (ed.), *Ethnicity, Identity and Music*, pp. 97–115.
Summit, Jeffrey A. *The Lord's Song in a Strange Land: Music and Identity in Contemporary Jewish Worship*, New York, 2000.
Taylor, Timothy. *Global Pop: World Music, World Markets*, London, 1997.
Turino, Thomas. *Nationalists, Cosmopolitans, and Popular Music in Zimbabwe*, Chicago, 1999.
Waterman, Christopher A. *Jùjú: A Social History and Ethnography of an African Popular Music*, Chicago, 1990.
Yang Mu. 'Music Loss Among Ethnic Minorities in China: A Comparison of the Li and Hui Peoples', *Asian Music* 27/1 (1995–6), pp. 103–31.
Zhu Jiesheng and Xu Yinping (eds.). *Huju Yinyue Jian Shu* [An Introduction to Huju Music], Shanghai, 1988.

· 2 ·

Music of a century: museum culture and the politics of subsidy

LEON BOTSTEIN

The predicament: a musical culture at the margins

From the perspective of the first decade of the current century, the career of high-art concert music during the twentieth century is not a story with a happy end. A significant number of contemporary participants in the world of so-called classical music, particularly journalists, look back at the twentieth century as an era of deepening gloom and decay.[1] The last century, it is argued, bequeathed to the next an unresolved and deepening crisis. The traditions of instrumental and vocal music cultivated in the public sphere since 1750 gradually lost their appeal and a significant hold on the public imagination. Despite striking developments in the transmission of music by electronic means throughout the twentieth century (thereby ensuring music's wide accessibility), classical music moved to the periphery of culture and politics. In particular, new music for the concert stage commanded less attention during the second half of the century than at any time in the previous two hundred years. The suggestion made by Carl Dahlhaus in 1972 that the Mahler revival of the 1960s might function as a bridge between the traditions of the nineteenth century and the avant-garde of the twentieth seems, in retrospect, not to have been prescient.[2] The embrace of Mahler coincided with a shift away from modernism. The accessible postmodernism of Philip Glass, Louis Andriessen, and Arvo Pärt has not succeeded in creating a resurgence of wide audience interest in new music, the brief success of Henryk Górecki's 1976 Third Symphony (*Symphony of Sorrowful Sounds*) notwithstanding.

The causes adduced for the decline of interest in classical music are many, ranging from aesthetic critiques, accounts of the deleterious impact of

1 The sources for this are numerous. See for example Norman Lebrecht's columns in the *Daily Telegraph* from 26 April 2000 and 1 February 2001, and Kyle Gann, 'Death Wish', in *The Village Voice*, 10 January 2001, as well as the writings in *The New York Times* by its chief music critics Edward Rothstein and Bernard Holland during the 1990s. For a different analysis see Charles Rosen's essay 'The Future of Music', *New York Review of Books* 48/20 (2001), pp. 60–5.

2 Carl Dahlhaus, 'Die rätselhafte Popularität Gustav Mahlers. Zuflucht vor der Moderne oder der Anfang der Neuen Musik?', in Heinz-Klaus Metzger and Rainer Riehn (eds.), *Gustav Mahler. Durchgesetzt?*, Munich, 1999, pp. 3–7.

early-twentieth-century modernism, and claims of a precipitous decline in cultural standards and taste in late-twentieth-century mass society. There is a consensus that a radical transformation in the patterns of musical life occurred, creating a sharp rupture with past practices and altering tastes and expectations. The onset of decline in the audience for so-called serious or classical music is dated most often to the late 1950s and early 1960s: in this account, the classical traditions of concert and operatic music continued to gain in audience size and prestige in the first half of the twentieth century, stimulated by access to new technologies of sound reproduction.[3] By the end of the century, however, in the major metropolitan areas of the United States only 1.5 per cent of the radio audience, representing a mere 350,000 people, listened to any classical music at all. Thirty-six per cent were tuning into to a mix of country and western, adult popular music (the official term for eclectic popular programming), and African-American urban music. There are currently only 145 stations out of a total of 13,500 in the United States categorized as featuring fine-arts programming, most of them offering a mixed daily fare in which classical music plays only a small role; few are dedicated to concert music and opera.[4]

The erosion in audience interest has also been measured in terms of age distribution. In North America, for example, the median age of listeners to classical radio has persistently remained in the range of 52–60, which is indeed ancient in terms of the radio-listening and CD-buying public (whose target age in terms of the marketing of popular music is more than thirty years younger). By the 1980s the typical subscriber to an orchestral concert series was described, quite properly, as middle-aged. In contrast to the subscription patterns of the later nineteenth century, attendance no longer constituted a family habit passed from one generation to the next, and there seemed to be few young people at concerts. The interactions within educated segments of society that encouraged audiences in the past to gather and socialize at public occasions of high-art music-making have shifted more to art museums, galleries, and movie theatres. The social allure of concert attendance has weakened. Social acquaintance and coherence, of the sort depicted in Franz Matsch's and Gustav Klimt's 1888 group portraits of the audience (each entitled *Auditorium at the Old Burgtheater*), could also be observed in *fin-de-siècle* concert halls;[5] by the end of the twentieth century anonymity within the audience had become the norm. Perhaps, as the radio statistics suggest, today's elderly audiences can be replaced by new

3 See Roland Gelatt, *The Fabulous Phonograph: 1877–1977*, New York, 1977.

4 Arbitron Inc. Statistics for 1998 and 2001. It is important to note that the radio marketing definition of 'classical music' is neither consistent nor narrow; it frequently includes repertoire considered by concertgoers as pops and crossover music.

5 See the reproductions in Colin B. Bailey (ed.), *Gustav Klimt: Modernism in the Making*, New York, 2001, pp. 74–5.

groups of the elderly. But given the decline of music education in schools and homes, the recruitment of successive generations of adult audiences remains an unsolved problem. In the era before recording, musical interest required some personal connection to the active making of music, and a musical literacy that connected the listener to live performance. Printed texts were central to this dynamics. In the absence of an effective surrogate to such literacy, classical concert music could be doomed even as a form of geriatric entertainment.

The median age and small size of the public for classical music seem plausible as evidence of decline in part because of the stark contrast with the expectations generated by late-twentieth-century mass consumer markets. Success in pop and rock music is measured in the many hundreds of thousands, if not millions, of listeners, viewers, and consumers. One can reasonably ask whether classical music ever had a younger or (in percentage terms) larger audience, particularly if the wider range of today's population and the shorter life expectancies in the past are taken into account. Nonetheless, within the confines of the urban nineteenth-century middle classes, music education – the acquisition of habits of domestic music-making and participation in amateur choral and instrumental groups linked to concert attendance – possessed a prestige and prominence not equalled in the twentieth;[6] the musical culture of the late eighteenth century had been embraced by and adapted to the industrializing nineteenth century. The aspiration to acquire skills connected to the classical tradition spanned generations and involved adults and children alike.[7] By contrast, the rapid growth of pop and rock music after the Second World War was almost wholly restricted to the young. As those who were young in the 1960s aged, however, they retained their interest in these repertories, and so an attachment to the wide repertoire of pop and rock – to its traditions – has become a characteristic of the middle-aged. Through recording, popular music has developed its own history and classical canon.

But the predicament faced by the classical-music tradition cannot be understood merely as a consequence of a late-twentieth-century youth culture. The ubiquity and popularity of sound films and television – narrative scripts with sound accompaniment – helped diminish the pre-1914 aura of the live public performance of instrumental music of longer duration. Insofar as symphonic concerts still feature large-scale works with explicit or implied narratives, the attraction to the concert experience as an engrossing and prolonged exercise of the imagination has become harder to sustain in the face of competition from modern cinema. Television, the video cassette and their successors, from the DVD to the computer, have only accelerated the displacement of the live

6 See Walter Salmen, *Das Konzert: Eine Kulturgeschichte*, Munich, 1988.
7 See Hans Engel, *Musik und Gesellschaft: Bausteine zu einer Musiksoziologie*, Berlin, 1960.

concert and its aura as an anachronism. Music that relies on repetition, atmosphere, mood, and colour in the manner pioneered by Liszt has lost its appeal as a unique opportunity to experience, in public, ordinary time transformed.[8]

In any case, erosion in the significance of the inherited musical culture was already being debated in the 1930s; a mix of technological and social change was held responsible for the weakening of nineteenth-century habits of musical education.[9] Starting with the generation born in the late 1930s, and despite the wider availability of formal schooling, middle-class children (particularly males) came of age without the same participatory connection to the traditions of concert instrumental and vocal music that their parents or grandparents had. This meant that, though numbers of children, teenagers, and adolescents in the West continued to rise after 1945, an ever-smaller percentage of young adults were potential future members of the audience for serious music.[10] By the end of the century new elites of literate, affluent individuals were indifferent to the legacy of high-art music. Consider, symbolically, the attitudes of post-Second World War American Presidents. Bill Clinton and George Bush (father and son) have never willingly attended a concert or bought a classical CD. But Harry Truman, an autodidact without the college education of other Presidents, wanted his daughter to be a concert singer; Richard Nixon played violin in the Whittier College orchestra, dabbled at the piano, and adored Eugene Ormandy; John Kennedy invited Pablo Casals to the White House; and Jimmy Carter (who listened constantly to classical music) cajoled Vladimir Horowitz into playing for him.

In North America, enrolments in university music courses dedicated to the Western classical heritage declined during the second half of the century. Periodicals directed at music lovers, such as *The Musical Leader* (1895–1967), *The Metronome* (1881–1965), *The Etude* (1883–1957), and *Musical America*, ceased publication.[11] Amateurism and the most rudimentary forms of music literacy in the classical tradition within the public as a whole became increasingly rare; they have been replaced by a thriving active engagement with popular music, centred on electric instruments (particularly the guitar) and the formation of countless rock bands by adolescents and young adults. And these shifts in taste and prestige during the final decades of the century coincided with a perceived

8 Leon Botstein, 'Hearing is Seeing: Thoughts on the History of Music and the Imagination', *Musical Quarterly* 79 (1995), pp. 581–9.

9 See for example Eberhard Preussner, 'Ausblick', in *Die bürgerliche Musikkultur*, Hamburg, 1935, pp. 199–210.

10 The analogy here is with sports. The personal experience of amateurism has remained indispensable to the formation of a spectator public, as the examples of soccer, tennis, and golf suggest. Insofar as concert-going and record-collecting are analogous to watching sports, a decline in amateurism will lead to an erosion in the numbers of spectators.

11 *Musical America* ceased publication in 1964, followed by a brief revival between 1987 and 1992.

failure of the concert tradition to reach diverse cultural groups, particularly in Europe and North America. In the United States, concert music fell into a politically and culturally charged chasm created by accelerating demographic changes. Attachment to high-art music had weakened among third- and fourth-generation descendants of the white Europeans (particularly the German and North European immigration from the nineteenth century) whose leadership had sustained the classical traditions as vehicles through which cultural continuities with Europe could be expressed.[12] For immigrants from Mexico and Latin America, and for African Americans, classical music was part of a cultural heritage that had little to do with them. This distance was exacerbated by the frequency with which classical music continued to be construed as aesthetically normative by its older, largely white, middle- and upper-class adherents; the failure to draw a large diverse audience was attributed by them to a general decline in standards of taste. The allegation of bias in this argument of decline seemed plausible since inherited white American (Anglo) and Central European cultural traditions were being displaced as the demography of North America diversified.

Classical music has never had a comfortable place in democratic culture, even in more homogeneous nations with egalitarian ideals. It has been strongly associated with the habits of the monarchy, the landed aristocracy and gentry of the eighteenth century, and the patronage of nineteenth-century robber-baron financiers;[13] it is still seen – with the exception of the occasional mass public encounter with selections from the standard Italian operatic repertoire – as entertainment characteristic of social ambition, wealth, and privilege. This socio-political linkage persists despite countervailing tendencies, including the Symphonic Pops concert format most successfully cultivated in Boston. A few close connections remain between late-nineteenth- and twentieth-century compositional conventions and popular taste, such as Hollywood film music from the soundtracks of early animation to the work of Max Steiner, E.W. Korngold, Ernst Toch, Bernard Herrmann, Lalo Shifrin, Miklós Rósza, and more recently John Williams and Tan Dun. But these links have not widened the interest in classical music. Neither did the extraordinary period between 1920 and 1960 when an intense interaction between jazz and classical musicians, even within the avant-garde, created seminal works within a distinctly American musical canon:[14] the 1930s and early 1940s (from which Aaron Copland's most popular scores date) were the high point of a musical populism in concert music.

12 Helen Lefkowitz Horowitz, *Culture and the City: Cultural Philanthropy in Chicago from the 1880s to 1917*, Lexington, 1976, and Milton Goldin, *The Music Merchants*, London, 1965.

13 See Ronald L. Davis, *A History of Music in American Life, Vol. II: The Gilded Years 1865–1920*, Huntington, 1980.

14 See Carol J. Oja, *Making Music Modern: New York in the 1920s*, New York, 2000.

By the end of the century even jazz had fallen victim to audience abandonment and apathy; like the classical tradition, it has been forced to seek refuge in universities and not-for-profit entities requiring subsidy. This dwindling interest in formerly prestigious and dominant musical traditions was not restricted to North America: in the final decade of the century it became palpable also among both the majority and the leading minority non-white populations of Britain, France, and Germany.

Meanwhile popular music, buttressed after the first decades of the twentieth century by highly successful and increasingly centralized patterns of ownership and marketing, became a commodity susceptible to easy mass distribution. The dance and the hit song were short forms well adapted to modern media, both in terms of the economics of radio time and the distribution of recorded materials, particularly before the long-playing record and the CD.[15] Popular music was able to assimilate diverse influences and project back a strong political component within an accessible, seemingly international style that cut across class and ethnic divides and became the unifying voice of a social group defined by generation. Elvis Presley is credited as the father of rock and roll because he applied jazz and bebop rhythms to the country music he grew up with, just as the Beatles borrowed heavily from black British and American jazz groups for their early compositions. Both put forth music that permitted a wide cross-section of the population around the world to appropriate it and invest it with personal significance, all with relative ease.

With its density, complexity, and experimentalism, classical music – and especially the more avant-garde music written between 1925 and 1975 – suffered by comparison. Even in the large-scale, more conservative twentieth-century orchestral repertoire (such as Mahler, Shostakovich, and Sibelius), the emphasis on the autonomy, structure, and independent logic of musical materials created a negative contrast to the successful synthesis in the popular world between commercial viability and political and social relevance; classical music could not shed its anti-democratic character as an opaque, if not obscure, preserve lacking clear social or political relevance.[16] And the suspicion of an incompatibility between mass democracy and the classical traditions was only reinforced by the dominant attitudes of leading musical modernists after 1945. On the one hand, contemporary music of the 1950s and 1960s, much of it inspired by the Second Viennese School (particularly Webern) and radical experimentalism (in the spirit of Ives, Cowell, and Cage), made little contact

15 See William Howland Kennedy, *Recorded Music in American Life: The Phonograph and Popular Memory 1890–1945*, New York, 1999.

16 For a more optimistic account of the past vitality and the future of classical music in American musical life see Richard Crawford, *America's Musical Life: A History*, New York, 2001.

with such traditional audiences as still existed for classical music; on the other, and despite its resistance to convention, new music gained few converts among the young, even in the tumultuous 1960s. Defenders of post-Webern modernism often revelled in its lack of connection to a larger public and its lack of susceptibility to easy listening.[17] But for those thrilled by the emotional intensity and subversive fashions of the Rolling Stones, cerebral arguments of the sort pioneered by T. W. Adorno against political and social tyranny as manifested in romantic musical conventions, jazz, and commercial pop music were not compelling. The dependence on philanthropy and the demeanour and etiquette of the concert hall marked the art-music tradition (even at concerts of new music) as old-fashioned and socially distant. Classical music signified snobbery and misplaced exclusivity.[18]

This mid-twentieth-century dynamic was only further reinforced by late-twentieth-century trends in cultural criticism, notably within the academy. The claims, following lines of argument developed by Shaftesbury and Schiller, that high-art musical culture possessed superior aesthetic or ethical value were cast into doubt by new interpretive strategies in musicology and criticism, in part encouraged by the example of cultural studies. Despite the presumed influence on such approaches from Adorno, his normative aesthetic biases gained little resonance: rural and urban musical forms outside the concert tradition (so-called folk and popular music) became objects of substantial research and close reading. In terms of analysis and criticism, they have assumed a prestige as cultural forms competitive with that of concert music.[19] But in this regard the career of new concert music in the later twentieth century stands in considerable contrast to the realms of the literary and the visual. In these fields there was a fertile interaction between popular culture and mass entertainment on the one hand, and the genres and techniques of high-art traditions on the other: the appropriation of everyday or common objects, technologies, and issues as materials for art-making is evident in the work of Andy Warhol, Roy Lichtenstein, and more recently Jeff Koons, Cindy Sherman, Nam June Paik, and Bill Viola, while popular culture also became a source for high-art practices in sculpture, photography, film, and video art. In new musical composition, however, such cross-fertilization never materialized in a vital and consistent way, with the exception of a few notable post-1975 developments.[20] Folk traditions

17 Consider Milton Babbitt's 1958 essay for the magazine *High Fidelity* entitled (by the editor) 'Who Cares if You Listen', reprinted in Oliver Strunk (ed.), *Source Readings in Music History* (rev. edn), New York, 1998, pp. 1305–11.

18 See for example Stephen Johnson, 'Larger than Live', *Guardian*, 19 January 2001.

19 See Kyle Gann, *American Music in the Twentieth Century*, New York, 1997, and Allen Forte, *Listening to Classical American Popular Songs*, New Haven, 2001.

20 Gann, *American Music*, pp. 291–324.

and popular genres may have found new status and attention within serious musical scholarship, but the synthesis between popular and art forms all but ceased during the mid-twentieth century.

In this respect, art music after 1945 stands in stark contrast to its own history. The dialectical and reciprocal connections between high-art traditions and popular and folk music, evident in the work of composers from Haydn to Brahms, Liszt, Stravinsky, Bartók, Janáček, Ives, Cowell, Copland, and Szymanowski, were decisively undermined by serialism despite its retention of rhythmic formulae derived from tonal practice.[21] From *Salome* to *Die Liebe der Danae*, Richard Strauss continued to make ironic references to popular music, but after 1918 he was considered isolated from the dominant trends of new music; in the modernist music of the 1950s such cross-referencing essentially disappeared. Equally, popular-musical traditions largely ceased to reference 'art'-musical models. The point is illustrated with particular clarity by the greatest late-twentieth-century success in the musical theatre, the work of Andrew Lloyd Webber. Late-nineteenth- and early-twentieth-century musical theatre owed much to the opera tradition: both Johann Strauss Jr. and Emmerich Kálmán depended on an audible farce-like interplay with high-art conventions, as did Frank Loesser and Leonard Bernstein. Lloyd Webber's scores, however, do not display explicit references to or parodies of either new or older operatic conventions. They do not demand recognition of an undercurrent of musical satire based in a history of music with which the audience is deemed familiar.

In sum, the traditions of classical high-art music increasingly appeared either obscure or peripheral within the cultural currents of the late twentieth century.[22] One further startling comparison underscores the point. Beginning in the 1870s, a substantial cadre of younger middle-class Europeans – many of them university students – embraced Wagner, both his music and the disparate ideologies his music inspired. Their parents' generation understood this as a form of rebellion and self-assertion. Wagner's extraordinary influence, for good or for ill, was debated regularly in homes and in the daily press; the central issues of the day, including national identity, the response to modernity, and anti-Semitism, were intimately bound up with Wagner's music and its influence over the minds of the young. In 1950s and 1960s North America, a comparable concern focused on rock and roll, while in the 1990s, controversy surrounded rap music and the music-based culture of hiphop. (Many young intellectuals today count hiphop as crucial to their political and cultural outlook.) As in the response to Wagnerism, controversy over rap and hiphop's

21 See Paul Griffiths, *Modern Music and After: Directions since 1945*, Oxford, 1995.
22 See Kurt Blaukopf, *Musical Life in a Changing Society* (tr. David Martinelli), Portland, 1992.

moral and political consequences and influence is divided along generational and racial lines; even the overt violence and brutality of hiphop can be compared to Wagner (in whose work, as Thomas Mann deftly revealed, incest was rendered palatable alongside considerable aspects of immorality and racism, no matter how well these dimensions were cloaked in myth[23]). The contradictions in Wagner's revolution are also present: hiphop articulates an argument of rebellion and critique, but its inherent aesthetic characteristics can be understood as undercutting the authenticity of its subversion. Like all its pop and rock precursors, hiphop is market driven and manipulative, demonstrating an enviable and brilliant capacity to pander to the tastes of the public and exploit opportunities for financial gain – and all in the name of a challenge to authority. This pattern is reminiscent of Wagner's strategy and claims for himself.

Whether hiphop can be considered a serious and significant movement is in this context irrelevant; the centrality of it and its rock and pop precursors as a cultural phenomenon is not in dispute, any more than is the importance of Wagner in late-nineteenth-century culture and politics – not only in German-speaking Europe, but in France, Britain, and Russia as well. But there is nothing in the realm of post-1945 contemporary instrumental or vocal music – inclusive of experimentalism and the avant-garde – that has remotely approximated the influence of Wagner in the nineteenth century or that of popular and rock music during the second half of the twentieth. And this decline in influence makes it all the more remarkable to observe the countervailing trends during the same period. In absolute numbers, there are more listeners to more concert music and opera than ever before. In North America and in Europe, the number of orchestras, opera companies, chamber ensembles, concerts, and concert series has remained remarkably high in urban centres, suburbia, and rural areas alike. There are summer festivals everywhere, and more classical music is available on recordings than ever before. The abandoning of public-school music programmes by state education boards in America has been countered by the active support of privately funded supplementary programmes in schools and in after-school programmes that teach instruments. Enrolments in music conservatories have remained buoyant and the production of new generations of classically trained performers with unparalleled technical proficiency has continued at a remarkable pace. More remarkably, the entire tradition of Western music from the eighteenth to the twentieth centuries has over the past quarter-century become integrated into the cultural habits of the middle class in several

23 See the 1905 short story by Thomas Mann, 'The Blood of the Walsungs', in *Death in Venice and Other Stories* (tr. H. T. Lowe-Porter), London, 1991, p. 292.

Asian nations, particularly Japan and South Korea. Interest in Western music continues to grow in China in a fascinating symbiosis with native Chinese musical traditions.

But despite all this, the sense of deterioration continues unabated. What is it that permits the robust and sustained presence of a concert life, performers, recordings, and concert organizations to coexist alongside the perceived marginalization of the high-art repertoire and its inherited performance traditions? The answer lies partially in the fact that over the course of the twentieth century concert performers and performing organizations have gradually assumed a dominant if not exclusive role as guardians of the past. They have become curators of a museum of historical performing art. They are only indirect and intermittent participants in the creation of new work. Their role in shaping a novel, aesthetic, contemporary sensibility is limited to re-creation. Even in the case of opera, a genre that has undergone a marked revival of interest in recent years, the overwhelming focus has been on a canon of works written between the mid-eighteenth century and the first half of the twentieth.

What is new is often limited to the manner in which the historical works is presented. The sustained interest of 'art'-music audiences in music from the medieval to the early classical periods, performed on period instruments, is perhaps the most striking evidence of a late-twentieth-century attitude to the concert tradition as an acoustic museum.[24] The more profound influence of the early-music phenomenon has been not in its ubiquitous offerings of pseudo-antique musical experiences (even to the point of costumed musicians and candlelight performances) but in how it has influenced more mainstream ensembles in repertory and performance practices. The premium placed on authenticity in performance fits neatly into the late-twentieth-century construct of concert life as existing under the obligation to preserve an accurate account of a vanished tradition historically and culturally potent in its own time. The twentieth century, in this view, witnessed the death of classical music as an active contemporary cultural form, and its rebirth as a museum catering to a limited public. Those few who seek it out desire a constructed point of contact with the past, perhaps as a theatrical opportunity for nostalgia, an oblique form of cultural criticism, or merely as entertainment.

The museum function

The perception that the concert and opera tradition is not viable as a living art has itself contributed to its relegation as a museum. New music and living

24 See the essays in Nicholas Kenyon (ed.), *Authenticity and Early Music*, Oxford, 1988, and Colin Lawson and Robin Stowell, *The Historical Performance of Music: An Introduction*, Cambridge, 1999, pp. 151–61.

composers within that tradition have a comparatively minor role in contemporary live performance, recording, and broadcast. The striking stability in the curriculum and pedagogical materials used in the teaching of instruments helps preserve the museum function. In elementary piano and violin instruction, including the popular Suzuki method, the strategy and structure of technical training are directed at developing the capacity to play rhythmic patterns, figurations, scales, intervals, and chords with accuracy and speed defined along traditional tonal lines; at more advanced levels, the sequence of violin methods and etudes from Kreutzer to Paganini has remained unchanged since the generation of the seminal early-twentieth-century pedagogues Auer, Sevčik, Crickboom, and Flesch.[25] With the exception of a few twentieth-century works, particularly those by Bartók, the standard concerto and sonata repertory in the advanced violin and piano classroom is strikingly similar to that which was in place in 1914, while in major international competitions high achievement and originality is defined by a standard repertoire from the eighteenth to the early twentieth century. In the 1998 violin finals of the prestigious Walter W. Naumburg Competition in New York, five out of six contestants chose to play the Brahms concerto and only one finalist, in any of the required genres, chose a twentieth-century work. And even that selection was hardly contemporary: the Schoenberg Fantasy op. 47, written in 1949.

The definition of technique in instrumental training, then, remains tied to a historical repertoire whose end point is the early twentieth century. The connection between the training of performance and the teaching of composition and improvisation has atrophied, rendering the performance of past music distinct from the capacity to manipulate the materials of music for the creation of new music. The close link between performance and composition, a mainstay of nineteenth- and early-twentieth-century practice (consider the cases of Brahms, Bruckner, Debussy, Rachmaninov, or Mahler), gave way to a significantly stricter separation of functions. As a young man, George Szell not only performed but composed (he was published by Universal Edition); so too did Bruno Walter and Otto Klemperer, while Jascha Heifetz, more modestly, followed in the path of Fritz Kreisler, writing popular tunes and making his own arrangements. Conversely, as pianists, Bartók and Shostakovich performed mainstream repertory as well as his own compositions. But as early as 1902 and 1905, only five per cent of the musicians giving recitals under management by the leading impresario in Vienna performed their own compositions,[26] and this pattern became increasingly entrenched as the century wore on. In the later half of the century there were of course composers who were also accomplished

25 Andreas Moser and Hans Joachim Nösselt, *Geschichte des Violinspiels*, Vol. II, Tutzing, 1967.

26 Leon Botstein, 'Music and Its Public', Ph.D. diss., Harvard University, 1985, Vol. V, appendix, table 1.

performers: Benjamin Britten, Olivier Messiaen, Michael Finnissy, and George Benjamin, for example. But with increasingly rare exceptions they restricted their performances to their own music, rather than pursuing an independent career as a performer. Other than a handful of conductors, notably Pierre Boulez and Leonard Bernstein, there were few musicians with parallel careers as top-flight composers and performers.

The advent of regular orchestral concerts can be dated to the second quarter of the nineteenth century, and if one peruses the repertoire in major centres of concert life, one can observe the gradual construction of a historical canon. By the mid-nineteenth century it was already clear that Beethoven had achieved unique status; his works provided the historical anchor in the repertory, while Mozart and Haydn were viewed essentially as precursors. (A Mozart renaissance would only occur in the 1890s; no Haydn revival would take place until after the Second World War.) Yet before 1900 orchestral concerts revealed a stable balance between historical and contemporary music. The composers of the mid-nineteenth century continued to be performer-composers who wrote material for their own performances. The major conductors of the early twentieth century routinely composed, not only famous ones such as Felix Weingartner and Wilhelm Furtwängler, but also lesser figures such as Robert Heger. Conversely, although Richard Wagner can hardly be considered a performer in the class of Liszt, his influence as a conductor earned him distinction as an important performer.

As the nineteenth century wore on, the incipient canon became increasingly resistant to facile expansion, despite the presence of new and contemporary music. As the audience widened and its level of musical literacy changed, its receptivity for and capacity to adapt to new music weakened: the repetition of the familiar led to the gradual exclusion of the new. Gustav Mahler's career provides a case in point. His music was viewed variously as innovative, derivative, and shocking. His penchant for integrating fragments from the everyday and his persistent habit of shattering the surface of sentimentality gave offence. His career and fame rested primarily on his role as an interpreter of the past, as a brilliant conductor of Beethoven, Mozart, and Wagner. Nevertheless, as the careers of Strauss and Elgar indicate, it was possible to be successful as a composer of new concert and opera music before the Second World War. That fact does not obscure the evidence of increasing conservatism on the part of the audience. The guidebooks to the concert repertoire published between 1887 and 1951 show a marked increase of attention to older music at the expense of contemporary repertoire.[27]

27 Compare Hermann Kretzschmar, *Führer durch den Konzertsaal*, Leipzig, 1887, with Max Burckhardt, *Führer durch die Konzertmusik*, Berlin 1909/1918, and Gerhart von Westerman, *Knauers Konzertführer*, Munich, 1951.

The processes of recording and broadcasting created unintended and novel commercial and structural barriers to the propagation of new music. An enlarged audience became familiar with music not by playing it themselves or remembering a live performance but by hearing a broadcast or, more importantly, by playing a record at home over and over again. It was repetition in listening, rather than through reading or playing, that generated familiarity. In the 1930s a generation grew up on 78 rpm recordings of the 'Eroica' Symphony in which one had to change sides for the fugue in the second movement, creating an expectation that such a break might actually be purposeful. Recording gradually influenced performance practices; though it flourished initially as a supplement to live performance, it quickly became the engine by which performing careers and the popularity of certain works were ensured. By the era of the long-playing record and the CD, the familiarity of audiences with a standard canonic repertoire was unparalleled – a familiarity however which was based not on musical texts but on repeated hearings of interpretations from a recorded library.[28]

By the last quarter of the twentieth century, music from the late 1700s to the early 1900s had come to be viewed as aesthetically normative. The task of future generations of professionals was redefined as preservation and restoration: the repertoire of the past demanded to be experienced, examined and re-examined. The closest analogue to the role assumed by the concert and opera traditions was the museum of art, whose character and public function, like that of the modern concert, was shaped during the second half of the nineteenth century; the National Gallery in London, the Louvre in Paris, the Pinakothek in Munich, the Metropolitan in New York, and the Hermitage in St Petersburg were created as repositories of treasures from the past, constantly restored, reinterpreted, banished to storage, exhumed, and rehung by a professional curatorial staff. But there is a crucial difference. When the expansion of the definition of history became difficult for older institutions, early-twentieth-century modernism either entered the major museums or (as in the case of New York's Museum of Modern Art and London's Tate Modern) became the subject of separate museums; either way it represents an integral part of museum culture. By contrast, it is strikingly hard for music written after 1945 to make the transition to a canonic status defined in terms of museum-worthiness; Schoenberg is still considered avant-garde. And the trend in concert programming in recent decades has been towards an even more restrictive construct of accessibility and worthiness. Classical music

28 See Robert Philip, *Early Recordings and Musical Style: Changing Tastes in Instrumental Performance, 1900–1950*, Cambridge, 1992.

has become prisoner in a prison of its own making: the obsession with masterpiece status. Unlike reading or seeing, listening – based on familiarity through recordings – does not seem to tolerate the encounter with new works, either from the past or present. Listeners seem unable to listen the way people read books and see pictures, judging as they go and willing to enjoy works of a wide range of quality, ambition and style. Furthermore, connoisseurship (and therefore the criteria for canonic status) in music still presumes the autonomy of musical meaning; the act of listening is understood normatively as possessing only marginal connections in terms of meaning to words and images.

The repertoire of established orchestras and choral societies confirms this historical pattern. In 1840s New York, Beethoven – whose works were already more popular in orchestral concerts than those of any other composer – was reasonably contemporary; in the 1950s, Beethoven still retained first place in popularity, occupying 12 per cent of the repertoire in major American orchestras. As regards the rest of the repertoire, in 1950 52 per cent of the repertoire was by composers from Mozart to Franck, a figure not very different from that for 1910, when well over 60 per cent of the repertoire of the Vienna Philharmonic was by composers from Bach to Brahms (with Beethoven occupying just over 17 per cent). In the last quarter of the twentieth century first performances of new works still occurred, but repeated performances and the inclusion within the standard repertory of new works became scarce. In the period 1895–1900, works by composers who were alive, or who had died within the previous fifteen years, constituted over 50 per cent of the repertoire of the New York Philharmonic, whereas by 1950 that percentage had dropped to less than 15 per cent.[29]

Despite the economic limitations and constraints experienced by the classical music industry in the late twentieth century, the reduction in the cost of producing CDs has resulted in the availability of more recorded music from the past and present than ever before. However, this library of recorded music (produced in small quantities and frequently with subsidy) continues to grow without significantly augmenting the traditional canon of live performance. The striking contrast between the function of the museum and concert life is that in the museum the repositories of historical material in storage and the receptivity of the public have occasioned revivals and revisions of history; apart

29 See John H. Mueller, *The American Symphony Orchestra*, Bloomington, 1951, pp. 182–252; Botstein, 'Music and Its Public', table 7; and Herta Blaukopf and Kurt Blaukopf, *Die Wiener Philharmoniker*, Vienna, 1986, pp. 218–20. An example of a slow but significant shift from a remarkable balance between new and historical repertoire to a more historical repertoire can be seen in the concerts given between 1882 and 1932 – 50 years – by the legendary Rosé Quartet in Vienna, whose commitment to new music was exemplary, as was its advocacy of the late Beethoven quartets (*In Das Rose-Quartet Fünfzig Jahre Kammermusik in Wien*, Vienna, 1932).

from scattered islands such as baroque opera and medieval music, the concert scene of the late twentieth century has witnessed a far less fluid and inclusive account of the past and permitted less in the way of revival or revision. Once-successful and highly regarded composers and individual works from the huge repository of the past, particularly from the nineteenth and early twentieth centuries, rarely return to the concert and opera stage once they have fallen outside the active repertory. The concert canon, even in historical terms, has gradually narrowed, excluding composers and works that, in an art museum, would be displayed and assessed as highly valuable.

It is ironic that the late twentieth century witnessed an impressive burgeoning of the academic study of music, resulting in more scholarship and publication on the history of music than in the nineteenth century. Yet the unprecedented production of critical editions, alternative versions, and scholarly publications, and the accumulation of new research on the past (all subsidized enterprises), have had less effect on the repertoire of concert life than one might have expected. Nonetheless, twentieth-century scholarly activity has helped legitimate the museum model within the high-art music tradition. Music journalism, from newspaper articles to programme notes, has been increasingly dominated by academics whose writing carries an authority based on scholarly research. Classical music, however, has not emulated the path pursued by art history, where the ongoing amassing of collections and serious scholarship have facilitated rediscoveries or advanced the range and character of exhibitions and the educational function of museums. The key difference is that, in contrast to music, a vital world of art-making outside the museum persists, which promises to increase and shape the scope of the museum over time. In music the rupture between the museum culture and the world of new music remains.

One explanation lies in the distinct trajectory of musical modernism during the first decades of the twentieth century. Modernist innovations in music might at first glance be considered analogous to contemporaneous movements in painting, sculpture, and literature. The extension of tonality and its subsequent abandonment can be understood as parallel to the rejection of realism and naturalism, and therefore equivalent to expressionism, abstraction, and non-objective art;[30] other varieties of musical modernism can be compared to the literary innovations of Robert Musil, Ezra Pound, and James Joyce, or the architectural shifts spearheaded by Adolf Loos, Frank Lloyd Wright, Le Corbusier, and the Bauhaus. But these comparisons are limited by the absence

30 See Stephen F. Eisenman, *Nineteenth-Century Art: A Critical History*, London, 1994, pp. 206–25 and 238ff.

of convincing correspondences between word, image, and sound. Furthermore, in architecture, literature, and the visual arts modernist innovations were subsumed into the larger culture, often as clichés of the post-1945 era. The progressive and radical developments in the style and character of concert music from the period 1910–60 did not make this transition in dissemination: the innovations of Stravinsky and Bartók might be heard faintly, at best, in the acoustic vocabulary of film, television, and advertising. It is not surprising, then, that in the final decades of the century a group of composers including Penderecki, Henze, Rochberg, and Del Tredici abandoned modernism. They returned to an older palette of musical expression, one that circumvented the radical innovations that appeared between 1920 and 1950. Consequently, the place in history and the repertory of the vital but once-disparaged twentieth-century conservative and neoclassical tradition, including Strauss, Britten, Sibelius, Shostakovich and a host of more minor figures, has experienced a striking reassessment as central and not marginal to the twentieth century.

The political economy of musical traditions

But will high-art music survive in this limited role as a museum preserve, a subordinate cultural phenomenon cut off from the living production of new contemporary aesthetic forms? In this regard one economic factor must be considered that helped propel the shift during the twentieth century of classical music from the centre to the periphery, notably within market economies. In their now-classic 1966 study of the economics of the performing arts, the economists William J. Baumol and William G. Bowen hit upon a characteristic that helped doom the inherited traditions of the performing arts to first practical, and then political and cultural insignificance.[31] In the twentieth century, they argued, nineteenth-century patterns of industrialization – particularly those of mass production and standardization – accelerated in intensity. They influenced value systems associated with private and public expenditure. As the unit cost of desirable goods and services continued to fall as a result of innovation, competition, and manufacturing efficiencies, items once regarded as luxuries became broadly affordable. Dishwashers and washing machines replaced the domestic labour once indispensable to the tasks of washing; the cost of such labour (apart from the work of women in families) had been out of the reach of most households, but the new gadgets were affordable. A virtuous circle developed: producers of consumer goods and services experienced greater aggregate profitability as unit costs fell and the scale of production increased, and the falling

31 William J. Baumol and William G. Bowen, *The Performing Arts: The Economic Dilemma*, Cambridge, MA, 1968.

price of new consumer technologies became a standard expectation. This pattern permitted discretionary goods to become, in cultural terms, essential, creating mass markets that helped in turn to determine the buying habits of consumers. Those habits establish the link between money and value, so defining a population's notions of acceptable and tolerable cost.

But Baumol and Bowen recognized that no such progressive efficiencies could be introduced into the traditional modes of concert music and opera production. A Verdi opera cannot be presented properly in the twentieth century in a more efficient and cost-effective manner than it was in the nineteenth, regardless of frugal budgeting. No comparable reduction in unit or aggregate cost can be introduced into the live performance of a Mahler symphony. One might perhaps substitute electronic instruments for acoustic ones in a Broadway pit, but not in live or even recorded accounts of music from the classical repertoire.[32] And if the labour intensity and inefficiency of opera and orchestral music cannot be reduced, neither can the acoustic experience of hearing be made more inexpensive to the end user by market means. The size of concert halls and opera houses cannot be enlarged beyond two to three thousand seats, the range established in the late nineteenth century, if the expectation of hearing non-amplified sound is retained. Even with halls with over two thousand seats, the resistance to efficiencies in concert and operatic music-making render it impossible to pay for the production of music through ticket income. (If consumers were to pay for all the expenses, then each ticket in a sold-out 2,700-seat Avery Fisher Hall for a routine New York Philharmonic concert would cost over $150.) Indeed, rather than falling, the real costs associated with concert life have increased considerably since the late nineteenth century: performers' legitimate expectations of a living wage have increased the aggregate cost of an orchestral concert or opera production. Relative to other goods and services, the cost of continuing the traditions of serious concert music has come to seem increasingly disproportionate, if not prohibitively expensive, to the consumer.

In terms of the priorities for private and public subsidy, higher relative costs coincided with the growing suspicion of cultural irrelevancy. These two perceptions conspired to make the classical traditions assume the appearance of unsustainable luxuries. For private philanthropists the level of support gradually came to exceed a reasonable sense of political, social, and cultural utility: Henry Lee Higginson required less money (in real value) to support the Boston

32 There have been recent successes, of course, with amplified concerts in stadiums with popularized repertoire and very expensive opera stars (the ubiquitous Three Tenors), but these can hardly be considered viable models for most concert and opera performance, and even under the best of circumstances, audience interest has been fickle. An attempt to stage *Aida* in Giants Stadium in New Jersey (complete with a huge floating sphinx blasting the fanfare around New York Harbour) in the early 1990s proved financially impractical and costly to its underwriters; it was never realized.

Symphony by himself in the 1880s than his numerous counterparts did a century later. And though the relative cost was greater, the perceived civic significance of the orchestra was less. In this way the escalating relative cost exacerbated in economic terms an already weak non-economic argument for public subsidy, particularly in post-Reagan America and post-Thatcher Britain: the competition for public tax support in democracies among activities not sustainable by marketplace economics, including aspects of health, education, and welfare, helped make support for classical music an implausible priority.

During the twentieth century technological innovation held the promise that this economic paradox for classical music might be solved. As availability of music increased via the radio and the gramophone, it was thought that a larger body of consumers would develop, thereby increasing demand and reducing the cost of performance. But broadcast and recording did not develop in ways that helped the economic structure of live concert performance: instead they benefited twentieth-century popular musical genres dependent on mixed and electronically enhanced sound – art forms which thrive independent of routine listener contact with live performance. A single studio session suffices, supported by periodic tours and appearances. This has only highlighted the quite antique and burdensome nature of the costs of live classical concert and operatic music. Even for those interested in classical music, going to concerts and keeping orchestras and opera companies alive can seem an irrational extravagance when one can buy a single recording of a Sibelius symphony and conclude that no further recording or live performance is required. An important new sub-group of adherents of classical music developed after 1950, record collectors and audiophiles who may not be regular concertgoers, just as concertgoers may not be regular purchasers of recordings.

Although the mid-twentieth century experienced a remarkable golden age in the broadcast and recording of classical music (especially between 1930 and 1980), these new formats of reproduction ceased to compete in the marketplace. When the CD supplanted the long-playing record in the 1970s and 80s, the recording industry experienced a brief Indian summer as old master tapes were digitally reformatted, new recordings were made, and audiophiles converted their collections. But from the recording industry's point of view a disadvantage of the CD is that, unlike the LP, it is relatively indestructible and does not require periodic replacement. It can also be copied readily by computer. And after the initial spurt, the demand for classical recorded music began to decline precipitously, for a quite small market (a sliver of the record-buying market as a whole) had been saturated. A few figures from the USA will make this clear:[33] in

33 These figures were provided courtesy of Sound Scan Reports 2000, USA.

2000, only two classical CDs issued by Sony, one of the major record labels, sold two hundred thousand copies – both of them pot-pourris of operatic highlights. Even CDs directed at a potentially larger market, entitled *Build Your Baby's Brain through Classical Music*, *Pachelbel's Greatest Hits*, *Mozart in the Morning*, or *The Best of Bach* sold only between ten and forty thousand units. High-quality recordings of individual works routinely sell between three hundred and two thousand copies. By the end of the century a die-hard community of collectors, numbering fewer than a hundred thousand, purchased more than one classical CD a year and subscribed to the magazines *Gramophone* (UK) and *Fanfare* (USA). Recordings of high-art music, including those issued in low-price categories (notably by the innovative Naxos label that specialized in bargain prices and rare repertoire), were routinely subsidized by performing artists and organizations.

As these sales figures suggest, the centralization of ownership in both the broadcast and recording industries and the demand for a competitive return on investment have made the profit margins of either recording or broadcasting classical music too meagre. The aggregate audience is too small. Likewise, the profitability of music publishing in the high-art field has declined, leading to a consolidation of ownership and the demise of independent firms. The value of the historic publishing houses remains in their back catalogues rather than in contemporary music. And few if any items of classical sheet music compete with popular sheet music in terms of profitability. Even the not-for-profit (subsidized) classical radio station has become vulnerable, since the average listener to classical music on the radio spends less than one hour listening and demands short, familiar, standard fare. Retail outlets selling recorded music see the classical inventory as dead weight, occupying valuable real estate without an appropriate return.

The failed competitive dynamic of the economics of live performance in the late twentieth century anticipated the dilemmas faced by the broadcasting and recording of concert music. Sales, just like earned income from tickets, play an ever more insufficient role in averting large losses. In line with Baumol and Bowen's thesis, there was a ceiling to the prices that can be charged, so that the volume and profits became too limited when compared to other opportunities for the use of capital. A comparable ceiling to philanthropy has surfaced as the costs of performance, broadcast, and recording appear excessive relative to the benefits from and prestige associated with other cultural activities and social services. As a result, by the end of the century the self-sustaining industries of recording, broadcast, and concertizing that had taken shape between 1900 and 1945 were in a state of collapse. In North America at least, the era when a corporation like NBC could justify carrying a full symphonic orchestra and luring the likes of Arturo Toscanini back to America to conduct it for the primary purpose of live broadcast was long gone:[34] commercial forms of music that required no state or private support set the standards for the entertainment industry and, more to the point, dominated and shaped reigning tastes. They were broadly attractive, efficient in cost, profitable, and cheap for the consumer. Arguments for public subsidy took on the character of special pleading for failed enterprises that were neither in the public interest nor aligned with public taste.

History since the 1960s has vindicated Baumol and Bowen's argument, which goes far to explain the death of the inherited musical culture. However, their analysis should not be read as normative. When they published their findings in the late 1960s, Baumol and Bowen were attempting to justify the need for systematic, tax-based support of the arts: condemnation of the inherited high-art culture of music for not competing successfully with mass entertainment was not their intent. Rather they argued that the expectation that concert music and opera could compete derived from a misunderstanding of the economic patterns and social fundamentals of the late nineteenth and early twentieth centuries, and that the economic symptoms used to diagnose the culture's dismal health were part and parcel of the aesthetic integrity of the inherited forms of music, dance, theatre, and opera.[35] In short, they argued, the discussion of the future of performing-art traditions had to be shifted back to the need for patronage, and away from the thoughtless application of market economics.

To understand the political economy of classical music one must consider music's historical relationship with structures of power and wealth. Between 1850 and 1950, when the most dramatic expansion in audience for music was under way, concert and operatic music remained as dependent as it had been before 1850 on patronage by church, state, landed aristocracy, and commercial elites. Nonetheless, in the mid-nineteenth century, a subsidiary but lively economic anomaly developed alongside patronage: goods and services associated with concert music, such as piano manufacturing, artist management, and sheet-music publication, became profitable and competitive as economic enterprises, but only as dependent elements in an overall system of patronage. Up to the advent of radio in the 1920s, the demand for live professional musical entertainment and for music in the home sustained performance-based businesses within the market economies of Europe and North America; in addition to publishers, instrument manufacturers, impresarios, and concert agents, leading

34 See Joseph Horowitz, *Understanding Toscanini: How He Became an American Culture-God and Helped Create a New Audience for Old Music*, New York, 1987.

35 See Hans G. Helms, 'Ökonomische Bedingungen der Musikalischen Produktion' (1971–2), in *Musik zwischen Geschäft und Unwahrheit*, Munich, 2001, pp. 27–82.

composers like Johannes Brahms and star performers like Anton Rubinstein, Hans von Bülow, and Jenny Lind were able to live well on their royalties or concert fees.

But patronage and subsidy remained indispensable to this new economic vitality. In North America (notably Boston, New York, and Chicago), concert halls and orchestras were the beneficiaries of private philanthropy. In Europe, the state at both local and national levels supported the institutional infrastructure of training and performance, and where the state was not the primary source of support, private patrons filled the vacuum (as the careers of Wagner, Tchaikovsky, Schoenberg, and Debussy reveal[36]). A specific illustration is provided by the musical institutions of Vienna. The city's first major concert hall, the Musikverein, was built in 1870 with proceeds from a state lottery, imperial subsidy and individual philanthropy; its principal recital hall, the Bösendorfersaal (opened in 1872), was a losing proposition, a marketing venture supported by a single patron, the piano manufacturer and civic leader Ludwig Bösendorfer. Again, the Konzerthausgesellschaft that built Vienna's second concert hall in 1913 illustrated (as Bayreuth had previously done) how patronage and subsidy worked to create an institutional infrastructure in which only a very few individual composers, publishers, managers, and performers could profit.[37] Even in the late nineteenth century, it was only the offshoots of the classical music tradition (particularly popular song, operetta, and dance music) that competed successfully for a mass market.

A contrasted case from the twentieth century is the non-market state-controlled economies of the Soviet Union and Eastern Europe before the fall of communism. Here classical music traditions flourished because of state support: concert music became a centrepiece of public culture as a result of an explicit government policy, with orchestras, opera and ballet companies, composers, and instrumentalists assuming a function (particularly during the Cold War period) as advertisements for and ambassadors of both national pride and communism to the non-communist world. Official socialist ideology held that the great nineteenth-century traditions of culture could be effectively democratized in a society free of class distinctions, and the socialist state accordingly took the place of past imperial and aristocratic support. In terms of education and state support for public entertainment, the concert and opera traditions held a near monopoly, and concert life constituted one of the few sustained

36 Ludwig II of Bavaria subsidized Wagner, Mme von Meck Tchaikovsky, Mahler Schoenberg, and various individuals (including Chausson) Debussy until his publishers could afford to offer him advances against future royalties.

37 Friedrich C. Heller and Peter Revers, *Das Wiener Konzerthaus: Geschichte und Bedeutung, 1913–1983*, Vienna, 1983.

opportunities for public gatherings in which control, censorship, and therefore fear were comparatively non-intrusive. As in Nazi Germany and previous periods of repression (such as under Metternich), public performance of instrumental music thrived in part because of music's apparent absence of ideological content and presumed surface of abstraction.

Nonetheless, particularly under Stalin and Hitler, efforts were made to lend music ideological significance by directives to living composers and new constructs of music history. It is astonishing and discomfiting to remember how invested Stalin was in what and how composers wrote. Few politicians in the twentieth century can compare to Stalin in his engagement with the aesthetic politics of new music: it was he who lured Prokofiev back to Russia (who in turn wrote a celebratory 1939 birthday ode, *Zdravitsa*), who rebuked and humiliated Shostakovich in 1936 in response to the success of the 1934 opera *Lady Macbeth of the Mtsensk District*, and who called Shostakovich personally at home in 1948 to ask him to represent the Soviet Union at an international conclave.[38] Yet it was in the same year that Stalin directed Zhdanov to decree aesthetic standards for the writing of new proper music. At stake in these interventions was a belief that a national culture needed to be created that reinforced and sustained the values of Soviet society; distinctions between high and low culture were artificial and invidious. Insofar as post-1936 Communist ideology could tolerate any Hegelian notion of the autonomy of the aesthetic, it became imperative that the highest aesthetic achievements be made accessible to all. The modernist individualism and experimentation that flourished initially under the rubric of a progressive historical dialectic in the 1920s were rejected; the music of Mossolov and Roslavets was vilified as a species of decadence and bourgeois individualism. Socialist Realism in music was designed to create a synthesis of neoclassicism and nationalism, an objective which took on particular urgency during the Cold War.[39]

Similarly, the role of the state in the support of musical culture in Wilhelmine and Weimar Germany helps explain the prominence of the politics of music in Germany during the 1920s and 1930s. The gulf between left and right mirrored itself in musical controversies. One of the consistent focal points of Nazi agitation in the late 1920s and early 1930s was the need to defend health in music against the avant-garde and renew a nationalist mission: the populism of National Socialism appropriated a conservative aesthetic in German musical circles that had appeared before the First World War. The aesthetics of fascism attacked two unrelated enemies. First, modernism was deemed the

38 Elizabeth Wilson, *Shostakovich: A Life Remembered*, Princeton, 1994, pp. 212–13.
39 See Levon Hakobian, *Music of the Soviet Age, 1917–1987*, Stockholm, 1998.

result of artificial abstract thinking; its qualities were characteristic of cosmopolitan, hyper-intellectualizing Jews, who were incapable of rootedness and the sense of blood and soil characteristic of a nativist nationalism. Second, the Nazis and their predecessors in the 1920s sought to counteract the commercial capitalist corruption of popular taste. Tempting but degenerate musical cultures from abroad were targeted (particularly jazz – the music of African Americans – and that of other lesser races, notably gypsies and Caribbean islanders). After seizing power, the Nazi regime supported composers, scholars, and music educators who pursued the objective of restoring active musical participation in traditional genres against the ravages of modern commerce; the nation required the sustenance of the communal institutions of music-making characteristic of the nineteenth century, particularly that of choral singing.[40] And it followed from this that music could not be left to the trends of a market economy: state subsidy was a political necessity. New music that exemplified a sound Aryan German aesthetic and morality was underwritten, as were ideologically structured celebrations of the German musical heritage, including the works of Mozart, Beethoven, Bruckner, Brahms, and Wagner. The Nazi enthusiasm for Richard Strauss and Hans Pfitzner was restrained: emphasis was placed rather on a new generation, including Werner Egk, Paul Graener, Boris Blacher, and Heinrich Sutermeister. But the best exemplar of the Nazi ideal was the post-1933 music of Carl Orff, particularly *Carmina Burana* of 1937. All the desired elements came together: a sense of community, accessible, compelling rhythms and sonorities, and an unambiguous assertion of a national tradition.[41]

Soviet communism and Nazism arrived at the same point from different directions. They shared the suspicion that twentieth-century modernism, with its rejection of tonality and surface comprehensibility, was little more than a species of manipulation and class-based self-deception. Both regimes (particularly the Soviet Union after the de-Stalinization of 1956) also demonized the commercial popular jazz and music, particularly from America, that was capturing the imagination of new generations. Thus, after 1945, the communist regimes of Russia and Eastern Europe subsidized new music and classical music education in the context of a campaign to suppress both modernism and foreign popular music; as a result, the popular music so derided by Marxist critics in the West as reflecting alienation and cultural fetishism took on, along with blue jeans and other symbols of commercial capitalist culture, a symbolism as

40 See Albrecht Dümling and Peter Girth, *Entartete Musik: Eine Kommentierte Rekonstruktion*, Düsseldorf, 1988, Fred. K. Prieberg, *Musik im NS Staat*, Frankfurt, 1982, and Michael H. Kater, *The Twisted Muse: Musicians and their Music in the Third Reich*, Oxford, 1997.

41 See Carl Niessen, *Die deutsche Oper der Gegenwart*, Regensburg, 1944.

forbidden goods of liberation and freedom. It should have come as no surprise that in the wake of the fall of Communism in the 1990s, the wave of enthusiasm for Western popular culture – particularly music – overwhelmed the high-art traditions that had flourished under state support.[42]

In the United States the necessity of state subsidy first became apparent in the wake of the Depression. Economic collapse eroded the American capacity to sustain the arts merely through private largesse. The Roosevelt administration considered musical culture significant enough to enact a programme of Federal support for composers and music education. Confident in the continuing interaction between popular and concert forms, American reformers placed particular emphasis on the documentation and research of folk music, with the cultivation of patriotism through indigenous music becoming a principal goal: the impulse provided by folk music to Hungarian, Russian, Spanish, French, Finnish, and Czech composers could perhaps be replicated for American composers. In this way the creation of an American sound and sensibility for the concert and opera stage became a national priority in the 1930s, and Roy Harris's rise to fame owed much to this climate. The expansion of American audiences for music lasted into the early 1950s, an achievement for which the policies of the New Deal can take some credit. But the expansion in public support also coincided with an increasing conservatism with respect to the repertoire of concert music: modernism, as Copland observed, was seen as challenging a symbiosis between the classical tradition and music that could be popular.[43] Nevertheless, well into the 1940s, the classical concert and opera traditions still seemed legitimate concerns of the body politic, appropriate candidates for subsidy as well as vital parts of a national culture.[44]

Before 1989, North America reflected the severest stage of loss of interest in classical musical traditions characteristic of capitalist economies and their attendant cultures; communist Europe demonstrated an artificially sustained alternative, with Western Europe representing an intermediary state of affairs. The mid-twentieth-century European pattern of government support of musical culture derived from a modified continuation of pre-First World War monarchical and aristocratic traditions. As early as the 1870s, when the Third Republic completed and opened the Palais Garnier, designed initially to

42 Leon Botstein, 'Music and Freedom: A Polemical History', in *The Paradoxes of Unintended Consequences*, Budapest, 2000, pp. 43–62.

43 Consider, for example, his account of his experiences during the composition of *Statements*, *El Salon Mexico*, and *The Second Hurricane*, in Aaron Copland and Vivian Perlis, *Copland: 1900 Through 1942*, New York, 1984, pp. 217–58.

44 See H. Wiley Hitchcock with Kyle Gann, *Music in the United States: A Historical Introduction* (4th edn), Upper Saddle River, NJ, 2000, pp. 233–59.

glorify Napoleon III's monarchy, public subsidy of artistic institutions and new work was regarded, even in incipient democracies, as in the national interest.[45] The continuation of state and taxpayer support for orchestras, conservatories, opera companies, and their venues long remained an integral (although weakening) part of the modern politics of European national identity. This still holds true for much of Scandinavia, particularly Finland. But among many members of the European Community, pressure to reduce the scale of the welfare state has brought pressure on the levels of subsidy traditionally made available to the infrastructure of the classical concert tradition. The allure, however illusory, of private philanthropy on the American model has become strong. Ironically, when conservatives achieved political power after 1980 (Thatcher, Reagan, and both Presidents Bush, for example), they privileged their advocacy of a free-market ideology over any desire to spur a cultural restoration; they opposed state subvention in matters of culture, even through the tax code, and thereby heightened the economic vulnerability of the high-art traditions. The attraction to a market economic logic, however, is a symptom of the increasingly marginal cultural and social significance of inherited musical traditions within Europe. American-style shifts in culture and taste are evident, even in the growing popularity of Broadway-style musical theatre. By the end of the twentieth century, only a limited number of key locations – particularly Germany, France, and Austria – are able to justify public subsidy of musical culture as a necessary economic strategy within a national tourist industry. For Austria, its chief value today is as an object of tourism focused exclusively on a distant past, a musical museum akin to castles and historic sites.

Since 1989, then, it has become more starkly apparent that high-art music has always stood apart from the logic of the market, depending for its vitality not on voluntary mass popularity but on systems of private not-for-profit investment and public subsidy – for whatever dubious political purposes. The demise in post-communist Eastern Europe and Russia of classical high-art traditions in terms of state support and audience interest has been amazingly rapid: the inundation of inexpensive commercial popular music and a wide range of television and video programmes, as well as the Internet, coincided with access to most forms of modern public entertainment. This, together with the sharp reductions in state subsidy, has eroded public participation in concert music in Eastern Europe and Russia. Music publishing has all but ceased. The once enviable music-educational infrastructure has weakened. State monopoly of the airwaves has given way to Western-style commercial competition. The

45 See Jane F. Fulcher, *The Nation's Image: French Grand Opera as Politics and Politicized Art*, Cambridge, 1987, and *French Cultural Politics and Music From the Dreyfus Affair to the First World War*, Oxford, 1999.

demands on impoverished governments for public subvention of social services has made sustaining the levels of state support for music enjoyed under communism unthinkable. The classical music tradition is now faced with the same challenges evident in Western Europe and North America.

At the end of the century, the principal exception to the trend (and a major source of musical tourism to Europe) was Asia, notably South Korea, Japan, and China, where interest in Western classical music has blossomed since 1945. Indeed the Asian and Asian-American population has become the leading source of high-quality music students in American schools and conservatories and of a new generation of orchestral musicians worldwide. The ubiquitous term globalization does, despite its abuse, reflect an undeniable historical trend. The political and economic integration of post-war Europe and the adoption of a common currency have created the prospect of increased fluidity of labour, open borders, and greater immigration from Asia, Africa, the Middle East, and Eastern Europe. The late-nineteenth-century cultural politics of nationalism are weakening, and an international style of popular musical culture has taken hold: in Europe and North America there is a growing interest in non-Western musical practices. As the pressures of a global economy on local circumstances continue to increase, domestic national subsidies for high-art traditions are under fire as serving too limited a population at too great a cost (the controversies of the 1990s in London and Berlin about how many orchestras and opera companies should be maintained are cases in point). As the demographics and habits of the younger European audience have begun to parallel those in North America, the interest of new generations in pre-1945 cultural habits is declining; the global spread of American-style commercial entertainment does not encourage a sustained, affectionate eclecticism inclusive of amateurism in the classical tradition and concert attendance.

Pessimistic diagnoses regarding the health of the inherited culture of high-art music in the twentieth century became widespread after 1975 and coincided with the rise of a current of neoconservatism and cultural nostalgia. A scathing critique of education and contemporary culture was launched throughout Europe and America. The decline of interest in classical music was viewed as a sign of debased cultural standards; even early-twentieth-century modernism once shunned by previous cultural conservatives was held up as superior and normative in terms of aesthetic quality and ethical and cultural value. But the late-twentieth-century neoconservative account of a decline in cultural standards in musical life represents a dubious nostalgia: the sense that a golden age in music has passed, and with it truly great singers, conductors, and instrumentalists (not to speak of composers), has helped undermine even the museum function of concert life. It is, however, equally logical to view the failure of the high-art tradition to satisfy economic and political expectations defined by mass consumerism as a vindication of today's standards. The real question is whether the expectations of a mass audience were ever plausible in the first place – that is, whether the idealist assumptions of American social reformers of the 1920s or communist policy-makers, that high-art music could be rendered central, through education, to the lives of members of the working and lower-middle classes, were ever reasonable.[46]

They may simply have been misguided aspirations. The traditions of high-art music have always required skills and capacities that are not easily generalized. Perhaps an analogy with mathematics can be made: what if the high-art concert music tradition requires, both for listening and active participation, training and understanding comparable to the study of higher mathematics? Most literate and highly schooled individuals (including the prominent neoconservative pundits) are perfectly well served by rudimentary algebra and arithmetic; they have no need to understand calculus, much less anything more arcane like number theory. In the same way, the public that gave Haydn his success in 1790s London may not be capable of transformation into a mass audience. And if that is the case, then the impression of a comparative decline in the fortunes of the high-art tradition may be false.[47] Likewise the economic fundamentals of the music world in which Mozart and Beethoven worked bear little resemblance to the standards by which the classical music industry is now being judged. The twenty-first century may be forced to abandon the illusions of mass democratization in taste, economic rationalization, and market self-sufficiency generated by the brief commercial success permitted concert and operatic life in the late nineteenth and early twentieth centuries. Nevertheless, the reality remains that in terms of cultural and political values, the will to sustain the level of private philanthropy and public subsidy necessary for a high-art musical culture that depends on patronage has weakened. The perception of economic weakness and lack of sufficient public interest underlines the marginalization of high-art musical culture over the course of the twentieth century.

Bibliography

Babbitt, Milton. Essay for the magazine *High Fidelity* (1958) entitled (by the editor) 'Who Cares if You Listen', reprinted in Oliver Strunk (ed.), *Source Readings in Music History*, rev. edn, New York, 1998, pp. 1305–11.

Bailey, Colin B. (ed.). *Gustav Klimt: Modernism in the Making*, New York, 2001.

46 See Gavin James Cambell, 'A Higher Mission Than Merely to Please the Ear: Music and Social Reform in America 1900–1925', *Musical Quarterly* 84 (2000), pp. 259–86.

47 See Simon McVeigh, *Concert Life in London from Mozart to Haydn*, Cambridge, 1993.

Baumol, William J. and William G. Bowen. *The Performing Arts: The Economic Dilemma*, Cambridge, MA, 1968.
Blaukopf, Herta and Kurt Blaukopf. *Die Wiener Philharmoniker*, Vienna, 1986.
Blaukopf, Kurt. *Musical Life in a Changing Society* (tr. David Martinelli), Portland, 1992.
Botstein, Leon. 'Hearing is Seeing: Thoughts on the History of Music and the Imagination', *Musical Quarterly* 79 (1995), pp. 581–9.
'Music and Freedom: A Polemical History', in *The Paradoxes of Unintended Consequences*, Budapest, 2000, pp. 43–62.
'Music and Its Public', Ph.D. diss., Harvard University, 1985.
Burckhardt, Max. *Führer durch die Konzertmusik*, Berlin, 1909/1918.
Copland, Aaron and Vivian Perlis. *Copland: 1900 Through 1942*, New York, 1984.
Crawford, Richard. *America's Musical Life: A History*, New York, 2001.
Davis, Ronald L. *A History of Music in American Life, Vol. II: The Gilded Years 1865–1920*, Huntington, 1980.
Dümling, Albrecht and Peter Girth. *Entartete Musik: Eine Kommentierte Rekonstruktion*, Düsseldorf, 1988.
Eisenman, Stephen F. *Nineteenth-Century Art: A Critical History*, London, 1994.
Engel, Hans. *Musik und Gesellschaft: Bausteine zu einer Musiksoziologie*, Berlin, 1960.
Forte, Allen. *Listening to Classical American Popular Songs*, New Haven, 2001.
Fulcher, Jane F. *French Cultural Politics and Music From the Dreyfus Affair to the First World War*, Oxford, 1999.
The Nation's Image: French Grand Opera as Politics and Politicized Art, Cambridge, 1987.
Gann, Kyle. *American Music in the Twentieth Century*, New York, 1997.
'Death Wish', *The Village Voice*, 10 January 2001.
Gelatt, Roland. *The Fabulous Phonograph: 1877–1977*, New York, 1977.
Goldin, Milton. *The Music Merchants*, London, 1965.
Griffiths, Paul. *Modern Music and After: Directions since 1945*, Oxford, 1995.
Hakobian, Levon. *Music of the Soviet Age, 1917–1987*, Stockholm, 1998.
Heller, Friedrich C. and Peter Revers. *Das Wiener Konzerthaus: Geschichte und Bedeutung, 1913–1983*, Vienna, 1983.
Helms, Hans G. 'Ökonomische Bedingungen der Musikalischen Produktion (1971/1972)', in *Musik zwischen Geschäft und Unwahrheit*, Munich, 2001, pp. 27–82.
Hitchcock, H. Wiley with Kyle Gann. *Music in the United States: A Historical Introduction* (4th edn), Upper Saddle River, NJ, 2000.
Horowitz, Joseph. *Understanding Toscanini: How He Became an American Culture-God and Helped Create a New Audience for Old Music*, New York, 1987.
Howland Kennedy, William. *Recorded Music in American Life: The Phonograph and Popular Memory 1890–1945*, New York, 1999.
James Cambell, Gavin. 'A Higher Mission Than Merely to Please the Ear: Music and Social Reform in America 1900–1925', *Musical Quarterly* 84 (2000), pp. 259–86.
Johnson, Stephen. 'Larger than Live', *Guardian*, 19 January 2001.
Kater, Michael H. *The Twisted Muse: Musicians and their Music in the Third Reich*, Oxford, 1997.
Kenyon, Nicholas (ed.). *Authenticity and Early Music*, Oxford, 1988.
Kretzschmar, Hermann. *Führer durch den Konzertsaal*, Leipzig, 1887.
Lawson, Colin and Robin Stowell. *The Historical Performance of Music: An Introduction*, Cambridge, 1999.

Lefkowitz Horowitz, Helen. *Culture and the City: Cultural Philanthropy in Chicago from the 1880s to 1917*, Lexington, 1976.
Mann, Thomas. *Death in Venice and Other Stories* (tr. H. T. Lowe-Porter), London, 1991.
McVeigh, Simon. *Concert Life in London from Mozart to Haydn*, Cambridge, 1993.
Moser, Andreas and Hans Joachim Nösselt. *Geschichte des Violinspiels*, Vol. II, Tutzing, 1967.
Mueller, John H. *The American Symphony Orchestra*, Bloomington, 1951.
Niessen, Carl. *Die deutsche Oper der Gegenwart*, Regensburg, 1944.
Oja, Carol J. *Making Music Modern: New York in the 1920s*, New York, 2000.
Philip, Robert. *Early Recordings and Musical Style: Changing Tastes in Instrumental Performance, 1900–1950*, Cambridge, 1992.
Preussner, Eberhard. 'Ausblick', in *Die bürgerliche Musikkultur*, Hamburg, 1935.
Prieberg, Fred. K. *Musik im NS Staat*, Frankfurt, 1982.
Rosen, Charles. 'The Future of Music', *New York Review of Books* 48/20 (2001), pp. 60–5.
Salmen, Walter. *Das Konzert: Eine Kulturgeschichte*, Munich, 1988.
Westerman, Gerhart von. *Knauers Konzertführer*, Munich, 1951.
Wilson, Elizabeth. *Shostakovich: A Life Remembered*, Princeton, 1994.

· 3 ·

Innovation and the avant-garde, 1900–20

CHRISTOPHER BUTLER

The first thing to grasp about artistic innovation and renewal is that it needn't come from an avant-garde, which usually groups together artists who are just a bit more self-conscious about 'progress', and more theoretically aware of the nature of art (or at least of that which they don't like). Nearly all the artists whose works still survive in the canon, however that may be institutionally or politically constituted, have made innovations, and even those who work within what is sometimes termed a 'consensus practice' will have been experimenting, more or less, with the boundaries of that consensus.

Indeed that is what a serious paradigm allows you to do. I am using 'paradigm' here in a loose sense, to mean the framework of ideas which help to define what is normal or usual in a practice. It was 'normal' for Georg Grosz to be taught the paradigms for realist biblical and historical narrative painting at his art school, as it was for musicians at the beginning of the century to understand and reproduce sonata form, with, as Hepokoski puts it, its 'melodic simplicity, squarely period phrasing, frequent cadences and balanced resolutions, symmetrical recapitulations', repetitions and so on.[1] Such textbook paradigms have a certain summarizing cultural authority, and this tends to be a property of those works which are part of the traditional canon, whether imitated in the life class or the counterpoint class. They are what comes before innovation, the traditional practice that confronts the individual talent. It takes a certain social awareness to locate the consensual, the accepted, and the 'normal' – and to that extent you have a clear idea of the risk and the value of going beyond it. Even Matisse, copying pictures in the Louvre and producing in turn an Impressionist work and a pointillist one, or Stravinsky producing in his Symphony in E flat a very traditional four-movement mixture of Tchaikovsky and Musorgsky and Ravel and Wagner, were at the same time making discoveries that would help to take them beyond convention. That was what they were intending.

It follows from this that the culture, and not just pedagogy, can change when an artist successfully goes beyond the paradigm. After Schoenberg's *Die*

1 James Hepokoski, *Sibelius: Symphony no. 5*, Cambridge, 1993, p. 5.

glückliche Hand (1910–13), we have an example of a new genre: expressionist drama in music. It is a work that explicitly challenges the 'laws' of art as imposed by the Academy, along with the order of society as a whole. In it, the artist figure of 'A Man' appears in the tattered clothes of a beggar; he has an open wound in his foot, and is therefore both Oedipal and Christ-like. His first words are the Nietzschean 'Yes, oh yes!', as he clambers out of a deep ravine, and contemplates 'The Workers' who foil his subsequent attempts to work at an anvil. But his hand rises, glowing, and he splits the anvil with his hammer, taking out of it a jewel-laden diadem. This visionary transformation of the artist/worker/hero-as-Siegfried combines two opposing characteristics: on the one hand Schoenberg's self-conscious conservativism in looking back to Wagner and the 'laws' of the past, and on the other his belief in the emancipation of the dissonance (that is, his treatment of dissonant harmonies on a par with the traditional consonances) as part of a necessary evolution within the language of music.

You can also make progress in a less ludicrously self-conscious manner, even if your attachment to consensus practices may seem to be a 'conservative' feature. The Fourth (1910–11) to Seventh (1924) Symphonies of Sibelius, the Fourth (1914–16) to Sixth (1924–5) of Nielsen, and even the Third (1921) of Vaughan Williams, are all formally innovatory, in various ways which were quite obvious at first performance, and posed quite new problems for an audience's understanding. Sibelius's Fourth Symphony, for example, is a synthesis of classicism and Romanticism but also has modernist characteristics, especially in the third movement, where there is an 'alternation of self-contained blocks of music with no apparent linking material'.[2] It is clear that works like these disrupted the narrative logic of the earlier symphony, and so have a number of characteristics in common with the work of other modernists; the earlier symphonies of all three of these composers had shown a far more comfortable embedding of the composer's identity in the community of nationalist tradition. And so we can now value the differences between Sibelius's Tchaikovskian First Symphony (1899) and the remarkable, thematically elusive one-movement structure of the Seventh as a demonstration that avant-gardists are not the only agents of aesthetic renewal. Both symphonies still move audiences, who are not in much doubt about the greater profundity of these composers' more experimental works. It is not just their 'reassuring conservatism' – as compared to the experiments of Webern or Ives or Varèse or even Antheil – which counts.

And in turbulent periods like this, music which takes an even more conservative stance can prosper. You don't have to be a Pfitzner, writing his *Palestrina* in

2 Ibid., p. 14.

1911–15.[3] After *Salome* (1903–5) and *Elektra* (1906–8), Richard Strauss seems quite consciously to have withdrawn from competition with the modernist procedures of others; in *Ariadne auf Naxos* (1911–12) he arguably anticipated the neoclassical developments of the 1920s.[4] The success of the conservative music of the period in tapping the universals of emotional response and admiration for virtuosity, as did Rachmaninov and Puccini, is obvious. Well-established musical genres can sustain some kind of social life, like Proust's aristocrats of the Faubourg St Germain, long after they have ceased to bear the burden of serious innovation. (And in some cases they can do both, as the later work of Fauré, and the remarkable survival of the symphony, both show.) Conversely, much of the overtly experimental work of this period retains very strong links to earlier paradigms.[5] Indeed it is an appreciation of the subtle links between tradition and innovation that can help to make experimental work more comprehensible, as for example in the metamorphoses of the Mahlerian march movement in Webern's *Six Pieces for Orchestra*, op. 6 (1909) and Berg's *Three Pieces for Orchestra* (1914–15).

This link to the past was strongly reaffirmed in early modernist experimentation, and it takes on a distinctively parodic and ironic mode in the neoclassicism of the 1920s.

Music and knowledge

The examples I have given so far mostly affect the form and rhetoric of musical works, but you can use a paradigm in many different ways, and nearly always to extend knowledge. This desire for what may be termed cognitive gain is often forgotten in accounts of artistic innovation, but art can parallel science even here. An obvious example of this process, and one which is for many people stereotypical of the early avant-garde – because of its opposition to conservative ('bourgeois') impercipience – is the investigation by the Impressionist school of painters into such matters as the nature of the actual colour of shadows, and indeed into the nature of light (most obviously in Monet's Rouen Cathedral and Seine and haystack series, painted at different times of day). This led to the discovery of natural constraints; it marks a genuine cognitive gain in terms of knowledge of nature. The Impressionists' effects of light challenged the hitherto conventional language of painting not only through better real-colour

3 See also Peter Franklin, *The Idea of Music: Schoenberg and Others*, London, 1985, pp. 117ff.

4 See Karen Forsyth, *Ariadne auf Naxos: Its Genesis and Meaning*, Oxford, 1982 (especially pp. 258ff. concerning the Vorspiel).

5 See Joseph N. Straus, *Remaking the Past: Musical Modernism and the Influence of the Tonal Tradition*, Cambridge, MA, 1990.

approximations, but also through the development of brush-stroke techniques which put pure colours side by side to be blended by the eye.

The conceptual change here – the motivating idea – is (partly) that we can move from the 'objective' realist representation of the object in an academic painting, to a position of 'subjective' attention to sensation or impression. This change is one of many which are of profound importance for modernism in general, one of whose leading characteristics is an insistence on the subjective point of view. Music could be Impressionist in the same sense: it could express different kinds of cognitive commitment to external reality, for instance through evoking or depicting real-life situations, or communicating a pantheistic attitude towards nature. Seen thus, musical Impressionism ranges from depiction of the baby's bath-time in Strauss's *Symphonia Domestica* (1902–3) to the atmospheric effects found in Delius's *Summer Night on the River* (1911), the 'tone-colour melodies' [*Klangfarbenmelodien*] of Schoenberg's 'Summer Morning by a Lake' (1909, the third of his *Five Orchestral Pieces*, op. 16),[6] the naturally climactic rising suns of Nielsen's *Helios* overture (1903), or the various evocations of nature in Debussy's *La mer* (1903–5), D'Indy's *Jour d'été à la montagne* (1905), and – as late as 1915 – Strauss's *Eine Alpensinfonie*.

The symphonic poem could also attempt to go beyond naturalistic impressionism by allying itself to advanced modernist thought, as in Strauss's *Also sprach Zarathustra* (1896).[7] Here the Schopenhauerian link between music and the will subserves not the degenerate death wish of *Tristan* but the anti-Wagnerian will-to-power of Nietzsche. Strauss's aim was not unambitious: 'to convey an idea of the evolution of the human race from its origin, through the various phases of development, religious and scientific, up to Nietzsche's idea of the superman'.[8] He represents science by a slow-moving fugue, thus suggesting through metaphor that it is learned, systematic, slow-moving, and complex, and somehow 'mathematical'. Another instance of the attempt to ally metaphorical meaning to autonomous music is the (impossible!) direction to the pianist in Debussy's '... des pas sur la neige ...' (from Book I of the *Préludes*, 1909–10): 'Ce rythme doit avoir la valeur sonore d'un fond de passage triste et glacé.' This is a piece which is technically modernist, in that it uses 'destabilising progressions to call formal continuity into question'.[9] But the Impressionist paradigm continues right through the modernist period in works like Falla's *Nights in the Gardens of Spain* (1909–15), and we should note that the thematic

6 The title 'Summer Morning by a Lake' dates from the 1949 revision of op. 16; the original title, added in 1912 at the request of the publishers C. F. Peters, was 'Colours' ('Farben').

7 For an account of this see John Williamson, *Strauss: Also Sprach Zarathustra*, Cambridge, 1993.

8 Richard Strauss, cited in Norman Del Mar, *Richard Strauss: A Critical Commentary on His Life and Works*, Vol. I, London, 1962, p. 134.

9 Arnold Whittall, *Musical Composition in the Twentieth Century*, Oxford, 1999, p. 26.

contents of the symphonic poem always have their representative and socio-political connotations: Sibelius perhaps makes a nationalist withdrawal from the modernist concern with the city in *The Bard* (1913) and the *Oceanides* (1914), D'Indy's *Jour d'été* is nationalist and also regional-pastoral, *Brigg Fair* (1907) is a Hardyesque bit of Merrie England, and so on.

The Impressionist motive thus allied itself to other types of thematic commitment, and particularly to the expression of nationalist or other cultural roots, as in the search for more or less 'authentic' and so 'primitive' folk song. Such researches could be technically emancipating, as in Bartók's collection and classification of folk music from 1904 to 1919, which 'revealed to men the possibility of a total emancipation from the hegemony of the major-minor system' in favour of a return towards church modes, and to ancient Greek and even more 'primitive' scales (notably the pentatonic).[10] Such interests have their origins in nineteenth-century nationalism and in the rise of anthropology, and they encounter modernism in different ways: Delius has one version of this in *Brigg Fair*, Stravinsky another – well enough disguised to avoid detection for some time – in *The Rite of Spring* (1911–13).[11] What differentiates the two is the growth of the modernist interest in ideas of the primitive; hence Nicholas Roerich's scenario for *The Rite*, and the appeal to unconscious folk memory by Stravinsky in *Les noces* (1914–23), which collaged together its texts in a very Joycean manner. The paradox is that Stravinsky made this primitivism more 'convincing' by making an astounding technical advance in his invention and notation of rhythms, way beyond anything to be found in folk music.

Even Schoenberg's experiments involved claims concerning a scientific investigation of the nature of reality:

> Justified already by historical development, the method of composing with twelve notes is also not without aesthetic and theoretical support. On the contrary it is just this support which advances it from a mere technical device to the rank and importance of a scientific theory.[12]

It is not so much the detail of the twelve-tone method that is at issue here, as the peculiar mixture of philosophical and quasi-scientific necessity that Schoenberg, together with such interpreters as Adorno, attributed to it. For Adorno, Schoenberg combined theoretical insight with a technique which not only enabled a new style, but also – and more importantly – led to a 'progressive'

10 Paul Griffiths, *Modern Music*, London, 1994, p. 57. Bartók's work is an excellent example of the balance between the imperatives of progress, and of assimilation of the new to the traditional.

11 On the more or less 'hidden' folk origins of much of the material of the *Rite* see Glenn Watkins, *Pyramids at the Louvre: Music, Culture and Collage from Stravinsky to the Postmodernists*, Cambridge, MA, 1994, p. 98 and the references given there.

12 Arnold Schoenberg, 'Composition with Twelve Tones' (1941), in Schoenberg, *Style and Idea: Selected Writings of Arnold Schoenberg* (ed. Leonard Stein, tr. Leo Black), London, 1975, pp. 218, 220.

cognitive gain. Adorno's thinking on this is conditioned by his concept of the 'historical force' which moulds music, and which music accordingly reveals. In twelve-tone music, says Adorno,

> The rules are not arbitrarily designed. They are configurations of the historical force present in the material. At the same time, these rules are formulae by which they adjust themselves to this force. In them consciousness undertakes to purify music of the decayed organic residue [of earlier styles]. These rules fiercely wage battle against musical illusion[.][13]

The trouble lies in the directness of the correlation which Adorno assumes between music and its social meaning. He equates musical 'illusions' with the 'illusions' of bourgeois 'false consciousness', and accordingly thinks that a purified music can have a liberating effect on consciousness. But it can't, because the relationship between music and consciousness is not one of this kind of message-delivering cause and effect. There is no more than a metaphorical similarity here.

A language of modern music?

Our story so far shows that any truthful picture of innovation is likely to be a collage. How then to give a unified account, which will also approximate to the 'progressive' model of science? The year 1909 saw the first performance of Rachmaninov's Third Piano Concerto and the composition of Schoenberg's *Five Orchestral Pieces*. It is perhaps natural to think that these two works 'speak a different language', one of which is more 'developed' than the other, and it is this linguistic model which has dominated academic discussion of musical innovation in the twentieth century. According to this view, there is an accepted, conventional, or 'academic' language of music at any one time, which innovators extend in various ways – for example, through the Wagnerian chromaticism that developed during the late nineteenth century towards twelve-tone music, resulting in the new set of rules for the syntactic combination of all of these twelve tones which Schoenberg apparently described to his pupil Josef Rufer, in the summer of 1921, as 'something which will assure the supremacy of German music for the next hundred years'.[14]

Before he got to this point, Schoenberg had disrupted other conventions for the language of music, while at the same time trying to keep a formal link to the Brahmsian tradition. For him the emancipation of the dissonance and the disruption of conventional harmonic/syntactic expectations led to a hugely

13 Theodor Adorno, *Philosophy of Modern Music* (tr. Anne G. Mitchell and Wesley V. Blomster), London, 1987, p. 64.

14 Joseph Rufer, *The Works of Arnold Schoenberg: A Catalogue of his Compositions, Writings and Paintings* (tr. Dika Newlin), London, 1962, p. 45.

fertile ambiguity, from which the musical sentence could take any turn. He saw discords as catachrestic additions to the rhetoric of music, very much as Joyce much later put the notion of a (culturally restricted) 'natural language' in question, by mixing together many of the world's languages in the super-saturated polyphony of *Finnegans Wake* (on which he was working from 1923).[15] It is this disruption of the syntactical order of a previously accepted language, hitherto thought 'natural', that causes the greatest distress. Schoenberg and others attacked the previously accepted tonal grammar of music, as Picasso and Braque attacked the accepted conventions of perspective in painting, and Joyce, Woolf, Faulkner, and others disrupted and put into question the history-and-realism derived causal logic of narrative.

The linguistic model facilitates a technical approach to modernist innovation, and helps to tell an apparently 'progressive' story of the loosening of the restrictive bonds of tonality, as Debussy, Schoenberg, Bartók and others enrich it with new strategies, and Schoenberg finally puts the whole system into question. The old language is conquered, and the death of tonality announced: in a lecture of 1932 Webern could promise to 'examine the state of tonality when it was in its last throes. I want to furnish you with proof that it is really dead. Once that is proven, there is no point in dealing any more with something that is dead.'[16] But twenty years later, Boulez would be declaring that Schoenberg, and his form of atonality with its terrible Romantic tendency to melody and accompaniment, was in turn 'dead'.[17]

As the example of Schoenberg shows, avant-gardists who aimed at a radical change of paradigm in the modernist period were more and more dependent upon being written into a progressive history of art, which sees changes in technical procedures as crucial. The many pictures painted by Braque and Picasso in this period can also be seen as breaking down the conventions for perspectival representation in a manner which can be made to seem entirely logical or 'progressive' in retrospect.[18] Each picture or musical work is analysed by critics as the 'appropriate' (or even 'inevitable') successor to another, so that the more and more emancipated treatment of the spatial interval or chord could free the pictorial space and musical narrative for new and contradictory implications, which in turn demanded further investigation. Schoenberg showed an acute

15 There are in fact in the modernist period relatively few cases of *linguistic* experimental discovery through the disruption of the grammar of a natural spoken language, so as to bring about stylistic changes. Mallarmé is the great precursor here – in an inflected language, which is easier – to be followed by Gertrude Stein's naive minimalist repetitions, Stramm's stripping away of grammatical connectives, Dada poetry, and Joyce's polysemy.

16 Hans and Rosaleen Moldenhauer, *Anton von Webern: A Chronicle of His Life and Work*, London, 1978, p. 88.

17 Pierre Boulez, 'Schoenberg is Dead', in *Stocktakings from an Apprenticeship* (tr. Stephen Walsh), Oxford, 1991, p. 212.

18 For an extended sequence of pictures see, for example, the exhibition catalogue *Picasso and Braque: Pioneering Cubism* (ed. William Rubin), New York, 1989.

awareness of this kind of history in attacking past 'laws' or 'codes' which he saw (with some exaggeration) as having 'legislated' for German music.

Useful though they are for purposes of academic exegesis, however, progressive linguistic models don't do nearly enough to explain the pluralist implications of experimental practices in their own time. The very idea of historical 'progress' is an essentially intolerant and illiberal one which may have misled many in the modern period, because an eclectic pluralism was in fact becoming dominant – with Strauss and Mahler so to speak on the Romantic and self-expressive side, Stravinsky on the 'objective' becoming neoclassical side, and Schoenberg awkwardly poised in between. All three traditions became and remain available, and it is nonsensically unempirical to invent a dialectic in which the Schoenberg school really bore the 'burden of history', while neoclassicism with all its cultural motivations isn't allowed to count. Imagine deciding which of Joyce, Woolf, or Lawrence, or Picasso, Kandinsky, Ernst, or Mondrian, was the more 'progressive' – let alone asking the same question of Wells, Shaw, and others who really did think of themselves as politically progressive at least – and then having to decide which kind of novel or canvas one 'ought' to produce, in the light of a choice between them! In all such cases the differences of technique are obvious, but the long-term cultural significance which will establish works in the canon is far less so – particularly given the growing dominance of American culture, which lets the far more eclectic methods of innovatory modernists like Ives, Varèse, and Cage into the picture. As Derek Scott puts it, 'Measured in terms of social significance, the twelve-bar blues has been of more importance to twentieth-century music than the twelve-note row.'[19] Just as tonal genres persist, so do rationalist modes of writing and representational modes of painting;[20] it is only a crippling aestheticist concentration on advances in technique – or its too-frequent corollary in the 1960s, the pursuit of the maximally systematic, unified musical work – and an ignorance of advances in more general kinds of conceptual thinking, that could lead us to believe that Schoenberg and his allies (or for that matter anyone else) were alone on the true or 'necessary' line of progress. There may be an obvious technical connection between *Tristan* and *Elektra* and *Erwartung*, but as I shall try to show below, what really *licenses* their similarities in technique is ideas about the representation of women and sex.

There are a number of different strands or genealogies to be looked at here. The major technical changes of *c.*1912 – the liberation from thematicism in Debussy's *Jeux*, the emancipation of dissonance in Schoenberg's *Pierrot lunaire*,

19 Derek Scott (ed.), *Music, Culture and Society: A Reader*, Oxford, 2000, p. 11.
20 See, for example, Brendan Prendeville, *Realism in Twentieth-Century Painting*, London, 2000.

and the revolutionary metrics and rhythms of *The Rite* – could and did lead off in all sorts of directions, not all of them atonal. All three were liberating, and all three posed new problems for composers of all sorts of persuasions. Technical changes like this worked within all sorts of frameworks of ideas, making possible, for example, the mystical meanderings of Skryabin and Szymanowski, the anguish of Berg's *Wozzeck* (1917–22), the urban savagery of Bartók's *Miraculous Mandarin* (1918–24), and many other scenarios.

Music and the unconscious

As is often pointed out, a study of the (progressive) 'grammar' of music can also fail to attend to the ways in which the music is actually heard. It doesn't pay nearly enough attention to the rhetorical effects of innovatory works upon the intelligent public. Alexander Goehr has summarized the effect of the major changes outlined above, as resulting in a music in which 'Continuity is fragmented or constructed of events unrelated to each other, pitch succession too complex to be memorable, and constructional procedures too difficult to be perceived as aural logic.'[21] It is important to realise that even trained musicians felt this. Thus Nielsen thought this of Schoenberg:

> an honourable musician . . . what I understand of him I find remarkable. So there's some reason to suppose that what I don't understand is also good. I just don't understand it. What I have against the very newest direction in music is that design itself, construction, development, the line are completely missing. For the most part we are left with a succession of trivia, fragments, a march on the spot.[22]

We need an analysis, then, of the reasons for the initial incomprehensibility of innovative work, and of the ways in which they can be overcome – even although atonality, like Cubism, looks as though it defies our 'normal' modes of perception.

In this context I mean by atonality what Jim Samson means: not just the use of discord, but the refusal to coordinate a work by reference to a central tonic.[23] It is a genuinely new paradigm, not the elaboration of an older one; and significantly, such procedures can allow the work to become to some degree about itself, rather than about such matters as an adequacy of representation or suggestion, or even particular emotional effects. Hence the emphasis by some

21 Alexander Goehr, cited in Whittall, *Musical Composition in the Twentieth Century*, p. 1.

22 Nielsen, interview with Axel Kjerulf in January 1922, cited in David Fanning, *Nielsen: Symphony no. 5*, Cambridge, 1997, p. 98. Compare a diary entry by Sibelius for 4 February 1914: 'Mahler's Fifth Symphony and Schoenberg's *Kammersymphonie*. I suppose that one can see things in this way. But it does hurt the ears. A result achieved by excessive cerebration.' (Cited in Hepokoski, *Sibelius: Symphony no. 5*, p. 17.)

23 Jim Samson, *Music in Transition: A Study of Tonal Expansion and Atonality, 1900–1920*, London, 1977, pp. 151ff.

on the 'reflexivity' of modernist, and postmodernist, experimental works: we seem to be asked to think about (the critical categories of) space and tonality. But the pleasure of Cubist painting depends not a little upon our appreciation of varying *grades* of tension between abstraction – which breaks the 'rules' or syntax of perspective, and leads to 'contradictions' – and our attempt to resist this abstraction in the search for a good old traditional representational function for the image. It is not surprising, then, that Roger Scruton has recently argued that our listening to atonal music similarly depends on the extent to which we can nevertheless impose, even if only locally, tonal types of response upon it.[24] This kind of consideration of the psychology of the work's effects can tell us more about the nature of innovation in the arts than technical analysis, because all technical changes ultimately need a psychological point or pay-off for an audience if they are to survive. (New but rhetorically ineffective new schemes are not too difficult to devise; Futurist music and much later serial music are good examples.)

For example, a listener to Debussy's *Prélude à 'L'après-midi d'un faune'* in 1894 might well have felt (correctly) that there wasn't a clear theme or melody that underwent a clear kind of variation or development. The piece seems fragmentary and unstable. The listener has to get used to the *idea* that in listening to this music, a concentration on the evocation of a mood, rather than on the telling of a thematic story, will do. It's not Liszt's *Les Préludes* (1849–55), to a story of life and death, it's the evocation of a very (or perhaps rather too vaguely) sexy state of mind, and we need a great sensitivity to minute shifts of feeling to get the point (as Debussy's opera *Pelléas et Mélisande* would confirm in 1902). The simplifying return to story for *L'après-midi* came only in 1912, in the choreography for the Diaghilev–Nijinsky ballet of the same name, by which time the mood and methods of the music had been well understood.

Similar problems of continuity came with *La mer*, which we can now hear as a highly organized symphonic work but which in its time clearly turned against the logic of the harmonic and thematic development to be found in the Austro-German classical symphony: another basic convention rejected. This can be more or less difficult, and more or less emotionally demanding: Debussy's *Jeux* is as radical as Stravinsky's *Symphonies of Wind Instruments* in disrupting formal continuity, but it is now much easier to follow, perhaps because it doesn't so much juxtapose its sections as continuously metamorphose its themes.[25] Robbed of an internal narrative logic, the audience has to look for something else which is typical of modernism – an emotional coherence which

24 Roger Scruton, *The Aesthetics of Music*, Oxford, 1997, pp. 294–307.

25 Schoenberg also thought (in 1949, with some hindsight into the history of modernism) that he too had learnt 'to link ideas together without the use of formal connections, merely by juxtaposition' (*Style and Idea*, p. 78).

can rationalize and put together apparently random associative fragments. And this move from causal narrative and logical argument to psychological association is one of the central developments of the period, supported by a radical, broadly Freudian reassessment of the nature of the person. Eliot's 'The Love Song of J. Alfred Prufrock' (1909–11, published 1915) also seems to express his ideas by mere juxtaposition and association, and so to have his mind all over the place; it's only when you tumble to what he is feeling, in *his* erotic reverie on a Boston afternoon (including an extreme sexual timidity which is preventing him from going to a tea-party), that you can appreciate that the various images and allusions of the poem make a psychological sense.

The new techniques were often used, then, in an attempt to express new notions of psychology and identity, and particularly of the flow of inner consciousness. This is partly a consequence of the extraordinary modernist turn to reliance upon point of view rather than on any form of 'omniscient' narration, and partly a consequence of new thinking about dreams, identity, and madness. There is an important stylistic match between mental disturbance and alienation, and an accompanying music which goes beyond conventional tonality. Once more there is a historical continuity between Impressionism, symbolism, and modernist experiment.

As a symphonic poem for string sextet, for example, Schoenberg's *Verklärte Nacht* (1899) develops the disturbing implications of Wagner's chromatic weakening of traditional harmony, which in *Tristan* had made the analogy between harmonic resolution (or the lack of it) and sexual fulfilment (or the lack of it) peculiarly explicit for most listeners. *Verklärte Nacht* is based on a poem from Richard Dehmel's *Weib und Welt* of 1896, which concerns a man and a woman walking though a wood at night. She confesses she is pregnant, but not by him, and is tormented by guilt. He comforts her, and accepts the child. She feels redeemed, and the night becomes transfigured. These events provide the basis for a five-part musical scheme – of introduction, confession, forgiveness, love duet, and apotheosis – whose operatic affiliations are obvious. Schoenberg recreates Wagner's 'short motives, with their possibility of changing the composition [*Satz*] as quickly and as often as the exact detail of mood requires'.[26] As Arthur Symons put it: 'Wagner's aim at expressing the soul of things is still further helped by his system of continuous, unresolved melody. The melody . . . is the whole expression of the subconscious life, saying more of himself than any person of the drama has ever found in his soul.'[27] Schoenberg thus approached a stream-of-consciousness technique. The main climax of the

26 Schoenberg in an interview of 1909, cited in Jelena Hahl-Koch (ed.), *Arnold Schoenberg, Wassily Kandinsky: Letters, Pictures and Documents*, London, 1984, p. 179.

27 From Symons' 'Bayreuth' (published in *Dome* 4 (September 1899), pp. 147–8), cited in Alan Robinson, *Poetry, Painting and Ideas, 1885–1914*, London, 1985, p. 246.

work comes in an operatic dialogue between the high strings (for the woman) and the low (for the man); the leitmotif technique used here had been described by Wagner himself in highly sexualized terms, with its themes 'restlessly emerging, developing, separating, then again reuniting, growing, diminishing, finally clashing, embracing and well nigh engulfing one another'.[28] *Verklärte Nacht* is a typically symbolist attempt to create this kind of fluctuating erotic response. Its interest in anxious self-division is of immense importance for later modernism, but it tends here to the gloomy, sigh-heaving, guilt-ridden mood of so much turn-of-the-century love poetry – a true *Nervenkunst* (art of the nerves). Love may transfigure, but the lovers still carry the heavy burden of cosmic pessimism, as they are 'borne along' by those 'nameless instinctual pressures' which Schoenberg's music attempts to express.

The 'discovery' of the unconscious (and the evidence offered for it by symbolist writers like Laforgue, as well as by Freud and Jung) gave rise in all the arts to technical changes aimed at an adequacy to this new theory of the nature of the person. Adorno endorses this new kind of subjectivity in Schoenberg's early atonal works: 'Passions are no longer simulated, but rather genuine emotions of the unconscious – of shock, of trauma – registered without disguise through the medium of music'; again, the first atonal works are 'psychoanalytic dream case studies'.[29] This, however, is not necessarily an improvement.

In pursuing the new subjectivity, writers could abandon the hitherto orthodox, grammatical, 'logical' forms of formal speech and writing, and turn towards the rhythms, abrupt topic shifts, associative patterns, mixtures of thought and sensory perception, syntactic disruptions, obsessions, and preoccupations which were believed to be present in pre-speech thought. *Pierrot lunaire* (1912), for example, uses fairly conventional symbolist texts, which it then disrupts for modernist expressionist purposes. In the programme book to the first performance the poem texts were described in Novalis's words as:

> tales where there would be no coherence, and yet associations – like dreams; poems that are simply euphonious and full of beautiful words, but with no meaning or coherence whatever . . . Such true poesy can have at most, an allegorical meaning, as a whole, and an indirect effect, like music.[30]

28 Richard Wagner on Act III of *Tristan und Isolde*, in 'Ludwig Schnorr von Carolsfeld' in his *Schriften*, VIII, 186; cited in Elliot Zuckermann, *The First Hundred Years of Wagner's Tristan*, New York, 1964, p. 19, an invaluable study of the influences I am sketching.

29 Adorno, *Philosophy of Modern Music*, p. 39.

30 It is hard to believe that Schoenberg thought Guiraud/Hartleben had really provided him with texts of anything like this kind. The fragmentation and dislocation are really brought about by his accompaniment, and the extraordinary range of emotionally contradictory speech acts demanded of the singer (screaming, groaning, crying, and so on).

Even an orchestral work like Webern's *Six Pieces for Orchestra*, op. 6 (described to Schoenberg on 16 June 1909 as 'In the instrumentation, almost entirely pure colours') was supposed to express a distraught, personal state of mind. Webern described the autobiographical basis of the work in a letter on 13 January 1913, a few weeks before the first performance, conducted by Schoenberg: 'The first piece is to express my frame of mind when I was still in Vienna, already sensing the disaster, yet always maintaining the hope that I would find my mother still alive . . . The third piece conveys the fragrance of the Erica [heather] . . . The fourth piece I later entitled *marcia funebre*', and it expresses his feelings as he walked behind her coffin to the cemetery.[31]

Some of the most culturally significant examples of such changes are to be found in the representation of the 'hysterical woman' in the literature, painting, and opera of this period, from *Pelléas* to *Salome* to *Elektra* – the last of whom is a '*wilde Katze*' who urges her attendants to eat fat and sweets and go to bed with their men, pities her sister Chrysothemis for her 'normal' desire to have children, and would rather breed a vulture in her own body. She is a riddling interpreter of dreams, and the 'hound' upon her mother Klytemnestra's traces. Similarly the anonymous woman of Schoenberg's *Erwartung* (1909) was conceived in a psychoanalytical context, and combines the new associative psychology, in a fragmented, disrupted text, full of unfinished sentences, with an equally radical disruption of tonal logic in the music which accompanies her;[32] the woman protagonist of the painter Kokoschka's play *Mörder Hoffnung der Frauen*, written in 1909, is equally hysterical, finding her most effective realization in Hindemith's operatic setting of this text (1919). These representations of women arose in a society in which female sexuality was seen as immensely threatening (hence for example Freud's intensely misogynistic, Schopenhauer-inspired desire to see women as inferior versions of men), and they have recently been much studied.[33] Susan McClary goes so far as to argue that in *Erwartung* 'atonality reigns in supreme, unchallenged lunacy'[34] and that 'the signs of their madness are usually among the favourite techniques of the avant-garde'. Women are at the 'extremes' and most successfully 'exceed the verbal component' of dramatic music; for her, this is 'genius', 'projected on to women'. On the basis of examining the metaphors in Schoenberg's *Theory of Harmony*, McClary even comes to the surely preposterous conclusion that his

31 Moldenhauer, *Anton von Webern*, London, 1978, p. 126.

32 See Christopher Butler, *Early Modernism: Literature, Painting, and Music in Europe 1900–1916*, Oxford, 1994, pp. 111–15, for a summary of the notion of the self involved in this kind of work.

33 See for example Bram Dijkstra, *Idols of Perversity*, Oxford, 1986, and Peter Gay, *The Education of the Senses*, Oxford, 1984, pp. 169–225.

34 Susan McClary, 'Excess and Frame: The Musical Representation of Madwomen', in *Feminine Endings: Music, Gender and Sexuality*, Minneapolis, 1991, pp. 80ff.

emancipation of the dissonance 'is self-consciously presented as the liberation of the female lunatic, of the genuine moment of desire and dread that had driven most nineteenth-century narratives'.[35]

Music and social meaning

My concern so far has been with musicians as *self-conscious innovators*, whose 'experimental' aims arise out of their thinking the newest thoughts, much as their contemporaries, Proust, Pound, Marinetti, Joyce, Stein, and Eliot did before the war, and Woolf, Tzara, Breton, and Beckett after it. This is because musicians like Debussy, Webern, and Schoenberg were serious readers of the ideas of their time; Webern, for example, reports his enthusiasm for Strindberg and Weininger in the summer of 1909.[36] Again, Stravinsky was so well connected that he must have picked up plenty of new ideas in conversation, but he too was a serious reader.[37] Delius too was typical of his generation in his interest in the 'modern'; hence his enthusiasm for Nietzsche, Whitman, and others. Musicians who worked with text, for song recitals, ballet scenarios, and opera, were involved with developing other modernist ideas: of myth, of memory and its functioning, of (cyclical) history, of symbol (as it developed from late-nineteenth-century symbolism into psychoanalysis), and of the declining, mythological status of religion, often along with a corresponding and compensatory interest in the occult.

In all these developments the place of musical expression within social formations is always also in question; we have already noted how Schoenberg's struggle for the 'internal' or technical evolution of 'music as language' went along with a view of music as an art embodying the struggle of the Wagnerian–Nietzschean genius who demands cultural changes on a far broader scale. But such exalted notions did not always lie behind modernist developments which, as the means of profitable communication within a mass society grew, changed the relationship between the 'high' and the 'low' cultures. Even *Pierrot lunaire* (1912) is as much cabaret act as song recital. In this period the 'high-cultural' status of traditional, 'classical' music is put into question. Popular music within

35 McClary, *Feminine Endings*, pp. 101, 107. It must be remembered that I am here concentrating on the relationship between innovatory technique and the new ideas, of the unconscious, of hysteria and so on, which motivate them. In a fuller story of the changing representation of women through the early-modernist period a much broader set of considerations would come to the fore, and we would for example have to pay considerable attention to relatively conservative works like Charpentier's realistic opera *Louise*; see, for example, Jane F. Fulcher, *French Cultural Politics and Music From the Dreyfus Affair to the First World War*, Oxford, 1999, pp. 77–97.

36 See Moldenhauer, *Anton von Webern*, p. 109.

37 As Stephen Walsh makes abundantly clear in his *Stravinsky: A Creative Spring. Russia and France 1882–1934*, London, 1999.

the classical style is nothing new (it is there, transformed, in Mozart), but under modernist pressures many musical works become far more obviously hybrid, as different styles are mixed together within a single work. The presence of popular elements disturbed many listeners to Mahler, because he seemed to bring about a potentially bathetic drop in the status of the symphony; but by the time of the cooperation between Diaghilev, Cocteau, Picasso, and Satie in *Parade* (1917), we are aware of a much larger transition within modernist culture towards the incorporation of the popular, on its own terms, into works not played in 'popular' surroundings, and with some typically modernist indications of ironic distance – rather like the Laforguian tone and the comic modifications made by Eliot to some of his most 'serious' allusions. Stravinsky's use of popular music in *Petrushka* (1910–11) and his rewriting of Pergolesi (and others) in *Pulcinella* (1919–20), and the (later) use by Les Six of popular forms and styles, all keep a kind of semi-parodic control of their popular elements.[38] This interaction is common to all the arts. It is obvious in the poems of Apollinaire (much set by the composers of Les Six), while in Cubist painting we can (now) see all sorts of 'pop art' elements in the slyly witty incorporation of popular material – newspapers, song titles, music, wine bottles – for apparently formal but actually often subversive purposes.[39]

Much early-twentieth-century music continued to be written for contexts which remained part of the abstract, 'philosophical', nineteenth-century concert-hall tradition of quartets, symphonies, symphonic poems, and so on, where innovations were far more likely to be 'internal', linguistic ones (as for example in the way that Bartók's string quartets move beyond those of his predecessors). But this was still part of what is now seen as a 'cultural politics' involving the negotiation of new relationships between the highbrow and the popular, and giving a place to avant-garde movements which clearly involved them in the politics of the time. Avant-garde artists (and their associates) are therefore seen in all sorts of ways: as outrageously confrontational and anti-bourgeois; or as a clique to be understood in relation to the (mere) politics of the art world; or as part of a self-perpetuating business within the museum/gallery complex, the usual battles of the opera house, or simply the fight to get published at all.[40] Or they may be seen as utopian revolutionaries, imagining the impossible as Schoenberg did, or as irrational, clownish, or pathetically marginal entertainers, irrelevant to the 'mainstream' of culture (as the Futurists were often seen), or as the rising generation in conflict with

38 See, for example, Watkins, *Pyramids at the Louvre*, pp. 134–215, 277–310, and Nancy Perloff, *Art and the Everyday: Popular Entertainment and the Circle of Erik Satie*, Oxford, 1991.

39 See Jeffrey Weiss, *The Popular Culture of Modern Art*, New Haven, 1994.

40 See, for example, Lawrence Rainey, *Literary Modernism: Literary Elites and Public Culture*, New Haven, 1998, who seems to disapprove of such attempts to make money.

its elders, involved in a Freudian psychomachia. And so on. There is a strong (leftist) tradition in academic criticism which *defines* the avant-garde as those artistic movements which are in a critical position with respect to the rest of society.

Innovators therefore do not take the risk of making experiments without a social purpose; they are involved to a greater (Stravinsky) or smaller (Ives) degree in acts of communication which are part of larger institutional arrangements, within which all of these changes have to have some use and some economic value. Musicians may be located within a fully institutionalized avant-garde – for example, the Futurist experimenters with their 'art of noise' – or be isolated drop-outs, or they may be inclined to various forms of compromise, and even to enter the embrace of a commercial culture (as did Stravinsky with Diaghilev, Korngold at the movies, and Weill on Broadway). They are all making changes which they calculate as more or less acceptable to institutions. And these latter also can change with them, as for example Diaghilev's crowded and crowd-pulling *Polovtsian Dances* (staged in 1909) metamorphosed themselves into the equally orgiastic but now avant-gardist uproar of *The Rite of Spring*.

Much recent scholarship has accordingly taken upon itself the demonstration of the ways in which works of art are not just concerned with the broadly philosophical universals of language, the self, and rationality which I have indicated, but are also at the same time involved with the expression or contestation of ideas which still trouble us – most notably those of class, gender, and ethnicity. This is obvious enough in the treatment of the 'hysterical' woman in all the arts and in early psychoanalysis; Lawrence Kramer argues that 'Far from being a slightly embarrassing extra, musical representation is one of the basic techniques by which culture enters music, and music enters culture, as communicative action.'[41] This makes musical semiotics a function of persuasive interpretation, despite the doubts of many that music without text can 'mean' in this way. The aim is to find features which are asserted to be common to music and to 'culture' (usually interpreted as the site of political conflict); the semiotician then interprets musical works as being representational, or communicative, or 'symptomatic' of some general political state of affairs by virtue of particular features. An example is the 'exotic' in Ravel's *Daphnis et Chloé* (1909–12), associated by Kramer with an 'Arcadian paradise', where 'eroticism and violence, the sacred and the profane' are intermixed with 'brilliant orchestration, intoxicating colour, sensuous harmonies', and which

41 Lawrence Kramer, *Classical Music and Postmodern Knowledge*, Berkeley, 1995, p. 68.

> is *precisely* of the kind that the culture of late nineteenth-century Europe associated with 'elemental drives' – and in that capacity *associated above all* with the sights and sounds that Europeans had found, selectively, to be sure, in the world of their colonial empires.[42] [emphasis added]

So for Kramer, the music '*embodies the cultural supremacy* by which Europe subsumes and organises the non-European world', because 'The category of the exotic is so bound up with the appropriative energies of commerce . . . that *no exotic pleasure can be entirely innocent*.'[43] The link here is between musical language and political process: in this 'typically exotic' work,

> The movement of melody is governed, neither by Classical techniques of fragmentation and development, nor by Romantic techniques of continuous growth and change, but by techniques of reproduction, iteration, similitude – techniques, we might suggest, strikingly similar to those by which commodities are identified and distributed.[44]

Ravel thus 'commodifies' sexual urges which basically arise from the European domination of colonial empires. But this interpretation hardly explains the contribution Ravel made to the history of music: basically it is designed to make a moral criticism and to stir up liberal guilt. It argues willy-nilly that the music should make us feel implicated in a suspect 'European cultural supremacy' with capitalist 'appropriative energies', and so give up our 'innocence' and feel guilt when we have such 'exotic pleasures'; even if we are attentive to the music's technique, we should find in it the methods which are those of the capitalist distribution and identification of 'commodities'. That may be more or less appropriate depending on what you think the proper functions of interpretation may be, but one thing it doesn't really do is describe the innovative ideas and intentions of its maker.

I am not sure that many listeners really do have thoughts of this kind when listening to *Daphnis et Chloé*; nor am I willing to be convinced by Kramer that I'm 'really' having them at some guilty level of unconscious complicity. Surely the response of many listeners is quite independent of this kind of critical-political sermonizing, simply because most of us already have fairly fully worked-out attitudes to imperialism, commodities, eroticism, and exoticism, and simply do not need to focus our no-doubt politically correct attitudes on a piece of music which is amazingly enjoyable on quite different levels (presumably political critics are not against our enjoying luscious tunes on the cellos or climaxes of *any* kind). And from the point of view of the explanation of innovation, this kind of interpretation is always in fact reactionary and regressive, since it refuses to

42 Ibid., pp. 202–4. 43 Ibid., pp. 211, 222. 44 Ibid., p. 216.

engage with the innovative and creative abilities of artists, in favour of seeing them as perpetually enmired in a drearily repetitive litany of failure to share the (usually leftist) critic's point of view. Such criticism is always implicitly totalitarian, distrustful of the decency of others, and intolerant of a diversity for which it always sees the same underlying explanation.

Conclusion: understanding innovation

If our aim is to understand the nature of artistic innovation, rather than sermonizing about it with reference to contemporary beliefs, we need to look very closely at the history of those ideas that were involved in conceptual changes, and are expressed in the different models, metaphors, and paradigms that underlie works of art. We typically find that there can be surprisingly diverse, and even contradictory, sources for a new theory about art. And so to understand an innovation, we always need to understand the type of intellectual model that the *individual* artist or scientist is using – just as we can ask whether Carnot was writing about heat as a physicist or as an engineer, we can ask whether Debussy/Maeterlinck or Proust or Eliot made Bergsonian assumptions about memory and the nature of the mind or the self, or ask how Freudian Strauss was in *Elektra* and Schoenberg in *Erwartung* (or Virginia Woolf was trying to be in *To the Lighthouse*). We can ask if Schoenberg's model for twelve-tone composition is really like that of linguistic grammar – in a quest for the rules of syntax – or whether it is in fact driven by larger concerns, such as the late-nineteenth-century demand for the total organization of all aspects of the work (something that also emerges in the work of Schenker and Adorno).

But we also need to go beyond that, and to see how these artists did not simply repeat these models or fall under their 'influence', but *changed* them. It is this adaptation that makes Proust a far more interesting, subtle, and informative writer on memory than Bergson, and the protagonist of *Erwartung* a far more surprising and thought-provoking individual than the cruelly systematized female patients described by Freud. This type of approach helps us to see changes in technique as motivated by changes in the conceptual models which license them. But what actually counts as progress, as opposed to the mere attempt at innovation by being different (remember we are talking about the canonic survivors here, not the many who fell by the wayside), is in the end indeed a matter of social and cultural acceptability: artists are no longer taught how to paint biblical history. This utility for survival includes an acceptability within the eclectic and yet canonic atmospheres of institutions – the museum, the concert hall, the public library, and notably the educational process. The innovatory music of this period can thus be thought of as a mode of public communication to which different groups in society had more or less access; hence for example the story of the arrival of jazz and Josephine Baker in Europe, to be welcomed by the modernists and (later) suppressed as decadent by the Nazis. But at this point we need not an account of innovation, but an empirical social history, as well as an account of music as something that can be interpreted as having meaning or significance for its audiences, then and now.[45]

The history-of-ideas approach tends to see innovative works as using conceptual frameworks which allow all sorts of *differing* social claims, and hence cannot be reduced by Adorno and his followers to a set of ideological repetitions of commonplaces analysed on Marxist principles. There are in fact many different kinds of avant-garde artists, who entered into a widely based and pluralistic conversation about new directions for art in this period. And it is at this point that the histories of science and art come apart. For science is most often practised in the context of rigidly patrolled beliefs: in positivism, in word–thing correspondence, in changing types of referential adequacy, in the attempt to pay attention to facts and evidence which is acceptable independent of the very different kinds of socio-cultural context we have touched upon above. Within the arts on the other hand, certainly since the beginning of a historically self-conscious twentieth century, the modernists seem to have opened up a deliberately relativist approach to different and even obviously opposed paradigms and styles. Incommensurability doesn't matter as much here as it does in science – though the differences between Schoenberg and Stravinsky *did* matter for the Adorno-inspired approach, indebted as it was to a supposedly 'scientific' Marxism. Despite their claims to be engaged in quasi-scientific 'research' (notably in the cases of Cubism and the Second Viennese School), artists are not really devoted to a collective and progressive discovery of truth, in which past experiments, made according to superseded paradigms, must be discarded.

Indeed it seems clear that the art of the past can go on revealing different aspects of the truth to us, even when it arises from assumptions which we believe to be false. The relationship of the innovative artist to the past has therefore often been one of *re*-discovery, so that his or her 'progress' may depend on breaking line and hopping over immediate predecessors so as to go even further back (as Pound, Eliot, and Stravinsky so notably did). That is why Robert Hughes can remark that 'Picasso, painting the *Demoiselles*, is the exact contemporary of Monet, painting his waterlilies at Giverny, and who can say

45 For example, Michael H. Kater, *Different Drummers: Jazz in the Culture of Nazi Germany*, Oxford, 1992.

which of them was the more "modern" artist?'[46] After all, Jackson Pollock later worked through Picasso to Monet in arriving at the 'all-over' technique of abstract expressionist painting.

In 1913 you could have heard the premieres of Debussy's *Jeux*, Stravinsky's *The Rite of Spring*, Schmitt's *La Tragedie de Salomé*, Vaughan Williams's *A Sea Symphony*, Webern's *Six Pieces for Orchestra*, op. 6, Fauré's *Pénélopé*, some of Debussy's second book of *Préludes*, Delius's *On Hearing the First Cuckoo in Spring*, Rachmaninov's *The Bells*, and Schoenberg's *Gurrelieder*. All are still of interest; all are innovative; all are absolutely individual, arising from unique creative abilities. Some represent genres on the rise, and others genres on the decline; some are no doubt more 'modern' – by some definition or other – than others. But all contribute something permanently valuable to the diverse and pluralist conversation of the concert hall.

Bibliography

Adorno, Theodor. *Philosophy of Modern Music* (tr. Anne G. Mitchell and Wesley V. Blomster), London, 1987.
Boulez, Pierre. *Stocktakings from an Apprenticeship* (tr. Stephen Walsh), Oxford, 1991.
Butler, Christopher. *Early Modernism: Literature, Painting, and Music in Europe 1900–1916*, Oxford, 1994.
Del Mar, Norman. *Richard Strauss: A Critical Commentary on His Life and Works*, 3 vols., Vol. I, London, 1962.
Djikstra, Bram. *Idols of Perversity*, Oxford, 1986.
Fanning, David. *Nielsen: Symphony no. 5*, Cambridge, 1997.
Forsyth, Karen. *Ariadne auf Naxos: Its Genesis and Meaning*, Oxford, 1982.
Franklin, Peter. *The Idea of Music: Schoenberg and Others*, London, 1985.
Fulcher, Jane F. *French Cultural Politics and Music From the Dreyfus Affair to the First World War*, Oxford, 1999.
Gay, Peter. *The Education of the Senses*, Oxford, 1984.
Griffiths, Paul. *Modern Music*, London, 1994.
Hahl-Koch, Jelena (ed.). *Arnold Schoenberg, Wassily Kandinsky: Letters, Pictures and Documents*, London, 1984.
Hepokoski, James. *Sibelius: Symphony no. 5*, Cambridge, 1993.
Hughes, Robert. *The Shock of the New*, London, 1980.
Kater, Michael. *Different Drummers: Jazz in the Culture of Nazi Germany*, Oxford, 1992.
Kramer, Lawrence. *Classical Music and Postmodern Knowledge*, Berkeley, 1995.
McClary, Susan. *Feminine Endings: Music, Gender and Sexuality*, Minneapolis, 1991.
Moldenhauer, Hans and Rosaleen. *Anton von Webern: A Chronicle of His Life and Work*, London, 1978.
Perloff, Nancy. *Art and the Everyday: Popular Entertainment and the Circle of Erik Satie*, Oxford, 1991.
Prendeville, Brendan. *Realism in Twentieth-Century Painting*, London, 2000.

46 Robert Hughes, *The Shock of the New*, London, 1980, p. 385.

Rainey, Lawrence. *Literary Modernism: Literary Elites and Public Culture*, New Haven, 1998.
Robinson, Alan. *Poetry, Painting and Ideas, 1885–1914*, London, 1985.
Rufer, Joseph. *The Works of Arnold Schoenberg: A Catalogue of his Compositions, Writings and Paintings* (tr. Dika Newlin), London, 1962.
Samson, Jim, *Music in Transition: A Study of Tonal Expansion and Atonality, 1900–1920*, London, 1977.
Schoenberg, Arnold. 'Composition with Twelve Tones' (1941), in *Style and Idea: Selected Writings of Arnold Schoenberg* (ed. Leonard Stein, tr. Leo Black), London, 1975.
Scott, Derek (ed.). *Music, Culture and Society: A Reader*, Oxford, 2000.
Scruton, Roger. *The Aesthetics of Music*, Oxford, 1997.
Straus, Joseph N. *Remaking the Past: Musical Modernism and the Influence of the Tonal Tradition*, Cambridge, MA, 1990.
Walsh, Stephen. *Stravinsky: A Creative Spring. Russia and France 1882–1934*, London, 1999.
Watkins, Glenn. *Pyramids at the Louvre: Music, Culture, and Collage from Stravinsky to the Postmodernists*, Cambridge, MA, 1994.
Weiss, Jeffrey. *The Popular Culture of Modern Art*, New Haven, 1994.
Whittall, Arnold. *Musical Composition in the Twentieth Century*, Oxford, 1999.
William, Rubin (ed.). *Picasso and Braque: Pioneering Cubism*, New York, 1989.
Williamson, John. *Strauss: Also Sprach Zarathustra*, Cambridge, 1993.
Zuckermann, Elliot. *The First Hundred Years of Wagner's Tristan*, New York, 1964.

· 4 ·

Music, text and stage: the tradition of bourgeois tonality to the Second World War

STEPHEN BANFIELD

The old world

In the opening scene of the American musical *Music in the Air* (1932), with music by Jerome Kern and words by Oscar Hammerstein, we see and hear a provincial German, Dr Walther Lessing, composing straight out of bed on a sunny morning. A linnet sings outside his window, represented by flute and piccolo in the pit orchestra. After silencing competition from his cuckoo clock, Lessing whistles the linnet's motif, harmonizes it on his on-stage house organ as the first two bars of a 2/4 polka, extends them to an eight-bar period, and stops to write it down, his scribbling represented by orchestral counterpoint to the motif. Trying it over on the organ, he is disturbed by children singing on their way to school, represented as more counterpoint to his music. They end abruptly as he calls on them to stop, with a two-quaver/crotchet rhythm from which he then tries, unconvincingly, to improvise a B section in the dominant for his polka. As he struggles with this at his desk, the pit orchestra telling us that an emotional, Wagnerian motif of a four-quaver upbeat in 4/4 is also very much on his mind (indeed it opened the scene before the curtain went up, and so was probably in his head as he awoke), yet another interruption occurs: his daughter bangs at the door with his breakfast tray. While she kicks, she also speaks: 'Father dear, let me in. Both my hands are full.' This is to the two-quaver/crotchet rhythm, followed by the four quavers, metrically repositioned. The pit orchestra imitates it, indicating, as do Lessing's muttered repetitions of her words while he writes, that it provides him with inspiration for the rhythmic continuity of his B section – which he now extends to eight bars leading back to the tonic and the A section, as we hear when he tries the whole thing over.

A clearer manifesto of the bourgeois musical experience could not be wished for. Tunes come from the sounds of nature and the speech of humans; incidental music mimics human actions and represents trains of thought and emotion; well-crafted melodies are formed by the struggle for good continuation (understood by the listener as it occurs) assisted by chance inspiration; composition means traditional, periodic dance tunes with tonal harmony, the harmony itself forming the glue between the diegetic layers of the drama as well as the continuum between music, text, and action, sound and sight, meaning and feeling. And all this was created by Kern and Hammerstein in order to appeal to and be immediately comprehended in all its detail by a commercial, non-musical audience wanting – and paying handsomely for – entertainment, not culture, but alive to wit and vocal beauty. Music, one might conclude, had found a gloriously efficient, effective, positive, and democratic role in that most complex (and lucrative) of twentieth-century art forms, popular musical theatre. It was a role, most commanding when most ancillary, that has continued in film and in some later musicals. But it has hitherto never held the place in the historiography of twentieth-century music that it should.

By 1900 tonality had become as integral a part of the bourgeois experience as the job, the fixed address, soap, or the three-course meal. There can have been few who did not occasionally take time or spend money to dance, sing, or listen to eight-bar phrases and perfect cadences, whether with oompah accompaniments or embedded in symphonic paraphernalia, or to laugh at a chromatic slide as a clown came to grief. The old tonal world of semantic consensus worked remarkably well; too well for its own good. A universal (or at least Western) language of musical signification had been comprehensively developed as a way of underscoring or setting text, underlining gesture or setting, or by extension analogizing narrative in instrumental music. A comprehensive code of expression, structure, and meaning – in short, a system – continued to suit most of music's artistic, social, and commercial obligations and had no intention of relinquishing its hold on Western culture. Tonality is the best single word for that system, with its keys and cadences, expressive and unifying calibration of major and minor scales, directional harmony, exquisite manners of voice-leading, and quadratic frameworks – that is, working in multiples of two and four – of metre, phrase, and period. And it was the quadratic framework shared by dance and song that for centuries gave tonal music a vital overlap with the other performance arts. Rhyme, step, and cadence interacted and coincided on the basis of the four-bar phrase and its multiples. Moreover, individual gestures, such as the trumpet signal, horn call, whistle, or drum beat, that had for even longer accompanied or signalled action, were early co-opted by the tonal system, which thereby became intrinsically pantomimic.

Song, dance (including the march), and pantomime (that is, the indication of an object or narrative, particularly movement, by analogical means) were tonality's affective channels. Song normally involves words, and both dance and pantomime involve music accompanying a show, real or imagined, observed or participated in. Hence tonality breasted its expressive heyday of around 1900 in a formidable *troika* of music, text, and stage. George Bernard Shaw wrote in the 1890s that 'during the last two centuries music has been so confounded with opera that even instrumental music has been either opera without words or else the expression in tone of a sort of poetry which the English express with great mastery in spoken verse'.[1] But such comments are insufficient to suggest to the twenty-first-century listener the vast generic hinterland that once surrounded and supported classical music in a hierarchical but continuous spectrum of taste and system of meaning.

Arenas and musical types

The hinterland was evident in any metropolis – London, Paris, Vienna, or New York – and its provinces. The arenas of bourgeois tonality were overwhelmingly those of the mass or casual public, encompassing the commercial theatre; the salon and drawing room; the parlour, restaurant, tavern, café, and street; the resort or spa, sporting a seaside promenade, populist concert hall, bandstand, palm court, ballroom, or festival town hall; and the civic gathering, in street or park, hall or church. To them must be added the new technological media: gramophone and player piano, cinema with its unprecedented mass public, and then radio. They complemented and amplified the reach of these arenas more than they ousted them, at least at first.

To the commercial theatre belonged the ballet, opera (at least in Italy), operetta, musical comedy, vaudeville, music hall, play with incidental music, and circus; and by semantic extension, as we shall see, the symphony, tone poem, and concerto in the concert hall, and the 'silent' or sound film score in the cinema. The salon (extending to elite, often matinée venues such as the Wigmore Hall in London) and drawing room supported the genteel song, pianoforte genre piece, and chamber music, while the parlour, restaurant, tavern, café, and street promoted proletarian song. The resort was the home of light music: the march, social dance, instrumental 'lollipop', and ballad. And the civic venue, witness to procession, mass meeting, and devotional gathering, housed military music, church music, the hymn, and oratorio. It will be clear that the *un*civic venue, namely cabaret with its provocative and subversive overtones, lay somewhat outside this scheme of things: one could argue that Bohemian meant modernist.[2]

1 George Bernard Shaw, *The World*, 14 March 1894, reprinted as 'English Music' in Dan H. Laurence (ed.), *Shaw's Music: the Complete Musical Criticism in Three Volumes*, Vol. III, London, 1981, pp. 161–2.

2 See Klaus Wachsmann and Patrick O'Connor, 'Cabaret', in Stanley Sadie and John Tyrrell (eds.), *The New Grove Dictionary of Music and Musicians* (2nd edn), 29 vols, London, 2001, Vol. IV, pp. 762–4.

There was a good deal of overlap between these arenas, which is the point: certain common musical types cut across them because the tonal formulae were so comprehensive. Those formulae worked themselves out in six basic types, all inherited from before the nineteenth century: the march, the waltz and its variants, the hymn, the romance, the fantasy, and what one might call the ditty – the catchy, rhythmic tune (such as a jig), short-breathed and colloquial, calling for rhyme and syllabic verbal wit to make it insidious.

Marches could be everything from military quicksteps and polkas to sonata-form expositions; waltzes anything from 'Daisy Bell' (words and music by Harry Dacre, 1892) to Delius's tone poem *Paris* (1899), Ravel's *La valse* (1920), or the symphonic dance of triumph from Richard Strauss's opera *Elektra* (1909). Hymns ranged from Sir Arthur Sullivan's 'Onward, Christian Soldiers' (still sung in English-speaking churches from black Africa to white Australia) to the main theme of the last movement of Mahler's Third or Ninth Symphony.[3] As for the romance, it might be the traditional guitar serenade with *bel canto* melody and oompah or finger-picked arpeggio accompaniment, found alike in Italian opera arias and anglophone popular song until at least 1900;[4] serenade accompaniments were modernized without parody by Fauré in many of his *mélodies*, having been a staple of the French art-song style at least since Gounod, and so continued through to Hahn and Poulenc (as they did in England from Stanford to Lennox Berkeley). Another type of romance in song was the more sentimentally sustained and nuanced accompaniment to an intimate melody, countermelody often interwoven: the English composer Roger Quilter offers good late examples of a type forged in the German Lied by Schumann. The genre was as happily instrumental as vocal; one may follow it through from Beethoven's slow movements, such as that to the 'Pathétique' sonata (which Elgar attempted consciously to match in emotional intensity in 'Nimrod' from his *Enigma Variations* [1899]), to a means of expression that covers the entire symphonic and operatic range in the later nineteenth century, including Mahler's 'feminine' second subjects (that of the first movement of the Sixth Symphony [1904] being a portrait of his wife Alma), much of the erotic writing in Wagner's highly romantic music dramas, and some of Richard Strauss's best moments, as late as the opening instrumental Sextet from *Capriccio* (1942).

3 Was this, in either or both cases, an echo of D. A. de Sola's Sephardic melody 'Adon olam'? See Emanuel Aguilar and Rev. D. A. de Sola, *Sephardi Melodies: Being the Traditional Liturgical Chants of the Spanish & Portuguese Jews' Congregation[,] London. Part I: 'The Ancient Melodies'*, Oxford, 5691–1931, p. 62

4 See Charles Hamm, *Yesterdays: Popular Song in America*, New York, 1979, pp. 62–88, 219–22, 294, 372.

The fantasy was the musical type in which tonal ingredients were apt to disintegrate just when their gestural and melopoetic efficacy was strongest. It could convey humour or horror, pantomime or melodrama, the natural (storm scenes in Sibelius), supernatural (fairies in Tchaikovsky), or subhuman (dragons in Wagner), all using disruptive, eccentric, ancient, or inchoate musical techniques that might derive from the baroque fugue or toccata, the classical symphonic introduction, development sections or transitions, or *divertimento* local colour. A famous example of pantomimic fantasy occurs in Act III of Wagner's *Die Meistersinger* as Beckmesser silently attempts to steal the prize song from Hans Sachs's work bench; sixty years later, in Eric Coates's orchestral Phantasy *The Three Bears*, the music for its eponymous subjects, stealthily re-entering their home to observe Goldilocks's depredations, is not much different – a familiar amalgam of diminished and half-diminished chords, sudden *sforzandi*, miniature *accelerandi* and tiny snatches of tune or rhythm that are broken off before they cadence. Finally, the ditty, often allied with fantasy in art music, ranged from the bassoon melody of Dukas's *The Sorcerer's Apprentice* to the sacristan's theme in Puccini's *Tosca*, the 'hook' of a Tin Pan Alley song such as 'Ta-ra-ra Boom-de-ay!', the universal signifier for silent-screen pathos 'Hearts and Flowers', the 'Hootchy Kootchy Dance',[5] or the immortal tag $\hat{1}$-$\hat{5}$-[$\sharp\hat{4}$]-$\hat{5}$-$\flat\hat{6}$-$\hat{5}$ [rest] $\hat{7}$-$\hat{1}$ – which must surely have originated in the later nineteenth century but whose etymology is, one imagines, as impossible to trace as that of 'OK'.[6]

Popular musical theatre and film

All these musical types played themselves out liberally on the popular stage as analogue or accompaniment to text (sung or spoken), gesture (acting or dance), or tableau. Just as later with film, music was ubiquitous even in 'straight' drama around 1900, but in the specifically musical theatre of the time it was positively triumphant. Popular musical theatre took a number of forms, all consolidated in the second half of the nineteenth century and most surviving into the twentieth with varying degrees of success, transformation, and longevity. One might list them in something approaching a descending order of respectability if not musical scope: comic opera, operetta, musical comedy, *opéra-bouffe*, vaudeville ('variety'), European burlesque, pantomime, music hall, minstrel show, cabaret,

5 See James J. Fuld, *The Book of World-Famous Music: Classical, Popular and Folk* (5th edn), Mineola, NY, 2000, pp. 276–7; Ralph P. Locke, 'Cutthroats and Casbah Dancers, Muezzins and Timeless Sands: Musical Images of the Middle East', *Nineteenth-Century Music* 22 (1998), pp. 20–53; pp. 33–4.

6 Fuld, *The Book of World-Famous Music*, p. 495, traces the phrase in print under the words 'Shave and a haircut, bay rum'. Richard Rodgers, in his autobiography, refers to it as 'Shave and a haircut: two bits': *Musical Stages: an Autobiography* (2nd edn), New York, 1995, pp. 17, 46.

café-concert, and circus. American burlesque (striptease) and the revue, by contrast, were twentieth-century outgrowths.

Systematic definitions would be tedious here, but some distinctions need to be understood.[7] Comic opera might be a sentimental costume drama such as Edward German's *Merrie England* (London, 1902), or a vehicle for satire as in the 'Savoy' operas of Gilbert and Sullivan (London, 1875–96). Vaudeville concatenated separate speciality acts that might range from classical or modern ballet to performing dogs, whereas the minstrel show was a precise blackface formula executed by four or more song-and-dance men. Music hall, which peaked around 1900, often included a compère and (as English pantomime still does) audience response, notably in sung refrains. Coinciding with the decline of participatory music hall, the consolidated refrain became a standardized thirty-two-bar unit in popular song forms by the 1920s, the preliminary 'verse' section withering like an appendix. But music hall's history, like that of vaudeville and its counterparts in other countries, is one of performers more than artefacts: Bert Williams and May Irwin in the USA, Marie Lloyd and Harry Lauder in Britain, Yvette Guilbert and Aristide Bruant in France, and Fritzi Massary in Austro-Germany were among the most famous singing entertainers, in one genre or another, of the early twentieth century.

Anything approaching a composer's score came into authoritative play only at the genteel end of the market, and even there a sought-after songwriter such as Jerome Kern had to wait several years before graduating from interpolating numbers into someone else's score to constructing his own in consultation with the 'book' writer of a musical comedy. Theatre orchestration remained the province of the musical director or specialist professional rather than the composer, and Hollywood almost never gave a songwriter the chance to write all the music for a musical film. When a score was more or less integral, as with the English musical comedies that succeeded the comic operas of Sullivan, it was often shared between two composers (such as the Edwardians Lionel Monckton and Howard Talbot), containing many short items separated by spoken sections and scenes, and aspiring towards opera in the through-sung finales and opening choruses (but seldom elsewhere). Edwardian musical comedy grafted both sentimentalism and music-hall titillation onto the tissue of 2/4 polkas, 6/8 country dances, and 3/4 waltzes – staples of late-nineteenth-century social dance – that Offenbach and Johann Strauss had bequeathed to Sullivan. But it was only with the introduction of Romantic underscoring accompanying key points of dialogue (in addition to or in place of moments of melodramatic

7 A convenient guide to most of the genres may be found in Richard Kislan, 'Forms of Musical Theater', in *The Musical: A Look at the American Musical Theater* (2nd edn), New York, 1995, pp. 11–110.

recitative in finales) that a composer for the popular musical theatre could begin to explore Wagnerian notions of musical motivation, Lehár leading the way with *The Merry Widow* (1905).

However limited in scope, the music of the popular stage was heard by enormous numbers of people. *The Times* for 14 February 1905 advertises twenty-five West End theatres, including six showing musicals, four variety, one extravaganza, and one circus; a simple calculation suggests that if thirty thousand people were frequenting them each night, two thirds of these lived in the metropolis of eight million, and one in five Londoners went to the theatre, then he or she was doing so more than once a week. In New York the Hammerstein dynasty of impresarios, beginning with Oscar I and including (in later life) his librettist grandson Oscar II, produced shows in an equally impressive number of popular auditoria which they also built and managed, marketing everything from vaudeville to grand opera, none of which would have brought in the public without music.

When film theatres wired for sound in the late 1920s, the composers and lyricists of Broadway became the songwriters of Hollywood. Kern, Hammerstein, Rodgers, Hart, the Gershwins, Harry Warren, and Irving Berlin all moved to the West Coast in the 1930s for longer or shorter periods. Without changing the way 'ordinary' music, its texts, and its dramatic correlatives affected audiences in the musical comedy or operetta, Hollywood nevertheless altered its dimensions considerably. First it made most of the music more or less plausibly diegetic – that is, it avoided having characters sing without cause. Second, it worked its material harder. Four or five songs per musical film were generally enough, not least because the film itself would be little more than half the length of an evening in the theatre. Dance breaks and production numbers tended to become longer, the AABA modulor being spun out to an extraordinary number of repetitions in Busby Berkeley routines. 'Book' scenes, depending on the studio, were more and more underscored, with background, dance, or chase material being extrapolated from the songs. As though in premonition of what sound film would require, Kern had done this on the stage in *Show Boat* (1927), the first musical in the modern canon; his orchestrator Robert Russell Bennett followed him to Hollywood, while other pioneers of the studio sound made their crucial contributions over the next three or four decades: Conrad Salinger, Roger Edens, Nelson Riddle. More than anyone, perhaps, these men preserved the workings of bourgeois tonality among radically changing patterns of singing, acting, and valuation, patterns reflecting the hegemony of Britain and the USA when it came to the business of music.

The Tin Pan Alley system

Long before the twentieth century, most popular 'hit' songs emerged from or were exploited in the commercial theatre, at least in Britain and its colonies and ex-colonies: ever since Shakespeare's day the London stage and its offshoots had been a powerful locus for music of the people. But in the early twentieth century you did not have to enter an auditorium, or even a circus tent, to hear a popular song. The bandstand in the public park, the pierrot stage on the seafront, and the street with its buskers and military bands all reproduced it from published sheet music, while an orgy of mechanical contrivances did so inescapably from punched holes, pins, or grooves: the early gramophone in the parlour, the polyphon (a giant musical box) in the pub, the steam organ at the fair, the barrel organ on the pavement, and the player piano in the arcade all churned out waltzes, polkas, marches, and ditties.

Fair organs were made in the Low Countries, northern Germany, and Paris; barrel organs were leased out by Italians on a weekly basis from city premises to their indigent virtuosi. Popular songs encountered in European cities and disseminated thence into the regions continued to appear in Italian (Luigi Denza's 'Funiculì – funiculà', actually written in St John's Wood, or 'O sole mio'), in French (Charles Trenet's 'Boum!'), and in German ('Lili Marleen'). England also produced hits, 'Don't Dilly Dally on the Way' being a notable early-twentieth-century one, and London was in many respects the leading base for the early recording industry. But radio developed from 1920 onwards, first in the USA and Canada; the leading player piano company, Aeolian, was American, and so were Wurlitzer and Hammond, the manufacturers who respectively pioneered the cinema pipe organ, ubiquitous in the 1930s both live and on the radio (and curiously unaffected by the arrival of sound film), and the domestic electronic organ. Above all, the configuration of the music industry that serviced all these machines and outlets was quintessentially American: Tin Pan Alley.[8]

Tin Pan Alley was a place, a section of 28th Street in Manhattan, but it was also a system and a style. The place was where a number of New York sheet-music publishers had their premises. The system was one of massive, raw commercial salesmanship between stage performers (crucial to a song's success), their managements, songwriters, and the song-pluggers who demonstrated the latest numbers on-site at jangly pianos and gave the area its name. It was partly the song-pluggers' style of performance that was jangly: this is how the young

8 See also the discussion of the Tin Pan Alley song stylists in Derek Scott's chapter in this volume (pp. 317–21).

George Gershwin earned his living, and as possessor of a voice which he himself described as 'small but disagreeable' he would have done all he could to sell a song not by vocal but by instrumental verve, the essence of which was relentless rhythm, catchy phraseology, and rich harmony. Capturing this last on the piano must have helped form the 'stride' piano idiom, while the 'novelty' style with its plentiful triplets, syncopations and parallel fourths ensured the ongoing brightness and dynamism. Other American songwriters cut their teeth on song-plugging, graduating to employment by a publisher to write songs, as Kern and Gershwin did with T. B. Harms (its boss, Max Dreyfus, very much a twentieth-century kingmaker).

The theatre could be crucial to songs' dissemination, and almost all of Gershwin's and Kern's songs were premiered there or, later, in the cinema. And for all the keyboard virtuosity of a song-plugger, what mattered were words and how they sat on a tune, which they increasingly had to clinch as a newspaper headline does its article, if they were to sell copies. Tin Pan Alley songs were about everyday concerns and situations, wryly conceived, and in a city full of immigrants, they characterized and demonized them. Coon songs parodied blacks; the Irish, Italians, Germans, and Jews were similarly treated.[9] Latin America, because exotic, was later given more positive treatment when tango rhythms (for the increasingly popular ballroom dancing) and languid crotchet triplets entered the popular musical lexicon.

Tin Pan Alley's style foundations were those of standard tonal practice. However, musical *négritude*,[10] that twentieth-century salve to the Anglo-Saxon conscience already long exploited in minstrelsy (for instance, with pentatonic melodies such as that of Stephen Foster's 'The Camptown Races'), began to overlay this with a new element, the sidelong rhythms of African-American syncopation. Ragtime songs developed out of polkas (two-steps) in the 1890s; Irving Berlin's 'Alexander's Ragtime Band' of 1910, while not in fact a ragtime song, focused a craze that later smoothed out the cross-rhythms into ballroom foxtrot features. One important concomitant of this was a new relationship of words to music. Triple-time lyric formations could be fitted to duple-time music: in 'The Lady is a Tramp' (*Babes in Arms*, 1937), Lorenz Hart's ten-syllable lyric lines such as 'I like the theater but never come late'[11] could have been set to four bars of triple time, end-stopped, with a syllable on each beat, but Richard Rodgers's musical period actually takes four bars of 2/2 time – the first crotchet beat of the first bar being silent, the second syllable of 'theater' syncopated as

9 See Charles Hamm, 'Irving Berlin and Early Tin Pan Alley', in Hamm (ed.), *Irving Berlin: Early Songs*, *Music of the United States of America* no. 2, Vol. I: *1907–1911* (Madison, WI, 1994), pp. xx–xxi, xxxiv–xxxviii.

10 See Paul Gilroy, '"Jewels Brought from Bondage": Black Music and the Politics of Authenticity', in *The Black Atlantic: Modernity and Double Consciousness*, London, 1993, pp. 72–100.

11 'Theater' counts as two syllables (thea-ter).

a minim in the centre of the second bar, and the word 'late' arriving with a cross-rhythmic foxtrot skip on the last crotchet of bar 3, which gives time for an instrumental 'response' or 'fill' in bar 4, also syncopated. Such rhythms – indeed whole tunes – were laid down first by composers, with lyricists adding words to them (Gilbert and Sullivan, in the art-music tradition, had worked the other way round), and this helps to account for the change in tone from poetic sing-song verse to the smart, casual, confidential economy of verbal expression found in the American popular ballad of the golden era, as Allen Forte has termed it.[12] P. G. Wodehouse, working with Kern, Gershwin, Porter, and others, was one of the most important lyricists of the new breed, and understood the reflexivity (the obverse of 'word-painting') that could be exploited when the music came first. (There is an example of it in the line cited above, when the note on the word 'late' arrives early.) At the height of the 'jazz age', in the mid-1920s, the waltz looked finished on this account and virtually a whole musical theatre score, *No, No, Nanette* (1925) by the American Vincent Youmans, could be written in duple time, its syncopation infectious in every number.

Opera, ballet and operetta

If Tin Pan Alley with its standardized hit songs represented the new downward pressures of consumerism on musical theatre, opera – an upward force in the northern countries – had in the later nineteenth century shown a remarkable power of percolation to the popular sphere; choruses and marches from *Il trovatore* or *Aida* and the *William Tell* overture were among the best-known pieces of music in the world around 1900, top stars such as Melba sang operatic material to indiscriminate audiences on worldwide tours, and even presentations of whole operas (with varying degrees of mutilation) could be hoped for in any town that aspired to an opera house, which many did regardless of whether opera actually took place in it.

But faced with the phenomenally rising scope of musical theatre entertainment (competitive forms existed in Paris, Berlin, Vienna, and Madrid as well as London and New York),[13] the old operatic culture was never fully embedded in the musical life of either of the two economic leviathans of the early twentieth century: the increasingly diasporic masses of the New World, and the still powerful populations of the British Empire. The newer musical culture would have to be anglophone, and though for a while it looked as though the Celtic muse

12 Allen Forte, *The American Popular Ballad of the Golden Era: 1924–1950*, Princeton, 1995.
13 See Andrew Lamb, *150 Years of Popular Musical Theatre*, New Haven, 2000.

might provide it (New York was awash with Irish tenors, and Victor Herbert was a powerful figure), Sullivan's fate in Britain – never quite a national hero – was symptomatic of this movement's overall failure, hastened by the German approach to high culture. This, increasingly philosophical and influential, managed to drive a most efficient wedge between the tastes and markets of different consumer groups in other countries. Thus Sullivan's comic operas were not respectable enough for them to carry British musical pride, while his concert works were too old-fashioned to stand up to Wagner.[14]

In Italy itself things went on much as before for quite a long time. Puccini's accomplishment, from *La bohème* onwards (1896), was what others aspired to: Charpentier with *Louise* (1900) in France, Smyth with *The Wreckers* (1906) in Britain, and Chadwick with *The Padrone* (1912) in the USA, not to mention Puccini's own compatriots Leoncavallo and Mascagni with *Pagliacci* (1893) and *Cavalleria rusticana* (1890). That is, he took realist or tragic melodrama and managed to pace it sufficiently fast that there was no obvious disjunction between how it would work on the stage as a straight play (*Tosca* and *Madama Butterfly* were based on successful recent plays) and how it flowed as opera. His acts were short, his music a deft procession of incidental effects and gestures and refrain- or ditty-like tunes woven seamlessly according to Wagner's techniques of motif and modulation. Everything was kept moving at a high emotional temperature (each harmony and snatch of melody having to have some particular quality of allure), and nothing went on for more than a few bars; film music later learnt much from such effectiveness. This was musical drama for an audience without a connoisseur's ability to savour and concentrate.

But opera, essentially a melodramatic art, had become the victim of its own success. Wagner in particular had shown not only how any dialogue could be set to music, any instrumental punctuation of recitative declamation turned into symphonic material, but also how even unsung thoughts and moods could be translated into symphonic terms in the spinning, combining, and transformation of motifs. Action, even words, were unnecessary when music could do all this, and the level of redundancy that the *Gesamtkunstwerk* entailed trammelled the spectator with its irresistibility; with every mien and gesture triggering sound, the inevitable destiny of this tonal fantasy was the Hollywood cartoon, where in turn it triggered laughter. Richard Strauss was perhaps the

14 For England's musical culture war with Germany, see Robert Stradling and Meirion Hughes, *The English Musical Renaissance 1840–1940: Constructing a National Music* (2nd edn), Manchester, 2001, pp. 115–63. Concerning the USA, see Frank R. Rossiter, *Charles Ives and His America*, New York, 1975, pp. 90–1; Alan Howard Levy, 'The Search for Identity in American Music, 1890–1920', *American Music* 2 (1984), pp. 70–81, p. 72; and Lawrence Levine, *Highbrow/Lowbrow: The Emergence of Cultural Hierarchy in America*, Cambridge, MA, 1988, p. 220. France's musical response to German superiority after 1870 is carefully considered in Michael Strasser, 'The Société Nationale and Its Adversaries: the Musical Politics of *L'Invasion Germanique* in the 1870s', *Nineteenth-Century Music* 24 (2001), pp. 225–51.

last composer fully to sustain the tonal expressivity of opera: indicative of the redundancy was his claimed ability to depict anything in musical terms; his mastery of declamation meant that he could also set anything to music (including stage directions, once or twice, by mistake). He took a Wilde play as libretto (*Salome*), as Debussy took Maeterlinck's *Pelléas et Mélisande*; as with Puccini, the texture and pacing of opera by implication were now identical to those of spoken drama. Strauss's librettist Hofmannsthal was a successful playwright, and *Der Rosenkavalier* has even been performed as a play without music.[15]

The danger with characters who no longer knew they were singing – another way of approaching the problem of operatic redundancy in this period – was that they no longer knew they existed;[16] it became necessary to reintroduce distancing and performative strategies. After Stravinsky, operatic composers such as Britten could take whatever elements of neoclassicism suited them, while Janáček found his own solutions, exploiting 'musical' quirks of vernacular speech (his characters tend to say everything twice) and deliberately misaligning the moment of utterance and the moment of feeling. Then again, Brechtian alienation – confronting the audience rather than overwhelming it – suited Kurt Weill in his early works. Weill's case is a seminal one, but its implications for twentieth-century music history have never been fully considered. He began his career with music as 'dirty' as he could make it, affronting every element of expressive decorum. Gradually affection began to creep back into his work, ironically the more so the further he got from his native land and language, exiled from Germany by the Nazis and writing for the French, English, and finally American theatre. With the emblematic 'Here I'll Stay' from the Broadway musical *Love Life* (1948) he finally embraced bourgeois sentiment; and a deeply moving song it is. Yet it could have appeared thirty years earlier in a German operetta.

Operetta and ballet avoided such crises, though in differing ways. Ballet automatically shed two layers of redundancy by doing without words and singing voices; one feels that a more innocent and indeed witty vocabulary of tonal gesture could flourish on the Franco-Russian stage because of this, in the full-length works of Delibes and Tchaikovsky, where music was the foil to the erotic beauty of moving bodies. It may have been no accident that it was in ballet that Ravel (*Daphnis et Chloé*, 1912) and Stravinsky (*The Firebird* [1910] and *Petrushka* [1911], if not *The Rite of Spring* [1913]) managed to carry audiences, indeed artistic history, with them through Impressionism into modernism.

15 Citizens' Theatre, Glasgow, September–October 1983, directed by Phillip Prowse.
16 See Edward T. Cone, 'The World of Opera and its Inhabitants', in *Music: A View from Delft*, Chicago, 1989, pp. 125–38.

One might compare this co-option of an appealing medium for subversive or elitist purposes with Austro-German attempts to harness melodrama with its heightened speech (old recordings make it clear just how close stage oratory was to singing a hundred years ago) as a vehicle for dissonance, which in a sense it always had been insofar as it conveyed the terrible. Schoenberg tried it in Claus the Fool's monologue (arguably the most effective part of *Gurrelieder*), in *Pierrot lunaire* and in many other places; so did Berg in *Lulu*. But perhaps only in Schoenberg's *A Survivor from Warsaw* did this yield people's music.

Operetta knew how to maintain the allure of the voice and a star's eroticism on stage where opera eventually failed. It enshrined the singing: female leads were still sopranos, trilling away in quite a different register from their interspersed dialogue, while their men commanded the 'book' with its verbal wit and suavity. Dance could be relied upon to bring them together as much as duetting. This strain of romanticism died hard, its embers still glowing in the relationship of Eliza Doolittle and Professor Higgins in *My Fair Lady* (1956), a piece played today on the operetta stages of continental Europe.

Programme music

Untexted music for most people in the earlier twentieth century was, like song, a matter of immediate musical gratification – and in family terms, for a 'lollipop' concert on the bandstand or in the winter garden had to be enjoyed by Granny as well as the kids, as did radio before the days of the transistor. Accordingly the period 1900–50 and beyond was awash with instrumental entertainment comprising operetta polkas, marches, and waltzes without the voice, ballet *divertissement* movements and suites without the dancers, stage monologues without actors, and orchestral 'songs without words'. Such light music rarely strayed far from ternary dance and song forms or ABAB marches, and revelled in tonal wit and cocky gesture, descriptive titles, fine tunes, short spans, and often a programmatic gimmick of some kind (such as in Albert Ketèlbey's 'In a Monastery Garden' or, later, Leroy Anderson's 'The Typewriter').

But starting with Beethoven's comments on his 'Pastoral' Sixth Symphony ('more feeling than painting'), the arbiters of musical culture – and particularly composers themselves – reacted to the success of programme music with an ambivalence that grew in proportion to its capabilities. Issues of representation and meaning in music accordingly came to a head not with what was texted and staged but what was not, that is, concert music. There is scarcely a composer of the period who did not first create powerful programmatic or referential tokens in their symphonic music and then suppress or deny them. Elgar dropped tantalising clues in most of his major works, most famously in the *Enigma*

Variations but also in the two symphonies and the Violin Concerto (he also composed an extraordinarily detailed tone poem in *Falstaff*); in almost the first book on him, Ernest Newman included an appendix on 'Elgar and Programme Music', in which he unmasked the hypocrisy that would have music 'pure' whose very attractiveness consisted in referential temptations of orchestral, formal, generic, dialectic, and titular coding.[17] When a Mahler symphony began, like the Second, with a minor-key march and ended with a chorus (by definition from an 'other' world in a symphony, regardless of its text), to construe it as being 'about' the pilgrimage from death to life could and can hardly be avoided.

Tchaikovsky with his 'fate' mottoes, Mahler with his hammer strokes, Rachmaninov with the 'Dies irae', Vaughan Williams with bold strokes of image and idiom in most of his symphonies, Ives with his quotations and style pluralisms, all complemented rather than contradicted Strauss and Respighi with their Romantic tone poems of minute descriptiveness; such features were often exactly those prized in opera or cantata but judged suspect without stage action or text, perhaps because they threw the spotlight not just on the composers' structural abilities but on their biographies as well. A programme that was not explicit was deemed personal and hence self-indulgent; the furore over Tchaikovsky's last symphony and death may actually have changed the climate for musical self-expression for ever. In short, composers quickly became ashamedly programmatic where they had once been unashamedly so. And it was Stravinsky who in the end exorcized the spectre of programme music, not just with his famous comment that music was incapable of expressing anything at all, but by concealing his own Romantic foundations, as Richard Taruskin has shown. When he wrote it in 1908, the *Scherzo fantastique* was about bees (Maeterlinck's, in *La vie des abeilles*); fifty years later, in the *Conversations*, it was not.[18]

The zenith of programmatic aptitude came with the 'struggle' symphony. We do no disservice to Sibelius's First (1899) if we hear swords on shields in the clashing cymbals of its finale, for Sibelius possessed a well-worn copy of Juhani Aho's novel *Panu*, published in 1897, and referred to it in sketches: the novel is about 'the final struggle between the Christian and heathen faiths in Finland'.[19] Clearly the Christians, with their chorale, vanquish the folk-dancing heathen, but in the symphony the authorial viewpoint is that of a tragic victory. (If Sibelius was on the pagan side that might have given further reason to

17 Ernest Newman, *Elgar*, London, 1906, pp. 177–85.

18 Richard Taruskin, *Stravinsky and the Russian Traditions: A Biography of the Works Through* Mavra, 2 vols., Oxford, 1996, Vol. I, pp. 6–8.

19 Erik Tawaststjerna, *Sibelius*, 3 vols., London, 1976–97, Vol. I, p. 201.

downplay the programme.) By the end of the nineteenth century, the 'struggle' symphony or tone poem (or concerto) could also form a highly plausible analogy with the *Bildungsroman*, the novel of personal character development, the portrait of the artist as a young man (seldom a young woman). Mahler's First (1889) is a good example, and it is worth remembering that while Mahler earned his living in the opera house he did not write for it, for some of the technical developments of nineteenth-century music – especially the enhanced continuum afforded by chromatic harmony and by the greater sustaining powers of instruments, of which Mahler's soaring string cantilenas are the peak – suggest a marriage with the reflective prose of the novel, not the dialogue and noisy action of the stage. The passage between cues 41 and 45 in Mahler's finale, where the violas violently bring the orchestra back to its striving senses – and Mahler's hero, the Titan, back to his – after the last romantic reverie, is surely the most suggestive interior monologue in music to that date. It could only be sung, *à la* Wagner, with the addition of a lot of redundant countermelody, and Mahler's eloquence is such that it needs no verbal or visual corollary at all.

However, the passage *could* be effectively acted or spoken as a stage monologue against the music, with a speech such as that of the poet Marchbanks at the end of Shaw's play *Candida* (1895), a rare *Bildungsroman* on the stage, Mahlerian irony and all. 'Out, then, into the night with me!' he cries. 'I no longer desire happiness: life is nobler than that.' And audiences and creators not susceptible to Mahler's symphonic contexts were already using music such as his (though less good) in precisely that way. They would do so increasingly as incidental music in the theatre, especially reflective or melodramatic underscoring, gained ground and eventually, when handed the *carte blanche* of technology, became film music.

Incidental music for stage and screen

'Silent' cinema, growing exponentially from its inception in the 1890s to the birth of sound film in the late 1920s, was not at all silent. It was accompanied by constant live music, not least because in the early days a film was often just one item on a variety-theatre programme and the orchestra was used to accompanying the turns. Beyond this, Prendergast cites three theories of (silent) film music: that it gave body to the screen 'ghosts' (Hanns Eisler), covered the sound of the projector (Kurt London), and articulated 'the rhythm of the film as an art of movement' (London again).[20] Walter Benjamin referred to 'the shock effect

20 Roy Prendergast, *Film Music: A Neglected Art*, New York, 1977, pp. 3–5.

of the film, which, like all shocks, should be cushioned by heightened presence of mind', a presence presumably assisted by musical commentary.[21]

Silent film must represent the nub of any argument about tonal music's commercial peak and aesthetic trough, for it found the widest audience.[22] It also perfected the visual corollary to nineteenth-century musical realism, offering in effect opera with surtitles but without singing, and taking on epic melodrama which thereby created a kind of musical novel; sound film took over this capability, adding popular song (the ballad) and dance, and drawing on operetta, 'straight' drama, and vaudeville traditions. Early film moguls were quite clear about the opportunity to create visual novels for a public without the patience, imagination or time to read literary ones: Adolph Zukor developed full-length feature films in order to attract a 'better' audience, by 'imitating the middle-class forms of the novel and legitimate theater' and thereby reconciling himself 'with the deepest strains in Jewish life where culture had always been held in special esteem'.[23] And nowhere is the anatomy of late-tonal music as a connected tissue of types, genres, and arenas from the gutter to the temple, from the ditty to the novel, and from the jingle to the symphony, better demonstrated than in how music in the silent film worked.

Essentially it paralleled music in the theatre where, in a tradition stemming from French nineteenth-century melodrama, incidental music was crucial to the success of a play; it set the emotional tone and lubricated the pace. The cheaper practice was to employ reach-me-down musical scraps such as 'four bars of "agit" '. These scraps were called *melos*[24] – the term could be plural, or singular as in Kern's use of it when underscoring speech in his musical comedies – and created melodrama in both senses of the word, that is, excitement for grandiose action on the stage and accompaniment to speech.[25] At the upper end of the market, music was commissioned with care from leading composers, as the star actor-manager Sir Henry Irving did at his Lyceum Theatre in London. Sullivan and German wrote Shakespeare scores for him; Stanford, Elgar, and Delius (*Hassan*) all supplied worthwhile orchestral music for West End plays, though today it never gets a chance to prove its power in a production. Others, such as Norman O'Neill, specialized as musical directors of London theatres for

21 Martin Marks, *Music and the Silent Film: Contexts and Case Studies, 1895–1924*, New York, 1997, p. 4. Marks's quotation is from Walter Benjamin, 'The Work of Art in the Age of Mechanical Reproduction', in *Illuminations* (ed. Hannah Arendt, tr. Harry Zohn), London, 1999, pp. 231–2.

22 See the Twentieth Century Club's accommodation figures for Boston, MA, in 1909–10, quoted by Lawrence Levine: legitimate theatres, 151,000 persons weekly; vaudeville and burlesque theatres, 206,000; cinemas, 402,000 (*Highbrow/Lowbrow*, p. 79).

23 Neal Gabler, *An Empire of Their Own: How the Jews Invented Hollywood*, New York, 1988, pp. 24, 26.

24 Presumably pronounced *mellows*.

25 See David Mayer and Matthew Scott, *Four Bars of 'Agit': Incidental Music for Victorian and Edwardian Melodrama*, London, 1983, pp. 49–72.

which they composed their own scores, in his case at the Haymarket: O'Neill's music for J. M. Barrie's *Mary Rose* (1920) – he also wrote a score for Maeterlinck's *The Blue Bird* (1909) – became famous, and he presented an illuminating Musical Association paper on how incidental music works.[26] In it he gave consideration to important scores by Bizet and Grieg, as well as to Humperdinck's *Königskinder* in its original guise as a melodrama (it later became a fine opera).

If melodrama wanted to be an opera when it grew up – as too did musical comedy – then film music wanted to become a symphony (and did, in the case of Vaughan Williams's *Antartica*).[27] But with the odd exception such as Saint-Saëns's integral score for *L'assassinat du Duc de Guise* (1908), film music in its youth was a thing of shreds and patches, issued first by producers as 'specific suggestions for music', then by publishers in the form of anthologies of pre-existent pieces or fragments for different dramatic situations, and finally, thanks to a brainwave by Max Winkler (a clerk in a New York music shop), as 'cue sheets' from a library: a sequence of pieces or extracts issued with the film with precise instructions on what to use where.[28]

All this entailed a highly indicative and systematic taxonomy of musical types and tonal effects; there was no room for doubt about what a particular piece or passage of music 'meant', which is why silent film belongs at the core of this chapter. The anthologies and handbooks of Giuseppe Becce contained music (some of it written by him) classified in layers such as the following:

DRAMATIC EXPRESSION (Main Concept)
1. Climax (subordinate concept)
   (Subdivisions)
   (a) catastrophe
   (b) Highly dramatic *agitato*
   (c) Solemn atmosphere; mysteriousness of nature.[29]

Winkler described how, in order to produce enough cue sheets, 'in desperation we turned to crime':

> Extracts from great symphonies and operas were hacked down to emerge again as 'Sinister Misterioso' by Beethoven, or 'Weird Moderato' by Tchaikovsky. Wagner's and Mendelssohn's wedding marches were used for marriages, fights

26 Norman O'Neill, 'Music to Stage Plays', *Proceedings of the Musical Association* 37 (1910–11), pp. 85–102, reprinted in Derek Hudson, *Norman O'Neill: A Life of Music*, London, 1945, pp. 124–38.

27 Korngold's Violin Concerto and other concert works were also formed from film scores; see Robert van der Lek, 'Concert Music as Reused Film Music: E-W Korngold's Self-Arrangements', *Acta Musicologica* 66 (1994), pp. 78–112.

28 Prendergast, *Film Music*, pp. 6–10.

29 Hans Erdmann, Giuseppe Becce, and Ludwig Brav, *Allgemeines Handbuch der Filmmusik*, Berlin, 1927, cited in Prendergast, *Film Music*, p. 6. I have regularized what appears to be scrambled tabulation in Prendergast.

> between husbands and wives, and divorce scenes: we just had them played out of tune, a treatment known in the profession as 'souring up the aisle'. If they were to be used for happy endings we jazzed them up mercilessly.[30]

By 1924 the musical director of several New York film theatres, Erno Rapée, could find it worth his while to publish *Motion Picture Moods For Pianists and Organists: a rapid-reference collection of selected pieces . . . adapted to fifty-two moods and situations*. This was an enormous anthology of about three hundred complete pieces ranging from nursery rhymes to national songs and including some of the best-known nineteenth-century music. Grieg featured prominently, but so did the obscure Otto Langey. In the margin of every page was an index of the fifty-two situations, so that one could flip directly from 'Doll' to 'Music-box', from 'Fire-Fighting' to 'Funeral', 'Gruesome', 'Joyful' or whatever as it arose on the screen. ('Fire-Fighting' included the 'card trio' from *Carmen*.)

A good improvising pianist could accomplish all this without a cue sheet, but an orchestra could not. Many musical directors of theatres, and even eminent conductors such as Eugene Goossens in a silent-film season with the LSO at Covent Garden (of all places) in 1922, compiled their own scores; Goossens found the 'numerous, indescribably weary, completely unknown' symphonies of August Enna perfect for his purpose.[31] Music specially prepared by a composer for a specific feature film in consultation with its director could not necessarily assume aesthetic precedence over this: Joseph Breil's score for D. W. Griffiths's *The Birth of a Nation* (1915), for example, contains a good deal of Liszt, Wagner and Tchaikovsky and many popular tunes such as 'Dixie' as well as his own music. It did however 'set standards of orchestration and cuing techniques'.[32]

Those standards were consolidated rather than obviated by the coming of sound film in 1927; the only musical revolution that this effected was, in addition to the incorporation of singing into the cinema when the musical went to Hollywood, the summary redundancy of thousands of theatre (i.e. cinema) musicians. Film music has perpetuated its techniques, even its styles, of romantic or melodramatic underscoring, soaring credit fanfares, indexical insertion of popular tunes, and predictable pastiche and parody (especially in cartoons) from that day to this. Art film can clearly pursue different aims, but the bourgeois commercial film represented, for the Austro-German tradition, that other side of the coin of modernist revolution, when a generation of Romantic opera, concerto, and operetta *maestri* arrived in Hollywood between

30 Max Winkler, 'The Origins of Film Music', *Films in Review* (December 1951), quoted in Prendergast, *Film Music*, p. 10.
31 Eugene Goossens, *Overture and Beginners*, London, 1951, pp. 182–6.
32 Prendergast, *Film Music*, p. 13.

the late 1920s and early 1940s: Max Steiner, Dimitri Tiomkin, Franz Waxman, Erich Korngold, and Miklós Rózsa were all professional émigrés from Europe, their names outweighing those of the native-born (David Raksin, Roy Webb, Bernard Herrmann, and Elmer Bernstein), and the appropriation of their skills in California attesting American supremacy like those of the German scientists in Nevada a decade later. Do we regret this? Would Steiner have been better off reserving his Wagnerian subtleties for operetta heroines, as he had in Vienna, rather than lavishing them on an outsize gorilla?[33] Not that he was old-fashioned; he and the other Hollywood film composers introduced modernism into their work. But they kept it where the public, and indeed the tonal tradition as a whole, has always preferred it: for the depiction of anguish.

Sacred and secular gentility

As popular music increasingly catered for people where they were rather than where their betters wanted them, it might be deduced that by 1900 not everyone was willing to subscribe to an upward cultural curve in this life; but most continued to aspire to heaven in the next, and music continued to play an important role in helping them to get there. It still does, for that dwindling number who so aspire a hundred years later, and the improvising church organist survives today as counterpart to the extinct cinema pianist. Attempts to capture the improvisatory spirit in anthem or cantata accompaniments and solo pieces, from Stainer's *Crucifixion* (1887) to Messiaen's organ cycles, offer a transcendent version of the film or theatre epic, playing out in musical terms the preparation or revelation of the divine mysteries to the suggestible faithful, just as film and theatre themselves have never hesitated to package the Bible for a commercial audience, whether via the Oberammergau Passion Play, Charlton Heston, or *Jesus Christ Superstar*.

Sacred music, Christian or Jewish (the two great bourgeois traditions operative in the West at the start of the twentieth century), had the most to fear from the loss of tonal inflection and mimesis, since for centuries it had used them to convey appropriate notions of the sublime and underline the preaching of the Word. It was understandably therefore a force for conservatism, and even today one may enter a church and experience processional or meditative music using much the same vocabulary of meanings as a hundred years ago, however updated (rumbling pedals, expanding chordal textures, long, satisfied tonics); or join in hymns with solid chord-by-chord harmonies, four-bar phrases, and subdued

33 For an account of the *King Kong* score see Christopher Palmer, *The Composer in Hollywood*, London, 1990, pp. 27–9; for a facsimile of Steiner's MS sketch of the closing music with its orchestral imitation of the spoken line 'Beauty Killed the Beast', see ibid., p. 20.

versions of dance rhythms, many favourites dating from the nineteenth century or earlier, standardized from sources covering many countries' vernacular traditions and at Christmas appealing almost equally to those outside the fold. The cultural politics of hymn-book editors such as Ralph Vaughan Williams who strove to effect this would deserve a study of their own. Much of this was also true, *mutatis mutandis*, of the synagogue.[34] Some of it – corporate spiritual enrichment through tonal rhetoric – even applies to school assemblies and football matches, their clients and charges still manipulated by the educational or ecclesiastical folklorists of a hundred years ago. And all of it was wholeheartedly applied to worship of the State rather than God in communist countries and movements; they had – still have? – their own tonal hymns of communal uplift, as indeed do most countries when it comes to a national anthem, blithely borrowing the musical syntax of Western imperialism however opposed to its legacy the state in question.

The decline of sacred music in the twentieth century would have taken place regardless of the musical pressures on tonality. But the former must have exacerbated the latter as fewer people, that diminishing army of choral amateurs, actually performed 'good' music in public[35] – performances which in the Protestant countries at least had gone right to the heart of European musical life with cyclical events in cities such as Düsseldorf and Birmingham, with Mendelssohn, Gounod, Dvořák, and Elgar all writing major works for the Birmingham Festival (which however did not survive the First World War). Thus oratorio, the concert mass, and the choral cantata, their lexicon of imagery ideally suited to maintaining the traditions of tonal drama and text-setting, lost generic force, despite impressive examples by Elgar (*The Dream of Gerontius*, 1900), Rachmaninov (*The Bells*, 1910), and Franz Schmidt (*The Book with Seven Seals*, 1937), and its continuing vitality in France and Switzerland (as in Lili Boulanger's psalm settings, Honegger's *King David* and *Joan of Arc*, and the works of Frank Martin). One can only wonder whether Skryabin, potentially so close to the yearning millions with his visionary programme of musical and human harmony, would have established his new world of cultural positivism had he lived longer and had the Great War not done its eschatological worst for spiritual consensus.

Away from the more traditional strongholds of the Roman Catholic church, where at least in theory (according to the 1903 *motu proprio* of Pius X) plainchant continued to suffice for most purposes, spiritual efficacy in music was

34 See Abraham Z. Idelsohn, 'Synagogue Song in the United States of America', in *Jewish Music: Its Historical Development*, New York, 1929, pp. 316–36.

35 See Dave Russell, 'Amateur Musicians and Their Repertoire', in Stephen Banfield (ed.), *Music in Britain: The Twentieth Century*, Oxford, 1995, pp. 145–76; pp. 145–9, for facts and figures on the decline of choral societies in Britain.

strongest at the lower end of the class spectrum and the more evangelical pole of the doctrinal one. Along with later evangelists, the American revivalists Moody and Sankey, beginning in the 1870s but building on earlier hymnody, had a tremendous impact far beyond their own country; their gospel songs, a kind of sacred counterpart to Stephen Foster, authorized the jaunty march or polka tune (sometimes bordering on ragtime) as the people's spiritual expression, as did countless Salvation Army bands on city streets, first in Britain and eventually worldwide. Long after adult sensibilities moved on, children perpetuated them in Sunday School hymns such as 'Jesus bids us shine'.[36] Not that adult sensibilities have moved on entirely; one remembered musical corollary to the twentieth century's abrupt end on 11 September 2001 will be 'The Battle Hymn of the Republic' sung in London's and Washington's cathedrals.

As for secular gentility, it must be remembered that, notwithstanding the theatre's ever-increasing scope (including cinematography), not everyone visited it in the early twentieth century. There were many who still disapproved (such as evangelical Protestants), who lived too far away, or were too poor, too ill, too old, or too young for ready access. Many genres were unsuitable for a family audience, and young women in particular were debarred from the very musical outlets in which they were being schooled at one remove through the songs, dances, romances, and fantasies they imbibed at the piano rather than on the stage – genteel songs, piano genre pieces, and their analogues for violin or cello, such as Saint-Saëns's *Le cygne* and Dvořák's *Humoresque*. This was the private sphere, its contiguity with the public not lost until genteel songs ceased being performed on the platform (ballads were interspersed with symphonies in metropolitan concert programmes well into the twentieth century, and into the twenty-first in the case of school concerts).

The 'royalty' ballad was every bit as commercial as the Tin Pan Alley song, though its financial workings were different, with publishers paying genteel professional singers to perform it at concerts or encouraging them to do so with a royalty on every copy sold. (Amateurs, by contrast, performed ballads 'without fee or licence' until performing rights began to be an issue with the growing reproductive technologies.) The distinction was not one of popularity but of class and race, as Hamm has explained with reference to the USA and the early work of Irving Berlin: there were 'genteel parlor songs . . . "of Heaven, Country, and Home"' for the representatives of white, Protestant culture, and there were 'rowdy stage songs . . . for working-class, ethnically diverse audiences', their lyrics 'humorous, ironic, sometimes deliberately crude, never sentimental or didactic'.[37] The division may have been less marked in Europe

36 Carey Bonner (ed.), *Child Songs*, Vol. I, Redhill, 1908, p. 64.
37 Hamm, 'Irving Berlin and Early Tin Pan Alley', pp. xvii, xix.

and the colonies and ex-colonies, but there was likely to be as much difference between a music-hall (or cabaret) song and a parlour ballad as between a parlour ballad and an art song. Where the early twentieth century is concerned, then, the important historical distinction is perhaps not popular versus 'classical' but proletarian versus genteel song – the latter, wherever it lay on the spectrum of taste between homespun and elite, sporting social or aesthetic pretensions, the former, however well-crafted, needing none.

This distinction helps make sense of the huge market for genteel songs and piano pieces. Only one small end of that market explored the Lied and *mélodie* traditions. It was perpetuated by Wolf, Strauss, Schoeck, and Schoenberg in the German-speaking world, Duparc, Fauré, Debussy, Ravel, and Poulenc in France, and Pizzetti and Casella in Italy; it was also transplanted without much change into English (by Parry, Stanford, Vaughan Williams, Butterworth, Gurney, Warlock, Ireland, and Finzi in Britain, and by Cadman, Carpenter, Hageman, Rorem, and Barber in the USA). Piano pieces, with their impressionistic or programmatic titles, inhabited a similar poetic world and were often written by the same composers, including Debussy, Fauré, Grieg, Macdowell, Zemlinsky, and Ireland. These genres for the concert or salon elite (the piano pieces, for example, could be quite difficult) shaded off into music for the home: Amy Woodforde-Finden's *Indian Love Lyrics* as exotic fantasy, musical furniture to complement an oriental rug or side table; Vaughan Williams's 'Linden Lea'; Easthope Martin's 'Come to the Fair'; and, at the piano, Ethelbert Nevin's 'Narcissus', Arndt's 'Nola', Confrey's 'Kitten on the Keys' and Mayerl's 'Marigold', keeping the idiom up-to-date and approaching stride piano, Gershwin and jazz. Radio probably killed the parlour ballad in the 1920s, as genteel song was transformed into the hit number, broadcast from the ballroom with dance-band accompaniment. Romance and novelty at the piano resurfaced in the educational market (with Walter Carroll, or Templeton's 'Bach Goes to Town'), though star performers from Russ Conway to Richard Clayderman helped preserve the allure of the ivories.

Devaluation

The overwhelming message from these perceptions of text, stage, and the tonal tradition from around 1900 to 1930 and beyond may seem to be one of continuities: between high and low, new and old, big and small, texted and untexted, abstract and referential, functional and 'pure', even good and bad music. Continuities there certainly were. Fauré wrote a gorgeous waltz melody as the finale's second subject in his Piano Quartet no 1 in C minor (1879, replacement finale 1883); its essence lies in the (major-key) phrase $\hat{5}$-$\hat{2}$-$\hat{3}$-$\hat{4}$-$\hat{5}$-$\hat{6}$-$\hat{5}$-$\hat{4}$-$\hat{5}$, floated on harmonies oscillating from and back to the dominant. Everything about it signifies beatific or innocent ecstasy. Twenty years later Puccini made Fauré's latent drama manifest when he used exactly the same phrase and harmonic gambit, in the same key (E flat), to encapsulate his heroine's moment of submission to Pinkerton in Act I of *Madama Butterfly* (cue 128), the moment in which she asks him 'to love me like a baby'. Another generation further on, in 1936, the phrase and its treatment recur, once again in E flat, set to the title words of the song 'Why Is There Ever Goodbye?' from Ivor Novello's London musical *Careless Rapture* – words which, together with those of the show's title, indicate clearly enough that ecstasy is still the expressive topic of the moment. Finally, in 1942, we find Kern using the same idea in his song 'Dearly Beloved' from the Columbia film musical *You Were Never Lovelier*, now transposed down to C major to fit the new chest-voice, 'belting' type of leading female singer.[38] Again the musical essence remains, as does the topic: the lyrics 'Dearly beloved, how clearly I see, / Somewhere in Heaven you were fashioned for me' offer another image of immortality in a moment of erotic perception.

A tonal formula thus retains its meaning across chamber music, opera, stage musical, and film.[39] But if meaning remains constant between Fauré in 1883 and Kern sixty years later, value does not. One might observe, cynically, that there is a curve from latency to blatancy between the four examples, as an embedded subject within a large-scale, abstract, instrumental form (Fauré) gives way in succession to a repeated motif underlining a specific moment in an operatic libretto (Puccini), a theme which, like its explanatory lyrics, is the sole focus of a song (Novello), and finally the melopoetic (words-and-music) hook of a 32-bar refrain (Kern). Moreover, Fauré is the one practitioner of the four who fully understands how precious such a musical moment is: the ecstasy is not even recapturable, he tells us in his recapitulation, which comes to a hiatus on a piano cadenza before veiled refractions of the theme re-gather into an acknowledgement of its passing. There is no restatement.

The curve is also reflected in the music's cultural currency. Fauré's quartet was premiered on St Valentine's Day 1880 before an elite subscription audience, its majority probably musicians, at the Société Nationale in the Salle Pleyel,

38 The song was composed as 'Serenata'; its autograph manuscript is in C major (I am grateful to Wayne Shirley of the Library of Congress for this information). In the film, it is first sung by Fred Astaire in D flat major, later by Rita Hayworth – or rather by Nan Wynn dubbing her vocals – in B flat major.

39 Following Philip Tagg, it might be referred to as a *museme* (Raymond Monelle, *Linguistics and Semiotics in Music*, Chur, 1992, pp. 286–7). Deryck Cooke, whose observations of expressive similarities across different styles and genres have perhaps been unfairly maligned, deals with it in summary form as (major-mode) $\hat{5}$-$\hat{6}$-$\hat{5}$, describing it in terms of 'joyful serenity, with a slight element of longing, or pleading', 'a burst of pleasurable longing' and 'the lover express[ing] his utter dependence on the beloved' (Deryck Cooke, *The Language of Music*, London, 1959, pp. 145–6).

Paris, and again under the same auspices on 5 April 1884, with the new finale.[40] The Salle Pleyel could accommodate around 450, a number roughly commensurate with its elegant ballroom appearance.[41] The Société's concerts were 'evenings of rare charm',[42] but the quartet's appeal was so rarefied that Fauré had difficulty publishing it.[43] Posterity regards it as a masterpiece: its value has accordingly been cumulative, a long-term investment of creative capital. *Madama Butterfly*'s first performance, at La Scala, Milan, on 17 February 1904, will have been to an international first-night audience of over two thousand,[44] its constituency a blend of critical expertise, social power, wealth, fashion, and perhaps cross-class enthusiasm, this last presumably in increasing evidence as the opera's repertoire performances gradually (and singly) accumulated over time and geographical space. In short, it became very popular – though it could be argued that as a transitory part of a through-composed score the passage under discussion began to acquire greater value, in terms of rarity, than the opera's highlights (such as 'One Fine Day', which was recorded from 1908 onwards by the likes of Enrico Caruso, Geraldine Farrar, and Emmy Destinn, so reaching tens of thousands more listeners than could find a way, or would care to go, to a staged performance of the whole opera).

As a separate number surrounded in the musical by spoken dialogue, 'Why Is There Ever Goodbye?' was conceived from the start as a quantifiably more detachable property, in terms of sheet-music sales (probably still greater than those of recordings in 1936), than anything from *Madama Butterfly*. At the same time it attracted large numbers to a star performance at the Theatre Royal, Drury Lane (the show opened on 11 September), given by Olive Gilbert who duly recorded it; the theatre seats over three thousand[45] and was filled to capacity for 296 performances.[46] The song is reprised in the score, which means that Charles Prentice, the show's musical director (and orchestrator), must have conducted it nearly six hundred times and it was heard by nearly a million pairs of ears in the theatre in under ten months; radio broadcasts, record playings, amateur performances of the song, and the subsequent national tour of the show multiplied this exposure. And given the simple, repetitive structure of

40 The first version of the finale does not survive; see Robert Orledge, *Gabriel Fauré*, London, 1979, pp. 60, 283. For the Société Nationale, see Elaine Brody, *Paris: The Musical Kaleidoscope 1870–1925*, New York, 1987, pp. 17–19.

41 The Salle Pleyel is illustrated in David Charlton, John Trevitt, and Guy Gosselin, 'Paris: §VI', in Stanley Sadie and John Tyrrell (eds.), *The New Grove Dictionary of Music and Musicians* (2nd edn), 29 vols., London, 2001, Vol. XIX, p. 110. I am grateful to Nigel Simeone for confirming its approximate capacity.

42 Charles Koechlin, *Gabriel Fauré (1845–1924)* (tr. Leslie Orrey), London, 1945, p. 6.

43 Orledge, *Gabriel Fauré*, p. 66.

44 *Grove* gives the seating capacity of La Scala as 2289; see Edward A. Langhans, 'Theatre Architecture', in Stanley Sadie (ed.), *The New Grove Dictionary of Opera*, 4 vols., London, 1992, Vol. IV, p. 715.

45 Ibid.

46 James Harding, *Ivor Novello: a Biography*, London, 1987, p. 135.

'Why Is There Ever Goodbye?', to have appreciated (memorized, been moved by) the phrase was to have grasped the whole. The song offered complete, instant gratification together with value for money: in a word, it was cheap, in terms of both the index of labour and the rewards for creator and consumer.

More or less the same will have been true of the Kern song, though as part of a Hollywood film released at Radio City Music Hall, New York, on 3 December 1942, and then nationwide and 'worldwide' shortly thereafter, it was heard by even greater numbers of people (and with a far greater level of reprise, as background underscoring) within an even shorter period.[47] It was also heard at considerably less financial cost (via a local cinema rather than a trip to the West End of London), and with minimum cultural effort. A musical-theatre audience had to muster the will to witness and applaud a live musical performer; a cinema audience took whatever was offered weekly, virtually all genres entailing the subliminal consumption of a musical background from which the temporary foregrounding of song in a musical film was effortlessly accomplished. Music had never come more cheaply than this, though its devaluation would later go much further.

Theories and dates of change

What happened to the styles, types, and capabilities of texted, staged, and referential music in the first third of the twentieth century? How are we to construe this shift of values across the bourgeois spectrum?

It was certainly part of modernism's programme to disrupt that spectrum, to put a stop to tonality's social promiscuity. We can sense this from two great novels from the first half of the century, Thomas Mann's *Dr Faustus* and E. M. Forster's *Howards End*. In a famous passage from the former, the twenty-year-old composer hero, Adrian Leverkühn, writes – the year is 1905 – 'Why must I think that almost all, no, all the methods and conventions of art today *are good for parody only*?'[48] This follows a description he has given of the semantics and rhetoric of what could be almost any late-Romantic symphony, or even the outer movements of Debussy's *La mer*. There are more than thirty personifications of tonal practice in the description: verbs that show instruments, melodies, chords, or the composer himself acting out a narrative, like characters on a stage. Tonal music, at least for the provincial bourgeois listener

47 Benjamin ('The Work of Art', p. 237) wrote: 'In 1927 it was calculated that a major film, in order to pay its way, had to reach an audience of nine million.' Even if it took six months to do this, it was still being seen by sixteen to eighteen times as many people as visited Drury Lane for *Careless Rapture* within the same period.

48 Thomas Mann, *Dr Faustus: The Life of the German Composer Adrian Leverkühn As Told by a Friend* (tr. H. T. Lowe-Porter), Harmondsworth, 1968, pp. 130–2.

of 1900, spoke and acted: appreciation was inseparable from its expressive narrativity. Moreover, its concern was sublimity, for in another passage we witness Leverkühn's mentor lecturing on melodic processes in Beethoven's op. 111: heaven, nature, eternity, consolation, pathos, and benediction are the states and objects invoked by verbal analogy. In 1910, Forster visited similar constructions on Beethoven's Fifth Symphony in an imagined contemporary performance at Queen's Hall, London. His bourgeois characters likewise hear speech ('Here Beethoven, after humming and hawing with great sweetness, said "Heigho", and the Andante came to an end') and drama ('the music [of the Scherzo] started with a goblin walking quietly over the universe, from end to end'), though the drama is not always serious: the goblins are followed by 'a trio of elephants dancing'.[49]

Both Mann and Forster could have classical music depicting and saying things because, a hundred years ago, that is what most people believed it did. Many still do. But modernism wanted something done about an audience that could hear elephants dancing in Beethoven's Fifth because it was used to them doing so to similar music in the circus and, indeed, the 'silent' animated film. New 'serious' music would abstract itself from the tonal analogue and repackage the old in intellectually purified ways: musical comedies and Gaiety Theatre chorus girls were among the objects on the Vorticists' blacklists.[50] And modernism was not the only revolution that displaced bourgeois musical traditions. Jazz (if one includes ragtime rhythms) arose to mock the classics from below at the same time as modernism was parodying or negating their principles from above; syncopation, blues harmonies, and what one might call 'dialect' instrumentation and performance techniques (to retain the analogy and indeed the association with speech) were its main weapons. Finally primitivism, that is a programme of modality, drones, ostinati, percussiveness, chested vocality, and much else besides, also ousted tonal decorum, starting in art music (Bartók, Vaughan Williams, Orff) and contributing perhaps more than any other impulse to the rock revolution whose *lingua franca* remains fully operational in and beyond 2001.

How then to construe the status of these revolutions? The first thing is to recognize the extent to which they were a northern European and North American phenomenon. As Ernst Roth pointed out, the great tradition of Italian opera carried on more or less unperturbed all through his inter-war years in Vienna as a young employee at Universal Edition, publisher of Berg, Schoenberg, Webern, Bartók, Janáček, Weill, Malipiero, and virtually every other modernist: the

49 Edward Morgan Forster, *Howards End*, Harmondsworth, 1941, pp. 31–2.
50 See Paul Edwards (ed.), *Blast: Vorticism 1914–1918*, Aldershot, 2000, p. 18.

young Puccini, Mascagni, Leoncavallo, Ponchielli, Giordano, and Cilea simply had to wait 'on the doorstep of the hall of fame' prepared for them by Verdi. 'The massive chain of mountains', Roth writes, 'seemed to be having on music the effect it has always had on the weather: the stormy, unsettled conditions which beset composers and publishers in the north were unknown in the south.'[51] Something similar must apply to Latin America, where urban modernism flourished while political revolutions took root but, perhaps because of this, life went on and 'ordinary' music retained its representative distinctiveness.

But in the more industrialized, imperially competitive north, ordinary music was doomed. One could argue that it simply got left behind in an era of rapid developments, or that it had nothing new to say and had already built up its maximum store of pieces and types. There is some truth in this, though it does not explain how, towards the end of his life, Rachmaninov could write such works as the Third Symphony and the *Symphonic Dances* in the old language, without a hint of staleness and with a genuinely true emotional quality (not untouched by Americanism). It does however confirm that the sounds of *Music in the Air* with which we began this chapter were very old-fashioned for 1932, their polka phraseology and harmonies showing little fundamental advance on those of Johann Strauss I. This was hardly music's fault, for its vernacular channels have seldom been the place for sustained progressivism – as Gershwin realised when he created *Porgy and Bess*, his most ambitious music, as an opera rather than a musical. Samples of the vernacular were of course appropriated by modernism for its own purposes; but when this happened, what was left behind lost aesthetic caste, if it had not already done so.

Dahlhaus called this residue *kitsch*, the problem of the *Trivialmusik* industry bequeathed to the twentieth century by the late nineteenth and the despair of Adorno when he contemplated the regressive listener to radio, film, and gramophone record. Such labels were a powerful way of putting the tonal consensus in its place. Kitsch, according to Dahlhaus, debases the tonal tradition because it 'has hybrid ambitions which far outreach the capabilities of its actual structures and sounds, and are manifested in effects without cause, empty attitudinizing, and titles and instructions for performance which are not justified by the musical results'.[52] Again, writing of the German equivalent of Tin Pan Alley songs (and in particular its refrains), Adorno found kitsch's task to be 'to awake, through the retention of old and superannuated formal types, the impression of an attested collective binding force'; this was achieved through

51 Ernst Roth, *The Business of Music: Reflections of a Music Publisher*, London, 1969, p. 56.

52 Carl Dahlhaus, *Between Romanticism and Modernism: Four Studies in the Music of the Later Nineteenth Century* (tr. Mary Whittall), Berkeley, 1980, p. 12.

the use of musical 'small change', that is, 'formulae which have become so familiar through over-use that they have become stereotypes'.[53]

But either of these descriptions (barring only Dahlhaus's final clause) might be as easily applied to a Donizetti *scena* as to a von Tilzer ballad, so they do not get us far beyond prejudice or what Benjamin called the 'ancient lament' about easy access to art.[54] They also theorize the consumer whilst forgetting that practical music could be servant as well as master, particularly in the theatre where actor-managers literally called the tune, players and conductor in the pit slipping in response 'into the comfortable patterns of making music which behaved in familiar ways and which therefore retained conventions long after their peak of fashion in high art music'.[55] A different set of labels might be fairer to the material, and here we should return to our 'ecstasy' phrase for a moment. Its four manifestations tell us, perhaps, that it became possible to buy into notions of sublimity (what else is ecstasy in music?) at less and less cost, and with less and less effort and discrimination. With the lowering of these barriers, the sublime and other aesthetic categories lost their sense of particularity.

'In 1914', Cyril Ehrlich writes, 'most people acknowledged an ascending order of popular, "middlebrow" and "highbrow" music, without question.' True: highbrow music had its canons of sublimity – of the sublime, the beautiful, and the picturesque, if we can map those favoured eighteenth-century artistic categories onto the musical types outlined earlier.[56] Ehrlich continues: 'It was common to pay at least lip-service to the necessity of improving taste: as intrinsically worthwhile, and as a necessary part of that social conditioning . . . which had begun in Victorian times.'[57] But ascending orders, in music as in life, implied that one had a place and knew it, however much one might aspire beyond it. And it could be argued that by 1900 the inherited world of tonality, with its understood texts and gestures and meanings, had something to offer those in most places – those, to adopt David Cannadine's analysis of class in Britain with its indubitable echoes in other countries, who inhabited a world

53 Max Paddison, *Adorno's Aesthetics of Music*, Cambridge, 1993, p. 27, referring to 'Schlageranalysen', *Anbruch* 11 (Heft 3, March 1929) and quoting the posthumously published essay of *c.*1932, 'Kitsch', both printed in Theodor Adorno, *Gesammelte Schriften*, Frankfurt, 1970–86, Vol. XVIII.

54 Benjamin, 'The Work of Art', p. 232.

55 Anne Dhu Shapiro, 'Action Music in American Pantomime and Melodrama, 1730–1913', *American Music* 2 (1984), pp. 49–72; p. 68.

56 William Crotch, painter as well as composer and scholar, is the most convenient authority for these terms (though he called the picturesque the 'ornamental'); see his 'On the Three Styles of Music – the Sublime, the Beautiful, and the Ornamental' (1831), reprinted in Peter le Huray and James Day (eds.), *Music and Aesthetics in the Eighteenth and Early-Nineteenth Centuries*, Cambridge, 1981, pp. 427–42.

57 Cyril Ehrlich, 'The Marketplace', in Banfield (ed.), *Music in Britain: The Twentieth Century*, pp. 39–53; p. 39.

of 'us' and 'them', of 'lower', 'middle' and 'upper', or of a seamless hierarchical web of positions and values from bottom to top.[58]

Ehrlich refers to 'the old profusion' of marketed music;[59] with it went what one might call the old way of listening. And I would argue that in that old way of listening, the sublime, the beautiful, and the picturesque were the province not only of those at the top of the ladder of taste (a position that required money and class to attain), but also of the more lowly, precisely because of the profusion of tonal music of all types and on all levels that the nineteenth century had generated. Each had their highbrow and lowbrow outlets, their 'great' and 'little' traditions (to adapt a distinction from folklore),[60] their site and its shadow. By contrast, in the new way of listening whose rise I have traced, the high and the low abandoned their separateness, their accepted hierarchy, and submitted to a levelling down and indeed a secularization that had to be rejected by the elite.

Thus the old sublime could encompass the great oratorio (Elgar, Mahler's Eighth) and the little hymn ('Land of Hope and Glory' or 'The Day Thou Gavest'); tragic epic on the old front was Verdi's *Aida* (great) versus 'Bredon Hill' recited or sung in Graham Peel's setting (little). The old picturesque was Strauss and his sheep in *Don Quixote*, Respighi and his legions, Wagner's Beckmesser pantomime in *Die Meistersinger* on the great side, Punch and Judy and circus knockabout on the little. The old beautiful was the great *bel canto* Bellini aria or its 'small' sentimental equivalent, 'Home, Sweet Home'. But in the new way of listening the forces of commodification – increasingly a matter of instant economic trade-off – brought the great and little traditions together and flattened them out as though their values and dimensions were the same. One size had to fit all where incorporated global business was concerned. The technological media, above all cinema, were partly responsible for this standardization, but one sees the same forces at work in popular musical theatre between the era of Gilbert and Sullivan and that of Cameron Mackintosh and Lloyd Webber.

The upshot was that everywhere the small – that reduction of values to the lowest common denominator of meaning that mass culture inevitably entailed – masqueraded as the big. The new sublime was the Rodgers and Hart love ballad ('My Funny Valentine', with its pseudo-tragic minor-key opening that sells out to the major by the end); tragic epic on the new front was *Show Boat*, its score in Act II tailing off into bits and pieces, some of them not even by Kern, as 'book' values took over from musical ones. The new picturesque was Eric Coates's *The Three Bears*, leading straight to Disney and mickey-mousing

58 David Cannadine, *Class in Britain*, New Haven, 1998.
59 Ehrlich, 'The Marketplace', p. 40.
60 Matthew Hodgart, 'Introduction', in *The Faber Book of Ballads*, London, 1965, pp. 11–12.

(*Snow White and the Seven Dwarfs*, 1937). The new beautiful was 'Tell Me, Pretty Maiden' or Kern's 'They Didn't Believe Me', the tangible influence of Bellini skewed by the cockiness of blackface minstrelsy. And so on.

And the date at which it all changed? The history of the 'ecstasy' phrase would suggest that it was a gradual process. Nevertheless, 1924 sounds attractive because it is when Puccini and Fauré died, and when Gershwin stormed the Aeolian Hall in New York with *Rhapsody in Blue*, climaxing Paul Whiteman's much-publicised 'experiment in modern music' with his first performance of a piece that combined tonal convention (tonal fustian, some would call it) with white jazz. Kern's reaction to the jazz age in that same year was different: he forbade dance-band arrangements to be made of his latest score, *Sitting Pretty*.

On the other hand, according to Virginia Woolf, it was 'in or about December 1910' that 'human character changed'. She continued: 'All human relations have shifted – those between masters and servants, husbands and wives, parents and children. And when human relations change there is at the same time a change in religion, conduct, politics, and literature.'[61] And music, she might have added. She would have been right, if we consider Richard Strauss's *Der Rosenkavalier* as it went into rehearsal for its first performance, at the Dresden Court Opera, on 26 January 1911, the epitome of aesthetic retreat as 'progressivism' fell out of the modernist race.[62] Another world premiere, the first ever at the Met in New York, on 10 December 1910, was hugely indicative of shifting cultural power: Puccini's *La fanciulla del West*, fusing opera and western, old world and new, with its unspoken challenge to American commercial music over the coming decades. A few months earlier Gustav Mahler, doyen of tonal expressivity, had overseen his last premiere, that of the Eighth Symphony (Munich, 12–13 September, with Mann in the audience), and sketched his last music, the Tenth Symphony. Again, in mid-December 1910 Igor Stravinsky was brought into collaboration with the designer Alexandre Benois on the ballet, *Petrushka*, with which he turned his back on the romance of *The Firebird* for fairground puppetry: this was pantomimicry with an objective vengeance entirely new for genteel purposes, however reliant on folk tradition. It jerked gesture and affective identification out of their accustomed grooves as forcefully as the syncopation and the 'coon-shouting' vocal style of 'Alexander's Ragtime Band' did the traditional relationship of text and music – and that, too, was composed 'in or

61 Virgina Woolf, 'Mr Bennett and Mrs Brown', in Rachel Bowlby (ed.), *A Woman's Essays (Selected Essays: Volume One)*, London, 1992, pp. 69–87; pp. 70–1. November–December 1910 was the date of the first Post-Impressionist Exhibition of painting in London, very much a rallying point for the Bloomsbury Group of which Woolf was a member; Edward VII had died the previous May, and Woolf's essay is about the demise of Victorian and Edwardian values in literature and the rise of new ('Georgian') ones.

62 Norman Del Mar dubs Strauss's earlier mature operas, the one-act *Salome* and *Elektra*, 'the stage tone poems', in *Richard Strauss: A Critical Commentary on His Life and Works*, 3 vols., London, 1962–72.

about December 1910' (it was published in March 1911).[63] And if 'Alexander's Ragtime Band' was wrenching the small-scale, confidential gesture from the reflective to the irresistible virtually within earshot of Mahler's strained sensibilities in his new abode, New York,[64] then back in Mahler's old home, Vienna, and partly reliant on his charity, Arnold Schoenberg was wrenching it in the opposite direction: towards the repellent, as evidenced by his op. 19 *Klavierstücke*, the first five of which were composed in February 1911 – shortly after his initial contact with the expressionist painter Wassily Kandinsky, whose first abstract *Composition* had just been completed.

1910 or 1924? It hardly matters, for despite these revolutions, tonal practice – certainly tonal meaning in its defining relationship to text and stage – continued; indeed it was growing rapidly throughout the first third of the twentieth century, as much of this chapter has indicated. What changed was its status. It travelled from the mastery of Wagner's music dramas to the servitude of Hollywood; from *The Ring* to *King Kong*. It was a story of commodification, which pricked the Romantic artist's bubble by practical or critical means and left him or her (but mostly him) best off pursuing the Romantic illusion as modernism of one kind or another. Schoenberg may have said that there were still plenty of fine tunes to be written in C major, but he did not write them.

Bibliography

Adorno, Theodor. *Gesammelte Schriften*, Frankfurt, 1970–86.

Aguilar, Emanuel and Rev. D. A. de Sola. *Sephardi Melodies: Being the Traditional Liturgical Chants of the Spanish & Portuguese Jews' Congregation [,] London. Part I: 'The Ancient Melodies'*, Oxford, 5691 – 1931.

Benjamin, Walter. *Illuminations* (ed. Hannah Arendt, tr. Harry Zorn), London, 1999.

Bonner, Carey (ed.). *Child Songs*, Vol. I, Redhill, 1908.

Brody, Elaine. *Paris: the Musical Kaleidoscope, 1870–1925*, New York, 1987.

Cannadine, David. *Class in Britain*, New Haven, 1998.

Charlton, David, John Trevitt, and Guy Gosselin. 'Paris: §VI', in Stanley Sadie and John Tyrrell (eds.), *The New Grove Dictionary of Music and Musicians* (2nd edn), 29 vols., London, 2001, Vol. XIX, pp. 100–11.

Cone, Edward. 'The World of Opera and its Inhabitants', in *Music: A View from Delft*, Chicago, 1989, pp. 125–38.

Cooke, Deryck. *The Language of Music*, London, 1959.

63 For the genesis, dating, early performance history and style of 'Alexander's Ragtime Band', see Charles Hamm, *Irving Berlin: Songs from the Melting Pot: The Formative Years, 1907–1914*, New York, 1997, pp. 102–36.

64 Well, not quite: Mahler stayed at the Hotel Savoy, whereas Berlin was living on East 18th Street. But like most visiting composers, Mahler duly pronounced upon American music in the press, referring to 'trashy' popular songs and ragtime. See his interview in *The Etude*, May 1911, reprinted in Zoltan Roman, *Gustav Mahler's American Years 1907–1911: A Documentary History*, Stuyvesant, NY, 1989, pp. 442–5.

Crotch, William. 'On the Three Styles of Music – the Sublime, the Beautiful, and the Ornamental' (1831), reprinted in Peter le Huray and James Day (eds.), *Music and Aesthetics in the Eighteenth and Early-Nineteenth Centuries*, Cambridge, 1981, pp. 427–42.
Dahlhaus, Carl. *Between Romanticism and Modernism: Four Studies in the Music of the Later Nineteenth Century* (tr. Mary Whittall), Berkeley, 1980.
Del Mar, Norman. *Richard Strauss: A Critical Commentary on His Life and Works*, 3 vols., London, 1962–72.
Edwards, Paul (ed.). *Blast: Vorticism 1914–1918*, Aldershot, 2000.
Ehrlich, Cyril. 'The Marketplace', in Stephen Banfield (ed.), *Music in Britain: The Twentieth Century*, Oxford, 1995, pp. 39–53.
Erdmann, Hans, Giuseppe Becce, and Ludwig Brav. *Allgemeines Handbuch der Filmmusik*, Berlin, 1927.
Forster, Edward Morgan. *Howards End*, Harmondsworth, 1941.
Forte, Allen. *The American Popular Ballad of the Golden Era: 1924–1950*, Princeton, NJ, 1995.
Fuld, James J. *The Book of World-Famous Music: Classical, Popular and Folk* (5th edn), Mineola, NY, 2000.
Gabler, Neal. *An Empire of Their Own: How the Jews Invented Hollywood*, New York, 1988.
Gilroy, Paul. *The Black Atlantic: Modernity and Double Consciousness*, London, 1993.
Goossens, Eugene. *Overture and Beginners*, London, 1951.
Hamm, Charles (ed.). *Irving Berlin: Early Songs*, 3 vols, Madison, WI, 1994.
Hamm, Charles. *Irving Berlin: Songs from the Melting Pot: the Formative Years, 1907–1914*, New York, 1997.
Yesterdays: Popular Song in America, New York, 1979.
Harding, James. *Ivor Novello: A Biography*, London, 1987.
Hodgart, Matthew. 'Introduction', in *The Faber Book of Ballads*, London, 1965, pp. 11–22.
Idelsohn, Abraham Z. 'Synagogue Song in the United States of America', in *Jewish Music: Its Historical Development*, New York, 1929, pp. 316–36.
Kislan, Richard. *The Musical: A Look at the American Musical Theater* (2nd edn), New York, 1995.
Koechlin, Charles. *Gabriel Fauré (1845–1924)* (tr. Leslie Orrey), London, 1945.
Lamb, Andrew. *150 Years of Popular Musical Theatre*, New Haven, 2000.
Langhans, Edward A. 'Theatre Architecture', in Stanley Sadie (ed.), *The New Grove Dictionary of Opera*, 4 vols., London, 1992, Vol. IV, pp. 709–22.
Laurence, Dan H. (ed.). *Shaw's Music: The Complete Musical Criticism in Three Volumes*, London, 1981.
Levine, Lawrence. *Highbrow/Lowbrow: The Emergence of Cultural Hierarchy in America*, Cambridge, MA, 1988.
Levy, Alan Howard. 'The Search for Identity in American Music, 1890–1920', *American Music* 2 (1984), pp. 70–81.
Locke, Ralph P. 'Cutthroats and Casbah Dancers, Muezzins and Timeless Sands: Musical Images of the Middle East', *Nineteenth-Century Music* 22 (1998), pp. 20–53.
Mann, Thomas. *Dr Faustus: the Life of the German Composer Adrian Leverkühn As Told by a Friend* (tr. H. T. Lowe-Porter), Harmondsworth, 1968.

Marks, Martin. *Music and the Silent Film: Contexts and Case Studies, 1895–1924*, New York, 1997.
Mayer, David and Matthew Scott. *Four Bars of 'Agit': Incidental Music for Victorian and Edwardian Melodrama*, London, 1983.
Monelle, Raymond. *Linguistics and Semiotics in Music*, Chur, 1992.
Newman, Ernest. *Elgar*, London, 1906.
O'Neill, Norman. 'Music to Stage Plays', *Proceedings of the Musical Association* 37 (1910–11), pp. 85–102.
Orledge, Robert. *Gabriel Fauré*, London, 1979.
Paddison, Max. *Adorno's Aesthetics of Music*, Cambridge, 1993.
Palmer, Christopher. *The Composer in Hollywood*, London, 1990.
Prendergast, Roy. *Film Music: A Neglected Art*, New York, 1977.
Rodgers, Richard. *Musical Stages: An Autobiography* (2nd edn), New York, 1995.
Roman, Zoltan. *Gustav Mahler's American Years 1907–1911: A Documentary History*, Stuyvesant, NY, 1989.
Rossiter, Frank R. *Charles Ives and His America*, New York, 1975.
Roth, Ernst. *The Business of Music: Reflections of a Music Publisher*, London, 1969.
Russell, Dave. 'Amateur Musicians and Their Repertoire', in Stephen Banfield (ed.), *Music in Britain: The Twentieth Century*, Oxford, 1995, pp. 145–76.
Shapiro, Anne Dhu. 'Action Music in American Pantomime and Melodrama, 1730–1913', *American Music* 2 (1984), pp. 49–72.
Stradling, Robert and Meirion Hughes. *The English Musical Renaissance 1840–1940: Constructing a National Music* (2nd edn), Manchester, 2001.
Strasser, Michael. 'The Société Nationale and Its Adversaries: The Musical Politics of *L'Invasion Germanique* in the 1870s', *Nineteenth-Century Music* 24 (2001), pp. 225–51.
Taruskin, Richard. *Stravinsky and the Russian Traditions: A Biography of the Works Through* Mavra, 2 vols., Oxford, 1996.
Tawaststjerna, Erik. *Sibelius*, 3 vols., London, 1976–97.
Van der Lek, Robert. 'Concert Music as Reused Film Music: E-W Korngold's Self-Arrangements', *Acta Musicologica* 66 (1994), pp. 78–112.
Wachsmann, Klaus and Patrick O'Connor. 'Cabaret', in Stanley Sadie and John Tyrrell (eds.), *The New Grove Dictionary of Music and Musicians* (2nd edn), 29 vols., London, 2001, Vol. IV, pp. 762–4.
Woolf, Virginia. 'Mr Bennett and Mrs Brown', in Rachel Bowlby (ed.), *A Woman's Essays (Selected Essays: Volume One)*, London, 1992, pp. 69–87.

·5·

Classic jazz to 1945

JAMES LINCOLN COLLIER

Precursors

Jazz has proved to be one of the most significant forms of music to arise in the twentieth century. Aesthetic considerations aside, it has been the source for the two most important forms of popular music in the West, and to a considerable extent elsewhere: the big dance band, which dominated popular music from about 1925 to 1945, and what is loosely called rock, in its various manifestations. Without jazz neither of these forms could have existed. As for 'classic' jazz, this term arose in the last twenty years or so of the twentieth century as a catch-all to subsume a variety of forms of music that existed before the arrival of 'modern' jazz in about 1945. The word 'classic' is a loaded one, chosen for its overtones of prestigious classical music, and reflecting the pressure during this period to assimilate jazz within the academic canon of great music; in this chapter, however, it is employed simply as a convenient term to cover pre-modern jazz, including Dixieland, swing and their variants, all of which share harmonic and rhythmic systems that are significantly different from those of modern jazz.

Jazz arose in the United States at the opening of the twentieth century out of a unique set of circumstances: the presence of a concentrated population of blacks and racially mixed 'Creoles' in the New Orleans area; rapidly developing systems of mechanical entertainment, including the player piano, sound recording, and radio; a craze for social dancing; and a dramatic shift in American attitudes occurring in about 1910–25. Broadly speaking, it is an amalgam of Western popular music and a music created in North America by black slaves of West African origin and their descendants. To simplify considerably, the more formal styles of West African music during the eighteenth and nineteenth centuries employed a repetitive, often fairly rapid beat, usually featuring two or as many as six repeated and interlocking metres. Percussive instruments were essential, but much of the music was vocal; in addition, a variety of wind and string instruments were employed. Scales were mainly pentatonic, with semitones being avoided (or, when they did occur, being widened to something like a three-quarter tone). Music was woven into virtually all aspects of West African life, accompanying work as well as religious and ceremonial events.

Most of the blacks brought as slaves to the New World were initially shipped to the Caribbean area, especially the sugar and tobacco islands; from here many were subsequently shipped to what would be called the United States. In the Caribbean most slaves worked in large gangs and lived in cabin communities, and could maintain much of their African culture, including their music. Although a considerable number of slaves in the American South worked in gangs on large plantations, by far the majority were scattered among the tens of thousands of small single-family farms on which most Americans dwelt until well after the Civil War. Such slaves lived in close proximity to the white families who owned them, sleeping and eating apart, but often working in the fields together, attending the same church (at least into the nineteenth century), and hunting together, with their children playing together in dusty dooryards.

Such blacks perforce became largely westernized. In particular, they sang standard hymns in church, sometimes played for the dances of their masters, and inevitably heard the popular music that was everywhere around them. Through a process of synergy, they melded Western and African forms to produce a black folk music with its own practices and conventions: a music that was neither African nor European, but *sui generis*. We understand it only murkily through the testimony of a handful of interested whites who studied it mainly in the mid- and late nineteenth century. It was largely vocal, either solo, or in groups – as in work songs and church 'spirituals' – and it usually had a repetitive ground beat and a rhythmic 'hitch', with some notes falling slightly ahead of or behind the beat. Widening of the semitones of the diatonic scales, usually by microtonally lowering the third and seventh degrees, appears to have been standard practice. Falsetto, melismata, and a coarsening of tone for emotional intensity were common.

From this music there developed three forms of importance to jazz. The first of these was the plantation melody. In North America there had always been considerable interest among whites in what was seen as the exotic black culture; this was especially true of black music, which was familiar yet strangely different. By the 1830s white entertainers in black face were having much popular success with parodic versions of black song and dance. Soon there evolved the minstrel show, an elaborately staged melange of songs, dances, jokes, and skits, purportedly showing black life on the plantation; blacks were usually presented as amiable ignoramuses, but occasional sentimental songs and sketches about the hardness of black life presented them in a more sympathetic light. Plantation melodies developing out of the minstrel tradition were widely popular and continued to be sung in the twentieth century. They were basically Western in form, but employed dotted rhythms, especially to produce the effect of the rhythmic hitch in black music; use of the sixth was frequent, probably in an attempt to capture the quality of the microtonal seventh, as a consequence of which the subdominant chord was sometimes used where a dominant might have been expected. Stephen Foster, author of 'Oh! Susanna', and 'My Old Kentucky Home', was the pre-eminent composer of plantation melodies, but there were many others, including some blacks such as James Bland, author of 'Carry Me Back to Old Virginny'. Related to plantation melodies were what came to be called 'Negro spirituals'. Like the plantation melodies, the spirituals were westernized versions of black church music, which in turn owed something to Western church music (although how much is debated). Spirituals like 'Nobody Knows the Trouble I Seen' and 'Swing Low, Sweet Chariot' were widely sung by whites in the twentieth century.

A second form to grow out of black folk music was ragtime. It probably began to evolve after the Civil War, when blacks were freer to work as entertainers, and may have begun as an attempt to recreate banjo music on the piano. St Louis and the surrounding area is generally thought to have been an early centre for ragtime, which is characterized by a liberal use of syncopation, but rhythmically more regular and rigid than the later jazz 'swing'. By the 1890s a number of composers were writing dense, complex rags which usually went through several strains in different keys, obviously modelled on the highly popular marches of the time. In this classic ragtime, the right hand played repetitive, pianistic figures, often employing imitation, over a rhythmic, 'striding' left hand which alternated chords with octaves, thirds, or single notes. Scott Joplin is considered the ragtime master, but there were many other composers in the genre, including Joseph Lamb and James Scott. By 1900 ragtime had become a popular craze in the United States and to some extent elsewhere; there developed simplified versions, especially the ragtime song, which was basically an ordinary popular tune incorporating a measure of ragtime syncopation and a more-than-usual use of the sixth. In the 1970s there was a significant ragtime revival in the United States, and the form continues to have practitioners.

The wide popularity of ragtime was abetted by the development of the player piano in the late nineteenth century; by 1919, almost half the pianos sold in the United States were players. Player pianos allowed listeners to hear at home the classic rags which were often too difficult for amateurs to perform. But even more important in making ragtime popular was a vogue for social dancing which developed early in the century. It has often been suggested that, like ragtime and the plantation melodies, the new dances had been taken from black culture, and no doubt black dancers contributed. However, it is more probable that the primary source for the new dances was European immigrants, who were arriving by the millions during this period: Americans were dancing the *schottische*, the mazurka, the polka, and the waltz throughout the latter part of the nineteenth century, and it seems evident that the new social dances, like the Texas Tommy, the Bunny Hug, the Buzzard Lope, and the ubiquitous Fox Trot, developed from them. The magnitude of the vogue for social dancing cannot be overestimated: people, especially the young, routinely went dancing several times a week. Workers even danced by their machines at lunchtime. These new dances had rhythmic hitches of their own: dotted rhythms seemed particularly suited to them, and by 1910 dotted rhythms were increasingly used in ragtime songs.

The third of the new forms was the blues. Once again it has been suggested that the blues developed well back in the nineteenth century, but firm evidence of them appears only after 1900. The first blues singers appear to have been males from the countryside, who accompanied themselves on the guitar; other accompaniments used were the banjo, piano, or a small instrumental group. The vocal line was built largely on a scale made up of the tonic, a microtonal or 'blue' third, the fifth, and a blue seventh; other notes were frequently used, but an adequate blues could be sung using no more than these four. In its standard form, the blues consisted of three sung lines of roughly two to three bars, followed by an instrumental phrase. (In the early country blues it is sometimes hard to draw bar lines.) Usually the second line repeated the first, and the third capped the statement:

> Captain, captain, I said you must be cross;
> Captain, captain, I said you must be cross;
> For it's twelve o' clock, and you won't knock off.

The blues, however, was a loose form and there were many variations, while in the country blues the metre would sometimes halt altogether. Frequently, phrases would begin on a high blue seventh and descend through the blue third to the tonic or below.

A vogue for the blues slowly grew through the 1910s, and by the 1920s it was in full swing. By this time the field was dominated by what are nowadays seen as the classic blues singers, such as Bessie Smith and Ma Rainey. Such singers worked in vaudeville and tent shows, and without electric amplification they needed powerful voices and an accompaniment louder than a guitar: many of them employed instrumental duets, trios, and even full jazz bands. In an attempt to profit from the vogue for the blues, many popular singers, including Alberta Hunter and Ethel Waters, were billed as blues singers, although their material was actually standard vaudeville songs. Conversely, while Smith and

Rainey sang the 'authentic' blues, employing the blue notes and the classic three-line lyric, they also used a lot of ordinary popular material.

Because blues were so often accompanied by jazz bands, the two came to be seen as one and the same, but there are differences: jazz does not routinely employ the blue notes standard in the blues, and has its own distinctive rhythmic qualities. The blues vogue was washed away by the swing-band movement of the 1930s, but it had a second life in the so-called urban blues of Big Bill Broonzy, Sonny Boy Williamson, and many others, principally in Chicago in the late 1930s and after.

The rise of jazz

Jazz owed something to all of these forms which had grown out of black culture, but it came more directly out of the music of the marching or 'brass' band. Such bands were everywhere in the United States from the post-Civil War period until well into the twentieth century; they still routinely perform at school and college sports events. The brass band was itself an outgrowth of the military band. It was designed for marching, but by the late nineteenth century had become a concert band, playing in village bandstands, big city concert halls, and at dances, as well as on football fields and in holiday parades. Most of these bands were associated with one of the many voluntary organizations which are a feature of American society – firemen's associations, fraternal organizations, burial societies, and many more – and inevitably they were mostly small and manned by amateurs. Typically they consisted of two or more cornets, at least one trombone, an assortment of alto and baritone horns, a tuba, and (despite the designation 'brass') a few clarinets and both snare and bass drums. However, there were also large, highly professional brass bands which played mostly concerts: the very popular John Philip Sousa Orchestra sometimes had seventy musicians. These bands played the standard marches, many of them written by Sousa himself, but as concert orchestras they also played arrangements of plantation melodies, popular hits, operatic arias, concertos featuring star soloists, and eventually rags.

Such bands were plentiful in New Orleans. This city was unique to the United States: initially it had been Catholic rather than Protestant, and French-speaking rather than English-speaking, facing the Caribbean rather than the Atlantic. It had drawn its culture from the libertarian spirit of eighteenth-century France, rather than from the more Calvinistic Britain. Music and dance were deeply woven into the city's social life; New Orleans had opera houses and concert halls when it was still emerging from the surrounding swamps. By 1900 Americans from the North had been filtering in for a century, and the

English-speaking Protestants dominated politically and economically, but the old French culture was still important.

The city was racially extremely mixed. There had always been racial mixing in the American South, with native Americans included, but in New Orleans the mixing had given rise to a social class, today inaccurately termed 'Creoles', who existed in a halfway house between the black slaves and the white masters. This mixed-blood group had in part risen naturally out of the propinquity of races, but a substantial number of them were descended from a group who had fled revolutions in the Carribbean island of Saint-Domingue after 1800. As we have seen, in the islands blacks were able to retain much of their old culture; it appears that these Saint-Domingue mixed-bloods brought with them a music that had a rhythmic hitch, or lilt, although precisely what it sounded like is difficult to know. Such evidence as we have suggests that this Creole music was an important ingredient in the formation of jazz. For one thing, by 1900 there were black musicians in cities all over America, and the blues and ragtime were being played in many southern cities, towns, and country villages; but the Creole music existed only in New Orleans, and only in New Orleans did jazz appear. Moreover, most of the dozen or so leading figures in the first generation of jazz musicians were Creoles. While it is by no means certain that the Creoles played the dominant role in the development of jazz, they certainly played a prominent one.

Whatever the case, by the late nineteenth century, blacks and Creoles were forming brass bands to play for picnics, dances, funerals, lawn parties, boxing matches, and other events. In the literature on jazz, formally organized groups like the Excelsior, Superior, and Eagle Orchestras are usually listed as the first jazz bands. These groups consisted of violin, cornet, trombone, clarinet, and some combination of drum, string bass, and guitar, though the instrumentation varied: for parades, for instance, a tuba would substitute for the string bass. There were also rough duos, trios, and quartets – usually a wind instrument or two against a small rhythm section – which worked in the honky-tonks (modest night clubs serving a mainly working-class black clientele) and elsewhere; larger, more polished groups played written music for dancing in clubs and restaurants for well-to-do whites.

How these bands sounded is uncertain. Rhythmically, the music was a halfway house between ragtime and the jazz swing to come. Drummers usually played repeated patterns of a crotchet followed by two quavers; basses played on first and third beats; banjos, where employed, stroked up and down; pianos employed the stride pattern of chords alternating with single notes or octaves. The rhythm section thus treated the first and third beats significantly differently from the second and fourth, and the effect was a rocking motion. Again, jazz had not yet become soloists' music; solos were few, and most frequently consisted of brief one- or two-bar 'breaks' played while the band dropped out. Nor, perhaps surprisingly, was this music improvised: not only were the occasional solos worked out in advance and played the same each time, but ensemble parts also tended to be fixed. The violin doubled the lead in the cornet, but, overpowered by the winds, was soon dropped. It is likely that the dominant texture of the music was not originally the characteristic polyphony of the Dixieland ensemble, but a sort of heterophony, with several instruments playing parallel lines; the standard polyphony probably evolved around 1910, with the cornet playing the lead, the trombone playing connecting links between phrases, and the clarinet playing rising and falling obbligati throughout. The slide trombone had recently come into vogue, replacing the valved instrument; portamenti were a popular comic novelty and were frequently employed. Saxophones were not generally used.

Among the most highly regarded of the early New Orleanians were the cornettists Freddie Keppard, Buddie Petit, and Joe 'King' Oliver; the clarinettists Sidney Bechet and Jimmie Noone; the trombonists Edward 'Kid' Ory and Honoré Dutrey; the drummer Louis Cotrell; the string bassist and guitarist Bill Johnson; and the pianist Ferdinand 'Jelly Roll' Morton. All but Oliver were Creoles. Coming along quickly were a number of white players, particularly the trombonist Tom Brown, his brother the bassist Steve Brown, the cornettist Ray Lopez, and others. Mexicans, like the clarinettist Lorenzo Tio, were also involved, as were a cadre of Sicilian immigrants, such as Nick Larocca.

This prototypical jazz began to spread out from New Orleans very early. Before 1905 itinerant New Orleanians were carrying it to towns along the Gulf Coast. In 1907 Bill Johnson travelled to the West Coast, decided that there was a market for this new 'hot' music there, and brought out other New Orleanians: as the Creole Orchestra they had some success playing for dances and eventually on the vaudeville circuit, where the music was presented primarily as a comic novelty, with the humour built around the jerky rhythms, trombone portamenti, and clarinet whinnies. In 1915 the group played the prestigious Winter Garden in New York, by which time there was some awareness of the new music, at least in show-business circles. Other groups also calling themselves Creole orchestras imitated Johnson's band to the point where he began billing it as the Original Creole Orchestra.

In the same year the Tom Brown band was heard in New Orleans by some travelling vaudevillians, who persuaded the manager of the popular Lamb's Cafe in Chicago to book it, and the success of the Brown band at Lamb's encouraged other clubs to book New Orleans bands. These were mostly white, but soon blacks like Bechet and the Johnson group were in Chicago and elsewhere in the North. By 1916 word of the new music, now called jazz (there were variant spellings of the word) was spreading, and in January 1917 a white group called the Original Dixieland Jass Band opened at Reisenweber's, an important New York restaurant. The roaring success of the ODJB in America's show-business capital quickly led to recording contracts: their Victor records were bestsellers and suddenly jazz was in vogue. Bands attempting to play the new jazz sprouted everywhere, some of them more authentic than others, for at first only the New Orleanians were able to really play jazz. However, the development of the music was slowed by America's entry into the First World War in April 1917, just as the ODJB records were first coming out: wartime energy shortages curtailed café and theatre performances in cold northern cities, and many Americans felt that going out dancing while men were in the trenches was unpatriotic. A short but sharp financial break after the war also badly hurt the recording industry, but by 1922 the economy was improving. Interest in the music, despite the slowdown in recording and club activity, had been growing; thousands of young musicians were trying to capture its infectious swing, while others were learning musical instruments for the express purpose of playing it. In 1923 jazz began to be recorded in quantity: the first recordings of Morton, Bessie Smith, Oliver, Bechet, and others appeared that year.

This was the most intense period of development in early jazz history. By now the New Orleanians were facing competition from other jazz bands, the best known being a spin-off from the ODJB which recorded under several names, but mainly as the Original Memphis Five; key members of this group were the cornettist Phil Napoleon and the trombonist Miff Mole. The group played in a bright, quick, musically competent style, with Mole being particularly admired for his great facility and imaginative high-speed playing. Two Chicago groups were also developing followings in the years after 1922. King Oliver had taken over the Creole Orchestra, which was made up almost entirely of New Orleanians, including Louis Armstrong on second cornet. It featured the leader's cornet, especially with the plunger mute, as in his celebrated 'Dippermouth Blues' solo (1923); Johnny Dodds, the clarinettist, had frequent solos, in the main pre-planned, while Armstrong also had an occasional solo, his brief solo on 'Froggie Moore' giving an indication of what was to come. Equal in popularity were the New Orleans Rhythm Kings, who included several northerners; the clarinettist Leon Roppolo was particularly admired for his fluid, rolling style.

Other groups, too, were catching up with the New Orleanians. In 1924 a mid-Western band called the Wolverines, featuring the cornettist Bix Beiderbecke, began to record. The group never achieved the popularity of the Memphis Five or the New Orleans groups, but it gained an underground reputation among musicians and serious jazz fans, especially for Beiderbecke's pure, ringing tone, somewhat clipped style, and rich music imagination: he soon became one of the most imitated musicians in jazz. Also in 1924 a black musical entrepreneur, Clarence Williams, was recording groups built around New Orleanians, among them Bechet and Armstrong. Bechet, now playing both clarinet and soprano saxophone, had already developed his mature style, intense and perfervid, and his 1923 'Wildcat Blues' and 'Kansas City Man Blues' were influential among musicians. Also in 1924 Williams teamed Bechet with Armstrong on several recordings; their very hot 'Cake Walking Babies' remains much admired.

By 1923, although jazz was still essentially ensemble music, the jazz solo was appearing with increasing frequency. The instrumental solo, of course, had been common in band concerts, classical music, and elsewhere: indeed, the wind instrument with a jazz trio in the honky-tonks was perforce a soloist. But the improvised solo was another matter. Bravura soloists in concert bands were expected to embellish their solos with turns and flourishes, but there was no tradition in brass band music, dance music, or early jazz for the wholly improvised solo. Sidney Bechet was often so far out in front of what was ostensibly a standard New Orleans ensemble that he appeared to be soloing; and although he worked out considerable proportions of his line in advance, he was certainly improvising to some extent. His example may have been significant, though it is also possible that jazz musicians were already improvising more frequently in live performance than they did in the formal circumstances of a recording. Since the early recordings represent the only reliable form of evidence, there is no way of being sure about this; what can be said with certainty, however, is that by 1923 Armstrong with Oliver, the saxophonist Coleman Hawkins with the Fletcher Henderson Orchestra, and the bass saxophonist Adrian Rollini with the popular California Ramblers, among others, were all playing occasional improvised solos on records. By 1924, although jazz was still ensemble music, the improvised solo had become a regular part of most jazz performances.

From a musical viewpoint, the New Orleans, or Dixieland, style reached its apogee in 1926–7, when Jelly Roll Morton, using mainly New Orleanians, began to record his Red Hot Peppers. Morton has been called the first jazz composer: his pieces were a mix of the standard New Orleans ensemble, arranged passages, solos, and carefully worked-out breaks. Especially admired are pieces like 'The Chant' and 'Black Bottom Stomp' (both 1926), which are not merely tunes but full compositions, rooted in Morton's piano style (itself developed out of march music), with different strains, changes of key, and careful orchestration. Also recording at this time were the Red Nichols's Five Pennies, which often included more than five members. The Five Pennies were innovative, using instruments new to jazz, like timpani and alto horns, and novel arranged passages; Nichols had developed a cornet style paralleling (and eventually influenced by) that of Beiderbecke, and with the trombonist Mole and clarinettist Jimmy Dorsey he had one of the finest front lines in jazz of the time, musically adept and imaginative.

But every major jazz history acknowledges that the greatest of New Orleans recordings were those made by Louis Armstrong between 1925 and 1928 in the 'Hot Five' series. (Names and personnel for these recordings varied over time.) The series began as a standard New Orleans ensemble, including some soloing, but it quickly became clear that Armstrong was the attraction, and increasingly the records featured him as soloist and vocalist. Early in the series he made exemplary solos in stop-time, where the band plays only the first beat of a bar, leaving Armstrong free to go as he pleases, although in fact he mainly follows the chords of the tunes; especially esteemed were his stop-time choruses on 'Cornet Chop Suey' (1926) and 'Potato Head Blues' (1927), the first of which is still copied by cornettists. By 1927, as we shall shortly see, the ensemble style was being pushed aside by a vogue for arrangements – a trend which suited the record company's interest in featuring Armstrong. Generally considered the greatest of the Hot Five series, and among the finest of all jazz records, are 'Tight Like This', 'Muggles', and especially 'West End Blues' (all 1928), which consist of strings of solos with occasional arranged passages and some New Orleans ensemble. Armstrong's opening cadenza to 'West End Blues', and his closing solo, reveal an artist in full maturity, possessed of a fine technique, a warm, full sound, a rich imagination, and a sense of dramatic construction rarely equalled and never surpassed in jazz. Armstrong did not, by himself, turn jazz from an ensemble into a soloist's music, but with the Hot Fives he showed that a jazz solo could be classified as art, however that term is used.

Second only to Armstrong, Bix Beiderbecke was during the same period making a series of highly influential records. Some of these, like 'Royal Garden Blues' (1929), were in the old ensemble style, but the most significant were essentially solo pieces with arranged passages; the construction of Beiderbecke's solo on Frankie Trumbauer's 'Singing the Blues' (1927) was particularly admired, and the solo was widely copied.

The hot dance band

The 1920s were a time of great change in the United States and much of Europe. Before, roughly, the First World War, American society had been dominated by the Victorian ethic, which demanded selflessness, self-control, and self-sacrifice for family, community, and the nation. However, by the end of the nineteenth century, what had begun as an ethic of selflessness had turned into a crusade for 'purity', which hoped to constrain not just pleasure, but the free expression of feeling. By the 1890s a backlash against Victorian purity was manifesting itself across the arts in America, including the novels of Stephen Crane and Theodore Dreiser, who took sex and working-class life as subjects, and the paintings of the Ashcan School depicting slums and saloon life. By 1913 intellectuals, writers, and artists, not only in the United States but in England, France, and elsewhere, were demanding a freer, more expressive life; many of them congregated in New York's Greenwich Village and similar bohemian enclaves. Very quickly these ideas spread. More and more, Americans felt free to have sex, even to cohabit, without marriage; to drink as they liked despite national Prohibition, which began in 1920; and to dance, go to parties, have fun. Duty to the self, rather than to the family and community, was the new cry: it was the individual, not the group, that mattered.

Jazz precisely exemplified the new attitudes. It was – or appeared to be – spontaneous, thrown off in the heat of emotion; as the solo style took over, it offered the image of a heroic individual making a personal cry. Jazz could not have made headway under Victorianism, but in the 1920s it fitted the mood of the nation. Not surprisingly, it was quickly taken up by intellectuals. To them, jazz was not only anti-Victorian in spirit; it also suited a growing belief that a decadent Europe, which had recently slaughtered millions of men to no purpose, was finished. In the eyes of many, a bright new America of skyscrapers, animated cartoons, and the erotic 'trot' dances was heralding a new way of living, even of being. Jazz was an integral part of the American package, and a number of critics, including Virgil Thomson, Carl Van Vechten, and Abbe Niles became strong supporters of it.[1] The most important of these early jazz critics was R. D. Darrell, who was later to make his mark as a record critic and discographer of classical music; from 1926 he was writing frequently about jazz, and within two or three years he was making judgements that still stand up today.

Also important to the growth of jazz were new systems of mechanical entertainment, especially sound recording and radio. Gramophone records allowed millions of Americans living at a considerable distance from big city clubs to hear the music; Beiderbecke, in Davenport, Iowa, learned to play jazz from records, and he was typical of many. Radio, first commercially broadcasting in 1920, was offering jazz bands by 1921. By the mid-1920s there was a significant amount of excellent jazz on radio; beginning in 1927, Duke Ellington made a national reputation broadcasting from the Cotton Club over the new radio

1 Virgil Thomson, in *Vanity Fair* 24/6 (1925) and 25/2 (1925); for R. D. Darrell, see all issues of *Phonograph Monthly Review*, 1/1–5/9 (1926–1931); for Abbe Niles, see all issues of *The Bookman* (1928 to January 1929).

'chains', or networks. However there was little consensus about what constituted jazz. Paul Whiteman was calling himself 'The King of Jazz', and to the majority of Americans of the time, the arranged music of his and similar bands, playing with a rhythmic bounce and offering jazz-like solos, *was* jazz. But a relatively small number of jazz fans, many of them college students, were establishing different criteria, in which the present-day connotations of the term are grounded, and reaching a shared sense of what we now see as the early jazz canon. By the late 1920s the general public, too, was developing a vague sense that jazz and commercial music were not the same, although many would not have been able to define the difference.

But by this time the general public, as well as many jazz fans, were shifting taste from the New Orleans or Dixieland ensemble to the bigger band playing from written or memorized arrangements, while featuring many improvised jazz solos. The 'swing' or big band is usually dated from 1935 to 1945, because that is the period of its dominance, but in fact it began much earlier. Up until the First World War, most dance music was provided by duets, trios, and quartets comprising some combination of piano, violin, drums, banjo, and wind instruments, mostly playing by ear. Then, in about 1916, a classically trained West Coast musician named Ferde Grofé decided to apply devices found in classical and march band music, like counterpoint and harmonized instrumental choirs, to dance music; he was soon hired by a San Francisco dance band leader named Art Hickman to make arrangements for his band. In about 1918 either Grofé or Hickman heard a saxophone duet in a vaudeville show (it was only as a vaudeville novelty that the saxophone had until then made an impact in the United States). Grofé promptly installed the saxophone duet in the Hickman band, making it the forerunner of the standard dance-band saxophone section. The Grofé system very quickly made Hickman's band celebrated on the West Coast; a trip east and some recordings were also successful, and other leaders looked his way. Most important of them was Whiteman, also classically trained, who hired Grofé away from Hickman. Within two or three years Whiteman's records were selling in their millions, and he had become internationally famous: year by year he expanded his orchestra, adding strings, double-reeds, and other instruments unusual in dance bands. He had many imitators, and by 1925, when in jazz the Dixieland style was reaching its apogee, the big arranged band was at the heart of popular music.

Many of the musicians in such bands were also capable of playing good jazz, and the groups occasionally offered jazz specialities; for the most part, however, their music was ordinary dance music with a lively, jazz-oriented beat and an occasional jazz solo. But through the 1920s the public taste for hotter music was growing, and some of the bands began playing a much hotter mix than the Whiteman-type bands offered. Perhaps the best of these was the Fletcher Henderson Orchestra. Armstrong had played with Henderson in 1924–5, and had drawn Henderson's men to his methods; by 1926, Coleman Hawkins, the trombonist Charlie Green, and others were providing the band with good jazz solos. Other bands contributing to the development of what would become the swing band were the Jean Goldkette group, with Beiderbecke, Jimmy Dorsey, and the violinist Joe Venuti; the Ben Pollack Orchestra, with the clarinettist Benny Goodman and the trombonist Jack Teagarden; the well-drilled Casa Loma Orchestra; and an enlarged Nichols' Five Pennies which at times included Goodman, Teagarden, Dorsey, and many others.

Many of the musical devices used by these bands, such as counterpoint and the playing-off of brass and saxophone sections, had been worked out by Grofé for Hickman and Whiteman. However, the early swing bands tried to capture in ensembles the swing feeling produced by the Dixieland groups in which many of their musicians had cut their teeth, and expected their soloists to play improvised jazz solos. These hot dance bands did not achieve the overwhelming popularity of the more commercial Whiteman groups, but they attracted relatively large followings, recorded frequently for major labels, and played major locations. In short, they constituted an important segment of American popular music. By 1927 Whiteman himself recognized the public desire for hot dance music, and added Beiderbecke and other important jazz musicians like Dorsey and Teagarden to provide jazz touches: Beiderbecke played solos on a third of the records made by Whiteman when he was with the orchestra.

Often seen at the time by the press as part of this movement, but to some extent outside it, was Duke Ellington. The Ellington band had evolved out of a group of Washington musicians who had worked together as teenagers. It eventually found work in a rough club in New York's Times Square area, adding the cornettist Bubber Miley and Bechet to provide the hot jazz which the original members were only learning. Miley had learned to use the plunger mute from hearing Oliver in Chicago; he added throat tones to produce a brass growl later emulated by Ellington's trombonists to create the characteristic 'jungle sound', as it was billed. In December 1927 the band, somewhat enlarged, opened at the Cotton Club, an elegant Harlem club meant for affluent whites, and it was here that Ellington developed the style – already evident in pieces like 'East St. Louis Toodle-oo' and 'Black and Tan Fantasy' (both 1927) – that made him famous. As has become increasingly clear, Ellington drew on many sources for his musical material, which he was not always careful to credit: 'Black and Tan Fantasy' was mainly worked out by Miley, while 'Creole Love Call' (1927) was taken almost intact from a King Oliver recording, and 'Mood Indigo' (Jungle Band, 1930) was written by Lorenzo Tio. Ellington was a self-taught pianist and had very little training in composition; as a consequence, he usually searched around for his own methods. But however he came to them, his compositions for his orchestra from 1927 on have long been considered among the finest works in big-band jazz.

Ellington's music was *sui generis*, not typical of the swing-band style. He did not play off the brass and saxophone sections as relentlessly as most did, but often wrote across the sections (as in the main theme to 'Mood Indigo', which is voiced for clarinet, muted trumpet, and trombone). He managed to hire some of the finest jazz soloists of his day, including the alto saxophonist Johnny Hodges and the trumpeter Cootie Williams, who took over the growling plunger-mute role from Miley, and he employed his soloists skilfully, working to their strengths and thus shaping their styles. But if musically the Ellington orchestra was somewhat at a tangent to the typical swing band, it was nonetheless seen by the public as one of the hot dance bands that was coming to play an important role in popular music.

With the rise of the hot dance band, the Dixieland style became moribund. Although Beiderbecke, Armstrong, and others continued to record in the old style, by 1926 they were working mainly in big dance bands. Following the trend, King Oliver added saxophones in 1925, but neither he nor Morton really adapted to the new style, and by the early 1930s both had fallen into obscurity.

Jazz piano

Because the piano can be played alone, it has tended to have its own course of development. When jazz arrived after the First World War, the ragtime players tried to adapt, and in the end created what became known as the stride style, which was basically ragtime played with the new jazz swing and a less formal, more varied approach. The ragtime bass of chords alternating with other figures was maintained, and although the right hand continued to play pianistic figures, these would now be varied from moment to moment as the performer chose: where the ragtimers had played set pieces, the stride pianists were improvising in the jazz manner. James P. Johnson has often been called the Father of Stride, and was certainly much imitated; his 'Carolina Shout' became a stride test piece. His student 'Fats' Waller played an infectious, swinging stride which, over time, became looser, with the bass sometimes much simplified. Other important stride players were Lucky Roberts, Willie 'The Lion' Smith, and Donald Lambert. Stride continues to have practitioners; the best-known of the latter-day stride players is probably Dick Wellstood.

The movement away from stride was driven by the example of Earl Hines, who frequently interrupted the stride bass with irregular figures; his right hand was also much freer than was customary in stride, often employing single-note or octave runs. Hines recorded with Armstrong on the important late Hot Fives, and went on to make a seminal series of solos in 1928. He was much admired and had many followers, one of the most important being Teddy Wilson, who had also begun as a stride player. Wilson soon gained a reputation as one who could work in the Hines manner, and by the early 1930s he was creating a style that over time grew increasingly spare, with the stride bass reduced to single notes or chords and the right hand frequently employed in runs.

During the 1930s the blind pianist Art Tatum emerged as perhaps the most admired pianist in jazz of the period. Blessed with a prodigious technique, Tatum – like Wilson originally a stride player – developed a rich, full style using sudden leaps into distant keys, many chord substitutions, and high-speed runs that astonished other pianists. However, the Tatum style was too difficult for any but the most accomplished pianists to attempt; during the late 1930s Wilson received much exposure with the Benny Goodman groups, so it was his playing that became the basic model for jazz piano during the remainder of the classic jazz period. Out of it grew the bop piano style of Bud Powell and others in the late 1940s.

The Depression

In 1929 the over-heated American stock market collapsed, revealing serious weaknesses in the economy which had existed for some time, and the nation slid rapidly into a deep depression. Eventually twenty-five per cent of workers would be unemployed and those still working would be on reduced wages. Production was down almost thirty per cent. Many people went to bed hungry at night; it was the worst calamity to hit the United States since the Civil War. Jazz, and the music business in general, was badly hurt. Dance halls and night clubs closed. Record sales plummeted from well over $100 million annually to $6 million in the early 1930s; virtually all of the small labels (many of which, like Paramount and Gennett, had recorded a lot of early jazz) were swallowed up by the majors, with the result that by the mid-1930s there were only three labels of any significance: Victor, Columbia, and Decca. New technologies were also having an effect: radio was free in the United States (once you had acquired a set), while talking pictures, which became practical at the time the Depression started, were driving out the old silent films and putting out of work thousands of musicians who had made their living accompanying them. Music-business executives now decided that people wanted dreamy romantic music into which to escape from their troubles, and sales of hot music fell accordingly.

Despite the problems, jazz continued to develop. For one thing, the dance bands increasingly found it economically important to add singers to their rosters. Through most of the 1920s the big dance bands did not typically carry singers, for without electric amplification only those with the strongest voices could carry over a noisy crowd in a dance hall or cabaret; when necessary, freelance vocalists might be hired for recordings, and in places like the Cotton Club the singers were brought in as individual acts, to be accompanied by the house band. But by the late 1920s Whiteman was carrying singers, and Ellington added a singer when he left the Cotton Club in 1931. Within a few years nearly all dance bands were employing at least one, and usually both 'boy' and 'girl' singers. As the 1930s progressed, leaders began adding vocal groups, and often comic male singers (like Glenn Miller's Tex Beneke), to sing novelty numbers. The trend towards vocalists would eventually have major effects on popular music.

From a jazz point of view, a more significant development was a subtle, but to jazz fans quite apparent, change in rhythm. Empirical studies have shown that intuitive analyses of rhythmic practices in jazz are usually wrong (though such research is at an early stage and it is advisable to tread cautiously in this area).[2] Nevertheless it may be said that jazz musicians usually divide beats unequally into what are termed *swing eighths* (that is, swing quavers, though the term is not used), in which the first of each pair is almost always longer than the second – usually in a ratio of about 3:2, though there is considerable variation. It is possible, but by no means certain, that after 1930 jazz musicians tended to lengthen the first quaver even more at the expense of the second one than the original New Orleans players had done. What is more certain, because evident in the recordings, is that in the 1930s the crotchet beat became increasingly 'democratized' – that is, instead of giving a different articulation to alternate crotchets, rhythm sections would play them all the same. Bassists began playing four beats to the bar, and pianists dropped the stride bass in favour of a more even manner; the guitar replaced the banjo and was played with a consistent downward stroke, giving all notes a similar quality. The total effect was to produce a more evenly flowing beat than had been the practice in the 1920s.

The early- to mid-1930s also saw the development of a type of jazz band that would have profound effects on popular music. There had always been small, hot jazz bands based in the blues, first in the New Orleans honky-tonks, then in Chicago and elsewhere, such as the Billy Banks Rhythmakers (a recording group which featured the leader's shouted blues vocals accompanied by very

2 Geoffrey L. Collier and James L. Collier, 'Microrhythms in Jazz', *Annual Review of Jazz Studies* 8 (1996), pp. 117–39.

hot jazz soloists). In 1936 a Chicago record producer put together the Harlem Hamfats by backing two blues singers with a small jazz band; the Hamfats were a recording group only, but had considerable success on jukeboxes with black audiences. Other groups followed the pattern, especially Louis Jordan and his Tympany Five, who by the 1940s were very popular with white audiences as well as black ones. The Jordan group often employed a shuffle beat, and almost always offered a comic and/or erotic blues-based vocal. Their wide popularity produced emulators, and very quickly these groups coalesced into the style later called rhythm and blues – and out of rhythm and blues, of course, came Bill Haley, Elvis Presley and the rock movement that followed. The rhythm-and-blues groups were not the only models for rock – the British groups also looked to the Chicago bluesmen like Broonzy and B. B. King – but they were the primary influence, and they in turn had grown out of jazz. Without jazz it is highly doubtful that anything like rock would have appeared.

Jazz goes abroad

For many years it was believed that jazz had always enjoyed a warmer reception, from both critics and popular fans, in Europe – especially Britain and France – than in the United States. Recent research has shown this supposition to be a myth: interest in 'jazz' proper outside the United States was virtually non-existent before the mid-1920s, and was confined to a tiny handful of ardent jazz fans and musicians until the 1920s were gone. The vogue for social dancing did exist in Europe, and many dancers wanted modern rhythms of the Whiteman type, but jazz as such, whether imported or home-grown, was almost entirely absent, despite brief visits by the ODJB and Sidney Bechet.[3]

However, some American jazz records had been exported, especially by Beiderbecke and Nichols; European musicians travelling on transatlantic liners heard jazz in New York and elsewhere, while members of the public returning from America brought back an awareness of the music. Among them was a Cambridge University student, Fred Elizalde, who in 1927 formed a group called the Quinquaginta Ramblers, modelled on the California Ramblers, including Adrian Rollini; the group did not succeed with the British public, but it can probably be called the first European jazz band. At about the same time, the editors of the British dance-band magazine *Melody Maker* began to cover American jazz, if without full understanding. In 1927 Hugues Panassié, often considered the first European jazz critic, discovered the music; in 1929 some *Melody Maker*

3 James L. Collier, *The Reception of Jazz in America*, Brooklyn, 1988. For further discussion of jazz in Europe during and after the First World War, see Susan Cook's chapter in this volume.

editors visited New York and their understanding of jazz grew. By the early 1930s there were at least a few Europeans of several nationalities capable of playing excellent jazz, among them the saxophonist André Ekyan, the violinist Sven Asmussen, the trumpeters Nat Gonella and Philipe Brun, and the pianist Stephane Mougin.

Then, in 1932, some Parisian students formed the Hot Club de France, with Panassié as its president, and in 1933 the club began putting on concerts, which by 1934 were built around the gypsy guitarist Django Reinhardt and the violinist Stéphane Grappelli. These two had taken as their model an important American group led by the violinist Joe Venuti and the guitarist Eddie Lang; Grappelli proved to be an excellent jazz musician, and Reinhardt very quickly developed an underground reputation as the first European to play on a level with the best Americans. And jazz in Europe got another boost in 1932 and 1933, when both Armstrong and Ellington made European trips. Nonetheless, the European audience for jazz remained small: even Armstrong was not able to work in Europe more than sporadically, and occasional concerts by the Hot Club de France, featuring Reinhardt and Grappelli, would typically draw four hundred people. As excellent as some European players were, they remained derivative: trumpet players followed Armstrong, Beiderbecke or Nichols; trombonists Teagarden; saxophonists Hawkins or Bud Freeman. Curiously, in view of the later European interest in 'trad' jazz, no attention was paid to the New Orleans style at this time; the Europeans had entered jazz as the Dixieland style was dying, and they had little awareness of Oliver, Morton, or the Armstrong Hot Fives. In sum, well into the 1930s the European jazz scene was small, if lively.

Interest in other parts of the world was even smaller. Ironically, Africans were simply unaware of the music. A few Americans, like the trumpeter Buck Clayton, made brief trips to Asia, but they inspired few followers: not until after the Second World War did Asia produce any significant jazz musicians. There was greater interest in South America, especially in the big port cities like Rio de Janeiro and Buenos Aires, where American cruise ships docked. A handful of fans there were collecting American jazz records in the 1930s, but home-grown players were rare: the Hispanic players in jazz at that time, such as Ellington's trombonist Juan Tizol, were invariably from the Caribbean nations.

The swing era

The opening of the Goodman Orchestra at the Palomar Ballroom in Los Angeles in 1935 has always been seen in the jazz literature as the key moment which sprung loose the swing bands. (The terms 'orchestra' and 'band' are interchangeable in this context, the former being normal in the recordings and advertisements of the time, the latter in ordinary conversation.) There is no question that the sudden success of the Goodman Orchestra in late 1935 brought a wave of publicity on which a gathering host of swing bands rode to public acclaim, but, as already explained, the swing bands of the 1935–45 period were in essence an extension of the hot dance bands which had developed in the late 1920s – some of which, like the Casa Loma, Ellington, and Henderson groups, had been working in the genre all along. Had there been no Depression, the one era would have flowed smoothly into the next. There has always existed an audience among American youth for some sort of rhythmic music, frequently as an adjunct to courtship, as for example the reels of the eighteenth century, the waltzes and polkas of the nineteenth, and ragtime and jazz in the early twentieth. Such young people existed in 1932 as well as 1935, but with money so short and the music business gripped by the belief that in the Depression only soft romantic music would sell, they must have found rhythmic music hard to obtain.

Goodman had been one of a cadre of highly skilled, professional musicians who could play jazz as well as other styles, and who worked in New York's radio and recording studios, and in pit bands. In 1934 he set about forming his own band, modelled on the earlier hot dance bands, particularly those he had played in, such as the Pollack and Nichols orchestras. (It is often said, for example by Alyn Shipton,[4] that the Goodman band was built around the arrangements of the Fletcher Henderson Orchestra, but although Henderson was indeed one of Goodman's major arrangers, he was but one of several, and contributed little during the formative period.) Goodman was soon appearing on a regular nationwide broadcast of dance music, which lasted for several months; a tour followed, ending with the Palomar engagement. The radio programme had helped to build an audience for the band among the young, and a California disc jockey had been playing its records. However, it was not just chance: the Goodman band had two brilliant soloists in the trumpeter Bunny Berigan and Goodman himself, a winning vocalist in Helen Ward, and played with verve and polish. And Goodman's success led similarly placed musicians to form bands of their own, among them Woody Herman, Artie Shaw, Count Basie, Jimmy and Tommy Dorsey (who had a joint band earlier), Glenn Miller, Charlie Barnet, and more. Swept along by the tide were the older bands of Ellington, Armstrong, Jimmie Lunceford, and Casa Loma.

4 Alyn Shipton, *A New History of Jazz*, London, 2001, p. 325.

The swing-band movement was a social as well as a musical phenomenon. The leaders became major celebrities, whose marriages, divorces, and attendant scandals were covered by gossip columnists. By 1937 movies were being built around the best-known of the 'name' bands, and fan clubs were formed, often with the aid of press agents. Young women, many of them teenagers, made themselves available to the bandsmen after the evening's dance. A great deal of money was made, but mostly by the leaders, dance hall managers, record companies, and band bookers: in the Depression young musicians could be hired for low wages, which helped to make these large bands financially viable. Star soloists (such as Goodman's trumpeter Harry James, Miller's Bobby Hackett, and Bob Crosby's Billy Butterfield) spun off their own bands. 'Jitterbug' dances were created specifically for swing; many of them grew out of the acrobatic dances done at Harlem's Savoy Ballroom. A uniform was evolved: short bobby socks, white buck shoes, and scalloped skirts for the girls; wide-lapel jackets with peg trousers for the boys.

By the late 1930s the swing bands had pulled the record industry, and the music business in general, out of the Depression: record sales were up to fifty million annually, and great dance halls, like Castle Gardens outside Cincinnati and the Meadowbrook in New Jersey, were filled night after night. Originally seen as dance bands, the swing bands were now being booked into theatres to play short concerts between movies. A certain peak was reached with the celebrated Goodman swing concert at the hitherto sacrosanct Carnegie Hall in 1938, which was highly publicized and received coverage from some classical music critics.

The music was another matter. In current jazz historiography it is usually said that the swing era was the only period during which jazz was truly popular.[5] It depends on how jazz is defined. At the time, both jazz fans and musicians scorned much of the music turned out by the swing bands. A minority even insisted that swing-band music was not jazz; for them, only the older Dixieland style qualified. And it is true that a substantial number of these bands, including the highly popular Guy Lombardo and Sammy Kaye bands, stuck to romantic, often syrupy ballads that had little to do with jazz except for a bouncy beat. Others, like the also very popular Tommy Dorsey and Glenn Miller Orchestras, mixed hot riff numbers with carefully crafted ballads at a ratio of perhaps two 'sweet' to one 'swing' number, as the terms then were. Even the hottest of the swing bands, like those of Crosby, Herman, Ellington, Goodman, Basie, and Barnet, had to play many ballads to meet dancers' requirements, although they tried to play them with a jazz beat and included jazz solos, as for example

5 For a fuller discussion see James L. Collier, *Jazz: The American Theme Song*, New York, 1993, p. 174.

Hodges's work on Ellington's 'Don't Get Around Much Anymore' (1940) or Berigan's exemplary solo on Goodman's 'Sometimes I'm Happy' (1935). In short, the bulk of the music produced by the swing bands lay in some middle area between what most knowledgeable fans then, and critics now, would see as jazz proper, and ordinary dance music. Of the fifty or so nationally popular swing bands, only a handful can be considered as essentially jazz bands.

The primary feature of hot swing music was the riff: a short figure, frequently two bars long, that was repeated a number of times with just enough variation to fit the chord changes. The interplay of riffs by saxophone and brass sections was at the heart of the music, although solos and more melodic passages were frequent. But the different bands handled these basic elements in different ways. The Benny Goodman band, for example, was less riff-based than some of the others. Goodman had a shrewd commercial sense but he thought of himself as a jazz musician first, and gave his soloists much space; they included some of the best of the time, among them Berigan, Cootie Williams, Harry James, the tenor saxophonist Vido Musso, and the guitarist Charlie Christian. Goodman held his band to high levels of musicianship, and played even the ballads with a jazz feel. By contrast, the Count Basie band was noted for the spare, light touch of its rhythm section and for the strength of its soloists, among them the tenor saxophonist Lester Young, the trumpeter Buck Clayton, and the trombonists Dickie Wells and Benny Morton. The band had grown out of loose-knit Kansas City jam sessions, and used a lot of 'head' (unwritten) arrangements built around sequences of riffs; it played many riff-based blues, but like the other bands had to play a certain number of ballads. The later Basie bands of the post-war era played a somewhat different, more modern style.

As for other bands, Charlie Barnet was an admirer of Ellington, and played a number of arrangements in the Ellington manner. However, his orchestra was best known for its riff tunes featuring the soloists. One of the most famous of all swing arrangements was Barnet's 'Cherokee' (1939), written by Billy May, which offered a more than usually complex interplay of trumpet, trombone, and saxophone sections. Again, the Bob Crosby band specialized in arranged versions of Dixieland, and probably offered a higher percentage of pure jazz than most of the swing bands; its cadre of soloists was among the best of its time and included the pianist Jess Stacy, the clarinettist Irving Fazola, and the trumpeters Billy Butterfield and Muggsy Spanier. Finally, the Woody Herman band at first called itself 'The Band That Plays the Blues', and offered many somewhat moody, blues-like numbers based on riffs, with much room for soloing; Herman sang many of the blues himself, and like the other groups it usually had two or three good soloists in its ranks. This early Herman band was different from the later one, discussed below.

But the Duke Ellington orchestra was once again *sui generis*. Where most swing-band leaders employed a corps of arrangers, Ellington continued to write most of the music for his group himself, drawing on many sources for his material. In 1939, however, he hired the young Billy Strayhorn who, until his death, wrote an incalculably large amount of the band's music under Ellington's direction. Ellington produced many fine works during the 1930s, especially a series of 'concertos' for various of his soloists, including 'Echoes of Harlem' and 'Clarinet Lament' (both 1936), but most critics agree that his music reached a peak in recordings made between 1940 and 1942. Contrast was always a key element in Ellington's work, and is particularly abundant in 'Harlem Airshaft' (1940), one of his many programmatic works: meant to depict the sounds and smells coming from a tenement airshaft, it is full of sudden disruptions and abrupt changes of direction. Ellington also liked to break rules: 'Main Stem' (1942) opens without preamble on a figure which jumps from a minor third to a sixth, reversing a standard jazz cliché. But perhaps the most notable piece from this period is 'Ko-Ko' (1940), which was originally intended to be part of a longer work; it is an exercise in pedal-point writing, with the various musical lines layered over the pedal becoming more and more dissonant, and with surprisingly little soloing.

By this time Ellington had become increasingly interested in what have been called his 'extended' pieces – longer works meant to reflect classical musical forms. His early extended works, such as 'Creole Rhapsody' (1931), were not well received by critics, but although he was occasionally discouraged, Ellington continued to devote more and more time to such works for the rest of his life. Their critical reception, however, remains mixed.

The Dixieland revival

The swing bands were at the centre of popular music in America and elsewhere until the end of the Second World War. However, two other related developments were more significant to jazz. The first of these was the Dixieland revival, while the second was small-band swing.

While the general public had long since lost interest in the old Dixieland, or New Orleans, style, many ardent jazz fans and musicians – who had been drawn to jazz when Dixieland was the only form it took – still favoured it, and it continued to be played in private jam sessions and occasionally in clubs. In 1936, when the swing-band movement was boiling up, it occurred to some members of the long defunct ODJB that there might be a new audience for their music. The band was reformed, made some records and radio broadcasts, and was well received; it might have gone on to some success, had it not broken up over internal disputes. But soon thereafter, *Down Beat*, the organ of the swing bands, started publishing a series of articles on the history of jazz, extolling the older music. In the winter of 1936–7, members of the Bob Crosby band, which was playing a big-band version of Dixieland, put together a small band to play in a Dixieland style. This 'Bobcats' group was a success, and at the same time, a club called Nick's opened in New York's Greenwich Village to feature the music. A small boom followed: some older records were reissued, some books discussing it appeared,[6] and a few small reviews were started to support it. In 1939, two more groups, the Summa Cum Laude Orchestra and the Muggsy Spanier Ragtimers, were also established to play Dixieland.

The best-known of these Dixielanders were a cadre around the guitarist Eddie Condon. A Chicagoan, Condon had a gregarious nature and good organizational sense, and for two decades from 1939 he led numerous recording sessions, radio broadcasts, and club performances, using many of the best of the older musicians (including the trombonists Teagarden and George Brunis, the clarinettists Pee Wee Russell and Edmond Hall, the trumpeters Wild Bill Davison, Bobby Hackett, Billy Butterfield, and 'Lips' Page, and many others). For much of this time he operated a New York club under his name, and the burgeoning Dixieland movement became entwined with it. The new Dixieland, however, was not intended as an exact reproduction of the older style: the musicians employed a swing rhythm little different from that of the big bands, and solos were no different from those in the big bands in which many of the musicians made their living. On the West Coast, by contrast, the cornettist Lu Watters was attempting to reproduce the older music much as it had originally been played, and he had some success with a band at the 1939 San Francisco World's Fair. A second band, led by the trombonist Turk Murphy, was spun off the Watters group, and others followed. These groups imitated Morton's Red Hot Peppers, Armstrong's Hot Fives, and especially Oliver's Creole Orchestra; eventually their repertories expanded. These New Orleans revivalist groups, then, were a second strand in the broader Dixieland movement, and a third strand was added when some researchers into early jazz found the ageing New Orleans cornettist Bunk Johnson, who claimed to have taught Armstrong (a claim which is almost certainly untrue). Johnson made recordings with other obscure New Orleanians of his generation; there was some national publicity, and the New Orleanians came north to record and to play in clubs.

Inevitably there was tension between these groups. Many Dixieland fans felt that only the original music was authentic; others scoffed at it as heavy-handed

6 Winthrop Sargeant, *Jazz, Hot and Hybrid*, New York, 1938; Wilder Hobson, *American Jazz Music*, New York, 1939; Frederick Ramsey Jr and Charles Edward Smith, *Jazzmen*, New York, 1939.

and sometimes badly played. But taken together, revival Dixieland proved to be a major element of jazz at this time. The independent label Commodore was started mainly to record it, and was followed by Blue Note and Riverside; soon the major labels were recording the Dixielanders, particularly those around Eddie Condon. From 1942–6 Condon organized a series of concerts in New York's Town Hall and Carnegie Hall, and a long series of the Town Hall concerts was broadcast, awakening many in the New York area – especially the young – to Dixieland. Also significant were a number of reissues of the earlier music, mainly from the 1920s, which began to appear in 1938 and became a steady stream in the early 1940s. Many of these were reissued in album sets of Armstrong, Morton, Beiderbecke, and others, complete with what appeared to be learned brochures; the resemblance of these sets to albums of symphonies and operas gave the older jazz a dignity and seriousness it had not always had before.

Through the 1940s and the 1950s, Dixieland showed considerable strength. It was widely popular on college campuses, where amateur Dixieland bands flourished; it is probable that Dixieland had as large an audience as did the modern jazz which surfaced after 1945. And this was particularly true outside the United States. Europeans belatedly became aware of the old New Orleans style and quickly took it up, in part because they had a greater sense of history than Americans did. Traditional – or 'trad' – jazz developed an important European following, especially in Britain and France, but elsewhere as well: Bunk Johnson's clarinettist George Lewis became a minor star in Europe. Europeans also quickly developed their own cadre of trad, or Dixieland, players, among them England's Humphrey Lyttleton and France's Claude Luter. And whereas this European trad, with its emphasis on tradition, followed the style of Lu Watters and similar groups in attempting to recreate the sound of the older music, the Europeans eventually developed their own style of Dixieland jazz, different in nuance if not in form from the American version.

Dixieland remains a far more significant part of jazz today than would appear from the jazz press and many jazz histories.[7] In the United States, the Sacramento Dixieland Jubilee draws 100,000 jazz fans annually – and this is only the largest of many similar Dixieland festivals. Dixieland venues continue to exist in major cities around the world, and the recordings of Condon, Watters, and others remain in production. The principal problem is that it is seen as a white movement, which it essentially is: some black musicians like Ed Hall worked in the genre in the 1940s, but few do any more. Because it is white, it

7 For example, Mark Gridley's *Jazz Styles: History and Analysis* (5th edn), Englewood Cliffs, NJ, 1994, a widely used text, virtually omits the Dixieland revival, while the listings in entertainment guides for New York City rarely include clubs devoted to Dixieland.

is, in the eyes of its critics, less authentic than the jazz more generally played by blacks.

Small-band swing

The Dixieland revival is best seen as one aspect of a larger movement which was at the heart of jazz of the swing era. While the big bands got the bulk of public attention, and get much space in standard jazz histories, far more significant jazz was being made by small groups consisting of one to three horns backed by a two-to-four-piece rhythm section. In fact, small groups playing improvised jazz in an informal manner had always existed: in the early New Orleans days, trios and quartets often played in the honky-tonks of the vice district, and elsewhere, while in the 1920s Jimmie Noone had made an important series of recordings, as the Apex Club Orchestra, with himself and a saxophone backed by a rhythm section. Others, like Johnny Dodds and Freddie Keppard, had also recorded in similar contexts. But by the mid-1930s, the small bands had been largely driven out by the big bands.

Renewed interest began with the first, somewhat cautious Goodman Trio recordings in 1935, with Teddy Wilson on piano and Gene Krupa on drums. The Trio recordings were successful, and there was pressure on Goodman to present the group on the bandstand, but there was also considerable fear that the public might object to the racial mixing: Wilson was black, which was not a problem in the studios, but at that time mixed bands were rarely presented live and almost never in major locations. Goodman was just becoming successful, but he risked it, and in the event the public appeared to be unconcerned. Over the next few years racial mixing in bands became increasingly common, and by the end of the Second World War in 1945 it had ceased to be an issue. Lionel Hampton, a black member of the later Goodman Quartet, was just one of those who explicitly believed that racial mixing in jazz opened the doors in the United States for racial mixing in sports and in American life in general.[8]

The commercial success of the Goodman Trio and succeeding groups encouraged musicians and promoters to present similar small groups, frequently featuring star soloists from the swing bands. The musicians were happy to have a chance to play 'pure' jazz and see their names on records; the promoters found it much cheaper to hire a small group than a fourteen-piece orchestra. The music of these groups largely consisted of improvised solos, although they frequently included riffs and brief arranged passages, often at the beginning and the end, to set off the solos. Material was usually made up of 'standards', that is,

8 Lionel Hampton, quoted in the *Saturday Evening Post*, 18 December 1954, p. 33.

well-known tunes from the popular repertory such as 'Sweet Georgia Brown', 'Way Down Yonder in New Orleans', and 'Whispering', as well as blues-based riff tunes. Some groups were spin-offs using personnel drawn from a swing band and were presented as an adjunct to it – as with the Bob Crosby Bobcats, a Dixieland group – while others, like the Artie Shaw Gramercy Five, were semi-permanent bands playing set repertory. But increasingly through the 1930s and into the 1940s, most of them were put together ad hoc for a specific recording date or dates, usually to feature a given soloist. In fact, most of the important work of major jazz figures was made with these small groups, not with the swing bands they made their livings in; this was true of Lester Young, Coleman Hawkins, Billie Holiday, Bobby Hackett, and many more.

The small bands gave rise to another phenomenon: the small 'independent' record company. Professional jazz musicians, used to pulling together performances at short notice, were capable of cutting as many as half a dozen three-minute 78 rpm recordings in a few hours. In the Depression, even star soloists could he hired to make records for small amounts of money, the necessary sidemen for even less. It was thus possible for a small promoter, or even an amateur jazz fan, to record a favourite soloist for a few hundred dollars. Following the example of Commodore, many other small labels were started, among them Keynote, Savoy, and Jump. Slightly later, independent labels were to be particularly important in recording the new bebop and other modern forms, of which the majors were wary. But even though Commodore and others made many important small swing-band recordings, the genre was popular enough for the majors as well; the small groups of Ellington, Goodman, Crosby, and Herman were recorded by major labels.

At the same time, similar small swing bands were being booked into clubs. Of particular significance were the half-dozen or so clubs along New York's 52nd Street (now remembered in jazz history as 'Swing Street'), the first of which opened with the ending of Prohibition in 1934; too small to house the popular big bands, they booked star soloists backed by rhythm sections. Performing regularly on 52nd Street were Lester Young, Billie Holiday, Coleman Hawkins, Roy Eldridge, Art Tatum, and various Dixieland groups. (By the early 1950s most of the 52nd Street locations had become striptease clubs.) Similar clubs existed in other American cities: by 1940 virtually all had several jazz clubs featuring small swing groups.

The best-known of these were the Goodman groups. The Trio mixed the sparkling piano of Wilson with Goodman's bright clarinet sound; soon Goodman added a further, similar voice with Lionel Hampton's bell-like vibraphone. There was later a Quintet, but possibly the most important of these groups was the Sextet, which in its classic form included the growl specialist

Cootie Williams and the electric guitarist Charlie Christian, who was already developing an advanced style which employed somewhat unusual harmonies and phrased against the grain of the metre. Christian did not invent the electric guitar – just who did is a matter of debate – but his exposure with the Goodman orchestra led to its popularization. Where the Goodman Quartets employed instruments with similar qualities, the Sextet used a much broader tonal palette, with a plunger mute against clarinet, electric guitar, and saxophone. Much of the material was original, often based on novel melodic lines worked out by Christian.

The success of the Goodman small groups encouraged Duke Ellington to record some of his own, using simple head arrangements, many of them by Billy Strayhorn; these featured his most important soloists, especially Hodges, Williams, the cornettist Rex Stewart, and the clarinettist Barney Bigard. Much of the material was based on the blues or simple chord sets, with one or two uncomplicated melodic lines breaking up the solos, and – as ever – contrast was a guiding principle, along with deft use of the Ellington tonal palette. Among the most important of the small-band recordings, however, was a long series produced by John Hammond under the direction of Teddy Wilson. From a wealthy and prominent family, Hammond had a strong determination not only to give jazz the place in American culture he thought it deserved, but also to break down racial walls: virtually all of his recordings were racially mixed. The majority of the sides with Wilson featured Billie Holiday, whom Hammond was promoting, but they included as sidemen many of the finest jazz musicians of the day of both races, among them Lester Young, Ben Webster, Harry James, Bunny Berigan, Goodman, Benny Morton, the drummer Cozy Cole, and more. In this series Holiday sang fewer of the pensive or gloomy songs she later became known for, in favour of bright, brisk pieces with a lilt. Commentators have often noted the way she and Young, with whom she had a personal relationship, interacted musically, as for example on 'Me, Myself and I' (1937).

Young himself also made many small-swing sides during this period. Probably the best-known of these are a series made with musicians drawn from the Basie band, under the title of The Kansas City Five (or Six). Young used a light, dry tone, which contrasted markedly with the heavy, full sound of Hawkins and his followers like Ben Webster. By 1940 Young was drawing to himself a lot of the young saxophonists; eventually a school of them developed to rival the one around Hawkins. Young was a very direct player, often hammering the tonic for several beats, but he was also able to fashion, almost at will, long, winding lines that swung hard. He remains a much admired figure in jazz, placed by some with Armstrong and Beiderbecke as pre-eminent in classic jazz.

Those mentioned above are only a fraction of the many hundreds of small swing-band records from this period. Taken together, they constitute one of the most important bodies of work in jazz, as significant as early Dixieland and the early bop that was shortly to come. They were far more varied than bop, with its limited instrumentation, set routines, and rigid harmonic formulae: there was more to distinguish both musically and emotionally between, say, a Hawkins/Eldridge Commodore recording and a Goodman Trio than between any of the bop groups following in the Gillespie/Parker mode.

But modern jazz was coming. Jazz musicians had always expressed interest in contemporary classical music, especially Debussy, Ravel, and Stravinsky. By 1940 or so, some swing band arrangers were attempting to incorporate ideas drawn from these and others into their work: Eddie Sauter was writing adventurous – in jazz terms – pieces for Goodman, such as 'Superman', while Ellington, though not a student of twentieth-century music, had always been pushing into new territory, as with 'Ko-Ko'. By 1944, and in some cases earlier, musicians in and around New York were beginning to hear of the experiments of Dizzy Gillespie, Charlie Parker, Thelonious Monk, and others, in Harlem jam sessions and with the short-lived Billy Eckstine big band; Herman and the hitherto lesser-known Boyd Raeburn and Claude Thornhill began introducing modern harmonies and rhythms into their bands' music. The largest splash, however, was made by Stan Kenton, who throughout the late 1940s and into the 1950s introduced one experimental band after another; some of these bands comprised as many as twenty players, and played loud and highly dissonant music for what was ostensibly a dance band. The Raeburn and Thornhill bands did not survive long, but the Kenton band was for a period the most popular of the remaining swing bands.

Both Herman and Basie were able to keep big bands going into the 1980s, but the swing era was really over by 1945. For a variety of reasons – social, economic, and musical – the big bands collapsed with a rush. For one thing, musicians' salaries were impelled upwards by wartime shortages of labour to the point where the bands could not be profitable. For another, the American mood was now for the light popular song, sung by young, good-looking singers of both sexes. Finally, the new bebop music made classic jazz seem outmoded. The harmonic innovations of the moderns had probably been inevitable, given the wide interest in Stravinsky and others, and might have been absorbed into swing; but the new rhythms of bop were hard for older hands to grasp, while young jazz fans were inevitably drawn to the new music. Yet classic jazz did not die with the swing bands. It continues to be played, not merely by veterans, but by a significant number of younger musicians. The audience for it, too, is large, as an examination of record-store shelves and performance lists will indicate.

At the beginning of the twenty-first century, classic jazz is a much larger part of the mix than either press attention or academic concern would indicate.

Bibliography

Collier, Geoffrey L. and James Lincoln Collier, 'Microrhythms in Jazz', *Annual Review of Jazz Studies* 8 (1996), pp. 117–39.
Collier, James Lincoln. *Jazz: The American Theme Song*, New York, 1993.
The Reception of Jazz in America, Brooklyn, 1988.
Gridley, Mark. *Jazz Styles: History and Analysis* (5th edn), Englewood Cliffs, NJ, 1994.
Hobson, Wilder. *American Jazz Music*, New York, 1939.
Ramsey, Frederick Jr and Charles Edward Smith. *Jazzmen*, New York, 1939.
Sargeant, Winthrop. *Jazz, Hot and Hybrid*, New York, 1938.
Shipton, Alyn. *A New History of Jazz*, London, 2001.

Discography

Louis Armstrong and His Hot Five. *Cornet Chop Suey* (OKeh, 1926)
Louis Armstrong and His Orchestra. *Potato Head Blues* (OKeh, 1927)
Louis Armstrong and His Savoy Ballroom Five. *Tight Like This* (OKeh, 1928)
Louis Armstrong and His Orchestra. *Muggles* (OKeh, 1928)
Louis Armstrong and His Hot Five. *West End Blues* (OKeh, 1928)
Charlie Barnet and His Orchestra. *Cherokee* (Bluebird, 1939)
Bix Beiderbecke and His Gang. *Royal Garden Blues* (OKeh, 1927)
Duke Ellington and his Kentucky Club Orchestra. *East St. Louis Toodle-oo* (Victor, 1927)
Duke Ellington and His Orchestra. *Black and Tan Fantasy* (Victor, 1927)
Creole Love Call (Victor, 1927)
Creole Rhapsody (Brunswick, 1931)
Duke Ellington and His Famous Orchestra. *Echoes of Harlem* (Brunswick, 1936)
Clarinet Lament (Brunswick, 1936)
Don't Get Around Much Anymore (as Never No Lament) (Victor, 1940)
Harlem Airshaft (Victor, 1940)
Ko-Ko (Victor, 1940)
Main Stem (Victor, 1942)
Benny Goodman and His Orchestra. *Sometimes I'm Happy* (Victor, 1935)
Billie Holiday and Her Orchestra. *Me, Myself and I* (Vocalion, 1937)
The Jungle Band. *Mood Indigo* (Brunswick, 1930)
Jelly Roll Morton's Red Hot Peppers. *The Chant* (Victor, 1926)
Black Bottom Stomp (Victor, 1926)
King Oliver's Creole Orchestra. *Dippermouth Blues* (Gennett, 1923)
Frankie Trumbauer and His Orchestra. *Singing the Blues* (OKeh, 1927)
Clarence Williams' Blue Five. *Wildcat Blues* (OKeh, 1923)
Kansas City Man Blues (OKeh, 1923)
Cake Walking Babies (OKeh, 1924)

· 6 ·

Flirting with the vernacular: America in Europe, 1900–45

SUSAN C. COOK

> 'What composer hasn't flirted with this seductive temptress?'
> Louis Gruenberg, 'Der Jazz als Ausgangspunkt', *Anbruch* 7 (April 1925).[1]

The remarks of Louis Gruenberg (1884–1964) quoted above appeared in a *Sonderheft* of the *Musikblätter des Anbruch*, the in-house organ of Universal Edition, widely known for its publications of new music. Devoted entirely to jazz, the issue included articles by critics and composers including Gruenberg, Darius Milhaud, and Percy Grainger, representing Germany and the United States (through Gruenberg's German-American residence and training), as well as France and Britain. While the authors did not agree on the extent of jazz's influence on their compositions or the works of others, they all acknowledged a fascination with and desire to utilize this kind of popular music as a transnational aspect of 1920s musical modernity.[2]

In identifying jazz 'as a point of departure' for the composition of new music, Gruenberg drew upon long-standing views of popular culture and its music as accessible, irresistible, and personified as female. Coming into its own in the 1920s, jazz was thus not unlike another social phenomenon of the time, the New Woman. Both were perceived as youthful, urban, and free from past conventions of propriety and morality. While more women did enter the public workplace during the 1920s, and often in ways that utilized modern technology, the new woman of the modern city was in many respects an overdrawn fiction. Similarly jazz and its seductive temptations were also potent fantasies

This chapter is offered in memory of Richard S. James and Mark Tucker, whose untimely deaths in 1993 and 2000, respectively, impoverished the field of musicology in ways too numerous to mention. It was my great fortune to have them among my peers during my graduate training at the University of Michigan. I remain indebted to both of them for what they taught me about music in the twentieth century.

1 'Wer [moderner europäischer Komponisten] hätte nicht schon mit dieser verführerischen versucherin geflirtet?' Louis Gruenberg, 'Der Jazz als Ausgangspunkt', *Anbruch* 7 (1925), pp. 196–9; p. 199.

2 For attempts to catalogue these works from the first decades of the twentieth century, see Susan C. Cook, *Opera for a New Republic: The Zeitopern of Krenek, Weill and Hindemith*, Rochester, 1988, especially chapter 4 and appendix A, and Heinrich W. Schwab, 'Zur Rezeption des Jazz in der komponierten Musik', *Dansk Årbog for Musikforskning* 10 (1979), pp. 127–77.

of modernism, fantasies that originated in the dichotomies of mind and body, classical and popular, cultural insiders and outsiders.

Popular music and the related term vernacular resist easy definition. At its most simple, popular music can be understood as the music of ubiquity, the music available to the largest number of people through the most available means of mass mediation and entertainments of any and all kinds.[3] Gendered feminine by Gruenberg and countless others, jazz in particular, and popular music in general, remained the central category of musical Otherness, an Otherness that accounted both for its desirability and its temptations. The popular, through its associations with the feminine, the body, and mass culture, promised something that was lacking within the privileged sphere of mindful high culture. In their desire to flirt with popular music, then, modernist composers in the 1920s shared sensibilities with composers, artists, and writers before them who had similarly transgressed national, racial, and class boundaries for aesthetic attributes of the Exotic that might likewise inform their 'serious' work. While the nature, details, and multiple meanings of the Exotic and frequently feminized Erotic Other shifted with respect to national boundaries and individual experience, it nonetheless remained firmly linked to inequitable power relationships that positioned the autonomous borrower above the things to be borrowed.[4]

But there was a difference between the nineteenth-century fascination with the Exotic and the twentieth-century fascination with the popular or vernacular: the latter was located not only outside but also within. While popular music has by its commercial nature been judged outside cultivated 'high culture', it also defiantly resides within a shared social world or habitus. It thus remains highly unstable, as suggested by the continual use of a pathological discourse throughout the twentieth century to discuss its presence: terms like 'dance craze', 'ragtime epidemic', and ' jazz germ' capture both the excitement of the novel and its perceived potential for cultural disruption. With the ascendance of minstrelsy as the dominant popular entertainment in the nineteenth century, popular music in the US became inextricably tied up with

3 I am grateful to Anahid Kassabian for the understanding of 'ubiquitous music'; see her essay 'Popular' in Bruce Horner and Thomas Swiss (eds.), *Key Terms in Popular Music and Culture*, Malden, MA, 1999, pp. 113–23.

4 My interpretation draws on the varied theoretical and historical perspectives of Edward W. Said, *Orientalism*, New York, 1979; Andreas Huyssen, 'Mass Culture as Woman: Modernism's Other', in Tania Modleski (ed.), *Studies in Entertainment*, Bloomington, 1986, pp. 188–207; Catherine Parsons Smith, '"A Distinguishing Virility": Feminism and Modernism in American Art Music', in Susan C. Cook and Judy S. Tsou (eds), *Cecilia Reclaimed: Feminist Perspectives on Gender and Music*, Urbana, 1994, pp. 90–106; Katharina von Ankum (ed.), *Women in the Metropolis: Gender and Modernity in Weimar Culture*, Berkeley, 1997; and Detlev J. K. Peukert, *The Weimar Republic: The Crisis of Classical Modernity* (tr. Richard Deveson), New York, 1992.

race and racialized identities that served to underscore the popular as second-class. As the recording industry emerged in the first decade of the twentieth century, industry representatives made crucial, if rarely unambiguous, marketing and programmatic distinctions between the 'novel' and the 'good'. While racially marked popular musics were present in recording catalogues from the beginning, recording companies and later radio licensing boards positioned the 'serious' over the 'light' in order to justify their commercial activities through providing audiences with morally 'good' or 'serious' music.[5]

While composers like Milhaud and Krenek celebrated popular music for its 'uncultured' primitivist vitality, the music's own creators increasingly argued for new kinds of legitimacy that would undo pernicious dichotomies that judged not only their musical creations but themselves as second-class. African-American composers, such as Scott Joplin and James Reese Europe, questioned the racialized terminology used to describe their music, and both expressed misgivings with the primitivist connotations of danger and excitement attached to ragtime by white, mainstream consumers. Scott Joplin and his publisher purposefully referred to his compositions as 'classic rags'. Europe and his Clef Club Symphony Orchestra gave performances in Carnegie Hall in 1912 and 1913 as a way of 'legitimizing the music of the negro',[6] while in the 1920s better-known experiments in recontextualizing popular music included Paul Whiteman's 'Experiment in Modern Music', which presented his 'symphonic jazz' along with George Gershwin's *Rhapsody in Blue*, again within the confines of the concert hall.

In the decade following the First World War, the United States took possession of modern life in the view of most Europeans, as images of American economic vitality and popular culture saturated post-war European life. With its New World status, America modelled a post-war life 'unencumbered by its burden of conventions' (as Edmund Wilson, Jr noted in the pages of *Vanity Fair*, not without genuine concern for those European traditions being left behind).[7] America was the locus for the emerging film industry, and especially the ascendance and continued development of syncopated social dance music and jazz, which first attracted international audiences in the nineteenth century through the minstrel show, the cakewalk, and orchestrated ragtime. New York City's skyscrapers increasingly became the architectural signs of the modern cityscape, and jazz dance music its urban soundscape.

5 Karl Christian Führer, 'A Medium of Modernity? Broadcasting in Weimar Germany, 1923–1932', *Journal of Modern History* 69/4 (1997), pp. 722–53.

6 Reid Badger, *A Life in Ragtime: A Biography of James Reese Europe*, New York, 1995, p. 73.

7 Edmund Wilson, Jr, 'The Aesthetic Upheaval in France: The Influence of Jazz in Paris and Americanization of French Literature and Art', *Vanity Fair* (February 1922), p. 49.

In the wake of a war that prevented an easy resumption of former lifestyles for most of Europe, artists re-examined their roles in society, their national identities, and their connections with audiences and patrons. A return to the immediate past was impossible, and the future was too unstable; for many, the present remained the sole option. With the advent of multiple mass media in the nineteenth century, it would have been the rare composer, critic, or musical citizen who could claim to have had no contact with the ubiquitous musics of popular culture. What was at stake were the ramifications of that contact, and individual responses carried different national resonances depending on pre-existing political realities and artistic currents. For composers of the 1920s, the challenge became how to approach this perceived and localized Other: what, precisely, should or could one borrow, and to what end?

Popular musics in their seeming vitality and connection with the victorious United States became a way for many composers to renegotiate the terms of the social contract between contemporary music and everyday life. Composers, both American and European, presented a range of responses, from limited appropriations of popular-music codes, to re-evaluating and calling into question its secondary status and validating its functional accessibility. The vast majority of new works that drew on the everyday power of popular music to resuscitate post-war art, however, did so in ways that retained the composer's modernist identities. The works remain unique interpretations of popular culture and its extra-musical meanings, rather than becoming that popular culture itself. Terms used in the 1920s, like *Kunstjazz*, present an image of two separate and unequal entities – art and 'something popular' – being forcibly mixed together. Thus even popular music's most articulate supporters perpetuated essentialized notions about popular culture and reinscribed the very dichotomies – high/low, timeless/timely, aesthetic/functional – they sought to dismantle. Composers retained their power as the privileged borrowers, often neglecting to acknowledge their sources or grant any real authority to them.[8] And it remains difficult, if not impossible, to talk about jazz or other popular musics without similarly perpetuating historically constructed hierarchical and inequitable positions.

There is also a further complication: what we mean today by the terms 'ragtime' or 'jazz', and what performers and composers meant in their time and particular geographic locales, are almost always at odds.[9] Our ears have

8 Bernard Gendron likens these composers, especially Darius Milhaud, to the privileged male *flâneur* or 'slummer' in their preoccupation with cultural Otherness. 'Jamming at Le Boeuf: Jazz and the Paris Avant-Garde', *Discourse* 12/1 (1989–90), pp. 3–27.

9 See Scott DeVeaux's 'Constructing the Jazz Tradition: Jazz Historiography', *Black American Literature Forum* 25/3 (1991), pp. 525–60, for an especially lucid discussion and critique of jazz historiography and scholarship.

been thoroughly conditioned by the availability of historic recordings and through scholarship that promotes originality and influence. In the 1920s the term 'jazz' could mean any and all popular music, regardless of origins or features. American imports were easily grafted onto pre-existing national and local practices, and the resulting hybrids, even when proclaimed or heard in their own contexts as 'true' to their imported models, appear corrupted to our contemporary sensibilities. Thus most recent jazz scholarship has had little interest in white ensembles like the Original Dixieland Jazz Band, the 'symphonic jazz' of Paul Whiteman and his Orchestra, or non-United States performers like London's Jack Hylton, even though these performers were extraordinarily popular and influential in the 1920s and 30s. Furthermore, many influential performers made few if any recordings, and even those who did were constrained by the limitations of the media; what we can hear may provide little sense of what audiences experienced.

Especially problematic for today's listeners is that improvisation, a hallmark of what we have come to identify as central to 'authentic' jazz, is missing almost entirely from these 1920s compositions that claim to draw from jazz; improvisation was not well understood by audiences or even performers until the end of the 1920s, and it remained at odds with the modernist conception of a fixed, autonomous work.[10] Thus many, if not all, of the compositions that celebrate jazz and other popular musics in their titles or descriptive programmes do so in ways that seem superficial or collapse genre distinctions as we know them. Common to these works, however, is a commitment to the moving modern body through the agency of social dances such as the foxtrot and tango, popular before the First World War, and the shimmy and charleston of the 1920s. Even the nineteenth-century waltz and the two-step, danced to the march, retained their power on the ballroom floor and in the popular imagination. Overwhelmingly, for composers and audiences well into the century, popular music – call it jazz, ragtime, cakewalk, two-step, waltz, or later, swing – was dance music, and it drew attention to bodies brought together in dance. Through participatory social dance many composers attempted to find a political and aesthetic meeting place between the inaccessible and often unpopular concert music and the functional and commercially successful space of popular music.

Given the central identity of popular music and jazz as dance music, then, it is not surprising that, as Anne C. Shreffler has pointed out, experiments with 'concert jazz' and some kinds of neoclassicism often existed in close proximity in the works of composers like Stravinsky, Milhaud, and Hindemith.[11]

10 The issue is complicated by uncertainties as to the extent to which improvisation was common in jazz until the mid-1920s; see James Collier's chapter in this volume.

11 Anne C. Shreffler, 'Classicizing Jazz: Concert Jazz in Paris and New York in the 1920s', in Hermann Danuser (ed.), *Die klassizistische Moderne in der Musik des 20. Jahrhunderts*, Basel, 1997, pp. 55–71.

Apologists of the 1920s frequently legitimated the use of popular music by identifying Bach suites and other functional music of the past as models. Both compositional responses could be negotiated through dances with their pre-existing rhythms, tempi and extra-musical affects. Be they triple-time minuets that conjured up disciplined aristocratic bodies of the past, or tangos that drew on racialized images of unchecked heterosexual passion and urban violence, dances provided ready and tantalizing models for reinterpretation. And the widespread discussion, throughout European and American culture, of jazz dance and its meanings meant that there was no way such borrowings could ever have been simply about 'the music itself'. 'Jazzy' works could not erase the attendant social implications of their models. The music of Erik Satie, Igor Stravinsky, Darius Milhaud, Paul Hindemith, Ernst Krenek, Kurt Weill, Constant Lambert, or Erwin Schulhoff remained inextricably linked to the social implications of their borrowed sources and their attendant fantasies about American culture, worked out within the circumstances of their own national identities.

Transnational popular musics

Unlike folk music, often idealized for its connection to a nostalgic rural past, popular music by definition speaks of the present. To be popular is to be up-to-date, and, in the 1920s, jazz was an aural representation of changing urban and industrialized environments, especially those of New York City, Paris, London, and Berlin, and to lesser extents Prague and Vienna. Although the United States served as a racial and national focal point for modern entertainments in the 1920s, Britain, France, Germany, and Austria had long competed as entertainment capitals and shared the fruits of their successes among themselves and with the United States. Such venues as the variety theatre, circus, music hall, vaudeville, cabaret, and *café-concert* emerged and developed throughout the late nineteenth century, continuing into the new century. These venues and their varied offerings shared musical and dramatic attributes while maintaining their own regional, national, or aesthetic identities, often in surprising ways.

Performers like British actor George Grossmith (1874–1935) demonstrate the multiple transnational interactions of popular culture and the difficulty of assigning direct influences or fixed social meanings. During his productive career Grossmith moved easily between London's Gaiety Theatre (where he gained a reputation for his knowledge of American song), Paris (where he performed in French), and New York City; he was best known for his comic roles that drew on British stereotypes of the upper-class fop. In 1912 Grossmith sang and danced 'The Argentine Tango' in *The Sunshine Girl* with leading lady Phyllis Dare. This number capitalized on the novelty of a controversial ragtime dance just beginning to be found on British dance floors. Imported from Paris where it had been popular since 1908, the tango was known to have developed among the underclass of Argentina: its steps, affect, and distinctive rhythms were associated in the popular imaginations of France, Britain, and the United States with an immodest display of heterosexual desire and aggressive, even brutal, masculinity. Through its proximity to other syncopated ragtime dances such as the one-step, the tango was also linked with African Americans for whom music and dance were 'natural' attributes of their second-class status. These dances and their syncopated music caused bodies to move in new and potentially threatening ways. Grossmith's comic persona tamed the dance while his performance, in gaucho costume with a rose in the teeth, provided a racialized image that echoes even today.

The Sunshine Girl opened in New York City the following year and Grossmith's role went to another British actor, Vernon Castle. Castle had appeared on the New York City stage since 1906, and had spent the previous season performing in Paris with his American wife Irene. He was related to Grossmith by marriage: Vernon's older sister, the actress Coralie Blythe, was married to Grossmith's younger brother, the actor Lawrence Grossmith. As a way to update the New York production, the Castles interpolated a ragtime one-step based on material they had devised and marketed in Paris, and within weeks they became the best-known performers of, and apologists for, racialized American ragtime dance as a participatory activity for the white mainstream. In doing so they drew on Vernon's British heritage not as a comic fop, but rather as the embodiment of a refinement in terms of class and race that aided their recuperation of dangerous ragtime dance through elegant demeanour and bodily control (Fig. 6.1). The couple's success depended as well on their relationship with African-American composer and bandleader James Reese Europe (1881–1919), well known in New York City; Europe became their music director and composed works expressly for their use, while his Society Orchestra became the first black ensemble of its kind to record.[12] He also kept them abreast of new dances, such as the foxtrot, that were being circulated within black popular culture by performers who had little access to the racially segregated entertainment market tapped by the Castles. The Castles' success, then, relied on their ability to negotiate and legitimate 'black' popular music through performances that drew on racialized notions of 'whiteness' and class refinement.

Before the enthusiasm for the jazz dances of the 1920s and the pre-war ragtime dance of the Castles and others, the cakewalk had earned a position of importance in turn-of-the-century Europe and fostered linkages between

12 For a complete discography, see Badger, *A Life in Ragtime*, pp. 235–40.

Figure 6.1: Irene and Vernon Castle in a ragtime dance pose. Source: J. S. Hopkins, *The Tango and Other Up-to-Date Dances* (Chicago, Saalfield Publishing Co., 1914). From the author's collection.

rhythmic vitality, bodily response, and race. Associated with pre- and post-slavery African-American dance practices, the cakewalk was commonplace in blackface minstrelsy where white performers utilized racial stereotypes to act 'black', and the cakewalk's virtuosic strutting and prancing movements became a standard feature of black theatrical productions of the 1890s, most notably in Will Marion Cook's *Clorindy, or the Origin of the Cakewalk* (1898). Its lilting, dotted melody and syncopation had much in common with the earlier minstrel-show tunes and 'coon songs' that continued to be central to popular-song repertories; works like Kerry Mills's 'At a Georgia Campmeeting' (1897), with its racially programmatic title and cover illustration (Fig. 6.2), became part of the varied programmes of John Phillip Sousa's band, while by 1899 the solo-piano ragtime of Scott Joplin and others began to appear in sheet music and entered the home and parlour repertories of mainstream America. Central to these intermingled popular repertories of marches, two-steps, coon songs, cakewalks, and piano ragtime was the presence of syncopation as the aural sign of racial difference, one that had the power to awaken a host of physical and mental responses that were soon exported to Europe: in 1900 Sousa's band performed their arrangements of marches, two-steps, and syncopated cakewalks at the Paris Universal Exposition and went on to tour Germany and Belgium. Subsequent European tours in 1901, 1903, and 1905 brought return engagements in England, France, and Germany, as well as appearances in Glasgow, Vienna, Prague, Copenhagen, and St Petersburg.

The racially marked music and movement of the cakewalk and ragtime quickly diffused throughout contemporary European culture. By 1902, foreign and local performers appeared in Parisian music halls, such as Nouveau Cirque and the Folies-Bergère, and cakewalk contests soon made the dance a recreational entertainment with far-reaching appeal. Dance instructions and images of white French citizens strutting arm in arm appeared in the popular press along with images of imagined Africans or real African Americans demonstrating the cakewalk's distinctive steps (Fig. 6.3). As both Glenn E. Watkins and Jody Blake demonstrate, this popular music and dance discourse took its place alongside ethnographic studies, travel guides, museum and exhibition displays, and other scientific and literary discussions.[13] This constellation of images and discourses collapsed differences between Africa and African Americans and became central to emerging French artistic modernism. In the 1920s, it spread beyond France in its celebration of modern life, modernist 'primitivism', and jazz.

13 Glenn E. Watkins, *Pyramids at the Louvre: Music, Culture, and Collage from Stravinsky to the Postmodernists*, Cambridge, MA, 1994, see especially chapters 3, 4, and 5; and Jody Blake, *Le tumulte noir: Modernist Art and Popular Entertainment in Jazz-Age Paris, 1900–1930*, University Park, MD, 1999.

Figure 6.2: Sheet music cover for Kerry Mills, 'At a Georgia Campmeeting' (New York, F. A. Mills, 1897), featuring racial stereotypes of the time. Source: Mills Music Library, University of Wisconsin-Madison, Americana Collection.

Figure 6.3: French postcard of 'The Elks' demonstrating the cakewalk as they performed it at the Nouveau Cirque, along with abbreviated instructions (postmarked 1904). From the author's collection.

Claude Debussy referenced the cakewalk as early as 1906–8, for the last movement in his piano suite *Children's Corner*, 'Golliwogg's Cake-Walk'; subsequent works such as 'Le petit nègre', and the piano *Préludes* 'Minstrels' and 'General Lavine – eccentric' from books I (1910) and II (1913) respectively, likewise draw on the cakewalk and its racial history. 'Le petit nègre', identified in a footnote as 'Danse nègre dite Danse du gateau', first appeared in Théodore Lack's 1909 piano tutor, and like 'Golliwogg's Cake-Walk' shares the distinctive four-bar introduction common in Joplin's solo piano rags, while dotted-quaver melodies frequently pit the right and left hands against each other in mild syncopation. 'Minstrels', by contrast, evokes the banjo, widely associated in the United States and Europe with African-American musical practices through its use on the minstrel stage; in the 1920s, the banjo continued to be used in jazz ensembles and together with the saxophone became a timbral and visual sign of African Americans and their distinctive musics (Fig. 6.4). Finally 'General Lavine – eccentric', with its marking 'Dans le style et le Mouvement d'un Cake-Walk', highlights the connections and contradictions between the military march and syncopated cakewalk: the opening drumrolls give way to a danceable melody and dotted-rhythm sections, but this cakewalk never completely breaks away from its march roots. Debussy's reinterpretations situate the cakewalk among children, perhaps because of the influence of the brother-and-sister cakewalk act known as 'Les petits Walkers', or because Africans and African Americans were more generally associated in contemporary discourse with primitive, natural, and childish popular entertainments. Durand et Fils's cover for *Children's Corner* prominently features a balloon decorated like the head and face of a Golliwogg, a character from the children's stories of Bertha Upton, whose features retained the grotesque stereotypes of minstrelsy.

Erik Satie's 'Ragtime du Paquebot' for the ballet *Parade* (1917) postdates Debussy's evocations by at least five years, and reflects the semantic, corporeal, and musical changes from turn-of-the-century cakewalk to pre-First World War ragtime song and dance, widely associated in the United States and Europe with Irving Berlin's ragtime songs, animal dances like the 'grizzly bear' popularized in Paris by Harry Pilcer and Gaby Deslys, and the 'modern dance' performances of the Castles. However, as Stephen Whiting demonstrates, the time gap does not accurately reflect Satie's long-standing professional involvement with popular entertainments and fondness for things American, which begins well before the emergence of the cakewalk.[14] Again, 'Le Tango (perpétuel)'

14 Steven Moore Whiting, *Satie the Bohemian: From Cabaret to Concert Hall*, New York, 1999; see also Robert Orledge, 'Satie and America', *American Music* 18/1 (2000), pp. 78–102.

Figure 6.4: Sheet music cover for Joseph Walker Sweeny, 'Jenny Get your Hoe Cake Done' (New York, Firth and Hall, 1840). Source: Mills Music Library, University of Wisconsin-Madison, Americana Collection.

from *Sports et divertissements*, composed in 1914 but not published until 1925, demonstrates Satie's knowledge of this dance and its Parisian pedigree; his characteristic marginalia juxtapose the dance's supposedly scandalous sexual display – 'The tango is the dance of the devil' – with performance indications of 'Moderately and with great boredom' suggesting how commonplace the risqué dance had become by 1914. His tango snapshot combines the dance's well-known rhythms – the habañera in the left hand against the semiquaver-quaver-semiquaver pattern in the right – with his own penchant for pungent harmonies and repetition.

Conceived by Jean Cocteau as a 'ballet réaliste', *Parade* was a large-scale collaborative effort combining the artistic and aesthetic contributions of Cocteau and Satie with Serge Diaghilev's Ballets Russes, Pablo Picasso's curtain, set, and costume designs, and the choreography of Léonide Massine. Cocteau's aesthetic of the everyday and celebration of popular French and American stimuli received its most extensive elaboration in his seventy-four-page pamphlet *Le coq et l'harlequin* (1918), but all of the collaborators could claim knowledge of popular culture and a shared dedication to new aesthetic principles. Combining the humour and parody of popular theatre and music-hall acts, *Parade*'s loose narrative throws into relief the hierarchical positions of popular culture and 'legitimate' theatre, for, as Whiting suggests, all of the acts presented were familiar to French audiences, just not within the context of the Théâtre du Châtelet.[15] Audience response to this decontextualization was mixed; critics generally attacked the work, finding it unpatriotic in the post-war age.

As identified in the published arrangement for piano four hands, 'Rag-time du paquebot' appears appropriately in 'Petite fille Américaine', the second and longest single section of the ballet. Ostensibly based in Cocteau's mind on cinematic images of Mary Pickford, Pearl White, and the American Wild West that necessitated the use of gunshot sound effects, Maria Chabelska's performance provided a collage of 'American girl' images, from cakewalking to playing in the sand. Satie's score for this section uses a large-scale ternary organization and combines a variety of cakewalk and ragtime dance elements; a four-bar introduction, after an extensive interruption, gives way to the quoted refrain from Irving Berlin's 'That Mysterious Rag' (1911), published in Paris in 1913, juxtaposed further with bitonal cakewalk sections.[16]

Igor Stravinsky's explorations of syncopated dance music in *Ragtime for Eleven Instruments*, *Piano-Rag-Music*, and especially *L'histoire du soldat* (composed between 1917 and 1919) are roughly contemporaneous with Satie's *Parade*. While created in Switzerland, far from from Satie and the energies of Paris,

15 Whiting, *Satie the Bohemian*, p. 473. 16 Ibid., pp. 477–8.

the works demonstrate Stravinsky's like-minded interest in the 'everyday' of Franco-American culture as a response to Germanic excess, views that he shared with Swiss-French writers like novelist C. F. Ramuz. Ernst Ansermet, who conducted *Parade*, was a shared connection with Satie having ostensibly provided Stravinsky with source material – probably sheet music that he purchased while on tour in the United States with the Ballets Russes. While the *Ragtime* and *Piano-Rag-Music* suggest Stravinsky's reliance on solo-piano sheet music as a model, the *Ragtime for Eleven Instruments* utilizes the chamber forces of orchestrated ragtime and dance bands. Picasso's cover illustration for the piano arrangement features an iconic banjo player along with a violinist (this instrument was commonplace in dance orchestras of all kinds both in the United States and Europe throughout the 1920s); while no banjo appears in the ensemble, the cimbalom provides a timbral double for the banjo's distinctive sound.

Given the multiple time signatures and unbarred sections throughout the work, *Piano-Rag-Music* quickly loses its connection to dance practices and becomes an abstraction of syncopated energies and rhythmic gestures. Its difficulty, appropriate for its dedicatee Artur Rubinstein, may also indicate the growing recognition amongst post-war audiences of the virtuosic performance demands of jazz; this is no longer the child's play of Debussy's cakewalks. Dance returns, however, in *L'histoire du soldat*, with its timeless yet timely story to be read, played, and danced, and with the tango, waltz, and ragtime of the 'Three Dances' capturing the affective qualities of these social dances – the tango and ragtime using percussion to highlight their rhythmic syncopation in contrast to the older waltz that remained viable as a social dance. In all three dances the violin plays a key role, again acting as the dance band's appropriate leader.

In 1917 the Victor Talking Machine Company, which had recorded the orchestrated ragtime of James Reese Europe and his orchestra in 1913–14, released 'Livery Stable Blues' and 'Dixie Jass [sic] Band One-Step', recorded by the five-member Original Dixieland Jazz Band; the presence of 'jazz' in the name has given this white ensemble's release a historical prominence in the semantic and musical shift from ragtime to jazz. Likewise their use of the terms 'blues' and 'one-step' present a transition from the pre-war dances of ragtime to the emerging practices of the blues that became increasingly important in the 'jazz age' of the 1920s.[17] The blues emerged from post-enslavement vocal traditions of field hollers and sung stories and began to make its way into printed

17 For discussion of the origins and early development of the blues see James Collier's chapter in this volume (pp. 126–7).

sheet music, such as W. C. Handy's 'Memphis Blues' (1912) and 'St Louis Blues' (1914), as well as into the instrumental repertories of Jelly Roll Morton, James Reese Europe, and the Original Dixieland Jazz Band. The 1920 release of black vaudeville singer Mamie Smith's 'Crazy Blues' sold unexpectedly well and helped identify a new audience for this vocal repertory that could also function as slow dance music. The emotional affect of sorrow, suffering, and loss, three-line rhyming stanzas, use of flat sevenths and major/minor thirds, and the repeated twelve-bar harmonic pattern with its teleological return to the tonic, became increasingly standardized, especially in the performances by popular vaudeville entertainers. As the 1920s continued, composers, critics, and others increasingly set the spontaneity, vocality, and emotional intensity of the blues in opposition to the speed, machine-like virtuosity, and polyphonic texture of jazz.

1917 also marked the entry of the United States into the First World War. While the war severely limited entertainment options, the American military provided a new conduit for the transnational sharing of popular culture. Given its political alliance, France became the first beneficiary of imported popular music, once more associated with African Americans through the performances of segregated army bands; perhaps the best-known of these all-black largely volunteer units was the 369th Infantry Band, led by none other than James Reese Europe. Given his prominence in New York City, Europe played a central role in recruiting African-American musicians for segregated bands that performed for both military and civilian audiences.

As ragtime trots and one-steps replaced cakewalks in the pre-war years, ragtime repertories expanded to include dances like the shimmy and charleston. The term 'jazz' came into wider usage, replacing 'ragtime' to identify the music associated with these new embodied practices of post-war culture. While performance ensembles varied in size, the jazz band came to be identified in the 1920s with a small group of virtuosic soloists who drew on the unique timbral possibilities of solo brass and reed instruments – trumpet, clarinet, and especially the saxophone – as well as the harmonic and rhythmic support of the piano, banjo, and trap drum set. Arrangements typically exploited energetic contrapuntal textures interspersed with the occasional virtuosic solo. Some ensembles utilized improvisation, while others presented carefully rehearsed arrangements; most offered a variety of musics including orchestrated ragtime and blues, early polyphonic jazz, and arrangements of spirituals, marches, and regional popular songs.

With the end of the war and the re-establishment of international contacts, American popular music, now almost uniformly identified as jazz, spread via live performance, increased numbers of recordings, and new musical compositions. A number of African-American musicians who had served in segregated army bands remained in France and became part of the emerging Parisian expatriate community. James Reese Europe's own Hellfighters band remained together after the war, returning to the United States and then Europe to tour; Europe himself died during one of these tours, after being stabbed by the band's mentally unstable drummer. Touring veteran Will Marion Cook returned to France and Britain in 1919 with his thirty-six-member Southern Syncopated Orchestra that included the clarinettist Sidney Bechet, while the Original Dixieland Jazz Band played a long-term engagement in London. London had other stars like Billy Arnold, who arrived from the United States in 1920, and later Jack Hylton, both of whom led influential touring ensembles.

The growing viability of the recording industry and later radio added to the accessibility and diffusion of popular musical culture in the post-war years. European-owned companies like Pathé and subsidiaries of American labels increasingly marketed Americanized popular musics as well as recording touring American musicians. Pathé, for example, recorded both Europe and his Hellfighters ensemble and Louis Mitchell's Jazz Kings.

Post-war responses

Jean Wiéner (1896–1982) encouraged the French enthusiasm for American popular music during the decade of the 1920s, even before the more celebrated appearance of Josephine Baker and *La revue nègre* in 1925. Not unlike any number of conservatory-trained performers and composers before and after him, Wiéner supplemented his income playing piano at various entertainment venues. By 1921, he was performing at the former Bar Gaya, a locus for Cocteau and his collaborators as well as for foreign visitors, including young composers from Germany, Czechoslovakia, and the United States, for whom Paris remained the source of things both chic and risqué; following the success of the Cocteau–Milhaud ballet *Le boeuf sur le toit* (1919), the Bar Gaya was renamed in honour of that work. Wiéner shared his performances with the Belgian pianist Clément Doucet and the saxophonist and banjoist Vance Lowry, who had performed in London before coming to Paris.[18] Wiéner's musical tastes were wide-ranging, and he organized a series of concerts that showcased the broad spectrum of post-war musics: the first Concert-Wiéner, in December 1921, featured Billy Arnold's American Novelty Jazz Band on a bill with an arrangement of Stravinsky's *The Rite of Spring* for mechanical piano. The ensemble's

18 Tobias Widmaier, 'Der weisse Neger vom "Boeuf sur le toit": Jean Wiéner und die Jazzrezeption im Umkreis der "Six"', *Neue Zeitschrift für Musik* 154 (1993), pp. 34–6.

make-up and repertory were similar to that of the Original Dixieland Jazz Band, with whom they had performed in London (where they also recorded for the British subsidiary of Columbia). As with *Parade*, Wiéner attempted to recontextualize and thus legitimate the popular by presenting it in concerts side-by-side with other new works; while critics now applauded his equalizing efforts, their reviews consistently voiced primitivist images of jazz's unchecked rhythmic and racial vitality.

Wiéner's compositions provided further examples of his interest in mixing musics and showed his particular fondness for the blues, which he often used for the traditional slow second movement, as in the *Sonatine syncopée* (1923), dedicated to American jazz bands. *Trois blues chantes* (1924) for voice and piano contains a free textless vocal part. In 1924 he received a commission from the musically astute Princesse Edmond de Polignac, the American heiress Winaretta Singer, paying homage to her with his *Concerto franco-américain*. His operetta *Olive chez les nègres, ou Le village blanc* was premiered at the Music-Hall des Champs-Elysées in 1926, and provided a model for other composers, while the 1929 *Album Wiéner-Doucet* contains two blues, a rag and a foxtrot composed by the duo pianists for their own performances; they continued to present popular music within a concert venue well into the following decade.

Josephine Baker was not yet twenty years old when she arrived in Paris in 1925 as part of *La revue nègre*. Under the direction of white American entrepreneur Caroline Dudley, *La revue nègre* was in the tradition of earlier all-black theatricals and combined up-to-date song-and-dance acts with images of southern plantation life in the tradition of minstrelsy; pianist Claude Hopkins led the revue's five-member jazz band, recruited from New York City. Baker opened the revue dancing the charleston, one of the latest in jazz dances that, like the shimmy, could be presented as a solo. Her performance was anachronistically set on a plantation and her costume portrayed her as an overgrown pickaninny, another throwback to pre-war minstrelsy and coon songs. The revue closed with 'La Danse des sauvages', the creation of veteran music-hall producer Jacques Charles, which proved to be the most popular number; semi-nude, Baker and her partner Joe Alex enacted a jungle *pas de deux*. As American critic Janet Flanner noted, Baker's performance redefined jazz for its largely white, male, French audience as the beautiful, objectified, and highly sexed black female body.[19] Following the revue's tour in Berlin, where Baker similarly drew praise from most critics, she returned to Paris and to a lucrative contract with the Folies-Bergère. Hopkins's ensemble disbanded, but individual members remained to perform throughout Europe. As male critics proved

19 Janet Flanner, *Paris Was Yesterday*, New York, 1972, pp. xx–xxi.

to be unable to deal with Baker as anything but a highly desirable savage, she became another incarnation of the Erotic Exotic, her performances throughout Europe representing jazz and its dances as savage and sexually excessive.

While audiences embraced Josephine Baker as the 'black Venus', desirable precisely because she did not fit pre-existing notions of the idealized feminine, Paul Whiteman claimed 'to make a lady out of jazz'. Whiteman had also performed during the war as part of a Navy band and afterwards made the conscious decision to cultivate popular music. His first successful recording in 1920 introduced his self-styled 'symphonic jazz', which made increasing use of Ferde Grofé arrangements for a larger ensemble, including strings, and featured syncopated arrangements of well-known concert repertory. Whiteman's approach to 'jazzing the classics' became popular in the United States and Europe, although critics found the arrangements with their often comic or tongue-in-cheek combination of popular-music codes and concert music aesthetically troubling. His orchestra performed in London in 1923, and he returned for a second Continental tour in 1925–6. Like Sousa, Whiteman's race afforded him access to touring markets, to recording contracts, and to the press, as in his self-aggrandizing *Jazz* (1926), that were generally unavailable to African-American artists.[20] Not unlike the Castles, Whiteman presented his music within a context of 'refinement' that clearly, if subtly, perpetuated notions that jazz and other popular musics required the ministrations of white composers, arrangers, or dancers to make them acceptable for a concert setting and wide popular consumption. Together Baker and Whiteman show the complicated and often contradictory meanings of popular culture as they literally played out on the stages of the United States and Europe.

Post-war Germany faced a set of circumstances markedly different from Britain, France, or the United States as its defeat and subsequent revolution provoked a crisis of national and cultural identity. In its first five years of existence, the new Weimar Republic faced crippling economic problems including the near-collapse of its currency, loss of territory, and occupation by foreign troops. As was true of elsewhere, however, the United States presented a model for post-war rebuilding, giving rise to the phenomenon of *Amerikanismus* that, while pronounced, was also inconsistent.[21] Industrialists, like those who visited Detroit's River Rouge automobile plant, lauded Henry Ford's model of factory efficiency and shared his enthusiasm for the free market; members of the avant-garde and political left, however, had little use for capitalist materialism

20 Paul Whiteman and Mary Margaret McBride, *Jazz*, New York, 1926.

21 See Frank Trommler, 'The Rise and Fall of Americanism in Germany', in Frank Trommler and Joseph McVeigh (eds.), *America and the Germans: The Relationship in the Twentieth Century*, Philadelphia, 1985, pp. 332–42, and Gesine Schwan, 'Das deutsche Amerikabild seit der Weimarer Republik', *Aus Politik und Zeitgeschichte* B/26 (1986), pp. 3–15.

and worker regimentation, and instead celebrated other aspects of American life and its idealized political system.

Images of American jazz proliferated throughout German expressive culture, where its extra-musical Otherness elided with both pre-war expressionism and the 1920s spirit of *Neue Sachlichkeit* (a term first used in the context of political, social, and economic ideology, which came to be used more generally for art, literature, and culture at large).[22] Within expressionism, jazz was embraced for its shock value, decadence, and supposed renunciation of culture; within post-war *Neue Sachlichkeit*, jazz again symbolized a break with the past, but now without the emotionalism associated with expressionism. In its more general usage this 'new sobriety' or 'new objectivity' favoured urban culture, modern technology, and new leisure entertainments for which jazz and its 'mechanistic' rhythm became the synecdoche.

Until 1924, when the Weimar Republic achieved some measure of economic stability, few foreign musicians ventured to perform in Germany, which therefore remained largely isolated from the post-war manifestations of popular culture elsewhere. However, indigenous German popular entertainments, like revues, *Kabaretts*, and other theatrical venues, began to feature material marked by ragtime dances, such as the foxtrot, by 1919, and local musicians did their best to update their material from what contact they had. American composer George Antheil (1900–59) provided early first-hand exposure: through the support of his patron Mary Curtis Bok, he debuted in Berlin in 1922 to great success with his repertory of virtuosic piano works, like the *Sonata sauvage* (1922–3) and *Jazz Sonata* (1922–3), celebrating both machines and American jazz. By 1926 Berlin boasted a Jazzband-Musiker-Union of five hundred members, with local ensembles – like Weintraub's Syncopators, the Comedian Harmonists, and a host of others performing in *Kino-Varieté* (shows performed during movie intermissions) – boasting their jazz credentials.[23] Some groups claimed particular authenticity and notoriety through the presence of African-American performers.[24] Composers like Friedrich Hollaender and Mischa Spoliansky, who

22 See Thomas W. Kniesche and Stephen Brockmann (eds.), *Dancing on the Volcano: Essays on the Culture of the Weimar Republic*, Columbia, SC, 1994, especially the essays by Jost Hermand, 'Neue Sachlichkeit: Ideology, Lifestyle, or Artistic Movement?', pp. 57–67, and Cornelius Partsch, 'Hannibal ante Portas: Jazz in Weimar', pp. 105–16; Marc A. Weiner, '*Urwaldmusik* and the Borders of German Identity: Jazz in Literature of the Weimar Republic', *The German Quarterly* 64/4 (1991), pp. 475–87; and Beeke Sell Tower, *Envisioning America: Prints, Drawings, and Photographs by George Grosz and his Contemporaries 1915–1933*, Cambridge, 1990.

23 Heribert Schröder, *Tanz- und Unterhaltungsmusik in Deutschland, 1918–1933*, Bonn, 1990, p. 310.

24 For documentation on the presence and kinds of popular music entertainers active in Germany during this time see Fred Ritzel, '"Hätte der Kaiser Jazz getanzt . . .": US-Tanzmusik in Deutschland vor und nach dem Ersten Weltkrieg', in Sabine Schutte (ed.), *Ich will aber gerade vom Leben singen: Über populäre Musik vom ausgehenden 19. Jahrhundert bis zum Ende der Weimarer Republik*, Reinbeck bei Hamburg, 1987, pp. 265–93, and especially Schröder's *Tanz- und Unterhaltungsmusik in Deutschland 1918–1933*. Rainer E. Lotz

collaborated on *Kabarettrevues* written with Rudolf Nelson, Marcellus Schiffer, Kurt Tucholsky, and others, provided opportunities for local and touring performers and demonstrated their knowledge of current idioms of the tango, foxtrot and charleston in their up-to-date shows. Josephine Baker starred in Hollaender's *Kabarettrevue*, *Bitte Einsteigen*, in 1928, but his best-known work, 'Ich bin von Kopf bis Fuss' (performed by Marlene Dietrich in the 1929 film *Der blaue Engel*) was a Boston, a waltz variation that regained popularity in the post-war years.

Before Josephine Baker first came to Berlin following the triumph of *La revue nègre*, Sam Wooding and his band appeared with *The Chocolate Kiddies Revue*, a show that opened in May 1925 and ran intermittently for two years. Wooding had performed with a segregated Army band and after the war returned to the United States, where he organized his own ensembles in New York City. Like *La revue nègre*, *The Chocolate Kiddies* drew on the stereotypes of all-black theatricals with images of Harlem, plantation life, and minstrel caricatures.[25] Although the revue featured numbers by Duke Ellington, it lacked a star of Baker's quality. Wooding and his ten-member ensemble, however, achieved success apart from the staged revue, and toured extensively with their repertory of early big-band jazz arrangements of German and American popular songs, Negro spirituals, and even a syncopated arrangement of Tchaikovsky's '1812' overture in the style of Paul Whiteman (whom Wooding admired). Between 1925 and 1927 they performed throughout Germany, in Stockholm, Copenhagen, Eastern Europe, Switzerland, Spain, Russia, France, and South America; they also played live over the Berlin radio and recorded for Vox, before leaving Berlin in 1930.[26] Besides Wooding, white performers like American banjoist Michael Danzi and violinist Alex Hyde performed and recorded in Berlin. Danzi performed with a number of highly regarded German bandleaders including Erno Rapée, who worked in Mischa Spoliansky's revues and later at New York's Radio City Music Hall. He also played in the premiere of Weill's *Aufsteig und Fall der Stadt Mahagonny*.[27]

Scholarly attention to jazz, as suggested by *Anbruch*'s special issue, had appeared since 1925, and the music and its influence continued to be widely discussed by critics, composers, and others throughout Europe. With the publication of *Jazz* by André Coeuroy and André Schaeffner in 1926, jazz – its

has also documented the crucial presence of African-American performers in Germany before and after the First World War in *Black People: Entertainers of African Descent in Europe, and Germany*, Bonn, 1997; its accompanying CD provides some sense of the syncopated repertories available on recording.

25 A photograph of band members with a poster of the revue appears in Tower, *Envisioning America*, p. 95.

26 These recordings were rereleased on *Sam Wooding and His Chocolate Dandies* (Biograph).

27 Michael Danzi, as told to Rainer E. Lotz, in Lotz, *Michael Danzi: American Musician in Germany 1924–1939*, Schmitten, 1986.

meaning and influence – increasingly became a topic for debate.[28] In Germany, Alfred Baresel became an impassioned proponent. In an essay that appeared in *Auftakt*'s jazz issue in 1926, he claimed that jazz could provide a kind of musical salvation;[29] in his *Das neue Jazzbuch*, which first appeared in 1925 and was revised and expanded in 1929, he provided both historical information and practical advice on how to arrange or '*verjazzen*' pre-existing tunes in the style of Wooding and Whiteman.[30] Paul Bernhard's *Jazz: Eine musikalische Zeitfrage* appeared in 1927 and, like Baresel, described *Kunstjazz* works by contemporary French and German composers as crucial to the development of new music.[31]

While much has been made of the hyper-modernity of the Weimar Republic with Berlin as its microcosm, the new Republic's avant-garde was fragile at best. Opposition to post-war change and republican ideology, present from the beginning, grew in virulence. Not surprisingly, jazz and its extra-musical associations of republican modernity and *Amerikanismus* had its detractors in Germany from the start. For them, it became a musical representation of the defeat of German *Kultur* through the invasion of anti-Germanic influences; the announcement in 1927 by Bernhard Sekles, director of Frankfurt's Hoch Conservatory, that his institution would become the first of its kind to offer jazz instruction provided a specific rallying-point against Americanized modernity. Classes, including solo instruction and ensembles, began in January 1928 under the direction of composer Mátyás Seiber (1905–60), a former student of Kodály whose performance credentials included playing with a shipboard orchestra on voyages to North and South America. Within the year, Seiber's ensemble gave concerts, performed on the Frankfurt radio, and assisted in the Frankfurt premiere of Weill's *Die Dreigroschenoper* during the 1928–9 season.

The storm of protest that greeted Sekles's announcement focused almost exclusively on jazz as a non-German influence that exacerbated the problematic aspects of modern Weimar life and culture. In his initial announcement Sekles had voiced his hope that the Hoch's courses would provide a 'transfusion of fresh Negro blood', an image that provoked racist Eugenic fears about cultural contamination, racial miscegenation, and the necessity of maintaining ethnic purity that had already been raised during the Ruhr occupation of 1923–5;[32] French-controlled Senegalese troops were among the occupying troops and had provoked a public outcry about 'Die schwarze Schmach' (the black disgrace) due to widely circulated, although rarely corroborated, claims that these

28 André Coeuroy and André Schaeffner, *Le Jazz*, Paris, 1926.
29 Alfred Baresel, 'Jazz als Rettung', *Auftakt* 6 (1926), pp. 213–16.
30 Alfred Baresel, *Das neue Jazzbuch*, Leipzig, 1929.
31 Paul Bernhard, *Jazz: Eine musikalische Zeitfrage*, Munich, 1927.
32 Karl Holl, 'Jazz im Konservatorium', *Frankfurter Zeitung*, 25 November 1927.

African soldiers were regularly raping young German women. Besides equating deviant heterosexuality with men of colour, these stories presented the unbearable image of the culturally elite Germania now occupied and controlled by her intellectual and cultural inferiors.[33] Sekles, who was Jewish, became one of the first high-profile music officials to lose his job after Hitler's accession to power in 1933. His experiment at the Hoch perpetuated in the minds of National Socialists a logical connection between jazz, as the music of African Americans, and the Jews with their access to, if not control of, the popular commercial marketplace.

Compositional responses

Loosely based around Satie as a mentor and sharing his interest in popular French culture, the individual members of Les Six presented a variety of responses to popular culture based on their own experiences in pre- and post-war France. Georges Auric dedicated his 1920 piano foxtrot *Adieu, New York!* to Cocteau, and its dotted melody captures the spirit of this easy-tempo walking dance with its combination of two or four steps per bar of music. Germaine Tailleferre's Violin Sonata (1923) makes no obvious claims to jazz dances, but the second-movement scherzo with its mixed metre of 3/8 + 2/8 evokes Satie's tuneful music hall and the 5/4 metre of the Half and Half (a dance popularized by the Castles before the war). Arthur Honegger's syncopated and rhythmically exciting *Sonatine* for clarinet and piano, although published in 1925, was composed in Paris and Zurich during 1921–2.

Maurice Ravel, although significantly older than the members of Les Six, gave a ragtime duet to his black Wedgwood teapot and the *chinoiserie* cup in *L'enfant et les sortilèges* (1925). His collaborator Colette provided the characters with suitable 'American' dialogue with references to racialized modernity ('Black, and strong. Black and chic'); Ravel's ragtime, old-fashioned by mid-1920s standards, suggests a throwback to Debussy's visions of cakewalks and childhood. The second movement ('Blues') from his Sonata for violin and piano (1927), with which he toured the United States, is more in keeping with 1920s resources as popularized by Wiéner. Ravel utilizes the lowered seventh associated with blues harmonies, while the violin imitates both an accompanying banjo and the singing voice.

Whereas jazz would give rise to the *Zeitoper* in response to a perceived crisis in post-war German opera, French opera composers other than Ravel did not generally find American popular music useful. As Danièle Pistone demonstrates,

33 Rosemarie K. Lester, 'Blacks in Germany and German Blacks', in Reinhold Grimm and Jost Hermand (eds.), *Blacks and German Culture*, Madison, 1986, pp. 113–34.

however, American dance music was central to the post-war revitalization of French comic *opérette*, especially following the success of Wiéner's *Olive* and of Vincent Youmans's *No, No Nanette* (1923) at the Mogador Music-Hall;[34] composers Raoul Moretti, Vincent Scotto, Maurice Yvain, and Georges Van Parys, in particular, created successful works that incorporated American dance and syncopated music. But the best-known and most sustained experiment from Paris in the 1920s is the large-scale collaborative ballet *La création du monde*, which drew upon the first-hand racial, national and cultural experiences and fantasies of collaborators Darius Milhaud, Blaise Cendrars, and Fernand Léger.

Milhaud first heard Billy Arnold's band while in London for the premiere of *Le boeuf*, an experience he later identified as revelatory;[35] his *Caramel mou* (1920), described as a shimmy, and *Trois rag-caprices* (1922), dedicated to Wiéner, represented his first responses to the new sounds. A subsequent concert tour of the United States in 1922 provided opportunities to hear African-American ensembles and to purchase recordings; Milhaud celebrated this 'authentic' exposure in his autobiography *Notes sans musique*, though he provides few specifics about performers or works.[36] He claimed to recreate what he heard in Harlem through a pared-down ensemble of winds, brasses, four strings, piano, and saxophone: brasses, woodwinds, and saxophone receive prominent solos, with contrapuntal and fugal sections suggesting Milhaud's attempt to notate the contrapuntal textures and improvisational energy of early jazz bands, while fast, syncopated sections contrast with slow sections implying the blues codes promoted by Wiéner.[37] But while Milhaud's own experience of American jazz was central to the work's success, *La création du monde* also drew on the artistic and aesthetic contributions of his older and at the time better-known collaborator Cendrars, who in 1921 published *L'anthologie nègre*, a compilation of African legends, stories, folklore, and humour culled from a vast array of pre-existing French-language sources, which became a central literary text in post-war artistic primitivism. Cendrars's scenario for the ballet was a composite of creation myths drawn from his African source material, presenting the communal generation of human and animal life; the sculptural costume constructions by Léger, some of which were ten feet tall and required the dancers to perform on stilts, subsumed the individual dancers' bodies. Commissioned

34 Danièle Pistone, 'Opera in Paris during the Roaring Twenties', *Opera Quarterly* 13 (1998), pp. 55–67.

35 Darius Milhaud, *Notes without Music*, New York, 1953, p. 118. 36 Ibid., pp. 136–7.

37 Milhaud later gave a lecture recital on 'Les ressources nouvelles de la musique (jazz-band et instruments mécaniques)' (*L'esprit nouveau* 25 (1924)); this presented, in an evolutionary fashion, his Black Swan recordings and Wiéner's transcriptions of blues for piano as the *Ur*-material from which both his *Trois blues chantes* and Stravinsky's works developed. His lecture (which may have been the basis for his subsequent articles published in *Anbruch* and elsewhere) culminated in a piano four-hand version of *La création du monde* performed by Milhaud and Wiéner; the programme for this lecture is reproduced in Wiéner's autobiography *Allegro Appassionato*, Paris, 1978, p. 106.

by Rolf de Maré's Ballets Suédois, who rivalled the Ballets Russes, *La création du monde* shared the programme with Cole Porter's sole ballet *Within the Quota*, on an American theme of immigration. The scenario and backcloth by Gerard Murphy presented a cavalcade of American images from millionaires to the African-American vaudevillians already well known in Paris; Porter's score, orchestrated by Charles Koechlin, likewise combined syncopation and tuneful melodies heard by the audience as American jazz.[38]

Prague, the capital of the post-war First Czechoslovak Republic, had an active new music community centred on Alois Hába and a vibrant entertainment and theatrical scene;[39] as was true of the new republic in general, Czech composers were particularly drawn to Parisian activities and attitudes. Josephine Baker included Prague, Budapest, and Croatia in her 1928 tour to great acclaim, and while this was the exception (few other touring performers of the 1920s played in Prague), journals like *Auftakt* carried reviews of foreign performances. As early as 1919, Erwin Schulhoff (1894–1942) composed his *Fünf Pittoresken* for piano, four movements of which are based on ragtime dance models including the foxtrot, one-step and maxixe. He dedicated the work to Georg Grosz, whose artwork from the time revels in images of popular culture and with whom Schulhoff associated while living in Germany during the early 1920s. An avid dancer himself, Schulhoff continued to find ragtime and jazz dances a source of political and artistic inspiration throughout the decade, especially in works for solo piano such as *Ironies* (1920), *Ragmusic* (1922), *5 Études de jazz* (1927, with individual movements dedicated to Zez Confrey, Paul Whiteman, and Alfred Baresel), *6 Esquisses de jazz* (1928), *Hot Music* (1929), and *Suite dansante en jazz* (1931); notable ensemble works include the Suite (1921) for chamber orchestra, the Second String Quartet (1929), *Hot sonate* (1930) for saxophone and piano, the 'jazz concerto' *HMS Royal Oak* (1930), and the Second Symphony (1932). Schulhoff's increasingly radical politics in the 1930s led to his death in a German internment camp following the occupation of Czechoslovakia.

Bohuslav Martinů left Prague for Paris in 1923; his *3 Skizzy moderné tancu* (1927) for piano, ballet *La revue de cuisine* (1927), *Jazz Suite* (1928) for small orchestra, and piano *Préludes* (1930) all combine French-inspired blues movements with dances such as charlestons, tangos, and foxtrots. Jaroslav Ježek (1906–42) served as music director for Prague's Free Theatre from 1928–39, during which time he led its jazz orchestra and wrote songs and incidental music, including dance numbers, for its repertory of political satires; his film

38 See Robert Orledge, 'Cole Porter's Ballet *Within the Quota*', *Yale University Library Gazette* 50 (1976), pp. 19–29.

39 See Brian Locke, '"The Periphery is Singing Hit Songs": The Globalization of American Jazz and the Interwar Czech Avant-Garde', *American Music Research Center Journal* 12 (2002), pp. 25–55.

scores and works written for performance outside the theatre showed an affinity for jazz idioms consistent with his radical avant-garde aims. (In 1939 he emigrated to the United States.) Finally Emil Burian (1904–59), like Ježek, had important connections with Prague theatre, working as an actor and director before leading a cabaret jazz band and founding his own experimental theatre in 1933; he led its resident jazz band until the German occupation and his subsequent exile to an internment camp. In the wake of Josephine Baker's presence in Prague, Burian published a monograph, *Jazz* (1928), which demonstrates his indebtedness to Parisian constructions of modernist primitivism. He also drew attention to compositions by his peers that utilized jazz idioms, as he had done in his *Koktarly* (Cocktails) (1926), his operatic theatre piece *Bubu from Montparnasse* (1927), and *Jazz-Requiem* (1928).

African-American performers, like the cakewalk team of Dora Dean Babbidge and Charles Johnson, performed in Germany by 1903, and composers associated with Austro-Germanic popular entertainments drew freely on American popular culture in their pre-war repertories. However, no Germanic composer of Debussy's reputation or standing did so. After the First World War Paul Hindemith became one of the first to turn to popular music, a development that resulted from his initial activity as a professional performer; this began before his induction into the military in 1917, and continued afterwards (as a member of the Amar Quartet he championed French music and had the opportunity to travel outside Germany). His enthusiasm for popular culture was integral to his concept of *Gebrauchsmusik* (which was based on the reformulation of functional music and promotion of amateur music-making together with the use of contemporary media), and was highly influential given his public performance career and later association with the Donaueschingen and Baden-Baden Chamber Music Festivals and the Berlin Hochschule.

Hindemith referenced popular dance idioms in a number of unpublished piano works composed between 1917 and 1921, such as the *Ragtime (wohltemperiert)* (1921). Three published works from 1922 – *Tuttifäntchen*, the *Kammermusik* no. 1, and the *Suite 1922* – show his fondness for the foxtrot, a dance that continued to have a particular power for German composers throughout the 1920s; the *Kammermusik* no. 1, with its 'Finale: 1921', the *succès de scandale* of the 1922 Donaueschingen Chamber Music Festival, quotes from an existing foxtrot,[40] while the contrapuntal and soloistic treatment of the ensemble demonstrates Hindemith's awareness of polyphonic jazz arrangements. Following the success of the *Kammermusik* no. 1, Hindemith composed his *Suite 1922* in the manner of a baroque keyboard suite with its collection of

40 Michael Kube identifies a probable source for the pre-existing foxtrot in 'Paul Hindemiths Jazz-Rezeption – Stationen einer Episode', *Musiktheorie* 10/1 (1995), pp. 63–72.

contrasting dances: it opens with a march (in the manner of the nineteenth-century grand march that began balls), followed in turn by a shimmy, the waltz-like Boston, and an especially virtuosic Ragtime to be played in a *Neue Sachlichkeit* spirit of machine-like regularity. Hindemith's self-drawn cover for the published edition depicted a street scene in keeping with the modern Republican cityscape and his urban dance music.

Other composers working in Germany who were influenced by popular music included Louis Gruenberg, born in Brest but raised in the United States, who studied in Berlin with Busoni before returning to the United States at the outbreak of the First World War. After the war he re-established contacts in Germany, where his self-described 'American idiom' works were influential for their models of *Kunstjazz* – even though in 'Jazz as Departure' he suggested that only composers 'whose blood, upbringing and heart is American' would be able to utilize all jazz's resources;[41] his *The Daniel Jazz* for voice and chamber orchestra, on a text by Vachel Lindsay, received an important hearing at the 1925 Venice meeting of the ISCM. Other compositions from the time include the *Jazzberries* (1925) for solo piano, the *Jazz-Suite* (1925) for chamber ensemble and *Jazzettes* (1926) for violin and piano. *Jazz-Masks* (1929) for piano uses pre-existing works by Chopin, Mendelssohn, Rubinstein, and Offenbach, not unlike Paul Whiteman's 'jazzing the classics' arrangements.

Ernst Krenek's opera *Jonny spielt auf*, meanwhile, was the unexpected success of the 1926–7 opera season, with a story and score that embodied a multitude of issues circulating in Germany regarding popular music and the future of German musical culture. While Krenek identified a trip to Paris in 1924 as central to his formulation of the work, he had explored tango and foxtrot rhythms in two early piano works, the 'Tanzstudie' and 'Toccata und Chaconne', both of 1922. His 1924 opera *Der Sprung über den Schatten* also utilized foxtrot and tango rhythms and extolled the liberating power of social dance. Following his trip to Paris, Krenek accepted a position at the opera house in Kassel that provided him with valuable production experience and tested his aim to create works that spoke to a modern audience. Four houses rejected *Jonny* before Walther Brügmann, general manager of the Leipzig Neues Theater, agreed to produce it during the 1926–7 season, where it brought the opera house national attention. Krenek's convoluted story pits his eponymous hero Jonny, an African-American jazz violinist and bandleader, against Max, a repressed composer of dissonant, unpopular modern music; Max's opening solo in which he praises his mountain retreat – 'Du schöner Berg' – makes clear whose musical aesthetic Krenek

41 Louis Gruenberg, 'Der Jazz als Ausgangspunkt', p. 199 ('der dem Blute, der Erziehung und dem Herzen nach Amerikaner ist'). Erwin Schulhoff took exception to Gruenberg's Americanist claims in 'Eine Jazz Affaire', *Auftakt* 5 (1925), pp. 220–2.

satirized. The Jonny–Max relationship is complicated by additional characters including Anita, an opera singer, and Daniello, an Italian violinist, who present the respective stereotypes of emotional working womanhood and racialized male sexuality. Max realizes the error of his compositional ways, returns to accompany Anita on her tour of the United States, and the opera ends with Jonny literally on top of the world playing for the cast while they proclaim the power of American popular dance music.

While Krenek's work addressed concerns about opera's viability and accessibility in a new age, the character of Jonny disturbingly displays the racial primitivism underlying the stereotype of black male sexual aggression current during the Ruhr occupation. Not surprisingly, the image of a black man and his powerful music interacting with a white German woman led to riots at the Munich premiere and considerable comment in the press: supporters, however, hailed it as a *Zeitoper*, an opera of its own time, and so the answer to the post-war operatic crisis. The production called attention to its modernity through a Parisian setting, use of on-stage popular music, radio broadcasts, and an animated film depicting Max's taxi ride to the train station; the complicated staging directions for the final scene in the train station even call for the on-stage arrival of an express train that then disappears as Jonny begins his apotheosis playing atop the railroad station clock – which then turns first into a whirling globe, and finally into a record disc inscribed '*Jonny spielt auf*: Ernst Krenek, Opus 45'.

Krenek's appropriation and assimilation of jazz and dance idioms in the score was extensive, including dominant-seventh chords and major/minor blue notes, prominent use of saxophone and banjo, and scenes built around clearly identifiable dance rhythms and affects; Krenek also incorporated musical references to spirituals and minstrelsy to add further to Jonny's racialized character. While much of the appropriated popular music appears as on-stage source music to characterize specific locales, other codes are assimilated into larger musical structures, and Krenek reused material in convincingly dramatic ways. The most popular number was 'Jonny's Triumph-Lied', in which Krenek recreated a spiritual as Jonny likens himself and his performative power to the harp-playing David of the Hebrew Scriptures; Universal Edition published a piano-vocal arrangement of the 'Triumph-Lied', and it was recorded by several popular musicians. *Jonny* was extremely popular in Germany and Eastern Europe (Prague produced it in the first season, and forty-five opera houses the following season, making it the most performed work of its time); however, it was not successful at its 1928 Paris premiere, where it was judged passé. The New York premiere in January 1929 was hampered by American racial politics that required rewriting the text and casting Jonny not as African American but rather as a white performer in blackface, in the manner of the currently popular performer Al Jolson.

Following *Jonny*, Krenek continued his aesthetic and musical experiments in his one-act 'burleske Operette' *Schwergewicht, oder die Ehre der Nation*, which spoofed the current interest in boxing and whose main character, Gaston, a French dance instructor, allowed for the easy incorporation of dance idioms; his *Kleine Symphonie* (1928) similarly uses the habañera rhythms associated with the tango in the third movement and features banjo, guitar, and mandolin. Thereafter, however, Krenek divorced himself from popular idioms, adopting an increasingly elitist aesthetic and, in time, the serial methods of the same Schoenberg whom he had earlier critiqued.

Like Krenek, Kurt Weill shared post-war concerns about new audiences and new artistic commitments. While a student in Berlin in the early 1920s, Weill joined the radical artistic collective *Novembergruppe* and began to experiment with popular-music idioms. By 1926, he was writing about this music in his columns for *Der deutsche Rundfunk* and had made contacts with contemporary playwrights, like Yvan Goll, who were interested in up-to-date theatrical techniques. His opera *Royal Palace* (1926), on a libretto by Goll, incorporated a filmed sequence with accompanying music in a ragtime foxtrot idiom that used the saxophone. In 1927 Weill scored a notable success with his *Mahagonny-Songspiel*, which was written on a commission from the Baden-Baden Chamber Music Festival and featured both topical subject matter and an accessible song style; this initiated a working relationship with playwright Bertolt Brecht.

In 1928 Weill composed *Der Zar lässt sich photographieren* to serve as a suitable one-acter to be paired with his successful expressionist work *Der Protagonist* (1925), on a libretto by Georg Kaiser. Weill likened the comic, satiric tone of *Der Zar*, again on a text by Kaiser (who had by 1928 abandoned his tragic tone), to that of an operetta: a Tsar visiting Paris attempts to get his photograph taken by a famous female photographer Angèle, but both the Tsar's attempt to seduce his photographer and a simultaneous assassination plot involving character disguises and slapstick fail, and the opera ends with him being photographed none the wiser as to what has transpired around him. Weill's score consisted of self-contained numbers that utilized an anachronistic male chorus in the pit, commenting on the action and emphasizing its comic nature; the Tsar's public political persona and his desire to be a private citizen in Paris are characterized by contrasting march idioms and the down-to-earth melodic appeal of foxtrots. However, the centrepiece of the work (and the feature most commented upon at the time) was the 'Tango-Angèle', which used an on-stage gramophone and a pre-existing recording to accompany the singers, the dance's seductive quality aptly mirroring the Tsar's attempts to woo his would-be assassin disguised as the famous Angèle. The Dobbri Saxophone Orchestra of Berlin, a mixed ensemble of violins, brass, banjo, and piano, recorded the tango, and it was later commercially released on the Parlophon-Beka label.

But perhaps the best-known German work created during the 1920s in response to questions about artistic categories and obligations is Weill's *Die Dreigroschenoper*.[42] Written in collaboration with Brecht, who characteristically claimed to be the dominant partner, *Die Dreigroschenoper* combined a satiric parody of old-fashioned operatic conventions with large-scale use of dance rhythms. In keeping with its small-scale, revue-theatre-like orientation, the six-member ensemble of accomplished studio musicians performing as 'The Lewis Ruth Band' provided the accompaniment. As in *Der Zar*, Weill utilized dance rhythms, although Brecht's Epic Theatre and its renunciation of a unified, internally consistent structure calls into question an easy relationship between the social conventions of these dances and the texts to which they are attached. It seems likely, however, that audiences of the time would have found textual–musical connections, whether satiric, parodic, or even simplistic, in the foxtrot of the 'Kanonen-Song', and even more so in the tango of the 'Zuhälter-Ballade' sung by former lovers Pirate Jenny and Mackie Messer.

Hindemith's *Zeitoper Neues vom Tage* (1929) followed on from Krenek's and Weill's successes, with an up-to-date story and a score featuring jazz dance rhythms and the timbres of saxophone and banjo. Hindemith collaborated with the noted revue lyricist Marcellus Schiffer, with whom he had worked earlier on his one-act chamber opera *Hin und züruck*. The comic-satiric story turns the conventional romance plot on its head as the central married couple move towards divorce, only to decide to remain married at the end. Like *Jonny spielt auf*, it is set in Paris, suggesting yet again the German perception of Paris as the locus of modernity. Like Weill, Hindemith organized the work on the model of an eighteenth-century number opera and brought in jazz dance references, in particular the foxtrot and Boston, as ways to characterize the individual numbers and their everyday dramatic quality; a scene set in a revue theatre, where the married couple opt for commercial success and perform their marital squabbles for an audience, features saxophone and banjo.

Other works also followed in *Jonny*'s wake, combining musical and extra-musical images of jazz and the United States, and often making use of techniques associated with cinema and documentary theatre. Wilhelm Grosz, like Krenek a student of Franz Schreker, composed *Jazzband* (1924), the Second Dance Suite (1926), and the pantomime-ballet *Baby in der Bar* (1927),

42 For a general introduction see Stephen Hinton (ed.), *Kurt Weill: The Threepenny Opera*, Cambridge, 1990.

all of which utilized jazz dances in extended ways, before creating *Achtung! Aufnahme!*, his *Zeitoper*; composed to a libretto by Béla Balász, who had supplied the story for the 1926 German film *The Adventures of a Ten-Mark Bill*, *Achtung! Aufnahme!* similarly explores aspects of the current film industry. Grosz emigrated to England in 1934 and later wrote popular songs such as the 1934 tango foxtrot 'Isle of Capri' and 'Red Sails in the Sunset' (1935). Again, George Antheil, who returned to Europe following the embarrassment of the 1927 Carnegie Hall performance of *Ballet mécanique*, composed his own Americanist *Zeitoper*, *Transatlantic* (1930); set in the United States and dealing with a presidential election marred by scandal and intrigue, *Transatlantic* included the by then *de rigeur* scene set in an entertainment venue, with numbers identified as a tango and a cut-time shimmy. The staging requirements, in particular the last act with its twenty-seven scenes played on four simultaneous sets followed by a filmed episode, borrowed on the innovations of Berlin director Erwin Piscator; its theatrical demands, while demonstrating its modernity, hampered the work's staging elsewhere after its successful Frankfurt am Main premiere.

The critic and composer H. H. Stuckenschmidt, who shared Krenek's fondness for Paris, America, and popular music, introduced Schoenberg to *Jonny spielt auf*. Schoenberg, who had composed popular songs for Ernst von Wolzogen's Überbrettl Kabarett, responded to Krenek's criticism of an inaccessible avant-garde with *Von heute auf morgen* (1930), an anti-*Zeitoper* comic one-acter which used saxophone, mandolin, and guitar but did not adopt dance idioms nor highlight these particular instrumental timbres. Its story presents a gendered corrective to the temptations of popular music: a husband's misguided attraction to his wife's modern girlfriend forces the wife to respond in kind, until the husband realizes his foolishness and chooses marital fidelity over the momentary excitement of a flirtation. Schoenberg's student Alban Berg used tango rhythms and jazz affects such as muted brass and strings plucked 'à la banjo' in his concert aria *Der Wein* (1929); once again the tango underscores the work's eroticism, both in its texts and in its hidden references to Berg's beloved Hanna Fuchs-Robettin.

Although a total of fifty-six houses produced *Jonny* in its first three years, it was not produced in England; a reviewer for the [London] *Times* at the 1930 Viennese premiere claimed that the work 'would not pass the censor in England in its present form'.[43] While London had its share of entertainment venues offering up-to-date fare, this critical assessment suggests a reticence on the part of British composers to undo their musical categories in the manner of their continental colleagues. Notable exceptions were William Walton

43 '"Jazz" Opera in Vienna', *The Times*, 4 January 1928.

(1902–83) and Constant Lambert (1905–51), who identified strongly with the French experiments of Les Six and shared Satie's bohemian interests. Walton's entertainment *Façade*, on poems by Edith Sitwell and dedicated to Lambert, received its first public performance in 1923; Sitwell's texts experiment with sounds and meanings, and Walton's six-member ensemble including clarinet, saxophone, trumpet, and percussion utilize a host of social dances past and present in their settings, ranging from an opening hornpipe and tango-pasodoble to the closing valse and foxtrot. Frederick Ashton choreographed the work in 1931. As for Lambert, his enthusiasm for jazz-based theatrical productions playing in London in the early 1920s led him to compose his *Elegiac Blues* (1927) in memory of the black singer Florence Mills, whom he had heard in one of these shows accompanied by Will Vodery and his band. *The Rio Grande* (1927) for chorus, orchestra, and solo piano, on a poem by Sacheverell Sitwell, features tango rhythms in its evocation of hispanic America, while the *Concerto for Piano and Nine Players* (1931), written in memory of Philip Heseltine (the composer Peter Warlock), incorporates elements of jazz improvisation.

The high expectations for jazz and popular music as the salvation of post-war musical culture were not realized, especially in the aftermath of the American stock-market crash of 1929, the rise of National Socialism, and the subsequent devastation of the Holocaust and the Second World War. A discomfort with the schisms between different musical traditions and the artificial nature of stylistic labels continued, however, along with the concern about modernism's inaccessibility and aesthetic difficulty; the identifications of 'third stream', 'crossover', and 'world' musics, and 'new Romanticism' represent comparable but more recent attempts by composers and performers to question and redefine insider/outsider positions of cultural power and prestige in the face of waning audience interest and the increasingly rigid repertories of concert music. But if, as Gruenberg suggested, jazz was reduced to a seductive temptress in the 1920s, in the decades since then her fortunes have changed. Not unlike much of Euro-American womankind, jazz has fought for and achieved prestige and legitimacy and the right to tell her own history. The new place of jazz is demonstrated in a growing body of scholarship that takes popular music seriously and challenges the inequitable practices of high modernism.

Bibliography

Ankum, Katharina von (ed.). *Women in the Metropolis: Gender and Modernity in Weimar Culture*, Berkeley, 1997.

Badger, Reid. *A Life in Ragtime: A Biography of James Reese Europe*, New York, 1995.

Baresel, Alfred. 'Jazz als Rettung', *Auftakt* 6 (1926), pp. 213–16.

Das neue Jazzbuch, Leipzig, 1929.

Bernhard, Paul. *Jazz: Eine musikalische Zeitfrage*, Munich, 1927.
Blake, Jody. *Le Tumulte noir: Modernist Art and Popular Entertainment in Jazz-Age Paris, 1900–1930*, University Park, MD, 1999.
Coeuroy, André and André Schaeffner. *Le Jazz*, Paris, 1926.
Cook, Susan C. *Opera for a New Republic: The Zeitopern of Krenek, Weill and Hindemith*, Rochester, 1988.
DeVeaux, Scott. 'Constructing the Jazz Tradition: Jazz Historiography', *Black American Literature Forum* 25/3 (1991), pp. 525–60.
Flanner, Janet. *Paris Was Yesterday*, New York, 1972.
Führer, Karl Christian. 'A Medium of Modernity? Broadcasting in Weimar Germany, 1923–1932', *Journal of Modern History* 69/4 (1997), pp. 722–53.
Gendron, Bernard. 'Jamming at Le Boeuf: Jazz and the Paris Avant-Garde', *Discourse* 12/1 (1989–90), pp. 3–27.
Gruenberg, Louis. 'Der Jazz als Ausgangspunkt', *Anbruch* 7 (1925), pp. 196–9.
Hermand, Jost. 'Neue Sachlichkeit: Ideology, Lifestyle, or Artistic Movement?' in Thomas W. Kniesche and Stephen Brockmann (eds.), *Dancing on the Volcano: Essays on the Culture of the Weimar Republic*, Columbia, SC, 1994, pp. 57–67.
Hinton, Stephen (ed.). *Kurt Weill: The Threepenny Opera*, Cambridge, 1990.
Holl, Karl. 'Jazz im Konservatorium', *Frankfurter Zeitung*, 25 November 1927.
Huyssen, Andreas. 'Mass Culture as Woman: Modernism's Other', in Tania Modleski (ed.), *Studies in Entertainment*, Bloomington, 1986, pp. 188–207.
''Jazz' Opera in Vienna', *The Times*, 4 January 1928.
Kassabian, Anahid. 'Popular', in Bruce Horner and Thomas Swiss (eds.), *Key Terms in Popular Music and Culture*, Malden, MA, 1999, pp. 113–23.
Kube, Michael. 'Paul Hindemiths Jazz-Rezeption – Stationen einer Episode', *Musiktheorie* 10/1 (1995), pp. 63–72.
Lester, Rosemarie K. 'Blacks in Germany and German Blacks', in Reinhold Grimm and Jost Hermand (eds.), *Blacks and German Culture*, Madison, 1986, pp. 113–34.
Locke, Brian. '"The Periphery is Singing Hit Songs": The Globalization of American Jazz and the Interwar Czech Avant-Garde', *American Music Research Center Journal* 12 (2002), pp. 25–53.
Lotz, Rainer E. *Black People: Entertainers of African Descent in Europe, and Germany*, Bonn, 1997.
Michael Danzi: American Musician in Germany 1924–1939, Schmitten, 1986.
Milhaud, Darius. 'Les ressources nouvelles de la musique (jazz-band et instruments mécaniques)', *L'esprit nouveau* 25 (1924), [n.p.].
Notes without Music, New York, 1953.
Orledge, Robert. 'Cole Porter's Ballet *Within the Quota*', *Yale University Library Gazette* 50 (1976), pp. 19–29.
'Satie and America', *American Music* 18/1 (2000), pp. 78–102.
Partsch, Cornelius. 'Hannibal ante Portas: Jazz in Weimar', in Thomas W. Kniesche and Stephen Brockmann (eds.), *Dancing on the Volcano: Essays on the Culture of the Weimar Republic*, Columbia, SC, 1994, pp. 105–16.
Peukert, Detlev J. K. *The Weimar Republic: The Crisis of Classical Modernity* (tr. Richard Deveson), New York, 1992.
Pistone, Danièle. 'Opera in Paris during the Roaring Twenties', *Opera Quarterly* 13/2 (1998), pp. 55–67.

Ritzel, Fred. '"Hätte der Kaiser Jazz getanzt . . .": US-Tanzmusik in Deutschland vor und nach dem Ersten Weltkrieg', in Sabine Schutte (ed.), *Ich will aber gerade vom Leben singen: Über populäre Musik vom ausgehenden 19. Jahrhundert bis zum Ende der Weimarer Republik*, Reinbeck bei Hamburg, 1987, pp. 265–93.

Said, Edward W. *Orientalism*, New York, 1979.

Schröder, Heribert. *Tanz- und Unterhaltungsmusik in Deutschland, 1918–1933*, Bonn, 1990.

Schulhoff, Erwin. 'Eine Jazz Affaire', *Auftakt* 5 (1925), pp. 220–2.

Schwab, Heinrich W. 'Zur Rezeption des Jazz in der komponierten Musik', *Dansk Årbog for Musikforskning* 10 (1979), pp. 127–78.

Schwan, Gesine. 'Das deutsche Amerikabild seit der Weimarer Republik', *Aus Politik und Zeitgeschichte* B/26 (1986), pp. 3–15.

Shreffler, Anne C. 'Classicizing Jazz: Concert Jazz in Paris and New York in the 1920s', in Hermann Danuser (ed.), *Die klassizistische Moderne in der Musik des 20. Jahrhunderts*, Basel, 1997, pp. 55–71.

Smith, Catherine Parsons. '"A Distinguishing Virility": Feminism and Modernism in American Art Music', in Susan C. Cook and Judy S. Tsou (eds.), *Cecilia Reclaimed: Feminist Perspectives on Gender and Music*, Urbana, 1994, pp. 90–106.

Tower, Beeke Sell. *Envisioning America: Prints, Drawings, and Photographs by George Grosz and his Contemporaries 1915–1933*, Cambridge, 1990.

Trommler, Frank. 'The Rise and Fall of Americanism in Germany', in Frank Trommler and Joseph McVeigh (eds.), *America and the Germans: The Relationship in the Twentieth Century*, Philadelphia, 1985, pp. 332–42.

Watkins, Glenn E. *Pyramids at the Louvre: Music, Culture, and Collage from Stravinsky to the Postmodernists*, Cambridge, MA, 1994.

Weiner, Marc A. '*Urwaldmusik* and the Borders of German Identity: Jazz in Literature of the Weimar Republic', *The German Quarterly* 64/4 (1991), pp. 475–87.

Whiteman, Paul and Mary Margaret McBride. *Jazz*, New York, 1926.

Whiting, Steven Moore. *Satie the Bohemian: From Cabaret to Concert Hall*, New York, 1999.

Widmaier, Tobias. 'Der weisse Neger vom "Boeuf sur le toit": Jean Wiéner und die Jazzrezeption im Umkreis der "Six"', *Neue Zeitschrift für Musik* 154 (1993), pp. 34–6.

Wiéner, Jean. *Allegro Appassionato*, Paris, 1978.

Wilson, Edmund, Jr. 'The Aesthetic Upheaval in France: The Influence of Jazz in Paris and Americanization of French Literature and Art', *Vanity Fair*, February 1922, pp. 49, 100.

·7·

Between the wars: traditions, modernisms, and the 'little people from the suburbs'

PETER FRANKLIN

> Why? Who is the German philistine that he should be upset by Dadaism? It is the German intellectual who explodes with rage because his formally perfect, schmalz-bread soul has been left to bake in the sun of ridicule . . .
>
> Raoul Hausmann in *Der Dada*, 1919

> . . . in the University of Vienna there are thirty policemen continually on duty – we wondered how we should like our own lecture-rooms to be patrolled in this manner . . . The only time we saw real happiness in public was in the State Opera House where a great crowd had assembled to hear Richard Tauber in *Der Evangelimann*. That voice lifted them above the things of this life; the audience sat entranced . . .
>
> A British journalist, writing in September 1936[1]

The cultural richness of the inter-war period – whether the focus is on Europe, Russia, Scandinavia, or America – simultaneously defies and incites linear history. It defies it because of the extent to which it is marked by diversity and contestation. The cultural high ground was so effectively fought over that narrative accounts are bound to be partial, marked by a bias that is itself a historical residue of the period. Linear history is nevertheless incited precisely by the generally assumed underlying directionality marshalling the complexities of cultural life in a Europe 'between' catastrophes. One inevitably turns to Weimar Germany to illustrate the point. Its European and even global importance was attested by the many musicians, artists, writers, and scientists who continued to flock there to study, listen, and observe. With hindsight, everything that happened during the Weimar period pointed with such macabre logic towards 1933 and the arrival of the National Socialists that the imposition of an alternative narrative seems almost a moral obligation. That alternative has familiarly construed modernism and the various avant-garde movements as representing a more sympathetic cultural trajectory – both critical and oppositional – above and around the accumulating evils of the period.

1 Quotations taken respectively from Anton Kaes, Martin Jay, and Edward Dimendberg (eds.), *The Weimar Republic Sourcebook*, Berkeley, 1994, p. 482, and Diana Napier-Tauber, *Richard Tauber*, London, 1949, p. 177.

To believe that, however, may be to subscribe to a version of the same Romantic idealism that had led the conservatively political Hans Pfitzner to preface the score of his 1917 opera *Palestrina* with a quotation from Schopenhauer attesting to the 'guiltless' and transcendent qualities of the life of the mind. Espousing alternative cultural-political, and even party-political, interests to those of Pfitzner (who was blaming Jews and 'cultural bolsheviks' for all that he disliked in contemporary music as early as 1920[2]), modernist music historians once knew why it was that he, whose creatively active life-span roughly matched that of Richard Strauss, came to be 'forgotten' and why so many of the contemporaries he detested, Schoenberg and his pupils not least, should now be admired: 'regressive' adherence to tonality versus 'progressive' exploitation of dissonance and atonality was the most used formula.

That was before postmodernist historiography encouraged us to think again: to re-examine a work like *Palestrina* and the conservative polemics of its composer, which were manifestly as significant 'historically' as the works and ideas we have chosen subsequently to cherish, for whatever estimable reasons. Pfitzner inspired prominent critical opposition and support; he focused debate and helped define positions and affiliations. The opera's first production was taken by Bruno Walter on a 'propaganda tour' to Switzerland during the First World War 'to demonstrate to the world the high level of German operatic art',[3] as a result of which it acquired an almost iconic status and held the German stage well into the 1950s. But to acknowledge the passionate commitment and relative cultural success of a composer like Pfitzner, both in *Palestrina* and in the consistently tonally oriented works that followed it, is also necessarily to accept the partiality of Nicolas Slonimsky's once unexceptionably linear assertion that the 'inevitable product of chromatic harmony as practiced [sic] by Wagner and Liszt was the decay of governing tonality'.[4] It is similarly to realize that we want history and criticism to be separate enterprises at the very moment in which we grasp that they have not been.

A further example, remaining in the world of Germanic musical theatre, focuses the problem in a slightly different way. One does not have to be a music historian to enjoy the surprises and unsuspected interconnections that are afforded by Richard Burbank's magnificent 1984 year-by-year chronology, bearing the authoritative title *Twentieth-Century Music*; it followed in the line of Slonimsky's own treasure-trove, *Music since 1900*. A representative year like 1925, solidly in the middle of the inter-war period, is divided up by Burbank

2 In Hans Pfitzner, *Die neue Aesthetik der Musikalischen Impotenz*, Munich, 1920; see Peter Franklin, 'Audiences, Critics and the Depurification of Music: Reflections on a 1920s Controversy', *Journal of the Royal Musical Association* 114 (1989), pp. 80–91.

3 Bruno Walter, *Theme and Variations: An Autobiography*, London, 1947, p. 247.

4 Richard Burbank, *Twentieth-Century Music*, London, 1984, p. xii.

into subsections: 'Opera', 'Dance', 'Instrumental and Vocal Music', 'Births, Deaths and Debuts', and 'Related Events'. There is no partisan bias in his choice of works and events. The opera premieres briefly described include Wolf-Ferrari's *Gli amanti sposi*, Zandonai's *I cavalieri de Ekebu*, Ravel's *L'enfant et les sortilèges*, Stanford's *The Travelling Companion*, and Busoni's *Doktor Faust*. But the longest entry (by some eleven lines) is that for the Berlin premiere, on 14 December 1925, of Alban Berg's *Wozzeck*. The negativity of some of the critical response to it is duly recorded, but the key central sentence reads, fairly enough in one sense, 'It is considered to be one of the most important operas of the century.'[5]

At this point a partisan historical narrative surfaces rather welcomely to ground the bewildering relativity of the catalogue of all those 1925 premieres. What that catalogue might nevertheless tell us, around and behind that surfacing critical narrative of musical modernism, is quirkily reinforced by both what is included in subsequent sections, and what is left out. We are told, for instance, that March 1925 saw the first electronic recording of classical music by Alfred Cortot (playing Chopin and Schubert). But for an example of what is omitted altogether we might turn to the events which were staged that year in Berlin in connection with the centenary of the birth of Johann Strauss II, including, in September, Erich Wolfgang Korngold's popularly successful new adaptation of *Eine Nacht in Venedig*. In October a special gala at the Municipal (Charlottenberg) Opera concluded with the second act of *Die Fledermaus*, conducted by the Pfitzner and Mahler advocate, Bruno Walter; the next day saw an uncut State Opera performance of *Der Zigeunerbaron*. Leading the star-studded cast at all three events was the tenor Richard Tauber.[6] I will return to his career as offering a valuable path through the musical-cultural landscape of the period.

Mapping the terrain

> The great entrance [of the Schloss] facing the Lustgarten is quite shot up; one of its columns lies shattered on the ground; the iron doors hang askew, bent and shot through. The balcony over them, from which the Kaiser made his speech on 4 August 1914, hangs down, smashed . . . During the playing out of these bloody events Christmas trading carried on undisturbed. Barrel-organs play in the Friedrichstrasse, street-pedlars offer indoor fireworks, cinammon cakes and tinsel. The jewellers on Unter den Linden are all open, without a care in the world, their windows brightly lit. In Leipziger Strasse the usual Christmas

5 Ibid., p. 118. 6 Napier-Tauber, *Richard Tauber*, pp. 98–9.

> crowds flock to Wertheim's, Kayser's, and so on. Quite certainly in thousands of homes the Christmas trees will be lit, and the children will be playing under them with the presents they have had from Daddy, Mummy, and their dear Aunt.[7]

Before embarking upon Tauber's path – that of a successful performer rather than a composer, theoretician, or critic (we will encounter many along the way) – we would do well to survey the terrain that lies before us. In 1918 it was in many respects quite literally a battlefield. Physically, psychologically, and sociologically Europe was scarred by the First World War in ways that had not begun to be envisaged at its outset in 1914. Key images might be those of the disfigured ex-soldiers that sit begging on street corners in Georg Grosz's mordant images of Berlin, their limbs and often parts of their face shot away, while fat bankers and corrupt clergymen revel in the financial and spiritual capital they have reaped from the war.[8] Grosz was a member of the Communist Party and one of the *Neue Sachlichkeit* or 'new objectivity' artists of the 1920s, whose affiliations were with politically committed music, cabaret and theatre people on the Left. Their representatives extended from the Dadaists or from Bertolt Brecht and his musical collaborators to 'agitprop' theatre troupes; all saw in the Russian Revolution an inspiring model that the short-lived November 1918 revolution in Germany had sought to emulate.

The artists' so-called *Novembergruppe*, which aimed to keep alive the political ideals of that attempted revolution, marked a historical moment in which modernism still had the potential to develop as a deliberately politicized cultural 'opposition' movement.[9] But in that same year of 1918, Rachmaninov and Stravinsky, both members of the Russian aristocracy and opponents of the Revolution, had severed their ties with their native country; Stravinsky – as significant a representative of musical modernism in the period as Schoenberg – was a signatory to a declaration issued by Russian artists in France bewailing the 'martyrdom' of their homeland and repudiating the 'sinister' Bolsheviks.[10]

From the beginning of the period, the myth of an artistic modernism embracing common objectives is dispelled by any closer consideration of its protagonists' circumstances, politics, and affiliations. Where the anti-bourgeois Kurt Weill and Hanns Eisler represented the politically committed far Left, aiming to mobilize the working class in opposition to capitalism and the rise of

7 Extract from Count Harry Kessler's diary for 24 December 1918. Quoted in Anton Gill, *A Dance between Flames: Berlin between the Wars*, London, 1993, p. 26.

8 Georg Grosz (ed.), *The Face of the Ruling Class*, London, 1984, p. 26.

9 See Peter Gay, *Weimar Culture: The Outsider as Insider*, Harmondsworth, 1974, p. 110.

10 Burbank, *Twentieth-Century Music*, p. 87.

fascism, Stravinsky's plea on behalf of 'Russian citizens of the liberal professions' seemed intended more for middle-class idealists for whom the Bolshevik Revolution was the embodiment of the 'politics' they opposed. 'Music', as a cultural metaphor for a universal language of humane idealism, was practically deconstructed by the ever-proliferating and increasingly mutually antagonistic groupings, movements, and class affiliations that characterize the cultural politics of the period. Nor were the methods of artistic revolution clear: against the populist tendencies of revolutionary socialists must be set the idealist-isolationist programme of Schoenberg's 1918 Viennese Verein für musikalische Privataufführungen (Society for Private Musical Performances), whose crusading zeal on behalf of new music discarded the wider audience-educating purpose of the pre-war Vereinigung schaffender Tonkünstler (Creative Composers' Association) (1904–5) in favour of attentive gatherings of willing initiates and devotees. The Society's rules required members to refrain from applause and excluded the critics, who were seen by Schoenberg as a retrogressive and insufficiently professional group who tended to confirm the worst prejudices of middle-class concertgoers without extending their sympathies or adding to their knowledge.

The exuberantly crusading, contestatory, and decentring musical-cultural enthusiasms of the early 1920s spawned a proliferation of groupings, associations, specific-interest festivals, and journals. The International Society for Contemporary Music (1922), Varèse's International Composers' Guild (1922), the modernist Donaueschingen Chamber Music Festival (1921), the high-status and relatively conservative Salzburg Festival (1920), and the journals *Musikblätter des Anbruch* (Vienna 1919), *Music & Letters* (London 1920), and *Melos* (Berlin 1920) all came into being in the early post-war years. Each played a part in the institutionalization of the modernist musical discourse of tonal 'collapse' and stylistic 'experimentation', as of the relevant critical oppositions and exclusions.

Significant amongst the exclusions were the very spheres of musical-cultural practice in which tonality had manifestly not 'collapsed', been superseded by serialism, or disfigured and ironized in the modes of ostensibly 'wrong-note' tonal pastiche found in the neoclassicism of Stravinsky, the witty performances of the Russian Prokofiev and members of 'Les Six' in Paris or, later, in the sinewy quasi-tonality of Hindemith. In this respect a primary excluded area was that of recreative musical practice. The old music-historical narrative of modernism's advance through pioneering composers, works, and styles was rooted in Romantic idealism, for all its rejection of Romantic manners, and had little interest in the history of music as socio-cultural practice. As a result it gave little hint of the extent to which the major institutions of European culture – the concert halls, the opera houses, for example – managed more or less to function throughout the First World War and rapidly relaunched themselves in its wake.

Post-war continuities and new media

The repertoires and even many of the performers in major concert series and opera seasons looked hardly different in the inter-war years from how they had before 1914. The re-establishment of such institutions was often a key issue of national pride and sensed national identity as the nightmare of the war receded. If anything, the audience for traditional 'classical music' continued to expand during the period of Furtwängler's association with the Berlin Philharmonic (from 1922). Mechanical recordings began to play a significant role, extending concert halls and opera stages into virtual space accessible in every urban living room. The arrival of the phonograph, and then of radio (from 1923 in Germany[11]), at prices the 'man in the street' could afford – as he undoubtedly could by the later 1920s and probably earlier – introduced what Adorno and Horkheimer would call the 'culture industry' (*Dialectic of Enlightenment*, 1947). The derision and critical intent with which they did so helps to explain the other great repression of the conventional narrative of musical modernism and the collapse of tonality: the whole sphere of popular culture, with its myriad venues, media, and modes of dissemination and its own patterns of change and development, not to mention the range of its 'products' (from the *Schlager*, or hit-song, to the operetta world of Johann Strauss and Offenbach, with its own contemporary composers like Oscar Straus and Franz Lehár).

Recreative performance and the popular sphere intersected most productively, however, in and around the new medium of film. Although silent film had been growing as a form of popular entertainment before the war, it was during the 1920s that purpose-built movie theatres made their first really self-confident appearances in German as in other European cities. America was the powerhouse of a new, international movie-industry that, before the arrival of sound, had few problems with language barriers. But film was also one of the key art forms of Weimar Germany, and some of its most famous productions – *The Cabinet of Dr Caligari* (Robert Wiene 1919), *Nosferatu* (F. W. Murnau 1921), and *Metropolis* (Fritz Lang 1926) – played a role in shaping the new medium and almost popularizing the world of German expressionist drama and design. During the course of the decade an ever-expanding body of musicians was

11 See Christopher Hailey, 'Rethinking Sound: Music and Radio in Weimar Germany', in Bryan Gilliam (ed.), *Music and Performance during the Weimar Republic*, Cambridge, 1994, pp. 13–36.

involved in accompanying film performances, from the humble improvising pianist to full orchestras playing elaborately manufactured scores comprising prescribed or specially chosen extracts from existing music. (More rarely, the music was specially written.)

In the presence of film, music took on an encyclopedic character, possessed of all the representational and associative significance that was both scorned and theoretically 'managed' by the factionalized music critics and theorists of high culture, be their sympathies traditionalist or modernist. From the bold modernist experimentation of Meisel (for *The Battleship Potemkin*, 1925) to the medleys of salon items, opera extracts, the latest hit songs, and operetta numbers of the improvising pianist, music for films reflected the wider musical experience and diversity of the period with a comprehensiveness that was matched by no other musical or music-related medium. Only with the advent of sound film at the end of the 1920s would the almost metamusical practice of film scoring be preserved in ways that were merely hinted at in the rapidly scattered or destroyed manuals, printed cue-sheets, and specially prepared scores of the 'silent' era.

In amongst the music plundered by the film accompanists would have been examples of popular songs and the imported, city-night-life-evoking jazz and ragtime that was extending the image of so-called 'negro music', hitherto represented by the sentimentalized songs and spirituals that were being collected and published before this period. As it permeated the popular music scene, 'jazz' (in whatever fake or bowdlerized form) simultaneously became the emblematically embodied sound of popular pleasure and a key signifier of the threat such pleasure posed to traditional high culture, often figured as a foreign or external threat to Culture itself. Associated with the primitive and unbridled, jazz was both the liberating sound of a new world of unfettered freedom and sensuality, and the harbinger of a polluting infection of violent 'primitivism'. Both sides of the Weimar-period discourse about jazz – a discourse echoed in different ways right across Europe – are evoked in a passage from Hermann Hesse's 1927 novel *Der Steppenwolf*, whose central character (Harry Haller) is in early middle age and suffering a culturally located form of what we might now call a 'mid-life crisis':

> From a dance-hall there met me as I passed by the strains of lively jazz music, hot and raw as the steam of raw flesh. I stopped for a moment. This kind of music, much as I detest it, had always had a secret charm for me. Jazz was repugnant to me, and yet ten times preferable to all the academic music of the day. For me, too, its raw and savage gaiety reached an underworld of instinct and breathed a simple, honest sensuality . . . Compared with Bach and Mozart and real music it was, naturally a miserable affair; but so was all our art, all

our thought, all our makeshift culture in comparison with real culture. [. . .] Amiably and unblushingly negroid, it had the mood of childlike happiness. There was something of the Negro in it, something of the American, who with all his strength seems so boyishly fresh and childlike to us Europeans.[12]

Class, race and *Zeitoper* jazz

Allusions to jazz and other forms of 'light' music (meaning popular entertainment or dance music) in works by high-culture modernists have often been read as 'reflections' of or homages to the world of mass culture. In practice they should probably be interpreted equally as having sought to absorb or appropriate such material in a spirit that was as much nervous as it was liberal. As stylistic imports, the complex implications of such allusions paralleled those of the potentially paternalistic (occasionally even condescending) incorporation of 'folk' material into such different musical worlds as those of the ethnographically punctilious Béla Bartók in Hungary or the nationally cherished Ralph Vaughan Williams in England. Both composers constructed a musical persona in which modern and traditional elements were joined, in a many-faceted discourse, with the politics of nationalism – which were increasingly conditioning the mass music-education policies of many European countries.

The Carinthian melody in Berg's powerfully Romantic–expressionist Violin Concerto (1934–5) bears comparison with such appropriations in the music of each of the above-mentioned composers and with the beer-garden dance music in Berg's *Wozzeck* (Act II, scene iv). Both establish a performatively critical distance from the worlds of real Carinthians or dancing, drunken soldiers, rather in the way that Stravinsky's 1938 'Dumbarton Oaks' Concerto – to take just one example – distances itself from the entertainment music it evokes, fusing baroque *concerto grosso* form with the rhythms and mannerisms of urban jazziness for the delectation of a rich American patron and an elite audience of 'modern-music' buffs. All three works insist upon the category of 'serious' music and construct an audience whose attitude towards popular mass culture was highly ambivalent.

The issues were resonantly thematized in a key operatic work of the period whose smash-hit premiere took place in 1927, just two years after that of *Wozzeck*. *Jonny spielt auf* (Johnny Strikes Up) did more than just appropriate or adapt 'jazz-band' idioms.[13] As virtually the defining example of the genre

12 Hermann Hesse, *Steppenwolf* (tr. Basil Creighton), London, 1965, pp. 46–7.

13 For a fuller description see Susan Cook's discussion in the present volume (pp. 178–80), and for further discussion J. Bradford Robinson, 'Jazz Reception in Weimar Germany: In Search of a Shimmy Figure', in Gilliam (ed.), *Music and Performance during the Weimar Republic*, pp. 107–34.

of *Zeitoper* (operas dealing with modern urban life and replacing the swords and spears of Wagnerian mythology with automobiles, steam trains, and telephones), *Jonny* made the reputation of its composer, Ernst Krenek. A pupil, in both Vienna and Berlin, of Franz Schreker – of whom more later – Krenek's earlier and indeed subsequent affiliations were with high modernism and subsequently more conventional forms of anti-conventionality. The message of *Jonny*, however, was different. Depicting the confrontation of high and low art through the characters of the composer Max and the negro jazz musician Jonny (and more specifically through the symbolism of the stolen Amati violin which Jonny uses for his jazz), the opera's final chorus announces the end of the old world: 'The new world's coming shining across the sea to take over old Europe with the dance!'[14]

It was, in its way, as new and exciting as it sounds, and yet on a deeper level it documents the institutionalization of discourse about the high–low divide which the Nazis would subsequently seek to administer with such devastating commitment. Two related contradictions in particular make *Jonny* a key German work of the late 1920s, beyond the statistical facts of its success as a 'jazz opera' preaching cultural renewal through popular dance; the first is internal to the work, the second related to its reception. That Max's bourgeois world of idealistic modernism and Jonny's world of popular jazz fail to fuse is revealed not only by the apparently either/or nature of their opposition, but also by the fact that the opera's musical manners and rhetoric are clearly *not* 'renewed' by the jazz idiom. Outside the *coup de théâtre* finale, the route to genuine renewal is signalled only in those moments when Jonny and his love, the Parisian hotel maid Yvonne, express their ironic (dis-)affection in the anti-operatic performance of a vaudeville-style song-and-dance routine with recurring refrain; it is the 'lower orders' (one of them a racially marked outsider) who threaten the 'higher' form in which they appear. That the liberal message (evidently what Krenek 'intended') was compromised by its demonstration of what high culture feared from mass culture is emphasized by the way in which the period discourse of racism spiralled out of and back onto *Jonny* in curious ways.

Second, although Hanns Eisler found *Jonny* 'stodgy and petty-bourgeois',[15] the dominant conservative response was to brand the opera a manifestation of threatening negro-jazz decadence. Its moral authority in that respect was retrospectively confirmed in the shameful caricature image of the negro Jonny playing his saxophone and wearing a Star of David (equating 'black', 'jazz', and 'Jewishness') that appeared on the front cover of Hans Severus Ziegler's pamphlet accompanying the 1938 Nazi 'Entartete Musik' exhibition in Düsseldorf.

14 Author's translation.
15 John Willett, *The New Sobriety: Art and Politics in the Weimar Period 1917–33*, London, 1978, p. 167.

No less revealing in this context, however, is the unembarrassed account by the first Munich Jonny (Alfred Jerger) of how the disruptive racist jeers that greeted his appearances in the theatre gave way to relieved cheers after the performance, when he appeared at the stage door, out of make-up, to reassure the hecklers that he was 'really' white after all.[16] The opera that threatened cultural norms could also be seen to reinforce them, depending upon the circumstances.

Cultural politics and merchandising in Vienna

Oddest of all the anomalies of *Jonny*'s reception was the furore in Vienna, where its premiere took place only a few weeks distant from that of another, very different opera by Jewish composer Erich Wolfgang Korngold: *Das Wunder der Heliane*. The continuing, if waning, cultural power of opera was demonstrated by the linked merchandising at the time of the premieres of two new kinds of cigarette (cheaper 'Jonnys' and more lavishly and decadently packaged 'Helianes'). Less amusing was the anti-*Jonny* campaign in which young Viennese brownshirts found their orchestrated opposition to the *Neger-oper* (negro opera) supported by the leading conservative music critic in Vienna, who happened to be both a Jew and Erich Korngold's father.[17]

Once again aesthetic conservatism seems to map directly onto right-wing political conservatism, or at least onto the kind of idealistic 'anti-politics' that provided the comforting space in which darkly real political impulses could breed unchecked by critical anxiety. Philosophers of the Marxist Frankfurt Institute for Social Research (founded in 1923), particularly Adorno and Horkheimer, would consistently link cogently argued analyses of the manipulative and commodifying character of mass-cultural entertainment with their criticism of the kinds of bourgeois high art (Wagner, Richard Strauss) which shunned the lonelier, but still potentially redemptive, path of an artistic modernism that defined itself precisely by rejecting bourgeois gratification and approval – and the financial security such approval brought with it. It is precisely into this compelling equation that *Jonny spielt auf*, whose fashionable success in opera houses across Europe netted Krenek and his Viennese publisher (Universal Edition) such un-modernist rewards, introduces a confusingly random term.

One might even propose a certain community of purpose and effect, differentiated more by the class affiliations than the conflicting political outlook of their audiences, between works like *Heliane* and *Jonny*, subsuming

16 Jerger's account is quoted on the sleeve of the 1964 Philips recording of *Jonny Spielt auf* (SAL 3498).

17 Brendan G. Carroll, *The Last Prodigy: A Biography of Erich Wolfgang Korngold*, Portland, OR, 1997, pp. 197–9.

both in an expanded notion of 'popular' culture defined by its opposition to high modernism. As a quasi-symbolist mystery play deploying all the musical and scenic techniques of late-Romantic transformation and transfiguration opera – its post-*Parsifal* relatives are Strauss's *Guntram* and *Die Frau ohne Schatten* and Pfitzner's *Palestrina* – *Das Wunder der Heliane* seems entirely a product of the world of Krenek's Max, light years removed from that of Jonny's jazz and *Zeitoper* naturalism. Yet its failure in comparison with *Jonny* or even Korngold's own earlier *Die tote Stadt* (1921) did not convert him to the martyr's path of modernism, in the manner of Schoenberg. Instead, it reawakened his earlier, often mischievously sceptical attitude to Second Viennese School earnestness. That scepticism now led him to turn his back on aesthetic pretensions (although he believed *Heliane* to be one of his finest works), and to fall in with Max Reinhardt's nostalgic and ostensibly apolitical revivals of Viennese operetta. It was an association that would lead in turn to his first Hollywood commission in 1934: an arrangement of Mendelssohn's *A Midsummer Night's Dream* music for the Warner Brothers' film version of Reinhardt's celebrated staging of the play. A series of film scores followed, one of the most unlikely of which – *The Adventures of Robin Hood*, with Errol Flynn and Olivia de Havilland – almost literally saved Korngold's life: it afforded him, at the time of Hitler's *Anschluss* of Austria in 1938, the physical and financial security to get the rest of his family, along with other friends and acquaintances, out of Austria and the clutches of the Nazis.

That chain of events does not of itself 'redeem' those movies or their scores as somehow harbouring greater moral weight or significance than the not dissimilar movies that ordinary Germans and their all-too-ordinary masters were enjoying in Nazi Berlin, Munich, or Vienna. It does, however, emphasize the multivalent complexity of that ever more widely available sphere of popular artistic entertainment whose catholic embrace included, by the late 1920s, aspects of traditional high culture, early-twentieth-century modernism, and the more sentimental and 'escapist' manners of operetta, popular Italian opera, hit-songs or *Schlager*, and mass-entertainment cinema. The threat to inherited high-culture orthodoxy often confused and pained its first generation adepts; Korngold himself occasionally bemoaned the relative 'worthlessness' of his work in Hollywood as compared to the products, however commodified, of his 1920s aspirations to 'great composer' status.

The symphony and the embattled survival of the 'Great Composer'

That many were eager to consume Greatness is demonstrated by the way in which the Finnish symphonist Jean Sibelius began at that period to consolidate his international reputation as the seeker of inspiration in Nature: he fostered a visionary cragginess of appearance that was celebrated in photographs whose number increased in inverse proportion as his output dwindled into the famous 'silence' that followed *Tapiola* in 1925. Careful attention needs to be paid (and has been, by James Hepokoski among others) to the musical content of and the forms of popular response to those symphonies. The 1920s and 30s were significant decades not only for continuing symphonic composition (including the last symphonies of Sibelius and the first seven by Shostakovich), but also for enthusiastic symphonic reception, latterly aided by gramophone recordings. That the Sibelius symphonies were written off by Adorno and other high modernists as 'nationalist', essentially popular and therefore lacking in genuine contemporary relevance, contrarily stresses their relevance, along with such other symphonies as Shostakovich's Fourth, Fifth, and Seventh: they became sites of musical expression and experience in which power and nostalgia, 'heroic' engagement, escape, lamentation, or euphoric communal celebration could be figured in ways that were immediately decipherable in the concert hall or the newly available privacy of 'home listening', but endlessly refractable, negotiable, or even deniable in verbal commentaries and critical discourse.

The modernist discussion of popular symphonies seemed often designed to block or neutralize their sympathetic critical elucidation; the same could be said of high-culture discussion of operetta, *Schlager*, or popular Italian opera, for reasons that were as passionately felt as they were marked by fears of sinister manipulative intent. The expression of those fears could, as we have seen in the case of jazz, betray curious and often compromising forms of psychological anxiety. A case in point would be the spiritedly ironic and yet oddly ambivalent psychosexual analysis of recent musical history which the German modernist critic Adolf Weissmann published in 1920, with quirkily erotic illustrations by Michael Fingesten, as *Der klingende Garten, Impressionen über das Erotische in der Musik*. His treatment of 'modern' musical development as a history of the ever-changing and ever more unbridled and explicit expression of eroticism began, and possibly ends, as almost a homage to the decadent Nietzscheanism of the 1890s, reinterpreted in the spirit of Freud. The ambivalent tone of his cultural criticism was nevertheless sharpest in the essay on Puccini, where Weissmann's humorously liberal frankness about and enthusiasm for musical sensuality gave way to satirical disapproval:

> Puccini is a master of the art of persuasion. In the hotels and cafes he whispers in the Kapellmeister's ear: With my notes you will conquer. In New York, London, Berlin, Paris – the same spectacle of seduction by Puccini's cantilenas . . . the refinement in the mix of passion and brutality – which sounds a thousand notes of remorse over the lost delicacy of *Bohème* and yet which is the real

> Puccini – through its success the opera-writer contaminates the world. Even in Germany it scares all metaphysics out of people's souls – people who don't experience intoxication [*Rausch*] but want to imagine it of themselves in order to get its effect.
>
> *Puccinismus* has become a sickness . . .[18]

Once again the manipulative and even 'contaminating' popular sphere, opposed by modernists and conservatives alike, proves to have embraced a wide diversity of genres and social 'classes' of music, whose sole common feature was the keenly sensed threat posed by their increasing economic and cultural power. Perhaps, indeed, a truly 'alternative' linear history of the period, the one that does the most justice to the changing economic and social circumstances of musical practice and experience that mark it, would cut a descending path through the parallelisms and simultaneities of modernist and conservative positions and aspirations: 'descending', that is, particularly in terms of the pre-war class structure and the various aesthetic manners and ideals that helped to define it. Many followed that path, sometimes willingly, sometimes driven by economic and political forces beyond their control. Richard Tauber did so in an interestingly representative way.

Tauber: a 1920s superstar

Whereas composers could take refuge in the hope that their unplayed works would one day find an audience, performers were (and are) more closely constrained by the tastes and enthusiasms of their time. A professional singer must to some extent temper his or her idealism to cultural and economic circumstances. The gradual expansion of the paying popular audience for music had been a feature of European musical history since the eighteenth century, perhaps earlier, but the threat to conventional musical culture and the canon that audiences' changing tastes had always been understood to represent seemed to be realized with renewed force in the 1920s and 30s. This was undoubtedly true in Austria and Germany. While the early recording and commodifying of voices like that of Enrico Caruso could be held to have played a part in preserving and 'freezing' moments of cultural practice for the delectation of all, the career trajectory of Richard Tauber reveals something more dynamic about the processes of change that were already at work.

Its main span fits quite closely into the inter-war period. Born in Linz in 1891, the son of actors, his route to eventual success had been mapped initially by enthusiastic aspiration rather than the discovery of a natural talent. His parents'

18 Adolf Weissmann, *Der Klingende Garten: Impressionen über das Erotische in der Musik*, Regensburg, 1920, pp. 55–6.

early separation and divorce afforded him wide experience of the stage, musical and non-musical (the two alternated or were linked in most theatres), as he spent time with both his mother and his father, who in 1903 was engaged by the Court Theatre in Wiesbaden. There the young Tauber developed an idolizing devotion to the tenor Heinrich Hensel, for whom he acted as dresser for a while. Wagner played a significant part in this devotion, and Tauber later claimed to have smuggled Hensel's *Lohengrin* costume out of the theatre and had himself photographed in it.[19] It was Hensel who eventually helped his father to send him to study at the Hoch Conservatory in Frankfurt. He excelled at piano, composition, and conducting; for a time he even attempted to earn money as a silent-film accompanist, until his father intervened. Aspirations to study singing were thwarted largely by his inappropriate devotion to Wagner as a source of audition material. It was the teacher Carl Beines in Freiburg who eventually took him on, having persuaded him that his light tenor voice was unsuited to Wagner but potentially perfect for *bel canto*.

Tauber's passionate imaginative commitment to the world of fantastic musical theatre and Wagner was, of course, common in that period, when theatre and opera catered to the emotional needs of a middle-class audience with a voracious appetite for dramatic sensation. The way in which that audience would subsequently flow into the wider and even less 'exclusive' one for the newly expanding medium of film – clearly seen as an advancing threat by composers and entrepreneurs of high-culture opera – is appropriately signalled not only by Tauber's brief pianistic connection with the cinema, but also by his fascination for photography and film (the latter would lead him to acquire his own camera and projector equipment long before such things were common domestic property). Some of his earliest operatic roles, alongside Mozart and the rest, were at Dresden in recently composed operas by Richard Strauss (*Der Rosenkavalier*, *Ariadne auf Naxos*). Given the developing sense of the danger posed by film to conventional theatre and opera, it is interesting that Strauss's own agreement to participate in a film version of *Der Rosenkavalier* in 1925 was secured in part by Hofmannsthal's judicious assurance that it would not threaten the 'real' opera but rather whet people's appetite for it.[20]

By 1915, when Tauber (who was exempted from military service) had more or less sightread his way through *Ariadne* at short notice, under Strauss's baton, he was, impressively enough, beginning to achieve his dream. Thanks to its conductor Ernst von Schuch, the important opera house in Dresden was closely associated with the foremost living German opera composer (it had staged the

19 Napier-Tauber, *Richard Tauber*, pp. 31–2.

20 See Peter Franklin, 'Movies as Opera (Behind the Great Divide)', in Jeremy Tambling (ed.), *A Night in at the Opera: Media Representations of Opera*, London, 1994, pp. 77–110; pp. 91–2.

premiere of *Salome*, amongst other Strauss operas), whose own high-culture career path from Wilhelmine modernist to conservative-idealist President of Goebbels's *Reichsmusikkammer* in 1933–4 shadowed the development of one significant stratum in the multi-layered historical picture that I have been building up. But Strauss was not the only living opera composer in whose works Tauber sang. D'Albert (*Tiefland*, *Die toten Augen*) was in his repertoire, as was Kienzl (*Der Evangelimann*); so too, even more interestingly, were Franz Schreker and Erich Wolfgang Korngold. During the 1920s Tauber sang Fritz in Schreker's highly successful 1912 opera *Der ferne Klang*, and created the role of Elis in Vienna, when *Der Schatzgräber* was first performed there in 1922. He was also to become a celebrated Paul in Korngold's 1920 hit *Die tote Stadt*.[21]

The word 'hit' is appropriate to all three of the last-mentioned operas. Their composers were both associated in slightly different ways with pre-war 'new music' in Vienna; Schreker was a '*Neutöner*' friend of Schoenberg and had conducted the first performance of *Gurrelieder*, while Korngold had been praised as a child prodigy by Mahler and partly trained by the conductor and composer Alexander Zemlinsky, another friend of Schoenberg's. Although they became forgotten in the wake of the Second World War, their considerable period significance was in a sense attested by the critical opprobrium that their new works began to reap in the later 1920s. Before Nazi anti-Semitism uprooted or (in Schreker's case) effectively killed all the above-mentioned composers, modernist and traditionalist critical narratives together turned upon composers such as Schreker, with his 'regressive' fairy-tales and operatic 'penny-dreadfuls' composed to his own libretti, and his intoxicating use of sound-colour. Korngold fared even worse, given his compromised position as the son of Vienna's leading anti-modernist critic. His Straussian and Puccinian *Die tote Stadt*, seven years prior to *Das Wunder der Heliane*, even included its own foregrounded '*Schlager*', specifically introduced as a debilitatingly nostalgic sentimental song ('Glück das mir verblieb'); appropriately enough, Tauber recorded it in Berlin with Lotte Lehmann in 1924. (This was a nostalgic year, in which Thomas Mann's *Der Zauberberg*, with its extended meditation on the pre-1914 German mentality, was first published, selling an unprecedented number of copies; in Vienna, Alma Mahler published her edition of Mahler's letters and the facsimile of the uncompleted Tenth Symphony.)

There was a little of Tauber in all three of his Korngold and Schreker roles. His susceptibility to sentimental songs, like Paul in *Die tote Stadt*, shaped the latter part of his career and the character of his fame. He must also have had something special to give to Schreker's Fritz, the poor boy in *Der ferne Klang* who goes off to

21 See Carroll, *The Last Prodigy*, p. 151.

search for the 'distant sound' that will secure his success as a composer; similarly to Elis the minstrel in *Der Schatzgräber* – the opera which Schreker completed, as he noted optimistically on the manuscript, on '12 November 1918 (on the day of the declaration of the German-Austrian Republic and the union with the German Reich!)', and which went on to achieve widespread success in German opera houses during the Weimar Republic.[22] The songs which Elis sings, accompanying himself on a magical lute, reach people's hearts, but the lute seems symbolically to perform its own modernist self-critique in that its strings vibrate not only in sympathy with human pain but also in response to the nearby presence of precious stones, jewels, and gold. The idealist artist is thus condemned to attract unwanted worldly rewards for his artistic integrity and emotional honesty; in *Der Schatzgräber* the blame symptomatically falls upon Els, the forest *femme fatale* with whom Elis falls in love.

Schreker's proto-modernist tendency to provide Music itself with both concrete and symbolic roles in his operas was accompanied by an intriguing turn-of-the-century tendency to figure its gender as problematically feminine, as if buying in to the modernists' critical penchant for the discursive feminization not only of his own music but also of the whole popular sphere. In a quite literal way, Els is very nearly the death of Elis: her sexual feelings are fixed so firmly upon a horde of stolen jewels, like the Queen who had once owned it and 'dreams about it . . . as if it were a lover', that she uses her attractiveness to seduce male admirers into obtaining pieces of the jewellery in various underhand ways, before having them murdered (hence her initial interest in Elis and his lute). In *Der ferne Klang*, Fritz's abandoned girlfriend Grete is condemned to a still more revealingly complex history before she re-encounters Fritz as the relatively successful composer of the opera we have been watching. Her initial attempt to follow him had led her into prostitution, first rather grandly in Venice but subsequently on the streets of the modern city where Fritz's opera is being premiered. She has heard part of it from the gallery (or was it a cheap Stehplatz?), been 'swept away' and collapsed – hence her removal to the nearby café where, in Act III, we hear snatches of *Der ferne Klang* drifting from the nearby theatre. But the ailing Fritz's problem proves to be greater: his continuing sense of dissatisfaction is dispelled, all too late, by the realization that he had wrongly ignored the beauty of Nature – and the girl he had left behind. He dies in her arms as the curtain falls.

While brief synopses hardly do justice to the musical and dramatic complexity of such works, they convey something of their outwardly sentimental and even

22 See Matthias Brzoska, 'An Opera for the Republic: *Der Schatzgräber*', booklet accompanying the CD set of Franz Schreker: *Der Schatzgräber under Gerd Albrecht* (Capriccio 60010–2, 1989), pp. 11 and 22, and Christopher Hailey, *Franz Schreker 1878–1934: A Cultural Biography*, Cambridge, 1993, pp. 99–109, p. 142.

proto-cinematic character, as seen from the viewpoint of critical modernism during the gathering political and economic crises of the middle and late 1920s. Grete is almost literally turned from Romantic Muse into the most ordinary of listeners who, as Brecht memorably suggested, flocked to bourgeois opera to be 'transported into a peculiar doped state, wholly passive . . . involuntary victims of the unchecked lurchings of their emotions',[23] to submit, in fact, to what Grete herself longingly recalls as 'die wilde Musik' – although for her it has acted benignly, giving her back the liberating dignity of recollection. This is not the place to consider the extent to which Schreker's self-conscious scenarios might have plotted an alternative, albeit vulnerably consumable form of modernism. Their evidently proto-cinematic qualities, musical ones not least, explain how they came to incite the kind of criticism that Korngold more intentionally courted during the same period, particularly following the failure of *Das Wunder der Heliane*. His own rather deliberate move into operetta – followed, as it turned out, by a highly successful defection to Hollywood – prompts further consideration of the other highly successful contemporary opera composer (*too* successful from Adolf Weissmann's perspective) with whom Tauber was closely associated in the 1920s. That was Puccini.

It is almost inevitable that he should have sung most of Puccini's major tenor roles. The composer had died in 1926, leaving unfinished his last opera *Turandot*, which nevertheless rapidly achieved worldwide success in Alfano's completed version. Tauber appropriately created the role of Calaf at the German premiere of *Turandot* in Dresden (1926) under Fritz Busch (it was to have been sung by Kurt Taucher, who developed a throat infection just days before the performance). Tauber's November 1926 recordings of 'Non piangere Liù' and 'Nessun dorma' (as 'O weine nicht, Liù' and 'Keiner schlafe') must have been amongst the earliest recordings of music from that opera, which so resonantly explored the redeeming power of love in a context of totalitarian state brutality, relished by a bloodthirsty chorus and wielded by another great *femme fatale* of that most fatal period.

A relevant, if historically compromised, supplement to early musical-historical accounts of the period is found in the very last book, published in Berlin in 1932, by the Austrian Jewish music critic Richard Specht: he had been a close friend of Mahler (and written two books about him), and a thoughtful supporter of Viennese modernism. It was a critical biography of Puccini, dedicated to Alma Mahler, in which Specht sought to make amends for his earlier Germanic inability to comprehend the ethos of modern Italian opera, and for his readiness to subscribe to the discourse of German modernism which

23 John Willett (ed.), *Brecht on Theatre* (2nd edn), London, 1974, p. 89.

demonized Puccini as a populist whose operas one might only enjoy, as it were, in private, or with suitably condescending irony in public. By 1932 Specht had come to believe that the apostles of 'advanced' music 'have no idea how sterile musical radicalism really is in the long run':

> [they] preach the gospel according to Schoenberg while secretly enjoying the intoxication of Puccini, whose 'unchaste' style they would be glad enough to imitate if only they had sufficient powers of invention; but they really ought to consider for a while the question of where the more honest artistic ideals are to be found – in the much abused Puccini, or in the many present-day musicians who are rather playing tricks [*Unfug verüben*] with music or else suffering from the malady of 'a progressive philosophy of life'.[24]

Puccini himself had been interested in and was well aware of what was happening in 'new music' (his knowledge of Schoenberg and Stravinsky is occasionally detectable in the opera's musical language and scoring). He had nevertheless nailed his colours very firmly to the mast of 'emotionalism' when he wrote to his librettists, Adami and Simoni, from Torre del Lago at the outset of the *Turandot* project:

> Put all your strength into it, all the resources of your hearts and heads, and create for me something which will make the world weep. They say that emotionalism is a sign of weakness, but I like to be weak! To the strong, so called, I leave the triumphs that fade: for us those that endure![25]

Whether we like it or not, the Weimar period was marked by the increasing success and wider dissemination of the music of such 'weakness'. Richard Tauber was one of the singers who sailed no less deliberately on the crest of its wave. His second wife, Diana Napier, suggests that it was around the time of the premiere of *Turandot* (she in fact dates the trend from the *Wozzeck* and Johann Strauss year of 1925) that Tauber began to include music by Johann Strauss and Franz Lehár in his solo programmes, alongside more conventional Lieder-recital material that included Schumann, Richard Strauss, Grieg, and operatic arias.[26]

But there was more to it. Certainly money, although Tauber was as ineffectual and irresponsible in the management of his financial affairs as he was stylish in manner and appearance. The hyper-inflation period around 1923 prompted him to demand the payment of some of his fees in gold, but he recklessly refused to enter into royalty agreements with the producers of his highly

24 Richard Specht, *Giacomo Puccini: The Man, his Life, his Work* (tr. Catherine Alison Philips), London, 1933, p. 179.

25 Giuseppe Adami (ed.), *Letters of Giacomo Puccini* (tr. Ena Makin), new edn rev. and introduced by Mosco Carner, London, 1974, p. 268.

26 Napier-Tauber, *Richard Tauber*, pp. 79–80.

successful gramophone recordings until well into the 1940s. There was also, as with Korngold and others, a deliberate and intentional aspect to Tauber's move into the popular and sentimental world of Viennese operetta. He was to play a key role in Lehár's later career, from his first appearance in *Frasquita* in 1923 – and more specifically from his bestselling recording in that year of its main hit, 'Hab' ein blaues Himmelbett'. Although not explicitly written for him, that song became the model for the focal '*Tauberlied*' of subsequent Lehár works and of adaptations made not only for Tauber, but with his close collaboration: Diana Napier (Tauber) suggests that her husband worked with Lehár on the detailed composition and nuancing of these songs, one of the most famous of which was 'Du bist mein ganzes Herz' (better known in English as 'You Are My Heart's Delight'), created specifically for the Berlin revival of *Die gelbe Jacke* as *Das Land des Lächelns* in 1929.[27] Tauber was famous not only for his effectively poised and paced performance of these songs, but also for his fondness for bringing the house down by encoring them in different languages or from unexpected places in the theatre; on occasion he would appear in a box or even in the central aisle of the stalls, singing amongst his public. They loved him for it, whether in the theatre or in extempore performances at public events like the 1929 Berlin Six Day Cycle Race, where Tauber was spotted in the grandstand of the vast Sportpalast, wearing his usual evening dress and monocle, and was coaxed down into the main arena for a brief performance.[28]

It is clear that he enormously enjoyed what amounted to a 1920s version of superstardom. During that first 1923 run of *Frasquita* in Vienna – for what Tauber sensed to be the unsnobbish audience of the Theater an der Wien, as compared with that at the Staatsoper – he began to develop ideas which he is reported to have voiced later in an undated interview:

> Modern music – Yes, I am able to separate the singer from the composer – I appreciate modern music. Stravinsky, Alban Berg, Schönberg, Krenek – I am sympathetic and I appreciate the technical construction, the almost mathematical accuracy of such compositions, the new harmonies. I enjoy reading a score by the great moderns. But such music cannot be sung – perhaps it should not be played? The modernist 'paints' his music instead of feeling it. It is like a magnificent piece of machinery. The technical construction may be perfect – but it has no soul. It is made, manufactured, not born.[29]

What is interesting here is not simply the way in which the Romantic ideology of inspirational authenticity is expressed by someone who himself occasionally composed, and who clearly 'manufactured' the *Tauberlieder* with Lehár to a

27 Ibid., p. 93. 28 Ibid., pp. 104–6. 29 Ibid., p. 103.

high degree of precision; it is specifically how that ideology is now reserved for a specifically popular and *performative* musical style.

After his death, another journalist ventured an ambitious assessment of the Tauber phenomenon, recalling the Berlin premiere of *Das Land des Lächelns* in 1929, and

> the 'little people' from the suburbs who nightly filled the theatre to capacity. Tauber, Lehár and the brothers Rotter [the producers] were providing an escape in a period of political disintegration of the German Reich. While the shadows of economic collapse and of civil war were rapidly falling over the capital, Tauber sang at the Metropol Theatre and gave the Berliners a little ray of sunshine, which they so eagerly sought. He was the 'Squire' of the proverbial *Castle in Spain* into which everyone followed him, most of all those who did not openly admit it. He was not only an artist but a significant expression of the sociological character of the times.[30]

Diana Napier herself pondered what it was that so endeared her husband to his public, probing further what she might almost have called the sociological character of his popularity, not least in his later years in England and with reference to the sentimental films in which Tauber starred in the 1930s. She quotes W. J. Elton from a 1935 edition of *Film Weekly* in which he proposed that 'family appeal' was behind the universality of Tauber's success:

> Would you take grandma to see Bing Crosby? Would you take mother to see Mae West or banjoist Bobby to hear a star such as Chaliapine? Naturally you wouldn't!
>
> On the other hand, would you have any fears about taking these assorted members of your family to see Richard Tauber in *Blossom Time*, or in his new film *Heart's Desire*?[31]

Whether affectionately or ironically intended, Elton had probably put his finger on it. Tauber's celebrated, almost childlike enthusiasm for what he did carried his audiences with him, into a commodified and startlingly democratized performance of all that 'music' (of the 'beautiful', 'good', and 'classical' kind) had signified in European culture for the past century. Its emotional universality was as urgently needed as ever, but it had been secured at a price: the price of appearing to deny the fundamental character of the sensuality and physicality it expressed, the price of shared criticality, or opposition, even of politics. So great was the need, and so powerful the cultural trope, that its emollient and affirmative qualities, like Tauber's own, proved too welcoming, too ready to appease the most terrifying of unwanted guests in the name of

30 Ibid., p. 121. 31 Ibid., p. 174.

'what fate ordains'. The formula is that of Chinese Sou Chong, who realizes at the end of *Das Land des Lächelns* that he must 'silently bear' the pain of his beloved Lisa's return to the pre-war Vienna from which he had hoped to woo her. Tauber, too, 'loathed discords in music no less than in life and always tried to avoid anything which would make people sad; not the least of his concerns was to keep unpleasant things away from himself'[32]: Diana Napier's fond diagnosis helps to explain why Tauber, like Erich Korngold (who heard the news in Hollywood), was so shocked by Hitler's *Anschluss* of Austria in 1938 that he shut himself into his room for a full three days.

Here at least the modernist analysis would appear vindicated; it is even more so by the fact that Lehár performances (like those of Puccini) continued in blithely sinister fashion after Tauber had been made stateless. One Jewish tenor was deemed hardly to matter when others were prepared to take his place – and so the next batch of Berlin Lehár recordings were made in 1939, with Anton Dermota re-recording Tauber's 'Dein ist mein ganzes Herz'. (Other Lehár highlights were recorded by Elisabeth Schwarzkopf and Rupert Gollwitsch.) There is a gloomy appropriateness about the fact that Tauber's 1936 wedding present to Diana Napier, in the year of the Berlin Olympics, had been the rights to an operetta of his own, called *The Singing Dream*.

We smile and shake our heads at the faded and fated poignancy of it all, but might do so no less at the hubris of the modernists' certainties, or of the idealist-socialist artist Käthe Kollwitz's response to a performance in December 1918, under Richard Strauss, of Beethoven's Ninth Symphony – a work whose Bayreuth and Nazi appropriation in subsequent decades exemplifies the promiscuity of musical signification. 'I was carried away', wrote Kollwitz, 'swept up out of the partisan dust to heights of purest joy. Yes, in the Ninth there is socialism in its purest form. There is humanity, glowing darkly like a rose, its deepest chalice drenched with sunlight.'[33]

Humanity eclipsed, or the undoing of 'music'

Before Tauber's forgotten percentage of Jewish blood precipitated the last phase of his career – he would eventually assume British nationality – he had already made his cinematic debut in what was billed as the first fully sound film made in Germany: *Ich glaub nie mehr an einer Frau* (1930). In this he completed his journey from high art to sentimental kitsch. It was also a journey *through* the new media: he had been in the first wave of performers to cement their fame by means of the gramophone and to become a familiar voice on the radio.

32 Ibid., p. 103. 33 Gill, *A Dance between Flames*, p. 36.

To encounter Tauber, his monocle firmly in place, in one of Berlin's hotel cafés or cabarets, with friends like Anton Kuh or Erich von Stroheim, would have been to be confronted with the simultaneities and stark contradictions of that fleetingly wild, decadently liberal Weimar Berlin in which one could attend a Furtwängler concert before satisfying more or less any desire with the help of willing prostitutes and bold transvestites, in pornographic cinemas or nude reviews. In the suburbs and woods youthful *Wandervogel* athletes and communal folksong singers were being courted or denounced by fascists, communists, theosophists. The picture of music in the period is always a montage of unlikely fragments. Until 1934 Franz Schreker managed the Berlin Musikhochschule and taught at the Prussian Academy of Arts alongside composers as divergent as Schoenberg, Busoni, Hindemith, and Pfitzner; meanwhile Otto Klemperer at the Kroll Oper was outraging brownshirt conservatives with Stravinsky's *Oedipus rex* and his 1929 constructivist-designed, modern-dress production of Wagner's *Der fliegende Holländer* (which Siegfried Wagner denounced as *Kulturbolshewismus*). And still the 'little people' – the same little people who would later stand by as Jewish shop and synagogue windows were smashed on *Kristallnacht* – were flocking to the Metropol to see Tauber in Lehár.

Perhaps it was appropriate that he should have spent the last decade of his life, the war years, based in England, where the high-versus-popular art equation remained still uncomplicated by the middle term of an effectively organized 'modernist' movement until the Britten, Auden, and Tippett generation began to make its presence felt in the mid-1930s. Until then manifestations of modernism were still reckoned a largely 'foreign' and 'European' affair whose brief incursions into concert programmes or the creative imagination of Vaughan Williams (as in the 1935 Fourth Symphony) were not infrequently written off as semi-pathological aberrations. The popular musical theatre was still, on one level, dominated by the 1920s nostalgic sentimentality of Ivor Novello – with strong family ties to that of Lehár – which had managed without too much difficulty to accommodate the socialist Celtic revivalism of Rutland Boughton, whose Glastonbury Festival opera *The Immortal Hour* had run for 216 consecutive performances at the Regent Theatre, King's Cross, in 1922–3. With its faery folk and druids, it conjured up a grown-up J. M. Barrie fantasy world whose final vision was of a pastoral Land of the Ever Young, where 'The lordly ones . . . play with lances / And are proud and terrible, / marching in the moonlight / With fierce blue eyes'.

Tauber's eyes tended to be anything but fierce, when they were not evoking the sparkle of pre-1914 Vienna. Although his habitually rather stiff stage movements, latterly made worse through illness, did not transfer well to the cinema screen, something of his charisma was caught in the 1937 film of

Pagliacci (it was a cherished project to film a complete opera), and in his portrayal of a rather stout and sad Schubert in the earlier *Blossom Time* (1934). His death in 1948, just one year before those of Pfitzner and Richard Strauss, marked a cultural cadence more resonantly final than that brought about by the First World War. Most of the theatres in which he had triumphed were completely destroyed or were bombed-out shells, like the main Munich and Vienna opera houses. The crassly administered culture of Goebbels and his high-art associates, amongst whom Strauss and Wilhelm Furtwängler had been numbered along with the acolytes of Bayreuth, had martyred '*Entartet*' (decadent) modernism so effectively that its critical triumph in the post-war years was assured. Some came to believe that no other outcome was conceivable after the deliberate prostitution of high art and its traditional ideals during the Third Reich; the circumstances that led to Anita Lasker-Wallfisch playing the Schumann *Träumerei* to Dr Mengele in Auschwitz saw to that.[34] Yet the continuities between operetta and the mid-twentieth-century musical, like those between the world of early-twentieth-century opera and that of mass-entertainment cinema (as traced in the careers of men like Korngold and Tauber), remind us that it was the coexistence of those forms with the conflicting dissonances of many modernisms that made up the larger dialectical harmony, if such one may call it, of European musical culture between the wars.

Bibliography

Adami, Giuseppe (ed.). *Letters of Giacomo Puccini* (tr. Ena Makin, new edn rev. and intr. Mosco Carner), London, 1974.

Adorno, Theodor and Max Horkheimer. *Dialectic of Enlightenment* (tr. John Cumming), London, 1979.

Allen, Roger. 'The thought of Wilhelm Furtwängler: A Study of the Politics of the Unpolitical', D. Phil. thesis, Oxford University, 2000.

Brzoska, Matthias. 'An Opera for the Republic: *Der Schatzgräber*', booklet accompanying the CD set of Franz Schreker: *Der Schatzgräber* under Gerd Albrecht, Capriccio 60010–2, 1989.

Burbank, Richard. *Twentieth-Century Music*, London, 1984.

Carroll, Brendan G. *The Last Prodigy: A Biography of Erich Wolfgang Korngold*, Portland, OR, 1997.

Currid, Brian, '"A Song goes Round the World": The German *Schlager* as an Organ of Experience', *Popular Music* 19 (2000), pp. 147–80.

Franklin, Peter. 'Audiences, Critics and the Depurification of Music: Reflections on a 1920s Controversy', *Journal of the Royal Musical Association* 114 (1989), pp. 80–91.

'Movies as Opera (Behind the Great Divide)', in Jeremy Tambling (ed.), *A Night in at the Opera: Media Representations of Opera*, London, 1994, pp. 77–110.

34 Anita Lasker-Wallfisch, *Inherit the Truth 1939–1945*, London, 1996, p. 79.

Gay, Peter. *Weimar Culture: The Outsider as Insider*, Harmondsworth, 1974.
Gill, Anton. *A Dance between Flames: Berlin between the Wars*, London, 1993.
Grosz, Georg (ed.). *The Face of the Ruling Class*, London, 1984.
Hailey, Christopher. *Franz Schreker 1878–1834: A Cultural Biography*, Cambridge, 1993.
'Rethinking Sound: Music and Radio in Weimar Germany', in Bryan Gilliam (ed.), *Music and Performance during the Weimar Republic*, Cambridge, 1994, pp. 13–36.
Hesse, Hermann. *Steppenwolf* (tr. Basil Creighton), London, 1965.
Huyssen, Andreas. *After the Great Divide: Modernism, Mass Culture and Postmodernism*, London, 1988.
Kaes, Anton, Martin Jay and Edward Dimendberg (eds.). *The Weimar Republic Sourcebook*, Berkeley, 1994.
Lasker-Wallfisch, Anita. *Inherit the Truth 1939–1945*, London, 1996.
Napier-Tauber, Diana. *Richard Tauber*, London, 1949.
Pfitzner, Hans. *Die neue Ästhetik der Musikalischen Impotenz*, Munich, 1920.
Robinson, J. Bradford, 'Jazz Reception in Weimar Germany: In Search of a Shimmy Figure', in Bryan Gilliam (ed.), *Music and Performance During the Weimar Republic*, Cambridge, pp. 107–34.
Specht, Richard. *Giacomo Puccini: The Man, His Life, His Work* (tr. Catherine Alison Philips), London, 1933.
Walter, Bruno. *Theme and Variations: An Autobiography*, London, 1947.
Weissmann, Adolf. *Der Klingende Garten: Impressionen über das Erotische in der Musik*, Regensburg, 1920.
Willett, John (ed.). *Brecht on Theatre* (2nd edn), London, 1974.
The New Sobriety: Art and Politics in the Weimar Period 1917–33, London, 1978.

· 8 ·

Brave new worlds: experimentalism between the wars

DAVID NICHOLLS

> Rich with a wealth of harmonics, the tremulous chorus mounted towards a climax, louder and ever louder – until at last, with a wave of his hand, the conductor let loose the final shattering note of ether-music and blew the sixteen merely human blowers clean out of existence. Thunder in A flat major. And then, in all but silence, in all but darkness, there followed a gradual deturgescence, a *diminuendo* sliding gradually, through quarter tones, down, down to a faintly whispered dominant chord that lingered on (while the five-four rhythms still pulsed below) charging the darkened seconds with an intense expectancy. And at last expectancy was fulfilled. There was a sudden explosive sunrise, and simultaneously, the Sixteen burst into song . . .
>
> Aldous Huxley, *Brave New World* (1932)[1]

> The sound of a truck at fifty miles per hour. Static between the stations. Rain. We want to capture and control these sounds, to use them not as sound effects but as musical instruments . . . it is now possible to control the amplitude and frequency of any one of these sounds and to give it a rhythm within or beyond the reach of the imagination . . . we can compose and perform a quartet for explosive motor, wind, heartbeat, and landslide . . .
>
> John Cage, 'The Future of Music: Credo' (?1940)[2]

Prologue: Brave New Worlds

If one major facet of nineteenth-century music was its obsession with the subjective Romantic legacy of E. T. A. Hoffmann (1776–1822) – of the 'sublime master' whose 'high self-possession [is] inseparable from true genius', who 'leads the listener imperiously forward into the spirit world of the infinite' and seals into his work 'wonderful enchanting pictures and apparitions . . . with magic power'[3] – then its antithesis is found in the increasingly objective

1 London, 1994, Chapter V/1. Further references to *Brave New World* will be to this Flamingo edition and will be given in parentheses in the text.

2 In John Cage, *Silence*, London, 1968, pp. 3–6.

3 Extracted from E. T. A. Hoffmann, 'Beethoven's Instrumental Music' [1813], in Oliver Strunk (ed.), *Source Readings in Music History*, rev. edn, New York, 1998, pp. 1193–8.

scientific scrutiny to which music was subsequently subjected. The best-known example of such scrutiny is *The Sensations of Tone* by Hermann von Helmholtz (1821–94), first published in German in 1863 and in English translation in 1875; the dissemination period of Helmholtz's work thus rather amusingly coincides with that of Wagner's later operas, including *Tristan und Isolde* (first performed 1865), *Siegfried*, and *Götterdämmerung* (both 1876). Helmholtz was a scientific polymath: his principal contributions to the study of music lay in such areas as the anatomy of the ear, the physiology of hearing, wave patterns, tuning systems, and especially the analysis of overtones in relation to timbre and such acoustic phenomena as combination tones. When first published, *The Sensations of Tone* provoked controversy (especially in its English translation, which was not always true to the original) but overall it provided a very solid base for later developments.

Among the more iconoclastic statements made by Helmholtz in his book – one that was particularly prophetic of a major area of twentieth-century musical exploration – was that

> the construction of scales and of harmonic tissue is a product of artistic invention, and by no means furnished by the natural formation or natural function of our ear, as it has been hitherto most generally asserted . . .
>
> just as people with differently directed tastes can erect extremely different kinds of buildings with the same stones, so also the history of music shews us that the same properties of the human ear could serve as the foundation of very different musical systems.[4]

Other, equally prophetic, aspects of scientific progress – in the broadest sense of that phrase – also had an impact in other musical spheres during the second half of the nineteenth century: for instance, by 1850 Theobald Boehm (1794–1881) had radically redesigned the flute, Adolphe Sax (1814–94) had patented the saxhorn and saxophone, and metal-framed pianos were the norm. The phonograph was invented in 1876, the microphone in 1878, the telegraphone (forerunner of the tape recorder) in 1898, and wireless transmission in 1900; the same period saw the erection of such acoustically influential buildings as the Boston Music Hall (1863), the Paris Opéra (1869–75), the Grosser Musikvereinssaal of Vienna (1870), and the Bayreuth Festspielhaus (1876). Subsequently, between 1895 and 1915, W. C. Sabine published a series of important papers on the scientific study of room acoustics, dealing principally with such matters as sound decay and the prediction of reverberation time.

All of these developments were symptomatic of the spirit of positivism that swept through society during this period. Unsurprisingly, this spirit served

4 Hermann von Helmholtz, *The Sensations of Tone* (tr. Alexander J. Ellis), 3rd edn, London, 1895, pp. 365–6.

as an inspiration to several generations of music theorists and explorers on both sides of the Atlantic, and was presumably a major factor in the tendency for creative artists increasingly to define their aesthetic standards via the manifesto: from Busoni and Debussy through to Cage and Partch, composers sought to expand on what Bojan Bujić has termed 'the "progressive" implications of Helmholtz's observation of the nature of our tonal system' and accordingly to define a number of brave new musical worlds.[5] What distinguishes these artists from the majority of their predecessors is the aesthetic stance they adopted. Most artists find an individual aesthetic locus through personal negotiation of three contrary cultural forces: the burden of tradition (retrospection), the temptations of other traditions (extraspection), and an image of the future (prospection). Thus the prospective vision of modernist composer Arnold Schoenberg was very much rooted in the Austro-German tradition in which he matured; extraspective influences were minimal. Maurice Ravel, meanwhile, though having a clear attachment to French tradition, formed his image of the future through such extraspective influences as contemporary popular music and the folk music of Spain. Composers more keenly affected by positivism, however, leaned heavily towards empirical prospection, largely shunning the immediate past and present; extraspective influences – if they occurred at all – were likely to be from more distant places and times. One of the more paradoxical results of such tendencies is the not infrequent juxtaposition in radical music of determinism and aleatoricism, formalism and primitivism.

Before the crash: 'ending is better than mending'

Aldous Huxley (1894–1963) wrote *Brave New World* in 1932, as a direct result of his first visit to America, six years earlier. During his voyage across the Atlantic, Huxley had read Henry Ford's book *My Life and Work*; much of what he experienced in California following disembarkation seemed, in David Bradshaw's words, 'perfectly in tune with Fordian principles' of mass production, conveyor-belt assembly lines, and job demarcation.[6] Huxley – apparently thrilled (and also presumably fascinated) by the vulgarity he discovered in America – described California as 'Materially, the nearest approach to Utopia

5 Bojan Bujić, 'Introduction' [to] '3.1[:] Psychology of Music and the Theory of *Einfühlung* (Empathy)', in Bojan Bujić (ed.), *Music in European Thought, 1851–1912*, Cambridge, 1988, p. 277.

6 David Bradshaw, 'Introduction' to Aldous Huxley, *Brave New World*, [p. vii]. Bradshaw's essay – on pp. [v]–[xiv] of the Flamingo edition – and the quotations it cites provide the basis of this paragraph. The quasi-Keynesian catchphrase 'Ending is better than mending' is part of a hypnopaedic text used to indoctrinate children in Huxley's dystopian World State: see, for instance, *Brave New World*, pp. 43ff. Incidentally, one of the principal (anti-establishment) characters in the novel is named Helmholtz Watson.

yet seen on our planet', and prophesied that 'the future of America is the future of the world'. As has been generally recognized – not least by the author himself in *Brave New World Revisited* (1958) – Huxley's 'satire on the global diffusion of the American way of life' is a worryingly accurate vision not so much of 'this year of stability, A. F. 632' (i.e. 2495, 632 years after the birth of Henry Ford) but rather of the second half of the twentieth century.

However, in one area – that of culture – Huxley's predictions were not entirely accurate. True, it has recently been suggested that the compulsory study of Shakespeare be dropped from the Cambridge English Tripos, reminding us of the Savage's remark – apropos *Othello* – 'Have you read it too? . . . I thought nobody knew about that book here, in England' (*Brave New World*, p. 199). Furthermore, the amusing description of 'the newly opened Westminster Abbey Cabaret' (ibid., p. 67), cited in part at the head of this chapter, can easily be likened to 1990s youth culture: Huxley's *soma* equates to ecstasy, while the synaesthetic experience of 'London's finest scent and colour organ' accompanying Calvin Stopes and his Sixteen Sexophonists, as 'four hundred couples . . . five-[step] round the polished floor' (ibid.) of a recently liberated performance space, is remarkably redolent of a rave. But Huxley assumed that high culture would be completely obliterated in the World State: on the one hand, His Fordship Mustapha Mond, Controller of the Western European Zone, defends the prohibition of Shakespeare on the basis that 'it's old [and w]e haven't any use for old things here . . . Particularly when they're beautiful' (pp. 199–200). On the other, his subsequent comment that 'we don't want people to be attracted by old things. We want them to like the new ones' is rooted in the premiss that there is a price to be paid for the stability of the World State. 'You've got to choose between happiness and what people used to call high art'; 'our world is not the same as Othello's world. You can't make flivvers without steel – and you can't make tragedies without social instability' (pp. 201, 200).

Rather surprisingly for someone so erudite and sophisticated, Huxley – either involuntarily or deliberately – apparently saw and heard in California in 1926 only the most superficial and banal manifestations of contemporary culture: the 'sea of melodic treacle' performed in motion-picture studios 'to play the actors into an appropriate state of soul'; the 'thousands of feet of art and culture' [*sic*] turned out each day by the studio labs; the 'announcements of rival religious sects, advertising the spiritual wares that they would give away or sell on the Sabbath'; and 'The Charleston, the fox-trot . . . the jazz bands, the movie palaces, [and] the muffins at breakfast'.[7] Although Huxley

7 Quotations extracted from the section titled 'Los Angeles. A Rhapsody', in Aldous Huxley, *Jesting Pilate: The Diary of a Journey*, London, 1940, pp. 229–37.

also mentions 'the joy . . . of trooping out on summer evenings with fifty thousand others to listen to concerts in the open air',[8] he would unfortunately have been unable to encounter the activities of Henry Cowell's New Music Society of California. Cowell (1897–1965) had founded the society in 1925, but was concertizing in Europe during Huxley's sojourn in California: thus Huxley missed both of the society's first two concerts. The programme of 22 October 1925 included 'ultra-modern' music by Dane Rudhyar (1895–1985), Edgard Varèse, Carl Ruggles, and Schoenberg; its successor – on 20 November 1926 – again featured works by Rudhyar, Ruggles, and Schoenberg, as well as pieces by Darius Milhaud, Alfredo Casella, and Cowell himself.

Despite the non-meeting, there is however one tiny but significant connection between Huxley and Cowell. In *Jesting Pilate*, Huxley describes an actress in the film studio he was visiting: she 'walked back to her chair. Reopening her book, she went on quietly reading about Theosophy.'[9] In the earlier part of the twentieth century, Theosophy was as ubiquitously trendy as is feng shui nowadays, and since around 1913, Cowell had been involved with both Theosophy and Theosophists. His first contact was through John O. Varian, a charismatic mystic, poet, and inventor, who became a kind of surrogate father to him. In 1914, Varian settled in a Theosophical colony at Halcyon, situated on the California coast; during the next ten or so years, Cowell visited Halcyon on many occasions, and although he never became a Theosophist *per se*, he was actively involved in the life of the community, collaborating frequently with Varian, setting his poetry and drawing influence from his Irish mythological tales. Indeed, some of Cowell's best-known pieces – including the tone-cluster piano piece *The Tides of Manaunaun* (*c.*1917) – resulted from this collaboration.[10] Subsequently, in 1925, Cowell visited the Chicago studio of Theosophist Djane Herz, whose circle included Cowell's (Theosophist) friend Dane Rudhyar, as well as Ruth Crawford who was later to marry Cowell's teacher Charles Seeger. Herz, Rudhyar, and Crawford were all devotees of the music of Alexander Skryabin, and herein lies a further (presumably accidental) connection with Huxley and Brave New World. For if Calvin Stopes, the Sixteen Sexophonists, and the Westminster Abbey Cabaret's scent and colour organ resemble anything – real or imagined – in the first (rather than the last) quarter of the twentieth century, it would be Skryabin's unfinished and sensorially overloaded *Mysterium*, which was intended to include 'colored lights, processions, and scents' and would culminate in an 'ecstatic abyss of sunshine'.[11]

8 Ibid., p. 234. 9 Ibid., p. 230.
10 For further details see Steven Johnson, 'Henry Cowell, John Varian, and Halcyon', *American Music* 11/1 (1993), pp. 1–27.
11 See Faubion Bowers, *The New Scriabin*, London, 1974, pp. 94–100, 124–6.

Mysterium is about as distant from positivism as could be imagined; it does serve to remind us, though – *contra* Huxley – that many of the more advanced musical developments of the twentieth century had their origins in Europe. Following the publication of *The Sensations of Tone*, one of the first to realise that 'ending [was] better than mending' was Ferruccio Busoni, whose *Sketch of a New Esthetic of Music* appeared in English translation in 1911. Although Busoni followed through few if any of the treatise's ideas in his own music, he advocated a number of radical alternatives to traditional tonality and temperament. He stated that he had established '113 [different] scales (within the octave C–C)' (though he fails to list them) and notes that 'the gradation of the octave is *infinite*', specifically mentioning the 'tripartite tone (third of a tone)'. Additionally, he drew attention to Thaddeus Cahill's dynamophone (*recte* telharmonium), 'a comprehensive apparatus which makes it possible to transform an electric current into a fixed and mathematically exact number of vibrations'.[12] The telharmonium, first exhibited in New York in 1906, was one of the earliest – and conceptually one of the most fantastic – examples of the synthetic music machines imagined in Huxley's *Brave New World*, and provided solutions to many of the problems inherent in the electrical generation of sound. Rather oddly, though, given that it weighed two hundred tons, it disappeared before the First World War and has subsequently been known only by reputation.

Busoni was of partly Italian extraction, and his *Sketch of a New Esthetic of Music* was first published in Trieste (though in German). Clearly, turn-of-the-century Italian music was not limited exclusively to *verismo*, but also contained a boldly radical prospective strain, of which Futurism – which emerged in 1909 – is the best-known and most prominent element. Although it began as a purely literary movement, with the publication in *Le Figaro* of Marinetti's 'Futurist Manifesto', it soon spread to the other arts, notably painting.[13] In music, the results were mixed: Balilla Pratella's 'Manifesto of Futurist Musicians' (1910) is little more than a rant against the musical establishment; Bruno Corra's 'Abstract Cinema – Chromatic Music' (1912) – though concerned mainly with visual effect – contains some Skryabinesque suggestions regarding a 'music of colours'. Paradoxically it was a non-musician, Luigi Russolo, who wrote the highly influential manifesto *The Art of Noises* in 1913 (substantially expanded in 1916), and went on to create both an orchestra of noise instruments – *intonarmori* – and a selection of pieces using them. Sadly, like

12 The quotations appear respectively on pp. 92, 93, and 95 of Ferruccio Busoni, 'Sketch of a New Esthetic of Music', in *Three Classics in the Aesthetic of Music*, New York, 1962, pp. 73–102.

13 The various texts cited here appear in Umbro Apollonio (ed.), *Futurist Manifestos*, London, 1973; see also the complete text of Luigi Russolo, *The Art of Noises* (tr. and ed. Barclay Brown), New York, 1986. Reconstructions and recordings of Futurist and Dada music have been issued on *Futurism and Dada Reviewed* (Sub Rosa Records, 1988).

Cahill's telharmonium, the *ululatori* (howlers), *rombatori* (roarers), *stropicciatori* (rubbers), *gorgoliatori* (gurglers), and other *esotici* have not survived; tantalizingly, they maintain a virtual existence through Russolo's detailed writings, a fragment of the score for *Risveglio di una città* (*The Awakening of a City*, 1913), contemporary concert reports, and even a few photographs. Their impact, though, has been huge: as Barclay Brown notes, 'Russolo anticipated – indeed, he may have precipitated – a whole range of musical and aesthetic notions that formed the basis of much . . . avant-garde thought', including the so-called machine music of the 1920s, the all-sound works of John Cage, the *musique concrète* of Pierre Schaeffer, and graphic notation. Even the frog chorus towards the close of Ravel's *L'enfant et les sortilèges* (1925) was inspired by one of Russolo's instruments.

When Russolo declared that 'We must break out of this limited circle of sounds [i.e. those of conventional music] and conquer the infinite variety of noise-sounds'[14] among those listening attentively were the Dadaists. Although music was not an integral part of Dadaism, the activities of its constituents certainly contributed to the general prospectivist thrust. Noise-music was part of Dada's crazy cabarets; in 1913, Marcel Duchamp had created his *Musical Erratum* by randomly drawing notes from a hat; and in 1924, Tristan Tzara advocated that 'musicians smash [their] instruments'. In the 1917 Erik Satie–Jean Cocteau ballet *Parade*, meanwhile, the original score – in addition to the standard wind, brass, and strings – called for typewriters, sirens, aeroplane propellers, lottery wheels, and other 'noise-instruments', though not all made it into performance. According to Roger Shattuck, 'It was probably Diaghilev himself, then living in Rome and hobnobbing with the futurists, who tossed in the idea of sound effects.'[15]

All of these influences converge in the person of Edgard Varèse, a friend of Russolo, Satie, Picasso, and Cocteau (among a cornucopia of others), and also fully versed in the theories of Futurism, Dadaism, and every other -ism present in pre-war Europe (though he was careful to distance himself from any 'school', especially Futurism). Along with Dane Rudhyar and Leo Ornstein (1892 or 93–2002), Varèse – who travelled to America in late 1915 – was among the first to transmit the latest radical European ideas to the New World. Only three months after he had arrived in New York, Varèse told the *New York Telegraph* and *Morning Telegraph* that 'Our musical alphabet must be enriched . . . We also need new instruments very badly . . . I refuse to submit myself only to sounds that have already been heard. What I am looking for are new technical mediums

14 *The Art of Noises*, p. 25.

15 Roger Shattuck, *The Banquet Years: The Origins of the Avant Garde in France, 1885 to World War I*, rev. edn, New York, 1968, p. 153.

which can lend themselves to every expression of thought.'[16] Although it would be almost half a lifetime before Varèse was able – in *Déserts* (1950–4), *La Procession de Vergès* (1955), and *Le Poème électronique* (1958) – to explore fully the electronic resources he so clearly desired, his works of the 1920s (all of which were premiered in the United States) show him pushing existing acoustic resources to their limits. *Amériques* (1920–1), *Offrandes* (1921), *Hyperprism* (1922–3), *Octandre* (1923), *Intégrales* (1923–5), and *Arcana* (1926–7) are all, to some extent, redolent of the music by Debussy and especially Stravinsky that Varèse had encountered before leaving Europe. But in their titles – which often evoke the world of scientific exploration rather than artistic creation – and more particularly in the degree to which they exploit the noise-world of percussion instruments (*Octandre* is the exception), they mark out new and unique musical territory, suggesting both Russolo's 'Art of Noises' and Cage's later vision of 'the all-sound music of the future'.[17] The opening of *Hyperprism*, though extreme, is not exceptional: trombones and horns – five of the meagre nine wind instruments constituting the work's conventional line-up – gradually elaborate a single melodic line, against a boisterous backcloth of drums, tambourine, cymbals, tamtam, triangle, anvil, slap stick, Chinese blocks, Lion Roar, rattles, sleigh bells, and siren. Varèse – as Morton Feldman memorably put it – 'was one of the legendary performers. His instrument was sonority.'[18]

Varèse's achievement in the 1920s was not limited solely to composition, however. Painfully (and personally) aware of the difficulties faced by composers of new music, he instigated two organizations devoted to the performance of contemporary work: the International Composers' Guild (1921–7) and the Pan American Association of Composers (1928–34). The former – very much under his control – oversaw the premieres of pieces by the Second Viennese School, as well as Americans including Cowell and Ruggles, and Varèse himself. The latter organization – in effect run in Varèse's absence by Cowell, and substantially bankrolled by Charles Ives – introduced to venues throughout the Americas and Europe a complementary roster of works by composers from North, Central, and South America. Cowell's promotional and entrepreneurial activities during this period were by no means restricted to the PAAC: his involvement in the New Music Society of California has already been noted, and this was complemented by his founding in 1927 of *New Music Quarterly* (again supported financially by Ives), whose earliest editions saw into print such

16 Quoted in Fernand Ouellette, *Edgard Varèse*, London, 1973, pp. 46–7.
17 From John Cage, 'The Future of Music: Credo', pp. 3–6.
18 Morton Feldman, 'Predeterminate/Indeterminate', in *Essays* (ed. Walter Zimmermann), Kerpen, 1985, pp. 47–9.

pieces as Ruggles's *Men and Mountains*, Rudhyar's *Paeans*, four of Crawford's Preludes for piano, and the second movement of Ives's Fourth Symphony.

Cowell's own work of the 1910s and 20s was at times remarkably radical. His sometime teacher, Charles Seeger, had encouraged him to examine systematically his use of innovatory compositional techniques, as well as to compose a repertory of works that would explore those selfsame innovations. Among the products of this project were the treatise *New Musical Resources* and the Rhythm–Harmony Quartets (1917–19). *New Musical Resources*, though only published in 1930, had been substantially completed over a decade earlier, and became a fertile source of ideas for such later composers as Conlon Nancarrow (1912–97) and Karlheinz Stockhausen (born 1928).[19] In the Rhythm–Harmony Quartets, meanwhile, Cowell's Helmholtz- and Seeger-inspired identification of the relationship between frequency and rhythm led to some extremely complex cross-rhythms and, accordingly, notation. At its simplest, Cowell's system for the *Quartet Romantic* saw a plain major triad, consisting of the fourth, fifth, and sixth partials of a given fundamental, generate cross-rhythms of 4:5:6; higher partials generated accordingly more complex rhythmic relationships, including – for instance – $1\frac{1}{2}:3:3\frac{3}{4}:5\frac{1}{3}$ and $1\frac{1}{2}:3:4\frac{1}{2}:7\frac{1}{2}$ in bars 162 and 163.

Cowell's achievements were not wholly *ab origine*, however: *New Musical Resources* was heavily influenced by Seeger's ideas (a comparison with Seeger's posthumously published 'Tradition and Experiment in [the New] Music'[20] is instructive) and also drew in its final form on the work of, among others, the Russian experimental musicologists Georgy Rimsky-Korsakov, Nikolai Garbuzov, and Georgii Konius. Cowell's development of tone clusters, meanwhile, was – as Michael Hicks has convincingly demonstrated – heavily indebted to the example of Ornstein.[21] Incidentally, mention of Rimsky-Korsakov, Garbuzov, and Konius serves to remind us that before Stalin's brutal suppression of artistic prospection in the emerging Soviet Union, Russian musicians were as much at the forefront of musical modernism as were their European and American contemporaries, as the music of Nikolay Roslavets and the extraordinary example of *The Foundry* (*Zavod*) (1926–8) by Alexandr Mosolov conclusively demonstrate.

As might be inferred from the preceding paragraph, one dimension of 1920s radicalism not often emphasized is its internationalism: Ornstein, Varèse,

19 Henry Cowell, *New Musical Resources*, with notes and an accompanying essay by David Nicholls, Cambridge, 1996. The Rhythm–Harmony Quartets are published by C. F. Peters Corporation. On Cowell's influence on Nancarrow and Stockhausen, among others, see Kyle Gann, 'Subversive Prophet: Henry Cowell as Theorist and Critic', in David Nicholls (ed.), *The Whole World of Music: A Henry Cowell Symposium*, Amsterdam, 1997, pp. 172–90.

20 Included in Charles Seeger, *Studies in Musicology II: 1929–1979* (ed. Ann M. Pescatello), Berkeley, 1994, pp. 39–266.

21 Michael Hicks, 'Cowell's Clusters', *Musical Quarterly* 77 (1993), pp. 428–58.

theorist Joseph Schillinger (1895–1943), and electronics wizard Lev Termen (Léon Thérémin) (1896–1993), among many others, were temporary or permanent immigrants to America at this time, while Europe was in turn startled in the earlier 1920s by the music of the young American George Antheil. Notable *succès de scandale* of his included the *Airplane Sonata* (1921) and especially the *Ballet mécanique* (1923–5), one version of which – in post-*Parade* fashion – called for anvils, saws, car horns, and aircraft propellers. Another remarkable émigré was the Australian Percy Grainger, whose well-known, tuneful folksong arrangements conceal a wealth of innovative practices, such as his elastic scorings (which must surely have influenced Cowell). Later in his career, Grainger advocated and experimented with what he termed 'free music', which – in Cagean fashion – sought to create music released from 'the tyranny of the performer'. The machines Grainger and his assistant Burnett Cross constructed 'were remarkable devices and would have made Heath Robinson and Roland Emmett envious'; among the names he devised for his creations were 'The Inflated Frog Blower', 'The Crumb-catcher and Drain Protector Disc', and 'The Cross-Grainger Double-decker Kangaroo-pouch Flying Disc Paper Graph Model for Synchronizing and Playing 8 Oscillators'.[22] Clearly, Grainger does not fit comfortably into any of the radical groups outlined above; in this (though for rather different reasons) he resembles another gloriously loose cannon, Charles Ives, most of whose radical ideas were conceived in complete isolation from the cultural world at large. Unencumbered by the restrictions of conventional performers and performance practices – 'My God! What has sound got to do with music!' he once remarked[23] – he could imagine, on the one hand, such systematically formulated works as the *Tone Roads* (1911–15), *Largo Risolutos* (1906), *In Re Con Moto et al.* (1913), and – ultimately – the gigantic Fourth Symphony (*c.*1910–16). On the other hand, there is the protean, protoplasmic, musical substance which (at various times) became temporarily fixed as the notation of parts of the 'Concord' Sonata (1904–15, rev. 1919), *Emerson Transcriptions* (?1917–22), *The Celestial Railroad* (?1925), and – for the last forty or so years of his life – the *Universe Symphony* (principally 1911–28). The grand vision of this last work links it with such other unfinished monuments as Skryabin's *Mysterium*, Schoenberg's *Die Jakobsleiter* (1917–22), and Varèse's *Espace* (*c.*1929–40).[24] A further link between the works by Ives, Skryabin, and Varèse is that, in different ways, they attempted

22 On Grainger and his Free Music, see John Bird, *Percy Grainger*, London, 1982, pp. 230–7, from which the quotations are drawn.

23 Charles Ives, *Essays Before a Sonata and Other Writings* (ed. Howard Boatwright), London, 1969, p. 84.

24 On the connections between these (and some other) works, see Philip Lambert, 'Ives's *Universe*', in Philip Lambert (ed.), *Ives Studies*, Cambridge, 1997, pp. 248–59.

to escape from the spatial and social confines of the conventional concert hall, thus anticipating other developments in the music of the later twentieth century.

After the crash: 'the more stitches, the less riches'

Notwithstanding the temporary retreat to the ivory tower attempted – at Hoffmann's suggestion – by some artists during the nineteenth and early twentieth centuries, music and Mammon have always been uncomfortably but inextricably linked. Consequently, one may easily point to the parallel expansion of musical radicalism and capitalist exploitation during the 1920s, as well as to the perhaps inevitable result of the latter: the worldwide financial collapse of the late 1920s and early 1930s, with all it implied for artistic innovation. Huxley's hypnopaedic aphorism, quoted above, was intended to argue in favour of Fordian wealth creation via the production of new goods (rather than the repair of existing goods): 'Every man, woman and child compelled to consume so much a year. In the interests of industry' (*Brave New World*, p. 44). But the aphorism can also be interpreted in opposite fashion: the more goods are created, the greater the likelihood of over-production and thence economic recession.

Despite this, the effects of the Wall Street Crash were not immediately obvious in the brave new musical worlds that had been created during the 1920s. The PAAC and *New Music* – to name but two organizations – continued to expand their roster of activities during the early 1930s. The former's most impressive achievement was probably the concert given in Paris on 6 June 1931, which included Cowell's *Synchrony*, Ives's new chamber-orchestra version of the *First Orchestral Set*, Ruggles's *Men and Mountains*, and pieces by Amadeo Roldán (1900–39) and Adolph Weiss (1891–1971). *New Music*, meanwhile, prior to Cowell's arrest and imprisonment in 1936, grew from a quarterly edition of new scores to embrace an orchestra series, rental library, and a number of recordings.

The effect of recession was, though, felt more keenly at an individual level. Some composers turned their efforts towards humanitarian issues: Ruth Crawford, for instance, while sustaining the dissonant, heterophonic, ultra-modern facets of her compositional language until 1933 (in such works as the String Quartet (1931) and Three Songs (1930–2)), set two overtly political texts in the *Ricercari* of 1932–3, before moving on to folksong arrangement. Varèse, after composing the highly influential, all-percussion piece *Ionisation* (1931) and the partly electronic *Ecuatorial* (1934), retreated between 1935 and 1947 to a desert both metaphorical and, in part, literal, his only new pieces being *Densité 21.5* for solo flute (1936) and the aforementioned, unfinished *Espace*.[25] Cowell, despite his prospective experiments in the early 1930s with the electronic rhythmicon, devised in collaboration with Lev Termen, turned increasingly to transcultural extraspection. In Europe, meanwhile, Messiaen temporarily rejected the futuristic swoopings of the six ondes martenot he had employed in *Fête des belles eaux* (1937), and returned instead to the comparative safety of voice and piano in *Chants de terre et de ciel* (1938), and organ in *Les Corps Glorieux* (1939). Most tragically of all, back in America, Harry Partch – unable to find institutional or other support for his experiments in monophony and temperament – became between 1935 and 1939 a hobo, an experience detailed in the journal 'Bitter Music'.[26]

Such brave new musical worlds as managed to struggle into existence during the remaining years before the Second World War also tended to subsist on an individual, rather than collective, basis. And significantly, perhaps – *contra* Huxley in *Jesting Pilate* – prospective artistic activity increasingly occurred on America's West Coast, rather than on the East Coast or in Europe. Despite the limitations of his peripatetic lifestyle, Partch – who had returned to the United States in 1935 after spending a period in Europe financed by the Carnegie Corporation – managed to build on his earlier work (not least in the notations included in 'Bitter Music'), and to experience much that would prove useful in later years (notably the material for *Barstow: Eight Hitchhikers' Inscriptions* (first version, 1941) and *U.S. Highball: A Musical Account of Slim's Transcontinental Hobo Trip* (first version, 1943)). Having at the start of the 1930s largely codified the intonational system that underpinned all of his subsequent music – a system that goes way beyond the experiments in microtones found in the works of Alois Hába (1893–1973) and Julián Carrillo (1875–1965) – he could also start to build instruments. These included, before 1940, an adapted viola, an adapted guitar, a kithara, and the Ptolemy – this last a keyboard instrument that one Carnegie Corporation official caricatured as 'not only resembl[ing] an adding machine, but . . . seem[ing also] to be a combination of a typewriter, checkerboard, Mah Jong and chocolate fudge'.[27] (The description is reminiscent of some of Grainger's more elaborate names for his free-music machines – except that it was the instruments' inventor, rather than an unsympathetic bureaucrat,

25 Varèse's literal desert was that of New Mexico. By a curious parallel, New Mexico served as the location of the Savage Reservation to which Bernard Marx takes Lenina Crowne in chapters VI to IX of *Brave New World*. Huxley's knowledge of New Mexico came from his friendship with D. H. Lawrence, who spent his last years there; Huxley himself lived in California's Mojave Desert during much of the Second World War. On Varèse during this period, and *Espace* in particular, see a further literary source: Henry Miller's 'With Edgar [*sic*] Varèse in the Gobi Desert', in *The Air-Conditioned Nightmare*, London, 1973, pp. 109–19.

26 See Harry Partch, *Bitter Music: Collected Journals, Essays, Introductions, and Librettos*, Urbana, 1991, pp. 3–132.

27 See Bob Gilmore, *Harry Partch: A Biography*, New Haven, 1998, p. 114.

who coined the latter.) A further achievement of these years was a sixth version of 'Monophony is Expounded', an early incarnation of the text that eventually became Partch's literary magnum opus, *Genesis of a Music*.[28]

Two of Partch's friends and contemporaries, John Cage and Lou Harrison, meanwhile, relied principally on an amalgam of modern dance and invented instruments to further their prospects. Each had studied with both Henry Cowell and Arnold Schoenberg (the latter having taken up residence on the West Coast in 1934); and each profited in different ways from the unlikely combination of freedom and stricture learnt as a consequence. Cage was the more overtly bold of the two. Impressed by Varèse's *Ionisation* and intrigued by Oskar Fischinger's suggestion that every object possesses an audible spirit waiting to be freed, he experimented with a plethora of percussive forces, variously drawn from the orchestral battery, the household, the junkyard, and from other cultures. Having realized early on in his studies with Schoenberg that he had no feeling for harmony, Cage sought a method of structuring music based instead on duration. In this he was aided by his work with dancers (who used 'counts' to measure out their movements) and by his knowledge of Cowell's recent music (in which – notably in the *United Quartet* of 1936 and *Pulse* of 1939 – Cowell had built extended forms from simple mathematical formulae).

These tendencies coalesced in the 1939 *First Construction (in Metal)*, which sports a durational micro-/macrocosmic 'square-root form', based in the proportions 4:3:2:3:4, and whose six percussionists play such instruments as orchestral bells, Turkish cymbals, anvils, oxen bells, cowbells, thundersheets, brake drums, water gong, Japanese temple gongs, and Chinese cymbals. Cage's personal vision of a brave new world – in many ways an accurate prophecy of his future direction as a composer – is elegantly summarized in 'The Future of Music: Credo', probably written in 1940, quoted in part at the head of this chapter, and as different as could be imagined from Huxley's populist, mass-consumption vision of 'the latest synthetic music' (*Brave New World*, p. 67). Drawing heavily on both Russolo's *The Art of Noises* and the recently published book *Toward a New Music* by Mexican composer Carlos Chávez, Cage's manifesto proposed, *inter alia*, a desire to use all available sounds in musical composition, the anticipation of – and search for – electronic instruments and music, and the establishing of new methods of notation and of organizing sounds.

Cage's other main innovation of this period lay in his development – again much influenced by Cowell's work, notably in such pieces as *A Composition* and

28 Harry Partch, *Genesis of a Music*, 1st edn, Madison, 1949; 2nd edn, enlarged, New York, 1974.

The Banshee (both 1925) – of the prepared piano, in which mutes of various kinds are placed between the strings of the piano, fundamentally altering its timbres. Among his better-known prepared-piano works are the short dance score *Bacchanale* (1940) and the extended concert work *Sonatas and Interludes* (1946–8). Cage also employed proto-electronic sounds, in an attempt to create 'a music produced through the aid of electrical instruments'.[29] For instance, he uses variable-speed turntables and frequency-tone recordings in *Imaginary Landscape no. 1* (1939), and oscillators, a recording of a generator, a buzzer, an amplified coil of wire, and other paraphernalia in *Imaginary Landscape no. 3* (1942), as well as radios in *Credo in Us* (1942). One consequence (possibly unforeseen, but nonetheless profound) of Cage's writing for such unconventional forces as percussion, prepared piano, and proto-electronic instruments was a loosening of the traditional ties between notation, execution, and perception: the sound produced by – say – a middle C prepared with a bolt or eraser is quite different to that implied by its notation.

Harrison's work of the 1930s paralleled that of Cage: he wrote for percussion – for instance in the *Fifth Simfony* (1939), *Canticle #1* (1940), and *Song of Quetzalcoatl* (1941) – and later similarly altered the sound of the piano, in his case by inserting thumb tacks into its hammers, creating the 'faux harpsichord' tack piano. Further variation on traditional keyboard practice is found in the work of Conlon Nancarrow who, catching sight of a throwaway remark in Cowell's *New Musical Resources* – which noted that 'these highly engrossing rhythmical complexes could easily be cut on a player-piano roll'[30] – devoted much of his mature compositional life to an increasingly complex series of studies for that very same instrument.

Epilogue: Brave New Worlds revisited

In *Brave New World Revisited* (1958), Aldous Huxley – in David Bradshaw's words – 'surveyed contemporary society in the light of his earlier predictions' (*Brave New World*, p. xiii). Significantly, although Huxley discusses such issues as overpopulation, propaganda (in both democracies and dictatorships), persuasion (both chemical and subconscious), and brainwashing, he says nothing about culture in general or music in particular. In *Brave New World*, the World Controllers had made the choice between 'happiness and what people used to call high art. We've sacrificed the high art. We have the feelies and the scent organ instead' (p. 201). But by 1958, Huxley must have realised that his vision of a culture reduced to the lowest common denominator – the 'all-super-singing,

29 'The Future of Music: Credo', lines 17–18. 30 Cowell, *New Musical Resources*, pp. 64–5.

synthetic-talking, coloured, stereoscopic feely. With synchronized scent-organ accompaniment' (*Brave New World*, p. 151) – had been unequivocally refuted by reality. Indeed, far from high-art music having been sacrificed for the common good, Cage and his colleagues in the so-called New York School had moved firmly in the direction of indeterminacy, and the international avant-garde was alive and kicking quite viciously.

However, the legacy of prospective radicalism was by no means completely incompatible with Huxley's original dystopian vision. Towards the conclusion of *Brave New World*, Huxley's anti-hero, Helmholtz Watson, is voluntarily exiled to the Falkland Islands, believing that 'one would write better if the climate were bad. If there were a lot of wind and storms, for example . . .' (p. 209). Differences in climate and location notwithstanding, Watson's Falklands might well be equated with the New Mexico desert of Lawrence, Varèse, and *Brave New World*'s Savage, as well as with Huxley's own Mojave Desert and Pala – the fictional Pacific utopia which is the subject of his last novel, *Island* (1962). For all of these remote places stand, with marvellous irony, as metaphors for the 'unknown land, more glorious and more beautiful than . . . our constricted world' of which E. T. A. Hoffmann wrote in 1813.[31] Radical prospection may have been born in the objective scientific scrutiny of Hermann von Helmholtz, but it seemed able to flourish only in the isolated, Romantic, utopian self-indulgence craved by his fictional namesake, Helmholtz Watson.

Thus the grand vision of Ives's *Universe Symphony* is rooted in cyclic pitch structures, chord-scale systems, and durational counterpoint, yet was composed in complete isolation, and intended for performance 'in valleys, on hillsides, and on mountain tops'.[32] In *Espace*, Varèse wished to compose 'rhythms in space as well as rhythms in time' and to break 'our present chromatic scale of halftones . . . into almost infinite gradations of vibration'. The project was largely conceived during the composer's 'desert' period, yet he 'imagined a performance of the work being broadcast simultaneously in and from all the capitals of the world . . . All men could have listened simultaneously to this song of brotherhood and liberation.'[33] Harry Partch's Helmholtz-inspired study of temperament led to him devising a tuning system based on a forty-three-fold division of the octave, and to him creating instruments capable of playing in such a system. But his Beethovenian cussedness and stubbornness were major factors in his inability to attract institutional support; and in his final vision

31 Hoffmann, 'Beethoven's Instrumental Music', p. 1198.

32 For details of the sketches of the *Universe Symphony*, and their realisation, see Larry Austin, 'The Realization and First Complete Performances of Ives's *Universe Symphony*', in Lambert (ed.), *Ives Studies*, pp. 179–232. For its intended performance venue, see Henry Cowell and Sydney Cowell, *Charles Ives and his Music*, New York, 1955, p. 201.

33 Quotations extracted from Ouellette, *Edgard Varèse*, pp. 132–3.

of corporeality – a performance practice in which 'sight and sound, the visually dynamic and dramatic, [are] all channelled into a single, wholly fused, and purposeful direction' – Partch created not only a hermetically sealed aesthetic world (a kind of Pala) inaccessible to any but its initiates and inhabitants but also, rather curiously, a synæsthetic experience not dissimilar to that of Huxley's Sixteen Sexophonists. More recently, a parallel to Partch's situation is found in the work of La Monte Young, with its just intonation, its specialized performers (The Theatre of Eternal Music), and its specially created utopian performance spaces, the Dream Houses.[34]

Huxley took the title of his most famous book from a line spoken towards the end of Shakespeare's most dazzling and magical play, *The Tempest* (1611). The enchanted island on which *The Tempest* is set 'lies literally in the Mediterranean between Tunis and Naples'[35] but has often been equated with the New World that, in the early seventeenth century, was being explored and colonized by both England and several other European powers. The Neapolitan travellers who are shipwrecked on Shakespeare's 'desert' island, 'Uninhabitable and almost inaccessible –'[36] encounter its current inhabitants: 'two Milanese castaways (Prospero and Miranda), two remarkable natives (Caliban and Ariel) and assorted spirits unlike anything [they] . . . have ever seen'.[37] Prospero, the deposed Duke of Milan, is a magician; indeed, the storm that opens the play is one of his illusions, and it is his magic that controls much of the subsequent action. One of the travellers, Gonzalo, later asserts that all of the Neapolitans have 'found' themselves during their time on the island;[38] and while this may seem 'overtly optimistic . . . he correctly judges that most of them [have been] radically changed by the experience'.[39] Prospero himself, meanwhile, finally vows to relinquish his magical powers, in order that he may better manage his imminent role as restored Duke of Milan.

So, perhaps, it may be that the ultimate fate of artistic visionaries such as Luigi Russolo, Charles Ives, Edgard Varèse, and Harry Partch, is temporary or permanent exile to some barren place, some *Island*, either literal or metaphorical, in the Old World or the New, where – like Prospero – they can practise in splendid isolation their particular form of magic. We, like the Neapolitan

34 For a summary of these aspects of the work of Partch and Young, see David Nicholls, 'Transethnicism and the American Experimental Tradition', *Musical Quarterly* 80/4 (1996), pp. 569–94. The Partch quotation is drawn from 'Statement' (regarding *And on the Seventh Day Petals Fell in Petaluma*), reproduced in Thomas McGeary, *The Music of Harry Partch: A Descriptive Catalog*, Brooklyn, 1991, pp. 17–18.

35 For extensive commentary on this and other aspects of the play, see Virginia Mason Vaughan and Alden T. Vaughan, 'Introduction' to William Shakespeare, *The Tempest* [The Arden Shakespeare, Third Series], Walton-on-Thames, 1999, pp. 1–138. The present quotation appears on p. 4.

36 *The Tempest*, II.i. 37. 37 *The Tempest*, 'Introduction', p. 5.

38 *The Tempest*, V.i. 208–13. 39 *The Tempest*, 'Introduction', p. 5.

travellers, come by chance (or is it design?) into contact with their work, and – both individually and collectively – are changed as a result. Whether (and in what circumstances) our latter-day Prosperos choose to relinquish their powers, and forgo their exile, in exchange for worldly success is, of course, another matter entirely. But regardless of the length of the exile, we can still marvel at its results, and – like Prospero's daughter Miranda – proclaim

> O wonder!
> How many goodly creatures are there here!
> How beauteous mankind is! O brave new world
> That has such people in't.
> (*The Tempest*, V.i.181–4)

Bibliography

Apollonio, Umbro (ed.). *Futurist Manifestos*, London, 1973.

Austin, Larry. 'The Realization and First Complete Performances of Ives's *Universe Symphony*', in Philip Lambert (ed.), *Ives Studies*, Cambridge, 1997, pp. 179–232.

Bird, John. *Percy Grainger*, London, 1982.

Bowers, Faubion. *The New Scriabin*, London, 1974.

Bradshaw, David. 'Introduction' to Aldous Huxley, *Brave New World*, London, 1994.

Bujić, Bojan (ed.). *Music in European Thought, 1851–1912*, Cambridge, 1988.

Busoni, Ferruccio. 'Sketch of a New Esthetic of Music', in *Three Classics in the Aesthetic of Music*, New York, 1962, pp. 73–102.

Cage, John. *Silence*, London, 1968.

Cowell, Henry. *New Musical Resources*, with notes and an accompanying essay by David Nicholls, Cambridge, 1996.

Cowell, Henry and Sidney Cowell. *Charles Ives and his Music*, New York, 1955.

Feldman, Morton. 'Predeterminate / Indeterminate', in *Essays* (ed. Walter Zimmermann), Kerpen, 1985, pp. 47–9.

Gann, Kyle. 'Subversive Prophet: Henry Cowell as Theorist and Critic', in David Nicholls (ed.), *The Whole World of Music: A Henry Cowell Symposium*, Amsterdam, 1997, pp. 171–222.

Gilmore, Bob. *Harry Partch: A Biography*, New Haven, 1998.

Helmholtz, Hermann von. *The Sensations of Tone* (tr. Alexander J. Ellis), 3rd edn, London, 1895.

Hicks, Michael. 'Cowell's Clusters', *Musical Quarterly* 77/3 (1993), p. 77, pp. 428–58.

Huxley, Aldous. *Brave New World*, London, 1994.

Brave New World Revisited, London, 1994.

Jesting Pilate: The Diary of a Journey, London, 1940.

Ives, Charles. *Essays Before a Sonata and Other Writings* (ed. Howard Boatwright), London, 1969.

Johnson, Steven. 'Henry Cowell, John Varian, and Halcyon', *American Music* 11/1 (1993), pp. 1–27.

Lambert, Philip. 'Ives's *Universe*', in Philip Lambert (ed.), *Ives Studies*, Cambridge, 1997, pp. 233–59.

McGeary, Thomas. *The Music of Harry Partch: A Descriptive Catalog*, Brooklyn, 1991.
Miller, Henry. *The Air-Conditioned Nightmare*, London, 1973.
Nicholls, David. 'Transethnicism and the American Experimental Tradition', *Musical Quarterly* 80/4 (1996), pp. 569–94.
Ouellette, Fernand. *Edgard Varèse*, London, 1973.
Partch, Harry. *Bitter Music: Collected Journals, Essays, Introductions, and Librettos*, Urbana, 1991.
Genesis of a Music, 1st edn, Madison, 1949; 2nd edn, enlarged, New York, 1974.
Russolo, Luigi. *The Art of Noises* (tr. and ed. Barclay Brown), New York, 1986.
Seeger, Charles. *Studies in Musicology II: 1929–1979* (ed. Ann M. Pescatello), Berkeley, 1994.
Shattuck, Roger. *The Banquet Years: The Origins of the Avant Garde in France, 1885 to World War I*, rev. edn, New York, 1968.
Strunk, Oliver (ed.). *Source Readings in Music History*, rev. edn, New York, 1998.
Vaughan, Virginia Mason and Alden T. Vaughan. 'Introduction' to William Shakespeare, *The Tempest* [The Arden Shakespeare, third series], Walton-on-Thames, 1999, pp. 1–138.

· 9 ·

Proclaiming the mainstream: Schoenberg, Berg, and Webern

JOSEPH AUNER

Of all the new musical developments in the years following the First World War, none has been entangled in more controversy than the claim made by Arnold Schoenberg, Anton Webern, and Alban Berg that their music, and 'the method of composing with twelve tones related only to one another' on which much of it was based (otherwise known as serialism), represented the culmination of the mainstream of the Austro-German tradition and thus, by implication, of the mainstream of music in general. All three composers maintained that theirs was the one true path, and drew on historical, national, and even metaphysical arguments to justify their claims. Schoenberg's 'National Music' (1931) traced his lineage from Bach and Mozart, through Beethoven, Wagner, and Brahms, concluding, 'I venture to credit myself with having written truly new music, which being based on tradition, is destined to become tradition'.[1] In a series of lectures from 1932–3, Webern pushed the origins of 'The Path to Twelve-Tone Composition' back past the Netherlanders all the way to Gregorian chant; insisting on the historical inevitability and necessity of twelve-tone composition, he charted a progression from the breakdown of the system of the church modes, through to Wagner's chromatic harmony, the end of tonality, and finally to twelve-tone composition, writing, 'It's my belief that ever since music has been written, all the great composers have instinctively had this before them as a goal.'[2] And in the essay 'Why is Schoenberg's Music so Difficult to Understand?', published in 1924 in celebration of his teacher's fiftieth birthday, Berg not only insisted on Schoenberg's pre-eminent place among contemporary composers and his status as 'classic', but laid claim to the future as well: by 'drawing the farthest conclusions' from 'all the compositional possibilities provided by centuries of music', Schoenberg had ensured 'not only the predominance of his personal art, but what is more that of German music for the next fifty years'.[3]

1 Arnold Schoenberg, 'National Music', in *Style and Idea: Selected Writings of Arnold Schoenberg* (ed. Leonard Stein, tr. Leo Black), Berkeley, 1984, p. 174.

2 Anton Webern, *The Path to the New Music* (ed. Willi Reich, tr. Leo Black), Vienna, 1975, p. 42.

3 Alban Berg, 'Why is Schoenberg's Music so Difficult to Understand?', in Willi Reich, *Alban Berg* (tr. Comelius Cardew), New York, 1905, pp. 189–204; pp. 202, 204.

Yet the vehemence of such assertions is a clear sign of the intensity of the opposition they expected, and indeed received, from all sides. Claims to the mainstream are by their very nature implicated in counter-claims of marginalization. And for Schoenberg, Berg, and Webern, these efforts to marginalize them came from many different directions. To the relatively small circles of listeners who had actually heard their music, as well as to the considerably larger numbers who knew them only by reputation, Schoenberg and his school had become associated with the most extreme radicalism and hypermodernity. Through their writings, well-publicized concert scandals, and the first performances in the 1920s of many of their 'expressionistic' works, the three had come to represent a rejection of the past and a deliberate spurning of the audience. Hans Mersmann in his 1928 history of modern music brands Schoenberg as 'the single greatest revolutionary in music of our time . . . he breaks all boundaries, destroys all that music previously affirmed'.[4] But to many composers of the younger generation and the critics who championed them, Schoenberg, Berg, and Webern appeared outmoded and out of step with the 'New Music'. In contrast to composers like Weill, Eisler, Krenek, Hindemith, Milhaud, and Stravinsky, and with all the associated slogans and catch phrases that were emerging, such as neoclassicism, *Neue Sachlicheit* [new objectivity], and *Gebrauchsmusik* [music for use], it was easy to portray the Viennese triumvirate as distant indeed from the mainstream. Perhaps most strikingly, this expulsion to the margins was often self-inflicted. In a newspaper notice from February 1933 concerning his lecture on 'New Music, Outmoded Music, Style and Idea', Schoenberg remarks: 'I stand, with my pupils Berg and Webern, alone in the world. The younger generation of composers, who should regard me as their forerunner, have stopped at nothing to fight against me and my music and have done their utmost to free themselves from me.'[5]

If Schoenberg's, Berg's, and Webern's claims to the mainstream were controversial when they were initially made, how much more problematic they appear from the perspective of our own *fin de siècle*! The extreme passions their music and writings have provoked in partisans and detractors have only intensified in the hundred years since the first performances of their works. In order to evaluate such claims and counterclaims in the midst of so much contradictory evidence, a crucial first step is to examine our understanding of the idea of a musical 'mainstream'. This is particularly important from present perspectives when the whole notion of a mainstream, together with its corollary master

4 Hans Mersmann, *Moderne Musik seit der Romantik*, Potsdam, 1928, p. 132 (author's translation).
5 'Arnold Schönberg, der Kürzlich in Wien einen Vortrag hielt . . .', *Bohemia*, Berlin, 18 February 1923 (author's translation).

narratives of the canon, universal values, and progress, have been significantly undercut epistemologically, as well as by simple observation of the diversity of the current musical scene:[6] do we locate the mainstream in continuities of musical style, through subsequent compositional developments, by statistical studies of performances and publications, or in the discourses of institutional power and influence? The way in which we define the musical mainstream thus determines the kinds of material and evidence we will consider, and accordingly will have a profound impact on our conclusions. Through his focus on the development of compositional techniques, and on the continuities of forms and genres, Donald Tovey's 1938 essay, 'The Main Stream of Music', can serve as an example of what has arguably become the dominant way of defining the term in historical and theoretical studies. Tovey's notion of the mainstream insisted on the timeless quality of the masterworks that made it up, which he reluctantly acknowledged were primarily German: 'musical history is full of warnings against facile attempts to trace the qualities of music to the non-musical history of the time. The musical composer is the most detached of all artists.'[7]

Questions of compositional technique and musical structure are, of course, central to how the composers of the Second Viennese School defined their own relationship to tradition and to how they have been viewed by others. But such structural concerns need to be seen in counterpoint with the full range of their activities, including their writings, teaching, involvement with performance, institutional affiliations, and interactions with contemporary developments.[8] That these aspects have tended to be de-emphasized can be attributed to one of the founding myths of modernism, namely its opposition to mainstream culture and society:[9] Theodor Adorno, who is responsible for the most influential account of the Second Viennese School, made their isolation a measure of the ultimate authenticity of their music.[10] Moreover, such isolation was not only acknowledged by Schoenberg and his pupils, but was at times even embraced. In an unpublished note from 1928 entitled 'Alone at last', Schoenberg described his shame, guilt, and depression when he had found himself in the years after the war, 'suddenly surrounded, hemmed in, besieged, by a circle of admirers

6 Robert Morgan, 'Rethinking Musical Culture: Canonic Reformulations in a Post-Tonal Age', in Katherine Bergeron and Philip V. Bohlman (eds.), *Disciplining Music: Musicology and its Canons*, Chicago and London, 1992, pp. 44–64.

7 Donald Tovey, *The Main Stream of Music and Other Essays*, Cleveland, 1964, p. 347.

8 See Martin Thrun, *Neue Musik im Deutschen Musikleben bis 1933*, Band 75: 'Der Orpheus – Schriftenreihe zu Grundfragen der Musik', ed. Martin Vogel, 2 vols., Bonn, 1995.

9 Andreas Huyssen, *After the Great Divide: Modernism, Mass Culture, Postmodernism*, Bloomington, 1986, pp. 53–4.

10 Max Paddison, *Adorno's Aesthetics of Music*, Cambridge, 1993, p. 105.

I had not earned'. Now that they were gone, having fallen away 'like rotten fruit', he rejoiced in his solitude – 'Finally alone again!'[11]

Yet rather than accepting such a statement as reflecting the reality of the situation for Schoenberg, Berg, and Webern in the 1920s and 30s, it should be viewed much more as a strategic act. Ultimately, there is little to be gained by attempting to resolve the question of their relationship to the mainstream, since this will be renegotiated retrospectively by each generation. Instead the focus here will be to consider why and how the tension between the mainstream and the margin became such a central part of the identity of Schoenberg and his school. This chapter will argue that their desire simultaneously to seize the mainstream and challenge it was a powerfully productive force for each of the composers, evident in every aspect of their works, writings, and institutional roles. Such a dialectical stance is evident in the familiar formulations of Schoenberg as the 'conservative revolutionary', and in the competing figures of Moses and Aron from his 1930–2 opera – with the isolated Moses as keeper of the incommunicable truth and Aron dominated by the urge to be understood. A public engagement with history and tradition provided not only legitimation and material, but also means for demonstrating the degree to which they had opened up new territory. But just as importantly, this inherently critical, dialectical stance towards the mainstream allowed them to engage productively with contemporary aesthetic and cultural developments, new technologies, and new audiences, while preserving their purported isolation. Thus through the act of proclaiming the mainstream their music continually evolved and expanded, while the very notion of the mainstream was contested and redefined.[12]

Institutions and performances

On 21 June 1932 a concert took place in the main hall of the Musikverein in Vienna that almost seems to have been designed to illustrate the many facets of Schoenberg's, Berg's, and Webern's complex relationship to the mainstream. The concert included two works by Schoenberg, the early tonal chorus *Friede auf Erden* (Peace on Earth), op. 13, and his recently completed film music for an imaginary film, *Begleitungsmusik zu einer Lichtspielszene* (Accompaniment

11 Arnold Schoenberg, 'Alone at Last!' [Endlich allein!], 4 February 1928, Arnold Schoenberg Centre, Vienna; published by permission of Lawrence Schoenberg. See also Schoenberg, 'How One Becomes Lonely', in *Style and Idea*, pp. 52–3.

12 For further discussion of the twelve-tone method and aesthetic developments in the music of Schoenberg, Berg, and Webern, see Robert Morgan, *Twentieth-Century Music: A History of Musical Style in Modern Europe and America*, New York, 1991, pp. 187–219.

to a Film Scene), op. 34; the Viennese premiere of Berg's concert aria, *Der Wein*, featuring the soprano Ruzena Herlinger; and Mahler's Second Symphony. In the light of present-day perceptions of their elitism, it is noteworthy that the event was part of a series of Workers' Symphony Concerts, and featured Anton Webern conducting the Vienna Symphony Orchestra, together with two choral groups (including the workers' chorus Freie Typographia). But virtually every aspect of the event is equally striking in the degree to which it challenges common perceptions of their position in the musical life of the time.

The first thing to note is the fact of the performance itself. Although music by Schoenberg, Berg, and Webern undoubtedly occupied a minority position on the concert stages during these years, as it does today, their works were widely performed and they themselves were active in speaking and writing about music to ever-broader audiences. All three were very involved with various performing and educational institutions, and worked with many of the most prominent performers and conductors of the day. Of course, to establish the fact that their works did receive many performances during these years does not constitute a measure of their success. It is undeniable that many performances of works by Schoenberg, Berg, and Webern were met with incomprehension and even hostility. But at the same time, it is clear that the prevailing view of their isolation has caused us to overlook the considerable number of successes they had as well. A review of the Workers' Symphony Concert that appeared in a Dresden newspaper was generally very complimentary about the pieces, Webern's conducting, and what the concert represented for the musical life. Of *Friede auf Erden*, the critic Otto Janowitz wrote that it was 'simply a beautiful work', while the film music was 'interesting, coloristically and musically'. Although he had some reservations about Berg's piece, he calls him 'the aristocrat of the school', and comments on the 'unusual manner and depth' of his creativity.[13]

That each of them had had to travel a considerable distance to reach their new positions of authority is undoubtedly a major reason for their vigour in proclaiming the mainstream. Indeed a defining characteristic of the Weimar period in general was the 'outsider as insider', marked by the sudden prominence of those formerly on the fringes of political, cultural, and social life: accordingly, in taking such public roles they sought to preserve an oppositional stance towards these institutions and organizations. The same productive tension and ambivalence characterized Schoenberg, Berg, and Webern's position

13 Otto Janowitz, 'Im Arbeiter-Sinfoniekonzert hörte man . . .', *Dresdener Neueste Nachrichten*, 18 February 1923, Steinger Sammlung, Berlin.

in relation to the mainstream. For example, the June 1932 concert was held in celebration of the tenth Festival of the International Society of Contemporary Music, which was going on at the same time;[14] both Berg and Webern had held important posts in the ISCM, and at the time of the concert Webern was the president of the Vienna section. The concert, however, was not officially connected to the ISCM festival, since Schoenberg had prohibited his works from being performed at ISCM concerts after being offended by an incident at the Venice festival in 1925; according to Stuckenschmidt, when Schoenberg had overrun his rehearsal time for the *Serenade*, op. 24, he was asked by Edward Dent, the President of the ISCM, 'if he thought he was the only composer in this festival. Schoenberg said yes.'[15]

Their formation of the Society for Private Musical Performances (Verein für musikalische Privataufführungen) is perhaps the best example of the complexity of Schoenberg, Berg, and Webern's relationship to the public sphere. Between 1919 and 1921 the Society presented over a hundred concerts, the result of enormous expenditures of energy by all three composers.[16] In an attempt to challenge the power of critics, to eliminate the 'corrupting influence of publicity', and to avoid the disruptions that had accompanied many performances, programmes were not announced in advance, only members were admitted, and any expressions of approval or disapproval were banned. As a result, the Society is often seen as a rejection of the mainstream and a precursor of a self-enforced withdrawal of new music to the academy after the Second World War. But the larger purpose of the society was to reform concert life and ultimately increase the audience for modern music. And in this pedagogic aim Schoenberg, Berg, and Webern were continuing efforts with which Schoenberg had been involved as early as 1904 with the Society of Creative Musicians, which proclaimed as its purpose 'to create such a direct relationship between itself and the public; to give modern music a permanent home in Vienna, where it will be fostered; and to keep the public constantly informed about the current state of musical composition'.[17]

The emphasis on extensive rehearsal and frequent repetitions of works resulting in a high level of performance for the musicians together with a greater familiarity with the works for the audience were the central aims of the later Society. Thus while the number of people who were officially involved with the Society was small, about 320 members in 1919, the ultimate impact through

14 Programmes for the other concerts, dated June 16, 17, 20, 21, are given in Nicolas Slonimsky, *Music Since 1900*, 5th edn, New York, 1994, pp. 347–8.

15 Hans and Rosaleen Moldenhauer, *Anton von Webern: A Chronicle of His Life and Work*, New York, 1979, p. 370; Hans Stuckenschmidt, *Schoenberg: His Life, World, and Work*, New York, 1978, pp. 308–9.

16 Joan Allen Smith, *Schoenberg and His Circle: A Viennese Portrait*, New York, 1986, pp. 81–102.

17 Willi Reich, *Schoenberg: A Critical Biography* (tr. Leo Black), New York, 1971, p. 19.

the composers involved, and just as importantly through performers such as Rudolf Serkin, Rudolf Kolisch, and Eduard Steuermann, has been considerable. The approach to performance practice established at the Verein is accordingly a significant aspect of the Second Viennese School's attempt to redefine the mainstream. The reduction of the social dimension of the concert experience, the emphasis on structure over surface appearance (a central motivation for the use of chamber-music reductions of orchestral works), and the notion that performance practice must adapt to present-day circumstances and musical developments, were all important parts of this legacy. In an unpublished essay entitled 'Styles of Musical Interpretation', Steuermann describes interpretation as an ongoing process shaped by the performer's cultural milieu. He accordingly places great emphasis on a commitment to contemporary music, both for its own value and as a means of better understanding the past: 'the true immersion in the music of the present brings us closer to past epochs.' Echoing Schoenberg's remarks about the relationship of style and idea, he writes: 'For the modern artist there is only modern music! It becomes music only if it is modern music. The performing artist exists to be a mirror, a circuit, a microphone, a transformer, so as to establish contact between eternity and the living moment.'[18]

At this time Schoenberg was living in the Viennese suburb of Mödling, where he also taught privately; his only institutional affiliation from these years was with a school run by the progressive educator Eugenie Schwarzwald, where he offered a seminar in composition in 1917. His situation changed dramatically at the end of 1925, when he was offered the directorship of a masterclass in composition as Busoni's successor at the Prussian Academy of the Arts in Berlin. The move coincided with a period of considerable compositional productivity, a very large number of writings, and many important performances throughout Europe and in the United States. Schoenberg himself conducted many concerts, and others were presented by figures such as Furtwängler and Scherchen; the *Accompaniment to a Film Scene*, for example, was premiered under Otto Klemperer on 6 November 1930 in a symphony concert at the Kroll Opera in Berlin.

Significantly, this performance was preceded a few months earlier by a radio broadcast with the Frankfurt Symphony under the direction of Hans Rosbaud. Although he had reservations about the technical limitations of the new medium, as well as concerns about how it would transform the act of listening, Schoenberg saw the radio as an ideal means for bypassing the critics and

18 Clara Steuermann, David Porter, and Gunther Schuller (eds.), *The Not Quite Innocent Bystander: Writings of Eduard Steuermann*, Lincoln, 1989, pp. 91–2, 117.

musical experts to reach listeners directly;[19] he used the radio for broadcasts of his works, and for lectures aimed at helping listeners understand his music. That such efforts had an impact is clear in a review of a broadcast lecture on the Variations for Orchestra, op. 31, from 22 March 1931, prior to a concert performance under Rosbaud:

> On Sunday morning it was not just any musician – not even just one of the most famous composers – but Arnold Schoenberg who, in the Frankfurt station of Southeast Radio and South Radio, allowed us to take a deep look into his workshop, into the ways and principles of his work. The most influential stimulus in the new music movement, the first master of a compositional method emancipated from the tonal system and the principles of construction of the classic-romantic era, explained and analyzed in rough outlines his Variations on his own theme for orchestra.[20]

Berg's fortunes also changed dramatically after the war. The success of *Wozzeck* marked the major turning point in his career. After an extended period of composition, he had completed the opera in 1922, and published the piano score at his own expense the next year. Following the successful performance in 1924 of the concert suite *Drei Bruchstücke aus 'Wozzeck'*, in Frankfurt under Scherchen, Erich Kleiber conducted the premiere at the Berlin Staatsoper at the end of 1925; despite the controversies that surrounded the performance, it was revived for a second season in Berlin, and then staged in many opera houses throughout Europe and beyond. Webern's professional life, too, got on firmer footing in the 1920s through a publication arrangement with Universal Edition (starting in 1920) and more regular conducting positions in Vienna, including the Workers' Symphony Orchestra and Vienna Workers' Chorus (1922–34). Webern conducted his first concert for the Austrian radio in 1927, and thereafter conducted twenty radio concerts over the next eight years. Performances of his works also became more frequent in Europe and abroad: for example, the Symphony, op. 21 was premiered on 18 December 1929 in New York at a League of Composers concert, and was again performed at the ninth ISCM festival in Oxford, included in a concert with Gershwin's *An American in Paris*. On 13 April 1931 the first all-Webern concert took place, featuring performances of tonal, atonal, and twelve-tone works by the Kolisch Quartet and Eduard Steuermann, and shortly after this event Webern was awarded the Music Prize of the City of Vienna.[21]

19 See Christopher Hailey, 'Rethinking Sound: Music and Radio in Weimar Germany', in Bryan Gilliam (ed.), *Music and Performance During the Weimar Republic*, Cambridge, 1994, pp. 13–36.

20 Cited in Joseph Auner, 'Arnold Schoenberg Speaks: Newspaper Accounts of His Lectures and Interviews, 1927–1933', in Walter Frisch (ed.), *Schoenberg and His World*, Princeton, 1999, pp. 265–82; p. 276.

21 Biographical information on Webern from Anne Shreffler, 'Anton Webern', in Bryan Simms (ed.), *Schoenberg, Berg, Webern: A Companion to the Second Viennese School*, Westport, 1999, pp. 251–314, and Bailey, *The Life of Webern*, Cambridge, 1998.

The idea of the Second Viennese School, tradition, and contemporary developments

That the 1932 Workers' Symphony Concert brought Schoenberg together with his two most famous students is not coincidental but reflects the fundamental part that teaching played in defining and perpetuating the mainstream. Berg and Webern also had important pupils, but it was Schoenberg's role as a teacher in Vienna, Berlin, and later in the United States that became an integral part of the public identity of the group. In addition to his direct involvement with a large number of students, Schoenberg also published extensively on all aspects of music, and still more of his teaching materials have been published posthumously. Over the course of his life, Schoenberg had contact with hundreds of students, among them many figures who have had a significant impact on the composition, criticism, and performance of music in the twentieth century. But in the 1920s and 30s the focus was increasingly on Berg and Webern, and it was as a group of three composers that the Second Viennese School took shape.[22]

The formation of the Second Viennese School became central to their mainstream claims and had significant ramifications for how they positioned themselves in reference to the Austro-German tradition as well as to contemporary trends. Many factors contributed to the deserved reputation of Berg and Webern as the most important students, including their compositional achievements, their prominent roles in the Society for Private Musical Performances, and their adoption of the twelve-tone technique. It is no coincidence that the limitation to three and the emphasis on Vienna allowed for clearer connections to the earlier Viennese school of Mozart, Haydn, and Beethoven. Analogies with the First Viennese School became increasingly common in writings about Schoenberg, Berg, and Webern: for example Adolph Weiss's essay on 'The Twelve-Tone Series', from the 1937 collection *Schoenberg*, compares the different approaches to the twelve-tone system by the three composers to the way in which 'Beethoven, Mozart, Haydn and others used practically the same harmonic formulae, those of the diatonic system.'[23] And the appeal to tradition became a central part of the group's identity. Numerous examples could be cited from the writings of all three composers in the inter-war years challenging the radical label and arguing for their connections to the past. This strategy took many forms, such as Berg's guide to *Pelleas und Melisande* (1920) which demonstrated how Schoenberg preserved a classical approach to form, or his

22 See Joseph Auner, 'The Idea of the Second Viennese School', in Simms (ed.), *Schoenberg, Berg, Webern*, pp. 1–36.

23 Adolph Weiss, 'The Twelve-Tone Series', in Merle Armitage (ed.), *Schoenberg*, New York, 1937, pp. 76–7.

'Credo', published in 1930, which compares Schoenberg's historical position to Bach's.[24]

This turn to the past arose from many sources. All three composers were deeply engaged with the music of the Austro-German tradition, as I will discuss further below, and their music similarly is fundamentally shaped by a profound interaction with this musical tradition. The renewed interest in traditional forms and genres as a means of ensuring comprehensibility reflected pronounced shifts in their own compositional aesthetics. Their image as isolated radicals came increasingly into conflict with the realities of their professional successes and ties to the musical establishment. But at the same time the evocation of tradition after the war also served important strategic purposes in how they sought to define their position and the mainstream itself. The need to proclaim a mainstream in the 1920s and 30s thus reflects the emergence of many competing trends, styles, and schools, as well as the increasing impact of the new technological and social developments that were profoundly changing the nature of the music and music-making; the perception of competing movements and schools had been much less strongly pronounced in the years before and immediately following the First World War. One sign of this was in the programming for the Society for Private Musical Performances: consistent with the statement in the prospectus that 'no school shall receive preference', concerts included works by Debussy, Ravel, and Stravinsky.[25]

Yet with the many slogans and trends circulating in these years around such terms as neoclassicism, polytonality, *Gebrauchsmusik*, and *Neue Sachlichkeit*, and the direct challenges from the younger generation such as Krenek, Hindemith, and Weill, it became necessary to stake out a clearly defined party platform.[26] That Schoenberg sought in effect to position his school against all other contemporary trends clarifies why it became so important to lay claim to the mainstream of the Viennese classical tradition. Schoenberg's *Three Satires*, op. 28 (1926), for example, defines the boundaries between his school and the 'quasi-tonalists' and those who 'nibble at dissonance' without drawing the full conclusions; 'those who allege to aspire to "a return to . . ."'; folklorists; and 'all " . . . ists", in whom I can see only mannerists'. Again, Webern's *The Path to the New Music* defines the new music as twelve-tone composition, 'for everything else is at best somewhere near this technique, or is consciously opposed

24 Alban Berg, '*Pelleas und Melisande* Guide', tr. Mark DeVoto, *Journal of the Arnold Schoenberg Institute* 16 (1993), pp. 270–92; p. 273. Berg, 'Credo', *Die Musik* 22/4 (1930), pp. 264–5.

25 The complete prospectus is printed in Smith, *Schoenberg and His Circle*, pp. 245–8.

26 See Scott Messing, *Neoclassicism in Music: From the Genesis of the Concept Through the Schoenberg–Stravinsky Polemic*, Ann Arbor, 1988; Susan Cook, *Opera for a New Republic: The Zeitopern of Krenek, Weill, and Hindemith*, Ann Arbor, 1988; Stephen Hinton, *The Idea of Gebrauchsmusik: A Study of Musical Aesthetics in the Weimar Republic (1919–1933) with Particular Reference to the Works of Paul Hindemith*, New York, 1989.

to it and thus uses a style we don't have to examine further, since it doesn't get beyond what was discovered by post-classical music, and only manages to do it badly'.[27] The controversies that have surrounded their claims to the mainstream have not only served to define their own position, but functioned as a central point of reference for many of the other developments over the century, as Stephen Hinton has observed: 'In the minds of most his contemporaries and in the composer's own mind Schoenberg's music embodied the very antipode of *Neue Sachlichkeit* and *Gebrauchsmusik*.'[28]

That the Workers' Symphony Concert included Mahler's Second Symphony can also be understood as making the point of the triumvirate's Viennese affiliations. The inclusion of the early tonal chorus *Friede auf Erden* served a similar ideological function. Schoenberg felt that his early music would prove his understanding of and respect for tradition, as evidenced by a letter about *Friede auf Erden* to the conductor Werner Reinhart from July 1923:

> I may say that for the present it matters more to me if people understand my older works, such as this chorus 'Peace on Earth'. They are the natural forerunners of my later works, and only those who understand and comprehend them will be able to hear the latter with any understanding beyond the fashionable minimum. And only such people will realize that the melodic character of these later works is the natural consequence of what I tried to do earlier . . . *I do not attach so much importance to being a musical bogeyman as to being a natural continuer of properly understood good old tradition*![29]

As this formulation suggests, the emphasis on tradition by the Second Viennese School also had significant national and political dimensions as the label of revolutionary became associated with Bolshevism and anarchy.[30] In 1922 Schoenberg described Berg and Webern as 'real musicians, not Bolshevik illiterates, but men with a musically educated ear'.[31] Perhaps the clearest examples of the relationship of their national claims to the political context are Webern's lectures on *The Path to the New Music* from early in 1933, after Hitler's election to the chancellorship. By demonstrating the inevitability of their compositional developments and their links to the tradition of Beethoven and Brahms, Webern tried to refute the label of '"cultural Bolshevism" . . . given to everything that's going on around Schoenberg, Berg and myself (Krenek too). Imagine what will be destroyed, wiped out, by this hate of culture!'[32] Many of the school's writings from the 1920s and 30s stress their allegiance to

27 Webern, *The Path to the New Music*, p. 32. 28 Hinton, *The Idea of Gebrauchsmusik*, pp. 102–3.

29 Quoted in Reich, *Schoenberg: A Critical Biography*, pp. 146–7 (Schoenberg's emphasis).

30 For more on the political aspects of neoclassicism see Richard Taruskin, 'Back to Whom? Neoclassicism as Ideology', *Nineteenth-Century Music* 16 (1993), pp. 286–302.

31 Stuckenschmidt, *Schoenberg: His Life, World, and Work* (tr. Humphrey Searle), p. 283.

32 Webern, *The Path to the New Music*, p. 19.

the German tradition, most explicitly Schoenberg's 'National Music' (1931), which describes his works explicitly in national and even militaristic terms as 'a living example of an art . . . produced on German soil, without foreign influences . . . able most effectively to oppose Latin and Slav hopes of hegemony and derived through and through from the traditions of German music'.[33]

But if the idea of the Second Viennese School necessitated the formation of such firm aesthetic, stylistic, political, and national boundaries, their compositional activities, writings, and mainstream aspirations represent a much more ambivalent reaction to contemporary developments and other national traditions. Indeed among Schoenberg, Berg, and Webern's works from the 1920s and 30s are significant points of contact with virtually every compositional and aesthetic development in the inter-war period. This is evident at the most general level in the neoclassical characteristics of their turn away from expressionist angst to a more objective and detached emotional character, and in the use of smaller ensembles, thinner textures, and baroque and classical genres and forms. (It was just these features that would earn such condemnation from Boulez and others after the Second World War.) The Workers' Symphony Concert, however, illustrates a more profound engagement with a broad range of contemporary debates about the relationship of high culture to entertainment music and popular dance forms, the urge for art with a social function, and the desire to respond to the technologies of recording, radio, and film.

Berg's *Der Wein* is a particularly clear example of this stylistic permeability, with its references to jazz scoring, quasi-tonal harmonies, and dance rhythms, in particular the tango. Berg interrupted work on his opera *Lulu* to compose the concert aria when he received the commission from the Viennese soprano Ruzena Herlinger in the spring of 1929.[34] A setting of three poems by Baudelaire, in Stefan George's translation, the aria has many similarities to the opera in its scoring, in Berg's handling of the twelve-tone system, and his writing for the voice; it has important links to the sphere of the *Zeitoper*, as does Schoenberg's own foray into the genre with *Von heute auf morgen*, op. 32 (1929). At the same time, the twelve-tone structure of Berg's aria, *Lulu*, and Schoenberg's opera obviously sets them apart from related works by Hindemith, Krenek, or Weill. It is precisely the complex and even contradictory way that these pieces simultaneously participate in and challenge their genre that is most typical of the Second Viennese School's relationship to the compositional and aesthetic trends of the time. Similarly, Schoenberg's compositions for the workers' choral groups, such as those that performed at the Workers'

33 Arnold Schoenberg, 'National Music', in *Style and Idea*, p. 173.

34 George Perle, 'Alban Berg', in Oliver Neighbour, Paul Griffiths, and George Perle (eds.), *The New Grove Second Viennese School*, New York, 1983, p. 170.

Symphony Concert, were also meant as exemplars and critiques of the idea of communal music.[35] Of the Six Pieces for Male Chorus, op. 35, Berg wrote:

> it also appears that you (you who have always shown the younger generation the way) for once wished to *show* something *after the fact*, thereby demonstrating that the simple forms generally associated with the low 'communal music' can also *lay claim* to the highest standards of artistry and skill and that their level need not be so debased as to make them suited to be sung only by children or on the street.[36]

As for the *Accompaniment to a Film Scene*, op. 34, it was conceived independently of any specific film or scenario, beyond the sparse programmatic outline, 'threatening danger, fear, catastrophe', indicated in the subtitle. The work was generally well received, though not without protests, a fact that caused Schoenberg some concern, as he wrote to his pupil Heinrich Jalowetz who had conducted it in 1931: 'What you told me about the performance pleases me very much . . . People do seem to like the piece: ought I to draw any conclusions from that as to its quality? I mean: the public apparently likes it.'[37] Schoenberg's irony here reflects the fundamental conflict he felt between the Weimar ideal of art serving the public and his sense of the moral and spiritual mission of the artist – a conflict evident in every aspect of the *Accompaniment to a Film Scene*. On a practical level, the attractions of the marketplace must have played a role in his accepting the commission to contribute to a special series for the Heinrichshofen publishing house, which specialized in scores for the thriving German silent-film industry. Yet while the relatively small orchestra, expanded percussion section, and stripped-down textures reflect the practices of silent-film scoring, the work's complexity, and dissonant, twelve-tone language would have prohibited its performance in a theatre.

This should not be thought of as a miscalculation, but rather, as some critics of the time noted, as a challenge to the new medium: despite its title, op. 34 is not an example but rather a critique of film music. Schoenberg had seen in moving pictures a danger for opera and theatre, and he protested against the vulgarity of the majority of films. But, as with many of his contemporaries, he also had high hopes for the possibilities film offered. In 1927, the year of the first full-length talking film, *The Jazz Singer*, he envisioned film 'as a completely new and independent instrument for innovative artistic expression'. Rejecting marketability of wide mass appeal as the sole factor determining production,

35 Joseph Auner, 'Schoenberg and his Public in 1930: The Six Pieces for Male Chorus, op. 35', in Frisch, *Schoenberg and His World*, pp. 85–125.

36 Juliane Brand, Christopher Hailey, and Donald Harris (eds. and tr.), *The Berg–Schoenberg Correspondence, Selected Letters*, New York, 1988, pp. 412–13. Emphases in original.

37 Erwin Stein (ed.), *Arnold Schoenberg: Letters* (tr. Eithne Wilkins and Ernst Kaiser), Berkeley, 1987, pp. 147–8.

and concentrating on true and deep ideas and emotions, Schoenberg believed film in Germany could rise to the level of its poetry and music.[38]

Historical necessity and twelve-tone composition

Crucial to the role of twelve-tone composition in the Second Viennese School's claim to the mainstream was that the method was both integrally related to tradition and an extension of it to a higher level of development. In 'My Evolution' Schoenberg described his atonal works as part of a coherent, unbroken development, still tied to the 'ancient "eternal" laws of musical aesthetics' and 'no more revolutionary than any other development in the history of music'.[39] In similar terms, Schoenberg spelled out the historical origins of twelve-tone composition in a letter to Webern containing suggestions for his planned lectures that became *The Path to the New Music.*

> I would recommend your possibly arranging the analyses in such a way (by the choice of works) as to show the logical development towards 12-tone composition. Thus, for example, the Netherlands School, Bach for counterpoint, Mozart for phrase formation, but also for motivic treatment, Beethoven, but also Bach for development, Brahms and possibly Mahler for varied and highly complex treatment.[40]

But central to their conception of this historical mainstream was that they had the obligation to continue these developments to an ever higher degree, with the goal being – in the formulation from the 1933 version of 'New Music, Outmoded Music, Style and Idea' – '*to take advantage of the musical space in all its dimensions so that the greatest and richest content is accommodated in the smallest space*'.[41]

Thus the mainstream for Schoenberg, Berg, and Webern represented a difficult balancing act between claiming to represent both a 'truly new music' and 'properly understood good old tradition'. Perhaps the most obvious way they approached this challenge was in their recompositions and arrangements of works by Bach, Brahms, Handel, and others, in which they updated the style of earlier works through orchestrations that would clarify motivic relationships, or through more extensive harmonic and formal transformations. Examples of the former include Webern's orchestration of the Fugue (Ricercar) from Bach's *Musical Offering*, and Schoenberg's version of the Prelude and

38 Arnold Schoenberg, 'Art and the Moving Pictures', in *Style and Idea*, pp. 153–7.
39 Arnold Schoenberg, 'My Evolution', in *Style and Idea*, p. 86.
40 Moldenhauer, *Anton von Webern*, p. 374.
41 Arnold Schoenberg, 'Neue und Veraltete Musik, oder Stil und Gedanke', *Stil und Gedanke: Aufsätze zur Musik* (ed. Ivan Vojtêch), Frankfurt am Main, 1976, p. 467 (author's translation).

Fugue in E flat, BWV 552 (1928); Schoenberg's Cello Concerto (1932–3), based on Monn's 1746 Concerto per Clavicembalo in D major (one of the works for which Schoenberg prepared a basso continuo realization for the *Denkmäler der Tonkunst in Österreich*) reflects a more thoroughgoing process of updating. In a letter to Pablo Casals he described bringing Monn's piece forward through time almost, but not quite, into the present:

> I think I've succeeded in making the whole thing approximate, say, to Haydn's style. In harmony I have sometimes gone a little (and sometimes rather more) beyond the limits of that style. But nowhere does it go much further than Brahms, anyway there are no dissonances other than those understood by the older theory of harmony; and: it is nowhere atonal.[42]

If the arrangements can be thought of as retrospectively working with the objects from the past to bring them up to the modern standards, then the twelve-tone method was an attempt to remake the tradition from the inside.

The basic idea of twelve-tone composition can be explained easily enough. In Schoenberg's most extensive statement, 'Composition with Twelve Tones', he defines the method as based on 1) 'the constant and exclusive use of a set of twelve different tones'; 2) an avoidance of creating 'false expectations' of tonality by refraining from the use of tonal harmony and octave doubling that might suggest a root or tonic; 3) the treatment of 'the two or more dimensional space as a unity', which involves the use of the row to generate melodic and harmonic material; 4) and the use of the basic set along with its inversion, retrograde, and retrograde inversion in any transposition, resulting in the forty-eight possible row forms.[43] But to understand why and how the method became the central means for Schoenberg, Berg, and Webern to present their mainstream claims involves, as Carl Dahlhaus wrote, the reconstruction of the 'problems as the solution to which . . . dodecaphony acquired a significance that would hardly have been accorded to it if it had been merely a technique, a procedure capable of being described in a few sentences'.[44]

Schoenberg characterized the method of composing with twelve tones as the product of an extended period of searching for a new way of composing: one that would both replace the system of tonality and formulate 'laws and rules', thereby allowing conscious control of the new means he had 'conceived as in a dream' in the freely atonal pieces. That this was a considerable struggle for Schoenberg reflects both the technical challenges he faced in formulating the 'laws and rules', but also the fundamental reconfiguration of his ideas about

42 Stein (ed.), *Arnold Schoenberg: Letters*, p. 171.

43 Arnold Schoenberg, 'Composition with Twelve Tones', in *Style and Idea*, pp. 218–27.

44 Carl Dahlhaus, 'Schoenberg's Poetics of Music', in *Schoenberg and the New Music* (tr. Derek Puffett and Alfred Clayton), Cambridge, 1987, p. 80.

the nature of art and creativity this necessitated. Indeed, he had already begun experimenting with twelve-note chords and the systematic completion of the aggregate during the composition of *Die glückliche Hand* (1910–13), just as Berg had done in the *Altenberg Lieder* and Webern in the Bagatelles, but it would be a number of years before they developed both a technical and an aesthetic basis for working systematically with twelve tones.

Following the completion in 1916 of the Four Orchestral Songs, op. 22, it was seven years before the publication of Schoenberg's next completed new work (the Piano Pieces, op. 23). When asked why Schoenberg might have composed so little during this period Marcel Dick, the violist of the Kolisch Quartet, attributed it to his concentration on the development of the twelve-tone system, claiming 'they were perhaps the most productive years of his life'.[45] Although no works were published in the intervening years, Schoenberg worked on a massive choral symphony that evolved into the oratorio *Die Jakobsleiter*. In *Die Jakobsleiter*, the Piano Pieces, op. 23, and the *Serenade*, op. 24 he experimented with ordered and unordered collections of various length, using a technique he described as 'working with tones of the motif'.[46] The Suite for Piano, op. 25, completed in 1923 and published in 1925, is the first piece to be twelve-tone throughout, while the Wind Quintet, op. 26 (1924) was the first to use a single row for all the movements.[47] After an initial presentation to a small group in 1921, he called his students and friends together in February 1923 to present the method publicly, an occasion motivated in large part by Schoenberg's concern to defend his claim to be the originator of twelve-tone composition against the Viennese composer Josef Hauer, who was working with related techniques.

Webern had been in contact with Schoenberg during the period when he was moving towards twelve-tone composition and had already experimented with it prior to the official unveiling. But while it is clear that there was some mutual influence, Schoenberg was reluctant to share all of his discoveries. In *The Path to the New Music* Webern describes visiting Schoenberg in 1917 when he was composing *Die Jakobsleiter*: 'He said that he was "on the way to something quite new". He didn't tell me more at the time, and I racked my brains – "For goodness' sake, whatever can it be?"'[48] Webern first attempted working with a twelve-tone row in the sketches for the song 'Mein Weg geht jetzt vorüber' (1922), though it was not used in the finished piece;[49] his first completed twelve-tone composition was a short piano piece entitled *Kinderstück* (1924, published

45 Smith, *Schoenberg and His Circle*, p. 181.

46 Schoenberg, 'Composition with Twelve-Tones (2)', in *Style and Idea*, p. 248.

47 For details on Schoenberg's development of the twelve-tone method, see Ethan Haimo, *Schoenberg's Serial Odyssey: The Evolution of His Twelve-Tone Method, 1914–1928*, Oxford, 1990.

48 Webern, *The Path to the New Music*, p. 44.

49 Shreffler, 'Anton Webern', p. 285.

posthumously), but the String Trio, op. 20 (1926–7), was the first twelve-tone work he published, and his first large-scale instrumental work in thirteen years. Like Webern, Berg too was kept in the dark about the details of the system. He wrote to his wife in April 1923 that Schoenberg had started showing him his secrets,[50] and used twelve-tone rows in the Chamber Concerto (1925), though much of the material of the piece was not row-derived. His first 'strict' twelve-tone composition was the setting of the poem 'Schliesse mir die Augen beide' (1925), of which he had previously produced a tonal setting in 1907.

Twelve-tone composition and defining the mainstream

Beyond what it offered as a compositional resource, the idea of twelve-tone composition served many purposes in defining the school and clarifying their relationship to tradition. In contrast to Bartók, Stravinsky, or Milhaud, for example, whose music was not consistently associated with specific compositional approaches, the Second Viennese School was firmly linked to twelve-tone composition in the mind of the public. The story of the break with tonality and the discovery of twelve-tone composition dominates many of Schoenberg's later writings, such as 'Composition with Twelve Tones' and 'My Evolution'. Webern equated undertaking twelve-tone composition with entering into a marriage or the revelation of divine truth, writing that in 1921, 'Schoenberg expressed the law with absolute clarity . . . Since that time he's practised this technique of composition himself (with one small exception), and we younger composers have been his disciples.'[51]

The function of twelve-tone composition as a visible marker of their identity as a group and of their relationship to the musical tradition also explains Schoenberg's insistence throughout his life on his 'priority' as the discoverer of the method. The importance he placed on this claim for defining his place in the mainstream of music history was played out publicly in his controversy with Thomas Mann about the dangers he saw in attributing the method to the fictional protagonist of Mann's novel, *Dr Faustus*, Adrian Leverkühn. In February 1948 he sent Mann 'A Text from the Third Millennium', which imagined an encyclopedia entry from the distant future that attributed the technique and thus the role as progenitor of subsequent historical events to Mann (while at the same time getting in a few digs at the neoclassical composers around Nadia Boulanger):

50 Smith, *Schoenberg and His Circle*, p. 200.

51 Webern, *The Path to the New Music*, p. 41.

> Probably Mann was in contact with Schoenberg about this time; Schoenberg was living in Vienna, only a few minutes' flight from Munich, where Mann lived. He probably invented the twelve-tone theory at that time (1933), and as he had given up composing himself, he allowed Schoenberg to use it and publish it under his own name. Mann's liberal nature never mentioned this violation of his rights. But it seems that they became enemies in the last years of their lives, and now Mann took his property back and attributed its origin to a person whom he had created himself (Homunculus). So the great American music came into the position of being able to profit from Mann's theoretical invention, and this led to all the progress in American music from the fusion of this with Budia Nalanger's modal methods of producing real old music which works like new music.[52]

As Schoenberg's sarcastic comments make clear, an important aspect of the role of the twelve-tone method in establishing and maintaining a tradition was the degree to which it could be codified. For practical and aesthetic reasons, the contextual, intuitive compositional approaches in the years before the war resisted theoretical formulation; while a developed literature has arisen in recent years, none of the composers themselves articulated a theory of 'atonal' composition.[53] In contrast, although all three composers remained ambivalent about the idea of twelve-tone composition as a set of rules or a compositional system, they nevertheless presented the method in ways that others could adopt. The idea of the twelve-tone method as an approach that could be codified and that offered cohesion and organization is also reflected in the new weight that they placed on the compositional process as a public act. They carefully preserved and dated large amounts of sketch material and often referred to sketches in their writings. This marks a significant departure from the years before the First World War when rapid, apparently effortless composition, especially in the case of Schoenberg, became a sign of the emotional authenticity and expressive immediacy of the music. But with the rise of twelve-tone composition, the creative process increasingly involved extensive sketching, row tables, and various twelve-tone devices.[54] All three composers used sketches as evidence of the unity and compositional logic of their works for a sometimes uncomprehending public. The strategy of making public the world of the creative process may shed light as well on the significance of the arrangements and recompositions for Schoenberg, Berg, and Webern. Here the compositional act is made visible by superimposing it explicitly on a pre-existing canvas, i.e. the original work.

52 Stuckenschmidt, *Schoenberg: His Life, World, and Work*, pp. 547–8.
53 See Ethan Haimo, 'Atonality, Analysis, and the Intentional Fallacy', *Music Theory Spectrum* 18/2 (1996), pp. 167–99.
54 Ibid.

An integral part of the mainstream function of the twelve-tone method was a new relationship to the listener that began to emerge during and immediately following the war years, a development shared by many artists of the time. Several factors contributed to this transformation in their thought, including their desire to reach a broader public, their awareness of the new audiences being created, and the demands of their new positions. The war itself undoubtedly had a significant impact on how they saw their social role: all three composers saw periods of military service during the First World War, and the impact of the experience is evident in many aspects of their work and thought, such as Berg's strong identification with the downtrodden character Wozzeck, Schoenberg's jovial barracks-style chamber work *Die eiserne Brigade* (1916), and in many less obvious ways.

A central goal of twelve-tone composition was the idea of comprehensibility: indeed Schoenberg wrote, 'Composition with twelve tones has no other aim than comprehensibility.'[55] Schoenberg wrestled with defining the idea of comprehensibility in an unfinished theoretical work entitled *Coherence, Counterpoint, Instrumentation, Instruction in Form*, dating from 1917, significantly the same time as he was composing *Die Jakobsleiter.* Most important from the present perspective is the way Schoenberg defines comprehensibility in terms of the size of the desired audience: 'The *more comprehensible* a form and a content, the *larger the circle* of those *affected* by it. *The more difficult to comprehend*, the *smaller.*'[56] Schoenberg had of course discussed the audience in his earlier writings, but in most cases it was to dismiss their relevance to the composer. In 'Why Are New Melodies So Hard To Understand?', from 1913, for example, he points out many features of his music that pose difficulties for the listener, but concludes: 'why should the rights of the slow thinking be respected?'[57] In the 1917 treatise he is also careful to differentiate comprehensibility from coherence, arguing that 'the limits of comprehensibility are not the limits of coherence'. Accordingly, coherence can result from connections 'inaccessible to consciousnesses', or that may have an effect only on 'those more experienced or trained'.[58] But the crucial difference from his earlier stance is that he then goes on in the rest of the treatise to present systematically all the compositional means for creating coherence and comprehensibility, and always with the question of the size and nature of the audience as a central concern:

55 Schoenberg, 'Composition with Twelve Tones', p. 215.

56 Arnold Schoenberg, *Coherence, Counterpoint, Instrumentation, Instruction in Form* (ed. Severine Neff, tr. Severine Neff and Charlotte M. Cross), Lincoln, 1994, p. 9.

57 Bryan Simms, 'New Documents in the Schoenberg–Schenker Polemic', *Perspectives of New Music* 16/1 (1977), p. 115.

58 Schoenberg, *Coherence, Counterpoint, Instrumentation, Instruction in Form*, p. 9 (translation modified).

> *Comprehensibility* depends on the degree to which the essential or inessential features held in common are conspicuously or inconspicuously used or worked out.
>
> It can be reduced to a minimum if the performer is little concerned with his listeners' capacities of comprehension; it must be striven for to the utmost if the author addresses himself to many listeners or to those of limited capacity.[59]

In many writings of the time Schoenberg makes it clear that there was an intimate relationship between the nature of the musical idea, the means of presentation, and the intended audience. Webern wrote in similar terms about the importance of reaching the listener in his orchestration of Bach's Ricercar by revealing the motivic coherence: 'Is it not worth while to awaken this music asleep in the seclusion of Bach's own abstract presentation, and thus unknown or unapproachable by most men? Unapproachable as music!'[60] This is of course not to say that Schoenberg, Berg, or Webern shared the political agendas of the official Social Democratic cultural policy, or of composers such as Weill and Eisler who advocated a social function for art; indeed there is evidence that they opposed these trends to varying degrees, both aesthetically and ideologically. But if there is no doubt that Schoenberg took advantage of the mass media for the purposes of propaganda and for the dissemination of his music, it is also clear that he confronted the more fundamental problem of writing music that would be accessible to the broader public created by these technologies. That Schoenberg did in fact take into consideration the conditions of performance and the intended listeners and performers is particularly evident in his many choral works from the 1920s and 30s, including his tonal and relatively conventional folksong arrangements, the Three Folksongs for Mixed Choir, op. 49 (published in 1930 in the state-sponsored *Volksliederbuch für die Jugend*), and in a more complex way in the Six Pieces for Male Chorus, op. 35 (1929–30), with their hybrid tonal/twelve-tone structure. The Six Pieces arose from a commission from the Deutsche Arbeiter-Sängerbund (the primary national organization of workers' choruses), and two of the movements (no. 4, 'Glück', and no. 6, 'Verbundenheit') were published by the *Deutsche Arbeiter-Sängerzeitung*. The pieces were widely performed, including a presentation in December 1932 of 'Verbundenheit' by the workers' chorus Freie Typographia, the same group that had sung *Friede auf Erden* at the Workers' Symphony Concert the preceding June.

Schoenberg's formulation of a theory of coherence in terms of the audience can clarify why traditional forms and genres became so central to the twelve-tone works of the Second Viennese School. In a section of the 1917 treatise

59 Ibid., p. 19.
60 Anton Webern, 'From the Correspondence', *Die Reihe* 2 (1955); English edn, 1958, p. 19.

entitled 'Understanding = Recognition of Similarity' he writes: 'To understand a thing, it is necessary to recognize that in many (or, if possible, in all) of its parts; it may be similar or even identical to things or parts that are familiar.'[61] This can refer to aspects of repetition, variation, and development within a work, but also involves establishing relationships between a work and other works already known to us: 'If a person is meant to understand what another is saying to him, the first presupposition', Schoenberg writes, 'is that the speaker use such signs or means of expression as are known to the listener; for example, the words of a language familiar to him'.[62] Thus in marked contrast to the extreme reduction of conventional material during the atonal period in pieces like *Erwartung*, op. 17, Berg's Four Songs, op. 2, or Webern's Five Pieces for String Quartet, op. 5, there was a re-emergence in the 1920s and 30s of traditional compositional approaches at every level of organization, including melodic phrase structure, homophonic and polyphonic textural types, conventional rhythms (march, waltz, dance styles), standard forms (sonata, minuet and trio, rondo, variation), and established genres (dance suite, trio, string quartet, concerto, and number opera). Variation forms were particularly well suited to an understanding of comprehensibility based on the 'recognition of similarity'; besides free-standing works such as Schoenberg's Variations for Orchestra, op. 31 (1928) and Webern's Variations, op. 30 (1940), there were variation movements in many works by all three composers, including Berg's Violin Concerto, Webern's Symphony, op. 21, and Schoenberg's Suite, op. 29.

Serial structure and musical character

A crucial feature of the twelve-tone method for its role in defining the mainstream was its flexibility in allowing each composer to pursue his own compositional concerns within a consistent framework. The three composers came to twelve-tone composition through very different paths; thus it is not surprising that they each developed the system in very individual ways, in terms of both its fundamental assumptions and the musical results. These differences have also helped make the status of the school somewhat resilient in the face of changing fashions since the Second World War. Several generations of composers with shifting compositional concerns have been able to find continuing sustenance in the school by turning their attention from one to another of the composers, or by seeking points of contact with particular stages in their development; this is most obvious in the transition from the strong interest in Webern by

61 Schoenberg, *Coherence, Counterpoint, Instrumentation, Instruction in Form*, p. 11.

62 Ibid., p. 13, and see Alan Lessem, 'Schoenberg, Stravinsky, and Neo-Classicism: The Issues Reexamined', *Musical Quarterly* 68 (1982), pp. 527–42.

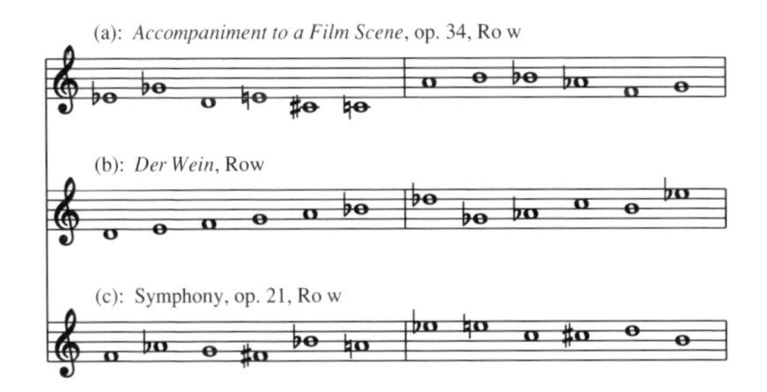

Example 9.1: Rows of Schoenberg's *Accompaniment to a Film Scene*, Berg's *Der Wein*, and Webern's Symphony, op. 21.

avant-garde composers in the 1950s and 60s to the Berg revival in the 1970s and 80s, paralleling the resurgence of neo-Romantic and eclectic elements in new works of the time.

The depth of their differences in approach to twelve-tone composition is evident at once by looking at the rows they employed in their works (see Ex. 9.1). To counter the impression that the row was simply a reshuffling of the chromatic scale, Schoenberg emphasized that the ordering of the twelve tones was the 'first creative thought', with far-reaching implications for every aspect of the piece.[63] The close relationship between twelve-tone composition and the earlier idea of composing with the tones of the motive is clear in Schoenberg's claim that 'The basic set functions in the manner of a motive', thus becoming the source for all the melodies and harmonies developed in the piece. By the same token, he de-emphasized the need for the row itself to be heard in the composition as a 'theme or a melody' that would be characterized by 'features of rhythm, phrasing, construction, character, etc'.[64] In the *Accompaniment to a Film Scene*, for example, a linear statement of the row does not appear until bar 9; instead the piece opens with fragmentary motives in the wind instruments against soft string tremolos. On the other hand, in pieces such as the first movement of the Fourth String Quartet, op. 37, linear thematic statements of the row do play an important role.

Because of the emphasis on the basic set as a source of motives, Schoenberg tended to structure the rows to produce a great deal of variety in the intervals of the three- and four-note subsets that made up the row. In the row of the *Accompaniment to a Film Scene* (Ex. 9.1a), the first two trichords produce the set 014, the half-step plus a minor third so common to Schoenberg's work, while the two trichords in the second half of the row are 012 (a semitone cluster) and 013. Throughout the piece these three-note motives appear in various

63 Schoenberg, 'Composition with Twelve Tones', p. 219. 64 Ibid.

transformations, particularly in the stylistically retrospective conclusion which recalls the '*Muss es sein?*' [Must it be?] theme of the last movement of Beethoven's final string quartet, op. 135. (Schoenberg discussed op. 135 as a prototypical twelve-tone piece in 'Composition with Twelve Tones'.) An overriding concern for Schoenberg in the construction of rows was their capacity for what is nowadays called 'hexachordal inversional combinatoriality', meaning that a row can be combined with one of its inversions, most often the inversion a perfect fifth below, without any pitches being duplicated. Accordingly, the inversion of the film music row starting on A♭ produces the following (A♭, F, A, G, B♭, B, D, C, D♭, E♭, G♭, E); the first six notes of the original row and the inversion together contain all twelve chromatic notes, and the same applies to the last six notes of each. Schoenberg thus was able to use the combinatorial pair of rows simultaneously to generate melodic and harmonic material without concern for doubling pitches.

In marked contrast to both Webern and Schoenberg, Berg's rows are often presented linearly in clearly audible form. The first vocal entrance in *Der Wein*, for example, consists of a complete linear statement of the row, followed by an inversion that is again made audible as such because the contour is inverted. Thus row statement and related thematic material can be used to define formal sections.[65] But the rows have a considerably different status in Berg's works due to his practice of combining twelve-tone and non-twelve-tone movements in a single work, such as the *Lyric Suite*, and of using new rows derived through various means; correspondingly, the row of *Der Wein* (Ex. 9.1b) is non-combinatorial, and the possibility of creating aggregates through the use of combinatorial rows, so central to Schoenberg's thought, plays little role in Berg's music. Instead, like the row of Berg's Violin Concerto, that of *Der Wein* is designed to allow a range of references to diatonic tonality: a D minor hexachord, a G♭ major triad, and an A♭ triad that can be either major or minor. This is even more explicit in the triadic Violin Concerto row (G, B♭, D, F♯, A, C, E, G♯, B, C♯, D♯, F), which also allows functional relationships between the component segments (G minor as tonic and its dominant; A minor as supertonic followed by its dominant.) But even where functional relationships are not part of the row, as in *Der Wein*, Berg often segments the row to produce chords that recall tonal progressions.

The marked tonal characteristics of Berg's rows reflect the changing status of tonality for the school. In Schoenberg's description of the twelve-tone system he often stressed the need to avoid tonal implications, as in 'Composition with

65 The discussion of Berg's twelve-tone music is indebted here and in the following to David Headlam, *The Music of Alban Berg*, New Haven, 1996.

Twelve Tones'. The question of tonality, however, clearly goes beyond purely structural concerns, being intimately bound up with how the Second Viennese School positioned itself in reference to contemporary developments, particularly Stravinsky's music and the bitter debates surrounding neoclassicism in the 1920s and 30s. But the reality of Schoenberg's, Berg's, and Webern's compositional practice is more complex: in keeping with their growing engagement with traditional forms and genres, and in turn with the listener, there was an increasing attempt to control and absorb the tonal tradition more explicitly into their works. In some cases the connections to tonality operate at the level of analogy, as in the use by all three composers of what are called hexachordal levels or twelve-tone areas, whereby the row or combinatorial pair of rows introduced at the opening serves as a sort of tonic. Webern writes in *The Path to the New Music*:

> The original form and pitch of the row occupy a position akin to that of the 'main key' in earlier music; the recapitulation will naturally return to it. We end 'in the same key'. This analogy with earlier formal construction is quite consciously fostered; here we find the path that will lead us again to extended forms.[66]

Tonal features also appear at a more surface level, and here an illuminating comparison between Berg and Schoenberg can be drawn. Unlike Berg's rows, Schoenberg's typically do not contain explicit tonal scalar passages or triads. But in some cases, major and minor triads and other tonal formations are available through pitches closely spaced in the row, as for example in the row of the Suite, op. 29 (E♭, G, F♯, B♭, D, B, C, A, A♭, E, F, D♭). Throughout the piece he partitions (divides up) the row in ways that foreground its triadic qualities;[67] in the third movement, for instance, this tonal potential moves to the surface with a set of variations of a tonal folk tune, anticipating Berg's use of tonal melodies in the Violin Concerto. In the light of Schoenberg's idea of the role of the listener discussed above, it is noteworthy that the Schoenberg pieces which deal in the most far-reaching way with the issue of tonality and twelve-tone composition are the Six Pieces for Male Chorus. The six movements of the choral pieces represent various approaches to both the challenge of finding a common ground with the listener, and that of finding common ground between tonality and twelve-tone compositional techniques. The final movement, 'Verbundenheit', is a tonal work, but the two halves are designed so that the second half is a strict inversion, transposed up a semitone, of the first half. On the other hand, the twelve-tone movements, such as 'Landsknechte', focus on a very limited

66 Webern, *The Path to the New Music*, p. 54.
67 For more on Schoenberg's links to tonality see Silvina Milstein, *Arnold Schoenberg: Notes, Sets, Forms*, Cambridge, 1992.

set of sonorities and have large-scale motions through hexachordal areas that mimic tonal behaviour. The first movement to be composed, 'Glück', integrates the two realms still more closely through an eight-note row that produces harmonies suggesting tonal chords and pitch centricity on A♭ and F.[68]

Berg's approach to the challenge of engaging with the tonal tradition through different means reflects the general permeability of his music. Quotations are common, including passages from Wagner and Zemlinsky in the *Lyric Suite*, folk tunes and references to popular idioms in *Der Wein* and the Violin Concerto, and many points of contact between pieces, such as the quotation in *Lulu* of passages from *Wozzeck* (a work which in turn draws on still earlier compositions by Berg). The tonal tradition is evoked in many ways in the Violin Concerto, from the structure of the row to the substantial quotation of the Bach chorale, 'Es ist genug!' The juxtaposition of twelve-tone and tonal materials in this work strikingly destabilizes the usual terms of the encounter through the use of a twelve-tone row that allows tonal triads and a Bach chorale that begins with a whole tone tetrachord; thus the most 'modern'-sounding part of the row, the last four pitches, is actually the most traditional. Accordingly, the function of the chorale as reconciling or heightening linguistic conflict has been interpreted in strikingly different ways, reflecting the dual nature of the mainstream claims.[69]

Even more so than Schoenberg's, Webern's rows do not function as themes or even as the source of motives in the conventional sense, but rather as a much more abstract background structure. Accordingly, his rows are not usually presented with distinct rhythms or contours, but are instead often disguised through voice crossing and large registral spans resulting from the pointillistic orchestration; the identity of the row as a theme is further obscured by Webern's tendency to use a much larger number of the available row transformations in the course of a piece. Yet if the row receded from the surface of Webern's music, he saw it as ensuring both unity and comprehensibility, and ultimately the historical legitimacy of the music. Anne Shreffler writes how in the early stages of twelve-tone composition Webern's almost religious faith in the row's power to unify gave him the freedom to construct music of 'unprecedented motivic density'.[70] In *The Path to the New Music* Webern discussed the function of the row in terms of Goethe's idea of the *Urpflanze* (primeval plant) from the *Farbenlehre*: just as Goethe viewed the shape of each individual leaf as well as

68 Robert Specht, 'Relationships Between Text and Music in the Choral Works of Arnold Schoenberg', Ph.D. diss., Case Western Reserve University, 1976, pp. 299–306.

69 Anthony Pople, *Berg: Violin Concerto*, Cambridge, 1991, pp. 98–102, and Joseph Straus, *Remaking the Past: Musical Modernism and the Influence of the Tonal Tradition*, Cambridge, MA, 1990, pp. 139–44.

70 Shreffler, 'Anton Webern', p. 287.

the abundance of forms and colours of plants as all derived from a single model, Webern regarded the row and all its permutations as 'a manifestation of this order in the aesthetic sphere'.[71] The mainstream claims for his twelve-tone compositions thus appealed to the highest source: nature.[72]

This concern for underlying unity and order is reflected in the derivation of Webern's rows from small generative cells. Webern's rows, in contrast to those used by both Berg and Schoenberg, tended to limit the choice of intervals; his general preference for the half-step is evident in the row of the Symphony, op. 21 (Ex. 9.1c).[73] In some cases this limitation is the result of generating rows systematically from a smaller collection using the twelve-tone procedures; in op. 21, the second half of the row is the retrograde of the first half transposed a tritone, and the fact that the resulting structure is thus a kind of palindrome has broad implications for how the work develops. Again, the row of the Concerto, op. 24 (1931), is based on a three-note set (B, B♭, D), followed by its retrograde inversion (E♭, G, F♯), its retrograde (A♭, E, F), and its inversion (C, C♯, A). In the String Quartet, op. 28 (1937), Webern shows that such techniques are also intimately related to the historical and mainstream claims of the works; here the row is derived from permutations of a tetrachord based on the BACH motive. Thus at the most basic level, the twelve-tone musical structure simultaneously appeals to and conflates nature, genius, and the Austro-German tradition.

More than half of the rows Webern used have the property of combinatoriality that was so central to Schoenberg's conception of twelve-tone composition. But Kathryn Bailey suggests that Webern was not so much interested in the combinatoriality for its own sake: rather this characteristic resulted from his use of highly symmetrical rows, which in turn tend to be combinatorial.[74] Webern's passion for order and unity is evident in the importance of symmetrical structures and strict contrapuntal devices in his music. The palindromic structure of the Symphony row, significantly based on the exact tritone division of the octave, is reflected in the appearance of small- and large-scale palindromes, as for example in the third variation of the second movement which contains palindromes at the level of the bar, as well as the overall eleven-bar length of the variation. Such symmetries play an important role in creating the crystalline quality of stillness so typical of Webern's music, and suggested by his remarks about an expedition in the mountains in a letter to Hildegard Jone from 1930:

71 Ibid., p. 295. 72 Julian Johnson, *Webern and the Transformation of Nature*, Cambridge, 1999.

73 My discussion of Webern's approach to twelve-tone composition is indebted to Kathryn Bailey, *The Twelve-Note Music of Anton Webern: Old Forms in a New Language*, Cambridge, 1991, pp. 13–29.

74 Ibid., p. 28.

> The day of the ascent there was bad weather, rain and fog, but nevertheless it was very beautiful. The diffused light on the glacier was quite remarkable (caused by the overcast sky and the fog). Just a few paces in front of you snow and fog blended together into a completely undifferentiated screen. You had no idea whether you were going up or down hill. A most favorable opportunity to contract snow-blindness! But wonderful, like floating in space.[75]

Webern's use of canon-in-inversion throughout both movements of the Symphony also produces mirror symmetries at every level of structure; Bailey describes the 'comprehensiveness and ingenuity' of the canonic structures of op. 21 as rivalling Bach's *Art of Fugue*.[76] Canon had emerged as an important structural device already in the vocal works written prior to Webern's adoption of the twelve-tone method, such as the Five Sacred Songs, op. 15, the final movement of which is a double canon in contrary motion, and the Five Canons on Latin Texts, op. 16. Webern's view of polyphony as the crowning glory of music reflects his studies of the compositional techniques of the Netherlanders under Guido Adler at the University of Vienna, where he completed a dissertation on Heinrich Isaac in 1906. That this urge towards unity and symmetry was intimately related to his sense of twelve-tone composition as the ultimate fulfilment and embodiment of the Austro-German tradition is evident in his endeavour to integrate as many different elements of the tradition as possible into his twelve-tone compositions. Thus Shreffler writes of the String Quartet, op. 28, whose row, as noted above, is itself generated from the BACH motive, as a 'homage to the German musical tradition' marked at the outset by Webern's choice of the 'most Beethovenian of genres'. In a letter to Stein from 1939 Webern discussed how the piece synthesized the main principles of the tradition: 'the "horizontal", or homophonic ("the classical cyclic forms [such as] sonata, symphony and so forth") and the "vertical", or polyphonic ("canon, fugue, and so on")'.[77]

The centrality in Webern's music of both the traditional formal types and the elaborate contrapuntal and symmetrical structures comes up against the fact that in many cases both features can be difficult to perceive audibly. This question of the audibility of musical structures was also an issue for Berg who wrote of *Wozzeck*, 'there is no one in the audience who pays any attention to the various fugues, inventions, suites, sonata movements, variations and passacaglias';[78] comparisons could also be made to Berg's use of large-scale palindromes in *Der Wein* and other works, along with complex numerical symbolism and secret programmes. But rather than a defect, the coexistence in the works

75 Bailey, *The Life of Webern*, Cambridge, 1998, pp. 130–1.
76 Bailey, *The Twelve-Note Music of Anton Webern*, p. 95.
77 Shreffler, 'Anton Webern', p. 299. 78 Perle, 'Alban Berg', p. 161.

of all three composers of what Bailey calls Webern's 'contradictory (complementary?)' predilections 'for symmetrical constructions and for concealment' is one of the defining features of their music.[79] Accordingly, for Webern, the contrapuntal structures and symmetries were not to be understood as a 'tour de force' of compositional ingenuity, but as having a deeper significance both for the historical claims of the works, and in the service of unity by creating 'as many connections as possible'.[80] This can be linked as well to his idea of the row providing a deep, mystical structure analogous to the hidden unity underlying the diversity of the natural world. Bailey reports that Webern kept minutely detailed accounts of his walks in the Alps, including times of departure and arrival and remarks on all the flora and fauna he encountered, as if there were some underlying patterns and meanings to be gleaned.[81]

The mainstream after 1933

If the Workers' Symphony Concert of June 1932 can be seen in many ways as affirming the mainstream claims of Schoenberg, Berg, and Webern, less than a year later their situation had profoundly changed. After Hitler's election as Chancellor in January 1933, it was only four months before Schoenberg and his family left Germany, settling briefly in France, and then emigrating to the United States in October. His last compositional work in Germany was to be the first two movements of the String Quartet Concerto, freely adapted from Handel's Concerto Grosso, op. 6, no. 7. This work, which he completed in France, marks a much more complex and ambivalent stance towards the Austro-German tradition, reflecting his reconversion to Judaism in July 1933 and the new sense of his identity suggested by such remarks as, from a letter to Webern, 'I have definitely separated myself from whatever binds me to the Occident.'[82]

Berg also experienced an enforced withdrawal from the mainstream. Despite the popularity of *Wozzeck*, performances became rare as the right-wing influence grew; he wrote to Webern in June 1933, 'My utter depression over these times has for a long time now impaired my ability to work.'[83] He completed the short score of *Lulu* in 1934, but his final work was the Violin Concerto, completed not long before his death from blood poisoning in December 1935. Meanwhile the rising influence of the Nazis in Austria meant that the

79 Bailey, *The Twelve-Note Music of Anton Webern*, p. 41.
80 Webern, *The Path to the New Music*, p. 56. 81 Bailey, *The Life of Webern*, p. 110.
82 Stuckenschmidt, *Schoenberg: His Life, World, and Work*, p. 370, and see Joseph Auner, 'Schoenberg's Handel Concerto and the Ruins of Tradition', *Journal of the American Musicological Society* 49 (1996), pp. 264–313.
83 Perle, 'Alban Berg', p. 186.

workers' musical organizations which had been Webern's main source of employment were disbanded; thereafter Webern survived through work for Universal Edition, a few grants from the *Reichsmusikkammer*, and a very small number of performances until his music was proscribed in 1938, the year of the Degenerate Music exhibition. If the idea of an Austro-German mainstream had splintered for Schoenberg, with Webern it appears to have solidified pathologically, as reflected by his sympathy with National Socialism.[84] As Shreffler writes: 'Given his fanatic reverence for authority, his extreme pan-German nationalism, and his conviction that the music of the Second Viennese School was the culmination of the great German musical tradition, it was perhaps predictable that he would share in the delusion of a great German Reich.'[85] At the close of the war, in 1945, Webern was accidentally shot by an American soldier in the town of Mittersill, near Salzburg, where he had gone to stay with family members.

In his later years, as the only surviving member of the triumvirate, Schoenberg returned to the affirmation of his relationship to tradition in writings such as 'My Evolution' and 'Composition with Twelve Tones'. But his American works are considerably more eclectic, both individually and as a group, than his earlier output, suggesting the breakdown of any sense of a single mainstream or of the possibility of a synthesis of diverse trends. And yet, in an open letter in response to greetings on his seventy-fifth birthday in September 1949, Schoenberg made clear in his somewhat broken English that, if he had given up on the present, he still held out hope for the future:[86]

> I have been given during these days much personal appreciation, which I have enjoyed immensely, because this showed me that my friends and other well-meaning people respect my aims and endeavors.
>
> On the other hand, I have for many years closed my account with the world, in bowing to the fact that I may not hope for plain and loving understanding of my work, that is: of all I have to express in music, as long as I am alive. However, I know that many friends have familiarized themselves thoroughly with my manner of expression, and have acquired an intimate understanding of my ideas. They then might be such who carry out, what I have predicted 37 years ago in an aphorism.
>
> 'The second half of this century will spoil by overestimation, all the good of me that the first half, by underestimation, has left intact'.
>
> I am somewhat embarrassed by so much eulogy. But, in spite of this, I find in it also some encouragement. Is it readily understandable, that one does not give up, though facing the opposition of a whole world?

84 Bailey, *The Life of Webern*, p. 170. 85 Shreffler, 'Anton Webern', p. 302.

86 Arnold Schoenberg, 'To become recognized only after one's death - - - - !' September 1949, Library of Congress; published by permission of Lawrence Schoenberg.

I do not know how the Great felt in similar situations. Mozart and Schubert were too young to be forced to occupy themselves with these problems. But Beethoven, when Grillparzer called the Ninth abstruse, or Wagner, when his Bayreuth plans seemed to fail, Mahler, when everybody named him trivial – how could these men continue to write?

I know only one answer: to say what man must know.

Once, when serving in the Austrian Army, I was asked whether I was really 'that composer', A. S.

'One had to be it', I said, 'nobody wanted to be, so I volunteered'.

Bibliography

Auner, Joseph. 'Schoenberg's Handel Concerto and the Ruins of Tradition', *Journal of the American Musicological Society* 49 (1996), pp. 264–313.

'Arnold Schoenberg Speaks: Newspaper Accounts of His Lectures and Interviews, 1927–1933', in Walter Frisch (ed.), *Schoenberg and His World*, Princeton, 1999, pp. 265–82.

'Schoenberg and His Public in 1930: The Six Pieces for Male Chorus, op. 35', in Walter Frisch (ed.), *Schoenberg and His World*, Princeton, 1999, pp. 85–125.

Bailey, Kathryn. *The Life of Webern*, Cambridge, 1998.

The Twelve-Note Music of Anton Webern: Old Forms in a New Language, Cambridge, 1991.

Berg, Alban. 'Credo', *Die Musik* 22/4 (1930), pp. 264–5.

'*Pelleas und Melisande* Guide', tr. Mark DeVoto, *Journal of the Arnold Schoenberg Institute* 16 (1993), pp. 270–92.

'Why is Schoenberg's Music So Difficult to Understand?', in Willi Reich, *Alban Berg* (tr. Cornelius Cardew), New York, 1965, pp. 189–204.

Brand, Juliane, Christopher Hailey, and Donald Harris (eds. and tr.). *The Berg-Schoenberg Correspondence, Selected Letters*, New York, 1988.

Cook, Susan C. *Opera for a New Republic: The Zeitopern of Krenek, Weill, and Hindemith*, Ann Arbor, 1988.

Dahlhaus, Carl. *Schoenberg and the New Music* (tr. Derek Puffett and Alfred Clayton), Cambridge, 1987.

Hailey, Christopher. 'Rethinking Sound: Music and Radio in Weimar Germany', in Bryan Gilliam (ed.), *Music and Performance During the Weimar Republic*, Cambridge, 1994, pp. 13–36.

Haimo, Ethan. 'Atonality, Analysis, and the Intentional Fallacy', *Music Theory Spectrum* 18/2 (1996), pp. 167–99.

Schoenberg's Serial Odyssey: The Evolution of His Twelve-Tone Method, 1914–1928, Oxford, 1990.

Headlam, David. *The Music of Alban Berg*, New Haven, 1996.

Hinton, Stephen. *The Idea of Gebrauchsmusik: A Study of Musical Aesthetics in the Weimar Republic (1919–1933) with Particular Reference to the Works of Paul Hindemith*, New York, 1989.

Huyssen, Andreas. *After the Great Divide: Modernism, Mass Culture, Postmodernism*, Bloomington, 1986.

Johnson, Julian. *Webern and the Transformation of Nature*, Cambridge, 1999.

Lessem, Alan. 'Schoenberg, Stravinsky, and Neo-Classicism: The Issues Reexamined', *Musical Quarterly* 68 (1982), pp. 527–42.
Mersmann, Hans. *Die Moderne Musik seit der Romantik*, Potsdam, 1928.
Messing, Scott. *Neoclassicism in Music, From the Genesis of the Concept Through the Schoenberg–Stravinsky Polemic*, Ann Arbor, 1988.
Milstein, Silvina. *Arnold Schoenberg: Notes, Sets, Forms*, Cambridge, 1992.
Moldenhauer, Hans and Rosaleen Moldenhauer. *Anton von Webern: A Chronicle of His Life and Work*, New York, 1979.
Morgan, Robert P. 'Rethinking Musical Culture: Canonic Reformulations in a Post-Tonal Age', in Katherine Bergeron and Philip V. Bohlman (eds.), *Disciplining Music: Musicology and its Canons*, Chicago, 1992, pp. 44–63.
Twentieth-Century Music: A History of Musical Style in Modern Europe and America, New York, 1991.
Neighbour, Oliver, Paul Griffiths, and George Perle (eds.). *The New Grove Second Viennese School*, New York, 1983.
Paddison, Max. *Adorno's Aesthetics of Music*, Cambridge, 1993.
Pople, Anthony. *Berg: Violin Concerto*, Cambridge, 1991.
Reich, Willi. *Schoenberg: A Critical Biography* (tr. Leo Black), New York, 1971.
Schoenberg, Arnold. *Coherence, Counterpoint, Instrumentation, Instruction in Form* (ed. Severine Neff, tr. Severine Neff and Charlotte M. Cross), Lincoln, 1994.
Stil und Gedanke: Aufsätze zur Musik (ed. Ivan Vojtêch), Frankfurt am Main, 1976.
Style and Idea: Selected Writings of Arnold Schoenberg (ed. Leonard Stein, tr. Leo Black), London, 1984.
Shreffler, Anne. 'Anton Webern', in Bryan Simms (ed.). *Schoenberg, Berg, Webern: A Companion to the Second Viennese School*, Westport, 1999, pp. 251–314.
Simms, Bryan. 'New Documents in the Schoenberg–Schenker Polemic', *Perspectives of New Music* 16/1 (1977), pp. 110–22.
Slonimsky, Nicolas. *Music Since 1900*, 5th edn, New York, 1994.
Smith, Joan Allen. *Schoenberg and His Circle: A Viennese Portrait*, New York, 1986.
Specht, Robert. 'Relationships Between Text and Music in the Choral Works of Arnold Schoenberg', Ph.D. diss., Case Western Reserve University, 1976.
Stein, Erwin (ed.). *Arnold Schoenberg: Letters* (tr. Eithne Wilkins and Ernst Kaiser), Berkeley, 1987.
Steuermann, Clara, David Porter, and Gunther Schuller (eds.). *The Not Quite Innocent Bystander: Writings of Eduard Steuermann*, Lincoln, 1989.
Straus, Joseph. *Remaking the Past: Musical Modernism and the Influence of the Tonal Tradition*, Cambridge MA, 1990.
Stuckenschmidt, Hans. *Schoenberg: His Life, World, and Work* (tr. Humphrey Searle), New York, 1978.
Taruskin, Richard. 'Back to Whom? Neoclassicism as Ideology', *Nineteenth-Century Music* 16 (1993), pp. 86–302.
Thrun, Martin. *Neue Musik im Deutschen Musikleben bis 1933*, Band 75: 'Der Orpheus – Schriftenreihe zu Grundfragen der Musik', ed. Martin Vogel, 2 vols., Bonn, 1995.
Tovey, Donald. *The Main Stream of Music and Other Essays*, Cleveland, 1964, pp. 330–52.
Webern, Anton. 'From the Correspondence', *Die Reihe* 2 (1955), English edn, 1958, pp. 13–22.

The Path to the New Music (ed. Willi Reich, tr. Leo Black), Vienna, 1975.
Weiss, Adolph. 'The Twelve-Tone Series', in Merle Armitage (ed.), *Schoenberg*, New York, 1937, pp. 76–7.

Archival and unpublished material

Janowitz, Otto. 'Im Arbeiter-Sinfoniekonzert hörte man . . .', *Dresdener Neueste Nachrichten*, 28 June 1932, Steininger Sammlung, Berlin.
Schönberg, Arnold, 'der kürzlich in Wien einen Vortrag hielt . . .', *Bohemia* 18 February 1923, Steininger Sammlung, Berlin.
'Alone at Last!' [Endlich allein!], 4 February 1928, Arnold Schoenberg Centre, Vienna.
'To become recognized only after one's death - - - - !' September 1949, Library of Congress.

· 10 ·

Rewriting the past: classicisms of the inter-war period

HERMANN DANUSER

In earlier periods in the history of music the past was either forgotten or else was present as a living, unconsciously handed-down tradition that was not specially thought about. It was only the increasing historical awareness in the eighteenth century, and particularly in the nineteenth, that enabled composers for the first time to forge links with the styles and practices of works that had been forgotten, while at the same time creating contemporary music with a historical subtext. Not by chance, these developments in composition coincided with the upsurge of historical awareness in concert life.

The formation and widening of a repertory that includes earlier works in their due place is a process that has continued to the present; the first half of the twentieth century saw at the same time the evolution of new forms of engagement by composers with the past. The present study is concerned solely with such historical references. It does not embrace other forms of engagement that introduced folksong into modern music as a reflection of popular culture; even if the tunes that are evoked, quoted, and put to new uses have ancient origins, it is not in such instances a matter of music from the past, but rather of music that is felt to be still alive today.[1] My first concern is with developing general characteristics of neoclassicism, particularly in connection with Stravinsky. Next I shall investigate the relationship to neoclassicism of those works whose titles end with the suffix '-ana' or '-iana' (a form of 'rewriting' primarily represented in Italy). By way of conclusion I turn more generally to questions of the relationship between 'national' and 'universal' classicism.

Classicisms old and new

In contradistinction to 'classicism' in music such as that of Vienna around 1800, which was recognized as such only in hindsight, true classicism always involves a retrospective relationship with earlier art. The richness of the term's

1 Hermann Danuser, 'Funktionswandel des Folklorismus', in Danuser, *Die Musik des 20. Jahrhunderts*, Laaber, 1984, pp. 48–61.

semantic field – and hence that of 'neoclassicism' – becomes apparent once the numerous major meanings of the concept of classicism are called to mind: among them are notions of period, ideals of style and form, generic models, and concepts of aesthetic perfection. These meanings are not only very varied between themselves, but are also defined in quite different fashions within individual cultural traditions. Consequently the concept of neoclassicism is likewise polyvalent, according to its points of reference within the semantic field of 'classicism'. It would therefore be vain to elaborate a single concept of neoclassicism within which the elements would all fall into place. Despite its widespread consequences for the period 1920–50, neoclassicism is not a concept defined by period, and despite the privileging of certain compositional practices, the concept is neither stylistic nor formal. Finally, in spite of its opposition to Romanticism and expressionism, it is not a new aesthetic concept either. Given this complexity with regard to historical realities, it is preferable not to pretend to construct a generalized ideal type but rather to adopt an open form of presentation that allows a description of the individual traits of neoclassicism.

Neoclassicism in music could not be based on direct reference to the practices of Graeco-Roman antiquity, as in the fine arts and literature of the period. Before and after the First World War, however, subjects related to classical antiquity were very frequently chosen for musical setting. This is unmistakable testimony to a break with the nineteenth century: the enthusiasm for themes from classical antiquity in operas, oratorios, and ballets reflected anti-psychological tendencies in drama that corresponded to the paring away of musical expression. In this process a central significance was taken on by the eighteenth century. On the one hand, the ancient world was often envisaged as reflected in the French classical period, which was itself a form of classicism (as in Ravel's *Daphnis et Chloé*). On the other hand, as represented by the early Viennese classics, the eighteenth century offered a plethora of possibilities for neoclassicism in its endeavour to break with Romanticism. In some instances this amounted to no more than returning to the ideas and musical style of the eighteenth century; in other instances, what was foregrounded was a concern for a modern vision of the antique that emphasized the unfamiliar. Never, however, did the post-Romantic classicism of the twentieth century take the same form as the pre-Romantic classicism of the eighteenth. The ideal of aesthetic simplicity on which Erik Satie's *Socrate* was based, for instance, was quite different from the 'edle Einfalt und stille Größe' ('noble simplicity and tranquil greatness') that the eighteenth-century art historian J. J. Winckelmann saw as essential to Greek art. *Socrate* was grounded in the nineteenth-century Greek Revival style – the basis of Satie's unsophisticated reverence for the Greeks – and in the 'simplicité' that Jean Cocteau in 1918 made the ideal of a post-Romantic and post-impressionist aesthetic.[2]

Satie became important for the neoclassicism of the 1920s far less through the thematic return to Ancient Greece than through the objectifying tendency of his 'musique dépouillée' (stripped-down music),[3] which set aside the artistic pretensions of music in order to renounce the aesthetic principle of expression. This was most immediately obvious when this tendency found expression in what Kolisch (referring to Stravinsky) called 'music about music'[4]; an example is Satie's Clementi parody, the *Sonatine bureaucratique* for piano (1917). Though a relationship with the ancient was neither aesthetically determinative nor of prime significance in what was produced, however, it was none the less a force in music history. And it is in the work of Stravinsky that this is particularly apparent: in his middle period – from the opera-oratorio *Oedipus rex* (1927) to the 'mélodrame' *Perséphone* (1934), and from the ballet *Apollon musagète* (1928) to *Orpheus* (1948) – a preference for ancient themes was the expression of a neoclassical aesthetic in music.

With respect to the many and varied ways in which neoclassicism had recourse to earlier music, a first question arises with regard to its relationship with historicism. Thanks to historicism, musical plurilingualism had long since emerged to replace the 'bilingualism of European composers' (to use the expression coined by Heinrich Besseler to describe the situation resulting from Monteverdi's distinction between *prima* and *seconda pratica*).[5] For with the advent of historicism composers saw themselves as ever more pressingly confronted with the possibility of reverting to earlier styles, genres, and patterns of musical thought. In general terms the past, in part reawakened and in part still present, was an abiding factor in the repertory of concerts and operas: this was predominantly the case from as early as about 1900. Consequently every composer with any awareness of history was confronted with a plurality of styles no longer shaped solely by generic considerations. These he might, like Max Reger, take into account, or else he could, like Claude Debussy, dismiss them from his mind in favour of unfettered modernism.

The eighteenth century was, besides, no longer seen as providing the foundation for the following era. Instead, along with the seventeenth century, it was regarded as a period in opposition to Romanticism. For an understanding of neoclassicism it is essential to distinguish between the various ways in which earlier music could serve as a pattern for contemporary composition, especially

2 Jean Cocteau, *Le coq et l'arlequin: notes autour de la musique*, Paris, 1979, pp. 43ff.

3 René Chalupt, 'Quelques souvenirs sur Erik Satie', *La revue musicale* 214 (1952), pp. 39–46; p. 45.

4 See Theodor Adorno, *Philosophy of Modern Music* (tr. Anne G. Mitchell and Wesley V. Blomster), London, 1987, p. 182.

5 Heinrich Besseler, *Die Musik des Mittelalters und der Renaissance*, Potsdam, 1931, p. 3.

as regards what may be termed 'substantive' and 'formalist' neoclassicism. The relationship between the German neo-baroque and Stravinsky is a case in point. The stock of the neo-baroque rose because its anti-Romantic attitude offered a substantive contribution to the understanding of the music of a circumscribed period – the seventeenth century and the earlier part of the eighteenth – in which neoclassicism sought stylistic and generic models for contemporary composition. Romantic historicism was an important precondition for the neo-baroque, in so far as it could be freed from its aesthetic foundations and transferred to a neo-baroque aesthetic (as was the case with Reger, through a purging from his music of the modern principle of utmost differentiation in expression). On the other hand, even at first when recourse to the eighteenth century was preponderant, 'formalist' neoclassicism did not recognize models for the present in any particular period of the past. It used music, irrespective of its origins, as material for its defamiliarizing compositional practices. Since this neoclassicism, as a new form of classicism, sprang from the spirit of the new music, it could even be open to the influences of the nineteenth century: Stravinsky, for instance, was not in the least obliged to modify his anti-Romantic aesthetic when looking to Beethoven or Tchaikovsky. Historicism was of no more consequence for him than for Busoni, another pioneer of neoclassicism who wanted to purge musical materials of the historicity characteristic of their period; Busoni adumbrated the notion of a 'young [or new] classicism' in the winter of 1920 in a letter to Paul Bekker, who had defended him against Pfitzner.[6] In the early days of neoclassicism, primarily as a consequence of productive misunderstandings, this became a conceptual marker for a young generation of composers.

Any historical characterization of neoclassicism must face up to the question of why composers in the first quarter of the twentieth century could so frequently and in such varied ways confront eighteenth-century music without their exerting an historical influence in any way comparable with that of Stravinsky from the mid-1920s. Insofar as we take neoclassicism to be classicism in the spirit of new music, the explanation is that for a long time, and particularly in France, classicism and modernism had been diametrically opposed: Debussy's position in the musical life of Paris is clear testimony to this. Neoclassicism in the sense suggested here implies, however, sweeping aside this opposition, even taking as equivalents what appeared irreconcilable antagonisms. Certainly the way had already been prepared, though not so much in Camille Saint-Saëns's modernistically tinctured (but extraordinarily wide-ranging) classicism as in Maurice Ravel's classically conceived

6 Ferruccio Busoni, 'Junge Klassizität', in *Von der Einheit der Musik. Von Dritteltönen und Junger Klassizität, von Bühnen und Bauten und anschließenden Bezirken. Verstreute Aufzeichnungen von Ferruccio Busoni*, Berlin, 1922, pp. 275ff.

modernity, exemplified for instance in the piano suite *Le tombeau de Couperin* (1914–17).

The historical moment when neoclassicism was able to emerge from a many-faceted preliminary phase of oscillation between traditional classicism and modernism and become the predominant force in contemporary music was, however, not reached until three conditions were met: expressionist modernism had to run its cycle; avant-garde experimentation had to start losing its artistic attractions and social legitimacy; and there had to emerge the possibility of a form of contemporary music that would be accessible to wider segments of the public thanks to its recourse to familiar stylistic means and forms. After the catastrophe of the First World War a fundamental rejection of the aesthetic of Romantic music was widely felt to be necessary. What at the time was of prime importance in terms of influence was the way Stravinsky and Schoenberg changed direction: they were seen by the musical public as two composers who had broken radically with tradition around 1910. But in the 1920s, albeit in different and indeed antagonistic fashions, they each went back to the past, creating works that were to set the agenda for classicism – neotonal in one case and dodecaphonic in the other – for the ensuing decades. In this connection the differences between Schoenberg and Stravinsky should not be seen as strictly antithetical. In 1928 Arthur Lourié, writing from a Stravinskyan perspective, set up the idea of an expressionist 'neo-gothic' in opposition to a 'neoclassicism' that privileged objectivity,[7] while Adorno, writing in 1949 from a Schoenbergian position, developed a 'philosophy of new music' that borrowed from intellectual history the concepts of 'progress' versus 'restoration'. The fact is that beyond all the profound differences in aesthetics and compositional techniques, neoclassicism – especially that of the 1920s – can be understood as striving for a new unity between classicism and modernity in music by recourse to the past. This applies to all the significant composers involved, including Hindemith.

A certain community between Schoenberg's twelve-tone system and Stravinsky's recourse to historical forms became possible only when both had run their course. Looking back, Stravinsky himself spoke of three schools of neoclassicism – Schoenberg's, Hindemith's, and his own – which determined the course of music history from 1930 to 1945.[8] In the mid-1920s, as became clear after the International Society for Contemporary Music's 1925 meeting in Venice, distinctions that had generally been flexible since the Armistice began to harden. In aesthetics and compositional techniques, a polarization emerged between

7 Arthur Lourié, 'Neogothic and Neoclassic', *Modern Music* 5/3 (1928), pp. 3–8; pp. 3ff.
8 Igor Stravinsky and Robert Craft, *Memories and Commentaries*, London, 1981, p. 122.

dodecaphonic atonality serving Romantic principles of expressivity on the one hand, and on the other a neotonality aiming at objectification and forswearing all subjective expression. That is why for a long time it was not clear to the general public that Schoenberg, on solving the formal problems of his twelve-tone music, was himself at first a classicist.

In his *Chorsatiren*, op. 28, of late 1925, Schoenberg showed how far his own new art was rooted in tradition. He made an acerbic attack on all the believers in '-isms' and denounced the adherents of 'new classicism'; in his view these disciples of Stravinsky – on whom he poured scorn as a 'little modernsky' – were going back to Bach just because it was the whimsical fashion, and because they wanted to write in a classical tonal style instead of accepting the consequences of a logical, objective system of musical composition. After all, Stravinsky had been turning since around 1920 from a 'Russian' phase to a 'neoclassical' one, a complex process involving a shift from a vocal-folkloristic manner to an instrumental and historical style. This evolution marked anything but a clean break, as Schoenberg insinuated in the polemical opening lines of his little cantata *Der neue Klassizismus* of 1925:

> Nicht mehr romantisch bleib' ich,
> Romantisch haß' ich;
> von morgen an schon schreib' ich
> nur reinstes Klassisch!

(I am not Romantic any longer; I loathe Romantic; from tomorrow onwards all I write is purest classic.)

The complexity of Stravinsky's metamorphosis, which exerted an extraordinary influence far beyond his own work, is shown by the way he moved towards the Octet for wind instruments (1922–3), his first original work in the neoclassical style. According to Rudolf Stephan,[9] neoclassicism can be taken as a principle of musical formalism in which the sources of the musical materials subjected to parody and defamiliarization are unimportant. If this is so, the birth of neoclassicism may be set right back in the second decade of the twentieth century, which establishes continuity between Stravinsky's 'Russian' and 'neoclassical' phases. The strongest evidence for this is *The Soldier's Tale*, the marching and dancing patterns of which are so defamiliarized as to call to mind Kolisch's phrase 'music about music'. Yet Stravinsky himself mentioned the Polka, his 1915 piano work for four hands, as the piece that spurred Alfredo Casella – later to become a spokesman for neoclassicism – to

9 Rudolf Stephan, 'Bach und die Anfänge der Neuen Musik', *Melos* 2 (1976), pp. 3–7; also in his *Vom Musikalischen Denken: Gesammelte Vorträge* (ed. Rainer Damm and Andreas Traub), Mainz, 1985, pp. 18–24.

write his *Pupazzetti* (1915), and which showed the way ahead for composition in the next decade.[10] For *Pulcinella* (1920), a ballet with songs, Stravinsky took up pieces of eighteenth-century music that were ascribed (some mistakenly, as it happens) to Pergolesi. This artistic procedure was no less important for the initiation of neoclassicism than for Stravinsky's breakthrough into new music. Before then Diaghilev had offered orchestration commissions to other composers, among them Vincenzo Tommasini, for *Le donne di buon umore* (1917, after the sonatas of Domenico Scarlatti), and Ottorino Respighi, for *La boutique fantasque* (1919, after Rossini). Yet the new epoch did not open until Stravinsky made his versions, redeveloping the original material with mixtures of harmonic reinterpretations, unresolved discords, and idiosyncratic instrumentation. The possibility of using adaptations of earlier music in ballet had, then, been available for some time, but Stravinsky was the first to grasp the opportunities for neoclassical parody.

Stravinsky produced the two works most typical of this revolution in 1920–1: the one-act *opera buffa Mavra* (after Pushkin) and the musically more substantial *Symphonies of Wind Instruments* of 1920 (dedicated to the memory of Debussy). *Mavra* represented a programmatic turning point. In terms of both intellectual history and compositional techniques, the abandonment of the basic concepts of the 'Russian' period could hardly have been more violently signalled than through the intentional 'Russian neoclassicism' of *Mavra*, with its reversion to Glinka's Russo-Italianate operatic style; for the allegorical ballet *Le baiser de la fée* (1928) Stravinsky would similarly look back to Tchaikovsky. In Stravinsky's eyes Glinka and Tchaikovsky both embodied a particular musical tradition of his former homeland that had universal and hence classical validity. This was a consequence of their resistance to the Russian nationalism and folklore that he too was now renouncing, for musical as well as for political and ideological reasons.

It remains an open question how far Stravinsky's exile and the need to oppose the Marxist interpretative framework then dominant in the USSR contributed to the formation of a neoclassical theory of music. Following the philosopher Pierre Souvtschinsky and with the help of Roland-Manuel, Stravinsky presented this in its fullest form in his 1939 Harvard lectures, *Poetics of Music*. A theory of universal neoclassicism is rigorously structured on concepts of 'order' and 'form'; it appears in the challengingly bald axiom, 'Composing, for me, is putting into an order a certain number of these sounds according to certain interval-relationships.'[11] National classicisms were developing about

10 Igor Stravinsky and Robert Craft, *Dialogues and a Diary*, London, 1968, p. 72.

11 Igor Stravinsky, *Poetics of Music in the Form of Six Lessons* (tr. Arthur Knodel and Ingolf Dahl), Cambridge, MA, 6th edn, 1982, p. 37.

the same time, looking back to underlying ancient national styles and aspiring, for instance in Italy and in Spain, to contribute to the establishment of a sense of national identity. During his 'Russian' phase Stravinsky had also identified extraordinarily with metaphysical and mystical thought from his homeland. But as he turned to neoclassicism he allowed elements from earlier Russian music no greater role in his works than musical material from any other source that yielded grist to his mill.

Though the eschewal of large orchestral forces was characteristic of neoclassicism from the outset, a start had already been made with works of the Russian period after *The Rite of Spring*. The severe yet extremely vivid coloration of a setting exclusively for wind, in contrast to string tone, had likewise been tried out on a larger scale in the *Symphonies of Wind Instruments*, before Stravinsky used it to greatest effect in his Octet. On 18 October 1923, just a few months after the premiere of the particularly Russian *Les noces*, the first performance of the Octet was received by the Parisian avant-garde with a *scandale du silence*. This reaction, no less striking than the riot at the premiere of *The Rite of Spring* a decade earlier, was testimony to the work's unexpected novelty. Stravinsky also showed he was setting out in a new direction by departing from his usual chariness about interviews and trying instead to foster an understanding of the Octet by the publication of his own remarks on it. Though the structural role of counterpoint – 'Form, in my music, derives from counterpoint' – may be overstated in his article on the Octet,[12] he was nonetheless right to draw attention to its quite new significance in his neoclassical compositions.

For the sequence of this work's three movements – Sinfonia, Thema with Variations, and Finale – Stravinsky looked mainly to eighteenth-century models. The Rondo of the Finale, however, develops a quasi-baroque theme in imitation of the rhythmically irregular pattern of the khorovod, a Russian line-dance. A link in form and rhythms with Stravinsky's earlier methods, it is related to the khorovods in *The Firebird* and *The Rite of Spring*.[13] Preceded by a slow introduction, the Allegro moderato does not employ the pedal points that Stravinsky used to favour, but in its strict counterpoint reveals an innovation: the production of formal progress by means of constantly changing contrapuntal patterns. The form is developed in sections through the contrapuntal elaboration of the seven-bar main theme, as also of the syncopated countertheme at rehearsal number 10; the reprise-like repetition of the main theme in

12 Translated in Eric Walter White, *Stravinsky: The Composer and his Works* (2nd edn), London, 1977, pp. 574ff.

13 Ernst Ludwig Waeltner, 'Aspekte zum Neoklassizismus Strawinskys: Schlußrhythmus, Thema und Grundriß im Finale des Bläser-Oktetts 1923', in Carl Dahlhaus et al. (eds.), *Bericht über den Internationalen Musikwissenschaftlichen Kongreß Bonn 1970*, Kassel, pp. 265–74.

the home key of E flat brings a traditional sense of closure. All this exemplifies neoclassical compositional practice with familiar musical material.

The initial consternation of the public when faced with the unexpected turn of events soon gave way to general celebration. Stravinsky was applauded too when he struck out in another new direction and, both as conductor and pianist, started performing his own compositions across the world. This was the motivation behind a number of piano works – the Concerto with wind instruments (1923–4), the Sonatas (1924), the Serenade in A (1925), the *Capriccio* with orchestra (1928–9), and a little later the Concerto for Two Pianos (1931–5), which he used to play with his son Soulima. A plurality of stylistic elements is evident in this group of works, ranging from Johann Sebastian Bach and his son, Carl Philipp Emanuel, to the overture in the French manner (at the opening of the Piano Concerto), Beethoven (in the slow movement of the Sonata), and Weber-like virtuoso developments (in the *Capriccio*). The range becomes wider still with the major neoclassical works like *Oedipus rex* (stylistically related to both Handel and Verdi) and the *Symphony of Psalms* (1930). These works cannot be characterized with the cliché favoured by contemporary critics: 'back to . . .' This is all the more the case because Stravinsky's compositional practice – whether it now separates stylistic elements that used to be linked or joins together those that were previously kept apart – never aims at restoring the styles of the past or at a copycat rewriting, no matter how strongly the models may shine through in the newly constructed music.

A powerful interpretation of Stravinsky's neoclassicism emerges from the Russian formalist theory developed in the first decade of the twentieth century by Viktor Sklovsky, Jury Tynjanov, and others.[14] A merit of such an approach is that it defends authentic neoclassicism from the polemical charge of merely restoring old styles, while also distinguishing it from the 'moderate' modernism that developed from it and became an influential force in the 1930s and 40s. Central to formalism are the concepts of 'parody', 'deformation', and 'defamiliarization'. They refer both to technical procedures for changing pre-existing structures and forms that have become mechanical through habit, and to the aim of transforming aesthetic experience and eliciting a new response. As regards compositional practice and aesthetics, what happened was that the novelty of the early neoclassical works upset a public accustomed to listening to contemporary music within an exclusively late-Romantic aesthetic, and also accustomed to the older compositions that Stravinsky was harking back to. In the 1923–4 Piano Concerto, for instance, he took as his point of reference the

14 Victor Erlich, *Russischer Formalismus*, Frankfurt am Main, 1973, pp. 189ff.

rhythmical regularity of J. S. Bach's music, defamiliarizing it with cross-accents and irregularly shaped phrases. Not only did he make the old appear in a new guise, with on the one hand unsuspected affinities with jazz, and on the other a mechanical, stiff uniformity of performance style contrary to the still universally accepted principles of rubato; by such means he also created something authentically new.

In the exact sense of the Russian formalists, the impact of neoclassicism was not widespread: it remained essentially centred on Stravinsky, particularly on his works up until the mid-1930s. Where it became a major current in contemporary music, principles of parody and defamiliarization became obscured because of a constant compulsion towards innovation, within which historical references became just another available style. In a historical context marked by an aversion to Romanticism and nineteenth-century values generally, the work of teachers like Nadia Boulanger, who taught generations of composers (particularly Americans) in Paris, fell on fertile ground and contributed to the determination of the history of neo-tonal music in the second quarter of the twentieth century by a moderate form of neoclassicism.

As regards its international diffusion, how far individual composers and individual neoclassical movements were 'universal' (like Stravinsky) or 'national' in orientation remains a difficult question calling for further investigation. According to Eric Salzman,[15] the idea of neoclassicism that crystallized into a style of synthetic neo-tonal music was most successful in those regions where late-nineteenth-century classicism itself had the quality of an artificially imposed construct, that is to say outside the sphere of central European musical culture where Brahmsian classicism was original and new. If this is correct, then it would be possible to recognize some differences in the development of neoclassicism in individual countries. Thinking in this way about origins would, however, be risky. In 1920 Casella, Milhaud, and Hindemith set out from different points to make their contributions to the development of music in Italy, France, and Germany before becoming, a little later, exponents of neoclassicism. In Italy neoclassicism came from the rejection of verismo opera and a desire to promote instrumental music; in France it sprang from a reaction to the primacy of German music's expressive aesthetic; in Germany itself it began with distaste for the expressive principles and formal canon of the classical and Romantic periods, including expressionism. Such a diversity of origins certainly provides some explanation for the general trend of developments in neoclassicism.

15 Erik Salzman, *Twentieth-Century Music: An Introduction* (2nd edn), Englewood Cliffs, NJ, 1974, pp. 43ff.

Reclaiming national traditions and the idea of '-ana' works

In the first dictionary of technical terms in the history of music, *Terminorum musicæ diffinitorium* (written in 1472–3 and printed in 1495), Johannes Tinctoris described the composer as an editor: 'Compositor est alicuius novi cantus æditor.'[16] Here 'editor' (from the Latin 'edere') does not mean 'editor' in the modern sense, but rather 'progenitor', 'begetter', in other words 'author' or 'creator';[17] all the same, the conflation of author and editor is less far-fetched than may at first appear to those whose thinking is formed by nineteenth- and twentieth-century concepts of originality. The domain of arrangements has long been the object of historical research,[18] and the idea of 'music about music' has won fresh relevance in the postmodern era,[19] as have the multifarious techniques of quotation and collage favoured by the avant-garde; the principle of 'borrowing' has been particularly debated in American musicology.[20] All this working with pre-existing musical material – all this 'rewriting' – reveals that the frontiers between 'creating' and 're-creating', between invention and imitation,[21] are far more elastic than would be readily admitted by those aesthetic theorists who make a fetish of originality.

Editing and composition come together in a particular fashion in a group of works – literary in the first place, then musical – that are characterized by a particular sort of title. It consists of a person's name followed by the suffix '-ana' or '-iana'. Lexically it derives from the fact that when materials left by an author on his death – his Remains, to use an English designation commonly employed in the eighteenth and nineteenth centuries – were gathered and

16 Johannes Tinctoris, *Terminorum musicæ diffinitorium* (facsimile of the 1495 Treviso incunabulum), Kassel, 1983, A.iiii. 'Æditor' is an orthographical variant of 'editor'. For what follows, cf. Hermann Danuser, 'Der Komponist als Editor: Zur Geschichte und Theorie musikalischer Übermalung in den "ana"-Werken', in Felix Meyer (ed.), *Klassizistische Moderne: Eine Begleitpublikation zur Konzertreihe im Rahmen der Versanstaltungen '10 Jahre Paul Sacher Stiftung': Werkeinführungen, Essays, Quellentexte*, Winterthur, 1996, pp. 331–51.

17 On the concept of 'author', see Hans-Georg Gadamer, 'Wege des Verstehens: Die Deutung von Autorschaft', *Neue Züricher Zeitung*, no. 239 (13/14 October 1984), p. 69. See also Hermann Danuser, 'Urheber und Mehrer: Aspekte der Autorschaft bei Weber/Mahlers komischer Oper *Die drei Pintos*', in Friedhelm Krummacher and Heinrich W. Schwab (eds.), *Weber – Jenseits des 'Freischütz': Referate des Eutiner Symposions 1986*, Kassel, 1989, pp. 41–58; also Danuser, *Gustav Mahler und seine Zeit*, Laaber, 1991, pp. 120–34.

18 See the collective volume *Bearbeitung in der Musik: Colloquium Kurt von Fischer zum 70. Geburtstag*, Bern, 1986.

19 Adorno, *Philosophy of Modern Music*, p. 182 (n. 35), links the 'inclination to write music about music' to two impulses: an atrophy of the creative perspectives of tonal musical material, and a 'collapse of what was once commonly known as "melody"'.

20 See e.g. Howard Mayer Brown, 'Emulation, Competition and Homage: Imitation and Theories of Imitation in the Renaissance', *Journal of the American Musicological Society* 35 (1982), pp. 1–48; J. Peter Burkholder, 'The Uses of Existing Music: Musical Borrowing as a Field', *Notes* 50 (1994), pp. 851–70; and Andreas Giger, 'A Bibliography on Musical Borrowings', ibid., pp. 871–4.

21 See Hans Ulrich Reck (ed.), *Imitation und Mimesis*, Cologne, 1991.

published posthumously, the volume would generally bear some such title as 'miscellanea' or 'collectanea' followed by the author's name. Subsequently this was shortened to just the author's name with the suffix '-ana'. According to Erich Haase, this literary form comprises:

> posthumous publications of miscellanies by a famous person whose name they bear; [these works with the suffix 'ana'] offer, in fragmentary form and in a readable sequence, comments and judgments on assorted scholarly topics, anecdotes, jokes, together with personal information, observations, comments, moral and religious meditations and sometimes even poems.[22]

The first published collection of '-ana' was *Scaligerana*, of 1666. It is a collection of characteristic snippets by Joseph Scaliger, the classical scholar who had died in 1619,[23] and the volume's success established the genre: collections of '-ana' appeared not only in France but other European lands (*Baconiana* appeared in England in 1679, *Conringiana* in Germany in 1708, and *Burmanniana* in the Netherlands in 1710).

The idea of fictional '-ana' led to one of the major original compositions in German Romanticism: *Kreisleriana* was the name Robert Schuman gave to his op. 16 of 1838, a set of eight fantasias for piano. Unlike the '-ana' musical works that bear the name of a historical composer, Schumann's title refers to a fictional musician, the hero of one of the tales in E. T. A. Hoffmann's literary work *Fantasiestücke in Callots Manier*. Rather than 'music about music', *Kreisleriana* is 'music about literature', a piano cycle inspired by nineteenth-century Romantic fantastic fiction that was itself a response to the highly imaginative etchings of the seventeenth-century artist Jacques Callot (1592–1635). If no difficulty arises over the true begetter of *Kreisleriana*, some certainly does with Tchaikovsky's Orchestral Suite no. 4 (op. 61, 1887), the work that inaugurated the series of '-ana' compositions in the sense of 'music about music': based on music by Mozart,[24] it bears the title *Mozartiana*, and Tchaikovsky's input amounts to the selection and orchestration of the pieces and their combination into a multi-movement work. Following Tchaikovsky, Carl Reinecke, a German composer who was another of Mozart's admirers, composed a work with the same title; his op. 253, '*Mozartiana*. Eight Little Piano Pieces on themes by Mozart', was published in two volumes in Leipzig in 1901.

22 Erich Haase, 'Spielarten Autobiographischer Darstellung in den -ANA', in Günter Reichenkron and Erich Haase (eds.), *Formen der Selbstdarstellung: Analekten zu einer Geschichte des literarischen Selbstportraits: Festgabe für Fritz Neubert [zum 70. Geburtstag am 2. Juli 1965]*, Berlin, 1965, p. 125.

23 Anthony Grafton, *Joseph Scaliger: A Study in the History of Classical Scholarship*, 2 vols., Oxford, 1983–93; and Haase, 'Spielarten Autobiographischer Darstellung', p. 134.

24 For composers' creative responses to Mozart, see Thomas Seedorf, *Studien zur kompositorischen Mozart-Rezeption im frühen 20. Jahrhundert*, Laaber, 1990, and also Wolfgang Gratzer and Siegfried Mauser (eds.), *Mozart in der Musik des 20. Jahrhunderts: Formen ästhetischer und kompositionstechnischer Rezeption*, Laaber, 1992.

The vogue for '-ana' compositions reached its high point between the First World War and the middle of the twentieth century. It is an expression of 'modernist classicism', a concept that I consider more productive than Adorno's negative idea of 'neoclassicism' (which he formulated only when the movement itself had become exhausted) because it stands not for restoration but for modernity.[25] Italy was clearly the centre of this development: '-ana' works were written by Alfredo Casella, Gian Francesco Malipiero and Ottorino Respighi, the most important representatives of the *generazione dell'ottanta*, the Italian composers born around 1880.[26] Luigi Dallapiccola, who was somewhat younger, also contributed to the genre, albeit in his own way.

First came Malipiero. His *Cimarosiana* for orchestra in 1921 was followed up decades later by his *Vivaldiana*, also for orchestra, in 1952, and his *Gabrieliana*, for chamber orchestra, in 1971. There are clear links between the increased effort put into the preparation of new editions of old music after the Great War and the compositional developments under discussion: in the preface to his *Vivaldiana* Malipiero acknowledges how after managing to resist umpteen times he had just this once surrendered to the temptation of going beyond the strict confines of literal transcription when preparing an edition and given way to the impulse to add his own contribution as a composer.[27] Respighi reinforced the new trend with his *Rossiniana* of 1925. This orchestral suite is described as a *trascrizione libera* of piano pieces by Gioacchino Rossini – the *Quelques riens* from the twelfth volume of his *Péchés de vieillesse*. The four movements are 1) 'Capri e Taormina (Barcarola e Siciliana)', 2) 'Lamento', 3) 'Intermezzo' and 4) 'Tarantella "puro sangue" (con passaggio della Processione)'. Most other composers of '-ana' think that they have done enough to acknowledge the contribution made by the creator of the original music if they fashion a title that includes his name; on this occasion, however, the work's dual origin is made quite explicit by its attribution to 'Rossini–Respighi (1925)'.

Such '-ana' works, as is plainly the case with the *Rossiniana*, cannot be understood in isolation: they stand in a wider historical context along with similar compositions without '-ana' in their titles. What Respighi did in *Rossiniana* was not in fact unprecedented. Since adaptations and pastiches were welcome in ballet at that time, he had turned to Rossini's *Péchés de vieillesse* six years earlier, when working on *La Boutique fantasque*. Stravinsky's score for *Pulcinella*

25 Adorno, *Philosophy of Modern Music*, pp. 206ff. His concept of 'neoclassicism' reflects the anti-historicism characteristic of serialism in the period immediately after the Second World War: see Hermann Danuser and Gianmario Borio (eds.), *Im Zenit der Moderne: Die internationalen Ferienkurse für neue Musik Darmstadt 1946–1966. Geschichte und Dokumentation*, 4 vols., Freiburg im Breisgau, 1997.

26 Dietrich Kämper, 'Nationale und internationale Aspekte in der italienischen Musik des frühen 20. Jahrhunderts', *Revista de Musicologia* 16/1 (1993), pp. 631–9.

27 Gian Francesco Malipiero, unpaginated Foreword, dated 28 October 1952, to *Vivaldiana per Orchestra*, pocket score (R. 666), published by Ricordi, Milan.

(1920), often hailed as we have seen as the origin of neoclassicism and a pioneering work in its modernization of historical material, is really part of the same generic development, as is Tommasini's orchestration of Scarlatti sonatas for *Le donne di buon umore* (1917). It was not, however, as a ballet score that Casella composed his *Scarlattiana* of 1926, a work for piano and chamber orchestra that in its seven movements took up numerous themes from several different keyboard sonatas by the earlier composer. It became well known in German-speaking lands, and for the centenary of the Vienna Philharmonic Orchestra in 1942, in the middle of the Second World War, Casella wrote his *Paganiniana*, a virtuoso divertimento for orchestra based on pieces and themes by the renowned violinist.

Though excessive significance should not be attributed to '-ana' compositions within the total output of the musicians who wrote them, they nonetheless cast light on a paradigm shift in Italian musical history. After the First World War, the younger generation of composers sought to win for instrumental music a status comparable to that of opera. Paradoxically, it was nothing other than the overwhelming international success of Italian opera from the nineteenth century up until Puccini and the verismo composers that prepared the way for change, namely the emergence of a school of instrumental music founded in the national tradition. With the exception of *Rossiniana* and *Gabrieliana* it was music from the eighteenth century, in every instance by Italian composers, that was selected for adaptation. In this way modernist classicism in music, as in other arts, manifested a nationalistic tendency: turning back to a great era in Italian musical history was to be a precondition of its renewal in the present day. Though the works in question differ markedly in detail as well as in their employment of a variety of sources, this music took a stand against 'German-dominated' Romanticism. Inevitably, given the climate of the time, it also had intellectual affinities, to some degree deliberate, with the fascism of Mussolini. In this respect the controversy over *Scarlattiana* prompted by Casella's article in the January 1927 issue of *Anbruch* is instructive: Casella adduced a link between the goal of modernist classicism – 'successfully using anew the pure old forms' – and developments in fascist Italy since 1922,[28] while in detailed responses Malipiero and Ernst Krenek stressed the need for a pluralistic attitude.[29]

28 [Alfredo Casella], 'Scarlattiana: Alfredo Casella über sein neues Stück', *Anbruch* 11 (1929), pp. 226–8. See Fiamma Nicolodi, 'Musica e Musicisti nel Ventennio Fascista', *Contrappunti* 19 (1984), pp. 244–57; Anna Marian Morazzoni, 'Der Schönberg-Kreis und Italien: Die Polemik gegen Casellas Aufsatz über "Scarlattiana"', in Rudolf Stephan and Sigrid Wiesmann (eds.), *Bericht über den 2. Kongreß der Internationalen Schönberg-Gesellschaft: 'Die Wiener Schule in der Musikgeschichte des 20. Jahrhunderts', Wien, 12. bis 15. Juni 1984*, Vienna, 1986, pp. 73–83; and Jürg Stenzl, *Von Giacomo Puccini zu Luigi Nono. Italienische Musik 1922–1952: Faschismus – Resistenza – Republik*, Buren, 1990, pp. 125–38.

29 Ibid., pp. 79–81.

Within the context of a composer's total output '-ana' works generally represent just one possibility, however interesting, of creative recourse to existing music: they take their place alongside other classical ideas and practices. In the case of Heitor Villa-Lobos, however, they amount to a major part of his work. Here the '-ana' title, linked with the name of J. S. Bach, is in the plural, applying to a whole series of works, and joined to an adjective referring to the composer's native land: *Bachianas brasileiras*, a group of nine works in all, is related to the single-movement *Chôros*, of South American inspiration, that caused a furore among the Parisian avant-garde of the 1920s. It was only after returning home in 1930 that Villa-Lobos composed the multi-movement *Bachianas brasileiras*. His aspiration was to enrich the struggling national musical patrimony of Brazil with the finest Western music as represented by the name of Bach.[30] Orchestration and formal layout are extremely varied: no. 1 is for eight cellos (1930); no. 2 for chamber orchestra (1930–8); no. 3 for piano and orchestra (1938); no. 4 for piano or orchestra (1930–41); no. 5 for voice and cellos or piano or guitar (1938–45); no. 6 for flute and bassoon (1938); no. 7 for orchestra (1942); no. 8 for orchestra (1944); and no. 9 for chorus or string orchestra (1945). What these works all share is the aesthetic concept programmatically expressed in the title *Bachianas brasileiras*: the linkage of South American popular folklore with European traditions of high art. This is reflected in the twofold structure of the titles of individual movements: each couples a term from the European musical tradition with a Brazilian dance or song. For instance, the successive movements in *Bachianas Brasileiras* no. 4 are: 1) Prelúdio (Introduça), 2) Coral (Canto do Sertão), 3) Ária (Cantiga) and 4) Dança (Miudinho). The individual parts of this work were written between 1930 and 1941.

Instead of referring back to a historical personage (or, as in the case of Schumann, a fictional character), the *Bachianas brasileiras* reveal a further possible form of reference in the '-ana' form when they invoke the 'myth of Bach' or his image as 'a master of the baroque'. In this case, specific motifs, elements, structures, and movements from Bach's works are not in fact transformed into 'music about music': the variety in the ordering of movements into suites and the grouping of these into the complete nine-part *Bachianas brasileiras* is an expression of the principle of intermingling inherent in the '-ana' concept. By referring to Bach, Villa-Lobos adheres furthermore to a basic trend in European modernist classicism in which arrangements of Bach by Webern, Schoenberg, Stravinsky, and many others, not forgetting Hindemith's *Ragtime wohltemperiert* and *Ludus tonalis*, were to exert an overpowering stylistic influence.

30 Giselher Schubert, 'Zur Charakteristik von Heitor Villa-Lobos', in Dieter Rexroth (ed.), *Zwischen den Grenzen: Zum Aspekt des 'Nationalen' in der Neuen Musik*, Mainz, 1979, pp. 62–72.

If we now cast our minds back over the '-ana' compositions that have been discussed here, the range is astonishing: it is scarcely less extensive than the domain of '-ana' as a literary genre. These musical 'retouchings', to use a term commonly applied to Mahler's performing versions of the classics, bring to light something that was hidden, forgotten and suppressed, as composers 'edit' or 'bring out' the earlier text. But unlike editors of literary works, who are subordinate to their sources, composers of '-ana' works do not set about their task without at the same time, to a greater or lesser degree, altering it, changing its coloration. Thus an abiding characteristic of musical 'retouching' becomes obvious. From the outset Stravinsky's arm's-length treatment of historical material had a destructive aspect; he did not – and this can hardly be pure chance – compose a single work with '-ana' in its title. If in the fine arts retouching has for centuries implied the correction, if not the destruction, of the lower layer of paint, as is the case with a palimpsest, there is in '-ana' works, by contrast, an aspiration to 'cast light' that is fundamental to the concept of 'edition' in general. Musical 'retouching' involves the most varied aspects of the historical text: key, melodic lines, sound patterns, form, and other dimensions of the music, whether taken singly or in combination.

There is in the '-ana' form an inherent tendency towards heterogeneity, as exemplified by the contemporary collage and montage practices of the visual arts (as well as by the later aesthetic of the 'open work'). However, this tendency was fettered and reined in by the composers of '-ana' works, who saw themselves as under affectionate obligations to the predecessors whose works they were 'retouching'. Like editors, who voluntarily circumscribe personal ambition, they gave particularly apt expression to the ambivalent historical character of modernist classicism that combines within itself past and present, history and the concerns of today.

From neoclassicism to modernist classicism

I have already observed that it is one of the peculiarities of music that, unlike the other arts, it cannot look back to or link with an ancient musical tradition recognised as classical. In literature, the fine arts, and architecture, works have survived from ancient times, albeit sometimes in fragmentary form or as ruins, and since the Renaissance classicizing artists and theorists have often returned to them. This is something music cannot do: its evolution since the twelfth century took place without the 'classical-universal' background that was characteristic of the other arts, which is why in Hegelian aesthetics it was a Christian–Romantic art. Consequently musical paradigms – Netherlandish–Burgundian music in the fifteenth and sixteenth centuries, Italian in the seventeenth and eighteenth and Austro-German in the nineteenth – sprang from national cultures without the encumbrance of a heritage from antiquity, and could themselves aspire to international or even universal significance.

As regards subjects, for which music too could have recourse to antiquity, twentieth-century composers turned to ancient sources more eagerly than their nineteenth-century counterparts. Throughout history, classical texts have normally been translated for musical setting; two exceptions, by virtue of their abnormal nature, serve to prove the rule. Though in his *Prometheus desmotes* – 'Prometheus Chained' – of 1968 Carl Orff set the (abridged) Greek original of Aeschylus's tragedy, this late work appears to be indebted primarily to the humanism of Germanic responses to the Greeks, like his earlier settings of tragedies. Stravinsky, on the other hand, had long before emphasized historical distance with his opera-oratorio *Oedipus rex*, in which Jean Cocteau's two-act French-language adaptation of the Sophoclean tragedy was presented in Latin translation: he underlined its universal significance not by carefully reconstructing it in the original language, but through a double translation – from Greek into French and then back into Latin (the latter by no means 'correct'). This was a modern, artificial staging of the problem of translation.[31] Generally, however, texts from the ancient languages, especially Greek, were set to music in modern translation: examples are the adaptations by Hofmannsthal and Claudel (*Electra* after Sophocles, *Alcestis* after Euripides, and the *Oresteia* trilogy after Aeschylus) that provided German and French libretti for Richard Strauss, Egon Wellesz, and Darius Milhaud. These and similar versions became, as also in other languages, part of the national literature in question, for the role of translation in the development of the national languages can hardly be exaggerated. But they also point, through their common link with classical antiquity, to a universal European patrimony. And this ambivalent conjunction is reflected in music:[32] the tension between what may with some exaggeration be called 'ancient universalism' and 'modern nationalism' allowed a range of divergent practices.

Alongside the concept of Graeco-Roman classicism, there is another form of classicism closely associated with the nation. It was the view of the German writer Martin Walser that the classicist is 'first a classic for his nation'; the only criterion for classicism that he accepts is 'usefulness'.[33] The sense of this

31 Hellmut Flashar, *Inszenierung der Antike: Das griechische Drama auf der Bühne der Neuzeit 1585–1990*, Munich, 1991, pp. 147–51.

32 See Hermann Danuser, 'Primordial and Present: The Appropriation of Myth in Music', in Gottfried Boehm, Ulrich Mosch, and Katharina Schmidt (eds.), *Canto d'Amore: Classicism in Modern Art and Music 1914–1935* [Catalogue of the Public Art Collection/Gallery of the Paul Sacher Stiftung, Basel, in the Basel Kunstmuseum, 27 April to 11 August 1996], Bern, 1996, pp. 298–314.

33 Martin Walser, 'Was ist ein Klassiker?', in Gottfried Honnefelder, *Warum Klassiker? Ein Alamanach zur Eröffnungsediton der Bibliothek deutscher Klassiker*, Frankfurt am Main, 1985, pp. 3–10; pp. 5ff.

interpretation is shown in the reversion on countless occasions to themes from national history and mythology through which attempts were made to establish links throughout the twentieth century, particularly in the 1930s and 40s. In this respect the full ambiguity of our pair of concepts was manifest even at the time of the First World War, when there was a tense relationship between exoticism with its international tendencies, and folklore with its national bias.[34]

Paris served as an international focus where, in a milieu eager for exoticism, several composers wrote those works that their native countries would later hail as summits of their national music: Manuel de Falla for Spain, Alfredo Casella for Italy, and Igor Stravinsky for Russia. While de Falla went back to Spain and Casella to Italy, however, the October Revolution forced Stravinsky to remain in exile abroad. With *Mavra*, his *opera buffa* of 1921–2, and the completion in 1923 of *Les noces*, he bade farewell to his Russian phase, in whose wide international resonance a deeply imbued nationalism was by no means the least important factor. Instrumental works such as the Octet (1922–3), the Concerto for Piano and Wind (1924), and the Piano Sonata (1924) instead laid claim to universality on account of their orientation towards historical models that had become completely generalized, because their influence had been exerted over so long a period. Subsequently the ballet *Apollon musagète*, the opera-oratorio *Oedipus rex*, and the *mélodrame Perséphone* showed Stravinsky turning towards modernist classicism on a thematic level too.[35]

In the musical history of the 1930s and 40s it is possible, in general terms, to discern a displacement of emphasis onto national subjects with works which in content often assumed the form of 'confessional' operas.[36] De Falla's scenic cantata *Atlántida* (1926–46, incomplete), like three operas from the 1930s – Hindemith's *Mathis der Maler*, Krenek's *Karl V*, and Schoenberg's *Moses und Aron* – present themes from national history with religious dimensions: Spanish Catholicism is portrayed mystically in *Atlántida* and *Karl V*, *Mathis der Maler* depicts the religious disputes of the German Reformation in the form of a *Künstleroper*, while with *Moses und Aron* Schoenberg returned to his roots in Judaism.

Subject elements attain to artistic expression in music only when linked with style. An example is the representation of a 'German' musical world in the first movement of the *Mathis der Maler* Symphony (linked closely with the opera), which Hindemith himself recorded with the Berlin Philharmonic on

34 Hermann Danuser, 'Funktionswandel des Folklorismus', in Danuser, *Die Musik des 20. Jahrhunderts*, pp. 48–62.

35 Richard Taruskin, *Stravinsky and the Russian Traditions: A Biography of the Works through* Mavra, 2 vols., New York, 1996.

36 Danuser, *Die Musik des 20. Jahrhunderts*, pp. 234–46.

9 April 1934.[37] A polyphonic development of the phrase from four bars before rehearsal number 12 leads to a contrapuntal texture at number 16, where the most important thematic elements of the movement are heard simultaneously. The striking triple presentation of the apt first line of the hymn ('Es sungen drei Engel ein süßen Gesang') creates the impression of a reprise, because the pitch relationships are the same as in the rising major thirds at the start (D♭, F, A). In dramatic terms, however, the development is directed towards the climax that is reached with the third repeat (number 17). The 'himmlische Musizieren' (celestial music-making) evoked in the hymn, made visible in Grünewald's Isenheim Altarpiece, is realized through a setting for full orchestra that combines the expanded hymn tune (clarinets and first trumpet) with the second theme in the flutes and oboes, ringing out in simultaneous counterpoint:[38] the clarity of the orchestration, the stabilization of key above the D minor pedal point, the broadening of the tempo ('Breit'), as well as the emphasis conveyed by rhythmic augmentation, all contribute to the effect of an inherent monumentality. After the 'wild' twenties, Hindemith's musical idiom appears to have consolidated, to have become grounded in classicism in a way that is personal yet at the same time linked with a national theme through the presentation of a German hymn in a setting unashamed of its craftsmanship.

Stylistically this modernist classicism represented a departure from turn-of-the-century musical modernism, the development of which had brought about the crisis of new music around 1910. In a wider sense, it also represented a turning away from the two major paradigms of nineteenth-century music: German instrumental music and Italian opera, which had together determined the development of both music and aesthetic thinking about it ever since the deaths of Beethoven and Rossini.[39] Those paradigms were linked with a national and cultural context, but became commonplaces of universal validity among the elites. In the twentieth century, by contrast, even radical compositions such as Schoenberg's *Pierrot lunaire* and Stravinsky's *The Rite of Spring* had their origins in elements that were national, not to say regional, despite the internationalism of their influences. Modernist classicism, like every aesthetic concept, resists the confines of stylistic definition, a point that is all the more salient because of the way music historians have parcelled up the various phenomena of classicism – the different tonal experiments of Stravinsky, Hindemith, and

37 Paul Hindemith, *Mathis der Maler [Symphonie]*. Recorded 1934; new digital reissue, in *Stravinsky conducts Stravinsky; Hindemith conducts Hindemith* (Teldec, 1993).

38 David Neumeyer, *The Music of Paul Hindemith*, New Haven, 1986, pp. 85–99.

39 Carl Dahlhaus, *Nineteenth-Century Music* (tr. J. Bradford Robinson), Berkeley, 1989; Bernd Sponheuer, *Musik als Kunst und Nicht-Kunst: Untersuchungen zur Dichotomie von 'hoher' und 'niederer' Musik im musikästhetischen Denken zwischen Kant und Hanslick*, Kassel, 1987.

Bartók, the dodecaphonic atonality of Schoenberg – into a single category.[40] The fact is that all these phenomena were originally linked through a common aversion to the aesthetic that had, around the turn of the century, raised the ideal of absolute music into an aesthetic religion of musical metaphysics.

With Stravinsky, stylistic reversion took on a universalizing quality. Eighteenth-century squabbles about the national character of various musical styles were forgotten, and the influence on future developments of Italian origins were seen in a European context. Hindemith,[41] Bartók, and other composers introduced eighteenth-century principles into their works in an innovative way, regardless of national stylistic categories. They sought to avoid anything recalling nineteenth-century symphonic traditions, such as procedures of the 'organic' development of motives. Yet historically even this compositional principle proved ambivalent, for there were at the same time attempts to allow national, not to say nationalistic, claims to emerge, as we have seen for example in the case of Casella. Around 1930, however, it became less urgent to draw a line under the aesthetic ideals of the nineteenth century, and so forms from that era (such as the symphony and the large-scale concerto) won renewed importance. With his Piano Concerto of 1942 Schoenberg looked back to the great Romantic examples of the form, instead of the more modest baroque model. This is an expression of the repeated change of historical reference that is part and parcel of an international network of relationships in modernist classicism.

The example of Schoenberg shows how the terminology of national and universal categories could change without the related meanings also necessarily changing. Schoenberg subscribed to the universalizing claims of German cultural hegemony without apparently being conscious of any contradiction between such 'Romantic' notions and the essentially international aesthetic of modernism. With his dodecaphonic technique – that is, with a 'modern', rational, and hence universally applicable procedure – he thought in the 1920s that he had made a discovery which would secure for the German musical tradition over the next century the primacy which it had enjoyed up until the First World War.[42] But conservatives, whose extreme nationalistic aspirations included

40 This matter of content marks a significant difference between the historiography of music and the fine arts: the interpretation of Schoenberg's twelve-tone works, an exemplary manifestation of twentieth-century modernism, has for decades been seen as a special form of musical 'classicism', while an equivalent understanding of the abstract works of Klee and Mondrian is only recent (Gottfried Boehm, 'An Alternative Modern: On the Concept and Basis of the Exhibition', in Boehm, Mosch, and Schmidt (eds.), *Canto d'Amore*, pp. 15–38).

41 Giselher Schubert, 'Kontext und Bedeutung der "Konzertmusik" Hindemiths', in Constantin Floros et al. (eds.), *Zur Musik des 20. Jahrhunderts*, Hamburg, 1980, pp. 85–114.

42 Arnold Schoenberg, *Berliner Tagebuch. Mit einer Hommage à Schönberg vom Herausgeber Josef Rufer*, Frankfurt am Main, 1974, p. 48: 'Als ich [Rufer] ihn [Schönberg] im Sommer 1921 – es war in Traunkirchen

no element of universality, were not satisfied with this attitude: instead they became even more inclined to hate Schoenberg as a Jew and a modernist.[43] From 1922 Schoenberg had been watching without any illusions the growth of anti-Semitic tendencies. The coming to power of the Nazis struck at the foundations of his identity as a 'German musician', and he sought safety in exile. In the United States he was no longer either able or willing to adhere to the concept of 'German music' that had been corrupted by the Nazis, though it still left its mark on his thought and his compositional style. Thereafter he spoke instead of classical music.[44]

In all these instances, as we have seen, universal and national factors come into play on both a stylistic and an ideological level, but the relation between them changes. From 1920 to 1950, the idea of modernist classicism was understood in terms of national connections. But from the standpoint of today it is clear that the music created under its sign drew on a range of other sources. Neither a national nor a universalist orientation guarantees musical success, nor does it exclude it. That is why much music of a classical stamp has deservedly perished – music that gave in to the temptations of nationalism in a manner analogous to the architectural classicism of the dictators. Other works of modernist classicism, however, have survived as musical testimony to the age when a searing flame of destructive nationalism spread from Germany to engulf the world.

Modernist classicism, to sum up, is one of those basic categories in the historiography of art and music that are not so much defined as given meaning in the light of a rewriting of the past: penetrating surveys, such as those of Scott Messing, Wolfgang Rathert, and Volker Scherliess,[45] show the enormous historical breadth that this category has encompassed. In earlier historical writing about music the two concepts that it links together were regarded as clear-cut contraries. 'Modernism' and 'classicism' were seen as mutually exclusive, as illustrated by the antagonism between the supporters of Wagner and those of

am Traunsee – zum üblichen Abendspaziergang abholte und das Gespräch auf seine Arbeit kam, sagte er: Mir ist heute etwas gelungen, womit ich die Vorherrschaft der deutschen Musik für die nächsten hundert Jahre gesichert habe.'

43 Eckhard John, *Musikbolschewismus: Die Politisierung der Musik in Deutschland, 1918–1938*, Stuttgart, 1994.

44 Arnold Schoenberg, 'On revient toujours' [1948], in *Style and Idea* (ed. Leonard Stein, tr. Leo Black), London, 1975, pp. 108–10; and 'Arnold Schönberg und die Idee einer deutschen Musik', in Peter Becker, Arnfried Edler, and Beate Schneider (eds.), *Zwischen Wissenschaft und Kunst*, Mainz, pp. 253–61.

45 Scott Messing, *Neoclassicism in Music: From the Genesis of the Concept through the Schoenberg–Stravinsky Polemic*, Ann Arbor, 1988; Wolfgang Rathert, 'Vom Klassizismus zur Postmoderne: Anmerkungen zur Musikgeschichte des 19. und 20. Jahrhunderts', in Meyer (ed.), *Klassizistische Moderne*, pp. 40–59; Volker Scherliess, '"Torniamo all'antico e sarà un progresso" – Creative Longing in Music', in Boehm, Mosch, and Schmidt (eds.), *Canto d'Amore*, pp. 39–62, and *Neoklassizismus: Dialoge mit der Geschichte*, Kassel, 1998.

Brahms in the second half of the nineteenth century. But if historians are to avoid making the antagonisms of the past the basis of their own understanding, what initially appears to be the oxymoronic notion of 'modernist classicism' or 'classical modernism' can be helpful. Simply at the level of terminology, it signals an endeavour to revaluate the phenomenon that has generally been treated in German-language musical historiography under the negative title of 'neoclassicism'. For if the concept of 'classicism' has pejorative undertones[46] (because it is seen as derivative and therefore in opposition to the principles of modernity), then this holds with even more force for the concept of 'neoclassicism': the tautological double reversion – to an earlier classicism and, beyond that, an earlier one still – appears to designate a second- or even third-hand artistic phenomenon. In establishing the category of aesthetic modernism, musical historiography (which has since 1950 been dominated by the avant-garde) has brushed aside modernist classicism – one of the most influential phenomena of musical history in the first half of the twentieth century – by means of the pejorative label 'neoclassicism'.

Both the concepts comprised under 'modernist classicism' are of wide-reaching importance for the history of culture and art in Europe and beyond. In music, classicism exerted its influence from the eighteenth century to the twentieth, whereas modernism did so in the nineteenth and the twentieth. Their relationship in the twentieth century leads one to ask whether the 'classical' branch of contemporary musical culture is better understood as opposed to radical modernism, or as part of it. If this question is to be answered, both basic concepts must be defined differently and more precisely than usual.

'Classicism' needs to be prised away from the prejudices that have crushed it under the mutually antagonistic values of a pure classical ideal on the one hand, and a pure modernist one on the other. In the first case it inevitably falls behind the level of earlier classics on which it is stylistically dependent; in the second it is seen as a contemporary form of artistic creation concerned with craftsmanship and tradition but failing to appreciate the logical and innovative premises of modernism. These evaluations, which on both sides are developed from 'pure' stances, do not stand up any more. At the end of a century of turmoil, these contrary ideals – unblemished classicism and pure modernism – have long since forfeited their historical force. What has replaced them is an understanding that awareness of tradition is integral not only to classicism but also to a modernism no longer seen as in opposition to the past. And conversely,

46 E.g. Stefan Kunze, 'Cherubini und der musikalische Klassizismus', in *Analecta Musicologica. Veröffentlichungen der Musikgeschichtlichen Abteilung des Deutschen Historischen Instituts in Rom*, vol. XXIII, Laaber, 1974, pp. 301–23; p. 303.

if a readiness to respond reflectively to tradition is characteristic of classicism, then tradition – now seen not in terms of precisely fixed criteria but as a series of points of reference – may be expected to contribute vitally to the artistic production of the twenty-first century.

The revision of the concept of 'modernism' in the light of the postmodernism debate also leads to a new evaluation of neoclassicism. Today the ideal of modernism as a single-minded drive for progress is no longer credible: there is scepticism about the idea that new music ended its heroic phase in the 1920s, emerging from a blind alley only with the development of serialism after the Second World War. And when musicology looks beyond the limited horizons of a chronicle of composers' methods, it seems absurd to imagine that modernism in music stalled just as titanic modernizing tendencies emerged in European society in the wake of the First World War. Neoclassicism is rather part of a more comprehensively and adequately understood musical modernism.

In art history, heed has long been taken of the relationship between neoclassical tendencies and totalitarian politics.[47] Some catching up is needed in musicology, which has not explored political interpretations of classical ideals in the 1930s and 40s with similar rigour. Precise political stances cannot be unambiguously ascribed to classicism and modernism, with one expressing a 'leftist', democratic stance and the other a 'right-wing', even totalitarian one; in reality all forms of musical modernism were probably more closely aligned with elitist values than a well-meaning but ill-informed historiography has cared to admit. Yet here, as in musicology generally, the question has to be asked: does the light cast by a composer's intentions really contribute anything solid to the understanding of a work of art? Can the music of Schoenberg, Webern, or Stravinsky really be evaluated only when these composers' political attitudes are borne in mind? Do not critics in this post-Marxist period who necessarily link Webern's later work with his enthusiasm for Hitler short-circuit the methodological problem? Issues of the weight to be attached to contextualization require more serious consideration: it ought not to be given such prominence on ideological grounds that a critical evaluation of musical objectives is no longer viable. If historians interpret modernist classicism too readily in terms of the propaganda slogans of the day, such as Jean Cocteau's cry for a 'rappel à l'ordre',[48] then other, deeper artistic impulses will not be recognized. Only those critics who step back from an

47 Kenneth E. Silver, '*Esprit de Corps*': *The Art of the Parisian Avant-Garde and the First World War, 1914–25*, Princeton, 1989; and Gottfried Boehm, 'An Alternative Modern', pp. 15–17. Among the many other discussions of the topic, attention may be drawn to Luciano Canfora's 'Classicismo e fascismo', *Quaderni di Storia* 2 (1976), pp. 15–48.

48 See Richard Taruskin's review essay, 'Back to Whom? Neoclassicism as Ideology', *Nineteenth-Century Music* 16 (1992), pp. 286–303.

all-embracing and deterministic political interpretation of this phenomenon in cultural history will be able to achieve an evaluation that respects its aesthetic presuppositions.

Translated by Christopher Smith

Bibliography

Adorno, Theodor W. *Philosophy of Modern Music* (tr. Anne G. Mitchell and Wesley V. Blomster), London, 1987.

Bearbeitung in der Musik: Colloquium Kurt von Fischer zum 70. Geburtstag, Bern, 1986.

Becker, Peter, Arnfried Edler and Beate Schneider (eds.). 'Arnold Schönberg und die Idee einer deutschen Musik', *Zwischen Wissenschaft und Kunst*, Mainz, 1995.

Besseler, Heinrich. *Die Musik des Mittelalters und der Renaissance*, Handbuch der Musikwissenschaft, Potsdam, 1931.

Boehm, Gottfried. 'An Alternative Modern: On the Concept and Basis of the Exhibition', in Gottfried Boehm, Ulrich Mosch and Katharina Schmidt (eds.), *Canto d'Amore: Classicism in Modern Art and Music 1914–1935* [Catalogue of the Public Art Collection/Gallery of the Paul Sacher Stiftung, Basel, in the Basel Kunstmuseum, 27 April to 11 August 1996], Bern, 1996, pp. 15–38.

Brown, Howard Mayer. 'Emulation, Competition and Homage: Imitation and Theories of Imitation in the Renaissance', *Journal of the American Musicological Society* 35 (1982), pp. 1–48.

Burkholder, J. Peter. 'The Uses of Existing Music: Musical Borrowing as a Field', *Notes* 50 (1994), pp. 851–70.

Busoni, Ferruccio. *Von der Einheit der Musik. Von Dritteltönen und Junger Klassizität, von Bühnen und Bauten und anschließenden Bezirken. Verstreute Aufzeichnungen von Ferruccio Busoni*, Berlin, 1922.

Canfora, Luciano. 'Classicismo e fascismo', *Quaderni di Storia* 2 (1976), pp. 15–48.

[Casella, Alfredo]. 'Scarlattiana: Alfredo Casella über sein neues Stück', *Anbruch* 11 (1929), pp. 225–8.

Chalupt, René. 'Quelques souvenirs sur Erik Satie', *La revue musicale* 214 (1952), pp. 39–46.

Cocteau, Jean. *Le coq et l'arlequin: notes autour de la musique*, Paris, 1979.

Dahlhaus, Carl. *Nineteenth-Century Music* (tr. J. Bradford Robinson), Berkeley, 1989.

Danuser, Hermann. *Die Musik des 20. Jahrhunderts*, Laaber, 1984.

'Der Komponist als Editor: Zur Geschichte und Theorie musikalischer Übermalung in den "ana"-Werken', in Felix Meyer (ed.), *Klassizistische Moderne: Eine Begleitpublikation zur Konzertreihe im Rahmen der Versanstaltungen '10 Jahre Paul Sacher Stiftung': Werkeinführungen, Essays, Quellentexte*, Winterthur, 1996, pp. 331–351.

Gustav Mahler und seine Zeit, Laaber, 1991.

'Primordial and Present: The Appropriation of Myth in Music', in Gottfried Boehm, Ulrich Mosch and Katharina Schmidt (eds.), *Canto d'Amore: Classicism in Modern Art and Music 1914–1935* [Catalogue of the Public Art Collection/Gallery of the Paul Sacher Stiftung, Basel, in the Basel Kunstmuseum, 27 April to 11 August 1996], Bern, 1996, pp. 298–314.

'Urheber und Mehrer: Aspekte der Autorschaft bei Weber/Mahlers komischer Oper *Die drei Pintos*', in *Weber – Jenseits des 'Freischütz': Referate des Eutiner Symposions 1986*, ed. Friedhelm Krummacher and Heinrich W. Schwab, Kassel, 1989, pp. 41–58.

Danuser, Hermann and Gianmario Borio (eds.). *Im Zenith der Moderne: Die internationalen Ferienkurse für neue Musik Darmstadt 1946–1966. Geschichte und Dokumentation*, 4 vols., Freiburg im Breisgau, 1997.

Erlich, Victor. *Russischer Formalismus*, Frankfurt am Main, 1973.

Flashar, Hellmut. *Inszenierung der Antike: Das griechische Drama auf der Bühne der Neuzeit 1585–1990*, Munich, 1991.

Gadamer, Hans-Georg. 'Wege des Verstehens: Die Deutung von Autorschaft', *Neue Züricher Zeitung*, no. 239, 13/14 (October 1984), p. 69.

Giger, Andreas. 'A Bibliography on Musical Borrowings', *Notes* 50 (1994), pp. 871–4.

Grafton, Anthony, *Joseph Scaliger: A Study in the History of Classical Scholarship*, 2 vols., Oxford, 1983–93.

Gratzer, Wolfgang and Siegfried Mauser (eds.). *Mozart in der Musik des 20. Jahrhunderts: Formen Ästhetischer und Kompositionstechnischer Rezeption*, Laaber, 1992.

Haase, Erich. 'Spielarten autobiographischer Darstellung in den -ANA', in Günter Reichenkron and Erich Haase (eds.), *Formen der Selbstdarstellung: Analekten zu einer Geschichte des literarischen Selbstportraits: Festgabe für Fritz Neubert [zum 70. Geburtstag am 2. Juli 1965]*, Berlin, 1956, pp. 123–43.

John, Eckhard. *Musikbolschewismus: Die Politisierung der Musik in Deutschland, 1918–1938*, Stuttgart, 1994.

Kämper, Dietrich. 'Nationale und internationale Aspekte in der italienischen Musik des frühen 20. Jahrhunderts', *Revista de Musicologia*, 16/1 (1993), pp. 631–9.

Kunze, Stefan. 'Cherubini und der musikalische Klassizismus', in *Analecta Musicologica. Veröffentlichungen der Musikgeschichtlichen Abteilung des Deutschen Historischen Instituts in Rom*, Vol. XXIII, Laaber, 1974, pp. 301–23.

Lourié, Arthur. 'Neogothic and Neoclassic', *Modern Music* 5/3 (1928), pp. 3–8.

Messing, Scott. *Neoclassicism in Music: From the Genesis of the Concept through the Schoenberg–Stravinsky Polemic*, Ann Arbor, 1988.

Morazzoni, Anna Marian. 'Der Schönberg-Kreis und Italien: Die Polemik gegen Casellas Aufsatz über "Scarlattiana"', in Rudolf Stephan and Sigrid Wiesmann (eds.), *Bericht über den 2. Kongreß der Internationalen Schönberg-Gesellschaft: 'Die Wiener Schule in der Musikgeschichte des 20. Jahrhunderts', Wien, 12. bis 15. Juni 1984*, Vienna, 1986, pp. 73–83.

Neumeyer, David. *The Music of Paul Hindemith*, New Haven, 1986.

Nicolodi, Fiamma. 'Musica e Musicisti nel Ventennio Fascista', *Contrappunti* 19 (1984), pp. 244–57.

Rathert, Wolfgang. 'Vom Klassizismus zur Postmoderne: Anmerkungen zur Musikgeschichte des 19. und 20. Jahrhunderts', in Felix Meyer (ed.), *Klassizistische Moderne: Eine Begleitpublikation zur Konzertreihe im Rahmen der Versanstaltungen '10 Jahre Paul Sacher Stiftung': Werkeinführungen, Essays, Quellentexte*, Winterthur, 1996, pp. 40–59.

Reck, Hans Ulrich (ed.). *Imitation und Mimesis*, Cologne, 1991.

Salzman, Erik. *Twentieth-Century Music: An Introduction* (2nd edn), Englewood Cliffs, NJ, 1974.
Scherliess, Volker. *Neoklassizismus: Dialoge mit der Geschichte*, Kassel, 1998.
'"Torniamo all'Antico e Sarà un Progresso" – Creative Longing in Music', in Gottfried Boehm, Ulrich Mosch and Katharina Schmidt (eds.), *Canto d'Amore: Classicism in Modern Art and Music 1914–1935* [Catalogue of the Public Art Collection/Gallery of the Paul Sacher Stiftung, Basel, in the Basel Kunstmuseum, 27 April to 11 August 1996], Bern, 1996, pp. 39–62.
Schoenberg, Arnold. *Berliner Tagebuch. Mit einer Hommage à Schönberg vom Herausgeber Josef Rufer*, Frankfurt am Main, 1974.
Style and Idea (ed. Leonard Stein, tr. Leo Black), London, 1975.
Schubert, Giselher. 'Kontext und Bedeutung der "Konzertmusik" Hindemiths', in *Zur Musik des 20. Jahrhunderts*, Hamburg, 1980, pp. 62–72.
'Zur Charakteristik von Heitor Villa-Lobos', in Constantin Floros et al. (eds.), *Zwischen den Grenzen: Zum Aspekt des 'Nationalen' in der Neuen Musik*, ed. Dieter Rexroth, Mainz, 1979, pp. 85–114.
Seedorf, Thomas. *Studien zur Kompositorischen Mozart-Rezeption im Frühen 20. Jahrhundert*, Laaber, 1990.
Silver, Kenneth E. *'Esprit de Corps': The Art of the Parisian Avant-Garde and the First World War, 1914–25*, Princeton, 1989.
Sponheuer, Bernd. *Musik als Kunst und Nicht-Kunst: Untersuchungen zur Dichotomie von 'hoher' und 'niederer' Musik im musikästhetischen Denken zwischen Kant und Hanslick*, Kassel, 1987.
Stenzl, Jürg. *Von Giacomo Puccini zu Luigi Nono. Italienische Musik 1922–1952: Faschismus – Resistenza – Republik*, Buren, 1990.
Stephan, Rudolf. 'Bach und die Anfänge der Neuen Musik', *Melos* 2 (1976), pp. 3–7.
Vom Musikalischen Denken: Gesammelte Vorträge (ed. Rainer Damm and Andreas Traub), Mainz, 1985.
Stravinsky, Igor. *Poetics of Music in the Form of Six Lessons* (tr. Arthur Knodel and Ingolf Dahl), Cambridge, MA, 6th edn, 1982.
Stravinsky, Igor and Robert Craft. *Dialogues and a Diary*, London, 1968.
Memories and Commentaries, London, 1981.
Taruskin, Richard, 'Back to Whom? Neoclassicism as Ideology', *Nineteenth-Century Music* 16 (1992), pp. 286–303.
Stravinsky and the Russian Traditions: A Biography of the Works through Mavra, 2 vols., New York, 1996.
Tinctoris, Johannes. *Terminorum musicæ diffinitorium* (facsimile of the 1495 Treviso incunabulum), Kassel, 1983.
Waeltner, Ernst Ludwig. 'Aspekte zum Neoklassizismus Strawinskys: Schlußrhythmus, Thema und Grundriß im Finale des Bläser-Oktetts 1923', in Carl Dahlhaus et al., *Bericht über den Internationalen Musikwissenschaftlichen Kongreß Bonn 1970*, Kassel, pp. 265–74.
Walser, Martin. 'Was ist ein Klassiker?', in Gottfried Honnefelder (ed.), *Warum Klassiker? Ein Alamanach zur Eröffnungsediton der Bibliothek deutscher Klassiker*, Frankfurt am Main, 1985, pp. 3–10.
White, Eric Walter. *Stravinsky: The Composer and his Works* (2nd edn.), London, 1977.

Music of seriousness and commitment: the 1930s and beyond

MICHAEL WALTER

The variety of compositional styles, the multiplicity of the functions of music, the verdict that Schoenberg's music was destined for the happy few who could understand it (and that Richard Strauss's was destined for the happy few who could afford it), the lamented lack of a relationship to society and 'the people', the lack of genre consciousness in the works of many composers in the 1920s, their flirting with the vernacular or the apparent banality of their music – all these perceptions led inevitably to a quest for greater seriousness in music and a new sense of social commitment. The new seriousness was meant to supersede the arbitrariness of musical styles and reinstate composition as a coherent manifestation of high cultural values or as a timeless emanation of the art of music. It was, in short, to replace the alleged social irresponsibility of the 1920s.

The scandals provoked by Schoenberg's and Stravinsky's music before the First World War had been a symptom of the dispersion of a hitherto more or less consistent stylistic language. Together with Stravinsky's *The Rite of Spring*, Schoenberg's non-tonal works had been the first compositions which seemed to jettison the musical tradition of the nineteenth century. In hindsight, a work like Richard Strauss's *Der Rosenkavalier*, mirroring in 'its ahistorical anachronisms' the 'disunities of modern life',[1] equally served to undermine a sense of coherent compositional development. The emergence of a plethora of disparate musical styles and techniques meant that there was no longer a perceived tradition: any composer could be progressive and regressive at the same time, and in this way compositional options presented themselves less in the form of a linear development than of a maze in which tradition seemed to play no part.

The fragmentation of any sense of a musical mainstream, and thus of a clear orientation for composers, reached its peak in the 1920s; it was all the more striking since parts of this former tradition still existed. There was the repertory of the opera houses and concert halls (mostly works of the late eighteenth

1 Bryan Gilliam, *The Life of Richard Strauss*, Cambridge, 1999, p. 89.

and nineteenth centuries), and music was still being composed in this tradition. In Italy, for example, Mascagni's *Nerone* was premiered at La Scala, Milan on 16 January 1935, while Giordano composed patriotic hymns (*Inno nazionale*, 1932; *Inno Imperiale*, 1936). In Germany Strauss's *Die schweigsame Frau* was premiered in 1935, his *Friedenstag* in 1938, and *Capriccio* in 1942. Pfitzner composed, among other works, his Violin Concerto, op. 44 (1935), the Symphony in C major, op. 46 (1940), and the String Quartet in C minor, op. 50 (1942). Despite their various individual styles, these and other composers represented the outgrowths of the nineteenth century: Pfitzner's music was plainly late Romantic, whereas Strauss conceived of his works as the last manifestations of the Wagnerian tradition, and Mascagni and Giordano stood for the still-surviving tradition of Italian verismo. None of these outmoded composers was influential in the 1930s, but they functioned as reminders of a lost ideal of musical seriousness.

The return to seriousness was not the only concern of the composers of the 1930s; they also had to cope with the aftermath of the First World War and the new political climate, along with the economic problems that this entailed. Obviously, in their quest for a new seriousness, composers could no longer count on the old elitist audience of the nineteenth century. They had to face the task, already set out after the First World War and the Latin American revolutions but culminating in the 1930s, of reaching 'the people' with 'serious' music. The concept of 'the people' was central to the nationalistic political climate of the 1930s: by no means a new concept, it went back to the nineteenth century but was at the same time the basis of the 'modern' political goals of the 1930s, as represented by the 'new deal' in the USA, the forging of a new socialist society in the Soviet Union, or the alleged modernity of the fascist dictatorships. These clashing concepts of a retrospective nationalism on the one hand and modernity on the other led to paradoxes that were not solved before the end of the Second World War. Nevertheless, given the disorientation caused by the music of the 1920s, it was natural that composers should invoke the concept of 'the people' or 'the nation' as a justification for their works. The idea of 'nation' had connotations of historical continuity and could function as a surrogate for a compositional tradition that lacked credibility, while composing for 'the people' promised a new route to social legitimation. When Aaron Copland wrote in 1941 that 'new music in future will no longer be confined to the sphere of the special society' but 'must interest the general public through the usual concert channels and the usual interpreters: pianists, singers, chamber organisations, choral societies, and so forth',[2] he expressed a feeling

2 Aaron Copland, *The New Music 1900–1960*, London, 1968, p. 106 [revised and enlarged version of the author's *Our New Music*, New York, 1939].

already shared by many European composers in the 1930s, notwithstanding their different political circumstances.

Emotions, traditions, nationalisms

The crucial paradox of modernity being bound to past notions of nationhood was solved by the idea of a new emotional impact of music, as revealed by three important manifestos. The key text of Soviet Socialist Realism was to become Maxim Gorky's essay *On Socialist Realism* (1933), which was politically promulgated by Andrei Zhdanov (voicing the opinions of Stalin himself) at the First All-Union Congress of Soviet Writers in 1934.[3] Zhdanov defined the goal of Socialist Realism as 'to depict reality in its revolutionary development', and he expected 'works attuned to the epoch'.[4] In January 1934 Stalin's famous slogan appeared in the *Sovietskaya muzïka* (the journal of the Union of Composers): 'the rise of cultures national in form and socialist in content has to take place'.[5] Soon it became clear that the appropriate compositional forms should nonetheless rely on 'Romanticism', and explicitly on Musorgsky's works as the allegedly canonical symbols of Russian nationalism (according to Lenin's principle of 'learning from the classics'[6]). In this way, modern revolutionary concepts of content were bound to outdated concepts of form in order to ensure the 'optimistic' nature of art.

One of the practical results of the politics of Socialist Realism was the infamous condemnation of Shostakovich's *Lady Macbeth of the Mtsensk District*. This had been premiered triumphantly in Leningrad on 22 January 1934, despite its use of heterogeneous musical models, its employment of montage or collage techniques, plurality of styles and forms, and musical irony.[7] It was not until 28 January 1936, when *Pravda* printed the notorious anonymous article 'Confusion instead of Music',[8] that Shostakovich's opera was excoriated as a muddle rather than real music: in the opinion of the author, who also criticized its dissonant harmonies, the ability of good music to affect the masses had

3 See H. G. Scott (ed. and tr.), *Soviet Writers' Congress 1934: the Debate on Socialist Realism and Modernism in the Soviet Union*, London, 1977.

4 Quoted in Boris Schwarz, *Music and Musical Life in Soviet Russia: 1917–1970*, London, 1972, p. 110.

5 Quoted in Marina Frolova-Walker, '"National in Form, Socialist in Content": Musical Nation-Building in the Soviet Republics', *Journal of the American Musicological Society* 51 (1998), pp. 331–71; p. 334. For popular folklorism see Richard Stites, *Russian Popular Culture: Entertainment and Society since 1900*, Cambridge, 1992, pp. 78–81.

6 See Dorothea Redepenning, '"... volkstümlich nach Form und Inhalt ..." Überlegungen zur russisch-sowjetischen Oper', in Udo Bermbach (ed.), *Oper im 20. Jahrhundert. Entwicklungstendenzen und Komponisten*, Stuttgart, 2000, pp. 305–7.

7 See Erik Fischer, *Zur Problematik der Opernstruktur: Das Künstlerische System und seine Krisis im 20. Jahrhundert*, Wiesbaden, 1982, pp. 119–51.

8 Rumour had it that Stalin himself had given Zhdanov, then leader of the Communist Party in Leningrad, instructions to write the article.

been sacrificed for formalistic pretentiousness.[9] Although dealing only with Shostakovich's opera,[10] the article was directed against all avant-garde composers. In contrast to *Lady Macbeth*, Ivan Dzerzhinsky's *Tikhiy Don* (*The Quiet Don*, 1935) – which consisted of a simple, remarkably non-modern lyricism drawn from folksong idioms as well as of monotone marching-step rhythms, and which lacked ensembles – was approved by Stalin himself; it served as an often-imitated model (called 'song opera') for a Soviet opera compliant with Socialist Realism, although the operas that followed its example were altogether unsuccessful. The tenor of the attacks on avant-garde composers in *Pravda* and elsewhere was a wish for a deeper emotional involvement on the audience's part (so-called 'healthy emotions'), and for a seriousness that allegedly was not possible with 'objective' (or 'formalistic') music.

In 1936 there appeared a manifesto by some young French composers who were united by their opposition to neoclassicism, though their aesthetic principles were diverse in other respects; it included as one of its main points a reference to Berlioz as an icon of modern music as well as the great French past:

> While the conditions of life become more and more hard, mechanical, and impersonal, music must without delay bring its spiritual force and its generous effects to those who love it. A group of friends, Yves Baudrier, André Jolivet, Daniel-Lesur, and Olivier Messiaen, [i.e.] the Jeune France, resumes the title which once elevated Berlioz to fame, and undertakes the dissemination of youthful works that are equally far from academic and revolutionary triteness. The tendencies of this group will be diverse: it will be united by instigating and propagating a music that is alive in the same elan of sincerity, liberalness, and artistic conscience.[11]

Although the authors' ideas had nothing in common with Socialist Realism, their manifesto again stressed the emotional impact ('spiritual force') of music and the national past. Symptomatically, Messiaen began his preface to *La nativité du Seigneur: neuf méditations pour orgue* (The Birth of the Lord: Nine Meditations for Organ, 1935) with these sentences: 'Emotion and sincerity above else. But conveyed to the listener by means which are clear and true.'[12] Notwithstanding

9 A slightly revised version of the opera was premiered in 1963 as *Katerina Izmaylova* and hailed as 'an example of applying the principles of socialist realism in musical composition' (L. Lebedinskij in his preface to the score of the 1963 version, Moscow, 1965; quoted in Fischer, *Zur Problematik der Opernstruktur*, p. 153); see also Laurel E. Fay, 'From *Lady Macbeth* to *Katerina*: Shostakovich's Versions and Revisions', in David Fanning (ed.), *Shostakovich Studies*, Cambridge, 1995, pp. 160–88. 'Formalism' was officially defined as 'the separation of form from content' (see Schwarz, *Music and Musical Life in Soviet Russia*, p. 129).

10 A week later Shostakovich's ballet *The Limpid Stream* was attacked in a second article.

11 Quoted in Serge Gut, *Le groupe Jeune France: Yves Baudrier, Daniel Lesur, André Jolivet, Olivier Messiaen*, Paris, 1984, pp. 16–17.

12 This and the following quotations from the preface of the score are translated by G. Levinson.

their conforming with the specific political landscape of France, where the Popular Front regime tried to forge new ties between music and the people, these words could have been written by almost any composer in the 1930s.

Nowhere was a sense of the loss of tradition and the desire for a new and yet traditional musical mainstream (one that would in effect slip over the 1920s) more evident than in a notorious Italian manifesto of 17 December 1932. It was published in three leading Italian newspapers (*Il Popolo d'Italia*, *Il Corriere della Sera*, *La Stampa*) and was signed by the composers Respighi, Pizzetti, and Zandonai, among others.[13] The manifesto was unmistakably anti-modernist and inveighed against 'atonal and pluritonal hullabaloo, objectivism [i.e. neoclassicism] and expressionism'. According to the manifesto, Italian music was still in a state of chaos and experimentation; the Italian audience was intimidated by the mass of reform programmes, not knowing 'which voice and which direction it should follow'. Music should again have human content instead of being a mechanical game and a cerebral sophistry. The manifesto proclaimed the validity of the Italian musical tradition and lamented the loss of music that had an emotional impact on the audiences. However, the ambiguity of the concept of *italianità* is obvious in the case of Alfredo Casella, who was in fact the main target of the manifesto, for he too had for years proselytized in favour of a specific musical *italianità*, emphasizing in particular Italian music from the sixteenth to the eighteenth centuries. What is more, he had exemplified his attitude in neoclassical works like the *Concerto romano* (1926). Like Casella and nearly all other Italian composers, the signatories were followers of Mussolini, who had demanded the emergence of a new art out of fascism in 1927; his girlfriend Margherita Sarfatti saw in *realismo fascista* a sort of 'romantic realism'.[14]

Reinventing traditions

Falling back on national traditions of serious music was impossible for nations that lacked such traditions, particularly the countries of the Iberian peninsula, the Latin American countries, and the USA. As a consequence, resort was made instead to indigenous folk traditions. Already in the early 1930s (the years of the Spanish Second Republic), the Spanish government fostered national folklore art and *zarzuela*. The Falange and later the Francoist state called for music based on popular, folkloristic themes and classical musical forms, at the same time

13 The complete Italian text may be found in Fiamma Nicolodi, *Musica e Musicisti nel Ventennio Fascista*, Fiesole, 1984, pp. 141–3; see also John C. G. Waterhouse, 'The Emergence of Modern Italian Music', Ph.D. diss., Oxford University, 1968.

14 See Jürg Stenzl, *Von Giacomo Puccini zu Luigi Nono. Italienische Musik 1922–1952: Faschismus – Resistenza – Republik*, Buren, 1990, p. 36.

condemning the Spanish avant-garde of the years 1914 to 1936.[15] The predicament of Portugal with regard to its tradition was still greater; the composer Ivo Cruz searched for a 'brilliant musical past'[16] with predictably meagre results. More realistic was the blunt statement of the composer Armando Leça in 1933: 'As we do not have any musical masterpieces of Portuguese universality, we must make do with folksongs.'[17]

As a result of its colonial context, music in nineteenth-century Latin America had merely imitated European music. In the 1920s and 30s, however, certain composers started to conceive their music as an expression of their national culture. The Mexican post-revolutionary period (early 1920s to mid-1930s) saw in an 'Aztec renaissance' the evocation of a pre-colonial past. The most influential Mexican composer, Carlos Chávez, a friend of Aaron Copland, tried to maintain an explicitly national character in some of his compositions: a few of Copland's own works, such as *El salón México* or his music for a puppet show, *From Sorcery to Science* (1939), were influenced by Chávez, but it was mainly Chávez's suggestion of the 'possibility of directing the musical affairs of the nation' that impressed Copland.[18] Chávez's 'Mexican' tendency influenced only about a quarter of his works, with a peak in the 1930s (he returned only sporadically to this kind of music in subsequent years). The study of early pre-Columbian instruments and of Aztec music led him to employ folk instruments and to incorporate the supposed traits of this music into such works as the Aztec ballets *El fuego nuevo* (1925), *Caballos de vapor* (1926–7), and *Xochipilli-Macuilxóchitl* (1940, scored for four wind and six percussion players using a variety of Indian drums). His 'Mexican' works also include the ballet *Los cuatros soles* (1925), the 'sinfonia proletaria' *Llamadas* (1934), *El Sol* (1934) for chorus and orchestra, and a symphony based on Indian themes (*Sinfonia India*, 1935–6). Chávez's compositional style was marked by complex rhythms and irregular metres, and as a whole it was austere in its combination of modernism and 'primitivism'; in this way, as Gerard Béhague puts it, 'his attempts at reconstructing pre-conquest Indian music ultimately constituted a pretext for writing music of a new character – all of it in line with the prevailing nationalist ideology'.[19] Because of the

15 See Gemma Pérez Zalduondo, 'El nacionalismo como eje de la politica musical del primer gobierno regular de Franco (30 de enero de 1938–8 de agosto de 1939)', *Revista de Musicología* 18 (1995), pp. 247–73, and 'The Concepts of "People" and "Nation" in the Republican and Francoist Musical Projects' (my thanks to Gemma Pérez Zalduondo for sending me her paper in advance of publication).

16 Quoted in Teresa Cascudo, 'Nationalism and Music during the 30's: the Portuguese Case', paper presented at the conference 'Nation, Myth and Reality: Music in the 1930s', Royal Holloway, University of London, October 1998 (my thanks to Teresa Cascudo for sending me her paper in advance of publication).

17 Quoted in Cascudo, 'Nationalism and Music during the 30's'.

18 Quoted in Howard Pollack, *Aaron Copland: The Life and Work of an Uncommon Man*, New York, 1999, p. 224.

19 Gerard Béhague, 'The Hispanic World, 1918–45', in Robert Morgan (ed.), *Modern Times: From World War I to the Present*, Englewood Cliffs, NJ, 1993, pp. 231–56; p. 232.

abstract and non-popular nature of his music, however, Chávez did not succeed in his professed intention to reach the people through the incorporation of folk elements.

As late as at the beginning of the twentieth century, the American tradition of serious music had in essence been a branch of the European tradition. It was not until the 1920s that composers like Aaron Copland and George Antheil tried to compose works with an obvious American character, which they achieved either by using jazz elements or by turning to the (Anglo-American) folk tradition. This 'American consciousness' became more intensive after the beginning of the Great Depression and the outbreak of the Second World War. The financial crisis of 1929 demonstrated how easily progress (and not just economic progress) could change into crisis: its value could no longer be taken for granted, nor could it be seen as everlasting. Analogously, musical modernism came to be seen as having no value in itself. The public had comparatively little interest in radical experimental compositions, and Krenek recalled how the radical émigré composers from Europe were compelled to 'be more attentive about reality'.[20] This was also true of the left-wing Composers' Collective of New York, whose members 'acknowledged that their modernist idiom was not communicating to the masses'[21] and turned instead to working with folksongs. What is more, the Works Progress Administration (Federal Music Project) gave musicians employment and provided opportunities for the performance of their music; as a corollary not only did the number of composers increase, but so did their sense that they were composing for the American people. Hence composers referred to indigenous musical elements and strove for a new 'national' music.

Though Roy Harris had studied with Nadia Boulanger in Paris during the 1930s, his Third Symphony (1939) was considered one of the masterpieces of purely American music, establishing a distinctively American style with its combination of hymn-like tunes, fanfares, and chorale-like brass passages: this style was soon to be imitated. Harris clearly saw his mission in being an American composer, and he simplified his style 'through a more obvious and naive use of folk and patriotic materials and motives'.[22] His Fourth Symphony (1941) was based on folksongs, and his Sixth (1944) on Lincoln's Gettysburg Address. Even Henry Cowell, who had been a radical composer in the 1920s, changed his style to a more folkloristic one in the 1940s.

20 Ernst Krenek, 'Amerikas Einfluß auf eingewanderte Komponisten', *Musica* 13 (1959), pp. 757–61; p. 759.

21 Carol J. Oja, 'Marc Blitzstein's *The Cradle Will Rock* and Mass-Song Style of the 1930s', *Musical Quarterly* 73 (1989), pp. 445–75; p. 459.

22 Richard Franko Goldman, 'American Music: 1918–1960 (i) Music in the United States', in Martin Cooper (ed.), *The Oxford History of Music, X: The Modern Age, 1890–1960*, London, 1974, pp. 569–638; p. 615.

Similarly Aaron Copland (another Boulanger pupil), presumably influenced by the emerging interest of the Composers' Collective in American folk music, abandoned his 'abstract' style of the 1920s and turned to more folk-inspired compositions. The first of these was the already mentioned *El salón México* (the orchestral version of which was premiered in 1936 under the direction of Chávez). Copland used Mexican folk tunes in *El salón México*, albeit not unaltered: in Howard Pollack's words, he 'freely deleted and changed pitches. He also varied rhythms, often prolonging or shortening a note or adding or omitting a rest.'[23] Often he alluded to indigenous melodies rather than quoting them. This is also true of his most successful work of the 1930s, the ballet *Billy the Kid* (1938), in which he incorporated material derived from six cowboy songs. Although the American story of Billy the Kid suggested the incorporation of such tunes, Copland at first refused to use them, presumably because he saw them as incompatible with his aim of writing artful, serious music. (As I shall argue, the examples of Prokofiev, who avoided simple quotation, and Tippett, who failed with the quotation of spirituals, show that Copland was right about this.) Cowboy tunes 'are often less than exciting', Copland wrote at the time of the ballet's premiere, and for this reason he had soon found himself 'hopelessly involved in expanding, contracting, rearranging and superimposing' them.[24]

In adapting the tunes to his own melodic and rhythmic requirements, Copland converted the folk elements into a means of aesthetic expression without corrupting his own style. This is especially true with regard to his irregular or uncommon metres (like the 5/8 rhythm in the *Mexican Dance*). The resulting musical style bears the stamp of 'American music': listeners are likely to get the impression of American music even if they do not recognise the melodic allusion. Although in *Lincoln Portrait* (1942) short quotations of American tunes can also be identified, Copland's American style is essentially an 'as if' style. It is not important whether or not a particular melodic fragment played by the oboe 'is almost certainly a folksong';[25] what matters is that it sounds like a folksong allusion. In the next of his so-called 'western ballets', *Rodeo* (1942), Copland incorporated folksongs 'in their entirety and in relatively traditional settings', so turning his technique upside down; but he also coined his own original music in the folk style 'to the point that one cannot be sure, without consulting the original sources, where a folk tune leaves off or resumes'.[26] The stylistic coherence of the music, in short, results not from the quotations but from Copland's ability to yield an impression of American authenticity.

23 Pollack, *Aaron Copland*, p. 299. 24 Quoted in Pollack, *Aaron Copland*, p. 320.
25 Neil Butterworth, *The Music of Aaron Copland*, London, 1985, p. 90 (referring to *Lincoln Portrait*).
26 Pollack, *Aaron Copland*, p. 367.

This meant that he was equally able to allude to non-American tunes by giving them an American touch through their 'jazzy treatment',[27] or to include folk-like materials such as the oboe melody in the section 'Corral Nocturne' (which Copland insisted was not a quotation). In his most famous ballet, *Appalachian Spring* (1944), he cited only a single American song – the Shaker melody 'Simple Gifts' – as the theme of four variations; nevertheless the music as a whole is still heard, in Neil Butterworth's words, as having 'its roots in the countryside of New England' and as a 'strong expression of national feeling'[28] (and this despite the fact that the music depicts neither the Appalachians nor the spring[29]). In fusing a modified vernacular style with his own, European-derived means of expression, Copland was able to forge a musical style which bore the convincing impression of being both authentic and distinctively American. At the same time he demonstrated his ability to 'say what I had to say in the simplest possible terms'.[30]

In Germany, however, where the 1920s had seen attempts to forge new styles through engagement with jazz and popular music, what might almost be seen as the reverse process took place. After the failure of his cooperation with the *Jugendbewegung*, his breaking-off with Brecht due to ideological differences in 1930, and the breakdown of political stability, Hindemith realised that the composer's problem was not the relationship of artist and society but the role of the artist within society. The experience of his *Gebrauchsmusik* ('utility' or 'common use' music) works in the 1920s had shown him the dangers of subsiding to a lesser artistic level and of being (ab)used for political ends, and for this reason he attempted to return to the great and serious tradition represented by German music. While he was working on the opera *Mathis der Maler* (whose plot centres on the painter Mathias Grünewald), his publisher described Hindemith's attitude as follows: 'He is very enthusiastic with the subject which can become *the* German opera . . . Grünewald's fate as an artist who went his own way in a misunderstood manner, and resisted the foreign influence of the Italian Renaissance, is a parallel to his own personality and is therefore extraordinarily intriguing for him.'[31]

Hindemith did not comply with National Socialist doctrines; from 1934 he was constantly attacked by Nazi officials, and he left Germany in 1938. However, his symphony *Mathis der Maler* (which is based on material from the opera of the same name and was first performed in 1934) shows a clear

27 Butterworth, *The Music of Aaron Copland*, p. 93. 28 Ibid., p. 101.
29 See Pollack, *Aaron Copland*, p. 390. 30 Copland, *The New Music 1900–1960*, p. 160.
31 Quoted in Gudrun Breimann, *'Mathis der Maler' und der 'Fall Hindemith'. Studien zu Hindemiths Opernlibretto im Kontext der kulturgeschichtlichen und politischen Bedingungen der 30er Jahre*, Frankfurt, 1997, pp. 62–3.

relation to the official conception of 'modern music' in the Third Reich.[32] This holds especially for the first movement ('Engelskonzert' or angels' concert), with its 'monumental-pathetic effect of the trombone choruses and the transfiguring ending',[33] allusion to antiquity through its archaic polyphony, chorale-like Lieder, and pentatonic and church-mode features. The work was enthusiastically welcomed by German audiences and experienced an immediate success. However the most striking new feature of Hindemith's music in the 1930s was the quotation of folksongs, not only in the *Mathis* symphony and opera but also in his Concert Music for Piano, Brass, and Harps, op. 49 (1930), his funeral music for King George V (1936, where he quoted the chorale 'Vor deinen Thron tret ich hiermit' as set by Bach), and his viola concerto *Der Schwanendreher* (1935, second version 1936), which he described as based on 'old folk-songs'. These songs, however, were not popular traditional songs;[34] rather they were selected for their uncommon modality, which Hindemith saw as evoking a sense of the 'dignity' of the (German) people's art. To this extent Hindemith did not share the basic approach of the folkloristic composers.

In Hindemith's opinion, musical art-works had to be uncomplicated and characterized by a clear formal design. As an expression of ethical values, they should also be timeless and universal, rather than tied to a single epoch. (It is one of the paradoxes of this attitude that it was expressed in works that are so obviously of their time.) Hindemith tried to absorb the musical techniques and forms of the tradition of tonal music in his works, which resulted (compared to his earlier works) in a more tonal and diatonic but also more abstract style. It is no coincidence, then, that it was at this time that Hindemith wrote his *Unterweisung im Tonsatz* (1935–7), in which he strove for a universal doctrine of tonality. Hindemith's *Unterweisung* documents the turning point of music history around 1930. His notion of tonality, although a theoretical one, claims to include all possible chord structures and connections, even the most complex. Implicitly, then, he rejected the experiences and historical reflections that underwrote the new music of the first quarter of the century.[35] Hindemith's music in the 1930s and 40s tended to be as academic as his *Unterweisung im Tonsatz*, losing much of the fresh and imaginative quality so typical for his

32 See Erik Levi, *Music in the Third Reich*, Basingstoke, 1994, p. 110.

33 Claudia Maurer Zenck, 'Zwischen Boykott und Anpassung an den Charakter der Zeit. Über die Schwierigkeiten eines deutschen Komponisten mit dem Dritten Reich', *Hindemith-Jahrbuch/Annales Hindemith* 9 (1980), pp. 65–129; p. 119.

34 Hindemith's source was Franz Böhme's *Altdeutsches Liederbuch* (1877); it is doubtful whether even German audiences knew the meaning of 'Schwanendreher' (guardian of poultry), addressed in the song 'Seid ihr nicht der Schwanendreher?' which forms the basis of the last movement.

35 See Hermann Danuser, *Die Musik des 20. Jahrhunderts*, Laaber, 1984, p. 228.

music in the 1920s. In Arnold Whittall's words, striving for works of a timeless validity often led to 'sadly dull and colourless' results.[36]

Music by the people, music for the people

In composing oratorios or oratorio-like works such as the Soviet mass cantatas, a composer was able to express a commitment to the people and a serious ambition at the same time. Such works stood in the tradition of Bach's and Handel's oratorios, and the participation of numerous singers in the choruses could be interpreted as a musical representation of the people. But all these works were aesthetically more or less problematic. This is true, for example, of Michael Tippett's oratorio *A Child of Our Time* (completed in spring 1941 but not performed until March 1944): its form is primarily related to the tradition of English oratorio, but with interspersed negro spirituals reminiscent in their function of the chorales in Bach's Passions.

In the early 1930s Tippett had no explicit concern about the relationship between his music and society (although he briefly joined the Communist Party in 1935). His famous Concerto for Double String Orchestra (1939) is a unique and confident synthesis of different stylistic elements, with its flexible rhythms, beats of irregular lengths, rhythmic polyphony, jazz features, use of harmony (still triadic) as tonal colouring, inclusion of folksong and modality, and echoes of English renaissance and baroque music. But in the course of the decade Tippett became increasingly aware of the realities of other people's lives and sought to express this compassion in his music, and when a German diplomat was shot by a Polish Jew in Paris in November 1938, Tippett responded with a first draft of *A Child of Our Time*.[37] As he explained:

> The Jews were the particular scapegoats of everything . . . For these people I knew somehow I had to sing songs . . . I felt I had to express collective feelings and that could only be done by collective tunes such as Negro spirituals, for these tunes contain a deposit of generations of common experience.[38]

The text of the oratorio was written by Tippett himself, who was at this time under the influence of Jungian psychoanalysis. Despite the obvious political slant, he treated the subject as a primarily psychological one: peace, in Tippett's Jungian interpretation, is the symbol of a new synthesis of the irrational elements within ourselves. However, there are also obvious references to actual political circumstances, as for example in no. 4 (The Narrator, Bass Solo: 'Now

36 Arnold Whittall, *Music since the First World War* (2nd edn), New York, 1988, p. 75.
37 The title stemmed from a story by Ödön von Horváth published in 1938.
38 Michael Tippett, *Moving into Aquarius* (2nd edn), St Albans, 1974, pp. 152–3.

in each nation there were some cast out by authority and tormented, / made to suffer for the general wrong. / Pogroms in the east, lynching in the west . . .'). A third layer of reference is presented by such apparently artless spirituals as 'Go down, Moses, 'way down in Egypt land'. But these three textual layers – symbolic or mystical allusions to psychoanalysis, political references, and spirituals – are hardly in accordance with one another, and so give rise to the impression of a textual patchwork rather than an organic whole. Although the spirituals were conceived (and should be thought of) as integral parts of the oratorio, there remains a stylistic gap over which many of Tippett's commentators have expressed reservations: only once did Tippett try to reduce the stylistic distance between his own essentially chromatic compositional style and the spirituals, when he employed a tango-like rhythm in no. 6 (Tenor Solo, 'I have no money for my bread').

Tippett's lack of virtuoso demands on the choral singers reflected his striving for oratorio-like simplicity; Whittall describes the result as an 'atypical stodginess of rhythm', an effect created in part through the imitations and sequential patterns that result from the frequent use of word repetition.[39] One can take *A Child of our Time* as an illustration of the problems inherent in composing a serious work *about* the people and *for* the people at the same time: the latter required a more popular and simpler music, in clear contradiction to the complex compositional techniques considered to be essential for serious music. More successful in this respect than Tippett's oratorio was Carl Orff's oratorio-like 'scenic cantata' *Carmina burana* (1937). With its vigorous hammering rhythms (the two pianos are used as percussion instruments), mostly strophic organization, sometimes massive yet sometimes delicate sonorities, simple harmonic structure, and homophonic choruses with uncomplicated tunes, Orff achieved a singular musical directness. Instantly, he was accused of musical primitivism.[40]

Meanwhile, in the Soviet Union, the immediate consequence of the *Pravda* review of *Lady Macbeth* was that Shostakovitch withdrew his Fourth Symphony (1936); he had been warned by an official that it would otherwise be necessary to 'resort to administrative measures'[41] (because of the 'formalist' nature of the work). An additional reason was presumably the resistance of the orchestra during the rehearsal of the third movement. By contrast his Fifth Symphony,

39 See Arnold Whittall, *The Music of Britten and Tippett: Studies in Themes and Techniques*, Cambridge, 1982, p. 73.

40 'His [Orff's] music does not arrive at larger musical forms; Orff is satisfied with an overemphasis of a simplicity which nearly looks primitive with regard to melody and rhythm.' (Herbert Gerigk, 'Aus dem Musikleben', *Nationalsozialistische Monatshefte* 8 (1937), pp. 650–3; p. 652. Gerigk was a highly influential National Socialist Critic.)

41 Isaak Glikman's words, quoted in Laurel E. Fay, *Shostakovich: A Life*, Oxford, 2000, p. 95.

premiered in November 1937, was a great success.[42] 'Among the reviews', he wrote, 'one gave me special pleasure, where it said that the Fifth Symphony is the creative answer of a Soviet artist to just criticism'.[43] But the work can also be seen as a solution to the symphonic problems of his Fourth Symphony with its diverse, contradictory and hardly integrated elements.[44]

Even if a composer did not use avant-garde ('formalistic') techniques it was difficult to meet the central criteria for Socialist Realism in orchestral music. Purely instrumental music was generally distrusted for not being able to depict Socialist reality. Thus it is not surprising that there was a decrease in the writing of such works in the Soviet Union after 1932. A much safer way to compose symphonies was to employ choruses set to appropriate texts, often with a simplistic musical texture. Large orchestrations were the ideal counterpart of the masses, brass passages conveyed the impression of the required heroism, and folk-music idioms (or allusions to them) could symbolize the non-Slavonic nations of the Soviet Union. Stylistically, most of these compositions represented 'a plateau of safe conservatism'.[45]

However, the problem with Socialist Realism was not so much the concept itself as its control by political means; it should not be forgotten that, as an aesthetic concept, Socialist Realism was not far from opinions already voiced by leading composers. When Prokofiev finally returned to the Soviet Union (or rather, in his politically unconcerned opinion, to Russia) in order to settle permanently in Moscow, he thought he could solve his creative crisis through being newly inspired by Russian speech and culture – in other words, by the nation and by the people. In an article in *Izvestiya* of 16 November 1934, he suggested that a Soviet composer should compose grand music, the idea and the technical dimension of which would match the grandeur of 'our' epoch; from such music would emerge a specifically Soviet style of composition which would show 'our true selves' to foreign countries.[46] In order to find a basis for communication with audiences, he continued, one has to compose music appropriate for the millions of people who are not used to (serious) music: 'Above all,' he said, 'it must be melodious; moreover, the melody must be simple and comprehensible, without being repetitive or trivial . . . The simplicity should not be an old-fashioned simplicity, but a new simplicity.'[47] This was in

42 See Richard Taruskin, 'Public Lies and Unspeakable Truth: Interpreting Shostakovich's Fifth Symphony', in David Fanning (ed.), *Shostakovich Studies*, Cambridge, 1995, pp. 17–56.

43 D. Shostakovich, 'Moi tvorcheskiy otvet', *Vechernyaya Moskva* (15 January 1938), p. 3; quoted in Laurel E. Fay, 'The USSR, 1918–45', in Robert Morgan (ed.), *Modern Times: From World War I to the Present*, Englewood Cliffs, NJ, 1993, pp. 141–61; p. 156.

44 See Fay, 'The USSR, 1918–45', pp. 156–7.

45 Schwarz, *Music and Musical Life in Soviet Russia*, p. 116.

46 Quoted in Daniel Jaffé, *Sergey Prokofiev*, London, 1998, p. 133.

47 Quoted in Jaffé, *Sergey Prokofiev*, p. 133.

fact not so different from what Prokofiev had said in a *New York Times* interview in 1930: 'We want a simpler and more melodic style for music, a simple, less complicated emotional state, and dissonance again relegated to its proper place as one element of music . . . I think we have gone as far as we are likely to go in the direction of size, or dissonance, or complexity in music.'[48]

In 1934 Prokofiev thought he had achieved his goal with the suites derived from his incidental music to Alexander Tairov's *Egyptian Nights*, and from his *Lieutenant Kijé* score. The latter was originally intended for a film based on the military career of a fictitious lieutenant; in the event the film did not materialize, and the composer put together the *Lieutenant Kijé* suite from the music he had composed for it. Prokofiev achieved a specific ironic distance from the plot by 'reconstructing in music the "Early Empire" style'.[49] For example, he composed his own melody for the romance 'My Grey Dove' instead of adapting the popular tune of this poem; again, in the music to 'Kijé is Getting Married', he used the sound of a cornet instead of a trumpet (which would be more typical for the dance-like tune), so giving the entire melody an ironic touch. It is true and authentic but at the same time it is not; it is a 'popular' tune but at the same time it is the foil for a series of artful variations. The cornet episodes are contrasted with a sort of 'official' and pompous wedding music, a contradiction which leads to an unreal atmosphere.

When the storm broke over Shostakovich's *Lady Macbeth*, Prokofiev was on tour abroad and he did not take the debate very seriously, although during the course of it he was accused of having denounced Soviet music as provincial. Since Prokofiev maintained that Soviet composers should not ignore the opinion of Western colleagues, his 'survival during Stalin's policy of terror' is indeed 'surprising',[50] even if one takes into account the fact that he was courted and privileged by propagandistically minded officials as a renowned composer who had voluntarily returned from abroad. There were reasons for it, however: already in his earlier works Prokofiev's melodic style had often been diatonic, so that his music was superficially in accordance with Soviet non-formalistic demands, and this remained the case of works like the ballet *Romeo and Juliet*, composed in 1935–6, and his most famous piece, *Peter and the Wolf*, 1936 – although in the latter case the objective to provide an introduction to the instruments of an orchestra for young children may have been more important for the form of the music than any political requirements. In any case, despite his brave words, Prokofiev was capable of accommodation: he composed a *Cantata for the Twentieth Anniversary of the October Revolution* (1936–7,

48 Quoted in Jaffé, *Sergey Prokofiev*, pp. 120–1.
49 Tatiana K. Egorova, *Soviet Film Music: An Historical Survey*, Amsterdam, 1997, p. 28.
50 Jaffé, *Sergey Prokofiev*, p. 148.

for some five hundred performers), set to texts by Marx, Lenin, and Stalin, though the work was accused of vulgarity and was not performed until 1966. And in 1938 he began to compose a Soviet opera with a heroic subject, which was to become *Semyon Kotko*[51] (named after the protagonist, a young partisan; the plot is set at the time of the Civil War). But he declined to write it in the form of a 'song opera', arguing that a new Soviet opera required a new model, and instead adopting a restrained musical style with recitative-like melodic devices and rhythmic speech moving smoothly from speaking to singing. Predictably, the opera was accused of being 'formalistic' and disappeared from the repertoire after its 1940 premiere.

Coming increasingly under political pressure (his friend Meyerhold had been arrested and was finally shot in February 1940), Prokofiev accepted the request to compose a radio-cantata *Zdravitsa* (*Hail to Stalin*) to celebrate Stalin's sixtieth birthday; this time the work complied both textually and musically with Stalin's personal taste, and therefore with the tenets of Socialist Realism. Similarly, and also in 1940, he tried to comply with the wishes of the Soviet Committee on Artistic Affairs in his opera *War and Peace*. In this way, having started with a commitment to the new Soviet audience in 1933, Prokofiev ended up seven years later with a commitment to the mandates of dictator and state.

New systems, new media

Born in 1908 and a devout Catholic, Olivier Messiaen became 'organiste titulaire' at the Paris church de la Sainte Trinité in 1931. Although it was not his first composition, *La nativité du Seigneur* (which dates from the same year) was deemed his first masterpiece. What is more, it was in *La nativité* that his idiosyncratic harmonic and rhythmic system became manifest for the first time. Messiaen's early works for orchestra (*Les offrandes oubliées*, 1931, *Le tombeau resplendissant*, 1932, *Hymne au Saint-Sacrement*, 1933, and *L'ascension*, 1935) were also in essence religious pieces, like *La nativité*, even though intended for the concert hall.

It is only at a first glance that Messiaen seems to be a special case. The reference to religion or *Weltanschauung* can be understood as a substitute for the lost musical tradition, just as in the case of other composers. In 1933, for example, Kurt Weill (working with Max Reinhardt and Franz Werfel) sketched *Der Weg der Verheissung* (revised by L. Lewisohn in 1935–6 as *The Eternal Road*), a biblical play first performed in 1937; again, Stravinsky – who had rejoined the

51 See Simon Morrison, 'Sergei Prokofiev's "Semyon Kotko" as a Representative Example of Socialist Realism', MA diss., McGill University, Montreal, 1992.

Orthodox Church in 1926 – composed his *Symphony of Psalms* in 1930 and two out of his three Slavonic sacred works in 1932 (*Simvol' verï*; Symbol of Faith) and 1934 (*Bogoroditse devo*; Blessed Virgin),[52] while he worked on his Mass from 1944–8. Other examples of *Weltanschauungsmusik* were Bartók's *Cantata profana* (1930), Schoenberg's *Moses und Aron* (1932), Krenek's *Karl V* (1933), and Hindemith's *Mathis der Maler* (1935).[53] Even Mario Castelnuovo-Tedesco alluded to the Jewish faith in his Second Violin Concerto (1931, subtitled *The Prophets*): its three movements characterize the prophets Isaiah, Jeremiah, and Elijah. It may be true that, as Paul Griffiths says, Messiaen's music 'makes its effect in the first place by virtue only of what it parades in sound and time, not by the intentions that may crowd around it',[54] but it is also true that the precondition of Messiaen's success was a climate in which religious music was accepted as an artistic expression, beyond any liturgical function it might have.

Messiaen's compositional means were rather different from those of other composers. He used transposable modes, 'expanded pedal groups . . . forming a musical whole (rhythm, harmony, melody)', and rhythmic formulae in which 'to any rhythm may be added one-half of the smallest note-value of the rhythm, either by a note or by a dot', as well as 'progressive expansion and contraction of intervals'.[55] In other words, he created his own unique musical system, setting it out in the preface to *La nativité* (which anticipated his 1944 treatise, *Technique de mon langage musical*). Apart from these technical explanations, harmony was for Messiaen primarily a means of expressing timbre, a colouristic device. He was obsessed with bird songs, and from the time of his *Quatuor pour la fin du temps* (1941, composed during his time as a prisoner of war in Germany) he often used imitations of them as motivic material. His compositions were also strongly influenced by Greek and Hindu rhythms of the thirteenth century (*deçî-tâlas*), as well as by some of Stravinsky's rhythms in *The Rite of Spring*;[56] begining with the *Quatuor pour la fin du temps*, Messiaen also used 'non-retrograde' rhythms (that is, rhythms which can be read from left to right or from right to left and remain the same). But this creation of a new musical style was only possible because Messiaen believed in and insisted on the theological bearing of his works. Their extra-musical and mystical meaning (Messiaen often associated his themes with a specific theological concept) liberated him from the ties of a possibly regressive reference to musical tradition.

52 The third of these works was *Otche nash'* (Our Father), already composed in 1926.

53 See Albrecht Riethmüller, 'Die Dreißiger Jahre: Eine Dekade kompositorischer Ermüdung oder Konsolidierung? Zusammenfassung der Diskussion', in Christoph-Hellmut Mahling and Sigrid Wiesmann (eds.), *Bericht über den Internationalen Musikwissenschaftlichen Kongreß Bayreuth 1981*, Kassel, 1984, pp. 176–7.

54 Paul Griffiths, *Olivier Messiaen and the Music of Time*, London, 1985, p. 51.

55 Preface to *La nativité du Seigneur*.

56 See Olivier Messiaen, 'Le rythme chez Igor Strawinsky', *Revue musicale* 191 (1939), pp. 91–2.

If a new relationship with religion was one element in the realignment of music in the 1930s, another was provided by advances in technology. In a certain sense, film music in the 1930s was a direct sequel to the tradition of late-nineteenth-century music; it was said that Erich Wolfgang Korngold, who had been successful as an opera composer in Europe before emigrating to Hollywood in 1938, set films to music 'as if they were opera librettos (without singing)',[57] relying on Wagnerian and Straussian techniques. In this way the Hollywood composers used the emotional vocabulary of Romantic music to mediate the protagonists' emotions to the audience. And although political circumstances in the Soviet Union were profoundly dissimilar to those in the USA, much of the film music composed there was not so different (or, to put it another way, the American composers' music could have fitted Soviet doctrines). The musical style often went back to Tchaikovsky, Rimsky-Korsakov, Musorgsky, or Glinka. Most important and internationally recognized was the collaboration between Sergei Eisenstein and Prokofiev in *Alexander Nevsky* (1938) and *Ivan Grozniÿ* (*Ivan the Terrible*, 1942–5). Prokofiev was interested in the musical techniques and technology of sound film, and had visited the Hollywood studios in 1938; consequently his film music was influenced by Hollywood techniques. At the same time, in using large hymnic passages, traditional Lied and dance forms, in alluding to folkloristic melodic material, and in picking up the tradition of nineteenth-century Russian opera in *Ivan the Terrible*, Prokofiev's music also conformed to the demands of Socialist Realism, as well as expressing his personal desire for a more popular music.

Even to serious composers like Copland it was obvious that 'an entirely new public for music had grown up around the radio and phonograph';[58] by the 1930s radio had become a mass medium in America, Europe, and the Soviet Union, and an overwhelming influence on people's musical experiences. Speaking directly to listeners in their own homes, recorded and broadcast music acquired a particular kind of reality or authenticity, and it is here that the comparison between popular and 'serious' music becomes telling. A new, intimate relationship could be forged between performer and audience. In her famous song 'Ich bin die fesche Lola' (from the film *Der blaue Engel*; *The Blue Angel*, 1930), for instance, Marlene Dietrich proved that her special style was to sing deficiently; she was not able to sing in tune or in rhythm, she could not perform proper changes of register, or even pronounce German in the accepted manner (she had the accent then characteristic of the Berlin working classes). But all these defects added up to a special, artless, in a word authentic style. Even 'hot

57 Wolfgang Thiel, *Filmmusik in Geschichte und Gegenwart*, Berlin, 1981, p. 163.
58 Copland, *The New Music 1900–1960*, p. 160.

jazz' and swing represented this authenticity in their (really or supposedly) improvised sections. It is this which was responsible for the special effect of popular music: the impression of authenticity representing musical and human truth – in short, exactly the features that were sought by 'serious' composers.

The end of an epoch

The 1930s marked the real end of nineteenth-century musical life insofar as – despite all the efforts of serious composers – the dominance of serious music, of music as a cultural representation of society, had obviously reached its end. The most popular song at the beginning of the 1940s was not from an opera, a ballet, or a symphony: it was 'Lili Marleen', which had become a global hit as a result of worldwide broadcasting and its expression of a mood of melancholy that was shared by the public. The musical genres embraced by the general public were popular ones, the aim of which (like that of film music) was to communicate human emotions, and popular music took on a particular emotional significance at a time when entertainment became an important (and often the only) means of assuaging the rigours of life.

Quantitatively, serious music for the concert hall or opera house had come to occupy only a small niche. Aiming at cultural predominance, it had dissolved into a host of contradictory impulses. It aimed to reach the people, thereby bringing about a newly reunified musical culture, and this was only possible through compositional simplicity; but at the same time serious music needed a certain complexity in order to be seen as a continuation of the nineteenth-century tradition, which was essential if it was to achieve the status to which it aspired. What is more, reaching a wide public entailed composing in more or less nationally specific idioms, further contributing to the fragmentation of styles, and so contradicting the aim of creating a new mainstream of serious music. But now, for the first time in history, there was a new popular music spread worldwide by means of film, radio, and record. (Glenn Miller's 'Chattanooga Choo-Choo' was the first million-seller ever; the Comedian Harmonists first became famous by way of their recordings, not their performances; even Harris's Third Symphony won popularity as the first American symphony distributed on 78s). This music achieved what serious composers had hoped for in vain: it was heard by millions of people, entertaining and touching them with an emotional authenticity which serious music only rarely managed to evoke. In this way there was, after all, a new musical mainstream, albeit a fast-changing one: popular music.

Although controversies concerning musical progress did not exactly come to an end, they became virtually obsolete, because the new age of mechanical reproduction meant that people could choose 'their' music according to their wishes. In this sense music history – conceived as never-ending compositional progress manifesting itself in constantly new techniques and aiming at a Hegelian 'truth' – came to an irreversible halt. Indeed tonality, the focus of controversies about musical progress earlier in the century, was no longer a central issue: whether it was swing or the music of younger composers like Tippett or Messiaen, harmony had come to be little more than a component of sonority or tone colour. Atonality was no longer a question of creed, but merely a response to musical need under certain circumstances, and in the same way there was a shift to rhythm as another core property of music. Of course, the rhythms of jazz had nothing in common with Messiaen's intricate rhythmical devices. But, like the new emphasis on sonority, both were symptoms of a shift in musical perception which was to dominate the rest of the century.

Bibliography

Béhague, Gerard. 'The Hispanic World, 1918–45', in Robert P. Morgan (ed.), *Modern Times: From World War I to the Present*, Englewood Cliffs, NJ, 1993, pp. 231–56.

Breimann, Gudrun. *'Mathis der Maler' und der 'Fall Hindemith'. Studien zu Hindemiths Opernlibretto im Kontext der kulturgeschichtlichen und politischen Bedingungen der 30er Jahre*, Frankfurt, 1997.

Bruhn, Siglind. *The Temptation of Paul Hindemith: 'Mathis der Maler' as a Spiritual Testimony*, Stuyvesant, NY, 1998.

Butterworth, Neil. *The Music of Aaron Copland*, London, 1985.

Cascudo, Teresa. 'Nationalism and Music during the 30s: the Portuguese Case', paper presented at the conference 'Nation, Myth and Reality: Music in the 1930s', Royal Holloway, University of London, October 1998.

Copland, Aaron. *The New Music 1900–1960*, London, 1968.

Danuser, Hermann. *Die Musik des 20. Jahrhunderts*, Laaber, 1984.

Darby, William and Jack Du Bois. *American Film Music: Major Composers, Techniques, Trends, 1915–1990*, Jefferson, NC, 1990.

Egorova, Tatiana K. *Soviet Film Music: An Historical Survey*, Amsterdam, 1997.

Fay, Laurel E. 'From *Lady Macbeth* to *Katerina*: Shostakovich's Versions and Revisions', in David Fanning (ed.), *Shostakovich Studies*, Cambridge, 1995, pp. 160–88.

Shostakovich: A Life, Oxford, 2000.

'The USSR, 1918–45', in Robert P. Morgan (ed.), *Modern Times: From World War I to the Present*, pp. 141–61.

Fischer, Erik. *Zur Problematik der Opernstruktur: Das künstlerische System und seine Krisis im 20. Jahrhundert*, Wiesbaden, 1982.

Frolova-Walker, Marina. '"National in Form, Socialist in Content": Musical Nation-Building in the Soviet Republics', *Journal of the American Musicological Society* 51 (1998), pp. 331–71.

Gerigk, Herbert. 'Aus dem Musikleben', *Nationalsozialistische Monatshefte* 8 (1937), pp. 650–3.

Gilliam, Bryan. *The Life of Richard Strauss*, Cambridge, 1999.
Goldman, Richard Franko. 'American Music: 1918–1960 (i) Music in the United States', in Martin Cooper (ed.), *The Oxford History of Music, X: The Modern Age, 1890–1960*, London, 1974, pp. 569–638.
Griffiths, Paul. *Olivier Messiaen and the Music of Time*, London, 1985.
Gut, Serge. *Le groupe Jeune France. Yves Baudrier, Daniel Lesur, André Jolivet, Olivier Messiaen*, Paris, 1984.
Hamm, Charles. *Yesterday: Popular Song in America*, New York, 1979.
Jaffé, Daniel. *Sergey Prokofiev*, London, 1998.
Kater, Michael. *Different Drummers: Jazz in the Culture of Nazi Germany*, New York, 1992.
Krenek, Ernst. 'Amerikas Einfluß auf eingewanderte Komponisten', *Musica* 13 (1959), pp. 757–61.
Levi, Erik. *Music in the Third Reich*, Basingstoke, 1994.
Manvell, Roger and John Huntley. *The Technique of Film Music* (rev. and enlarged by Richard Arnell and Peter Day), London, 1975.
Messiaen, Olivier. 'Le rythme chez Igor Strawinsky', *Revue musicale* 191 (1939), pp. 91–2.
Morrison, Simon. 'Sergei Prokofiev's "Semyon Kotko" as a Representative Example of Socialist Realism', MA diss., McGill University, Montreal, 1992.
Nicolodi, Fiamma. *Musica e musicisti nel ventennio fascista*, Fiesole, 1984.
Oja, Carol J. 'Marc Blitzstein's *The Cradle Will Rock* and Mass-Song Style of the 1930s', *Musical Quarterly* 73 (1989), pp. 445–75.
Pollack, Howard. *Aaron Copland: The Life and Work of an Uncommon Man*, New York, 1999.
Redepenning, Dorothea. '". . . volkstümlich nach Form und Inhalt . . ." Überlegungen zur russisch-sowjetischen Oper', in Udo Bermbach (ed.), *Oper im 20. Jahrhundert. Entwicklungstendenzen und Komponisten*, Stuttgart, 2000, pp. 305–7.
Riethmüller, Albrecht. 'Die Dreißiger Jahre: Eine Dekade kompositorischer Ermüdung oder Konsolidierung? Zusammenfassung der Diskussion', in Christoph-Hellmut Mahling and Sigrid Wiesmann (eds.), *Bericht über den Internationalen Musikwissenschaftlichen Kongreß Bayreuth 1981*, Kassel, 1984, pp. 176–7.
Schuller, Gunther. *The Swing Era: The Development of Jazz 1930–1945*, New York, 1989.
Schwarz, Boris. *Music and Musical Life in Soviet Russia: 1917–1970*, London, 1972.
Scott, H. G. (ed. and tr.). *Soviet Writers' Congress 1934: the Debate on Socialist Realism and Modernism in the Soviet Union*, London, 1977.
Stenzl, Jürg. *Von Giacomo Puccini zu Luigi Nono. Italienische Musik 1922–1952: Faschismus – Resistenza – Republik*, Buren, 1990.
Stites, Richard. *Russian Popular Culture: Entertainment and Society since 1900*, Cambridge, 1992.
Taruskin, Richard. 'Public Lies and Unspeakable Truth: Interpreting Shostakovich's Fifth Symphony', in David Fanning (ed.), *Shostakovich Studies*, Cambridge, 1995, pp. 17–56.
Thiel, Wolfgang. *Filmmusik in Geschichte und Gegenwart*, Berlin, 1981.
Tippett, Michael. *Moving into Aquarius* (2nd edn), St Albans, 1974.
Waterhouse, John C. G. 'The Emergence of Modern Italian Music', Ph.D. diss., Oxford University, 1968.

Whittall, Arnold. *The Music of Britten and Tippett: Studies in Themes and Techniques*, Cambridge, 1982.
Music since the First World War (2nd edn), New York, 1988.
Wicke, Peter. *Von Mozart zu Madonna: Eine Kulturgeschichte der Popmusik*, Leipzig, 1998.
Zalduondo, Gemma Perez. 'The Concepts of "People" and "Nation" in the Republican and Francoist Musical Projects', paper presented at the conference 'Nation, Myth and Reality: Music in the 1930s', Royal Holloway, University of London, October 1998.
'El nacionalismo como eje de la politica musical del primer gobierno regular de Franco (30 de enero de 1938–8 de agosto de 1939)', *Revista de Musicología* 18 (1995), pp. 247–73.
Zenck, Claudia Maurer. 'Zwischen Boykott und Anpassung an den Charakter der Zeit. Über die Schwierigkeiten eines deutschen Komponisten mit dem Dritten Reich', *Hindemith-Jahrbuch/Annales Hindemith* 9 (1980), pp. 65–129.

· 12 ·

Other mainstreams: light music and easy listening, 1920–70

DEREK B. SCOTT

Problems and definitions

It should be stated at the outset that light music and easy listening are not diluted forms of heavy music and difficult listening prepared for those with delicate musical digestions. The music discussed in this chapter produces effects and valorizes moods, identities, and ideas that no other music does. When, for example, the crew of HMS *Amethyst* sailed down the Yangtse under fire from Chinese guns during the Second World War, they chose to demonstrate British composure by singing 'Cruising Down the River' (Beadell/Tollerton, 1945).[1] Three types of easy listening need to be distinguished, and in none of these cases does that necessarily entail the meaning 'facile', nor imply that it is appropriate to describe the music as easy technically. First, there is the type that is often tightly controlled but perceived as cool, sophisticated, relaxed, and classy, which ranges from the crooners to the more varied song stylists like Frank Sinatra. Second, there is the type that evokes a nostalgic mood and whose present reception therefore differs from its original meaning (it is usually categorized as nostalgia or, in France, as *rétro*); an example would be a song like 'The Trail of the Lonesome Pine' (MacDonald/Carroll, 1913) sung by Laurel and Hardy, the corny and sentimental quality of which may now be valued as offering an experience of something vulnerable and human that high art generally guards against. Third, there is the apparently easy listening that proves emotionally difficult listening, as often occurs in the French *chanson réaliste*.

These types can be, in turn, distinguished from light music, if that term is restricted to music that relates more closely to the Western classical tradition. There are, of course, inevitable overlaps, especially where 'updating' of classical pieces is undertaken, as in Perry Como's hit of 1945, 'Till the End of Time' (Kaye/Mossman), based on Chopin's Polonaise in A flat. The terms lounge music, 'loungecore', or cocktail music refer to music that also overlaps with what I have described as type one of the 'easy' category. As I write, Andy Williams's 1967 recording of 'Music to Watch Girls By' (Ramin) is a

1 Here and throughout, authors of songs are identified as composer/lyricist.

loungecore favourite. Lounge music also embraces gentle bossa and samba rhythms, 'classical' arrangements of Beatles tunes, and atmospheric orchestral film scores by composers such as James Barry and Ennio Morricone. The orchestras of Cyril Stapleton, John Schroeder, and John Hatch are all well versed in this repertoire. The aim is to create a mood that lends sophistication to an environment in which people wish to drink and relax. Lounge music is distinct from muzak, which is not intended to be listened to; the latter was originally developed (by Planned Music, Inc., whose tradename 'Muzak' is) to provide a sound environment that encouraged greater working efficiency – which clearly would not happen if workers were listening to the music rather than concentrating on their jobs.

While light music is often seen as downmarket classical, easy listening is often regarded as upmarket pop. That is why both genres meet in the middle – but it is the middle approached from different directions. The identification of a middlebrow taste began in the 1920s, continued in the 1930s, and was perceived by some critics in the next decade as more of a threat to high art than was lowbrow taste. However, as discussed at the end of this chapter, the closing decades of the twentieth century were witness to the 'disappearing middle', and even those styles once regarded as raw and proletarian, like Rockabilly, are jumping genre categories (Gene Vincent appears in one of the HMV Easy compilations).

The label easy listening is now applied to music that was not, until the 1980s, marketed as a particular product, yet this is the sort of music that, from Adorno onward, has been condemned by critics as the music industry's most unchallenging, manipulative commodity. The tendency has been to interpret the twentieth-century music industry in terms of the mass-production model associated with Henry Ford, and to see standardized material rolling off the assembly belt.[2] However, as Keith Negus has emphasized, the music business has always been alert to changing niche markets and, indeed, 'most of the recordings issued throughout the twentieth century were never simply marketed to or purchased by a "mass" audience'.[3] Antoine Hennion, surveying the music industry in France, considered that its business staff did not so much manipulate the public as 'feel its pulse'.[4] In sum, light music and easy listening represent a broad field of musical production and consumption.

In Pierre Bourdieu's model, the field of cultural production is subject to struggles resulting from two principles of hierarchization: the heteronomous

2 David Ewen uses the assembly-belt metaphor in *Panorama of American Popular Music*, Englewood Cliffs, NJ, 1957, p. 29.

3 Keith Negus, *Music Genres and Corporate Cultures*, London, 1999, p. 17.

4 Antoine Hennion, 'The Production of Success: An Anti-Musicology of the Pop Song', *Popular Music* 3 (1983), pp. 158–93; p. 191; cited in Negus, *Music Genres and Corporate Cultures*, p. 18.

principle that is responsive to external demands (favourable to those who dominate the field economically) and the autonomous principle ('art for art's sake').[5] The positions carry differing amounts of prestige, celebrity, or honour. Light music and easy listening often yield high-society success (Andrew Lloyd Webber became Lord Lloyd Webber of Sydmonton), and this adds to its connotations of sophistication. However, it increases the scorn of the autonomous sector (Andrew Lloyd Webber® is a registered trademark) and of those in the heteronomous sector who seek success as 'one of the people' (often as rock, blues, or country musicians). Musicals are at the top of the economic hierarchy in terms of status because only a limited number can be performed in major cities at the most prestigious theatres. Stephen Sondheim, however, provides an illustration of struggles within the field: if his show fails with the audience it damages him for some but raises his status for others.

The following survey, which is organized by genre, is highly selective: limitations of space make it necessary to illustrate with reference only to selected figures, genres, and countries, and to restrict the mention of songs and stage works to those about which a specific point is made. However, that is not to imply that what I am omitting is of little importance or less distinctive than what I choose to discuss – the Finnish tango, Greek film music, and Spanish *zarzuela* spring immediately to mind, and there was, of course, Swedish light and popular music before Abba.[6]

Light classical music

Light music is a term that, for much of the twentieth century, embraced a great deal of the musical terrain now known as easy listening, such as the music of dance bands. It was also used to indicate music related to a classical idiom – especially to light opera or *opérette* – rather than jazz; this style was commonly described as 'light classical', but it was always more than watered-down classical. From its earliest manifestations (the music of Josef Lanner and the elder Johann Strauss in Vienna), it bore a distinctive character and developed its own unique features, such as falling leading-notes and an emphasis on the sixth degree of the scale.[7] A simple listing of composers' names will demonstrate the ubiquity and familiarity of this repertory, particularly in the English-speaking world.

5 Pierre Bourdieu, *The Field of Cultural Production: Essays on Art and Literature* (ed. Randal Johnson), Cambridge, 1993, pp. 40–6.

6 See Olle Edström, 'The Place and Value of Middle Music', *Svensk Tidskrift för Musikforskning* 1 (1992), pp. 7–60.

7 See Peter van de Merwe, *Origins of the Popular Style: The Antecedents of Twentieth-Century Popular Music*, Oxford, 1989, pp. 223–76, and Derek B. Scott, 'Music and Social Class', in Jim Samson (ed.), *The Cambridge History of Nineteenth-Century Music*, Cambridge, 2001, pp. 544–67; p. 550.

The enormously popular British composer Albert Ketèlbey (1875–1959) wrote short descriptive pieces, several of which evoke exotic locales, for example *In the Mystic Land of Egypt* (1931); they were made available in a variety of arrangements, ranging from full orchestra or military band to piano or organ solo, and, as in the nineteenth-century 'descriptive fantasia', the music is designed deliberately to serve the narrative. Ketèlbey's contemporary Eric Coates (1886–1957), in later life famous for his march *The Dam Busters* (1954), had been composing light orchestral suites since before the First World War, and his music was heard frequently on BBC radio: 'Knightsbridge', from his suite *London* (1933), and 'Calling All Workers' (1940) became familiar as signature tunes. The next generation of British light music composers included Vivian Ellis (b. 1903) and Ronald Binge (1910–79), who enjoyed great success with 'Elizabethan Serenade' (1951), while Malcolm Arnold (b. 1921) has also been an important contributor to light music through both his film scores and his orchestral dance sets. David Rose (1910–90) was British-born but spent almost his entire life in America, making a success of demure light orchestral pieces like *Holiday for Strings* (1943) as well as scoring a raunchy hit with *The Stripper* (1961). In the first decades of the twentieth century, the German-Irish composer Victor Herbert (1859–1924) and Czech composer Rudolf Friml (1879–1972) were among those writing light music in the USA, while a composer of distinctively American light music was Leroy Anderson (1908–75), who arranged for the Boston Pops Orchestra and composed the popular *Sleigh Ride* (1950) and *Blue Tango* (1951). In Europe there were the likes of Gabriel Pierné (1863–1937), Paul Lincke (1866–1946), Hugo Alfvén (1872–1960), Fritz Kreisler (1875–1962) – primarily known as a violinist – and Jonny Heykens (1884–1945).

In the 1930s, radio provided work performing light music for some of the many out-of-work musicians who had played in orchestras accompanying silent films in the larger cinemas before the introduction of the 'talkies' in 1927 (the first mass-distribution film with integral sound was *The Jazz Singer*). Ironically, a decade later, film scores were to provide part of the staple diet of light orchestras; one has only to think of the 'Warsaw Concerto' (Richard Addinsell) from *Dangerous Moonlight* (1941), or 'The Dream of Olwen' (Charles Williams) from *While I Live* (1947). In the 1950s, such orchestras added music from TV shows to their growing screen-music repertoire.

One of the most famous light orchestras was that of [Annunzio Paolo] Mantovani (1905–80), an accomplished classical violinist who came to attention broadcasting with his Tipica Orchestra in the 1930s. His New Orchestra of 1951 was a sensation. He and Ronald Binge, both of them skilful arrangers, created a luxurious texture from forty players, employing devices such as the 'cascading strings' first heard in his 1951 recording of 'Charmaine' (Pollack/Rapee, 1926). The pioneer of the sentimental massed-string sound was George Melachrino, but Mantovani was the first to exploit recording-studio effects. Other leaders of light orchestras were Alfredo Campoli, Harry Horlick, Jack Byfield, and Dorothy Summers. Besides playing on their own, these orchestras accompanied singers of ballads, light opera, and musicals, as well as instrumental soloists: Eddie Calvert's trumpet solo version of 'O mein Papa' (Burkhard, 1948) was recorded with Norrie Paramor and his orchestra in 1953. There were numerous orchestras in the second half of the century (including those of Frank Chacksfield, Percy Faith, Stanley Black, Henry Mancini, Bert Kaempfert, Paul Mauriat, and James Last) that developed out of this tradition. In the 1960s, however, Herb Alpert and the Tijuana Brass were already providing the new sort of easy-listening instrumental music, like *Spanish Flea* (Wechter, 1966), that was largely to supplant light orchestral music, while the light instrumental ensemble music of the 1970s would be represented by the rock-influenced styles of Mike Oldfield's *Tubular Bells* (1973) and Jean-Michel Jarre's *Oxygène* (1977).

The continuing popularity of the Anglo-American drawing-room ballad style is represented by songs like 'Roses of Picardy' (Weatherly/Haydn Wood, 1916); the continental equivalent usually had an operetta-like quality, as in 'Wien, du Stadt meiner Träume' (Sieczynsky, 1916) and 'Parlez-moi d'amour' (Lenoir, 1923). As a result of the folksong movement, there were also ballads relying on folk sources (Marjory Kennedy-Fraser's *Songs from the Hebrides*, 1909–27) or emulating folk styles ('Up from Somerset', Weatherly/Sanderson, 1913). During the 1930s, some singers of this material were taking to the variety theatre, as did baritone Peter Dawson (1882–1961). This style of music also continued to resonate in songs from operetta, for example, 'We'll Gather Lilacs' from Ivor Novello's *Perchance To Dream* (1945).

The piano still dominated music in the home in the 1920s; for the dissemination of jazz, however, recordings were vital, and the gramophone (invented in the late nineteenth century but initially a rare commodity) had achieved great popularity by 1930. Yet, though the ballad declined, it never died out, and women composers were still involved in this genre: 'Bless This House' – later a favourite of the Welsh tenor Harry Secombe – was by May Brahe (words by Helen Taylor, 1927). Some famous ballad singers from abroad were in Britain in the 1930s: the African-American bass Paul Robeson stayed for a while, and the Austrian tenor Richard Tauber [Ernst Seiffert] (1892–1948), hero of many a Lehár operetta, settled in Britain following the *Anschluss* and took British nationality.

The Northern Irish tenor Josef Locke [Joseph McLaughlin] (1917–1999), furnishes an example of how these singers earned a living. On the advice of another Irish tenor, John McCormack, he visited London to audition with the bandleader and impresario Jack Hylton in 1945 and was immediately booked. The next year he was in the seaside resort of Blackpool, the first of nineteen holiday seasons there. He toured variety theatres and released his first records in 1947, which included six songs associated with him throughout his career. One was 'Hear My Song, Violetta', originally a German tango song 'Hör mein Lied, Violetta' (Klose/Lukesch), adapted by Harry Pepper. The others were English, American, Irish, Austrian, and Italian: 'The Holy City' (Weatherly/Adams), 'I'll Take You Home Again Kathleen' (Westendorf), 'Galway Bay' (Colahan), 'Goodbye' (Stolz/Graham), and 'Come Back to Sorrento' (Aveling/de Curtis). In his first year of recording, then, he had fixed what was to be his unchanging repertoire, a mixture of religious and secular ballads, operetta, and songs of Ireland. His vocal techniques included an Italianate portamento and sobbing catch in his voice, and he enjoyed decorating a melodic line. Locke performed little on film, but that medium was another outlet for such singers. The Italian-American tenor Mario Lanza (1921–59) enjoyed some of his biggest hits as a consequence of his film appearances: 'The Loveliest Night of the Year' (Webster/Aaronson, 1951, based on a waltz by Juventino Rosas, *Sobre las Olas*) was from the film *The Great Caruso* in which he starred as the eponymous character.

It was not just solo singers that were found concentrating on the light operatic and ballad repertoire. Webster Booth's career as a tenor soloist took a new direction when he met Anne Ziegler [Irene Eastwood] during the filming of Gounod's *Faust* (the first English colour film, 1936), in which they were playing the leading roles. They began touring concert halls and variety theatres singing duets, and were undoubtedly influenced by the public's enthusiasm for Nelson Eddy and Jeanette MacDonald, especially their recording of 'Indian Love Call' from the 1936 film version of Friml's *Rose Marie* (1924).

Vaudeville and variety theatre

Variety theatre and vaudeville (the usual American term) played host to a range of musical styles. As F. F. Procter established an ethos of respectability in New York, so did Oswald Stoll in London. The music halls became 'palaces of variety' and offered a similar fare to American vaudeville (acrobats, dancers, singers, magicians, comedians, and so on), but their differing regional characters did not suddenly disappear. Harry Lauder espoused a Scottish idiom, and George Formby sang songs in a Lancashire accent. Variety theatres declined in popularity in the 1920s and 1930s because of competition from radio and films, and suffered a further decline in the 1950s, attributable, in part, to the rise of television. A sense of the power of the latter is gleaned from the fact that during 1954–5 a TV series signature tune, 'The Ballad of Davy Crocket' (Blackburn/Bruns), became the fastest-selling song in the history of the record industry (more than twenty versions were released).[8] Variety theatres survived longest, and still survive today, at seaside holiday resorts. In the 1920s and 1930s, some weathered the economic storms by putting on revues instead of a programme of individual 'turns', while others became cinemas – even Paris's famous Moulin Rouge was a cinema during 1929–33.

The Moulin Rouge had been a *café-concert* and dance hall from 1899 to 1903; then it was turned into a *music-hall* (the French term is hyphenated) where people dined during the show. It burned down in 1915 and, because of the war, was not rebuilt. In 1924, it reopened in art deco style with the revue *New York – Montmartre*. From 1925, its revues were dominated by one of its former dancer-singers who was currently the star of the Casino de Paris, Mistinguett [Jeanne Bourgeois] (1875–1956).[9] However, it began to lose more and more of the French character of its entertainment in responding to the demand for American popular music; in 1937, after its spell as a cinema, Teddy Wilson and his orchestra were there with the revue *Cotton Club de New York*.

In the late 1920s jazz and jazz-influenced music became established as the dominant type of popular music; hundreds of thousands of Americans toured Europe, bringing records with them that increased the European interest in jazz. The ground had been laid by the growing numbers of touring jazz musicians, white and black. Most famous was Josephine Baker (1906–75), the daughter of a black mother and white Jewish father, who came to Paris as part of *La revue nègre* (1925) and became an emblematic figure of the 1920s 'jazz age' in Paris;[10] French songs became a significant part of her repertoire, one of the best known being 'J'ai deux amours' (Scotto/Koger/Varna, 1930). A home-grown celebrity was Maurice Chevalier (1888–1972), who was a *café-concert* singer before being taken up by Mistinguett and becoming a major star of the *spectacles de variétés*; he achieved international fame after appearing in the Hollywood film musical *The Love Parade* (1929).[11] Perhaps the most popular of all male singers in France, however, was the Corsican tenor Tino Rossi (1907–83), whose 'Petit Papa Noel' was the first winner of a French Gold Disc award in 1945. Jean Sablon (b. 1906) was the first French crooner, though never far from cabaret and chanson, while Charles Trenet (b. 1913) was influenced by American swing, but remained rooted in French *music-hall*; Charles Aznavour

8 Joseph Murrells, *Million Selling Records from the 1900s to the 1980s: An Illustrated Directory*, London, 1984, p. 89.

9 Originally spelt Mistinguette, the final 'e' was dropped, since it was not pronounced; thus she was Mistinguett' around 1908 and Mistinguett shortly after.

10 See Elaine Brody, *Paris: The Musical Kaleidoscope 1870–1925*, London, 1988, pp. 242–3.

11 James Harding, *Maurice Chevalier: His Life 1888–1972*, London, 1982, pp. 99–103.

(b. 1924) also succumbed to American influence in both his songwriting and his style of singing.

During the 1930s, showbands began to top the bill at variety theatres; it was a development that helped to prevent many of the theatres from becoming cinemas. Since showbands were to be looked at, not danced to, they developed routines and set pieces: for example, at the end of 'He Played His Ukulele as the Ship Went Down' (le Clerq), Jack Hylton's band 'sank on stage'.[12] Piano acts were also in demand in variety, and they ranged from pianists specializing in syncopated music (like Billy Mayerl and Charlie Kunz) to those playing in a light classical vein, like the Polish duettists Rawicz and Landauer. In the second half of the twentieth century there was still a demand for pianists – for example Winifred Atwell and, of course, Liberace.

The most acclaimed vaudeville artist of the first half of the twentieth century was undoubtedly Al Jolson [Asa Yoelson] (1886–1950), who had moved from Lithuania to the USA with his family in 1893. His 1912 recording of 'Ragging the Baby to Sleep' (Guilbert/Muir) was the first popular song to sell over a million discs. He starred in *The Jazz Singer*, and his undiminished selling power was evident in the later 1940s when Decca released three albums of his songs. It might be thought that, by then, the blackface entertainment in which Jolson specialized was embarrassingly outmoded. However, the immensely popular British TV *Black and White Minstrel Show* did not commence until 1960, and theatrical spin-offs from that show were still taking place in the 1980s.

Dance bands

The BBC's Variety Department was responsible, in addition to variety entertainment, for dance bands, operettas, revues, and cinema organs; these were all beneath the dignity of the Music Department. Whether 'variety' is an apt umbrella term or not, there was a lot of shared repertoire. Some dance bands dipped into the repertoire of light orchestras: Jack Hylton's band played Coates's *The Selfish Giant*,[13] and Paul Whiteman played 'Dance of the Hours' from Ponchielli's *La gioconda*. Until Jimmy Kennedy added words to provide Henry Hall with a novelty record for Christmas 1932, *The Teddy Bears' Picnic* was a light orchestral intermezzo of 1907 by the American composer John Bratton. Some performers felt equally happy in a dance-band or light-orchestral context: one such was Gracie Fields (1898–1979), who ran the gamut from music-hall comedy to light classical.

12 Ian Whitcomb, *After the Ball: Pop Music from Rag to Rock*, New York, 1994, p. 171.
13 Brian Rust, *The Dance Bands*, London, 1972, p. 61.

The first modern dance band in Britain was led by Archibald Joyce, who recorded for HMV in 1912. The new bands were little affected by the visit of the self-consciously anarchic Original Dixieland Jazz Band in 1919, but it was different when Paul Whiteman and his Orchestra appeared in the revue *Brighter London* at the London Hippodrome in 1923. Whiteman (1890–1967), originally a violinist in the Denver Symphony Orchestra, had the first million-selling dance band disc with 'Whispering' (Malvin Schonberger/John Schonberger) in 1920, and famously commissioned and premiered Gershwin's *Rhapsody in Blue* in 1924. The demand for syncopated music grew, and dancing while dining out was made possible by the introduction of dance floors into hotels and restaurants. Those with expertise in this style were in demand: in 1920, for example, the proprietor of the Embassy Club in London enticed Bert Ambrose (1897–1971) back from New York, where he had been performing with an American band. Dance halls with names such as Palais and Astoria sprang up everywhere.

As Europe was emerging from the First World War, John Philip Sousa and James Reese Europe were among the first to popularize American syncopated dance music there. There was so much demand for this type of music that some bandleaders concealed their identities in order to record for different companies; Ben Selvin made thousands of records using pseudonyms between 1919 and 1934. Singers were often Broadway stars, like Helen Kane, or radio stars, like Vaughn de Leath. There were also popular radio bands, like that of Vincent Lopez; the BBC engaged a resident band in 1926, led briefly by Sidney Firman, then Jack Payne and, lastly, Henry Hall. Eventually, bandleaders on both sides of the Atlantic were given their own TV shows – Fred Waring in the USA, and Billy Cotton in the UK. Singers who later had flourishing solo careers often began by singing refrains with dance bands: Perry Como worked with Ted Weems's band for a while, and Bing Crosby gained experience with Whiteman.

In the late 1920s some British critics and musicians wished to define jazz in a particular way, stressing the importance of its stylistic innovations and its improvised solos.[14] However, for many white people jazz simply meant syncopated dance music – the most widely broadcast and recorded type of which was that played by all-white, all-male bands. A further polarization surfaced in the mid-1930s, setting 'purist' jazz fans, keen on the 'hot', against those who preferred the 'sweet'. 'Sweet' music was associated with the gentle, lyrical style of Guy Lombardo and his Royal Canadians; this smooth, sophisticated music was soon favoured in plush hotels in many of the world's larger cities.

14 See Derek B. Scott, 'The "Jazz Age"', in Stephen Banfield (ed.), *Blackwell History of Music in Britain: The Twentieth Century*, Oxford, 1995, pp. 57–78; p. 61.

Black musicians were becoming more visible in white bands in Europe, if not the USA (Ben Bernie did include trumpeter Bill Moore in his band at the Hotel Roosevelt in the late 1920s, but only by passing him off as Hawaiian); Billy Cotton employed trombonist Ellis Jackson, and Garland Wilson played piano with Jack Payne. Black singers also became more prominent: Alberta Hunter joined Jack Jackson's band at the Dorchester Hotel, London, in 1934. Benny Goodman was the first white American musician to perform openly and publicly with a black musician – first Teddy Wilson, then Lionel Hampton. However women, black or white, were noticeably absent as instrumentalists or composers where dance bands were concerned, though there were a few exceptions: Ivy Benson, for example, had several hit records in the 1940s with her All Girls Band (which included trumpeter Gracie Cole). Female vocalists were a different matter, and were frequently employed to add glamour to an all-male band.

The band most concerned to keep abreast of dancers' needs was that of Victor Silvester (1901–78), winner of the World Ballroom Dance Championship in 1922, and author of *Modern Ballroom Dancing* (1928). Because most dance bands chose a tempo they thought appropriate for the tune, not the dance, or treated tempo too flexibly, Silvester persuaded Parlophone to release some piano records in 'strict tempo'. Their success encouraged him to form his Ballroom Orchestra in 1935, a small band comprising saxophone doubling clarinet, bass, drums and, unusually, two pianos, one playing melodically while the other provided what he called 'lemonade' – high trickling notes between chords. Later, he put together a second orchestra called 'Silver Strings' for Latin-American dances and Viennese waltzes. He moved with the times, responding to American swing and the presence of GIs in the UK by making recordings with a Jive Band. Sales of his records exceeded those of every other bandleader by 1955.[15]

War was declared just as the new style associated with Benny Goodman, known as swing, was beginning to make an impact. Some bands began to play swing, but many were decimated by the call-up: virtually the entire brass section of Ambrose's band disappeared, and re-emerged in the Squadronaires, the RAF Dance Orchestra. During the war, the music of Glenn Miller, which did most to popularize swing, became an ever-increasing influence, especially when he was stationed in Britain with his massive Army Air Force Band in 1944. For Gunther Schuller, the formula 'worked to death' by swing bands was: a relentless four-to-the-beat bar; riffs constructed to fit any of the primary triads; and the fade-out ending.[16] Miller is accused of making a career out of

15 Sid Colin, *And the Bands Played On: An Informal History of British Dance Bands*, London, 1977, p. 75.
16 Gunther Schuller, *Early Jazz: Its Roots and Musical Development*, New York, 1986, pp. 276–7.

this formula, but why the formula sometimes worked and sometimes failed is unexplained. Besides, swing was not just about music. It was about being young and sexy, about certain fashions in clothes (sports jackets for men, pleated skirts and bobbysox for women) and about new dances (jitterbugging); popular singers associated with this lifestyle were Dinah Shore (b. 1917), Jo Stafford (b. 1920) known as 'GI Jo', Vera Lynn (b. 1919), and Anne Shelton (1923–94). In the mid-1940s, big-band boogie-woogie was popularized by Harry James in the USA, and was soon added to the repertoire of those playing swing. By this time, jazz purists were looking elsewhere – specifically, to the sound of Kansas City (Count Basie).

After the war, jazz split into revivalist and modernist camps. The scorned middle ground was now 'Archer Street jazz', which described jazz played for gain rather than from conviction (Archer Street in London was a kind of open-air labour exchange for musicians). At the dawn of the 1960s, another struggle to distinguish good 'authentic' jazz from bad 'commercial' jazz was that of traditional (or 'trad') versus 'traddy-pop'. The outcomes of such struggles affect aesthetic status: Kenny Ball and Acker Bilk are found today in the easy listening section at record stores, but revivalist Ken Colyer is not.

The Tin Pan Alley song stylists

The term 'song stylist' emphasizes the singer's personal manner and interpretative skills; Fred Astaire was more of a straight singer, whereas Bing Crosby, Frank Sinatra, and Judy Garland were 'stylists'. They countered the formal predictability of Tin Pan Alley songs (so named after the area in New York where commercial songwriting was concentrated), which usually consist of a fairly unimportant verse, and a thirty-two-bar chorus built on a favourite structure of AABA (like 'Smoke Gets in Your Eyes', Harbach/Kern, 1933) or ABAC (like 'White Christmas', Berlin, 1942).[17] Harmonically, Tin Pan Alley incorporated elements of European light music (for example, added sixths and unresolved sevenths) into an American popular style.

Rudy Vallee and 'Whispering' Jack Smith may have been the first crooners, but Bing [Harry] Crosby (1904–77) became the most celebrated. The Tin Pan Alley style dominated all American entertainment media, and Crosby showed what profits could be made when different media – records, radio, films – were used to promote each other. There was also musical cross-fertilization: Charles

17 For an extended discussion of the musical and lyrical style of Tin Pan Alley songs, see Charles Hamm, *Yesterdays: Popular Song in America*, New York, 1979, pp. 361–77 (and for big-band arrangements, pp. 384–5); Stephen Banfield, 'Popular Song and Popular Music on Stage and Film', in David Nicholls (ed.), *The Cambridge History of American Music*, Cambridge, 1998, pp. 314–22; and, for Schenkerian analysis, Allen Forte, *The American Popular Ballad of the Golden Era: 1924–1950*, Princeton, 1995. See also Banfield's discussion of Tin Pan Alley in his chapter in this volume (pp. 97–9).

Hamm attributes the new emphasis on strings in the accompaniment to songs of the 1930s to the influence of Hollywood film scores.[18] Crosby was the most popular recording artist until challenged by Frank Sinatra; the musical debate thrown up by their different singing styles featured in the film *High Society* (1956). Crosby's strong points were an accomplished use of the microphone, a relaxed swing, and a warm, resonant voice. He often varied the melody gently but, at the same time, was not free from mannerisms – especially, the overuse of the device of decorating a note with a mordent; David Brackett has provided a detailed discussion of Crosby's vocal technique alongside a perceptive analysis of the different reception and critical discourses surrounding Crosby's and Billie Holiday's recordings of 'I'll Be Seeing You' (Fain/Kahal, 1938), which were both released in 1944.[19] In the early 1930s, when dance band records announced simply 'with vocal refrain', the singer remaining anonymous, admirers of Crosby sought out records featuring his distinctive voice, and in this way helped to elevate the status of the popular vocalist.

The same was true of Al [Albert] Bowlly (1899–1941), who was born in what is now Maputo, Mozambique, but made his first recordings and built his reputation in Berlin. From there, he was invited by Fred Elizalde to join his band at the Savoy Hotel as vocalist and guitarist. With Lew Stone's band, he further refined his technique, recorded, broadcast on radio, appeared in variety theatres, and became a 'crooner' to rival Bing Crosby. He disliked the term 'crooning', preferring 'modern style singing', the title of a book issued under his name (but probably ghosted) in 1934.[20] The book observes that the modern intimate style of singing depends on the microphone, which gives a new timbre to the voice, amplifying previously unheard harmonics. The techniques described are characteristic of Bowlly: for example, a slight portamento, an added grace note, a fresh attack, and a dragging behind the tempo followed by a catching up. His technique is heard to advantage in 'The Very Thought of You' (Noble), recorded with Ray Noble's New Mayfair Orchestra in 1934. Bowlly spoke Afrikaans as well as English, and recorded several records in the former language in 1930 for the South African market.

The outstanding African-American Tin Pan Alley stylist was Nat 'King' Cole (1916–65), originally the pianist of a jazz trio. His recordings of 'Mona Lisa' (Evans/Livingston, 1950) and 'Too Young' (Dee/Lippman, 1951) consolidated his reputation as a singer, and also made Nelson Riddle's name as an arranger. Cole regarded his transition from his early days as a small-group jazz musician to his later career as a popular singer as 'adjusting to the market', and complained,

18 Charles Hamm, *Music in the New World*, New York, 1983, p. 367.
19 David Brackett, *Interpreting Popular Music*, Berkeley, 2000, pp. 34–74.
20 Al Bowlly, *Modern Style Singing ('Crooning')*, London, 1934.

'as soon as you start to make money in the popular field, they scream about how good you were in the old days, and what a bum you are now'.[21] However, only so much adjusting to the market was possible for singers such as Cole. Like Tony Bennett and Andy Williams, he was doing well until the mid-1960s – 'Ramblin' Rose' (Joe and Noel Sherman) was a big hit for him in 1962 – but the development of new forms of popular music had a considerable and negative impact on the demand for easy listening:[22] rock 'n' roll made the first dent in this market, and disco a second, larger dent in the 1970s.

Frank [Francis] Sinatra (1915–98), born the son of Italian immigrants in Hoboken, New Jersey, has been described as representing the consummation of the tradition of the American popular singer.[23] In 1939, he sang with Harry James's band, then for the next three years with Tommy Dorsey. He went solo, but exhausted himself and, by the beginning of the 1950s, was in decline. When he rebuilt his celebrity after signing to Capitol in 1953, it was due to the respect he commanded as a song stylist. He aimed to be different from Crosby and, in particular, developed a much wider dynamic range, thus moving away from crooning. Sinatra was the first to develop the technique of moving the microphone towards and away from himself to adjust for his vocal dynamic level.[24] He also picked up elements of jazz performance techniques from his big-band days, although he rarely departed far from a song's melody when improvising; some of the credit for the jazz-like swing of Sinatra's much-admired album *Songs for Swingin' Lovers* (1956)[25] should go to Nelson Riddle, who made effective use of devices such as riffs, call and response, and stabs, arranging for a big band in which strings and piano are romantically prominent. This album offers plentiful examples of Sinatra's technique, showing his ability to inflect a melodic line in a personal manner: pulling a note behind the beat here, pushing a note before the beat there, and producing a rhythmic kick by adding accents to certain words. At the same time, he was not without debt to the Italian singing tradition; in relation to this, Henry Pleasants has commented on 'his legato attack [. . .], his handling of portamento and rubato, and his sensitive modulation of vowel sounds'.[26] In 'Old Devil Moon' (Lane/Harburg), for instance, he makes an Italian elision of vowels, running 'me' and 'it' together when he sings, 'soon begins bewitching me, It's that old devil moon.'

21 Quoted in 'Cole, Nat "King"', in Colin Larkin (ed.), *Encyclopedia of Popular Music* (3rd edn), 8 vols., London, 1998, pp. 1159–61; p. 1160.

22 For an account of the causes of the 'rock revolution' and whether they were primarily social or born of power struggles within the music business, see Richard A. Peterson, 'Why 1955? Explaining the Advent of Rock Music', *Popular Music* 9 (1990), pp. 97–116.

23 Henry Pleasants, 'Sinatra, Frank', in Stanley Sadie and John Tyrrell (eds.), *The New Grove Dictionary of Music and Musicians* (2nd edn), 29 vols., London, 2001, Vol. XXIII, pp. 416–7; p. 417.

24 Gene Lees, *Singers and the Song*, New York, 1987, p. 107.

25 Capitol Records (1987).

26 Pleasants, 'Sinatra, Frank', p. 417.

Sinatra's vocal range easily encompassed two octaves: 'Too Marvelous for Words' (Whiting/Mercer) ends with a top F, while 'How About You?' (Lane/Freed) ends with a low F. Schuller comments on his ability to make 'a musical totality of a song rather than a series of vaguely connected phrases',[27] relating it to Dorsey's lyrical trombone playing: 'Like Dorsey in his trombone solos, Sinatra would carry phrases across bar lines or phrase joinings, balancing out weak points in songs or dramatizing their best structural elements.'[28] His performance of 'You're Getting To Be a Habit with Me' (Warren/Dubin) offers examples of his subtle restructuring of phrases:

> I used to think your love was something that I
> Could take [*breath*] or leave alone, [*breath*]
> But now I couldn't do without my supply, [*no breath*]
> I need you for my own.

A voice with an even wider dynamic range than Sinatra's was that of the vaudeville-reared Judy Garland [Frances Gumm] (1922–69), and it was coupled to a dramatic performing manner; Garland was prepared to take more and greater liberties with a song than most of her contemporaries in order to convey a passionate, vibrant immediacy. For some this is gloriously 'over the top' or perceived as camp (a similar reception has been accorded to Shirley Bassey); an example would be the interpretation of 'Come Rain Come Shine' (Arlen) that Garland recorded in 1956.[29] On the other hand, the enthusiasm with which she sang 'Chicago' (Fisher, 1922) was irresistibly infectious.[30]

Other esteemed singers of the late 1940s and 50s not so far mentioned include Margaret Whiting, Peggy Lee, Billy Eckstine, Doris Day, Dean Martin, Sammy Davis Jr. (the last two being members of the Sinatra 'rat pack'), Frankie Laine, David Whitfield, Keely Smith, Harry Belafonte, Rosemary Clooney, Johnny Mathis, and Connie Francis; further names from the late 1950s and 60s include Alma Cogan, Petula Clark, Brenda Lee, Gene Pitney, Dionne Warwick, Dusty Springfield, and, broadening into the easy listening repertoire, Freddy Quinn [Manfred Petz] (Germany), Kyu Sakamoto (Japan), Françoise Hardy (France), and Nana Mouskouri (Greece). There is a noticeable increase in the number of female singers of this music and a corresponding decline in men: rock music had become the genre with which many younger male singers identified, and the Tin Pan Alley style consequently began to be 'feminized'. The point can be made through a comparison of Dinah Shore's interpretation (accompanied by André Previn) of 'I've Got You Under My Skin' (Porter),[31] recorded in 1960,

27 Gunther Schuller, *The Swing Era: The Development of Jazz, 1930–1945*, New York, 1989, p. 689.
28 Ibid. 29 Capitol Records.
30 Listen to the live recording of 1960, reissued on *The Greatest Divas Collection* (HMV, 1999).
31 Capitol Records (1960), rereleased on the album *Sophisticated Ladies*.

with Sinatra's on *Swingin' Lovers*. The contrast between the silky, seductive, and feminine on the one hand, and the energetic, hot, and masculine on the other, demonstrates how the same song can be interpreted in ways that carry different yet equally meaningful connotations of gender.

Operetta and musical theatre

The beginnings of light operatic music are found in *opéra-bouffe* and, especially, the work of Offenbach. Viennese operetta and the Savoy Operas of Gilbert and Sullivan were influenced initially by Offenbach, but soon established characters of their own.[32] Vienna lost some of its sparkle in the 1920s: Austria was without an empire after the First World War and suffering from economic depression. Franz Lehár (1870–1947) began to take an increasingly melancholy view of the world in operettas like *Paganini* (1925) and *Friederike* (1928). Berlin was wealthier and, having become increasingly cosmopolitan, was taking over as the European centre for operetta. Many operetta composers were Jewish, however, and soon had to make an escape, compromise, face persecution, or worse; Léon Jessel (1871–1942), composer of the delightful *Schwarzwaldmädel*, was tortured at the age of seventy by the Gestapo, and died a few weeks later.[33]

In Austria, the popularity of Viennese light music, especially waltzes and operetta, was for a while an effective barricade against jazz. In *Die Csárdásfürstin* (1915), by Emmerich Kálmán (1882–1953), Hungarian gypsy music performs a role similar to that which would later be taken by African-American music: it suggests that a greater emotional and physical freedom is within the grasp of the operetta's bourgeois characters. Eventually, musical features associated with the Black American (flattened thirds and sevenths, the saxophone) would replace those of the Hungarian gypsy (augmented seconds and fourths, the violin) for creating moments of erotic *frisson*: Kálmán's *Die Herzogin von Chicago* (1928) gives centre stage to the culture clash between Austro-Hungarian dance music and jazz. From here on, jazz influence was to be found in other Viennese operettas, until the clampdown on 'degenerate' music following the *Anschluss* in 1938, when the country was ruthlessly 'Nazified' within a matter of weeks.[34]

In France, Maurice Yvain (1891–1965) was writing songs for the revues at the Casino de Paris in the 1920s, including 'Mon homme' (Willemetz) for Mistinguett; it was sung as 'My Man' by Fanny Brice in *Ziegfeld Follies of 1921*,

32 For expanded studies of operetta and musical theatre in the twentieth century, see Richard Traubner, *Operetta: A Theatrical History*, London, 1984, and Andrew Lamb, *100 Years of Popular Musical Theatre*, New Haven, 2001.

33 Traubner, *Operetta*, p. 299; for operetta in Berlin in the 1920s, see pp. 237–9, 257–62, and 282–3.

34 Berta Geissmar, *The Baton and the Jackboot: Recollections of Musical Life*, London, 1944, pp. 324–31.

and John Moore contends that it 'provided the formula for the torch song',[35] the song of aching love for the undeserving. American torch songs were disposed to taking on bluesy elements, as in 'Can't Help Lovin' Dat Man' from *Show Boat*. No doubt it was a combination of these associations that made 'My Man' seem a suitable vehicle for Billie Holiday. Yvain enjoyed a measure of international success with his operetta *Ta bouche* (1922), but his inclination towards America meant that a more typically French operetta composer was, ironically, the Venezuelan Reynaldo Hahn (1875–1947), with works like *Ciboulette* (1923).

In the UK, the Welsh composer and actor Ivor Novello [David Ivor Davies] (1893–1951) did most to sustain the Viennese style of operetta in works like *Glamorous Night* (1935) and *The Dancing Years* (1939); Noel Coward (1899–1973) had written his operetta *Bitter Sweet* in just such a style in 1929. Vivian Ellis's *Bless the Bride* (1947), however, was set in Victorian England and, in the following decade, the American musical of the 1920s was to be the subject of affectionate parody in Sandy Wilson's *The Boy Friend* (1953).

Early-twentieth-century operetta composers in the USA were Victor Herbert, Rudolf Friml, and Sigmund Romberg (1887–1951), a Hungarian who composed operettas in a Viennese character, for example *The Student Prince* (1924) and *The Desert Song* (1926). European qualities began to weaken with the success of *Shuffle Along* (1927), by Eubie Blake and Noble Sissle, and *Show Boat* (1927) by Jerome Kern (1885–1945) – the first white musical to assimilate African-American elements and (in Oscar Hammerstein II's libretto) tackle racial laws. George Gershwin [Jacob Gershvin] (1898–1937) and his brother Ira successfully integrated the blues idiom and dance-band style into the stage show with *Girl Crazy* (1930), which contains songs like 'Embraceable You' and 'I Got Rhythm'.[36] *Porgy and Bess* (1935, libretto by Du Bose Heyward and Ira Gershwin) was consciously intended and described as an 'American Folk Opera' and, as a measure of his serious intentions, Gershwin orchestrated it himself. This ran counter to the then-standard practice of employing professional orchestrators; Robert Russell Bennett (1894–1981), for example, made a considerable contribution to the Broadway sound through orchestrating over three hundred shows, including musicals by Berlin, Gershwin, Kern, Loewe, Porter, and Rodgers.[37]

Kurt Weill (1900–50) was not alone in grappling with political issues; there was often a political edge to Gershwin (for example, *Of Thee I Sing*, 1931 and

35 John Moore, '"The Hieroglyphics of Love": The Torch Singers and Interpretation', in Richard Middleton (ed.), *Reading Pop: Approaches to Textual Analysis in Popular Music*, Oxford, 2000, pp. 262–96; p. 263.

36 Banfield, 'Popular Song and Popular Music on Stage and Film', p. 328.

37 See Robert R. Bennett, *The Broadway Sound: Autobiography and Selected Essays of Robert Russell Bennett* (ed. George Ferencz), New York, 1999.

Let 'Em Eat Cake, 1933), and much that was stronger in *The Cradle Will Rock* (1937) by Marc Blitzstein (1905–64). Weill had to familiarize himself quickly with the style and conventions of the American musical, but by the time he composed *Lady in the Dark* (1940) there were few doubts of his being a major voice on Broadway. The 'Moritat' from *Die Dreigroschenoper* can be used to illustrate Weill's ambiguous position as a composer for the stage. The song can be heard as an example of Weimar political satire, in a context of *neue Sachlichkeit* ('new objectivity') and experimental theatre. Yet Bobby Darin's version 'Mack the Knife' (1959) occupies a quite different position; its bowdlerized gruesomeness becomes 'tongue in cheek', it reaches for 'hit parade' success as an American popular song, and falls comfortably into the lower-status category of easy listening. The argument may be extended to explain the lower status of Weill's New York works as compared to his Berlin works – though the latter did not lack influence on Broadway, as John Kander and Fred Ebb's *Cabaret* (1966) demonstrates.

Annie Get Your Gun (1946) and *Oklahoma* (1943) established the quasi-realistic American musical in content and style, though the composers of both were Jewish: Irving Berlin [Israel Baline] (1888–1989) was born in Siberia, while Richard Rodgers [Rogazinsky] (1902–79) was the son of Russian-Jewish immigrants. For twenty-four years (1919–42) Rodgers collaborated exclusively with Lorenz Hart. Though their works have not held the stage, they are full of songs that became standards. Rodgers dominated Broadway for twenty years with his next collaborator, Oscar Hammerstein II. *Oklahoma* set the agenda for the integrated or holistic musical in which the music, whether for song or dance, advances rather than holds up the action (there is a parallel with developments in opera at the end of the eighteenth century). Rodgers and Hammerstein both had original qualities to offer, the latter with his lyrical ingenuity and the former with his desire to avoid the predictability of Tin Pan Alley song form. *Oklahoma* was turned into an extremely successful film in 1955, as were others of their musicals, most notably *South Pacific* (1949, film 1958), *The King and I* (1951, film 1956) and, most popular of all, *The Sound of Music* (1959, film 1965).

Cole Porter (1891–1964) achieved a notable success with *Kiss Me Kate* (1948, with a libretto based on Shakespeare by Bella and Samuel Spewack), which was the first Broadway musical to find acceptance in European opera houses.[38] However, the conductor and composer Leonard Bernstein (1918–90) brought opera and the musical yet closer together in *Candide* (1956), based on Voltaire's satirical story of that name; his compositional skill is also evident in the ensembles of *West Side Story* (1957), an adaptation of *Romeo and Juliet*, where

38 Kurt Gänzl, *The Blackwell Guide to Musical Theatre on Record*, Oxford, 1990, p. 345.

different musical styles are used to characterize the rival gangs (the Sharks are given Latin styles). A further innovation in this work concerns the use of dance. In operettas and musicals, dances are usually part of the action (in film parlance, 'diegetic'): the on-stage characters *know* they are dancing. But in *West Side Story*, the fight scenes are choreographed, as if in a ballet. This musical, together with Lerner and Loewe's *My Fair Lady* (1956), erected a theatrical barricade against the rock revolution that long proved insurmountable.

Stephen Sondheim (b. 1930) came to attention as the lyricist for *West Side Story* and, in the next decade, as the author-composer of *A Funny Thing Happened on the Way to the Forum* (1962). In 1971, *Follies* showed his talent for pastiche, though Stephen Banfield adds the important rider that it contains 'deep layers of irony';[39] since then, he has tended to prove increasingly demanding for audiences and singers. *Sweeney Todd, the Demon Barber of Fleet Street* (1979) revealed its ambiguous position on Broadway when it was chosen for production by New York City Opera in 1984. While more threatening dramatically and more unified musically than Lloyd Webber's macabre equivalent, *Phantom of the Opera*, it is not as melodically memorable (excepting its opening ballad, based on that horror-movie favourite, the *Dies irae*). At the same time, that helps to give Sondheim a certain status, for as one reviewer explained, 'If you say you find the man's tunes dull and lifeless, they say that he's aiming for a higher art.'[40] His work possesses what Bourdieu would call charismatic consecration, a high reputation without commercial success. There is no doubting Sondheim's attention to compositional craft, as illustrated for example by the subtlety of his use of triple time in *A Little Night Music* (1973).[41] However, Sondheim's compositional skills are not always the equal of his musical ambition. Although he writes ensembles, their voice leading is often awkward, as in bars 17–27 of the opening ensemble in *A Little Night Music*. He also seems to have little understanding of vocal register: the vocal writing at the conclusion of Act I is gruelling.

Whereas Sondheim's popular roots are in Tin Pan Alley, those of Andrew Lloyd Webber (b. 1948) are in rock and pop. His first musical, and first collaboration with lyricist Tim Rice, was *Joseph and the Amazing Technicolour Dreamcoat* (1968), originally a short school production but later turned into a full-length show. Their next effort, *Jesus Christ Superstar*, was released as an album (1970) before its premiere in 1971, as was *Evita*. Lloyd Webber then began working

39 Stephen Banfield, 'Sondheim, Stephen (Joshua)', in Sadie and Tyrrell (eds.), *New Grove* (2nd edn), Vol. XXIII, pp. 701–3; p. 701.

40 Scott Fosdick writing in the *News American* in 1985; quoted in Gerald Bordman, *American Musical Theatre: A Chronicle* (expanded edn), New York, 1985, p. 692.

41 Stephen Banfield, *Sondheim's Broadway Musicals*, Ann Arbor, 1993, pp. 228–39.

with other writers and, in the case of *Cats* (1981), setting T. S. Eliot (except for the show's hit song, 'Memory'). He possesses a talent for parody and pastiche that has sometimes been described in harsh terms. However, as John Snelson remarks, it allows him to create 'the sense of an individual sound world for each of his shows' – the rock style of *Superstar*, the operatic elements of *The Phantom of the Opera* (1986), and the Hollywood sound of *Sunset Boulevard* (1993).[42]

There are sometimes awkward word stresses in Lloyd Webber's vocal writing and, as with Sondheim, no firm sense of his composing for established voice types. Christine's role in *Phantom*, for instance, demands a compass of two octaves and a sixth, but for the most part she sings in a narrow mezzo range. Characterization is rarely more than two-dimensional: the quick vocal flourish at the end of 'Think of Me' illustrates nothing about Christine's character, but merely signifies that she is an opera singer. In fact, almost every time her music rises above the stave it is simply to function as a sign for opera. But while Lloyd Webber may have a tendency to exploit well-worn devices, such as pushing the music up a semitone to freshen the effect of a repeated refrain, he possesses a skill for melody that frequently avoids the predictable: songs from his shows have appealed to – and been hits for – singers of all ages, from Cliff Richard (b. 1940) to Boyzone. His commercial success might suggest that he is simply good at spotting what the public wants, but such a claim sits uncomfortably with the surprising subject matter he has chosen for his musicals. The reason *Superstar* began life as a recording was that nobody was willing to produce it.

The 1980s witnessed the revitalizing of the West End musical, though not all shows were British. Claude-Michel Schönberg's *Les Misérables* (libretto by Alain Boublil) was first performed in Paris, but it was its rewritten London version of 1985 (translated by Herbert Kretzmer) that went on to succeed around the world: this reduced the span of Hugo's novel and introduced more theatricality. Even more spectacular was Boublil and Schönberg's second triumph, *Miss Saigon* (1990). Towards the end of the twentieth century, alongside revivals like Kander and Ebb's *Chicago*, the rock/pop musical became more common, whether using original material, like Willy Russell's *Blood Brothers*, or existing pop songs (*Mamma Mia* is based on music by Abba).

Chanson and cabaret

There are, broadly, three types of chanson: the *music-hall* chanson, the *opérette* chanson, and the *chanson réaliste* associated with the poet-composer-performers

42 John Snelson, '(2) Andrew Lloyd-Webber', in Sadie and Tyrrell (eds.), *New Grove* (2nd edn), Vol. XV, pp. 30–2; p. 31.

of artistic cabaret (the trend-setting example being Aristide Bruant). Chansons of all types are subsumed under the label *variétés*, a term that embraces all forms of French light music.

Edith Piaf [Gassion] (1915–63) started as a street singer but it was her transformation into a *réaliste* singer that opened up her market. When she was booked for her first nightclub appearance by Louis Leplée, she had to abandon her *opérette* couplets and the ballads made popular by Tino Rossi; moreover, though she might have learned about stage manner from music-hall star Marie Dubas, she was not able to include any of the latter's comic songs, becoming from now on trapped in the guise of *tragédienne*.[43] Instead of being Denise Jay or Huguette Hélia (her previous pseudonyms), her new name *piaf*, the Parisian slang for sparrow, suggested an authentic voice of the streets in defiant opposition to the music business. Jean Cocteau wrote the introduction to her autobiography, and described the effect of her singing: 'The soul of the street filters into every room in the town.'[44] There is evidence here of the bohemian artist's love of socially marginal art. However, it jars with Piaf's open statement of her admiration for Damia, a *tragédienne-chanteuse*, and her indebtedness to Dubas.[45]

Cocteau believed that Piaf's singing offered an unmediated aesthetic experience: 'it is the rain that falls ... it is the wind that blows'.[46] Perhaps only a woman's voice, informed by the ideology of gender, could be thought to offer such a communion with nature. He also compares her to the nightingale, that famous non-verbal songster. Yet Piaf herself stressed the importance of words to her singing: 'To sing is to bring to life; impossible if the words are mediocre, however good the music.'[47] She had all the techniques of the *diseuse* – declamation, hushed confession, shouts, choked tones – as well as a wide dynamic range and command of lyrical techniques, such as cantabile phrasing, portamento, and the gradual application of vibrato to a held note. Her musical interpretive skills are revealed in her control of dynamics within phrases and ability to attack and leave notes in various ways, while her intensity is conveyed by a rapid vibrato and her dramatic flair by a variety of vocal timbre, as well as by hesitations and other manipulations of tempo. Some prefer the early Piaf on the grounds that later songs and performances are too melodramatic; but melodrama has always been there, even in *chansons réalistes* like 'Elle fréquentait la rue Pigalle' (Maitrier/Asso, 1939). It became stronger in later songs but, to take as an example 'La belle histoire d'amour' (Piaf/Dumont, 1960), her transition from the

43 Gene Lees was assured by Charles Aznavour that Piaf had a raucous sense of humour and would have liked to sing comic songs; *Singers and the Song*, p. 43.

44 Edith Piaf, *The Wheel of Fortune: The Autobiography of Edith Piaf* (tr. Peter Trewartha and Andrée Masoin de Virton), London, 1965, p. 9.

45 Ibid., p. 57. 46 Ibid., p. 9. 47 Ibid., p. 56.

harsh implacable verse to the reminiscence of love in the refrain creates an emotional impact few have equalled. Piaf's voice has a 'grain' in the meaning Barthes gave to the word:[48] you can hear the body in her performance – the teeth, tongue, nose, and throat (as in 'L'accordéoniste', recorded live at the Olympia in 1955).

Words have always been regarded as important in the chanson tradition, and a style of singing arose in which expression of words takes priority (Yvette Guilbert was the first to be celebrated as a *diseuse*, in the 1890s). Georges Brassens (1921–82), who sang folk-like songs to a guitar accompaniment, was a winner of the Académie Française's Grand Prix de Poésie (1967); his lyrics have a deliberate, sometimes archaic, poetic manner that produces an ironic effect in what Peter Hawkins calls 'a low-prestige, popular form such as *chanson*'.[49] Together with Léo Ferré (1916–93), he elevated the literary style of chanson; they both attained publication in the publisher Segher's *Poètes d'aujourd'hui* series, and Ferré was prouder of being number 93 in that series than of being number 1 in the same publisher's *Poésie et chansons* (though he was given to describing himself with heavy irony as an *artiste de variétés*).[50] The odd status of chanson means, however, that Brassens and Ferré are found in neither the recent edition of *New Grove* nor Colin Larkin's eight-volume *Encyclopedia of Popular Music*.

Jacques Brel (1929–78) was born in Brussels, but his career as a chansonnier took off in Paris; he was influenced by Trenet, Ferré, and Brassens, and had important musical collaborators in François Rauber, Gérard Jouannet (his pianist), and Jean Corti. The acclaim that greeted his London concert of 1964 was partly due to his dramatic stage presence. He sang only in French, believing that translations were 'an emasculation of the chansonnier's craft'.[51] One can see his point if his suicidal 'Le moribund' (1961) is compared with its 'translation' 'Seasons in the Sun' (a hit for the Kingston Trio in 1963), or 'Ne me quitte pas' (1959) with 'If You Go Away'.[52] The latter proved one of his most popular chansons and was covered by Dusty Springfield and Shirley Bassey among others. Mort Shuman's off-Broadway cabaret revue *Jacques Brel Is Alive and Well and Living in Paris* (1968) gave his reputation a further boost; Scott Walker in the USA, David Bowie in the UK, and the Canadian Leonard Cohen all found Brel inspirational (though, unusually, it was Brassens that influenced the English satirical singer-songwriter Jake Thackray). His subject matter was

48 'The Grain of the Voice', in Roland Barthes, *Image–Music–Text* (tr. Stephen Heath), London, 1977, pp. 179–89.

49 Peter Hawkins, *Chanson: The French Singer-Songwriter from Aristide Bruant to the Present Day*, Aldershot, 2000, p. 128.

50 Ibid., p. 104. 51 Alan Clayson, *Jacques Brel: The Biography*, Chessington, 1996, p. 108.

52 A discography is contained in Olivier Todd, *Jacques Brel: une vie*, Paris, 1984.

wide-ranging: he sang about vagrancy, cruelty to animals, the passing of time, and death. He also delighted in irony and character studies, with 'Les bourgeois', for example, being sung in the character of a young man who despises the bourgeois life, yet is finally absorbed by it.

Barbara [Monique Serf] (1930–98) made her reputation as *la dame de minuit* at the cabaret *L'Ecluse* in the late 1950s, mixing her own chansons with those of Brassens, Brel, and others. She was, at that time, strongly influenced in the delivery of some chansons by the *diseuse* technique of Yvette Guilbert (though her voice had a range and flexibility well beyond that of Guilbert). She became a fully-fledged *auteur-compositeur* in this male-dominated genre, and her music could be as imaginative as her lyrics: 'L'aigle noir' (1970), for instance, takes the form of a continually modulating chaconne. 'Nantes', a moving account of the death of her father, is in F sharp minor, framed by F minor; the semitonal slip downward on the return to F minor is given a chilling effect by the simultaneous entry of a bowed bass doubling the voice.

Cabaret had begun in France, but spread rapidly elsewhere in the early twentieth century.[53] In the 1930s cabarets flourished in Vienna and Zurich, though the Nazis were closing them down in Berlin and Munich. Cabaret thrived in the days of the Weimar Republic (1918–33), when it advanced an attack on all kinds of oppression, including sexual – as in the case of Mischa Spoliansky's 'gay rights' song 'Das lila Lied' (with words by Kurt Schwabach). The film *Der blaue Engel* (1930), concerning a cabaret of that name, made Berlin-born Marlene [Maria Magdalene] Dietrich (1901–92) a huge star. The music was by Friedrich Holländer (1896–1976), one of the most prolific of German cabaret composers, who had previously collaborated with the political satirists Walter Mehring and Kurt Tucholsky. Dietrich was primarily an actress, subsequently moving to the USA, and did not begin performing as a solo cabaret artist until 1953; she had the theatrical flair of Piaf, but was hampered by a limited vocal technique. Peter Bogdanovich remarked of her performance of 'Where Have All the Flowers Gone?' (Seeger, 1961) that it was 'not just another anti-war lament but a tragic accusation against us all'.[54]

Lale Andersen [Lieselotte Bunnenberg] (1905–72) had the big success of the war years with the *Kabarettschlager* (cabaret hit) 'Lili Marleen', Norbert Schnultze's 1939 setting of a poem written by Hans Leip in 1915. Her first recording in 1939 had verses in both German and English, and had a gentle orchestral accompaniment. By contrast her second version, from 1940, was more militaristic in manner, entirely in German, and included a male-voice

53 For an overview of twentieth-century cabaret, see Lisa Appignanesi, *Cabaret: The First Hundred Years* (rev. edn), London, 1984.

54 Quoted in Sheridan Morley, *Marlene Dietrich*, London, 1978, p. 70.

choir. The song was covered by singers of various nationalities: Suzy Solidor, Greta Keller, Marlene Dietrich, and Anne Shelton – interestingly, like Andersen, these were all noted for their low alto voices and erotic charge, though here they were singing a man's song to a woman.

Cabaret was first established in London with the Cave of the Golden Calf in 1912, but only took off when George Grossmith adopted the New York style of cabaret and produced *Midnight Follies* at the Hotel Metropole, where cabaret was seen as an 'adjunct to the meal'.[55] Noel Coward was an admired performer of his own songs in such cabarets. There is no real equivalent to chanson in the UK, but Tom Jones's 'Delilah' (Reed/Mason, 1968) has the narrative, the drama, the 'in character' delivery, and the triple time typical of many chansons; not surprisingly, it climbed straight to the top of the French charts.

Popularity charts and song contests

Popularity charts and competitions often challenge accepted critical evaluations. The biggest UK hit of 1965, for example, was not the Beatles' 'Ticket to Ride', but Ken Dodd's 'Tears' (Capano/Uhr, originally recorded by Rudy Vallee in 1929). In 2001, Channel Four in the UK broadcast a television programme devoted to the 'Easy Listening Top Ten', which consisted of 1) Frank Sinatra, 2) Burt Bacharach, 3) Nat 'King' Cole, 4) Andy Williams, 5) The Carpenters (Richard and Karen), 6) Englebert Humperdinck [Arnold Dorsey], 7) Dusty Springfield, 8) Dean Martin, 9) Dionne Warwick, and 10) Tony Bennett. None of these is found in Roy Shuker's much-used textbook *Understanding Popular Music* (1994, revised 2001).

Usefully highlighted here is the significance of Burt Bacharach (b. 1928), who was classically trained and had received composition instruction from Milhaud, Martinů, and Cowell. He was Marlene Dietrich's musical director on her international tours during 1958–61, while from the mid-1950s he wrote songs with Hal David (b. 1921) in New York's Brill Building on Broadway. A huge early hit was 'Magic Moments' (1957), recorded by Perry Como in 1958. The finest interpreters of the David/Bacharach songs, however, have tended to be female, the most admired being Dionne Warwick (b. 1940) and Dusty Springfield [Mary O'Brien] (1939–99). Bacharach composes in an eclectic style, frequently with a Latin-American flavour.

The 'Easy Listening Top Ten' was based on record sales and weeks in the record charts. But for more than half of the twentieth century it was sheet-music sales that counted most, and these generated multiple recordings; from 1946 to

55 Christopher Pulling, *They Were Singing*, London, 1952, p. 228.

1955, of all the music featured in the Music Publishers' Association sheet-music charts, only seventeen had just a single recording to their credit. However, there were eighteen such cases in the year 1959 alone,[56] providing circumstantial evidence of a growing feeling that one particular record was the 'real' song. This must be linked to the production of a record being seen as an essential part of the song, as a consequence of increasingly sophisticated studio technology.[57] The idea established itself because record-buying was enjoying a boom: sales figures show that the turnover of the record industry in the USA more than trebled between 1950 and 1960.[58]

One of the most prestigious European song contests is the San Remo Song Festival in Liguria, Italy: Domenico Modugno (b. 1928) was launched to fame in 1958 after winning first prize with 'Nel blu, dipinto di blu' [Volare] (Migliacci/Modugno), a million-selling hit for both himself and Dean Martin. Some San Remo songs were more restricted geographically in their popularity: for example, Antoine's 'La tramontana' (Pace/Panzeri) of 1968 found its warmest welcome in Italy and France. Others were taken up with great success in English translation; Dusty Springfield's 'You Don't Have to Say You Love Me' (1966) was the English version of 'Io che non vivo' (Pallavicini/Donaggio), the San Remo winner of 1965.

The Swedish contest, the Melody Festival, acts as a qualifying competition for the song to be entered for the Eurovision Song Contest, and has been the subject of a study by Alf Björnberg. After 1970, Björnberg found, the accompaniment of songs began to shift from light orchestra to a big-band sound with reduced strings, while by 1980 a rock-group sound dominated. Before 1970, the usual song type employed the thirty-two-bar Tin Pan Alley form, but thereafter shorter pop structures took over. At the same time, there remained more in the way of reference to older popular music and even classical harmonic practice than there was in pop of the same period. Finally, Swedish features (like 'tra-la-la') were abandoned in favour of Anglo-American pop vocal sounds (like 'wow').[59]

56 Statistics in Brian Henson and Colin Morgan, *First Hits: The Book of Sheet Music 1946–1959*, London, 1989, p. 245.

57 A brief account of the growing importance of studio production practices from the 1950s on is given in Keith Negus, *Producing Pop: Culture and Conflict in the Popular Music Industry*, London, 1992, pp. 87–9.

58 Record sales increased from 200 to 650 million dollars; figures (to the nearest five million) from Murrells, *Million Selling Records*, p. 7.

59 Alf Björnberg, 'En liten sång som alla andra Melodifestivalen 1959–1983', *Skrifter från Musikvetenskaplliga Institutionen* 14 (Göteborg, 1987), pp. 227–32, and 'Sounding the Mainstream: An Analysis of the Songs Performed in the Swedish Eurovision Song Contest Semi-Finals 1959–1983', in K. Roe and U. Carlsson (eds.), *Popular Music Research: An Anthology from NORDICOM-Sweden*, Göteborg, 1990, pp. 121–31.

Love themes rather than social issues have dominated the lyric content of the Eurovision Song Contest, except where the sentiment is sufficiently universal, as in Germany's winning entry of 1982, 'Ein bißchen Frieden' (Meinunger/Siegel), sung by Nicole (Hohloch). Germany's confusion about the cultural position occupied by the Eurovision Song Contest was evident in 1956, its first year. There were then two German entries, one a thoughtful *Kabarettschlager*, in keeping with the country's most distinctive contribution to popular song, and the other a Bill Haley-style rock 'n' roll number. Much of Björnberg's analysis holds true for the Eurovision Song Contest, too, but this contest did continue to ensure massive sales for the music of artists in countries that could otherwise scarcely compete with the Anglo-American record industry. Moreover, the stylistic hegemony that Anglo-American music exercised from the mid-1960s began to be challenged by a reawakening of interest in national musical traditions in the 1990s – such as 'Nocturne' (Løvland/Skavian), Secret Garden's winning entry for Norway in 1995, and 'The Voice' (Graham), Eimear Quinn's winning entry for Ireland the following year.[60]

The dispersal of the middle ground

The days when a taste preference for easy listening might have been ascribed to an aspiring semi-detached suburban social stratum have now passed; one has only to recall the manner in which Demis Roussos's 'Forever and Ever' was able to feature as a marker of taste in Mike Leigh's *Abigail's Party* of 1978. Max Weber noted long ago the loose fit between status group and social class.[61] Indications of status (for example, etiquette or taste in music) can be imitated and, towards the end of the nineteenth century, what art was appreciated and what was shunned began to be an important status marker.[62] The 'three zones of taste' model (highbrow, middlebrow, and lowbrow) dominated the years 1920–80, and even informs Pierre Bourdieu's critical treatise on taste.[63] The zones began to crumble around 1980 – significantly, at the same time as the easy listening market disintegrated. In the 1990s, for instance, high status was more likely to be obtained by displaying a cosmopolitan 'omnivorous'

60 For a history of the Eurovision Song Contest, see Jan Feddersen, *Merci, Jury! Die Geschichte des Grand Prix Eurovision de la Chanson*, Vienna, 2000.

61 'Class, Status, Party', in Hans Gerth and C. Wright Mills (eds.), *From Max Weber: Essays in Sociology*, London, 1991, pp. 180–95.

62 See Lawrence W. Levine, *Highbrow/Lowbrow: The Emergence of Cultural Hierarchy in America*, Cambridge, MA, 1988, and Richard A. Peterson, 'The Rise and Fall of Highbrow Snobbery as a Status Marker', *Poetics* 25 (1997), pp. 75–92.

63 Pierre Bourdieu, *Distinction: A Social Critique of the Judgement of Taste* (tr. Richard Nice), London, 1984.

taste than by exclusive adherence to what was formerly categorized as high-brow.[64] This does not fundamentally challenge Bourdieu's ideas, however, since the manner in which different groups consume music continues to be permeated with features that perpetuate the importance of social distinction in matters of taste (for instance, consumption can be at 'face value', ambivalent, or ironic).

In the late 1960s, rock music became all-consuming, absorbing and fusing with so many other styles that it eroded the possibility of light music remaining a separate category; in some cases, such as that of the Beatles' *Sgt. Pepper's Lonely Hearts Club Band*, rock came to occupy the space of a popular 'art music' that had formerly been the particular province of light music. British composer Anthony Hedges, who had previously enjoyed success with his light orchestral music on radio, was informed by the BBC at the dawn of the 1970s that his light music compositions would no longer find an outlet there, since light music was extinct.[65] Easy listening also began to lose its identity as something distinguishable from pop: for example, some Beatles songs – 'Yesterday', 'When I'm Sixty-Four' – fell effortlessly into the easy listening category (and may be heard, in instrumental arrangements, throughout departure lounges the world over), as did an increasing amount of country music. In the late 1970s, the popular 'middle' type of music was being kept alive mainly by Barry Manilow, the Carpenters, and Barbra Streisand. But the way middlebrow taste has now become dispersed can be illustrated by reference to the rock band U2: the band has an image of being uncompromising, 'authentic' rock musicians, yet is in reality a huge business enterprise encompassing records, tours, radio, television, and associated merchandise, with sales in over a hundred markets estimated to generate £230 million in 2001.[66] For that to be possible, it is clear that the band's appeal must cut across the old zones of taste.

Although light music and easy listening no longer occupy the middle ground, the experiences and values they represent will always have a place in the musical terrain. The film music of John Williams (b. 1932), for example, has obvious links with light music. And in the 1990s there was both a light music revival, led by Ronald Corp and the New London Orchestra, and an easy listening revival. Moreover, these values and experiences are not only available through revivals, but are also being continually reworked and renewed: as light music

64 See Richard A. Peterson and Albert Simkus, 'How Musical Taste Groups Mark Occupational Status Groups', in Michele Lamont and Marcel Fournier (eds.), *Cultivating Differences: Symbolic Boundaries and the Making of Inequality*, Chicago, 1992, pp. 152–68, and Richard A. Peterson and Roger M. Kern, 'Changing Highbrow Taste: From Snob to Omnivore', *American Sociological Review* 61 (1996), pp. 900–7.

65 Personal communication to the author.

66 Figures from Rory Godson, 'Why McGuinness Is Good for U2', *The Sunday Times*, Section 9: Culture, 3 June 2001, p. 6.

was followed by easy listening, so the latter has been succeeded by chill-out music. Despite this, there are aspects in which little seems to change. 'Groove Armada have fallen asleep', exclaimed the *Guardian* newspaper when reviewing their new chill-out album *Goodbye Country* on 7 September 2001. Half a century earlier, the familiar wisecrack about Dean Martin was 'Any easier, he'd have been asleep.'

Bibliography

Appignanesi, Lisa. *Cabaret: The First Hundred Years* (rev. edn), London, 1984.

Banfield, Stephen. 'Popular Song and Popular Music on Stage and Film', in David Nicholls (ed.), *The Cambridge History of American Music*, Cambridge, 1998, pp. 309–44.

'Sondheim, Stephen (Joshua)', in Stanley Sadie and John Tyrrell (eds.), *The New Grove Dictionary of Music and Musicians* (2nd edn), 29 vols., London, 2001, Vol. XXIII, pp. 701–3.

Sondheim's Broadway Musicals, Ann Arbor, 1993.

Barthes, Roland. *Image–Music–Text* (tr. Stephen Heath), London, 1977, pp. 179–89.

Bennett, Robert R. *The Broadway Sound: Autobiography and Selected Essays of Robert Russell Bennett*, ed. George Ferencz, New York, 1999.

Björnberg, Alf. 'En liten sång som alla andra Melodifestivalen 1959–1983', *Skrifter från Musikvetensklapliga Institutionen* 14 (Göteborg, 1987), pp. 227–32.

'Sounding the Mainstream: An Analysis of the Songs Performed in the Swedish Eurovision Song Contest Semi-Finals 1959–1983', in K. Roe and U. Carlsson (eds.), *Popular Music Research: An Anthology from NORDICOM-Sweden*, Göteborg, 1990, pp. 121–31.

Bordman, Gerald. *American Musical Theatre: A Chronicle* (expanded edn), New York, 1985.

Bourdieu, Pierre. *Distinction: A Social Critique of the Judgement of Taste* (tr. Richard Nice), London, 1984.

The Field of Cultural Production: Essays on Art and Literature (ed. Randal Johnson), Cambridge, 1993.

Bowlly, Al. *Modern Style Singing ('Crooning')*, London, 1934.

Brackett, David. *Interpreting Popular Music*, Berkeley, 2000.

Brody, Elaine. *Paris: The Musical Kaleidoscope, 1870–1925*, London, 1988.

Clayson, Alan. *Jacques Brel: The Biography*, Chessington, 1996.

Colin, Sid. *And the Bands Played On: An Informal History of British Dance Bands*, London, 1977.

Edström, Olle. 'The Place and Value of Middle Music', *Svensk Tidskrift för Musikforskning* 1 (1992), pp. 7–60.

Ewen, David. *Panorama of American Popular Music*, Englewood Cliffs, NJ, 1957.

Feddersen, Jan. *Merci, Jury! Die Geschichte des Grand Prix Eurovision de la Chanson*, Vienna, 2000.

Forte, Allen. *The American Popular Ballad of the Golden Era: 1924–1950*, Princeton, 1995.

Gänzl, Kurt. *The Blackwell Guide to Musical Theatre on Record*, Oxford, 1990.

Geissmar, Berta. *The Baton and the Jackboot: Recollections of Musical Life*, London, 1944.
Godson, Rory. 'Why McGuinness Is Good for U2', *The Sunday Times* (Section 9: Culture), 3 Jun 2001, p. 6.
Hamm, Charles. *Music in the New World*, New York, 1983.
Yesterdays: Popular Song in America, New York, 1979.
Harding, James. *Maurice Chevalier: His Life 1888–1972*, London, 1982.
Hawkins, Peter. *Chanson: The French Singer-Songwriter from Aristide Bruant to the Present Day*, Aldershot, 2000.
Hennion, Antoine. 'The Production of Success: An Anti-Musicology of the Pop Song', *Popular Music* 3 (1983), pp. 158–93.
Henson, Brian and Morgan, Colin. *First Hits: The Book of Sheet Music 1946–1959*, London, 1989.
Lamb, Andrew. *100 Years of Popular Musical Theatre*, New Haven, 2001.
Larkin, Colin (ed.). *Encyclopedia of Popular Music* (3rd edn), 8 vols., London, 1998.
Lees, Gene. *Singers and the Song*, New York, 1987.
Levine, Lawrence W. *Highbrow/Lowbrow: The Emergence of Cultural Hierarchy in America*, Cambridge, MA, 1988.
Moore, John. ' "The Hieroglyphics of Love": The Torch Singers and Interpretation', in R. Middleton (ed.), *Reading Pop: Approaches to Textual Analysis in Popular Music*, Oxford, 2000, pp. 262–96.
Morley, Sheridan. *Marlene Dietrich*, London, 1978.
Murrells, Joseph. *Million Selling Records from the 1900s to the 1980s: An Illustrated Directory*, London, 1984.
Negus, Keith. *Music Genres and Corporate Cultures*, London, 1999.
Producing Pop: Culture and Conflict in the Popular Music Industry, London, 1992.
Peterson, Richard A. and Kern, Roger M. 'Changing Highbrow Taste: From Snob to Omnivore', *American Sociological Review* 61 (1996), pp. 900–7.
Peterson, Richard A. and Simkus, Albert. 'How Musical Taste Groups Mark Occupational Status Groups', in Michele Lamont and Marcel Fournier (eds.), *Cultivating Differences: Symbolic Boundaries and the Making of Inequality*, Chicago, 1992, pp. 152–68.
Peterson, Richard A. 'The Rise and Fall of Highbrow Snobbery as a Status Marker', *Poetics* 25 (1997), pp. 75–92.
'Why 1955? Explaining the Advent of Rock Music', *Popular Music* 9 (1990), pp. 97–116.
Piaf, Edith. *The Wheel of Fortune: The Autobiography of Edith Piaf* (tr. Peter Trewartha and Andrée Masoin de Virton), London, 1965.
Pleasants, Henry. 'Sinatra, Frank', in *The New Grove Dictionary of Music and Musicians* (2nd edn), 29 vols., London, 2000, Vol. XXIII, pp. 416–17.
Pulling, Christopher. *They Were Singing*, London, 1952.
Rust, Brian. *The Dance Bands*, London, 1972.
Schuller, Gunther. *Early Jazz: Its Roots and Musical Development*, New York, 1968.
The Swing Era: The Development of Jazz, 1930–1945, New York, 1989.
Scott, Derek B. 'The "Jazz Age" ', in Stephen Banfield (ed.), *Blackwell History of Music in Britain: The Twentieth Century*, Oxford, 1995, pp. 57–78.
'Music and Social Class', in Jim Samson (ed.), *The Cambridge History of Nineteenth-Century Music*, Cambridge, 2001, pp. 544–67.

Shuker, Roy. *Understanding Popular Music* (2nd edn), London, 2001.
Snelson, John. '(2) Andrew Lloyd-Webber', in *The New Grove Dictionary of Music and Musicians* (2nd edn), 29 vols., London, 2001, Vol. XV, pp. 30–2.
Todd, Olivier. *Jacques Brel: une vie*, Paris, 1984.
Traubner, Richard. *Operetta: A Theatrical History*, London, 1984.
Van de Merwe, Peter. *Origins of the Popular Style: The Antecedents of Twentieth-Century Popular Music*, Oxford, 1989.
Weber, Max. 'Class, Status, Party', in Hans Gerth and C. Wright Mills (eds.), *From Max Weber: Essays in Sociology*, London, 1991, pp. 180–95.
Whitcomb, Ian. *After the Ball: Pop Music from Rag to Rock*, New York, 1994.

· 13 ·

New beginnings: the international avant-garde, 1945–62

DAVID OSMOND-SMITH

No previous convulsion had so profound an impact upon the musical life of Europe at large as did the Second World War. In as much as they could, combatant nations clung to a vestige of the familiar and well-loved. Despite the emigration to the United States of a dismayingly large percentage of those who commanded a measure of cultural authority, opera houses and concert halls struggled to assert 'business as usual' in the face of daunting circumstance, and awaited better times. In consequence, the late 1940s and early 1950s were devoted to the restoration not just of the fabric of Europe's devastated cities, but of long-established cultural institutions. As was to be expected, the music-loving middle classes returned with gratitude to their cultivation of an authoritative classical repertoire.

But for the generation of young European musicians who had passed their formative years amongst the constrictions of the later 1930s and early 1940s, the imperative was now to make their own the more radical currents of pre-war culture to which they had been denied access. The situation was particularly acute in Germany – subject since 1933 to stringent regulation of the culturally permissible by Goebbels's *Reichsmusikkammer*. Although Italian fascist cultural policy, as directed during the immediate pre-war years by the minister of culture, Giuseppe Bottai, had proved somewhat more encouraging of a carefully regulated innovation, its younger generation felt itself similarly cut off.[1] The élan of French cultural life of the 1920s and 30s (strongly neoclassical and pro-Stravinsky) had been brought sharply to heel under German occupation, leaving Olivier Messiaen as a solitary beacon for younger composers with an interest in the modernist tradition. Britain, meanwhile, had found insular security in traditional aesthetic values and the cult of the pastoral idyll.

The engines of the avant-garde

The revival of concert-hall activity therefore did little to give younger composers a sense of potential function within post-war musical life. To create that

1 Cf. Fiamma Nicolodi, *Musica e Musicisti nel Ventennio Fascista*, Fiesole, 1984.

sense, they needed a milieu responsive to their work, and sources of support and patronage. The need for a sympathetic milieu was met by specialized festivals of contemporary music – notably those of Donaueschingen, Venice, and Palermo – and by events at which an international body of young musicians might meet and fraternize, such as the summer schools at Darmstadt and Dartington. But although individual patrons – Paul Sacher in Basel, Suzanne Tezenas in Paris – continued to play a part in supporting new work, the creation of a framework within which young composers could develop their vision became, to an unprecedented degree, the responsibility of certain of the European radio stations. This was not merely a matter of providing a source of employment for young composers: the possibility of sustaining an 'avant-garde' within media-based culture was profoundly dependent upon the radio. It had been evident since the start of the century that the patrons of urban concert halls and opera houses were only rarely disposed to sympathize with the more radical aesthetic adventures of their contemporaries. But broadcasting allowed musical innovators to postulate the existence of a diffused network of listeners who did not have to be brought together in one place. Furthermore radio was free: access to it was open in the same way as, at the start of the twenty-first century, access to the Internet is free to all who can afford the equipment and the phone bill (and paying for radio equipment in the 1940s and 50s was less economically exclusive than is its contemporary equivalent). Therefore challenging cultural products could quite literally be 'broadcast': seed could be scattered in all directions in the hope that some of it would sprout and grow.

A crucial example in this regard was provided by the British Broadcasting Corporation, which in 1946 founded the Third Programme.[2] Its example was widely influential, most obviously on Italian Radio's Terzo Programma, inaugurated in 1950, while the French RTF began to foster experiment through the foundation, in 1948, of the Club d'Essai that was to form a base for Pierre Schaeffer's experiments in *musique concrète*. But it was the radio stations of the newly established West German Bundesrepublik – above all the Südwestfunk in Baden-Baden and the Westdeutscher Rundfunk in Cologne (until 1956 part of the Nordwest deutscher Rundfunk) – that became seminal forces in the creation of an international avant-garde. In part this was a product of politics. The Third Reich had centralized its national radio service, the Reichsrundfunk, under Goebbels; the victorious Allies considered it wise to decentralize, restoring regional radio stations that thereafter kept a competitive eye upon each other's achievements. After only partially successful attempts at revival in 1946 and 1947, the Donaueschingen festival – the only one in Germany devoted to contemporary music – was reinstated in 1950 by the

2 Cf. Humphrey Carpenter, *The Envy of the World*, London, 1996.

Südwestfunk, under the direction of Heinrich Strobel. At its inception in the 1920s, Donaueschingen had been focused upon chamber music, but now the Südwestfunk Radio Symphony Orchestra, under the meticulous direction of its conductor Hans Rosbaud, was made available to the festival each year, and in consequence young composers were able to conceive of writing substantial orchestral works without having to run the gauntlet of the concert-hall Establishment. As well as promoting its own concert series for new music, 'Musik der Zeit', the Westdeutscher Rundfunk enabled Herbert Eimert to found the Studio für Elektronische Musik in 1951. Other concert series that allowed for the commissioning of new work were the Bayerischer Rundfunk's 'Musica Viva' in Munich, and the Norddeutscher Rundfunk's 'Das Neue Werk' in Hamburg.

But such instances of the broadcasting of live performances formed only part of the impact of radio upon new music during the 1950s. Recording onto electronic tape, first demonstrated at the 1935 Berlin Radio Fair, had become rapidly and universally adopted in the late 1940s, bringing with it a radical shift in aesthetic perspectives. Tape, like film in the great days of the silent cinema, is a medium that can be cut and rejoined. Sound materials – whether 'composed' electronically as in the Cologne studio, or recorded from diverse 'live' sources and transformed as appropriate, as in the Paris studio – can be structured into a sequential montage. But unlike the images of silent cinema, they can also be superposed to create a counterpoint of complex sound-layers whose origin is less important than is their interactive potential. Such was the approach of the first American experimenters in tape music, Vladimir Ussachevsky and Otto Luening, collaborating from 1951 not at a radio station but at the Music Department of Columbia University in New York. Luciano Berio heard the first public performance of their work at the New York Museum of Modern Art in 1952, and returned to Milan determined to create a similarly 'open' approach in the studio which he and Bruno Maderna eventually succeeded in persuading the Italian Radio to set up there in 1955. (It is no accident that, apart from the two major metropolitan centres of cultural activity, Paris and New York, two further magnets for innovative young musicians were precisely Cologne and Milan – not because their radio stations engendered everything of worth that developed in those cities, but because their presence helped to create a buoyant and experimental cultural atmosphere.)

That music for radio (or for radio drama) might thus develop its own aesthetic was one of the great innovatory hopes of the 1950s, given concrete focus when the European Broadcasting Union, meeting on Capri in 1948, inaugurated the Prix Italia for a musical work with text, and for a dramatic work with or without music. In practice, juries generally proved resistant to works with a strong electroacoustic basis (so that the 'radiophonic representation' *Ritratto di Cittá* produced in 1955 by Berio and Maderna on a text by Roberto Leydi in their new Milan studio had to be proffered as a curiosity outside the main competition). 'Radio opera' looked for a while as if it would become a genuine genre – as with Henze's Kafka-based *Ein Landarzt* (1951, but presented in the 1953 session, where it won the RAI prize) or Antheil's *The Wish* (1955) – and reached a genuine high-point in 1961 with Maderna's *Don Perlimpin* and Castiglioni's Lewis Carroll-based *Attraverso lo specchio*. But it never reached the heights of radio drama with music that were achieved by Dylan Thomas's *Under Milk Wood* (music by Daniel Jones), which won the 1954 prize, or Muriel Spark's *The Ballad of Peckham Rye* (music by Tristram Cary), the winner in 1962.[3]

The more radical perspectives opened up by tape music may not have won the hearts of Prix Italia juries, but they did rapidly impact upon the concert hall – and particularly upon the new approaches to orchestral writing that the Donaueschingen festival did so much to foster. The orchestra during the 1950s began to be viewed by younger composers as a source for multiple layers of dense sound, counterpointed with or responding to each other, as in the classic instance of Stockhausen's *Gruppen* (1955–7), or the *Quaderni* that Berio brought together to form *Epifanie* (1959–62). Furthermore, the interface between tape music and instrumental music rapidly became a crucial area for exploration and aesthetic debate during the later 1950s, obliging musicians to confront the profound qualitative differences between music emanating from speakers, and music performed live.

There would be substantial historical and musical justice in calling the 1940s and 50s the 'radiophonic' era. But it was one of the great international meeting-points for young musicians, more fundamentally, that conferred upon the post-war generation a distinct (if at times rather glibly applied) critical identity. That the Darmstadt summer schools should have taken on an almost symbolic significance within the sphere of post-war reconstruction is hardly surprising. The town of Darmstadt had been razed almost to the ground by British air raids on 11–12 September 1944: over seventy per cent of the population were left homeless. As the mayor, Ludwig Metzger, struggled to deal with the crisis in the ensuing year, he was approached by the young musicologist Wolfgang Steinecke with a proposal that seemed remote from the basic practicalities with which Metzger was concerned: Steinecke insisted that the reconstitution of a coherent presence for the German Bundesrepublik at the heart of post-war Europe depended as much upon cultural revival as upon rebuilding the material bases of life. The town of Darmstadt was in ruins, but the castle of Kranichstein,

3 Cf. Angela Ida De Benedictis, 'Arte *alla* Radio – Arte *per* la Radio: il Caso Premio Italia', in De Benedictis, 'Radiodramma e arte Radiofonica. Storia e Funzioni della Musica per Radio in Italia', Ph. D. diss., Università di Pavia, 2001, pp. 55–123.

in the countryside nearby, stood undamaged, and Steinecke successfully urged Metzger to allow its use for summer courses that would give young Germans the opportunity of re-establishing roots in the music of the last fifty years. He obtained financial help for the project from the occupying American forces' Theatre and Music Officer, Everett Helm, and accordingly, in 1946, the first Internationale Ferienkürse für Neue Musik took place.[4]

The German press noted with some satisfaction the absence of Schoenberg's music from the first Ferienkurse, and although the 1947 session included a performance of his Second String Quartet, it was little understood. Yet by 1948 the tide had turned. The fourth-based opening theme of the Allegro from Schoenberg's First Chamber Symphony became the Ferienkurse's 'motto', printed on all publications, and the assiduous, if doctrinaire, René Leibowitz lectured on twelve-tone technique. Perhaps more prophetically, Peter Stadlen gave the first German performance of Webern's Variations, op. 27. The Darmstadt melting-pot had begun to bubble. (More quietly and more eclectically, the Bryanston Summer School was founded in the same year by William Glock, moving to Dartington in 1953.)

Over the next five years, the seminal character of these summer meetings became ever more clearly established. In 1949 it was the turn of Josef Rufer to teach twelve-tone technique (already by no means a Darmstadt monopoly, as was witnessed by the First International Dodecaphonic Congress, held earlier that year in Milan as a postscript to the Palermo ISCM festival[5]). But more crucially, Messiaen was invited to Darmstadt as guest of honour, and during his stay began work on the *Quatre études de rythme* that were to exercise so strong an influence upon the new generation of composers over the next few years. By 1950 some of the dramatis personae were beginning to establish themselves: T. W. Adorno attended for the first time, as did the young Luigi Nono. But Darmstadt was still by no means a closed shop: Varèse attended for the first and only time (an encounter that Nono was not quickly to forget), and with Scherchen's performance of his *Ionisation* inaugurated the summer school's propensity for lively protest and aesthetic dissent. Krenek was given much attention; Henze's Second Symphony was performed. And in 1951 two other central Darmstadt protagonists paid their first visit: Bruno Maderna and Karlheinz Stockhausen. By now the Schoenbergian filiation was more explicit; Schoenberg had himself agreed to come from America to teach, but was too ill to attend. However, Scherchen gave the first performance of the 'Dance around

4 The record given throughout this chapter of what occurred at Darmstadt is indebted to Antonio Trudu's chronicle, *La 'Scuola' di Darmstadt*, Milan, 1992.

5 Cf. Maria Grazia Sità, 'I festival', in G. Salvetti and B. M. Antolini (eds.), *Italia Millenovecentocinquanta*, Milan, 1999, pp. 117–36; pp. 126–7.

the Golden Calf' from *Moses und Aron*, as well as of Nono's *Polifonica-Monodica-Ritmica*. And as if proposing a clear declaration of intent, Darmstadt hosted the Second Dodecaphonic Congress.

So far, one powerful creative presence had remained absent. Pierre Boulez already had a formidable body of compositions to his credit, and the publication in 1950 of his Second Piano Sonata had attracted widespread comment. (It was rapidly to become an obligatory rite of passage for the pianistic Young Turks of Europe and America.) In 1952, Messiaen returned to Darmstadt to teach, bringing with him his formidable young protégé, whose confrontational apologia for Webern, 'Schoenberg Is Dead', had just been published by William Glock in *The Score*.[6] Messiaen's wife, Yvonne Loriod, played the first movement of the infamous but much-admired sonata. But visitors for that year were also confronted, on the third evening, by an extraordinary concert that included the premieres of Stockhausen's *Kreuzspiel* (with Maderna playing percussion, and the audience in active revolt), Maderna's *Musica su due dimensioni* – the first work to attempt the combining of live instrumental and electronic sound – and Nono's *España en el corazòn*, the first part of *Epitaffio per Federico Garcia Lorca*, conducted by Maderna (and so warmly applauded that it had to be repeated). The omnipresence of Maderna – a musician of generous and catholic tastes – was to do much to preserve the summer schools from becoming excessively doctrinaire over the next decade.

If the figurehead at Darmstadt from 1948 to 1952 had been Schoenberg, from 1953 through to the end of the decade it was to be Anton Webern – whose accidental death in 1945, shot by an American soldier, had left his music almost entirely unexplored save by a handful of enthusiasts. His work had been heard at Darmstadt before: four pieces had been heard between 1948 and 1952, and Adorno had given a (somewhat condescending) talk on him in the Dodecaphonic Congress of 1951. But in 1953 a whole memorial evening was dedicated to him on what would have been his seventieth birthday, featuring performances of opp. 5, 7, 9, 11, and 23. Eimert gave a brief address (taking issue with Adorno's valuation of two years before), and read appreciations from the absent Boulez and Karel Goeyvaerts, while Stockhausen propounded an enthusiastic analysis of the first movement of the Concerto, op. 24. Nono countered by denouncing technical fetishism: for him Webern instead personified 'the *new man*, who possesses the absolute confidence that permits him to mould the inner life with tension'[7]. Stockhausen and Nono argued long

6 Pierre Boulez, 'Schoenberg is Dead', *The Score*, 6 May 1952; repr. in *Stocktakings from an Apprenticeship* (tr. Stephen Walsh), Oxford, 1991, pp. 15–19.

7 Cf. Trudu, *La 'Scuola'*, p. 85. For a slightly different version, see Luigi Nono, *Écrits* (ed. Laurent Feneyrou), Paris, 1993, p. 351.

into the night over their respective interpretations of their hero – this time in private, though future years were to see more public confrontations. The critic, Albert Rodemann, wrote a long account of the Webern evening for the *Darmstädter Tagblatt* with the prophetic title 'Ein Unbekannter bildet Schule' (an unknown composer builds up a school).

The Nono–Stockhausen debate heralded enduring questions as to whether the Webern cult that dominated the work of the European avant-garde over at least the next five years was not, as Paul Griffiths has aptly suggested, a 'creative misunderstanding'.[8] (The same might indeed be said for Darmstadt's interpretation of the man who was so tellingly to undermine the Webern cult at the end of the 1950s: John Cage.) The incisive polemics launched by Boulez in the name of Webern saw in him the bearer of the pan-serial tools, governing not only pitch motifs but also rhythm, dynamics, and other dimensions, that would allow the creation of 'a universe in perpetual expansion' – a literally endless proliferation of new materials, never repeating themselves but each a link in a transformational chain. Yet it is hard to imagine anything further from the spirit of Webern than perpetual expansion. On the contrary, once Webern had received 'the law' from Schoenberg's hands, and thus found himself empowered to return to instrumental writing from the Symphony, op. 21, on, his concern was to revalidate, in the most refined and concentrated manner, the closed, organically integrated forms of the past.

A tale of two cities: Paris and New York

The establishment of the Webern cult at Darmstadt offers an appropriate point at which to pause and survey the wider scene. For distinctive as the role of radio stations and summer schools was during this period, a more traditional form of cultural geography also continued to assert itself. Although Darmstadt was pivotal to the development of a self-conscious avant-garde in Germany and Italy in the early 1950s, the same cannot be said for other European countries, especially France. For three centuries, Paris had regarded itself as the cultural capital of Europe. Although after 1945 it never regained the self-evident centrality that it had enjoyed in the early decades of the century, it made a number of attempts to regain lost momentum. A natural focus for such efforts was the conductor Roger Desormière, whose devotion to new work was of long standing. He now began to programme works by Messiaen (the *Trois petites liturgies*) and the young Boulez (whose *Le soleil des eaux* was one of the last pieces that Desormière prepared for performance before illness forced him into premature retirement in 1950). A more formidable reassertion of the centrality

8 Paul Griffiths, 'Webern', *The New Grove Dictionary of Music and Musicians*, London, 1980, 20 vols., vol. XX, p. 279.

of Paris came in 1954 when, backed by the patronage of Suzanne Tezenas, Boulez started his Domaine Musical concerts, for many years the most single-minded and meticulously executed concert series devoted to the avant-garde in Europe.

If Paris continued to exert a gravitational force, this was also due to Messiaen's emergence as the pre-eminent composition teacher of the post-war years. Quite apart from Boulez, who had studied with him for a year in 1944–5 and continued to be closely associated with him thereafter, Goeyvaerts joined his class from 1947–50, Barraqué from 1948–51, and Stockhausen from 1952–3. While Goeyvaerts and Stockhausen were to have a significant impact upon the early development of the Darmstadt ethos, Barraqué never attended. His remarkable Piano Sonata (1950–2) is almost as significant a monument of post-war French serialism as is the extraordinary flow of works that Boulez had produced in the previous few years; yet it had little impact at the time – as much as anything because of Barraqué's fastidious and unassertive temperament. The other focus for young Parisian composers was René Leibowitz, whose stormy teaching relationship with Boulez may have been of short duration, but who successfully fostered the development of other French serialists such as Michel Phillipot.

A further contribution to the distinctive mix of creative possibilities offered by Paris in the early 1950s was Pierre Schaeffer's Groupe de Recherche de Musique Concrète (GRMC). Schaeffer, although the son of musicians, was a polymath and radio technician who, in 1942, had participated in the establishment of Radiodiffusion Française's experimental Club (later Studio) d'Essai. Although equipped only with disc recordings, he there began experimenting with creating structures from recorded sounds or noise in a projected *Symphonie des bruits*: an approach greatly facilitated in the immediate post-war years by the introduction of magnetic tape. A series of 'Etudes' produced in 1948 led to the *Symphonie pour un homme seul* of 1950, produced in collaboration with Pierre Henry, and to the establishment in 1951 of the GRMC. Schaeffer left the GRMC in the charge of Henri in 1953, intent upon other broadcasting projects, but returned in 1958 to reform the Groupe (now 'de Recherches Musicales', or GRM) with Mâche and Ferrari. The emphasis of the GRMC/GRM upon developing a disciplined attention to the qualities of complex sound – considered independently of its source or of its acoustic analysis – was, throughout the 1950s, to provide an important counter-balance to the concept of 'composed' sound being developed contemporaneously at the Cologne studios by Eimert and Stockhausen.

That Paris could still fulfil at least part of its traditional role as an international magnet is evident from the career of Iannis Xenakis. Escaping from the threat of death for his activities in the Greek Resistance, Xenakis settled in Paris in

1947, where he found encouragement and support from Messiaen (as well as working as assistant to the architect Le Corbusier). But it is a testimony to the uncertain support offered to new composition by the Parisian orchestral establishment after Desormière's retirement that the series of extraordinary 'stochastic' orchestral works that he produced there during the 1950s, whose 'clouds' of musical particles were calculated by aspects of probability theory, were taken up not by French conductors, but by Rosbaud at Donaueschingen (*Metastasis*, 1955) and Scherchen at Munich (*Pithoprakta*, 1957).

If Paris could no longer regard itself as the self-evident centre of the Western cultural world, this was in part due to the rise of a formidable rival. Both the East and West Coasts of the United States had benefited substantially from the inflow of immigrant musicians during the 1930s, but when it came to offering a sustained challenge to Paris, it was New York that established an unassailable position. Such pillars of the European avant-garde as the radio stations and the musical summer schools and festivals played little part in this development. Instead, like nineteenth-century Paris, New York was sufficiently rich and sophisticated to support – even if with crumbs from the table of the artistic establishment – a provocative bohemian fringe, loosely but amiably focused upon John Cage. Central to the achievements of Cage, Earle Brown, and Morton Feldman was the stimulus provided by the New York school of abstract painters. Although 'Abstract Expressionism' (a term coined by the *New Yorker* art critic, Robert Coates, in 1945) has undoubted evocative power when applied to painters such as Jackson Pollock and Willem de Kooning, it is of little help in grasping the aspirations of this group of composers. On the other hand, such alternative labels as 'All-Over' and 'Field' art do convey with some precision the determination of Feldman and Christian Wolff to create quiet, abstract structures that provided a drastic corrective to the emotional masturbation of the symphony concert. (A similar mission was taken up – if with somewhat different technical means – by Aldo Clementi in Italy at the start of the 1960s.)

The fact that the canvases of the New York school bore so vividly the traces of the bodily actions that made them seemed to provoke an inverse reaction in the New York composers: they began to make graphic scores that would provoke the human body into performance. Morton Feldman was first into the field with the *Projections* series (1951–2), but then retreated to precise notation, leaving Earle Brown, from *December 1952* on, to map out its potential over the next decade. Graphic scores were one of many means employed by the New Yorkers to challenge the metaphysical notion of the musical 'work', conceived and notated in solitude by a composer, and reproduced with deferential fidelity by the concert-hall performer. Cage himself was a natural performer – one who, like Oscar Wilde, saw little point in exaggerating the boundary between art and life. He also understood very well how to draw a performance from others similarly gifted, like David Tudor and in due course Cathy Berberian. In effect, he resurrected an honourable but atrophied tradition: the composer sets up a performance situation with a few discrete indications, and then trusts the performer to perform. Dismissed as 'neo-Dada' when first he impinged upon the Germanic musical world, Cage's Zen prescriptions nonetheless undermined the mystique of composition with such serene affability that it has never quite recovered.

New York also possessed, either within the five boroughs or linked by a wider East Coast network, a group of universities that saw it as one of their tasks to protect the more intellectually rigorous forms of musical experiment. Although by no means a typical 'academic' composer, Elliott Carter taught at the Peabody Conservatory, Baltimore (1946–8), at Columbia University (1948–50), and at Queens College, New York (1955–6). Whereas the avant-gardes on both sides of the Atlantic nourished themselves on mutual response and exchange, Carter remained very much his own man. His studies with Nadia Boulanger in Paris before the war had given him firm roots in the modernist mainstream, so that he was not greatly exercised by attempts to assert an American 'alternative' to the European tradition. But the solutions that he developed from the First String Quartet (1950–1) on testified to a highly individual sense of instrumental 'dramaturgy'. Untrammelled by the developing post-Webernian consensus of his European contemporaries, he developed means to achieve the simultaneous articulation of metrically distinct layers into a meticulously organized superabundance that would have given pleasure to the mentor of his teenage years, Charles Ives. His major works of the period – the Sonata for flute, oboe, cello, and harpsichord (1952), the orchestral Variations (1954–5), the String Quartet no. 2 (1959), and the Double Concerto for harpsichord, piano, and two chamber orchestras (1961) – were achievements so distinctive as to gain widespread applause, though little direct imitation.

More consistently devoted to the academic environment was Milton Babbitt, working at Princeton. During the war he had consolidated his systematic approach to pitch-set theory; now he sought to extend the serial principle to other parameters. The difficulties in achieving performed precision in these matters drew him towards the realization of his ideas by computer. He spent much time in the mid-1950s exploring the potential of RCA's Mark II synthesizer in New York, but began producing complete compositions for the medium only in the early 1960s. Babbitt and Roger Sessions meanwhile joined forces with Luening and Ussachevsky from 1959, to form the Columbia/Princeton Electronic Centre. Nor were East Coast academics alone in their curiosity regarding electronic resources. Cage and his collaborators devoted a good deal of energy to stockpiling sound materials at Louis and Bebe Barron's private studio in Greenwich Village. A montage of these, assembled by Cage according to the dictates of the I Ching and funded by the architect Paul Williams, became *Williams Mix* (1952), Cage's first electronic work.

The sense of cultural topography established by these centres of activity was not, of course, exclusive. But those outside the ambit of Paris, New York, Milan, and 'the marvellous German radio stations' (as Nono called them) often had to endure a remarkable degree of isolation and miscomprehension; the stoic perseverance of Elisabeth Lutyens in England is a case in point. For those obliged to earn their living elsewhere – like, for instance, Goeyvaerts and Henri Pousseur in Belgium – the existence of an international gathering of fellow musicians at Darmstadt each year became a vital source of stimulus. The 'international', however, only became truly global towards the end of the 1950s, as Japanese musicians began to make their mark. Ever since the war, they had resumed their scrutiny of Western developments. Yoritsune Matsudaira's highly individual synthesis of *gagaku* and serialism captured attention early in the 1950s through the offices of the International Society for Contemporary Music, and this led to a series of commissions: from Darmstadt in 1957 (*Umai*), and from the Südwestfunk in 1960. Toru Takemitsu's *Requiem* (1957) similarly attracted widespread attention. The drawing of Japan into the international network was confirmed when, in 1958, Matsudaira himself came to Darmstadt to speak on Japanese music. The avant-garde was rapidly acquiring a third capital: Tokyo.

Aesthetics and technique: Boulez vs. Cage

Looking back, it may appear that the agenda for much of what followed in the 1950s was set not at Darmstadt, but by the encounters between 1949 and 1952 between John Cage and Pierre Boulez. Although of differing ages (Cage was thirteen years older), each was in the process of defining a unique artistic profile that was to provide a continuous source of challenge to those around them. Setting those profiles side by side may therefore provide a frame for the concerns of the later 1950s.

When Boulez arrived in German-occupied Paris in 1943 at the age of eighteen, he threw himself into a rapid and definitive assimilation of the modernist aesthetic in music, poetry, and painting. In 1944 he entered Messiaen's advanced harmony class at the Conservatoire, but also joined the private analysis seminars to which Messiaen admitted his more promising students, delving into Debussy, early Schoenberg, and Stravinsky's *Rite of Spring*. In 1945 he attended a private performance of Schoenberg's Wind Quintet conducted by

René Leibowitz. Fascinated, he and other members of Messiaen's class subsequently asked Leibowitz for further insight into how the work was written. Leibowitz was happy to respond: as well as expounding general serial principles, he analysed for them Webern's Symphony, op. 21, of which Boulez made his own score (printed copies being unavailable). Intensely responsive to literature, he threw himself into the poetry of Rimbaud, Mallarmé, and Char, into Artaud and Joyce, and into the painting of Klee.

By the age of twenty-one the foundations of an aesthetic and technical framework of formidable inner consistency were in place, and in a first great spurt of creative energy from 1946 through to the early 1950s, Boulez explored the potential of this new terrain. Its first fruits included the pithy, violent Sonatine for flute and piano (1946), whose serial manipulations are still sufficiently traditional to be easily analysed by the curious. But by the epoch-making Second Sonata for piano of 1948, such straightforward procedures had dived beneath a ferociously dense musical surface. Dodecaphonic note rows had given place to a cellular proliferation rooted in the serial principle, but not mechanically replicating it. That Boulez was conscious even at this early stage in his career of having arrived at a complete technical and poetic vision – of sufficient authority that his task for many years thereafter was to put his energies as composer and conductor at its service – may be guessed at from the concluding words of his 1947 setting (subsequently much revised) of René Char's *Le visage nuptial.* Boulez's choice of texts is never casual, and this one reads like a warning to the world:

> Dans la stupeur de l'air où s'ouvrent mes allées
> Le temps émonderà peu à peu mon visage,
> Comme un cheval sans fin dans un labour aigri.
> Écartez-vous de moi qui patiente sans bouche.[9]

Stepping rapidly beyond any remnant of Schoenberg's post-Brahmsian, panthematic view of the serial principle, which in his hands had metamorphosed into a subcutaneous generator of radical 'difference', Boulez had in his grasp the technical means to create a music that set its face against the infantilistic pleasures of repetition. Repeating the familiar had long been anathema to the radical aesthetic tradition given voice by Baudelaire and Rimbaud. But as the post-war generation understood with desolate clarity, intuitive attempts at novelty (such as those favoured by the surrealist tradition) seemed fated merely to reiterate negatively what was to hand. The creative imagination therefore needed to exist in tension with something that was experienced as alien, as

9 'In the stuporous air where my paths open up / Bit by bit, time will de-husk my face, / Like a horse harshly, endlessly ploughing. / Move aside from me: taciturn, I bide my time.'

counter-intuitive. Setting up a maze of serial games that compelled one to take constant leaps into unknown territory – to find a way of living with and through the unfamiliar – was the means to this end. From this standpoint, Schoenberg's own obsession with guaranteeing the 'organic' integrity of the post-tonal work appeared as an anachronism, a regression from the fine leap into the dark of his expressionist atonal masterpieces – and yet, despite himself, he had offered the post-war generation the seeds of a new creative praxis.

The complex and assertive thrust into unknown territory that was *Le visage nuptial* proved, despite repeated revisions, dauntingly difficult to perform. But Boulez's next engagement with Char's poetry, *Le soleil des eaux* (1948), had an easier career. Derived from the music that he wrote for a radio broadcast of Char's play, it combined the wry charm (not a characteristic frequently evidenced by Boulez's music) of 'Complainte du lézard amoureux' with the entirely characteristic power of 'La sorgue'. Plainly, Boulez was not aiming at a post-Webernian pastorale: the poems exert their power as psychological metaphors (of 'impossible' love and Nietzschean will respectively), and as such are given the same meticulously sensitive attention that he was subsequently to devote to his final Char cycle, and to Mallarmé.

If the serial musical work was 'a universe in constant expansion', the musical workshop on the contrary demanded a clear sense of limits, and in particular of the limits beyond which the serial principle becomes a parody of itself. The necessity of finding out by experience where the limits lay became clear to Boulez while he was working on his *Livre* for string quartet (1948–9) – particularly on its last movement, where the experiments contemporaneously pursued by Messiaen in his *Modes de valeurs et d'intensités* fused with Boulez's own analyses of Webern to point a path towards the necessary experiment of total serialism. This experiment was accomplished in 1951–2 with the composition of *Polyphonie X* and *Structures 1a* for two pianos, the latter being a walk into the pan-serial wilderness that Boulez had thought to call (borrowing a title from Paul Klee) 'At the Edge of Fruitful Land'. From there, he could return – confident of what it felt like to assent to the minimalization of choice within the compositional process – to a finely judged balance between the generative power of the serial principle and the composer's obligation to take creative responsibility through choice, as was in effect achieved by *Structures 1b*.

Even more persuasive in this regard was his third Char cycle, *Le marteau sans maître* (1953–5). Built from three interpenetrating cycles, of two, three, and four movements respectively, each of them proposing settings and commentaries upon a poem of exceptionally compact density, *Le marteau* quickly established itself as one of the key works of the 1950s avant-garde: in part because of its taut, athletic vigour, but also because it inhabited an arresting and distinctive sound-world. The ensemble of alto flute, xylorimba, vibraphone, percussion (much of it metallic), guitar, viola, and contralto created an amalgam of Boulez's favoured non-Western sound-types: the resonances not merely of South-East Asian gamelan, but of African hammered wood. Thus might Boulez attempt to keep himself 'violent and friend to the bees of the horizon'.[10]

John Cage's early career lies outside the scope of this chapter.[11] But in 1946 he had started work on his *Sonatas and Interludes* for prepared piano (and also enrolled in Daisetz Suzuki's class in Zen Buddhism at Columbia University); the work crowned a decade of experiment with percussive sound within fixed, additive rhythmic frames. The success of its first performance in New York in 1949 prompted the Guggenheim Foundation to offer Cage a bursary for work abroad. Cage went to Paris, and at the suggestion of Virgil Thomson, called upon Boulez. The two, no doubt guided by the attraction of opposites, struck up a friendship: Boulez organised a private, but well-attended, performance of *Sonatas and Interludes* at the house of his patron, Suzanne Tezenas, while Cage helped encourage several of Boulez's most important scores into print, including, crucially, the Second Sonata. They kept up a correspondence[12] after Cage's return to New York, in which Boulez detailed his move towards total serialism, while Cage advanced along his chosen path with *Music of Changes* (1951). In this work, the properties of each individual note were determined by charts derived from the I Ching, navigated by tossing a coin; the element over which Cage chose to assert compositional control was the constant modification of tempo within a given number of bars.

Thereafter, Cage found increasing fulfilment in harnessing the reverential attention traditional within the concert hall to the task of opening oneself to chance events. He found a sympathetic milieu for his ideas not only amongst the younger composers – Morton Feldman, Earle Brown, and Christian Wolff – who gravitated to him in New York at the start of the 1950s, but also among the younger generation of New York painters, notably Robert Rauschenberg and Jasper Johns. His partnership with the dancer Merce Cunningham, exploring how sound and movement might coexist without undue mutual determination, led him towards the multimedia events subsequently to be labelled 'happenings', of which the first took place in 1952 at Black Mountain College, a radical art summer school in North Carolina. (Rauschenberg, who studied at Black Mountain, became an important collaborator in the Cage–Cunningham

10 René Char, *La sorgue*, from *Le soleil des eaux*.

11 See David Nicholls' chapter in the present volume (chapter 8).

12 Jean-Jacques Nattiez (ed.). *The Boulez–Cage Correspondence* (tr. Robert Samuels), Cambridge, 1993.

performances.) That same summer, Cage also prevailed upon David Tudor to play Boulez's Second Piano Sonata at Black Mountain; in consequence, when Boulez visited New York in the autumn as music director for the Compagnie Renault-Barrault, his name was already well known in Abstract Expressionist circles, and drew many of the New York painters to his concerts.

The enthusiastic response of Abstract Expressionists to the intense textures of the Second Sonata provides pause for thought concerning the differing reception and patronage of avant-garde painting and music. We have already noted that the serial machinations governing the Sonata lie well below its ferocious surface. This will trouble only the scholarly analyst: what is important about the serial 'principle' (which is, in practice, reinvented work by work) is that it allows the generation of fresh, unpredictable musical material in such abundance – like paint thrown by Pollock across a canvas – that composers can address themselves to accommodating its provocations within the larger scale. As Boulez's Sonata demonstrated, working on a big time-scale, and concerning oneself with global densities and rarefactions, gestural agglomerations, and frozen refusals of the same, is perceptually more challenging and disorienting than are the equivalents in the large-scale paintings that were being produced contemporaneously by New York's Abstract Expressionists. When working inside one of his huge canvases laid out on the floor, Pollock was undoubtedly as fervently absorbed by the global challenges of its developing structure as was Boulez amidst his serial charts. But while the perceiver's eye can travel to and fro 'all over' the aggressive turmoil of a Pollock canvas without any threat to subjective temporal continuity, the same is not the case when listening to Boulez: the ear is swept along without being able to recuperate and integrate. And although much criticized for being 'merely' the cumulative consequence of a long series of actions, each responding to the aggregate of those previously performed, Pollock's canvases bore the static traces of a real body's dynamism. By contrast, Boulez – and in due course other vivid, gestural composers such as the Stockhausen of the mid-1950s, and then Berio – seemed to be inventing, by techniques that were reputed by non-practitioners to be coldly mathematical, imaginary bodies given over to violently erotic and/or aggressive action. Such disconcerting disparities mark a dividing of the ways for new painting and new music during the second half of the century: the New York painters of the 1950s established for themselves a degree of financial success, and a tradition of patronage, that European composers could only envy.

While in New York, Boulez wrote an article for *New York Herald Tribune* hailing Webern as '*the* threshold to the music of the future'. In his review of a concert that included *Structures 1a* and *1c*, the *New York Times* critic, Arthur

Berger, countered that Boulez appeared to have learnt little from his proclaimed model as far as control of texture and nuance were concerned. In retrospect, Boulez would probably have agreed – at least as regards the experiments of *Structures 1a*. But the observation points up a basic difference between what New York musicians were learning from Webern, and what European 'post-Webernians' found illuminating. Morton Feldman and Christian Wolff were both deeply responsive to the spare sensitivity of Webern's sound-world. But Feldman in particular was quite uninterested in serial dogma, and insisted that he had otherwise learnt more from the New York painters. Accordingly, he went on to produce throughout the 1950s numbered sequences of works with pointedly abstract titles – 'Projections', 'Intersection', 'Extensions', and 'Durations'.

By the time that his 1952 trip to New York came to an end, Boulez could see plainly that the chance-welcoming, painterly atmosphere that prevailed there ran counter to his own artistic convictions. In effect, Cage and Boulez had crossed paths at the one stage where, as well as finding a certain relish in each other's company, they could take a bemused interest in each other's creative concerns: *Structures 1a* and *Music of Changes* were as musically close as they were ever to come. Although Boulez understood the implications and motivations of Cage's position, he set his face squarely against the worship of 'raw' chance. From then on, his correspondence with Cage ceased, and the infiltration of Cagean influence into the European avant-garde was met with the stringent polemics of which Boulez was so effective a practitioner.

Children of Darmstadt: Nono and Stockhausen

At different periods, Boulez and Cage exercised a profound impact on those who made the pilgrimage to Darmstadt each summer, but their careers developed independently of the summer school. Such was not the case for the other two central figures of the mid-1950s avant-garde, Nono and Stockhausen. For each, Darmstadt was an essential springboard, and a frequent battleground. It was Nono who coined the optimistic but deceptive phrase 'the Darmstadt School'; ironically, it was also he who, in 1960, first felt obliged to abandon Darmstadt to its own devices – or perhaps more accurately to Stockhausen, who for many years to come treated it as a personal fiefdom.

If Boulez absorbed, stepped beyond, and discarded with almost contemptuous speed the precepts of his Conservatoire training, the early career of Luigi Nono seemed instead to demonstrate that one could make one's mark within Germany's 'New Music' with remarkably little conventional training.

The grandson of a painter, caught up throughout his teenage years in the diffused and unfocused cultural enthusiasms of an affluent Venetian family, Nono began to develop a technical curiosity only in 1944, when his father asked the head of the Venice Conservatory, Gianfranco Malipiero, to advise his twenty-year-old son on the improvement of his rudimentary musical knowledge. Even then, two further years were to pass before Nono finally resolved to gain a real technical grasp by studying Hindemith's *Unterweisung im Tonsatz*, and was referred by Malipiero to Bruno Maderna. The chance to play Pygmalion evidently intrigued Maderna: he took the twenty-two-year-old under his wing. But rather than guide him through the *via crucis* of theoretical counterpoint and harmony, Maderna instead co-opted him as research assistant as he delved into renaissance musical publications in Venice's Biblioteca Marciana. Concurrently, he initiated him into the strangely congruent serial games of his own contemporaries. Nono's first major work, the canonic variations on the series of Schoenberg's *Ode to Napoleon* (1950), echoed this precipitate double immersion. Another crucial influence in the four hectic years between starting serious musical study and first presenting his work in public at Darmstadt was Hermann Scherchen, who came to Venice in 1948 to give a conducting course. On Malipiero's advice both Maderna and Nono attended – and as was his habit, Nono threw himself into a devoted informal discipleship, following Scherchen around Europe from one concert to the next.

Nono's very lack of 'Conservatoire' values gave him a free-ranging openness to other influences. In Scherchen's conducting class there was a Brazilian composer, Eunice Catunda, who opened further new horizons; she introduced him to the poetry of Lorca, but also – being half native Brazilian – to the rhythms and songs of the Mato Grosso. Despite his introductory *hommage* to Schoenberg, the works by which Nono was to capture the attention of Darmstadt were rooted in this exotic repertoire. *Polifonica-Monodia-Ritmica*, with which Nono confirmed his emergent status in 1951, was based upon melodic modules taken from a ceremonial Brazilian song to the goddess of the sea (and not, as was commonly supposed at the time, the first fruits of an earnest devotion to Webern). The *Epitaffio a Federico Garcia Lorca* of 1952 – the year that Nono and Maderna enrolled in the Communist Party – returned to the same source, adding to its second part *Bandiera rossa* (The Red Flag), treated in similar fashion. The pitch material of these works is calculatedly limited, and never dodecaphonic. Finding his own response to the 'problems of rhythm' whose solution also seemed, in their profoundly different ways, imperative to Boulez and Cage, Nono was above all concerned with the superposition of borrowed rhythmic modules. That determination to create anew from 'found' material, which Nono likened to his studies of fifteenth-century procedures with Maderna, again manifested itself in *La victoire de Guernica*, where every aspect of the material derives from *L'internationale*, although the song is never directly quoted.[13]

Even at this early stage, Nono seemed blessed with that uncanny talent that finds vivid artistic potential in the technically 'unsophisticated'. Nothing could be further from Boulez's meticulous serial complexities than this juggling with fragments of beloved objects, musical and literary. But in their raw enthusiasm, the results captured the German imagination (to which intensity of conviction untroubled by doubts as to its propriety was as seductive as it was hard to achieve). Much of Nono's subsequent work of the 1950s, starting with *Incontri*, used as its pitch basis the all-interval series generated by alternating between chromatic scales that progress upward or downward from a pivotal pitch: not, therefore, an idiosyncratic, pre-composed germ-cell from which grew the characteristics of a particular work, but a raw pitch 'material' upon which the aesthetic needs of the moment could be stamped.

Nono had the habit of producing a chain of related works, and then abruptly changing direction. *Canti per tredici* and *Incontri* (1955), both of them purely instrumental, interrogated the spare expressive weight of individual notes. But they were followed by a series of major choral works: *Il canto sospeso* (1955–6), *La terra e la compagna* (1957), *Cori di Didone* (1958), and *Sarà dolce tacere* (1960). All set texts of central importance for Nono: the letters of young Resistance fighters facing execution in *Il canto sospeso*, the austere beauty of Ungaretti's poetry in the *Cori di Didone*, and Cesare Pavese's stringent honesty about the partisan fight against fascism. Yet these texts were split up, syllable by syllable, and passed from voice to voice. What in principle results is delivery of the poem by a single, collective voice (except in that portion of *La terra e la compagna* where two texts are articulated simultaneously). But the bourgeois ideal of shared choral affirmation of cardinal texts depended upon a choir being able to deliver them with conviction – which even professional choirs found desperately hard in the post-Webernian idiom. Boulez had quickly grasped the problem, and save for the high ideals of his 1952 reworking of *Le visage nuptial* (and the cautious pragmatism of his 1958 reworking of *Le soleil des eaux*) relied upon the highly skilled female soloists to whom much of the best vocal writing of this generation went. Nono, too, developed a fine understanding of the lyrical potential of the female voice, but his burning conviction that the remaking

13 Cf. the interview between Nono and Enzo Restagno, in Restagno (ed.), *Nono*, Turin, 1987.

of social relations and of artistic praxis went hand in hand obliged him to continue the struggle with the 'collective' idiom of choral writing up to 1960, before turning to the more practical but – however vivid the voices recorded – more impersonal medium of the tape collage.

In 1960, the director of the Venice Biennale, Mario Labroca, took the bold step of inviting Nono to take on that other grand institution of middle-class cultural ideals, the opera house, into which no other member of the post-war avant-garde had yet ventured without first modifying the more radical components of their musical language (as had, for instance, Hans Werner Henze or Giselher Klebe). Like Nono's choral works, *Intolleranza 1960* (1960–1) is now a work honoured more by critical reference than by performance, but at the time it opened new perspectives – and awakened old memories. Enthused by Angelo Ripellino's studies of the theatrical experiments of revolutionary Russia, Nono fashioned a string of contemporary images into a rudimentary plot: a migrant worker longs to return home, but is surrounded by the capitalist exploitation of natural resources, in this instance a dammed river that bursts its banks and carries all before it in an apocalyptic finale. Nono's favoured materials – aggressive blocks of sound, spare pointillist textures, and impassioned solo lines – were thrown into a vigorous mix with abstract projections by his painter friend, Emilio Vedova. This raw, rhetorical demonstration of how one might achieve a militant music theatre was not lost on a younger generation – notably Giacomo Manzoni, who was to keep alive for another decade the ideal of a post-war music theatre bearing contemporary witness.

If during the early 1950s it was widely held that the most continously challenging figure among the European avant-garde was Boulez, by the latter half of the decade that honour had passed in many eyes to Stockhausen. The extraordinary fertility of Stockhausen's imagination, which made of each new work a technical project breaking into unexplored territory, meant that no one could afford to ignore him; most were prepared to discount the showman-like propensity to astonish, and the as yet infrequent lapses into kitsch that were in due course to alienate the more fastidious of his contemporaries. His studies with Messiaen, and his contacts with Boulez in Paris, had prompted him to step beyond the isolated points of *Kreuzspiel* to the more fluid, vivid idiom of *Kontra-Punkte* (1952–3), his first published score. Returning to Cologne, he threw himself over the next three years into producing intensive 'studies' within two favoured media: piano and electronics. The Cologne Studio at the Westdeutscher Rundfunk, under the direction of Herbert Eimert, offered Stockhausen the chance to explore meticulous control, building up sounds from sine tones. At first the seductions seemed twofold: on the one hand the promise of 'new sounds', and on the other the possibility of exact articulation of serial structures that defied exact performance. In fact, neither of these proved to be the central strength of the new medium. It was when Stockhausen worked with electronic manipulation of the pre-recorded voice that he produced the first uncontested masterpiece of the new medium: *Gesang der Jünglinge* (1955) which, with its five spatially separated one-track tapes, marked out a new ease in dynamizing acoustic space that has remained one of the genuine strengths of electronic resources. The extent to which the recorded human voice compensated for the lack of a physically present performer was confirmed when Luciano Berio entered the field, elaborating upon Cathy Berberian's recorded voice in *Omaggio a Joyce* (1958) and *Visage* (1961).

The other solution to the 'impersonal' loudspeaker was to explore interactions between taped sound and live performance. We have seen that Bruno Maderna had first explored this territory with *Musica su due dimensioni* of 1952.[14] But suddenly in the late 1950s everyone returned to the fray. Pousseur established a dialogue between three orchestral groups and tape in *Rimes* (1958–9); Berio explored a continuum between live sound and progressive transformations on tape in *Différences* (1958–9). Stockhausen's competitive spirit was unleashed: *Kontakte* (1959–60) for electronic sound from four speakers, piano, and percussion was a vivid chain of sonic 'moments' that explored an encyclopedic variety of responses between electronic and live sound.

In 1954, Strobel invited Cage and Tudor to appear at the Donaueschingen Festival, where their performances were angrily denounced as childish neo-Dada. However, they also called in to Cologne to show Stockhausen some of the work of the New York school. Stockhausen was fascinated, and was from then on to make himself a bridgehead for the Cage group, encouraging Steinecke to invite first Tudor in 1956, and eventually Cage himself in 1958, into the citadel of Darmstadt. The first fruits of their contact were the *Klavierstücke* V–X (1954–5) in which, responding to Tudor's encouragement, Stockhausen relaxed the almost impossible demands of constantly differentiated serial dynamics into a more performer-friendly idiom. From then on, a flattered Tudor performed Stockhausen and, with few exceptions, abstained from Boulez. Stockhausen proposed a further piano piece to Tudor at Darmstadt in 1956, one that would involve the performer to an unprecedented degree. *Klavierstück* XI was a single large sheet of paper on which were set out nineteen

14 Recomposed in 1958 as more convincing technical possibilities became available; cf. Mario Baroni and Rossana Dalmonte (eds.), *Bruno Maderna: Documenti*, Milan, 1985, p. 205.

musical fragments to be played in any order, each conditioning the interpretation of whichever was played next. Such para-Cagean latitudes were to be greatly enlarged upon in the next decade – though it would seem that this experiment was conducted without detailed knowledge of pre-existing examples from New York. Boulez, who had already begun to explore the possibility of alternative performance routes through a fixed conceptual structure in his plans for the Third Piano Sonata, expressed dismay at such compositional vagaries.

But between 1955 and 1957, Stockhausen was also engaged in a far more sophisticated adventure: the simultaneous articulation of different movements through time. The first of these, the vivid *Gruppen* (1955–7), expanded upon the dynamization of acoustic space explored in *Gesang der Jünglinge* by dividing an orchestra into three dialoguing ensembles positioned around the auditorium, each with a conductor to guide them through their own set of serialized tempi. The second, *Zeitmasse* (1956) for woodwind quintet, oscillates between 'groups' strictly coordinated by a conductor, and others determined by what a performer can comfortably execute in one breath – a dialectic usually brought to resolution in the rehearsal room, rather than made a generator of musical structure. But drawing artistic conclusions from rethinking the materials and praxes of music was rapidly becoming central to the fascination that Stockhausen exerted upon his fellow musicians. In 1957, he held Darmstadt in his thrall by propounding a 'unified' theory of musical sound, seeking to develop the consequences of the (acoustically unquestionable) fact that the principal musical parameters – pitch, rhythm, timbre – can all be viewed as patterned manifestations of pulsed energy.[15] (Boulez was not slow to point out that the ear did not tell the same story as did the theorizing brain.)

But for Stockhausen, the attractions of the New York school remained formidable. Earle Brown, who had first come to Darmstadt in 1957 and whose *Four Systems* were played there by Tudor and Cage in 1958, had been developing graphic scores for five years; inspired by Calder's mobiles, he had also begun to experiment with 'open form' from *Twenty-five Pages* (1953) on. Such issues now set Stockhausen upon new paths. In 1959 he produced the graphic *Zyklus* and the eminently 'open' *Refrain*, and backed up his new enthusiasms with a series of lectures. In 1960 he sent from his mountain retreat at Paspels (where he was working on *Carré*) a lecture on 'Ambiguous Form',[16] to be performed *à la* Cage by Heinz-Klaus Metzger, who was proffered specific points of licence at which he might interpolate his own comments, sarcastic or otherwise, but

15 Karlheinz Stockhausen, 'Sprache und Musik', *Darmstädter Beiträge zur Neuen Musik* 1 (1958), pp. 57–81.

16 Karlheinz Stockhausen, 'Vieldeutige Form', in *Texte zur Musik II*, Cologne, 1964, pp. 245–61.

was instructed to sound gongs or tam-tams as he reverted to Stockhausen's text. It was an apt prelude to the new decade.

Choice vs. chance

For pan-serialism, 1955 was a year of critical review. Boulez had already caused some dismay by his attacks on the 'lunatic sterility' and aural dryness of those seduced into imitating *Structures 1a* too literally.[17] Post-Webernian orthodoxy now gained a theoretical reservoir through the new journal *Die Reihe*, which printed the most significant discussions presented at Darmstadt. But it was from Xenakis, in an essay published the same year in Scherchen's new *Gravesaner Blätter*, that it received its most penetrating critique to date. As Xenakis observed, a totally serialized polyphony 'has as its macroscopic effect an uncalculated and unforeseeable dispersion of sounds over the complete extent of the sonic spectrum'.[18] If instead one tried to extend the serial principle to the generation of large-scale perspectives (control of comparative density and so forth), it tended to confound the cogency of the serial interactions required for the generation of individual notes. Xenakis, however, was a student of mathematical probability, and so could pithily assert that 'le hasard se calcule' (chance may be calculated) – an axiom which he put into aesthetic practice in the first of his stochastic orchestral works, *Pithoprakta* (1955–6), where a seething cloud of musical atoms combine to generate a constantly shifting global shape.

Behind both Boulez's creative mitigation of the extremities of total serialism and Xenakis's calculation of stochastic processes lay a stringent perception of aesthetic responsibility. They were surrounded by the attempts in many different fields to absorb the full intellectual and ideological implications of a universe and a human mind that appeared to be equally the products of chance. If it was still art's task to 'imitate nature', then Boulez or Xenakis could indeed be deemed to be constructing a mimetic artefact that reflected the buzzing anarchy of natural contingency, whether in the mind or in the external world. Merely allowing contingency to invade the concert hall as an object of contemplation was too passive and complacent a path, however. If the inwardness dear to the Western tradition was not to be devalued once it was viewed as the product of chance, then the composer was obliged to produce, by an act of will, a simulacrum of contingency to which – being mediated by a human mind – the listener could actively assent, and make his or her own.

17 Boulez, 'Recherches maintenant' (1954), in *Stocktakings from an Apprenticeship*, pp. 15–19. Cf. also *Conversations with Célestin Deliège*, London, 1976, p. 64.
18 Iannis Xenakis, 'La crise de la musique serielle', *Gravesaner Blätter* 1 (1955), pp. 2–4; p. 2.

So when the Stockhausen–Tudor alliance allowed Cagean influences to infiltrate the European avant-garde, Boulez felt obliged to fight back. Tudor's performance and analysis of parts of *Music of Changes* at Darmstadt in 1956 provoked fierce argument between Boulez and Stockhausen. Boulez went away to prepare his response. The result, entitled 'Alea',[19] had to be read out at the 1957 summer school by Heinz-Klaus Metzger (a practised bearer of provocative tidings), since Boulez himself was ill. It acknowledged the logic of searching out a form that evades literal self-repetition at each performance: Boulez's own Third Sonata aspired to demonstrate that, like a complex building, a musical form may be a structure through which there is more than one route. But those routes, like everything else in the work, must remain the fruit of conscious choice, even though the rigours of such choice can prove extreme. As so often, Boulez seemed to be making daunting demands of his fellow musicians. The exceptionally acute combinatorial intuition, that allowed him to sense which moves within the multi-dimensional serial game would generate vitality and immediacy, had served him well. Few others from the post-war generation were content to work with Boulez's painstaking rigour – but few others generated results of such freshness and resilience over time.

In 1958, Boulez was scheduled to teach ten seminars on instrumental technique at Darmstadt, but preparations for Donaueschingen, where his highly experimental elaboration upon Henri Michaux's curse-poem *Poésie pour pouvoir* was to be premiered, obliged him to cancel. Stockhausen could not resist the opportunity: he persuaded Steinecke to invite Cage instead.[20] Cage, still raw from his unsympathetic reception at Donaueschingen in 1954, accepted with relish. The *jeunesse dorée* of the avant-garde flocked to Darmstadt in eager anticipation, nor did Cage disappoint. He delivered three characteristic lecture-compositions: the first placing Cagean dicta, carefully timed, into the silences of *Music of Changes*; the second distancing himself from excessive obligation by deprecating Stockhausen's timid embrace of chance in *Klavierstück* XI; and the third, composed according to I Ching principles, combining 214 questions, nineteen cigarettes smoked with studied precision, and a handful of quotations. With Tudor, he gave a piano-duo programme of works by the New York School. Walks in the woods yielded a variety of fungi, whose preparation and cooking he demonstrated to students with characteristic panache.

19 Boulez, 'Alea' (1957), in *Stocktakings from an Apprenticeship*, pp. 26–38.

20 Joan Peyser, *Boulez*, New York, 1976, p. 139. But it should be noted that acccounts differ: Trudu, *La 'Scuola'*, p. 125, n. 6, credits Maderna with the idea – a less piquant, but equally plausible, possibility.

The furore caused by these manifestations proved deeply seductive to Stockhausen, and deeply alienating to Nono who, in introducing his composition course that year, insisted in neo-Hegelian fashion that 'we do not live by chance, we don't do anything by chance'.[21] Rather like Boulez two years earlier, he went away to prepare his attack for the following year. When it came, the belligerent 'The Presence of History in the Music of Today' caused a final, ferocious rupture with Stockhausen – who was by now advocating graphic scores, and encouraging the provocations of *enfants terribles* like Cornelius Cardew and Sylvano Bussotti. Nono was unsparing:

> It requires too much courage and strength to look one's own epoch in the face, and to take the decisions that it demands. It is much easier to hide one's head in the sand: 'We're free because we have no will; we're free because we're dead; dead as stones' . . . joking aside, we're free because the blind-fold that covers our eyes was put there by ourselves.

And acknowledging the formidable interpretative panache of Severino Gazzelloni and David Tudor, he derided the scores 'sprouting like mushrooms' all around, whose notational experiments served only to incite these two virtuosi to improvise – thereby lending the composers a borrowed glory that they scarcely merited.[22]

A further remarkable maker of performances came to Darmstadt the following year to open up new horizons by means of another of Cage's performance vehicles. Cathy Berberian had caught Cage's imagination with some 'domestic clowning' when he was in Milan to make *Fontana Mix* at the RAI studio in 1958. Displaying extraordinary agility, she would leap precipitately from one vocal style to another. Cage asked Berberian for appropriate texts, which he then fragmented and ordered, leaving her free to choose different types of vocalization for each strand of the work.[23] Her performance of the resultant score, *Aria*, at Darmstadt in 1959 liberated the imagination of many of the younger composers present, for whom the voice had not previously offered more than a fallible dodecaphonic *bel canto*. Now they were free to lend immediacy to their imaginings by incorporating anything and everything of which the voice was capable.

Those deeply entrenched in Adornian critical traditions reconciled themselves over the ensuing years to proliferating compositional licence by professing to hear in it echoes of heroic Beckettian laughter in the face of the inner void. But Boulez knew Cage too well to be thus deceived. Characteristically,

21 Luigi Nono, *Écrits*, p. 355. 22 Ibid., pp. 158–65.
23 Cathy Berberian: private communication with the author, Rome, May 1981.

he set about measuring his distance both creatively and theoretically. In 1957, as he perceived the tide turning against his ideal of what a composer might be, he had begun the *Improvisations sur Mallarmé I & II* that were to form the core of his grand, elegiac Mallarmé cycle, *Pli selon pli*. The third *Improvisation* was added in 1959, and the concluding *Tombeau* commenced. In 1960 he wrote a first version of the introductory *Don* for soprano and piano, but withdrew it, replacing it in 1962 with a new work for soprano and orchestra based on the same poem. *Pli selon pli* was the summation and closure of a creative season. It was an essay not merely in technical refinement, but also in how music may interrogate text, and promote a reading of it far removed from the *longeurs* of literary criticism. Both *Don* and *Tombeau* follow in the path of Debussy's response to Mallarmé: both are autonomous works which exist alongside the poems that they evoke. They assert fraternal relations not just by their title, but by setting a single line from each poem (the first in the case of *Don*, the last in the case of *Tombeau*). But they enclose three sonnet-settings that are meticulous, line-by-line readings. The poems demand careful scrutiny of this kind; any more straightforward *mise en musique* would be gratuitous, for this is by no means lyric poetry. All are sonnets recording loss: of the opportunity to affirm life, of creative opportunity. They are stoic and exact in rendering experiences common to all unsentimental maturity. Just as the art of the consumer society began to persuade itself of the possibility of being a perennial teenager, Boulez bade farewell to the 'rivière trop tot parti, d'une traite, sans compagnon'[24] of his explosive youth of a decade before.

Confronted with the chimeric ebullience generated by Stockhausen's increasing hegemony at Darmstadt, Boulez also drew himself up to deliver a theoretical *compte rendu*: his 1960 lectures, published as *Penser la musique aujourd'hui*.[25] Precise, doctrinaire and confrontational, they provided a touchstone for his admirers, but greatly irritated many of those younger composers who caught the scent of new freedoms in the air. Boulez continued to speak and conduct at Darmstadt until 1965, but regarded with a basilisk eye the encroaching latitudes all around him.

In one essential regard Darmstadt had indeed changed. On the evening of 15 December 1961, Wolfgang Steinecke and his wife left a gathering of friends to go home. Opening the door of his car, he was hit by a passing vehicle and gravely injured. He died eight days later. As was often observed afterwards, chance – that issue of constant preoccupation for the argumentative

24 'River that set out too soon, at a single bound, companionless'; René Char, 'La sorgue'.

25 Published in English as *Boulez on Music Today* (tr. Susan Bradshaw and Richard Rodney Bennett), London, 1971.

nucleus of composers whose interactions he had facilitated – here intervened with disconcerting directness to signal a parting of the ways. Through the 1960s the composers who had animated Darmstadt under his aegis were to pursue profoundly different trajectories. It is likely that not even Steinecke's amiable persistence could have persuaded these competing egos into further dialogue.

What had unified them was a radicalism of aesthetic purpose. For the modernist tradition of the nineteenth and twentieth centuries, the great sin against the human spirit was that of boredom. It was a sin brilliantly and definitively epitomized by Baudelaire in his great poem, 'Le Voyage'. Repetitions and returns – forms that achieved closure by recapitulation, by submitting gratefully to the gravitational force of 'home keys', styles that knowingly acknowledged that desire through the manipulation of neo-baroque and neoclassical topoi – were not merely pardonable indulgences; they were denials of the quintessential potential of human life. They ministered – either resignedly or in calculation – to the regressive streak present in every human and massively encouraged by the popular culture of the years after the Second World War.

Confronted by this perverse proliferation of the democratic principle into the realm of artistic experience, the avant-garde continued to refine the tools necessary for the generation of what they hoped would be a pristine newness, a 'vierge, vivace et bel aujourd'hui'[26] that neither the idealized nature to which suburban man made occasional placatory trips, nor a culture intent upon persuading him that his appointed destiny was to consume enviably, could offer. They did so in the conviction that sooner or later enough people would revolt against the blasphemy of a commodified life to constitute a genuine spearhead towards the 'new man' of whom Nono saw Webern as a prophet. If for the present that calculation appears to have miscarried – forcing its advocates to camouflage themselves as one of a hundred 'minority interests' allowed to scurry unmolested among the crumbs of the consumer society's feast – the problem that they sought to address has mercifully refused to go away. Baudelaire's redeeming faculty of boredom and self-loathing remains active (for how otherwise could the vast commercial apparatus that peddles the narcotic of repetition flourish so mightily?). In setting their faces against the dissolution of passion into what Ezra Pound scathingly called 'a willingness-to-oblige',[27] students of 1950s modernism might yet echo the curse-poem of Henri

26 'Virgin, vital and beautiful today' (Stéphane Mallarmé, *Plusieurs sonnets*); one of the lines set by Boulez in *Pli selon pli*.

27 'Epitaph' from *Lustra*, in *Selected Poems* (ed. T. S. Eliot), London, 1928.

Michaux that echoed so disconcertingly through Boulez's (withdrawn) *Poésie pour pouvoir*:

> . . . J'ai mis une flaque dans ton œil qui ne voit plus
> Un insecte dans ton oreille qui n'entend plus
> Une éponge dans ton cerveau qui ne comprend plus
> . . .
> Je rame
> Je rame
> Je rame contre ta vie
> Je rame
> Je me multiplie en rameurs innombrables
> Pour ramer plus fortement contre toi
> Tu tombes dans le vague
> Tu es sans souffle
> Tu te lasse avant même le moindre effort
> Je rame
> . . .
> JE RAME[28]

Bibliography

Baroni, Mario and Rossana Dalmonte (eds.). *Bruno Maderna: Documenti*, Milan, 1985.

Boulez, Pierre. *Stocktakings from an Apprenticeship* (tr. Stephen Walsh), Oxford, 1991.

Conversations with Célestin Deliège, London, 1976.

Boulez on Music Today (tr. Susan Bradshaw and Richard Rodney Bennett), London, 1971.

Carpenter, Humphrey. *The Envy of the World*, London, 1996.

De Benedictis, Angela Ida. 'Radiodramma e Arte Radiofonica. Storia e Funzioni della Musica per Radio in Italia', Ph.D. diss., Università di Pavia, 2001.

Griffiths, Paul. 'Webern', in *The New Grove Dictionary of Music and Musicians*, 1980, 20 vols., Vol. XX.

Nattiez, Jean-Jacques (ed.). *The Boulez–Cage Correspondence* (tr. Robert Samuels), Cambridge, 1993.

Nicolodi, Fiamma. *Musica e Musicisti nel Ventennio Fascista*, Fiesole, 1984.

Nono, Luigi. *Écrits* (ed. Laurent Feneyrou), Paris, 1993.

Peyser, Joan. *Boulez: Composer, Conductor, Enigma*, New York, 1976.

Restagno, Enzo (ed.). *Nono*, Turin, 1987.

Sità, Maria Grazia. 'I festival', in G. Salvetti and B. M. Antolini (eds.), *Italia Millenovecentocinquanta*, Milan, 1999, pp. 117–36.

28 '. . . I have put a splash in your eye, which can no longer see / An insect in your ear, which can no longer hear / A sponge in your brain, which no longer understands / I row (/toil/exert myself) / I row / I row against your life / I multiply myself into innumerable rowers / To row more strongly against you / You fall into vacancy / You are breathless / You tire before even the slightest effort / I row . . . I ROW.'

Stockhausen, Karlheinz. 'Vieldeutige Form', in *Texte zur Musik II*, Cologne, 1964.
'Sprache und Musik', *Darmstädter Beiträge zur Neuen Musik* 1 (1958), pp. 57–81.
Trudu, Antonio. *La 'Scuola' di Darmstadt*, Milan, 1992.
Xenakis, Iannis. 'La crise de la musique serielle', *Gravesaner Blätter* 1 (1955), pp. 2–4.

· 14 ·

Individualism and accessibility: the moderate mainstream, 1945–75

ARNOLD WHITTALL

> God forbid that there should only be radicals in this world . . . [I]t may be that the conservative composer is very necessary for an overall, general balance and correct rate of development. What we do want is probably a kind of controlled instability. In other words, it takes all sorts to make a world of contemporary music.
>
> Roberto Gerhard, 'The Contemporary Musical Situation', 1956[1]

No serious aesthetic analysis can be conducted on the principle that individualism and accessibility are incompatible. The history of the arts offers countless examples of works which are highly personal to their creators yet far from innovative in matters of style and technique. Doing something new with existing styles and techniques is a more common phenomenon in the arts than the kind of individuality that seems to succeed in avoiding all significant connections with other creators, whether from past or present; and this is as true of the years immediately after 1945 as of those just before 1914.

The era of the Cold War, though not without military confrontations, was also a time of reconstruction, of steadily improving communications: and those improving communications – perhaps symbolized most acutely for musicians by Stravinsky's return visit to Russia in 1962[2] – only rarely gave prominence to cultural events of a specialized, radical nature. Even though the liberating effect on the musicians of Poland or Hungary of their limited contacts with the Western avant-garde was considerable, and the impact of the cultural 'thaw' of the late 1950s on, for example, Lutosławski, was dramatic,[3] it is not always easy to distinguish genuine enthusiasm for the avant-garde from the more basic need for artistic freedom and access to all kinds of cultural production. Soviet-style repression may have been deplored in the West, but this did not mean that the 'free world' rejected conservatism in artistic expression. It was China (with its

1 Meirion Bowen (ed.), *Gerhard on Music: Selected Writings*, Aldershot and Burlington, VT, 2000, p. 27.

2 Robert Craft, *Stravinsky: Chronicle of a Friendship* (2nd edn), London, 1994, pp. 313–41.

3 See Steven Stucky, *Lutosławski and his Music*, Cambridge, 1981, especially chapter 3 (pp. 60–83), and Charles Bodman Rae, *The Music of Lutosławski* (3rd edn), London, 1999, especially chapters 3 and 4 (pp. 49–116).

satellite North Korea) rather than the Soviet Union that remained culturally inscrutable, inspiring fear of the unknown. Nevertheless, with Japan, Hong Kong, Singapore, and South Korea demonstrating their ability to produce performing musicians with internationally marketable skills in the interpretation of Western music, even the (non-Marxist) Far East was not a pure embodiment of cultural 'otherness', and several of the West's most prominent composers, including Messiaen and Britten, successfully absorbed elements of oriental technique and expression into their styles.[4]

This early mention of 'prominent composers' indicates that this chapter will be focused on creators of music, rather than the institutions which received their creations, and that only a small number of composers, deemed prominent on grounds of quality, will be considered. Such canon-dependent selectivity proceeds from the conviction that there is little to be gained by listing the maximum number of relevant composers without any supporting musical analysis; while it was undoubtedly one of the defining attributes of the period that so many 'moderate' composers were given relatively frequent hearings, the pre-eminence of those discussed here was not, and has not (so far) been, seriously challenged, and to this extent it is the nature of their contribution that is most salient in helping to define this aspect of musical identity during the years in question. It can also be argued that these were the composers who did most to ensure that there was not a more determined drift – by other composers and listeners alike – away from what will be termed here the 'moderate mainstream', and towards its coexisting (but never absolutely separate) complement, the 'modernist mainstream'.

Towards a moderate mainstream

The end of the Second World War is often seen by music historians as embodying a pervasive feeling of exhaustion which prompted a partial reaction in favour of the radically new, and the notion of 'Year Zero' – of a birth, rather than some kind of rebirth – acquires a powerful symbolic significance.[5] In practice, however, while the Year Zero concept might have stimulated a certain number of radically inclined composers, with Elliott Carter (b. 1908) the most senior, its usefulness tended to be dissipated by the natural conservatism inherent in musical institutions devoted to education, or to the commercial promotion of performances. It was therefore especially significant

4 See Robert Sherlaw Johnson, *Messiaen*, London, 1975, and Paul Griffiths, *Olivier Messiaen and the Music of Time*, London, 1985; also Mervyn Cooke, *Britten and the Far East*, Rochester, NY, 1998.

5 For example, see Paul Griffiths, *Modern Music and After: Directions Since 1945*, Oxford, 1995, especially pp. 3–20.

that, during the immediate post-war years, there was a strong commitment to reviving and developing modernist ideals, by demonstrating that modernism's most cherished principles need not be compromised by exploring accommodations with the genres (and therefore the institutions) which more moderate or conservative composers also supported. Genres and institutions found themselves able to encompass such radical differences as between Karajan and Boulez as conductors, or Shostakovich and Stockhausen as composers of works for symphony orchestra: and, to this extent, the most crucial change of all between 1945 and 1975 – consequent on increasing economic prosperity – was the steadily increasing opportunity for an unprecedented diversity of attitude and expertise. The fact that Boulez would conduct Bartók but not Shostakovich did not result in the suppression of the latter's music: for every Boulez there was a Rostropovich whose tastes – as cellist and, later, conductor – ranged from Britten to Berio, and beyond. There nevertheless remained a distinction, however blurred and imprecise, between availability and accessibility. The willingness of audiences to trust the judgement of Rostropovich when it came to playing Berio or Lutosławski, because they so enjoyed his Bach and Dvořák, did not mean that the new composers replaced the old at the heart of the musical canon. Rostropovich was admired, or at any rate tolerated, for his catholicity, but the more radical works he performed were not admired as wholeheartedly as the more familiar and conventional ones.

Changes in popular music can also be seen as a factor constraining the development of any increasing market share for 'art' music during the period 1945–75. The songs and dance music by the likes of Irving Berlin, Jerome Kern, and Cole Porter so popular in the 1940s were, like much contemporary jazz, closer to the technical procedures and expressive world of classical composition than to the unchained Dionysiac rituals of rock and roll, and although enthusiasts for the more genteel forms of pre-rock popular music might not have migrated any more consistently or permanently into appreciation of the classics than did their rock-generation successors, the powerful commercial context within which the new pop music emerged and prospered was not predicated on 'crossover' – always excepting occasional points of contact with electronic or minimalist techniques, which were in any case greater after 1975 than before. To this extent, the degree of convergence evident in 1940s America between the ballets of Aaron Copland and the musical theatre of Rodgers and Hammerstein was something of a special case.[6]

6 See Howard Pollack, *Aaron Copland: The Life and Works of an Uncommon Man*, London, 2000, pp. 372–7.

The moderate mainstream of serious composition, then, was not formed from the fusion of popular and serious styles. As a result, a study of the presence, and nature, of the interactions between moderation and innovation which did so much to preserve that mainstream during the third quarter of the twentieth century focuses most naturally on the accommodations achieved between conservatism and progressiveness, the former renewing itself through limited contact with the latter in ways for which Benjamin Britten's music in and after *The Turn of the Screw* (1954) provides one essential paradigm.[7] Quite different degrees of contact are involved here – with respect, for example, to matters of tonality and the emancipation of the dissonance – than are relevant to those composers, including Stravinsky, who can be associated with the modernist mainstream.

Canons of accessibility

In the later 1940s it was not surprising that Britten's opera *Peter Grimes*, a large-scale composition in an established genre and a style grounded in traditional techniques, should have achieved far greater success, in terms of frequent performance and general critical and popular acclaim, than works aiming at more comprehensive innovation, like the then-recent scores of Boulez.[8] As with all such comparisons, however, innovativeness cannot simply be equated with individualism. The perception of individuality is one of the core variables of reception, made more complex by the possibility that informed awareness of allusions and influences can serve to enhance the individuality – the result of one individual absorbing or alluding to a variety of sources and associations – of any particular work; for example, the linking of *Peter Grimes* with a range of connections from late Verdi to Gershwin draws attention to Britten's ability to make such heterogeneous associations serve his own purposes, and to throw his own musical identity into still clearer relief.[9] Conversely, there is an assumption that compositions apparently lacking such fruitful connections with other, relatively familiar music will be less accessible than those whose links with some aspects of tradition are more explicit. Even so, the concept of accessibility is more complex than that of individualism, since the listener's judgement as to whether a work is accessible or not depends on that work being made accessible – available – in the first place, and that act of making accessible,

7 See Patricia Howard (ed.), *Benjamin Britten: The Turn of the Screw*, Cambridge, 1985, and Peter Evans, *The Music of Benjamin Britten* (2nd edn), Oxford, 1996, chapter 10, pp. 203–22.

8 See below, pp. 380–2.

9 See Philip Brett (ed.), *Benjamin Britten: Peter Grimes*, Cambridge, 1983, pp. 136–9.

whether as score or performance, is likely to have involved commercial as well as aesthetic judgements.

Musical life in the modern era is made up of multiple strands of relatively active or passive participation and reception. Between 1945 and 1975 there was a considerable enhancement of the inherent, and inherently ambiguous, polarization of 'art' music between entertainment and education – an enhancement which came about through the invention of the long-playing record and the acceptance that public-service broadcasting could include extensive provision for minority tastes. The decision-making of those responsible for releasing gramophone records, as well as for the performances that were often taking place in rebuilt or new concert halls and opera houses, was obviously not governed entirely by the notion that the new and challenging should remain inaccessible at all costs. But the kind of aesthetic adventurousness and ambition demonstrated by those operating the BBC Third Programme in London or certain radio stations in Germany could not simply be transferred to the more commercial arenas of concert and opera promotion or recording. Here the new and challenging not only tended to need special subsidy, but always remained subordinate either to the old and well-tried or to music which combined newness with familiarity. Probably the most striking instance during the period 1945–75 of this latter category, worldwide, was the music of Mahler – effectively 'new', in the sense of generally unfamiliar before the mid-1950s, but proclaiming its kinship with the genres and expressive codes of earlier symphonic music even as it made an undeniably personal contribution to the continuation and further development of those genres and codes. It is therefore notable that those living composers who were most highly regarded for their ability to combine individualism and accessibility – Britten and Shostakovich above all – were often perceived as having Mahlerian traits.[10]

At the same time, however, there was more to the accessibility of Mahler than awareness among audiences that his music was not literally new. In attempting to define these qualities, the historian or critic inevitably attempts to speak for the mass audience whose acceptance of the composer is the 'historical' reason for his significance. Such history is all about perceptions, and to declare that

10 See Donald Mitchell and Philip Reed (eds.), *Letters from a Life: Selected Letters and Diaries of Benjamin Britten*, London, 1991, pp. 352–3, 499, 552; and Laurel E. Fay, *Shostakovich: A Life*, New York, 2000, pp. 43, 93, 185. For a summary account of Ivan Sollertinsky's Mahler study (1932) see Eric Roseberry, *Ideology, Style, Content and Thematic Process in the Symphonies, Cello Concertos and String Quartets of Shostakovich*, New York, 1989, pp. 507–20. For earlier references, see Donald Mitchell and Hans Keller (eds.), *Benjamin Britten: A Commentary on his Works from a Group of Specialists*, London, 1952, and Robert Simpson (ed.), *The Symphony 2: Elgar to the Present Day*, Harmondsworth, 1967, p. 198. There is also some discussion of the significance of Mahler for both composers in Ludmila Kovnatskaya, 'Notes on a Theme from *Peter Grimes*', in Philip Reed (ed.), *On Mahler and Britten: Essays in Honour of Donald Mitchell on his Seventieth Birthday*, Woodbridge, 1995, pp. 172–85.

the essence of Mahler is the contrast between intimate emotion and grandiose assertion is to describe the music in terms which are believed to explain its appeal. With Mahler the nineteenth-century tendency to intensify the contrasting representations of joy and sorrow reached its symphonic fulfilment, and the increasing popularity of this music after 1945 provided a context for contemporary composers able to aspire to comparable modes of expression. Alongside Mahler, Sibelius could appear constrained, Strauss complacent, the sense of intense personal suffering less immediate; whereas the suffering Mahler could represent the very paradigm of post-war angst, the vulnerability of faith and hope in a time of continuing political uncertainty, complemented by the possibility of a triumphant reassertion of control. 'Art' music may be peripheral to a world dominated by military confrontations and political processes, but it can absorb and transcend the emotions aroused by awareness of the tensions which living in such a world creates. It can do this by treating tradition as sacred, or as corrupt, or as something to be acknowledged with scepticism, even irony: and if, in the interests of accessibility, it welcomes a close relation to tradition, because it believes tradition remains open to individual reinterpretation, then those elemental states of joy and sorrow so palpably present in Mahler are likely to remain the principal sites of creative activity.

Such a construction of cultural practice places 'art' music after 1945 within the framework of post-Romantic modernity, or of neo-Romanticism, a move which rings true to the extent that the kind of neoclassicism so vital and prominent between 1920 and 1950 went into decline when Stravinsky himself migrated towards the modernist mainstream, adopting twelve-tone serialism and moving much further into realms of austerity and formal discontinuity than those more moderate composers – Britten, Copland, Shostakovich – who profited from serial thinking without turning away from traditional genres, or from modes of expression rooted in that fundamental polarity between consonance and dissonance which radical music sought to destroy.[11] Nevertheless, the claim that compositions by moderates are likely to be immediately accessible, those by modernists inaccessible, is vulnerable to the counter-argument that modernist music is no less accessible as the expression or representation of feeling. While few musicians might claim to be able to hear, in real time, either the detailed tonal unfolding of a 'common-practice' composition or the serial framework of a twelve-tone one, all listeners are likely to be struck by the expressive, emotional aura of any composition of substance, moderate and modernist alike. The technical elements of moderation to be emphasized here are therefore those which represent explicit procedural connections with

11 Stephen Walsh, *The Music of Stravinsky* (2nd edn), Oxford, 1993, pp. 217ff.

certain traditions: first, the distinction between consonance and dissonance (even though this was no longer as absolute as tended to be the case before 1900); second, the identifiable presence of motivic or thematic statement and development; and third, the consistent use of rhythmic, metric regularity.

In addition, the compositions discussed in the following sections refer not only to tonality but also to the established genres of tonal composition, as sources to be critiqued, and even destabilized, but not disrupted – still less destroyed. The moderate music of the mid-century years acknowledged the forms and textures of the tonal past, as well as many of its compositional procedures, even when significant intersections between the moderate and the modernist can also be detected. It cannot be guaranteed that such music will by definition be accessible to – its technical features immediately perceptible by – all listeners, however informed or inexperienced; still less is there the implication that such a style of moderation ensures a certain value for the work in question. The persistence of technical and generic traditions after 1945 was a challenge to moderate composers as much as an opportunity. Those composers could depend on a greater degree of immediate accessibility than that provided by more radical music, but for that very reason they were more vulnerable to odious comparisons – to accusations of failing to do justice to the noble heritage handed down by the great masters of the past.

This accusation was levelled at Mahler himself, of course, not least by those who regarded Sibelius as a more powerful precedent and a more stimulating early-twentieth-century model;[12] it might even be possible to trace a basic separation in moderate music from the years 1945–75 in terms of its adherence either to the relatively 'Romantic' aspects of Mahler or the relatively 'classic' aspects of Sibelius. And a basic opposition can also be found in modernist music, between that which focuses on discontent and pessimism, and that which offers utopian visions of new worlds, the former representing the disorientation of loss, the latter a sense of joy at being freed from the shackles of tradition. Where the two types of music can intersect is in their evocation of certain elemental topoi – lament, for example – and it remains a point of some interest as to whether moderate music will tend to evoke generic and topical associations more penetratingly through closeness to tradition than modernist music can do through distance.

Such comparisons need to be approached with scepticism. Can we really argue that the laments in Shostakovich's late quartets, or Britten's late vocal works, are more vivid, more affecting, than those in Maxwell Davies's *Worldes Blis* (1969) or Birtwistle's *Melencolia I* (1976)? The differences are not matters

12 Robert Simpson, *Sibelius and Nielsen*, London, 1965, pp. 4–5.

of quality, but of style: even so, Shostakovich and Britten are certainly more accessible than Maxwell Davies and Birtwistle, in the terms defined above. And it is their music that the later stages of this chapter will consider in some depth, along with some of the critical responses to which it has given rise, after briefer accounts of the most prominent moderates whose careers were in most cases over well before 1975.

Some prominent moderates

Strauss and Vaughan Williams

By 1944, his eightieth year, Richard Strauss's position within the moderate mainstream was less significant than that of younger composers, like Hindemith or Prokofiev, whose influence had spread more widely and whose styles were less obviously linked to the late-Romantic gestures of the nineteenth century. Yet the new works by Strauss that appeared during the last five years of his life (1944–9), and which were accepted as moving and important, reinforced the authenticity of his personal reinterpretation of tradition, and the continued viability (both aesthetic and commercial) of such sustained commitments to accessible styles and genres that – in the absence of new work by the still-living Sibelius – informed the later symphonies of Vaughan Williams, Prokofiev, Shostakovich, and many others. Strauss's example was so important because it proved that even the more backward-looking, explicitly conservative sector of the mainstream need not be infected with academicism: the sliding triadic chromaticisms that are so unaffectedly expressive of personal vulnerability and aspirations to serenity in *Metamorphosen* (1945) and the *Four Last Songs* (1946–8) could also serve to articulate the bleak vision of spiritual and social nothingness at the end of Vaughan Williams's Sixth Symphony (completed in 1947, revised 1950), as well as the more sharply outlined austerity and ultimate serenity of Stravinsky's *Orpheus* (1947), and – at the other extreme – the ecstatic spiritual release of the *Turangalîla-symphonie* (1946–8), Messiaen's uninhibited hymn to sacred and secular love. The fact that the Stravinsky represents that composer's persistent engagement with the fractured formal designs of modernism as authentically as the Vaughan Williams embodies that composer's struggle to preserve the 'moderate' continuities of hierarchic organicism does not prevent them from having certain common qualities. As noted earlier, it was, and remained, an essential facet of twentieth-century musical multivalence that moderate and modernist mainstreams were not mutually exclusive.

Richard Strauss's *Four Last Songs* epitomize accessible originality. The style of this music had evolved over the past half-century and more, while remaining faithful to the syntax and expressive aura of German late Romanticism, and resisting the more radical consequences of expressionism and neoclassicism alike.[13] One reason why the arching melodic phrases of the final section of 'Beim Schlafengehen' form such an unmistakably Straussian gesture is their closeness to the sublimely renunciatory spirit of *Der Rosenkavalier*'s great trio, composed three and a half decades earlier. At the end of his life, Strauss remembers his own most personal portrayal of age ceding to youth, and this allusion is scarcely less tangible than the direct quotation of *Tod und Verklärung* in 'Im Abendrot'. Despite such explicitness, however, ambiguity and instability are also of the essence. For example, at the beginning of 'Frühling' there is a spirit of restlessness evident both in the tension between the orchestra's 6/8 metre and the voice's 3/4, and also in the strongly chromatic harmony, whose initial alternation of C minor and A flat minor chords is the first step in a tonal journey that ends, not in C, but in A major. Structuring the tonality of a movement around third relations goes back at least as far as Beethoven's 'Waldstein' Sonata (1803–4), and became part of the common stock of Romantic harmony, in Schubert, Brahms, and Wagner, but the device appears at its most Straussian at points where the still greater intensity of dissonance is avoided, and chromaticism is offset by an emphasis on pure triadic consonance. The solemn, hymn-like music that ends 'Im Abendrot' enriches rather than destabilizes the basic E flat tonality with motions from E flat major to C flat major (both in second inversion) before the diatonic corrective of the final full close in E flat.

The presence maintained by Strauss's music during the decades after his death had much to do with the continued appeal of well-established operas and concert works of high quality. It had little to do with his continued relevance as a compositional model; and although the extent of his willing complicity in National Socialist ideology continued to be debated – more vigorously since 1975 than before[14] – his music was not found distasteful for the degree to which its embrace of instinctive, hedonistic emotionalism might have been felt to embody a significant and reprehensible aspect of German national character. On the one hand, he was seen as superior to the crudely primitive Orff or the drily academic (later) Hindemith; on the other, it was assumed that German composers who genuinely looked to the future – whether moderately, like Hartmann and Henze, or radically, like Schnebel and Stockhausen – would

13 See Timothy L. Jackson, '*Ruhe, meine Seele!* and the *Letzte Orchesterlieder*', in Bryan Gilliam (ed.), *Richard Strauss and His World*, Princeton, 1992, pp. 90–137. Also Timothy L. Jackson, 'The Metamorphosis of the *Metamorphosen*: New Analytical and Source-Critical Discoveries', in Bryan Gilliam (ed.), *Richard Strauss: New Perspectives on the Composer and His Work*, Durham, NC, 1992, pp. 193–241.

14 See in particular Michael Kennedy, *Richard Strauss: Man, Musician, Enigma*, Cambridge, 1999, pp. 269ff.

easily avoid any association with the Straussian ethos and all that it represented. From a later perspective, such arguments appear simplistic in the extreme, but at the time they made sense, not least because the failure of German music to continue the Straussian project – at least at the same level of artistic achievement – seemed inevitable and just.

The idea that composers in other countries, referring to very different traditions, might nevertheless usefully be aligned with Strauss can still arouse resistance. Yet the turbulent, at times exalted lamentation of *Metamorphosen* and the stoical serenity of the *Four Last Songs* were such vivid responses to the cultural temper of the times that it would have been astonishing if parallel initiatives could not be found on the part of composers working from quite different stylistic perspectives. With Ralph Vaughan Williams (1872–1958), only eight years Strauss's junior, those perspectives had little to do with nineteenth-century Romanticism, and little even to do with the British Romantic heritage that culminated in Elgar. The invigorating originality of Vaughan Williams's *Fantasia on a Theme of Thomas Tallis* (1910) was the result of reaching back to Tudor models in order to create a new, twentieth-century national tone that was capable of positive accommodation with the mainstream genres which sustained the 'international' style. Although Vaughan Williams's music may never have achieved Strauss's level of international prominence, it has reached out well beyond the composer's native shores.[15]

Two of Vaughan Williams's most substantial and important compositions from the end of the Second World War bear witness to the validity of the comparison with Strauss's late focus on the complementary topics of serenity and lamentation. On the one hand, the Symphony no. 6 is as potent an emblem of the age of the Cold War as many works by Shostakovich, beginning in a spirit of turbulent unease and ending in icy gloom and despair. On the other hand, the long-term evolution of the stage work (called 'morality' rather than opera) based on Bunyan's *The Pilgrim's Progress* (completed in 1949, first staged in 1951) offers a wealth of Christian imagery, and expresses Christian beliefs about the ability of fallible humans to achieve eternal redemption. The capacity of extended tonality, allied to traditional formal and rhythmic practices, to serve diverse emotional states in vividly memorable ways is as explicit in the English composer as it is in Strauss, and as late as Vaughan Williams's own *Four Last Songs* (1954–8), to words by his second wife Ursula, there are quite unambiguous echoes of the methods and materials of those large-scale symphonic and operatic conceptions; for example, the references to darkness and despair

15 See Michael Kennedy, *The Works of Ralph Vaughan Williams*, Oxford, 1964, and Alain Frogley (ed.), *Vaughan Williams Studies*, Cambridge, 1996.

at the end of no. 1, 'Procris', summon up the Sixth Symphony's concluding opposition between E flat major and E minor. Yet, as with Strauss, Vaughan Williams's Indian summer of compositional success after 1945 did not lead to his enthronement as a model for young composers. Even the more progressive Britten had difficulty fulfilling that role, at a time when radical models, from Schoenberg and Webern to Boulez and Stockhausen, were far more attractive to most young composers than moderate traditionalists.

Poulenc, Hindemith, and Prokofiev

Francis Poulenc (1899–1963), Paul Hindemith (1895–1963), and Sergei Prokofiev (1891–1953) were all born later than Strauss and Vaughan Williams, yet none of them survived beyond the early 1960s, and none (save possibly Poulenc) surpassed the compositional achievements of the inter-war years. Poulenc's post-war music represents a degree of retreat from, or contrast with, the character of his earlier work, and the topos of lament looms large.[16] For a composer with Poulenc's background in French anti-Romanticism (Ravel, Satie) and neoclassicism this mode of expression would never be as unrestrained as it was for those touched by Mahler and expressionism. Yet it is not fair to accuse Poulenc of excessive emotional constraint: the Preface to the score of his last stage work *La voix humaine* (1959) states that 'it is necessary to move suddenly from despair to calm, and vice versa', and although the work's final stages are governed by an atmosphere well described in the score as 'très calme: morne et résignée', that does not exclude a brief *fff* outburst, marked 'très violente'. Such moments are briefly destabilizing rather than fundamentally disruptive, even so, and it is the sober, tonally rooted processional style that dominates, as also in the final stages of the full-length opera *Dialogue des Carmélites* (1953–6), marked 'extraordinairement calme'.

These two late stage works can, to a degree, represent the topoi of psychic despair and spiritual conviction respectively, although, with their relative lack of ambiguity, they have arguably proved less durable than several of Poulenc's less ambitious scores. A manic depressive, his genius was less for the intensive exploration of single expressive states, and more for the kind of interactions between regretful melancholia and wry good humour that can be heard in one of his last works, the Oboe Sonata (1962). The ending of the sonata's final 'Déploration' – the work is dedicated to the memory of Prokofiev – can stand as an exemplary demonstration of Poulenc's use of clouded triadic resolution, allowing major and minor thirds to clash, and adding a major seventh to the final tonic chord. The instruction 'triste et monotone' reinforces the composer's

16 See Wilfrid Mellers, *Francis Poulenc*, Oxford, 1993.

desire for a downbeat, reticent effect, but there is nothing thin or unfocused about such clearly defined musical thinking.

Writing at the end of the 1960s, a few years after Hindemith's death in 1963, Ian Kemp declared that

> Hindemith's current reputation is at a low ebb, and this is principally because his conservatism is at odds with contemporary musical values. His music lacks that element of the irrational, the 'divine madness' evidently a *sine qua non* for the creative artist in the mid-twentieth century; and if greatness is equated with a capacity to stimulate later styles, Hindemith's negligible influence on younger composers can be regarded as another nail in his coffin.[17]

These comments reflected the increasing tendency for most younger music critics of the time to downgrade the moderate mainstream; by the late 1960s it was common to take Britten and Shostakovich for granted, and to regard the fringe rather than the centre as the principal site of significant development. In such a context, Hindemith was easily written off as both dull and pretentious, not least because a central factor in determining the character of his later music, as Kemp explains, was his determination to practise the principles set out in his textbook *The Craft of Musical Composition*. Not only did this preach adherence to tonality, albeit of an 'extended' kind: it gave theoretical substance to the 'restoration', in Hindemith's own music, 'of the triad to a position of central harmonic importance, in a language neither artificial nor nostalgic'.[18]

As both Kemp and David Neumeyer have shown, Hindemith's 'conservative' gospel did not prevent him from developing a degree of rapprochement with more progressive, even twelve-tone chromaticism, and 'it is entirely possible that Hindemith, in company with a good number of other composers, felt freer to explore Schoenberg's legacy after his death in 1951, since they would now be less threatened by any association with its ideology'.[19] Like Britten and Shostakovich, and unlike Stravinsky, Hindemith did not pursue such developments to the extent of abandoning all foundations in triadic harmony, in keeping with his conviction that 'what is held to be "atonality" necessarily turns out to be another aspect of tonality'.[20] Yet in aiming to preserve a traditional basis of accessibility and comprehensibility in his later music he did not at the same time revert to the more expressionistic spirit of his earlier work: in the preface to his 1948 revision of the song cycle *Das Marienleben* he wrote of 'the ideal of a noble music', and Kemp uses this to underline the 'serenity' and 'calm at the centre of his post-*Mathis* music, the quality that distinguishes it most readily from the often tense and agitated music of the 1920s, and, for that

17 Ian Kemp, *Hindemith*, Oxford, 1970, p. 55. 18 Ibid., p. 43.
19 David Neumeyer, *The Music of Paul Hindemith*, New Haven, 1986, p. 243.
20 Ibid., p. 240, quoting Hindemith's, *A Composer's World*.

matter, from the music of the majority of his contemporaries'.[21] Again, therefore, we confront the possibility of a style that is individual and accessible, yet which lacks the vital spark, or the cultural relevance, to maintain a permanent and prominent place in contemporary musical life.

The difficulty Hindemith had in matching the power and memorability of that earlier style is brought home in the case of the 1952 revision of the opera *Cardillac*, which simply 'weakens the directness and bite of the original'.[22] At its best, as in the opera after Thornton Wilder, *The Long Christmas Dinner* (1960), Hindemith's later music can be both 'tender and translucent', with 'a sextet of almost Schubertian delicacy harmonized exclusively in triads',[23] and the work's ending is the more effective for avoiding explicit tonal closure in favour of a dissolving fade-out. Nevertheless, despite the evidence of more dissonant and intense harmonic activity to be heard for example in the Tuba Sonata (1955) and the motet 'Vidit Joannes Jesum' (1959), which 'permitted considerable ambiguity in the definition of the principal tonality',[24] Hindemith had left it too late to follow through the implications of these more radical possibilities; as Kemp puts it, 'the final bars of his last work, the Mass for unaccompanied chorus . . . draw poignant beauty from a triadic tonal language . . . Although he may secretly have come to regret his conservatism, it was inescapable.'[25] For Neumeyer, the Mass refutes any allegation 'that Hindemith abandoned his theoretical principles in the last music', or 'that he compromised them for the sake of remaining fashionable'.[26] But Kemp's assessment is more downbeat, diagnosing a loss of touch with the spirit of the times so complete 'that his music can already [in 1970] be seen with some detachment as belonging to a past era'.[27] It is just possible that, in a twenty-first century more sympathetic to classical values, Hindemith's time will come again.[28]

'Because Prokofiev had traditional leanings and was not an iconoclastic, radically inventive composer, his music may not have actively engaged subsequent composers in the same way as Schoenberg's or Stravinsky's.' Neil Minturn's concluding assessment has similarities with Kemp's verdict on Hindemith, and is based on the conviction that 'Prokofiev's traditional temperament makes him an awkward fit into a century with both an ever-accelerating rate of change in virtually all areas of human endeavor and an obsession with innovation.'[29] This somewhat uninflected view leaves out of account a number of Soviet and Eastern European symphonic composers who were 'engaged' by Prokofiev's

21 Kemp, *Hindemith*, p. 40. 22 Ibid., p. 51. 23 Ibid., p. 53. 24 Neumeyer, *Hindemith*, p. 241.
25 Kemp, *Hindemith*, p. 55. 26 Neumeyer, *Hindemith*, p. 251. 27 Kemp, *Hindemith*, p. 28.
28 For a notable attempt at a more contextual approach to the critical interpretation of Hindemith, see Kim H. Kowalke, 'For Those We Love: Hindemith, Whitman, and "An American Requiem"', *Journal of the American Musicological Society* 50 (1997), pp. 133–74.
29 Neil Minturn, *The Music of Sergei Prokofiev*, New Haven, 1997, pp. 207–8.

lack of obsession with innovation;[30] nor does it seek to distinguish between the receptivity of composers and that of other classes of 'consumer'. But this does not affect the conclusion that Prokofiev's achievements before 1945 far outweighed the efforts of his final decade, when he was beset by failing health as well as ideological persecution. It is on a range of compositions from the 'Classical' Symphony (1916–17), *The Love of Three Oranges* (1919), *Romeo and Juliet* (1935–6), and *War and Peace* (1941–3, with revisions 1946–52), to the piano sonatas nos. 6 to 8 (1939–44) and the Symphony no. 5 (1944) that his abiding reputation is founded. There is only one undoubted masterwork from the post-war years, the Symphony no. 6 (1945–7) – if the ongoing reshaping of *War and Peace* is discounted – and it is a work that sums up the technical and expressive qualities of Prokofiev's genius to powerful effect. The Piano Sonata no. 9 (1947), the Cello Sonata (1949), and the Symphony no. 7 (1952) all risk blandness by comparison, not least in their lack of rhythmic interest. A juxtaposition of the beginning and ending of the Piano Sonata no. 9 demonstrates this reliance on regular patterning, while also revealing the degree to which chromatic dissonance can still effectively expand and delay the most clear-cut basics of tonal construction; in particular, the opening out of a conventional II–V–I cadence at the end has a bitter-sweet, valedictory quality that could be speaking as poignantly of the composer's awareness of failing creative powers as of his wider political and ideological dilemmas.

Minturn has sought to encapsulate Prokofiev's distinctiveness in terms of 'the play between the familiar and expected, on the one hand, and the surprising and unaccountable, on the other',[31] and to explain these inherent oppositions by a systematic exploration of the way 'wrong notes' function to enrich, even as they contradict, triadic diatonicism. Nevertheless, as Prokofiev's Sixth Symphony well illustrates, the musical result of these strategies is made memorable by qualities in the materials themselves which are much closer to archetypally twentieth-century topics and generic allusions than Hindemith's calm nobility. Not only is Prokofiev's later music unremittingly secular, but it sets up a clear-cut opposition between melancholy and exuberance, thereby calling straightforward affirmation into question, even though tonal resolution takes place.[32] This strategy is a fundamental feature of musical moderation during the Cold War decades, and it is basic to the moods, and the techniques, which Britten and Shostakovich deployed so brilliantly throughout this period. It is one of the tragedies of twentieth-century music that Prokofiev himself, dying

30 For a pioneering preliminary survey, see David Fanning, 'The Symphony in the Soviet Union, 1917–1991', in Robert Layton (ed.), *A Guide to the Symphony*, Oxford, 1995, pp. 292–326. See also Harlow Robinson, *Prokofiev: A Biography*, London, 1987.

31 Minturn, *Music of Prokofiev*, p. 207.

32 See Arnold Whittall, *Musical Composition in the Twentieth Century*, Oxford, 1999, pp. 146–50.

in 1953 at the age of sixty-one, did not survive to build more substantially on the impressive foundations of his Fifth and Sixth Symphonies.

Copland and others

In 1946 Aaron Copland (1900–1990) completed his Symphony no. 3, 'an end of war piece . . . intended to reflect the euphoric spirit of the country at the time'.[33] The triumphalist apotheosis of the 'Fanfare for the Common Man' with which the symphony ends was the most blatantly affirmative of all Copland's major musical statements, and it came in the middle of a decade in which his music achieved its most spectacular successes: *Rodeo*, *Lincoln Portrait* (both 1942), *Appalachian Spring* (1943–4), Symphony no. 3 (1944–6), *In the Beginning* (1947), Clarinet Concerto (1947–8), and *Twelve Poems of Emily Dickinson* (1950), not to mention several important film scores, comprise a remarkable body of work, in a style which (as suggested earlier) came as close as any to blending popular and serious in a productively intimate synthesis. Howard Pollack is right to describe *Appalachian Spring* as 'an astonishing absorption of the vernacular'.[34] The challenge was to maintain substance and depth in such an idiom, and the judgement that the Third Symphony has 'no real depth',[35] while countered by other responses to its 'astounding depth and monumentality',[36] indicates that the problem was soon felt to be a real one. In principle, therefore, Copland's adoption in the Piano Quartet (1950) of a more chromatic style, influenced by twelve-tone thinking but retaining tonal features in a way that has reminded some commentators of Bartók, might have marked the beginning of a new and valuable phase in his work – at a time before even Stravinsky had begun serious engagement with serial procedures, and probably reflecting Copland's admiration for Dallapiccola.[37]

By no means all of Copland's later compositions follow up the features found in the Piano Quartet (the opera *The Tender Land* of 1952–4 is the most substantial exception). But the only one of those works generally agreed to match the confidence and scope of his earlier music is the *Piano Fantasy* (1957). It is easy to conclude that social and personal factors, from the composer's confrontation with the McCarthy tribunal in the early 1950s to the gradual loss of creative vitality which preceded the onset of Alzheimer's disease after 1975, serve to explain both the darker, more stressful character of such works as *Connotations* (1962) and the more withdrawn reflectiveness of *Inscape* (1967) or the short piano piece *Night Thoughts* (1972). Such factors nevertheless need to be placed beside his commitment to the value of 'big-sounding, healthy-sounding

33 Pollack, *Copland*, p. 410. 34 Ibid., p. 399. 35 Ibid., p. 418. 36 Ibid., p. 412.
37 Ibid., pp. 446, 461–2.

music',[38] which the compositions of the 1940s displayed in abundance, and which is much less evident in the later works. Copland's predispositions were such that he might be expected to be uneasy with forthright expressions of sorrow and lament. At the same time, the kind of emphatic affirmation that worked in the Third Symphony would not seem 'healthy-sounding' in the post-war years, and for every critic who found 'majesty' in the 'anxious and angry vision'[39] of *Connotations* there would be another for whom *Inscape* was intolerably 'dry and pedantic'.[40] In this context, the character of *Night Thoughts (Homage to Ives)*, with its extended G major tonality and its harmony rooted in higher consonance, embodies an overriding commitment to moderation, and a simple yet magical gravity of spirit suggesting an affinity with the Gallic understatement of the later Poulenc.

It is idle to speculate on the possibility that Copland might have been more successful after 1950 had his embrace of new developments (like Carter's) been more complete. But there is no doubt whatever that the American composers who remained most closely identified with traditional tonality and forms (outside the realm of popular music, of course) failed even more decisively to win either critical or popular praise. Not only was there relatively little enthusiasm for the later symphonic music of Roy Harris, Walter Piston, Howard Hanson, and William Schuman, but Samuel Barber's large-scale neo-Romantic operas (*Vanessa*, 1956–7 and *Antony and Cleopatra*, 1966) had little initial success – though later revivals, especially of the latter, have somewhat redressed the balance.[41] In a not untypical twentieth-century irony, Barber might simply have been premature in trying to do something that other composers would manage to do more effectively in the heyday of eclecticism and pluralism after 1980. But his failure was the more significant, given the memorability and emotional depth of other post-war works, such as *Medea* (1946), *Knoxville: Summer of 1915* (1947), the Piano Sonata (1949), and the Piano Concerto (1962). In any case, such backward-looking, nostalgic essays were put in their place not by the radical visions of Babbitt, Sessions, or Carter, but by the lighter expressiveness and parodic exuberance of works by Leonard Bernstein (*Trouble in Tahiti*, 1952; *Chichester Psalms*, 1965) and David del Tredici (especially *Final Alice*, 1976). Such works depend to some extent on those deliberate associations with earlier tonal music which, in America, were pioneered by George Rochberg and William Bolcom, and whose consequences were more significant after 1975.[42] This is music that can equally well exploit the Ivesian principle that the electric shock

38 Ibid., p. 530. 39 Ibid., p. 501. 40 Ibid., p. 507.

41 See Barbara B. Heyman, *Samuel Barber: The Composer and His Music*, New York, 1992.

42 See Jonathan W. Bernard, 'Tonal Traditions in Art Music Since 1960', in David Nicholls (ed.), *The Cambridge History of American Music*, Cambridge, 1998, pp. 545–66.

of stylistic juxtaposition creates a special musical energy, or develop the post-modern perception that the more completely composers appear to identify with a borrowed style, the freer they are to be themselves.

In a class of their own: Britten and Shostakovich

Works of 1945–6

Of the composers chosen for detailed discussion in this chapter, only Shostakovich and Britten can be said to have prospered throughout the period from 1945 to 1975. Such a sustained level of creative achievement is the more remarkable, given that both were already widely admired by the middle of the 1930s: despite being often taken for granted, and devalued, by critics and authorities with more progressive sympathies, especially after 1960, their cultural prominence was never seriously eroded, either in their own countries or worldwide. 'Cultural prominence' implies functioning as a pillar of the establishment, and that function intensified the conflict between the roles of insider and outsider, which Britten and Shostakovich both lived out in very different ways.[43]

In the aftermath of the Second World War, English critics did not resist the temptation to link cultural events with the wider world: the *Musical Times* for July 1945 declared that 'the reopening of Sadler's Wells Theatre on June 7 was the first positive sign in London music that peace is upon us'.[44] That said, however, there was little concern to set up associations between the onset of peace and the specific nature of the opera performed, Britten's *Peter Grimes*. Reviewers avoided weighty observations about the devastating nature of conflicts within small societies, those 'little wars' which are the result, not of simple oppositions between the wholly good and the irredeemably evil, but of more ambiguous mixtures of rights and wrongs, affecting both sides. Nor, as far as I can discover, were there any public sneers about the irony of inviting a pacifist composer to mark not only the onset of peace but what, for most people, was a more decisive mood of victory. Whatever its textual subject matter, *Peter Grimes* had the kind of music that seemed right for the moment, and in his comment that 'the song of the fisher folk at work on the nets is a choral lyric, and one of great attraction and originality',[45] the *Musical Times* reviewer identified that

43 The most comprehensive biographical study of Britten is Humphrey Carpenter, *Benjamin Britten: A Biography*, London, 1992; for the music, see Evans, *The Music of Benjamin Britten*. On Shostakovich's life, see Fay, *Shostakovich*.

44 William McNaught, '*Peter Grimes*', *Musical Times* 86 (1945), pp. 215–16; p. 215. For other early reviews, see Brett, *Grimes*, pp. 153–62. For an exhaustive study of the opera's genesis, see Paul Banks (ed.), *The Making of Peter Grimes*, Rochester, NY, 1996.

45 McNaught, '*Grimes*'.

particular connection between individuality and a non-radical musical style which is the source of *Grimes*'s enduring success. That individuality, however, could cut both ways, and prompt disapproval too. A month later, the *Musical Times* radio columnist, W. R. Anderson, came up with a prophecy that proved to be wildly inaccurate: '*Wozzeck* . . . probably influenced Mr Britten: perhaps not consciously. His style reminds one a little of that, and also of streaks of Shostakovich, but it seems to be largely personal. I think his opera is likely to fare as did Crabbe's poetry, being highly praised by critics, and missing the public mark.'[46] By October, however, the journal was providing announcements of performances planned in four other countries, as this 'largely personal' music began to proclaim its accessibility in a triumphant voyage of public conquest.

Both the individuality and the accessibility of *Grimes* can be encapsulated in that 'song of the fisher folk' which opens Act I. This choral lyric has a melody of the greatest simplicity, emphasising triadic intervals, and with a degree of repetitiveness that would not be out of place in a popular song. At the same time, the harmonic context is not that of hymnic or chorale-style convention, and the music's originality lies in the way its tensions and contrasts (as well as its generic allusions) move between 'orthodox' and 'unorthodox', with an overall coherence that results from bridging such extremes. This way of working with basic tonal, triadic elements is to be heard at the very beginning of the opera, as the Prologue is launched in a spirit of neoclassical bustle (mocking the self-importance of the coroner Swallow). The principle of moving from diatonic to chromatic in this manner is far from new; but Britten uses a routine procedure with enough energy and flair to make it not merely accessible but gripping – a *coup de théâtre*. As even Anderson conceded, however many influences one might detect, the effect 'seems to be largely personal'.

That this can still be said more than half a century later is not only because *Peter Grimes* is still performed, and has become – by the standards of twentieth-century compositions – very well known. Britten was able to maintain the momentum fuelled by that success – coming, as it did, as a new stage in a career which had already made him, by the age of thirty, one of the most prominent British composers of the time. Britten's productivity, coupled with his profile as performer and festival promoter, sustained the accessibility and approachability of his music over the three decades between the premiere of *Grimes* and his death in 1976; to a far greater extent than Vaughan Williams, who was seventy-three in 1945, it was Britten who provided the yardstick against which other British composers tended to be judged. This was especially so from the late 1950s, when Vaughan Williams had died and LP recordings of Britten's

46 W. R. Anderson, 'Round About Radio', *Musical Times* 86 (1945), pp. 238–40; p. 240.

operas and other works began to emerge with some frequency. Here were the foundations of that 'Britten industry', often regarded with scepticism after his death, but which – certainly in the 1960s and 1970s – was symptomatic of a cultural context in which the possibility of prosperity was not denied to the proponents of 'high art'.

In his occasional public pronouncements, Britten was inclined to proclaim the need for accessibility rather than remoteness, simplicity rather than complexity: 'I believe in the artist serving society. It is better to be a bad composer writing for society than to be a bad composer writing against it. At least your work can be of *some* use.'[47] It is understandable that, on portentous public occasions like his acceptance of the first Aspen award in 1964, Britten did not make a point of claiming that his primary motivation in writing music was self-expression and self-satisfaction, or of inveighing against audiences for their timidity and conservatism. But it is difficult to prove that the relative accessibility of his music was more the result of a social conscience than of 'selfish' aesthetic predilections. Whether or not he lacked that blend of confidence and cussedness that kept Tippett at a greater remove from concerns about the practical and accessible despite an equally intense commitment to the concept of art as a social force, Britten never found himself seriously threatened with being ignored or misunderstood, at least for any length of time. By 1945 his music had reached, and thereafter maintained, a higher level of achievement than that of the great number of his British near-contemporaries who might be defined as more or less moderate in style and technique, but whose music – however accessible in principle – failed to achieve anything like the prominence accorded to Britten, at least on the British scene, throughout the second half of the twentieth century.

The contrasts between the cultural circumstances of Britten and Shostakovich were probably never greater than in the years immediately after 1945. As Richard Taruskin has claimed, the years between the denunciation of *Lady Macbeth of the Mtsensk District* (1936) and the death of Stalin (1953) were 'his period of misery, but also of his most highly acclaimed and publicized works' – essentially, the Fifth and Seventh Symphonies – and 'Shostakovich's zenith as an international figure came in 1949, when he was sent as his country's cultural ambassador to the Waldorf Peace Conference held in New York to protest against the gathering Cold War'.[48] In Taruskin's view all the later debate, arising from the posthumous publication of the composer's controversial 'testimony', as to the degree (if any) of Shostakovich's sincere acceptance

47 Carpenter, *Britten*, p. 441.

48 Richard Taruskin, 'Hearing Cycles', Aldeburgh Festival Programme Book, 2000, p. 65. For references to the composer's suicidal state of mind at this time, see Fay, *Shostakovich*, pp. 162–4.

of Marxist principles and practices is best resolved by the judgement that the composer was 'neither dissident nor modernist',[49] and that he 'found a way of maintaining public service and personal integrity under unimaginably hard conditions'. One palpable musical result of this was a new emphasis on the composition of chamber music, and 'an increasingly resolute denial of optimism' after 1945.[50]

Shostakovich completed five symphonies during the decade to 1945 (nos. 4 to 8), but his string quartets seemed to dig more deeply and range more widely. Even if the Quartet no. 2 (1944) is 'an entertainment', and, like the Fifth and Seventh Symphonies, 'an exercise in heroic classicism', the Third Quartet (1946) is very different. In Taruskin's judgement, 'Shostakovich had found his surrealistic, disquieting and inimitable quartet voice at last. And the genre, precisely because it allowed the impression of intimate rather than hortatory communication, and gave a composer back a private rather than a public voice, gradually displaced all the others in its importance to him.'[51] Taruskin goes into more detail about what this voice means:

> The Shostakovich quartet 'voice', like Beethoven's, is an amalgam of generic and specific signifying devices: always allusive, but always elusive as well – code without key. The horrors broached in the Third Quartet (or rather its second half), and the tight-lipped reticence with which it ends, can all be linked with the events and moods of the just-concluded Patriotic War. But they can be read in many other contexts as well. Some are personal. Some are political.[52]

This memorably captures the music's special tone – after all, no one would say that Britten's Second Quartet, composed in September and October of 1945, was 'linked with the events and moods' of the Second World War. But that is not to devalue the 'purely musical' allusions which link the funeral march of Shostakovich's fourth movement to a nexus of Romantic precedents, ranging from the 'trio' section of Schubert's string quintet to the main theme of Schoenberg's Quartet no. 1, op. 7. This is music whose moderate mainstream status is affirmed by the way in which diatonic stability provides a context for destabilizing chromaticism: however powerful the emotional charge, the essential organicism and goal-directedness of the structure are not disrupted. Both the 'horrors' and the 'tight-lipped reticence' of which Taruskin speaks are 'keyed' to tonality, and few contemporary works offer as powerful a demonstration as this quartet of the truth that post-tonal modernity did not have a monopoly over unsparingly intense musical expression. Small wonder that a performance of the work many years later had the effect on the composer that

49 Richard Taruskin, *Defining Russia Musically*, Princeton, 1997, p. 496. 50 Ibid., p. 491.
51 Taruskin, 'Hearing Cycles', p. 67. 52 Ibid.

it did: 'when we finished playing he sat quite still in silence like a wounded bird, tears streaming down his face. This was the only time I saw Shostakovich so open and defenceless.'[53]

Two late quartets

Eric Roseberry has provided a broad survey of parallels between Britten and Shostakovich, in support of his argument that 'the concept of requiem, of the search for peace, eternal rest in the face of violence and death' is 'a theme as close to Shostakovich's heart as it was to Britten's'. Roseberry concludes that 'in the case of both these composers, death becomes the gateway to ideals that we can cherish while we are still alive', and that 'their sense of realism and high-mindedness, their commitment to life in the context of a deeply tragic sense of our mortality are worthy of our salute'.[54] Roseberry also provides various technical pointers to reinforce his theme of shared concerns and common procedures, and a degree of affinity is certainly not in doubt. Yet it should not be forgotten that Shostakovich frankly resisted the 'offer of consolation in the hereafter' which he felt to be contained in the *War Requiem*, nor that what Laurel Fay terms the 'stark realism' and 'denial of spiritual redemption' of works like the Symphony no. 14 and the Quartet no. 15 are 'profoundly disturbing'.[55] Even so, it would be an absurd over-simplification to claim that Britten's later music is essentially optimistic, Shostakovich's unremittingly pessimistic: just as there is an element of consolation in Shostakovich's commitment to the enhancement of traditional values in the extended forms of his late compositions, so Britten never escaped the sense of 'profound sadness that any celebration of peace, or love, which he might undertake, had to be tinged with regret, with the acknowledgement that such blissful states were unstable if not utterly unreal'.[56] These are the topics which underpin the following discussion of the last string quartet of each composer.

There could scarcely be a more obvious difference between Britten and Shostakovich than the fact that the string quartet, and symphonic music in general, appeared to mean far more to the Russian than to the Briton. Nevertheless, Britten's third quartet (1975) is as 'representative' a work – technically and emotionally – as Shostakovich's fifteenth (1974), and both offer ample material for

53 Recollection of the Beethoven Quartet's violist, Fyodor Druzhinin, in Elizabeth Wilson, *Shostakovich: A Life Remembered*, London, 1994, p. 442.

54 Eric Roseberry, 'A Debt Repaid? Some Observations on Shostakovich and His Late-Period Recognition of Britten', in David Fanning (ed.), *Shostakovich Studies*, Cambridge, 1995, pp. 229–53; pp. 238, 253.

55 Fay, *Shostakovich*, p. 263.

56 Arnold Whittall, 'Britten's Lament: the World of *Owen Wingrave*', *Music Analysis* 19 (2000), pp. 148–66; p. 165.

readings focused on individuality and accessibility. Whereas the Shostakovich begins and ends with unambiguous diatonicism, the Britten begins with the refusal of clear-cut tonality and ends with the undermining of what could have been clear-cut cadential closure. This does not make the Britten an atonal work, however: it is rather that both quartets employ a 'moderate' language of extended tonality, within which the dialogue between diatonic and chromatic, unambiguous and ambiguous, is used to very different formal ends.

Shostakovich's six movements are all slow, and all have six-flat key signatures, but their generic prototypes – Elegy, Serenade, Intermezzo, Nocturne, Funeral March, and Epilogue – are well contrasted. Britten's five movements offer even more basic differentiations, the titles of the first four – Duets, Ostinato, Solo, Burlesque – avoiding formal generic attribution, and that of the finale – Recitative and Passacaglia (La Serenissima) – bringing together two genres which are not paired in traditional practice. The obvious implication, that neither work seeks to place itself firmly in the classic tradition of four symphonically structured movements, needs countering with the suggestion that, for these composers, seriousness and substance were not exclusively vested in that tradition. Both were perfectly capable of using the 'abstraction' of symphonic design as the basis for profound 'topical' discourse, but in these works a more intense, economical mode of formation was required.

'Economical' might seem an ironic term to apply to Shostakovich's thirty-five-minute piece, yet its entire character is determined by the way a ruminative, apparently expansive opening not only resists generic predictability but also invites subsequent contradiction at all levels. The resistance is first apparent in the way the imitative texture of the opening section (to Fig. 6 in the score) 'fails' to function as an orthodox fugal exposition: even its potential as a developmental dialogue is challenged. The first violin's relatively expansive counterpoint to the restricted second violin chant does not motivate a general opening-up of the textural and emotional range, and after Fig. 4 the four lines are reduced to little more than oscillations – an effect which is less static than it might be because it coincides with a harmonic shift, from E flat to D flat, the first step on the way to the C basis of the movement's second section.

The first movement's first section therefore provides the music's fundamentals: in melody, narrow chant versus more expansively lyrical material; in harmony, a rootedness whose very modal purity invites destabilization; in rhythm, a basic regularity which can be subject to unpredictable expansions and foreshortenings. In the final stages of the movement these elements are at work with a freshness and control which, despite having so much in common with so many other works by Shostakovich, has nothing in the least mechanical about it. This is the living language of tradition, and the quartet's subsequent movements project these fundamentals through the wide range of textural and formal models implied by their titles, confirming their immense dramatic potential. Thus, the hacking, guitar-like pizzicatos and dissonant chords of the second movement show that this is no sweetly romantic Serenade but a mocking, diabolical seduction; the short Intermezzo has strongly contrasted elements of cadenza and recitative, and offers not relaxation but connection, projecting the E flat to D flat progression of the first movement's first section across its entire length. Likewise, the sinuous accompanying arpeggios that begin the Nocturne are too unstable to suggest serenity, just as the main melody fails to escape the lamenting chant-like motives which bind the work's main melodies together. As the Nocturne texture disintegrates, a march-like menace takes its place (Fig. 55), even before the Funeral March proper begins.

This fifth movement is notable for shunning the cumulative, remorsely collective assertiveness of the more public, orchestral manifestations of the genre. Much of it is monodic, though the solo lines reach out beyond the registral confines of merely vocal expression: the effect is of a grief as personal as it is unrestrained, and although the dotted march rhythms are consistently present, the form is inherently unstable, the phrase structure breaking down into recitative-like prosody. This anticipates the fantasy-like formal flexibility of the Epilogue, which not only reasserts the E flat centre, and recalls earlier materials, but recontextualizes its recollections as if to embody a movement forward to new levels of darkness and despair. There is even the momentary disorientation of the thudding pizzicato chords which, though triadic, are foreign to the prevailing harmony. Because of that harmony, however, the disorientation itself is accessible to the listener, and the experience of the work as a whole is satisfying: far from inducing suicidal thoughts, this music of sorrow is a monument to the composer's memory, a strong and permanent structure which rejects the silence of oblivion.

The purely formal strengths of Shostakovich's last quartet have much to do with cyclic processes, the recurrences and enrichments of the various elements which ensure that the music's unifying forces are never fundamentally undermined. This does not entail mechanical symmetry, as the new aspects and diverse yet balanced form of the Epilogue make clear. But it is a conception profoundly resistant to modernist disintegration. In this context, if no other, Britten is the more radical – not because he actually embraces modernism, but because his rejection of it is less consistently explicit. Perhaps because of his favoured operatic and dramatic topics, he became practised in deflecting and delaying the emergence of significant unity; while Shostakovich challenges, diversifies, but ultimately reasserts his central E flat in the Quartet no. 15, Britten progresses through a logical tonal scheme (very basically, from G and

C to A and E – a symmetrical octatonic tetrachord), which is treated with a scepticism that does nothing whatever to suggest that it is perfunctory, still less redundant. Just as Shostakovich's allusion to a Mahlerian funeral march reinvents the genre in his own terms, so does Britten's allusion to a Mahlerian *Ländler*. Allusion enhances individuality: and in Britten's case, the absence of integrated motivic working is compensated for by a pervasive textural homogeneity, itself promoted by his liking, especially in his later works, for an element of heterophony. Britten's progression in the third quartet from tonal ambiguity to tonal clarity indicates that local harmonic events have greater autonomy than in Shostakovich's more explicitly centripetal design. In both quartets, however, exact or varied repetition are essential form-building elements, allied to rhythmic regularity and balanced phrase-structure.

Britten was hardly a more 'original' composer than his Russian contemporary, but it is probably the case that his style reflected a wider variety of sources and influences – or that those influences continued to affect his thinking for longer than was the case with Shostakovich. In the Third Quartet, however, the only obvious references outside Britten's own very personal idiom are the Mahlerian allusions of the Burlesque movement, and even these are more generic than literal. (It is, after all, the second movement of Mahler's Ninth Symphony, not the third, the Rondo-Burlesque, that is a *Ländler*.) It is then to be expected that the progression to tonal clarity, and the last-minute challenge to that clarity, will be reflected in a progression of tone or mood as well as texture. In considering the nature of this progression, the dangers of hermeneutic naivety are immense, but they must be confronted if anything useful is to be said about the inevitability as well as the subtlety of Britten's achievement.

Most fundamental to the sequence offered by the first two movements is the opposition between suggestions of siciliana or barcarolle in the flowing lines of 'Duets' and the quick-march assertiveness of 'Ostinato'. Appropriately, the first movement's structural progression from C to G is veiled, and the musical mood is far from monolithic, with the final bars encapsulating a confrontation between turbulence and passion on the one hand and subsiding reticence on the other; textural homogeneity here is underlined by rhythmic unisons and compound melody, and the sense of common purpose could have something to do with a mood which avoids the bleakness of utter despair. There is greater bleakness in the grimly jaunty mechanics of the second movement, if only because this can appear to be trying to shrug off its angry, melancholy aura, and even to take refuge in the spiritual comfort of a soft chorale. The ambiguous ending makes a precarious homogeneity out of the ostinato bass and the chorale, and provides a brilliantly effective transition to what is commonly referred to as the quartet's still centre – 'Solo'. The solo sections of the third movement are certainly 'very calm', as Britten's indication instructs, and this serenity, this apparent attainment of peace after stormy seas, is carried over into the ecstatically improvisatory central episode, as if to suggest a kind of transfigured spiritual freedom. At the same time, the extended tonal movement within the 'calm' sections, coupled with their glacially sparse textures, has something of that unreal, and even dangerous detachment which is one of the writer Aschenbach's attributes in *Death in Venice*, the opera to which the Third Quartet is a pendant. The great irony of Mann's story, and Britten's opera, is that, while passion might indeed lead to 'the abyss', 'pure detachment' seems even more likely to provoke a surge of damaging passion than to prevent it; hence the appropriateness of the way in which the quartet's fourth movement, 'Burlesque', brings the music back down to earth with a vengeance – back to rough, fierce reality. Yet this music ought not to provoke the smiles appropriate to a genial parody. It seems deadly serious in the way its traditional basics of harmony and form are attacked from within, stability and instability equally assertive, equally prominent. Here, as in the way the finale moves away from its carefully prepared, serene diatonicism into darker regions of doubt, is the evidence as to how Britten, like Shostakovich, could turn the personal use of traditional devices, on which his special accessibility relies, to musical ends of exceptional quality and memorability.

The ending of the 'Passacaglia' is perhaps the more impressive because the introductory 'Recitative' seems contrived. Unlike the recitative-like phrases which abound in Shostakovich's last quartet, Britten's references to the opera proclaim their quotation marks too literally. One of the triumphs of *Death in Venice* is in the way certain elements of staginess – not only Aschenbach's direct addresses to the audience, but the ritual-like artificiality of the events which promote his disgrace and death – appear more inevitable and effective than any more naturalistic or realistic treatment of the story, or any attempt to downplay the inner drama on which it depends, could hope to do. It is this sense of action as internal which the steady tread of the 'Passacaglia' restores. This is supremely restrained music, yet it builds to heights of poetic eloquence intensified by the sorrowing turns of chromatic inflection and the troubling dissonances created by the heterophonic alignments. Inevitably, Britten comes quite close in places to that sense of superimposing complementary, conflicting lines that is the essence of modernist counterpoint (see bar 89f.), but even here the inexorable, processional passacaglia bass draws all the upper lines into a powerfully expressive combination, a fusion from which illusory diatonic resolution and the final, open-ended chromatic dissonance can emerge with equal conviction. In the end, Britten rejects the full, unfettered emancipation of the dissonance which was so fundamental an element for Schoenbergian modernism; for him, the difference between consonance (lower or higher) and dissonance was the difference between musical life and death.

Conclusion: centres and extremes

The criteria set out in this chapter prompt the conclusion that, in terms of individuality and accessibility between 1945 and 1975, Britten and Shostakovich were in a class of their own: while both confronted rather than evaded the darkest situations and states of mind, the corresponding strengths of their musical thinking have the power to console rather than depress. Even so, it can be argued that the most vital current of musical production during this period was the modernist mainstream – the kind of less moderate stylistic and technical transformations found to varying degrees in Stravinsky, Carter, Tippett, Messiaen, Lutosławski, Dutilleux, and Ligeti, to name but seven. Of course, some of the composers on this list travelled less far down the road towards an embrace of avant-garde notions than others. But it is not difficult to diagnose a general aura of decline in the power of moderate thinking, and the most prominent example of a composer who regressed from progressiveness to conservatism hardly offers a convincing case for the defence. The early expressionism of Krzysztof Penderecki (b. 1933) found favour as the intensely concentrated expression of grief in face of the horrors of Auschwitz and Hiroshima, but was tempered at quite an early stage by his aspiration to find a contemporary equivalent for the ritual solemnity and dramatic vividness of Bach's Passions. The *St Luke Passion* (1963–5) won initial acclaim for the gap-bridging way in which it brought dissonant clusters alongside tonal triads to express the universal scope of its subject matter. The conjunction of expressionism and melodrama had an undeniable post-Bergian punch, but Penderecki's subsequent retreat into a rambling, overblown, unrelieved, and anonymous kind of neo-Romanticism, such as pervades the forty minutes or so of the Violin Concerto no. 1 (1976–7), seems to fulfil all one's worst apprehensions about the negative results of rejecting stylistic and technical progress: the contrast between this concerto and the short, pungently expressionistic orchestral work that Penderecki wrote a couple of years earlier – *The Dream of Jacob* – is especially instructive.

The polarized tensions between liberation and oppression conventionally attributed to culture in the 1960s made many composers of significance rely more on their instincts than their intellects, and drove them to progress either towards 'true' liberation, or towards the freedom to be constrained. This would explain why it became increasingly difficult to achieve and sustain the kind of balance between the personal and the traditional found in Shostakovich and Britten: after all, even they accepted an element of revitalization from serial technique, but without taking the decisive step of suppressing rooted centricity of harmony, the consonance/dissonance distinction, and traditional generic and formal content. But critical generalization on this level inevitably lacks nuance and flexibility, so it is useful, in seeking a balance, to note one particular view of Britten's status, written immediately after his death. In a memorial essay, the composer Robin Holloway (b. 1943) characterized the crucial difference between the music of the 1970s and that of the 1940s in terms of 'the malaise of music at large – the flight to the extremes that leaves the centre empty'. Holloway went on:

> I wouldn't want to say that Britten's style is itself central, but I think it can show the way better than any other to a possible pulling-together. In particular the combination of lucidity, emptiness and tightness in the latter works, can reveal common ground between the most unexpected and related sources. This music has the power to connect the avant-garde with the lost paradise of tonality; it conserves and renovates in the boldest and simplest manner; it shows how old usages can be refreshed and remade, and how the new can be saved from mere rootlessness, etiolation, lack of connexion and communication.[57]

This eloquent apostrophe – with its particular echoes of the kind of concerns found in Kemp's late-1960s assessment of Hindemith[58] – is evidently more prospective than retrospective in tone. Nor is it that of a disinterested commentator, but a cry from a composer himself experiencing the discomfiting circumstance of being encouraged to live on 'the extremes' when 'the centre' is more instinctively appealing. Holloway's caveat, that 'Britten's style' was not in itself 'central', reflected the more immediate perceptions of the mid-1970s, when the idea that any style might be truly 'central' seemed implausible (this was the time when, locally, Maxwell Davies was as prominent as Tippett, and, internationally, avant-gardists and retrogressives were equally adept at gaining new commissions, if not frequent follow-up performances and a place in the canonic 'standard repertory'). The reality which emerges in retrospect is that, between 1945 and 1975, the most accessible styles were, in general, the 'central' styles, by all criteria other than those of professional participants on the contemporary scene. The assumption which Holloway reveals, that it was precisely because of Britten's ability to connect extremes that his style was not as central for composers as his aesthetic stance, can itself be interpreted as an involuntary acknowledgement of the gap between criteria relevant for composers and those relevant for most other musicians and music-lovers. Unsurprisingly,

57 Robin Holloway, 'Benjamin Britten, 1913–1976', *Tempo* 120 (1977), pp. 5–6.
58 See above, pp. 375–6.

the wider world of musical appreciation and consumption found it easier to live with a concept of the mainstream than did the coterie of engaged professionals.

And yet the sense of decline persists. Composers disinclined by temperament to challenge or ignore the conventional expectations of audiences and promoters were in one sense reassuring, as upholders of established, living traditions, but after 1945 they found it difficult to offer audiences a music that was optimistic, serene, celebratory. To uphold tradition in a world of austerity and uncertainty was to enhance uneasiness and instability, and to underscore that tradition's vulnerability to trivialization and decay. Such upholders of tradition, in the years after 1945, were arguably at their finest and most powerful when they were inspired by what David Fanning terms 'the apparently irreconcilable legacies of the Classical and Romantic traditions', and by their capacity to 'coexist and lend one another new profundity of meaning'. Fanning is actually referring to the finale of Shostakovich's Tenth Symphony (1953), by way of leading to his conclusion about the symphony as a whole: 'From the epic tragedy of the first movement, to the naked violence of the second, to the enigmatic defiance of the third, to what? To a coexistence of the Mahlerian poles of utopia and catastrophe, of idealism and nihilism.'[59] Yet even in Shostakovich's symphonic masterwork, the moderating hand of a living tradition kept modernist disintegration at bay. It was younger composers, with less well-established styles than a Shostakovich, who were more likely to experience the magnetic attraction of Holloway's 'extremes'.

In his 'Introduction' to Volume 10 of the *New Oxford History of Music*, Martin Cooper struck a pessimistic note not so different in character from that of Robin Holloway, though the context is quite different. Cooper declared that 'this whole period' – 1890–1960 – 'has been marked by a refusal on the part of the public, at first resolute and all but absolute, and still only cautiously yielding, to interest itself in New Music'. He added that 'up to 1950 the New Music was accepted by the public in direct proportion to the number of its links with the old',[60] and argued that 'this picture of a sharply divided musical world, in which a small number of *avant-garde* pioneers, almost out of sight of the main body of performers and listeners, who concern themselves with musical archeology and indiscriminate truffle-hunting, is something entirely new.'[61] It was nevertheless the unprecedented availability of music which filled

59 David Fanning, *The Breath of a Symphonist: Shostakovich's Tenth*, London, 1989, p. 76.
60 Martin Cooper, 'Introduction', in Martin Cooper (ed.), *The New Oxford History of Music, X: The Modern Age, 1890–1960*, Oxford, 1974, p. xvii.
61 Ibid., p. xviii.

Cooper with alarm, so that 'the accepted institution of music as a background to other activities, and even to no activity at all, plainly dulls the listening faculty itself, eventually blurring the line that divides passive listening from active listening': such dumbing-down, he added, seemed an appropriate outcome to a situation in which 'European music, which once expressed man's idea of what he *should* be, his aspirations, now reflects what in his own eye he *is*; and it seems likely that this will continue to be true of music in the future.'[62]

Even at the time, Cooper's pessimism seemed excessive, ignoring the visionary qualities of Tippett and Stockhausen – or, by implication, discounting them because they were not expressed in more accessible, traditional terms. But his fears that the music of the moderate mainstream had been lost, or was in danger of being lost between the extremes of the avant-garde and enthusiasm for 'early' (pre-1914) music, accurately reflected a widespread perception of the 1970s, when the greatest exponents of compositional moderation – Britten and Shostakovich – were regarded as either in decline or wavering on the verge of capitulation to modernism, while no obvious successors of stature were apparent. With hindsight, it is apparent that the explicit embrace of comprehensibility and positive thinking evident in minimalism, in its various experimental and 'holy' guises, was already becoming a force to be reckoned with; the earlier works of Glass and Reich were becoming known, while Górecki's Third Symphony, though not an instant success, was written in 1976. The evolution of late-twentieth-century pluralism was well under way as Cooper wrote, and not the least of its achievements was to make space in which the moderate mainstream of the mid-century years could retain a prominent position.

Bibliography

Anderson, W. R. 'Round about Radio', *Musical Times* 86 (1945), pp. 238–40.
Banks, Paul (ed.). *The Making of Peter Grimes*, Woodbridge, 1996.
Bernard, Jonathan W. 'Tonal Traditions in Art Music since 1960', in David Nicholls (ed.), *The Cambridge History of American Music*, Cambridge, 1998, pp. 548–66.
Bowen, Meirion (ed.). *Gerhard on Music: Selected Writings*, Aldershot, 2000.
Brett, Philip (ed.). *Benjamin Britten: Peter Grimes*, Cambridge, 1983.
Carpenter, Humphrey. *Benjamin Britten: A Biography*, London, 1992.
Cooke, Mervyn. *Britten and the Far East*, Rochester, NY, 1998.
Cooper, Martin (ed.). *The New Oxford History of Music, X: The Modern Age, 1890–1960*, Oxford, 1974.
Craft, Robert. *Stravinsky, Chronicle of a Friendship* (2nd edn), London, 1994.

62 Ibid., p. xix.

Evans, Peter. *The Music of Benjamin Britten* (2nd edn), Oxford, 1996.
Fanning, David. *The Breath of a Symphonist: Shostakovich's Tenth*, London, 1989.
'The Symphony in the Soviet Union, 1917–1991', in Robert Layton (ed.), *A Guide to the Symphony*, Oxford, 1995, pp. 292–326.
Fay, Laurel E. *Shostakovich: A Life*, New York, 2000.
Frogley, Alain (ed.). *Vaughan Williams Studies*, Cambridge, 1996.
Griffiths, Paul. *Olivier Messiaen and the Music of Time*, London, 1985.
Modern Music and After: Directions since 1945, Oxford, 1995.
Heyman, Barbara B. *Samuel Barber: The Composer and His Music*, New York, 1992.
Holloway, Robin. 'Benjamin Britten, 1913–1976', *Tempo* 120 (1977), pp. 5–6.
Howard, Patricia (ed.). *Benjamin Britten: The Turn of the Screw*, Cambridge, 1985.
Jackson, Timothy L. 'The Metamorphosis of the *Metamorphosen*: New Analytical and Source-Critical Discoveries', in Bryan Gilliam (ed.), *Richard Strauss: New Perspectives on the Composer and His Work*, Durham NC, 1992, pp. 193–241.
'*Ruhe, meine Seele!* and the *Letzte Orchesterlieder*', in Bryan Gilliam (ed.), *Richard Strauss and His World*, Princeton, 1992, pp. 90–137.
Johnson, Robert Sherlaw. *Messiaen*, London, 1975.
Kemp, Ian. *Hindemith*, Oxford, 1970.
Kennedy, Michael. *Richard Strauss: Man, Musician, Enigma*, Cambridge, 1999.
The Works of Ralph Vaughan Williams, Oxford, 1964.
Kovnatskaya, Ludmila. 'Notes on a Theme from *Peter Grimes*', in Philip Reed (ed.), *On Mahler and Britten: Essays in Honour of Donald Mitchell on his Seventieth Birthday*, Woodbridge, 1995, pp. 172–85.
Kowalke, Kim H. 'For Those We Love: Hindemith, Whitman, and "An American Requiem"', *Journal of the American Musicological Society* 50 (1997), pp. 133–74.
McNaught, William. 'Peter Grimes', *Musical Times* 86 (1945), pp. 215–16.
Mellers, Wilfrid. *Francis Poulenc*, Oxford, 1993.
Minturn, Neil. *The Music of Sergei Prokofiev*, New Haven, 1997.
Mitchell, Donald and Hans Keller. *Benjamin Britten: A Commentary on his Works from a Group of Specialists*, London, 1952.
Mitchell, Donald and Philip Reed. *Letters from a Life: Selected Letters and Diaries of Benjamin Britten*, 2 vols., London, 1991.
Neumeyer, David. *The Music of Paul Hindemith*, New Haven, 1986.
Pollack, Howard. *Aaron Copland: The Life and Works of an Uncommon Man*, London, 2000.
Rae, Charles Bodman. *The Music of Lutosławski* (3rd edn), London, 1999.
Robinson, Harlow. *Prokofiev: A Biography*, London, 1987.
Roseberry, Eric. 'A Debt Repaid? Some Observations on Shostakovich and His Late-Period Recognition of Britten', in David Fanning (ed.), *Shostakovich Studies*, Cambridge, 1995, pp. 229–53.
Ideology, Style, Content and Thematic Process in the Symphonies, Cello Concertos and String Quartets of Shostakovich, New York, 1989.
Simpson, Robert. *Sibelius and Nielsen*, London, 1965.
(ed.). *The Symphony 2: Elgar to the Present Day*, Harmondsworth, 1967.
Stucky, Steven. *Lutosławski and his Music*, Cambridge, 1981.
Taruskin, Richard. *Defining Russia Musically*, Princeton, 1997.
'Hearing Cycles', *Aldeburgh Festival Programme Book* 2000, pp. 60–9.

Walsh, Stephen. *The Music of Stravinsky* (2nd edn), Oxford, 1993.
Whittall, Arnold. *Musical Composition in the Twentieth Century*, Oxford, 1999.
'Britten's Lament: the World of *Owen Wingrave*', *Music Analysis* 19 (2000), pp. 145–66.
Wilson, Elizabeth. *Shostakovich: A Life Remembered*, London, 1994.

· 15 ·

After swing: modern jazz and its impact

MERVYN COOKE

The decline of the big bands

Early jazz had taken some years to reach a wide international audience, and the furore caused by the visit of the Original Dixieland Jazz Band to London in 1919 was an indication that the new music was destined to become notorious on account of its associations with behaviour both rebellious and, in the case of Prohibition in the United States, illegal.[1] For most of its subsequent history, jazz was tainted by extra-musical associations: although it is often tacitly assumed that this music of African-American origin scandalized a predominantly white audience, the perceived link between jazz and moral decay was fostered as much by those middle-class African Americans for whom the blues – 'the Devil's music' – had always been an uncomfortable reminder of the social problems from which they had at least in part managed to escape.[2] The development of diverse jazz styles after the Second World War, and their impact on perceptions of the music as both art and commerce, were significantly affected by the prejudices and partisanship of an earlier generation of commentators and consumers.

Even the definition of jazz was contested. A concerted attempt to legitimize swing as 'jazz' was made in the pages of the journals *Down Beat* and *Metronome* in the early 1940s,[3] in defiance of those purists who looked askance at any jazzy style that downplayed the role of improvisation and other techniques explicitly associated with the music's African-American heritage (such as blues structures, blue notes, and 'dirty' timbres). Such purism showed little awareness of, or sympathy towards, the conflicting demands on performing musicians of commercial viability and a desire for increased technical experimentation, both of which were to be defining factors in the burgeoning of new and contrasting

1 For contemporaneous reviews of the ODJB's London visit, see Jim Godbolt, *A History of Jazz in Britain 1919–50*, London, 1984, pp. 6–14.

2 See John Gennari, 'Jazz Criticism: Its Development and Ideologies', *Black American Literature Forum* 25/3 (1991), pp. 449–523; p. 451.

3 Scott DeVeaux, 'Constructing the Jazz Tradition: Jazz Historiography', *Black American Literature Forum* 25/3 (1991), pp. 525–60; p. 537.

jazz styles after the mid-1940s. At the same time, the concerns over the effect on the jazz tradition of commercialization, which were expressed during the heyday of swing, may not have been entirely misplaced, and a convenient example of what is at issue is provided by the Glenn Miller band.

Miller had secured for himself an enviable position at the head of the record charts in the late 1930s, and in the early 1940s his band starred in two commercially successful movies. His perennially popular *In the Mood* and *Moonlight Serenade*, both recorded in 1939, are still commonly regarded as 'jazz'; indeed, the insistent riffs of *In the Mood* exemplify one of the most characteristic clichés of the big-band style. However, the cloyingly sentimental *Moonlight Serenade* (suggestive of jazz only in its prominent use of saxophones) has dated markedly as popular tastes have changed – hence its almost *de rigueur* use as a period establisher in modern movies with a nostalgic wartime setting. With hindsight, Miller may be viewed as the first high-profile bandleader to pander to popular taste at the expense of musical substance (a criticism also frequently levelled at Armstrong in the 1930s, when the stunning creativity he had displayed in the late 1920s appeared to have atrophied); Miller's music is competent but unimaginative, and has been aptly dismissed by Ian Carr as 'polished sterility'.[4] As early as 1946, Rudi Blesh noted that commercialism in big-band swing was 'a cheapening and deteriorative force' on the history of jazz that might prove 'not only hostile, but fatal' to its future development.[5]

There were problems of a different nature in the case of Duke Ellington. In 1943, like Benny Goodman five years earlier, Ellington and his band appeared at New York's prestigious Carnegie Hall; there they performed their 'tone parallel to the history of the American Negro' entitled *Black, Brown and Beige*, by far the most ambitious extended structure yet essayed in a jazz idiom. It failed to satisfy either jazz or classical critics, however, both camps judging this singular achievement by applying entirely different (and equally inappropriate) criteria.[6] The muted critical response discouraged Ellington from further exploration of extended structures: his later large-scale compositions were invariably couched in the format of a loosely connected suite of movements, which gave the illusion of extended form without addressing any of the structural challenges raised by the pioneering *Black, Brown and Beige* (of which Ellington subsequently recorded only extracts). Nevertheless, his band made further annual appearances at Carnegie Hall until 1952; it also played at New York's Metropolitan Opera House in 1951, and the future of jazz in

4 Ian Carr, *Miles Davis: A Critical Biography*, London, 1982, p. 26. For an assessment of Miller from a popular music perspective, see Donald Clarke, *The Rise and Fall of Popular Music*, London, 1995, pp. 221–7.

5 Rudi Blesh, *Shining Trumpets: A History of Jazz*, New York, 1946, pp. 11–12.

6 For contrasting criticisms of *Black, Brown and Beige*, see Mark Tucker (ed.), *The Duke Ellington Reader*, New York, 1993, pp. 153–204.

the concert hall was then assured. In subsequent decades, this emphatic placing of select jazz on a high artistic pedestal was to disturb the conscience of a younger generation of purists who resented any suggestion that their music should become canonic – or, indeed, display any affinity with the 'European' compositional techniques that so many of the leading lights in jazz had studied and self-evidently wished to emulate.[7]

The more esoteric nature of Ellington's style undoubtedly helped his music survive when populist big-band idioms fell by the wayside in the late 1940s. Several factors contributed to this collapse, some practical and others aesthetic. It had been virtually impossible for even the most famous bands to maintain consistent personnel during the years of military conscription; there was a dire wartime shortage of the shellac used in the production of gramophone records; a heavy cabaret tax was levied in the United States; and a succession of strikes mounted by the American Federation of Musicians in 1942–4 and 1948 imposed severe economic hardships on its members. The strikes had another important consequence, being partly responsible for the rise to fame of popular singers (including Bing Crosby and Frank Sinatra, the latter first attaining stardom with Tommy Dorsey's band in the early 1940s), who had not been prevented from recording during the AFM's periods of industrial action. Some post-war listeners came to regard the big bands as a costly extravagance, while others did not wish to be reminded of a style of music inevitably associated with times of war – an association intensified by the fact that several prominent bandleaders (such as Miller and Artie Shaw) had devoted their services to the military and were universally familiar from uniformed publicity photographs. This picture of decline was reflected even outside America: in those countries of continental Europe liberated by Allied forces in 1944–5, swing had suffered from the brutal eradication of Jewish and African-American music perpetrated by the Nazi party – a situation paralleled in the USSR and Japan.[8] And in the UK, the growth of post-war jazz was at first stunted by the continuation of a long-term and ludicrously short-sighted Musicians' Union ban on visits by US performers between 1935 and 1954.[9]

The bebop 'revolt'

With the advent of bebop in the 1940s, modern jazz was born. The style may have taken its name either from a pair of nonsense syllables commonly used

7 For provocative discussions of the alleged canonization of jazz, see DeVeaux, 'Constructing the Jazz Tradition', and Krin Gabbard, 'Introduction: The Jazz Canon and its Consequences', in Gabbard (ed.), *Jazz Among the Discourses*, Durham, NC, 1995, pp. 1–28.

8 See Michael H. Kater, *Different Drummers: Jazz in the Culture of Nazi Germany*, New York, 1992.

9 See 'Jazz Comes to Britain by Stealth', chapter 14 of Godbolt, *Jazz in Britain*, pp. 236–53.

in scat singing, or as an onomatopoeic reference to the dislocated accents of bop's innovative drumming techniques. On its first appearance, bop appeared to be a veritable stylistic revolution. Ross Russell described it as 'the music of revolt: revolt against big bands, arrangers . . . – against commercialized music in general. It reasserts the individuality of the jazz musician.'[10] In subsequent debates between staunch advocates of traditional pre-war jazz and adherents of the new style (who called the traditionalists 'mouldy figs'),[11] it became evident that bop was considered by many not to be jazz at all. The adoption of the label 'modern jazz' by the boppers (at precisely the time when Ellington had stopped using the term 'jazz' altogether on account of its limited usefulness and potentially restrictive stylistic implications) was nevertheless a clear attempt to demonstrate that bop was a logical continuation of the precepts and qualities of earlier jazz, and not as radical a departure from them as many initially believed.

Bop was first promulgated in small-ensemble recordings made by trumpeter Dizzy Gillespie and saxophonist Charlie Parker in 1945, its earliest manifestations (at Harlem's legendary Minton's Playhouse, Monroe's Uptown House and elsewhere) having been permanently lost in the black hole of the AFM's recording ban. Its harmonic vocabulary was extended by the experimentation of both Gillespie and pianist Thelonious Monk – whose considerable talents as a composer were later to be somewhat belied by his often clumsy piano-playing and on-stage eccentricities – while its style of melodic improvisation drew much from the influence of guitarist Charlie Christian, who died prematurely in 1942. The style was also explored in a big-band context, notably under the leaderships of Billy Eckstine and Earl Hines, and later by Gillespie (often with a Latin flavour).

Initially, the new music was not popular. On the surface, bop appeared to be characterized by a wilful distortion of traditional musical values: its style of improvisation (based on chains of melodic cells and often termed 'formulaic' by analysts) seemed far removed from the melodic memorability of swing, which had been based largely on the popular-song repertoire, while bop's ostensibly complex harmonic language and frenetic speed left even some professional musicians fazed. In fact, bop retained at least three defining elements of the swing style – riffs, walking bass lines, and propulsively swung cymbal rhythms – all of which were to remain prominent features of mainstream jazz throughout the second half of the twentieth century. And part of bop's appeal to younger

10 Ross Russell, 'Bebop', in Martin Williams (ed.), *The Art of Jazz*, New York, 1959, p. 202.

11 Often incorrectly attributed to critic Leonard Feather, the term 'mouldy figs' was coined by Sam Platt in a letter to *Esquire* magazine in June 1945; see Feather, 'Goffin, *Esquire*, and the Moldy Figs' [1986], in Robert Gottlieb (ed.), *Reading Jazz*, London, 1997, p. 733. See also Bernard Gendron, '"Moldy Figs" and Modernists: Jazz at War (1942–1946)', in Gabbard, *Jazz Among the Discourses*, pp. 31–56.

performers, who later adopted it as their *lingua franca*, came from the idiom's essential simplicity: its harmonic structures were mostly decorations of standard chord progressions borrowed from existing songs, its 'complex' chords were often created merely by superimposing dissonant added notes on familiar harmonies (and by improvising more on these extensions than the triads underpinning them), and its infamous rhythmic unpredictability – pioneered in the work of drummers Kenny Clarke and Max Roach – was conceived as local disruptions of an unwaveringly secure underlying pulse.[12]

Bop's basic structure – a statement of the 'head' theme, followed by a succession of improvised solos before a concluding statement of the head – could hardly have been more straightforward. The head–solos–head format was to prove an enduring phenomenon in jazz, and Paul Berliner has offered a persuasive view of why jazz musicians continue to rely on what is essentially a formal straitjacket. Following on from trumpeter Red Rodney's remark that the audience will accept anything as long as it is based on a 'standard' (i.e. a familiar tune forming part of the mainstream repertory, which in the 1950s expanded to incorporate numerous bop themes), he comments:

> In this regard, the conventional format of jazz arrangements serves the interests of listeners by reminding them of the structures on which artists base their intricate improvisations. [Trumpeter] Doc Cheatham always plays 'the melody of each tune first before I improvise, so that the audience knows what I'm doing.' . . . By extension, repeating the melody at the close of a band's rendition encapsulates solos in familiar material, usually of a simpler lyrical nature, temporarily relaxing the demands upon listening and providing the rendition with a satisfying shape overall. [Saxophonist] Lee Konitz adds that repeated performance of the same pieces over the years allows serious fans to appreciate the uniqueness of the most recent version in relation to the history of past performances.[13]

While of continuing fascination to aficionados ('serious fans' who 'appreciate . . . uniqueness'), a thorough comprehension of this refined sense of structural variety can be too demanding and esoteric for both casual listeners and classical musicians schooled in different organizational principles, for whom the surface simplicity of the rigid ternary pattern can all too easily seem unimaginative. In this way, bop's most important structural legacy did little to help those who wished to establish jazz as a middle ground between popular and art musics,

12 Charlie Parker, as part of his attempt to claim originality for bop, declared that it was different from earlier jazz because it had 'no steady beat' (quoted in DeVeaux, 'Constructing the Jazz Tradition', p. 556, n. 12). Parker's view that bop was 'something entirely separate and apart from jazz' was not shared by Gillespie: see Mervyn Cooke, *Jazz*, London, 1998, p. 116. For a concise summary of the principal elements of the bop style, see ibid., pp. 116–23.

13 Paul Berliner, *Thinking in Jazz: The Infinite Art of Improvisation*, Chicago, 1994, p. 458.

and the situation intensified the split between the cognoscenti and opponents of the new idiom.

Bop's resurrection of the twelve-bar blues and its heavy emphasis on solo improvisation reflected the (predominantly black) boppers' desire to wrench jazz away from the 'polished sterility' of the pre-composed music of the (predominantly white) swing bands, and steer it vigorously back towards its African-American origins.[14] It marked a self-conscious shift away from jazz as entertainment music to jazz as artistic (and sometimes political) statement, a move most obviously reflected by the new music's incompatibility with conventional dancing. Ralph Ellison explained how this led to a number of 'myths and misconceptions' on the boppers' part:

> that to be truly free they must act exactly the opposite of what white people might believe, rightly or wrongly, a Negro to be; that the performing artist can be completely and absolutely free of the obligations of the entertainer, and that they could play jazz with dignity only by frowning and treating the audience with aggressive contempt; and that to be in control, artistically and personally, one must be so cool as to quench one's own human fire.[15]

As LeRoi Jones put it:

> In a sense the term *cultists* for the adherents of early modern jazz was correct. The music, bebop, defined the term of a deeply felt nonconformity among many young Americans, black and white. And for many young Negroes the irony of being thought 'weird' or 'deep' by white Americans was as satisfying as it was amusing. It also put on a more intellectually and psychologically satisfying level the traditional separation and isolation of the black man from America. It was a cult of protection as well as rebellion.[16]

This attitude in due course became a significant influence on the broader artistic experiences of the Beatniks in the 1950s and 1960s.[17]

The stark shift in emphasis was difficult, if not impossible, for the wider listening public to negotiate. Bop fell neatly between two stools: on the one hand, it was often not melodically memorable enough to assure its commercial success; on the other hand, its structures seemed entirely alien in conception

14 For commentary on the vital role played by white musicians in shaping the development of jazz, see Gene Lees, *Cats of Any Color: Jazz, Black and White*, Oxford, 1994; Richard M. Sudhalter, *Lost Chords: White Musicians and Their Contribution to Jazz 1915–1945*, Oxford, 1999; and Gerald Early, 'White Noise and White Knights: Some Thoughts on Race, Jazz, and the White Jazz Musician', in Geoffrey C. Ward and Ken Burns, *Jazz: A History of America's Music*, New York, 2000, pp. 324–31.

15 Ralph Ellison, 'Minton's' [1959], in Gottlieb, *Reading Jazz*, p. 553. For Gillespie's reminiscences of the aura at Minton's Playhouse in the early years of bop, see ibid., pp. 555–72.

16 LeRoi Jones [Amiri Baraka], 'Bop', in Gottlieb, *Reading Jazz*, p. 871. The extract is taken from Jones's book *Blues People: Negro Music in White America*, New York, 1963, a seminally important text on the history of jazz and the first to be written by a black commentator.

17 See Gennari, 'Jazz Criticism', p. 487 and n. 17, p. 512.

to those for whom Ellington's music remained a high point of intellectual achievement in jazz. It also engendered social disquiet: as the style spread in the 1950s (attaining a large following in Europe after visits of American musicians to pioneering French jazz festivals in 1948–9), so did public unease at its apparently inextricable association with the consumption of hard drugs – the means by which some boppers took their personal isolation from society to its self-destructive extreme. In the UK, the ongoing promotion of bop at London's Carnaby Club by saxophonists John Dankworth and Ronnie Scott was almost curtailed in 1950 after the venue was raided on the pretext of a drugs search; heroin accelerated Parker's death in 1955, and affected most of the leading bop performers at some stage in their careers. Subsequently, the image of the genius Parker as dope-ravaged pauper became just as strongly romanticized in the popular imagination as that of the genius Ellington as tuxedo-clad classicist.

Mainstream and cool jazz in the 1950s

Alongside the burgeoning of bop, jazz continued to be partly defined by its more commercially viable 'mainstream'. As Scott DeVeaux has pointed out, this label was 'first applied (retroactively) to swing, but quickly used to describe any body of music neither so conservative as to deny the possibility or desirability of further development, nor so radical as to send that development in uncontrollable directions'.[18] Populist jazz styles persisted in the 1950s, and even Parker found it expedient to make recordings with saccharine pre-arranged string accompaniments. So did singer Sarah Vaughan, who was well versed in bop techniques (she recorded with Parker and Gillespie in 1945 after serving as pianist in Hines's big band and as vocalist in Eckstine's) but also knew how to win herself a wider following by a canny choice of repertoire and accompaniment. Singers continued to secure commercial success far more readily than instrumentalists; Ella Fitzgerald's 'songbook' recordings (issued by Verve between 1956 and 1961), for example, remain bestsellers on account of their easy-going nature, supreme technical confidence, and mainstream popular-song repertoire. More thought-provoking was the work of Billie Holiday, whose genius for recomposing melodies as she sang them was unique and inimitable; her stormy private life and drug-related death in 1959 paralleled the misery of many bop performers, and this biographical mystique has continued to attract popular attention as much as – if not more than – her musical skills. A select group of big bands survived in the 1950s, performing modernized forms

18 DeVeaux, 'Constructing the Jazz Tradition', p. 550.

of swing: chief among them were the very different ensembles led by Count Basie (the most blues-rooted of all bandleaders), Stan Kenton (whose West Coast 'progressive jazz' seemed at the time to be boldly experimental, but has not stood the test of time well), Harry James (formerly Goodman's principal trumpeter), Woody Herman, and Charlie Barnet. Basie's trumpeter Thad Jones, together with drummer Mel Lewis, continued to develop the Basie style with resourcefulness and imagination well into the 1970s, showing in the process how the essentially sectionalized structure of big-band arrangements easily permitted the insertion of bop-style solo improvisations. Sometimes tinged with nostalgia, traditional big-band jazz remained marketable, as demonstrated by Goodman's fortieth-anniversary appearance at Carnegie Hall in 1978.

Of the various alternative styles of jazz that had established themselves by 1960, the closest to bop was one of many styles falling loosely under the label 'hard bop' (sometimes known as 'funk' or 'soul jazz'). In the hands of leading exponents such as drummer Art Blakey's Jazz Messengers, hard bop exploited the head–solos–head structure by making the head melodies catchier than they had ever been before, and by infusing improvisations with powerful blues inflections and strongly propulsive backbeats. Appropriately, the leading record label promoting this style was Blue Note; with hits such as trumpeter Lee Morgan's *The Sidewinder* (1963), it showed how solid jazz with simple yet memorable riffs was still easily capable of achieving impressive sales. Some hard bop was dismissed as another 'sell-out', for reasons outlined by DeVeaux:

> [B]y the 1950s, the earthier and less prestigious functions of [jazz] had been passed on to rhythm and blues. At the same time that musicians and critics were struggling to make a case for jazz as art music, the more commercially minded hard bop musicians strove mightily to win back audiences alienated by bebop's intellectual pretensions with hard-swinging grooves and a folky sensibility that wore its ethnicity on its sleeve.[19]

Other instrumentalists in the 1950s coaxed jazz in directions different from those offered by bop and more traditional idioms, breaking away from the structural limitations of bop by readmitting elements of pre-composition to varying extents. Pianist John Lewis promoted with his famous Modern Jazz Quartet (1951–74), featuring vibraphonist Milt Jackson, one of many brands of so-called 'cool' jazz: the group experimented with baroque contrapuntal techniques and harmonies directly recalling the classics, using (for example) prominent first-inversion chords – jazz having always preferred stronger root-position harmonies – and directional bass lines as reminiscent of Bach as they were of jazz walking basses. A representative example of the MJQ's laid-back

19 Ibid., p. 548.

counterpoint is their fugal piece 'The Rose Truc', originally written as part of the film score *No Sun in Venice* in 1957, in which entries of the fugue subject are pre-determined and the elusive counter-subjects evidently improvised around them. Like Ellington, Lewis and his associates had no qualms about presenting their live performances in the sanitized ambience of the classical concert hall.

Also responsible for promoting a style of modern jazz greatly appreciated by white intellectual audiences was West Coast pianist Dave Brubeck, whose quartet made legendary appearances at US university campuses from 1953 onwards. With their album *Time Out* (1959), which included Paul Desmond's 'Take Five' (the first jazz instrumental recording to sell over a million copies), the Brubeck Quartet netted an enormous popular following – though the album's bold experiments in additive rhythms were felt by Brubeck's label, Columbia, to be too challenging for commercial success, and accordingly the recording was issued only on condition that he also record a set of standards (*Gone with the Wind*).[20] Both Brubeck and Bill Evans were widely influential on later performers for their radical rethinking of keyboard voicings (which had grown clichéd in the hands of second-rate bop pianists); in the case of Evans, his deep knowledge of classical piano repertoire significantly affected both his harmonic idiom and his performing technique.

Counterpoint, now carefully pre-planned rather than the ebullient and spontaneous heterophony of the old New Orleans style, became the trademark of much cool jazz. The phenomenally popular crooner and trumpeter Chet Baker, for instance, who flourished on the West Coast from 1952 onwards and in terms of systematically marketed adolescent appeal was the jazz equivalent of James Dean, indulged in polished contrapuntal duets with fellow spirits such as baritone saxophonist Gerry Mulligan. Baker's treatment of popular standards (of which by far the most famous was 'My Funny Valentine'), although cool in mood and appropriately unflamboyant in technique, showed bop to be an abiding influence: the head–solos–head structure prevailed, and the improvisational techniques were broadly similar. This is also true of the most renowned of all cool groups, the nonet led by trumpeter Miles Davis in 1948–50 which recorded a group of sides for Capitol, later assembled in 1957 as an LP entitled – with the clear benefit of hindsight – *The Birth of the Cool*.[21] Although the spirited and sometimes disjointed melodic idiom of bop is self-evident in several of these pieces (not surprisingly, since most of the group were bop performers

20 See Darius Brubeck, '1959: The Beginning of Beyond', in Mervyn Cooke and David Horn (eds.), *The Cambridge Companion to Jazz*, Cambridge, 2002, p. 199.

21 For two contrasting critical assessments of *The Birth of the Cool*, see André Hodeir, 'Miles Davis and the Cool Tendency', in Bill Kirchner (ed.), *A Miles Davis Reader*, Washington and London, 1997, pp. 22–37, and Max Harrison, 'Sheer Alchemy, for a While: Miles Davis and Gil Evans', in ibid., pp. 74–103.

and Davis had himself served an apprenticeship with Parker in 1945–8), much of the music is pre-arranged; it explores rich textures and sonorities strongly reminiscent of later Ellington, as reinterpreted by arranger Gil Evans (who drew on his experience of working for Claude Thornhill's innovative band in 1941–8). In addition to the new emphasis on pre-composition, Davis's associates – who, after the nonet disbanded, developed their own types of cool across the United States – were influenced by the example of tenor saxophonist Lester Young, who had shown how a clean instrumental timbre could be just as eloquent as the increasingly strained and strident sonorities cultivated by some bop expressionists.

Davis, Coltrane, and the birth of free jazz

The two instrumentalists who transformed bop from the inside, and in the process acquired for themselves (for very different reasons) huge popular followings, were Miles Davis and tenor saxophonist John Coltrane. Davis's nonet was short-lived, partly because Capitol refused to back the venture further,[22] and for the remainder of the 1950s he continued to work within a lively bop style – at first with a quintet featuring Coltrane (notably on a series of albums for Prestige in 1951–6) and then with a sextet including alto saxophonist Julian 'Cannonball' Adderley and Bill Evans. This augmented ensemble recorded *Kind of Blue*, one of the most influential jazz albums of all time, in 1959. The album acquired a degree of mystique on account of the sextet's apparent lack of prior rehearsal, and was musically significant in part for its promotion of modal techniques (already encountered occasionally in earlier albums by Davis, Bill Evans, and others), which saw a move away from improvising on rapidly changing chord sequences towards improvisation based on the notes of pre-determined scales. This innovation did little to dispel the by now somewhat predictable adherence to the head–solos–head structure, but it did radically change the tonal palette and harmonic rhythm of jazz; so influential were the new modal techniques, and side-effects such as the changing role of the bass line (which at times retained the surface characteristics of the walking bass, but increasingly anchored long stretches of harmonic stasis by the simple devices of bass riffs and pedals), that they were to remain seminal features of both acoustic jazz and jazz-rock in the 1970s. In the 1960s, Davis formed a virtuosic second quintet (featuring pianist Herbie Hancock, saxophonist Wayne Shorter, bassist Ron Carter, and teenage drummer Tony Williams) that brought the sophistication of bop rhythm-section playing to seemingly unsurpassable heights, and at the

22 See Miles Davis with Quincy Troupe, *Miles: The Autobiography*, New York, 1989, p. 131.

same time began to explore techniques that would soon crystallize in Davis's style of jazz-rock.[23]

Coltrane's propensity for frenetic chromaticism created sometimes extreme harmonic tension with the chord changes underlying his improvised solos and made him rather ill-suited to the modal restraints he was forced to adopt when collaborating with Davis on *Kind of Blue*. According to Nat Hentoff, Coltrane commented that it had been Monk's insistence that he play longer and longer solos 'to find new conceptions' that led him to 'go as far as possible on one phrase until I ran out of ideas'; obsessed with harmonic details, he at times felt himself to be 'making jazz through the wrong end of a magnifying glass'.[24] Although Coltrane was relatively at home in a hard-bop style (see, for example, his 1957 Blue Note album *Blue Train*), it was in other directions that his future stylistic development lay. Pushing tonality to its limits in his post-bop idiom, Coltrane espoused two ground-breaking trends in the early 1960s: free jazz and cross-cultural borrowings from world music (chiefly Indian). But it was his deep spirituality, culminating in the prototypical concept album *A Love Supreme* (1964), that made him a popular guru for both blacks and white hippies: the recording sold half a million copies within a year of its release. Again, jazz continued to speak most strongly to a wide lay audience when it showed itself to have an appealing extra-musical dimension – in this case a born-again religiosity that, escalating outside Coltrane's personal control, led to his virtual canonization in a Californian church established in his honour and using *A Love Supreme* as its liturgy.[25]

The vertiginous spontaneity of Coltrane's notorious large-ensemble album *Ascension* (1965) was inspired by the prior efforts of fellow saxophonist Ornette Coleman in originating a type of avant-garde jazz that constituted potentially the most self-destructive watershed the music had yet encountered. Given that bop had, for all its 'revolutionary' characteristics, still found it necessary to assert its status as a modernized continuation of a well-established jazz tradition, with Coleman all that was conventional in jazz seemed in danger of abrogation. Looking back at his early album *The Shape of Jazz to Come* (1959), it now seems clear that in some technical matters – the simple use of bass riffs to anchor complex and at times near-atonal harmony, or the pre-composition of

23 A thorough analytical investigation into these aspects of Davis's 1960s music has been carried out by Charlie Furniss in his M.Phil. dissertation, 'The Origins of Miles Davis's Jazz-Rock Style in his Music of 1965–68', Nottingham University, 2000.

24 Nat Hentoff, 'John Coltrane' [1976], in Gottlieb, *Reading Jazz*, p. 623.

25 See Lewis Porter, Michael Ullmann, and Ed Hazell, *Jazz: From its Origins to the Present*, Englewood Cliffs, NJ, 1993, p. 313. The album was the subject of a ground-breaking article in jazz analysis by Porter, 'John Coltrane's *A Love Supreme*: Jazz Improvisation as Composition', *Journal of the American Musicological Society* 38 (1985), pp. 593–621.

intense unison head melodies – Coleman was exploring territory not dissimilar to the freely exploratory music of Davis's 1960s quintet; the latter developed the 'time no changes' concept, by which conventional rhythmic propulsion was maintained while fixed chord progressions (the 'changes' in jazz parlance) were temporarily abandoned. Considerably more radical in its apparent randomness was Coleman's double-quartet album *Free Jazz* (1960), featuring cornettist Don Cherry and reed-player Eric Dolphy. Ironically, it had taken a wholesale eradication of conventional structural techniques for jazz players to produce music that could now fill an entire side of an LP without interruption, as was the case in both *Free Jazz* and *Ascension*. (The parallel with Schoenberg's liberating plunge into free atonality in 1909 is striking.)

Coleman's *Free Jazz* gave the avant-garde movement its name and explicitly suggested the socio-political dimension later inextricably associated with it. Even more than had been the case with bop, free jazz reflected LeRoi Jones's assertion that 'the irony of being thought "weird" or "deep" by white Americans' was in itself meaningful, putting on a still more 'intellectually and psychologically satisfying level the traditional separation and isolation of the black man from America'. Significantly, that increasing 'separation and isolation' – and, indeed, the equally drastic and partly self-induced ostracization of white free-jazz musicians from their native cultural mainstream – ultimately resulted in the relocation of many important musicians to Europe where their new brands of music could be given free rein and receive the kind of critical accolades denied them in the United States.

Jazz at the movies

In the mean time, critical and popular perspectives on jazz in general had broadened markedly during the 1950s. A creative use of jazz techniques had become universally familiar in movie soundtracks, for example, in stark contrast to the music's role in pre-war cinema, when it was exclusively diegetic in function so that scenes featuring black performers could be neatly excised by district censors in the United States. With Alex North's sultry, jazz-inflected score to *A Streetcar Named Desire* (1951) and Elmer Bernstein's screaming riffs accompanying scenes of drug abuse in *The Man with the Golden Arm* (1955), an association between jazz and low-life continued to prevail in the popular imagination; jazz may now have become relatively commonplace for movie-going audiences, but Hollywood told them in no uncertain terms that its resonances were just as sleazy and potentially immoral as they had been in the early days of sex, alcohol, and drugs. (The deaths of many prominent musicians from substance abuse, and the fact that Sinatra played a jazz-drummer junkie in *The Man with the Golden*

Arm, seemed to prove the point.) The inevitable link between jazz and urban decay persisted at least until Bernard Herrmann's score to *Taxi Driver* (1975); the notion that jazz – albeit of a certain, coolly restrained, type – might equally signify wealth and refinement only began to emerge in film music during the 1980s. Even then, films based on the lives of real or fictional jazz musicians – for example, Bertrand Tavernier's *'Round Midnight* (1986), Clint Eastwood's *Bird* (1988), and Spike Lee's *Mo' Better Blues* (1990) – continued to dwell on the darker side of their subjects.[26]

Some jazz musicians explored more creative applications of their music in films of the later 1950s. In 1957, Miles Davis improvised a music track for Louis Malle's *L'ascenseur pour l'échafaud* (Lift to the Scaffold) which showed how abstract, fragmentary cues – some of them modal – could create oddly disquieting atmospheres; Lewis's MJQ scored Roger Vadim's *Sait-on jamais* (*No Sun in Venice*) in the same year, achieving a similar effect with very different musical means. The Davis–Malle collaboration was a significant influence on the use of jazz in later realist cinema, where it flourished notably in Eastern Europe; an example is the work of Polish pianist Krzysztof Komeda for the early films of Roman Polanski, such as *Knife in the Water* of 1962. Cinema's potential for disseminating popular jazz styles was demonstrated by *Black Orpheus* (1958), which featured music by the Brazilian songwriter Antonio Carlos Jobim and did much to stimulate interest in bossa nova ('new wave'). This cool Latin jazz was promoted by the versatile saxophonist Stan Getz among others, and became a commercial phenomenon in the early 1960s with the success of the hit songs 'The Girl from Ipanema' and 'Desafinado'. In spite of the production of film scores by jazz musicians of the stature of Ellington (*Anatomy of a Murder*, 1959) and Charles Mingus (*Shadows*, 1959), it remained rare for the music to be used in narrative cinema for anything other than plots concerning crime or violence.

Symphonic jazz and the Third Stream

Musicologists and critics rarely paid serious attention to film music in the 1950s and 1960s, so it had to be elsewhere that jazz musicians sought to strengthen appreciation of their art on deeper intellectual levels. One of the most obvious compliments paid to jazz by classical musicians had been the steady succession of jazz-inspired compositions to flow from the pens of leading composers in both Europe and the United States. Beginning with Debussy's and Stravinsky's

26 See Gennari, 'Jazz Criticism', pp. 516–17. For an overview of jazz in the cinema, see Krin Gabbard, *Jammin' at the Margins: Jazz and the American Cinema*, Chicago, 1996.

flirtations with ragtime, interest in symphonic jazz not surprisingly centred on Paris, with Milhaud's *La création du monde* (1923) an early high point. In the 1920s it was expected that American composers would study in Paris, hence Aaron Copland's exposure to both neoclassical Stravinsky and Parisian symphonic jazz during his years there; he took both idioms to the United States when he travelled home in 1924. Copland's early symphonic jazz, best represented by *Music for the Theater* (1925) and the Piano Concerto (1926), was his first attempt at creating an American nationalism in concert music, and was bolder in conception than Gershwin's Broadway-rooted symphonic jazz. At the time, Copland hoped that jazz would become 'the substance not only of the American composer's fox trots and Charlestons, but of his lullabies and nocturnes',[27] but he soon chose to abandon the marriage between jazz and concert music in favour of a more rarefied use of national folk materials. His protégé Leonard Bernstein, however, followed directly in his mentor's footsteps, with *Prelude, Fugue and Riffs* (written for jazz clarinettist Woody Herman in 1949) showing a clear debt to Stravinsky's own idiosyncratic homage to big-band jazz, the *Ebony Concerto* (premiered by Herman's band in 1945). The piano-and-percussion scherzo of Bernstein's Second Symphony, *The Age of Anxiety* (also dating from 1949), is a manically jazzy set-piece typical of the emotional ambivalence characterizing much symphonic jazz: it depicts a group of young hedonists 'convinced that they are having a good time; but there is an element of desperation that negates that feeling'.[28]

Symphonic jazz has become so fully absorbed into the mainstream repertory of colourful mid-twentieth-century orchestral music that it is difficult for the modern listener to recapture the intensity of the debate surrounding its artistic viability at the time. In 1947, for example, the *Esquire Jazz Book* published the conflicting views of Bernstein and swing drummer Gene Krupa. Krupa, obsessed with 'authentic' jazz, deemed Gershwin 'pretentious' and declared his own intention to compose a concerto for 'swing band and symphony' that kept the jazz and classical players separate as if to symbolize their incompatibility. Bernstein, while admitting (somewhat archly) that jazz elements had been insufficiently absorbed by both Gershwin and Stravinsky, noted that jazz had provided the 'serious composer' with a solution to 'the two problems of being original and of being American'. He urged readers to explore more recent music by Copland, Roy Harris, Roger Sessions, William Schuman, and Samuel Barber:

27 Aaron Copland, 'Jazz Structure and Influence', *Modern Music* 4/2 (1927), pp. 9–14, quoted in Aaron Copland and Vivian Perlis, *Copland: 1900 through 1942*, London, 1984, p. 119.

28 Leonard Bernstein, press conference for performance of Symphony No. 2 at the Berlin Festwochen, August 1977, repr. in liner notes to the composer's recording with the Israel Philharmonic Orchestra, Deutsche Grammophon, CD reissue 445 245–2, n.d., p. 9.

'analyses and diagnoses notwithstanding, the great synthesis goes irrevocably on'.[29]

Towards the end of the 1950s, Gunther Schuller (a classically trained horn player, composer, and conductor who had played in the *Birth of the Cool* sessions) made a determined attempt to establish a fresh style of partly pre-composed jazz – conceived more from a jazz perspective than a classical viewpoint, in that improvisation was often a vital ingredient – that would once and for all show that the two musical worlds were not incompatible. To describe the synthesis he coined the term 'Third Stream' during a lecture at Brandeis University in 1957, and was later alarmed when it appeared in a *New York Times* headline in 1960 and became a controversial buzz-phrase. The sudden notoriety of third-stream music took him by surprise, as he had predicted that the two major streams would continue to flow in their separate directions and thus keep the purists happy on both sides:

> I had hoped that in this way the old prejudices, old worries about the purity of the two main streams that have greeted attempts to bring jazz and 'classical' music together could, for once, be avoided. This, however, has not been the case. Musicians and critics in both fields have considered this Third Stream a frontal attack on their own traditions.
>
> Characteristically, the jazz side has protested against the intruder more vigorously than its opposite partner.[30]

Clearly annoyed by his critics, Schuller retorted that third-stream music

> certainly does not expect to generate easy acceptance among those whose musical criteria are determined only on the basis of whether one can snap one's fingers to the music . . . At its best Third Stream can be an extremely subtle music, defying the kind of easy categorization most people seem to need before they can make up their minds whether they should like something or not.[31]

Among the distinguished composers and jazz musicians who espoused Schuller's cause were Milton Babbitt, clarinettist Jimmy Giuffre, bop trombonist J. J. Johnson, John Lewis, and George Russell (whose *Lydian Chromatic Concept of Tonal Organization* was a milestone of 1950s jazz theory).[32] Continuations of the symphonic-jazz tradition conceived along broadly similar lines had also been evident outside the United States, and included Swiss composer Rolf Liebermann's twelve-tone *Concerto for Jazz Band and Symphony Orchestra* (1954) and a notable British collaboration between Dankworth and Mátyás

29 The Krupa–Bernstein debate is reprinted in Gottlieb, *Reading Jazz*, pp. 774–84.

30 Gunther Schuller, 'Third Stream' [1961], in *Musings: The Musical Worlds of Gunther Schuller*, New York, 1986, p. 115.

31 Ibid., p. 116.

32 George Russell, *The Lydian Chromatic Concept of Tonal Organisation*, New York, 1953 [2nd edn, 1959].

Seiber (*Improvisations for Jazz Band and Symphony Orchestra*, 1958), which featured twelve-tone symphonic writing alongside jazz improvisations and big-band swing.

Schuller went on to establish a unique third-stream department at the New England Conservatory, of which he became President in 1967. Its 1981 publicity brochure claimed that Third Stream represented 'a beautiful brotherhood/sisterhood of musics that complement and fructify each other', a phenomenon that is 'quintessentially American'.[33]

Fusions and redefinitions

The future of jazz was highly uncertain at the start of the 1960s, the stylistic and cultural waters surrounding it having been muddied by numerous apparently incompatible trends.[34] Outside the Third Stream, few musicians chose to follow the example of Ellington in attempting to combine recognizable jazz elements with a sophisticated attitude to composition. (That came later, when a new generation of jazz musicians graduated from university and college music courses in the 1970s.) A glaring exception was bassist and composer Charles Mingus, who mixed esoteric experimentation with earthy African-American elements in such seminal albums as *Mingus Ah Um* (1959) and *The Black Saint and the Sinner Lady* (1963), and whose epic composition *Epitaph* was posthumously realized by Schuller in 1989.

The striking growth of free jazz in the 1960s, while partly an expression of the times (both in paralleling aleatory techniques in classical music, and in its more outspoken political connotations), seemed to mark the abrupt end of jazz's sometimes frustrating quest for popular acceptance. At the same time, free jazz came closer to avant-garde classical music than at any other time: the Blue Note album *Unit Structures* (1966) by pianist Cecil Taylor, for example, with its Webern-like *Klangfarbenmelodie*, apparently mathematical precision, and non-jazz instrumentation (e.g. the inclusion of an oboe), was still further removed from the popular notion of jazz than Coleman's chaotic *Free Jazz* had been six years previously. For those who subscribed to a teleological view of musical history, jazz seemed finally to have caught up with art-music

33 Gunther Schuller, 'Third Stream Revisited' [1981], in *Musings*, pp. 119–20. For a list of representative third-stream works composed since the 1950s, see Schuller's own entry on 'Third Stream' in Barry Kernfeld (ed.), *The New Grove Dictionary of Jazz*, London and New York, 1988; one-volume reprint, 1994, p. 1199.

34 As Berliner noted, these trends remained distinct even in the 1990s as a result of 'discrete camps of musicians with specialized loyalties to one or another of the tradition's idioms' (*Thinking in Jazz*, p. 279).

experimentation after four decades of assimilating a compendium of classical techniques.[35]

Never before had the question 'is it jazz?' seemed so relevant, or the answer so resoundingly negative. Leading exponents of free jazz formed themselves into cliques in Chicago and elsewhere; free from the burdens of commercial success (which many seemed to go out of their way to avoid), the movement was imbued with a deep artistic and political seriousness that belied the fact that no one really wanted to listen to its music. Some American free-jazz artists, such as the Art Ensemble of Chicago and Sun Ra's Myth-Science Arkestra, gained wider exposure through the incorporation of theatrical elements in their performances. Others emigrated to Europe, where they were to exert a powerful influence on trends in modern European jazz, some learning to temper their often aggressive originality with an admixture of more popular elements. Once again, Europe proved itself to be a forum more receptive to innovation in jazz (perhaps because of its less rigid categorization of idioms) than its country of origin, with labels such as Italy's Black Saint offering numerous recording opportunities to American musicians in the 1970s.

A bitter opponent of free jazz was Miles Davis, in spite of the increasing freedom evident in his own music in the 1960s. In a blindfold listening test published in *Down Beat* in 1968, and later in his autobiography, he unfairly blamed white audiences for hyping black free jazz because 'they don't want to have to admit that a black person could be doing something that they don't know about'.[36] With his own brand of post-bop (both live and on record) playing to dwindling audiences, Davis resented his label Columbia's mass marketing of ascendant rock stars – among them Blood Sweat & Tears and Chicago, who signed with Columbia in 1968 and 1969 respectively – while jazz was relegated to the catalogue's margins and, as Davis put it, 'withered on the vine'.[37] He persuaded the label's president, Clive Davis, to rethink its marketing policy, and reconfigured his own musical style to draw heavily on the surface characteristics of rock (or, more accurately, rhythm and blues) in an attempt to capture the attention of the swathes of youthful listeners who were no longer enticed to listen to jazz. Although certain techniques associated with Davis's

35 See for example Schuller, writing in 1977: 'There is a view, shared by many jazz historians and writers, that the history of jazz parallels in its broad outlines that of Western classical music – only on a much briefer time scale: what took nearly nine centuries in European music is concentrated into a mere six decades in jazz' ('The Avant-Garde and Third Stream', repr. in *Musings*, pp. 121–33; p. 121). For a contrary view, see DeVeaux, 'Constructing the Jazz Tradition', *passim*.

36 Davis and Troupe, *Miles: The Autobiography*, p. 241. All Davis's *Down Beat* blindfold tests, which were conducted by Leonard Feather, are reprinted in Kirchner, *A Miles Davis Reader*, pp. 123–39. Davis's condemnation of Don Cherry, John Tchicai and Archie Shepp appears on p. 135, where he misidentifies Shepp as Ornette Coleman: 'Ornette sounds the same way. That's where Archie and them got that shit from; there sure ain't nothing there.'

37 Davis and Troupe, *Miles: The Autobiography*, p. 287.

new style – such as 'straight' (i.e. not swung) rhythms, modal improvisations, and static bass riffs – had increasingly surfaced in his acoustic jazz of the earlier 1960s, he now intensified these elements in prolonged, open-ended structures featuring prominent electric sonorities, chiefly electric bass and multiple electric keyboards. Later known as jazz-rock fusion, the style (boldly termed 'New Directions in Music' in Columbia's publicity) was launched by the album *In a Silent Way* and the extraordinarily intense double-album *Bitches Brew*, both recorded in 1969 using creative tape-editing techniques that were radically to change musicians' attitudes towards studio work.

Jazz-rock fusion was almost as much about image and packaging as it was about musical substance.[38] Jazz had long been in danger of seeming too exclusive or elitist, no matter in which new direction it headed: largely pre-composed ensemble jazz was too close to classical formalism, the improvisations of Davis and Coltrane were too complex to follow, and the hard-core avant-garde seemed to be purveying meaningless noise, its secrets only revealed to an inner core of cognoscenti. Furthermore, mainstream jazz now seemed squeaky-clean, having lost its association with youthful rebellion and illicit activities. Davis's fusion albums deliberately and successfully seduced rock fans with heady electronics and 'concept' orientation (in which flamboyant sleeve artwork played a vital role), and in live performances he and his sidemen adopted a trendy manner of dress to make themselves directly comparable with rock superstars; Davis even assumed the fashionable soubriquet 'Prince of Darkness'. Over-hyped, these ventures nevertheless drew on the most far-reaching of Davis's earlier techniques and represented a significant stylistic advance in jazz, much to the consternation of purists who lamented Davis's calculated 'sell-out'.[39]

Columbia's gamble paid off handsomely: sales of *Bitches Brew* comfortably broke all previous records for jazz, and Davis instantly found himself playing live to thousands of 'mostly white hippies' alongside popular bands such as The Grateful Dead.[40] Biting the hand that fed him, however, Davis blamed inept marketing on Columbia's part for the failure of his album *On the Corner* in 1972, and resented their spectacular success with Herbie Hancock's funky *Headhunters* in 1973. By this time, Davis's creativity was dwindling, and while he was self-consciously trying to justify his rambling electronic soundscapes

38 For a detailed survey of fusion, see Stuart Nicholson, *Jazz-Rock: A History*, Edinburgh, 1998.

39 For an outspoken attack on Davis's later work, see Stanley Crouch, 'On the Corner: The Sellout of Miles Davis' [1995], in Gottlieb (ed.), *Reading Jazz*, pp. 898–914. A more positive view, which includes criticism of Crouch's position, is offered by Gary Tomlinson in his 'Cultural Dialogics and Jazz: A White Historian Signifies', *Black Music Research Journal* 11/2 (1991), pp. 249–64.

40 Davis and Troupe, *Miles: The Autobiography*, p. 290.

with reference to influences as diverse as Sly Stone and Stockhausen, it was left to his younger sidemen from the 1969 sessions to capitalize on the artistic potential of his recent innovations. Apart from Hancock, whose career balanced work as a hard-bop pianist with other phenomenal pop successes such as *Rockit* (which reached number one in the charts in 1983), Davis's one-time keyboard players Joe Zawinul and Chick Corea both led highly successful fusion groups from the 1970s into the twenty-first century. With the collaboration of Wayne Shorter, Zawinul's Weather Report in particular produced a stream of albums (also for Columbia, whose market dominance shaped fusion consumption across the globe in the 1980s) that showed how melodic memorability, harmonic experimentation, unpredictable pre-composed structures, and popular appeal were not incompatible. British guitarist John McLaughlin's Mahavishnu Orchestra (also recorded by Columbia) and his smaller acoustic ensemble Shakti both added Indian philosophy and world-music elements to the heady stylistic mix.

Neither avant-garde jazz nor more conventional acoustic jazz, both of which seemed as elitist as the classics in the 1970s and 1980s, could compete for popularity with the multifarious and highly colourful offshoots of fusion. The latter's impact on film and television music was considerable, with some composers adapting their style to embrace its characteristics as a way of updating the funky big-band sound that Henry Mancini had already popularised in his music to the television series *Peter Gunn* (1958) and, later, the series of *Pink Panther* movies. Third-stream pioneer Lalo Schifrin, for example, brought a type of fusion – sometimes termed 'urban cool' – to the big screen in scores such as *Bullitt* (1968), and composed influential rock-tinged music for television series such as *Mission: Impossible* (1966) and *Starsky and Hutch* (pilot episode, 1975); Schifrin's musical education was typical of his generation, since he balanced a classical training with Messiaen at the Paris Conservatoire with wide experience as both bop pianist and arranger for Gillespie. Film composer Jerry Goldsmith combined Stravinskyan octatonicism – which jazz musicians call the 'diminished scale' – with jazz-rock in his title music to *Escape from the Planet of the Apes* (1971), part of one of the most successful movie franchises of the era. Limited doses of free jazz found a commercially viable outlet when included as single tracks on otherwise mass-appeal fusion albums, such as Weather Report's *Mr Gone* (1978) and the Pat Metheny Group's *Offramp* (1981); conversely, avant-garde pioneer Ornette Coleman adopted popular electronics with the foundation of his own fusion band, Prime Time, in 1975.

In the United States, trumpeter Wynton Marsalis (who won Grammy awards for both classical and jazz recordings in 1984) did much to rescue mainstream acoustic jazz from incipient oblivion. Other notable performers, principally pianists, continued to pursue dual careers in both fusion and acoustic jazz in the 1980s. Unfortunately, Marsalis was unaccountably intolerant of fusion – his much-publicized personality clash with Miles Davis seemed to epitomize the schism between purism and populism in jazz – and at times appeared to be preoccupied with a historically aware quest for rediscovering the spirit of 'authentic' jazz at the expense of bolder experimentation. One positive result of the rise of this jazz neoclassicism has been the ongoing systematic preservation of the American jazz heritage, although this suggests a process of canon-formation which makes many commentators distinctly uncomfortable – even as they appreciate the need to preserve, through transcription and performance, material which might otherwise disappear.

The vital position of jazz in twentieth-century music was officially recognized in 1987 when the US Congress declared it to be a national treasure. The formal resolution stated, in flamboyant terms, that jazz had brought 'to this country and the world a uniquely American musical synthesis and culture through the African-American experience'; that it was 'an outstanding artistic model of individual expression and democratic cooperation within the creative process'; a 'unifying force' bridging numerous social gaps; 'a true music of the people' with 'a historic, pervasive, and continuing influence on other genres of music'; and 'a true international language adopted by musicians around the world as a music best able to express contemporary realities from a personal perspective' – the point of all this being that, even in the late 1980s, its country of origin lamented that a 'great American musical art form has not yet been properly recognized nor accorded the institutional status commensurate with its value and importance'.[41]

Jazz in Europe embraced popular fusion in its own complex stylistic mix to create a synthetic style that continues to attract a substantial middle-of-the-road audience. The major success story in this regard was the label ECM (Edition of Contemporary Music), established by Manfred Eicher in Cologne in 1969: the label's house style was one of the most distinctive and enduring of all musical idioms to emerge during the last quarter of the century. It proved flexible enough to embrace lyrical acoustic jazz by major US performers (such as pianist Keith Jarrett), popular fusion artists (guitarist Pat Metheny), free jazz with a liberal dose of world music (Don Cherry), and distinctively European jazz blending folk elements with aspects of fusion and the avant-garde (including the Norwegian saxophonist Jan Garbarek, whose bestselling 1993 album

41 The full text of House Congressional Resolution 57 is reproduced in Berliner, *Thinking in Jazz*, appendix A, p. 759, and in Robert Walser (ed.), *Keeping Time: Readings in Jazz History*, New York, 1999, p. 333.

Officium showed that it was still possible for a single crossover project simultaneously to attract the attention of huge numbers of classical and jazz listeners). Although the term 'crossover' has become popular when describing the continuing erosion of perceived social and artistic barriers affecting the packaging and consumption of music, 'fusion' (if it had not become so tainted by the heated debates between jazz purists and jazz-rockers) would perhaps be a more appropriate word to describe the often satisfying and broadly appealing stylistic amalgams that continue to characterize jazz – much in the spirit of its origins as a perennially fertile cultural hybrid.

Bibliography

Berliner, Paul. *Thinking in Jazz: The Infinite Art of Improvisation*, Chicago, 1994.
Blesh, Rudi. *Shining Trumpets: A History of Jazz*, New York, 1946.
Brubeck, Darius. '1959: The Beginning of Beyond', in Mervyn Cooke and David Horn (eds.), *The Cambridge Companion to Jazz*, Cambridge, 2002, pp. 177–201.
Carr, Ian. *Miles Davis: A Critical Biography*, London, 1982; 2nd edn, *Miles Davis: The Definitive Biography*, London, 1999.
Clarke, Donald. *The Rise and Fall of Popular Music*, London, 1995.
Cooke, Mervyn and David Horn (eds.). *The Cambridge Companion to Jazz*, Cambridge, 2002.
Cooke, Mervyn. *Jazz*, London, 1998.
'Jazz amongst the Classics, and the Case of Duke Ellington', in Mervyn Cooke and David Horn (eds.), *The Cambridge Companion to Jazz*, Cambridge, 2002, pp. 153–73.
Copland, Aaron and Vivian Perlis. *Copland: 1900 Through 1942*, London, 1984.
Copland, Aaron. 'Jazz Structure and Influence', *Modern Music* 4/2 (1927), pp. 9–14.
Davis, Miles with Quincy Troupe. *Miles: The Autobiography*, New York, 1989.
DeVeaux, Scott. 'Constructing the Jazz Tradition: Jazz Historiography', *Black American Literature Forum* 25/3 (1991), pp. 525–60.
Early, Gerald. 'White Noise and White Knights: Some Thoughts on Race, Jazz, and the White Jazz Musician', in Geoffrey C. Ward and Ken Burns (eds.), *Jazz: A History of America's Music*, New York, 2000, pp. 324–31.
Furniss, Charlie. 'The Origins of Miles Davis's Jazz-Rock Style in his Music of 1965–68', M.Phil. diss., Nottingham University, 2000.
Gabbard, Krin (ed.). *Jazz Among the Discourses*, Durham, NC, 1995, pp. 1–28.
Jammin' at the Margins: Jazz and the American Cinema, Chicago, 1996.
Gendron, Bernard. '"Moldy Figs" and Modernists: Jazz at War (1942–1946)', in Krin Gabbard (ed.), *Jazz Among the Discourses*, Durham, NC, 1995, pp. 31–56.
Gennari, John. 'Jazz Criticism: Its Development and Ideologies', *Black American Literature Forum* 25/3 (1991), pp. 449–523.
Godbolt, Jim. *A History of Jazz in Britain 1919–50*, London, 1984.
Gottlieb, Robert (ed.). *Reading Jazz*, London, 1997.
Jones, LeRoi [Amiri Baraka]. *Blues People: Negro Music in White America*, New York, 1963.

Kater, Michael H. *Different Drummers: Jazz in the Culture of Nazi Germany*, New York, 1992.
Kernfeld, Barry (ed.). *The New Grove Dictionary of Jazz*, London, 1988; one-volume reprint, 1994.
Kirchner, Bill (ed.). *A Miles Davis Reader*, Washington, 1997.
Lees, Gene. *Cats of Any Color: Jazz, Black and White*, Oxford, 1994.
Nicholson, Stuart. *Jazz-Rock: A History*, Edinburgh, 1998.
Porter, Lewis. 'John Coltrane's *A Love Supreme*: Jazz Improvisation as Composition', *Journal of the American Musicological Society* 38 (1985), pp. 593–621.
Porter, Lewis, Michael Ullmann and Ed Hazell. *Jazz: From its Origins to the Present*, Englewood Cliffs, NJ, 1993.
Russell, George. *The Lydian Chromatic Concept of Tonal Organisation*, New York, 1953.
Schuller, Gunther. *Musings: The Musical Worlds of Gunther Schuller*, New York, 1999.
Sudhalter, Richard M. *Lost Chords: White Musicians and Their Contribution to Jazz 1915–1945*, New York, 1999.
Tomlinson, Gary. 'Cultural Dialogics and Jazz: A White Historian Signifies', *Black Music Research Journal* 11/2 (1991), pp. 249–64; repr. in Katherine Bergeron and Philip V. Bohlman (eds.), *Disciplining Music: Musicology and its Canons*, Chicago, 1992, pp. 64–94.
Tucker, Mark (ed.). *The Duke Ellington Reader*, New York, 1993.
Walser, Robert (ed.). *Keeping Time: Readings in Jazz History*, New York, 1999.
Williams, Martin (ed.). *The Art of Jazz*, New York, 1959.

Discography

Brubeck, Dave. *Gone with the Wind* (Columbia, 1959)
Time Out (Columbia, 1959)
Coleman, Ornette. *The Shape of Jazz to Come* (Atlantic, 1959)
Free Jazz (Atlantic, 1960)
Coltrane, John. *Blue Train* (Blue Note, 1957)
A Love Supreme (Impulse!, 1964)
Ascension (Impulse!, 1965)
Davis, Miles. *L'ascenseur pour l'échafaud* (Fontana, 1957)
Birth of the Cool (Capitol, 1957 [rec. 1949–50])
Kind of Blue (Columbia, 1959)
In a Silent Way (Columbia, 1969)
Bitches Brew (Columbia, 1969)
On the Corner (Columbia, 1972)
Ellington, Duke. *Black, Brown and Beige* (Victor, 1943)
Anatomy of a Murder (Columbia, 1959)
Garbarek, Jan. *Officium* (ECM, 1993)
Hancock, Herbie. *Headhunters* (Columbia, 1973)
'Rockit' from *Future Shock* (Columbia, 1983)
Metheny, Pat. *Offramp* (ECM, 1981)
Miller, Glenn. *In the Mood* (Bluebird, 1939)
Moonlight Serenade (Bluebird, 1939)

Mingus, Charles. *Mingus Ah Um* (Columbia, 1959)
The Black Saint and the Sinner Lady (Impulse!, 1963)
Modern Jazz Quartet. *No Sun in Venice*, a.k.a. *Sait-on jamais* (Atlantic, 1957)
Morgan, Lee. *The Sidewinder* (Blue Note, 1963)
Taylor, Cecil. *Unit Structures* (Blue Note, 1966)
Weather Report. *Mr Gone* (Columbia, 1978)

· 16 ·

Music of the youth revolution: rock through the 1960s

ROBYNN STILWELL

The story usually goes something like this:

> *Once upon a time, in the early 1950s, black rhythm and blues and white country music were married in the southern United States and gave birth to rock and roll, a blast of youthful energy that disrupted the stultifying blandness of a self-satisfied and conservative affluent post-war society. Parents were horrified, but the kids were more open-minded and rebellious than previous generations, and the course of musical events was completely and irrevocably changed. After a few short years of revolution, many of the major players were sidelined for various reasons (most of which are open to a reading of conspiracy by the US government afraid of the growing power of teenagers and African-American culture), and music entered a dead zone between 1958 and 1963, during which nothing of any interest or import happened. This all changed with the rise of the Beatles, the British blues boom, and the flowering of real revolution – political, sexual, racial, artistic – which was heralded by the arrival of the rock god in his many guises and reached its pinnacle in the hedonistic festival culture of the late 1960s. Afterwards came decadence and decline, only to be shaken up by a new revolution in which the Bicentennial of American Independence and the Silver Jubilee of Elizabeth II in England were disrupted by the arrival of punk. The Goths were at the walls.*

But that's a story for another night.

Like most myths and legends, this fairy story tells us more about the culture that tells it than it does about the historical events on which it is based. It is the classic Western tale of rise and fall, whether of the individual or the civilization. How much of the truth of those historical events survives? Are any of these truths recoverable at this late date? These may seem foolish questions about something that happened within living memory, but that is indeed largely where it exists – in the living memory of people who experienced the events along highly personal pathways, in oral histories, in the words of journalists and critics who very often had their own agendas. The same is true of many movements, of course, but the convergence of music history, socio-political history, and technological and economic development in the case of rock and roll is particularly volatile, even more so than at the similar birth of jazz some half a century earlier.

Part of the difficulty in dealing with the history of rock and roll is that myth-making is very much part of the ideology. Rock and roll is the last bastion of the Romantic ideal, melding the European drive towards self-expression with the American ethos of individualism, raising to godlike status those charismatic lead singers like Mick Jagger and Jim Morrison, or guitarists like Eric Clapton and Jimi Hendrix. They must suffer for their art and in their music tell a genuine truth in an 'authentic' musical style. But this ideology only arose in the mid-1960s, well into what is perceived as the 'history' of rock and roll, and all that comes before it is coloured by this outlook. As the legend begins to be told, it is, like any story, told in the light of concerns of the present. That which does not fit is left aside, even hidden.[1]

So does our fairy story contain any truth? Certainly it does, but it also seems a very partial, idealized truth. Although the project of this chapter is to present a history of rock and roll up to the 1969 Woodstock festival (a symbolic enough moment at which to end), its underlying aim is to question the easy 'truths', to point out possible alternative readings of received wisdom, to question how the romance relates to both musical style and social history.

The prehistory and contexts of rock and roll

In most histories of the twentieth century, whether musical or general, there is a sense of a break at mid-century; the upheaval of the Second World War, and the social, economic, political, and technological changes that happened afterwards, certainly contribute to such a perception. However, in the case of popular music, the perceived stylistic revolution of the rock era – usually dated from the huge success of Bill Haley and the Comets' 'Rock Around the Clock' in 1955, helped along by its use in the film *Blackboard Jungle* – is a little overstated; one can hear music from as early as the late 1920s which in a later time might be labelled rock and roll, and the styles that would feed into the 'new' sound were developed throughout the 1930s and 40s, largely in the southern United States, predominantly by African Americans, but also by rural whites.

The fairy tale says that rock and roll was the melding of black and white; a variant is that the music is black and was only appropriated by whites. There

1 The Britpop movement of the mid-1990s was an excellent example of this, striving to re-present a distinctively English musical past in which the strong blues element was effectively erased (artists like The Rolling Stones, The Animals, and Eric Clapton were marginalized, while The Beatles' American sources were also underplayed). The explanation of this rewriting of the 1960s lay in the threat posed to the British music industry during the 1990s by the dominance of American grunge.

is certainly truth in both readings, but each is incomplete and far simpler than the reconstructable history. That the situation is clearly more complex can be highlighted by bringing up the issue of the Latin element, so fundamental to the style of rock and roll. The famous 'Bo Diddley' rhythm, one of the stylistic markers of 1950s rock and roll, is a variation of the clavé (3+3+3+3+2+2) beat that originates in the Caribbean, as does the basic rumba/habañera (3+3+2) rhythm that underlies many early rhythm and blues (hereafter 'R&B') and rock songs, including 'The Twist'. A Caribbean rhythm of this kind is the product of Hispanic and African mixing; but Hispanic music comes to the New World already 'pre-mixed' in the multi-cultural world of medieval Spain, where gypsy, North African, Arabic, Jewish, Iberian, Celtic, and Southern European styles all coexisted and intermingled.[2] The question arises clearly with Hispanic music: how long does the mixing have to go on before it is recognized as something distinctive in itself? The question is no less pertinent in the case of rock and roll – clearly not just a matter of black and white, but of browns and greys as well – but because the history is so recent and the politics so raw, it is a vexed one.

In a study of Caribbean music, Peter Manuel concisely sketched out the issue:

> For the last two centuries, scholars (and pseudoscholars) have argued about the degree to which black communities in the Caribbean and the United States have been able to retain elements of their traditional African cultural roots. A persistent white view had been that Africa had little particular culture to begin with, and that the slaves had lost touch with that as well. Anthropologist Melville Herskovits challenged this conception in his *The Myth of the Negro Past* (1941), and in his wake, scholars have devoted many volumes to documenting or claiming the existence of African-derived elements in modern Afro-American and Afro-Caribbean cultures. Such writing has also criticised the tendency to regard slaves as passive victims of circumstance, instead stressing the ways in which slaves and free blacks fashioned their own culture – 'the world the slaves made', as the subtitle reads in historian Eugene Genovese's influential *Roll, Jordan, Roll* (1974). In recent decades, the scholarly pendulum may have swung a bit too far in the direction of emphasizing the ability of slaves to retain and construct their own cultures.[3]

This binary view of black and white has led to the frequent use of the term 'hybridization' which implies a simple cross between two things. However,

2 The common denomination of 'African' is problematic in itself, because of course Africa is a huge continent with many musical cultures. Since most of the slaves brought to the New World were from West Africa, it is the traditions of West African tribes which are conflated as 'African'.

3 Peter Manuel, with Kenneth Bilby and Michael Largey, *Caribbean Currents: Caribbean Music from Rumba to Reggae*, Philadelphia, 1995, p. 6.

culture is rarely that simple, and music almost never is. Manuel proposes an alternative:

> A key concept in the formation of Caribbean culture and music is identified by the rather inelegant term *creolisation*, which connotes the development of a distinctive new culture out of the prolonged encounter of two or more other cultures. The process is also described as 'syncretism', although 'creolisation' is particularly appropriate in the Caribbean, due to the long usage of the term *creole* there and its ability to suggest some of the complex sociocultural issues also involved in the process. In linguistic terms, a creole language is one evolved through the blending of two or more prior languages; the creole language subsequently becomes a native tongue to later generations, who may forget or lose contact with the original languages. The process is more than, say, the mixing of blue and yellow to make green, since people are active, creative agents, not inert chemicals, and the new human product, whether a language or a musical style, takes on a life of its own.[4]

The term seems to fit the situation in the Caribbean quite well, as Manuel points out, but in his description we find nothing that would make it exclusive to the Caribbean; on the contrary, it could fit the situation in the American South as well. The only caveat is that it is not *one* musical style that arises, but many, and the strength of the different strains varies from style to style and place to place. An example of such different 'weightings' of influence can be found in Louisiana, where Cajun music and zydeco share a number of traits, though zydeco is more strongly tinged with blues and R&B, and Cajun music tends to have more waltzes.

Another political factor affecting the myth is that the birthplace of rock and roll, although it cannot be pinned down to one particular city, is in the South: the Mississippi River from St Louis through Memphis down to the New Orleans delta, Texas, and the Smoky and Blue Ridge mountain ranges of Kentucky and Tennessee. From colonial times, the North and the South have been different cultures, settled by different groups of immigrants, driven by different economies and different values; but the industrial, mercantile, and religiously Puritanical North has always politically and economically dominated the rural, agricultural, more hedonistic (even in its religious practices) South. After the American Civil War (1860–5), the South was literally a defeated and occupied country, and the histories, musical and otherwise, have tended to be told by those of a different culture,[5] leading to misunderstandings

4 Manuel, *Caribbean Currents*, p. 14.

5 A significant contribution to a history of the South by the South can be found in the relatively recent publication of *An Encyclopedia of Southern Culture*, ed. Charles Reagan Wilson and William Ferris, 4 vols., New York, 1989, which not only offers a distinctive interpretive orientation but also contains many entries on musical practice.

and misinterpretations as fundamental as the perceived musical segregation between black and white.[6]

Many of the social factors contributing to the rise of rock and roll emerged in the decades before the 1950s. The increased migration of poor blacks and whites North and West in the 1930s, in search of employment due to the Depression and the agricultural disaster of the Dust Bowl, created new cultural and racial mixings and fostered feelings of uprootedness. The Second World War likewise created a need for racial mixing as well as female entry into the workplace in the face of national emergency, and once the walls of segregation were breached it was difficult to turn back; this probably only accelerated changes already in place. The post-war industrial boom also encouraged emigration from the South.

The generally perceived blandness of American society in the 1950s is reinforced by media representations of the time, such as the family-based television situation comedy (for instance, *Father Knows Best*, *Leave It to Beaver*, *The Adventures of Ozzie and Harriet*, *The Donna Reed Show*), and of later periods, such as the wave of 1950s nostalgia in the 1970s (*Happy Days*, *Grease*). However, these representations were perhaps more a kind of social control than a reflection of truth, a subtler containment of anxiety over the changing dynamics of race, gender, generation, and class than the political tensions of the Cold War and the fear of nuclear holocaust evidenced by popular science fiction and monster movies. More recent representations of the era, such as the television series *M*A*S*H* (1972–83), Billy Joel's song 'We Didn't Start the Fire' (1989), and particularly the film *Pleasantville* (1998), have focused on this dichotomy.

The 1950s have often been cited as having 'invented' the teenager, as increased affluence and changing social values extended childhood through the teen years. Most adolescents no longer had to go to work; allowances from parents and afternoon and weekend jobs meant that they had a disposable income and relatively few responsibilities, and more and more went to college, especially girls. All of these changes go at least as far back as the previous post-war upheaval and musical revolution, the 'jazz age' of the 1920s, but in the 1950s it was happening on a much larger scale. Jazz itself had developed into something more self-consciously artistic, first with bebop and then cool jazz and modalism; the intellectualism, the increasing sophistication, and the proliferation of various styles were moving jazz away from the dance floor and

6 Most assume that whites listened to black music but not vice versa. For example, refuting the assumptions of musical segregation to a surprised British interviewer on the series *All Back to Mine* (Channel 4 [UK], 2000), musician Gil Scott Heron remembered growing up in Tennessee listening to a variety of music by black and white artists, including Elvis Presley. Rufus Thomas has spoken often of listening to *The Grand Ole Opry* on radio; his daughter Carla's 1960 hit 'Gee Whiz' certainly shows country influences, including a fiddle solo, and she later recorded in Nashville.

a popular audience. It was becoming 'parents' music', something that very few generations have been able to stomach.

Just as the development of affordable gramophones helped jazz cross boundaries of class, race, and geography, a number of technological developments of the late 1940s and early 1950s created a context in which the coming revolution could occur. One was the cheap and relatively indestructible 45 rpm single, which replaced large, heavy, brittle 78s. Another was the opening up in post-war America of many more radio frequencies for commercial broadcasting, and FM radio, the improved quality of which allowed broadcasting in the newly developed stereo format. By the end of the 1960s, a split would open up between singles-driven AM radio, easily accessible on cheap, portable transistor radios and associated with Top 40 and adolescent listeners, and the album-oriented, stereo-quality FM radio that would foster the development of a connoisseur listenership of rock and roll – much the same as had happened in jazz twenty years earlier. But in the early 1950s it was the AM stations, which could broadcast over astonishing distances depending on weather conditions, that were opening listeners' ears to a wide variety of styles. Many of these styles had been around for some years, but they were now reaching new audiences across social and geographical boundaries.

Musical origins and revolution

The term 'rock and roll' has been attributed to the legendary Cleveland disc jockey Alan Freed, but like 'jazz' before it, the term is, in some Southern African-American communities, a euphemism for sex. Charlie Gillett mentions several songs from the late 1940s and early 1950s, including Roy Brown's 'Good Rockin' Tonight' (1947) and The Ravens' 'Rock All Night Long' (1948), in which the dual meaning of rock and roll as both sex and dance is exploited.[7] However, the phrase appears in songs dating back to the 1920s and had been used as a song title as early as 1934 in the recording 'Rock and Roll' by The Boswell Sisters, a New Orleans trio of white women who certainly sound 'black' by most modern criteria of accent and performance style (Ella Fitzgerald has even been quoted as wanting 'to sound like Connie Boswell'[8]). The creole nature of what would become rock and roll was established years before the 'rock and roll era'.

Rock and roll is effectively an umbrella term for the various styles of music emerging from the South in the 1950s, disseminated by radio, records, and

7 Charlie Gillett, *The Sound of the City: The Rise of Rock and Roll* (rev. and expanded edn), London, 1983, p. 3.

8 David Hajdu and Roy Hemming, *Discovering Great Singers of Classic Pop*, New York, 1991, p. 66.

jukeboxes. The fairytale nomination of R&B and country as the 'parents' of rock is true as far it goes, although in practice these musics, while perceived as separate, had been coexisting and cross-fertilizing for many years before the 1950s. It may be one of those 'unrecoverables' to determine to what extent they were actually separate traditions in the South before the advent of recording. In the 1920s, recording companies eager to capitalize on the new technology sent scouts out into the field to find and record new talent. Recordings were divided into different marketing categories, and white artists were marketed to white audiences on one label, whereas black artists were marketed to black audiences on another. This was the beginning of the so-called 'race record' practice. However, there is strong anecdotal evidence that this division was an artificial one; the Carter Family, for instance, recorded 'River of Jordan' in 1928, a song that had been taught to them by a family friend who happened to be black, and although the white singer Jimmie Rodgers has been hailed as the 'father of country', he was considered by many musicians, black and white, to have been a blues singer. The famous 'Leadbelly' (Huddie Ledbetter), considered at the time of his recordings in the 1940s to be a blues singer, was closer to the folk or country balladeer (sometimes called a 'songster') than what is now recognized as blues; this may also indicate a slippage of terminology in the intervening years.

R&B and country had common antecedents in gospel music; although this is considered by many from outside the South to be a wholly African-American phenomenon, there is an identifiable white gospel tradition. While separation may again be purely superficial and based on skin tone rather than musical content, there are stylistic differences, often gradations rather than sharp differences. For instance, group singing with close harmony is fundamental to both styles, but in the white tradition the voices tend to be homophonic or imitative, whereas the call-and-response pattern, which evolved into the leader and backing group, is more prevalent in the black tradition (though certainly not unknown in white traditions, particularly in the practice of 'lining out', a mnemonic device in which the leader sketches out the shape and words of a line for a congregation that may be illiterate). Both styles are often heavily ornamented, though the preferred full-voiced or falsetto timbres of the black tradition allow for greater flexibility in swoops, runs and timbral shading than does the white tradition's reedy, nasal tone, which lends itself more to slides, breaks, and yodelling inflections. But again, these are all just tendencies rather than hard and fast divisions.

In rural cultures within which gospel singing is not merely worship but also social activity, the singing styles influence and are influenced by other kinds of singing, and these lie at the heart of R&B and country singing. One of the finest R&B singers of the 1950s, Sam Cooke, began his career as the lead singer of the gospel quartet The Soul Stirrers (from 1950 until his departure to become a solo singer in 1957); gospel quartet singing, blended with the nonsensical but musical syllables of jazz 'scat' singing, is probably at the base of the northern, urban practice of 'doo-wop' singing performed by groups of young black (and Italian) men on the street corners of cities like Philadelphia and New York, and having influence far beyond its 'pure' stylistic manifestations. Little Richard's flamboyant delivery was heavily influenced by black Baptist preaching and female gospel singers including his grandmother, while Elvis Presley sang gospel through his formative years; with The Jordanaires backing him up, he helped bring the black gospel quartet sound to a popular audience (even though they were white). Even the close, head-voiced harmonies of the Everly Brothers are clearly traceable to the shape-note singing traditions of the Appalachian mountains and Deep South.

Chicago boogie-woogie and New Orleans R&B are other major tributaries to rock and roll. The bands were often configured like a swing big band or a small jazz combo; the music was harmonically simpler, usually based on the twelve-bar blues, but more rhythmically energetic (one of the alternative names of the style is 'jump blues') and more typically vocal. The piano was a prominent feature, functioning more as a rhythm than a melodic instrument, as typified by such figures as Clarence 'Pinetop' Smith, Meade Lux Lewis, Professor Longhair (Henry Roland 'Roy' Byrd), and Antoine 'Fats' Domino. Domino, like Bill Haley, was older than the rock and roll audience that would take up his music, with an established musical career before the 'revolution'; his rolling, compound rhythms had an enormous stylistic impact on the 1950s in such songs as 'Blueberry Hill', 'Ain't That a Shame', and 'Walking to New Orleans'. The piano would remain a key instrument through the 1950s for artists like Ray Charles (who was classified more as R&B than rock and roll, despite the lack of a clear difference between the styles), Little Richard, and Jerry Lee Lewis – the latter being one of the few white exponents of the piano, whose flamboyant and destructive approach to the instrument prefigured the violent guitar virtuosi of the next decade, Pete Townshend and Jimi Hendrix.

Country music is often perceived as the poor white-trash relation of rock and roll, but stylistically it is difficult to consider it as such. Most of the major white figures of rock and roll began as country singers in some way or another. Hank Williams, one of the leading exponents of country music, prefigures the stereotypical rock and roll hero more than any other artist of the 1950s: he revolutionized country-music style; he wrote and performed his own songs, which reflected both a genuine personal feeling – one of the primary components of what would come to be called 'authenticity' – and the wider emotional concerns of his peer group under social pressure (in his case, young family men who migrated North in search of jobs and longed for the family and homes left behind in the South). He lived a fast, hedonistic lifestyle that included heavy touring and substance abuse, and died young from his excesses.

The Texas Swing style of bands like Bob Wills and the Texas Playboys drew on big-band jazz, but also on jump blues and other Southern dance styles, while key early figures like Bill Haley and the Comets, and even Chuck Berry, were essentially Texas Swing. One of Bill Haley and the Comets' big hits was 'See Ya Later, Alligator', a New Orleans R&B tune, and many of Chuck Berry's tunes (such as 'Maybelline', 'Promised Land', and 'You Never Can Tell') are based on the rhythms of a Cajun two-step. This latter fact again underlines the difficulty of saying anything substantive about race and musical style, since Cajun music (unlike its close relative zydeco) is a largely Celtic music. Blues artist Jimmy Witherspoon states simply, 'Chuck Berry is a country singer. People put everybody in categories, black, white, this. Now if Chuck Berry was white ... he would be the top country star in the world.'[9] Similarly, Ray Charles has recorded country songs throughout his long career. It is curious that Elvis Presley, a white man, is recognized for playing black music, but the converse does not hold true.

The Everly Brothers came from a family of country musicians; the boys' first real exposure came when they were children on their parents' radio show (1945–57). Conversely, Conway Twitty, who started out as one of a flood of Elvis imitators, became a major star of country music, and Sam Phillips' famous Sun Records roster included Elvis Presley, Jerry Lee Lewis, Johnny Cash, and Charlie Rich. Although there was considerable stylistic consistency, the first two are considered rock and roll musicians, while the latter two went on to their greatest successes in country – yet another example of how 'the history' of rock and roll has been refracted through hindsight, and of how the artificial construct of the charts (like record-company practices earlier in the century) has divided music by perceived audience rather than style. Elvis Presley had the greatest success as a 'crossover artist' in the twentieth century not necessarily because he changed styles, but because his musical styles were heavily influenced by country, gospel, and R&B, the styles which fed into 'rock and roll'. 'Crossing over' from one chart to the other reflects airplay on radio stations that have particular stylistic allegiances and record sales; the charts are marketing tools and do not reflect who actually listens. And this means that the charts can be used to manipulate public perceptions. For instance, David Brackett has

9 Quoted in Arnold Shaw, *Honkers and Shouters: The Golden Age of Rhythm & Blues*, New York, 1978, p. 215.

written about the elimination of the specialist R&B charts in the early 1960s, which was put forward as a kind of liberal 'mainstreaming', recognizing the crossover success of black artists; the effect, however, was their suppression, as the specialist charts allowed a kind of exposure otherwise hard to come by.[10]

Like the Everly Brothers, Buddy Holly had been a country musician in the Texas Panhandle area around his native Lubbock before radio introduced him to the variety of new styles being lumped together under the rubric of 'rock and roll'; his distinctive 'hiccuping' vocal style, particularly the nasal vocal production and pitch breaks, grew out of white rural folksong and gospel traditions. Holly and his group The Crickets had perhaps the greatest influence of any 1950s artists on the next decade, not so much in terms of musical style as of structure. It is with The Crickets that the fundamental rock combo solidified into drums, bass, lead guitar, and rhythm guitar (with the singer usually doubling on either bass or rhythm guitar), and that two other key figures rose in importance: the internal songwriter and the record producer. Holly wrote or co-wrote many of his songs, a number of them with his producer Norman Petty, and later Holly would produce on his own. For over fifty years, the standard division of labour in popular music had been between songwriter and performer; with rock and roll that division began to blur until, by the end of the 1960s, performance of someone else's composition was held to be not just 'inauthentic' but even in some way dishonest.[11] The improved technology of sound recording would also raise the profile of the producer: initially an engineer, the producer eventually became an artistic contributor on a par with the songwriter, arranger, and musicians. This revolution was led partly by novelty producer Mitch Miller (who, ironically, loathed rock and roll), and especially by two young songwriters, Jerry Leiber and Mike Stoller, who crafted distinctive hits for The Coasters, The Drifters, and Elvis Presley.

Buddy Holly and the Crickets made an especially strong impact in England, where they were among the few early rock acts to tour (1958). The four- or five-man combo was to become the norm for the British music boom of the next decade; their very name, 'The Crickets', inspired The Beatles, while George Martin, along with Leiber and Stoller, Phil Spector, and Brian Wilson in the US, expanded the role of the producer to the point where they could have a style as distinctive and a name as bankable as an auteur film director.

10 'The Politics and Practice of "Crossover" in American Popular Music, 1963 to 1965', *Musical Quarterly* 78 (1994), pp. 774–97.

11 This division of labour remains in effect in country music to this day, making it difficult for songwriters to 'cross over' into performance. Some artists like Clint Black and Garth Brooks, who grew up singing and playing rock as well as country, may be changing this prejudice, although the highly successful songwriter Matraca Berg (an attractive woman with a fine voice whom one would think a good candidate) has not had the same success despite her best efforts.

Economic interlude

By 1958, Elvis Presley was in the Army and Buddy Holly was dead (along with Ritchie Valens, one of the few Hispanic Americans to have wide mainstream success in the entire history of American popular music[12]), while Jerry Lee Lewis's marriage to his thirteen-year-old cousin Myra had triggered a staunch moral backlash that effectively stalled his career. Another key figure would soon be sidelined: in 1961 Chuck Berry was imprisoned under the Mann Act for transporting an underaged girl across state lines for immoral purposes. According to the myth, music was entering a time of stagnation and triviality. This is a view that prioritizes a particular kind of music that did not really come into existence until 1963, when the arrival of The Beatles is said to have ended the 'dead zone'; this is one of the most obvious inconsistencies in the dominant narrative of rock and roll, according to which The Beatles served as a kind of collective saviour, rescuing 'real' music from the doldrums. One of the few histories of rock and roll that acknowledges the partiality of this mythical moment was the 1997 BBC/PBS documentary series *Dancing in the Street*; at the end of one episode about American rhythm and blues, Motown, Stax, and girl groups, footage of the Beatles landing in New York appears with the voiceover: 'It is said that they saved rock and roll; the question is, from whom?'

A more balanced historical view would acknowledge that the period around 1960 was one of economic and racial upheaval. Old practices in the music industry were forced to change with the advent of new technologies, new media, and new listening patterns, while increasing awareness of racial divisions and civil rights led to a reshaping of the musical landscape. With the arrival of the 45 rpm single and the 33⅓ rpm album, increased exposure of recordings on radio and television, and the wide variety of musical styles that were gaining popularity through such exposure, sheet music and even live performance receded as the definition of a piece of music; according to Reebee Garofalo, 1952 was the first year in which record sales outstripped sheet music in sales revenue.[13] The recorded performance took precedence, a process that had already begun in jazz but became increasingly important as performance styles varied more widely, especially when the performers were also the songwriters.

12 Valens's bestselling record, 'La Bamba', was based on a traditional Mexican wedding song (legend has it that Valens learned it phonetically, having never learned Spanish himself). Its rhythm and chord changes were the basis for 'Twist and Shout' (Bert Russell/Phil Medley), made famous first by the black R&B group The Isley Brothers and later by The Beatles; adaptations of the 'La Bamba' groove persisted throughout the 1960s (The Kingsmen's 'Louie, Louie' is a classic example) and still occasionally show up as a retro throwback (Matchbox 20's 'Damn' or Liz Phair's 'Happy', for example), giving it a status similar to that of 'I Got Rhythm' in jazz.

13 Reebee Garofalo, *Rockin' Out: Popular Music in the USA*, Boston, 1992, p. 84.

One of the most reviled practices of the 1950s was in large part a result of the collision between previous practice and the new musical landscape with its heightened racial awareness. The common practice of white artists covering hits by black musicians has often been read as a purely racist strategy, intended to protect vulnerable white ears from the barbarism of 'primitive' black music, but more importantly to rob black musicians of their rightful royalties. There is no doubt that the music industry had a long history of economic discrimination against black musicians, starting from the earliest days of the segregated 'race' records and extending to the dubious partnerships between white – often Jewish – managements and black musicians (such as that between Irving Mills and Duke Ellington), which caused particular racial tensions between the two minority groups. But to read this practice as purely racially motivated is to miss its continuity with practice going back to the 1930s, when sheet music was the dominant mode of dissemination. In those days, when a record started to have success, other record companies would rush out their own versions of the song; it was not unusual for two or more different recordings of the same song to sell well. And all of them served to publicize the principal saleable commodity, that is, printed sheet music. But two things were different in the rock and roll era. First, the recordings that initiated a song's success were often by black artists, while the major recording companies had mainly white artists on their rosters; and second, listeners and critics were beginning to develop the feeling that it was the *recording* that really mattered in terms of ownership – and it was certainly what mattered in terms of profits. To be sure, many of the white covers could be considered musically inferior to the black originals – Pat Boone's version of Little Richard's 'Tutti Frutti' is usually cited as a particularly egregious musical misconception – but others may be more appropriately considered 'different'. The Everly Brothers' version of 'Lucille', for instance, is certainly not like Little Richard's, but their close, swooping harmonies have an appeal different from, but arguably equal to, his gospel wails.

There is also the fact that it was at this time that the practice self-destructed. Many of the white covers were failures; the black originals outsold them and have superseded them in historical accounts. Although the result of the practice was racist, it was primarily an economic strategy, and in the end, it was destroyed by the public's increasing awareness of and sensitivity to black musical styles. Ironically, one of the last of the major 'covers' was a black cover of an earlier black recording which became one of the most important recordings of the entire century: Hank Ballard's original version of his song 'The Twist' had not met with success upon its release in 1958, but in 1960, a high-school student dubbed Chubby Checker re-recorded it in a version so close to the original that Ballard himself, upon hearing it, thought that it was his own record. Although the light-skinned Checker has been seen as a 'compromise' from the darker-skinned and more overtly sexual Ballard, he was also an unusually charismatic performer, and his recording shot to the top of the charts not once but twice – first when the teenagers bought it, and again a year later when an older, more affluent audience discovered it. 'The Twist' is a straight twelve-bar blues in a rumba rhythm, making it *the* quintessential twentieth-century dance tune.

The expansion of radio airplay in the 1950s was immense, but the exposure of rock and roll through television and film was also crucial. Television echoed radio in one of the most successful and long-running of all American television shows, *American Bandstand*, which started as a local show in Philadelphia in 1952, just prior to the rock and roll revolution, and went national in 1957, running until 1989. The kids who danced on the show became teen idols in their own right for several generations, and its eternally youthful host, Dick Clark, has entered American popular culture mythology as a Dorian Gray figure. Clark was one of the few figures to emerge unscathed from the payola scandals of the late 1950s; in what is now seen as a witch-hunt aimed at stemming the tide of rock and roll, the US Congress investigated the widespread but illegal practice of payola (bribes paid by record company representatives to ensure airplay). The investigation effectively ended the careers of most of the country's major disc jockeys, including Alan Freed.

In its early days in America, the television variety show represented the last gasp of vaudeville and gave many artists their first visual exposure to the nation. However, rock and roll was not just a musical but a social revolution, one that seeped into other genres as well, particularly the situation comedy. By the late 1950s, the 'sitcom' was primarily about projecting an idealized image of the American family[14] – which often, of course, included an adolescent or two. *The Adventures of Ozzie and Harriet* (1952–66) was a typical example of the 1950s family sitcom, set in suburbia where the father came home from an unspecified office job to his homemaking wife and two handsome teenaged sons, David and Ricky. Ironically, the real-life family that starred on the show had a strong musical history obscured by the carefully constructed suburban normality: in the 1930s and 40s Ozzie Nelson had been a successful bandleader, while his actress wife, Harriet Hilliard, had sung with the band. So it was not surprising that their younger son, Ricky, brought rock and roll into the American living room, on the show and therefore in real life. Ricky Nelson formed an important link between the first wave of rock and roll and the late 1950s explosion of teen idols singing a more polished, commercial form of it. He was an unusually

14 See, for instance, Alexander Doty, 'The Cabinet of Lucy Ricardo: Lucille Ball's Star Image', *Cinema Journal* 29/4 (1990), pp. 3–18.

beautiful young man whose wholesome image made him seem less threatening to mainstream audiences; his appeal to teenagers, especially girls, was increased when he picked up a guitar and began to sing on the show, promoting his career as a musician as well. His rockabilly style was midway between Elvis Presley and the Everly Brothers, and early hits like 'Hello, Mary Lou' and 'Traveling Man' have regained a level of 'authentic credibility' in recent years. That authenticity was originally lost largely because Nelson became associated with the burgeoning numbers of 'squeaky-clean' pretty boys – some of whom had limited musical skills – who filled the void left by the departure of the initial rock and roll heroes from the scene, and perhaps also because his music, like that of the Everly Brothers, became increasingly categorized as 'country', a style which never had the cachet of its black relative, R&B. Ironically, it was Nelson's early death in 1985, in a plane crash eerily resembling the one in which Ritchie Valens and Buddy Holly died, that led to a re-evaluation of his music. It has often been observed that, thanks to rock's Romantic ideology, dying is a good career move: John Lennon's reputation as the most 'authentic' talent in the Beatles was solidified after his death, whereas Paul McCartney's more traditional, craftsmanlike felicity with tunes has subsequently been denigrated, possibly because he has continued writing and is thus seen to be 'diluting' his legacy.

Ricky Nelson was not the only sitcom star to become a teen idol; Paul Petersen, the son on *The Donna Reed Show*, trod a similar path, but was eventually outstripped by his on-screen sister, Shelley Fabares. Indeed the rock and roll cliché of the 1950s sitcom is so ingrained that when the 1990s sitcom *Roseanne* did a mock flashback to its 1950s roots, one of the key plot threads was about the young son, DJ – nicknamed 'the Deej' in tribute to the 1950s sitcom icon Beaver 'the Beave' Cleaver from *Leave It to Beaver* – and his desire to play 'the rock and roll music'. (His mother supports this, while his father wants his boy to play football, a more manly pursuit, satirically highlighting the long-standing American anxiety about music and masculinity.) Other teen idols came from the Italian neighbourhoods of New York and especially Philadelphia, helped along by *American Bandstand*'s Dick Clark; they included Fabian, Frankie Avalon (the star of numerous films in the *Beach Blanket* series), and James Darren, who starred in the *Gidget* series and became known more as an actor than a singer until a unique career twist brought him back to his musical roots when he starred as nightclub singer Vic Fontaine in the last year of *Star Trek: Deep Space Nine*. In Britain, the young Cliff Richard began his career as a singer in the mould of Elvis Presley but quickly moved (like his model) into the movies, as did Tommy Steele and Jim Dale, both of whom went on to highly successful careers in musical theatre. For three decades, since Al Jolson in *The Jazz Singer*, popular singers had been courted by the movies; just because the style changed did not mean industry practice did.

Rock and roll sparked a number of quickly made films, some of which were little more than filmed variety shows (rather like Paramount's *Big Broadcast* series from the 1930s); others recapitulated the arguments about jazz versus classical music from the movies of the 1930s and 1940s – except that now the new music, rock and roll, was opposed to the 'old' new music, jazz. Other movies took an almost sociological approach, with a journalist or academic – an anthropologist or an ethnomusicologist (as in *Bop Girl Goes Calypso*, 1957) – investigating this strange new phenomenon, only to be won over by its vitality in the end. Although there was an almost hysterical tone (whether for or against rock and roll) to some of the films of 1955–6, by 1958 the pattern had settled back into the boy-meets-girl formula of the classic Hollywood musical. The only difference was that the leads were now identifiably the new breed of teenager, and the music had been assimilated into the mainstream.

Life in the 'dead zone'

The twist at the end of James Darren's acting career, from former teen idol to nightclub singer, might seem inexplicable if one saw the arrival of rock and roll as a cataclysmic event which changed the musical scene irrevocably; but then Darren always was a bit of a crooner. The career of his more famous near-namesake from New York, Bobby Darin, demonstrated even more clearly the stylistic plurality of the late 1950s and early 1960s: after bursting on the scene in 1958 with the rocking 'Splish Splash', Darin quickly returned to the style he had grown up singing and became a sort of junior Sinatra, with a swinging style that appealed across the generations. He won a Grammy for his version of Kurt Weill's 'Mack the Knife', recorded only eight months after 'Splish Splash', and would later turn to the folk-protest idiom.

By 1960 Tin Pan Alley, the publishing district which had been home to the songwriters of the early part of the century (George Gershwin, Irving Berlin, Cole Porter, and Jerome Kern, among many others) had shrunk to the famous Brill Building, 1619 Broadway, and around the corner at 1650, where Aldon Music was housed. A new generation of young songwriters – particularly teams like Jerry Leiber and Mike Stoller, Doc Pomus and Mort Shuman, Burt Bacharach and Hal David, Barry Mann and Cynthia Weil, Jeff Barry and Ellie Greenwich, Neil Sedaka and Howard Greenfield, Carole King and Gerry Goffin – were writing in a new style, heavily influenced by R&B but also by the longer tradition of American popular song. Although these songwriters, some of them still teenagers, were mostly Jewish and from New York (and therefore very much in line with an earlier generation of songwriters), many of their songs were recorded by black singing groups.

Ahmet Ertegun, the Turkish-born head of Atlantic records, had grown up listening to jazz. Later he discovered gospel and R&B, and his label recorded and promoted black music in the 1950s and early 1960s in a way no other major label did. Ruth Brown, Joe Turner, The Clovers, The Coasters, Ray Charles, and Aretha Franklin (as well as Bobby Darin) were among the major Atlantic artists, but around 1960 the pivotal group was The Drifters, a singing group who recorded numerous hits penned by Brill Building writers and produced by Leiber and Stoller. Often based on a synthesis of gospel vocals with a Latin beat and songs whose lyrics commented subtly on current social conditions ('Up On the Roof', 'Under the Boardwalk', 'On Broadway'), the success and style of their songs provided a template for the music that flourished in this supposed 'dead period'. Young entrepreneurs, like Leiber and Stoller's protégé Phil Spector and Aldon publisher Don Kirshner, were having great success with equally young female singing groups like the Crystals, the Chiffons, and the Ronettes. Most of these groups were black.

Two other independent recording labels started in the late 1950s which were not only hugely successful, economically and musically, but also brought under particular scrutiny the charged issues of race and identity: they were the Detroit-based Motown Records, which was founded in 1958 by songwriter Berry Gordy, Jr. and was by the end of the 1960s the most successful black-owned business in the United States; and the Memphis-based Stax, which was founded in 1959 by brother-and-sister team Jim Stewart and Estelle Axton (a fiddler and a banker respectively). Both Motown and Stax recorded black artists, and both developed distinctive sounds to the extent that the label names also became stylistic markers: Motown's backbeat tambourine or handclaps and reverberant piano made their recordings as recognizable as Stax's slight rhythmic delay on beat two and Hammond B3 organ. Both moreover were family businesses with an operating approach that covered all aspects of their artists' careers and even lives; Motown especially ran everything 'in house'. They had a stable of songwriters like a mini-Brill Building, including the hugely successful team of Brian Holland, Lamont Dozier, and Eddie Holland; Barrett Strong and Norman Whitfield; and William 'Smokey' Robinson, who wrote with several different partners and was also a highly successful performer with his group The Miracles. Motown even had a 'charm school', an extended version of the A&R (Artist and Repertoire) divisions of most recording companies. Not only were the artists – most of them young, poor African Americans from the Detroit area or similar – styled and matched up with songs; they were taught how to conduct themselves in public, how to speak to journalists, and of course how to dance (by Cholly Atkins, the man who created many of the dance steps made famous by the likes of the Temptations, the Four Tops, and the Supremes). Gordy's ambition was that his artists should assimilate into mainstream American culture, and to a very great extent he succeeded.

Although Stax was white-owned, its music has been considered, then and now, to be more 'authentically' black. This is despite the fact that half of its famous house band – the musicians who played on the majority of their records – were white: guitarist Steve Cropper (who also wrote or co-wrote many Stax classics, including 'Knock on Wood', 'In the Midnight Hour', and 'Dock of the Bay') and bassist Donald 'Duck' Dunn, who replaced original bassist Lewis Steinberg in 1964 but is usually considered part of the classic lineup. These two, together with drummer Al Jackson and organist Booker T. Jones, had numerous instrumental hits as 'Booker T. and the MGs', including 'Green Onions', one of the few truly classic instrumentals of the rock era. Easy racial assumptions of authorship and authenticity are thoroughly confounded by Stax and Motown.

The late 1950s and early 1960s also saw the development of a particularly localized, originally instrumental rock[15] music style on the beaches around Los Angeles: surf music. The man credited with originating the style was guitarist and surfer Dick Dale; his extra-thick strings, repeating and sliding notes, and high reverb, as heard on hits like 'Let's Go Trippin'' (1961) and 'Misirlou' (1962), were highly distinctive, and were certainly an influence on John Barry's orchestration of one of the most widely heard guitar solos in history: the James Bond theme. In 1963, another key instrumental surf hit was the Surfaris' 'Wipe Out', hardly more than an articulation of a twelve-bar blues pattern but with a kicky energy and a famous drum solo. In the early 1960s, however, vocals were added to an already distinctive musical style by two different groups, at about the same time. The duo of Jan and Dean had tight, Everly-styled harmonies; the five-member family group of The Beach Boys – brothers Brian, Carl, and Dennis Wilson, cousin Al Jardine, and family friend Mike Love – developed an even more extraordinary sound of close, five-part harmonies, inspired by musical leader Brian Wilson's love for The Four Freshmen (a barbershop-like group that enjoyed some popularity in the 1950s, though they were not in any way 'rock and roll'). Despite the group's deceptively simple lyrics about girls, cars, high school, and the joys of surfing, Wilson's ear for complex harmony, arrangement, and production made The Beach Boys' music among the most sophisticated of the 1960s, and the competition between The Beach Boys and The Beatles led to ever-increasing experimentation on both sides.

15 Although there is an unspoken consensus that 'rock and roll' refers to anything up to the British Invasion and 'rock' to everything thereafter, I have categorized surf music as 'rock' because it does not fit into the styles usually categorized as 'rock and roll'.

The British Invasion

1963–7 is a period associated with the term 'The British Invasion'. This term originates, of course, from an American perspective, but the irony is that 'the British were coming' armed with American music; moreover, despite the term 'British', the vast majority of the musicians were from England and not the Celtic regions of the UK (though Liverpool, it is true, has strong links with both Wales and Northern Ireland). Post-war England was a very different place from the United States, where the horrors of war had never really touched and where relatively good economic times made the bad times easy to forget. By contrast, England had to rebuild after the extensive bombing, and shortages meant that food rationing continued until 1954. But films continued to disseminate American music, and records became easier to obtain. In the mid-1950s, kids who could not afford guitars and drums fashioned their own makeshift instruments (markedly reminiscent of the mountain string bands of Appalachia and the Smoky Mountains) and began to imitate the records they heard; thus was the skiffle boom born. Skiffle was essentially an acoustic, low-tech version of rock and roll. Lonnie Donegan's seminal recording of the Leadbelly tune 'Rock Island Line' (1954) was stylistically very close to country music, but as we have seen, country music was one of the main tributaries to mainstream rock and roll – though most English listeners would have had little or no awareness of this stylistic variant because the dissemination of American music was erratic and partial.

Elvis Presley, Chuck Berry, and Buddy Holly and the Crickets had a galvanizing effect on the music scene in England, although the effects would not reach back to America for several years. Buddy Holly seems to have had particular influence; this can partly be attributed to the fact that he toured there, but his thin, eccentric vocal style also seems to have had an affinity with the preferred voice in English popular music for several preceding decades. The trendy coffee bars that in America were associated with jazz and beat culture (and later folk) were home to skiffle and later rock and roll in England. And as the economy improved and more instruments became available, skiffle groups transformed into rock and roll groups – the most famous of these being The Quarrymen, later to become The Beatles.

Although The Beatles were undoubtedly the most important group of the 1960s in terms of impact, they did not spring up in isolation. Their greatest strength was not in innovation but in synthesis: even if they had not cited their influences, their early records give proof of their eclectic tastes – the above-mentioned artists, plus girl groups (both the Motown groups and those who worked with Phil Spector), The Everly Brothers, and even Broadway musicals. In the early days, a large part of their repertoire was cover versions (The Isley Brothers' 'Twist and Shout', The Marvelettes' 'Please Mr. Postman', ''Til There was You' from *The Music Man*), but their own early originals bear the stamp of their sources almost as clearly. 'Love Me Do', which sounded so strange to so many ears in 1963, would never have happened without The Everly Brothers, mimicking the feel of tracks like 'Wake Up, Little Susie' and 'Till I Kissed Ya' and the close, spiralling harmonies of 'Cathy's Clown'. Early on, The Beatles had been matched with a former classical oboist, George Martin, as their producer, and Martin's knowledge of classical music, his experience as a producer of both classical and comedy/novelty recordings, and the group members' own skills, interests, and enthusiasm created an increasingly sophisticated stylistic synthesis in the mid-1960s. The Beatles also capitalized on the kind of teen frenzy that Elvis and the teen idols had provoked a few years earlier, but orchestrated it to even greater heights, setting the stage for the arrival of full-fledged Beatlemania in 1963. The mayhem in Britain was as much a factor as the music in the impact of their arrival in America, but it was the music that gained the first real 'adult' audience for the new style.

Running parallel to, but to a large extent separate from, the pop-rock boom spearheaded by The Beatles was the British blues boom. The Rolling Stones took their name from a Muddy Waters song and formed a stylistic bridge between The Beatles on the 'pop' end of the rock spectrum, and the blues on the other. Mick Jagger and Keith Richards formed a songwriting duo that challenged John Lennon and Paul McCartney for supremacy of the airwaves in the mid-1960s, although the rivalry whipped up between the two hugely popular bands was more a product of the media than of any real animosity; this was an early example of how the British media, in particular, emphasizes attitude and ideology over musical content.

Until the late 1950s, blues had been to a large extent known only as a precursor of jazz or, later, R&B; the thriving Chicago blues style (a harder, straighter, amplified version of the Southern Delta or country blues) was somewhat isolated from the musical mainstream. It was ironic then, but perhaps not surprising, that the recovery of the blues tradition took place thousands of miles away from its birthplace in the American South, in a place culturally far removed. American servicemen and merchant seamen stationed in or travelling to England brought recordings over, which was one of the reasons why Liverpool – a major port – became such a hotbed of musical activity. The first serious book on the blues was written by a white Englishman: until recently, Paul Oliver's *Blues Fell This Morning* (a rich cultural history based around the blues as a record of the black experience in the United States) was still the definitive book on the subject, compiled by a man who knew the music only from records. But Paul Oliver was not the only white Englishman finding a resonance with the blues. The young Eric Clapton was one of many who picked up a guitar in the late 1950s, but he became the first rock-guitar god, fronting the band The Yardbirds; after his departure from the band, his slot would be filled by two more soon-to-be-legendary guitarists, Jeff Beck and Jimmy Page.

With the blues boom came the introduction of virtuosity into rock and roll, most obviously in the privileging of the guitar solo; however it was present in vocalists as well. While the blues musicians from the area around London – The Yardbirds, John Mayall, and Alexis Korner among others – were drawn to the Chicago blues of artists like 'The Three Kings' (BB, Albert and Freddie), those further north showed more influence from more vocally-driven R&B: The Animals from Manchester, The Them from Belfast, and The Spencer Davis Group from Birmingham, who notably adopted the Hammond B3 organ so popularized by the Stax house band. Each of these groups was fronted by an unusually charismatic and versatile singer who would continue to make well-received music for at least the next three decades. Eric Burdon of the Animals was a prototypical bad boy, with none of the refined edges of his predecessors Elvis Presley or even Mick Jagger, and with a particularly rough blues delivery; Van Morrison of The Them had then and would continue to develop a remarkably flexible vocal style blending R&B with Celtic phrasing, also shaped by his saxophone playing. And like Morrison, Stevie Winwood of the Spencer Davis Group was a multi-instrumentalist; he played guitar and organ as well as writing and singing the rock vocal classic 'Gimme Some Lovin'' at the tender age of sixteen. Winwood, along with Clapton and Rolling Stone bassist Bill Wyman, championed a revival of the original blues musicians who had inspired them, recording with Howlin' Wolf and Muddy Waters, among others.

It was through this interest in the blues and its perceived status as an authentic expression of personal experience, as well as of an oppressed culture, that the notion of 'authenticity' entered the ideology of rock music. It was perhaps overdetermined by the many stylistic tributaries to rock and roll: 'telling it like it is' from the blues; 'speaking from the heart' from country; 'testifying' from gospel; and a sense of historical continuity and responsibility from folk music, as we shall see below. This is not to deny that such 'authenticity' (an unacknowledged synonym for 'integrity') exists; it is merely to point out the inherent Romanticism of such an idea. This notion, hardly in existence at the beginning of the decade, would come so to dominate rock discourse that at times it seems as if ideology rather than style determines musical categorization.

The American response

As we have seen above, popular music in the United States was hardly 'dead' before the British Invasion, but it did change afterwards. Guitars and the rock combo came back into fashion. But something was happening in America that would make the American rock of the 1960s different from that of the British and have an impact back on Britain.

In the 1930s, left-wing political activists had taken up folk music as a way of constructing community and as a didactic tool. Woody Guthrie was one of the most prominent of these modern balladeers, recognised for his clear and direct but poetic language, most famously in 'This Land Is Your Land', which was simultaneously patriotic and a protest song. During the Second World War, such political activism was channelled into the war effort or put on hold until a more auspicious time; Guthrie himself fell very ill and was confined to a sanatorium in 1952 (he died in 1967). In the late 1950s, however, folk music rose in popularity again, this time taken up by a largely college audience more interested in its musical qualities, though the whiff of political radicalism has appealed to college students generation after generation. Groups like the Weavers, the Chad Mitchell Group, and the Kingston Trio were the norm, performing close-harmony versions of traditional ballads.

Bob Dylan (born Robert Zimmerman in rural Minnesota) came to New York City's bohemian Greenwich Village in January 1961 with his guitar, harmonica, and love of Woody Guthrie, and began singing in the coffee bars and clubs which were beginning to feature folk music. Dylan was not the only young singer-songwriter on the scene, but he quickly became the most prominent, being noted, like Guthrie before him, for his lyrics and, more controversially, for his idiosyncratic vocal style. But Dylan had enormous success relatively quickly, and his allegorical and allusive poetic style had a profound impact on popular music, easily on a par with The Beatles – and in fact The Beatles often cited Bob Dylan as an influence on *them*, because he showed that popular music could be about more than the adolescent topics of romance, sex, dancing, and cars. Among others affected by Dylan's success were a couple of students from Flushing Meadows, New York who had been childhood friends and, as 'Tom and Jerry', had even had a minor rock and roll hit called 'Hey, Schoolgirl' back in 1957. They were Eng. Lit. Masters' student Paul Simon and Mathematics doctoral student Art Garfunkel. Simon was the primary songwriter; Garfunkel helped work out the harmonies and contributed one of the purest natural voices in twentieth-century popular music. Simon was Dylan's only real rival as a songwriter in the folk movement, but their tremendous popular success was undoubtedly boosted by their vocal blend, closely modelled on that of the Everly Brothers.

Along with its social consciousness, folk brought to rock a kind of musical Puritanism, exemplified by the infamous uproar at the Newport Folk Festival in 1965 caused by Bob Dylan playing with electric instruments. Folk was supposed to be acoustic, preferably played by one person, the singer-songwriter, so that the connection between performer and audience was transparent, unmediated. Dylan's backing band, soon to be known simply as The Band, had played with Southern rocker Ronnie Hawkins as The Hawks before joining Dylan, and went on to be one of the most musically acclaimed bands of the rock era. Even though, ironically, all but one of them were Canadian (the exception was Arkansas-born drummer and lead singer Levon Helm, later a critically acclaimed actor as well), The Band created a sound that was perceived as 'authentically' American. Indeed songwriter Robbie Robertson's emotive songs such as 'The Night They Drove Old Dixie Down' (famously performed acoustically by Joan Baez), 'The Weight' and 'King Harvest (Has Surely Come)', redolent as they were of the American rural past, sounded to many like genuine folksongs.

The East Coast folk movement was protest-based, but also intellectual and philosophical (one of Simon and Garfunkel's tunes was called 'A Simple Desultory Philippic', and even The Band's music had a kind of studied historicism); perhaps influenced more by the Beach Boys' sophisticated sound and the burgeoning hippie culture of California, the West Coast folk movement was more 'lifestyle'-oriented. The Mamas and the Papas, and The Byrds, featured complex four- and five-part harmonies, and their songs, as well as their well-publicized lifestyles, were about love, personal freedoms, and drugs (though usually covertly). Even an apparently poppy little song like The Associations' 'Along Comes Mary' (1965) could be about marijuana if one listened carefully enough. But the folk movement also paved the way for politics to enter popular music in a more volatile way. The shock of the black power movement and its expression in soul music – a consciously rebranded form of R&B, as will shortly be explained – was cushioned to some extent by the fact that social comment and protest had been a very important part of the music scene in America throughout the decade. In a way, it was Bob Dylan's 'Blowin' in the Wind', and 'For What It's Worth' by the group Buffalo Springfield, that made Marvin Gaye's 'What's Going On?' and James Brown's 'Say It Loud – I'm Black and I'm Proud' viable in popular culture.

The folk movement's poetics merged with the blues-borne concept of personal authenticity to foster the rise of the confessional singer-songwriters at the end of the 1960s, and prominent among them were two artists who had been part of the Brill Building scene at the beginning of the decade: Carole King and Neil Diamond. King recorded one of the bestselling and most influential albums of the era with *Tapestry* (1971), an album which presented her versions of songs she had written during the previous decade, along with newer, more personal songs. Known as a particularly charismatic performer, Diamond also epitomized many of the stylistic cross-currents and ideological contradictions of rock music, mixing a love of high-energy gospel and Latin-based rock music with deep, angst-like introspection. He has been one of the few rock artists whose Jewishness and continuity with earlier, pre-rock-era popular entertainment were never completely covered over, as his starring role in the 1980 remake of *The Jazz Singer* highlighted.

Stax and especially Motown were highly successful throughout most of the 1960s, keeping African-American music high on the charts and competing well with the British Invasion. However, though the Civil Rights Act of 1964 closed one chapter of the Civil Rights Movement, it opened another, and new sectors of the American public – particularly an alliance between politicized youth of varied ethnicities and racial minorities – had their impact on music. The assimilationist tone of Motown quickly acquired an archaic and reactionary quality; the relative rawness of Stax conversely was seen to take on an air of increased 'authenticity', with Otis Redding going from 'Mr Pitiful' to demanding 'Respect'. That song was better known from the cover version by the great, gospel-trained Aretha Franklin (a recording closely associated with the rise of the women's rights movement), but it had more obvious racial overtones when sung by a black man, who was seen to be disenfranchised not only by white society but also by the stereotypically matriarchal black American household. Southern gospel and blues elements fused with harder, faster rhythms to create the music called 'soul' – a word in many ways synonymous with authenticity, embracing sincerity, personal integrity, and even a feel for the beat that was racialized. (This turned the negative, age-old stereotype about black people 'having rhythm' into a positive one; characteristically, however, it at the same time reinforced the Western mind–body split, with the supposedly 'inferior' body being displaced onto blacks.) Redding's horn arrangements harked back to the days of the R&B big band, while James Brown's gradual abandonment of long-phrased melodies and conventional harmonies for complex rhythmic structures and short, contrapuntal layers of riffs were building towards a full-blown funk style in the early 1970s. This style would rebound on Motown at the end of the decade, particularly with the Temptations' smash hit 'Papa Was a Rolling Stone', which melded James Brown's rhythmic riffing with a touch of Otis Redding's social commentary.

Musical developments in the 1960s were pushed not only by social forces but also by a spirit of experimentation and by continual technological advances: the emergence of stereo for commercial recordings, the four-track and eventually the eight- and sixteen-track studio with the concomitant rise in importance of the mix, and the advent of FM radio broadcasting. All these factors also led to a shift of focus from the single to the album, something that had really begun as early as the 1950s with Frank Sinatra's mood-setting, proto-concept albums like *In the Wee Small Hours* (1954) and *Songs for Swinging Lovers* (1955). (It is important to remember that artists like Frank Sinatra were still selling well throughout the decade, and that The Beatles were challenged for album chart supremacy by the pop-mariachi band Herb Alpert and the Tijuana Brass.) And it was in the new recording studio, with its capabilities for overdubbing, that recording began to supplant live performance as the primary text. Whereas the emphasis in 1950s recordings had been on capturing the excitement of a live performance, in the 1960s artists began to create music that could not be played live. Two key players in this regard were The Beatles, with their adventurous producer George Martin, and The Beach Boys, led by Brian Wilson. As already mentioned, a rivalry developed which pushed studio technique ever further: The Beach Boys' complex contrapuntal single 'Good Vibrations' (1965) spurred The Beatles on in their album *Revolver* (1966), while The Beach Boys responded with *Pet Sounds* (1966), which apparently put a real fright into John Lennon and Paul McCartney, resulting in the seminal *Sergeant Pepper's Lonely Hearts Club Band* (1967).

This illustrates how, although there was a perceived schism between American and British music in the 1960s, the era was in reality considerably more complex than this. The North/South, blues/pop dichotomy in Britain is one example of this: on the one hand American, and particularly African-American, influence was very strong, but on the other there was a redefinition of a kind of eccentric Englishness (The Kinks, Chad and Jeremy, even The Who and some of The Beatles's music-hall adaptations). In the United States, by contrast, race, region, and lifestyle created other faultlines. However, throughout the decade, one can divine a common trend towards the formation of a rock ideology founded in an idealized Romanticism with a heavy stress on personal expression, and in a socio-political awareness that led to radical activism on race, class, or gender issues, or against the war in Vietnam. This did not preclude a simultaneous elevation of hedonism, however, as a utopian peace was portrayed as fostering free love and championing the use of mind-expanding drugs. Drugs had been part of the music scene in America for quite a long time – alcohol, marijuana, and heroin in particular having been associated with jazz from its earliest days – and during the Prohibition Era of the 1920s, jazz was an integral part of the illicit world of organized crime and illegal alcohol (at least in the mythology of popular culture). During the 1960s drugs came out of the shadows, starting with the amphetamine habits of the sharp-dressed, scooter-riding 'mods' of London. But it was for the use of sedative and hallucinogenic drugs like marijuana and LSD that young people began arguing as a right and as an alternative to the 'uptight' adult world. The shadow of heroin addiction and the deaths of Janis Joplin, Jim Morrison, and Jimi Hendrix were as yet over the horizon.

The prospect of an alternative reality together with the urge towards personal expression fostered the rise of the virtuoso, while the advent of psychedelia – an attempt to recreate musically the experience of hallucinogenic drugs – and the utopian ideals of community (together with advances in amplification!) led to a number of massive music festivals in the last years of the decade: Monterey, Isle of Wight, Altamont, Woodstock. It was at these festivals that some of the great rock virtuosi really rose to prominence: Jimi Hendrix at Monterey, Carlos Santana at Woodstock. The Who (who had begun as a R&B cover band, became the darlings of the mods, and would help launch the wave of progressive rock at the end of the decade) emerged as one of the most important acts on the festival rounds because of their flamboyance; their controversial, stage-destroying performances undoubtedly provoked Jimi Hendrix's burning of his guitar at Monterey. They also headlined at Woodstock, while at the Isle of Wight they performed extracts of their 'rock opera' *Tommy*. Albums like *Tommy* and *Sergeant Pepper* heralded a shift that led music into the next decade: following the pattern of the bebop movement in jazz twenty years earlier, the influence of classical and avant-garde aesthetics led to the rise of progressive rock.

A perspective on historiography

Storytelling is important in the creation of mythology, and the Romantic ideology of rock has given rise to a number of 'histories' that read more like hagiographies. Relatively few books have been written about the history of rock and roll as a musical style (exceptions, to varying degrees, include those by Bradley, Garofalo and Gillett[16]). Wilfrid Mellers's own musicological allegiance to Romantic ideology, although coming from a different direction, resulted in an effort to elevate The Beatles to the pantheon of 'great composers' through detailed technical analysis; the emphasis on the tortured genius has, however,

16 Dick Bradley, *Understanding Rock 'n' Roll: Popular Music in Britain 1955–1964*, Buckingham, 1992; Garofalo, *Rockin' Out*; Gillett, *The Sound of the City*.

primarily produced biographies, most of them written by journalists. The extent to which musicians are considered godlike and untouchable may be discerned by the reaction to Albert Goldman's biographies of Elvis Presley and John Lennon: they have been perceived as historically inaccurate and even vindictive, but the vitriol with which they were attacked by fans and the media testifies to the intense feeling that these two figures – perhaps *the* icons of the rock and roll era – engender.

Scholarly work on rock music started not in music but in sociology. Simon Frith's pioneering work typified a (mainly British) approach primarily concerned with the ways in which people use music – what they listen to, how they listen, how and to whom they talk about it; such work tended to focus on specific subcultures consisting of relatively small, self-contained, and self-identifying audiences. However satisfying and fascinating the findings of these studies, however, they have a number of drawbacks. For one thing, they have almost all been based in Britain, where the dynamics of popular culture are significantly different from America (though this distinction has rarely been acknowledged). They also cannot be extrapolated to larger, more heterogeneous audiences, which means that the 'mainstream' has often been neglected and even derided; this is one of the great dangers of the sociological approach, which can reinforce and even replicate the mythology without perhaps questioning its historical accuracy.[17]

Musicological work on rock, which only began to develop a decade after Mellers's work, has tended to be in one of two camps. Detaching music from its context and analysing it as a continuation of the classical 'masterwork' tradition has resulted in a number of theory-based projects, from Schenkerian graphs of popular songs to a whole host of studies on progressive rock: because this music aspired towards the 'art' tradition anyway, it lends itself relatively well to this kind of analysis (though no amount of graphing can explain *why* the musicians had such aspirations).[18] The other and possibly more productive path, exemplified by the work of Robert Walser and Philip Tagg, is less heavily trodden: it strives to understand the music as *both* a musical *and* a cultural text.[19] Whereas this might be seen as aiming to combine technical analysis with

17 An excellent example where the researcher seems to have become so wrapped up in the mythology that he fails to question it is found in Dick Hebdige's landmark book on punk, *Subculture: The Meaning of Style*, London, 1979.

18 For several examples of Schenkerian graphs, see John Covach and Graeme Boone (eds.), *Understanding Rock: Essays in Musical Analysis*, New York, 1997 (articles by Mathew Brown, Lori Burns, and Walter Everett).

19 See Philip Tagg, 'Analysing Popular Music: Theory, Method and Practice', *Popular Music* 2 (1982), pp. 37–67, and 'Open Letter: "Black Music", "Afro-American Music" and "European Music"', *Popular Music* 8 (1989), pp. 285–93; Robert Walser's *Running with the Devil: Power, Gender, and Madness in Heavy Metal Music*, Hanover, 1993. John Covach ('We Won't Get Fooled Again: Rock Music and Musical Analysis', *In Theory Only* 13 (1997), pp. 119–41) offers a thorough critical overview and bibliography of the theoretical writing on popular music, also arguing in favour of a culturally informed application of musical analysis.

the kind of culturally oriented approach represented by Frith's work, there is a difference: sociology is based in the social sciences and has a quantitative orientation, whereas Walser's or Tagg's approaches draw rather on cultural studies. Key to the cultural studies approach is the assumption that one can never adopt a neutral position 'outside' a cultural text, because any author is always part of the cultural process; the best one can hope for is an awareness of the forces that are shaping one's own perceptions, or of those whose interpretations one is reading.

What this might entail can be illustrated through consideration of Eileen Southern's landmark *Music of Black Americans*, first published in 1971. This is a comprehensive history encompassing both art and popular musics, one of the few studies that traces the continuities rather than policing the multitudinous style boundaries that seem to have become more entrenched as the century wore on. Yet a fundamental division remains, as indicated by the title. However historically necessary and however much of a disciplinary remedy the book was when it was published, it reinforced the essentialist idea that music and race are somehow completely codependent. In a 'coda' to the second edition (1983), Southern concluded:

> Again and again black musical styles have passed over into American music, there to be diluted and altered in other ways to appeal to a wider public or to be used as the basis for developing new styles. There was the transformation of the slave songs, for example, into Ethiopian minstrel songs and, on another level, the assimilation of jazz elements into the music of a Gershwin or a Stravinsky. The black composer's response to such a transfer has been simply to invent a new music: thus spirituals were replaced by gospel; traditional jazz, by bebop; rhythm 'n' blues, by soul – to cite a few examples. The old is never totally discarded, however, but absorbed into the new. In summary, black music constantly renews itself at the same time as its innovations are being absorbed into the general language of Western music. And that is as it should be.[20]

This is certainly in line with the mythology of popular music in the twentieth century, and it is by no means historically inaccurate. But the implications are problematic, not least in separating the music of 'black Americans' from 'American music' as well as 'Western music'; it demonizes the mainstream, and even 'Western music', as a bland and uninteresting, 'inauthentic' space. Southern's statement also implicitly reiterates the mantra of 'blacks innovate, whites appropriate', one of the most common elements of the mythology, and perhaps the most difficult to deal with in any meaningful way. In the first place, the history of the music has been so convoluted that an unequivocal assignment of colour to any stylistic feature is impossible. The second problem is that a

20 Eileen Southern, *The Music of Black Americans: A History* (2nd edn), New York, 1997, pp. 553–4.

term like 'dilute' brings with it a rhetorical force that becomes evident if we ask: dilute with what? If 'black' musical style is being mixed with something else ('white' style?) that undoubtedly has its own aesthetic criteria, would it not be better to describe this as a process of hybridization, or better, creolization, than of dilution? There is no escaping the fact that Southern's statement is a political one based on a specific historical and racial perspective, and she is making it from an unassailable position: any refutation of, or even engagement with, it can be accused of racism.

Race has always been a central issue with rock and roll, and the rise of rock was historically contingent with the Civil Rights movement in the USA. But another revolution of the same period did not have the same impact on rock; if anything, the Romantic ideology prioritized masculine experience and the masculine display of power and control, whether musical or sexual. Women were marginalized in the practice of rock, and they have certainly been marginalized in the writing of its history, making it impossible to reintegrate their history smoothly even in this revisionist approach. Therefore, we must conclude that . . .

. . . it's a man's world

In the 1957 film *Bop Girl Goes Calypso*, a pony-tailed young woman named Judy Tyler sings a rousing rock number. She has attitude and charisma to put most of her rocking male contemporaries – especially the cinematic ones – to shame. Her jeans and plaid cotton shirt and her loud, belting voice (or that of the singer who dubbed her, it is unclear which) are in stark contrast to the passive pop princesses of the day. Those girls, like Connie Francis or Annette Funnicello, wore pretty party dresses and represented the ideal, virginal good girl. They sang about their romantic (and asexual) dreams and their broken hearts; their innocence or, conversely, their victimization was their badge of safe femininity, as were their pitch-accurate, unforced voices. When Tyler lets go, her voice goes out of tune in a remarkably liberating way. She doesn't have a great voice, but she's a great singer. This ranging beyond conventional tuning is not uncommon in blues or R&B, but for a white girl in the 1950s, her willingness to go out of tune breached a kind of social protocol that highlighted the stifling containment of other girls of her race and age. And Judy Tyler is more than just an interesting anomaly, she's a historiographical problem. If she was a construct of the film, then the fact that there was no one else like her would make her as speculative as the film's larger contention that rock and roll was a temporary fad about to be replaced by the new calypso revolution (!).

But what if she is the unexpected remnant of a kind of singer captured almost accidentally on celluloid but now lost to history?

The recapitulation of 'great man' strategies in histories (like the 'masterpiece' strategies of analysis) marginalizes the participation and experience of women in music. Ironically, rock's tributaries – blues, R&B, and country – are all kinds of music in which women have long participated in great numbers and with significant impact. The first recorded blues singers were women; the men only began to be recorded a few years later. Yet it was the men's music that was taken by later writers to be the 'authentic' expression (the women were read as providing commercialized entertainment and therefore inherently 'inauthentic'), and artists such as Robert Johnson were taken to be the starting point for the British blues boom. Again, in R&B, singers like Ruth Brown and Big Mama Thornton, who recorded Leiber and Stoller's 'Hound Dog' before Elvis Presley, sang in a forthright and even assertive manner and had a number of hits in the 1950s, but have largely been written out of the histories – and certainly out of the mythology. And in country, the women entered as mountain folk singers and white gospel singers, but also often played instruments: Maybelle and Sarah Carter of the Carter family were perhaps the most famous of these, beginning a line that extends through their daughters (Janette, Anita, Helen, and June Carter Cash) and granddaughters (Carlene Carter and Roseanne Cash – the latter a stepchild, but part of the family music-making tradition). The mountain tradition also included Dolly Parton and, through its virtuosic, experimental, and later commercialized offshoot of bluegrass, younger artists like Alison Krauss and the Dixie Chicks. The list goes on. Country trailblazer Kitty Wells was actually a Western singer,[21] and Patsy Cline a bluesy pop singer with a country sensibility, while Loretta Lynn took up the hard honky-tonk of Hank Williams from a distinctly female perspective that resulted in such revolutionary songs as 'You Ain't Woman Enough to Take My Man' (1966), 'Your Squaw is on the Warpath' (1969), and particularly 'The Pill' (1975). These songs might be considered proto-feminist, but stemmed mainly from Lynn's straightforward and practical take on life – a kind of strength and independence not uncommon among poor white Southern women but unknown or at least unacknowledged in more mainstream society.

It seems that the 1950s were largely devoid of white female rock singers. This is not to dismiss the cultural significance of pop singers like Francis, whose vocal style prefigured the placid-but-tortured quality of Karen Carpenter some fifteen years later, or especially Brenda Lee, whose punchy style and slightly

21 Although allied with 'country' music by the charts, 'Western' music was actually a form of popular music invented by the movies, fostered by the figure of the singing cowboy like Roy Rogers, and reflecting another American myth – that of the lonesome cowboy riding the range and singing to his cattle.

tomboyish image seems the closest model for 'Judy Tyler'. But in fact, Lee is the only survivor of historiographical purge that has only recently been recovered– rockabilly singers like Janis Martin, Wanda Jackson, and Lorrie Collins are being excavated by music historians.[22] Restoring these girls (because they were all teenagers) to their position in history is obviously an uphill battle against the weight of rock mythology, as they still remain so obscure, even when one does some digging; Lee was spared complete obliteration because she continued a successful chart career in country music well into the 1960s, but perhaps more importantly, she was a novelty – a tiny girl who sang like the big boys.

The girl groups of the early 1960s were important in breaching the gender as well as the race barrier: it was perhaps easier to accept girls if they were black, and blacks if they were girls. Many of them were groomed to be as pretty and nice as the white girls of the 1950s, though the Ronettes, led by Ronnie Spector (wife of Phil), and the all-white Shangri-Las had a tougher, sexier image. Singers like Dusty Springfield and Lulu had success in Britain, and to a lesser extent in the US, with a brand of pop R&B not far from Motown or Stax; understood in the context of the times, however, one of the most striking figures is the petite, big-eyed Lesley Gore whose 'It's My Party (And I'll Cry If I Want To)' (1963) becomes a perverse proclamation of self-determination in what was for many young women a stifling era, and whose 'You Don't Own Me' (1963, on the album *Lesley Gore Sings of Mixed-up Hearts*) becomes positively revolutionary.

For many girls of this period, participation in rock culture was primarily through fandom. Beatlemania was the most prominent 'wave', very much orchestrated and developed by the group themselves.[23] Although the intensity and scale of Beatlemania seems extreme, prefiguring the later [Bay City] Rollermania of the 1970s and the heavily strategic marketing of boy bands in the 1990s (particularly in Britain), it was part of a process of escalation going back through Elvis to Frank Sinatra and Rudy Vallee: it is really the actor and dancer Rudolf Valentino who, in the 1920s, provided the model for such fan hysteria – and even that can be traced back to the actors and musical virtuosi of the nineteenth century, where so much of the mythology of the inspired author-performer has its origins. There are even medieval tales of hysteria at religious events that bear a striking resemblance to the behaviour at rock concerts, with adolescent girls screaming and fainting with emotion. In cultures where their voices and emotions were strictly governed, these sanctioned events clearly offered some sort of outlet.

22 See David Sanjek, 'Can a Fujiyama Mama Be the Female Elvis? The Wild, Wild Women of Rockabilly', in Sheila Whiteley (ed.), *Sexing the Groove*, London, 1997, pp.137–67; and Mary A. Bufwack and Robert K. Oermann, *Finding Her Voice: The Saga of Women in Country Music*, New York, 1993.

23 Tamara Levitz, 'Twist and Shout: The Female Voice and the Silencing of the Beatles', unpublished paper presented at the Cross(over) Relations Conference, Eastman School of Music, 1996.

For most of the early period of rock and roll, the most influential role for women was behind the scenes. They did often not rise very high within the record companies – as company founders, Estelle Axton of Stax and Florence Greenberg of Scepter were very much the exception. Women did, however, find places as publicity or A&R people: one of the most important and influential A&R people in the rock era was Motown's Suzanne de Passe, who later branched out into film and television production. Even women with the notional rank of 'secretary' could be important as talent spotters and screeners but, predictably, their contributions were rarely acknowledged. Nor were women often journalists, though Annie Leibowitz began working as a photographer at *Rolling Stone* in 1970, broke through with the 1975 Rolling Stones tour, and became one of the most important portraitists of the latter part of the century. It is true that the women writers of the Brill Building formed one of the few substantial populations of women in rock history, but the significance of this is qualified by the fact that they were, without exception, paired with a male writing partner to whom, without exception, they were married. Allison Anders's 1996 film *à clef*, *Grace of My Heart* is a thinly veiled fictionalization of Carole King's life, and effectively highlights the way in which men still determined women's careers: each musical phase of the main character's life is governed by a relationship with a different man – except for the last one, which holds out the possibility of an independent existence.

Other than in all-girl singing groups or as backing vocalists hired as much for their looks as their singing ability, women had little presence as performers – though bassist Carole Kaye, who played extensively on sessions for Phil Spector and The Beach Boys, was a notable exception. Only with the 'folkie' girls of the 1960s, particularly Joan Baez and Joni Mitchell, did they begin to attract serious attention from the (predominantly male) writers of rock history; like the singer-songwriters of the latter part of the decade, they were seen as 'authentic' because they wrote their own songs and sang with a direct quality that evoked sincerity. In the late 1960s, however, more women started to come to the fore. Prime among these was a white girl from Texas, Janis Joplin. Her blues influences have been recognized widely, but listening to songs like 'Mercedes Benz' or 'Me and Bobby McGee' makes it clear that her country roots ran just as deep; because of the racialized myth of authenticity (black sources are 'more authentic' than white sources), this side of her style has often been ignored. As a woman, too, her appearance was under constant scrutiny: she was often and bluntly described as 'ugly'. This made her experimentation with and finally death from hard drugs less appealing than that of her male counterparts, Jim Morrison and Jimi Hendrix, and she has not benefited (if that is the right word) from the tragic glamour of the rock and roll martyr to the same degree.

Jefferson Airplane was unusual in having a female lead singer, Signe Anderson, and when Anderson left after only one album (*Takes Off*, 1966), Grace Slick became the lead singer. Here women were still conflated with their bodies as 'front' and as voices, but Slick was especially assertive in both her looks and her vocal style. Christine McVie joined the blues band Fleetwood Mac on a much more integral level, not only as a singer but also as a keyboardist and songwriter; in fact, by the time the band was at the top of the charts in the mid- to late 1970s, McVie was perhaps its dominant member, sharing leadership with the new guitarist Lindsey Buckingham. By that time, too, Stevie Nicks was part of the band, contributing songs and singing lead. At the same time, Fleetwood Mac exemplifies the way in which women were generally brought into groups as the girlfriend or wife; Christine was married to bassist John McVie, while Buckingham and Nicks had a long-standing relationship. Similarly, Grace Slick was in a long-standing relationship with Paul Kantner in Jefferson Airplane that would produce a daughter, China.

There is no denying that Slick, Nicks, and Christine McVie were all of great importance to the success of their bands, but it is probable that none of these women would have been brought into the group without their personal connections. Even solo artists were often known more for their romantic links than their own music: Joan Baez's relationship with Bob Dylan is one example, but Marianne Faithfull's with Mick Jagger is the most extreme. Baez eventually stepped out of Dylan's shadow, but Faithfull, partially hindered by a serious drug problem, is hardly ever remembered as the promising recording artist of the mid-1960s that she was. By the time of Woodstock, then, women were beginning to become a little more visible in rock music. But as in society at large, their roles were still marginal, subservient, and judged in terms of their relationship to men.

Bibliography

Brackett, David. 'The Politics and Practice of "Crossover" in American Popular Music, 1963 to 1965', *Musical Quarterly* 78 (1994), pp. 774–97.

Bradley, Dick. *Understanding Rock 'n' Roll: Popular Music in Britain 1955–1964*, Buckingham, 1992.

Covach, John. 'We Won't Get Fooled Again: Rock Music and Musical Analysis', *In Theory Only* 13 (1997), pp. 119–41.

Covach, John and Graeme Boone (eds.). *Understanding Rock: Essays in Musical Analysis*, New York, 1997.

Dawson, Jim. *The Twist: The Story of the Song and Dance that Changed the World*, London, 1995.

Doty, Alexander. 'The Cabinet of Lucy Ricardo: Lucille Ball's Star Image', *Cinema Journal* 29/4 (1990), pp. 3–18.

Frith, Simon. '"The Magic that can Set you Free": The Ideology of Folk and the Myth of the Rock Community', *Popular Music* 1 (1981), pp. 159–68.
Performing Rites: On the Value of Popular Music, Cambridge, MA, 1996.
Sound Effects: Youth, Leisure, and the Politics of Rock 'n' Roll, New York, 1981.
Garofalo, Reebee. *Rockin' Out: Popular Music in the USA*, Boston, 1992.
Gillett, Charlie. *The Sound of the City: The Rise of Rock and Roll* (rev. and expanded edn), London, 1983.
Goldman, Albert. *Elvis*, New York, 1981.
Elvis: The Last 24 Hours, New York, 1991.
The Lives of John Lennon, New York, 1988.
Hajdu, David and Roy Hemming. *Discovering Great Singers of Classic Pop*, New York, 1991.
Hebdige, Dick. *Subculture: The Meaning of Style*, London, 1979.
Levitz, Tamara. 'Twist and Shout: The Female Voice and the Silencing of the Beatles', unpublished paper presented at the Cross(over) Relations Conference, Eastman School of Music, 1996.
Manuel, Peter, with Kenneth Bilby and Michael Largey. *Caribbean Currents: Caribbean Music from Rumba to Reggae*, Philadelphia, 1995.
Marcus, Greil. *Mystery Train: Images of American in Rock 'n' Roll Music* (4th rev. edn), New York, 1997.
Mellers, Wilfrid. *Twilight of the Gods: The Music of the Beatles*, New York, 1973.
Oliver, Paul. *Blues Fell This Morning* [also published as *The Meaning of the Blues*], London, 1960.
Peterson, Richard A. 'Why 1955? Explaining the Advent of Rock Music', *Popular Music* 9 (1990), pp. 97–116.
Shaw, Arnold. *Honkers and Shouters: The Golden Age of Rhythm & Blues*, New York, 1978.
Southern, Eileen. *The Music of Black Americans: A History*, New York, 1971, 1983, and 1997.
Tagg, Philip. 'Analysing Popular Music: Theory, Method and Practice', *Popular Music* 2 (1982), pp. 37–67.
'Open Letter: "Black Music", "Afro-American Music" and "European Music"', *Popular Music* 8 (1989), pp. 285–93.
Walser, Robert. *Running with the Devil: Power, Gender, and Madness in Heavy Metal Music*, Hanover, 1993.
Wilson, Charles Reagan and William Ferris (eds.). *An Encyclopedia of Southern Culture*, 4 vols., New York, 1989.

Discography

The Association. 'Along Comes Mary' (Warner Bros., 1965)
Baez, Joan. 'The Night They Drove Old Dixie Down' (Vanguard, 1971)
Ballard, Hank. 'The Twist' (King, 1958 [some list as 1959, but the song was around definitely in 1958])
The Band. 'King Harvest (Has Surely Come)' (Capitol, 1968)
'The Night They Drove Old Dixie Down' (Capitol, 1968)
'The Weight' (Capitol, 1968)

The Beach Boys. 'Good Vibrations' (Capitol, 1965)
Pet Sounds (Capitol, 1966)
The Beatles. 'Love Me Do' (Parlophone, 1963)
'Please Mr. Postman' (Parlophone, 1963)
Revolver (Parlophone, 1966)
Sergeant Pepper's Lonely Hearts Club Band (Parlophone, 1967)
'Till There Was You' (Parlophone, 1963)
'Twist and Shout' (Parlophone, 1963)
Berry, Chuck. 'Maybelline' (Chess, 1959)
'Promised Land' (Chess, 1959)
'You Never Can Tell' (Chess, 1959)
Booker T. and the MGs. 'Green Onions' (Stax, 1962)
Boone, Pat. 'Tutti Frutti' (Dot, 1956)
The Boswell Sisters. 'Rock and Roll' (Victor, 1934)
Brown, James. 'Say It Loud – I'm Black and I'm Proud' (Polydor, 1969)
Brown, Roy. 'Good Rockin' Tonight' (DeLuxe, 1947)
Buffalo Springfield. 'For What It's Worth' (Atco, 1967)
Carter Family. 'River of Jordan' (RCA Victor, 1928)
Checker, Chubby. 'The Twist' (Cameo-Parkway, 1960)
Dale, Dick. 'Let's Go Trippin' (Del-Tone, 1961)
'Misirlou' (Del-Tone, 1962)
Darin, Bobby. 'Mack the Knife' (Atlantic, 1958)
'Splish Splash' (Atlantic, 1958)
Domino, 'Fats'. 'Ain't That a Shame' (Imperial, 1955)
'Blueberry Hill' (Imperial, 1956)
'Walking to New Orleans' (Imperial, 1956)
Donegan, Lonnie. 'Rock Island Line' (Decca, 1954)
The Drifters. 'On Broadway' (Atlantic, 1963)
'Under the Boardwalk' (Atlantic, 1964)
'Up on the Roof' (Atlantic, 1962)
Dylan, Bob. 'Blowin' in the Wind' (Columbia, 1963)
The Everly Brothers. 'Cathy's Clown' (Warner Brothers, 1960)
'Lucille' (Warner Brothers, 1961)
'Till I Kissed Ya' (Cadence, 1959)
'Wake Up, Little Susie' (Cadence, 1957)
Floyd, Eddie. 'Knock on Wood' (Stax, 1966)
Franklin, Aretha. 'Respect' (Atlantic, 1967)
Gaye, Marvin. 'What's Going On' (Motown, 1971)
Gore, Lesley. 'It's My Party (and I'll Cry If I Want To)' (Mercury, 1963)
Lesley Gore Sings of Mixed-Up Hearts (Mercury, 1963)
'You Don't Own Me' (Mercury, 1963)
Guthrie, Woody. 'This Land Is Your Land' (first recorded Smithsonian, 1940)
Haley, Bill and the Comets. 'Rock Around the Clock' (Decca, 1955)
'See Ya Later, Alligator' (Decca, 1955)
Howlin' Wolf. *The London Sessions* (Chess, 1971)
The Isley Brothers. 'Twist and Shout' (Sundazed, 1962)
Jefferson Airplane. *Takes Off* (RCA, 1966)

Joplin, Janis. 'Me and Bobby McGee' (Columbia, 1971)
'Mercedes Benz' (Columbia, 1971)
Little Richard. 'Lucille' (Specialty, 1957)
'Tutti Frutti' (Specialty, 1955)
Lynn, Loretta. 'The Pill' (MCA, 1975)
'You Ain't Woman Enough to Take My Man' (MCA, 1966)
'Your Squaw Is On the Warpath' (Decca, 1969)
The Marvelettes. 'Please Mr. Postman' (Motown, 1961)
Matchbox Twenty. 'Damn' (Atlantic, 1996)
Nelson, Ricky. 'Hello, Mary Lou' (Imperial, 1958)
'Traveling Man' (Imperial, 1959)
Phair, Liz. 'Happy' (live, 1996)
Pickett, Wilson. 'In the Midnight Hour' (Atlantic, 1965)
Presley, Elvis. 'Hound Dog' (RCA, 1956)
The Ravens. 'Rock All Night Long' (Mercury, 1948)
Redding, Otis. 'Dock of the Bay' (Stax, 1968)
'Mr. Pitiful' (Stax, 1964)
'Respect' (Stax, 1965)
Simon and Garfunkel. 'A Simple Desultory Philippic' (Columbia, 1967)
Sinatra, Frank. *In the Wee Small Hours* (Capitol, 1954)
Songs for Swinging Lovers (Capitol, 1955)
Surfaris. 'Wipe Out' (Decca, 1963)
The Temptations. 'Papa Was a Rolling Stone' (Motown, 1972)
Thomas, Carla. 'Gee Whiz' (Stax, 1960)
Thornton, Willa Mae. 'Big Mama', 'Hound Dog' (Peacock, 1953)
Tom and Jerry (Simon and Garfunkel). 'Hey Schoolgirl' (Big, 1957)
Valens, Ritchie. 'La Bamba' (Del-Fi, 1959)
Waters, Muddy. *The London Sessions* (Chess, 1971)
The Who. *Tommy* (MCA, 1969)

· 17 ·

Expanding horizons: the international avant-garde, 1962–75

RICHARD TOOP

Darmstadt after Steinecke

When Wolfgang Steinecke – the originator of the Darmstadt *Ferienkurse* – died at the end of 1961, much of the increasingly fragile spirit of collegiality within the Cologne/Darmstadt-centred avant-garde died with him. Boulez and Stockhausen in particular were already fiercely competitive, and when in 1960 Steinecke had assigned direction of the Darmstadt composition course to Boulez, Stockhausen had pointedly stayed away.[1] Cage's work and significance was a constant source of acrimonious debate, and Nono's bitter opposition to him[2] was one reason for the Italian composer being marginalized by the Cologne inner circle as a structuralist reactionary. Other Cologne figures were starting to assert their creative personalities, and look for their place in the sun: Argentinian-born Mauricio Kagel, whose *Anagrama* (1959) had upstaged the premiere of Stockhausen's *Kontakte* at the 1960 ISCM Festival in Cologne, was starting to rebel against Stockhausen's assumptions of supremacy; the Hungarian György Ligeti, disenchanted by the incessant conflicts, had left Cologne for Vienna just at the moment where his own distinctive compositional voice was starting to emerge in the orchestral work *Apparitions* (1960); and Gottfried Michael Koenig (b. 1926), who had been Stockhausen's right-hand man in the electronic studios since the mid-1950s, and whose *Klangfiguren II* (1956) had been the only work one could think of setting beside *Gesang der Jünglinge*, would shortly leave for Holland.

These territorial power struggles and secessions offered a paradoxical yet symbolic upbeat to a decade whose central theme was to be openness. Orthodoxies would continue, but as the number of composers affiliated to the notion of an avant-garde swelled dramatically – even globalized – every form of authority and exclusiveness would be questioned. As the 1960s progressed, both hope and disenchantment grew in harness with one another, mirroring

1 Cf. Inge Misch and Markus Bandur (eds.), *Karlheinz Stockhausen bei den Internationalen Ferienkursen für Neue Musik in Darmstadt 1951–1996*, Kürten, 2001, pp. 262ff.

2 Cf. Luigi Nono, 'Geschichte und Gegenwart in der Musik von heute', in *Melos* 27 (1960), pp. 69–75.

the political dreams and discontents that erupted in the abortive uprisings of 1968. In Europe, at least, 1968 marked a crucial turning point: a collapse of utopian thinking, which diversified into furious protest and denial on the one hand and resignation or capitulation on the other, the latter paving the way for the most 'retro' elements of mid-1970s postmodernism.

Initially, though, this was also a period of enormous achievement and excitement. Boulez referred contemptuously to the 'dreadful and regular epidemics'[3] that seemingly created new fashions on an annual basis. Naturally, as the ranks of the 'avant-garde' grew, so too did epigonism: multiplying numbers does not necessarily multiply talent and originality, or at least, not by the same factor. But it was precisely the proliferation of ideas that characterized the 1960s, not the systematic working-out of a consistent radical position that had preoccupied the avant-gardes of the previous decade. In some respects Boulez, whose own compositions in the fourteen years separating *Pli selon pli* (1961) and *Rituel in memoriam Bruno Maderna* (1975) would scarcely match his earlier triumphs, was now out of step with the times. In the wake of the modernist 'grand narratives' of the 1950s – serialism and its derivatives, indeterminacy, and electroacoustic music – there was certainly ample scope for the acts of consolidation rather than innovation that Boulez now appeared to endorse, but the mood of the era did not favour them. Initially, works by young Boulez disciples and protégés such as *Diaphonies* (1964) and *Triade* (1965) by Gilbert Amy (b. 1936), or *Equivalences* (1963) by Jean-Claude Eloy (b. 1938), impressed through their superior craft and elegance; but before long, the predictable melange of mellifluous harmonies, limited aleatory elements, and massed metallophones was seeming like a new academicism (starting with *Faisceaux-Diffractions* (1970), Eloy too would break out into quite new directions), and increasingly, it was to the ever-unpredictable Stockhausen that young composers looked, as the prophet of times to come. Purism gave way to pluralism.

Another respect in which the European avant-garde detached itself from the post-Webernism of the preceding decade was its espousal of large forms and dramatic gestures. If there was any trace of a Webernesque 'Andacht zum Kleinen' at the start of the 1960s, it soon disappeared. Though the individual movements of Boulez's *Pli selon pli* may not have exceeded fifteen minutes in length, the overall one-hour span demonstrated a new sense of scale, almost doubling the length of those Stockhausen works (*Gruppen* (1957), *Carré*, and *Kontakte* (both 1960)) which had previously set the benchmark for temporal and gestural ambition. Stockhausen himself would soon up the stakes with the

3 Pierre Boulez, *Boulez on Music Today* (tr. Susan Bradshaw and Richard Rodney Bennett), London, 1971, p. 21.

1965 version of *Momente*, and above all with the massive electroacoustic composition *Hymnen* (1967), which lasts almost two hours (over two hours in the version with soloists). Without quite aspiring to these dimensions, Berio's works from this period, such as *Passaggio* (1962), *Epifanie* (1964), and *Laborintus II* (1965), moved up around the half-hour mark, as did Kagel in works like the orchestral *Heterophonie* (1961), and *Tremens* (1965), or Ligeti in his *Requiem* (1965).

More significant than duration, though, was the broadening of themes and emotional scope. The move from the studio/laboratory mentality of the 1950s avant-garde to a more theatrical orientation may have been partly an outcome of the avant-garde's growing impact and cultural status, but it also reflected an increasing willingness to address major human and social themes, as in the works by Berio mentioned above and in Stockhausen's *Hymnen*, with its utopian aspiration of unifying all peoples through music. The 'big statement' also becomes clear in Xenakis's works of the late 1960s, such as the orchestral works *Terretektorh* (1966) and *Nomos Gamma* (1968), in which the orchestral players are to be placed amidst the audience, the ballet score *Kraanerg* (1969), and the tape composition *Persepolis* (1971). Once again, this is not just a matter of duration or large forces, but of subject matter: *Kraanerg*, for instance, was inspired in part by predictions that around 2020, eighty per cent of the world's population will be aged under twenty-five, and that 'a biological struggle between generations will sweep the planet',[4] destroying all known social frameworks.

However, the spirit of 1960s modernism is not adequately conveyed by its more glamorous and dramatic products alone. Almost equally characteristic was the 'do-it-yourself' attitude which many composers extrapolated from Cage's work – an approach which viewed the whole notion of the 'great work' with some scepticism. Pluralism and cosmopolitanism notwithstanding, the 1960s saw a clear polarization between the modernist activities of American and European composers (in passing, it may be noted that the two most durable new tendencies introduced during this time – live electronics and minimalism – both emanated from the United States). Moreover, within the United States a sharp split emerged between an 'orthodox' modernism fostered within university music departments, embodied by composers such as Milton Babbitt (b. 1916) and Elliott Carter (b. 1908), and more experimental activities pursued largely without reference to educational institutions, this split being encapsulated in the New York distinction between 'uptown' and 'downtown' composers.

4 'une lutte biologique entre les générations déferlant que toute la planète . . . ', composer's note to Erato [vinyl] recording.

New national schools

The Boulez–Nono–Stockhausen triumvirate that appeared to dominate Darmstadt in the late 1950s may have been international, but the nations involved were the same ones that had dominated nineteenth-century music: France, Italy, and Germany. In fact, quite apart from the New York School around Cage, avant-gardes had already begun to emerge during the 1950s in countries as diverse as Sweden, Holland, England, Spain, and Japan. An emphatic multi-nationalism, however, became clearer from the early 1960s onwards. Initially, the most striking instance of this was the Polish 'sonorist' school that emerged rapidly from 1956 onwards, after the loosening of Socialist Realist stylistic restrictions: by 1961, younger composers like Krzysztof Penderecki and Henryk Górecki, and older ones like Witold Lutosławski and Kazimierz Serocki (1922–81), had already made an international impact with works which laid emphasis on colourful and novel sonorities and were characterized by abrupt, almost cinematic changes of texture. In the course of the 1960s, comparable but more limited Eastern European avant-gardes appeared in Czechoslovakia (Marek Kopelent (b. 1932), Rudolf Komorous (b. 1931), and Zbynek Vostrak (1920–85)), and Yugoslavia (Milko Kelemen (b. 1924), and above all Vinko Globokar (b. 1934), who was to play a major international role both as composer and as virtuoso trombonist). Yet while the emergence of these schools may reflect the waning influence of official communist arts ideologies, the simultaneous rise of a Cuban avant-garde, headed by Leo Brouwer (b. 1939), was made possible by Castro's liberal view of all forms of 'radical' expression.[5]

In many cases, these modernist schools provided a major revitalization of national musical culture, though rarely in a nationalist sense. In England, the early works of Peter Maxwell Davies, Alexander Goehr, and Harrison Birtwistle – who, together with the composers and performers Elgar Howarth and John Ogdon, made up the so-called 'Manchester School' – marked a clear break with current British practice, yet while superficially espousing a European sound-world, Davies and Birtwistle in particular established links back to earlier English avant-gardes ranging from Dunstable to Bull. But alongside the Manchester trinity, there were many other persuasive forces, including David Bedford (b. 1938), who had studied with Nono, but was more obviously influenced by the music he had heard on visits to the Warsaw Festival, and subsequently by radical developments in rock music. By the late 1960s,

5 Cf. Fidel Castro, 'Words to the Intellectuals', in Lee Baxandall (ed.), *Radical Perspectives in the Arts*, Harmondsworth, 1972, pp. 267–98.

early works by Brian Ferneyhough (b. 1943) and Michael Finnissy (b. 1947) brought the first intimations of what was ultimately to become known as 'new complexity'.

Particularly significant was the engagement of several Asian (and especially Japanese) composers with Western avant-garde techniques, not least because they brought a new sensibility into play, and in some instances showed how non-Western art musics could offer new perspectives to Western 'new music' without resort to the 'exoticism' practised by French composers, in particular, in the first part of the century. While some younger composers such as Tōru Takemitsu and Jōji Yuasa (b. 1929) initially resisted overt references to Japanese art-music traditions, not least because of its associations with a discredited Imperial system,[6] *Bugaku per orchestra* (1961) by Yoritsune Matsudaira (b. 1907) transposed aspects of *gagaku* (the ancient Japanese court music) into a serial and aleatory context, while the *Nirvana Symphony* (1958) by Toshiro Mayuzumi (1929–97) drew on elements of Buddhist chant. A comparable reinterpretation of Korean court music was pursued by Isang Yun (1917–95) in works like *Loyang* (1962) and *Réak* (1966). Such pieces induced many Western composers to consider whether aspects of non-Western music, past or present, might not open new avenues for them. One of the first to do so was Messiaen, whose *Sept Haïkaï* (1962) for piano and small orchestra followed a visit to Japan, and includes Matsudaira among its dedicatees; the fourth movement, entitled '*Gagaku*', is Messiaen's attempt to effect his own recreation of the ancient genre. An intriguing and in some respects paradoxical case history relating to Asian influence is provided by the Australian avant-garde that evolved in the course of the 1960s. Peter Sculthorpe (b. 1928), while clearly affected by aspects of Polish sonorism, insisted on the importance of Asia as a source of inspiration, and used elements of Balinese and Japanese music in many works before turning to native Australian traditions; similarly, early works by Richard Meale (b. 1934) drew on concepts from Japanese culture, while espousing a harmonic language derived from Boulez.

Composing with textures

There had already been moments in the 1950s, in both orchestral and electronic music, where the sheer number and complexity of sounds present meant that the individual sounds could no longer be heard, except as part of an overall texture or tendency. Stockhausen had already commented on this in relation

6 Toru Takemitsu, *Confronting Silence*, Berkeley, 1995, p. 53.

to parts of *Gesang der Jünglinge* (1956) and *Gruppen*, and other notable instances occur in his *Carré*. But such moments, in Stockhausen, nearly always comprised exceptions or extremes – they are not the *raison d'être* of the work in question. In a work like Xenakis's *Pithoprakta* (1956), on the other hand, the manipulation of sound masses through applications of probability theory was precisely the point at issue (the programmatic, almost autobiographical dimension of the piece is not one that Xenakis was willing to comment on at the time).[7] Here there were indeed figures, but only as the fixed outcomes of random distributions: the figures had no importance in themselves, except in relation to an overall distribution of clouds of sounds.

Pithoprakta may be a relatively rare example of the avant-garde work that really is ahead of its time, albeit only by a few years. Even in Xenakis's own work it had no immediate major successors, though elements are resumed in the tape composition *Diamorphoses* (1957) and in *Syrmos* (1959) for eighteen strings. But by 1961, the notion of a purely 'textural' music in which figuration of any kind served only to articulate global sonic processes was very much in the air, primarily among composers who, wherever they happened to be living at the time, were of Eastern European origin. Two 'emblematic' textural works from 1961 – Ligeti's *Atmosphères* and Penderecki's *Threnody for the Victims of Hiroshima* – serve to highlight both common practice and essential differences. Both seek to neutralize harmony through the use of chromatic clusters, and both operate with dense bands of sound characterized by changing width, register, and timbre. However, *Atmosphères* consists of one continuous section, with a brief coda-epilogue at the end, whereas the slightly shorter *Threnody* comprises half a dozen clearly contrasted sections, each of which also employs contrast within a more restricted range. The Polish work makes use of a wide variety of novel string techniques, many of them involving aleatory elements, whereas the intricate 'micropolyphony' of *Atmosphères* is fully notated and eschews 'extended techniques' until the coda, where the wind players breathe through their instruments without producing a pitched sound. Broadly speaking, one could describe Ligeti's piece as 'organic', and Penderecki's as 'tachiste' – a description applicable not only to Penderecki's other early works (within which *Fluorescences* (1962) represents an extreme of experimentation) but to Polish sonorism in general: to Lutosławski's *Jeux vénitiens* (1961) and *Trois poèmes d'Henri Michaux* (1963), Serocki's *Segmenti* (1961), Górecki's *Genesis* cycle (1961–2), and Wojiech Kilar's *Diphthongos* (1964). Here the primary intention is often (though not always) to provide a glittering array of unusual sonorities.

7 Cf. Nouritza Matossian, *Xenakis*, London, 1986, p. 58.

Ligeti's organicist position (continued in the graphically notated *Volumina* (1962) for organ) is paralleled by *Fasce* (1961) and *Spiegel II* (1962) by Friedrich Čerha (b. 1926) – the remainder of the remarkable *Spiegel* cycle, apparently conceived in the early 1960s, was not actually carried through until 1970 – and works by the young Swedish composer Jan Morthensen (b. 1940), whose book *Nonfigurative Musik* included an adulatory preface by Heinz-Klaus Metzger.[8] Another 'textural' path was pursued by Aldo Clementi (b. 1925), under the influence of informal abstractionism in painting: in his work of the early 1960s, typified by the three pieces entitled *Informel* (1961–3), harmony and melody are almost completely neutralized in favour of an opaque but constantly shifting surface. However, next to Ligeti, perhaps the finest exponent of an organic textural style was a composer whose work was, at the time, almost completely unknown: Giacinto Scelsi. A reclusive Sicilian aristocrat, deeply influenced by Buddhism, he produced two remarkable works in 1958: *I presagi*, a work for wind ensemble which reanimated the spirit of Varèse's ensemble pieces from the 1920s within a hieratic, ritualistic context, and above all the *Quattro pezzi per orchestra*, each of whose four movements centres on a single pitch, subjected to constant changes of timbre, intonation, and (chromatically blurred) octave doublings, producing music of quite unique and ominous intensity. However marginal they may have appeared at the time, Scelsi's preoccupations are actually quite close to those of both Stockhausen and the 'texturalists'. Scelsi's harmony-less 'single notes' are, in effect, smudged unison clusters; as for Stockhausen (who appears to have been completely unaware of Scelsi), in 1960 he began work on *Monophonie*, a 'one-note' orchestral work which, had he ever completed it, might have come fascinatingly close to Scelsi's aesthetic.

Collage, quotation, and irony

Perhaps the clearest indication of a break with 1950s avant-garde purism was the degree to which composers became willing to introduce stylistic 'foreign bodies' into their work, often in form of direct, collage-like quotations. The European pioneer here was the Cologne-based Bernd Alois Zimmermann, whose opera *Die Soldaten* (1960), *Dialoge* for two pianos and orchestra (1960, rev. 1965), and piano trio *Présence* (1961) introduced quotations ranging from Bach to (with intentional irony) Stockhausen, within a highly serialist framework. For Zimmermann, such quotations had a metaphysical dimension, deriving from St Augustine and from the composer's own notion

8 Jan Morthensen, *Nonfigurative Musik*, Stockholm, 1966.

of the 'spherical shape of time'. For other composers, the sheer provocation of confronting 'old' and 'new' music, or turning the former into the latter, was attractive enough in its own right. A characteristic early example is the quintet *Modulation I* (1966) by the Zimmermann pupil Johannes Fritsch (b. 1941), also closely associated with Stockhausen; the opening artfully fuses quotations from Beethoven, Brahms, Berg, and Schoenberg in such a way that everything sounds familiar, yet not actually like a quotation. The most celebrated European instances of a collage/quotation-based composition are probably the third movement of Berio's *Sinfonia* (1968) and Stockhausen's *Hymnen*, but the strategies of the two works are quite different. Berio creates an intricate web of exact quotations from Bach to the mid-1960s, grafted onto the scherzo of Mahler's *Resurrection Symphony*, which is almost constantly present in full or more fragmentary form. In *Hymnen*, on the other hand, a wide range of national anthems is used as a 'familiar' basis for constant musical transformation – an approach which Stockhausen describes, with some justification, as 'meta-collage'.

A comparable, and ultimately more drastic phenomenon in the US occurs in the work of George Rochberg (b. 1918). Up to the early 1960s, Rochberg had typified the accomplished American academic composer; he was a serialist with a distinctly Schoenbergian orientation whose Second String Quartet (1961), in particular, was widely admired. In 1964, following the death of his son, Rochberg claimed that for him, writing serial music had become a meaningless activity,[9] and in *Contra mortem et tempus* (1965) he adopted a 'collage-assemblage' approach, combining passages from works by many composers, from Berg and Webern to Boulez and Rochberg himself. Here virtually all the quotations are atonal; in subsequent works, such as the Third String Quartet (1972), Rochberg moves from quotation to a 'polystylistic' approach to composition whose stylistic references extend back to Beethoven. A comparable progression (or regression, depending on one's point of view) may be observed in the work of George Crumb, who attained a considerable level of popularity in the late 1960s and 70s with works such as *Vox balaenae* (1971) and the Lorca cycle *Ancient Voices of Children* (1970).

Such characteristics obviously beg questions concerning the borderlines between pluralism and postmodernism. While the latter, in terms of music, is often regarded as a particular outcome of 1960s pluralism which emerges in the early and especially mid-1970s, there are certain works from the 1960s, especially from Italy, which seem to fulfill all the conditions of ahistoricity, irony, and double meanings established by subsequent theoreticians such as the

9 George Rochberg, sleeve note to the Composers Recordings Inc recording of 'Contra mortem et tempus' (*ca.* 1968).

architect Charles Jencks.[10] Perhaps the most striking musical precursor is Paolo Castaldi (b. 1930), whose *Anfrage* (1963) for two pianos consists entirely of cut-out quotations of tonal and atonal repertoire, with rather Satie-esque verbal instructions which are also collages from other sources. The tonal excerpts are provided without key signatures, but are to be played literally as they appear on the score page, without 'tonal reconstruction'; only the atonal quotations escape the indignity of arbitrary distortion. More modest examples by the same composer are *Grid* (1969) for solo piano, in which the melodic/harmonic content of Liszt's third *Liebestraum* is grafted onto the rhythmic structure of Chopin's E major Etude, op.10, no. 3, and *Elisa* (1967), in which a characteristically complex 'structuralist' rhythmic notation (partly appropriated from Bussotti's *Pour Clavier*) is used to simulate a painstaking but painfully inept rendering of Beethoven's *Für Elise*. Comparable tendencies are found in certain works by Niccolo Castiglioni (1932–96), notably the enormous *Sinfonie guerrière et amorose* for solo organ (1967), which embraces every organ genre from Darmstadt to the fairground.

In fact, the kind of ironic evaluation of musical material often associated with postmodernism was already widespread among the 1960s avant-garde. Two companion pieces by Ligeti, *Aventures* (1963) and *Nouvelles aventures* (1965), deliberately sought to push the 'hyper-expressive' dimension of wide-leaping post-Webern vocal styles to the point of absurdity, and the same strategy is pursued at the beginning of the 'Dies irae' of his *Requiem*. This bizarre insertion into what is innately a highly serious work could be regarded as a latter-day 'alienation effect' (in the Brechtian sense); comparable instances are found (alongside straightforward examples of gleefully malicious satire) in several works by Maxwell Davies, including *Revelation and Fall* (1966), *St Thomas Wake* (1969), and *Vesalii icones* (1969). However, the primary exponent of ironic equivocality was undoubtedly Mauricio Kagel, who in terms of the 'Cologne school' might be regarded as playing Mephistopheles to Stockhausen's Faust. Virtually every piece of Kagel's has some unsettling aspect, whether it be the 'too high' tuning up note that begins *Heterophonie*, the seeming contradiction between the highly serious musical content of *Match* (1964) for two cellos and percussionist and its visual effect as a droll sports contest, or the way that the instruments of Praetorius's *Syntagmum musicum* are resurrected to function as an avant-garde ensemble in *Music for Renaissance Instruments* (1966). The climax of Kagel's earlier work is probably provided by *Staatstheater* (1970), in which the entire institutional apparatus of a state opera house is dissected, using its own means against it.

10 Cf. Charles Jencks, *What is Post-Modernism?*, London, 1986.

The New York School and Fluxus

The 1960s saw increasing divergences of opinion within the group of composers around Cage. Put simply, Cage and Christian Wolff (now supplemented by the Japanese composer Toshi Ichiyanagi (b. 1931)) continued to espouse an 'egoless' view of composition, while Earle Brown and, above all, Morton Feldman sought to establish recognizable and relatively consistent artistic personalities. A significant indicator of this was the approach to notation. In the eight years that separate *Atlas eclipticalis* (1961) and *Cheap Imitation* (1969), Cage produced almost no work in anything resembling a notated score format. Rather than producing 'works', he preferred to create particular situations (albeit documented with a 'work title') that gave rise to the production and perception of sounds, with no particular bias towards instrumental (or vocal) performance. Some of these scores, following the model established in *Fontana Mix* (1958), involved the random superimposition of plastic sheets with graphic elements; others were purely verbal, such as *Variations V* (1965), subtitled 'remarks re an audio-visual performance'.

Brown's scores from *Available Forms I* (1961) onwards mix spatial notation with graphic elements; some, like *Available Forms I & II* and *Novara* (1962), are open forms, while others are 'through-composed', though sometimes incorporating 'mobile' elements. They are notable for their economy and pragmatism, embodying the composer's dictum that 'Good notation is what works'.[11] The twelve-minute *String Quartet* (1964) is notated on just three pages, and the twenty-minute *Centering* (1973), for violin and small orchestra, on only fifteen.

On the other hand Feldman's music, while maintaining the slow pace and soft dynamics that had emerged as a personal trademark during the 1950s, moved towards ever more exact notation. The graph notation of the 1950s (always just one practice out of many) reached a peak with the orchestral *Out of Last Pieces...* (1961), but was then largely abandoned, its last use being in *The King of Denmark* (1964) for solo percussionist. *Durations* (1960–1), an important set of five pieces for various small ensembles, is ironically titled, insofar as durations are the one area where the performers have significant freedom. However, with the *Vertical Thoughts* series (1963), durations too started to be more exactly specified. Moreover, as with so many other modernists in the 1960s, Feldman evolved a very distinctive harmonic vocabulary, not in the conventional sense of chord 'progressions', but in terms of personal sonorities.

The New York School's exploration of new notations spread rapidly through the European avant-garde from the end of the 1950s onwards. The motivations seem to have ranged from exploration to pragmatism, from serious attempts

11 In John Cage (ed.), *Notations*, New York, 1969, unpaginated.

at notational reform to mere fashion. Publishers undoubtedly latched on to the latter: in the mid-1960s, Universal Edition was advertising its New Music catalogue in terms of 'stabiles' (i.e. relatively conventionally notated scores), 'mobiles', and 'musical graphics', and the latter (notably examples by Sylvano Bussotti, Roman Haubenstock-Ramati, and Anestis Logothetis) regularly provided eye-catching promotional material – though the new formats demanded by graphic and texturalist composers soon led to scores becoming too large and expensive for anyone but professionals to contemplate buying them. While such 'musical graphics' scarcely outlived the 1960s, they played an important role in loosening distinctions between composition and improvisation, extending the traditional polarity between 'action notation' and 'result notation' by adding an 'incitement to activity' category. They also had a relatively brief but significant impact on the strategies of secondary-school music educators (evident, for instance, in the influential work of John Paynter in the UK).[12] Some aspects were absorbed into contemporary modernist practice, but the general level of resistance from musicians outside specialist circles meant that, as the avant-garde gained access to larger, more institutionalized performance bodies, the incentive to pursue notational innovation receded.

By 1960, Cage's influence had extended beyond the musical world, as normally defined; the classes in composition he gave in the late 1950s at the New School for Social Research in New York were attended not so much by aspiring composers as by visual artists and poets, some of whom, like Allen Kaprow, had already been instrumental in evolving the 'happenings' genre. One outcome of this was Fluxus, a multimedia anti-art movement presided over by George Maciunas, in which, unusually, music played a major role. While Fluxus notionally began in Wiesbaden (Germany), in 1962, its general preference for brief, provocative, and humorous 'events', strung together to form a 'show', seemed more characteristically American. One could probably make a distinction between 'cool' Fluxus, embodied in the succinct texts that comprise George Brecht's *Water Yam* collection (the 'score' of *Saxophone Solo* (1962) comprises the single word 'Trumpet') and 'hot' Fluxus, characterised by the ritualistic, often masochistic 'actions' of the Korean Nam June Paik (b. 1932), who subsequently became one of the most significant early video artists.

Cage himself had highly equivocal feelings about Fluxus, admiring aspects of the work of Paik and Alison Knowles (b. 1933), but being disturbed both by the violence of Paik's performances and the insistence on frivolity of many other

12 Cf. John Paynter and Peter Aston, *Sound and Silence: Classroom Projects in Creative Music*, Cambridge, 1970, as well as the numerous 'new music' scores for school use published by Universal Edition (London and Vienna).

participants. On the other hand, many of the Darmstadt avant-garde (particularly Kagel and Ligeti) were particularly intrigued by Paik, who was active in Cologne around 1960, and Stockhausen actually incorporated Paik into the initial performances of his theatre piece *Originale* (1961). Ligeti wrote one explicit Fluxus piece (the near-silent *Trois Bagatelles* (1961) dedicated to David Tudor), and his 'mute' lecture *Die Zukunft der Musik* (1961) and *Poème symphonique* for a hundred metronomes (1962) also have clear Fluxus affiliations. For a while, Maciunas avidly sought closer links with the European avant-garde, but then rejected them with equal vehemence.

Electroacoustic music – tape music and live electronics

In the course of the 1960s, technological leadership in the area of electroacoustic studio composition passed to the US, mainly by virtue of innovations in synthesizer technology which European studios were relatively slow to adopt. In the early 1960s, the primary agent here was the Columbia-Princeton Studio headed by Milton Babbitt, and therefore initially oriented to a fairly orthodox serialist approach in which pitch and rhythmic relationships took clear precedence over the search for new concepts of timbre (though the sound-world of early pieces by Bulent Arel (1919–91) and Mario Davidovsky (b. 1934) is sometimes reminiscent of work done at the Milan studios around the same time). However, despite the recognition achieved by two early works for voice and tape – *Vision and Prayer* (1961) and *Philomel* (1963) – relatively little of Babbitt's subsequent work involved the use of electronics.

In Europe, Stockhausen remained committed to the 'classic' studio medium; *Telemusik* (1966) is perhaps the most perfect example of the genre from this period, while *Hymnen* (1966–7) is certainly the most ambitious. Nono, who had initially rejected electronic music on ideological grounds (as 'inhuman') eventually came to regard it as an important vehicle for conveying Marxist ideology, starting with *La fabbrica illuminata* (1964). But for the rest, leading European avant-gardists mainly rejected it. After composing *Visage* (1961), a remarkable 'scena' for female voice and electronic music, Berio, who had been an early pioneer, virtually abandoned electronics (there is a brief but typically brilliant electronic episode in *Laborintus II* (1965)); Boulez, after the relative debacle of *Poésie pour pouvoir* (1958), wrote no further electroacoustic works for another couple of decades. An attempt in the early 1960s to attract newly emerging composers such as Castiglioni, Clementi, and Franco Donatoni (1927–2000) to the Milan studios had no ongoing consequences, though Maderna continued to work there. Perhaps the only significant 1960s extension of the electronic purism of the 1950s was the work undertaken by Gottfried Michael Koenig at the Instituut voor Sonologie, where he completed the *Terminus* series (1962–7) begun in Cologne, and produced the *Funktion* cycle (1968–9), in which matters of aesthetic pleasure are almost entirely subordinated to the imperatives of algorithmically based research (though the abrasive sound of the results also represents a characteristic late-1960s 'aesthetic'). Nevertheless, a large number of electronic studios continued to be active throughout the 1960s; in addition to those already mentioned, mention should be made of the studios at Mills College (where Pauline Oliveros realised several remarkable early works) and Dartmouth in the United States, at Nippon Radio in Tokyo, and at Swedish Radio and Polish Radio.

From the early 1960s, the orientation of the Paris *musique concrète* studios (Groupe de Recherches Musicales) changed. Pierre Schaeffer remained influential as a theorist, primarily through the publication of his *Traité des objets musicaux* (1966),[13] but the work produced at the GRM and elsewhere in France moved away from research towards a new aesthetics, and from clinical etudes to a more poetic, even pictorial approach. This change is exemplified by the work of Luc Ferrari (b. 1929), whose first brief tape pieces were impeccable etudes *à la* Schaeffer (*Etude aux sons tendus*, *Etude aux accidents* (both 1958)). In 1960 came a more extended work, whose provocatively programmatic title *Tête et queue du dragon* (Dragon's Head and Tail) foreshadowed major trends in the years to follow (provocation was to remain a central aspect of Ferrari's music). Leaving the GRM in 1963, Ferrari engaged with what he called 'anecdotal music' – a sort of composer-processed sound reportage – examples of which are *Music Promenade* (1964) and *Presque rien* no. 1 (1970). By this time, several other young composers such as François-Bernard Mâche (b. 1935) and the initially Cage-influenced François Bayle (b. 1932) had joined the studio, followed shortly after by Bernard Parmegiani (b. 1927). The latter two became, along with Pierre Henry, the principal exponents of *musique concrète*, though their most significant work dates from the mid-1970s onwards.

Arguably the most characteristic development in this area after 1962, however, took place outside the studios, and it had its origins in Cage. To the end of his life, Cage insisted that his most important contribution was the 'silent' piece *4′33″*, but in terms of influence on musical practice *Cartridge Music* (1960) may have stronger claims. This highly indeterminate score (on transparent sheets) is conceived in terms of 'amplified small sounds', produced by inserting various objects into a gramophone pickup; from this modest beginning grows the whole history of 'live electronic music'. What this new genre sought to do

13 Pierre Schaeffer, *Traité des Objets Musicaux*, Paris, 1966.

was to abolish the distinction between electronic music (or *musique concrète*) as 'studio practice', and live concert performance. It did this by using selected equipment from the studios to modify instrumental or other sounds electronically in a live performance context, as opposed to juxtaposing live instruments and tape – a practice already well established by the late 1950s. Even in the hands of composers with a slightly less radical aesthetic agenda than Cage's, live electronic music was 'experimental' in the sense that its outcomes could scarcely be foreseen (it only became a 'precise science' with the advent of computer technology in the late 1970s). Of the established European composers, only Stockhausen was immediately attracted to live electronic music; in fact, it became a central aspect of his work during the years 1964–70, most notably in *Mikrophonie I* (1964), a virtuoso display piece for six performers and one tam-tam, and *Mantra* (1970) for two pianos, the piece in which he established the method of 'formula composition' which dominated his work from that time on, as well as a sequence of works written for his own performing ensemble. But in the United States, live electronics was the basis on which a younger generation of composers, such as David Behrman (b. 1937), Larry Austin (b. 1930), and Allan Bryant (b. 1931), established a new performance practice. Here experimentation, instrument building, and a measure of improvisation went hand in hand, and circuit design was often part of the composition process. An important technological factor here was the replacement of valve technology by transistors. This dramatically reduced the physical size of electronic instruments; by the end of the 1960s, the sci-fi laboratory ambience of the RCA Mark II synthesizer at Columbia-Princeton had largely been displaced by instruments which could sit on a table top.

Minimalism and psychedelia

In the course of the early 1960s there emerged a new tendency (with marginal links to live electronic practice) which in some respects broke more radically with modernist orthodoxies than even the New York School around Cage had done. Initially described variously as 'static music', 'hypnotic music', and 'repetitive music', it came to be known as 'minimalism'. The origins of minimalism are normally traced back to La Monte Young:[14] to the startlingly long durations of his String Trio (1959), and above all to one of his Fluxus-oriented pieces, a *Composition #7 1960* which consists only of the notes F# and B, and the instruction 'to be held for a very long time'. There is a limit, perhaps, to

14 Cf. Michael Nyman, *Experimental Music: Cage and Beyond*, 2nd edn, Cambridge, 1999; Wim Mertens, *American Minimal Music*, London, 1983; Keith Potter, *Four Musical Minimalists: La Monte Young, Terry Riley, Steve Reich, Philip Glass*, Cambridge, 2000.

what one should extrapolate from a simple polemical gesture. However, the diatonic interval, the implied stasis and the long duration all anticipate fundamental characteristics of minimalism. What is lacking here, however, is the element of obsessive repetition that is generally associated with the three other principal early exponents of minimalism: Terry Riley, Steve Reich, and Philip Glass. Mertens indicates that both Riley (who, like Young, had early affiliations to Fluxus) and Reich made use of tape loops (a guarantee of repetition) in early music for film-soundtrack productions,[15] and presumably Riley's 'all-night concerts' in Sweden in 1963 rested at least in part on the insistent 'looped' figures that became his trademark in the mid-1960s. The first notated documentation of a minimalist/repetitive school came with two works by Riley from 1964: *Keyboard Studies* and *In C*, the latter work being the one that first established international awareness of this new tendency. While *Keyboard Studies* assumes a high level of keyboard proficiency, *In C*, for any number of instruments, is defiantly anti-virtuosic: it consists of a sequence of fifty-three fairly simple diatonic figures, gradually moving from C via E minor towards F, which can be repeated any number of times by each player before moving on to the next figure. Throughout a performance, which typically might last forty to fifty minutes, the tempo is coordinated by a pianist playing the top two Cs on the instrument in a regular quaver pulse.

Reich's first characteristic works were machine-based: initial experiments used electronic 'gates',[16] while *It's Gonna Rain* (1965) and *Come Out* (1966) used tape-loops of brief spoken phrases (which also act as diatonic pitch motives), gradually drifting out of phase with one another to produce psychoacoustic illusions reminiscent of moiré patterns (and indeed of the 'Op-Art' of painters such as Bridget Riley that surfaced at much the same time, though there is no persuasive evidence of direct influence). This 'phase-shifting' technique was then transferred to live instrumentalists in *Piano Phase*, *Reed Phase*, and *Violin Phase* (all 1967). The 'mechanical' aspects of Reich's early music reflect a very different aesthetic to that of Young and Riley: whereas both Young and Riley aimed to induce a trance-like state (Young's famous assertion 'If my music doesn't transport you straight to heaven, then I've failed' is only slightly hyperbolic), Reich, as he emphasized in his early writings, was concerned that the listener followed every detail of what was happening, and the same holds good for the additive processes that Glass used in pieces like *Music in Fifths* and *Music in Contrary Motion* (both 1969).

The open instrumentation of *In C* notwithstanding, the performance practice of early minimalism was largely centred on the composers themselves. Riley

15 Mertens, *American Minimal Music*, pp. 37, 48.
16 Steve Reich, *Writings about Music*, New York, 1975, pp. 18ff.

was essentially a solo performer, often using tape-delay systems to build up a mesmeric sonic tapestry, while Young, Reich, and Glass all formed their own ensembles. Moreover, with the exception of Reich, the composers generally declined to make their scores easily available for performance by others. As for the widespread popularity eventually gained by these composers, it did not come immediately; the first disc releases came out on small, specialist labels, and it was not until the 1968 release of *In C* that a substantial international following developed. That album, while issued on the 'classical' Columbia Masterworks label, had cover art reminiscent of contemporaneous psychedelic rock albums, and a quote from respected classical critic Alfred Frankenstein on the front cover was complemented by on the back by a 'rave' from Paul Williams, editor of the psychedelia-orientated US rock magazine *Crawdaddy*, declaring that 'what we have here is a "trip" '.

This, coming at the height of 'flower power' and epic levels of LSD consumption, symbolized a relatively brief point of intersection between the 'rock' and 'art' avant-gardes and their audiences that was by no means restricted to minimalism. Stockhausen, whose photo appeared at the top left of the Beatles' *Sergeant Pepper* album, attended several Grateful Dead concerts during his months in California in 1968, and had a large following among progressive-rock aficionados. Conversely, members of the Grateful Dead formed a Rex Foundation which, even thirty years later, was funding recordings of radical 'complexist' works. Moreover, the feedback-based improvisations of rock guitarist Jimi Hendrix were, in many respects, just as much instances of 'live electronic music' as the work of groups such as Sonic Arts Union or Musica Elettronica Viva.

Death of the author: improvisation and collective composition

However characteristic minimalism may seem of a certain 1960s ethos, there were two significant respects in which it swam robustly against the tide of the times. One was its essentially affirmative character (arising from its strong preference for diatonic, major-mode figures), which came at a time when 'progressive' art was assumed to have a critical content, and all suggestions of affirmation were widely regarded within the avant-garde as reactionary. The other was the relatively constrained, regimented role of performers in minimalist works. Even in Riley's *In C*, the freedom of performers to proceed through the materials at their own pace was offset by the constraints of an unflinchingly regular and regulatory pulse. In works by Reich and Glass, the performers were absolutely locked into an ultra-disciplined, mechanistic rhythmic grid.

While both Reich and Glass have portrayed their early works as being, in part, a reaction against prevailing serialist orthodoxies, in retrospect it is hard to believe that this was the whole story, or even a significant part of it. It may have been an issue for the composers, but scarcely for their target audiences, for whom the existence of serialism, even if acknowledged, would have been a non-issue: if audiences were to be 'weaned away' from anyone, it would have been Janis Joplin rather than Pierre Boulez. It was another story for those composers who chose in the early 1960s to move from structuralism, via Cagean indeterminacy, to improvisation. One of the first examples was provided by Franco Evangelisti (1926–80), who from the mid-1950s had produced works in which rigorously conceived structures were subverted from within by aleatory structures. Around 1963, after completing the orchestral work *Random or Not Random*, he renounced composition, supposedly (as he claimed to his publisher and former fellow-student Hans Swarsenski) because he had devised a system within which any possible composition was foreseeable, and therefore uninteresting. In the wake of this drastic decision, he formed the Gruppo Nuova Consonanza, a collective of mainly younger composers working in Rome at the time, initially including Roland Kayn (b. 1933), Frederic Rzewski (b. 1938), Ivan Vandor (b. 1932), and also, more surprisingly, the highly successful film composer Ennio Morricone (b. 1928).

Rzewski and Vandor soon seceded to form their own group Musica Elettronica Viva, along with Allan Bryant, Alvin Curran (b. 1938) and Richard Teitelbaum (b. 1939); MEV then became the model for numerous other groups, especially in America, such as Sonic Arts Union (more a composer collective than a 'group') and the California Time Machine. Though initially generated from a 'concert-hall' avant-garde, the stylistic boundaries of such 'free improvisation' were never clearly delineated, and became less so. This was, after all, a period in which influential younger jazz performers such as Ornette Coleman and Cecil Taylor were already pioneering 'free jazz' within comparably small ensembles, as indeed were some rock groups (and the actual name California Time Machine could easily have been that of a 1960s rock group). Nevertheless, the general assumption underlying such groups was that a knowledge of the structuralist repertoire, detached from its generative methods, could be the basis for a richer and more 'relevant' new form of musical communication.

A similar course was followed by the Englishman Cornelius Cardew, who had worked as Stockhausen's assistant on the realisation of *Carré*. In 1959, Cardew wrote a Third Piano Sonata that was a high point of late-1950s structuralism; then, under the influence of Cage, he composed a sequence of highly indeterminate scores, such as *Autumn '60* and *Octet '61*. The latter caused a minor sensation in England when issued as a musical supplement in the *Musical Times*, at a time when this journal's supplements more characteristically consisted of diatonic Anglican church anthems. From 1963–7 Cardew worked on *Treatise*, an exquisitely drafted 193-page graphic score with (as a matter of principle) no performance instructions. Thereafter he moved on to improvisation, joining the AMM group established by Lou Gare, Eddie Prevost and Keith Rowe (it is symptomatic of the authority attaching to composer participation that AMM is often regarded as having been Cardew's creation, or at least led by him; there is no reason to suppose this was actually the case).

To a degree, Stockhausen too followed this course. His major work of the early 1960s, *Momente* for soprano, thirteen instrumentalists, and chorus (1962–5, completed 1972), is an open-form work; so too are the live-electronic works *Mikrophonie I*, *Mixtur* (both 1964) and, to a degree, *Stimmung* (1968). But starting with *Plus-Minus* (1964), Stockhausen also produced what he called 'process compositions'. These were pieces in which the scores and/or parts indicated only strategies for the transformation of materials – given in some detail for *Plus-Minus*, but left completely open in *Kurzwellen* (1968), where the materials to be transformed are found at random on short-wave radio receivers. Presumably sensing that such pieces required a new oral tradition to establish proper performance practice, Stockhausen formed a small live-electronic ensemble to realize these pieces, two of whose members (Johannes Fritsch and Rolf Gehlhaar (b. 1943)) were also gifted young composers. The extreme extension of this strategy is found in the cycle of text-compositions *Aus den sieben Tagen* (1968).

The live performances and recordings of the latter at Darmstadt in 1969 gave rise to considerable controversies (including issues of authorship) which in retrospect give cause to reflect on the role of 'new-music virtuosi' during this era. Back in the late 1950s, Stockhausen had praised performers such as the flautist Severino Gazzelloni, and especially the pianist David Tudor, for their 'co-creative' spirit.[17] This co-creativity had many dimensions: for instance, the willingness to make decisions in relation to variable or open formal structures, to interpret highly ambiguous notations, and above all to extend the limits of their instrument. The latter might operate in conventional terms (such as the extra fifth the young Heinz Holliger added to the top of the oboe range, or Harry Sparnaay's even more radical expansion of bass clarinet tessitura), but more typically it involved an exploration of new timbres, and especially the transitional territory between pitch and noise (which was inherently at odds with the nature of inherited Western notation, and naturally led towards quasi-improvisation). The result, in Europe at least, was a panorama of solo performer

17 Karlheinz Stockhausen, *Texte zur Musik II*, Cologne, 1964, p. 69.

categories, ranging from relatively conventional 'servants of the music', such as the pianists Alfons and Aloys Kontarsky and the cellist Siegfried Palm, via 'personality cult' performers such as percussionist Stomu Yamashta, to increasingly radically inclined virtuoso composer-performers such as Globokar and Holliger.

Another symptom of the collectivist spirit of the mid- and late 1960s was the proliferation of 'collective compositions' that not only involved many composers, but to some degree sought to efface notions of individual authorship. Given the rather rosy view of Maoism that was widespread in the time (a copy of the Little Red Book was standard equipment for the dissenting university student), there may be conscious parallels here with the 'composer committees' in China that produced works such as the *Yellow River* and *Butterfly Lovers* concertos, even though the artistic outcomes are worlds apart. Three particular instances may give some idea of the breadth of intentions and applications:

- In 1963, eleven composers associated with the GRM in Paris collaborated in a *concert collectif*, for which six of them provided a number of 'base sequences', both as recordings and as notated scores. All but one of these six composers, plus four others, then went on to compose individual compositions lasting about eight minutes, which were elaborated from one or (in most cases) more of these sequences. One could see this as a radical extension of the theme(s) and variations principle within an essentially athematic, high-modernist context.
- In 1967, at the Darmstadt Summer School, the twelve young composers in Stockhausen's composition class (many of them well on the way to establishing significant individual creative personalities) collaborated with Stockhausen to produce a four-hour performance entitled *Ensemble*. Following discussions, Stockhausen provided an overall framework and composed eight inserts 'intended to function as clear temporal demarcations, giving the ENSEMBLE orientation points in respect to past and future'.[18] Stockhausen's aim was to establish a completely new kind of collaborative compositional practice.
- In 1970, five young Dutch composers – Peter Schat, Jan van Vlijmen, Misha Mengelberg (all b. 1935), Reinbert de Leeuw (b. 1938) and Louis Andriessen (b. 1939), the latter still relatively unknown – collaborated with two young authors to produce the 'collective opera' *Reconstructie*, a rereading of the Don Juan myth with intermittent reference to Mozart, in which the Don represents voracious American capitalism in South America, the Commendatore

18 Rolf Gehlhaar, *Zur Komposition Ensemble*, Mainz, 1968, p. 70.

is Che Guevara, and Leporello is transformed into an unflattering representation of the Dutch philosopher Erasmus. The score engages, often ironically (or rather, 'dialectically'), with all kinds of contemporary styles, both popular and 'high art'. One of its main aims was to affront the establishment, both local and international; in this, it succeeded to a considerable degree. This reflected a situation in which, following the uprisings of 1968, the political responsibilities of artists had become a matter of considerable debate.

Political engagement before and after 1968

In the 1950s, Luigi Nono was almost alone among 'radical' composers in espousing an overtly leftist stance. The riot that erupted during an explicitly anti-fascist scene at the premiere of his opera *Intolleranza 1960* may not have been the only scandal of that era, but it was probably the only one where (right-wing) demonstrators yelled out 'Viva la polizia!' Even so, works such as this and the subsequent cantata *Canti di vita e d'amore: sul ponte di Hiroshima* (1961) could still be interpreted in terms of humanitarian rather than party-political concerns. With *La fabbrica illuminata* (1964) for soprano and four-track tape, this ceased to be the case: the piece was a direct attack on appalling working conditions in northern Italian Fiat factories, and the 'inhuman' capitalist interests that they reflected. In subsequent works such as *Ricorda cose ti hanno fotto in Auschwitz* ('Remember what they did at Auschwitz' – derived from music for Peter Weiss's play *Die Ermittlung*) (1966), *A floresta è jovem e cheja de vida* (1966), or the *Contrappunto dialettico alla mente* (1967), attacks on American involvement in South America and Vietnam were so explicit as to make Nono a *persona non grata* at institutionally funded Western European new music festivals (especially in West Germany, where allied occupation troops were still in residence). But ideologically, Nono's influence on the European avant-garde was decisive: it forced all composers to reflect on social responsibilities as well as aesthetic ones.

One of the more surprising and public converts was Hans Werner Henze. After the debacle of his attempted entry into the avant-garde with the *Concerto per il Marigny* (1956), Henze had conspicuously broken his ties with it: his *Kammermusik 1958*, using the same ensemble as Schubert's Octet, was clear evidence of this. The exquisitely crafted lyricism of a work like the Rimbaud setting *Being Beauteous* (1963) is stylistically closer to Frank Martin than to any of the Darmstadt practitioners. Yet three years later, following his opera *Die Bassariden*, Henze underwent an artistic crisis; not for the first time, he felt alienated from the bourgeois culture which, nevertheless, his work exemplified. The student uprisings of 1967–8 led Henze not only to espouse left-wing causes, but also to radicalize his style:[19] it is hard to reconcile the extreme vocal histrionics of the *Versuch über Schweine* (1968) or the nihilistic ambience of *Der langwierige Weg in die Wohnung von Natasha Ungeheuer* (1971) with the lyrical opera composer of a few years earlier. In these politically oriented works, Henze pursued what he terms a 'musica impura':[20] a music whose style is deliberately inconsistent, since different styles are necessary to symbolize different social strata or reflect different ideologies.

A yet more intransigent path was pursued by three younger German composers, Helmut Lachenmann, Hans Joachim Hespos (both b. 1938), and Nicolaus A. Huber (b. 1939). Hespos's political position was essentially a radical anarchist one, whereas Huber and Lachenmann were 'idealistic socialists' (Lachenmann's early works include a *Salut für* [Christopher] *Caudwell*). Their music was conceived as, among other things, a frontal assault on bourgeois values, including musical ones; it not only 'extended' conventional playing techniques in a manner typical of the 1960s avant-garde, but also set out to eradicate any trace of inherited ('bourgeois') notions of beauty attaching to particular instruments – a trait which led to Lachenmann in particular being depicted journalistically as a *Verweigerungsmusiker* (literally, a 'denial musician').[21] Globokar adopted a similar position – his *Laboratorium* (1973) is a particularly drastic instance of this – and for a while so too did Kagel, whose *Acustica* (1970), for 'experimental sound sources', is a ruthless investigation of what the composer has called *Scheissklänge* ('shit sounds'), a notion that naturally invites comparison with contemporary German production in the visual arts.

However, left-wingers did not have a monopoly on dissent and resistance. Under communism, the writing of overtly religious works was also an act of political defiance. Penderecki's *Stabat mater* (1962), subsequently absorbed into his *St Luke Passion* (1965), provided a benchmark, while also highlighting the problems associated with avant-garde affirmations: after ten minutes of clusters, interspersed with diatonic chant, the work ends with a sustained but incongruous triad. The highly dissonant, experimental side of the 1960s was well suited to the expression of critical or tragic sentiments, but much less so to positive assertions of any kind of belief. Thus it was quite feasible for Ligeti to write a *Requiem* (1965), or Penderecki a *Dies irae* (1967), but for the time being a *Magnificat* or *Te Deum* seemed hard to imagine. When Messiaen, in the wake of his brilliant but controversial orchestral work *Chronochromie* (1960), returned

19 Cf. Hans Werner Henze, *Musik und Politik – Schriften und Gespräche 1955–1975*, Munich, 1976, p. 149.
20 Ibid., pp. 186ff.
21 Cf. Helmut Lachenmann, 'Die Gefährdete Kommunikation', in *Musik als Existentieller Erfahrung: Schriften 1966–1995*, Wiesbaden, 1997, pp. 110ff.

to writing works with an explicit theological programme in which birdsong was not the only major element, the stylistic disparities from earlier works like the *Turangalîla-symphonie* soon became apparent, whether in the modal chant melodies of *Couleurs de la cité céléste* (1963) or the unabashedly tonal cadences that dominate the last movement of the massive oratorio *La transfiguration* (1969). In Germany, Kagel and especially Dieter Schnebel (b. 1934) espoused an 'acoustic theology'[22] in which expressions of faith were radically detached from the traditional musical vocabulary of affirmation. The most extreme assertions of this position include Kagel's *Hallelujah* (1968), and two works by Schnebel: the *Choralvorspiele* (1968/9) for organists and trombonists, at the end of which the trombonists take their chorale fragments outside the 'sacred space' implied by the organ and into the open air, and *für stimmen (missa est . . .)* (1958–68), a choral work in the final section of which the human voices are joined (on tape) by those of animals. Such ventures were, however, relatively short-lived. The 'crisis of communication' implicit here ultimately had consequences for left-wing composers too; they had to make a decision between writing radical works in notional support of a proletariat that had no interest in such music (though there is some evidence that Nono managed to overcome this problem), or adopting more 'accessible' styles (as did Cardew, explicitly following Maoist models, and Rzewski).

In comparison, such concerns were scarcely at the forefront of American new music, though there were notable exceptions. When in 1969 *Source Magazine* published twenty composers' responses to the question 'Have you, or has anyone else ever used your music for social or political ends?'[23] only five (including Robert Ashley (b. 1930) and Frederic Rzewski, but not John Cage!) asserted clear socio-political intentions. In Ashley's case, this was clear even in an early piece like *The Wolfman* (1964); Rzewski's engagement became more apparent in the course of the 1970s, starting with pieces like *Attica* and *Coming Together* (both 1972). The situation of American composers was, however, a special one. Worldwide, the US was identified by most leftist composers as a primary target, and it seems fair to observe that the ethical and practical problems involved in attacking a geographically remote nation (e.g. the US from Europe) are much less than those of attacking even limited aspects of one's own country's political system. The most widely remarked instance of such internal US criticism was Sal Martirano's (1927–95) *L.'s G.A.* (1968), for 'gassed-masked politico, helium bomb and two-channel tape', in which the protagonist attempts increasingly

22 Cf. Rainer Fanselau, 'Mauricio Kagels akustische Theologie', *Musik und Bildung* 13/12 (1981), pp. 744–9; Dieter Schnebel, 'Geistliche Musik heute', in *Denkbare Musik*, Cologne, 1972, pp. 420–30.

23 'Events/Comments – is new music being used for social or political ends?', in *Source: Music of the Avant-Garde* 6 (1969), pp. 7ff.

autistic renditions of Lincoln's Gettysburg Address. A more broadly based, but no less apocalyptic critique is *Kingdom Come* (1970) by Henry Brant (b. 1913), while George Crumb's very striking *Black Angels* (1968) for amplified string quartet has been identified by the composer as a critical response to the war in Vietnam.[24]

A postscript on documentation and dissemination

Die Reihe, in effect the 'house journal' of the Cologne/Darmstadt avant-garde, published in Vienna by Universal Edition, ceased publication in 1962, almost exactly at the moment when *Perspectives of New Music* began in the United States. The contrast between the two is instructive: *die reihe* largely lost its *raison d'être* once the Darmstadt avant-garde's reputation was solidly established and its members started to fall out with one another, whereas the American publication was, from the start, a classic academic journal, and continues as such to this day. Moreover, it soon became clear that *Perspectives* espoused a rather more rigorous notion of 'theory' than its predecessor had done. In the course of the 1960s, several of the European avant-gardists published books which described their composition techniques with varying degrees of precision – the first two volumes of Stockhausen's *Texte zur Musik* (1961–2), Boulez's *Penser la musique aujourd'hui* (1963), Xenakis's *Musiques formelles* (1968),[25] and Pousseur's *Fragments théoriques I* (1970)[26] – but these turned out to be accounts of highly divergent personal practices, not contributions to establishing common practice. In contrast, Babbitt's extended article 'Twelve-Tone Rhythmic Structure and the Electronic Medium',[27] published in the first issue of *Perspectives* (1962), became the virtual foundation stone for a whole school of American theoretical writing, primarily allied to university departments.

In the same issue of *Perspectives*, Elliott Carter expressed concern that the increasing dependence of new American composition on 'the protection of the universities' could lead to a situation where it would be 'destroyed as a public communication'.[28] How far this happened remains a matter of debate, but there is no doubt that seen from outside, much new endeavour seemed to be polarized between the faculty concert and the SoHo loft (or equivalent), in contrast to the heavily subsidized public presence of new European music at institutional

24 Composer's programme note.

25 English version Iannis Xenakis, *Formalized Music: Thought and Mathematics in Composition*, Bloomington, 1971; rev. and expanded edn, Stuyvesant, NY, 1992.

26 Henri Pousseur, *Fragments théoriques I sur la musique expérimentale*, Brussels, 1970.

27 Milton Babbitt, 'Twelve-Tone Rhythmic Structure and the Electronic Medium', *Perspectives of New Music* 1/1, pp. 49–79.

28 Elliott Carter, 'The Milieu of the American Composer', *Perspectives of New Music* 1/1, pp. 149–51.

festivals or on the radio (the effectiveness of the latter having been somewhat curtailed since the 1960s by the introduction of FM stereo broadcasting, which improved quality but greatly reduced the range of access which had previously been a key contributor to the cosmopolitanism of European new music).

In the 1950s, very little 'new music' had made its way onto the relatively novel medium of the LP. This started to change significantly in the early 1960s. Significant early landmarks included three ten-inch LPs of electronic music from Cologne (by Eimert, Koenig, Krenek, and Stockhausen) from Deutsche Grammophon; two discs of Parisian *musique concrète* (Boîte à musique); the Warsaw Festival's documentation of new Polish works from 1963 onwards; a three-disc set by Italian RCA, mainly conducted by Maderna and including works by Berio, Boulez, Brown, Haubenstock-Ramati, Penderecki, Pousseur, and Stockhausen (1965); Cage's *Indeterminacy* lecture (Folkways 1959) and his 25th Anniversary concert, including the notorious premiere of the *Concert for Piano and Orchestra*; and perhaps most remarkably of all, the Time-Mainstream series directed by Earle Brown, which covered both the New York School and the Darmstadt avant-garde. Later in the 1960s, the series of discs issued in conjunction with *Source* magazine drew attention to a slightly younger generation of US experimental composers, such as Robert Ashley, David Behrman, and Alvin Lucier, while Behrman himself was chief producer for the CBS Odyssey label. Definitive official sanction was provided in 1969 by Deutsche Grammophon's decision to issue a six-disc set entitled *Avant-Garde*, which had three successors in subsequent years; by this stage, those with ears to hear had plenty to listen to.

Bibliography

Babbitt, Milton. 'Twelve-Tone Rhythmic Structure and the Electronic Medium', *Perspectives of New Music* 1/1 (1960), pp. 49–79.

Boulez, Pierre. *Boulez on Music Today* (tr. Susan Bradshaw and Richard Rodney Bennett), London, 1971.

Cage, John (ed.). *Notations*, New York, 1969.

Carter, Elliott. 'The Milieu of the American Composer', *Perspectives of New Music* 1/1 (1960), pp. 149–51.

Castro, Fidel. 'Words to the Intellectuals', in Lee Baxandall (ed.), *Radical Perspectives in the Arts*, Harmondsworth, 1972, pp. 267–98.

Fanselau, Rainer. 'Mauricio Kagels akustische Theologie', *Musik und Bildung* 13/12 (1981), pp. 744–9.

Gehlhaar, Rolf. *Zur Komposition Ensemble*, Mainz, 1968.

Henze, Hans Werner. *Musik und Politik – Schriften und Gespräche 1955–1975*, Munich, 1976.

Jencks, Charles. *What is Post-Modernism?* London, 1986.

Lachenmann, Helmut. *Musik als Existentieller Erfahrung: Schriften 1966–1995*, Wiesbaden, 1997.
Matossian, Nouritza. *Xenakis*, London, 1986.
Mertens, Wim. *American Minimal Music*, London, 1983.
Misch, Inge and Markus Bandur (eds.). *Karlheinz Stockhausen bei den Internationalen Ferienkursen für Neue Musik in Darmstadt 1951–1996*, Kürten, 2001.
Morthensen, Jan. *Nonfigurative Musik*, Stockholm, 1966.
Nono, Luigi. 'Geschichte und Gegenwart in der Musik von heute', *Melos* 27 (1960), pp. 69–75.
Nyman, Michael. *Experimental Music: Cage and Beyond*, 2nd edn, Cambridge, 1999.
Paynter, John and Peter Aston. *Sound and Silence: Classroom Projects in Creative Music*, Cambridge, 1970.
Potter, Keith. *Four Musical Minimalists: La Monte Young, Terry Riley, Steve Reich, Philip Glass*, Cambridge, 2000.
Pousseur, Henri. *Fragments théoriques I sur la musique expérimentale*, Brussels, 1970.
Reich, Steve. *Writings about Music*, New York, 1975.
Schaeffer, Pierre. *Traité des Objets Musicaux*, Paris, 1966.
Schnebel, Dieter. *Denkbare Musik*, Cologne, 1972.
Stockhausen, Karlheinz. *Texte zur Musik II*, Cologne, 1964.
Takemitsu, Toru. *Confronting Silence*, Berkeley, 1995.
Xenakis, Iannis. *Formalized Music: Thought and Mathematics in Composition*, Bloomington, 1971; revised and expanded edn, Stuyvesant, NY, 1992.

· 18 ·

To the millennium: music as twentieth-century commodity

ANDREW BLAKE

> In response to the new challenges created by the internet and the converging of communications media, the industry is working very hard on systems of encryption and watermarking and collaborates with the government to set up a strong legal framework and to educate the public about the value of music.
>
> Frances Lowe, Director, British Music Rights, The Performing Rights Society[1]

> It is sickening to know that our art is being traded like a commodity rather than the art that it is.
>
> Lars Ulrich, drummer of heavy metal band Metallica[2]

> There was this bloke and there was me and we really got along. Our friendship was founded on our mutual passions for pop music, indolence and substance abuse. We would sit around together, heroically stoned, and play records all day long: punk records, soul records, horny disco records like 'Hot Stuff' by Donna Summer . . .
>
> Dave Hill, music journalist[3]

Twentieth-century listening and its spaces

Artists, fans, and the music business share an uneasy but symbiotic partnership. Dave Hill's homosocial friendship, exploring music not through performance but through listening to purchased recordings, is a deeply twentieth-century subjectivity, reflecting the basic premise of much musical entertainment since the invention of sound recording. This involves a set of paradoxical relationships. For one thing, 'music' is a phenomenon that can and perhaps should be considered and enjoyed in and for itself – but to facilitate this enjoyment it has

1 Frances Lowe, 'It's the Wild Wild Net', *PRS Statement* (Spring 2000), p. 5.
2 Lars Ulrich, quoted on http://www.paylars.com, during a heated debate about hard-disk-sharing software and copyright.
3 Dave Hill, 'Doing what comes Naturally', *Independent Magazine*, 8 April 2000, p. 31.

become a commodity, bought, sold, and consumed, to the regret of many composers and performers such as Lars Ulrich. However, the relationship between music and the flow of capital was threatened in the last quarter of the century by another difficult relationship – between the producers of recordings for sale, and the makers of equipment to reproduce those recordings: record companies depended on the purchase of discrete objects produced by a manufacturer who held copyright on behalf of composer and performer, by a consumer who also had to purchase hardware to play these objects. The recording and broadcasting industries provided these record players and radios, but also developed carriers of musical information which could be erased and reused. From blank tape to hard-disk-sharing Internet software, this side of the music industry provided commodities which allow the domestic user to copy commercial recordings without respecting copyright, and as these technologies developed to allow more perfect copying, they threatened to destabilize what Francis Lowe saw as the 'value' of music.

'Listening to music', then, which for the purposes of this chapter means hearing sonic information abstracted from the conditions of its production, was among the twentieth century's most characteristic practices; so also was the purchase of hardware to receive broadcasts and to play software media such as vinyl discs, compact cassettes, and compact discs (CDs) containing sonic information. The technologies of radio broadcasting and sound recording displaced the listener from the musical practitioner, creating a new skill – that of critical listening without visual stimulus – which at its mid-century height facilitated a demand for recordings not just of concert musics from symphonies to jazz, but also of audio-visual forms such as film scores, musicals, and opera, and which made such apparent oddities seem desirable commodities.

Music made for non-participants had of course been routine in public life well before the gramophone appeared; professional performance had long been associated with the rituals of the church and the armed forces, as well as entertainment such as the opera, the concert, and the music hall. Domestic music-making, on the other hand, had been perforce by amateur participants singing and playing. But at the end of the nineteenth century, through the new musical machines, music made by professionals, and abstracted from the conditions of its production, invaded the private space of the home for the first time. This new relationship with sound was serviced by the manufacturers of receiving, recording, and replaying equipment, and by broadcasting and record companies. A new category of human experience, *listening* to music, appeared, and a new category of human subject, 'the listener', was created.

From the first appearance of those machines, however, the listener had a double, a schizophrenic other self, in Western Europe and the United States at least: s/he was both an informed critic or enthusiastic fan of the efforts of others, and a consumer category. On the one hand, in order to enable the skill of listening, a body of music criticism and journalism grew; titles like Percy Scholes's *The Listener's Guide to Music* (1919) and *The Listener's History of Music* (1923–9) record not only the construction of 'the listener' but also the way in which listening became a site for self-improvement. On the other hand, in order to service the new technologies and experiences, music was commodified and reified, made into an intangible abstract thing, the easier to be bought and sold. A significant shift in the balance between these two aspects took place throughout the century, though at different speeds depending on local economic and political conditions. In the United States music was always a commodity category, though structured within notions of high and low art, while in the communist countries the listener was an entrenched category serviced by national musical corporations until the 1990s, and music was hardly commodified at all before that point;[4] in Western Europe the shift towards pure commodification accelerated in the final quarter of the century. As symbolic of this shift we may note the fate of two British publications. *The Listener*, a BBC magazine dedicated to critical listening strategies and responses to broadcast sound, was closed in 1976, a generation after its parent company had started to make images as well as sounds for broadcast; *The Record Collector*, meanwhile, remained an important magazine, helping the enthusiast to explore the byways of this particular consumer artefact.

This critical listener and consumer was imagined, and implicitly addressed, as male. The technologies of recording and broadcasting gradually transfigured the home, providing an alternative to the domestic piano, and therefore displacing one aspect of skilled femininity. Indeed, when broadcasters imagined their female audiences, even the skill of listening was denied them. The head of BBC local station Radio Essex gave the following invocation in 1985: 'We call our average listener Doreen. She lives in Basildon. She isn't stupid but she's only listening with half an ear, and doesn't necessarily understand long words.'[5] In the case of the BBC's deliberately highbrow network, the Third Programme (later Radio 3), the assumption was reversed: material was provided for an educated male who was imagined to be listening with both ears.[6] Furthermore, modes of music diffusion governed by listener choice such as record and tape players and their associated amplifiers and loudspeakers, and especially the more upmarket forms of these devices known collectively as hi-fi, are among the few domestic technologies associated with masculinity,

4 Yugoslavia, going its own way under Tito, was a partial exception to this rule.
5 Stephen Barnard, *On the Radio*, Milton Keynes, 1989, p. 43.
6 William Glock, *Notes in Advance*, Oxford, 1987, is written on this assumption.

as are collections of recordings.[7] It was accepted that listening to the sounds of the contemporary world was an important personal and social attribute. In the nineteenth-century city Baudelaire's imagined *flâneur*, the male observer, enjoyed the shape of modern urban life, by wandering the streets and seeing;[8] the twentieth-century equivalent, also implicitly male, was content to retire to a small room, close the curtains from the visible world, and listen. He knew the value of music, and was prepared to pay for it.

We should note the role played by broadcasting in the creation of the generic boundaries which informed the notion of the critical listener. Radio, meanwhile, was the linchpin that ensured that Western classical music topped the generic hierarchies: while the commercial stations in the United States and the monopolist European stations such as the BBC adopted different strategies, each tended to solidify classical music as an elite consumer category. In the United States, broadcasts of mainstream repertoire by star conductors with European backgrounds, such as Arturo Toscanini and Leopold Stokowski, helped to create a conservative concert public, with Toscanini constructed as a broadcasting and recording artist thanks to his work with the NBC Symphony Orchestra (a band put together for radio broadcasts), while Stokowski's fame came in part from his conducting of Disney's 'edutainment' cartoon *Fantasia*.[9] The BBC's insistence from its foundation in 1926 that the corporation's cultural mission was to educate as well as to entertain led to its subsidy of classical music (including new music), which began in the late 1920s, enjoying a high point in the mid-1960s to mid-1970s, and which survived in attenuated form at the end of the century.[10] From the 1920s onwards, then, the place of classical music was guaranteed by broadcasting – and thanks to the reach of imperial and trading relations, it was guaranteed worldwide: the association of Western art music and new technology helped to underline the enthusiasm for its continuance by the founders of Sony, who built their first machines in the rubble of post-war Tokyo. (Sony co-founder Akio Morita had long been a devotee both of records featuring music by Bach and Mozart, and the Victrola gramophone which played them.[11]) The radio broadcasting of complete works made acceptable the practice of 'listening' to musics which had heretofore been actively

7 Nick Hornby's novel *High Fidelity*, London, 1995, filmed under the direction of Stephen Frears in 1999 (Touchstone), may be taken to exemplify this 'collector's masculinity'. Fandoms are explored in Lisa Lewis (ed.), *The Adoring Audience*, London, 1992, and Matthew Hills, *Fan Cultures*, London, 2002.

8 For discussion of this persona, see Richard Sennett, *The Fall of Public Man*, London, 1986, pp. 205–18.

9 Michael Chanan, *Repeated Takes: A Short History of Recording and its Effects on Music*, London, 1995, p. 82.

10 Andrew Blake, *The Land Without Music: Music, Culture and Society in Twentieth Century Britain*, Manchester, 1997, pp. 52–70; Jennifer Doctor, *The BBC and Ultra-Modern Music 1922–1936: Shaping a Nation's Tastes*, Cambridge, 1999; Glock, *Notes in Advance*, pp. 26, 35, 45, 58, 59, 197.

11 John Nathan, *Sony: The Private Life*, London, 1999, p. 19.

seen as well as heard: to operas and musicals, to church music divorced from its ritual setting and spiritual meaning, and to dance musics meant for active participation rather than armchair appreciation. These broadcasting innovations, transfiguring the home, also affected the ways in which concert life and the record industry developed.

Despite the increasing importance of the domestic sphere as the site of musical reception, however, public space remained important in the commercial diffusion of music. During the century new types of venue from small jazz and folk clubs to sports stadia for globally successful rock bands became important extensions of the existing venues for dance, music-hall or vaudeville entertainment, and concert music, each of which relies on a sense of people-in-public as active and informed listeners or participant consumers. But from the 1950s on the music business also provided music which is avowedly not for active participation, nor for 'the listener', but designed to be only semi-audible, even when loud.[12] Through the jukebox, in-store radio, in-pub MTV, shopping-mall muzak and so on, people massed as 'the general public' were narcotized into certain predictable forms of behaviour – modes of purchasing and consumption which are associated through the music with an easily transferable sense of lifestyle and life-cycle. Thanks to these public diffusion technologies, commodity-music became pervasive in this semi-audible form during the later twentieth century; it was hard to find urban public spaces anywhere in the world without it.

However the category of the semi-audible had already emerged earlier in the century, in film music. Coming into being at around the same time as sound recording but developing separately as a technology until the 1920s, film helped to transfigure the awareness of sound in public space. The development of 'talkies' from the late 1920s led to increasing opportunities for composers, who responded by transposing aspects of folk, popular, and classical musical traditions in a way foreign to the concert hall. Film in India, for instance, quickly developed a collagistic hybrid soundtrack whose composers and performers had to be adept in Western and Eastern performance styles. However, comparatively few noticed these tendencies or made much of them: music was judged as more or less appropriate to the films' dramatic and emotional structures, and seldom studied in its own right. Music here was indeed semi-audible: experienced rather than actively listened to.

When listening *was* encouraged, however, the changing presence of music in public spaces contributed to the changing of genre boundaries. The spaces devoted to certain types of music had economic, political, and cultural

12 See Joseph Lanza, *Elevator Music*, London, 1995, for an eloquent defence of the genre.

consequences. At the Cotton Club in late-1920s Harlem, the Duke Ellington Orchestra, a black band playing at a whites-only club in a black residential area of New York, helped to create 'jazz' as an exotic consumer category which was sold on to an increasingly Americaphile Europe. Again, in the 1960s the Vienna Staatsoper guarded the culture of an international, conspicuously consuming, middle class – and helped the Decca label to record much of the standard operatic repertoire for sale. Meanwhile the outdoor festival, notably events such as the first Woodstock (1968), helped to create 'rock' as a category almost separate from pop, in which sales were based on albums rather than the less profitable singles. During the late 1980s, outdoor 'raves' produced a new quasi-independent popular musical form, in which the listener was addressed principally through the production of pseudo-mnemonic recordings, mixed by DJs as if they were performing live, in order to function domestically as a memory of, and substitute for, the experience of raving.[13]

Public space, especially when permeated by the semi-audible sonics of muzak, denies the singularity or agreed mutuality associated with 'the listener', who must first choose the listened object. But alongside the flourishing of muzak, developers of the technologies which diffuse music addressed this problem with astonishing success, providing a series of increasingly effective portable musical sources to enable 'the listener' to function, and to preserve 'his' listening autonomy, even in the most crowded, impersonal public space. Small portable reel-to-reel tape recorders appeared in the 1950s, and transistor technology enabled the construction of the first pocket-sized radio, marketed by Sony in 1957.[14] In the 1970s the compact cassette Walkman, and in the 1990s its digital derivatives, 'personal' CD and minidisc players (each, again, pioneered by Sony), provided small, relatively cheap, portable, and – thanks to their use of headphones rather than loudspeakers – intensely personal sonic environments.[15] Adorned by a Walkman the listener could listen to one world while observing another – for example the sounds of a rapper from South Central Los Angeles on a sunny beach in Goa. Through such experiences the listener's identity could be reinforced in most circumstances, and the manufacturers of playback equipment and magnetic media had increased personal choice while facilitating the withdrawal of people physically 'in public' into their own, private, listening worlds.[16]

13 Clubs such as Cream (in Liverpool), Renaissance (originally from Mansfield, UK), and London's Ministry of Sound have launched CD series; the latter also sells a wide range of fashion and other associated merchandising.

14 Nathan, *Sony*, p. 35.

15 See Paul Du Gay, Stuart Hall, et al., *Doing Cultural Studies: The Story of the Sony Walkman*, London, 1997; Michael Bull, *Sounding Out the City: Personal Stereos and the Management of Everyday Life*, Oxford, 2000.

16 It is worth noting that the great symbolic personal technology of the 1980s, the mobile telephone, precisely reversed this tendency, turning the speaker's domestic life into public property.

Hi-fi and the culture of 'authenticity'

The Walkman was deliberately marketed as a tool for the diffusion of popular music; nevertheless the cumulative development of successive recording formats in the second half of the century – including the long-playing vinyl disc, the compact cassette and the audio CD – replicated the impact of broadcasting, confirming the hegemony of the Austro-German symphonic tradition by enabling the listener to hear long stretches of music without interruption, and so enabling domestic record consumption to mimic the radio broadcast as much as the ritual concentration of the concert hall. The hegemony of concert performance (and in particular the concert tradition of Western classical music), as reinforced by broadcasting, helped to determine even the format of audio software: at the insistence of the then chairman of Sony, Norio Ohga (himself a conductor of Western classical music), the time available for music reproduction on a CD, co-developed by Philips and Sony, was set at a maximum seventy-four minutes in length – a limit chosen purely in order to accommodate a complete performance of Beethoven's Ninth Symphony.[17]

Equally important to the technological development of playback equipment has been the underlying notion of discrete performance, in which the tape or disc and what it contains are seen as, precisely, *media*, transmitting a performance which has taken place elsewhere in real time, rather than as products in their own right. The developing recording and broadcast technologies were characterized, through successive waves of improvement in frequency response, as increasingly 'faithful' to performance, and many musicians responded to this perceived fidelity:[18] in the mid-1950s, for instance, the American big band leader Stan Kenton re-recorded much of his work from the 1940s (including such titles as 'Artistry in Rhythm'), because he wanted to link his music to the new developments in sound recording and reproduction technology which were labeled 'hi-fi' – in other words, as having higher fidelity in both frequency and dynamics to the original performance. No sooner had the album *Kenton in Hi-Fi* hit the streets, however – and gone to the top of the album charts – than early experiments in stereo recording were making mono hi-fi technologically obsolete, and Kenton recorded much of his 1940s work yet again for the new medium, often using smaller groups of instrumentalists to take advantage of the subtleties of detail which stereo could offer.[19]

17 Nathan, *Sony*, pp. 130–40.

18 Chanan, *Repeated Takes*; see also Pekka Gronow and Ilpio Saunio (tr. Christopher Moseley), *An International History of the Recording Industry*, London, 1998.

19 *Stan Kenton in Hi-Fi* (Capitol, 1956) was rereleased on CD under the same title by Capitol (1992), with some alternative takes and later-1950s examples in stereo.

Herbert von Karajan's four complete recordings of the Beethoven symphonies, likewise, relate to the introduction of new recording technologies. The first cycle, recorded in the early 1950s with the Philharmonia Orchestra in London for EMI, was made just as the twelve-inch vinyl LP was replacing the 78 rpm disc as the common recording format. The early 1960s Deutsche Grammophon issues, played by the Berlin Philharmonic Orchestra, celebrated that company's embracing of stereophonic recording. A mid-1970s Berlin Philharmonic set was recorded in the acoustic of the orchestra's Berlin Philharmonie concert hall, using Deutsche Grammophon's recording studio specially constructed in the building, and utilizing multitrack recording techniques imported from rock music. The final set under Karajan's baton, made in the early 1980s, again with the Berlin Philharmonic Orchestra for Deutsche Grammophon, used the new digital recording technologies and was the first complete Beethoven set to appear on CD.[20] Fidelity was, it was claimed, increased by each of these recordings: as with Kenton's choice to re-record in hi-fi, it was the aim of Karajan and his recording engineers each time both to make the music sound more like itself, and to be associated with technological modernization.

Prominent in this tendency to 'fidelity' was the emergence of a musical archaeology. In one sense the preservation of material from the past had always been part of the development of music technology, and the early twentieth century saw the preservative recording of a vast amount of material from folk traditions all over the world. Some of this recording was by composers such as Vaughan Williams and Bartók, who wanted new sources for their own music. However, at least since the popularity of Felix Mendelssohn's Bach performances in the 1840s, the classical repertoire had built a more passive sense of its own past. As, especially in the United States, the broadcast repertoire froze into a celebration of the music of the eighteenth and nineteenth centuries, and as the more adventurous twentieth-century composers developed styles to which audiences were hostile (and which were therefore unprofitable), broadcasting and recording companies' search for new repertoire looked to the further past. Doubtless influenced by the folk revival's insistence on performances as close as possible to the imagined original, Deutsche Grammophon's 'Archiv' project (and others, from the 1950s onwards) assembled a library of performances of music written before the mid-eighteenth century: here the idea of 'high fidelity' was extended beyond hi-fi's purely technical relationship to the sound source, reflecting scholarly notions of how the music had sounded in its

20 Nathan, *Sony*, p. 140; Blake, *The Land Without Music*, pp. 18–19.

original moment of performance.[21] Such performances of 'early music' using lower pitch, folk-related vocal techniques, violins with gut strings, valveless horns, keyless flutes, and so on were christened by their adherents 'authentic', and labelling them as such created a niche sales category as well as a performance practice. This 'authenticity' was subsequently extended: as the excitement of the early-music movement waned, the attention of many of its practitioners moved through the eighteenth and nineteenth centuries, and even into the early twentieth. By the 1980s 'authentic' performances of work by Beethoven were commonplace, and of Elgar frequent (the New Queen's Hall orchestra was established specifically to perform early-twentieth-century music in 'authentic' period style).

Meanwhile, however, such scholarly concerns were being challenged by the increasing orientation of Western governments away from the subsidized pseudo-nationalization of taste, and towards the alleged advantages of the free market. This led among other things to the end of broadcasting monopolies in much of Europe, and the appearance of new radio and television channels interested in ratings rather than the upholding of canons of public taste. Genres which could be identified with demographic and purchasing categories were enthusiastically promoted, especially in radio, and stations dedicated to jazz, album rock, and classical music became commonplace (as they had been in the United States for most of the century). In Britain, Classic FM started to broadcast in 1992, and found an audience big enough to please its advertisers by reversing the careful work of Reithian broadcasters: it played not complete works but excerpts from narrative-tonal compositions, including orchestral film music. At exactly the same time that pop was turning away from the album and towards the concept-packaging of collections of tracks, Classic FM promoted compilations such as *Classics from the Ads* and *Classics for Lovers*, all under the soothing general soubriquet of 'the world's most beautiful music'. Classical charts appeared. Classical music had become pop.[22]

Pop had always been made with radio in mind: singles were usually marketed in 'radio edit' form, mixed so as to sound acceptable on the small loudspeakers built into cheap radio sets. In other words, pop was made for the radio rather than the other way round: there is no sense of 'fidelity' to anything other than the ideal of maximizing broadcasting time and therefore increasing sales figures. As a side effect of this commercial strategy, pop singles also sounded

21 Much of the scholarly debate – and some idea of the importance of the study of past performance practice to academia as well as to performance practice – can be disinterred from Nicholas Kenyon (ed.), *Authenticity and Early Music: A Symposium*, Oxford, 1988.

22 Classic FM was not alone in this tendency. A range of strategies were employed to make classical performers such as violinist Nigel Kennedy more like pop stars; see Blake, *The Land Without Music*, pp. 68–9.

good when played on small, low-powered domestic playback equipment of the sort to be found in teenagers' bedrooms, such as the Dansette record player or small radio-cassette units. By contrast, rock, which ostentatiously claimed to disregard such commercial imperatives, used studio technologies such as multitrack recording and artificial reverberation and delay, which made the 'album' into a sonic artefact distinct from the potentialities of live performance. From the mid-1960s, multitrack tape could be assembled from fragmentary performances (a band need not play simultaneously in the studio), and any errors could be corrected in minute detail. The same multitracking and editing technology permeated the production of classical recordings, which both problematized the sense in which they could be understood as (authentic) reproductions of performances, and encouraged audiences to expect the same note-for-note perfection in live performance as on disc. But for rock and pop there was simply no longer any archetypal perfect realization beyond the final master tape, mixed down to two-track stereo from the multitrack, from which the album was cut: nothing to which the term 'hi-fi' could express faithfulness, except the sounds of the album – the commodity – itself.

However, during the 1990s even this comparative point of stability began to collapse. The potential for remixing which had always been inherent in music based on multitrack recording (whether the multitracks were on tape or computer hard disk) threatened in its turn the conceptual stability of the 'album', whose charts were dominated increasingly by compilations and remixes. This was in part due to the increasing influence in popular music of forms like dub (which originated in Jamaica in the 1960s), techno (from 1980s Detroit), and drum 'n' bass (originating in 1990s London), each of which uses studio techniques without any necessary reliance on the vagaries of human performance beyond samples originated by performers.[23] Nonetheless, while dance genres, dominated by producers and DJs, constantly evolve into subgenres, they are still accompanied by taxonomies whose language implies certainty and authenticity, even when this is perforce reduced to an insistence on certain tempi or the use of various brands of analogue synthesizer.[24] In all these musics there is little sense of 'the album' or 'the single' as a finished product; instead all music seems malleably subject to further sampling, remixing, or other manipulation to realize yet more, different, music. Both 'authenticity' and 'authorship' are at issue here in a discourse that sees such boundaries as at best contingent, and

23 Neither drum 'n' bass nor other forms of dance music, as sound-worlds or ensembles of techniques, deny the possibilities of live performance. 1998 Mercury Prize winners Roni Size and Reprazent mixed live performance and sequenced data, as did French techno act Rinôçérôse, among many other examples.

24 See Alexei Monroe, 'Thinking about Mutation: Genres in 1990s Electronica', in Andrew Blake (ed.), *Living Through Pop*, London, 1999, pp. 146–58.

which therefore threatens the stability of the commodity category of music imprinted onto discs or any other permanent medium.

The establishing of such taxonomies and genre boundaries, while important to the ideological category of 'the listener', has always been vital to the music industry, and vital in particular to some ideas of what 'hi-fi' exists to reproduce. B & W Loudspeakers, a British company started in 1967 by two classical-music enthusiasts, developed their products with the intention of providing acoustically transparent renderings of live musicians' capabilities. At sales demonstrations, a live musician – say, a cellist – would perform, at some point a recording made by the same musician would replace her after a notated rest, and those present were challenged to tell when the live performance stopped and the speakers took over. B & W's focus on this notion of authentic high fidelity meant that their products were taken seriously by music producers and sound engineers: many classical recordings carry the imprimatur 'monitored using B&W speakers'.[25]

A comparison with the recordings used to demonstrate equipment made by Arcam, another British company formed by a small group of enthusiasts some ten years later, signals an important shift in tastes and expectations. Rather than demonstrating that a live cello will sound like a recording and vice versa, Arcam provided for their consumers lists of commercial recordings which they claimed would best demonstrate the capabilities of their equipment. Coincidentally, all the music cited in their promotional material is Anglo-American mainstream popular, jazz, or classical (examples include pop/rock by George Michael, Crowded House, REM, Sheryl Crow, Madonna; jazz from Pat Metheny and Sonny Rollins; and the Academy of St Martin in the Fields, conducted by Sir Neville Marriner, playing Vivaldi).[26] What seems important here is the accurate transmission not of nuanced *performance* but of nuanced *sonic information* to the listener, a form of 'authenticity' which now fetishizes the disc and the amplification equipment rather than the performance. This attitude owes something to the notion of hi-fi, but nothing to any sense of genre hierarchy – indeed hierarchies of musical value are produced here not by genre, but through the ability of equipment to generate accurate transmission of what is recorded (e.g. clear deep bass notes or unsibilant vocals). Clearly, among the important facets of Arcam's marketing strategy is to present to the consumer an uncontroversial, easily accessible list of test recordings, signalling that their products – however technologically advanced – are not designed for

25 E.g. Mahler Symphony no. 7, performed by the City of Birmingham Symphony Orchestra conducted by Simon Rattle (EMI Classics, 1992); see the website http://www.bandwspeakers.co.uk

26 See any issue of Arcam's quarterly publication *Arcam File*; the company's website is http://www.arcam.co.uk

the reproduction of an elite musical tradition, but will improve the sound of any (middlebrow) music.[27]

Patterns of discrimination: genres, labels, niches

Early-twentieth-century recording was all in effect middlebrow, dominated by star performers of the light-classical and opera repertoire such as Dame Nellie Melba and Enrico Caruso, who in 1904 became the first recording artist to sell a million copies.[28] Apart from Italian opera arias, the classical repertoire was at that time difficult to record: alongside problems of balance for orchestral works (partly solved from the 1920s by the use of electric microphones and multichannel mixing) were those of length, the maximum playing time on one side of a twelve-inch 78 rpm record being six minutes – too little for most sonata-form movements even without the repeated exposition. Where jazz musicians responded by fitting their arrangements and improvised performances to the time available (and the 'side', later the 'track', became common parlance for an individual piece of music), classical music remained a problem for recording until the 1950s. Heroic efforts to record the classical repertoire onto multiple sets of 78 rpm records, often using subscription clubs to fund individual recording sessions (organized by innovative record producers such as Walter Legge[29]), gave way to mass-production orthodoxy as the early-1950s success of the vinyl disc revolving at 33⅓ rpm meant that most symphonic movements (and many complete works) could be presented on one side of a disc; the advent of stereo, and its take-up for commercial recordings in the late 1950s, then increased the level of detail possible. This helped to ensure the success of British label Decca's opera series, headlined by the first complete studio recording, in stereo, of Wagner's *Ring* cycle (*Das Rheingold*, the first of these recordings, was released in 1957).[30] The early impact of stereo – in particular the detail which was available through sonic placement – also aided in the popularization of long symphonies with large orchestral forces by the likes of Bruckner, Mahler, and Shostakovich. This in turn, thanks to the continuing high status of classical music, led to the late-1960s rock 'concept album' and to the subsequently derided subgenres of rock opera, such as

27 Arcam are sponsors of the *Gramophone Film Music Good CD Guide* (3rd edn), ed. Mark Walker, Harrow, 1998. My thanks to Gemma Bryden for this reference.

28 Chanan, *Repeated Takes*, 14. However, note there is no entry for Caruso in either Peter Gammond, *The Oxford Companion to Popular Music*, Oxford, 1991, or Donald Clarke (ed.), *The Penguin Encyclopaedia of Popular Music*, London, 1989; for some Anglo-Americans, it seems, the conflation of opera with popular music is still too difficult.

29 Elisabeth Schwarzkopf, *On and Off the Record: A Memoir of Walter Legge*, London, 1982, pp. 57–60.

30 The producer's account of this recording project is John Culshaw, *Ring Resounding*, London, 1975.

The Who's *Tommy*, and 'progressive rock' (for instance Yes's *Tales from Topographic Oceans*).[31]

Occasionally, new typographies and taxonomies have been simply invented by a music business in search of new marketing strategies. 'World music' was a late 1980s sales category invented for local pop musics (not ethnomusicology or local high-culture musics); however, since the success at this time of acts such as the Bhundu Boys and Ofra Haza, world-music charts have tended to be 'crossover' (with Western input into production, composition and/or performance) rather than genuinely local.[32] More usually, however, musical taxonomies have been produced through forms of organized mediation such as academic criticism, journalism, and fan cultures. Until late in the twentieth century, academic musicology concentrated on the Western classical tradition, inventing 'ethnomusicology' as a sideline, and leaving the detailed classification of popular musics to journalists and fans who eagerly filled the gap with an abundance of critical and adulatory writing. This adulation fiercely policed boundaries within and among the genres: a discourse of value, ranged around the binary 'commercial-popular' versus 'authentic-popular', attempted to preserve the status of the informed listener as against the mass consumer.[33] Chart pop was routinely denigrated in music journalism aimed at adults, while the blues, jazz, album rock, punk rock, hiphop, reggae and ragga, and electronic dance music which does not privilege vocals, were allotted positive value by different (though overlapping) groups of adherents. And this informed discrimination enjoyed a symbiotic relationship with the concerns of the music business. Since the 1950s, popular music has fragmented into a wide variety of genres and subgenres, and the post-Fordist capitalism of the music business has addressed the tastes of a variety of informed and discriminating consumers as niche markets. The global 'pop chart' of the 1940s, which included jazz and dance music as well as formulaic pop songs, has also fragmented: both in the United States and worldwide there are now not only pop charts, representing singles and albums, but also charts for dance, blues and soul, country, and classical musics.

Charts are of course no more and no less than sales registers, a crucial part of the music business's ability to invest for the future, and as much a means of constructing as of reflecting demand. Like academic and journalistic critics, the

31 A conspectus of the aesthetic, ethical, and economic pressures in play at this moment can be gleaned from Blake, *The Land Without Music*, pp. 125–76; Brian Martin, *Listening to the Future: The Time of Progressive Rock*, Chicago, 1998; Paul Stump, *The Music's All that Matters: A History of Progressive Rock*, London, 1997; Edward Macan, *Rocking the Classics: English Progressive Rock and the Counterculture*, New York, 1997; Sheila Whiteley, *The Space Between the Notes: Rock and the Counterculture*, London, 1992.

32 Timothy Taylor, *Global Pop: World Music, World Markets*, London, 1997, pp. 2–3, p. 11.

33 A useful discussion of authenticity, in relation to an avowedly commodified music scene, is Sarah Thornton, *Club Cultures: Music, Media and Subcultural Capital*, Cambridge, 1995.

charts work within an assumed Anglo-American hegemony in which, despite the success of the Beatles and other British acts, the dominant partner was American for most of the century, and American forms such as blues and its rock 'n' roll derivatives became quasi-universal. This is partly, doubtless, thanks to the aesthetic attractions of these forms, but perhaps more importantly because of the twentieth-century success of American-led communications industries. By the end of the century, however, American hegemony was partly illusory. The organisations making and marketing recordings were no longer simply reducible to companies based in nation states; most of the music business was owned by concerns whose holdings were as European and/or Japanese as they were American. Nonetheless the illusion had force because most of the bestselling acts, globally, were indeed American. At the BRIT (British Record Industry Trust) awards ceremony in 1993, all categories were won by Americans – which produced the short-lived genre 'Britpop' as a chauvinistic local response to this perceived hegemony.

By the end of the century, such prize events, with televised award ceremonies, had emerged as important arbiters of popular taste and future sales success alike, and here too there is a significant symbolic shift away from 'the listener' and towards 'the consumer' as the imagined recipient of musical information. Typically working with shortlists drawn from major-label recordings, these televised awards supplemented, and to an extent supplanted, the patterns of discrimination offered by journalism and fan culture. As with prizes for literature and art (such as the Booker or Turner prizes), music awards such as the BRITs or the Mercury Prize in Britain, or the Victoires de la Musique in France, replaced print magazines such as the British *New Musical Express* (*NME*), or the French *Les Inrockuptibles*, as taste-formers. Through this strategy the global music-diffusion industry celebrated its achievement by awarding prizes to the already-successful, and then selling the winners' products to an even wider public. Effective as they became in targeting mass as well as niche markets, however, the pace and direction of technological change helped to ensure that the major labels did not maintain total monopoly in the production, distribution, and exchange of music.

Small, independent labels have come and gone throughout the century, serving niche markets too small, local, or otherwise specialized for the major-label companies. In the UK a crop of small labels sprang up whenever there was musical innovation (often shadowed by illegal 'pirate' radio stations, eager to broadcast what cannot be found on mainstream radio). In the late 1960s labels such as Chrysalis and Charisma mixed business with pleasure, serving the middle-class bohemianism of the rock underground; the major labels countered by setting up independent-looking labels such as Harvest (EMI) and Vertigo

(Philips/Polygram). At least one independent, Virgin, had become a major label in its own right within a decade of its 1971 launch (its first release was Mike Oldfield's quirky but best-selling *Tubular Bells*). The same process occurred during the mid-1970s heights of punk rock, and thereafter many labels set out to keep so small they could not be mistaken for majors: the British 1990s punk rock label Slampt!, for instance, was set up in Newcastle to serve the interests of the listener, providing music by bands with a certain following, with no thought for profit; having fulfilled its own brief, it went out of business at the end of the decade.

In the field of classical music a number of small labels served a similar function: examples include Kairos, NMC, and Metier. Even in the last fifteen years of the century, however, it was possible for record companies to grow and develop: the Naxos label, for example, grew from a small label into a considerable company, thanks to changing structures of demand and technological development. The 1980s saw a boom in demand for classical music, marketed as a luxury item for conspicuous consumption in the era of Margaret Thatcher and Ronald Reagan; this was facilitated by record labels' recycling of their existing catalogues onto CD. The record companies' massive investment in CD production facilities meant that by 1986 available capacity had lowered the unit production price of a CD so far that compilation CDs became commonplace as giveaways with music magazines; general knowledge of this low unit cost led to consumer complaint over CD prices, which were routinely fifteen per cent more than the vinyl or cassette equivalent. Complaint was especially strong in relatively poor South-East Asia, where CDs were priced the same as in the United States, and where in 1986 Naxos launched a range of new digital recordings of mainstream classical repertoire recordings at one third of the major labels' prices; the label was launched in the United States and Europe in the following year. Naxos used comparatively cheap East European or South-East Asian artists and recording facilities; and because they paid fees rather than performance royalties to the artists, the company was able to offer the result for less than half the price charged by major labels for the same material performed by artists on the Western Europe/USA concert circuit. The major labels, caught by punitive royalty agreements, 'competed' not by offering new cheap digital recordings of their own, but by recycling old products at marginally lower prices. The deaths of star conductors Karajan, Leonard Bernstein, and Georg Solti increased this tendency to recycle, and diminished major-label investment in new artists.

Instead of repeating mainstream repertoire with new performances, Naxos diversified into more obscure twentieth-century compositions (such as symphonies by Arnold Bax, and operas by Hans Pfitzner); avant-garde 'classics', such as John Cage's music for prepared piano; the rerelease of archival material (including a series of Toscanini performances originally broadcast in the 1940s); and subsidiary labels offering jazz, new age, and world music, together with 'audiobooks' of classic fiction, read to the accompaniment of music from the company's backlist. The label then moved into the present, firstly recording music by living composers with strong local followings, such as the Scot James MacMillan and the Finn Einojuhani Rautavaara; early in 2000 Naxos actually commissioned ten new string quartets from Peter Maxwell Davies, all to be released at the same price as their renditions of Beethoven or Elgar. So this independent mainstream-repertoire label began to operate simultaneously as a multi-niche label, in the same way as the much bigger Decca, with star classical conductors (Solti), star contemporary composers (Harrison Birtwistle), and star rock acts (The Rolling Stones) had done in the 1960s. The operation of the free market, in this instance, encouraged diversity and innovation.

The ECM label provides a similar story. Under the control of Manfred Eicher, trained as both a jazz and classical musician, who founded the company in 1969 and produced the majority of its recordings, ECM developed a distinctive jazz 'house style', a relaxed modernism, experimental without the puritanical denial of narrative structure shared by most free improvisers; it subsequently began to offer new composed music, and to act as distributor for small jazz and new-music labels from Norway and the United States. ECM has throughout its history been a hi-fi label, offering faithful transcriptions of real-time performances, with high recording values achieved through venue choice (offering genre-sensitive natural reverberation) and high-quality performance often recorded direct to stereo, rather than the bland precision of multitrack recording. Cross-subsidy within the label – for example from *Officium*,[34] in which saxophonist Jan Garbarek improvised over medieval vocal music performed by the Hilliard Ensemble, and which was sold at premium price despite its success – enabled the recording of work by cult composers such as the Georgian Giya Kancheli.

The many late-twentieth-century dance-music labels which flourished after the 'acid house' moment of 1987–8 seemed particularly well placed to go beyond the replication of existing cultural relations. Indeed the bewildering pace of generic fragmentation, qualified only by the temporary resolution of genres through compilations and the shifting reputations of DJs, imply that all this is simultaneously niche-market music targeted at an already-knowing listener, and product released as a quantum leap into an unknowable and uncontrollable market, one of whose imponderables is the shifting nature of musical

34 Jan Garbarek and the Hilliard Ensemble, *Officium* (ECM, 1993).

subjectivity itself. Labels such as the German Mille Plateaux (named after a work by French post-Freudian theorists Gilles Deleuze and Felix Guattari), and the British Ninja Tune, each have a stable of artists, remixers, and producers who conform very roughly to a label sound, but who are always pushing music into different directions. Mille Plateaux's products incorporate a Deleuzian dance aesthetic which denies the focused subjectivity of 'the listener'; in the case of Ninja Tune, music as such is subordinate to an imagined, and partly realized, multimedia futurism which deliberately acknowledges both the importance of the visual in contemporary music, and the importance of the participant observer (rather than the seated, concentrating, but otherwise passive 'listener') in the making of the musical/audio-visual event.[35]

Not all genres attempt to embody such trajectories, however; much small-label recording is dedicated to the preservation of genres often considered obsolete. Punk and its successors did not need long recording time in expensive studios, or massive financial support for tours. It survived as a genre, and continued to reproduce itself despite major-label indifference as young acts offered themselves to genre-specific labels such as Epitaph or Fat Wreck Chords in the United States, or Ars Mundi in Poland, which survived partly through a set of 'non-commercial' practices in which musicians and label owners alike accept that in pursuit of their musical ideals they are unlikely to make a fortune. Much folk and jazz, like punk, is often organized at a semi-professional level, in which practitioners and enthusiasts alike cross-subsidize their enthusiasm. This includes recording and distribution of music through 'bedroom businesses' such as the British label, Matchless Recordings, which maintains a catalogue of free improvisations by established performers in the genre, recorded straight to stereo from public performance, from a cottage in a village in Essex.[36]

Glocalization: selling the world music

Generic survival, revival, and innovation remain more likely in the smaller labels than with global players, and among small-label sites on the Internet as well as in shops; indeed, according to Epitaph Records the very survival of American punk rock is due to the global market which the World Wide Web has created. So, in a form discarded by the major labels and mass media, punk rock survived in a market which was fragmented and discontinuous but also global, as it is with recordings of locally and ethnically specific musics which

35 The Coldcut video *Let us Play* (Zen, 1997) contains documentary material exploring this vision; the CD *Let Us Replay* (Zen, 1998) includes a CD-ROM track which tries to demonstrate it.

36 Matchless Recordings, 2 Shetlock's Cottages, Matching Tye, near Harlow, Essex, CM17 0QR, UK.

originate from outside the West. These sell to known audiences, including in major 'multicultural' Western cities, but as often serve local populations through intermediate technology. Cheap to buy and to copy to and from, the compact cassette was developed by Phillips in the 1960s as a modest alternative to the reel-to-reel recording tape developed in the 1940s, which was used by the recording industry and favoured by the hi-fi enthusiast. Indeed, the format's indifferent sonic capability meant that few specialist hi-fi manufacturers attempted to make cassette playback/recording machines (one Japanese firm, Nakamichi, filled that gap in the market to the virtual exclusion of others). But the cassette's cheapness as a medium – with equally cheap playback machines readily available – simultaneously helped the exposure of the rest of the world to Anglo-American pop, and enabled small recording and manufacturing operations, recording local music, to challenge the majors' hegemony.

The compact cassette did not, however, necessarily benefit local markets. By the end of the 1970s EMI and Decca had withdrawn from Ghana thanks to local cassette cultures, which were copying tapes illegally for retail; consequently, by the end of the 1980s, there was no technologically developed recording industry there.[37] In India, on the other hand, low-cost cassette-based recording labels were unambiguously a success story. They flourished in the last quarter of the century, where India's biggest label, the local (i.e. Indian-owned) HMV, saw its proportion of sales (mainly of film scores with songs in Hindi) fall from 80 per cent to less than 15 per cent during the 1980s; while Polygram's Music India sold about 8 per cent, most else was small-scale, low-cost, and served the tastes of local or regional genres and languages.[38] The gradual growth of CD posed little threat of a comeback either by Polygram or Bollywood, as by the later 1990s CD players, writers, and media were almost as low in price as cassettes. But not quite – and in Eastern Europe as well as in the 'Third World', the compact cassette remained an important mode of diffusion at the end of the century.

The survival of local music industries has as often been due to governmental strategy as to the operations of market forces. A range of political strategies offered local music protection. In most of the communist world, classical and folk musics were propagated officially, through broadcasts on state radio, and recordings by state-sanctioned ensembles sold through labels such as Electrecord (Romania) and Melodiya (Russia).[39] Jazz and rock music, generally dismissed as bourgeois decadence by official propaganda, often had a genuinely

37 Peter Manuel, *Cassette Culture: Popular Music and Technology in North India*, Chicago, 1993, p. 30.

38 Ibid., p. 71.

39 Two examples from Communist-era Romania's Electrecord label, each released in 1977, indicate the range of official musical discourses. One album presents George Enescu's *Rapsodia Română* nos. 1 and 2, op. 11, alongside his *Poema Română*, op. 1, played by the Symphony Orchestra of Romanian Radio under

subversive existence; the leader of the Czech 'velvet revolution' of 1989, Vaclav Havel, stressed the importance of the Czech rock underground led by acts such as Plastic People, and their Western models such as the Velvet Underground, to the eventual defeat of Communism.[40] And while Anglo-American music only became a commodity in Eastern Europe after 1989, in much of the Western world music was protected as commodity as well as archaeology. Public policy in Britain from the 1930s to the 60s fostered local popular-musical cultures which were Americanized in style but British in personnel; as well as the trade-union control of the number of performances by visiting Americans, a series of 'needle time' agreements controlled the amount of time broadcasters could give to recordings, thus maintaining the employment of local musicians. It is hard to imagine the emergence of The Beatles without this protection. Similarly, in both Australia and Canada, local 'contact rules' restricting the amount of overseas content in radio broadcasting helped to preserve and foster local talent; in Canada's case, while French-language stations (mimicking those of France itself) were clearly trying to preserve Francophone Canada as a cultural space, the English-language stations were as clearly attempting to foster the development of local musicians. Similar strategies (though with fewer strictures about language) have been adopted in Sweden, which has in consequence arguably punched above its weight in world popular music since the 1970s triumphs of Abba.

Such regulations, whatever their effects on the market, did not mean the preservation in aspic of local performing styles. Scandinavian death metal, Romanian progressive rock, Polish punk rock, and French rap were each derived from Anglo-American forms, but were developed with local distinctiveness to address and sell within local markets. Globalization spoke with many languages and many more accents. And yet it remained globalization: leading Polish ensemble Brathanki (whose music encompasses a wide range of pop and folk attributes) were signed to the Columbia label – owned by Sony, whose late-century company philosophy is indeed encapsulated by the key phrase 'global localization',[41] often abbreviated to 'glocalization'. Despite the importance of music within local cultures (which can be serviced by recording), the marketing of 'world music' even on dedicated and enthusiastic specialist labels such

Iosif Conta; the sleeve-notes earnestly document Enescu's place at the head of the 'Romanian School' (ST-ECE 0817). Another presents Dumitru Farcaş, with small ensemble, playing Transylvanian folk music for the clarinet-like taragot; here, the sleeve quotes at length from approving reviews of Farcaş's playing in German, Swiss, and French newspapers (ST-EPE 01334).

40 See Lou Reed, 'Interview with Vaclav Havel', in Hanif Kureishi and Jon Savage (eds.), *The Faber Book of Pop*, London, 1995, pp. 696–709.

41 http://www.sony-europe.com

as Globestyle, promulgated a westernized sense of what music was, divorcing sound from context in exactly the way radio broadcasting and recording had done to Western opera, religious, or dance music: this is music for 'the listener'. Similarly, through aspects of the folk-roots movement, and of festivals such as WOMAD (World of Music and Dance), the westernization of 'world music' can be traced to collaborative, hybrid projects such as Afro-Celt Sound System,[42] removing sonic information from its local-cultural context and placing it within that of product innovation for the listening consumer.

'Multiculturalism', then, in the form of mutual exploration and discovery, has been important to the development of the musical commodity, removing music from its place of origin and placing it before an audience moved by an aestheticized, and occasionally political, interest in 'the Other' as the repository of an imagined authenticity lost to the industrialized and secularized West. This was the place of jazz in France and Scandinavia in the 1930s, or of Bulgarian choral music in late-1980s Western Europe as the Cold War ended. However, such narrow aesthetic, political, ethnographic, or archaeological tendencies became dissipated because by the end of the century world cities such as Paris, New York, and London were not unicultural, or indeed in any obvious sense national, but home to shifting and diverse populations each of which had some tendency to hybridize (the binaries collapsed in the face of the unanswerable question: 'other' than what?). Thanks to broadcasting and recording, musics did not any longer belong solely to specific ethnic or political groups: by making music from everywhere available in much of the world, the twentieth century's technologies put an end to such cultural secrets. The fluid boundaries among linguistic and political groups in large cities offered space for development of new forms and new markets, as for example the 1980s revival in New York of klezmer, an East European Jewish popular form touched by the other folk musics of East Europe – and in its turn touching the jazz of the African-American clarinettist Don Byron.

Copyright from sheet music to samples: whose music?

While pop charts have since the 1950s oscillated between a search for novelty and the stability of performance formats such as the boy- or girl-group, rock has had to deal with its own history, and with an audience which has, like many of the acts themselves, grown older without giving up the tastes formed in

42 *Afro-Celt Sound System* (Real World, 1996).

their teens and early twenties. The last quarter of the twentieth century saw the emergence of a consumer category known as album rock or adult-oriented rock (together with radio stations dedicated to the broadcasting of older material, such as Nostalgie FM in France). In this way the work of rock artists such as REM was placed into the lifetimes and life-cycles of their listeners, thus aiding both the sales of new product and the recycling of old.[43] And this pop demographic indicates the increasing importance of catalogues as the principal driver of music-business profits. Much of the music recorded since the advent of stereo has had at least three lives: a first one as new product, a second one as lower-priced catalogue item, and a third one when rereleased in different formats such as compact cassette, CD and minidisc. Even more impressive are the intangible earnings of music through broadcast royalties paid to the copyright holders (usually the publisher on behalf of the composer, and the record label on behalf of the performer). Because of copyright, back catalogues of commonly performed or broadcast music are in themselves valuable: the Beatles' Northern Songs has been auctioned several times, and is currently owned by Michael Jackson.

A few successful artists, such as Madonna, Pink Floyd, David Bowie, and Frank Zappa, have exercised total copyright control over their own material. More usually, however, the composer has promoted his or her rights in the marketplace through collective organizations; the French SACEM, founded in 1850, was the first of these.[44] Fees from performing and mechanical rights are typically collected on behalf of composers and publishers through a series of worldwide agreements between organizations such as the PRS and MCPS in Britain, and ASCAP and BMI in North America. World Trade negotiations, increasingly important since the 1989 fall of Russian and European communism, have grappled with the notions of intellectual property, moral rights, and copyright because of their general importance to a world structured by the industrial patenting of items such as medicines and GM foods as well as 'creative' work; composers and record companies have continued to benefit. Despite the power of musicians' unions in much of the West, performers have been much less well protected globally; for instance, they have no rights to royalties in the United States.[45]

The other strand in the music business, however, offered a number of ways through which the individual music consumer could avoid the payment of rights for music: tape and disc recording, and Internet download. In the early

43 These positions are developed in Blake, *Living Through Pop*, *passim*.

44 Dave Laing, 'Copyright and the International Music Industry', in Simon Frith (ed.), *Music and Copyright*, Edinburgh, 1993, pp. 24–37; p. 24.

45 Ibid., p. 29.

1970s the recording business ran a campaign against the sale of blank tape; in much of the world all blank tape sold carried a levy, paid to the recording companies. The concerns of the record business increased exponentially with the appearance of the first digital audio format, DAT, in the mid-1980s. Cassette copying degrades the original; digital copying is exact, and increased the pirates' ability to simulate the original. Eventually, all sides of the industry agreed that domestic DAT recorders would incorporate a copycode system which would prevent the endless duplication of perfect copies; similar restrictions were built into the digital minidisc recorders sold from the end of the 1990s. But by this time, the industry was by no means as sharply divided into recording and reproduction strands. Polygram was bought by Philips, and CBS by Sony: in each case the owner was convinced of the synergy of having both hardware and software products in the same company – which meant that, for example, new formats such as minidisc could be released with a range of recordings, each of which would earn money for the holding company. Each company would also provide soundtracks for its own movies. This attempted oligopoly was not entirely successful; disappointed with the financial results of their aggrandisement, Philips sold Polygram to drinks manufacturer Seagram in 1998. Sony, meanwhile, had launched a combination DVD player/games console, Playstation 2 – which signalled a more general move away from 'music alone' to multimedia as the domestic-entertainment concept of the early twenty-first century.

Furthermore, by the end of the century it had become difficult to define a singular 'author' or other owner of moral rights. Pastiche was ubiquitous – for example in the Abba-esque work of boy/girl pop group Steps, or Michael Kamen's score to Hollywood action movie *Die Hard 2: Die Harder*, which owes a great deal to Sibelius's *Finlandia* – and so were the technologies of sampling and remixing in pop, in acts such as Fatboy Slim or Basement Jaxx. The serious question 'are they composers or arrangers, and what rights are they therefore entitled to?' was surrounded by a series of equally vexed questions about the moral rights of those whose work they clearly, and with acknowledgement, used. Legal patterns of sub-ownership which identify samples such as drum riffs confirm the fragmentation and instability of the late-twentieth-century musical commodity. Meanwhile the Internet's growing use for both legal and illegal transactions presented the downloader as composer/arranger, or the hacker as liberator, realizing the Attali-esque prediction of 'composition' as a universal propensity at the potential expense of the entire structure of the music business, unless it can produce a new guardian to secure the composer–performer–consumer relationship: not education, or critical journalism, but copy-protection software. That, however, is the twenty-first century's problem.

Multimedia: the end of 'music'?

> [M]usic video is about the changing ratio, in rock and youth cultures, between sound and vision . . . in a larger context in which visual media and images are competing with, if not displacing, musical and aural images.
>
> Lawrence Grossberg[46]

Multimedia is a term still hard to define at the beginning of the twenty-first century. But from the point of view of this chapter, one significant shift should be registered. At the same time as companies were moving towards commercial synergy by producing hard- and software, the technologies of production were also becoming more synergistic, and music was becoming an integrated part of a general audio-visuality. From the late 1980s one of the leading magazines of the recording profession, *Studio Sound*, began to carry reports on audio-visual production technologies. In the 1990s Sony Professional, the production-technology arm of the company, invested more in developing technologies for the moving image, and sound alongside image, than in pure sound carriers such as DAT or minidisc: one product of this tendency was the VAIO (Visual-Audio Integrated Output) computer system, a PC-based rival to the Apple Macintosh. The late twentieth century was a world in which professional producer technology was increasingly oriented to the audio-visual, and in which the synergy of music, effects, and voice soundtracks was as immediate on computer games as it was in the sonic virtual reality of cinema surround-sound systems such as Dolby Digital; increasingly versions of these systems became available for use in home cinema and computer games.

All these innovations tend to the destabilizing of 'the listener'. Listening was founded by the invention of the gramophone, established in the 1930s heyday of radio, but threatened by the domestic invasion of the moving image in the 1950s. By the late 1980s the portable sonic environment – the Walkman or portable radio – had offered a reinvention of the listener. However, one wave of innovation which was foreshadowed at the end of the century – new portable interconnective technologies such as radio- and Internet-connected mobile telephones – implies another reconfiguration of sound/space and public/private relations, in which the listener is replaced once more by the *flâneur/flâneuse*, someone who looks in at other people and organizations, while less sure of the boundaries of his or her own identity. All this adds up to the end of music *as we know it*. The popular music genres and subgenres that have been quickest to embrace the new technologies,

46 Lawrence Grossberg, 'The Media Economy of Rock Culture: Cinema, Post-modernity and Authenticity', in Simon Frith and Andrew Goodwin (eds.), *Sound and Vision: A Rock Video Reader*, London, 1993, p. 186.

which we can group under the umbrella term dance music, are a long way from the twentieth-century idea(l) of the listener: theirs is a music deliberately designed to be appropriated in a moment of interactive and synaesthetic performance, in which the body and mind of the dancer are as responsive to drugs and the built, lit, and otherwise designed environment of the dance floor as to the pulses and phases of the DJ's arrangements of various pre-recorded musical tracks. Music here has been restored to its place – an honourable place – within, rather than abstracted from, the lived practices and rituals of life.

With film, and latterly television, there has been a similar shift. Image and music consorted through most of the century in partnerships which implied the dominance of the visual. 'The listener' survived because film was public, and because television was generally semi-visible as well as semi-audible (and until the 1980s sounded worse than transistor radios); music was a problem for television, a mass medium which could not afford to appeal simply to a high-culture audience or to 'youth'. Only perhaps in India, with the largest cinema industry in the world, were local musical cultures seriously threatened by popular-music soundtracks taken from audio-visual sources (indeed, the influence of Bollywood was far more pervasive than that of the global music business: Indian mass culture is always-already audio-visual).[47] The key transitional moment elsewhere was the emergence of music video. Video was established in the late 1970s as a domestic medium, despite the hostility of Hollywood; then in the early 1980s, at around the time of the racist 'disco sucks' campaign in the United States, MTV (Music Television) appeared, with music videos its main programming. MTV was subsequently paradigmatic of global capitalism, in its development from presenting only white pop/rock to a more ethnically representative mix, and in continuing (Anglo-)American hegemony but developing regional niche markets – including European, Scandinavian, and Asian versions, much of whose presentation is in a multi-accented 'MTV English'. For all this niche programming, however, MTV principally sold chart pop, but more importantly, MTV and its advertisers *sold*: in which pursuit, image was everything. Crucial to MTV, advertising strategies aimed at the young person's spending power were an important aspect of all of television's second quarter-century.[48] MTV presented music to buy to, not to listen to, a domestic equivalent of shopping-mall muzak: music here was a lifestyle accessory, a decorative aspect of dress, and not something to do, or to take seriously as a critical project for self-realization.

47 Manuel, *Cassette Culture*, p. 8.
48 Cf. Simon Frith, 'Youth/Music/Television', in Frith and Goodwin (eds.), *Sound and Vision*, p. 73.

Music, as Jacques Attali has claimed, has a unique propensity for prefiguration.[49] Semi-audible music had been consistently prefigured in the music of left-field composers from Erik Satie onwards. 'Ambient music' emerged as a category when in the 1980s, influenced by the minimalism of La Monte Young, Terry Riley, Philip Glass, and Steve Reich, Brian Eno started to make music for deliberately sub-audible presentation, and during the 1990s the label 'ambient' was revived for music in 'chill-out rooms' at dance events. David Toop has characterised much 1990s music as working without narrative: one does not have to listen to it consecutively, but can drift in and out of conscious connection with it, so that the listener becomes the dreamer.[50] In the hands of performers such as Bang on a Can, Eno's post-minimalist aesthetic was presented at 'classical' concerts, while Glass's symphonies on themes from the music of Eno and David Bowie reworked, without comment, the relations between classical and popular music.[51]

Glass's dramatic work also crosses the film/art boundary. Film has used a variety of musics, from the post-Wagnerian (Erich Wolfgang Korngold's *The Sea Hawk*, 1940), through orchestral with modernist tinges (Bernard Herrmann, *Psycho*, 1960), jazz (Sonny Rollins, *Alfie*, 1963), and soul (Isaac Hayes, *Shaft*, 1971), back to the Romantic orchestra with 'space opera' (John Williams, *Star Wars*, 1977), and on to postmodern avant-garde-influenced orchestral (Don Davis, *The Matrix*, 1999). All of these provide diegetic heightening of drama through scores which were hardly functional in their own right and hardly ever taken seriously before the end of the century, partly because the composers themselves often regarded such work as moonlighting (Herrmann, for example, regarded his film work as a sideline and was consistently frustrated at his critical failure as a concert composer). This is indeed a complex issue, partly because from the 1970s on film was also used as a form of music video, to sell already-existing pop, either through actual pop soundtracks such as *American Graffiti* (1973) or through compilations of music used in and 'inspired by' movies; by the end of the 1990s it was common for two albums to be released – a representation of the film's orchestral soundtrack score, and a compilation of related pop – and for each to be released by the same audio-visual holding company (such as Sony or Polygram) that owned rights to all the music used in the film as well as to the film itself. The soundtrack album, however compromised by the needs of pop sales divisions, is arguably the last stand of the concept album; it

49 Jacques Attali, *Noise: A Political Economy of Music* (tr. Brian Massumi), Manchester, 1984.

50 David Toop, *Ocean of Sound: Aether Talk, Ambient Sound and Imaginary Worlds*, London, 1995.

51 Glass (based on music by David Bowie and Brian Eno), *Low Symphony* (Point, 1993); *Heroes Symphony* (Point, 1997); Bang on a Can, *Music for Airports* (music by Brian Eno, Point, 1998). Point Music is Glass's own company; its distribution is through Polygram.

helped both to boost pop sales and – in the case of big orchestral soundtracks – to reinvent the label 'classical music'.[52]

However, all did not disappear into lifestylized audio-visuality, with music reduced to the semi-audible; in many ways the contrasts between sound and vision have been clarified, rather than obscured, by the late-century innovations. The increasing abundance of film-related music for the listener signals the increasing importance of sound in film in the last quarter of the century, an importance determined in part by changing technologies. The development of Dolby digital and other increasingly powerful forms of surround sound, together with more sophisticated and detailed mixing techniques which allow the separation of music, sound effects, and dialogue, in effect led to the expansion of the flat screen from two to three dimensions. In consequence cinematic music, which when recorded in mono and mixed under the dialogue was perceived as an emotion-heightening blur, became far more impressive, and could indeed be listened to at the expense of the image, even when in the cinema; this new clarity in turn led to a revival of academic, journalistic, and fan interest in film music. Domestic technologies such as wide-screen television were accompanied by multichannel sound systems which replicated this new sonic clarity – this new listenability – in the home.

Nonetheless, however festooned with audio and visual effects, film remained at the century's end much as it had been at its start: an ordered narrative told through a sequence of images, supported by dialogue and music, watched and heard by a passive audience. Towards the end of the century composers began to write commissioned computer or video game scores, which echo the experimental compositions of the 1960s in their subventions of musical narrative and the roles they expect of the participant player – the same chunks of music can be used in different parts of the game, so that (depending on his or her game-playing ability) the player becomes an arranger, and in Attali's terms arguably a composer. The game's soundtrack writer, by extension, is still an artisan (as was Herrmann, beholden to the will of the director and producer), and the status of the commodity (identified as the game, not its music) reduces that of the composition, as does film music in general, to that of component.

At the start of the twenty-first century, then, the technologies of musical entertainment were in a crisis which challenged their basic premise: that 'music' is a phenomenon which can and should be bought and sold as a commodity. The music business was trying to reinvent itself for the information age.

52 Walker, *Gramophone Film Music Good CD Guide* 3rd edn, Harrow, 1998, pp. 10–11. It is worth noting that DVD has opened the possibility for the more intensive study of film music; the region 1 DVD of *The Matrix*, for example, includes a complete run of the movie with music soundtrack but no dialogue, with commentary by the composer in the appropriate gaps.

In January 2001 the multimedia publisher Time Warner, owner of the Warner record label and Warner Brothers films, announced the completion of its merger with the Internet service provider AOL (America On Line). A year earlier, just after proposing this merger, Time Warner had also made a bid for EMI, whose music-recording interests include the massive back catalogue necessary for the launch of a major Internet diffusion system. This potential copyright-led media giant did not in fact come into being, thanks to American and European commercial, legal, and political opposition. Meanwhile, also in early 2000, the heavy-metal band Metallica sued Napster, an Internet company whose software enabled users to share music files on their hard disks without making copyright payments. 335,435 Napster subscribers were cited by name as abusers of their copyright (as Metallica saw it); though this and subsequent legal action closed Napster down, similar software programs remained openly available. Some form of encryption may eventually emerge, and make the Time Warner dream of Internet diffusion for profit a reality; meanwhile Toop's dreams, and Attali's prophecies, may turn out to signal a nightmare end for a music business that expanded resolutely throughout the twentieth century on the basis of the industrial production of discrete artefacts. Music, as a phenomenon isolated by the technologies of sound broadcasting and recording, was one of the most successful commodities of the century, but while it remained an identifiable, composable, and performable category, this isolated status was under threat at the century's end. And yet the gradual collapse of the musical commodity into multimedia offers new possibilities not just for music and musicians, but for the emergence of a new participant – who is no longer simply a listening subject, but who looks, hears, and interacts, and in this way knows the 'value' of music.

Bibliography

Attali, Jacques. *Noise: A Political Economy of Music* (tr. Brian Massumi), Manchester, 1984.
Barnard, Stephen. *On the Radio*, Milton Keynes, 1989.
Blake, Andrew. *The Land Without Music: Music, Culture and Society in Twentieth Century Britain*, Manchester, 1997.
(ed.). *Living Through Pop*, London, 1999.
Bull, Michael. *Sounding Out the City: Personal Stereos and the Management of Everyday Life*, Oxford, 2000.
Chanan, Michael. *Repeated Takes: A Short History of Recording and its Effects on Music*, London, 1995.
Clarke, Donald (ed.). *The Penguin Encyclopaedia of Popular Music*, London, 1989.
Culshaw, John. *Ring Resounding*, London, 1975.
Doctor, Jennifer. *The BBC and Ultra-Modern Music 1922–1936: Shaping a Nation's Tastes*, Cambridge, 1999.

Frith, Simon and Andrew Goodwin (eds.). *Sound and Vision: A Rock Video Reader*, London, 1993.
Gammond, Peter. *The Oxford Companion to Popular Music*, Oxford, 1991.
Gay, Paul du, Stuart Hall et al. *Doing Cultural Studies: The Story of the Sony Walkman*, London, 1997.
Glock, William. *Notes in Advance*, Oxford, 1987.
Gronow, Pekka and Ilpio Saunio. *An International History of the Recording Industry* (tr. Christopher Moseley), London, 1998.
Grossberg, Lawrence. 'The Media Economy of Rock Culture: Cinema, Post-modernity and Authenticity', in Simon Frith and Andrew Goodwin (eds.), *Sound and Vision: A Rock Video Reader*, pp. 186–205.
Hill, Dave. 'Doing What Comes Naturally', *Independent Magazine*, 8 April 2000, pp. 30–4.
Hills, Matthew. *Fan Cultures*, London, 2002.
Hornby, Nick. *High Fidelity*, London, 1995.
Kenyon, Nicholas (ed.). *Authenticity and Early Music: A Symposium*, Oxford, 1988.
Laing, Dave. 'Copyright and the International Music Industry', in Simon Frith (ed.), *Music and Copyright*, Edinburgh, 1993, pp. 24–37.
Lanza, Joseph. *Elevator Music*, London, 1995.
Lewis, Lisa (ed.). *The Adoring Audience*, London, 1992.
Lowe, Frances. 'It's the Wild Wild Net', *PRS Statement*, Spring 2000, pp. 4–5.
Macan, Edward. *Rocking the Classics: English Progressive Rock and the Counterculture*, New York, 1997.
Manuel, Peter. *Cassette Culture: Popular Music and Technology in North India*, Chicago, 1993.
Martin, Brian. *Listening to the Future: The Time of Progressive Rock*, Chicago, 1998.
Monroe, Alexei. 'Thinking about Mutation: Genres in 1990s Electronica', in Andrew Blake (ed.), *Living Through Pop*, London, 1999, pp. 146–58.
Nathan, John. *Sony: The Private Life*, London, 1999.
Reed, Lou.'Interview with Vaclav Havel', in Hanif Kureishi and Jon Savage (eds.), *The Faber Book of Pop*, London, 1995, pp. 696–709.
Scholes, Percy. *The Listener's Guide to Music: With a Concert-Goer's Glossary*, London, 1919.
The Listener's History of Music, 3 vols., London, 1923–9.
Schwarzkopf, Elisabeth. *On and Off the Record: A Memoir of Walter Legge*, London, 1982.
Sennett, Richard. *The Fall of Public Man*, London, 1986.
Stump, Paul. *The Music's All That Matters: A History of Progressive Rock*, London, 1997.
Taylor, Timothy. *Global Pop: World Music, World Markets*, London, 1997.
Thornton, Sarah. *Club Cultures, Music, Media and Subcultural Capital*, Cambridge, 1995.
Toop, David. *Ocean of Sound: Aether Talk, Ambient Sound and Imaginary Worlds*, London, 1995.
Walker, Mark (ed.). *Gramophone Film Music Good CD Guide* (3rd edn), Harrow, 1998.
Whiteley, Sheila. *The Space Between the Notes: Rock and the Counterculture*, London, 1992.

· 19 ·

Ageing of the new: the museum of musical modernism

ALASTAIR WILLIAMS

The cultural event that most conspicuously marked the turn of the millennium in Britain was the opening of London's Tate Modern, the refurbished power station that is now, spatially, the world's largest museum of modern art. The building itself is significant since it marks a transformation from an industrial utility to a cultural space; together with its contents, it signifies a commitment to modern art at the end of the twentieth century. It is even able to include a replica of Marcel Duchamp's celebrated urinal – an object designed to test institutional limits. So reconstructed, museums no longer instil a dominant view of culture, nor do they display artists as overbearing bastions of authorial rectitude: they are more likely to present contrasting outlooks and leave spectators to find ways of accommodating them. Like the exhibits in the Tate, modernist musical artefacts cannot survive without support, yet their institutions can evolve and need not be governed by the curatorial attitudes normally associated with museum culture. Institutions, like music, are embodiments of human ideas and are therefore potentially mobile and subject to interpretation.

Institutions and performers

The most remarkable institution of twentieth-century music must surely be IRCAM (Institut de Recherche et Coordination Acoustique/Musique). Adjacent to the Centre Georges Pompidou in central Paris, IRCAM is devoted to the technical and creative advancement of music. Remarkably, it derives from the vision of one man, Pierre Boulez, whose stature as a musician enabled him to secure funding from the French government for the development of a music research institute. Since the pioneering days of the 1950s, Boulez had believed that musical life was locked into a museum culture that discouraged technical advances in instrument design and educated performers to reproduce the conventions of the classical repertoire. Advances in sound technology, he

I am grateful to Irvine Arditti for discussing pertinent issues with me. I should also like to thank colleagues at Keele for providing materials used in the course of writing this chapter.

felt, offered few compositional resources because they served the same system, geared to producing quality recordings of a stagnant repertoire.[1] In Boulez's opinion, the solitary efforts of individual composers were likely neither to transform such a mindset nor to develop the technology that would enhance musical creativity. It was more probable, he argued, that such advances, like other late-twentieth-century innovations, would be generated by collaborative team efforts. Accordingly, he based IRCAM on the model of a scientific research institute with different specialists pooling their expertise.

Boulez secured funding for IRCAM in 1974 and the building was completed in 1977. Built underground, it contains studios, laboratories, offices, and a concert hall in which the reverberation time can be modified by moving electronically adjustable wall panels, and in which the three sections of the ceiling can be moved separately according to performance requirements. The institute was originally established with departments devoted to areas such as electroacoustics, computer music, and extended instrumental techniques, with each domain directed by an established figure. In 1980, however, after three years of running at full capacity, the institute entered a crisis, with all five directors resigning. Boulez responded by reconfiguring the organization into two sectors, one musical and one scientific, with a pedagogical unit coordinating the two. The new structure reflected the subsuming of electroacoustics within computer music, even though it was research in Berio's electroacoustic department that had led to the development of the important 4X computer. In recent years Boulez has distanced himself from the day-to-day running of IRCAM, even though his influence on its behalf remains vital.[2]

Rarely in its history has music received patronage on the scale that IRCAM, with its extensive public funding, has enjoyed. It is thus a privileged institution and has, not surprisingly, triggered much debate. Born in the 1970s, IRCAM consolidated the modernist belief in technical advance at a time when its authority was being questioned elsewhere by the success of minimalism and pop art. It tended to reinforce the idea that modernist values are dependent on powerful institutions that seek to exclude other voices, particularly those deriving from popular music.[3] This controlling tendency was confirmed, in the initial stages at least, by its commitment to developing powerful mainframe systems instead of exploring the increasing potential of micro-computers – and there was a degree of self-protection in this stance, since micros, and

1 For more on Boulez's frustrations with music's institutions, see Jonathan Harvey, 'IRCAM', in William Glock (ed.), *Pierre Boulez: A Symposium*, London, 1986, pp. 239–46.

2 For more on the history and development of IRCAM, see Dominique Jameux, *Pierre Boulez* (tr. Susan Bradshaw), London, 1991.

3 This point is consistently made in Georgina Born, *Rationalizing Culture: IRCAM, Boulez, and the Institutionalization of the Musical Avant Garde*, Berkeley, 1995.

more recently the Internet, encourage desktop composition and dissemination without requiring institutional affiliation. This said, IRCAM's ability to pursue research without an immediate need for commercial delivery remained vital in an age driven by marketing, and its willingness to commission composers from all over the globe has been important for the continued health of musical life.

While IRCAM was becoming established in the mid-1970s, the Darmstadt summer school, which had cradled so much new life in the 1950s, was witnessing the ageing of the avant-garde and the emergence of a new generation. The turning point in the 1970s was the so-called neo-Romanticism of composers such as Manfred Trojahn, Detlef Müller-Siemens and, above all, Wolfgang Rihm. Casting off the fetters of what they considered to be an ageing avant-garde, this group offered a more inclusive aesthetic in the pursuit of musical freedom and intensity. The ensuing debates triggered a response from the eminent musicologist Carl Dahlhaus who was critical of what he considered to be indiscriminate mixtures of the beautiful and the ugly, the significant and the trivial, though he noted a concern with tone colour that could be traced to post-serial music.[4]

More traditional Darmstadt values were represented by Brian Ferneyhough, who became a major figure at the summer courses in the 1980s. This decade also saw attention given to previously neglected figures such as the American Morton Feldman, a guest composer in 1984 and 1986, and the Italian Giacinto Scelsi, whose music received special attention in 1986, while interest in Luigi Nono also revived at this time. Alongside such revaluations, the 1980s also saw heated debates about minimalism, and in 1994 a concert was devoted to the music of La Monte Young.[5] No less significant was a symposium in the same year devoted to the writings and music of the major philosopher and cultural critic Theodor Adorno, an event that demonstrated that modernism was becoming increasingly reflexive and willing to examine the interests and functions served by its own discourses. Finally, the dismantling of the Berlin Wall in 1989 heralded a much wider European participation at Darmstadt.

The ageing of Darmstadt was of course part of the means by which high modernism became sedimented into history. The importance of this process was recognized by the opening of the Paul Sacher Foundation, Basel, in 1986. Initially based on the collections of its wealthy patron, the Foundation acquired the

4 Quoted in Achim Heidenreich, 'Ein Rhythmus im Alltäglichen. Zu Wolfgang Rihm', in Rudolf Stephan et al. (eds.), *Von Kranichstein zur Gegenwart: 50 Jahre Darmstädter Ferienkurse (1946–1996)*, Stuttgart, 1996, pp. 487–93; p. 489.

5 For an overview of Darmstadt 1982–94, see Christopher Fox, '1982–1994: L'Atelier Énorme', in Rudolf Stephan et al. (eds.), *Von Kranichstein zur Gegenwart*, pp. 461–7.

estates of Stravinsky and Webern in the 1980s and now houses the archives of many of the composers mentioned in this chapter, including Berio, Birtwistle, Boulez, Carter, Feldman, Ferneyhough, Gubaidulina, Lachenmann, Ligeti, Nancarrow, Rihm, and Rochberg. Both reflecting and shaping the writing of twentieth-century music history, it provides a major international resource for music scholars.

Contemporary music depends not only on a responsive cultural climate, but also on the accumulated expertise of ensembles dedicated to that repertoire. The need for specialist groups such as Ensemble InterContemporain, the London Sinfonietta, and the Arditti String Quartet clearly indicated that new music required performers who were familiar with the idiom, or prepared to learn, and used to interpreting certain notational conventions. This was no less true outside modernism since the minimalists Philip Glass and Steve Reich also founded ensembles specializing in their own music. Such ensembles, in whatever genre, create conventions on which scores rely, and hearing new sounds inevitably stimulates composers to explore further. Since the 1980s, moreover, performers have been able to use readily available CD technology to cater for a specialist and geographically dispersed audience.

Because composers rely on specialized performers, many of them foster close associations with new-music ensembles, and none more so than Boulez, who brings a wealth of conducting experience to twentieth-century music. He established himself as a conductor in the 1960s, with a view to furthering his desire to create a climate that would push public taste beyond a curated canon and encourage interest in modern music. It was not just the listening public that he set out to reform; he also attempted to overcome the animosity to new music of institutions such as symphony orchestras steeped in the classical repertoire (though it is only fair to point out that individual players frequently transcended such limitations). Much progress was made on both fronts during Boulez's sojourn from 1969–75 as Chief Conductor of the BBC Symphony Orchestra, and with such aspirations, it is not surprising that, in 1975, Boulez founded the Ensemble InterContemporain as an intrinsic part of IRCAM. The group has two main functions: one is to perform music generated by IRCAM and to take part in developments of electronic techniques, while the other is to perform what might be called the modernist repertoire from Webern to Ferneyhough. Boulez's overall hopes for the acceptance of modern music have been dashed by the crisis in modernism; nevertheless the ensemble has established a formidable reputation, recorded and performed extensively, and done much for the public perception of IRCAM. Working closely with Boulez, it has achieved a degree of flexibility and accuracy that would have been impossible in less favourable conditions.

In Britain the London Sinfonietta, founded in 1968 and at the time of writing directed by Oliver Knussen, is likewise dedicated both to the performance of established twentieth-century music and to fostering new scores. In the first capacity, it has mounted festivals celebrating the work of Schoenberg, Webern, Britten, Tippett, Stravinsky, Ravel, and Varèse. In the second, it has been instrumental in supporting both established British composers such as Birtwistle and younger talents such as Thomas Adès (b. 1971), while also providing performances for senior figures such as Elliott Carter. Even though it is now usual for orchestras to have an education programme, the Sinfonietta has been pioneering in this respect since 1983, working both in schools and in the wider community. At the time of writing, for example, it is providing resources on Boulez and his compositional techniques for curriculum-based school projects.[6]

The Arditti Quartet was founded in 1974, close to the inception of IRCAM, and thus celebrated its twenty-fifth anniversary in 1999. Revealing just how indebted new music is to committed performers, the quartet places great value on individual preparation so that all the players are aware of one another in rehearsal. Normally, the composer will give advice on a new score and, where the music significantly extends the bounds of traditional notation, may well offer guidance from the start. The Ardittis' dedication is exemplified in their approach to Brian Ferneyhough's Second String Quartet, of which Irvine Arditti comments, 'We worked on that not bar by bar, but beat by beat, and I think in those days, in 1980, we spent about sixty hours learning the piece. It was some twelve minutes long.'[7] Unlike, say, a Haydn quartet, Ferneyhough's Second Quartet is not fully immersed in tradition, so problems need to be solved, procedures invented, and traditions established which – though not beyond dispute – carry a residue of the music that is not present in the notation. Such circumstances encourage us more than ever to think of the score as something that requires imagination from performers to bring it into being. Indeed it was Irvine Arditti's performance of the first sixteen of Cage's *Freeman Etudes*, which brought the seemingly impossible into the realms of possibility, that inspired Cage to complete the set.[8] By pushing string playing beyond established limits, Arditti and his colleagues feed the imaginations of composers and enhance their creative freedom. Much of the music discussed in this chapter depends on such commitment from performers.

6 For more on the London Sinfonietta, see http://www.londonsinfonietta.org.uk

7 Irvine Arditti, 'Irvine Arditti in Interview with Max Nyfeller', programme for Huddersfield Contemporary Music Festival, 1999, p. 51.

8 See James Pritchett's liner notes to Irvine Arditti's recording of Cage's *Freeman Etudes*, Books One and Two (Mode, 1993).

Composers 1: Boulez, Carter, Ligeti, Berio, Nono, Stockhausen, Cage

Chapters 13 and 17 were devoted to a pioneering group of composers who made reputations for radical innovation early in their careers. This section charts their subsequent development. Mainly associated with the initial years of the Darmstadt summer courses and mainly born in the mid-1920s, these figures made such an indelible impression on music in the second half of the twentieth century that their careers after those heady years in many ways define the trajectory of modernism. The two Americans, John Cage and Elliott Carter, were born some years before the main European group, but both were established mid-century and Cage's 1958 visit is part of Darmstadt legend.

Pierre Boulez, who was born in 1925, made his mark as a composer and polemicist; subsequently, as we have seen, he also secured an international reputation as a conductor before founding a major institution. These different roles not only show what a multi-talented figure he is, but also demonstrate that music flows through a number of channels and cannot be understood in only one dimension. Along with Mahler, Wagner is the figure from the orchestral repertoire that most engages Boulez's empathy (milestones in his conducting career include *Parsifal* in 1966 and *The Ring* between 1976 and 1980, both at Bayreuth), and it is arguable that the gestural and theatrical tendencies of both these composers have affected Boulez's own compositions since the mid-1970s. Such influences are not direct, however, because – unlike, say, Wolfgang Rihm – Boulez refuses to import stylistic references into his own music, instead insisting that material should be generated by the compositional process.

Although Boulez continued to compose even during the busiest phases of his conducting career, his output diminished. While this might not seem surprising, Boulez candidly attributed the situation to an impasse in contemporary composition, admitting, in his words, that 'orchestral conducting was the consequence and not the cause of the compositional silence'.[9] The solution of course was the founding of IRCAM, described by Boulez as 'an institution which is to have musical research as its function, acoustics as its subject, and the computer as its instrument',[10] in a programme that exerted huge pressure on himself to create something of significance that would embody the intersection of music and science. That something was *Répons*, but before turning to this, we should note premieres in the 1970s of an early version of *... Explosante-fixe ...* (1972–4) and of *Rituel in memoriam Bruno Maderna* (1974–5), an orchestral work written in memory of the Italian composer and conductor, which has proved to be one of Boulez's most approachable scores. His œuvre is

9 Quoted in Jameux, *Pierre Boulez*, p. 169. 10 Ibid.

distinguished by its 'work-in-progress' status, and even the earliest pieces are liable to be revisited. *Notations* offers an example: in its 1945 incarnation it comprises a group of twelve piano pieces, four of which have so far been transformed into a set of orchestral pieces, *Notations* I–IV (1977–8), that offer glittering studies in modern orchestration. Boulez intends to complete all twelve.

Répons is another incomplete work: three versions were performed between 1981 and 1984 before the score was, at least temporarily, consolidated in its present form. It is written for a small orchestral ensemble, electronic equipment, and soloists who play the following instruments: cimbalom, piano 1, xylophone doubling with glockenspiel, harp, vibraphone, and piano 2 doubling with synthesizer. A computer is used to distribute and transform the sounds of the soloists, which are heard through six loudspeakers, while the soloists and speakers are grouped around the ensemble, allowing complex trajectories of spatialized sound. As far back as 1958, in *Poésie pour pouvoir*, Boulez had tried to achieve an organizational continuum between acoustic and electroacoustic resources, and had been sufficiently frustrated in his efforts not to explore electronic resources again until developments at IRCAM enabled him to pursue his ideal. The instrument that brings this aim to fruition in *Répons* is the 4X computer, which enables live electronic processing of sounds, so ensuring that there is not a timbral gap of the sort often experienced between pre-recorded tape and an instrumental ensemble. This sonic continuity is heard to dazzling effect with the entrance of the soloists, whose arpeggiated chords are expanded to vast spatial spirals by the 4X.

This very audible, dramatic effect is a manifestation of Boulez's tendency throughout his œuvre to proliferate an underlying idea. *Répons* is built from five generative chords, which are multiplied and transformed to form its sometimes luxurious web of sound. The same chords provide the material for *Dérive* (1984), which also shares *Répons*'s trilled textures. Recent compositions include another version of . . . *Explosante-fixe* . . . (1991–3), this time for MIDI flute, two solo flutes, ensemble, and electronics; *Incises* (1994) for piano; and *Sur Incises* (1996) for three pianos, three harps, and three keyboard percussionists. *Répons* remains the major work by Boulez of the past twenty years, and has fulfilled its tough obligation to create an aesthetic justification for IRCAM's attempts to overcome the schism between acoustic and electronic music. Despite a dwindling flow of music in recent years, Boulez remains a giant figure in contemporary music because his activity on so many fronts has done so much to transform musical institutions.

Elliott Carter (b. 1908) – one of the few contemporary composers held in high esteem by Boulez – has been an energetic composer throughout three of the four quarters of the twentieth century, and his output in the last quarter was both prolific and significant. Modernism in American music is broadly split between an experimental tradition (of which Cage was a leading exponent), keen to leave behind a European past, and a form of modernism that – like its European counterpart – is concerned with advancing musical material, though from the perspective of American experience. David Schiff argues that 'Carter's mature style dares to bring together these seemingly irreconcilable musical sources', and by doing so combines freedom of invention with intellectual challenge.[11] Dramatized instrumental roles are a regular feature of Carter's music and Schiff chooses the Third Quartet, which is divided into separate metric pairings of instruments, as a metaphor for the gap negotiated in Carter's music between Europe and America.

With a decline in the institutions of modernism especially marked in the United States since the 1980s, it is from Europe that most of Carter's commissions have come in the last twenty years, mainly from ensembles such as the London Sinfonietta and the Ensemble InterContemporain: it was perhaps recognition of this interest, and of the resources offered by the Sacher Foundation, that prompted him to accept an invitation from Paul Sacher to deposit his sketches in Switzerland.[12] In Carter's late style we see the dramatic contrasts so characteristic of his earlier music played out in less confrontational ways.[13] This fluidity is evident in *Night Fantasies* for piano (1980), in which all-interval twelve-note chords are used to convey, according to Carter, 'the fleeting thoughts and feelings that pass through the mind during a period of wakefulness at night'.[14] Shifting modes are also found in the piano piece *90+* (1994), written for the ninetieth birthday of the Italian composer Goffredo Petrassi, in this case underpinned, Carter says, by 'ninety short, accented notes played in a slow regular beat'.[15] The 1980s and 90s also produced oboe, violin, and clarinet concertos, the Fourth and Fifth String Quartets, and two substantial orchestral trilogies: *Three Occasions* (1986–9) and *Symphonia: Sum Fluxae Pretiam Spei* (1993–7). The former puts together three separately composed pieces, all with Ivesian titles: *A Celebration of Some 100 × 150 Notes* (which includes Ivesian fanfares), *Remembrance*, and *Anniversary*. The three components of *Symphonia* – 'Partita', 'Adagio tenebroso', and 'Allegro scorrevole' – can also be played separately; together they constitute a symphony that ends with weightless sonorities instead of a synthesizing statement. 'Adagio tenebroso'

11 David Schiff, *The Music of Elliott Carter* (2nd edn), London, 1998, p. 7.

12 Carter comments on this decision in Jonathan W. Bernard, 'An Interview with Elliott Carter', *Perspectives of New Music* 28/2 (1990), pp. 180–214; pp. 206–7.

13 For a discussion of style in late Carter, see Arnold Whittall, *Musical Composition in the Twentieth Century*, Oxford, 1999, p. 262.

14 Elliott Carter, Preface to *Night Fantasies* for piano, New York, 1980.

15 Elliott Carter, programme note to *90+* for piano, London, 1994.

is generally considered to be one of Carter's darkest meditations, and for Schiff it 'seems to encompass all the suffering of the twentieth century'[16] – a century nearly encompassed by Carter's life. Of all the music considered in this chapter, Carter's makes the strongest claim to represent a mainstream modernism.

The ways in which modernism has survived and transformed itself, after many of the beliefs that held sway at its height in the 1950s have foundered, are of central importance for this chapter. György Ligeti is interesting in this respect because his output has successfully traversed both eras, meeting the demands of both modernism and postmodernism without the one being obviously subsumed by the other. From the vastly reduced resources of texture scores such as *Atmosphères* (1961) – which took a sideways look at constructivist composition, using dense, imperceptible micro canons to produce highly perceptible transformations in texture – Ligeti has gradually reclaimed the resources of melody and rhythm. The opera *Le grand macabre* (1974–7) is often seen as a turning point in this incremental process because of its return to harmonic progression, particularly in the final scene.

Subsequent scores draw on a range of influences, as exemplified by a renewed engagement with the musical past evident in the Horn Trio (1982), intended as a homage to Brahms, in which 'horn fifths' progressions evoke classical horn writing. Nevertheless, this heritage is heard from a skewed perspective and integrated into Ligeti's own musical language, separating it from more eclectic tendencies that, in his view, theatricalize the past.[17] Ligeti also acknowledges, through a quirky version of phase shifting, the impact of minimalism, notably in 'Selbstportrait mit Reich and Riley (und Chopin ist auch dabei)', one of three pieces for two pianos, *Monument–Selbstportrait–Bewegung*, from 1976. The phase shifts of minimalism might be described as aural illusions since their beats are not notated but arise instead from simultaneous metrical processes.

Such illusions are an important part of Ligeti's compositional technique and have been enriched by diverse influences since the 1980s. These include the metric complexities of Conlon Nancarrow's Studies for Player Piano: by punching patterns into paper rolls for player piano, or pianola, Nancarrow was able to achieve levels of metrical intricacy that would surpass the capacities of human pianists. It is this idea of simultaneous rhythmic levels that appeals to Ligeti, who had already touched on it in his *Poème symphonique* for a hundred metronomes (1962), and who is also attracted to the simultaneous metric processes that occur in the polyphonic percussion playing of several sub-Saharan African nations. Neither Nancarrow nor African polyphony appear in

16 Schiff, *The Music of Elliott Carter*, p. 319.

17 György Ligeti, *Études* (tr. David Feuzeig and Annelies McVoy), notes to *György Ligeti: Works for Piano*, played by Pierre-Laurent Aimard (Sony, 1996), pp. 11–12.

recognizable form; instead they are used as points of departure for Ligeti's own polymetres, which combine to create a kaleidoscopic texture. Another trait in the later scores, particularly evident in the Horn Trio (1982), is the use of natural harmonics to create the distorted effects that, in one dimension or another, distinguish most of Ligeti's music.

A range of techniques appear in the five-movement Piano Concerto (1985–8).The first movement is a polymetric *moto perpetuo*, based around displaced hemiola patterns, where, as the composer comments, 'the rhythmic events, too complex to be perceived in detail, hang in a suspended state'.[18] The second movement contains characteristic extremes of register, jarring clusters, and Bartók-like superimposed modal systems, along with the folk-inflected 'night sounds' of slide whistle and alto ocarina. Ligeti has been preoccupied since the mid-1980s with piano etudes, which explore in detail many of the techniques found in the Concerto: so far he has produced two books of studies, the first (1985) containing six and the second (1990) a further six and two added subsequently, and a third book is under way. 1990 also saw the Violin Concerto, in which we hear more of Ligeti's capacity for complex textures and strange tunings – the latter notably in a passage in the second movement where ocarinas and recorders carry the melody.

Ligeti is one of the most eloquent of the composers discussed in this chapter; and this capacity to verbalize his musical thinking has undoubtedly contributed to the interest taken in his work, strengthened the position he occupies in contemporary culture, and (arguably) also added to the clarity of his music. The following comment situates his aesthetic in the middle of many currents: 'Now with the Piano Concerto I offer my aesthetic credo: my independence both from the criteria of the traditional avant garde and from those of fashionable postmodernism.'[19] Ligeti means by this that his music is dependent neither on abstract compositional schemes nor on references to a range of styles. Instead, it has found a path between these extremes by absorbing a range of influences into internally-generated, audible musical processes.

Like Ligeti, Luciano Berio has retained widespread admiration since becoming a well-known figure in the post-war avant-garde. Though very much involved in the Darmstadt of the 1950s, he experienced the faltering of modernism less acutely than others because he was not principally a system builder and had long been comfortable with multiplicity. His affinity with vocal music and gesture not only guarded against structural obsessions but also lent itself to music theatre in the 1960s and 70s, and his output included a number

18 György Ligeti, 'On My Piano Concerto' (tr. Robert Cogan), *Sonus: A Journal of Investigations into Global Musical Possibilities* 9/1 (1988), pp. 8–13; p. 9.
19 Ibid., p. 13.

of scores that engage the genre of opera – although the composer insisted that they were not operas. The first, ironically enough, was called *Opera* (1969–70), while the second two were both collaborations with Italo Calvino: *La vera storia* (1977–81) and *Un re in ascolto* (1979–84). Because Berio believed that opera in the traditional sense of a sung story was no longer viable, it is appropriate that *Un re in ascolto* (A King Listens), which is loosely based around Shakespeare's *The Tempest*, takes theatrical representation as its subject matter and dramatizes the process of staging a play. The weakening of the producer's control is staged with his collapse at the end of the first act and in his eventual death – a death paralleled, the composer suggested, by the music 'dying structurally alongside him'.[20]

In the last years of his life Berio also continued his string of *Sequenzas* – pieces that characterize a particular solo instrument – with compositions since 1980 for clarinet, saxophone, trumpet, guitar, bassoon, and accordion. He also continued to elaborate these scores into compositions for solo instrument and ensemble in the *Chemins* series, completing *Chemins* VI for trumpet and ensemble in 1996. This series shows a willingness to revise existing ideas that was even more marked in Berio's disposition to work with material by other composers, most famously in the third movement of *Sinfonia* (1968–9), which builds on a symphonic movement by Mahler. Later work in this vein includes *Rendering* (1989), which combines Berio's own ideas with orchestrations, or restorations, of fragments from what would have been Schubert's Tenth Symphony, along with an arrangement for baritone and orchestra of six early songs by Mahler (1987). Such practices show Berio to be aware, like contemporary critical theory, of just how intertextual creative acts are.

Berio and Ligeti have managed to respond in idiosyncratic ways to changing priorities in modern music. With Luigi Nono we encounter a more uneven career trajectory that culminates in the highly regarded scores of the 1980s. A prominent figure in the early days of Darmstadt, Nono was never confined by formalist ideals and became the most politically committed composer of his generation, with well-known scores such as *Il canto sospeso* (1956) and the opera *Intolleranza 1960* (1960–1) employing modernist techniques to convey themes of social injustice. These sympathies remain active in his second opera, *Al gran sole carico d'amore* (1975), which takes revolutionary struggle as its topic. But at this time his music also turned in a new direction, prompting much debate about whether this amounted to an abandonment of a politicized aesthetic. This issue is important for a more general understanding

20 Luciano Berio, 'Eco in ascolto: Luciano Berio Interviewed by Umberto Eco' (tr. David Osmond-Smith), *Contemporary Music Review* 5 (1998), pp. 1–8; p. 7.

of modernism at the close of the twentieth century, and will be considered after introducing music from Nono's later years.

. . . sofferte onde serene . . . (1974–6), composed after *Al gran sole carico d'amore* for Nono's pianist friend Maurizio Pollini, uses electronic resources not for political realism, but for the exploration of sound. The tape part expands the live piano performance and includes recordings of the instrument's mechanism. Nono acknowledged the influence on this music of the Venetian bells that reached his home from across the lagoon, and such floating sounds are an important component of his late style. Sounds from nowhere – islands in space – are the core of the landmark string quartet *Fragmente–Stille, an Diotima* (1980), one of the few works without electronics from the last decade. The fragments and silences of the title are much in evidence in music that is predominantly quiet and often high – music that slows time and sounds from the threshold of existence. Friedrich Hölderlin, the author of *Diotima* and other poems from which Nono liberally inserted fragments in his quartet is present in a silent capacity: the composer was adamant that these quotations are not to be read out, recommending instead that 'the players should "sing" them inwardly'[21] – a quixotic instruction that might be interpreted as an indication that the players should use the quotations to access a certain emotional intensity in the music, which will be conveyed to the audience.

Composed shortly after the quartet, *Das atmende Klarsein* (1980–1) for small chorus, bass flute, live electronics, and tape utilized the electronic studio of Südwestfunk at Freiburg im Breisgau, and this resource, along with an associated group of performers, was to prove invaluable in the following years. The floating vocal textures and electronically modified instrumental sounds, which include breathing and fingering, herald the sound world of *Prometeo* (1981–5), an unstaged opera based on the myth of Prometheus, with a libretto by Massimo Cacciari. Eschewing narrative direction in favour of reflections on the god who brings fire to humankind at terrible personal cost, the opera unfolds at a predominantly slow tempo through timbral associations, using high vocal textures, microtonal inflections, and electronic modifications. This sound world is also present in subsequent works such as *Omaggio a György Kurtág* (1983–6), while the dispersal of orchestral units in *Prometeo* is also a feature of the large orchestral piece *No hay caminos, hay que caminar* (1987). This title is extracted from an inscription found on a cloister wall in Toledo, which in full means 'Wayfarers, there are no ways, only faring on.'

Versions of this inscription appear in the titles of several late works, and the idea of a journey without established paths offers some insights into Nono's

21 Luigi Nono, notes to *Fragmente–Stille, An Diotima*, Milan, 1980.

turn away from overt political themes. Another pointer is offered by Walter Benjamin's celebrated essay 'Theses on the Philosophy of History', which forms the basis of Cacciari's *Il maestro del gioco*, a prose poem that appears in *Prometeo*. Famously, Benjamin talks of redeeming past suffering and of breaking open the continuum of history. Such ideals surely link Nono's early and late styles, suggesting that the strident calls for political action became transformed into an awakening utopianism.[22] The matter is well put by Helmut Lachenmann, a Nono pupil, when he comments: 'The silence into which Nono's late works lead us is a *fortissimo* of agitated perception.'[23] Formulated like this, we find in Nono a rejection of modernist formalism, alongside a heightening of modernism's critical charge at just the time when its institutional prestige started to wane. So Nono's late style finds space for (again in Lachenmann's words) an 'unprotected creative process' in which the familiar is estranged by heightened perception.[24]

Espousing a mysticism far removed from Nono's imagination, no composer demonstrates the contrast between the post-war years of dynamic invention and subsequent consolidation better than Karlheinz Stockhausen (b. 1928). Perhaps the most adventurous innovator of the 1950s, since 1977 Stockhausen has devoted his musical energies to work on the opera cycle *Licht*, scheduled for completion in 2002.[25] Conceived on a vast scale, *Licht* will comprise seven operas, one for each day of the week, six of which are complete at the time of writing. The sequence of composition was *Donnerstag* (1978–80), *Samstag* (1981–4), *Montag* (1984–8), *Dienstag* (1988–91), and *Freitag* (1991–6), while *Mittwoch* was premiered in 2000, so the cycle will finish when *Sonntag* is completed. Stockhausen has approached this mammoth task in a practical manner by allowing sections to stand as pieces in their own right: *Klavierstück* XII, for example, is to be found in *Donnerstag* and *Klavierstück* XIV in *Montag*. Furthermore, the orchestra used in *Donnerstag* has been replaced in later operas by synthesizers and electronic resources, thereby making production more manageable.

As one would expect from such a versatile approach to production, the operas do not possess a sense of unfolding drama, but dwell instead on the cosmic themes that underpin the cycle. These are found in the three central characters: Michael, who embodies dynamic action, Luzifer, who embodies idealism, and Eve, who embodies wisdom – each of these qualities being associated

22 For more on Nono and Benjamin, see Mário Vieira de Carvalho, 'Towards Dialectical Listening: Quotation and Montage in the Work of Luigi Nono', *Luigi Nono (1924–1990): Fragments and Silence*, *Contemporary Music Review* 18/2 (1999), pp. 37–85.

23 Helmut Lachenmann, 'Touched by Nono', *Luigi Nono (1924–1990): The Suspended Song*, *Contemporary Music Review* 18/1 (1999), pp. 17–30; p. 27.

24 Ibid., p. 28.

25 For an overview of Stockhausen's music, including *Licht*, see Robin Maconie, *The Works of Karlheinz Stockhausen* (2nd edn), Oxford, 1990.

with a musical formula. These characters can be split into several personae, with the same person being represented, sometimes simultaneously, as a mime artist, a singer, and an on-stage instrumentalist. Since the on-stage instrumental parts need to be memorized, they make great demands on performers, and Stockhausen has found players equal to this task by drawing on an inner circle of family and acquaintances. There is fine music in *Licht*, as exemplified in the huge role of the solo trumpet, played with virtuosity by Stockhausen's son Markus, found in Michael's journey around the earth in the second act of *Donnerstag*. But this inspired writing is let down by stereotyped representation of the world cultures that Michael encounters on his journey. Unfortunately, such miscalculations are never far away on a more general level, since *Licht*'s celestial images rely on the kind of essentialized gender roles that have been hotly contested in the later twentieth century. However, Stockhausen's creativity remains impressive, even if his grand vision is not always convincing.

This section opened with Boulez, and so it seems appropriate to close it with the figure with whom Boulez shared so many interests in the early 1950s and so few in subsequent years.[26] That figure is John Cage, a composer and inventor whose diverse activity was sustained by the prospect of letting sounds speak for themselves with as little interference as possible from intentions and traditions: *4′ 33″* (1952), which simply invites audiences to listen to the sounds around them, offers the best-known example of this aesthetic. We have seen that after the system-building of the 1950s, many composers have explored broader conceptions of meaning and identity in music, and the same can be said, in an oblique way, of Cage, despite his willingness to subject the richest of semantic resources to the distancing of chance procedures. Generalizing, there are two main strands in Cage's output from the late 1970s to his death shortly before what would have been his eightieth birthday. One strand comprises a series of instrumental compositions, of sometimes extreme virtuosity; the other (which I will examine first) constitutes major multimedia works such as *Roaratorio* and the five *Europeras*, both of which draw on existing materials that contribute strongly to the meaning of the music.

During the 1970s Cage wrote a series of mesostic poems: poems, that is, with a keyword in capital letters running through the middle of the typescript. The results include a series of readings of James Joyce's *Finnegans Wake*, with the words 'JAMES JOYCE' running through the centre. 'Writing for the Second Time through *Finnegans Wake*' forms the basis of *Roaratorio* (1979), a radio play commissioned by Westdeutscher Rundfunk. With a view to recreating Joyce's

26 Shared interests are conveyed in Jean-Jacques Nattiez (ed.), *The Boulez–Cage Correspondence* (tr. Robert Samuels), Cambridge, 1993.

text in a different medium, Cage made recordings of sounds referred to in the novel and also recorded at places mentioned in Ireland. These sounds, along with recordings of Irish traditional musicians and the composer's reading of his mesostic text, were mixed down to a stereo tape for radio broadcast, using the facilities at IRCAM (in concert performance the text can be read and the traditional music played live). The result on the CD recording, which used sixty-two-track tape, is a jumble of sounds of varying density fading in and out, with Cage's expressionless reading taking place in the sometimes inaudible background.[27] The experience is neither about Joyce nor an interpretation of him; it is better understood as a presentation of him.[28] However, by drawing on a specifically Irish-American identity that emphasizes predominantly rural sounds and recognizably traditional music, even such an unorthodox presentation relies on established meanings more than Cage's aesthetics might lead us to suppose.

Issues of identity and tradition also arise with the five *Europeras*, Cage's major multimedia offerings of the 1980s. The Joyce-like compound *Europera* combines the words 'Europe' and 'opera' and sounds like 'your opera' when spoken. *Europeras* 1 and 2 (1987) were Cage's response to a commission from the Frankfurt opera, while *Europeras* 3 and 4 (1990) and *Europera* 5 (1991) were written on a less grand scale, with piano accompaniment making them suitable for performances outside the opera house. Cage found the material for *Europeras* 1 and 2 by plundering the New York Metropolitan Opera's archives for repertoire operas that were out of copyright. These provided vocal and instrumental lines that could be combined using chance procedures, yielding arias to be sung in no particular order by the nineteen singers. Sets and costumes were also extracted from archives and distributed randomly, while lighting was organized by chance operations that made any highlighting of a character accidental. *Europeras* 1 and 2 are therefore collages of independent events and components, and because the quantity of chance decisions that fed them was so huge, a more technological solution than Cage's tried and tested coin-tossing procedures was required: a computer program was designed to simulate the chance procedures of the I Ching on a large scale. The result was a typically Cagean paradox: a very precise set of instructions generated by random means themselves derived from a computer. And the contradictions do not stop there, for the *Europeras* are caught in a tension between a genre associated with intense expression and the automated procedures Cage applied in order to defamiliarize learned responses. For some critics and listeners, these

27 Cage, *Roaratorio: An Irish Circus on 'Finnegans Wake'* (Mode, 1992).
28 For discussion of this distinction, see James Pritchett, *The Music of John Cage*, Cambridge, 1993, pp. 190–1.

scores give permission to cast off the fetters of tradition; for others they map a growing indifference to bourgeois culture.

After reaching the age of sixty, Cage felt free to develop a number of techniques that he had explored earlier in his life.[29] With *Roaratorio* and the *Europeras* we have looked at a strand in Cage's output that developed from earlier multimedia events. His already cited *Freeman Etudes* for solo violin, on the other hand, echo the strictures of instrumental compositions such as *Music of Changes* for piano (1951). Composed in two groups (1977–80/1989–90), these thirty-two studies were assembled by using procedures determined by star charts; the resulting music is so difficult that the violinist is forced to make decisions in order to render the music playable. In the final years of his life Cage wrote a series of so-called 'number compositions', which also hark back to another characteristic of his earlier music: sparse isolated sounds. Using a widely adaptable time-bracket method of composition, these pieces comprise fragments of specified duration ranges that occur during given time ranges in performance. The resulting music, taking *Four* (1989) as an example, is still, with gaps and single notes fading in and out, sometimes forming chords, sometime occupying lonely space. Cage completed some of his most significant projects in the last twenty years of his life, and even though these refined earlier techniques, he never lost his ability to perplex.

Discourses

The most innovative work in post-war modernism – what might be called high modernism – took place in the 1950s and 60s. During these decades composers such as Stockhausen extended serial technique beyond pitch to include rhythm and duration, and also pursued these organizational possibilities into the electroacoustic studio. The overriding concern was with developing new musical techniques, a project that was pursued not only in composition but also in the related articles that composers and theorists wrote in journals such as *Die Reihe*. The most prolific and outspoken of these essayists was Boulez, who was equally dismissive of music's nineteenth-century institutions and of composers inclined to ignore developments in serialism. Despite this dependence on the written medium, high modernism ironically saw itself as concerned far more with how to do things than with what they meant. It formed this outlook in opposition to Romantic aesthetics, which associates music with extra-musical ideas, but in so doing encountered the paradox that technical advancement is of course an aesthetic in itself, not an avoidance of aesthetics; and one,

29 Pritchett makes this point; ibid., p. 174.

when pursued in isolation, that ignores the range of ways in which music signifies.

As a consequence, much of the rethinking that has occurred since the height of modernist constructivism has concerned itself with the aesthetic considerations that were originally ignored. In a lecture from 1960, given at Darmstadt, we already find Boulez asking: 'Were we not set on a course that could lead only to what might seem to be a perfect "technological" rationality but was in fact a monumental absurdity?'[30] And this absurdity was spelt out in Ligeti's analysis of the opening piece of Boulez's *Structures*, Book 1 (1951–2).[31] Responding to these dilemmas, much of Boulez's subsequent work has been devoted to overcoming the contradictions generated between imposed form and individual moments that can pull in other directions – as can be seen in later works such as *Répons* and the orchestration of *Notations*, where we find a creative play between an underlying order and its expansive proliferations.

The new was built on the prospect of inventing a future through rejecting a past; nevertheless it was also a continuation of 'art' music, harking back to this tradition even as it jettisoned many of its tenets. One facet of the past that modernism was keen to develop was the notion that music enjoys a critical distance from everyday concerns: in a twentieth-century context new techniques might display an affinity with technological advancement, but music was also seen as offering a freedom that lay outside the constraints of mass production. Nevertheless, a combination of technical invention and critical values proved hard to sustain – a point forcefully made by Theodor Adorno in an address delivered at Darmstadt (as early as 1955) and later published as 'The Ageing of the New Music', in which he berated composers for hiding behind systems. Just one example of his large output on aesthetics and music criticism, this essay resists the modernist tendency to focus on technique by understanding music as a medium of subjectivity beset by all the dilemmas of modernity. Even though the article has been criticized for the vagueness of its references,[32] the ageing of the new remains an acute issue for modernism after the initial waves of innovation.

The inventions of the 1950s looked to a new future and this is perhaps the most significant reason, together with its critical impulse, why 1960s modernism was able to form a surprising alliance with new social movements. The 1970s proved to be a more difficult decade during which belief in

30 Pierre Boulez, 'Putting the Phantoms to Flight', *Orientations: Collected Writings by Pierre Boulez* (ed. Jean-Jacques Nattiez, tr. Martin Cooper), London, 1986, p. 66.

31 György Ligeti, 'Pierre Boulez: Decision and Automatism in *Structure 1a*' (tr. Leo Black), *Die Reihe* 4 (1960), pp. 36–62.

32 Notably by Heinz-Klaus Metzger, 'Just Who is Growing Old?' (tr. Leo Black), *Die Reihe* 4 (1960), pp. 63–80.

modernism faltered, even though we have seen how it was then that many of its present-day institutions were established. The decade also saw something of a rethink, with modernism widening its semantic resources to include references to other musics, as we have already seen in connection with Darmstadt. However, this was a time of transition not just for modernism, but for a whole range of cultural practices. Most notably, it was a time when the youth culture of the 1960s became absorbed into mainstream values: rock music, which like new music sought an authenticity that would defy commercialization, saw its message of freedom becoming increasingly used as a marketing tool. And as gender studies became more sophisticated, critics and academics became increasingly sceptical of a music that so ostentatiously celebrated its male guitar heroes. Nor did progressive rock provide an escape from this impasse: as it became more like 'art' music, it increasingly reinstated the outdated ideologies of Romanticism, for which it was brutally condemned by punk rock with its anarchic impulses. Finally, the transition from the 1970s to the 80s saw conservative regimes installed in the UK and USA that had little sympathy for the aspirations of the 1960s. The result, in these countries at least, was that the public funds that had subsidized much modernist music became tighter throughout the 1980s and 90s, as free-marketeers insisted that culture should pay its way, with the consequence that modernism was reduced to a specialist sector.

A changed political climate has obviously not helped modernism; nevertheless internal contradictions and increasing theoretical understanding of aesthetic discourses have also affected its trajectory. In order to understand this cultural shift, it is instructive to see how these debates have been played out in the domain of architecture. Here the high-modernist aesthetic was most marked in the so-called international style which used new materials, such as reinforced concrete, and promoted efficient design over the needs of those who would occupy the buildings. The ideal is flawed because such inhabitants rarely conduct their lives in accordance with the systems that were supposed to channel their needs. Formalist architecture has been strongly criticised by, amongst others, Charles Jencks, who points out that buildings cannot just be about their own form because their colour, texture, and shape will interact with the surrounding buildings and environment.[33] Extrapolating from this, we can say that modernism is situated by its surrounding discourses, even if it chooses to work from a narrow aesthetic base.

Such insights derive from critical theory, which saw intense development in the last quarter of the century, both drawing on the reflexive powers of

33 Charles Jencks, 'The Emergent Rules', in Thomas Docherty (ed.), *Postmodernism: A Reader*, Hemel Hempstead, 1993, pp. 281–94.

modernism and turning its attention to those same generative discourses.[34] Most criticisms and modifications of modernism focus on the ways in which its obsession with technique serve to disguise particular interests. How, they ask, does modernism portray gender, how does it relate to popular culture, and what is the listener to make of its focus on production? On close inspection, modernism reveals a number of contradictory values. One such paradox is embodied by a constructivist aesthetic which, on the one hand, might appear to strengthen the control of a composer while, on the other hand, allowing the composer to be marginalized – as Cage repeatedly demonstrated – by a system unfolding with a logic of its own. And we have already seen how elaborate compositional schemes leave a gap, of sometimes creative significance, between the compositional structure and what a listener may make of the music in performance. For this reason, a listener presented with a stream of sounds that shun a familiar organizational logic needs to find strategies for interpreting that experience. In so doing that listener, in the language of poststructuralism, treats the score more as a text than as a work, by creating meaning instead of simply decoding authorial intention.[35]

The same listener may of course hold views on gender and popular music that deviate from the prevailing modernist postures, which derive from institutions dominated by men. From the perspective of gender studies, modernism's narrowly constructivist aesthetic creates the illusion of a self-controlling subjectivity that reins in music's sensory, somatic qualities so that a hard-won institutional prestige is not tainted by feminine associations.[36] In the same vein, this doctrine of autonomy, it is argued, also rejects what is often seen to be the 'feminine' dependency of popular music.[37] However, while there is no disputing that the history of modernism has been excessively populated by men, attempts to convey it as an obsessively controlled discourse encounter problems because one of the most interesting facets of modernism is its continual dialogue with particulars that escape systematic control: with elements, that is to say, that undermine a closed subjectivity.

Before concluding this section with a more general consideration of postmodernism, I want to examine transformations in the discourses of modernism by reference, as a concrete example, to the values represented by discipline-specific journals. The American journal *Perspectives of New Music* was founded

34 For more on applications of critical theory to musicology, see my *Constructing Musicology*, Aldershot, 2001.

35 The key essay on this topic is Roland Barthes, 'From Work to Text', in *Image–Music–Text* (tr. Stephen Heath), London, 1977, pp. 155–64.

36 For a feminist view of modernism, see Susan McClary, 'Terminal Prestige: The Case of Avant-Garde Music Composition', *Cultural Critique* 12 (1989), pp. 57–81.

37 For more on this association, see Andreas Huyssen, 'Mass Culture as Woman: Modernism's Other', in *After the Great Divide: Modernism, Mass Culture and Postmodernism*, London, 1986, pp. 44–62.

in 1961 along lines similar to *Die Reihe*, the journal in which many key early Darmstadt debates had appeared. The initial advisory board was made up entirely of composers, including Igor Stravinsky, Darius Milhaud, and Roger Sessions, while committed modernists such as Milton Babbitt, Elliott Carter, and George Perle all exerted strong influence in these early editions. The emphasis was on the intersection between modernist composition and theory, with both composers and theorists writing primarily on compositional systems and techniques – and thereby demonstrating (as I put it) more interest in how things work than in what they mean. Nor has the journal abandoned this strand, as a recent edition, which includes 'A Symposium in Honor of Milton Babbitt', demonstrates.[38] Nevertheless, true to the peculiar alliance of modernist rigour and hedonism that emerged in the 1960s, *Perspectives* has covered Cage and the experimentalists as well as minimalism.

From the mid-1980s, established concerns vie in its pages with influences that have transformed the field of contemporary composition and music theory. Recent issues devote sections to critical theory and to feminist music theory, with Susan McClary, in the latter, proposing cultural studies as the ground on which the contextualizing concerns of feminism and the technical preoccupations of music theory might meet.[39] A shift from means to meaning is also marked in a collection of essays published in 1994, all taken from the journal, entitled *Perspectives on Musical Aesthetics*. Amongst other things, it includes a series of essays by Benjamin Boretz, one of the founding editors, that reveal a crisis of confidence in modernism and in the Western canon. Arguing that masterpiece culture is based on symbolic autonomy and thus echoing much recent musicology, Boretz wishes to emphasize that music is something 'done by and among people' and thereby relates to specific human circumstances.[40]

Recent music scholarship has expanded not only the scope of interpretive methodologies at its disposal but also the range of contemporary music it examines. This diversity is well reflected in *Contemporary Music Review*, a journal founded in 1984. The eclectic range of topics is illustrated by the special issues devoted to 'Flute and Shakuhachi' and to 'Music and Mysticism', while significant space was devoted to music and the cognitive sciences.[41] This breadth

38 'A Symposium in Honor of Milton Babbitt', *Perspectives of New Music* 35/2 (1997), pp. 5–136.

39 'Critical Theory of Music', *Perspectives of New Music* 31/2 (1993), pp. 6–71; 'Toward a Feminist Music Theory', *Perspectives of New Music* 32/1 (1994), pp. 6–85; Susan McClary, 'Paradigm Dissonances: Music Theory, Cultural Studies, Feminist Criticism', *Perspectives of New Music* 32/1 (1994), pp. 68–85.

40 Benjamin Boretz, 'Interface I–V: Texts and Commentaries on Music and Life', in John Rahn (ed.), *Perspectives on Musical Aesthetics*, New York, 1994, p. 125.

41 'Flute and Shakuhachi', Jo Kondo and Joaquim Bernitez (eds.), *Contemporary Music Review* 8/2 (1994); 'Music and Mysticism', Maxwell Steer (ed.), *Contemporary Music Review* 14/1–2 and 14/3–4 (1996); 'Music and the Cognitive Sciences', Stephen McAdams and Irène Deliège (eds.), *Contemporary Music Review* 4, 2 vols., (1989), also Ian Cross and Irène Deliège (eds.), *Contemporary Music Review* 9 (1993).

serves to demonstrate that current musical production and reception take place in a space that is pervaded by debates about methodology, textuality, identity, and meaning.

The space that such critical responses inhabit is often called postmodernism. Like modernism, postmodernism is also a contradictory affair, and much is gained from understanding it as a transformation of the same condition rather than as its successor. Postmodernism touches new music with the arrival of chance procedures in the 1960s, since, as we have seen, they undermine traditional notions of authorial intention. At the same time, however, such procedures are compatible with a modernist focus on technique, since chance operations are formal: with their arrival, we see music standing somewhere between determinate procedures and open textuality. Just as significant, however, is what might be called the semantic broadening of modernism, since as music becomes more referential and more willing to look beyond its own internal configurations, so it creates a level of meaning that is more obviously pitched at a semiotic level rather than a purely syntactic one. Put differently, as music become more reflexive, so its components increasingly participate in an intertextual and intercultural matrix.[42] And such expanded horizons are by no means limited to composition. Musicology, too, has become more sensitive to the range of ways in which music signifies and has sought to contextualize musics and discourses that were once considered autonomous. In so doing, it has challenged the selective reception history of early-twentieth-century modernism on which high modernism was based. Hence, as this volume testifies, the Second Viennese composers and Stravinsky are now understood within rich historical traditions instead of being valued primarily as inventors of new techniques. In this sense, the expanded horizon of postmodernism is more a reinterpretation of modernism than its abandonment.

Composers 2: Ferneyhough, Birtwistle, Davies, Schnittke, Gubaidulina, Rihm, Saariaho, Saunders

We have seen that the prevailing response of established composers to the decline in modernism's fortunes was to consolidate their previous achievements, while moving beyond narrowly systematic concerns. In this section we encounter a more diverse collection of composers who came to prominence after the 1950s. It is possible to find shared concerns amongst them, particularly with regard to their ways of working through the tensions between tradition

42 This argument is made in my 'Adorno and the Semantics of Modernism', *Perspectives of New Music* 37/2 (1999), pp. 29–50.

and restructuring that are the hallmarks of modernity, but they do not share the underlying sense of purpose that propelled the previous group to international significance. The most direct link with high modernism is provided by Brian Ferneyhough, whose music provides the principal exception to the general softening of structural obsessions since the 1950s. (Other British composers associated with this branch of new music, sometimes known as the new complexity, include James Dillon and Michael Finnissy.) Of all the composers discussed in this chapter, Ferneyhough has retained the most faith in the achievements of the 1950s, despite hailing from a later generation, so it is fitting that he should have initially found acceptance in Germany and became a major figure at the Darmstadt summer courses, particularly in the 1980s.

It should not, however, be assumed from this description that his music is without passion or urgency, though it is certainly forbidding on first hearing and even more so in its written format, due to the sheer density of information and detail. Generally written in short note-values, which give them a very black appearance, his scores are characterized by the extensive beaming used to articulate particular gestures and to create direction. Out of this mass of detail, often audible gestures arise such as the rhythmic unisons that open his Second Quartet (1980). The composer's own account of processes in this piece explains how the opening is meant to convey the idea of a 'super instrument' by adding instruments, one by one, to the opening violin to create a textural thickening of sound, into which he then introduces micro-variations such as different articulations of the same rhythm.[43] The underlying aesthetic orientation from which such practices arise is that, because most unfiltered musical statements fall into pre-established meanings, it is only by generating events from complex, unexpected intersections of objects that new energies can arise.

The complexity of Ferneyhough's music enables considerable intricacy to be achieved when writing for a solo instrument, and it is of course more practical for one person to devote significant time to learning convoluted music than it is for a large group. Established solo pieces from the mid-1970s include *Unity Capsule* (1975–6) for solo flute, *Time and Motion Study I* (1971–7) for bass clarinet, and *Time and Motion Study II* (1973–6) for cello and electronics. Solo instrumental compositions have remained an important medium for Ferneyhough: later pieces in the genre include compositions for piano (*Lemma–Icon–Epigram*, 1981); piccolo (*Superscriptio*, 1981); violin (*Intermedio all Ciaconna*, 1986); guitar

43 Brian Ferneyhough, *Collected Writings* (ed. James Boros and Richard Toop), Amsterdam, 1995, pp. 119–20. For a detailed account of Ferneyhough's compositional procedures, based on sketch material, see Richard Toop, 'Brian Ferneyhough's *Lemma–Icon–Epigram*', *Perspectives of New Music* 28/2 (1990), pp. 52–100.

(*Kurze Schatten II*, 1985–8); and double bass (*Trittico per Gertrude Stein*, 1989). This concentrated medium also spills into pieces for soloist and ensemble, with *Terrain* (1991–2) for violin and eight instruments exemplifying Ferneyhough's daunting challenges for the soloist.

A series of chamber works from the 1980s, including the Second, Third, and Fourth String Quartets (the latter incorporating a solo soprano), demonstrate the increasing refinement of Ferneyhough's inventive capacity. 1982 saw the composition of *Carceri d'Invenzione* I (for chamber orchestra), which initiated a cycle of compositions by that name. The title, which means 'Dungeons of Invention', is derived from a series of etchings by Giambattista Piranesi that touched on a number of Ferneyhough's compositional concerns, inspiring him to consider how seemingly oppositional forces might be interlocked in the compositional process.[44] These preoccupations derive from systematic procedures that have their roots in the 1950s, although Ferneyhough's preference is to sieve complex material into smaller constituents, rather than to continually expand events in the manner of Boulez. Such concerns may seem narrow in an age of eclecticism; nevertheless they clearly provide a vital resource for Ferneyhough's imagination; his obsessions with system encourage, rather than inhibit, unexpected configurations, creating situations where, as Jonathan Harvey puts it, 'hyper-intellectual meets manic raver'.[45]

Twenty years ago, as now, composers such as Boulez and Ligeti would have featured in any survey of modern music; however, Harrison Birtwistle would have been less prominent.[46] Birtwistle's reputation advanced substantially in the 1980s, and *Secret Theatre*, a mixed ensemble piece written for the composer's fiftieth-birthday concert in 1984, is often seen as the turning point in his career: it received much critical acclaim and sums up his characteristic techniques. 1986 saw the premiere of *Earth Dances*, a large orchestral score, and it was in the same year that *The Mask of Orpheus* (1983) – a music drama started in 1973 – finally reached the stage. *Secret Theatre* is an apposite title for a Birtwistle score because drama is central to his musical imagination and permeates even instrumental pieces: *Tragoedia* (1965) for wind quintet, string quartet, and harp is concerned with the ritual and formal aspects of Greek tragedy, while the five woodwind, five brass, and three percussionists called for in *Verses for Ensembles* (1969) follow directions in the score to move around a four-tier stage in performance, dramatically enacting musical events. *Secret Theatre* itself establishes an interplay between a melodic

44 Ibid., pp. 131–2. 45 Foreword to ibid., p. xii.

46 For comprehensive discussions of Birtwistle's œuvre, see Robert Adlington, *The Music of Harrison Birtwistle*, Cambridge, 2000, and Jonathan Cross, *Harrison Birtwistle: Man, Mind, Music*, London, 2000.

'cantus' and a mechanically repetitive continuum, with the collisions, mergers and separations of the two factions being dramatically underscored by staged movements.

It is apparent from such instrumental scores that Birtwistle is less concerned with character portrayal than with the formal procedures of drama – a priority that extends to stage works such as *The Mask of Orpheus*, where the three main characters of the Orpheus myth are represented in triplicate by masked singers, masked mime artists, and puppets. Dramatically, this device taps into Birtwistle's central musical preoccupation with, in his words, 'going over and over the same event from different angles so that a multi-dimensional musical object is created, an object which contains a number of contradictions as well as a number of perspectives'.[47] His next stage drama, *Gawain* (1989–91), based on the Middle English romance of *Sir Gawain and the Green Knight*, yielded plenty of opportunities for such procedures, with scenes such as the Green Knight's appearance at King Arthur's court, his decapitation, and Gawain's seduction all experienced from several perspectives. This said, there is more of a narrative thread in *Gawain* than in *The Mask of Orpheus*, since Gawain gains self-knowledge on his journey to the Green Knight's chapel and returns to King Arthur's court refusing to accept a hero's welcome.

Retelling events, according to literary theory, enables us to see that they are constructed from particular viewpoints and are therefore open to interpretation; however such textual flexibility encounters some resistance from Birtwistle's preference for conveying archetypal situations by detached procedures. The advantage of such mechanisms is that, by leading both composer and audience away from hackneyed expectations, they can potentially release unexpected responses; the disadvantage is that they downplay human subjectivity in a manner that is somewhat at odds with an age fascinated by identity. After all, what may look like an underlying fundamental – a peep behind history – may be entirely historical: it may, that is to say, be an embodiment of modern alienation. Despite such cavils, dramatic situations clearly inspire Birtwistle's musical imagination; since *Gawain* he has composed two further operas, *The Second Mrs Kong* (1993–4) and *The Last Supper* (1998–9).

Birtwistle and Peter Maxwell Davies are often paired together on account of their shared British nationality, shared student experiences, and similar age. They also share an interest in music drama, even though in the later part of the century their responses to the tensions between tradition and modernity have diverged, with Davies looking to continue the symphonic tradition.

47 Quoted in Nicholas Snowman, 'Birtwistle the Dramatist: Some Reflections', programme to *Gawain*, Royal Opera House, London, 1991.

We see him turning in this direction with the orchestral score *Worldes Blis* (1966–9), which is described by the composer as 'a conscious attempt to reintegrate the shattered and scattered fragments of my creative persona'.[48] A new stage in this development was reached with the composition of the First Symphony (1973–6), which inaugurated another six symphonies (the Seventh was premiered in 2000 at the BBC Proms), and a wealth of concertos. The latter include the ten Strathclyde concertos written for members of the Scottish Chamber Orchestra, an ensemble with which Davies has enjoyed close links since the mid-1980s.

In Davies's recent music rigorous musical arguments jostle with evocations of the Scottish Orkney community in which the composer has chosen to settle, drawing on a range of resources, including chant, quasi-serialist procedures, the classical tradition, and folk. For example, two types of material – one derived from the overture to Haydn's opera *L'Isola Disabitata* and the other from Jan Albert Ban's *Vanitas* – are heard at the opening of the Fifth Strathclyde Concerto for violin, viola, and string orchestra (1991), before being absorbed into the musical process. The Fourth Symphony (1989), on the other hand, eschews such intertextuality, even though the influence of Sibelius is evident in the compression of four movements into a single form, and in the underlying developmental flow. Different sound-worlds certainly sit alongside each other in the 'choreographic poem' *The Beltane Fire* (1994), where Arnold Whittall finds 'expressionistic symphonism and material evoking either solemn hymnody or exuberant folk-dance', suggesting to him a conjunction between what he calls 'a "supranational" modernist manner and vivid representations of local people and places'.[49] It is in such intersections that Davies most directly addresses late-twentieth-century worries about the erosion of traditions and communities.

Such concerns are of pressing urgency to Alfred Schnittke and Sofia Gubaidulina, two strong individualists whose lives nevertheless share core experiences. Both endured an intolerable Soviet regime and both experienced deep apprehension at what the collapse of the same system left behind. Schnittke comments: 'The enormous problems in Russia which are building up just now will remain and possibly *never* be resolved.'[50] Gubaidulina, for her part, observes that 'We are existentially shaken by what has happened to our country.'[51] Both composers sustained themselves financially by writing film

48 Quoted in Paul Griffiths, *Modern Music and After*, Oxford, 1995, p. 155.

49 Arnold Whittall, 'A Dance of the Deadly Sins: *The Beltane Fire* and the Rites of Modernism', in Richard McGregor (ed.), *Perspectives on Peter Maxwell Davies*, Aldershot, 2000, pp. 138–58; p. 139.

50 Schnittke, quoted in Anders Beyers (ed.), *The Voice of Music: Selected Interviews with Contemporary Composers*, Aldershot, 2000, p. 241.

51 Gubaidulina, quoted in ibid., p. 45.

music, both experienced ambivalence towards modernist systems, both have prompted comparisons with Shostakovich, both chose to live in Germany after the collapse of Communism, and both convey religious feelings in their music, fuelled in Gubaidulina's case by a deep-rooted mysticism. These shared life experiences, nonetheless, fuel very distinct musical identities.

Despite attempting, against all the odds, to keep abreast of developments in the West, Schnittke was frustrated by what he saw as the self-denial of constructivist composition and was not afraid to look elsewhere, notably to the Western canon, for expressive immediacy. His ties to the past are, however, complex since the polystylism for which he is famous is torn between a clashing pluralism and a yearning for the certainties of tradition. Both these characteristics are strongly present in the *Concerto grosso* no. 1 (1977), his best-known composition, in which a prepared piano and recognizably modernist techniques are heard alongside baroque figurations and a Tango. His desire for custom is more explicit in the Fourth Symphony (1984), in which chants from Russian Orthodox and Jewish litanies, amongst others, offer shelter from the confusion of modern life.

Redemption is an explicit theme in Gubaidulina's violin concerto *Offertorium* (1980) – the work, premiered by Gidon Kremer, that made her an international figure – in which the central theme is sacrificed and resurrected; similarly, for the composer, the three personae of *The Seven Words of Christ* – cello, bayan (a Russian folk accordion), and orchestra – represent the Holy Trinity.[52] All Gubaidulina's music is religious in inspiration; however, because it is not designed for the formal ceremonies of the church its meaning is not explicit, and so its intensity leaves interpretive space for the listener. In the Second Quartet (1987) this spirituality takes the form of a meditation around sustained sonorities, while *Zeitgestalten* (1994) creates an opulent tapestry of sound enriched by two electric basses.

We have seen that Ligeti, Boulez and, from a later generation, Ferneyhough feel that there should be a distinction between internal and external musical processes, drawing a firm line between their aesthetic and the eclecticism that has continued since the late 1970s. In doing so, they attribute primary importance to internal structural organization and less significance to the intertextual relations between a musical score and the range of discourses in which it is situated. This stance closes down horizons, while avoiding the hazards associated with mixing materials and traditions. Ligeti in particular distinguishes himself from neo-Romanticism – a nomenclature for a style of composition that rejects the structural obsessions of modernism and embraces the emotional

52 Gubaidulina, quoted in ibid., p. 50.

resources of Romanticism. Arguing in favour of such stylistic expansion, the British composer Robin Holloway, a Schumann admirer, considers that composers should be at liberty to take inspiration from composers and styles of their own choice rather being expected to follow the established examples of modernism.[53] At its most pronounced, this tendency involves a figure such as the formerly constructivist American George Rochberg turning to the emotional resources of Mahler and late Beethoven in his Third String Quartet (1972). An inclusive aesthetic is, however, hard to categorize because its nature is to suggest multiple possibilities.

Neo-Romantic is one of the labels, amongst others, that has been applied to Wolfgang Rihm, the leading German composer of his generation, even though his output is too diverse to be contained by this, or any other, category. Commenting on his relationship to history, in a typically extreme statement, Rihm boldly declares that 'Tradition can only ever be "my tradition".'[54] One reading of this pronouncement is that both the canon and modernism have become disembedded from the traditions that provided them with established meaning and have, consequently, become more open to interpretive practice. This loosening allows Rihm to take whatever he wants from music history, though it is generally a European past he looks to, reserving particular enthusiasm for the freedom of Schumann, the early atonal works of Schoenberg, and the fluidity of Debussy; influences which provide inspiration for a style that seeks directness, on occasion through violent or expansive gestures. Rihm's music sometimes filters tradition, sometimes distorts it, and sometimes finds refuge in it, while in all cases ensuring that references are heard through a thick semantic grid.

Rihm gained success in his early twenties and has continued to be a prolific composer. Scores from the mid-1970s such as *Dis-Kontur* (1974), *Sub-Kontur* (1975), *Klavierstück* no. 5 (1975), and the Third String Quartet (1976) gave him a reputation for drawing on late-Romantic style and challenging the stylistic strictures of high modernism.[55] *Sub-Kontur* is a large orchestral piece in sonata form, characterized by tempestuous sonorities and eruptions of ecstatic tonal harmony, both combined with a proportional tempo scheme reminiscent of the composer's one-time teacher, Stockhausen. The Third String Quartet, *Im Innersten*, alludes to a wide variety of sources from the genre and elsewhere; its second movement winds down to a Mahlerian adagio that functions as a

53 Robin Holloway, 'Modernism and After in Music', *Cambridge Review*, June 1989, pp. 60–6; p. 64.

54 'Musikalische Freiheit', in Wolfgang Rihm, *Ausgesprochen: Schriften und Gespräche* (ed. Ulrich Mosch), 2 vols., Winterthur, 1997, Vol. I, p. 23.

55 For more detailed discussion of Rihm, see Williams, *New Music and the Claims of Modernity*, pp. 136–45.

refuge from the surrounding music, while being touched by the same events. (Interestingly, Rihm appears not to envisage a full-blown Romanticism in this passage, since he discouraged the Arditti Quartet from using portamenti and wide vibrato in performance.[56]) His admiration for Schumann is clearly evident in the three pieces that comprise *Fremde Szenen* I–III (1982–4), subtitled *versuche für klaviertrio, erste folge*. In the second of these scenes, lyric lines and flowing piano textures reminiscent of Schumann's chamber works are cut into by sometimes violent modernist gestures, or transformed by frenzied repetition. The music can be understood as an attempt to harness the abundance and diversity of Schumann, to experience subjectivity as a succession of moods.

The European tradition is obviously important to Rihm and probably never absent from his imagination, but its influence is not always direct. In the 1980s he was influenced by the late style of Nono, with its isolated islands of sounds, though he has not emulated the latter's use of live electronics; spaces and silences characterise *Kein Firmament* (1988) for an ensemble of fourteen players, in which the energy Rihm always seeks is reduced to small gestures that are associated through timbral links, interrupted by fierce accents, and heard across empty spaces.[57] The sound-world, though not the tonal references, of his large orchestral scores from the 1970s is also felt here with the presence of bass clarinet, contrabassoon and double bass. This intensity is transferred to a continuous line with *Gesungene Zeit* for violin and orchestra (1991–2), in which the violin spins a high line that is coloured by what the composer calls an orchestral *Doppelgänger*. With the consistent top register generating a certain urgency, Rihm's suggestion that he is trying to make 'strands of thought audible', to make something that is both ephemeral and palpable, is helpful and appropriate.[58] During the 1990s, he was engaged, amongst other things, with a project entitled *Vers une symphonie fleuve*, the fourth version of which was written in 1997–8. Punning on Adorno's essay 'Vers une musique informelle', which ponders the prospects of a music beyond formal constraints, Rihm's title conveys the idea of a form in motion (flooding beyond the confines of the single work).[59] The range covered by Rihm's output shows just how inclusive modern music can be: it can, like the Third Quartet, operate though a combination of internal

56 Personal conversation with Irvine Arditti, 8 August 2000.

57 For a useful discussion of this piece, see Rudolf Frisius, notes to recording of Wolfgang Rihm: *Kein Firmament* and *Sine Nomine* (CPO, 1992).

58 Wolfgang Rihm, 'Time Chant' (tr. Mary Whittall), notes to recording, DG, 1992. The suggestion that the orchestra is a *Doppelgänger* is made by Rihm in the same place.

59 'Mitteilungen zu *Vers une symphonie fleuve*', in Rihm, *Ausgesprochen*, Vol. II, pp. 402–3. See also John Warnaby, 'Wolfgang Rihm's Recent Music', *Tempo* 2/3(2000), pp.13–15.

and intertextual associations or it can, like *Kein Firmament*, work within a more defined environment. This eclectic style rocks rigid distinctions between modernism and postmodernism, suggesting that the future and the past can intersect on multiple horizons.

Composers teach as well as compose, and so it is appropriate to end this section by mentioning Kaija Saariaho (b. 1952) and Rebecca Saunders (b. 1967), one-time pupils of, respectively, Ferneyhough and Rihm. Saariaho also studied with Klaus Huber and attended computer-music courses at IRCAM; the computer has remained important to her, as has Paris where – though of Finnish origin – she has chosen to live. Her work is characterized by subtle inflections of harmony and timbre, often enhanced by interactive electronics, as seen in *Lichtbogen* (1985–8) for chamber ensemble and electronics, in *Nymphéa* (1987) for string quartet and electronics, and in the solo song cycle *Lohn* (1996) for soprano and electronics.

After studying in Germany, Saunders has established more of a reputation there, notably in Darmstadt, than in her native Britain; although her music does not sound like Rihm's (she was also taught by Nigel Osborne), it clearly has affinities with his regard for gestural directness, for extremes (witness the shrill whistles in *CRIMSON*) and for inclusion. In Saunders's music, instruments achieve a presence that often includes the mechanical sounds that performers are normally encouraged to minimize, and the sounds are heard as humanly produced, while generating other allusions of a less specific nature. The titles of both *CRIMSON – Molly's Song 1* (1995) and *Molly's Song 3 – shades of crimson* (1996), however, make such allusions more concrete: they refer to Molly's monologue from James Joyce's *Ulysses*. So when Saunders, speaking of the latter piece, tells us that it 'seeks to sustain a musical energy strong enough to withstand the assaults of a succession of destructive events', she does so in the context of a polymorphic passage celebrated as an example of *écriture féminine*, thereby offering a response to Joyce far removed from the mid-century fascination with his formal procedures.[60]

Survival

The range of recent developments makes modernism less easy to define, even if it remains possible to identify a stream of music that flows in modernist channels. Such music will, typically, encourage reflection on its own procedures, mechanisms, and content, and will contain elements that identify it as indebted

60 Quoted in Robert Adlington, 'Into the Sensuous World: The Music of Rebecca Saunders', *Musical Times* 140/1868 (1999), pp. 48–56; p. 56. My comments on Saunders are indebted to this informative article.

to the conventions of 'art' music – though it will not necessarily espouse bourgeois values of conflict and resolution. There is no reason to think that modern music will not continue to invent new methods of organizing musical material, but it is just as likely to develop new ways of connecting with multiple discourses. The intersection of acoustic instruments and live electronics is also likely to be a key concern for technical development, and may well lead to music-making becoming a more obviously collaborative affair. This said, there is ample scope for creativity without electronic resources, thereby avoiding the hazard of computer programs tugging the compositional process in a particular direction.

At its zenith, modernism achieved prominence not because it was popular but because it was considered important. For all its radicalism and frustration with nineteenth-century institutions, it occupied the institutional space of high art and derived prestige from that position, particularly by retaining the mystique of the individual craftsman in an age of mass production. Its position was therefore always precarious in a world that might at any moment decide to dispense with 'high art', and as the world becomes more inclined to do just that, so the modernist musical 'world' takes on the configuration of one global community amongst countless others. People do not, however, only subscribe to just one such community: they interact with a variety of traditions and cultures that cross-pollinate one another, thereby making modernism a more hybrid culture (as the Tate Modern testifies).

From such a pluralist perspective, not all the odds are stacked against the survival of a transformed modernism. For one thing, as already mentioned, the relative ease with which CDs can be produced makes music with a small following viable. For another, the World Wide Web provides new opportunities for the dissemination of music without support from recording companies or publishers; composers working in electronic media are already able to place sound files and scores on the Internet, to be downloaded by people with similar interests. Information technology enables global access and has thereby increased the potential audience for modernist music, which need no longer be a primarily North American and European phenomenon. The technological revolution that facilitates such possibilities is very different from the production-based wave of innovation that characterized the 1950s, because such soft technology focuses primarily on the distribution of knowledge. For this reason, it is likely that modernist music will be driven not only by new compositional techniques but also by innovative patterns of circulation.

Nevertheless, even functioning as a specialist interest rather than a dominant form of culture, modernism still requires some form of support – preferably from institutions willing to create space for music of intrinsic value that is not driven by mass sales. For if modernism can no longer sustain claims to be the only authentic musical voice of the modern age, it can still explore creatively matters such as the intersection of identity and difference that are of shared concern in the modern world. In doing so, it may well push human subjectivity in directions that are less easily envisaged in realms that face the responsibilities of everyday practicality. A sector of music that can turn the energy of innovation towards the experiences that pragmatism is prone to marginalize will fulfil a vital aesthetic need and has every chance of survival.

Bibliography

Adlington, Robert. 'Into the Sensuous World: The Music of Rebecca Saunders', *Musical Times* 140/1868 (1999), pp. 48–56.

The Music of Harrison Birtwistle, Cambridge, 2000.

Adorno, Theodor. 'The Ageing of the New Music' (tr. Robert Hullot-Kentor), *Telos* 77 (1988), pp. 95–116.

'Vers une musique informelle', in *Quasi una Fantasia* (tr. Rodney Livingstone), London, 1992, pp. 269–322.

Arditti, Irvine. 'Irvine Arditti in Interview with Max Nyfeller', programme for Huddersfield Contemporary Music Festival, 1999, p. 51.

Barthes, Roland. *Image–Music–Text* (tr. Stephen Heath), London, 1977.

Berio, Luciano. 'Eco in Ascolto: Luciano Berio Interviewed by Umberto Eco' (tr. David Osmond-Smith), *Contemporary Music Review* 5 (1998), pp. 1–8.

Bernard, Jonathan W. 'An Interview with Elliott Carter', *Perspectives of New Music* 28/2 (1990), pp. 180–214.

Beyers, Anders (ed.). *The Voice of Music: Selected Interviews with Contemporary Composers*, Aldershot, 2000.

Boretz, Benjamin. 'Interface I–V: Texts and Commentaries on Music and Life', in John Rahn (ed.), *Perspectives on Musical Aesthetics*, New York and London, 1994, pp. 116–42.

Born, Georgina. *Rationalizing Culture: IRCAM, Boulez, and the Institutionalization of the Musical Avant Garde*, Berkeley, 1995.

Boulez, Pierre. 'Putting the Phantoms to Flight', in Jean-Jacques Nattiez (ed.), *Orientations: Collected Writings by Pierre Boulez* (tr. Martin Cooper), London, 1986, pp. 63–83.

Carter, Elliott. Preface to *Night Fantasies* for piano, New York, 1980.

Programme note to *90+* for piano, London, 1994.

Cross, Jonathan. *Harrison Birtwistle: Man, Mind, Music*, London, 2000.

Danuser, Hermann. 'Neue Musik', in *Die Musik in Geschichte und Gegenwart* (1997), Vol. VII, pp. 75–122.

Ferneyhough, Brian. *Collected Writings* (ed. James Boros and Richard Toop), Amsterdam, 1995.

Fox, Christopher. '1982–1994: l'atelier énorme', in Rudolf Stephan et al. (eds.), *Von Kranichstein zur Gegenwart: 50 Jahre Darmstädter Ferienkurse (1946–1996)*, Stuttgart, 1996, pp. 461–7.
Griffiths, Paul. *Modern Music and After*, Oxford, 1995.
Harvey, Jonathan. 'IRCAM', in William Glock (ed.), *Pierre Boulez: A Symposium*, London, 1986, pp. 239–46.
Heidenreich, Achim. 'Ein Rhythmus im Alltäglichen. Zu Wolfgang Rihm', in Rudolf Stephan et al. (eds.), *Von Kranichstein zur Gegenwart: 50 Jahre Darmstädter Ferienkurse (1946–1996)*, pp. 487–93.
Holloway, Robin. 'Modernism and After in Music', *Cambridge Review*, June 1989, pp. 60–6.
Huyssen, Andreas. *After the Great Divide: Modernism, Mass Culture and Postmodernism*, London, 1986.
Jameux, Dominique. *Pierre Boulez* (tr. Susan Bradshaw), London, 1991.
Jencks, Charles. 'The Emergent Rules', in Thomas Docherty (ed.), *Postmodernism: A Reader*, Hemel Hempstead, 1993, pp. 281–94.
Lachenmann, Helmut. 'Touched by Nono', *Contemporary Music Review* 18/1 (1999), pp. 17–30.
Ligeti, György. 'Pierre Boulez: Decision and Automatism in *Structure 1a*' (tr. Leo Black), *Die Reihe* 4 (1960), pp. 36–62.
'On My Piano Concerto' (tr. Robert Cogan), *Sonus* 9/1 (1988), pp. 8–13.
Maconie, Robin. *The Works of Karlheinz Stockhausen* (2nd edn), Oxford, 1990.
McClary, Susan. 'Paradigm Dissonances: Music Theory, Cultural Studies, Feminist Criticism', *Perspectives of New Music* 32/1 (1994), pp. 68–85.
'Terminal Prestige: The Case of Avant-Garde Music Composition', *Cultural Critique* 12 (1989), pp. 57–81.
Metzger, Heinz-Klaus. 'Just Who is Growing Old?' (tr. Leo Black), *Die Reihe* 4 (1960), pp. 63–80.
Nattiez, Jean-Jacques (ed.). *The Boulez–Cage Correspondence* (tr. Robert Samuels), Cambridge, 1993.
Nono, Luigi. Notes to *Fragmente–Stille, An Diotima*, Milan, 1980.
Pritchett, James. *The Music of John Cage*, Cambridge, 1993.
Rihm, Wolfgang. *Ausgesprochen: Schriften und Gespräche* (ed. Ulrich Mosch), 2 vols., Winterthur, 1997.
Schiff, David. *The Music of Elliott Carter* (2nd edn), London, 1998.
Schöning, Klaus (ed.). John Cage: *Roaratorio. An Irish Circus on Finnegans Wake*, Königstein, 1982.
Snowman, Nicholas. 'Birtwistle the Dramatist: Some Reflections', programme to *Gawain*, Royal Opera House, London, 1991.
Toop, Richard. 'Brian Ferneyhough's *Lemma–Icon–Epigram*', *Perspectives of New Music* 28/2 (1990), pp. 52–100.
Vieira de Carvalho, Mário. 'Towards Dialectical Listening: Quotation and Montage in the Work of Luigi Nono', *Contemporary Music Review* 18/2 (1999), pp. 37–85.
Warnaby, John. 'Wolfgang Rihm's Recent Music', *Tempo* 213 (2000), pp. 12–19.

Whittall, Arnold. 'A Dance of the Deadly Sins: *The Beltane Fire* and the Rites of Modernism', in Richard McGregor (ed.), *Perspectives on Peter Maxwell Davies*, Aldershot, 2000, pp. 138–58.

Musical Composition in the Twentieth Century, Oxford, 1999.

Williams, Alastair. 'Adorno and the Semantics of Modernism', *Perspectives of New Music* 37/2 (1999), pp. 29–50.

Constructing Musicology, Aldershot, 2001.

New Music and the Claims of Modernity, Aldershot, 1997.

· 20 ·

(Post-)minimalisms 1970–2000: the search for a new mainstream

ROBERT FINK

> The conventional wisdom is that Minimalism – an idiom of clear, non-decorative lines, repetition, and great tonal simplicity which arose in the 1960s and 70s – was the last identifiable new style in music history. Actually, there has since been an accelerating series of new styles, many of them building on minimalist roots toward greater and world-music-inspired complexity.
>
> Kyle Gann[1]

> My music is very much an example of what's happened to music at the end of the twentieth century. We're in a kind of post-style era. Composers my age and younger, we are not writing in one, highly defined, overarching expression, like Steve Reich or Luciano Berio would write.
>
> John Adams[2]

After the last new style

As a label for trends in music history since 1970, the term 'post-minimalism' has, at first, a seductively familiar ring – if by 'music history' we mean the succession of compositional styles conceptualized as a linear progression, most memorably analogized by Donald Francis Tovey as 'the mainstream of music'. If 'post-minimalist' is a music-historical adjective of time, like 'post-Romantic' or 'pre-classical', then the familiar narrative strategies of classical music might still apply: an early style (minimalism) progresses – either through evolutionary ramification or dialectical synthesis – to another, later one (post-minimalism). The stream flows on.

So argues Kyle Gann, in the epigraph above and in his 1997 survey *American Music in the Twentieth Century*. But, as Gann acknowledges, minimalism is most often seen not as the beginning of a new drama of stylistic evolution, but as *finis Terrae musicologicae*, as the 'last identifiable new style in music history'.

1 Kyle Gann, course catalogue listing for Music 217, 'New Musical Currents Since Minimalism', Bard College, Fall 1998.

2 John Adams, as quoted in Stewart Ocksenhorn, 'John Adams: Opera Can (and Must) Be Relevant', *Aspen Times* 117/90 (1998).

Minimalism occupies this lonely promontory because it can be read as the final chapter of the post-Cagean experimental tradition (which, as the 'New Determinacy', is where it appears in Michael Nyman's 1974 survey, *Experimental Music*). If, as Leonard Meyer argued in 1967,[3] Cage and his followers represented the incipient collapse of a four-hundred-year tradition of humanistic music, the 'end of the Renaissance', then minimalism is truly the last gasp, *the end of the end* of the Renaissance. After the collapse, Meyer hypothesized the end of music history: no more mainstream, no stylistic progression, just an indefinite period of 'fluctuating stasis' during which many styles would flourish, artists would feel free to shift among them, and the main criterion of success would be elegance, not originality. This is quite a good prediction of what we now call 'postmodernism' in the arts. Is post-minimalism, then, simply post(modern)-minimalism? This is the position that composer John Adams (b. 1947) takes, placing himself on one side – the 'post-style era' – of an unbridgeable historical chasm. On the other side are 'older' composers like Luciano Berio (1925–2003) and, interestingly enough given Adams' penchant for pulsed repetition, a founding minimalist like Steve Reich (b. 1936).

To an even younger composer like Rhys Chatham (b. 1952), who cheerfully confesses to starting out a 'hardcore minimalist', the distinction is clear:

> The modernist project of this century was concluded, give or take a few years, during the sixties with the phenomenon of minimalism, the apogee of modernism, which succeeded in deconstructing music to its basic signifiers: a beat, a chord, a sound. The music of the seventies heralded the beginning of the post-modern period . . . Rather than using our freedom to define a personal playing style or mode of music that would immediately be identifiable, and incidentally, saleable, I felt it would be more interesting to directly explore the nature of this freedom by composing a series of pieces, greatly varied in style.[4]

For Chatham, 'post-minimalism' is anything and everything that happened after minimalism, the last modernism, burnt itself reductively out, taking the very idea of an identifiable, marketable style (and the musical mainstream) with it.

As will become clear below, my account of minimalism and its aftermath is a smaller, more provisional narrative woven from alternating strands of these two grand historical hypotheses. For some composers, including its original practitioners, minimalism *was* an evolutionary or dialectical starting point,

3 Leonard B. Meyer, *Music, the Arts, and Ideas: Patterns and Predictions in Twentieth-Century Culture*, Chicago, 1967.

4 Rhys Chatham, *Composer's Notebook 1990*, http://perso.wanadoo.fr/rhys.chatham/Essay_1970-90.html

the beginning of a new mainstream. At the same time, minimalists, post-minimalists, and critics alike continue to struggle with the radical possibility that minimalism really was (for good or ill) an unrepeatable deconstructive gesture, the end of the stylistic line. Is a coherent post-minimalist style even possible? Or is it just selling out?

Minimalism triumphant

It is impossible to understand the birth of 'post-minimalism' in the 1970s in isolation from the unanticipated popularity of the music that was originally called 'trance', 'hypnotic', 'repetitive', and even 'neo-primitive'. Post-minimalism as a style begins in the shadow of 'minimalism' as a brand.

Between 1968, when Columbia Masterworks plucked Terry Riley's 1964 *In C* out of the California counterculture, and 1981, when Philip Glass, fresh from the European triumph of his second opera, signed an exclusive classical recording contract with CBS Records, the breakthrough of minimalism into mainstream consciousness was as swift as it was unpredictable. Even arbitrary: the choice in 1968 of Riley over the equally trippy La Monte Young (who had recorded some vocal pieces for Columbia but, unlike the easy-going Riley, refused to do overdubs) guaranteed that for the next twenty years the public face of minimalism would be dominated not by extended microtonal drones but by pulsed modular repetition. Hence the rise of rhythmic process music: Riley's sequel, *A Rainbow in Curved Air* (1969); an influential European tour by Glass and Reich in 1971; the 1973 major-label recording of Reich's *Drumming*. By 1974 Glass's four-hour *Music in Twelve Parts* had been performed in an uptown New York recital hall and released on the British pop-rock label Virgin; finally, in the summer of 1976, New York saw the simultaneous sold-out premieres of Reich's *Music for Eighteen Musicians* and Glass's *Einstein on the Beach*.

The period between 1974 and 1982 was the cultural apogee of pulse-patterned minimalism: before 1974, highly reductive music could still be dismissed as marginal experimentation; after 1982, nobody really thought the music sounded 'simple' any more. But the elaborate pulsed process music that broke into mainstream consciousness in the late 1970s as 'minimalism' was (confusingly enough) actually the first stirrings of post-minimalism, already an evolutionary shift away from the early reductionism of its founders. Certainly neither Reich nor Glass now sees his music of the 1970s as 'minimal', nor did downtown New York critics at the time. Both composers had begun self-consciously to experiment with functional harmony, and with a new richness of instrumental resources. This was especially true of Reich, whose late-1970s work was consistently called 'lush', 'sensuous', even (by one disappointed early supporter) 'sappy'.[5] The emphasis on an impersonal music structured by clearly audible process began to recede: both Reich and Glass began to use more processes that changed faster, and to intervene unpredictably in their unfolding.

To take a classic instance, Reich's *Music for Eighteen Musicians* is supposedly based on the cycle of eleven pandiatonic chords which opens and closes the work; in the interim, each chord's pitches are prolonged and used as the basis for a short 'variation'. These mini-pieces *are* minimal, with audible additive and subtractive process. But not only are the chords hard to hear as such (most of the verticalities have several common tones with their neighbours); Reich's realization of the cycle on a larger scale is strikingly arbitrary – one chord is barely touched, while another is developed through two complete variations. The composer even breaks his own rules, wilfully violating the cycle to create the large-scale dominant-to-tonic bass progression at the centre of his work. Minimalism's basic contract with the listener had been Reich's disarming promise that he was not interested in hidden structures, that 'all the cards were on the table'. Post-minimalists preferred to keep at least a few up their sleeves.

Post-minimalism (still branded at this point as 'minimalism') no longer appeared to mainstream composers as a forbidding experimental *aesthetic*; popular success and its new hospitality to traditional notions of craft and compositional voice now made it an attractive *stylistic* choice.[6] An extraordinary number of older European composers, many of them committed modernists, found themselves drawn into the deep gravitational well of Riley, Reich, and Glass between 1976 and 1980. György Ligeti (b. 1923) was humorously forthright in his 1976 *Selbstportrait mit Reich und Riley (und Chopin ist auch dabei)*; in that same year the Belgian serialist Karel Goeyvaerts (1923–93) composed *Pourque les fruits mûrissent cet été* (May the Fruits Ripen this Summer), a tribute to the improvisatory modular repetition of *In C*, transposed to dorian mode and wittily scored for renaissance instruments (a discreet repeated D on the lute takes the place of Riley's infamous piano octaves). For pillars of the post-serialist avant-garde like Simeon ten Holt (b. 1923) and Hans Otte (b. 1926), the rise of minimalism was a call to extended meditation, at the piano, on musical first principles. Massive keyboard rituals like Otte's twelve-part *Buch der Klänge* (1979–82) and ten Holt's evening-long *Canto Ostinato* for four pianos (1977–9) were radical departures from the Boulez–Cage axis of Continental musical orthodoxy. Though hardly 'minimal' in the reductive 1960s sense, their glacial time-scale, lush tonality, and repetitive modular structure would have been inconceivable without the example of Reich and Glass circa 1976.

5 See Tom Johnson, *The Voice of New Music (New York City 1972–82)*, Eindhoven, 1989, p. 374.

6 Timothy A. Johnson, 'Minimalism: Aesthetic, Style, or Technique?', *Musical Quarterly* 78 (1994), pp. 742–73.

Otte's work may have been more directly influenced by the expatriate Californian John McGuire, a long-time resident of Cologne who was also working on an extended process piece for keyboards. McGuire's *48 Variations for Two Pianos* (1976–80) is built on a slow, hour-long descent through four cycles of fifths, over which McGuire sets what he calls 'a bundle of slowly gliding melodic waves of different length, superimposed upon one another so as to render audible a flow of continuously shifting melodic and rhythmic symmetries'.[7] As described, classic minimalism; but since McGuire's waves, realized in a diaphanous Debussy-like tapestry of sound, stand in the complex ratio of 8:12:18:27 – a set of ratios themselves then transformed along a 'temporal cycle of fifths' – what one actually hears is a gorgeous contrapuntal web of pulsations over a hypnotically slow-moving progression of (mostly) consonant harmonies: that is, 1970s post-minimalism.

Born in 1942, McGuire is one of a group of American composers who began their careers within earshot of *In C* and Reich's first phase pieces: Daniel Lentz (b. 1942), Ingram Marshall (b. 1942), William Duckworth (b. 1943), Stephen Scott (b. 1944), Janice Giteck (b. 1946), John Adams, and Paul Dresher (b. 1951). Dresher is young enough to have studied with Terry Riley, as an apprentice tape-delay work like *Liquid and Stellar Music* (electric guitar, live tape loops, 1981) demonstrates; but for the rest of this generation, minimalism was something picked up by ear. These post-minimalists have thus been more concerned with sound and feeling, less with rigour and experiment. Process is still important, as is an extended time-scale and the avoidance of climaxes, but often there is a yen for what Lentz once called 'pretty pieces': rich, reverberant sonic landscapes, the lushness for its own sake of *Music for Eighteen Musicians*.

Scott's work with bowed piano (*Minerva's Web*, 1985), Marshall's atmospheric combination of foghorns and tape-delayed brass (*Fog Tropes*, 1982), Duckworth's meditations on Appalachian shape-note singing (*Southern Harmony*, 1980–1) – all use some kind of complex repetitive process, but hide their rigour behind a pulsating veil of beautiful sound. Often, as in Giteck's *Om Shanti* (1986), meditative spirituality and healing are engaged; the influence of Pauline Oliveros (b. 1932), her Sonic Meditations, and the musicians associated with the reverberant recordings of her Deep Listening Ensemble (Stuart Dempster, David Gamper, Panaiotis, Ellen Fullman) is clear. There is also a parallel with the lessons that British composers drew from 1960s minimal music. Michael Nyman has identified a minimalist-enabled 'cult of the beautiful' that swept over British experimental circles around 1970, exemplified in the work of John White (b. 1936) and Gavin Bryars (b. 1943).[8] Molasses-slow meditations

7 Liner notes to John McGuire, *48 Variations for Two Pianos* (Largo, 1987).
8 Michael Nyman, *Experimental Music: Cage and Beyond* (2nd edn), Cambridge, 1999, p. 135.

on familiar hymnody like Bryars' *The Sinking of the Titanic* (1969–) and *Jesus' Blood Never Failed Me Yet* (1971–93) have little in common with the whirring precision of early Reich and Glass; yet they are recognizably 'post-minimalist' when they use additive process and an extended time-scale to transform tonal clichés into luminous fields of sound.

The string orchestra parts for the 1975 first recording of *Titanic* were conducted by a young American friend of the composer, recently relocated to San Francisco, named John Adams. Adams began his mature career by rejecting both serialism and post-Cage conceptualism, only to surrender to the late 1970s pull of repetitive music, a style he associated as much with Bryars as with Reich and Glass. The slow-motion string chorale of *Christian Zeal & Activity* (1973) is clearly influenced by Bryars; *Phrygian Gates* (1977), on the other hand, sits perfectly alongside McGuire's contemporaneous work, hiding its equally complex rhythmic processes underneath elaborate 'waves' of virtuoso figuration and then setting the whole cascading gravely around the cycle of fifths. But *Phrygian Gates* is already more 'post-minimalist' than McGuire's *Variations.* Adams' shifting figuration has a driving, nervous intensity, and the 'gates' of the title – instantaneous shifts of mode – snap open and shut with disconcerting suddenness. His string septet *Shaker Loops* (1978), still securely post-minimalist in its modular 'loop' structure, went one step further: channelling the forward momentum of motoric figuration through long sequences of rising melodic tension, the work's third movement, 'Loops and Verses', builds to an unforgettable moment of ecstatic harmonic release.

By dangling what Tom Johnson once disparaged as 'the climax carrot' before audiences, Adams set the stage for a revolutionary break with 1970s post-minimalism. *Grand Pianola Music* (1982), scored for a deliberately crass ensemble of two pianos and wind band, made that break explicit. The last movement begins post-minimally, filling the aural space with delicate out-of-phase arpeggios from the two keyboards. The figuration speeds up and ramifies, but it is not until Adams yanks the rug out with a blatant and brassy major triad that we realize we've been had: the meditative opening was in fact prolonging a dominant-seventh chord, which in resolving to the tonic completes the hoariest cliché of tonal music. A series of Beethoven quotations ensues, culminating in a hilariously boozy parody of Beethoven's 'Ode to Joy'.

Adams called the movement 'On the Dominant Divide', and it does seem that 1982 was a watershed moment for both him and post-minimalism. For Adams, having bid farewell to what he called minimalism's 'endless prairies of non-event', the trail was open to a powerful fusion of post-minimalist process, the post-Romantic symphony, and (for a while) postmodern operatic pastiche. For the next generation of American composers to grow up 'after minimalism', the path forward would actually lead back, to the 1960s radicalism at the heart of the original minimalist aesthetic.

Banging on a can: the post-minimalism of resistance

Louis Andriessen (b. 1939), youngest scion of a musical dynasty, committed Marxist, and, as the leader of the 'New Hague School', long-time *provocateur* within Dutch new-music circles, was a key mentor and father figure for the generation of post-minimalist composers born in the 1950s and early 1960s. Andriessen's own compositional role model has always been Stravinsky, from whom he inherited not only a powerful rhythmic drive, but also a restless desire to test himself dialectically against whatever stylistic trends cross his path. (Like Adams, Andriessen has always considered himself more a fox than a hedgehog.) After a precocious brush with total serialism, Andriessen spent the first half of the 1960s exploring the limits of the European avant-garde, and the second half in musico-political agitprop. Highpoints included the 'postmodern' collage works *Anachronie I* and *II* (1966–9); a 1970 sit-in at the Concertgebouw that landed the composer in jail; and *Volkslied* (1971), which transformed the Dutch national anthem note by note into the Marxist *Internationale*. In 1972, Andriessen's anti-institutional love of popular music, in particular free jazz and American rhythm and blues, led him to found De Volharding ('perseverance'), a mixed ensemble of classical and jazz musicians. His music for the Volharding ensemble, pieces like *On Jimmy Yancey* (1973) and *Workers Union* (1975), fused Stravinsky, jazz, and boogie-woogie piano; they also had some of the raw, amplified abrasiveness of mid-1960s minimalism. But it was with *Hoketus* (1975–7), composed largely during his year-long seminar on American repetitive music at The Hague's Royal Conservatory, that Andriessen's engagement with minimalism began in earnest.

Hoketus now looks like an attempt to rewrite music history, to construct an alternative post-minimalism in which American Pop would not triumph over, but synthesize dialectically with European modernism. Andriessen was emphatically not one of those European composers who surrendered to 1970s post-minimalism as a relief: the work's relentless *fortissimo* and obsession with a single additive rhythmic process were distinctly 'retro' for 1975. Polemically, the other key features of early pulse-pattern minimalism are replaced by their high modernist opposites: the harmonic material is unremittingly dissonant, and the beat is jerky and irregular rather than flowing. The ensemble, dominated by highly amplified keyboards, drums, and electric guitars, had its roots in rock, but not the trippy, mellow, progressive kind evoked by Riley and Glass. *Hoketus* sounds more like a workout by the MC5 – or the Ramones.

Andriessen's punk-meets-Stravinsky take on minimalism was overtly political and confrontational: witness works like *De Staat* (1973–6), a setting of Plato's proscription of 'new' music from his ideal Republic, and *Mausoleum* (1979), on inflammatory texts by the anarchist Mikhail Bakunin. By the 1980s, a coherent compositional position had begun to take shape which, paraphrasing art critic Hal Foster, we might designate as a 'post-minimalism of resistance'.[9] Radical left-wing politics would validate fusing the rigour of early minimalism with the 'progressive' dissonance of European modernism; the resulting mixture would itself be validated by reference to the rhythmic complexity and raw countercultural power of African-American popular music. This mixture was imbibed directly – along with a predilection for loud hockets – by Andriessen's British student Steve Martland (b. 1958), as the programmatic titles of works like *Babi Yar* (1983), *American Invention* (1985), and *Shoulder to Shoulder* (1986) demonstrate.

The post-minimalism of resistance has been most effectively disseminated by the closely knit composers of the 'Bang on A Can' (BOAC) collective, Michael Gordon (b. 1956), David Lang (b. 1957), and Julia Wolfe (b. 1959), who take their name from the series of marathon free-for-all concerts of new music they have sponsored in New York since 1987. Andriessen figures prominently in their pantheon, along with left-wing iconoclasts Frederic Rzewski (b. 1938), Conlon Nancarrow (1912–97), and Harry Partch (1901–74). Aggressive, guitar-driven, amplified chamber-music like Lang's *Are You Experienced?* (1987–8), Wolfe's *Lick* (1994), and Gordon's *I Buried Paul* (1996) are logical products to come from the first generation of composers to grow up post-minimalist in the post-Beatles era. Add global media and the ubiquity of world music to the mix and out come fusions like Gordon's *Trance* (1995). *Trance* features a guitar-and-horn-driven ensemble stomping its Andriessen-like way through complex syncopated polyrhythms, anchored to an implied rock backbeat. Gordon himself makes the analogy between the 'independent interlocking units going on simultaneously' and musical information overload: 'all the different thoughts in one's head that go on – like being able to hear all the music that's going on everywhere in the world, in one's head, at the same time'.[10] (The penultimate movement drowns the pulse in a sludge of overdubbed indigenous trance music from around the globe, making the analogy spookily concrete.) Contemporary critics dubbed this resistant and omnivorous style 'totalism'; what else could one say about impresarios whose first BOAC marathon knowingly placed Reich's *Four Organs*, the *ne plus ultra* of early minimalism, next to Milton Babbitt's twelve-tone *Vision and Prayer*?

9 Foster defined the 'postmodernism of resistance' (and its dialectical other, the 'postmodernism of reaction') in his introduction to Hal Foster (ed.), *The Anti-Aesthetic*, Port Townsend, WA, 1983, pp. ix–xvi.

10 Liner notes to Michael Gordon, *Trance* (Argo, 1996).

The 1990s success of totalism had mostly to do with the virtuosity and marketing savvy of the BOAC collective, but their concerns interlocked with those of another, older set of downtown musicians, many of whom were attempting in their own way to chart a resistant course from the radical reductionism of the 1960s; the extended just-intonation drones of La Monte Young's Theater of Eternal Music, conspicuously absent from the popular conception of minimalism, provided a common starting point. It is now generally accepted that it was violinist Tony Conrad (b. 1940) who first interested Young in the mathematical intricacies of tuning, but Conrad soon abandoned music to concentrate on video. Phil Niblock (b. 1933) used analogue and later digital electronics to guide live performers through the infinitesimal gradations of frequency his drone works demanded: a typical work might allow a piercingly amplified and overdubbed F♯–G♯ dyad to converge on a unison G over the span of half an hour. As Kyle Gann points out, totalists have consistently been fascinated by the fact that the mathematical complexities of the overtone series can be mapped into complex, repetitive structures of rhythm – a relationship made vividly concrete by Niblock's work, which seethes with the rhythmic pulsation of difference tones and clashing upper partials.[11] Young himself became obsessed with the interference and reinforcement patterns generated by rapid strumming on a grand piano in just intonation, as he added wings onto the rambling edifice he called *The Well-Tuned Piano*; by the 1980s the work lasted five hours in performance. Perhaps the only musician to surpass Young in this regard was the legendarily flamboyant Charlemagne Palestine (b. Charles Martin, 1947): after propping a crowd of teddy bears on his specially tuned and lit Bösendorfer Imperial, and fortifying himself periodically with cognac, Palestine attacked the keyboard in late 1970s performance works like *Strumming Music* and *The Lower Depths*, exploring the outer reaches of both the overtone series and human endurance.

By the 1980s Niblock, Palestine, and Conrad had all left the new music world to concentrate on visual art, and it is only on recent reissues of rare 1970s recordings that their anticipation of the New York totalist sound becomes clear. On the other hand, the legacy of La Monte Young was flourishing in late 1970s punk rock. It had been ten years since John Cale took his amplified viola drones from the Theater of Eternal Music to another downtown musical collective, the Velvet Underground. The Velvet's 'Heroin' (1967), with its droning perfect fifth, overtone noise, and thudding rock beat, was a pioneering stylistic fusion; by the late 1970s, Young protégés like Rhys Chatham and Arnold Dreyblatt (b. 1953) were consciously cross-breeding microtonal drones, overtone music,

11 Kyle Gann, *American Music in the Twentieth Century*, New York, 1997, pp. 355–6.

and the incipient punk of the Ramones. Dreyblatt worked with his self-fashioned 'Orchestra of Excited Strings', which by 1981 contained detuned guitars and pianos, multiple double basses strung with piano wire, monochords, magnetic zithers, and a specially built portative organ to sustain his complex tuning system of twenty tones to the octave. In performances that Dreyblatt called 'Nodal Excitations', the performers would rhythmically excite the long, amplified strings while touching harmonic nodes, producing a jangling, throbbing mass of upper partials. The results sometimes had an eerie sonic resemblance to the high-overtone fuzz of electric guitars run through overdriven speakers.

The full-on fusion of microtonal minimalism and punk rock was carried out by Rhys Chatham and Glenn Branca (b. 1948). Chatham had slight priority, and perhaps the better pedigree: he had been the musical director of the Kitchen, a key Downtown performance space, and his grasp of overtone theory went back to his stint as La Monte Young's piano tuner. After hearing the Ramones live in 1976, Chatham took up the electric guitar, started playing in a punk band, and by 1977 had produced a *Guitar Trio* for three electric guitars, electric bass, and drums; works like *Drastic Classicism* (four guitars, bass drums, 1980) and *Die Donnergötter* (six guitars, bass, drums, 1984) exploited the ability of multiple electric guitars at high volume to produce complex 'overtone melodies'.

Other totalists were attracted to multiple guitars, most notably Lois Vierk (b. 1951) whose extraordinary *GO Guitars* (1981), taking its name from the Japanese word for 'five', twists five electric guitars into a hyper-kinetic version of the Japanese *gagaku* ensembles she has studied for almost two decades. (Vierk is attracted to multiples; her 1981 *Tusk* is scored for eighteen trombones.) But it was Branca who turned microtonal punk into a powerful cultural force. Theatrically rather than musically trained, he was interested in punk as spectacle, starting two noisy bands, Static and Theoretical Girls, in the late 1970s; like Chatham, he became fascinated by the sonic and ritualistic possibilities of massed guitars. In 1981, he staged 'Symphony no. 1', subtitled *Tonal Plexus*, in a New York City parking structure. The four-movement work, scored for massed guitars, winds, keyboards, and percussion, was, by all accounts, a terrifying spectacle (it climaxed with a pair of percussionists hammering with two-by-fours on a sixty-gallon oil drum); but calling the piece a 'symphony' – by which Branca meant an instrumental work with the dramatic and ritualistic ambitions of Beethoven or Bruckner – was an immediate public-relations coup. It was at this point that Branca encountered just intonation, and a string of microtonal guitar symphonies followed, often using detuned or specially constructed instruments. Branca's genius was to fuse the raw energy of punk with the arcana of tuning theory and his own uniquely Gothic sense of theatre

(Symphony no. 2 is called 'The Peak of the Sacred'; no. 6, 'Devil Choirs at the Gates of Heaven'). Heard live, his works are perhaps the most shattering experiences avant-garde music has to offer, combining the gut-churning power of La Monte Young's amplified drones and the head-banging intensity of punk with a romantic sense of large-scale unfolding that Branca shares with Adams.

In recent years Chatham and Branca have been engaged in a somewhat childish contest to see who can write for the largest ensemble. Chatham's *An Angel Flies Too Fast to See* (1989), which calls for a hundred guitars, has achieved multiple performances; Branca's millennial *Hallucination City*, for two thousand guitars, has not. Branca now prefers to write for traditional orchestra, but graduates of his guitar ensemble – perhaps the most famous are Thurston Moore and Lee Ranaldo of the seminal noise-rock band Sonic Youth – continue to seek a resistant post-minimalism under the guise of 'alternative' rock.

Minimalism institutionalized: the post-minimalism of reaction

The May–June 1983 issue of *Saturday Review* carried a long feature article on Philip Glass, which by itself would hardly be worthy of mention: by 1983 Glass had been profiled in *Time* (twice), *Newsweek* (twice), *Horizon*, *Esquire*, and the *New York Times*. What was shocking was the full-page advertisement for Cutty Sark whiskey that graced the magazine's inside front cover – with Glass's familiar mug peering out over a scotch on the rocks. He has never been forgiven. But was the transgression in doing the ad, or in the institutional success that the ad celebrated? Glass was at that moment the most famous and successful living composer in America, having sold almost 100,000 copies of his CBS debut album, *Glassworks*. But Reich was not far behind: *Music for Eighteen Musicians* had sold over 100,000 copies on ECM and been named one of the ten best pop albums of 1978, and five years later Reich was asked to rescore *Tehillim* for the New York Philharmonic. John Adams' rise was even more meteoric: in 1983 he was the composer in residence at the San Francisco Symphony. By 1985, when his *Harmonielehre* was premiered to rave reviews, pulse-pattern 'Minimalism' and the classical music establishment were in the throes of a brief, intense love affair, with Adams firmly planted in America's symphony halls and Glass in the opera houses of the world; even Reich was producing oratorios and orchestral works to order.

Post-minimalism – now encompassing Adams, Glass, Reich, the 'mystical' Pärt and Górecki, neo-Romantics like Corigliano and MacMillan, even a paleo-Romantic mystic like Hovhaness – was being openly marketed by multinational media conglomerates as a synthetic mainstream, a 'New Tradition': 'Minimalism,' wrote Mark Swed, 'a remarkably enduring style, now some 30 years old, has also evolved into a mainstream way to bring traditional harmony, melody, and rhythmic appeal back into music, yet make it sound fresh.'[12] For a composer like Michael Torke (b. 1961), a derivative post-minimalist style could be the key to precocious success; the twenty-four-year old dropped out of graduate school to fulfil the commissions pouring in from choreographers and conductors for more bouncy, professional-sounding orchestral works like *Ecstatic Orange* (1985). Torke had wit and talent, as the deconstruction of classical clichés in a work like *Ash* (1989) made clear. But in 1994, it was the empty bombast of Torke's *Javelin*, commissioned for the Atlanta Olympics, that topped the Billboard 'classical crossover' chart.

The composer as (mass-market) hero; an embrace of classical music institutions; an explicit return to tonal harmony and neo-Romantic pastiche – in the hands of its founders and followers, minimalism seemed to have turned into what Hal Foster would undoubtedly have analogized to 1980s neo-Romantic painting or corporate postmodern architecture: a 'post-minimalism of reaction'. Not surprisingly, those in favour of a more resistant route out of minimalism tried to refocus attention on the style's early, anti-establishment days. Tom Johnson complained in a 1982 *Village Voice* article that La Monte Young, the 'original' minimalist, had been overshadowed by what he sardonically called 'the famous minimalists',[13] and it is true that Young had dropped out of sight – but the reason was not neglect. He had been given an art-world institution all to himself.

Those who wanted to champion La Monte Young as avatar of a resistant post-minimalism had to reconcile themselves with two inconvenient facts. Young and his wife, visual artist Marian Zazeela, had since the early 1970s been formal disciples of the Indian classical singer Pandit Pran Nath, with all the overtones of submission to authority and guru-worship that implied. Even more difficult to harmonize with a left-wing agenda was Young's relationship to the wealthy de Menil family, Houston petroleum magnates whose daughter channelled some of their extracted surplus into the non-profit-making Dia Foundation. Between 1979 and 1985, Young, Zazeela, Nath, and a rotating staff of assistants and followers lived inside their 'Dream House': the permanent sound-and-light installation housed in the six-storey New York City brownstone that was purchased, remodelled, and staffed by the Foundation for their exclusive use. Even a sympathetic observer like Robert Palmer called

12 Mark Swed, 'Contemporary Composers: The New Tradition', *BMG Encore* [record club newsletter] I-C/47/0 (*c.*1995), p. 2.

13 Tom Johnson, 'The Original Minimalists', *Village Voice*, 27 July 1982, pp. 68–9.

6 Harrison Street a Bayreuth-like 'monument to Young'.[14] In this way, Young avoided the compromises with classical music institutions and the mass media that made Glass, Reich, and Adams seem so 'reactionary' – but only, it may be argued, by completing the transformation of his drone music into a different type of commodity, the kind of expensive conceptual art object suitable for collecting and investment during the overheated 1980s art market. The base-superstructure relationships entailed became painfully obvious when the oil money dried up and the Foundation's priorities were rearranged: Young and Zazeela were thrown into the street with whatever tapes and materials they could salvage.

But the die had been cast; Young continues to this day to treat his huge archive of tapes more like precious art objects than recordings for dissemination. This has brought him into violent conflict with Tony Conrad, one of the original 1960s members of what Conrad now calls, with bitter anti-capitalist irony, the 'Dream Syndicate'. In interviews, demonstrations, and pastiche works like *Slapping Pythagoras* (1995) and *Early Minimalism* (1994–6), Conrad has passionately attacked as reactionary and elitist Young's later attempts to assert sole control (compositional as well as financial and physical) over early group creations whose very value Conrad understands to be their postmodern deconstruction of the traditional role of 'composer'. It is undeniable that Young went on to develop this early drone music into intricate and extended compositions that are uniquely free from commercial pressures, and uniquely his; yet Conrad's caricature of an isolated and pampered egomaniac playing the role of 'great artist' to the hilt for a few rich patrons has enough truth in it to sting. There is, it seems, more than one way to sell out.

(Post-)minimalist music theatre

One of the most penetrating critiques of minimalist art accused it of betraying 'pure' painting and sculpture for the conceptualist play-acting of theatre.[15] One might, without the accusatory tone, make the same observation about music: musical theatre has consistently fostered post-minimalisms of all stripes, from the thornily resistant to the resplendently reactionary.

Philip Glass has always considered himself primarily a theatre composer; for many onlookers, the impact of a work like *Einstein on the Beach* (1976) was as much about the theatrical imagination of Robert Wilson as it was about Glass's music. Wilson's plotless, slow-motion surrealism was on full display in *Einstein*.

14 Robert Palmer, 'A Father Figure for the Avant-Garde', *The Atlantic Monthly* 247/5 (1981), p. 48.

15 Michael Fried, 'Art and Objecthood', in Gregory Battcock (ed.), *Minimalist Art: A Critical Anthology*, New York, 1968, pp. 116–47.

He constructed a series of abstract, slowly changing stage pictures, then filled them with Einstein clones, an avuncular African-American bus driver, even Patty Hearst brandishing a machine gun. His non-narrative 'libretto' took the disjointed writings of a developmentally disabled fourteen-year-old and combined them with found texts invented by the work's original cast. (All the solo parts are speaking roles; it was Glass, in rehearsal, who gave the singing chorus their self-referential repertoire of counting and *solfège* syllables.) But as in all of Wilson's work, the form of the piece was rigorous and abstract. The opera's five hours are divided into three acts, each with two scenes; the six dramatic sections present the three scenic ideas of the work (1. train; 2. trial; 3. field) in the order 1–2, 3–1, 2–3, creating the theatrical hemiola (2 × 3) vs. (3 × 2). This minimalist process theatre meshed perfectly with Andrew de Groat's abstract dance patterns and Glass's own polyrhythmic process music. The whole exceeded the sum of the parts: Wilson's archetypical imagery gave Glass's music a new mythic depth and cultural resonance, while Glass's music (and the physical demands of live musical theatre) energized and focused Wilson's notoriously glacial theatrical pacing.

After its premiere at New York's Metropolitan Opera House, *Einstein on the Beach* single-handedly reinvented 'opera', long the most conservative of high-art genres, as a site for experimental composition with (not always singing) voices. Opera as radical cultural challenge had long been the singular obsession of the American experimentalist Robert Ashley (b. 1930), who studied speech pathology and acoustics, and constructs vast, non-linear, rhythmically-precise theatrical structures based on the sound of his own voice. His trilogy of 'television operas' (*Perfect Lives*, 1978–83; *Atalanta*, 1985; *Now Eleanor's Idea*, 1993) have the loose, cool, randomness of an evening of TV: hilarious shaggy-dog allegories with historical figures like Bud (Powell, the 'world's greatest piano player') and Max (Ernst) are draped over a rigid temporal structure derived from the twenty-four-minute time-span of the typical situation comedy. Ashley's musical material has the blank, repetitious banality of Satie: most of the rhythmic patterns in *Perfect Lives* are sampled from stereotyped dance beats stored in an old Gulbransen 'Palace' electric organ.

Technologically enabled theatrical surrealism combined with spoken word performance became a preferred habitat for many post-minimalist composers, as in the case of Paul Dresher's work with San Francisco techno-wizard George Coates (*The Way of How*, 1981, and *SeeHear*, 1984). But perhaps the most famous practitioner of this synthesis is performance artist Laurie Anderson (b. 1947), whose work, like Ashley's, is founded on the timbre and rhythm of her speaking voice; 'O Superman', a dark meditation on power, regression, and loss of self which un-spools over the pulsing of Anderson's own sampled vocalizing, became an unlikely British pop hit in 1981. In works like the evening-length multimedia performance *United States* (1983), Anderson has explored both the wonder and the alienation of technology, refracting off-kilter stories and observations through complex systems of electronics, minimalist repetition, and her trademark vocal processing.

Steve Reich has confessed that he loathes both the artificiality of words set to music and the sound of classically trained operatic voices; nor was Reich interested in himself becoming a vocal performer like Ashley or Anderson. But the advent of the MIDI-controlled digital sampler allowed him to capture and then trigger recorded voices in a musical context, using the pitches and rhythms of everyday speech for musical material. (He had been anticipated by guitarist-composer Scott Johnson (b. 1952), whose 1982 album *John Somebody* pioneered this technique.) In works like *Different Trains* (1988) and the 'video opera' *The Cave* (1993), Reich combined sampled and looped speech with instruments and, in the opera, a wall of video screens, creating live multimedia theatre works with the documentary immediacy of early tape pieces like *It's Gonna Rain* (1964). But not all post-minimalist music theatre was as sternly deconstructive of opera-house values as the work of Ashley and Reich. With the success of Glass's second opera, *Satyagraha* (1980), scored for full orchestra and traditional operatic voices, it became clear that minimalism's strong rhythmic pulse and broad, impersonal swathes of tonal repetition lent themselves quite naturally to a revival of the grand operatic style. *Satyagraha*, sung in Sanskrit and based on the early life of Mahatma Gandhi, is a mytho-historical opera in the tradition of both Metastasio and the Risorgimento, full of choral pageantry and heroic resistance to oppression. In this and subsequent operatic works, most notably the 'Rome' act of Wilson's *The CIVIL warS* (1983), Glass has reaffirmed what nineteenth-century operatic masters like Rossini and Verdi knew: that simple musical structures, realized with conviction on a large scale, can amplify the primal power of the human singing voice, and may well underpin operatic spectacle more effectively than more complex, more inherently instrumental conceptions.

Nothing makes this point better than the crowning masterpieces of 'reactionary' post-minimalism, the John Adams–Peter Sellars–Alice Goodman collaborations *Nixon in China* (1985–7) and *The Death of Klinghoffer* (1990–1). For *Nixon*, Goodman and Sellars constructed a brilliant postmodern libretto which, on the deepest level, takes nothing less than the power of mass mediation as its subject. At his first entrance, Nixon muses that 'News . . . has a kind of mystery'; Sellars and Goodman explore that mystery, swooping vertiginously up and down the many levels of simulation involved in the US President's historic visit to Red China. Many of the crowd scenes restage events once staged for television cameras, precisely duplicating the 1972 camera angles; the proscenium stage becomes a surrogate TV screen. Adams responds to this riot of mediation with virtuoso postmodern pastiche: his music for Sellars' restaging of Madame Mao's melodramatic propaganda ballet *A Red Detachment of Women* is priceless, composed in equal parts of *The Butterfly Lovers*, Gershwin in Hollywood, and Wagner's *Ring*. He also proves himself the equal of Musorgsky as a setter of the vernacular. Goodman's libretto is filled with elaborate poetic speeches and quickly moving diplomatic conversations, like the darkly hilarious meeting between Nixon, Kissinger, Chou-En Lai, and Mao in Act I, scene 2; Adams consistently rises to the challenge, using stretches of pulsating 'minimalist' repetition to set up a rhythmic grid upon which slight variations of word accent and placement can be plotted with pinpoint precision.

Adams has recently been exploring music-theatrical hybrids, most notably the impressive *El Niño* (1999–2000), a millennial 'nativity oratorio' on pre-Christian, biblical, and contemporary Chicana poetry. In performance, the multimedia work places uncostumed singers, dancers, and musicians in front of a film by Peter Sellars, alternately gritty and abstract, that defamiliarizes the traditional Christmas story by reimagining it within contemporary Latino Los Angeles. This juxtaposition of live performers and cinematic imagery has also been explored extensively by Philip Glass in his 'Cocteau trilogy'; the best known is the 'opera' *La belle et la bête* (1994), produced by replacing the entire soundtrack of Cocteau's 1946 film with a live operatic score precisely lip-synched to the original dialogue. But Glass's most influential work, especially in the pop world, is arguably the soundtrack for Godfrey Reggio's *Koyaansqatsi* (1982), and the collaboration of English composer and critic Michael Nyman (b. 1944) with avant-garde film-maker Peter Greenaway was equally influential. Scores like *The Draughtsman's Contract* (1982) and *Drowning by Numbers* (1988) place Nyman in the tradition of Bryars' Portsmouth Sinfonia and its fascination with familiar canonical works imperfectly remembered and reproduced. In Nyman's music, systematic process dismembers short passages from Purcell and Mozart and then reassembles the pieces into autistic repetitive music, very much akin to the obsessive symmetries of plot and imagery in Greenaway's disturbing films.

A new mainstream?

At the end of the twentieth century, post-minimalism confronted a wave of historicism. Reissues on CD of long-lost works by Riley, Palestine, and even (in fiercely contested bootleg form) La Monte Young competed for shelf space with lavish boxed sets devoted to the 'collected works' of Reich and Adams.

Millennial speculations about the future of classical music often turned to minimalism, and the musicologist Richard Taruskin's review of the Reich box set the tone: 'it seems a good bet that Steve Reich will turn out to be the oldest twentieth-century composer in whom twenty-first-century musicians will find a kindred spirit'.[16] Taruskin saw Western art music undergoing a 'systemic evolution' in which minimalism was a key first step. Kyle Gann agreed, arguing that minimalism was a 'pre-classic' style, like Florentine monody or the Mannheim symphony, and thus evolutionarily destined for greater (or at least more complex) things.[17]

Is post-minimalism a new mainstream? The fractured story of the preceding pages, with its multiple and mutually antagonistic post-minimalisms, might argue in the negative. But we may recognize in minimalism the beginning of a new mainstream musical style, *if* we also recognize that the mainstream in question flows mainly outside the narrow levees of 'classical' music. The future belongs to minimalism's stepchildren: ambient and electronic dance music.

The new mainstream thus flows mostly outside the scope of this narrative. But, by way of conclusion, the landmarks of its channel can at least be sketched in. Brian Eno (b. 1948), one-time member of the progressive rock band Roxy Music, collaborated with Gavin Bryars on *Discreet Music* (1975), using process and tape-delay systems to create soft environmental washes of sound; the album *Ambient 1: Music for Airports* (1978) gave the new genre a name. Eno, Stockhausen, and progressive rock were key influences on German bands like Tangerine Dream and Kraftwerk. Kraftwerk's minimalist 'man-machine' aesthetic led them to electronic musical instruments, in particular the analogue synthesizers and robotic percussion tracks featured on *Trans-Europe Express* (1977). By 1982, Kraftwerk plus hiphop on the streets of Brooklyn had created a futuristic dance music called 'electro'; electro plus the equally robotic style of dance music called 'Eurodisco' (Giorgio Moroder, Donna Summer) cross-bred with indigenous forms of disco, soul, and funk to create a stripped-down, electronic dance-club music called variously 'garage' in New York, 'house' in Chicago, and in Detroit, where the robo-futurist influence of Kraftwerk was particularly strong, 'techno'. By 1988, Detroit techno and Chicago house, ignited by the first explosion of interest in MDMA (Ecstasy), jumped from the underground dance scene to the mainstream of British pop.

After that, the techno deluge. Many key figures in the ambient and electronic dance-music scene openly acknowledge the influence of minimalism: for most of them, the exposure to pieces like *Koyaanisqatsi* and *Music for Eighteen Musicians*

16 Richard Taruskin, 'A Sturdy Bridge to the Twenty-First Century', *The New York Times*, 24 August 1997.

17 Gann, *American Music*, pp. 184–5.

came during the early 1980s, when the 'famous minimalists', Glass and Reich, were at their most famous. I have argued elsewhere that the canonical boundaries between the art and vernacular species of repetitive electronic music are so permeable as to be meaningless;[18] from the perspective of the early twenty-first century, I am willing to wager that new art music will come from interbreeding the post-minimalist descendants of the dance floor, the concert hall, the recording studio and the artist's loft. The levee may break; but the stream flows on.

> I mean, I'm fourteen years old, I'm at Birdland, I'm listening to Kenny Clarke, and then I'm on-stage at Queen Elizabeth Hall and there's Eno, and later when I was in Berlin doing *Music For Eighteen Musicians*, there was David Bowie, and now there's these Techno guys. I mean, it's a two-way street. It's that back and forth.[19]

Bibliography

Chatham, Rhys. 'Composer's Notebook 1990: Toward a Musical Agenda for the Nineties', http://perso.wanadoo.fr/rhys.chatham/Essay_1970-90.html

Fink, Robert. 'Elvis Everywhere: Musicology and Popular Music Studies at the Twilight of the Canon', *American Music* 16 (1998), pp. 157–60.

Foster, Hal (ed.). *The Anti-Aesthetic*, Port Townsend, 1983.

Fried, Michael. 'Art and Objecthood', in Gregory Battcock (ed.), *Minimalist Art: A Critical Anthology*, New York, 1968, pp. 116–47.

Gann, Kyle. *American Music in the Twentieth Century*, New York, 1997.

Johnson, Tom. *The Voice of New Music (New York City 1972–82)*, Eindhoven, 1989.

Johnson, Timothy A. 'Minimalism: Aesthetic, Style, or Technique?', *Musical Quarterly* 78 (1994), pp. 742–73.

Meyer, Leonard B. *Music, the Arts, and Ideas: Patterns and Predictions in Twentieth-Century Culture*, Chicago, 1967.

Nyman, Michael. *Experimental Music: Cage and Beyond* (2nd edn), Cambridge, 1999.

Palmer, Robert. 'A Father Figure for the Avant-Garde', *Atlantic Monthly*, May 1981, p. 48.

Strickland, Edward. *Minimalism: Origins*, Bloomington, 1993.

Swed, Mark. 'Contemporary Composers: The New Tradition', *BMG Encore* [record club newsletter] I-C/47/0 (*c.*1995), p. 2.

Taruskin, Richard. 'A Sturdy Bridge to the Twenty-First Century', *The New York Times*, 24 August 1997.

18 See Robert Fink, 'Elvis Everywhere: Musicology and Popular Music Studies at the Twilight of the Canon', *American Music* 16 (1998), pp. 157–60.

19 Steve Reich interviewed by David Paul in *Seconds* 47 (1998).

· 21 ·

History and class consciousness: pop music towards 2000

DAI GRIFFITHS

This chapter begins in the late 1970s – not with Abba, or Queen, or *Evita*, all of which were internationally successful at the time, but with punk rock. Even when dealing with ostensibly popular music, there remains a tension between critical and populist versions of music history, and some history books devote much space to punk while others avoid it.[1] Here pop music towards 2000 is depicted, in a necessarily selective way, as being in the front line of a shift in critical thought from class-based critique to identity politics. Through staying power pop music became established as art form; a case is also made here for a looser discursive model based in movement and creative dialogue, focusing on remix and cover. The perspective of the chapter starts from Britain and jumps around with dates, though the reader may sense a certain centre of gravity around the year 1985.

Punk

Punk rock is sometimes seen as a spearing of the bloated beast which pop and rock had become over the decade from 1965 to 1975. Above all others, The Sex Pistols supplied many of the great iconic moments, over the remarkably short period of time from their first single 'Anarchy in the UK', released on 19 October 1976, to their last concert in San Francisco on 14 January 1978. ('Ever get the feeling you've been cheated?' was singer Johnny Rotten's memorable last comment.) The Pistols provided great entertainment: spewing foul language over teatime telly, bagging the number one spot with an anti-monarchy rant at the time of the Queen's jubilee, annoying British town councils and American rednecks, and eventually supplying for pop hedonism, in Sid and Nancy, its ultimate Romeo and Juliet script. For all that, the critical

1 Greil Marcus has devoted books to punk, and his *The Dustbin of History* (Cambridge, MA, 1996), Chuck Eddy's *The Accidental Evolution of Rock 'n' Roll: a Misguided Tour through Popular Music* (New York, 1997), and Jon Savage's *Time Travel: Pop, Media and Sexuality 1977–96* (London, 1996) are important backgrounds to this chapter. The single paragraph on punk at pp. 500–1 of Donald Clarke's *The Rise and Fall of Popular Music* (Harmondsworth, 1995) can stand for a contrary view.

response to The Sex Pistols has tended towards art and political theory. In one version, associated with the manager of The Sex Pistols, Malcolm McLaren, designer Vivienne Westwood, and British critic Jon Savage, the Pistols are positioned in an art-school context, with precedents in The Who or David Bowie. In another version, fostered again by the assiduous McLaren and artist Jamie Reid but associated especially with the American critic Greil Marcus, the band is set in a historical lineage which stretches back to the modernist art movement Dada in 1915 and passes through the Situationist International and French politics of 1968. In a recent film directed by Julien Temple, *The Filth and the Fury* (2000), however, the remaining Sex Pistols appeared to emphasize their association less with suburbia, Jon Savage's great theme, than with British, urban, white, working-class experience. So a relatively simple pop phenomenon like The Sex Pistols can be and has been interpreted in many ways. That said, in the sales charts of the day, punk records had relatively little impact. Greil Marcus's entry on UK punk for the canon-forming *Rolling Stone Illustrated History of Rock and Roll* has a special symbol for its discography, found nowhere else in the eighty-eight chapters which end with discographies: a star meaning 'best-selling or influential', with chart positions, again almost uniquely, not included.[2] Such a tension between relative commercial failure and critical esteem is expressive both of punk and of its time.

An important factor about punk was its ability, even at its appearance, to be defined and described as a self-contained genre. In popular music, genres are important, acting as a shorthand to capture both the sound itself and elements of production and reception around it. Punk drew attention to its difference from the rock genres of the day: heavy metal, progressive rock, and glam rock. Notable in punk's self-definition was its challenge to the orthodoxies of the industry: inspired with a do-it-yourself attitude, punk was the catalyst for a wave of small-scale independent record labels. The key British punk bands, The Sex Pistols and The Clash, did sign to major labels, but in the case of The Pistols, the splendid drama of jumping from EMI to A&M (wittily captured in 1977 at the very end of their 'EMI') and thence to Virgin summed up an insouciance about corporate fidelity. And for The Clash, signing to CBS in January 1977 was at the time a great touchstone of 'selling out' (and still the matter of earnest debate in Don Letts' 1999 film *Westway to the World*); 'Complete Control', their single of 1977, was even *about* their record deal. In the UK a number of labels emerged from punk – Rough Trade, Factory, Mute, 4AD – and their story mapped itself across the 1980s. For bands, punk embodied

2 Greil Marcus, 'Anarchy in the U. K.', in Anthony DeCurtis and James Henke with Holly George-Warren (eds.), *The Rolling Stone Illustrated History of Rock and Roll*, London, 1992, pp. 594–608.

an idea about the de-skilling of pop music that had major consequences, not least a challenge to stable ideas about masculinity and genius which had become quickly lodged in pop's imagery: The Slits' Peel Sessions (1977–8) remain the sound of this moment. (The idea that a recorded *radio session* was a performative moment – as expressive as a live performance or a studio recording, and a mediation between them – is a great punk legacy.) 'This is a chord, this is another, this is a third: now form a band', announced a fanzine – another punk invention.[3]

The sound of punk rock was immediately recognizable as such, though it was a construction which took a basic version of the rock sound, mediated through heavy metal, with The Clash showing the way to a merging with other roots forms, notably reggae. Punk's occasional proud parade of energy over technique recalled American garage bands of the 1960s. The very opening of The Mekons' '32 Weeks' of 1978 is a great example: 'Too fucking fast!' someone shouts out as they start again, *much* slower. 'I don't know the words', Johnny Rotten bluntly points out on The Pistols' cover of 'Johnny B. Goode' (on *The Great Rock 'n' Roll Swindle* of 1977). For its audiences, punk had its own look and clothes in which the major theme appeared to be invention of personality and a tendency towards androgyny: 'Love Lies Limp' (1978) by Mark Perry's Alternative TV is a great statement of sex-insouciance, and The Buzzcocks carefully crafted the subject positions of their songs to avoid specificities of gender. Critically established as genre, any number of potentially contradictory subgenres appear in retrospect: for instance, the difference between US and UK punk was recognized as such, the former being conceived far more artily in bands such as The Patti Smith Group, Television, and Talking Heads, if not The Ramones. Even within the UK itself there was something of a difference between the London-based punk of The Sex Pistols, The Clash and The Damned, all urban flash, noise and loud colour, and the Manchester-based punk of The Buzzcocks, Magazine, The Fall, the poet John Cooper Clarke, and Joy Division: dour, boringly-dressed, witty.

Punk set itself in identifiable ways against the prevalent state of rock and pop at the time. But in order for this to be the case, it was necessary in some way positively to understand the past, and a sense of *knowingness* about pop music, irony, even, is crucial in punk's narrative. What does this knowingness about pop music mean and how is it manifest? A unifying element in 1960s bands was the *cover version*: most of the 'British Invasion' groups – The Beatles, The Animals, The Them, The Rolling Stones – engaged in, and often began from, the direct performance of already existing originals. Passing *reference to*

3 See Jon Savage, *England's Dreaming: Sex Pistols and Punk Rock*, London, 1991, p. 280.

music, as opposed to covering it, was as likely to be 'outside' pop music, to jazz or whimsically to the light classical music which was still a dominant musical language in British culture. Pop music in the 1960s, young and aimed at youth, needed the broader version of 'art' to sustain itself as musical form, 'art' not in the formal sense of art training or some given and linear idea of art history, but in a more contemporary sense of self-invention and authentic presence – a form of direct social intervention, a means of fostering or protecting self-identity in an age of mass culture. With pop music becoming more established, transitional figures are found in David Bowie and Bryan Ferry of Roxy Music, and in 1973 both Bowie (*Pinups*) and Ferry (*These Foolish Things*) issued albums consisting entirely of cover versions. On another record, *Young Americans* of 1975, we see Bowie seemingly trying to get close to John Lennon of The Beatles: so, he *covers* Lennon's song 'Across the Universe' (from *Let It Be* of 1970), he *co-writes and performs alongside* Lennon on the song 'Fame', and finally the title track 'Young Americans' makes *passing reference* to Lennon's section of The Beatles' song 'A Day in the Life' (from *Sergeant Pepper's Lonely Hearts Club Band* of 1967: the line 'I read the news today, oh boy').

That last element, knowing reference, was important during and immediately after punk: pop music was becoming confident enough in its internal content to be self-referential. US punk was steeped in the past: Patti Smith's debut album, *Horses*, was produced in 1975 by John Cale (who had played with the Velvet Underground, and produced the punk foreshadowers *The Stooges* in 1969, as well as the debut of Jonathan Richman and the Modern Lovers in 1972), while Lenny Kaye of Patti Smith's group had compiled volumes of garage bands in a series called 'Nuggets'. In the UK The Clash included in '1977' and 'Clash City Rockers' (1977/8) little digests of the state of pop at the time, while the cover of *London Calling* of 1979 cleverly echoed Elvis Presley's first album of 1956. It was almost as though pop music was becoming academic. 'Academic inspiration, you gave me none', Kevin Rowland informs Geno Washington in the Dexy's Midnight Runners hit of 1980, but 'academic' is interesting there, since Rowland was in some ways crisply academic, the song a flattering footnote to his Northern Soul hero. Again, Elvis Costello's *Get Happy!* of 1980, even more than its three preceding albums, shows a scholarly grasp of popular music, and the album is a great reference-maker: the track 'High Fidelity' opens with the first line of the Supremes song 'Some Things You Never Get Used To' (1968), while 'Love for Tender' starts with a beat lifted from the Supremes' 'You Can't Hurry Love' (1966), and 'Temptation' picks up on Booker T and the MGs' 'Time is Tight' (1969). Other such references include The Specials' first single 'Gangsters' (1979), which starts the same as, and adapts, Prince Buster's 'Al

Capone' (1965); The Jam's 'Start' (1980), which starts with a riff lifted from The Beatles' 'Taxman' (1966); Paul Weller's 'The Changingman' (1995), with the opening of the Electric Light Orchestra's '10538 Overture' (1971); and The Smiths' 'Rusholme Ruffians' (1985), with the riff of Elvis Presley's record '(Marie's the Name) His Latest Flame' (1961).

For these pop-conscious, post-punk *auteurs*, pop music constituted the referential landscape. When sampling arrived in the mid-1980s, technology enabled reference to inhabit the entire musical texture, but already among its critical vanguard, knowing pop was enough to occupy the space of music history or art history.

History, consciousness, and identity

The way in which pop music fitted into the musical or broader artistic and cultural landscape might be described through György Lukács' dichotomy, history and class consciousness – class-based terms crisply expressed in a 1968 record by The Rolling Stones, 'So what can a poor boy do, except join a rock 'n' roll band?' Then there was Jarvis Cocker of Sheffield's Pulp, setting consciousness against the military establishment in 1995: 'we won't use guns, we won't use bombs, we'll use the one thing we've got more of, and that's our minds'. Through pop music, art was becoming democratically available, nothing to do with school or conservatoire or college training: 'ain't bin to no music school', proclaimed a single by punk band The Nosebleeds in 1977. In Raymond Williams' terms, pop music can be seen as an emergent formation displacing a dominant classical music from its position of hegemony, making classical music residual as pop music became dominant;[4] again, you might see pop musicians as Gramscian 'organic intellectuals' – art schools in the UK often acting as prime training ground[5] – aiming through self-expression for some model of a free life. In so doing, they evoked fundamental twentieth-century concerns: tradition and individual talent, mass civilization and minority culture. Such concerns have to do with the way in which individuals, often displaced or under-educated or even in some sense untalented, express themselves alone or in groups in mass culture, with history as a central and defining battleground of consciousness and claim. There is for pop music a huge story, a healing, and great hope, that links the voice of Sam Cooke in 1960, admitting on 'Wonderful World' that he didn't know much about history (understandable considering his segregated

4 Raymond Williams, *Marxism and Literature*, Oxford, 1977, pp. 121–7.
5 See Simon Frith and Howard Horne, *Art into Pop*, London, 1987.

education[6]), to Chuck D of rap band Public Enemy, supplying for his autobiography in 1997 an inspiring, historical and motivational bibliography,[7] or the British band Asian Dub Foundation at the century's close, emerging from and subsequently supporting community education programmes (*Community Music*, 2000).

During the late 1970s and 1980s, however, class interpretation tended to give way to other forms of identity politics. Race and gender were embodied in 1960s civil rights legislation, but the markers of identity kept on moving against the background of a more affirmative action: sexuality (with disco a key genre in the 1970s) and age (with pop always closely tied to youth), as well as religion and nation. So from punk onwards the actual presence of women was a consistent theme, while rap was interpreted in racial terms from the start. A good example of a point of confusion is Patti Smith's track 'Rock 'n' Roll Nigger' from *Easter* (1978), which culminates in her voice at its most steely and inspiring, proclaiming Jimi Hendrix, Jesus Christ, and Jackson Pollock as all 'niggers'. The track adapted an earlier poem of hers called 'neo boy', which declared the word nigger 'no invented for the color', but applicable to 'the artist the mutant the rock n roll mulatto'.[8] And when she shouts out 'nigger' several times in the record, she sounds like the comedian Lenny Bruce, attempting to materialize the word, to flatten its effect or to reclaim it for non-offensive and even utopian usage. However, at a time of increasing awareness of the boundaries of identity, things were not so straightforward, and it appears that even at the time the liberal US press was uneasy.[9] Later, however, the word was reappropriated by several rap performers: the band Niggers with Attitude, Ice Cube's 'The Nigga Yo Love To Hate' (1990), A Tribe Called Quest's 'Sucka N***a' (1993) and Ol' Dirty Bastard's 'N***a Please' (1999). Debates such as this – which can be traced back to Sly and the Family Stone's 1971 admonition, 'Don't Call Me Nigger, Whitey' – sometimes involved state intervention in the form of bans and prohibitions, in which pop music, or at least the words of songs and the attitudes they described, could act as a template for social mores and the boundaries of expression, often played through the grid of identity politics.

The Spice Girls, at the close of the century, positioned themselves firmly as a gender issue, drawing attention to 'girl power' – though feminists were

6 Daniel Wolff, *You Send Me: the Life and Times of Sam Cooke*, London, 1996, pp. 31–2. See also Marcus, *Dustbin*, pp. 21–2.

7 Chuck D with Yusuf Jah, *Fight the Power: Rap, Race and Reality*, Edinburgh, 1997, pp. 267–9.

8 Patti Smith, *Early Work 1970–1979*, New York, 1994, p. 73.

9 See Victor Bockris, *Patti Smith*, London, 1998, pp. 148, 161. See also Lester Bangs, 'The White Noise Supremacists' [1979], in Greil Marcus (ed.), *Psychotic Reactions and Carburetor Dung*, London, 1988, pp. 272–82.

not too certain what to make of them, as suggested by Pratibha Parmar's film *The Righteous Babes* of 1998. And one might question the claim of *Spice Girls Present . . . the Best Girl Power Album . . . Ever!* (a compilation issued in 1997 after their first few international chart-toppers) to present musical images of female empowerment. First, a collection of 'mere' female vocal performances is undermined by a lack of attention to credits for instrumental support, songwriting, and production; the fact that nearly all of the acts are British or American, and certainly English-speaking, again introduces a masked specificity which rather belies gender's powerful and universal claim. Second, the collection seems to aspire towards being *The Best Black Girl Power Album . . . Ever!*: a good half of the selection are soul divas like Aretha Franklin or Tina Turner, disco acts like Gwen Guthrie or the Weather Girls, and more recent rap acts like Salt 'n' Pepa and Mary J. Blige. The Spice Girls may have fiercely wished to foster or project a gender-specific context, and it is true that, unlike an earlier generation of girl groups such as the Shirelles, Supremes, and Crystals, the Spice Girls were certainly and markedly known as individuals (almost like The Who in their day). In an age of managed global commerce, however, the most seemingly innocent presentation or, in this case, a claim to female empowerment as an authentic point of definition, became open to counter-claim as one mark of identity implied another.

An expressive story at the time, and essential in this period, is the impact of what suddenly seemed to appear in the 1980s with the title of world music. A vantage-point is provided by Paul Simon's hit record *Graceland* of 1986, the recording of which involved Simon's visiting apartheid South Africa in a way which (it was claimed) broke the terms of a 1980 United Nations cultural boycott, but which also gave employment and worldwide prominence to many of its black South African musicians. It's well worth listening to *Graceland*, since it presents a fine enactment of the possibilities and the limitations of cross-genre collaboration: the question of whether South African music is ever truly given a voice in *Graceland*, or whether it is heard always on Simon's terms, seemingly forces itself on the most distracted listener. In the track 'Homeless', for instance, there is a moment when Simon himself enters against what became famous vocal effects by the band Ladysmith Black Mambazo: their career took off instantaneously, but it's hard not to hear those effects as pigeon-holing Africa as a fascinating background to Simon's precise English verbiage. There is also very telling filmed evidence (found on the *Classic Album* video series, 1997) of Simon and producer Roy Halee recording performances 'live' at the African townships: nevertheless the recordings were carefully constructed at a studio in New York City. In live performance, too, the musicians accompanying Simon did just that, supplying interestingly diverse frames to the singer in the middle.

On the other hand, the musicians themselves stick doggedly and passionately in Simon's defence.

An instructive comparison can be, and has been, made with David Byrne, who employs Cuban musicians on what sounds to me (and to Tony Mitchell[10]) more like equal terms on his album *Rei Momo* (1989): through the label Luaka Bop, Byrne was also actively promoting compilations of this and other world musics. Alongside fixities of identity, flexibilities and masquerades also became possible. The country singer Garth Brooks issued several albums, produced in Nashville by Allen Reynolds during the decade after 1989, sales of which reached over a hundred million, and songs like 'The Dance' and 'Friends in Low Places' became genre standards. Nevertheless, in 1999 he invented an alter ego, Chris Gaines, carefully presenting Gaines' imaginary career as a 'greatest hits' collection which ended with a promise of a movie soundtrack.

Technology and authenticity

So far I have read the history of pop against a critical and political background; another way, closer to what sociologists call the 'production of culture' approach, is to see punk as simply one more embodiment of what had been *technologically* stable conditions in popular music, going back to the 1950s and the development of electric amplification and multitrack recording, with albums being issued in various 'analogue' formats (vinyl records and cassette tape), heard on radio and bought in record shops. One reason why the technological argument carries such force towards 2000 is that massive change really did occur during the 1980s. These revolved around one central change: from analogue to digital forms of information storage. This affected instruments, formats, and even the modes of dissemination that structure the music industry. Among the main developments four might be singled out. First is the gradual shift from 'playable' to 'programmable' technology: electric guitars and keyboards gave way to synthesizers and samplers, and drums to drum machines, leading to pop's karaoke moment. This happened alongside changes from analogue to digital production and reception. Some key pieces of technology were the Roland TR-808 drum machine (1980), Yamaha DX-7 keyboard (1983), and Akai S-1100 sampler (1986). A second development was that of video as an economical medium related to, but separate from, cinema and cinematic convention: MTV (Music Television) went on air in 1981. A third was the primacy, from 1979, of CD as reproductive format, which made possible a massive remarketing of already-available repertory; at the same time, through the practice of

10 Tony Mitchell, *Popular Music and Local Identity: Rock, Pop and Rap in Europe and Oceania*, Leicester, 1996, pp. 80–4.

DJs, vinyl acquired a different form of credibility (the Technics 1200 MK2 deck became available in 1980). The final development was the ability to download musical information from the Internet, which began to question even the very basis in copyright of the recording industry: MP3 download technology was widely available by 1999.

The consequences of these changes cannot be overestimated. By way of example, much of the backing instrumental sound of 'Relax' and 'Two Tribes' (1983–4), by the group Frankie Goes to Hollywood, was programmed by producer Trevor Horn and engineer Steve Lipson; on the hit 'Ride on Time' by Black Box (1989), even the vocals were sampled (from Loleatta Holloway's 'Love Sensation' of 1980). Again, in 'Sweet Dreams', a 1983 single by The Eurythmics, Annie Lennox's soulful vocal sounds like she wants to be rescued from a prison depicted by electronic sound. To the extent that such technology enabled artists to speak directly to listeners through the recording, the decision even to be in a group became optional; the band might serve a function only in relation to live performance, or to some possibly romantic idea of songwriting, or simply growing up with a bunch of mates. Bands like Blur or the Manic Street Preachers had elements of all of these, while other groups like The Fall became more like loose collectives around a central figure. In the alliance of medium and expression which is a fundamental theme of art history, pop records often simply demonstrated the potential of the new technology: the quickly repeated vocal stutters of records like Paul Hardcastle's '19' (1985) or Steve 'Silk' Hurley's 'Jack Your Body' (1987) exploited digital delay, while in records such as those of The Pixies (1987–91), most of which were produced by Gil Norton, Nirvana's *Nevermind* (1991), produced by Butch Vig, or the Wedding Present's *Seamonsters* (1991), produced by Steve Albini, the quiet bits seemed to get very quiet and the loud bits very loud.

If technology had rendered authenticity to some extent provisional or optional, then the period around 1985 represented a certain crisis for the earlier model of performer presence which had been established – and also romanticized – by the role of singer-songwriter. The singer-songwriter had emerged from a folk- or country-based model, but was given a particularly modern and literary energy in the late 1960s by Bob Dylan and Leonard Cohen. Singer-songwriters abounded: Joni Mitchell, James Taylor, Jackson Browne, Loudon Wainwright III, Bruce Springsteen, John Prine, David Bowie, Elvis Costello. In other cases, among them Carole King, Paul Simon, and Randy Newman, songwriters who belonged to an earlier model of 'industrial' songwriting, pitching songs for other singers or groups, were reinvented as singer-songwriters. Often too the central songwriters of bands were eventually recast as singer-songwriters: Lennon and McCartney, Jagger and Richards, Lou Reed and John

Cale, Stephen Stills and Neil Young, Van Morrison, Pete Townshend, Ray Davies, Don Henley, Bryan Ferry, Aimee Mann.

Bob Dylan remained the emblematic figure, though by 1985, following a series of records on religious themes, there appeared to be something of a crisis of confidence at Columbia Records; he was granted a major retrospective, called *Biograph*, at the same time that his new album, *Empire Burlesque*, was sent out to hit producer Arthur Baker. For an interview that year to accompany the retrospective, Dylan looked back to the band eventually captured on *Street Legal* (1978), comparing its saxophonist (Steve Douglas) with that of Bruce Springsteen's E Street Band (Clarence Clemons):

> I saw one review which accused me of going Vegas and copying Bruce Springsteen because I was using Steve Douglas . . . the saxophone thing was almost slanderous . . . I mean I don't copy guys that are under 50 years old and though I wasn't familiar with Bruce's work, his saxophone player couldn't be spoken of in the same breath as Steve Douglas who'd played with Duane Eddy and on literally all of Phil Spector's records . . . I mean no offence to Clarence or anything but he's not in the same category.[11]

This is a curious comment, in that sax solos aren't really what pop songs are there for, and from what I can tell *both* Steve Douglas, on great, kitschy Spector records like 'Da Doo Ron Ron' (1963), *and* Clarence Clemons, on hunky, sweaty records like 'Born to Run' (1975), just tooted away for a short while in between verses; the pop song hardly allowed room for an Ornette Coleman or Eric Dolphy. If anything, Spector's production de-saxed the sax much as it down-voiced the voices, rendering both as mere elements in the Wall of Sound's sonic assault, while Clemons was for many years properly one of the Springsteen band, a relatively rare position for a sax player. In contrast to his own persona in the mid-1960s or to the mercurial Neil Young in the early 1990s, Dylan, it would seem from this, began to see time itself – age, precedence, past achievement – as sufficient critical purchase over and above the immediacy of pop music here and now.

In the 1990s Dylan returned to his songwriting roots through albums of cover versions, some of which (*Good as I Been to You* and *World Gone Wrong*, 1992–3) were taken from Harry Smith's *Anthology of American Folk Music*. Here history became layered, fold on fold: recordings from the late 1920s, issued by Smith in 1952 (and reissued in 1997), documented songs and performance styles which now seem timeless, or at least multiply timed. Dylan's covers were consistent with a general retreat from technology into the comforts of 'real'

11 Bob Dylan, *Biograph* (1985), booklet, p. 25.

sounds, albeit with just enough electricity not to hinder capital's ability to reach mass audiences. Nothing illustrates this better than *Unplugged*, a series of concerts in which stars would perform their songs acoustically – for television! Springsteen himself simply put a slash through the 'un' of 'unplugged' for his 1992 release and carried on as usual – paradoxically since, on tours coinciding with *The Ghost of Tom Joad* (1995), he started asking audiences for silence while he performed. But there did seem to be a return to acoustic instruments: on the fringe independent scene in Britain, first albums by PJ Harvey (*Dry*, 1992), Tindersticks (1993), and Gorky's Zygotic Mynci (*Patio*, 1991–3) appeared to foreground the grain of an instrument, often strings, with music which sometimes recalled Captain Beefheart and the Magic Band's *Trout Mask Replica* (1970). Something similar informed 'alt-country' in the US, while certain markers – gospel (Madonna), Ireland (The Corrs), Asian percussion (Massive Attack) – became designer traces of the true and the real, almost as a counterpoint to the way that people's lives became more and more played through the screens of television and computers.

Perhaps a better or more genuine signal of the ageing of authenticity than the appearance of stars on *Unplugged* was the number of tribute albums which appeared: from 1987 a British record label called Imaginary released a whole series of tributes, often consisting of covers by alternative or independent acts. The tribute performance or album sometimes threw light on the present in an unexpected way: one for Leonard Cohen, *I'm Your Fan* (1991), illustrated a renegotiation of songwriting by bands like The Pixies or REM, while a tribute to The Carpenters, called *If I Were a Carpenter* (1994), showed with some fondness that scuzzy-sounding bands like American Music Club or Sonic Youth were actually imbued with the melodiousness of the 1970s duo. Then there were compilations, many of which seemingly merged authenticity with identity in a way unheard of until the later 1990s, including *Respect: a Century of Women in Music*, *Lesbian Favourites*, *Stand Up and Be Counted: Soul, Funk and Jazz from a Revolutionary Era*, *Sisters of Swing*, *Boyz of Swing*, *Independence Day: the Best New Women in Country*. Often they were tied to charity or activist concerns, with the 'Red, Hot' series raising AIDS awareness and contributing funds being perhaps the most sustained example and taking a variety of genres under its wing: *[Red Hot and] Blue* (the original of 1990, covering Cole Porter), *Country*, *Rio* (Brazilian), and *Cool* (jazz meets rap), as well as *No Alternative* (indie), *Offbeat* ('a sound trip'), and others. Other charity records were for ever more obscure causes: *Return of the Grievous Angel: a Tribute to Gram Parsons* was for Vietnam Veterans of America Foundation's 'Campaign for a Landmine Free World', and *Freedom of Choice: Yesterday's New Wave Hits as Performed by Today's Stars* for Planned

Parenthood Federation of America Inc., while *Hen Wlad fy Nhadau* – a cover of the seminal 1978 Welsh-language album by Geraint Jarman a'r Cynganeddwyr – was 'in support of a campaign for a Property Act to ensure that local people in Wales have control over their own communities and stop the needless tourist and capitalist developments'. While the link between the records and the cause was sometimes less than clear, response to Tori Amos's moving solo 'Me and a Gun' (1992) led to the setting up in the US of a Rape, Abuse, and Incest National Network. Compilations eventually began to be issued to reflect lifestyles and moods, these often marketing 'classical' music as a form of pop music. A charitable or directly political element to records has arguably outlasted the charity gig, though the latter seemed at one time all-engulfing, notably with Band Aid and Live Aid of 1984 and 1985.

Many of the conflicts around identity and technology were wrapped together in music video, a medium both separate from and parasitic upon cinematic convention. The supply of visual correspondence to music had precedence in the album cover, although this applied to music across genre divides. Album covers helped define the area in which pop art and pop music most closely corresponded: the 'feel' of *The Who Sell Out*, *Sticky Fingers*, or *Tales from Topographic Oceans* mattered, and constituted an aspect which CD, valiantly, and cassette, hopelessly, struggled to recapture. Music video was more determinedly an industrial pop form, with a firm divide between pop and opera on the one hand, and instrumental forms – classical, contemporary, and jazz – on the other. In fact, the relationship between the video for a record and the words of its song is often and reductively the key element available to criticism. Technological experimentation with the medium was a feature, and while examples such as the videos directed by Chris Cunningham in the late 1990s for Aphex Twin or Björk demonstrated to a remarkable extent the aesthetic potential of this most frankly industrial of formats, it was debatable whether such experimentation was the purpose of MTV as a broadcasting medium. Perhaps it was with the 'greatest hits' compilations of Madonna (the *Immaculate Collection* of 1990) or Michael Jackson (*History*, 1995) that the record collector finally had to face the idea that the video compilation might well represent the tracks in a more authentic state than their audio equivalents.

Sound and words

If the 1980s saw the stars of several 1960s heroes come down to earth, then the decade can be seen as the rise of Brian Eno, the triumph less of song as a realist or romantic statement and more of music as sound quality. Leaving Roxy Music in 1973, Eno began as early as 1975 to develop ambient sound.

From 1977 onwards he acted as studio catalyst and carrier of sound quality with, among many others, David Bowie (1977–9, and again in 1995), Talking Heads (1978–80), U2 (co-produced with Daniel Lanois and with spectacular success from 1984 onwards), and James (1993–4). Eno carries on the lineage of Phil Spector, Brian Wilson, and John Cale in emphasizing the quality of sound *on a record* rather than anything specifically belonging to a song. In this passage Eno links his practice and aesthetic of recording to Spector, who produced 'Be My Baby' for The Ronettes in 1963:

> I hate the way classical music is mixed, I think it's pathetic and completely antediluvian and quite unintelligent as well because it assumes that fidelity is important in making records. Fidelity is not an issue! What's important is making an experience that makes sense in a living room: if you're making a record, that's what you're doing. You're not giving someone a concert, you're giving them a record. There's no sense at all in which 'Be My Baby', for example, ever existed outside of the recording studio. There probably never was a performance of it outside of the studio, as far as I know. Coming up with the idea of creating a piece where drums and pianos occupy 98% of the, sort of, sonic spectrum, and the voice occupies about 2% of it, like this little bee, this sliver of glass in the middle of this great picture, it's brilliant.[12]

Since Eno's sound-worlds tended to have particular visual rather than verbal qualities and associations, these sounds were ripe for video and for TV or cinema adaptation – a tendency towards the bringing together of sound and vision which deepened during the period, almost as an aural correspondence to the synergies of media corporations. Records like Talking Heads' 'Houses in Motion'(1980), U2's 'Within You Without You' (1987), and especially U2's remarkable *Achtung Baby* of 1992 arguably set the agenda for sound quality at the time. And as if all this were not enough, in 1981 Eno and David Byrne compiled the album *My Life in the Bush of Ghosts*, prefiguring many of the issues of cultural reading which were to arise with sampling.

Good examples of the effect of a 'sound-centred' shift were found in two career trajectories of the time, those of Tom Waits and Suzanne Vega. Vega in particular is archetypal, starting with two albums of classic singer-songwriter material against a production style essentially designed to couch the songs in suitably soft surroundings. 'Luka' (from *Solitude Standing* of 1987) is the story of an abused woman living in an apartment above the songwriter: what's bad about the situation is in the words and the narrative, which is rendered in a non-expressive manner. In 1990 British DJs called DNA took the track 'Tom's Diner', the framing track of *Solitude Standing*, and remixed it as a dance

12 BBC Radio 1, *The Story of Pop*, December 1994.

track. Rather than wrangle over ownership, Vega threw herself into the idea of reinvention, even overseeing a compilation of several interesting versions of 'Tom's Diner' (1991). When she returned to the studio for *99.9 °F* (1992) she seemed to have taken the idea of sound quality to heart, with a stripped-out, industrial sound that challenged rather than complemented her vocal style. A comment by Eric Sadler of Public Enemy concerning the production process in rap – 'We stripped it apart like a car and put it back together totally again'[13] – applies equally to these recordings, in which the voice is one protagonist among many found sounds.

Not entirely detached from the shift towards sound quality is a change in status of the words themselves in the construction of songs, a development which can be dated back at least to Patti Smith's *Horses* of 1975. Whereas such 1960s bands as The Beatles, Rolling Stones, Beach Boys, Searchers, and Byrds had collectively controlled both words and music, by the early 1980s there was often a division of labour by which one member of the group alone (usually the singer) supplied the words. In one sense this was a return to the earlier Tin Pan Alley model where, for example, Burt Bacharach had supplied the music and Hal David the words. But where their whole aim had been to come together in the single lyric – cadences coinciding with rhymes, syllables with rhythms – it was now possible for music and words to remain more distant, as though the words were simply brought to music, and their coincidence a matter of chance rather than careful design. A good example, impossible for the earlier model of divided labour, is 'Girlfriend in a Coma' (1987) by The Smiths: over a bouncy band accompaniment Morrissey tells, separately as it were, a hideous scenario in which a girlfriend is unconscious but he finds it difficult seriously to respond. Michael Stipe of REM is a fine case of a writer in whose work 'anti-lyric' has rediscovered lyric on its own more flatly prosaic terms: good examples are heard throughout *Automatic for the People* (1992). For all their grimy urban detail, punks were surprisingly wedded to lyrical principles of euphonious line endings: songs like The Sex Pistols' 'Holidays in the Sun' (1977) or The Clash's 'White Man in Hammersmith Palais' (1978) rhyme throughout. With anti-lyric the governing approach, pop songs became filled with realist detail: 'microwave ovens' in the Dire Straits hit 'Money for Nothing' (1985) is a good example of a precise, true-to-life, contemporary reference, and the chorus ends with a hard non-rhyme: 'colour TVs'. The shift in sound and in the status of words showed how pop song continued to develop as a form during this period: nobody, however, could have predicted the sheer amount of verbiage which was to arise with the matter of the next section.

13 Tricia Rose, *Black Noise: Rap Music and Black Culture in Contemporary America*, Hanover, 1994, p. 80.

Rap

One of the great peculiarities of pop music throughout the period, and something that might not be so prevalent in the history of the novel or cinema, is that racial distinction remains a constant factor. This section concerns the fate of black music and has again to be taken back to the 1950s and 1960s to make sense. 'British Invasion' bands such as the Rolling Stones defined an aesthetic of self-expression through founding moments in cover versions, often of black originals. In some cases, a lot of money followed a commitment to continuing an established lyrical mode, as publishing copyright accrued more to songwriter than to performer: in one of many such cases, the songwriters of The Smiths, Morrissey and Johnny Marr, were taken to court over royalties by other members of the band soon after their split in 1987. This situation can arguably be followed back to the origins of rock and roll, with the bringing together in 1954 of white country and black rhythm and blues (R & B) by Elvis Presley and his producer Sam Phillips. Pop song as an art form was built on a racial premise which turned out not only to favour but even to reinforce, through copyright, a certain model of white supremacy. The consistent point about Presley's capping of all three US charts (pop, R & B, and country), starting in 1956 with 'Don't Be Cruel' backed with 'Hound Dog', is that the traffic went one way: it was possible for a white singer to top the r. & b. chart but not so easy for a black singer to inhabit country. This makes Ray Charles' series of country recordings tremendously important, notably the two volumes of *Modern Sounds in Country and Western Music* (1962), which reached numbers 1 and 2 in the US pop album chart.[14]

The British Invasion, in particular the American breakthrough of The Beatles in 1964, eclipsed the hitherto successful 'sweet' soul of The Drifters, The Coasters, and The Shirelles. Motown in particular was a commercially geared response, but the defining moment for what follows in black music is James Brown's recording of 'Papa's Got a Brand New Bag' in 1966, a dramatic reclamation of the performative space of black music. If by 'Cold Sweat' of 1967 Brown's records don't sound much like The Beach Boys or The Byrds, they also don't sound much like Motown hits or the particular Southern blend found in Aretha Franklin and Otis Redding, or even like earlier James Brown hits such as 'Please Please Please' (1956) or 'It's a Man's Man's Man's World' (1966). Funk, really, just sounded *new*. Around a first beat in the bar which Brown virtually deified as 'the one', a space opened which was assuredly not that of the lyric song, but a rhythmic gap which Brown's master band, in its varying personnel, would fill. Brown set the agenda for black music to follow,

14 See also the box set, *From Where I Stand: the Black Experience in Country Music* (1998).

with most of the surviving soul stars having to respond to funk in one way or another.

If soul to funk was something of a giant leap, then only relatively small steps were needed to take black music from funk in the late 1960s to hiphop in the early 1980s. However, at a crucial period, around disco's heyday in 1975, the key developments were not *on* record at all, but rather depended on things people did *with* records, that is to say, on the role of the disc jockey. The well-documented, if not recorded, DJ Kool Herc founded many of the practices which became standard: 'scratching' the record as though it were a percussion instrument, and carefully selecting the 'breakbeat' – a section of a funk record, usually in the middle, when voice and front-line instrumentation would drop out, leaving the rhythm section alone. By the time the first recorded hiphop appeared, Tanya Winley's 'Vicious Rap' (1980, but thought to date from 1978) and Sugarhill Gang's 'Rapper's Delight' (1979), there was still some confusion between live club performance (Sugarhill Gang used a live band, even though they may have been playing the music of a current disco hit) and DJ alone (Herc, Grandmaster Flash, and Afrika Bambaataa are regarded as the founding fathers). The mistrust which exists between 'live' musicians, albeit in rock music dependent entirely on electronic amplification, and the DJ – the suspicion, in other words, of the idea that selecting from pre-existing music is or at least generates a form of music – continues to this day. Rock guitarist Lemmy gave this reason for wanting to hit DJ Judge Jules in 2000: 'He kept going on and on like he was some kind of musician when all he does is play records.'[15]

The invention of the digital sampler infinitely expanded the range of selection, and made live breakbeat mixing simply an option for live performance. Sampling is a nerve-point of, on the one hand, the rhetoric and reality of technology as liberation and, on the other hand, a particular kind of authenticating practice whereby reference is explained as exemplar of identity. You *want* to say (as does Ben Thompson, echoing Kodwo Eshun) that 'in this brave new world of digital possibility, traditional ideas of authenticity are turned on their heads . . . and the way is paved for a heroic unification of the pulse of machinery and the power of human thought'.[16] Not so easy: the samples that figured the most, crucially, were precisely those of the funk moment, of James Brown's turning-back on sweet soul, of 'the one'. The significance of this tendency is

15 *New Musical Express*, 13 May 2000, p. 8.

16 Ben Thompson, *Seven Years of Plenty: A Handbook of Irrefutable Pop Greatness 1991–1998*, London, 1998, p. 39. See also Kodwo Eshun, *More Brilliant than the Sun: Adventures in Sonic Fiction*, London, 1998, pp. 187–93, and Jason Toynbee, *Making Popular Music: Musicians, Creativity and Institutions*, London, 2000.

hard to overestimate, and reflects a greater awareness of the politics of racial identity, by which the choice of breakbeat or sample became what Tricia Rose calls 'a means of archival research, a process of musical and cultural archaeology':[17] 'Rebel without a Pause', on Public Enemy's *It Takes a Nation of Millions to Hold us Back* (1988), opens with a direct sampled reference to the saxophone squeal of 'The Grunt' (1970), performed by James Brown's backing band The J.B.s. References like these give copyright credit to James Brown (important in that the chances of a performance of his like 'Cold Sweat' ever being covered were extremely limited); legal shifts concerning copyright declaration can be observed by comparing the sleeves of De La Soul's *Three Feet High and Rising* of 1989 and their next record, *De La Soul is Dead* of 1991: the latter has its major samples listed. In fact, for Public Enemy, the list of samples became a matter of cultural pride, the sleeve listing various genealogies alongside guides to street education.

What became of rap is open to debate. In one version, hiphop itself, in a fairly pure form, becomes an international phenomenon: France in particular has a burgeoning hiphop scene, captured on compilations called *Le Flow* (1998 and 2000). Even in its earliest recorded period, there was a pull between the 'rapper's delight' in verbal sound and syllable, and rap as statement or social comment, with Grandmaster Flash's 'The Message' (1982) setting the agenda. US hiphop went through a number of subgenre shifts: A Tribe Called Quest were typical of a somewhat softer rap style, with De La Soul, Queen Latifah, and Arrested Development balanced against the harder and more realist style of Run DMC and Public Enemy, allied in some respects with heavy metal. That in turn led to West Coast hiphop and gangsta rap of the early 1990s: Ice T, NWA, Ice Cube, Tupac Shakur, and the Notorious BIG. Following the death of the latter two rappers, young and caught in gangland wars, rap reached a calmer rapprochement, less male-dominated and with more soulful vocals, in the Fugees, Lauryn Hill, and Mary J. Blige. In another version, associated more with Europe, hiphop becomes one rap option among many, set largely in functional dance contexts and centred crucially on the DJ. From around 1986, these options began to progress at a remarkable rate of generic change: house, acid house, techno, ambient, jungle or drum and bass, UK garage. In these various forms the quality of sound mattered far more than MC statement, and a rapid and relentless drive to innovation and adaptation to technology lent it the air of modernist commitment.[18]

17 Rose, *Black Noise*, p. 79.
18 Ulf Poschardt, *DJ Culture* (tr. Shaun Whiteside), London, 1995.

Canon and movement, remix and cover

We left Bob Dylan in the 1990s, recording cover versions. In fact, what he did most of the time towards 2000 was tour constantly – the sleeve note to *World Gone Wrong* ends with a small satire on the relentlessness of these tours and the way they were given lavish titles for marketing purposes – and a big part of what it is to be a devotee of Dylan or any performer or band is in measuring live performance to the recorded version carried in the head: does it remain close to the original or does it change? Nothing illustrates this better than Dylan's 'Tangled Up in Blue', which exists in three commercially available versions (the 'official bootleg', 1974 but issued in 1991, *Blood on the Tracks*, 1975, and *Real Live*, 1994), as well as dozens of unofficial bootlegs and tapes which circulate among fans. Some, like the official bootleg, are close to the famous 1975 record; others are more remote, like one from July 1999 at Jones Beach Amphitheatre, and the difference between a faithful rendition of an original and its creative appropriation is a theme I want to explore towards the end of this chapter. In some ways it mirrors the state of technological play: the reissue programmes fostered by the change in format to the CD has resulted in a sense of canon in pop music – with fixed masterpieces and representative generic exemplars – while the availability of music on the Internet appears to contradict this, making everything massively available in rapidly recorded shows and fluid versions.

Remix: Massive Attack

With the arrival of CD, the longer time length available for high-quality sound resulted in the reissue of many 'classic' records with demo versions and studio out-takes drawing attention to the amount of construction which went into the final decision over a particular mix. A famous case was the Velvet Underground's 1969 album *Velvet Underground*, which is known in two versions: one mixed by Val Valentin which took its bearings from the pop sound of the day, and one mixed by Lou Reed himself which was dubbed the 'closet mix' because of its seemingly more claustrophobic sound quality. The emotion involved in decisions about mixing is well observed in Kevin Rowland's sleeve-note to the reissued 'Dance Stance' of 1979 (on the remixed Dexy's Midnight Runners compilation *It Was Like This*, 1996): 'the remix sounds like the original first single should have sounded like. We always hated the original mix of this, it was done without our knowledge and we were railroaded into releasing it.'

The first practice consistently to offer single tracks in multiple mixes appears to have been the dub sides of record issues in reggae, under innovative producers like Lee Perry and Prince Far I. Dub versions often consist of the removal of a vocal track and the addition of reverberation and studio effects: their instantaneous nature deconstructs the original both technically and aesthetically. Good examples are found in the box set of Lee Perry's music from the late 1970s, *Arkology* (1997). It includes five versions of Junior Murvin's 'Police and Thieves' of 1976, all credited to different authors: the 'original' (co-written by Murvin and Perry); a song called 'Bad Weed'; a version by Glen DaCosta called 'Magic Touch', which substitutes a sax solo for the vocal line; another by Jah Lion, called 'Soldier and Police War', which preserves the original in the background but adds another vocal on top (performed by Bongo Herman); and a final dub ('Grumblin' Dub') which fragments the original. An analogy sometimes made is that dubs present an X-ray of the original, and it is the final version of 'Police and Thieves' that sounds the most radical and suggests the more experimental edge of remixing.

During the 1980s alternative mixes continued to appear, often filling the twelve-inch vinyl singles produced for DJs and presenting different mixes for different functions; by the 1990s remixing was very much a central DJ technique. Remixing can be approached in two ways: from the point of view of the song (its availability or resistance to being remixed), and from that of the DJ – the question of whether s/he attempts to build a consistent remixing sound or approach, or simply responds to the track in question according to the particular demands of the song. This is not so far from decisions in cover versions, which can also be reduced to *rendition*, a faithful performance of the original not so far from classical performance, as against *appropriation*, a filtering of the original through the personality of the performer.

Taken together, the reissued set *Massive Attack: Singles 90/98* (1998) and the remix of Massive Attack's second album *Protection* (1994), issued a year later as *No Protection* by Massive Attack v. Mad Professor, offer a superb vantage-point for observing the development of remixing during the 1990s. Massive Attack was less a band than a collective of three musicians based in Bristol, and augmented on record by performers and producers, including vocalists such as Shara Nelson, Horace Andy, Tricky, Tracey Thorn, and Liz Fraser; the 'Bristol Sound' that emerged from Massive Attack was influential, leading to records by Portishead (*Dummy*, 1994), Tricky himself (*Maxinquaye*, 1995), and eventually via DJ Roni Size (Reprazent and Breakbeat Era) to drum and bass. The remixes of 'Karmacoma' from *Protection* demonstrate clearly what can be done with a recording that offers plenty of space for adaptation. 'Karmacoma' is far less a song to sing at the piano than a particular musical space created by the sound quality, words, and instrumentation. The remixes bring out different things. Portishead's remix almost defines or summarizes the sound that Portishead had developed in *Dummy*: cinematic sound effects and a fuzzy, Hendrix type of guitar solo. This is a great example of remix as appropriation, the original wrung through the remixer's aesthetic. If Portishead bring out a threatening underside to the track, Ben Young's 'Napoli Trip' brings out the otherness of some of the track's samples, returning Massive's eastern references to the east, and adding a new vocal from Almamegretta (something similar happens with State of Bengal's mix of 'Inertia Creeps'). By contrast, James Lavelle's remix for U.N.K.L.E. sounds more like a standard DJ production, with a confusion of samples and scratches and Tricky's vocal given greater prominence.

Remixes also offer a way of considering comparisons of the one DJ. In addition to remixing the entire second album (with the exception of one track 'Eurochild', and the live cover version of The Doors' 'Light My Fire'), Mad Professor contributes remixes of tracks from the third album, *Mezzanine* (1998), to the singles box set. As remixer, he brings a consistency of dub principles: his superb remix of 'Protection' from the second album is a good example, retitled 'Radiation for the Nation'. He emphasizes certain aspects of the original: an 'ordinary' bass line at the opening becomes a threatening-sounding fuzzy bass sound, while a percussive, triangle sound halfway through is magnified to a level almost bigger than the voice. Again, the effect is much scarier, and again less a song and more a sonic landscape. His own dense and boomy 'Karmacoma', by contrast, makes more reference to standard dub practice. By the late 1990s, remix styles had become so identifiable, notably in the case of Norman Cook (also known as Fatboy Slim), that the suspicion arose of a return to star status, not helped by the fact that the DJs were almost invariably men. This seemed to deflect from the readily available, instantaneous, and reactive nature of remix practice.

Cover: 'Eleanor Rigby'

Cover versions are useful in that they afford a central analytical standpoint, the song, from which to observe change in performance and recording, and very often changes in identity, locality, and genre too. A good example of the process in action is The Beatles' song 'Eleanor Rigby', which appeared originally on *Revolver* in 1966. Reissues during the 1990s of demos and out-takes of well-known albums served as a reminder of the amount of pre-production work which went into the most seemingly innocuous track: The Beach Boys' *Pet Sounds* of 1966, which often topped critics' lists, was reissued thirty years later across four CDs. Of 'Eleanor Rigby', the second such *Anthology* (1996) of Beatles reissues presented the recording overseen by producer George Martin of a double string quartet, over which McCartney sang his song; the track itself was suggestive of a change in the practice encountered earlier, since the other three Beatles are entirely absent. But more importantly, that particular string sound on a record is always a suggestion, it seems to me, of class, since the ability to play string instruments in a recognizably classical fashion implies a certain and quite extensive mode of tuition. The final recording, with McCartney's vocal intact, is a very British sound: it is the sound not only of class but also of class *distinction*. Listening in terms of critique, here is the sound of a working-class Liverpudlian voice superimposed upon an educated middle-class instrumental support; understood in these terms, when you think of how unlikely it would have been for the members of The Beatles to have been able to play string instruments and what it meant for them now to call the economic shots, what we hear is a very moving sound.

Just over three years later the 'Queen of Soul', Aretha Franklin, recorded 'Eleanor Rigby'. The sound of a white British man is replaced by a black American woman, and, rather suddenly, the appropriation invites us to think comparatively about their cultural condition. Some of the changes are unexpected: one thing which Aretha Franklin invariably does is to alter the religious connotation of what she sings, so that in this case McCartney's Liverpool Catholic is transmuted into Franklin's Baptist, and Father MacKenzie seems to undergo a kind of Lutheran conversion in mid-Atlantic. But within a year, possibly as a response to pressure from the black community following the assassination in 1968 of Martin Luther King, the Muscle Shoals house band – who played on Franklin's record, and most of whose members were white – were dismissed and replaced by musicians most of whom were black: *their* 'Eleanor Rigby' can be heard on a live album from 1971. Again, the musical content of the Franklin cover is almost negligible, but its cultural condition is extremely suggestive, because of the way it invites us to hear the sound of race, class, gender, religion. Aretha Franklin was at this time a kind of practical critical musicologist, reclaiming songs from white men trying to imitate gospel: between 1969 and 1970 she released superb covers of McCartney's 'Let It Be', Paul Simon's 'Bridge Over Troubled Water', and Elton John and Bernie Taupin's 'Border Song (Holy Moses)'.

Remixes and cover versions are useful positions from which to think critically about music. They hold certain things – the music, the score, the notes – consistent, but allow difference and change in all the markers of identity and subjectivity. One becomes aware also of the boundaries within which such change can occur: notice how Aretha Franklin is immediately tempted to see herself as the protagonist in the song ('I'm Eleanor Rigby'), and the fixed or given difference between what it is for a black woman to 'pick up the rice in a church' and for a white man to observe a woman so doing. She also alters the phrase-structure of the music, returning the five-bar phrases of the Beatles' original verses to groups of four bars, and so making the phrasing swing in a more symmetrical and standardized way:[19] this makes the cover seem like an original, and the original like a cleverly constructed cover. To use a cliché, what matters is not so much the two tracks as the space between them – the space of my choosing these tracks for discussion, my sharing it with you, our reflecting upon it, our using it as a platform from which to understand the workings of political power at a given time.

Having considered carefully the space between The Beatles' and Aretha Franklin's versions of 'Eleanor Rigby', it's open to anyone to revisit the song: why don't you do your own version? And this kind of analysis applies as well to references as to covers. A track by Sinéad O'Connor called 'Famine' (from the album *Universal Mother* of 1994) bulges with sample and reference, including the Irish politician Jack Lynch, the musical *Fiddler on the Roof*, and the Thelonius Monk standard, 'Straight No Chaser'; then, without great fuss or announcement, O'Connor integrates the chorus of 'Eleanor Rigby' – 'All the lonely people' – now with a dance-based sound and in a highly politicized setting which arguably returns the song to its Catholic Irish roots. It's another illustration of songs functioning not just as money-generating sources of copyright, but as traces of individuality in an endless and fluid negotiation, shifting across space and time.

Conclusion: history revisited

During the 1990s a new wave of groups appeared in the UK, lumped together as Britpop: Oasis, Blur, Suede, Elastica, Pulp. Slightly outside this group were other bands which arose from a tradition of independently produced pop music: Manic Street Preachers, Radiohead, PJ Harvey. One of the big themes of Britpop was the evocation of the 1960s – 'I wish it was the 60s', sang Radiohead's Thom Yorke on 'The Bends' (1995), wistfully but agonizingly – and this evocation often consisted (as we saw earlier with David Bowie) of trying to get close to the sources of 1960s pop music. Oasis covered and often referred to The Beatles, Blur's Damon Albarn appeared on TV alongside his hero Ray Davies of The Kinks to sing 'Waterloo Sunset', Suede's Brett Anderson was photographed alongside David Bowie for an *NME* cover, and Elastica made clear reference to songs by punk groups The Stranglers and The Wire, featuring Mark E. Smith of The Fall on a later release. But although they were evoking pop up to and including punk, it was noticeable how much it seemed like the practice of

19 My thanks to Matthew Baber for pointing this out.

punk and after. There was something touching in the way that pop music had become a vast bank of memory and information which the young generation had to sift through. But such self-invention and declared allegiance could be inspiring too, and inclusive of earlier generations in a way that the 1960s had refused.

Towards 2000 pop music developed in many remarkable directions, with diversity and inclusiveness. Pop music was, arguably, the supreme art form of the late twentieth century, albeit 'art' in its broadest, most generous, and utopian sense, while so many of the other art forms simply continued an earlier modernist commitment to the inner workings of art-form materiality. A closing scene: Courtney Love and the band Hole perform at the Glastonbury Festival in 1999, broadcast on television, ending with a superb run through the single and title track of their album issued that year, *Celebrity Skin*. The song is a scowling but energetic comment on Hollywood. Courtney Love herself, singing and playing guitar, is totally in charge, her guitar slung around – surely an inspiring role model for people everywhere but especially, one would think, for women, girls. The song and performance end noisily with lots of feedback; it looks as though the set is over, but Love herself is still at the microphone and clearly still enunciating something. Eventually the crowd quietens, and you can just hear what she's singing: fragments of the song 'She's Lost Control' from the debut album *Unknown Pleasures* of 1979 by the Manchester punk band Joy Division, followed by a line from Echo and the Bunnymen's 'Rescue' of 1980.[20] In that set and on that afternoon pop music was energy, excitement, immediacy, engagement; pop music was both community and mass communication; pop music was art and social comment; pop music was diversity and the progress of women; but pop music, at the century's close, was memory, mortality, recollection, history.

Bibliography

Bangs, Lester. *Psychotic Reactions and Carburetor Dung* (ed. Greil Marcus), London, 1988.
Bockris, Victor. *Patti Smith*, London, 1998.
Chuck D. [Ridenhour, Carlton] with Yusuf Jah. *Fight the Power: Rap, Race and Reality*, Edinburgh, 1997.
Clarke, Donald. *The Rise and Fall of Popular Music*, Harmondsworth, 1995.
DeCurtis, Anthony, and James Henke, with Holly George-Warren (eds.). *The Rolling Stone Illustrated History of Rock and Roll*, London, 1992.
Eddy, Chuck. *The Accidental Evolution of Rock 'n' Roll: a Misguided Tour through Popular Music*, New York, 1997.
Eshun, Kodwo. *More Brilliant than the Sun: Adventures in Sonic Fiction*, London, 1998.

20 My thanks to Louise Morgan and the Official Hole Website for the reference to 'Rescue'.

Frith, Simon and Horne, Howard. *Art into Pop*, London, 1987.
Marcus, Greil. *The Dustbin of History*, Cambridge, MA, 1996.
Mitchell, Tony. *Popular Music and Local Identity: Rock, Pop and Rap in Europe and Oceania*, Leicester, 1996.
Poschardt, Ulf. *DJ Culture* (tr. Shaun Whiteside), London, 1995.
Rose, Tricia. *Black Noise: Rap Music and Black Culture in Contemporary America*, Hanover, 1994.
Savage, Jon. *England's Dreaming: Sex Pistols and Punk Rock*, London, 1991.
Time Travel: Pop Media and Sexuality 1977–96, London, 1996.
Smith, Patti. *Early Work 1970–1979*, New York, 1994.
Thompson, Ben. *Seven Years of Plenty: a Handbook of Irrefutable Pop Greatness 1991–1998*, London, 1998.
Toynbee, Jason. *Making Popular Music: Musicians, Creativity and Institutions*, London, 2000.
Williams, Raymond. *Marxism and Literature*, Oxford, 1977.
Wolff, Daniel. *You Send Me: the Life and Times of Sam Cooke*, London, 1996.

Discography

Amos, Tori. *Little Earthquakes* (East West, 1992)
Asian Dub Foundation. *Community Music* (London, 2000)
The Beach Boys. *Pet Sounds* (Capitol, 1966)
The Beatles. *Revolver* (Parlophone, 1966)
Sergeant Pepper's Lonely Hearts Club Band (Parlophone, 1967)
Let It Be (Apple, 1970)
Black Box. 'Ride on Time' (deConstruction, 1989)
Bowie, David. *Pinups* (RCA, 1973)
Brooks, Garth. *In the Life of Chris Gaines* (Capitol, 1999)
Brown, James. *Star Time* (Polygram, 1991)
Byrne, David. *Rei Momo* (Luaka Bop, 1989)
Byrne, David and Brian Eno. *My Life in the Bush of Ghosts* (Polydor, 1981)
Captain Beefheart and his Magic Band. *Trout Mask Replica* (Reprise, 1970)
Charles, Ray. *The Complete Country and Western Recordings 1959–1986* (Rhino, 1998)
The Clash. *Story of the Clash vol. 1* (Columbia, 1988)
London Calling (Columbia, 1979)
Super Black Market Clash (Columbia, 1999)
Cooke, Sam. *The Man and his Music* (RCA, 1986)
Costello, Elvis and the Attractions. *Get Happy!* (F Beat, 1980)
Ice Cube. *AmeriKKKa's Most Wanted* (Priority, 1990)
De La Soul. *Three Feet High and Rising* (Tommy Boy, 1989)
De La Soul is Dead (Tommy Boy, 1991)
Dexy's Midnight Runners. *Searching for the Young Soul Rebels* (EMI, 1980)
It Was Like This (EMI, 1996)
Dire Straits. *Brothers in Arms* (Vertigo, 1985)
Dylan, Bob. *Blood on the Tracks* (Columbia, 1975)
Street Legal (Columbia, 1978)
Real Live (Columbia, 1984

Biograph (Columbia, 1985)
Empire Burlesque (Columbia, 1985)
Good as I Been to You (Columbia, 1992)
World Gone Wrong (Columbia, 1993)
The Bootleg Series Volumes 1–3: Rare and Unreleased 1961–1991 (Columbia, 1991)
Echo and the Bunnymen. *Ballyhoo* (Warner, 1997)
Electric Light Orchestra. *The Electric Light Orchestra* (Harvest, 1971)
The Eurythmics. *Greatest Hits* (RCA, 1991)
Ferry, Bryan. *These Foolish Things* (Island, 1973)
Frankie Goes to Hollywood. *Welcome to the Pleasuredome* (ZTT, 1984)
Franklin, Aretha. *Queen of Soul: the Atlantic Recordings* (Rhino, 1992)
Gorky's Zygotic Mynci. *Patio* (Ankst, 1994)
Hardcastle, Paul. '19' (Chrysalis, 1985)
Harvey, PJ. *Dry* (Too Pure, 1992)
Hole. *Celebrity Skin* (Geffen, 1998)
Holloway, Loelatta. 'Love Sensation' (Salsoul, 1980)
Hurley, Steve 'Silk'. 'Jack Your Body' (DJ International, 1987)
Jackson, Michael. *History* (Sony, 1995)
The Jam. *Sound Affects* (Polydor, 1980)
The JB's. *Food for Thought* (Polydor, 1972)
Joy Division. *Unknown Pleasures* (Factory, 1979)
Madonna. *The Immaculate Collection* (Sire, 1990)
Massive Attack. *Protection* (Circa, 1995)
Singles 90/98 (Circa, 1998)
Massive Attack vs. Mad Professor. *No Protection* (Circa, 1994)
The Mekons. '32 Weeks' (Fast, 1978)
The Modern Lovers. *The Modern Lovers* (Creation, 1992)
Nirvana. *Nevermind* (Geffen, 1991)
O'Connor, Sinead. *Universal Mother* (Ensign, 1994)
Ol' Dirty Bastard. *N***a Please* (Elektra, 1999)
Perry, Lee. *Arkology* (Island, 1997)
Pixies. *Death to the Pixies* (4AD, 1997)
Portishead. *Dummy* (Go!, 1994)
Presley, Elvis. *The Complete 50s Masters* (RCA/BMG, 1992)
Public Enemy. *It Takes a Nation of Millions to Hold Us Back* (Def Jam, 1988)
Pulp. *Different Class* (Island, 1995)
Radiohead. *The Bends* (Parlophone, 1995)
REM. *Automatic for the People* (Warner, 1992)
The Rolling Stones. *Beggars' Banquet* (London, 1968)
Sticky Fingers (Rolling Stones, 1971)
Sex Pistols. *Never Mind the Bollocks* (Virgin, 1977)
The Great Rock 'n' Roll Swindle (Virgin, 1979)
Simon, Paul. *Graceland* (Warner, 1986)
The Slits. *Peel Sessions* (Strange Fruit, 1998)
Sly and the Family Stone. *Stand!* (Epic, 1969)
Smith, Patti. *Horses* (Arista, 1975)
Patti Smith Group. *Easter* (Arista, 1978)

The Smiths. *Meat is Murder* (Rough Trade, 1985)
Strangeways Here We Come (Rough Trade, 1987)
The Specials. *Specials* (2-Tone, 1979)
Springsteen, Bruce. *Born to Run* (Columbia, 1975)
Unplugged (Columbia, 1992)
The Ghost of Tom Joad (Columbia, 1995)
The Stooges. *The Stooges* (Elektra, 1969)
Talking Heads. *Remain in Light* (Sire, 1980)
Tindersticks. *Tindersticks* (This Way Up, 1993)
A Tribe Called Quest. *Midnight Marauders* (Jive, 1992)
Tricky. *Maxinquaye* (Fourth and Broadway, 1995)
U2. *The Joshua Tree* (Island, 1987)
Achtung Baby (Island, 1992)
Vega, Suzanne. *Solitude Standing* (A&M, 1987)
99.9 F (A&M, 1992)
Velvet Underground. *Velvet Underground and Nico* (MGM, 1969)
Peel Slowly and See (Polydor, 1995)
Wedding Present. *Seamonsters* (RCA, 1991)
Weller, Paul. *Stanley Road* (Go!, 1995)
The Who. *Sell Out* (Track, 1968)
Yes. *Tales from Topographic Oceans* (Atlantic, 1974)

Compilations

1-2-3-4: Punk and New Wave 1976–79 (Universal, 1999)
Anthology of American Folk Music, ed. Harry Smith (Smithsonian Folkways, 1997)
Back in the Day: Old School Hip-Hop from the Block Party Era (Ace, 2000)
Back to the Old School: Sugar Hill Club Classics (Sequel, 1999)
Boyz of Swing (Polygram, 1996)
Freedom of Choice: Yesterday's New Wave Hits as Performed by Today's Stars (City Slang, 1992)
From Where I Stand: the Black Experience in Country Music (Warner, 1998)
Hen Wlad fy Nhadau (Ankst, 1990)
If I Were a Carpenter (A&M, 1994)
I'm Your Fan (East West, 1991)
Independence Day: the Best New Women in Country (BMG, 1998)
Le Flow vol. 1: the Definitive French Hip Hop Compilation (Delabel, 1998)
Le Flow vol. 2: the French Hip Hop Avant Garde (Delabel, 2000)
Lesbian Favorites: Women Like Us (Rhino, 1997)
No Alternative (Arista/Red Hot, 1993)
Nuggets: Original Artyfacts from the First Psychedelic Era 1965–1968 (Rhino, 1998)
Offbeat: a Red Hot Sound Trip (Wax Trax!/Red Hot, 1996)
Out of Time: the Very Best of the Imaginary Tribute Series (Imaginary, 1991)
Red Hot and Blue (Chrysalis, 1990)
Red Hot and Country (Mercury/Red Hot, 1994)
Red Hot and Rio (Red Hot, 1996)

Respect: a Century of Women in Music (Rhino, 1999)
Return of the Grievous Angel: a Tribute to Gram Parsons (Almo, 1999)
Sisters of Swing 98 (Polygram, 1998)
The Spice Girls Present the Best Girl Power Album in the World . . . Ever! (Virgin, 1997)
Stand Up and Be Counted: Soul, Funk and Jazz from a Revolutionary Era (Harmless, 1999)
Stolen Moments: Red Hot and Cool (Impulse!/Red Hot, 1994)

'Art' music in a cross-cultural context: the case of Africa

MARTIN SCHERZINGER

> The artistic challenge, one I accept, is to use the tools of Western progress and communicate messages of African heritage.
>
> Francis Bebey[1]

> When a note arrives in town from the village, the town returns it with electronic delay, with reverb, limiter and all the studio technology, but it is the same note that came from the village.
>
> Manu Dibangu[2]

(Re)constructing African music

In the interconnected global ethnoscape of the late-twentieth century, the aesthetics of 'art' and popular music alike increasingly bore the mark of hybridity and cultural crossover. It is a world in which once-secure musical boundaries became highly porous; in which transnational cultural exchanges produced an array of richly intersecting multicultural musical forms; indeed, a world in which 'polystylism' was itself considered a representative hallmark of a post-modern condition that challenged the very concepts of cultural authenticity and artistic originality. Collaborative avant-garde projects, like that between Philip Glass and the West African griot Foday Musa Suso, resulted in music that smoothly overlays discrete musical styles, in this case Glass's distinctively minimalist additive rhythms (already indebted to Indian classical music) with the cyclic patterning of the *kora*.[3] Elsewhere, European composers with minimalist leanings, like György Ligeti, extended the dense textures created by Central African polyphonic techniques by drawing out acoustically produced 'inherent

I would like to thank Akin Euba, Gyimah Labi, Daniel Avorgbedor, Bongani Ndodana, and especially Kofi Agawu for their helpful input into this chapter.

1 Quoted in Graeme Ewens, *Africa O-Ye! A Celebration of African Music*, London, 1991, p. 113.

2 Quoted in Angela Impey, 'Popular Music in Africa', *Africa: Garland Encyclopedia of World Music*, New York, 1998, pp. 415–37; p. 415.

3 Cf. 'Spring Waterfall' on Jali Kunda's CD *Griots of West Africa and Beyond* (1997). The *kora* is a form of harp (technically harp-lute) traditional in West Africa and common in commercialized 'world music'.

rhythms' in the context of Western musical instruments.[4] Relatedly, American postmodernists, like Mikel Rouse, wrote operas (such as *Failing Kansas* (1995) and *Dennis Cleveland* (1996)) that sound like creative transcriptions of the African rhythmic processes found in A. M. Jones's *Studies in African Music*.[5]

Experimentally minded Western musicians are equally indebted to other non-Western influences. On his *Rhythmicolor Exotica* (1996) percussion virtuoso Glen Velez draws on percussion techniques from around the world (such as the frame drumming from ancient Mesopotamia) to create sound collages that ostensibly articulate the surrounding mythologies associated with these techniques (such as Mayan creation stories). John Zorn, a self-declared product of the 'information age', composed rapid-fire successions of diverse musical styles; these 'blocks of genre' (ranging from commercial radio sounds to Japanese music) produce a shifting, restless, and 'decentred' sonic panorama, as for instance in 'Forbidden Fruit' with its volatile palette of fragmented references to pre-recorded music, quotations, and generic parodies. In popular music, ambient-oriented electronic projects, like *Deep Forest* (Eric Mouquet and Michel Sanchez, 1994), combined a range of ethnographically retrieved music samples with multiple layers of highly manipulated electronic tracks; Africanized techno-funk is coupled with lyrics based on the conversations of West African drummers on the proto-punk band Talking Heads' album *Remain in Light*;[6] Moby's dazzling multi-genre album *Play* is anchored by samples from Alan Lomax field recordings; sample-heavy dance tracks, like 'London Zulu' compiled by the techno outfit *Global Underground*, are consciously aimed to 'pick you up and dump you somewhere on the other side of the planet';[7] and celtic harp and whistle are joined by West African *kora* and *djembe* (Ghanaian hand drums) on Youssou N'Dour's collaboration with Breton harpist Alan Stivell.[8] Even Madonna, reinvigorating her sound with dance-based electronica, drew on a number of the world's cultures for sonic and

4 As for instance in Book I of Ligeti's *Etudes* for Piano (1985). The concept of 'inherent rhythms' was introduced by Gerhard Kubik in the early 1960s to refer to combinations of parts performed by several musicians; in his words, 'The image as it is heard and the image as it is played are often different from each other' ('The Phenomenon of Inherent Rhythms in East and Central African Music', *African Music Society Journal* 3 (1962), pp. 33–42; p. 33). The concept was influential in circles of both scholarship and composition, for instance probably influencing Steve Reich's notion of 'resultant patterns'.

5 A. M. Jones, *Studies in African Music*, London, 1959.

6 Talking Heads, *Remain in Light* (1980). It is likely that David Byrne's pastor-like ranting on the theme of water in the Talking Heads' 'Once in a Lifetime' is the result of his acquaintance with John Chernoff's account of how African drummers converse with one another in *African Rhythm and African Sensibility: Aesthetics and Social Action in African Musical Idioms*, Chicago, 1979: in 'Water No Get Enemy', Fela Anikulapo Kuti sings, '. . . if your head dey hot, na water go cool am. If your child dey grow, na water you go use. Nothing without water. Water him no get enemy' (Chernoff, *African Rhythm*, 72).

7 D. J. Sasha, *Global Underground: Arrivals* (1999), CD sleeve.

8 See, for example, 'A United Earth I' on the CD *Dublin to Dakar: A Celtic Odyssey* (1999).

visual inspiration on a recent tour.[9] In short, the polystylistic ethnoscape was practically a condition of musical life in late postmodernity.

It is tempting to acclaim this proliferation of cross-cultural artistic inventions as a newly democratic postmodern play of stylistic norms. But not all syncretic musical forms articulate equally with late postmodern modes of production, and it is necessary to differentiate these forms in terms of their social, cultural, economic, political, and musical specifics. To begin with, ethnically based musical borrowings took various stylistic forms. On the one hand, new marketing labels such as 'world beat' and 'world music' explicitly categorized diverse musical practices in terms of distinct cultural types – a development that has paradoxically spawned entirely new genres of music like 'ethnotechno' and 'goatrance'. On the other hand, existing Western metropolitan musical genres took on a progressively multicultural hue via stylistic cross-pollination with music from culturally remote regions. Likewise, musicians operating from *non*-Western *loci* increasingly appropriated or transformed Western styles and idioms to suit local purposes: for example, the 'Afrobeat' of Femi Kuti recalls American funk, blues, and hiphop, while South Africa's first major post-apartheid music genre, *kwaito*, is a fusion of various North Atlantic styles (techno, rave, rap, salsa) and homegrown styles (*mbaqanga*, *mbube*).[10] Occasionally these references to Western music were quite specific about their models: Vusi Mahlasela's album *Wisdom of Forgiveness* (1994) is substantially indebted to the work of Paul Simon, sounding practically like a follow-up to Simon's 1986 *Graceland* – right down to the boyish vocal timbre and the hopeful lyrics embracing a unifying feeling of cross-cultural empathy. Similarly, Wes Welenga's album *Wes* is an imitative echo of the keyboard-centred ambient music of Deep Forest (itself a paradigmatic example of 'ethnotechno'). Paradoxically, Welenga copies the sound of the *sampled* aspects of Deep Forest's music with his own voice.[11]

Despite the blurring of stylistic borders, these various syncretisms often operated under different rules and constraints in the late-capitalist economic and political order. They cannot simply be read as so many instances of laissez-faire postmodern pastichism or polystylism. Let me explain using the following well-documented examples. First, in addition to the well-known participation

9 Madonna's interest in non-Western music is also reflected on her song 'Cyber-Raga' on the CD *Groundwork: Act to Reduce Hunger* (2001), which was distributed exclusively by Hear Music and the Starbucks Coffee Company; it includes a text adapted from the Vedic mantra and the Mahabharata, accompanied by breakbeats, electronics, sitar, and tabla.

10 See, for example, TKZee Family's *GUZ 2001* (1999).

11 Wes Welenga, *Wes* (1998). Other examples of Africanized ethnotechno include the song 'Limbo' by the Sandoz Project, which features sampled vocals of the Nigerian Yoruba people, and 'AKA Electric' by Steel Porn Rhino, which employs songs from the pygmies of Central Africa; both tracks can be found on *Ethnotechno: Sonic Anthropology*, Volume 1 (1994).

of Ladysmith Black Mambazo on *Graceland*, Paul Simon hired the South African musicians Chikapa 'Ray' Phiri, Bakithi Khumalo, and Isaac Mtshali to perform the dance/funk rhythm section on his song 'You Can Call Me Al'. Musically speaking, this is a kind of cross-cultural dialogue of styles; the lyrics, arranged in a fuzzy word montage, articulate a postmodern constellation of ideas loosely related to the theme of lifeways in global modernity.[12] Similarly, Kevin Volans used transcriptions of the *Nyanga* pan-pipe dance of the Nyungwe people in Mozambique for the second and fourth movements of his string quartet *White Man Sleeps*; the sound is invigoratingly original, replete with acoustical illusions produced by the 'inherent' melodies of interlocking pan-pipe parts, which, in turn, elaborate typically African harmonic movements. Interestingly, in both these cases, the already hybridized pieces became the source for further musical exploration. Fifteen years after the release of *Graceland*, MDC produced a techno dance tune called 'Sunny Trumpets', which splices and pastes the opening trumpet riff of 'You Can Call Me Al' in various patterns, surrounding it in hypnotically motoric techno-dance rhythms with strongly accentuated offbeats and no words. Analogously, in 2000, Nelly Furtado employed a sample from the second movement of *White Man Sleeps* on the opening track ('Hey, Man!') of her album *Whoa, Nelly!*, where the words, sung in a laid-back girl-next-door vocal style, comment on the complexities of life in the modern world. Thus, in both of these cases, the 'African' input into the music, at least twice removed from its original context, seems to circulate in a new kind of signifying practice. The result is a hybridized hybrid: the African music has become a reference of a reference, caught in a seemingly endless free play of signification.

The problem is that while these rich recontextualizations produced fascinatingly complex cross-cultural intertexts, the economic realities underlying their production tended to benefit only some of the agents involved: despite their efforts to acknowledge their sources, both Simon and Volans are listed as the exclusive composers of the above works. And, once commodified, the copyright privileges that accrue to these pieces extend to the samples made by MDC and Furtado respectively. So, in 'You Can Call Me Al' Simon may voice the captivating realms of cultural interchangeability that have become possible in the new global order, and in 'Sunny Trumpets' MDC may conjure the spirited sound of Africanized trumpets, but, financially speaking, only the Westerners benefit from the borrowings. This is not to criticize the work of

12 For example, the third verse runs: 'A man walks down the street. It's a street in a strange world. Maybe it's the Third World. Maybe it's his first time around. He doesn't speak the language. He holds no currency. He is a foreign man. He is surrounded by the sound. The sound. Cattle in the marketplace. Scatterlings and orphanages. He looks around, around. He sees angels in the architecture. Spinning in infinity. He says Amen! and Hallelujah!' The title of this song resulted from a dinner engagement at which Pierre Boulez kept mistakenly calling Simon 'Al' (and his wife Peggy, 'Betty').

Simon or Volans (both of whom have made considerable contributions to the causes of African music and musicians), but to demonstrate the skewed logic of capitalism in a context of drastic economic and political inequality. According to Simon Frith, copyright law is implicated in economic exploitation on a global scale: 'from an international perspective, copyright can be seen as a key plank in Western cultural and commercial imperialism', used 'as a weapon . . . by the multinationals against small nations'.[13]

While global exchange of musical material across borders of drastic inequality often carries an imprint of economic exploitation – and there are countless examples of brazen appropriations of non-Western musics[14] – this is not inevitable, nor does it apply to every case. While current copyright law tends to protect Western musicians in most cases (if only because non-Western music is often regarded as in the public domain), the South African musicians involved in *Graceland* greatly benefited from the exposure. While ANC supporters picketed a performance in London because the concert defied the terms of the cultural boycott against South Africa (then still under white Nationalist Government control), the exiled South African activist musicians Hugh Masekela and Miriam Makeba wholeheartedly lent their support to it, even appearing on stage with Simon, because they recognized the strategic value for African musicians of participating in the tour. And indeed, in the late 1980s, major international labels began to sign up groups like Ladysmith Black Mambazo: numerous cross-cultural collaborations and exchanges resulted from their involvement with Simon. Even Laurie Anderson's intensely personal style was inflected by South African *mbaqanga* guitar riffs (performed by Bakithi Khumalo and Ray Phiri on her 1989 CD *Strange Angels*). The *Graceland* tour also brought international recognition to a host of African musicians *not* directly involved with Simon: vocal groups like the eight-piece Black Umfolosi from Zimbabwe, whose gospel-inflected a cappella singing resembles the *mbube* harmonisations of Black Mambazo, gained international recognition in the 1990s (the group is billed in the West in terms of its stylistic links with Ladysmith Black Mambazo). It has even been argued that Simon's music 'softened the more strident tonalities of the antiapartheid struggle'.[15]

13 Simon Frith (ed.), *Music and Copyright*, Edinburgh, 1993, p. xiii.

14 In his article 'The/An Ethnomusicologist and the Record Business', *Yearbook for Traditional Music* 28, 1996, pp. 36–56, Hugo Zemp describes various scandalous examples of Western musicians exploiting African and other musicians for profit. For an extended discussion of the role of transnational capital in the formation of global pop, see Timothy Taylor, *Global Pop: World Music, World Markets*, New York and London, 1997. For a discussion of the ethical and financial implications of sampling in electronic dance music, see David Hesmondhalgh, 'International Times: Fusions, Exoticism, and Antiracism in Electronic Dance Music', in Georgina Born and David Hesmondhalgh (eds.), *Western Music and Its Others: Difference, Representation, and Appropriation in Music*, Berkeley, 2000, pp. 280–304.

15 Veit Erlmann, *Music, Modernity, and the Global Imagination: South Africa and the West*, New York, 1999, p. 171.

Again on the positive side, the invention of 'world music' encouraged a dramatic increase in the number of commercial recordings of African music, a development that spawned renewed interest and activity in various African instrumental styles, including the *mbira* and *kora*. Today, young performers like Forward Kwenda and Musekiwa Chingodza sustain professional careers as mbirists in the United States and beyond, while *kora* soloists, duos, and trios regularly tour Europe and the United States. Arguably less positive from the point of view of African traditions, African performers frequently relocated to these regions, drawn by their technological resources: the Gambian *kora* player Foday Musa Suso, who blends the sound of the authentic *kora* with electronics and drums, currently resides in New York City, and Chartwell Dutiro, former *mbira* player for Thomas Mapfumo and the Blacks Unlimited, in London. At the same time, various African initiatives for the promotion of local music are attempting to compete with the established centres of production in New York and London. For example, a number of music festivals (including the SADC festival in Zimbabwe and the MASA festival in Ivory Coast) are forging musical connections within the continent, while in South Africa and Senegal sophisticated recording studios assist in the development of an infrastructure for the production and promotion of local talent.[16]

In this way the modern incarnation of traditional African music, bestowed with a kind of 'classical' prestige (replete with 'master' musicians), opened a significant global market for numerous African musicians towards the end of the century. Inevitably, however, these new modes of marketing, engineering, sound production, and styling affected the sound of African music. As the international 'world music' industry continued to modify and refine its expanding niche markets, a new demand for 'authentic' traditional African music was created in Europe and America. Old ethnomusicological recordings were repackaged to reflect historical authenticity, and new recordings underscoring the 'ritual' aspects of African music-making appeared. For example, Louis Sarno's *bayaka: The Extraordinary Music of the Babenzélé Pygmies* (1995) used wall-to-wall sounds of the jungle – insects, birds, monkeys – to provide a smooth sonic segue from track to track; the tracks include the sound of women yodeling and singing in the distance (probably with studio-added echo), *mondumé* (harp zither) music, drumming, and so on. The music *sounds* fascinating, mysteriously veiled by the jungle, and above all, remote. The same aesthetic of the imaginary informs some new *mbira* recordings, such as the 1998 release of *Pasi Mupindu (The World is Changing)* by Tute Chigamba's Mhembero Mbira Ensemble: this was recorded live in Highfield, Harare, with the microphones

16 Impey, 'Popular Music in Africa', p. 437.

held at some distance from the *mbiras*, presumably in order better to capture the overall ambience, and although some of the formal intricacies of the *mbira* playing are lost in the process, the resultant music *sounds* authentically African, like a ritual.[17] In this way, a peculiar marketing category instituted in the North Atlantic mediates the aesthetic angle of the music's sound.

While considerable attention has been devoted to the relationship of both African traditional and popular music to the international music market, very little attention has been paid to the relationship of African 'art' music to musical internationalism. Perhaps this is because 'art' music partially falls outside the international commodity sphere (and thus below the perception level of many commentators), or perhaps – as the Nigerian composer Akin Euba suggests – the very idea of African 'art' music does not tally with Western notions of what 'typifies' Africa:[18] the African production of musical idioms with a contemplative dimension is dismissed as inherently un-African. Popular and 'art' musicians alike recognize the incipient racialism implied by insisting Africans compose only 'African'-sounding music: as the Cameroonian saxophonist Manu Dibangu puts it, 'Yes, I am an African but is it the African they [audiences in the USA] want to hear or is it the musician? . . . If you judge everything by its color, nothing has changed.'[19] Likewise, South African trumpeter Hugh Masekela seeks to exercise musical discrimination based on purely aesthetic rather than racial considerations: 'We are all living in a universal world today and the criteria should be what is good music and what is bad . . . . But if people insist that music doesn't have enough bone in the nose, or the lips are not big enough, or the nose is not flat enough, at that point instead of being culture it becomes tribalistic or racial.'[20] African composers of 'art' music frequently voice similar views, and indeed, although the relevance of 'art' music in Africa is hotly contested,[21] it plays a fascinating role in the struggle for international cultural legitimacy precisely because it seems to defy ostensibly indigenous African practices at its very inception.

Having said this, however, it is not in practice possible to make clear distinctions between traditional, popular, folk, and 'art' music in Africa. Johnston Akuma-Kalu Njoku broadly defines 'art' (or, as he terms it, 'art-composed')

17 Ironically, the *Mhembero* Ensemble was founded only in the late 1980s, when Chigamba's daughter Irene finished a tour with the Zimbabwean National Dance Troupe; far from representing indigenous rituals of Zimbabwe, the troupe was formed with the aim of performing professionally.

18 Akin Euba, *Modern African Music: A Catalogue of Selected Archival Materials at Iwalewa-Haus, University of Bayreuth, Germany*, Bayreuth, 1993, p. 1.

19 In Graeme Ewens, *Africa O-Ye! A Celebration of African Music*, London, 1991, p. 7.

20 Ibid., p. 24.

21 See, for example, Abiola Irele's polemical essay, 'Is African Music Possible?', *Transition* 61 (1993), pp. 56–71; and Kofi Agawu's 'Analytic Issues Raised by Contemporary African Art Music', in Cynthia Tse Kimberlin and Akin Euba (eds.), *Intercultural Music*, Vol. III, Richmond, CA, 2001, pp. 135–47.

music as notated music composed for performances in concert halls and on stages aimed at audiences of contemplative listeners[22] – a tradition associated with 'Western'-influenced ensembles and genres, which in turn are associated with the aesthetics of beauty in sounding forms. Even with this kind of definition in place, however, the boundary between African 'art' music and other forms of African music remains hard to draw. For one thing, there are many examples of traditional African musical expressions that emphasize contemplative listening in the manner of Western 'art' music. For another, most African states instituted and funded various national musical ensembles, ballets, or cultural troupes after they gained independence, and although these projects largely functioned as symbols of national identity and unity in the wake of the colonial experience, they also encouraged just the kind of aesthetic paradigm advanced by Njoku in his description of 'art' music. In other words, the state-sponsored institutionalization of indigenous music reflects an attitude of pride and seriousness that parallels the aspirations of Western 'classical' music.

For example, soon after independence in Mali, the state sponsored several large orchestras representing the musical styles of each region of that country. Likewise, in the early 1980s Zimbabwe established the National Dance Company as well as various 'Culture Houses' representing cultural regions around the country. These new cultural formations significantly shifted the function of traditional music in modern Africa, and served contemporary aesthetic and political needs. The National Orchestra of Cameroon (founded in 1978), for example, strives to revive traditional forms of music in the context of a contemporary idiom; it frequently tours the various regions of Cameroon, presenting formal concerts and dances. Here traditional music serves as a public relations tool in the context of African nationalism. A similar case can be found in Angola, where the Ministry of Culture funded various folklore-oriented groups as well as a national orchestra called *Semba Tropical*, while in post-colonial Tanzania the National Dance Troupe (founded in 1964 by the Ministry of National Culture and Youth) developed a unique musical style that amalgamated regional styles from around the country; this nationalized form of music reflects the political doctrine of *Ujamaa*, a socialist-inspired doctrine attempting to eliminate tribalism. Even more ambitiously, the Pan-African Orchestra, founded in 1988 in Accra, Ghana, aims to construct a post-colonial African cultural identity that extends beyond regional differences: the music is a composite style derived from the indigenous traditions and resources of various ethnic groups in a number of African countries, including the twenty-one-string *kora*, west

22 Johnston Akuma-Kalu Njoku, 'Art-Composed Music in Africa', in Ruth Stone (ed.), *Africa: The Garland Encyclopedia of World Music*, Vol. I, New York, 1998, pp. 232–53; 232.

African drums, rattles and bells, animal horns, bow chordophones, and flutes. As suggested by the title of their first CD – *The Pan-African Orchestra, Opus 1* (1995) – this is music intended less for social participation than for listening. Furthermore, the orchestra has a designated conductor, a position currently held by Nana Danso Abiam, formerly the conductor of Ghana's National Symphony Orchestra, and in this respect resembles the structure of its Western counterpart more than it does a traditional African ensemble.

It is true that towards the end of the century, some of these national cultural projects were discontinued: as a result of the economic adjustment programmes instituted by the World Bank and the International Monetary Fund, for example, the National Dance Company of Zimbabwe was disbanded in the early 1990s. Other groups, however, continue to thrive. The Gambian National Dance Troupe, for example, is regularly engaged both domestically and internationally, while the Drummers of Burundi, comprised of court musicians attached to royal families, have gained an increasingly international profile. In fact, despite the nationalist and pan-Africanist ambitions of these musical projects, the new approach to indigenous music-making has increasingly become a resource for commodification by the international music industry: in the last decade alone, the drummers of Burundi have released three hugely successful CDs, while the dramatic traditional *kora* music and singing of Dembo Konte, Malamini Jobarteh, Kausu Kouyante, and Amadu Bansang Jobarteh have likewise received recent international acclaim. In these contexts, 'traditional' music – music that is not so much traditional as reinvented in the context of nation-building – is increasingly consumed in a manner approximating 'art' music in the West: it is music composed, conducted, and performed by professional musicians and aimed at a separate listening audience.

In this way the notion of commodified 'art' music is not antithetical or anomalous to contemporary Africa. It may be true that commodification of the African cultural sphere is not a desirable development, but this moral stance alone does not reckon with the fact that such commodification is already in practice under way in most parts of Africa. Politically speaking, there is a need to seek strategies for effectively combating drastic exploitation of African musicians in this inevitable process, rather than recoiling in alarm from the commercialization of African culture *per se*. And it may be this oppositional role that provides the best working definition of the 'art' music of Africa, interrogating the ethnically based expectations and desires of the 'world music' market without lapsing into the false view of African art viewed in terms of uncommodified pre-conquest utopianism. This means that, as with popular musical forms in Africa, the development of 'art' music is complex and contradictory, involving the incorporation *and*, paradoxically, the rejection of Euro-American musical styles, structures, and techniques. Thus the music's uneven relation to national politics, liberation struggle, and post-colonial national identity on the one hand is vividly counterbalanced by its demands for recognition in an international frame on the other.

What follows is a survey of aspects of locally produced African 'art' music as it intersects with popular and traditional musical forms in an era of transnational commerce. An essay of this length cannot hope to do justice to the scope of the topic and is thus necessarily selective; rather than making a vain attempt to represent the diversity of 'art'-musical production in Africa, I shall aim to identify some of its defining characteristics. Moreover, even though an 'art'-music tradition in many parts of Africa can be traced back to the nineteenth century,[23] I will approach the topic in the context of post-colonial Africa alone, and thus focus primarily on the final decades of the twentieth century. As a convenience I will divide this study into two major geographical zones, first north and west Africa, and then south and east Africa, in each case outlining the broader contexts of popular and 'traditional' musics against which the 'art' repertories need to be understood.

Unequal fusions: popular and 'art' musics of north and west Africa

Any account of music in north and west Africa in the late twentieth century cannot fail to mention the explosion of new musical forms resulting from the creative syntheses of styles. From the soaring melodies and bursting rhythmic fragments of Youssou N'Dour's Wolof-based *mbalax* to the sophisticated and lavish arrangements of Salif Keita's Manding-based big-band fusions, west African music in the 1980s and 1990s was essentially a music of crossover and metamorphosis. *Mbalax*, for example, drew on the rhythmic language of *sabar*, *bugarabu*, and *tama* drums, which were smoothly layered into the electronic sound world of guitars and synthesizers that typified Western popular music of the time.

N'Dour's remarkable vocalizations covered a range of eclectic topics, ranging from the subject of radiating toxic waste dumped in Africa by industrialized nations (on *Set*, 1990) to cover versions of Western rock music sung in Wolof (such as Bob Dylan's 'Chimes of Freedom' on *The Guide*, 1994); following N'Dour's example, Chérif Mbaw (a Senegalese singer-guitarist living in Paris) recorded his *mbalax*-derived album *Kham Kham* (2001), which combines

23 In Nigeria, for example, compositions in the Western 'art'-music tradition were performed under the auspices of the Lagos Philharmonic Society as early as the 1870s; see Njoku, 'Art-Composed Music', p. 233.

typically staccato vocals with restless guitar work, in his native Wolof. Despite the foreign language, these albums were popular successes in France, and their message did not go unnoticed: it may well have been the political dimension of N'Dour's lyrics that cost him his contract with Virgin Records, who dropped him after two albums. More generally, popular music in west Africa is a voice of resistance: for instance Femi Kuti, son of Afropop pioneer Fela Kuti, harnessed a pulsing music style that blends African with African-American music in the service of stinging political messages. He spares neither Western cultural imperialism nor African corruption in his critique: on *Blackman Know Yourself* he sings in a calculated pidgin English, 'We get the wrong people for government / Who force us to think with colonial sense / Na wrong information scatter your head / You regret your culture for Western sense.' And in a less overtly political but similarly eclectic spirit, Salif Keita (along with other 'electro-griots' like Ismael Lo) blended the styles of jazz, rumba, and the folk music of the Sahel region into highly westernized quasi-orchestral fusions.[24]

In anglophone west Africa, equally inventive genres emerged in the final decades of the century. Nigerian *fuji* music, a musical style based on multiple percussion parts and vocals (without guitars or bass), gradually superseded *juju* music in popularity. Alhadji Sikuru Ayinde Barrister even created an offshoot of this style called *fuji garbage*, which added a Hawaiian guitar and keyboards to the percussion-oriented ensemble; in the 1980s he toured both Britain and the United States extensively and to critical acclaim. Meanwhile dynamic new genres, like *bikoutsi*-rock, appeared in Cameroon: the high-energy music of Les Tetes Brulées (The Burnt Heads) drew on the subtle polyphonic *bikoutsi* music of the Beti people,[25] and by magnifying these percussion lines into delirious synthetic textures resembling futuristic hammering they crafted a sound as unique as their mohican hairstyles and retro-Africanist body paint. At the start of the 1990s the international market for African crossover music opened up to prominent female artists from west Africa as well. For example, Angelique Kidjo, whose debut album was a resolutely pan-African blend of Congolese *makossa* and *soukous*, Jamaican reggae, and Islamicized *zouk* woven into unique adaptations of traditional Beninoise folklore, achieved fame in France and beyond; likewise, Oumou Sangare from the Wassoulou region of southern Mali, along with Mbilia Bel and M'pongo Love from the Congo (formerly Zaïre), achieved international renown in the 1980s and 90s. This was also a time of unprecedented collaborations between African and Western musicians. N'Dour performed with Peter Gabriel, Bruce Springsteen, and Stevie Wonder; Ali Fakar Toure collaborated with Ry Cooder; Ismael Lo recorded music with Marianne

24 Ewens, *Africa O-Ye!*, pp. 57–65. 25 In ibid., p. 124.

Faithfull; Manu Dibango worked with Bill Laswell and Herbie Hancock for Celluloid; Fela Kuti's music was remixed by Laswell with Jamaican reggae artists; Salif Keita recorded with Joe Zawinul; Sting scored a hit with Algerian *rai* star Cheb Mami. The list goes on.

It is thus in a context of extensive creative innovation and experimentation that west African popular music evolved in the 1980s and 1990s: the translocation and amalgamation of musical styles from various quarters opened hitherto unexplored musical possibilities. Indeed, the transatlantic feedback between Africa, Europe, and other parts of the globe resulted in an international terrain of popular music that was irreducibly hybridized. Aside from the overt cross-culturalism of electronic world trance, for example, even mainstream DJs like Paul Oakenfold from Britain, spinning techno and house music in the dance capitals of the Western world, drew inspiration from the sound of African drumming ensembles;[26] in turn, African pop, stimulated by technology, global communications, migration, and capital investment, became a global phenomenon. But while African no less than Western popular music was increasingly layered with mutual influences and strategic borrowings, the path to success was more hazardous for African musicians than for their Western counterparts: the relationship between African artists and their commercial labels all too frequently followed the pattern begun by N'Dour in the 1980s. The Nigerian *juju* star King Sunny Ade, for example, was dropped by Island Records after three albums, and Thomas Mapfumo, the 'lion' of Zimbabwean *chimurenga* music, after two. Many foreign companies set up subsidiary bases in African countries (Nigeria, Ivory Coast, South Africa, Tanzania, Kenya, and Zimbabwe), but in reality the geographical centre of the corporate network comprising the recording industry was situated in Europe and the United States, as was the centre of mass music consumption. Music industries in Africa could not compete: while the 1980s witnessed a shift from vinyl to CD as the primary sound-carrying medium in the West, for example, African recordings are still released primarily on cassette, because CDs are simply not affordable to local consumers. Furthermore, lacking crucial resources and faced with increasing political, social, and economic instability, the music industry in Africa became increasingly vulnerable in the 1990s, with the once-thriving industries of Nigeria and Tanzania going into decline.[27]

26 In 'Somali Udida Ceb' (Somalia Don't Shame Yourself'), a song by Maryam Mursal mixed by Paul Oakenfold, the interest in African socio-politics is explicit; appearing on a CD entitled *Spirit of Africa* (2001), Oakenfold's mix forms part of a joint initiative of the Mercury Phoenix Trust (founded by the surviving members of the group Queen in memory of their singer Freddie Mercury) and Real World records to combat AIDS in Africa.

27 Impey, 'Popular Music in Africa', p. 417.

This structurally inscribed socioeconomic inequality was ideologically reflected in the aesthetic discourse surrounding late-twentieth-century marketing categories for popular music. As we have seen, the invention of 'world' music as a niche market constructed a demand for authentic-sounding African music, which in turn affected the production, marketing, styling, and engineering of African pop; as a result, the African products were 'indigenized' through a complex interplay of imagination, fabrication, sound, and fashion. But while both African and Western pop were at bottom equally hybridized musical expressions, critics have interpreted this hybridity in contrasted ways: the African elements in the music of 'rock' stars like Peter Gabriel, Paul Simon, and David Byrne are regarded as creatively enhancing their work, while the Western elements of 'world' musicians like Youssou N'Dour, Manu Dibango, and Sunny Ade are seen as compromising theirs. This places unique aesthetic constraints on African musicians: they are charged with betraying their roots in a way that Western musicians are not.[28] Seen this way, African music is confined to the condition of a historically unmediated raw material which can be manipulated to revitalize and enrich Western popular music.

In contrast, because it is not as vulnerable to the profit-driven markets of the international music industry, the 'art' music of Africa poses an intriguing challenge to the ideologies of race implied by this exclusionary scenario. As with popular music, the development of 'art' music in west Africa involves a complex layering of traditional practices into imported musical idioms, styles, and genres. The incorporation of non-African idioms into traditional musics and vice versa has a long legacy in this part of the world: all west African countries underwent a period of colonial domination during the late nineteenth and early twentieth centuries, which affected their musical soundscapes to varying degrees. The arrival of Christianity in Nigeria, for example, not only introduced church music (hymns, chants, canticles, cantatas, anthems, motets), but also contributed to the generation of new secular musical styles that drew on it, such as *highlife* and *juju*;[29] church music was adapted and reworked by Nigerian congregations, already well-versed in choral music, to reflect local conditions and aspirations. As the disjuncture between the colonial state and the African churches intensified in late colonial times, these adaptations increasingly incorporated traditional drumming, clapping, and dancing. This process of gradual re-Africanization was remarkably widespread throughout

28 N'Dour, for example, resists the curatorial role he is expected to play and emphasizes instead the importance of cultural blending: 'You can't really program music. A musical life should not have any limits . . . It's from . . . new experiences that interesting things happen' (Youssou N'Dour, 'Postcard: Youssou N'dour on Senegal', *Time* 158/14 (2001), special issue: 'Music Goes Global', p. 66.

29 Euba, *Modern African Music*, p. 4. Still today, various churches house Western orchestral instruments, which are occasionally used for concerts (Njoku, 'Art-Composed Music', p. 236).

twentieth-century Africa, ranging from the 'Spiritual churches' of Ghana to the 'Ethiopian churches' of South Africa. Arguably, the process of strategically borrowing cultural concepts and resources from the West for local purposes typifies modern Africa, and so it has become possible to speak of African *traditions* grounded in Western idioms or instruments: west African Christian hymn settings, Congolese guitar compositions, Zulu concertina music (commonly known as the *gxagxa* tradition), and, of course, African 'art' music.

West African 'art' music at the end of the twentieth century covers a broad spectrum of compositional approaches. Ranging from the non-modulating diatonicism of J. H. Kwabena Nketia's *Antubam* for cello and piano and Ayo Bankole's *Three Part-Songs* for female choir to the intensely dissonant quartal harmonies of Gyimah Labi's densely-textured *Dialects* for Piano, or the distinctive modal language of Joshua Uzoigwe's *Four Igbo Folk Songs*, African 'art' composition embodies a vast panorama of possibilities.[30] Despite the many references to high-life music and other distinctively west African popular idioms, however, and despite the use of quotations from folksongs, the *tonal* collections employed and the *harmonic* behaviour of the musical materials tends to derive from some or other Western modality: Okechukwu Ndubuisi's settings of folksongs for piano and voice, for instance, draw strongly on Western functional harmony. Indeed, the tonal dimensions of the original folksongs are substantially altered to suit the demands of key-based diatonicism, sometimes to the point of disregarding the tonal inflections of vernacular Igbo: in works such as 'Atuak Ukot Odo' and 'Onye Naku na Onuzo Muo', the short motives and conjunct melodic motions of the original tunes are lyrically transformed into continuous melodic lines in which the call-and-response structure is disguised by elision and overlapping of phrases.[31]

Rhythmically speaking, however, these pieces elaborate various cross-rhythmic ostinato patterns reminiscent of African drumming: one typical pattern of this sort, which Njoku describes as the 'Ndubuisi bass' (in the manner of 'Alberti bass') is a 12/8 arpeggiation figure with a rhythmic accent on every

30 J. H. Kwabena Nketia (b. 1921) is probably the world's leading African authority on African music and aesthetics living today. Nketia was a professor of music at UCLA and the University of Pittsburgh. He is also the Director of the International Center for African Music in Legon-Accra, Ghana. Ayo Bankole (1935–76) was a Nigerian composer who studied music at Cambridge and ethnomusicology at UCLA, holding a teaching position at the University of Lagos in the late 1960s and 70s and intermittently working as music producer at the Nigerian Broadcasting Corporation. The Ghanaian composer Gyimah Labi (b. 1950) studied composition with Ato Turkson and ethnomusicology with Kwabena Nketia at the University of Ghana, Legon; he then emigrated to the United States, where he currently resides. Joshua Uzoigwe (b. 1947) pursued his music studies at the University of Ibadan (Nsukka), and at Trinity College of Music (London); he also completed an MA in ethnomusicology under the guidance of John Blacking. Further information on African composers (compiled by Daniel Avorgbedor) can be found under their respective names in the *New Grove Dictionary of Music and Musicians*, 2nd edn (London, 2001), and details are therefore provided only selectively in this chapter.

31 Njoku, 'Art-Composed Music', p. 243.

second quaver. In these songs, Njoku argues, even the word-painting achieved by instrumental means is based on idiomatic Igbo verbalizations through drumming.[32] And the role of drumming in west African 'art' music extends to the domains of both style and idea. In other words, while some composers explicitly foreground the traditional instruments of west African drumming ensembles in their works, others derive compositional ideas from the structural behaviour of these ensembles. Gyimah Labi's crowded rhythmic polyphony exemplifies the former tendency: his Timpani Concerto is even scored for traditional instruments (bell, rattle, kidi, and sogo), along with two saxophones, a cowbell, and timpani, and they tend to articulate traditional African rhythmic patterns. The bell, for example, outlines a subtle variation of a typical west African time-line (with occasional interruptions and silences), while the soloistic timpani loosely approximates the behaviour of a west African master drum.

At the other end of the spectrum, the music of J. H. Kwabena Nketia is less overtly beholden to the multi-layered rhythms of west African drumming. Yet Nketia's work is frequently regulated by the underlying structural principles of traditional music. Nketia describes the organization of his compositions in terms of the 'traditional principle of achieving complexity through the combination of simple elements'.[33] In keeping with the tradition of assigning the 'role of master drummer to the lowest pitched instruments', he frequently places his principal rhythmic motifs in the lowest voices; the upper layers, by contrast, tend either to emphasize the lower ones (through octave doubling, polyphonic imitation, or rhythmic interlocking), or to draw out independent motivic possibilities that seem to comment on the bass movements. In the fifth movement from his Suite for flute and piano, for example, the piano elaborates lengthy spans of changing harmonic consonances in a steady *perpetuum mobile* punctuated by momentary interlocking rhythms, while the flute precariously vacillates between doubling the piano part (with unpredictable deviations!) and deriving new melodic and motivic ideas from various rhythmic patterns set forth by the piano. Thus, as was the case with Ndubuisi, Nketia's rhythmic language reflects traditional concepts related to west African drumming, while his tonal language is an unconventional reworking of Western diatonicism.

The same division of influence between African and Western elements seems to characterize the output of the internationally known Nigerian composer Akin Euba.[34] That is, the percussive, rhythmic, and timbral aspects of Euba's

32 Ibid., p. 244.

33 Kwabena J. H. Nketia, 'Exploring African Musical Resources in Contemporary Composition', in Cynthia Tse Kimberlin and Akin Euba (eds.), *Intercultural Music*, Vol. I, Bayreuth, 1995, pp. 221–39; p. 232.

34 The Nigerian composer Akin Euba (b. 1935) is Andrew W. Mellon Professor of Music at the University of Pittsburgh; his musical and academic training took place in England, the United States, and Nigeria. Euba is internationally renowned as both composer and scholar.

work are characteristically African, while his tonal language tends to be shaped by Western 'art'-musical practices, albeit distinctly modernist ones: in his *Scenes from Traditional Life* for piano, for example, melodic movement is defined by a twelve-tone row. It might be argued that the row is delicately infused with traditional African modalities of pitch construction – for instance, the tonal patterns of *dundun* drumming rarely include augmented fourths and minor seconds, which are equally scarce in Euba's composition – but the music is unambiguously organized on dodecaphonic principles. More striking is the way various melodic fragments incessantly lapse into extended passages of arpeggiated rhythmic ostinato as well as a host of familiar-sounding African rhythmic patterns intoned on repeated tones: the thematically consequential fragment opening the first movement is loosely derived from a west African time-line pattern, while the striking syncopated bass rhythm undergirding the third movement is derived from a west African highlife pattern.[35] This unusual approach to the piano exemplifies Euba's concept of 'African pianism' – an example of how a European instrument can be adapted for distinctly African aesthetic purposes. Euba outlines the key features of African pianism thus:

> Africanisms employed in neo-African keyboard music include (a) thematic repetition (b) direct borrowings of thematic material (rhythmical and/or tonal) from African traditional sources (c) the use of rhythmical and/or tonal motifs which, although not borrowed from specific traditional sources, are based on traditional idioms (d) percussive treatment of the piano and (e) making the piano 'behave' like African instruments.[36]

Other composers who have worked in this idiom include Gamel Abdel-Rahim, Halim El-Dabh, Kenn Kafui, Labi, Uzoigwe, and Nketia; Nketia, for example, explicitly models his *Twelve Pedagogical Pieces* for piano on distinct African styles ranging from music of the Anlo-Ewe (in *Volta Fantasy*) to popular highlife rhythms introduced into Ghana by the Kroo of Liberia (in *Dagomba*).[37] But in spite of the conscious 'Africanization' of the piano in a piece like Euba's *Scenes from Traditional Life*, the music of these composers ultimately reflects an allegiance to Western 'art' music. Or at least, their musical structures are generated by a divided paradigm, one in which the treatment of pitch is modelled

35 Uzoigwe, *Akin Euba*, pp. 68–9. 36 Euba, *Modern African Music*, p. 8.

37 In relation to this title, it should be noted that Nketia, Labi, Euba, Nzewi, and others have been actively involved in writing theoretical studies of traditional African music. In most parts of Africa this effort answers to a critical educational need: in the late-modern African context, where 'Western' classroom-based education is the norm, there is an almost total lack of textbooks that use musical examples from Africa.

on Western compositional procedures while the treatment of rhythm tends to draw on African ones.[38]

Occasionally, this division of labour is literally carried out in the context of a single work. In his opera *Chaka*, based on the dramatic poem by Léopold Sédar Senghor about the famous nineteenth-century Zulu chieftain of that name, Euba employs a massive cross-cultural instrumentarium: the African traditional instruments in the orchestra include Ghanaian *atenteben* (bamboo flutes), *agogo* (bell), rattle, slit drums, various fixed-pitch membrane drums, Yoruba hourglass, and kettle drums. These forces are deployed largely in a stylistically west African way, in which bell patterns derived from various dances (including the Ashanti *adowa* dance and the Ewe *atsiagbekor* dance) are creatively combined with a variety of polyrhythmic patterns. Throughout the two 'chants' of the opera, these sections of traditionalized African drumming are layered, woven, and juxtaposed with music composed for Western chamber ensemble. The Western instruments, by contrast, largely intone Western idioms: Euba exploits a range of Western compositional procedures ranging from twelve-tone technique (in the manner of Alban Berg) to the circulation of leitmotifs (in the manner of Richard Wagner). This basic dualism between African and Western styles, in turn, grounds an array of vocal styles ranging from African praise chanting and speech-song in free rhythm to haunting operatic escalations in the soprano's highest register.

Chaka's dizzying polystylistic excursions produce cross-cultural meanings that are rich and strange. The piece opens with a memorable horn motif outlining a perfect fifth and fourth before folding into a cadence. Thus, like Senghor's poem, the opera begins at a kind of end-point: Chaka's death. After a suggestive pause, the sounds of a well-known bell pattern, polyrhythmically coordinated with agile African percussion patterns, emerge as if in a memory; this tapestry of rhythm is spattered and smeared with gestural fragments from horns and winds. Then the musically hybrid texture, punctuated by solemn references to the opening motif, finally segues into a concluding section featuring the *antenteben* flutes. At one point, Euba incorporates a neo-African rendition of the *Dies irae* in a rhythmic 6/8, a theme later heard again in connection with Chaka's illustration of colonial oppression; here the brass emphatically elaborates the chant in a manner recalling Berlioz. This intertextual reference not only expands the theme of death beyond the figure of the dying Chaka towards the murderous dimensions of the colonial venture itself, but paradoxically also

38 On the other hand, Euba's widespread use of open forms as well as his innovative notation in *Four Pieces for African Orchestra* are reminiscent of experiments in the Western avant-garde. In reality, they are grounded in an effort to render an African idiom more precisely than traditional notation, a fact that paradoxically serves as a reminder of the non-Western basis for much Euro-American innovation.

reverses the logical sequence of Berlioz's thematic transformation: it is as if the more literal quotation in fact *derives* from the Africanized *Dies irae* in the prelude. The retrospective hearing encouraged by this kind of memory-menacing music poses a challenge to the history of relations between Africa and Europe. Indeed, Euba's opera can be described as a complex study in allusions to and quotations of stylistic idioms on both sides of the continental divide: for example, at one point in the first chant White Voice's self-righteous expression of redemption through suffering is mockingly accompanied by an organ sounding a cadential formula, and then, in the second chant, Euba presents a traditional African call-and-response song 'Ki lo se to o jo' ('Why Do You Not Dance?') for chanter and chorus.

Euba's bi-musical facility is a calculated challenge to Euro-American cultural dominance. While his polystylism functions in a less overtly deconstructive way than that of, say, Luciano Berio or Alfred Schnittke, his intertextual palette is more genuinely multifaceted. In the spirit of Senghor's now famous dictum, 'Assimilate but don't be assimilated,' Euba's work is motivated by an effort to forge encounters between Europe and Africa in mutually enriching ways. He writes in his book *Modern African Music* that 'The modern African composer has responded to the politics of imperial conquest by beating Europeans at their own game, and then rejecting the rules as irrelevant.'[39] But this rebellion in musical language cannot disguise the fact that such African composers have a paradoxical double voice, for without singing the praises of Western musical premises there can be no global recognition of the African voice. Moreover, the yearning to merge African and European aesthetics in Euba's œuvre is confounded by the almost alienated division of musical material: Western instruments harmonize; African instruments rhythmicize. Such a dual musicality risks recapitulating what Kofi Agawu calls the 'invention' of African rhythm no less than the vividly contrasting invention of European harmony:[40] stated in Theodor Adorno's terms, the pre-constituted stylistic oppositions presented by the music cohabit in a blocked dialectic.

Two types of 'art' music from north and west Africa confound the kind of aesthetic dichotomy found in the works discussed above. The first type involves the unbridled paraphrase of traditionally conceived music in the context of Western art-music instruments. The Sudanese composer Hamza El Din's *Escalay* ('Waterwheel') for string quartet is a classic example of this orientation: it is a creative transcription of El Din's composition by the same name for *oud*

39 Euba, *Modern African Music*, p. 9.

40 Agawu recognizes the way rhythmic processes are frequently foregrounded to signal the African dimensions of neo-African 'art' music: 'This "invention" of African rhythm has had the negative effect of discouraging explorations in the dimensions of melody, instinctive harmonization and timbrel density' ('Analytic Issues', p. 143).

(lute), an instrument of classical Arabic origin, combining Arabic influences with ideas growing out of the vocal music and drumming of traditional Nubia. The Kronos Quartet commissions, *Saade* ('I'm Happy') by the Moroccan composer Hassan Hakmoun and *Wawshishijay* ('Our Beginning') by the Ghanaian composer Obo Addy, also belong in this category: Addy specializes in traditional Ghanaian music and dance as well as various African/American fusions, rather than notated 'art' music, and his bands Kukrudu and Okropong – both founded in the 1980s – use no musical notation. (*Wawshishijay* was transcribed for Kronos by Chris Baum.[41]) But by shifting the music to a medium that lies at the heart of European high-'art' music, Addy's African music morphs into a contemplative Western form. Interestingly, Addy explicitly demystifies the vexing ideological dimension of an innately African rhythmic sense: 'American audiences are a little funny about me playing African music with white people in the band. But you can get a white person who is more rhythmic than an African.'[42] While it is true that Addy's work for the Kronos Quartet resists the polarities found in the art compositions by Euba, Nketia, and others, it potentially falls prey to a different kind of ethnographic essentialism that is encouraged by the packaging of the CD *Pieces of Africa* (1992), designed as it is to resonate with the curatorial ideology of 'world' music.

A second way African composers have confounded the widespread aesthetic dichotomy between rhythm and pitch involves the creation of tonal pitch fields that are neither African nor European in origin. Composers like Joshua Uzoigwe from Nigeria and Gamal Abdel-Rahim from Egypt, for example, have achieved this ideal principally through the use of modal constellations. In the 1950s and 60s Abdel-Rahim composed primarily in a Western idiom, but following a systematic study of traditional Egyptian music in the 1970s and 80s the composer began to cross-breed Western stylistic traits with Egyptian ones. Abdel-Rahim's musical language replaces the major/minor system with Egyptian folk *maqams* (or modes) and incorporates extensive use of rhythmic irregularities drawn from traditional music.[43] But the most important innovation in Abdel-Rahim's work is his extension of traditional monody into the context of polyphony. The composer governs the linear polyphonic weave by rules grounded in the typical intervallic structure of the modes: in works like his Rhapsody for Cello and Piano, for instance, extensive motivic transformations engender new modal fields, which, in turn, establish large-scale form through modal modulation.

41 Taylor, *Global Pop*, p. 59.

42 In Lynn Darroch, 'Obo Addy: Third-World Beat', *Northwest Magazine*, 20 August 1989, p. 4.

43 Samha, El Kholy, 'Gamal Abdel-Rahim and the Fusion of Traditional Egyptian and Western Elements in Modern Egyptian Music', in Kimberlin and Euba (eds.), *Intercultural Music*, Vol. I, Bayreuth, 1995, pp. 27–37; p. 29.

Like their contemporaries in popular music, west and north African composers of 'art' music are faced with considerable challenges in the new century. As Kofi Agawu and Abiola Irele have pointed out, various prohibitive material circumstances curtail its development on African soil.[44] Agawu notes that 'there is no patronage for composers of "art" music, few competent performers, few good performing venues, and practically no support of radio or television. Add to this the paucity of written music and – perhaps most significant for a composing tradition based on European models – the general unavailability of – perhaps even a lack of interest in – twentieth-century European music and you can see the formidable problems facing the post-colonial African composer.'[45] Irele even suggests that, in contrast to African popular music, an African 'art' music is neither possible nor desirable: he notes the extraordinary range and vitality of local musical life in Africa and contrasts the expressive power of various traditional and popular musical forms with the diminishing relevance of modern 'art' music in the West.[46] Irele correctly points out that the formal complexity of much *traditional* African music is the match of the West's high musical art and that these traditions have contemplative value: why then manufacture a contemplative idiom in the European image when one already exists in African traditions? He asks rhetorically, 'What novel contribution to the universal patrimony of music can be made by a work written for that wonderful instrument – say, a "Concerto for Kora and Orchestra" – that hasn't already been made by the organic fusion of oral utterance with song in the Manding epic of Sundiata?'[47]

One problem with this position is that, as we have seen, it is open to a perniciously essentialist interpretation (serious music is for whites, popular music for blacks). Another is that related fusions between the *kora* and Western instruments – which often means collaborations between musicians from different cultural traditions – are in fact already under way in various parts of the world. Philip Glass's collaboration with Foday Musa Suso on 'Spring Waterfall' is one such example. After listening to various kinds of world music, Suso composed the *kora* part using a digital delay and harmonizer; cascading layers of the *kora* were mixed into three tracks of piano music played by Glass in his characteristic minimalist style. The point is that not all 'fusions' are equal. As we have again seen, African music has become increasingly mired in the operations of the transnational music market, where it occupies a precarious and vulnerable place, and in this context musicians whose overwhelming allegiance is to the aesthetic dimensions of music have an urgent role to play in

44 See Irele, 'Is African Music Possible?', and Agawu, 'Analytic Issues'.
45 Agawu, 'Analytic Issues', p. 137. 46 Irele, 'Is African Music Possible?', p. 70. 47 Ibid.

keeping the world's ears open to precisely the value, complexity, and autonomy of which Irele speaks. And 'art' music is a potentially crucial frontier in this general struggle, acting perhaps paradoxically as a custodian of traditional African sound-worlds. In this respect at least, the contribution made by African composers – their insistence, in Agawu's terms, on playing 'in the same league as their European, American, and Asian colleagues'[48] – cannot be spirited away in the metaphorics of Irele's hoped-for 'organic' evolution.

Recontextualizing tradition: popular and 'art' musics of south and east Africa

Musical life in southern Africa underwent dramatic transformations in the final decades of the twentieth century. These changes reflected the drastically altered political landscape accompanying independence. In the Zimbabwean war of liberation, for example, popular music was used to encourage fighters in the guerrilla camps as well as to politicize and mobilize people living in the rural areas; known as *chimurenga*, these songs were disseminated locally via nocturnal gatherings (*pungwes*) involving local peasants and guerrillas who had established themselves in a particular area, as well as radio programmes (often broadcast from sites outside Rhodesia). While most *chimurenga* songs were based on a hybrid Euro-African style – a blend of pop, rock, *makwaya*, *jocho*, *jiti*, Ndebele songs, and Christian hymns – their African nationalist rhetoric extolling the value of indigenous art forms gradually became reflected in their stylistic idioms as well: in particular, *chimurenga* star Thomas Mapfumo's output of the 1980s and 90s was marked by a distinctively hypnotic reinvention of *mbira* music. In the song 'Chitima Ndikature' (from *Chamunorwa*, 1989), for example, the sound of the *mbira* is transposed to one of the guitar lines, while the second guitar intermittently outlines the characteristically descending melodic figures played by the index finger of the right hand on the *mbira*; the shuffling sound of the *hosho* (hand-held rattles) is emulated by the high-hat and the bass drum, while the bass guitar plays a pattern that emerges from the combined left-hand parts of the *mbira* lines. Mapfumo's lyrics address the problem of political injustice and exploitation on both local and global fronts: immersed in a lengthy Congolese war and faced with escalating inflation, the worst petrol and food shortages in decades, and an AIDS crisis of staggering proportions, the Zimbabwean government came under increasing attack towards the end of the millennium. Again, Oliver 'Tuku' Mtukudzi's infectious *chimurenga-mbaqanga-rumba* music of the 1990s stages a critique of the current governing powers in

48 Kofi Agawu, review of 'Akin Euba: An Introduction to the Life and Music of a Nigerian Composer, by Joshua Uzoigwe', *Research in African Literatures* 27/1 (1996), pp. 232–6; p. 236.

much the same way that traditional *chimurenga* musicians had done under threat from Rhodesian censors; songs like 'Wake Up' (on Mtukudzi's massive international hit *Tuku Music*, 1999) urge listeners to be attentive to current political developments via suggestion instead of outright statement.[49] The musical basis of the music hinges on the dampened string technique typical of *chimurenga* 'mbira-guitar', interlacing two polyphonic lines around an indigenous tune.

In a context where black people had long been denied equal access to political, cultural, and commercial mobility, popular music had a lengthy association with expressions of freedom and political defiance. In South Africa, for example, Mzwakhe Mbuli, dubbed the 'Poet of the Struggle', formed The Equals, a band whose township-derived music enlivened political rallies in the 1980s and early 90s. In apartheid South Africa the simple act of performing with musicians across the colour line was an act of defiance – the most well-known example of such inter-racial musicking being Juluka, a popular band founded on a collaboration between the white South African Johnny Clegg and the black South African Sipho Mchunu. While less extroverted in their political message than Mbuli and the Equals, Juluka combined lyrics that explicitly expressed the disruptions of the dispossessed with forceful Zulu-based *mazkhande* riffs and athletic dancing; they also drew on funk, reggae and *mbaqanga* styles. While South Africa had a long tradition of multiracial musical performance, particularly in African jazz circles, Juluka paved the way for collaborations between black and white musicians on the terrain of more visibly popular music. Further mixed bands like Mapantsula and Mango Groove appeared, and even Afrikaans-identified white bands like The Kalahari Surfers, The Cherry Faced Lurchers and the Gereformeerde Blues Band (mockingly named after the hyper-conservative Nederlandse Gereformeerde church) sang out against social oppression, political hypocrisy, and military conscription. Unlike the Zimbabwean case, South African music associated with political liberation tended to turn less towards indigenous musical idioms and more towards defiant genre-bending.

Of course not all innovative synthetic styles reflected political ambitions. Sipho 'Hotstix' Mabuse, for example, combined *mbaqanga*-derived 'bubblegum' pop with disco and soul to create an unabashedly popular jive music; although his 1987 album *Chant of the Marching* introduced a political dimension to the music, his popularity derived more from the new synthetic disco style than from the social message. Likewise, the unbridled bubble-gum music of Yvonne Chaka Chaka became massively popular in pan-Africa: on the strength of her 1988 album *Umbqombothi*, she was able to fill the seventy thousand seats

49 See the discussion of Tuku Beat in Jonathan Stock's chapter, pp. 33–5.

of Kinshasa's football stadium.[50] Despite the cultural boycott on South African music, some musicians managed to break into the international market in the 1980s and 90s. Mahlathini and the Mahotella Queens, for example, recorded with the Art of Noise in the 1980s and toured England and the United States as an independent outfit in the early 1990s; they combined a fast-paced brew of *mbaqanga* and synthesized Zulu music (known as *simanjemanje*) with dizzying dance steps. Mahlatini's legendary bass 'groaning' intoned powerful images of African pride and independence.

Following the achievement of material independence in 1994, the already thriving South African popular-music scene entered a renewed wave of eclectic innovation and experimentation. The unprecedented influx of musicians from across Africa, coupled with a growing music-festival culture, encouraged creative exchanges between local and international musicians, and in the process new musical genres were invented and old ones transformed. For example, the highly synthesized 1980s bubble-gum pop of divas like Chaka Chaka and Brenda Fassie morphed into the pulsating pop style known as *kwaito* in the 1990s; in this new era, the outrageously provocative Fassie (affectionately dubbed the 'Queen of *Kwaito*') mostly abandoned singing in English and adopted instead an innovative blend of Sotho, Xhosa, and Zulu. (Her 1998 album, *Memeza* or 'Shout', was the first South African album to go platinum on its first day of release.) *Kwaito* is a genre-defying style blending the programmed percussion and vibrant call-and-response vocals of 1980s bubblegum with British garage, American hiphop, and the new Jamaican ragga music; this inter-cultural mix, in turn, is framed by laid-back bass lines that can sound like Chicago-based house music in slow-motion. New *kwaito* bands like Bongo Maffin and TKZ Family raised their international profiles when they appeared on the Central Park SummerStage in 2001.

While most popular South African music of the 1980s and 90s was the hybridized result of transatlantic borrowing, blending, and metamorphosis, Africanized 'art' music in the region tended strategically to limit its aesthetic parameters to the structural configurations of specific indigenous idioms. The compositions for string quartet by the Zimbabwean composer and *kalimba* virtuoso Dumisani Maraire, for example, are creative paraphrases of traditional African forms.[51] In *Kutambarara* ('Spreading'), Maraire presents a well-known *kalimba* tune in the context of a string quartet along with a Western-styled

50 Ewens, *Africa O-Ye!*, p. 204.

51 The *kalimba* is a 'thumb piano' similar in technique (but quite different in structure) to the *mbira*. Dumisani Maraire was a master *kalimba* performer who spent many years at the University of Washington, Seattle teaching Shona music and culture; his Ph.D. thesis, from the University of Washington, examines Shona *mbira* music in the context of spirit possession. Before his death in 2000, Maraire lived in Zimbabwe, where he taught at the University of Zimbabwe, Harare.

choir; the *kalimba* is retuned to a diatonic scale and the music's Shona-based harmonic movement is reinterpreted as a functional progression. The four strings elaborate a multi-part texture derived from the *kalimba* lines, while Maraire sings messages in Shona about 'spreading . . . African concepts, perspectives, philosophies, traditions and cultures' to the increasingly jubilant response of the choir.[52] The musical works of the Ugandan composer, Justinian Tamusuza, are similarly rooted in paraphrase technique:[53] his pieces *Ekitundu Ekisooka* ('First Movement') for string quartet and *Abakadde Abaagalana Be Balima Akambugu* ('Mutual Lovers Are Always Successful') for soprano, tenor, and prepared piano, for example, are both based on specific Kigandan folksongs. In *Abakadde*, the voices, which sing in Luganda about the struggle for sustainable love in intimate relationships, are set in a kind of call-and-response contrast with the piano, which has been prepared in order to approximate the timbre of Kiganda xylophones; the music constantly, albeit irregularly, shifts between metric articulations of simple and compound time, with the downbeats implied by the melodies' staggered entrances tending to be disaligned with each other no less than with the piano part. These cross-penetrating contrapuntal lines, in turn, interact with patterns drawn out of the texture by a layer of cross-rhythmic accents in the piano and by changes in the microtonal vocal inflections of the voices. Tamusuza restricts his tonal language to two pentatonic collections (gently estranged by the piano preparations and the vocal inflections), forming a large-scale ABA′. The return of the opening section is punctuated by traditional hand-clapping.

The tendency towards unfettered transcription, paraphrase, and quotation of local African music became a hallmark of South African 'art' music in the 1980s and 90s. Unlike the 'art'-music tradition in west Africa (broadly speaking a tradition committed to integrating African and European musical structures), the new South African model was to identify local forms of African music *as* a self-contained form of 'art' music.[54] By the beginning of the 1980s, several varieties of South African music had entered the concert hall on both a local and global scale: before forming the rock-oriented band Juluka, Johnny Clegg and Sipho Mchunu had performed traditional music for Zulu mouthbow and guitar to an audience of contemplative listeners at venues such as the Market Theatre in downtown Johannesburg, while the then exiled jazz pianist

52 Dumisani Maraire, liner notes from *Pieces of Africa*.

53 Justinian Tamusuza (b. 1951) was trained in Kigandan traditional music before studying composition at Queen's University (Belfast) and Northwestern University (Illinois). He currently teaches at the Makerere University in Uganda.

54 One exception to this general rule is Hans Roosenschoon's *Timbila*, which combines the music of Venancio Mbande and the Chopi xylophone players with a symphony orchestra; the work was commissioned by the locally based Oude Meester Foundation in 1984, a time of particularly intense state-sanctioned oppression.

Abdullah Ibrahim performed in sit-down concert venues in Europe and the United States. Ibrahim's unique pianistic style – blending a motley array of distinctly South African idioms (from Sufi music to Xhosa music) – was harnessed to messages of political defiance and hope; in this way the concert piano became Africanized in both form and content (the comparison with Euba's concept of 'African pianism' is telling). Building on these foundations, South Africa had produced by the end of the 1990s a number of innovative musical genres approximating the condition of 'art' music, ranging from the Soweto String Quartet (performing African popular music) to the gospel group SDSA Chorale (showcasing the rich a cappella traditions of South Africa). In this way locally made music became increasingly classicized in the post-Apartheid era.

In southern Africa, local musicians have long adopted Western instruments (the guitar, the trumpet, the concertina, the piano, and so forth) in the service of African aesthetics, and the idea of performing indigenous idioms on Western *orchestral* instruments in the final decades of the twentieth century was an extension of this. Such reconceptualization of African music as 'art' music emerged in a complex historical conjuncture. First, the cultural boycott against South Africa in the apartheid years paradoxically produced an era of fervent artistic innovation grounded entirely in local resources. Second, in the context of growing anti-apartheid sentiment many of the arts actively experimented with imagining delineations of a genuinely post-apartheid South African cultural identity. Third, the emergence of new marketing categories in the music industries of the industrialized nations brought a potentially international profile to homespun forms of African music: for instance, the already-cited Kronos Quartet release *Pieces of Africa* was marketed and styled in terms representing an intersection between avant-garde-oriented new 'art' music and tradition-oriented 'world' music.

In apartheid South Africa, the minority government invested considerably in Western forms of culture, including the building of impressive institutions housing productions of symphonies, ballets, operas, and drama. Consequently, in the domain of music education, the central methodological and canonical reference point was European music. A coterie of white composers, largely supported by institutional bodies propped up by the apartheid state, created 'art' music reflecting and sustaining this ideological orientation.[55] However, in the 1980s and 90s, a number of calculated attempts to resist the then prevalent anti-African aesthetic surfaced within the art tradition, with composers like Kevin Volans, Michael Blake, Mzilikaze Khumalo, and Bongani Ndodana creating works prominently featuring African modes of music-making. Ndodana

55 Representative composers include Arnold van Wyk (1916–83) and Hubert du Plessis (b. 1922).

treats the source material grounding his music as an open-ended palette of ideas that can be freely combined; while his thematic lyricism and intricate rhythmic patterning is beholden to African music, the constant transformation of thematic material recalls European Romanticism. For example, Ndodana bases the first movement of his *Rituals for Forgotten Faces* (IV) for string quartet on the unmistakable *ughubu* bow playing of the late Princess Magogo. Vacillating unpredictably but incessantly between two fundamental pitches, the music evolves into a web-like array of motivic ideas. Sometimes these cannot be disentangled and become pure texture; at other times they sound forth in stark simplicity; or they mischievously evaporate, illusion-like, into silence. The chromatic pitch collection coupled with the free transformations of themes and ideas exceeds the language of the original *ughubu* bow, but by elaborating simultaneous layers of melodic-rhythmic groupings, even the non-traditional transformations sound like African modes of variation. Likewise, in the second movement of *Rituals*, Ndodana inhabits the terrain of African plucked lamellophones, once again complicating the distinction between cluster and figure, texture and polyphony, innovation and tradition.

Another example of music distinctly modeled on African idioms is the music of Michael Blake: his *Let Us Run Out of the Rain* (for two players at one piano or harpsichord or for percussion quartet), for example, is a refracted paraphrase of *Nsenga kalimba* music from Zambia. The music filters and recombines typical *kalimba* fingering patterns into novel fragments, which in turn articulate unpredictable formal episodes of call-and-response. By transferring the overtone-rich sounds of the *kalimba* to the time-worn blandness of the modern industrial piano, the music paradoxically conjures up the faded colours and open spaces of the southern African landscape. In some works Blake abstracts the process of paraphrasing African music still further: his *French Suite* for piano solo traces elusively skeletal references to the formal patterns produced by the *kora* and the *mbira* in the unfamiliar (and defamiliarizing) context of asymmetrically shifting rhythmic groupings. Blake's understated translations of African music into Western idioms deftly negotiate the borderline between quotation and abstraction, and, in the process, interrogate the opposition between the two.

Likewise, the pioneering work of Kevin Volans' African-inspired work is a critique of the commonplace figuration of African music in the metaphorics of 'folk' or 'world' music (and its attendant de-emphasis of 'pure' aesthetic value), drawing attention instead to the profound formal complexity and beauty of African music. In the words of the composer, 'I . . . did quite consciously want to elevate the status of street music and African music in South Africa.'[56] Volans'

56 Quoted in Timothy Taylor, 'When We Think about Music and Politics: The Case of Kevin Volans', *Perspectives of New Music* 33 (1995), pp. 504–36; p. 514.

strategy was to take a hands-off approach and allow the music to be heard *as* quotation: the source material is overt, vivid, literal, almost tangible. In his piece *Mbira*, for example, Volans simply presents ten full minutes of basically unaltered transcriptions of the mbira tune *Nyamaropa* (performed by Gwanzura Gwenzi) for two retuned harpsichords. Even the titles are pre-given: 'She Who Sleeps with a Small Blanket', 'Cover Him With Grass', and 'White Man Sleeps' are all taken from African song titles (the last a translation of *Nzungu agona*, one of the silent dance patterns of the Nyanga Panpipe Dance of the Nyungwe at Nsava, Tete, Mozambique). It is precisely because of the immediacy of this recognition that the African dances themselves recede from earshot and the listener is drawn to something else: released from their familiar context, the musical materials are experienced as a formal play of sound, giving rise to a purely 'aesthetic' hearing.

Again, in his string quartet *Hunting: Gathering*, Volans juxtaposes a variety of pieces of African music – *kora* music from Mali, *lesiba* music from Lesotho, an Ethiopian folk tune, and so on – in a musical pastiche that passes like a journey or a dream. In the middle of the second movement, the *mbira* tune 'Mutamba' appears in its traditional form; this was the song played by Zhanje for Pasipamire, the legendary spirit medium for Chaminuka, during the nineteenth-century Shona/Ndebele wars (legend has it that the song endowed Pasipamire with superhuman strength in the face of certain death). Volans then builds a set of variations on it, characteristically separating the two *mbira* parts by one pulse – a technique which, on a note-to-note level, is in keeping with Shona tradition. But in the context of the quartet the passage is striking for its gentle, almost Schubertian, melodic character. By placing the *mbira* music in the strings' most comfortable range, and by framing the passage with more abstract colouristic sections (such as angular leaping gestures in the violin, random fragments of pizzicato, desolate tapestries of extended harmonics, and suddenly outbursting double-stops), Volans draws attention to the intricate *melodic* and *harmonic* power of 'Mutamba'. Challenging the Eurocentric stereotyping of African music as 'rhythmic', he effectively downplays the musical exoticism of the *mbira*, and the passage in this way makes a unique aesthetic and political point.

The emergence of an Africanized 'art' music in southern Africa was an overdetermined confluence of contradictory historical factors. Consequently, the music paradoxically both aspires to cultural legitimacy in an international context *and* aims to resist the global juggernaut threatening local traditions. While its significance to the the overall cultural scene in Africa is contested and in doubt, African 'art' music has a substantial role to play in the context of global intercultural relations. First, the creative tension between local African musical traditions and Western 'art' music has the potential to encourage new directions in the evolution of international 'art' music in the twenty-first century. As Nketia argues, while intercultural encounters were considered idiosyncratic throughout most of the twentieth century, they came to be regarded as a 'distinct area of contemporary compositional practice . . . an alternative or complement to modernism' in its final decades;[57] since 1977, for example, an international composers' workshop hosted in Europe under the auspices of the International Music Council (UNESCO) has facilitated globally based intercultural contact between composers. Second, although its role has been systematically under-narrated, the importance of African music to the development of Western music in the twentieth century has been considerable: aside from the extensive quotations of African music in that of the West, African procedures and structures arguably lie at the heart of some of Europe's most ground-breaking musical production. Just as the figure of the 'primitive' in Pablo Picasso's middle-period work culminated in the radical abstractions of analytic Cubism, so European music's radically abstract mathematical formalizations in the twentieth century coincided with a fascination with African and other non-Western music. In this way the impact of non-Western music was felt in Western music's most 'formalist', and thus apparently culturally 'pure', musical production, no less than in its more overtly hybridized production: even Pierre Boulez's very first attempts at total serialism (the serial organization of all musical parameters) in the 1950s were carried out on the terrain of African music – in this case *sanza* music from the Cameroon, in his *Etude* for tape.

But what is really remarkable is the fact that almost all standard historical accounts have been wholly silent on the contribution of African music to both the formation and the displacement of Western music's various aesthetic categories: the work of the minimalist composers is generally interpreted within a wholly Western framework, despite the literal and overt references to African and other non-Western music and, in the case of Steve Reich, the composer's well-documented study of African drumming. African music, in short, has become a central reference point for defining a genuinely post-serialist aesthetic in the West. And yet, shorn of its African heritage, the conventional historical narrative emphasizes the music's abstract organization at the expense of any understanding of the complex intercultural negotiations of sound and meaning that gave rise to it. This is where the African 'art' music of the 1980s and 90s paradoxically reclaims a stake in the making of the world's musical history.

57 Nketia, 'Exploring African Musical Resources in Contemporary Composition', p. 224.

Bibliography

Agawu, Kofi. Review of 'Akin Euba: An Introduction to the Life and Music of a Nigerian Composer, by Joshua Uzoigwe', *Research in African Literatures* 27/1 (1996), pp. 232–6.

'Analytic Issues Raised by Contemporary Art Music', in Cynthia Tse Kimberlin and Akin Euba (eds.), *Intercultural Music*, Vol. III, Richmond, CA, 2001, pp. 135–47.

Chernoff, John Miller. *African Rhythm and African Sensibility: Aesthetics and Social Action in African Musical Idioms*, Chicago, 1979.

Darroch, Lynn. 'Obo Addy: Third-World Beat', *Northwest Magazine*, 20 August 1989, p. 4.

El Kholy, Samha. 'Gamal Abdel-Rahim and the Fusion of Traditional Egyptian and Western Elements in Modern Egyptian Music', in Cynthia Tse Kimberlin and Akin Euba (eds.), *Intercultural Music*, Vol. I, Bayreuth, 1995, pp. 27–37.

Erlmann, Veit. *Music, Modernity, and the Global Imagination: South Africa and the West*, New York, 1999.

Euba, Akin. *Modern African Music: A Catalogue of Selected Archival Materials at Iwalewa-Haus, University of Bayreuth, Germany*, Bayreuth, 1993.

Ewens, Graeme. *Africa O-Ye! A Celebration of African Music*, London, 1991.

Frith, Simon (ed.). *Music and Copyright*, Edinburgh, 1993.

Hesmondhalgh, David. 'International Times: Fusions, Exoticism, and Antiracism in Electronic Dance Music', in Georgina Born and David Hesmondhalgh (eds.), *Western Music and its Others: Difference, Representation, and Appropriation in Music*, Berkeley, 2000, pp. 280–304.

Impey, Angela. 'Popular Music in Africa', in Ruth Stone (ed.), *Africa: The Garland Encyclopedia of World Music*, Vol. I, New York, 1998, pp. 415–37.

Irele, Abiola. 'Is African Music Possible?', *Transition* 61 (1993), pp. 56–71.

Jones, A. M. *Studies in African Music*, London, 1959.

Kubik, Gerhard. 'The Phenomenon of Inherent Rhythms in East and Central African Music', *African Music Society Journal*, 3/1 (1962), pp. 33–42.

N'Dour, Youssou. 'Postcard: Youssou N'Dour on Senegal', *Time* 158/14 (2001), special issue: 'Music Goes Global', p. 66.

Njoku, Johnston Akuma-Kalu. 'Art-Composed Music in Africa', in Ruth Stone (ed.), *Africa: The Garland Encyclopedia of World Music*, Vol. I, New York, 1998, pp. 232–53.

Nketia, Kwabena J. H. 'Exploring African Musical Resources in Contemporary Composition', in Cynthia Tse Kimberlin and Akin Euba (eds.), *Intercultural Music*, Vol. I, Bayreuth, 1995, pp. 221–39.

Samha, El Kholy. 'Gamal Abdel-Rahim and the Fusion of Traditional Egyptian and Western Elements in Modern Egyptian Music', in Cynthia Tse Kimberlin and Akin Euba (eds.), *Intercultural Music*, Vol. I, Bayreuth, 1995, pp. 27–37.

Taylor, Timothy. 'When We Think about Music and Politics: The Case of Kevin Volans', *Perspectives of New Music*, 33 (1995), pp. 504–36.

Global Pop: World Music, World Markets, New York and London, 1997.

Uzoigwe, Joshua. *Akin Euba: An Introduction to the Life and Music of a Nigerian Composer*, Altendorf, 1992.

Zemp, Hugo. 'The/An Ethnomusicologist and the Record Business, *Yearbook for Traditional Music*, 28 (1996), pp. 35–56.

Discography

Laurie Anderson. *Strange Angels* (Warner, 1989)
Tute Chigamba. *Mhembero* (independent release, 1998)
D. J. Sasha. *Global Underground: Arrivals* (Bedrock Music, 1999)
Nelly Furtado. *Whoa, Nelly!* (Dreamworks, 2000)
Kronos Quartet. *Pieces of Africa* (Elektra/Nonesuch, 1992)
Jali Kunda. *Griots of West Africa and Beyond* (Ellipsis Arts, 1997)
Madonna. *Groundwork: Act to Reduce Hunger* (Hear Music and the Starbucks Coffee Company, 2001)
Vusi Mahlasela. *Wisdom of Forgiveness* (Shifty/BMG Records Africa, 1994)
Thomas Mapfumo and the Blacks Unlimited. *Chamunorwa* (Mango/Polygram, 1989)
Chérif Mbaw. *Kham Kham* (Elektra, 2001)
MDC. *Sunny Trumpets (Kenard Mix)* (Groovilicins, 2001)
Eric Mouquet and Michael Sanchez. *Deep Forest* (Sony, 1994)
Oliver Mtukudzi. *Tuku Music* (Indigo Records, 1999)
Youssou N'Dour. *Set* (Virgin, 1990)
Youssou N'Dour. *The Guide* (Columbia, 1994)
Youssou N'Dour and Alan Stivell. *Dublin to Dakar: A Celtic Odyssey* (Putamayo World Music, 1999)
The Pan African Orchestra. *Opus 1* (Real World Records, 1995)
Louis Sarno. *Bayaka: The Extraordinary Music of the Babenzélé Pygmies* (Ellipsis, 1995)
Paul Simon. *Graceland* (Warner, 1986)
Talking Heads. *Remain in Light* (Warner, 1980)
TKZee Family. *GUZ 2001* (BMG, 1999)
Glen Velez. *Rhythmicolor Exotica* (Ellipsis Arts, 1996)
Wes Welenga. *Wes* (Sony, 1998)

Compilations

Ethnotechno: Sonic Anthropology, Volume 1 (Wax Trax! Records, 1994)
Spirit of Africa (RealWorld, 2001)

· Appendix 1 ·

Personalia

PETER ELSDON WITH BJÖRN HEILE

Abba Swedish pop group. They became famous with their winning song in the 1974 Eurovision Song Contest, 'Waterloo'. During the 1970s, they were the world's most successful pop group, selling huge numbers of records. Their style was based on the use of multitracked vocals, set against backing tracks drawing on dance music of the time.

Abbado, Claudio (b. 1933) Italian conductor. He studied conducting in Milan and Vienna, becoming the music director at La Scala, Milan, in 1971, where he included 20th-century works in the company's repertory. He became principal conductor of the London Symphony Orchestra in 1979, and succeeded Karajan as chief conductor of the Berlin Philharmonic in 1990. Abbado's recordings encompass a wide range of music, including the symphonies of Beethoven, Brahms, and Mahler, and many operatic works.

Adams, John (b. 1947) American composer and conductor. He studied at Harvard with Kirchner and Sessions. His early pieces such as *Phrygian Gates* (1977) and *Shaker Loops* (1978) drew on the minimalist style of Reich and Glass. The large-scale pieces of the next decade, such as *Harmonium* (1981) and *Harmonielehre* (1985), extended these techniques with a command of large orchestral forces and a nod to the late-Romantic tradition. Adams's operas *Nixon in China* (1987) and *The Death of Klinghoffer* (1991) drew on contemporary political events. Significant works of the 1990s included the Violin Concerto (1993) and *El Niño* (2000). Adams was also particularly active as a conductor during the 1990s, appearing with prominent American and European orchestras.

Ade, 'King' Sunny (b. 1946) Nigerian performer, known as the 'King' of Juju music. After achieving huge popularity in his home country, he was promoted in Europe by Island Records during the 1980s. Ade's bands usually include multiple guitarists and drummers.

Adès, Thomas (b. 1971) English composer. He studied at Cambridge and rapidly established a reputation as a major figure on the international scene. His string quartet *Arcadiana* (1994) demonstrates his interest in rekindling classical models, while other works show an exploration of the kind of rhythmic complexities tackled by Nancarrow and Ligeti. Other works of particular importance include the chamber opera *Powder Her Face* (1995), the orchestral piece *Asyla* (1997), and the full-scale opera *The Tempest* (2004).

Adorno, Theodor (1903–69) German sociologist and critical theorist, much of whose writing concerns music. In the late 1920s he studied piano with Eduard Steuermann and composition with Alban Berg, and edited the journal *Musikblätter des Anbruch*. Books such as *Philosophy of New Music* (1949, tr. 1973) and *Introduction to the Sociology of Music* (1962, tr. 1976) gave theorized expression to such Schoenbergian principles as the polarity between a progressive 'art' musical culture and a regressive mass culture. He taught at the Darmstadt summer courses in the 1950s and 60s, so helping to link the pre- and post-war avant-garde. His belief that music encodes basic aspects of society influenced the development of a more socially conscious musicology (the 'New' musicology) in the 1980s and 90s.

Andriessen, Louis (b. 1939) Dutch composer who studied composition at the Royal Conservatory in the Hague, and then worked with Berio in Berlin. In the 1970s he turned towards the minimalism of Reich, Riley, and Glass, employing a distinctive instrumental sound dominated by winds, keyboards, and guitars. Pieces such as *De voldharding* (1972) and *Hoketus* (1977) were written for ensembles specifically formed to perform his music. Later works such as *De tijd* (1981), and *De Materie* (1989) brought his compositional concerns into larger-scale settings. Andriessen is now a prominent figure on the European scene both as a composer and teacher.

Ansermet, Ernest (1883–1969) Swiss conductor. He studied mathematics before taking up conducting, becoming principal conductor of the Ballets Russes in 1915. He premiered pieces such as Satie's *Parade*, and Stravinsky's *The Soldier's Tale* and *Pulcinella*. Ansermet was also particularly involved in championing the work of Britten and Bartók.

Antheil, George (1900–59) American composer and pianist. He studied composition with Bloch, and quickly gained notoriety in Paris, moving there in 1923. His *Ballet mécanique* (1927) is a major piece in the history of percussion music, employing unconventional instruments such as aircraft propellers. Antheil's early reputation waned, and he settled in the US in 1933, where he wrote many film scores and turned to a Romantic style of composition.

Arlen, Harold (1905–86) American composer. His work included writing for many Broadway productions such as *St Louis Woman* (1946) and *House of Flowers* (1954). He worked on the score for the film musical *The Wizard of Oz* (1939), contributing the music to 'Over The Rainbow' for singer Judy Garland. He also collaborated with lyricists Ira Gershwin and Johnny Mercer.

Armstrong, Louis (1901–76) American jazz trumpeter, born in New Orleans. He moved to Chicago to join King Oliver's Creole Jazz Band in 1922, then joined Fletcher Henderson in New York in 1924. From 1925 he made a series of recordings with his Hot Five and later Hot Seven groups, which changed the course of jazz, promoting Armstrong as a powerful solo voice with an unequalled melodic conception. In his later career he presented himself increasingly as a popular entertainer.

Babbitt, Milton (b. 1916) American composer and theorist. He studied mathematics and music at the University of Pennsylvania and at New York University, and worked with Sessions at Princeton. He joined the music faculty there in 1948, becoming Conant Professor of Music in 1960, as well as a member of the composition faculty at Juilliard School in 1973. Babbitt's work as both composer and theorist is chiefly connected with the exploration of serial techniques, his background in maths aiding the systematization of twelve-tone theory; he was not only one of the first American composers to adopt the innovations of the Second Viennese School, but was also instrumental in extending serial principles to parameters other than pitch. He was also a pioneer of electroacoustic music, as in *Philomel* (1964).

Baez, Joan (b. 1941) American singer and songwriter. Baez became popular during the 1960s, at a time when folk music in America was associated with political sentiment. She performed at many of the major festivals and popular music events during the 1960s, and was known for a pure, unornamented style of vocal delivery.

Baker, Josephine (1906–75) American singer and actress, dubbed 'the black Venus'. She gained huge popularity in Paris after moving there in 1925, performing in stage shows where she combined the erotic and the comic to great effect. After rising to a pre-eminent position in Parisian society she starred in films, and was associated with the French Resistance during the Second World War.

Barber, Samuel (1910–81) American composer, known particularly for his *Adagio for Strings* (1936), ballet score *Medea* (1946), Cello Concerto (1945), and Piano Sonata (1949). The *Adagio for Strings* was performed by Toscanini and the NBC Symphony orchestra in 1938 and became Barber's best-known work, taking on a special significance through its inclusion in a number of film soundtracks and even CD compilations of mood music.

Barbirolli, John (1899–1970) English conductor. He studied at the Royal Academy of Music, and worked as a cellist before beginning a career as a conductor with the British National Opera Company. After some time at Covent Garden, he became permanent conductor of the New York Philharmonic, succeeding Toscanini, and then worked with the Hallé Orchestra. Barbirolli was best known for his interpretations of Romantic works, and particularly British composers such as Elgar, Delius, and Vaughan Williams.

Barenboim, Daniel (b. 1942) Israeli pianist and conductor, who studied in Paris with Nadia Boulanger. His early career as a pianist was spent mainly in Europe, and he made a number of recordings with the English Chamber Orchestra. He came to prominence as a conductor during the 1960s, while continuing to work as a pianist (most notably with Dietrich Fischer-Dieskau and Janet Baker), and in

1967 married the cellist Jacqueline Du Pré. He was music director of the Chicago Symphony Orchestra, as well as conducting at Bayreuth during the 1980s.

Barry, John (b. 1933) English composer, most famous for his scores for the James Bond films, particularly *Dr No* (1962), and *The Living Daylights* (1987). He has won awards for *Dances with Wolves* (1990), *Out of Africa* (1985), and *Born Free* (1966).

Bartók, Béla (1881–1945) Hungarian composer, pianist, and folklorist, decisively influenced by his interest in Hungarian folk music; early pieces reflecting this influence include the First String Quartet (1909) and the opera *Duke Bluebeard's Castle* (1911). The works from the following decade, such as *The Miraculous Mandarin* (1924), explore dissonant harmony more intensively, while the Third and Fourth String Quartets (1927 and 1928) combine folk influences with an interest in symmetrical forms. The piano collection *Mikrokosmos* (many of the pieces from which were first performed in 1937) is the most comprehensive result of Bartók's interest in folk music. Of the later works, *Music for Strings, Percussion, and Celesta* (1936) and the Concerto for Orchestra (1944) have both become major pieces in the contemporary orchestral repertory. Active throughout his career as a pianist, he continued to conduct research into folk traditions in Eastern Europe and Turkey, publishing major studies of Hungarian and Romanian music.

Basie, Count (1904–84) American bandleader and jazz pianist. He began working in the stride piano style, influenced by James P. Johnson and 'Fats' Waller. In 1935 he formed his own group in Kansas City, which gradually expanded into the Count Basie Orchestra; this produced such hits as 'Jumpin' at the Woodside' (1938) and 'Taxi War Dance' (1939), and included the bassist Walter Page and drummer Jo Jones, who helped establish a distinctive swinging four-beat style. The Basie Orchestra went through a number of incarnations during the course of its leader's career, but Basie's style always remained distinctive.

The Beach Boys American pop group formed in 1961, consisting of three brothers (Brian, Carl, and Denis Wilson) joined by two others (Al Jardine and Mike Love); the songs were written by Brian Wilson. Their first hit was 'Surfin'', and after signing for Capitol in 1962 they had a series of successes, including the songs 'California Girls' and 'I Get Around', with their distinctive close-harmony sound. The 1966 album *Pet Sounds* is widely considered their best, although it was not a commercial success.

The Beatles English pop group, comprising John Lennon, Paul McCartney, George Harrison, and Ringo Starr (who joined in 1962). They began playing in their native Liverpool, taking the name 'The Beatles' in 1960, but it was when Brian Epstein began promoting them and George Martin subsequently signed them to Parlophone that their success really began: their 1962 'Love Me Do' was a huge hit in Britain, and subsequent songs followed up on that success. In 1964 they conquered America with 'I Want To Hold Your Hand', and they quickly became a phenomenon, mobbed by teenage audiences wherever they went. The McCartney/Lennon partnership was crucial to their success, and produced many of their most successful songs. Later albums pursued a more experimental approach, and though the group ceased playing live in 1966, *Sergeant Pepper's Lonely Hearts Club Band* (1967) was one of the most important albums of the decade, with innovative use of tape and electronic effects. The band split up in 1970, and hopes of a reunion were dashed by Lennon's assassination by a fan in 1980.

Bechet, Sidney (1897–1959) American clarinettist and saxophonist, born in New Orleans. He worked in local touring shows before joining Will Marion Cook's Southern Syncopated Orchestra, which toured Europe in 1919. Thereafter Bechet formed his own group, in which he specialized on the soprano saxophone, the first jazz musician to do so. He subsequently worked with Duke Ellington and Louis Armstrong, recording with Armstrong in the Clarence Williams Blue Five group. Bechet travelled widely, finally settling in Paris in 1951, but was not fully recognized in his home country during his lifetime.

Beiderbecke, Bix (1903–31) American cornettist, who was exposed to jazz in Chicago, and began playing with The Wolverines in 1924. He also formed an association with saxophonist Frankie Trumbauer, and both played in Paul Whiteman's orchestra. Beiderbecke died tragically young, due in large part to alcoholism. His style was founded on a sophisticated harmonic understanding and a distinctive clear sound.

Bennett, Richard Rodney (b. 1936) English composer and pianist. He studied at the Royal Academy of Music and then with Boulez, attending the Darmstadt Summer School. At the same time, he was pursuing a career as a film composer, his many film scores including *Murder on the Orient Express* (1975). His *Concerto for Stan Getz* (1990) was never performed by its intended soloist due to Getz's premature death, but illustrates Bennett's concern to fuse jazz and 'art' styles.

Berg, Alban (1885–1935) Austrian composer, a student of Arnold Schoenberg and the composer of two influential operas, *Wozzeck* and the unfinished *Lulu*. He had stronger Romantic tendencies than the other members of the so-called Second Viennese School, and his freely atonal works such as the Three Orchestral Pieces (1915) and *Wozzeck* (1922) combine a certain nostalgia with sometimes ironical reworkings of earlier styles; at the same time, like Webern, he was fascinated by constructive devices (the first of the Three Pieces is a palindrome). He adopted Schoenberg's serial system in 1927, with the *Lyric Suite* for string quartet, but his use of it was highly individualistic (as illustrated by his serial setting of Bach's chorale 'Es ist genug' in the Violin Concerto of 1935). *Lulu* also employs serial techniques, while incorporating something of the sound-world of jazz, but Berg did not complete the orchestration, and only in 1976 was the opera staged complete (in a version by Friedrich Čerha).

Berio, Luciano (1925–2003) Italian composer. He trained at Milan Conservatory and with Dallapiccola at Tanglewood and in 1955 joined Bruno Maderna in setting up the Studio di Fonologia of the RAI, the Italian broadcasting network;

he also held a variety of other positions, notably at the Juilliard school (1965–71) and IRCAM (1974–80). Although initially associated with Darmstadt-style multiple serialism, he quickly developed a personal voice characterized by clear musical gestures of almost corporeal immediacy, as in *Sinfonia* (1968–9) and *Coro* (1975–7); among his most notable achievements are his treatment of the voice, as in *Thema (Omaggio a Joyce)* (1958) and *Sequenza III* (1965–6), and his work in music theatre, as in the 'messa in scena' *Passaggio* (1961–2) and the 'azione musicale' *Un re in ascolto* (1979–84).

Berlin, Irving (1888–1989) American composer. Berlin had a highly successful career encompassing Broadway shows, popular songs, and film scores. His early work was influenced by ragtime, including the famous *Alexander's Ragtime Band* (1911); his musicals include *Face The Music* (1932) and *Annie Get Your Gun* (1946), while his songs include 'God Bless America', 'White Christmas', and 'You're Just In Love'. He also composed many film scores, including *Top Hat* (1935), *Carefree* (1938), and *Holiday Inn* (1942).

Bernstein, Elmer (b. 1922) American composer and conductor, who studied composition with Sessions and Wolpe, and after serving in the Air Corps began a career as a film composer. In scores for such films as *Walk on the Wild Side* (1962) he employed a jazz vocabulary in the context of an orchestral score; other notable scores include *The Great Escape* (1963), *To Kill A Mockingbird* (1963), and *The Magnificent Seven* (1960).

Bernstein, Leonard (1918–90) American composer and conductor. He studied composition with Piston at Harvard, and conducting with Koussevitzky at Tanglewood, and made a stunning debut with the New York Philharmonic in 1943; the following year his First Symphony was premiered. His compositions span the genres of the Broadway musical (*On the Town*, 1944, and *West Side Story*, 1957) and the concert-music tradition (*Prelude, Fugue, and Riffs*, 1949, and *Chichester Psalms*, 1965). In 1958 Bernstein became musical director of the New York Philharmonic Orchestra, and he formed a close association with the Vienna Philharmonic in later years. He had a reputation as an intensely passionate conductor whose physical expression of his art tended to polarize opinion.

Berry, Chuck (b. 1926) American singer and guitarist, whose 1950s hits such as 'Roll Over Beethoven' and 'Johnny B. Goode' encapsulated the rock and roll style of the time. His style was based mostly on the blues, and his guitar playing proved as influential as his songs.

Bhundu Boys Zimbabwean group, formed in 1980 by Biggie Tembo, Rise Kagona, David Mankaba, Shakie Kangwena, and Kenny Chitsvatsa, and strongly influenced by Thomas Mapfumo, the best known popular musician from Zimbabwe. Their style of music drew from the township style of South Africa, while incorporating their own unique 'jit' style of dance. They gained significant exposure in Britain through Radio 1 DJ John Peel, and their 1986 album *Shabini* was a considerable success. They signed to the WEA label in 1987.

Birtwistle, Harrison (b. 1934) English composer. He studied clarinet at the Royal Manchester College of Music, where his fellow students included Alexander Goehr and Peter Maxwell Davies. *Refrains and Choruses* (1957) was his first major work, showing the influence of Boulez and Stockhausen. *Punch and Judy* (1966) demonstrated Birtwistle's interest in cyclic structures, fusing elements of the traditional Punch and Judy show with Greek tragedy, while *Verses for Ensembles* (1969) required musicians to move about the stage while performing in a kind of instrumental theatre, and *The Triumph of Time* (1972) brought Birtwistle's concerns with temporality to the fore. His operas *The Mask of Orpheus* (1984), *Gawain* (1991), *The Second Mrs Kong* (1994), and *The Last Supper* (1999) are among the major British operatic works of the century.

Boulanger, Nadia (1887–1989) French teacher, conductor, and composer. She studied at the Paris Conservatoire with Fauré and Widor, and was initially active as a concert pianist, although she composed many songs and chamber works up until the 1920s. She made her first public appearance as a conductor in Paris in 1934, and went on to perform throughout Europe and America. Boulanger was of most importance as a composition teacher, her students including Bernstein, Copland, Sessions, and Harris.

Boulez, Pierre (b. 1925) French composer and conductor. He trained at the Paris Conservatoire, where he took part in Olivier Messiaen's analysis classes, quickly establishing himself as one of the leading composers of the Darmstadt circle through a rigorous adherence to multiple serialist techniques, as in *Structures I* (1951–2), but developing a more flexible and sensuous style in *Le marteau sans maître* (1963–5) and *Pli selon pli* (1957–62); thereafter he pursued a highly successful career as a conductor. A brilliant campaigner and organizer, he persuaded the French government to set up IRCAM (Institut de Recherche et Coordination Acoustique/Musique), the world's biggest institution devoted to new music, which he directed from 1977–92. His composition *Répons* (1980–4) is one of the most sophisticated explorations of IRCAM's techniques for spatial sound distribution.

Bowie, David (b. 1947) English rock singer and songwriter. Bowie changed his name early on in his career, and became well-known with the album *The Rise and Fall of Ziggy Stardust and the Spiders from Mars* (1970), featuring his alter ego Ziggy Stardust, an alien rock musician. Bowie declared his bisexuality at around the same time, and his music continued to explore the incorporation of different stylistic influences with albums such as *Aladdin Sane* (1973) and *Diamond Dogs* (1974); *Low* (1977) was a product of his collaboration with Brian Eno. In the 1980s and 90s Bowie was active as a producer, working with such artists as Iggy Pop and Lou Reed.

Brendel, Alfred (b. 1931) Austrian pianist who studied with Steuermann and Fischer, and has focused on the Austro-German repertory; his recordings of Beethoven, Schubert, and Mozart are particularly well regarded. He has recorded the complete Beethoven sonatas a number of times, with each recording demonstrating an increasingly sophisticated interpretation. Brendel is also known for his writings, which propound an analytical approach directed specifically towards performance.

Britten, Benjamin (1913–76) English composer, conductor, and pianist. He composed prolifically as a boy, studying at an early age with Frank Bridge; later he studied with John Ireland at the Royal College of Music, where his interests turned towards continental modernism; early successes included his *Variations on a Theme of Frank Bridge* (1937) and *Les Illuminations* (1939). In 1939, with the advent of war, he left for America, and on his return in 1942 he began working on the opera *Peter Grimes*; his operas, culminating in *Death in Venice* (1973) are central to his output, though his *War Requiem* (1962), which juxtaposed the text of the Requiem Mass with poems by Wilfred Owen, had considerable public impact. In 1948 Britten, together with his lifelong partner Peter Pears, founded the annual Aldeburgh Festival.

Brown, Earle (b. 1926) American composer, particularly associated with a group of composers working in New York during the 1950s that included Cage, Feldman, and Wolff; Cage did much to promote Brown's work through his contacts in Europe. His music demonstrates similar concerns to those of his colleagues, particularly in the use of aleatoric techniques and alternative forms of notation, such as in *Music for Cello and Piano* (1955) and *Available Forms II* (1962).

Brown, James (b. 1928) American soul singer, who began his career singing with gospel groups and then moved towards rhythm and blues; *Live at the Apollo* (1963) marked a major point in his career, demonstrating the intense and impassioned quality of his live performances. *Papa's Got a Brand New Bag* (1965) exemplifies Brown's use of riff-based song structures, a style that was hugely influential and became known as funk. Brown was notoriously demanding, and many of his sidemen became famous in their own right, including the bassist 'Bootsy' Collins and the saxophonist Maceo Parker. With the advent of sampling technology in the 1980s, Brown became probably the most sampled recording artist ever.

Busch, Fritz (1890–1951) German conductor. He studied at the Cologne Musikhochschule, and in 1918 became director of the Stuttgart Opera; he extended the repertory of the company, performing works by Hindemith, Busoni (*Doktor Faustus*), and Strauss (*Intermezzo*). Busch left Germany in 1933 and became director of music at the new opera house at Glyndebourne, also working in the US during the 1940s.

Busoni, Ferruccio (1866–1924) Composer and pianist in the Lisztian tradition, of Italian and Austrian parentage, well known for his concert transcriptions of music by Bach, Brahms, Liszt, Mendelssohn, Mozart, and Schoenberg. His compositions integrated elements of folksong, and include the unfinished opera *Doktor Faust* (1925).

Bussotti, Sylvano (b. 1931) Italian composer. He studied at Florence Conservatory under Luigi Dallapiccola, and attended the Darmstadt Summer School in 1958, quickly establishing himself as one of the most idiosyncratic members of the post-war avant-garde. His notoriety rests chiefly on his beautiful but cryptic graphic scores, his open espousal of homoeroticism and sadomasochism, and his unique blending of music, text, theatre, and dance, which he calls 'BUSSOTTIOPERABALLET'.

The Byrds American rock group. The Byrds became well known with 'Mr Tambourine Man' (1965), and many of their hits were covers of Bob Dylan songs; they were promoted as America's answer to the Beatles, and played a major role in popularizing what is now known as folk rock.

Cage, John (1912–92) American composer and writer, who studied with Cowell and Schoenberg. After initial explorations in twelve-note composition, Cage began experimenting with dance, percussion, and new sonorities (including noise) in works such as *First Construction (in Metal)* (1939). Drawing on Cowell, he invented the prepared piano, for which he wrote *Sonatas and Interludes* (1946–8). Drawn to Indian and Zen philosophy, Cage developed an aesthetics of silence, non-intentionality and indeterminacy, leading to his best-known works such as *Music of Changes* (1951), his silent piece *4′33″*, *Water Music* (1952), and the *Concert* for piano and orchestra. After explorations in diverse media and art forms, Cage finally returned to concert music in his 'number pieces'. Cage's influence stems not only from his music, but also from his philosophy and forceful personality.

Callas, Maria (1923–77) Greek soprano. Though brought up in America she studied in Greece, making her debut in Athens. She moved to New York in 1945 and was soon in great demand for some of the major roles in the operatic repertory. After performing Wagner early in her career, she subsequently concentrated on Italian opera, and was particularly respected for her work in this genre.

Cardew, Cornelius (1936–81) English composer. After studying at the Royal Academy of Music, he worked in Cologne as Stockhausen's assistant for three years. He was influenced by American avant-garde music, particularly the work of Cage, whose influence is reflected in the graphic score *Treatise* (1968). He was a founder member of the free improvisation group AMM, and of the Scratch Orchestra, a collective dedicated to playing experimental compositions. His turn towards Marxist politics during the 1970s went hand in hand with a move away from experimental techniques towards a more conventional tonal language.

Carter, Elliott (b. 1908) American composer, who studied at Harvard with Piston, and took lessons with Nadia Boulanger in Paris. Works in an accessible neoclassical style, such as the First Symphony (1942), gradually gave way to a more dynamic and challenging style, which reflected his engagement with the music of Ives. The First String Quartet of 1951 explored complex rhythmic techniques, and with his works of the 1960s Carter took on board the European avant-garde tradition, producing pieces of a much more fragmented, abstract nature; well-known examples include the *Concerto for Orchestra* (1969) and *Symphony of Three Orchestras* (1977).

Caruso, Enrico (1873–1921) Italian tenor who achieved huge fame throughout Europe and America. He made his name singing Italian opera in his home country, debuting at Covent Garden in 1902 and at the Metropolitan Opera in New York in 1903. It was around this time that he also began recording. From 1912 he appeared almost continuously at the Metropolitan Opera in New York, and his recordings were hugely popular.

Casals, Pablo (1876–1973) Catalan cellist, conductor, and pianist. He studied in Madrid and Brussels, and by the end of the 1890s had made his name as a major international performer. He formed a famous association with pianist Alfred Cortot and violinist Jacques Thibaud, recording trios by Beethoven, Haydn, Mendelssohn, and Schubert, and was known for his concentrated and intense approach to performance. He settled in France in 1936.

Casella, Alfredo (1883–1947) Italian composer, organizer, pianist and conductor, who studied at the Paris Conservatoire, where he worked with Fauré and befriended Ravel. While embracing both impressionism and expressionism, Casella is chiefly known for his neoclassical style, as represented in *Concerto romano* (1941). As an active teacher and organizer he had considerable influence on younger composers such as Malipiero and Castelnuovo-Tedesco.

Cash, Johnny (1932–2003) American singer and songwriter. After serving in the US airforce, he recorded for Sun records in Memphis, working with Elvis Presley and Roy Orbison. In 1968 he signed for Columbia Records, and his recordings for this label combine the lyricism of folk music with the country style for which he was best known. His recordings include live albums such as *Johnny Cash at San Quentin*, and work with Bob Dylan on *Nashville Skyline*.

Chávez, Carlos (1899–1978) Mexican composer, conductor, and teacher, who trained as a pianist but became best known as a composer. His role in Mexican culture included important teaching activities and government positions with responsibility for the arts. Chavez also spent time in New York, associating with Varèse, Cowell, and the International Composers' Guild.

Clapton, Eric (b. 1945) English rock and blues guitarist. Clapton began as a blues musician, and in the late 1960s formed the 'supergroup' Cream with Ginger Baker and Jack Bruce. Thereafter Clapton established himself as a solo artist, working both in mainstream pop (including singles such as 'Layla') and in the blues tradition, and remains active into the twenty-first century.

Coleman, Ornette (b. 1930) American saxophonist and composer. Coleman's arrival in New York in 1959 with his quartet caused a sensation in the jazz world; the style he espoused became known as free jazz, and was seen by many as a rejection of normative jazz practices. The recordings for Atlantic records of this time, such as *The Shape of Jazz To Come* (1959), and *Free Jazz* (1960), were among the most influential of the 1960s. His later work included compositions for orchestra, an electric group called Prime Time, and work with Pat Metheny on the album *Song X* (1985).

Coltrane, John (1926–67) American saxophonist. He began playing with rhythm and blues bands before working with some of the major jazz names of the time, including Thelonious Monk and Miles Davis; his work with Davis included playing on the legendary *Kind of Blue* recording (1959). Around this time he formed his own group, producing the album *Giant Steps* in 1959. His style developed rapidly from this point on, as he began to include the soprano saxophone in his playing, most notably in his version of 'My Favourite Things'. *A Love Supreme* (1964) was his most enduring work, a multi-part composition which served as an expression of Coltrane's deeply held religious beliefs. In his later years his approach came to be seen as distinctly avant-garde, with *Ascension* (1965) proving particularly controversial.

Cook, Will Marion (1869–1944) American composer and conductor. Cook began in musical comedy, but in 1918 created the New York Syncopated Orchestra, which toured through Europe and America; Sidney Bechet frequently performed with the orchestra. Later in his life Cook was active as a teacher and concert promoter.

Copland, Aaron (1900–90) American composer, pianist, and conductor. Copland was born in New York, studying privately with Rubin Goldmark, and later with Nadia Boulanger in Paris. His ballet *Grohg* (1925) was his first major work, but a performance of the Organ Concerto under Koussevitzky, with Boulanger as soloist, effectively launched his career. The initial reception of his music was frosty, and it was only when Copland began pursuing a deliberately accessible style with works such as *El Salón México* (1936) and *Appalachian Spring* (1944) that he enjoyed real success. By the 1940s he was regarded as one of America's leading composers, subsequently receiving many awards and decorations.

Corigliano, John (b. 1938) American composer, who studied with Luening at Columbia University (New York), and has worked in the media and as an educator. Corigliano is one of America's most popular living composers, and has won many awards for his music, including a Pulitzer Prize in 2001 for his Second Symphony. His style draws from that of fellow American composers such as Bernstein and Copland.

Cortot, Alfred (1877–1962) French pianist and conductor. He studied at the Paris Conservatoire, and then worked as an assistant conductor at Bayreuth, also conducting the first Paris performance of *Tristan und Isolde*. Cortot's reputation as one of the leading French conductors of his time has been eclipsed by his work as a pianist, both as a soloist and in the famous trio with Casals and Thibaud. Cortot was best known for his playing of the Romantic repertory, and made a large number of recordings.

Cowell, Henry (1897–1965) American composer, theorist, and promoter. Cowell's activities in promoting his own music and that of his contemporaries was important to the development of the radical American tradition: he was heavily involved in running the Pan American Association of Composers, and he founded the journal *New Music* in 1927. In his highly influential book *New Musical Resources* (1930), Cowell explored new harmonic, rhythmic, and timbral approaches to composition; among the concepts he propounded in the book were tone clusters (as used in piano pieces such as 'The Tides of Manaunaun'), dissonant counterpoint (as in the First String Quartet), and complex rhythmic proportions derived from the overtone series. Cowell's output varies widely in terms of technique and aesthetic, and later in his life he turned towards a more populist stance; one of the key features of his later output is the attempt to integrate musical elements from foreign cultures into his compositions.

Crawford, Ruth (1901–53) American composer. She trained in Chicago, and a number of her works were published by Cowell in the *New Musical Quarterly*. She then went on to study with composer and musicologist Charles Seeger, whom she subsequently married. In 1930 Crawford became the first woman to be awarded a Guggenheim Fellowship in composition. Later in her life she and her husband did much to study and preserve the American folksong tradition, and her son Pete Seeger became a major figure on the folk music scene in the 1960s.

Cream English rock band formed in 1966. Cream consisted of drummer Ginger Baker, bassist Jack Bruce, and guitarist Eric Clapton. All these musicians had backgrounds in the blues, but they produced a hard-edged sound, in many ways similar to the approach of Jimi Hendrix. The group's live performances and recordings often featured extended improvisations, and set something of a precedent for progressive rock.

Crosby, Bing (1904–77) American singer and actor. He appeared early in his career with the Paul Whiteman orchestra, and subsequently starred in film musicals such as *Holiday Inn* (1942). His appearance with Louis Armstrong in the film *High Society* (1956) made a particular impact, and he became one of the most popular of all American singers.

Crumb, George (b. 1929) American composer, who studied in Berlin with Boris Blacher, producing his first important works during the 1960s; he won the Pulitzer Prize for *Echoes of Time and the River* (1967). Many of his works take inspiration from contemporary events, a good example being *Black Angels* (1970) with its references to the Vietnam war.

Cui Jian (b. 1961) Chinese rock musician of Korean descent. He received a classical training, at one time playing trumpet in the Beijing Symphony Orchestra, but came to prominence as a rock guitarist and singer in the late 1980s; he was closely identified with the student protests in Tiananmen Square in 1989, appearing there in person. Predictably his profile was low in the aftermath of the Tiananmen Square massacre (4 June 1989), but he helped the government to raise funds for the Asian Games in 1990, and toured both nationally and internationally during the 1990s. His band featured traditional Chinese as well as Western instruments.

Davies, Peter Maxwell (b. 1934) English composer. He studied at the Royal Manchester College of Music, associating with fellow students Harrison Birtwistle and Alexander Goehr; he then worked with Petrassi in Rome, and with Babbitt and Sessions at Princeton. His early work often took medieval or renaissance music as its starting point; he developed a distinctive brand of musical theatre (*Eight Songs for a Mad King*, 1969), as well as composing symphonies and operas. He settled on the island of Orkney in 1971, and among his more recent works are ten 'Strathclyde' concertos for the Scottish Chamber Orchestra. As a co-founder of the 'Fires of London', Davies worked extensively as a conductor, generally performing his own music.

Davis, Carl (b. 1936) American composer and conductor. He studied in America and Copenhagen before beginning a career as a prolific film composer, a representative example of his work being *The French Lieutenant's Woman* (1981). He has also worked as a conductor, and written musicals and operas; he collaborated with Paul McCartney on *Liverpool Oratorio* (1991).

Davis, Miles (1926–91) American jazz trumpeter, one of the most influential and respected of all jazz musicians. Davis began his career playing with bebop saxophonist Charlie Parker, and recorded an influential nonet session in 1949, later entitled *Birth of the Cool*. After making a series of recordings during the 1950s for Prestige, Davis produced the 1959 album *Kind of Blue*, regularly cited as one of the greatest of all jazz recordings. At this time Davis's group included John Coltrane and Bill Evans; the 1960s saw another superlative incarnation of his band, with Wayne Shorter, Ron Carter, Herbie Hancock, and Tony Williams. Towards the end of the 1960s Davis turned towards jazz-rock fusion, with *Bitches Brew* (1969) proving highly influential. After disappearing from public view in the middle of the 1970s, Davis returned in 1980, gathering young musicians around him and working largely with electric lineups.

Debussy, Claude (1862–1918) French composer who studied at the Paris Conservatoire, where he was well known for his questioning of conventional compositional procedures. Wagner was an important initial influence, as was the gamelan orchestra he heard at the Universal Exposition in 1889. One of his first major works was the *Prélude à 'L'après-midi d'un faune'*, inspired by a poem by Mallarmé; the orchestral *Nocturnes* were completed in 1899, while his opera *Pelléas et Mélisande* was first performed in 1901. The two books of *Préludes* for Piano (1910 and 1913) have become a mainstay of the 20th-century piano repertory. Although Debussy's use of pentatonic and whole-tone modes was not in itself new, his employment of them alongside diatonic harmony which avoided conventional patterns of progression created a distinctive and innovative style, and was widely imitated.

Denisov, Edison (1929–96) Russian composer. He studied at the Moscow Conservatory on the encouragement of Shostakovich, gaining knowledge of the Western avant-garde at a time when few Russians were familiar with it. His role as a teacher at the Conservatory was thus of considerable importance, and his String Trio (1969) took its inspiration from Webern and Boulez; *Peinture* (1970) was indebted to Ligeti in particular, and marked an important point in the development of Denisov's language. The *Requiem* (1980) is among his best-known pieces.

Diaghilev, Sergei (1872–1929) Director of the Ballets Russes, which he established in 1909. The company commissioned and performed such major works as Stravinsky's *Firebird* (1910), *Petrushka* (1911), *Rite of Spring* (1913), *Pulcinella* (1920), and *Mavra* (1922), as well as Ravel's *Daphnis et Chloé* (1912), Debussy's *Jeux* (1913), and Satie's *Parade* (1917). The company's choreographers included Fokine, Nizhinsky, Nizhinska, and Massine.

Dibangu, Manu (b. 1934) Cameroonian saxophonist, who studied and lived in France before moving to Belgium. He developed a distinctive blend of jazz and Cameroonian *makossa* style, recording his first album in 1968. In 1971 his 'Soul Makossa' became a huge hit in America, and Dibango subsequently signed for Island Records. He has continued to develop his music since then, exploring reggae influences in particular.

Dietrich, Marlene (1901–92) American actress and singer. She was born in Germany and began her career working in stage shows. During the 1930s she made a number of films in Hollywood with director Josef von Sternberg; her best-known role was in *Destry Rides Again* (1939). Dietrich became a huge star, continuing to perform into the 1970s.

Dolmetsch, Arnold (1858–1940) English musician, a major figure in the development of period-instrument performance. He studied at the Royal College of Music, and in the 1890s began to collect early instruments, playing works by English composers such as Jenkins, Lawes, and Locke. He toured the US in 1902, demonstrating these instruments, and in 1915 published an influential book entitled *The Interpretation of the Music of the XVII and XVIII Centuries Revealed by Contemporary Evidence*.

Domingo, Placido (b. 1941) Spanish tenor and conductor. He studied in Mexico and made his American debut in 1961; he then worked with the Israeli National Opera, and as his stature grew appeared at La Scala and the Metropolitan Opera in New York. As one of the 'Three Tenors' (with Carreras and Pavarotti), he played a key role in the late-twentieth-century transformation of operatic highlights into mass culture.

Donatoni, Franco (1927–2000) Italian composer, who studied at the conservatories of Bolzano, Milan, and Bologna. Influenced at first by Petrassi, he was introduced to the avant-garde by Maderna; confounded by this experience,

Donatoni developed a music of self-negation, based on a grim understanding of randomness. After a personal and artistic crisis he developed a more transparent style characterized by clear linear development and delicate but motoric rhythms, as in *Spri* (1977) or *Le ruisseau sur l'escalier* (1980). He had a decisive influence on many younger Italian composers.

The Doors American rock band formed in 1965. The Doors established a distinctive instrumental sound, largely through the inclusion of an organ in the band's lineup, and became leading representatives of the 1960s counterculture with such hits as 'Light My Fire' (1967). The group was dominated by the self-destructive personality of its lead singer, Jim Morrison, whose death in 1971 effectively ended the group's career, although the remaining members continued to play together into the 1980s.

Dylan, Bob (b. 1941) American singer-songwriter (born Robert Zimmermann). He became active in the folk scene in New York's Greenwich Village early in the 1960s, modelling his style on Woodie Guthrie, and began recording for Columbia in 1962. His music became identified with the political protest movement, particularly with songs such as 'The Times They Are A Changin'', and 'Blowin' in the Wind'. However, he gradually moved away from such political concerns to more abstract imagery, and his appearance at the Newport Festival with an electric band in 1965 caused uproar among folk purists. Dylan subsequently pursued rather more introspective paths with albums such as *John Wesley Harding* (1968). He has influenced a whole generation of songwriters.

Eimert, Herbert (1897–1972) German theorist and composer. He studied in Cologne, where he received a doctorate in musicology. In 1951 he became the director of the NWDR Studio für Elektronische Musik in Cologne. Both in this position and as co-editor (with Stockhausen) of the seminal journal *Die Reihe*, he exerted a defining influence with his uncompromising commitment to multiple serialism, far eclipsing the impact of his compositions.

Eisler, Hanns (1898–1962) German composer who studied at the New Vienna Conservatory and privately under Arnold Schoenberg. Initially influenced by modernism and dodecaphony, as evidenced in his *Palmström* (1924), Eisler turned to more immediately accessible, mostly diatonic, idioms after joining the German Communist Party (in 1926, following his move to Berlin); well known for his collaborations with Bertolt Brecht, he also wrote marching songs and film music. During the Third Reich Eisler went into exile, eventually moving to the US, where he taught at the New School for Social Research and worked in Hollywood, writing the book *Composing for the Films* in collaboration with Adorno. After being expelled by the Committee for Un-American Activities, he settled in the GDR in 1948.

Elfman, Dannie (b. 1953) American film composer. His early career was as a rock musician and arranger, but he turned to film scoring in 1985, with his work on Tim Burton's *Batman* (1989) being particularly successful; his scores for the cartoon show *The Simpsons* are also well known, while recent work includes *Edward Scissorhands* (1990) and *Good Will Hunting* (1997).

Elgar, Edward (1857–1934) English composer. He began his career as a freelance violinist and organist, achieving his status as one of England's greatest composers only after years of relative obscurity. It was with a performance by Hans Richter of the *Enigma Variations* (1899) that he came to prominence; *The Dream of Gerontius* (1900) was not initially well received, but met with success in Germany and subsequently in Britain, while the *Pomp and Circumstance* marches (the first composed in 1901) confirmed his reputation. Among the major works which followed were the violin and cello concertos, two symphonies (a third was left unfinished, but was performed in a version completed by Anthony Payne in 1998), and a number of choral works. Elgar's style is essentially Romantic and his works are still popular, particularly in Britain.

Ellington, Edward Kennedy 'Duke' (1899–1979) American composer, bandleader, and pianist. Ellington first made his name through a lengthy engagement at Harlem's Cotton Club from 1927. As his band expanded in size, Ellington's compositions and arrangements grew more amibitious, while retaining a distinctive sound; pieces such as the 1931 *Creole Rhapsody* were among the first examples of extended compositions in jazz. Ellington worked into the 1960s, with tours of Europe and large-scale compositions. His influence as a composer and recording artist was huge, and many of his compositions are still played by jazz musicians today.

Eno, Brian (b. 1948) English rock musician, composer, and producer. He studied at art school and was a member of the successful band *Roxy Music*, in which he played synthesizers and used tape recorders as a means of treating sound. Subsequent projects included working with the guitarist Robert Fripp on *No Pussy Footing* (1973), and with David Bowie on *Low* (1977). Solo releases such as *Music for Films* (1978) and *Music for Airports* (1979) defined the genre of ambient music. During the 1980s Eno became an influential producer, working with U2 (*The Joshua Tree*), Laurie Anderson, and David Bowie.

Euba, Akin (b. 1935) Nigerian composer who studied composition and piano at Trinity College, London (1952–7) and ethnomusicology at UCLA (1962–6). He taught in Lagos and Ife before taking up a position at the University of Pittsburgh. His compositions fuse traditional African musical instruments and features (including call-and-response and polyrhythm) with Western approaches, including serialism; his opera *Chaka* (1970), based on the famous Zulu chieftain of that name, attracted considerable attention, but his most sustained contribution has perhaps been his 'African pianism' (as exemplified in the *Studies in African Pianism* nos.1–3 of 1987), an attempt to recreate for the Western instrument the percussive and rhythmic qualities of traditional African music. He has also written extensively on both traditional and new music in Africa.

Europe, James Reese (1880–1919) American bandleader and composer. He achieved success as a composer with a number of theatre productions, and worked with the Castles, but is best known for conducting the orchestra of the Clef Club, the black musicians' union in New York. Europe performed with this group at Carnegie Hall in 1912, and they recorded for Victor Records.

Evans, Bill (1929–80) American jazz pianist, who recorded with Charles Mingus and George Russell before joining the Miles Davis group, where he was involved in the recording *Kind of Blue* (1959). Evans was best known for his work in the trio format, and of his different lineups that with Paul Motian and Scott LaFaro was the most famous. His approach fused lyricism with a harmonic sophistication that became a benchmark for subsequent pianists.

Feldman, Morton (1926–87) American composer. Feldman began a career as a businessman, but turned to composition and associated with such New York composers as Cage, Brown, and Tudor. He avoided any adherence to compositional systems, instead preferring an abstract approach based largely on intuition; his early pieces such as *Projections* (1951) employ graphic scores, while some later works specify pitch but not rhythm, examples being *Pieces for Four Pianos* (1957). Feldman's later pieces employ conventional notation, and many run continously for extremely long periods of time, such as the Second String Quartet, lasting for between four and five hours.

Ferneyhough, Brian (b. 1943) English composer. He studied at the Royal Academy of Music with Lennox Berkeley, then with Ton de Leeuw in Amsterdam, moving to Germany in 1973, and more recently holding teaching positions in the US. He is a leading representative of what became known as the 'New Complexity', reflecting his interest in exploring the boundaries of both compositional and instrumental technique through pieces such as *Cassandra's Dream Song* (1970) and the large-scale *Transit* (1975).

Ferrier, Kathleen (1912–53) English contralto who made her reputation during the war years, becoming one of Britain's best-known vocal performers. Her operatic work was limited to Gluck and Britten's *The Rape of Lucretia*, but her Mahler performances were particularly renowned.

Finnissy, Michael (b. 1946) English composer and pianist. Finnissy studied at the Royal College of Music as well as in Italy, and has held a number of teaching positions in England. He is often described as a representative of the 'New Complexity', but his works are extremely varied and frequently reference other musical styles in a highly virtuosic manner; his *Gershwin Arrangements* (1988), for example, are 'transcriptions' which weave the original works into Finnissy's own language, creating a highly distinctive effect.

Fischer-Dieskau, Dietrich (b. 1925) German baritone, who studied in Berlin and made his debut in Germany in 1947; subsequent engagements included work at Bayreuth in the 1950s, as well as at the Salzburg festival. He performed in the premiere of Britten's *War Requiem*, but is best known for his interpretations of the Lieder of Schubert, Schumann and Wolf.

Fitzgerald, Ella (1917–96) American singer. She won a talent show at New York's Apollo Theatre in 1934, and went on to work with Chick Webb's band during the height of the swing era. She began a solo career in the 1940s, and went on to issue a series of influential recordings based on the work of major songwriters, including *Ella Fitzgerald Sings The Cole Porter Songbook* (1956) and *Ella Fitzgerald Sings the Duke Ellington Songbook* (1957). For many years she was widely regarded as the greatest living jazz singer, being particularly renowned for her scat singing.

Franklin, Aretha (b. 1942) American soul singer. Franklin recorded for Chess Records before moving to Columbia, singing a mix of different styles including gospel and blues. When she signed to Atlantic in 1967 a distinctive individual sound emerged, with covers of songs such as 'Respect' by Otis Redding (1967) as well as original soul numbers such as 'Think', and 'Since You've Been Gone'.

Furtwängler, Wilhelm (1886–1954) German conductor. He took up a post at Lübeck in 1911, and succeeded Nikisch as conductor of the Leipzig Gewandhaus, but was most closely associated with the Berlin Philharmonic. His approach contrasted sharply with Toscanini's, subordinating literalism to interpretative lyricism and phrasing, and he was best known for his interpretations of Beethoven, Brahms, and Wagner.

Gabriel, Peter (b. 1950) English rock singer, musician, and producer. Gabriel was lead singer with Genesis until 1975, but his solo career did not take off until the 1980s, particularly with the album *So* (1986). He played a key role in the promotion of world music in Britain and beyond, through his founding of the WOMAD (World of Music and Dance) festival, and the Real World record label.

Gardiner, John Eliot (b. 1943) English conductor who studied with Thurston Dart and Nadia Boulanger, and made his debut in 1966. He is known in particular for his work in the baroque and renaissance repertory, which reflects research into period-performance practices. He also founded the Orchestre Révolutionnaire et Romantique in 1990.

Garland, Judy (1922–69) American singer and actress. Garland made her name performing in films, most notably in *The Wizard of Oz*, from which came the song 'Over the Rainbow' (1939) with which she is still especially associated. Of her many later roles, *A Star is Born* (1954) is one of the best known.

Gaye, Marvin (1939–84) American singer and songwriter, who began working in doo-wop groups before signing to Motown in 1960. It was his soul recordings of the late 1960s that made his name, including 'I Heard It Through the Grapevine' (1968), which became the label's bestselling record up to that point. The 1971 album *What's Going On* dealt with issues of discrimination and poverty, and was one of the most influential soul recordings of the decade.

Gershwin, George (1898–1937) American pianist, composer, and conductor. He began working as a song-plugger, but quickly turned to songwriting, producing a hit for Al Jolson in 1920. One of his best-known works was *Rhapsody in Blue* (1924) an example of 'symphonic jazz' written for the Paul Whiteman orchestra; the piece retains considerable popularity today, as does the opera *Porgy and Bess* (1935). But Gershwin's most influential output was as a writer of musicals (*Of Thee I Sing*, 1931, was the first musical to win a Pulitzer Prize), and many of his songs – generally written in collaboration with his brother Ira – have been adopted by jazz musicians; the chord changes to 'I Got Rhythm' (from *Girl Crazy*, 1930) have formed the basis for numerous jazz compositions.

Gilels, Emil (1916–85) Russian pianist. Gilels studied in Moscow, coming to prominence by winning a competition in Brussels in 1938. He spent most of his career performing in his home country and around Eastern Europe, not appearing in America until 1955, where he was immediately acclaimed. He was best known for his performances of the late-Romantic repertory, as well as works by Russian composers including Rachmaninov and Skryabin.

Gillespie, John Birks 'Dizzy' (1917–93) American trumpeter and composer, along with Charlie Parker the principal exponent of the style known as bebop, which combined fast tempi with altered chord changes and complex melodic lines. Gillespie worked in many of the dance bands of the time, before developing bebop in jam sessions with Parker and Thelonious Monk, among others. He performed frequently with Parker, and went on to lead his own big band, creating a distinctive brand of Afro-Cuban jazz. Many of his compositions, such as 'Night In Tunisia' (1942), are now jazz standards.

Glass, Philip (b. 1937) American composer, particularly associated with the minimalist group of composers including Riley, Reich, and Young. Glass studied in Chicago and New York, although his interest in Indian music proved as important to his compositional style as his conventional studies. During the 1960s and 70s he wrote much of his music for his own ensemble. His most influential works have been the operas, including *Einstein on the Beach* (1976), *Satyagraha* (1980) and *Akhnaten* (1984). He has also collaborated extensively with artists from the popular field, notably Laurie Anderson and David Byrne.

Globokar, Vinko (b. 1934) Slovenian composer and trombonist, who studied at the Paris Conservatoire and took composition lessons with Leibowitz and Berio. His extraordinary virtuosity attracted composers such as Stockhausen, Berio, and Kagel to write pieces specifically for him (an example is Berio's *Sequenza* V), and it is as a performer that he is best known.

Godowsky, Leopold (1870–1938) American pianist and composer of Polish birth. Godowsky began performing at an early age in America, gaining popularity in Europe by the 1890s; his appearance in Berlin in 1900 established his reputation as one of the major performers of the day, and he performed throughout Europe and America. He made a series of recordings in London during the 1920s, but his career was cut short by a stroke.

Goehr, Alexander (b. 1932) British composer, son of the conductor Walter Goehr. While studying at the Royal Manchester College of Music he came into contact with fellow students Peter Maxwell Davies and Harrison Birtwistle; he subsequently studied with Messiaen in Paris, and works such as *The Deluge* (1959) established his reputation in Britain. While his early music built from the tradition of Schoenberg, his style has evolved towards a more varied and personal language, as represented by his opera *Behold the Sun* (1984). He has been particularly influential as a teacher of composition, holding teaching posts in both America and Britain.

Goeyvaerts, Karel (1923–93) Belgian composer. He studied composition at the Antwerp Conservatory (1943–7) and attended the Paris Conservatoire (1947–50), where he studied analysis with Messiaen and composition with Milhaud. Goeyvaerts achieved fame with his Sonata for Two Pianos (1951), frequently cited as the first multiple serialist work, and he exerted a crucial influence on Karlheinz Stockhausen. His subsequent disaffection with serialist techniques led him to adopt experimentalism, music theatre and, later, minimalist techniques.

Goldsmith, Jerry (b. 1929) American film composer and conductor, who wrote music for radio and television before going on to write film scores; these included *Planet of the Apes* (1968), *The Omen* (1976), *Star Trek, the Motion Picture* (1979) and *Gremlins* (1984).

Goodman, Benny (1909–86) American clarinettist, composer, and bandleader. He worked as a classical musician, but became famous for his big band, which achieved huge popularity during the swing era of the 1930s and 40s; it was the band's performances of 'hot' swing numbers that earned them their reputation. Goodman also worked in small-group formats, as well as commissioning a number of classical pieces, including Bartók's *Contrasts* (1938).

Górecki, Henryk (b. 1933) Polish composer. While his early music shows an interest in serial and avant-garde techniques, his later work is deeply lyrical, and employs a more conventional harmonic language, often featuring tonal and modal elements. It was only in 1992, with the phenomenal success of Dawn Upshaw's and David Zinman's recording of his Symphony no. 3 (1976), that Górecki's name became widely known.

Gould, Glenn (1932–82) Canadian pianist. Gould studied in Toronto and quickly became known in his native country, making his American debut in 1955; at the same time he began recording for Columbia, and his 1956 recording of the Goldberg Variations was immediately acclaimed. Gould came to prefer the privacy of the recording studio to the glare of the concert-hall lights, and in 1964 ceased public performance, but continued recording. He also produced radio plays and wrote extensively, particularly towards the end of his life. Gould is widely admired as an idiosyncratic performer whose intensely introspective approach was perfectly suited to the recording studio.

Grainger, Percy (1882–1961) Australian composer and pianist. Grainger grew up in Australia but studied in Europe, living for a time in London; he worked there as a pianist and folksong collector. Grainger's work as a composer became known from about 1910 onwards, but he remains best known for his arrangements and transcriptions of folksongs. His career as a concert pianist took him all around the world, and he also worked extensively as an educator.

Grappelli, Stéphane (1908–97) French jazz violinist (originally classically trained), who played with guitarist Django Reinhardt, the two co-leading the famous Quintette du Hot Club de France. He later moved to England, where he worked with such musicians as George Shearing and Yehudi Menuhin, and was regarded as one of the greatest of jazz violinists.

The Grateful Dead American rock group. The Grateful Dead are particularly associated with the psychedelic rock tradition which emerged from San Francisco during the latter part of the 1960s; they took part in 'acid trips' organized by Ken Kesey, and their style integrated diverse elements from rock and jazz to bluegrass and rhythm and blues. Despite their many successful recordings, The Grateful Dead were primarily a live band, whose performances often included extensive improvisations featuring lead guitarist Jerry Garcia. The band remained active until Garcia's death in 1995.

Grisey, Gérard (1946–98) French composer who studied with Messiaen in Paris, and then with Xenakis and Ligeti in Darmstadt. He was best known for his work in what became known as spectral composition, a technique based on harmonic analysis which was particularly influential in France during the 1980s; examples include *Les espaces acoustiques* (1985) and *Talea* (1985).

Gubaidulina, Sofia (b. 1931) Russian composer. She studied in Moscow, and has since become one of the major Russian composers of the latter part of the century. Her music deals with themes of spirituality and philosophy, and often incorporates elements of folk traditions. *Offertorium* (1980) for violin and orchestra and *Stimmen . . . Verstummen* (1986) are among the best known of her works.

Guthrie, Woody (1912–67) American folk singer who espoused left-wing politics and became especially known for his 'Dust Bowl Ballads'. He was a focus of the folksong revival of the 1960s, his singing and political activism inspiring a younger generation of musicians, in particular Bob Dylan. His son Arlo (b. 1947) was also a folk singer, working among others with Pete Seeger.

Haitink, Bernard (b. 1929) Dutch conductor. He studied in Amsterdam, working initially as a violinist, and subsequently as conductor of the Netherlands Radio Philharmonic Orchestra. He was appointed principal conductor of the Concertgebouw Orchestra in 1961, and has worked with major orchestras all over the world. His repertory is wide, but he is known particularly for his interpretations of Wagner and Bruckner.

Haley, Bill (1925–81) American rock singer. Haley's importance stems primarily from his music of the 1950s, which played a major part in establishing rock and roll as the dominant sound in American popular music. His most influential song was 'Rock Around The Clock' (1954).

Harnoncourt, Nikolaus (b. 1929) Austrian conductor and cellist, who studied in Vienna and played cello in the Vienna Symphony Orchestra before forming a viol consort. This led to work on Bach's Brandenburg Concertos with period instruments, and since then he has made a major contribution to the historical-performance movement. While he is best known for his work in the baroque repertory, he has also recorded classical works, working with the Concertgebouw Orchestra and the Chamber Orchestra of Europe, and has written on performance practice.

Harrison, Lou (1917–2003) American composer, best known for incorporating elements of non-Western musics into his own compositional language. He grew up in California and studied with Cowell in San Francisco, while helping to arrange performances of Ives's music. He worked with Cage on *Double Music* (1941), and much of his early music came from collaboration with dance companies. His output spans a wide range of different genres; particularly notable are the Piano Concerto (1985), written for Keith Jarrett, the *Pacifika Rondo* (1963), and the puppet opera *Young Caesar* (1971).

Harvey, Jonathan (b. 1939) English composer. He studied with Hans Keller in London and with Milton Babbitt at Princeton, later spending time at IRCAM in Paris. His *Mortuos plango, vivos voco* (1980) is a classic of electroacoustic music, transforming recordings of a cathedral bell and a boy soprano, while *Bhakti* (1982) integrates live ensemble with tape, drawing inspiration from Hindu writings. He has held teaching posts in Britain and America.

Hauer, Josef Mathias (1883–1959) Austrian composer and theorist, mainly remembered for claiming priority over Schoenberg in the development of twelve-tone technique, which he employed first in *Nomos*, op. 19 (1919); however his techniques did not involve strictly serial ordering. His esoteric aesthetic ideals, centring on a purely spiritual, objective music which he came closest to realizing in his *Zwölftonspiele* of the 1940s and 50s, are also in stark contrast to Schoenberg's.

Hawkins, Coleman (1904–69) American saxophonist who worked with the Fletcher Henderson Orchestra during the 1920s and 30s before forming his own group. Hawkins's recording of 'Body and Soul' (1939) was a major commercial success, and he was widely imitated as one of the finest saxophonists of his day; his harmonic sophistication was vital to the development of bebop.

Heifetz, Jascha (1901–87) American violinist of Russian birth. Heifetz studied at St Petersburg, making his debut in Berlin in 1912; he subsequently performed Tchaikovsky with Nikisch and appeared triumphantly at Carnegie Hall in 1917. He then settled in America, although his performing career took him all over the world. Heifetz was one of the most famous performers of his day, known for a virtuoso technique combined with a strong, sometimes forceful tone.

Henderson, Fletcher (1897–1952) American bandleader and arranger. In 1924 he formed a dance band which included jazz numbers in its repertory and was particularly notable for Henderson's hiring of 'hot' musicians such as Louis Armstrong; recordings such as 'Copenhagen' (1924) and 'Sugar Foot Stomp' (1925) mark important stages in the development of the big band. Many of the band's most famous arrangements were written by Don Redman, and some of them were later used by Benny Goodman (with whom Henderson worked after his own band folded in 1939).

Hendrix, Jimi (1942–72) American guitarist and singer. Hendrix was self-taught and developed an unusual technique, playing a right-handed guitar in a left-handed manner so that the instrument was effectively upside-down. After serving in the army he worked as a backing musician with a sequence of soul and blues performers, and developed his flamboyant and innovative technique during this time. Hendrix first became famous after coming to England and forming his group the Jimi Hendrix Experience; after the 1967 album *Are You Experienced?*, he made a now-legendary appearance at the Monterey Festival, which culminated in the burning of his guitar. He made another album, *Electric Ladyland* (1968), before his untimely death in 1972. Hendrix redefined electric guitar technique in a manner which influenced a whole generation of subsequent performers.

Henry, Pierre (b. 1927) French composer who studied with Boulanger and Messiaen, before joining the RTF studio, where he composed what came to be known as *musique concrète*. Along with Pierre Schaeffer, he created the *Symphonie pour un homme seul* (1950), the first extended electronic composition. Subsequently he worked in different studios around Europe.

Henze, Hans Werner (b. 1926) German composer. Henze studied at the Brunswick State Music School and later in Heidelberg with Fortner, who introduced him to modern music; initially influenced by neoclassicism, he was one of the first post-war composers to adopt dodecaphony, as in his *Whispers from Heavenly Death* (1948). Championed in the early days of the Darmstadt School, he was alienated by the increasingly dominant multiple serialist doctrines of the early 1950s; this is one of the reasons why he settled in Italy in 1953, where his music attained the more lyrical and sensuous quality exemplified by his opera *Elegy for Young Lovers* (1961). Henze's lifelong socialist persuasions came more to the fore as in *El Cimarrón* (1969–70), while in recent years his political motivations increasingly merged with more traditional forms, as in the *Requiem* (1990–2) or Ninth Symphony (1995–7).

Herrmann, Bernard (1911–75) American composer and conductor who studied in New York, and began a career writing for radio. He then moved on to film scores, becoming best known for his collaboration with Alfred Hitchcock; his output included *Citizen Kane* (1940), *Psycho* (1960), and *Vertigo* (1958). A would-be concert composer, Herrmann was known for orchestrating all his music himself, unlike other film composers of the time, and he used dissonance to particular effect, especially in the much-imitated score for *Psycho*.

Hindemith, Paul (1895–1963) German composer, teacher, and conductor, who worked initially as a violinist, thereafter taking up the viola and playing in the Frankfurt Opera, but in 1919 gained a publishing contract with Schott. His compositions developed from a romantic to a more contemporary, expressionist style, as in the *Kammermusik* no. 1 (1922) and the Third and Fourth Quartets (1920, 1921); subsequent works established a neo-baroque style. Hindemith taught in Berlin from 1927, completing his opera *Mathis der Maler* in 1935, but increasing problems with the Nazi regime led him to take up a position in Turkey, following which he settled in the US. His work as a teacher and writer was very influential, in particular his book *The Craft of Musical Composition* (1940).

Hofmann, Josef (1876–1957) American pianist of Polish birth, who toured Europe at a very early age, eventually establishing himself as a major performer throughout Europe and America; during the early decades of the century he was widely regarded as the finest living interpreter of the Romantic repertory, and Rachmaninov's Third Piano Concerto was dedicated to him. He was among the first classical musicians to make recordings.

Hogwood, Christopher (b. 1941) English fortepianist and conductor. Hogwood studied in Cambridge, and along with David Munrow founded the Early Music Consort (1967). In 1973 he set up the Academy of Ancient Music, which specialized in performing on period instruments, and he has performed and recorded extensively with this group.

Holliger, Heinz (b. 1939) Swiss composer, oboist, conductor, and pianist; he studied oboe in Paris and composition with Veress in Berne; he also had lessons with Boulez in Basel. Originally influenced by serialism, Holliger moved to a more immediate, ultra-expressionist style, before developing a more introverted idiom in his *Scardanelli-Zyklus* (1975–91). His radicalism as a composer contrasts with his work in many historical styles as one of the most sought-after oboists and a distinguished conductor.

Holly, Buddy (1936–59) American singer and songwriter, who recorded with his group the Crickets, his hits including 'That'll be the Day', and 'Oh Boy'. While he died tragically in a plane crash, his music survived and became extremely influential in the emerging rock and roll sound.

Honegger, Arthur (1892–1955) Swiss-French composer, one of a group of composers known as Les Six. He studied at the Paris Conservatoire, and his first compositions were performed around 1916; *Le roi David* (1921) established him as an important figure of the time. Later works include *Pacific 231* (1923), and five symphonies, all but the first dating from the 1940s.

Horowitz, Vladimir (1903–89) American pianist of Ukrainian birth. He studied in Kiev, making his debut in Berlin in 1926, but subsequently working mainly in America. Horowitz was known for an astonishing technique and magnetic stage persona, and for his interpretations of the late-Romantic repertory, particularly the music of Liszt.

Huber, Klaus (b. 1924) Swiss composer who studied with Burkhard in Zurich and Blacher in Berlin. Huber's complex aesthetics were based on his political as well as religious persuasions, and his belief that music should strive for utopian ideas led to a music which resists emotional immediacy, typified in his oratorio *Erniedrigt-Geknechtet-Verlassen-Verachtet* (1975–8). This uncompromising stance and his prodigious and committed teaching activities (at Basel and Freiburg, among other places) make him a far more influential figure than the performances and impact of his compositions might suggest.

Huber, Nicolaus (b. 1939) German composer. He studied with Bialas in Munich, worked with Riedl in the Siemens electronic studio in Munich and completed his studies with Nono in Venice. His early music combined multiple serialism with a critical reflection of music history. After having initially attempted to 'purify' music of its bourgeois heritage in the name of Marxist ideology, he eventually lost hope in the possibility of revolution and developed a more positive approach to tradition.

Ibrahim, Abdullah [Dollar Brand] (b. 1934) South African pianist and composer who became well known in his home country, where he worked with Hugh Masakela, before moving to Europe in 1963. It was Duke Ellington who arranged for Ibrahaim to record, and he appeared at numerous jazz festivals, subsequently moving to New York. His many recordings evidence an individualistic style which fuses jazz with South African influences.

Ives, Charles (1874–1954) American composer. Ives came to be seen as one of the most important American composers of the century, yet in his lifetime his music was little performed. He studied at Yale with Horatio Parker but thereafter pursued a successful career in insurance, composing only in his spare time. His works were highly experimental, particularly in the juxtaposition of different rhythmic and harmonic strands, sometimes resulting in a dense polyphonic web. Towards the end of his life he began to receive belated recognition for his work, and was awarded a Pulitzer prize in 1947 for his Third Symphony.

Jackson, Michael (b. 1958) American singer. While still a child he performed in the Jackson Five with his brothers and sisters, becoming their lead vocalist; their album *I Want You Back* (1969) was a huge success, but Jackson's solo career did not take off until the end of the 1970s. It was with producer Quincy Jones that he recorded *Off the Wall* (1979), and then the phenomenal *Thriller* (1982), the bestselling album of all time. His style fused soul and funk with elements of rock, including a distinctive vocal delivery and stunning dance routines. Subsequent recordings included *Bad* (1987) and *Dangerous* (1991), but because of personal problems Jackson largely disappeared from view in the later 1990s.

Janáček, Leoš (1854–1928) Czech composer who studied in Prague and was active as a choral conductor in his early years. His work was heavily influenced by Moravian folk music, and during his career he produced a number of folksong editions. Janáček's present-day reputation is based mainly on his large-scale works such as the *Glagolitic Mass* (1927), and the operas *Jenůfa* (1904) and *Katya Kabanova* (1921).

Jarre, Maurice (b. 1924) French composer, studying in Lyons and at the Paris Conservatoire. After working in theatre, he started composing for films. Since then his many scores have included *Lawrence of Arabia* (1965), *A Passage to India* (1984), and *Dead Poets Society* (1989); Jarre has become one of the most sought-after film composers, and worked with many of Hollywood's major directors.

Jefferson Airplane American rock group formed in 1965. Jefferson Airplane were prominent members of the psychedelic rock scene which emerged in San Francisco during the 1960s, and their 1967 album *Surrealistic Pillow* established them as the leading West Coast acid rock band. As with many other groups of the time, they drew from a wide range of influences, including jazz, blues, and Indian music, but they were unusual in featuring a female vocalist (Grace Slick).

Jobim, Antonio Carlos (1927–94) Brazilian composer, pianist, and guitarist. Jobim was the most famous exponent of the bossa nova style, and his best-known piece, 'Girl from Ipanema', was recorded by saxophonist Stan Getz and singer Joâo Gilberto, becoming a huge hit in 1962. It was largely through Jobim that bossa nova became so popular in the US during the 1960s.

Johnson, Robert (1911–38) American blues singer whose recordings, including 'Hell Hound On My Trail' (1933) and 'Kind Hearted Woman' (1936), form an important document of the Mississippi delta blues tradition. Johnson's songs played a major role in the rhythm and blues movement of the 1960s, being covered (not always with acknowledgement) by many British bands including The Rolling Stones, Cream, and Led Zeppelin. His complete recordings were reissued in 1990.

Jolivet, André (1905–74) French composer, one of the group of composers known as 'La jeune France' (which also included Messiaen and Daniel-Lesur). Jolivet's early music was particularly influenced by Debussy and Ravel, but exposure to the music of Schoenberg and Varèse proved important to the development of his style; his output includes chamber and vocal works, along with ballets such as *Ariadne* (1964), and *L'infante et le monstre* (1938).

Jones, Quincy (b. 1933) American producer and composer. He performed in dance and jazz bands at an early age, recording with Lionel Hampton; subsequently he worked as an arranger, writing for Count Basie among others, and during the 1950s studied with Nadia Boulanger. In the 1960s he wrote a number of film soundtracks, including *In the Heat of the Night* (1967), and among his television soundtracks were the Bill Cosby Show (1974). His work as a producer includes Michael Jackson's *Off the Wall* and *Thriller* albums.

Joplin, Scott (1867–1917) American composer, generally considered the greatest of the ragtime composers. After beginning as a cornet player, he studied piano and composition, publishing his first piano piece in 1899; *Maple Leaf Rag* (1899) sold huge numbers of copies for its time. As well as producing many other piano pieces, he wrote an opera, *Treemonisha*, but this was never performed complete in his lifetime. There was a revival of interest in Joplin's music around 1970.

Kagel, Mauricio (b. 1931) Argentine-German composer, film-maker and playwright, who studied literature and philosophy in Buenos Aires and received private tuition in music. He moved to Cologne in 1957 to work at the NWDR Studio für Elektronische Musik, and soon developed a very personal approach to experimental music theatre (which he calls 'instrumental theatre'), as evidenced in *Sur scène* (1959) and the opera *Staatstheater* (1971). At this time his radical experimentalism also led him to concentrate on music for often grotesque sound producers which had to be specially built (*Acustica*, 1970). Beginning with *Ludwig van* (1970) he engaged more closely with existing musical traditions, giving his music a more traditional surface without diminishing its subversive and often surreal wit.

Kante, Mory (b. 1951) Guinean performer. Kante came to prominence in Europe during the 1980s as a performer who fused the traditional *kora* sound of his native country with African dance forms. His recording *Courougnegne* (1981) established his popularity in the West, as well as proving a huge success in parts of Africa.

Karajan, Herbert von (1908–89) Austrian conductor who studied at the Vienna Music Academy, and made his debut in 1929 in Ulm. From 1938 he worked with the Berlin Philharmonic, finally succeeding Furtwängler as principal conductor in 1955; at the same time he held posts as director of the Salzburg Festival and director of the Vienna Staatsoper. A charismatic conductor and prolific recording artist who concentrated on the 18th- and 19th-century canon, Karajan was perhaps more than anyone responsible for establishing the mainstream tradition of orchestral conducting in the second half of the century.

Keita, Salif (b. 1949) Malian vocalist. By the 1970s Keita's reputation had spread throughout West Africa, and he became known both in America and Europe through his performances there. His recordings showcase a style which fuses traditional Malian music with contemporary production techniques.

Kern, Jerome (1885–1945) American composer who worked as a rehearsal pianist and song-plugger before beginning a career as a songwriter. His musical *Very Good Eddie* (1915) was his first major success, but the 1927 *Show Boat*, written with lyricist Oscar Hammerstein II, is probably his most highly regarded work. Many of his songs are staples of the Tin Pan Alley repertory, and pieces such as 'A Fine Romance' and 'All The Things You Are' have been widely interpreted by jazz musicians.

Khan, Nusrat Fateh Ali (1948–97) Pakistani singer. He is mainly known for performances of devotional Sufi music, but his work has included explorations of a number of different traditions. Khan recorded for Peter Gabriel's Real World label, as well as performing at the WOMAD festival, activities which helped make him well known in the West during the last two decades of the century.

Kidjo, Angelique (b. 1960) Nigerian singer who grew up in Benin, but moved to Paris in 1983 and played with jazz groups, recording *Parakou* for the Mango label in 1992. Her music is a combination of jazz and soul, with lyrics often in her native language.

Klemperer, Otto (1885–1973) German conductor. Klemperer studied composition and conducting in Berlin, and by 1920 had established himself as one of the leading German conductors. Seen as an exponent of the Austro-German conducting tradition exemplified by Mahler, Klemperer conducted contemporary music as well as the classics, and in 1927 became director of a new branch of the Berlin Staatsoper devoted to contemporary music; during the following three seasons he conducted performances of Stravinsky's *Oedipus rex*, Schoenberg's *Erwartung*, and Hindemith's *Cardillac*. In 1933 he moved to the US.

Knussen, Oliver (b. 1952) English composer and conductor. He completed his Second Symphony while still in his teens, and became well known with his fantasy opera based on a story by Maurice Sendak, *Where the Wild Things Are* (1979–83). He developed an eclectic compositional style that blends aspects of freely handled serialism with Carter-style tempo modulation, sometimes including overt or covert references to earlier twentieth-century composers. Since the 1980s he has developed a distinguished career as a conductor of contemporary music, working at first with the London Sinfonietta and subsequently with many European and American orchestras; he was artistic director of the Aldeburgh Festival from 1983 to 1998.

Kodály, Zoltán (1882–1967) Hungarian composer, ethnomusicologist, and educationalist. Kodály was closely associated with his compatriot Bartók, and both composers worked to create a style of music which drew inspiration from Hungarian folk traditions, as well as being active collectors of folksong. But Kodály's greatest influence was perhaps in education: The 'Kodály method' emphasizes the importance of early musical training and the role of choral singing in developing the ear, and has had a worldwide influence.

Kolisch, Rudolf (1896–1978) American violinist of Austrian birth. Kolisch studied in Vienna and formed the Kolisch Quartet, which performed works by many contemporary composers but was particularly associated with the music of Schoenberg, Berg, and Webern. Kolisch later moved to the US, where he taught at a number of colleges and universities.

Korngold, Erich Wolfgang (1897–1957) American composer of Austrian birth. The son of a leading Viennese music critic, he was a child prodigy, and his two operas *Der Ring des Polykrates* and *Violanta* were both completed in 1914. He taught in Vienna while continuing to compose, but thereafter moved to Hollywood, where he worked on the film score for *A Midsummer Night's Dream* (1934); subsequent film scores included *The Sea Hawk* (1940) and *King's Row* (1941). Korngold saw himself as primarily a concert composer, but it is as a film composer that he was hugely influential, and his technique of employing leitmotifs in this context was widely imitated.

Koussevitzky, Serge (1874–1951) American conductor of Russian birth. He studied in Moscow, working there as a double-bass player, and made his conducting debut in 1908. In 1909 he founded the Edition Russe de Musique, which published such composers as Stravinsky, Prokofiev, and Rachmaninov. In 1924 he took over the Boston Symphony Orchestra from Pierre Monteux. He was known for his performances of contemporary music; among the premieres he conducted were Stravinsky's *Symphonies of Wind Instruments* and works by Prokofiev and Honegger. He was also music director of the Tanglewood Summer School from 1940, where he taught conducting.

Kraftwerk German pop group. Their founding members Ralf Hütter and Florain Schneider-Esleben came together in 1968, with their breakthrough recording *Autobahn* being released in 1975. Their music was created using synthesizers, drum machines, and sequencers, and they were one of the first groups to use this new technology to generate commercially successful pop music. Subsequent albums such as *Trans-Europe Express* (1977) also proved influential, and Kraftwerk are often cited as precursors of the electronic dance music of the 1980s and 90s.

Kreisler, Fritz (1875–1962) American violinist and composer of Austrian birth. He studied in Paris and Vienna, and his performances with the Berlin Philharmonic and Nikisch in 1899 attracted much attention. He became well known as a soloist, touring Europe and America, and Elgar's violin concerto was composed for him. He later settled in the US. Although he was recognized for his immaculate and seemingly effortless technique, there was some controversy over his compositions, which he passed off as the work of forgotten eighteenth-century composers.

Krenek, Ernst (1900–91) Austrian composer and writer. He studied in Vienna and Berlin, and his early work proved popular enough to earn him a publishing contract. His most celebrated work is the opera *Jonny spielt auf* (1925), which capitalized on the popularity of jazz in Europe at around that time. Subsequent operas also enjoyed considerable success, building on the relatively conservative style that Krenek had by then developed. He later settled in the US and taught there for most of the rest of his life.

Kurtág, György (b. 1926) Hungarian composer and pianist who studied in Budapest, and whose early works evidence a particular debt to Bartók. His studies in Paris with Messiaen and Milhaud in 1957 brought some significant changes to his music, and he was particularly influenced by Webern; the song cycle *Bornemisza Péter mondásai* (1968) is one of the most substantial works from this time. Other well-known works include *Poslaniya pokoynoy R. V. Trusovoy* (1980), *Omaggio a Luigi Nono* (1979), and *Stele* (1994).

Kuti, Fela (b. 1938) Nigerian bandleader who studied in London, leading a group called Koola Lobitos, before moving back to Nigeria. Kuti referred to his music as

'Afrobeat' and took his group to the US, establishing links with a number of black militants there. He became a star in West Africa, although his radical politics caused him a number of problems in his home country.

Lachenmann, Helmut (b. 1935) German composer, who studied at the Stuttgart Musikhochschule and received tuition from Nono in Venice. Lachenmann at first followed the technical innovations of the post-war avant-garde, evident in his *Souvenir* (1959); beginning with *temA* (1968), however, he sought a more immediate musical expression through a focus on unusual instrumental and vocal techniques and noise production, which he called *musique concrète instrumentale. Accanto* (1975–6) inaugurated a further stage in which Lachenmann explored hitherto unheard sonorities, reflecting his forcefully articulated belief in 'music as existential experience'.

Ladysmith Black Mambazo South African choral group. They began performing professionally in the 1970s, but came to real prominence in the West with their work on Paul Simon's *Graceland* album (1985). They subsequently recorded for Warner Brothers, and remain a popular act in Europe and America.

Landowska, Wanda (1879–1959) Polish pianist and harpsichordist. She was particularly known for her harpsichord performances, and did much to promote the instrument at a time when it was still relatively little used. Landowska is particularly important to the historical-performance movement, and her research into historical performance practice provided a model for many later performers.

Leadbelly (1885–1949) American blues singer and guitarist who became prominent as a result of being recorded in the 1930s by the musicologist Alan Lomax for the Archive of Folk Song at the Library of Congress. These recordings are important documents of the early delta-blues style, and it was largely because of Lomax's work that Leadbelly found an audience later in his life.

Led Zeppelin English rock group formed in 1968, including guitarist Jimmy Page and vocalist Robert Plant. Their music, based on blues and rock riffs, formed an important bridge from hard rock to the heavy-metal genre of the 1980s, and Zeppelin's music was characterized by the use of distorted guitars with a bass-heavy rhythm section. Among their best-known hits is the song 'Stairway to Heaven' (1972), which became a rock standard.

Legrand, Michel (b. 1932) French composer and arranger, who studied in Paris, taking conducting lessons with Nadia Boulanger, before taking up a career as an orchestrator and songwriter; his 1958 recording *Legrand Jazz* featured jazz musicians Miles Davis and John Coltrane. He has also pursued a career as a film-music composer, his scores including *Lady Sings the Blues* (1972), *Yentl* (1983), and *Best Friends* (1982).

Lehár, Franz (1870–1948) Austro-Hungarian composer and conductor, most associated with the operetta form, and one of the most significant composers of light music of the early part of the century. Among his best known works are *Die lustige Witwe* (1905), *Der Graf von Luxemburg* (1909), and *Zigeunerliebe* (1910).

Leibowitz, René (1913–72) French theorist, teacher, conductor, and composer, who studied in Warsaw and Berlin before moving to Paris. He played an important role in disseminating the music of the Second Viennese School, conducting Schoenberg's music in Paris just after the war, and attracted such students as Boulez, Globokar, and Masson. He also taught at the Darmstadt Summer School, although his academic approach later came under attack, notably from Boulez.

Levine, James (b. 1943) American conductor and pianist. Levine studied piano with Serkin and conducting at Juilliard, thereafter working with the Baltimore Symphony Orchestra, and then the Cleveland Orchestra with George Szell. He became increasingly known for his operatic work, making his debut at the Metropolitan Opera in New York in 1971, and was appointed principal conductor there two years later. One of the most active conductors of the last decades of the century, he has also conducted at Bayreuth and recorded with the Vienna Philharmonic.

Liberace [Walter] (1919–87) American pianist and entertainer who made his concert debut at the age of seventeen, and soon after performed with the Chicago Symphony. He cultivated a showmanlike personality on stage, donning elaborate outfits; this endeared him to a wide audience and helped make him a star attraction. His repertory always included virtuosic pieces designed to showcase his keyboard technique.

Ligeti, György (b. 1923) Hungarian-German composer. He studied in Kolozsvár and Budapest under Farkas and Veress, but emigrated in 1956 to the West, eventually settling in Cologne where he studied at the NWDR Studio für Elektronische Musik and eagerly absorbed avant-garde styles. However, he quickly came to reject the orthodoxies of multiple serialism, instead developing his characteristic techniques for creating static, vast instrumental sonorities by combining cluster-based harmony with rapid, dense polyphony, as in *Atmosphères* (1961). Later on, he integrated more traditional compositional techniques such as melodic writing and counterpoint, developing an evocative music drawing from many sources, as in the ongoing series of piano studies (begun in 1985).

Lindberg, Magnus (b. 1958) Finnish composer whose compositional starting point was the complex serialism of Stockhausen and Babbitt, but whose style has become increasingly eclectic, drawing not only on the 'art' music tradition but also on free jazz, progressive rock, and non-Western musics. While much of his music is orchestral, some of it incorporates live electronics (e.g. *UR*, 1986 and *Related Rocks*, 1997), and he has also made use of rule-based computational software (*Engine*, 1996).

Little Richard (b. 1932) American rhythm and blues singer. Richard was heavily influenced by gospel music, but made his sound by drawing on rhythm and blues and jump blues, incorporating his own distinctive vocals which featured much use of his falsetto register. Million-selling hits such as 'Tutti Frutti' (1956) influenced performers like Jerry Lee Lewis, Jimi Hendrix, and Mick Jagger.

Lloyd Webber, Andrew (b. 1948) English composer. He studied at the Royal College of Music, and from the beginning of his career wrote music for shows. His collaboration with lyricist Tim Rice produced *Joseph and the Amazing Technicolour Dreamcoat* (1968), launching a hugely successful career that included *Evita* (1976), *Phantom of the Opera* (1986), *Cats* (1981), and *Sunset Boulevard* (1993). These shows all enjoyed great success at a time when the genre of the musical was generally thought to be in decline.

Loriod, Yvonne (b. 1924) French pianist. Loriod studied at the Paris Conservatoire with Milhaud and Messiaen, and was subsequently involved in the performances of much of Messiaen's music; she later became his second wife. Loriod also played the music of other contemporary European composers, performing *Structures* with Boulez in 1951, and making a number of important recordings.

Lutosławski, Witold (1913–94) Polish composer. He studied in Warsaw, and the music of Szymanowski was an important initial influence. The *Symphonic Variations* (1938) was one of his first pieces to be widely performed, but his career was interrupted by the Second World War, and his First Symphony (1947) was proscribed by Polish authorities due to its perceived modernist tendencies. Subsequently, he wrote in a more acceptable style publicly, while continuing his compositional development in private pieces. As the political climate thawed his reputation grew throughout Europe, with the Concerto for Orchestra (1954) becoming particularly well known; his aleatoric technique can be seen in pieces such as *Jeux vénitiens* (1961) and *Trois poèmes d'Henri Michaux* (1963). More recent works include *Mi-Parti* (1976), *Les espaces du sommeil* (1976), and the Third and Fourth Symphonies (the last completed in 1992).

Lutyens, Elisabeth (1906–1983) English composer, who studied in Paris and then at the Royal College of Music (London). Her style developed gradually, and built on a distinctive and rigorous use of chromaticism; later she wrote film music to support herself. After the war she adopted contemporary techniques such as serialism, often writing in a highly expressionist vein, as demonstrated by *Music for Orchestra I* (1955) and the chamber opera *Infidelio* (1954).

Maal, Baaba (b. 1960) Senegalese singer and guitarist. After working as a vocalist in Senegal, he studied for a time in Paris, releasing an influential series of albums during the 1980s. His mixture of a Senegalese style with modern production techniques and jazz and reggae influences has proved extremely popular in the West.

MacMillan, James (b. 1959) Scottish composer. MacMillan studied in Edinburgh, and his music has been heavily influenced by his interests in native Scottish culture and the Roman Catholic faith. *The Confession of Isobel Gowdie* (1990) was followed by the percussion concerto *Veni, veni Emmanuel* (1992), written for Evelyn Glennie, which has been widely performed. MacMillan's language encompasses tonal, atonal, and modal elements, often incorporating elements of folksong and plainchant that serve as germs for larger-scale musical structures.

Maconchy, Elizabeth (1907–94) English composer who studied at the Royal College of Music with Vaughan Williams and Wood, and subsequently in Prague with K. B. Jirák; she became known through her Piano Concerto of 1930. During her career she produced a wide variety of pieces for both professional and amateur performance, often characterized by a concern with thematic development.

Maderna, Bruno (1923–73) Italian composer and conductor who studied composition at the Rome Conservatory and conducting in Siena. He regularly visited and taught at the Darmstadt Summer School from 1949 on, becoming one of its guiding spirits. In 1955 he co-founded, and co-directed with Berio, the Studio di Fonologia Musicale of the RAI (Italian broadcasting network) in Milan. Maderna quickly adopted dodecaphony and multiple serialism in his Second Serenade (1955), yet he did not allow any particular system to dominate his music; he pioneered live electronics and aleatoric techniques as early as 1953 with his *Musica su due dimensioni*, and developed both further in the colossal *Hyperion* cycle (1962–9), which consists of a multitude of independent pieces for various instrumentations.

Madonna [Ciccone] (b. 1958) American singer and songwriter, now resident in Britain. She studied dance and worked in New York on a variety of different projects before releasing her first album in 1983. The single 'Like A Virgin' (1984) was a huge hit, and subsequent albums (including *Like A Virgin*, 1984, and *You Can Dance*, 1987) followed; frequently reinventing her media image, she became seen as an icon of postmodernism. In the 1990s she worked with a number of different producers, the outcomes including *Ray of Light* (1998) with William Orbit.

Mahler, Gustav (1860–1911) Austrian composer and conductor. Mahler's music became the subject of increasing attention during the 1970s, and he came to be seen as a bridge between late Romanticism and the expressive atonal music of Schoenberg; while his musical idiom was essentially post-Wagnerian, its use of a wide variety of different moods and styles points towards a kind of polystylism. Mahler's nine symphonies have become a major part of the twentieth-century symphonic repertory (a tenth was left unfinished, but was completed by Deryck Cooke); he also composed several large-scale song cycles, including *Das Lied von der Erde* (1909). He was an extremely influential conductor, directing the opera in Vienna, but left for New York in 1907 after becoming the subject of anti-Semitic attacks.

Makeba, Miriam (b. 1932) South African singer who came to prominence during the 1950s in South Africa, moving to the US in 1959. While her fame grew in the West, her outspoken condemnation of the South African regime meant her work was proscribed in her home country. After moving to West Africa, she appeared with Paul Simon on his tour of the *Graceland* album.

Mancini, Henry (1924–94) American arranger, composer, and pianist who worked as an arranger for dance bands before moving on to write film scores for Universal. His music for the TV series *Peter Gunn* was a huge success, and thereafter his services were in great demand; other notable film scores include *Breakfast at Tiffany's* (1961) and *The Pink Panther* (1963). Mancini drew on jazz in much of his music, creating a distinctive individual style.

Mantovani (Annuncion Paolo) (1905–80) British violinist of Italian birth who became a major figure in the British light-music circuit. After studying in Italy he moved to England, where he began a career playing for musicals and radio broadcasts. He was involved with a number of Noel Coward productions, and later toured widely with his own orchestra. He was also active as a composer of light music.

Mapfumo, Thomas (b. 1945) Zimbabwean vocalist. Mapfumo is the major figure of Zimbabwean popular music, blending traditional approaches with modern influences, and has a considerable international reputation. His exposure to American popular music, particularly that of Presley, Redding, and Cook, was vital to his development. His music uses some of the patterns of *mbira* (thumb piano) music, translating them into guitar patterns. Mapfumo has never fought shy of political rhetoric, which has sometimes led to problems in his home country, even resulting in a period of imprisonment.

Marley, Bob (1945–81) Jamaican reggae singer, songwriter, and bandleader. He made his first record in 1960, forming a group called the Wailers; Marley's work with producer Lee 'Scratch' Perry (now a legend in his own right) was crucial to the development of his style. He embraced Rastafarianism in the 1970s and became hugely popular in the West through albums such as *Catch a Fire* (1972) and *Burnin'* (1973).

Marsalis, Wynton (b. 1961) American trumpeter, composer, and bandleader, who studied both jazz and classical music, and has been highly succcessful in both fields, but is best known for his jazz playing. He joined Art Blakey's Jazz Messengers band in 1980, as well as touring with Herbie Hancock before beginning his own recording career. Technically he is regarded by many as the foremost jazz trumpeter of the last two decades. However his reassessment of older jazz styles and criticism of some forms of modern jazz has led to charges of narrow-mindedness from fellow musicians and critics, notably Keith Jarrett and Herbie Hancock. His directorship of the jazz programme at Lincoln Center makes him an extremely important figure in the American jazz scene, while his work as an educator is also influential. His oratorio *Blood on the Fields* (1994) won a Pulitzer prize.

Martin, George (b. 1926) English producer and composer who worked for EMI and then Parlophone records before producing the Beatles. He played a crucial role in their recordings, contributing string arrangements and helping to develop some of the unusual tape effects which marked out the group's later work. Later on he set up his own studios, subsequently producing such artists as Paul McCartney and Neil Sedaka.

Masekela, Hugh (b. 1939) South African trumpeter. He formed his first band in the 1950s, later forming the Jazz Epistles (which included pianist Abdullah Ibrahim). After taking the opportunity to study in the US, he quickly became well known on the jazz scene in New York. His career has encompassed a number of stylistic shifts, and his music has explored mainstream jazz, jazz funk, and a distinctive blend of township music and jazz.

Melba, Nellie (1861–1931) Australian soprano. She studied in Paris, and quickly became a major name, appearing throughout Europe and America and being associated particularly with the music of Puccini. In the early part of the century she was a huge star, known throughout Europe and America for her performances, and made numerous recordings.

Menuhin, Yehudi (1916–99) American violinist and conductor. He made his debut at a very early age, performing the Beethoven Violin Concerto at only 11 with Fritz Busch. Performances with Walter and the Berlin Philharmonic Orchestra followed, and he then settled in Paris with his family; his 1932 recording of Elgar's Violin Concerto, with the composer conducting, became particularly well known. His interests covered a wide musical range, and included explorations of jazz and Indian music, resulting in recordings with Stéphane Grappelli and Ravi Shankar. Menuhin was also an important figure as a teacher, establishing the first Menuhin talent school in 1963 (at Stoke d'Abernon, Surrey, UK), and in 1977 he founded Live Music Now!, an international organization that promotes concerts in such venues as prisons and hospitals.

Messiaen, Olivier (1908–92) French composer, organist, and teacher. He had a profound impact on twentieth-century music through both his compositions and his teaching. After studying in Paris, he took up a post as an organist there which he held for 60 years, and many of his early works, such as *L'ascension* (1935), were for organ. During the war he was captured and held in a concentration camp, where he wrote *Quatuor pour la fin du temps* (1941). After the war Messiaen taught at the Paris Conservatoire, where his many pupils included Boulez and Stockhausen; the *Turangalîla-symphonie* (1948) is one of his largest-scale works from this time, but his short piano piece *Mode de valeurs et d'intensités* (1949) had a far greater influence on young composers, since it suggested the possibility of total serialism. Messiaen's music was also concerned with integrating elements of birdsong, as exemplified by the *Catalogue d'oiseaux* for piano (1958); later works include *Saint François d'Assise* (1983), his only opera.

Milhaud, Darius (1892–1974) French composer. He studied in Paris and became best known for his attempt to blend the language of jazz with concert music in *La création du monde* (1923). His writing for percussion was particularly influential, with his Percussion Concerto (1930) being the first of its kind. In 1940 Milhaud emigrated to the US, where he held a number of teaching positions.

Miller, Glenn (1904–44) American bandleader and trombonist who worked with a number of dance bands in the late 1920s before organizing his own band in 1937. By the end of the decade, Miller's group had become one of the most popular of the swing bands, and had hits with 'In The Mood' (1939) and 'Chattanooga Choo Choo' (1941). Miller died in an air crash on the way to Europe, but a number of groups continued to play his music after his death.

Mingus, Charles (1922–79) American jazz bass player, pianist, and composer. Mingus began his career playing in the bands of musicians such as Louis Armstrong and Lionel Hampton, and worked with a number of bebop musicians during the early 1950s. He began running his own groups during the 1950s, which explored different facets of the jazz tradition from New Orleans style to gospel, blues, and free-form improvisation. Mingus blended these different elements together in a unique manner, taking an approach which demanded individuality and commitment from every musician. His best-known work includes recordings such as *Pithecanthropus Erectus* (1956) and the large-scale *The Black Saint and the Sinner Lady* (1963).

Mitchell, Joni (b. 1943) Canadian singer and songwriter. Mitchell came to prominence in the 1960s as a singer/songwriter, mostly performing solo. She performed at the famous Woodstock festival, but her most highly regarded work came during the 1970s, particularly with the album *Blue* (1971). She has also collaborated with jazz musicians such as Pat Metheny and Jaco Pastorius, and recorded an album devoted to the music of Charles Mingus.

Mitropoulos, Dimitri (1896–1960) Amerian conductor, pianist, and composer. He was born and studied in Greece, and made his name when he appeared with the Berlin Philharmonic, directing Prokofiev's Third Piano Concerto from the keyboard. He then toured Europe and was invited to conduct in Boston, subsequently gaining a post with the Minneapolis Symphony Orchestra. There he became an important figure in the promotion of contemporary music, performing music by Berg, Mahler, Krenek, and Sessions. He later became director of the New York Philharmonic, and worked with a number of European orchestras towards the end of his career.

Monk, Thelonious (1917–82) American jazz pianist and composer. Monk appeared on the jazz scene in New York around the time that Charlie Parker and Dizzy Gillespie were developing the bebop style. Monk worked with Coleman Hawkins and then with Gillespie, beginning his own recording career as a leader for Blue Note in 1947. His style developed into one of the most unique and eccentric in jazz, emphasizing angular, dissonant, and spare melodic lines, as reflected in his many compositions which have become jazz standards, including 'Straight No Chaser' and ''Round Midnight'.

Monteux, Pierre (1875–1964) American conductor of French birth. He studied at the Paris Conservatoire, and after working at the Paris Opéra became conductor of Diaghilev's Ballets Russes. With the company he took part in a series of major performances which included the Stravinsky ballets (notably *Firebird* and *The Rite of Spring*) as well as works by Ravel and Debussy. Subsequently he worked at the Metropolitan Opera in New York, and then with the Boston Symphony Orchestra. He returned to Europe to work with the Concertgebouw Orchestra in 1924, only later to move back to America and the San Francisco Symphony Orchestra.

Morricone, Ennio (b. 1928) Italian composer who studied with Petrassi and, after working both as an arranger and in the field of experimental improvisation, made a successful career writing film scores. Morricone produced scores for Sergio Leone's Westerns (including *Per un pugno di dollari*, 1964), and more recent works have included *The Mission* (1986) and *Cinema Paradiso* (1988).

Murail, Tristan (b. 1947) French composer. He studied in Paris with Messiaen, and established the Group de l'Itinéraire, which played an important role in performing contemporary works in France during the 1970s and 80s. Along with his compatriot Grisey, Murail pursued the technique of spectral composition. His studies at IRCAM assisted in this, and his works include *Treize couleurs du soleil couchant* (1979), *Gondwana* (1980) and *Désintégrations* (1983). Murail is also well known as a performer on the ondes martenot.

Nancarrow, Conlon (1912–97) American composer who studied with Sessions and Piston, but subsequently moved to Mexico City because of anti-communist sentiment in America. There he embarked on a series of studies for player piano, which explored rhythmic techniques of an otherwise unrealizable complexity. Nancarrow was little known until the 1970s when some of his work was published; subsequently the studies were recorded and became the focus of much interest from musicologists and composers.

N'Dour, Youssou (b. 1959) Senegalese vocalist. Since the 1980s N'Dour has been Senegal's best-known musician; among his albums, *Immigres* (1985) and *Nelson Mandela* (1986) were both significant in establishing his name in the West, where he became seen as a leading representative of 'World beat'. N'Dour has worked and toured with Peter Gabriel, and continues to perform extensively both in Europe and America.

Newman, Alfred (1900–70) American composer and conductor. He began a career as a performer at a very young age, working on Broadway and in touring shows; by 1930, he was engaged in work as a film composer, for which he became most famous. His best-known scores include *Wuthering Heights* (1939), *The Hunchback of Notre Dame* (1939), and *The Robe* (1953). Newman's Romantic style was highly influential in the genre, and continues to be much imitated.

Nikisch, Arthur (1855–1922) Austro-Hungarian conductor. Nikisch studied in Vienna and began working at the Leipzig Opera. He then took up a position with the Boston Symphony Orchestra, subsequently holding positions with the Berlin Philharmonic and Leipzig Gewandhaus. He was perhaps the most admired conductor of his day, particularly for his work in the Romantic repertory, and strongly influenced a number of twentieth-century conductors, including Furtwängler.

Nirvana American band, often categorized as 'grunge'. Nirvana formed in 1987, and their music was characterized by thick distorted guitar textures combined with the distinctive lyrics of Kurt Cobain. The group achieved huge popularity in the early 1990s, especially with the album *Nevermind* (1991). Cobain commited suicide in 1994, and the group subsequently split up.

Nono, Luigi (1924–91) Italian composer who studied at the Venice Conservatory with Malipiero. Mentored by Scherchen and Maderna, Nono became a leading force in the Darmstadt avant-garde, composing one of the first multiple serial pieces with *Polifonica – monodia – ritmica* (1951). However, following his entry into the Italian Communist Party, the emphasis of his music shifted from compositional technique to the expression of political concerns, as in *Il canto sospeso* (1955–6), a setting of texts by condemned prisoners of the European Resistance. He maintained that political engagement should be linked with the most advanced compositional means, such as electronics, which he used to great effect in pieces such as *La fabbrica illuminata* (1964). With his string quartet *Fragmente – Stille, an Diotima* (1979–80), Nono embarked on a phase of more intimate musical expression, without giving up his political motivations.

Nørgård, Per (b. 1932) Danish composer who studied in Copenhagen and subsequently with Boulanger in Paris. Among his best-known works, the symphonies are characteristic, exhibiting a style which combines a chromatic language with a slow unfolding of musical material. Active as a teacher, he has held positions at a number of conservatories in Europe from the 1960s.

Norrington, Roger (b. 1934) English conductor, best known for his work in period performance and his founding of the London Classical Players in 1978. His recordings of Haydn, Mozart, and Beethoven, as well as his work in the later Romantic repertory, typify a concern with detailed background research combined with the use of period instruments. Norrington has performed extensively both in Europe and America.

North, Alex (1910–91) American composer and conductor. After beginning his career writing scores for the theatre, he made his name as a film composer, particularly with *A Streetcar Named Desire* (1951), a score notable for its jazz influences. Among his many later works are *Spartacus* (1960), and *Who's Afraid of Virginia Woolf?* (1966); in 1967 he scored *2001: A Space Odyssey*, but the director, Stanley Kubrick, famously set aside North's score in favour of his temp track.

North's work drew on a range of instrumental forces, and he made no attempt to separate his writing for film from his continuing interest in concert music.

Novello, Ivor (1893–1951) British composer. Novello was the most popular composer of British musicals during the first half of the century; among them are *Glamorous Night* (1935) and *King's Rhapsody* (1949). But he probably reached more people through composing 'Keep the Home Fires Burning', a song which was popular with both British and American soldiers during the First World War.

Nyman, Michael (b. 1944) English composer. He studied in London, and was initially known as a writer on minimalism (he was the first commentator to apply this term to music). His early works are experimental in the tradition of Cage, and during the 1970s he wrote for his own ensemble, the Michael Nyman Band, following the example of composers such as Reich and Glass. Film scores play a major role in Nyman's output, which has increasingly concentrated on reworking older compositional styles in a distinctive fashion; the score for *The Piano* (1992) exemplifies this approach, taking its cue from the Romantic piano tradition.

Oliver, Joe 'King' (1885–1938) American jazz cornettist and bandleader. Oliver grew up in New Orleans, playing in several of the city's many brass and dance bands. He formed his own band in 1920 and took it to Chicago, where Louis Armstrong joined. Armstrong soon left to pursue his own career, but Oliver's band remained one of the most successful bands from New Orleans, with 'Dippermouth Blues' (1923) being one of its best-known recordings.

Orff, Carl (1895–1982) German composer and educationalist. After serving in the First World War he worked as both a conductor and a composer, achieving international fame with *Carmina Burana* (1937), a large-scale choral work based on 23 poems from late medieval times. Based in Munich after the Second World War, Orff was active as an educator, advocating children's participation in rhythmic ensembles and inventing percussion instruments for them to use.

Ozawa, Seiji (b. 1935) American conductor of Japanese origin. Ozawa studied in Tokyo, initially as a pianist, but then took up conducting, quickly winning prizes, and travelled to Europe. He came to the attention of Bernstein, who offered him a post as assistant conductor at the New York Philharmonic. Subsequently Ozawa worked with all the major American orchestras, holding posts with many of them; he has also performed opera in all the major houses of the world. Ozawa is best known for his interpretations of a range of contemporary music, including Debussy, Messiaen, and Takemitsu.

Parker, Charlie (1920–55) American saxophonist, a key figure in the development of bebop during the 1940s, along with Dizzy Gillespie and Bud Powell. Parker worked in Kansas City before moving to New York, where he played with various bands and participated in the now-legendary jam sessions at Minton's Playhouse; he came to be the leading saxophonist of his time, revered by fellow musicians despite all too apparent drug and alcohol problems. Although he died early,

Parker left an impressive body of recordings, and is generally regarded as one of the most gifted all of jazz improvisers.

Pärt, Arvo (b. 1935) Estonian composer. Pärt began writing music for film and theatre, while also writing concert music. He explored serial technique in his early works, as well as a brand of neoclassicism based in particular on Bach. However, during the late 1960s his musical direction changed and he became particularly interested in Gregorian chant; the pieces which followed employed a technique he called 'tintinnabuli', and included *Cantus in memoriam Benjamin Britten* (1977). In recent years Pärt's music has become particularly popular in the West, in no small part through the recordings of his works on the ECM record label.

Partch, Harry (1901–74) American composer and theorist. Partch spent part of his early life as a hobo travelling through America, and much of his life was punctuated by moves from place to place. His work was principally occupied with the exploration of unconventional tuning systems, as outlined in his book *Genesis of a Music* (1949); building his own instruments was an essential part of Partch's approach, with his creations including a microtonal marimba. Partch's best known works are his large-scale music dramas, such as *King Oedipus* (1952) and *The Bewitched* (1957). Since his death Partch's work has gradually become better known, including his theoretical work on tuning.

Penderecki, Krzysztof (b. 1933) Polish composer who achieved an international reputation in the 1960s. A typical example of his early style, *Threnody for the Victims of Hiroshima* (1960), is characterized by an unusual and dense approach to string writing; his later works became more lyrical and conventional, and include the First Violin Concerto (1976) and the *Polish Requiem* (1984).

Perahia, Murray (b. 1947) American pianist, now resident in London. He studied widely in America, including time spent working with Serkin and Casals, before embarking on a solo career; he performed with the New York Philharmonic in 1972, and then won the Leeds International Piano Competition. Since that time he has become one of the major international concert pianists, particularly known for his work in the baroque repertory and for his advocacy of Schenkerian analysis for the performer.

Petrassi, Goffredo (b. 1904) Italian composer who studied at the Conservatorio di S. Cecilia in Rome. Petrassi established himself as a distinguished composer with his *Salmo IX* (1934–6); his best known work, *Noche oscura* (1951), shows a pragmatic approach to compositional technique, freely combining dodecaphony with neoclassical and tonal elements. These characteristics made him one of the most influential Italian composers of the mid-century.

Pfitzner, Hans (1869–1949) German composer and conductor. His early works, such as the opera *Der arme Heinrich* (1893), were heavily indebted to Wagner; from 1907 he worked as a conductor in Strasbourg, being particularly known for his performances of German Romantic opera. In both his writings and his music,

Pfitzner opposed modernist trends, advocating both aesthetic and political conservatism. Among his best known compositions are the opera *Palestrina* (1915) and the cantata *Von deutscher Seele* (1921).

Piaf, Edith (1915–63) French singer and actress, who made her name working in Parisian nightclubs singing popular songs, and subsequently made a number of films; her greatest hit was 'La vie en rose' (1946). Piaf's popularity, based on emotional expression rather than technical ability, extended far beyond the Paris scene in which she worked; she appeared in both London and New York in the 1950s, and her records sold widely.

Piazolla, Astor (1921–92) Argentine composer, bandleader, and performer, best known for his innovative style of tango composition. He found major acceptance in America and Europe before being recognized in his home country. His music has recently been performed by classical musicians, notably the Kronos Quartet.

Pink Floyd English rock band formed in 1965; the original members were Syd Barrett, Nick Mason, Roger Waters, and Rick Wright. They began performing in London in the late 1960s, and were known for a psychedelic style which included the use of elaborate light shows. After the recording *Piper at the Gates of Dawn* (1967), Barrett was replaced by Dave Gilmour, and it was this lineup which recorded *The Dark Side of the Moon* (1973), one of the seminal albums of the decade and one of the bestselling records of all time. Later work included *The Wall* (1979), and although Waters left in 1983, the band continued with the album *A Momentary Lapse of Reason* (1987).

Pollini, Maurizio (b. 1942) Italian pianist who came to prominence after winning a number of competitions in the late 1950s, although it was not until the late 1960s that he achieved a major reputation and began recording for DGG. While he has recorded the works of the classical and Romantic period extensively, he is also known for his work in contemporary music, and has often collaborated with conductor Claudio Abbado.

Porter, Cole (1891–1964) American composer. Porter made his name writing for Broadway, his many famous songs including 'Night and Day', 'I Get A Kick Out Of You', and 'You're The Top'. The best-known of his musicals is *Kiss Me, Kate* (1948), and he also scored films such as *High Society* (1956).

Poulenc, Francis (1899–1963) French composer and pianist. He studied with various composers, including Koechlin, and his first major success was *Les biches* (1924), written for the Ballets Russes. He was known for a style characterized by an accessibility often lacking in other music of the time, and his *chansons* are particularly admired. Among his later works are a number of concertos and four operas, including *Dialogues des Carmélites* (1957) and *La voix humaine* (1958).

Pousseur, Henri (b. 1929) Belgian composer and theorist who studied at the Liège Conservatory. Pousseur's exposure to the post-war avant-garde at the Darmstadt Summer School led him to adopt multiple serialism, aleatoric techniques, and electronics, resulting in such notable works as *Scambi* (1957) and *Mobile* (1957–8). His lasting collaboration with the French writer Michel Butor led him to broaden his musical language through reference to historical styles, which he integrated within a complex harmonic system; a major result of his work with Butor was the opera *Votre Faust* (1960–8). He later pursued the ideal of a universal music through the inclusion of non-Western idioms in works such as *La rose des voix* (1982).

Powell, Bud (1924–66) American jazz pianist. Powell was one of a group of jazz musicians who pioneered the bebop style, along with Charlie Parker and Dizzy Gillespie. His piano style was founded on rapid right hand 'trumpet-style' lines and bare left-hand chords, and he was generally regarded as the foremost bebop pianist, although later in his life he worked little owing to health problems.

Presley, Elvis (Aaron) (1935–77) American rock and roll singer, actor, and sex symbol, known as the 'King' of rock; he had a huge impact on American popular culture of the 1950s and 60s. His early recordings for Sun Records reflected the influence of bluegrass style and rhythm and blues, but in 1955 'Colonel' Tom Parker became his manager and signed him to RCA; his first RCA recording ('Heartbreak Hotel', 1956) was a million-seller and Presley became an archetypal star, greeted with hysteria by teenage fans. Subsequently he starred in a number of films, including *Jailhouse Rock* (1957). Although the films continued up to 1970, his last years were difficult both personally and musically. His total record sales at the time of his premature death were estimated at 150 million.

Previn, André (b. 1929) American composer and conductor who studed piano in Berlin, playing jazz as well as classical music, and also writing for films. He took conducting lessons with Monteux while serving in the US army in San Francisco, and after establishing himself as a concert pianist quickly became a much-respected conductor; he is noted for his recordings of British music, particularly Vaughan Williams, which he made while conductor of the London Symphony Orchestra. In recent years Previn has concentrated on composition, and the diversity of his different musical activities has led to comparisons with Bernstein.

[The Artist Formerly Known as] Prince (b. 1958) American singer. Prince was one of the most distinctive black popular artists of the 1980s, creating a style which fused funk, rock, and blues. The album from a film in which he starred, *Purple Rain* (1984) made him into a top star, prompting comparisons with Michael Jackson.

Prokofiev, Sergei (1891–1951) Russian composer and pianist. He studied in St Petersburg with Rimsky-Korsakov and Tcherepnin, and then toured extensively as a pianist and conductor, mainly performing his own works. His early compositions were for the most part for the piano, and his concertos for that instrument caused controversy, blending often dissonant harmonies with a forceful percussive style of writing. Prokofiev moved to Paris after the 1917 revolution, and his works written during this time include *The Love for Three Oranges* (1921) and the Third and Fourth Symphonies. He returned to Russia during the 1930s – a propaganda coup for the Communist regime – but party officials were often critical of his approach, leading him to adopt patriotic themes in much of his work.

Puccini, Giacomo (1858–1924) Italian composer. While a large part of Puccini's career belongs in the previous century, his most influential operatic output dates from the beginning of the twentieth. Puccini had already made his name with works such as *Manon Lescaut* (1893) and *La bohème* (1896); *Tosca* (1900) was well received, but *Madama Butterfly* (1904) was initially a failure, while his later works included *Turandot* (left unfinished at his death). Puccini's style was deceptively modern and continues to form a hugely popular part of the operatic repertory.

Queen English rock band. The group formed in 1970, and consisted of vocalist Freddie Mercury, guitarist Brian May, bassist John Deacon, and drummer Roger Taylor. 'Bohemian Rhapsody', a mixture of rock and opera from the album *A Night at the Opera* (1975), was publicized by what is often described as the first music video, and remains the group's best-known number. They gave a famous performance at Live-Aid in 1985, and by the time that the flamboyantly gay Mercury died in 1991 Queen were one of the most popular British rock acts of the era.

Rachmaninov, Sergei (1873–1943) Russian composer, pianist, and conductor who studied piano in Moscow and began composing at a young age, winning a publishing contract early in his career. He completed his First Symphony in 1895 (although this was not well received) and subsequently began working as an opera conductor in Moscow. He made his London debut in 1899, and first toured America in 1909, performing his own music. Rachmaninov remains best known for his piano works, which include four concertos, sets of preludes and études, and two sonatas. His essentially Romantic style was founded on tonal harmony but made full use of the technical possibilities of the piano.

Radiohead English rock band. They formed in 1988, and took their cue from the grunge style being played by bands like Nirvana and Pearl Jam. Radiohead's own distinctive style began to develop on albums such as *The Bends* (1994) and particularly *OK Computer* (1997) – one of the seminal albums of the 1990s, ambitious in scope, and compelling in mood.

Rattle, Simon (b. 1955) English conductor. He began his career in the 1970s with the Bournemouth Symphony Orchestra, moving to the Liverpool Philharmonic and then the City of Birmingham Symphony Orchestra, with which he stayed until 1998. Rattle turned the CBSO into a world-class orchestra, making a series of critically acclaimed recordings, such as Mahler's Second Symphony (1988), as well as championing new British music. He has subsequently worked with the Vienna Philharmonic, and took up a post with the Berlin Philharmonic in 2002.

Ravel, Maurice (1875–1937) French composer. Ravel studied in Paris but notoriously failed to win the Grand Prix de Rome on five separate occasions. Like

Debussy, he was struck by the gamelan performances at the International Exposition in 1889, but took his main influences from Satie, Chabrier, and Debussy. His early works were performed in Paris, including *Ma mère l'oye* (1910) and *Daphnis et Chloé* (1912, for the Ballets Russes). After Debussy's death, Ravel became regarded as one of the leading French composers; his late works show an interest in exploring jazz influences, for instance in the Sonata for Violin and Piano (1927) and Piano Concerto in G (1931).

Redding, Otis (1941–67) American soul singer and songwriter, who released a series of recordings for Stax records from 1963 and made a legendary appearance at the Monterey Pop Festival in 1967. The release of his single '(Sittin' On) The Dock of the Bay' later that year established Redding's popularity to a wide audience, but tragically followed his early death in a plane crash.

Reich, Steve (b. 1936) American composer, perhaps the most highly regarded of the 'minimalist' composers who emerged from America, and particularly New York, during the late 1960s. He studied with Berio but had strong interests in African music and jazz. His early tape pieces such as *It's Gonna Rain* (1965), with two tape loops moving into and out of phase, provided much of the impetus for his later music; in the 1967 *Piano Phase* Reich translated this technique into an instrumental genre, with subsequent pieces such as *Drumming* (1971) extending these concerns. Reich performed with his own ensemble in both America and Europe, recording for DGG in 1974. His music of the later 1980s and 90s moved away from the abstraction of the early works; *Different Trains* (1988), for example, includes recordings of Holocaust survivors juxtaposed against multitracked string quartet.

Reinhardt, Django (1910–53) French guitarist and founding member (with violinist Stéphane Grappelli) of the Quintette du Hot Club de France; the quintet gained considerable popularity through their recordings, and Reinhardt became known as one of the best of the early jazz guitarists, later performing with many other jazz musicians such as the saxophonist Coleman Hawkins. His technique was unique because two fingers of his left hand had been damaged in a fire.

Richter, Sviatoslav (1915–97) Russian pianist. Richter was initially self-taught, working as an accompanist before formal studies in Moscow, where he made his debut in 1940. He became widely known in the West in the 1960s, with American and European tours and a number of acclaimed recordings. He is best remembered for his interpretation of the late Romantic repertory (particularly Liszt) and of Prokofiev, whose Sixth and Seventh Sonatas he premiered.

Rihm, Wolfgang (b. 1952) German composer, who studied composition with Stockhausen in Cologne, and with Klaus Huber in Freiburg, where he also studied musicology. Rihm broke early with the mostly technical concerns of the post-war avant-garde and created an idiom of great emotional immediacy, characterized by violent ruptures and allusions to earlier styles. With his

Sub-Kontur (1974) he became a model for many young composers who wanted to break away from what had become a habitual avant-gardism without simply reverting to traditionalism; major works include the Third String Quartet *Im Innersten* (1976), the ballet *Tutuguri* (several versions, 1980–3), and the opera *Die Eroberung von Mexico* (1987–91). In recent years Rihm has been striving for more suppleness and greater linearity, as in his *Vers une symphonie fleuve* (1994–8).

Riley, Terry (b. 1935) American composer and performer. After studying piano and composition in San Francisco, Riley made a living working as a pianist, all the while studying Indian music. A meeting with La Monte Young deeply affected his outlook and, after some time in Europe, he began working with tape-delay systems. His *In C* (1964), built on a series of repeated melodic phrases, is regarded as a seminal piece in the development of minimalism; later work included improvised performances incorporating tape delay systems (*A Rainbow in Curved Air*, 1968), and a large-scale piano work which employs a just-intonation tuning system (*The Harp of New Albion*, 1986).

Rimsky-Korsakov, Nikolay (1844–1908) Russian composer and teacher. While most of his work was produced in the previous century, his contribution to the development of Russian music in the twentieth century was highly significant, particularly through his influence on his pupil Stravinsky. In addition his colourful orchestration, disseminated though an influential textbook as well as his own music, influenced such composers as Debussy and Ravel.

Robeson, Paul (1898–1976) American singer and actor. He made his early career as a performer of black spirituals, and became extremely popular in the US, touring all around the country. He later performed around the world, becoming especially known for his role in *Show Boat*, and his performance of 'Ol' Man River' from that show.

Rodgers, Richard (1902–79) American composer. He formed an important collaboration with lyricist Lorenz Hart, and together they produced many songs and shows, although initially meeting with little success. Rodgers' collaboration with Oscar Hammerstein II resulted in *Oklahoma!* (1943) and *Carousel* (1945), two of the most influential film musicals, as well as *South Pacific* (1949) and *The King and I* (1951).

The Rolling Stones English rock group, formed in the 1960s and playing rhythm and blues; founder members Mick Jagger and Keith Richards were later joined by Bill Wyman on bass and Charlie Watts on drums. After signing with Decca they became one of the most popular acts of the mid-1960s, their first US no. 1 single being '(I Can't Get No) Satisfaction' (1965). Later albums such as *Their Satanic Majesties Request* (1968) attempted to follow something of the path the Beatles had taken with *Sergeant Pepper*. Known primarily as a performing band, the Stones continued touring into the 1990s, and while their style changed little, it remained enduringly popular.

Rosbaud, Hans (1895–1962) German conductor who studied in Frankfurt, and began working professionally in the 1920s. He was known in particular for his championing of modern music, including works by Hindemith, Schoenberg, Webern, Berg, and Stravinsky. After the war he worked in Baden-Baden and made many appearances at ISCM festivals, a particularly significant event being his direction in 1954 of both the concert and stage premieres of Schoenberg's *Moses und Aron*.

Rosen, Charles (b. 1927) American pianist and writer. Rosen studied at the Juilliard school of music, as well as taking a degree in French literature at Princeton University. In 1951 he made his debut in New York, since when he has performed a wide range of music from Bach to Boulez (in 1961 he premiered Elliott Carter's Concerto for piano and harpsichord), although he is best known for his work in the classical repertory. Rosen has been highly influential as a writer on music, his book *The Classical Style* (1971) being particularly admired.

Rostropovich, Mstislav (b. 1927) Russian cellist, pianist, and conductor. He studied in Moscow (where Shostakovich was one of his teachers), and travelled widely in the 1950s, appearing both in Britain and America, where he quickly built a reputation as a performer of international stature; among the works written for him were Shostakovich's Cello Concerto and Britten's Symphony for Cello and Orchestra. Since the 1960s he has also been widely active as a conductor, especially known for his performances of Russian music. He left the USSR in 1974, following his criticism of the regime's restrictions on cultural freedom.

Rósza, Miklós (1907–95) American composer of Hungarian birth. He studied in Budapest and in Leipzig, and after establishing a reputation as a composer of concert music, began writing film music. His influential scores include *The Thief of Baghdad* (1940) and *Ben-Hur* (1959).

Rubinstein, Artur (1887–1982) American pianist of Polish birth. He performed throughout Europe in the early decades of the century, although it was some time until he was widely accepted. By the 1930s he had achieved an impressive reputation in America, and he continued to tour widely until the 1970s. His interpretations of the classical and early Romantic repertory were always direct and modest, but he was best known for his performances of Chopin.

Ruders, Poul (b. 1949) Danish composer, who studied at the Royal Danish Conservatory but is mostly self-taught as a composer. His music has revolved round borrowing elements from different sources, often older music, and integrating them into his own idiom. His First Symphony (1989) marked an important stage in his career, typifying his then compositional concerns.

Ruggles, Carl (1876–1971) American composer. Ruggles took private lessons before producing his first major compositions during the 1920s; at this time he was closely associated with other American composers such as Cowell, Ives, and

Varèse, and representative pieces include *Men and Mountains* (1924) and *Sun-Treader* (1932). Ruggles' style retained elements of diatonic harmony but applied them in an unconventional manner.

Russell, George (b. 1923) American composer and theorist. Russell made a career as a jazz composer, writing for bandleaders including Dizzy Gillespie, while at the same time studying with Stefan Wolpe. His theoretical ideas, condensed in his book *The Lydian Concept of Tonal Organisation*, were influential among jazz musicians during the late 1950s and 60s, and had a direct impact on the development of modal harmony, particularly in the music of Miles Davis. In more recent times Russell has led his own band, employing both American and European musicians.

Russolo, Luigi (1885–1947) Italian inventor, painter, and composer. He was an important figure in the futurist movement, and in 1913 published a manifesto entited *L'arte dei rumori*. This argued for the importance of noise in music, and Russolo's compositions were at this time scored for a series of 'noise intoners'. He gave a series of concerts in Paris in 1921 to much controversy, and his ideas had some impact on the French composers who attended.

Saariaho, Kaija (b. 1952) Finnish composer. She studied with Ferneyhough and Huber before moving to Paris, where she worked extensively at IRCAM. Her music incorporates new instrumental techniques along with the use of electronics, exemplified by *Jardin secret II* (1984) and *Stilleben* (1988), a radiophonic composition. Larger-scale works include the violin concerto *Graal théâtre* (1994).

Santana, Carlos (b. 1947) American guitarist and bandleader. He began playing blues, but is best known for a style which fused rock with Latin influences. His group Santana became hugely popular and influential after playing the 1969 Woodstock festival, a position reinforced by the albums *Santana* (1969), and *Abraxas* (1970). During the 1970s he collaborated with jazz musicians such as Herbie Hancock, Wayne Shorter, and John McLaughlin.

Satie, Erik (1866–1925) French composer who studied at the Paris Conservatoire, and spent most of his life in that city, where he was known for his eccentric lifestyle. Much of his music prefigures the harmonic innovations of Debussy and Ravel; his *Gymnopédies* for piano (1888) were orchestrated by Debussy, while the 1914 *Sports et divertissements* featured short pieces combined with his humorous and eclectic texts. *Parade* (1917) was written for the Ballets Russes, and Picasso was involved in some aspects of the production. Satie was also involved with the Dada movement.

Scelsi, Giacinto (1905–88) Italian composer, a recluse of aristocratic origins, strongly influenced by Buddhism. While relatively little is known about his life, in the later decades of the century his music attracted increasing attention. His early work evidenced a concern with the prevalent modernist trends in composition, but from the 1950s onwards his music focused on subtle changes in intonation and timbre, often employing such techniques in the context of sustained pitches; an example is *Quattro pezzi (su una nota sola)* (1959).

Schaeffer, Pierre (1910–95) French composer, theorist, writer, and teacher. As a sound engineer working for Radiodiffusion Française he was instrumental in setting up the Club d'essai (1941) and, in 1951, the Group de Recherche de Musique Concrète (GRMC, later GRM); this was devoted to what Schaeffer called *musique concrète*, i.e. tape music using only pre-recorded sounds. His *Etude aux chemins de fer* (1948) is credited with being the first example of *musique concrète*, while his collaboration with Henry in *Symphonie pour un homme seul* (1950) represents one of the first major electronic works. Schaeffer's teaching activities at the Paris Conservatoire from 1968 and his magisterial theory of *musique concrète* in *Traité des objets musicaux* (Paris, 1966) ensured his continuing influence in the field of electroacoustic music.

Scherchen, Hermann (1891–1966) German conductor who became known for his performances of Schoenberg's *Pierrot lunaire*, and was subsequently extremely active in performing contemporary music through his work with many European orchestras. Among the pieces he is particularly associated with are Berg's Violin Concerto (which he premiered), and Schoenberg's *Moses und Aron* (through his editing of the score).

Schnabel, Artur (1882–1951) Austrian pianist and composer. He spent much of his career in Berlin, and was involved in performances of *Pierrot lunaire*, as well as performing the classical repertory and composing. His recordings for HMV in the 1930s are still highly regarded; he was best known for his interpretations of Beethoven. Influential as a teacher, Schnabel later settled in the US.

Schnittke, Alfred (1934–98) Russian composer who studied both in Vienna and in Moscow. After his concert piece *Nagasaki* was criticized by officials in 1958, Schnittke kept in touch with developments in modern music by studying scores by Stravinsky, Schoenberg, and Stockhausen, but his own music was little performed and it was not until the late 1980s that he achieved any kind of international recognition. His early symphonies, in particular, reflected many different techniques and styles, resulting in a kind of polystylism; the 1977 *Concerto Grosso* takes the baroque concerto as a starting point, while later works use material by Beethoven and Mahler.

Schoenberg, Arnold (1874–1951) Austrian composer, painter, teacher, and writer. He had little formal training in composition, and his earliest works, such as the string sextet *Verklärte Nacht* (1899), are late Romantic in style. From around 1908, with the Five Orchestral Pieces and *Erwartung* (both 1909), Schoenberg moved towards what is now called free atonality, and the sequence of melodramas *Pierrot lunaire* (1912) was toured through Europe, gaining considerable success at a time when modern music was being met with increasing hostility. In the next few years Schoenberg devised the system of composition he called 'composition with twelve tones' (serialism), major examples including the Variations for Orchestra

(1928) and the opera *Moses und Aron* (left unfinished at his death). His influence was disseminated not only through his own music, but through that of his pupils Berg and Webern. While Schoenberg spent much of his life in Vienna, he taught in Berlin between 1926 and 1933, when he emigrated to the US; there he was again active as a teacher, his students including John Cage.

Schreker, Franz (1878–1934) Austrian composer, teacher, and conductor. He studied in Vienna, and had his first pieces performed just before the turn of the century. He was best known for his operas, with *Der ferne Klang* (1910) and *Die Gezeichneten* (1918) establishing his reputation; *Der Schatzgräber* followed in 1920, and he subsequently took up a position at the Hochschule für Musik in Berlin. Schreker's music was in general harmonically conventional but incorporated chromatic and polytonal elements.

Schuller, Gunther (b. 1925) American composer, conductor, and writer. Schuller worked as a professional horn player, while also participating in jazz sessions, including work with Miles Davis around 1949. During the 1950s Schuller coined the term 'third stream' to describe a brand of composed music that attempted to integrate jazz elements, exemplified by his own compositions such as *Transformation* (1957) and the Concertino for jazz quartet and orchestra (1959). Schuller has also been influential as an educator and conductor.

Schwarzkopf, Elisabeth (b. 1915) German soprano. She studied in Berlin, and made her debut in 1938. She became particularly known for singing Lieder, with a reputation equivalent to that of Fischer-Dieskau. She performed at major venues around the world, recording extensively for EMI from 1950.

Sciarrino, Salvatore (b. 1947) Italian composer who studied art before turning to music, and worked in Rome with Franco Evangelisti. His music is known for its concern with unconventional instrumental techniques, often taking unusual instrumental sounds as the basis of the musical material. Sciarrino's works include *Canzoni da batello* of 1977 and *Tre notturni brillanti* (1975) for viola, along with the operas *Lohengrin* (1984) and *Perseo e Andromeda* (1990).

Sculthorpe, Peter (b. 1929) Australian composer who became known during the 1960s, having studied in Melbourne and then Oxford. After working in a serial style early on, he developed a more individual direction which focused on achieving clarity of texture; the series of *Sun Music* pieces from the 1960s exemplifies these concerns. Sculthorpe's music became increasingly divorced from European models, exploring non-Western musical influences (particularly Balinese) and subsequently native Australian ones.

Sessions, Roger (1896–1985) American composer. Sessions was something of a prodigy in early life, studying with Horatio Parker at Harvard and with Ernest Bloch in New York. He subsequently spent time in Europe, supported by Guggenheim Fellowships. His output consists mainly of symphonic music, mostly produced after 1950; after becoming friendly with Schoenberg later in his life, he adopted serial technique.

The Sex Pistols British punk band. They formed in 1975, largely at the prompting of Malcolm McLaren, and made a reputation for a brash performing style that favoured noise and violence over musical precision. Their first single 'Anarchy in the UK' was released in 1976, but they are best remembered for the controversy surrounding the 1977 'God Save the Queen' (which was banned on daytime radio but still rose to near the top of the charts), as well as the circumstances surrounding the arrest (for murdering his girlfriend) and death of their bassist, Sid Vicious [John Ritchie].

Shankar, Ravi (b. 1920) Indian sitar player and composer who began to tour the US and Europe in the 1950s, playing a major role in stimulating Western interest in Indian music: George Harrison of the Beatles studied with him, and he collaborated with Yehudi Menuhin and Philip Glass. Regarded as one of India's foremost musicians, Shankar has received numerous awards for his work.

Shostakovich, Dmitri (1905–65) Russian composer. Shostakovich studied at the Conservatory in Petrograd, initially specializing as a pianist. His First Symphony (1925) enjoyed considerable public success, and the piece was taken up by a number of prominent Western conductors, but by 1930 Shostakovich's work was being attacked for its 'formalism'. After a particularly fierce attack on his opera *Lady Macbeth of the Mtsensk District*, Shostakovich was forced to withdraw his Fourth Symphony, finding with the Fifth a compromise that appeared to the authorities to embody a patriotic spirit, while also being open to other interpretations. His subsequent symphonies are widely seen as a major achievement in a genre which waned in stature during the century.

Sibelius, Jean (1865–1957) Finnish composer whose output includes seven symphonies, a violin concerto, and a number of tone poems; much of it is dominated by a concern with his homeland, whether by kindling a nationalistic spirit or drawing on folk legend. Sibelius became known outside his home country in 1900, after a tour of the Helsinki Philharmonic Orchestra throughout northern Europe, attracting particular attention from British critics. The increasing classicism of his work contrasted with the modernist tendencies prevalent in European music of the time, and his music still enjoys great popularity.

Sinatra, Frank (1915–98) American popular singer and film actor. He began working as a vocalist with the Harry James band, and then with Tommy Dorsey, with whom he became hugely popular. In the early 1950s he established himself as a major figure with recordings for Capitol records, notably *Come Fly With Me* (1957); his film roles included many musicals such as *Guys and Dolls* (1955) and *High Society* (1956). His work of the 1960s featured jazz arrangements by well-respected writers. Sinatra was a highly influential singer, with a phrasing technique which was innovative for its time but has since been widely imitated.

Skryabin, Alexander (1872–1915) Russian pianist and composer. He studied in Moscow as a pianist, and then spent time in Paris, making his debut in 1896; he was active as a performer throughout his life, often performing his own music.

His works included *Poème d'extase* (1908) and *Prométhée* (1910), both orchestral pieces demonstrating an unusual blend of mysticism, religion, and cosmology. He developed an advanced conception of harmony, eschewing tonality in favour of diatonic elements used in unusual combinations, along with whole-tone and octatonic scales.

Sly and the Family Stone American funk group, which became famous with the 1968 single 'Dance to the Music'. Their mix of soul, doo-wop and funk was particularly successful at the 1969 Woodstock festival, and subsequent releases built on that reputation. However, in the later 1970s their reputation waned as their sound became more formulaic, coinciding with drug-related problems suffered by group members.

Smith, Bessie (1894–1937) American blues singer. Smith began by performing in minstrel shows, and moved on to the blues with a particularly successful 1923 recording of 'Down Hearted Blues'. She also worked with many of the jazz musicians of the time, including Louis Armstrong and Fletcher Henderson. Smith was the greatest of the so-called 'classic blues' singers, bringing a personal and emotional approach into the context of jazz.

Smyth, Dame Ethel (1858–1944) English composer. She studied in Leipzig and remained there for several years before returning to England, where she fought hard to have her work accepted. Nonetheless, there were significant successes, including her opera *The Wreckers*, premiered in 1906. Later in her life she received increased recognition and was awarded a number of honorary degrees.

Solti, Georg (1912–97) British conductor of Hungarian birth. He studied in Budapest, with Dohnányi, Bartók, and Kodály, and made his conducting debut in 1938. He left for Switzerland at the outbreak of the Second World War, and then moved to the Staatsoper in Munich. He quickly gained an international profile, moving in 1961 to Covent Garden, where he created a company widely seen as among the best in the world. His interpretations of *The Ring* were particularly well received, and he conducted the first studio recording of the complete cycle between 1958 and 1964. Much of his later life was taken up with work with the Chicago Symphony Orchestra.

Sondheim, Stephen (b. 1930) American composer. Sondheim is regarded as one of the foremost writers of musicals of the latter part of the century, and has composed a number of shows for Broadway; *Sweeney Todd* (1979) is the most ambitious and has also been one of the most successful. His musical language draws influences from jazz as well as classical composers such as Ravel and Copland.

Spector, Phil (b. 1940) American record producer and songwriter, particularly known for his work with his own label, Philles Records, which he formed in 1961. He employed dense production techniques to create a distinctive 'wall of sound', involving orchestration, percussion, and echo effects. The acts he produced included The Crystals and The Ronnettes, The Righteous Brothers, and Ike and Tina Turner.

Springsteen, Bruce (b. 1949) American singer and songwriter. Springsteen grew up modelling himself on Bob Dylan, and began his recording career in the 1970s with a number of albums featuring his backing group, the E Street Band. *Born To Run* (1975) was a major hit and was followed by a number of acclaimed recordings, culminating in *Born In The USA* (1984), which made him one of the most popular artists of the time.

Steiner, Max (1888–1971) American composer and conductor of Austrian birth. He trained in Vienna, working as a musical director for theatrical productions. After moving to New York, he worked on Broadway, and then began writing film scores; he rapidly became one of the most prolific of Hollywood film composers, writing more than 300 scores, and his thematic approach to film scoring (as exemplified in *King Kong*, 1933) was innovative and influential.

Steuermann, Eduard (1892–1964) American pianist and composer of Polish birth. He studied with Busoni in Berlin, and thereafter was involved in the first performance of *Pierrot lunaire*, as well as many of Schoenberg's later works; he was a frequent performer at Schoenberg's Verein für Musikalische Privataufführungen. He emigrated to the US in 1938 and taught at the Juilliard School of Music (New York).

Stockhausen, Karlheinz (b. 1928) German composer. He studied at Cologne Musikhochschule with Frank Martin, and after visiting the Darmstadt Summer School in 1951 became one of the most influential figures in the post-war avant-garde. He composed one of the earliest multiple serialist compositions (*Kreuzspiel*, 1953) and quickly moved on to electronics (*Studie 1*, 1953), aleatoric techniques (*Klavierstück 11*, 1957), and spatial music (*Gruppen*, 1955–7); later he experimented with group improvisation (*Aus den sieben Tagen*, 1968), live electronics (*Kontakte*, 1958–60) and other approaches. In 1963 he succeeded Eimert as director of the NWDR Studio für Elektronische Musik in Cologne, a post he held until 1973, when he became professor of composition at the Cologne Musikhochschule. Beginning with *Mantra* (1968), Stockhausen conceived his 'formula' technique, which enabled him to concentrate on melodic writing over longer time spans, culminating in his colossal opera cycle *Licht* (1977–2002), which consists of seven operas on the days of the week and expresses Stockhausen's increasingly opaque and New Age-influenced cosmology.

Stokowski, Leopold (1882–1977) American conductor of British birth. After studying at the Royal College of Music, and working as an organist and conductor, he made his major debut in Paris and then obtained a post with the Cincinnati Symphony Orchestra. It was with the Philadelphia Orchestra that Stokowski became best known, although he later formed a number of his own ensembles. He championed many works by contemporary composers, including Schoenberg,

Stravinsky, and Berg, and was also known for his complex transcriptions, particularly his orchestral version of Bach's Toccata and Fugue in D minor.

Strauss, Richard (1864–1949) German composer and conductor whose early symphonic poems, such as *Don Juan* (1889) and *Also sprach Zarathustra* (1896), were much influenced by the late Romantic tradition. But at the start of the twentieth century Strauss adopted a distinctively modern style; the operas *Salome* (1905) and *Elektra* (1909) featured proto-expressionist use of dissonance. Subsequent works included *Der Rosenkavalier* (1911) and *Ariadne auf Naxos* (1912), both of which exhibited more classicizing tendencies. Strauss was involved in setting up the Salzburg Festival in 1920, while under the Nazi regime he held but resigned the post of President of the Reichsmusikkammer. The effect of the war on his music is clear in *Metamorphosen* (1945), which laments the destruction of the Dresden Opera House, while other later works, nowadays highly regarded, include the Oboe Concerto (1948) and *Four Last Songs* (1948). Strauss was also well known as a conductor, with a somewhat dispassionate style.

Stravinsky, Igor (1882–1971) Russian composer and conductor. Stravinsky studied with Rimsky-Korsakov, and his first major success was a folkloristic ballet commissioned by Diaghilev, *The Firebird* (1910). He remained in France after the first performance, producing *Petrushka* (1911) and then *The Rite of Spring* (1913). *The Rite* marks one of the major moments in twentieth-century music, not only for a score which combined ostinati and innovative rhythmic devices to powerful effect, but also for a riotous first performance that became a legend. *The Soldier's Tale* of 1918 pioneered an influential form of stripped-down music theatre, while Stravinsky subsequently moved towards the style now known as neoclassicism (or modernist classicism): in works such as *Oedipus rex* (1927) and the 'Dumbarton Oaks' Concerto (1938), the models are classical but the language, while still recognisably Stravinskyan, has a baroque resonance. Stravinsky moved to the US when the war broke out, and after completing his opera *The Rake's Progress* (1951) – which coincided with Schoenberg's death – he began to explore serial technique, albeit in a highly idiosyncratic manner. In his performances of his own music, and also in his writing, Stravinsky expounded a literalistic performance style, advocating 'execution' rather than 'interpretation'.

Strayhorn, Billy (1915–67) American composer, arranger, and pianist. Strayhorn is best known for his work with Duke Ellington, whose band he joined in the 1940s as an arranger and second pianist. His collaborations with Ellington include such famous pieces as 'Take the "A" Train', 'Satin Doll', 'Chelsea Bridge', and 'Lush Life'.

Szell, George (1897–1970) American conductor of Hungarian birth. He studied in Vienna, appearing at a young age, and worked with Richard Strauss in Berlin. In 1937 he recorded the Dvořák Cello Concerto with Casals; thereafter he worked mostly in the US, performing with many of the major American orchestras before becoming musical director of the Cleveland Orchestra in 1946. His singlemindedness turned the orchestra into one of the best in the world, as his many recordings testify.

Szymanowski, Karol (1882–1937) Polish composer. After studying in Warsaw, Szymanowski became one of a group of young composers pressing to have their music performed in a prevailingly conservative climate. His early works owe something to Chopin, but his initial Romanticism changed following his visits to north Africa; he also drew on the music of Debussy and Ravel. Works such as his four symphonies and *Stabat Mater* (1926) combine a rich and sensuous harmonic approach with a colourful and vivid orchestral manner.

Takemitsu, Toru (1930–96) Japanese composer who received some teaching from Kiyose Yasuji but was largely self-taught; his early music was influenced by that of Debussy and particularly Messiaen. In 1964 he staged 'happenings' in collaboration with John Cage in Tokyo; ironically, Cage's main influence on Takemitsu was in awakening a serious interest in traditional Japanese music. His use of Japanese instruments from around this time represented an overt attempt to forge a distinctive national style, whereas the music of the 1970s, such as *Garden Rain* (1974) and *A Flock Descends into the Pentagonal Garden* (1977), combined conventional Western instrumentation with a distinctly non-Western sense of temporality. Takemitsu's debt to the work of Joyce is important in this regard, and later pieces such as *Riverrun* (1984) exemplify similar concerns. Takemitsu won many awards and travelled widely, teaching throughout the US and Europe.

Tan Dun (b. 1957) American composer of Chinese birth. He trained at the Central Conservatory (Beijing), where he encountered a wide range of Western contemporary music, and after moving to the US in 1986 became the leading voice for contemporary Chinese music in the West. Tan Dun's music has been concerned with integrating elements of Chinese musical culture into the context of contemporary composition, and among his recent works the series of Orchestral Theatre pieces have achieved particular recognition.

Tatum, Art (1909–56) American pianist. Tatum, who had only partial sight, became recognized as the leading jazz pianist of his time. He began in the stride style, but developed a characteristically soloistic and orchestral approach to the piano. His best known recordings are solo performances, such as his version of 'Tiger Rag', taken at an astonishingly fast tempo.

Tauber, Richard (1891–1948) Austrian tenor. After study at Freiburg, he debuted at Chemnitz in 1913 as Tamino in *Die Zauberflöte*, before being engaged by the Dresden Opera. Although an accomplished opera singer, he is remembered primarily as a singer of popular songs and an operetta star, for instance in Lehár's *Das Land des Lächelns*.

Taylor, Cecil (b. 1929) Taylor has been one of the most progressive of jazz pianists over the last forty years, and was among the first jazz musicians to explore free jazz in the late 1950s. During the 1960s, Taylor was often unable to earn a living as a musician due to his uncompromising approach, but he developed a much higher profile during the 1970s. His pieces are often intricately assembled, and witness an extraordinary piano technique. His many albums include *Unit Structures* (1966) and *Indent* (1973).

Theodorakis, Mikis (b. 1925) Greek composer who has produced songs, film scores, and original compositions, though his political activism has sometimes led to problems in his home country. The best known of his film scores is *Zorba the Greek* (1964).

Tiomkin, Dimitri (1894–1979) American composer and pianist of Ukrainian birth. He studied in St Petersburg and Berlin, and made his early career in Europe. He then moved to Hollywood, where he scored a large number of films in a generally Romantic idiom; examples are *High Noon* (1952) and *The Old Man and the Sea* (1958).

Tippett, Michael (1905–98) English composer who studied composition and conducting at the Royal College of Music. His early music shows a debt to the Austro-German symphonic tradition, yet has a distinctly English character, as in the Double Concerto (1939) and First Symphony (1945). *A Child of Our Time* (1941) had a considerable resonance in the context of war, and the operas *The Midsummer Marriage* (1952) and *King Priam* (1961) extended Tippett's reputation. At around this time his musical language became increasingly modern, exploring dissonant harmony in works such as *The Vision of Saint Augustine* (1965) and the Triple Concerto (1979); these consolidated his reputation as one of the major English composers of the century.

Torke, Michael (b. 1961) American composer. He studied in New York, and his early music exhibited a distinctive combination of jazz, pop, and minimalism; works such as *Vanada* (1984) illustrate this clearly, while subsequent pieces such as *Green* (1986) built a characteristically melodic style. More recent works, such as the Saxophone Concerto (1993) developed this style in the direction of larger-scale forms.

Toscanini, Arturo (1867–1957) Italian conductor who directed opera at La Scala from 1898 to 1913, concentrating on Verdi and Wagner. He then moved to New York to direct the Metropolitan Opera, where he worked with some of the best singers in the world, including Caruso. After returning to La Scala in 1920, he toured the US with the house orchestra, to much acclaim. In 1933 he refused to honour his engagements at Bayreuth because of the growing anti-Semitism of the German regime, and the main focus of his work turned again towards America. He worked with the New York Philharmonic until 1936, and then with the orchestra of the NBC (National Broadcasting Corporation), with which he recorded extensively and broadcast weekly. Toscanini was famous for his insistence on accuracy, demanding performance '*com'e scritto*', as it is written – a conception that resonated with Stravinsky's.

Touré, Ali Farka (b. 1949) Malian guitarist. His distinctive acoustic style became extremely popular following his performances in France during the 1970s. He has collaborated with such musicians as Ry Cooder and Taj Mahal, and has recorded extensively.

Tudor, David (1926–96) American pianist and composer. During the 1950s he was one of the leading interpreters of contemporary music, giving premieres of pieces by Cage, Boulez, Cowell, Kagel, Stockhausen, and Wolpe among others; he also worked with the Merce Cunningham Dance company, as well as teaching extensively. His compositions are based on live electronics, with sounds being generated and triggered within the environment of performance.

U2 Irish rock band which formed in 1977, with lead singer Bono, guitarist The Edge, bassist Adam Clayton, and drummer Larry Mullen. U2 came to prominence during the 1980s with a series of albums including *The Unforgettable Fire* (1984) and *The Joshua Tree* (1987); during this time their sound became increasingly individualistic, based on The Edge's distinctive guitar riffs with delay effects and Bono's passionate vocals. *The Joshua Tree* marked their rise to the status of international supergroup, a position which they continued to hold through a number of changes in musical direction in the 1990s, as documented by the albums *Achtung Baby* (1991) and *Pop* (1997).

Umm Kulthūm (1904?–75) Celebrated Egyptian female singer whose concerts and broadcasts brought the tradition of *tarab* (a genre of small-group performance with a high degree of extemporization and performance interaction) to unparalleled popularity across the Arab world in the decades after the Second World War; her work trod a fine line between a nationalist expression of traditional Arabic musical values and incorporation of European elements. In later life she become a major presence in Egyptian cultural life, sponsoring a series of concerts to help rebuild the Egyptian government's finances following the 1967 war against Israel.

Ustvol'skaya, Galina (b. 1919) Russian composer who studied in Leningrad with Shostakovich and Steinberg, and later taught there. Her early works focused on depicting programmes or scenes in a style reminiscent of Shostakovich; later pieces brought a more distinctive approach, favouring extremes of dynamic and texture, while some of her music evokes plainsong and chant. Ustvol'skaya's music gained increasing international recognition during the last two decades of the century.

Varèse, Edgard (1883–1965) American composer of French birth. He studied in Paris, moving to Berlin in 1907 and then back to Paris; in 1915 he left for the US, where he remained for the rest of his life. There he promoted contemporary music both as a conductor and through his founding in 1921 of the International Composers Guild; the Guild organized performances of music by Schoenberg and Stravinsky among others. Varèse's writing for percussion in *Ionisation* (1931) was extremely influential, demonstrating the possibility of constructing a coherent composition without pitched instruments. His style has often been described as using 'sound-masses', as in *Arcana* (1927) and *Déserts* (1954), the latter involving 20 performers together with a two-track tape consisting of sounds generated from percussion instruments. *Poème électronique* was composed for the Brussels Trade Exposition in 1958, and marked a milestone in the development of elecronic music. While Varèse's output was small, his influence remains considerable.

Vaughan Williams, Ralph (1872–1958) English composer and conductor who studied at the Royal College of Music and then Cambridge, and with Ravel in Paris. He drew on English musical traditions, including folksong and the work of earlier English composers, as exemplified by the *Fantasia on a Theme by Thomas Tallis* (1910). The *Pastoral Symphony* of 1922 marked the beginning of a significant engagement with the symphonic tradition; the symphonies which followed marked out important points of his career, in particular the Fourth Symphony of 1935 and Sixth Symphony of 1948. In the 1940s he embarked on writing a number of film scores, notably for *49th Parallel* (1941) and *Scott of the Antarctic* (1948), the latter becoming the *Sinfonia Antarctica*.

Velvet Underground American rock band, based in New York and associated with Andy Warhol; it included guitarist and vocalist Lou Reed and multi-instrumentalist John Cale (who collaborated with La Monte Young), and was unusual in having a female drummer (Maureen Tucker). Their music of the 1960s drew on a wide range of styles, from rhythm and blues to avant-garde concert music. Albums such as *The Velvet Underground and Nico* (1967) and *White Light/White Heat* (1968) developed a style based on dense, sometimes impenetrable textures, and although the band was not commercially popular it had a major long-term influence, in particular on David Bowie and on punk.

Villa-Lobos, Heitor (1887–1959) Brazilian composer. He studied in Brazil, and his early work involved much use of folksong. His early music marked a significant break with the academic style then current in Brazil, and in 1923 he moved to Paris. It was in Europe that he achieved real success, gaining the support of many major figures; he also became well known in the US through regular concert tours in the 1930s and 40s. The *Bachianas brasileiras* series is a particularly good illustration of his adaptation of Brazilian folk influences within a Western classical idiom. Villa-Lobos was also heavily involved in developing the Brazilian music education system.

Volans, Kevin (b. 1949) Irish composer of South African origins. After a first degree at University of the Witwatersrand, he studied with Stockhausen in Cologne during the 1970s; however, he returned to South Africa, teaching at Durban during the first half of the 1980s, and this is the period of what, at the time, he called his 'African paraphrases' (such as *Mbira* and *Matepe*) – works in which traditional African materials are interpreted through perceptions coloured by his involvement in the European avant-garde. He became well known through the Kronos Quartet's recording of *White Man Sleeps* (1986), which became one of the bestselling classical recordings of 1993. Perhaps in reaction to the pigeonholing of his work, his subsequent work is less overt in its African references.

Waller, Thomas 'Fats' (1904–43) American pianist, composer, and vocalist. Waller began his career as a pianist working in the stride tradition of his mentor James P. Johnson; he subsequently became known as a song writer and all-round entertainer, his hits including 'Honey Suckle Rose' (1929) and 'Ain't Misbehavin'' (1929).

Walter, Bruno (1876–1962) American conductor and composer of German birth, studying in Berlin and making his debut as a conductor in 1894. He worked with Mahler in Hamburg and then as his assistant in Vienna, and the older composer was a major influence on Walter's style and musical outlook: after Mahler's death Walter gave the premieres of *Das Lied von der Erde* (1911) and the Ninth Symphony (1912). He travelled widely, recording with the Vienna Philharmonic, and then moved to America in 1939; there he became known for his work with the New York Philharmonic, playing American music as well as standard symphonic repertory.

Walton, William (1902–83) English composer. He studied at Oxford but failed to pass his exams. He made his reputation with *Façade* (1929), which demonstrated a range of influences from jazz, the tango, and the foxtrot, to Stravinsky's *The Soldier's Tale*. The Viola Concerto of 1929 continued a steady compositional development, demonstrating a more sustained musical language, and was followed by the oratorio *Belshazzar's Feast* (1931), which proved a particular success. Walton also composed two symphonies and some film scores, particularly for patriotic films during the war.

Waxman, Franz (1906–67) American composer of German birth. He began scoring films in the late 1920s, moving to America in 1934; his scores included *The Bride of Frankenstein* (1935), and his Romantic manner was widely imitated, particularly in the horror-film genre.

Webern, Anton (1883–1945) Austrian composer, a pupil of Schoenberg and member of what is now termed the Second Viennese School; he studied at Vienna University, completing a doctorate on the sixteenth-century composer Isaac. Webern's music was initially in a late Romantic style but became more dissonant and abstract under Schoenberg's influence, with material typically compressed into short time-spans. His employment of serial technique was more systematic than Schoenberg's, his use of such devices as rhythmic canon and palindrome (perhaps honed by his study of Isaac) resulting in transparent textures often based on 'points' of sound. Accidentally killed by a US soldier in 1945, Webern had his greatest impact after Schoenberg's death, when the European avant-garde (especially Boulez) adopted him as a figurehead. The availability at the Sacher-Stiftung (Basel) of the large corpus of sketches and unfinished work underlying his small published output is likely to lead to a re-evaluation of his achievement.

Weill, Kurt (1900–50) German composer. Weill studied in Berlin with both Humperdinck and Busoni, his early works showing aspects of a neoclassical style fused with expressionist elements. His collaboration with dramatist Bertolt Brecht resulted in his most famous works, such as *The Threepenny Opera* (1928) and *Rise and Fall of the City of Mahagonny* (1929), which combined elements of cabaret and art culture; the financial rewards from these enabled Weill to concentrate solely on composition. He moved to the US in 1935 and remained there for the rest of his life, producing musicals for Broadway.

Weingartner, Felix (1863–1942) Austrian conductor and composer who studied in Graz and then in Leipzig. Working at first on opera in Berlin and Vienna, he built a career in both Europe and America as a symphonic conductor known for his clarity and control. He left many recordings, among them the symphonies of Beethoven and Brahms, as well as influential writings on conducting.

Wemba, Papa (b. 1952) Zairean singer. He became a huge star in his home country, with a style combining a popular Zairean sound along with his distinctive vocals. It was with his recordings of the 1980s, which feature synthesizers and drum machines, that Wemba became a popular artist in Europe.

Whiteman, Paul (1890–1967) American bandleader. Whiteman's band was famous in the 1920s, infusing the standard dance orchestra with jazz elements; he hired jazz soloists such as Bix Beiderbecke in order to be able to include improvised solos in his arrangements. Whiteman is also famous for commissioning Gershwin's *Rhapsody in Blue*.

The Who English rock group. They formed in London in 1964, and with some shrewd management adopted a 'mod' style which appealed to a very particular cross-section of the teenage audience. Guitarist Pete Townshend was known for his highly physical style, often resulting in instruments being smashed during performances. Their performance at the 1967 Monterey Pop Festival established them in the US, and they then embarked on a number of highly ambitious projects, including the rock operas *Tommy* (1969) and *Quadrophenia* (1979).

Williams, John (b. 1932) American composer. He studied in both New York and Los Angeles, and worked with Previn, among others, during the 1960s. It was at this time that he began writing film music, becoming best known for his scores for several films by Steven Spielberg: *Jaws* (1975), *Close Encounters of the Third Kind* (1977), and *Star Wars* (1977). His music builds on the style of earlier film composers such as Korngold, and is particularly effective in the context of action and science-fiction films.

Wolff, Christian (b. 1934) American composer of French birth. He moved to America in 1941, and was known as a member of the New York scene which included Cage, Feldman, and Brown. He was largely self-taught as a composer, and his approach involved allowing the performers to shape the course of music by affording them different kinds of choices in performance. Works such as

For 5 or 10 People (1962) reflect this approach, while later pieces move further towards improvisation.

Wolpe, Stefan (1902–72) American composer of German birth. He studied in Berlin and became associated with the Dada movement; his political ideals led him to write mainly for amateur groups, particularly later in his career. *Schöne Geschichten* (1927) is a chamber opera demonstrating the influence of Schoenberg and Berg, while a little later Wolpe studied with Webern and started using serial techniques. He moved to the US in 1938, and later pieces such as the Saxophone Quartet of 1950 reflect an interest in jazz, specifically in terms of incorporating improvisatory elements into his music.

Wonder, Stevie (b. 1950) American singer, songwriter, and keyboard player. Blind from birth, Wonder signed to Tamla Records at a very early age, displaying extraordinary talents as a multi-instrumentalist, singer, and songwriter. It was in his recordings of the 1970s, such as *Talking Book* (1972) and *Innervisions* (1973), that Wonder developed a distinctive style which drew on elements of Motown, funk, soul, gospel, and jazz; his music of this time is also characterized by the use of synthesizers and electronics. Wonder's career continued to develop through the 1980s and 90s.

Wyk, Arnold van (1916–1983) South African composer who studied at the Royal Academy of Music (London), before returning to South Africa in 1946; thereafter he worked at Cape Town and Stellenbosch Universities. He is representative of those South African composers who worked very much within the European tradition, adopting an extended tonal style. He composed vocal, orchestral, and chamber music, his most famous work being the late *Missa in illo tempore* (1979) for double chorus with boys' voices.

Xenakis, Iannis (1922–2001) French composer of Greek parentage. Xenakis studied engineering in Athens from 1940–6 while at the same time working for the Resistance. He entered France as an illegal immigrant and gained employment as the architect Le Corbusier's assistant; in Paris he studied with Honegger and Milhaud, and attended Messiaen's analysis course. Xenakis was one of the few avant-garde composers to reject any form of serialism, instead developing a very personal technique based on architectural structures 'translated' into music by means of complex mathematical procedures (he called this 'stochastic' music). His music is characterized by dense sound masses and extraordinarily expressive glissandi, as in his *Metastasis* (1953–4). In the following years, he adopted a number of scientific and mathematical principles such as kinetic gas theory leading to 'clouds of sound' in *Pithoprakta* (1955–6), or game theory in *Duel* (1959). He also applied his training as an engineer to electroacoustic music, with works such as *Persépolis* (1971) being influential.

Young, La Monte (b. 1935) American composer who studied in Los Angeles and at the Summer School in Darmstadt. Influenced by his studies of Indian music, Young's output was particularly important for the development of minimalism in the late 1960s, although his music is quite different from the mainstream minimalism of Reich, Riley, and Glass. After being involved in Fluxus-type events in New York in the 1960s, he founded the Theatre of Eternal Music, which included John Cale (who also played with the Velvet Underground); the music he produced with this group leant towards a radical use of repetition along with the employment of drones. *The Well-Tuned Piano*, which lasts over six hours, explores not only massive scale but also unusual tunings. More recent pieces have included *Chronos Kristalla* (1990) for the Kronos Quartet.

Zappa, Frank (1940–93) American composer and rock musician. Zappa formed The Mothers of Invention in 1964, and their first album *Freak Out!* (1966) capitalized on the psychedelic styles of the time, while containing strong elements of parody; his music drew on styles from rock, free jazz, and avant-garde concert music, to electronics and doo-wop. Ensuing albums pursued a similarly eclectic style, and Zappa continued to compose prolifically after the group disbanded; his output ranged from the (near) rock opera *Joe's Garage* (1979) to the album *Jazz from Hell* (1986), produced in his home studio using a Synclavier synthesizer. Achieving extensive international recognition, Zappa worked during the decade before his death with the London Symphony Orchestra, Ensemble Intercontemporain, and Ensemble Modern; his late works have become the object of considerable musicological attention.

Zemlinsky, Alexander von (1871–1942) Austrian composer and conductor who taught Schoenberg for a time, his other pupils including Webern, Berg, Korngold, and Horowitz. He was active as a pianist and conductor in Vienna, where he worked alongside Mahler, before moving to Prague and continuing an active career as a composer. His operas *Der Traumgörge* (1906) and *Der Zwerg* (1921) are characteristic of his style, which built on the thematic techniques of Brahms but remained within a broadly tonal framework.

Zimmermann, Bernd Alois (1918–71) German composer who studied philosophy, German literature, and music at Cologne, Bonn, and Berlin. Zimmermann adopted serialism in early works such as *Perspektiven* (1955–6), but is mostly remembered for his philosophical conception of time as a unity of past, present, and future; this was the basis of his 'pluralist' style, which consisted of collages of quotations drawn from very different sources, and was used to great effect in his celebrated opera *Die Soldaten* (1958–60) and the orchestral piece *Photoptosis* (1968). A troubled personality, he committed suicide shortly after finishing his disturbing 'ecclesiastical action', *Ich wandte mich und sah an alles Unrecht, das geschah unter der Sonne* (1970).

Zorn, John (b. 1953) American composer and saxophonist who first made his name in the free improvisation scene of 1970s New York. His development of 'game' pieces for free improvisers has been particularly influential in a musical territory where composition and planning are not generally thought useful. With his early groups, including Naked City and Painkiller, Zorn explored fusions of free jazz with speed metal, as well as combining snatches of widely disparate musical styles to extraordinary effect. Subsequently, the groups Masada and Bar Kokhba have explored Jewish musical culture through free jazz-inspired interpretations. *Kristallnacht* (1992) for string quartet marked a significant point in Zorn's career as a composer, and he remains a hugely influential figure on the New York scene, his musical activities covering a wide range of different projects.

Zwilich, Ellen Taaffe (b. 1939) American composer and violinist who studied with Sessions and Carter at the Juilliard School and in 1975 became the first woman to be awarded a DMA in composition. By this time she was receiving significant premieres, but she became internationally known in 1983, when her Symphony no. 1 was awarded a Pulitzer prize (again she was the first female musician to receive one). Her output has been largely orchestral (including many concertos), and her style has evolved from a rigorous atonality to an increasingly accessible idiom that reintroduces tonal elements and rhetoric within a contemporary context.

· Appendix 2 ·

Chronology

PETER ELSDON AND PETER JONES

Date	First performances/ recordings	Other musical	Other cultural	Socio-political
1900	Charpentier: *Louise* Debussy: *Nocturnes* Elgar: *The Dream of Gerontius* Fauré: *Prométhée* Mahler: Symphony no. 4 Puccini: *Tosca* Sibelius: *Finlandia*	The Paris Universal Exposition includes a performance by Sousa's band. Inauguration of Symphony Hall, Boston. Elgar is awarded an honorary degree by Cambridge University.	Dramatist and wit Oscar Wilde dies in Paris, where he has been exiled since 1897 following his conviction and disgrace for homosexual offences. The 'Fauvist' movement begins, led by Matisse. Cézanne: *Still Life With Onions* Chekhov: *Uncle Vanya* Freud: *The Interpretation of Dreams* Gorki: *Three People* Toulouse-Lautrec: *La modiste* Monet: *Water Lilies* Shaw: *Three Plays for Puritans*	The Boxer rebellion in China threatens to destabilize the country. As many as 1,500 foreigners are reportedly killed before an Allied force of British, American, German, and Japanese troops quells the rising. In Britain, a new political force is founded under the name of the Labour Representation Committee. In the South African war, British troops enjoy increasing success with the relief of Ladysmith, followed later by that of Mafeking and the formal annexation of the Transvaal.
1901	Debussy: *Nocturnes* (first complete performance)	Death of Verdi. Universal Edition publishers are established in Vienna.	Marconi transmits messages by wireless telegraph from Cornwall to Newfoundland.	Britain's Queen Victoria dies aged 82 after 64 years on the throne. She is succeeded by her son Edward VII.

Date	First performances/ recordings	Other musical	Other cultural	Socio-political
	Dvorak: *Rusalka* Elgar: *Cockaigne* Fauré: *Pelléas et Mélisande* Mascagni: *Le Maschere* Pfitzner: *Die Rose von Liebesgarten* Rachmaninov: Piano Concerto no. 2 (first complete performance) Skryabin: Symphony no. 1 Strauss: *Feuersnot*	Ravel is awarded the lower 2nd Grand Prix de Rome (effectively 3rd place). The German journal *Die Musik* begins publishing in Berlin. Tenor Jean de Reszke gives his final performances in New York.	Chekhov: *Three Sisters* Freud: *The Psychopathology of Everyday Life* Gauguin: *The Gold In Their Bodies* Kipling: *Kim* Maeterlinck: *Life of the Bee* Munch: *Girls on the Bridge* Picasso: *Blue Period* Shaw: *Caesar and Cleopatra* Weber: *The Protestant Ethic and the Birth of Capitalism*	The Boxer rebellion is formally ended with the signing of the Peace of Peking. China is to pay reparations to Western nations. Unrest in Russia explodes when more than 800 students are arrested after clashes with Cossacks in St Petersburg. The students' direct action is mirrored across Europe in countries as far apart as Belgium and Italy, as socialist and anarchist groups demand wholesale political reforms. In the United States, President William McKinley is shot dead in Buffalo. He is succeeded by Vice-President Theodore Roosevelt.
1902	Debussy: *Pelléas et Mélisande* Ives: *The Celestial Country* Mahler: Symphony no. 3 Ravel: *Jeux d'eau* Rimsky-Korsakov: *Servilia*	Mascagni tours America with his opera company. Caruso records for the Gramophone Company in a Milan hotel room.	D'Annunzio: *Francesca da Rimini* Barrie: *The Admirable Crighton* Conan Doyle: *The Hound of the Baskervilles* Gauguin: *Horsemen on the Beach* Gide: *The Immoralist* Kipling: *Just So Stories* Monet: *Waterloo Bridge* Rodin: *Roméo et Juliette*	The signing of the Peace of Vereeniging brings the Boer War to a close, with the British victorious. Unrest continues in Russia, where Sipyengin, the interior minister and head of the Tsar's secret police, is murdered by socialist revolutionaries. Following widespread riots, Tsar Nicholas offers to hold a private audience with more than 200 Russians from all walks of life in an attempt to defuse the situation.

	Schoenberg: *Verklärte Nacht* (1899) Skryabin: Symphony no. 2 Sibelius: Symphony no. 2 Smyth: *Der Wald* Wagner: *Götterdämmerung* (first French performance, directed by Cortot in Paris)		Verhaeren: *Les forces tumultueses*	The Triple Alliance between Germany, Austria, and Italy is renewed.
1903	Bruckner: Symphony no. 9 (unfinished; completed, revised, and directed by Ferdinand Loewe). Elgar: *The Apostles* Glazunov: Symphony no. 7 D'Indy: *L'Etranger* Verdi: *Ernani* (HMV; the first complete opera recording) Wolf-Ferrari: *Le donne curiose*	Ravel is once again passed over for the Prix de Rome. Controversy over the announcement of planned performances of *Parsifal* at the Metropolitan Opera in New York. Copyright objections are raised by Cosima and Siegfried Wagner. Schoenberg meets Mahler for the first time in Vienna. Victor produces the first of its Red Seal recordings. Pope Pius X issues a document giving guidelines about the performance of music in churches.	Oscar Hammerstein builds the Drury Lane Theatre, New York (later the Manhattan Opera House). Work begins on Liverpool Cathedral. New York Chamber of Commerce is built. Butler: *The Way of All Flesh* Hofmannsthal: *Elektra* James: *The Ambassadors* McCutcheon: *Kit Carson* (the world's first Western) Shaw: *Man and Superman*	The stability of Central and Eastern Europe is again threatened by a series of outrages. In Russia, peasants rampage unopposed through Kishinev killing scores of Jews, Alexander I and Queen Draga are murdered by a group of disaffected army officers, and up to 50,000 Bulgarians are massacred by Turkish troops in and around Monastir in response to the decision by the Macedonian Central Revolutionary Committee's decision to mount a revolt against Turkish rule. The United States leads the way into the modern world with the creation of the Ford Motor Company for the mass production of motor cars. The first heavier-than-air flight is made by Orville and Wilbur Wright in Dayton, Ohio.

Date	First performances/ recordings	Other musical	Other cultural	Socio-political
1904	Caruso: 'Vesti la giubba' (his first recording made in the US, which sells over a million copies) Debussy: *Estampes* Janáček: *Jeji pastorkyna* Mahler: Symphony no. 5 Puccini: *Madame Butterfly* Ravel: String Quartet, *Shéhérazade* Rimsky-Korsakov: *Pan Voyevoda* Schoenberg: *Six Orchestral Songs* Sibelius: Violin Concerto Strauss: *Symphonia Domestica*	Richard Strauss travels to the US for the first time, and conducts a programme of his own music in New York. The London Symphony Orchestra is formed, and gives its inaugural concert under Richter. Schoenberg founds the Society of Creative Musicians with Zemlinsky. Among the pupils he takes on for private teaching are Webern and Berg. Caruso gives his first performance in Berlin. Elgar is knighted. Death of Dvořák.	Barrie: *Peter Pan* Cézanne: *Mont Sainte Victoire* Chekhov: *The Cherry Orchard* Conrad: *Nostromo* Pirandello: *Il fu Mattia Pascal* Rousseau: *The Wedding*	Japan launches a surprise attack on Russian forces at Port Arthur, Korea, precipitating the Russo-Japanese war. The Japanese later consolidate their successes, occupying Seoul, Korean capital, and Dalny on Russian soil. At home, Tsar Nicholas pledges to improve the living conditions of the population, but warns that the rule of law will prevail. The US removes one of the last obstacles to the building of a Panama canal by buying a French company's concession to cross the continent at the isthmus. The British and French administrations sign a historic agreement aimed at resolving many outstanding economic and diplomatic differences.

1905	Debussy: *La mer* Glazunov: Violin Concerto Lehár: *Die lustige Witwe* Massenet: *Chérubin* Respighi: *Re Enzo* Saint-Saëns: Piano Concerto no. 2 Schoenberg: *Pelleas und Melisande* Skryabin: Symphony no. 3 Strauss: *Salome*	Fauré is appointed director of the Paris Conservatoire. Cortot–Thibaud–Casals trio forms. Rimsky-Korsakov is sacked from his position at the St. Petersburg Conservatory after signing a public letter calling for political reform. Later, he rejoins the conservatory when Glazunov takes over as director.	Cézanne: *Les grandes baigneuses* Freud: *Three Treatises on the Theory of Sex* Hofmannsthal: *Das Gerettete Venedig* Matisse: *La joie de vivre* Picasso: *Boy With Pipe* Strindberg: *Historical Miniatures* Wharton: *House of Mirth* Wilde: *De Profundis*	Russia is again in turmoil following defeats in the war against Japan and atrocities at home. In St Petersburg, troops and Cossacks shoot dead more than 500 workers marching to deliver a petition to the Tsar. Later, the entire country is paralysed by a general strike. In the far East, the Korean stronghold of Port Arthur finally falls to Japanese forces, and the Russians are finally forced to sign a peace treaty with Japan. Tsar Nicholas II concedes to widespread demands for reform and transforms the country from an absolute autocracy to a semi-constitutional monarchy.
1906	Delius: *Sea Drift* Handel: *Messiah* (recording issued in London on 25 discs) Ives: *The Unanswered Question* (composed) Mahler: Symphony no. 6 Patti: recording of 'Voi che sapete' from *The Marriage of Figaro* Puccini: *Madame Butterfly* (first American performance)	Skryabin visits the US for a short concert tour. Victor release a new version of the gramophone: the Victrola. Rubinstein makes his New York debut. Weingartner first performs with the New York Symphony Orchestra.	Claudel: *Partage de Midi* Derain: *Port of London* Pinero: *His House in Order* Sinclair: *The Jungle* Valéry: *Monsieur Teste* Wright: *Unity Temple*	Thousands of people die in a series of natural disasters around the globe. In Tahiti, upwards of 10,000 are killed when a fierce cyclone whips up 65-foot waves; more than a thousand are claimed in an earthquake which devastates San Francisco in the United States; and Mount Vesuvius erupts in Italy. Following further waves of unrest across the country, Russia's first elected Parliament, the Duma, is dissolved in July, and martial law is declared.

Date	First performances/ recordings	Other musical	Other cultural	Socio-political
	Rimsky-Korsakov: *The Miserly Knight* Strauss: *Salome* (first Berlin performance) Szymanowski: Concert Overture Wolf-Ferrari: *I quattro rusteghi*			
1907	Elgar: *The Wand of Youth* Rachmaninov: Symphony no. 2 Schoenberg: String Quartet no. 1, Chamber Symphony Sibelius: Symphony no. 5 Strauss: *Salome* (first US performance) Stravinsky: Symphony in E♭ Webern: Quintet	Busoni's *Sketch of a New Esthetic of Music* published. In Paris Diaghilev organises 'Five Historical Concerts of Russian Music from Glinka to Skryabin'. Controversy breaks out over Strauss's *Salome* at the Metropolitan Opera in New York: supporters of the house threaten to withdraw financial support. The piece isn't performed there again until 1934. Mahler conducts his last performance at the Vienna Opera, before leaving for America.	Exhibition of Cubist paintings in Paris Conrad: *Secret Agent* Derain: *Blackfriars Bridge*. *The Bathers* Gorki: *Mother* Picasso: *Les demoiselles d'Avignon* Munch: *Amor and Psyche* Rilke: *Neue Gedichte* Shaw: *Major Barbara* Synge: *Playboy of the Western World*	Britain sees further fierce clashes between suffragettes and their supporters and police, with 57 arrests being made including that of one of the movement's leaders, Christabel Pankhurst. A young Indian lawyer called Mohandas Gandhi calls a 'Satyagraha', or campaign of peaceful civil disobedience, against the passing of the Asiatic Law Amendment Ordinance in South Africa, which requires all Indians to submit to registration and restriction of movement.

		Buddy Bolden, credited as one of the first jazz musicians, is admitted to a mental institution in Jackson, where he remains for the rest of his life. Death of Grieg. First wireless broadcast of a piece of music.		
1908	Elgar: Symphony no. 1 Debussy: *Pelléas et Mélisande* (first US performance) Mahler: Symphony no. 7 Rachmaninov: Symphony no. 2 Ravel: *Rapsodie espagnole* Schoenberg: String Quartet no.2 Skryabin: *Poem of Ecstasy* Stravinsky: *Fireworks* Webern: *Passacaglia* (composed)	Strauss takes over from Weingartner as conductor of the Berlin court orchestra. Death of Rimsky-Korsakov Lee de Forest broadcasts phonograph music from the Eiffel Tower. Koussevitzky conducts the Berlin Philharmonic for the first time. Toscanini conducts *Aida* at the Metropolitan Opera in New York, his first American performance. Mahler conducts *Tristan* at the Metropolitan Opera in New York. Debussy conducts performances of the *Prélude* and *La mer* in London	Behrens: AEG Turbine Factory, Berlin (first steel and glass building) Bonnard: *Nude Against the Light* Brancusi: *The Kiss* Chagall: *Nu rouge* Forster: *A Room With a View* Grahame: *The Wind in the Willows* Matisse: *The Red Room* Monet: *The Ducal Palace*, *Venice*	Sultan Abdul Hamid II is forced to restore Turkey's constitution, suspended in 1876, following the success of the Young Turk revolutionary movement in spreading disaffection throughout the army. In the United Kingdom Herbet Asquith takes over as Prime Minister. In the troubled Balkan region of Europe, Austria annexes Bosnia and Herzegovina with Russian approval, and Bulgaria's Prince Ferdinand declares independence from the Ottoman Empire. Fritz Haber invents an industrial process for synthesizing ammonia.

Date	First performances/ recordings	Other musical	Other cultural	Socio-political
1909	Bartók: Second Suite for Small Orchestra Finck: recording of Tchaikovsky's *Nutcracker Suite* Rachmaninov: Piano Concerto no. 3, *The Isle of the Dead* Rimsky-Korsakov: *Le coq d'or* Saint-Saëns: *Samson et Dalila* Schoenberg: Piano Pieces Op. 11 (composed) Smetana: *The Bartered Bride* Strauss: *Elektra* Stravinsky: *Scherzo fantastique*	Serge Koussevitzky establishes the Russian Music Publishing House (Edition Russe de Musique), which goes on to publish Skryabin, Stravinsky, and Prokofiev, among others. A young Henry Cowell gives a demonstration at San Francisco Music Club of his 'tone clusters'. A private radio broadcast transmits Caruso singing from the Metropolitan Opera in New York. Diaghilev's Ballets Russes perform in Paris.	US Copyright Law is passed. Filippo Marietti first uses the term 'Futurism'. Sigmund Freud lectures in the US. Apollinaire: *L'enchanteur pourissant* (pseud) Bourdelle: *Hercules the Archer* Gide: *La Porte Étroite* Kokoschka: *Princess Montesquieu-Rohan* Matisse: *The Dance* Picasso: *Harlequin* Wells: *Tono-Bungay* Wright: Robie House, Chicago	In Britain, a fierce constitutional row breaks out over new Chancellor Lloyd George's radical budget; the proposals are rejected by the House of Lords, precipitating the dissolution of Parliament by Prime Minister Asquith. Serbs, led by Prime Minister Stojan Novakovic, demand the return of Bosnia Herzegovina from Austrian rule to full independence, prompting fears of further bloodshed in the Balkans. Frenchman Louis Blériot gains instant celebrity when he flies across the Channel in 43 minutes, landing at Dover Castle.

<table>
<tr>
<td>1910</td>
<td>Casella: Symphony no. 2
Elgar: Violin Concerto
Grieg: Piano Concerto (an ‘abbreviated’ recording is issued by Gramophone)
Korngold: Der Schneemann
Mahler: Symphony no. 8
Massenet: Don Quichotte
Strauss: Elektra (first London performance)
Stravinsky: The Firebird
Vaughan Williams: Fantasia on a Theme by Thomas Tallis, Symphony no. 1
Varèse: Bourgogne</td>
<td>James Reese Europe organises the Clef Club in New York, an organization for black musicians.
Francesco Balilla Pratella issues a ‘Manifesto of Futurist Musicians’.
Schoenberg’s paintings are exhibited for the first time.
Lee de Forest broadcasts Caruso singing an operatic selection from the Metropolitan Opera in New York.
Mahler performs in Paris for the first time.
Fauré makes his first visit to Russia, performing his own music.</td>
<td>The first talking picture is demonstrated by Thomas Edison in New Jersey.
‘Futurist Manifesto’ signed by Boccioni, Carra, Balla, and Severini.
Roger Fry organises a Post-Impressionist exhibition, in London.
Forster: Howards End
Griffiths: In Old California (first Hollywood film)
Kipling: If
Léger: Nues dans le foret
Modigliani: The Cellist
Russell/Whitehead: Principia Mathematica (vol. 1)
Rousseau: The Dream</td>
<td>Britain mourns the death of King Edward VII after nine years of rule. He is succeeded by his son, George V.
The Chinese army occupies Lhasa in Tibet, forcing the Dalai Lama to flee to India.
In a year that sees the uses of modern communications technology taken to new heights, murderer Dr Hawley Harvey Crippen is captured on a transatlantic steamer partly through the use of long-range radio.</td>
</tr>
</table>

Date	First performances/ recordings	Other musical	Other cultural	Socio-political
1911	Berg: String Quartet Debussy: *Le martyre de Saint-Sébastien* Elgar: Symphony no. 2 Mahler: *Das Lied von der Erde* Paderewski: recording of Chopin's Waltz in C sharp minor Ravel: *L'heure espagnole* Skryabin: Symphony no. 5 Sibelius: Symphony no. 4 Strauss: *Der Rosenkavalier* Stravinsky: *Petrushka* Webern: Four Pieces for Violin and Piano	Mahler conducts the New York Philharmonic for the last time in February (he dies in May). Schoenberg finishes his *Harmonielehre*, which he dedicates to Mahler. Solomon makes his London debut at the age of 8, playing Tchaikovsky's First Piano Concerto.	Diaghilev's Ballets Russes perform in London. Beerbohm: *Zuleika Dobson* Braque: *Man With Guitar* Brooke: *Poems* Chagall: *I and My Village* Klee: *Self Portrait* Lawrence: *The White Peacock* Renoir: *Gabrielle with a Rose* Rilke: *Duimo Elegies* Wells: *The New Machiavelli* Wharton: *Ethan Frome*	Civil war breaks out in China; in December the revolutionary leader Dr Sun Yat-sen is elected first President of the Chinese Republic. In Mexico rebels force the resignation of President Porfirio Diaz, whose dictatorial rule had lasted 45 years. He is replaced by a provisional government led by Francisco Madero. Britain is rocked by riots and direct action as strikes by transport workers spill onto the streets of London and Liverpool, precipitating the mobilisation of 50,000 troops.

1912	Leoncavallo: *La reginetta delle rose* Mahler: Symphony no. 9 Massenet: *Roma* Prokofiev: Piano Concerto no. 1 Ravel: *Daphnis et Chloé*, *Ma mère l'oye* (orchestral version) Schoenberg: *Pierrot lunaire* (first performed in Berlin and toured through Germany and Austria), Five Orchestral Pieces Strauss: *Ariadne auf Naxos* (revised 1916)	Luigi Russolo publishes *The Art of Noises*, calling for composition based on environmental sound sources. W. C. Handy publishes 'Memphis Blues', the first published blues piece. James Reese Europe and his Clef Club Symphony Orchestra perform in Carnegie Hall, New York. Stokowski makes his debut with the Philadelphia Orchestra.	'New Poetry' movement in the US. First performance of the ballet *Prélude à 'L'après-midi d'un faune'* by Diaghilev's Ballets Russes; Nijinsky's new stylized form of dancing is hailed as visionary and brilliant by some, but shocks others. Adler: *The Neurotic Condition* Duchamp: *Nude Descending a Staircase* Jung: *Theory of Psychoanalysis* Mann: *Death in Venice* Marc: *Tower of Blue Horses* Picasso: *The Violin* Shaw: *Pygmalion* Tagore: *Gitangali*	The world is stunned by the loss of over 1,500 passengers and crew on the maiden voyage of the 'unsinkable' liner, the SS *Titanic*. The *Titanic* hits an iceberg while steaming across the Atlantic in an attempt to win the coveted Blue Riband for the fastest crossing, and sinks in a matter of hours. War is declared between the Balkan League – comprising Serbia, Bulgaria, Montenegro, and Greece – and Turkey. Turkish forces are rocked by the ferocity of the onslaught, which is the result of the League's demand for independence from Turkey's occupying forces, and within a month the opposing sides are holding talks on the front lines outside Constantinople.

Date	First performances/ recordings	Other musical	Other cultural	Socio-political
1913	Charpentier: *Julien* Debussy: *Jeux* Elgar: *Falstaff* Prokofiev: Piano Concerto no. 2 Rachmaninov: *The Bells* Satie: *Coco-Chein* Schoenberg: *Gurrelieder* Strauss: *Der Rosenkavalier* (first US performance) Stravinsky: *The Rite of Spring* Webern: *Six Pieces for Orchestra*	First use of the word 'jazz' in print. The Grand Prix de Rome is awarded to Lili Boulanger, the first woman to receive the award. 1st Gesellschaft der Musikfreunde of Donaueschingen takes place, a concert series devoted to new music. The Academic Society of Literature and Music in Vienna presents a concert of music by Schoenberg (Chamber Symphony), Webern, Zemlinsky, and Berg, which results in a near riot. The first performance of Stravinsky's *Rite of Spring*, in Paris, provokes an uproar, directed largely at the choreography.	Armory Show, New York, introduces Post-Impressionism to the US. Alain-Fournier: *Le grand Meaulnes* Apollinaire: *The Cubist Painters* Lawrence: *Sons and Lovers* Proust: *Swann's Way* Wharton: *The Custom of the Country*	The Grand Vizier of Turkey, Kiamil Pasha, is deposed, and the war between the Balkan League and Turkey ends with the signing of a new treaty. However, Greece and Serbia declare war on their erstwhile ally Bulgaria, and a strained peace is only reached following the signing of the Treaty of Bucharest. In Britain, suffragettes mourn the death of Emily Davison who is trampled to death by the King's Horse, Anmer, during the Epsom Derby. The German Reichstag authorises a 25% increase in its army from 653,000 to 863,000.

		First recordings by a black band made by James Reese Europe. Russolo premieres his ensemble of 'noisemakers'.		
1914	Ives: *Three Places in New England* Nikisch: recording of Beethoven's Symphony no. 5. Rimsky-Korsakov: *Le coq d'or* Satie: *Sports et divertissements* Schoenberg: Five Orchestral Pieces (first US performance) Stravinsky: *The Rite of Spring* (first concert performance) Vaughan Williams: *London Symphony*	Concert of 'futurist' music takes place in Milan, Italy, presented by Marinetti and Russolo. James Reese Europe's Syncopated Society Orchestra is signed to Victor, the first African-American group to gain a record contract. Sibelius makes his first visit to the US, and is awarded an honorary doctorate by Yale. Schoenberg makes his first appearance in London, conducting the Five Orchestral Pieces and *Gurrelieder.* Works by living German composers are excluded from British concert programmes after the outbreak of war. ASCAP is established in New York. The fifth IMS congress meets in Paris.	Braque: *The Guitarist* Burroughs: *Tarzan of the Apes* James: *The Golden Bowl* Joyce: *The Dubliners* Jugo: *Niebl* Russell: *Knowledge of the External World as a Field for Scientific Method in Philosophy* Stella: *Battle of Lights, Coney Island*	Britain declares war on Germany. The catalyst for the crisis is the murder in Sarajevo of Archduke Ferdinand, heir to the Austro- Hungarian throne, although the direct cause of Britain's declaration is the refusal of Germany to honour an 1839 treaty guaranteeing the neutrality of Belgium. By the end of August, British and French troops are defeated in the battle for Mons in Belgium and Russian troops are routed on the Eastern front. By the end of the year, the war has spread to European colonies in Africa. Turkey declares war on Russia following her invasion of Armenia, and the Eastern front extends to Poland.

Date	First performances/ recordings	Other musical	Other cultural	Socio-political
1915	Bartók: *Sonatina* Debussy: *Etudes* Rachmaninov: *Vespers* Skryabin: *Prometheus* Sibelius: Symphony no. 5 Strauss: *Alpine Symphony* Wood: recording of the Prelude from Act III of *Lohengrin*	Varèse travels to America. King Oliver forms his jazz band in New Orleans. Jelly Roll Morton publishes 'Jelly Roll Blues'. The first issue of *The Musical Quarterly* appears. Death of Skryabin. Stravinsky makes his public debut as a conductor in Geneva, conducting *The Firebird*. Casals makes his first recordings for Columbia, including music by Bach. Grainger makes his US debut in New York. Dolmetsch publishes *The Interpretation of the Music of the XVIIth and XVIIIth Centuries.*	Buchanan: *The Thirty-Nine Steps* Duchamp: *The Bride Stripped Bare by Her Bachelors Even* Griffith: *The Birth of a Nation* Ford: *The Good Soldier* Kafka: *Metamorphosis* Kirchner: *Self-Portrait as Soldier* Lawrence: *The Rainbow* Maugham: *Of Human Bondage* de Mille: *Carmen* Mondrian: *Pier and Ocean* Pound: *Cathay*	In the war in Europe, the Germans mount a sea blockade of Britain; British and French troops launch an offensive on the Germans at Ypres, northern France; British, French and ANZAC forces storm the Gallipoli peninsula in the Turkish Dardanelles, later being repelled at a cost of 25,000 dead, 76,000 wounded and 13,000 missing; Germany and Austria partition Poland and occupy Belgrade in Serbia. Central Italy suffers a massive earthquake which kills 29,000.

1916	Korngold: *Violanta*. *Der Ring des Polykrates* Nielsen: Symphony no. 4 Prokofiev: *Scythian Suite* Strauss: *Ariadne auf Naxos* (revised) Wood: recording of Strauss's *Till Eulenspiegel*	Diaghilev's Ballets Russes perform at the Metropolitan Opera in New York. Death of Richter. German music is prohibited in Italy until the end of the war. Monteux cancels an engagement to conduct Strauss's *Till Eulenspiel* in New York due to anti-German sentiment.	The Cabaret Voltaire in Zurich perform a new 'art form' called Dada; Max Ernst, Jean Arp, and Francis Picabia claim to be using 'anti-art' to reform art. Andreyez: *He Who Gets Slapped* Brighouse: *Hobson's Choice* Griffith: *Intolerance* Joyce: *Portrait of the Artist as a Young Man* Monet: Water Lilies series O'Neill: *Bound East* Yeats: *Second Coming*	In Britain, military conscription is instituted and 2 million women are deployed to assist in war work. David Lloyd George succeeds Herbert Asquith as Prime Minister of the coalition war government. Germany intensifies its bombing of Verdun on the Western Front; Russia captures most of Galicia from the Austrians; and a new offensive is launched by the Allies in the Balkans. Irish republicans seize control of the Post Office in Sackville Street, Dublin; 794 civilians and 521 troops and police are killed or wounded in the ensuing fighting. Ulster Unionists vote in favour of partition.
1917	Bartók: *The Wooden Prince* Busoni: *Turandot* Debussy: Violin Sonata Glazunov: Piano Concerto no. 2 The Original Dixieland Jazz Band: 'Livery Stable Blues', 'Dixieland Jazz Band One-Step' Pfitzner: *Palestrina* Respighi: *Fountains of Rome* Satie: *Parade*	The Original Dixieland Jazz Band open at Reisenweber's restaurant in New York, attracting record company attention. Jascha Heifetz debuts at Carnegie Hall at the age of 16. He begins recording in the same year. Death of Scott Joplin.	Piet Mondrian launches *de Stijl* magazine in Holland. First use of term 'Surrealist', by Apollinaire of Picasso's costumes for Diaghilev's ballet *Parade*. Apollinaire: *Les mamelles de Tirésias* Bonnard: *Nude at the Fireplace* Eliot: *Prufrock and Other Observations* Hamsun: *Growth of the Soil* Modigliani: *Crouching Female Nude* Pirandello: *Right You Are If You Think You Are* Stella: *Brooklyn Bridge*	Tsar Nicholas II of Russia abdicates in the face of continuing revolt at home and huge war casualties. He is replaced as premier by Alexander Kerensky, who is soon ousted by the revolutionary Bolsheviks, led by Vladimir Lenin and Leon Trotsky. The United States enters the war to 'save democracy'. In Europe, the Allies launch an offensive against the Hindenburg Line at Arras; German aeroplanes kill their first civilians along the south coast of Britain, and later begin their bombardment of London; the first US troops land in France; and the Italian army collapses at Caporetto following the use of gas by the Germans. The British government announces that it is to give full support to the Jews in establishing a homeland in Palestine.

Date	First performances/ recordings	Other musical	Other cultural	Socio-political
	Stokowski: recording of Brahms's Hungarian Dance no. 1 Szymanowski: Symphony no. 3 (*Song of the Night*) Zemlinsky: *Eine florentinische Tragödie*			
1918	Bartók: *Bluebeard's Castle* Janáček: *Taras Bulba* Prokofiev: 'Classical' Symphony Satie: *Socrate* Schreker: *Die Gezeichneten* Strauss: *Die Frau ohne Schatten* Stravinsky: *The Soldier's Tale*	Schoenberg founds the Verein für musikalische Privataufführungen (Society for Private Musical Performances); its first concert includes music by Debussy, Mahler, and Skryabin. Rachmaninov leaves Russia. Death of Debussy. Karl Muck, the German conductor of the Boston Symphony Orchestra, is arrested and interned. Gigli makes his first performance at the Metropolitan Opera in New York. Prokofiev makes his American debut as pianist-composer, in a	Apollinaire: *Calligrammes* Cather: *My Antonia* Joyce: *The Exiles* Klee: *Gartenplan* Nash: *We Are Making a New World* Ozenfant and Le Corbusier: *Après le Cubisme* Pirandello: *Six Characters in Search of an Author* Spengler: *Decline Of The West* Strachey: *Eminent Victorians*	The First World War finally ends with the signing of the Armistice in November. The terms of the peace are harsh on Germany, and the Hapsburg empire is broken up into four 'new' nations: Austria, Czechoslovakia, Hungary and a confederation of Serbs, Slovenes, Croats, and Montenegrans (soon to become Yugoslavia). In Germany, the immediate result of the Armistice is open revolt, and Kaiser Wilhelm II is forced to flee to Holland. The human cost of the war is 10 million dead, with Germany and Russia bearing the brunt of casualties. In Russia, the Bolsheviks change their name to the Russian Communist Party and create a people's Red Army. In July, the Tsar and his family are bayoneted to death in a cellar in Ekaterinburg.

		programme of his own music in New York. Trumpeter and bandleader 'King' Oliver leaves New Orleans for Chicago. Richard Strauss and Max Reinhart plan the annual Salzburg Festival (which begins in 1920).		
1919	Debussy: Rhapsody for Saxophone De Falla: *The Three-Cornered Hat* Delius: *Eventyr* Elgar: Cello Concerto Europe: 'Memphis Blues' Fauré: *Ballade* Stravinsky: *Le chant du rossignol* Webern: Five Songs	Founding of German journal *Musikblätter des Anbruch* in Vienna. Founding of the new-music journal *Melos* by Hermann Scherchen. 50th anniversary celebrations of the Vienna Opera house: Strauss conducts Mozart, Beethoven, and Wagner. The US Supreme Court rules that the Victor/Columbia cartel is illegal. The Original Dixieland Jazz Band perform in London. Will Marion Cook's American Syncopated Orchestra perform in London and Paris, along with Sidney Bechet. James Reese Europe's band tour America.	Anderson: *Winesburg Ohio* Beckman: *The Night* Brancusi: *Bird in Space* Gide: *La symphonie pastorale* Huizinga: *Waning of the Middle Ages* Ibanez: *The Four Horsemen of the Apocalypse* Maugham: *The Moon and Sixpence* Picasso: *Pierrot and Harlequin* Shaw: *Heartbreak House*	Despite the onset of famine and hardship, and an unsuccessful Communist uprising in Berlin, Germany returns to some semblance of political stability when a republic is declared at Weimar. However, there is widespread anger in Germany at the punitive conditions of the Versailles treaty. British troops massacre many Indian protesters at Amritsar, the Sikhs' holy city, during an unlawful demonstration following a business strike called by the civil rights leader, Mohandas Gandhi. Captain John Alcock and Lt. Arthur Brown complete the first non-stop transatlantic flight in a Vickers-Vimy biplane.

Date	First performances/ recordings	Other musical	Other cultural	Socio-political
1920	Holst: *The Planets* Korngold: *Die tote Stadt* Milhaud: *Le boeuf sur le toit* Ravel: *Le tombeau de Couperin* (orchestration) Satie/Milhaud: *Musique d'ameublement* Smith: 'Crazy Blues' Stravinsky: *Pulcinella*, *Ragtime* Vaughan Williams: Symphony no. 2 Whiteman: 'Whispering'	The first Salzburg Festival takes place. The journal *Music and Letters* begins publishing in London. Stravinsky moves to Paris. Toscanini records and tours America with the orchestra of La Scala, Milan. Lev Termin invents the Theremin, an electric instrument played by moving the hand around a metal pole. The first commercial radio broadcast featuring music takes place in Detroit. Caruso makes his last recordings.	Antoine Pevsner and Naum Gabo issue the Realistic Manifesto, containing the principles of European Constructivism. Gris: *Guitar, Book and Newspaper* Kafka: *The Country Doctor* Lewis: *Main Street* Mansfield: *Bliss* Matisse: *Odalisque* Smith: *Christ Bearing the Cross* Wells: *Outline of History*	Violence erupts in Ireland on 'Bloody Sunday' (21 November) as the IRA kill 14 soldiers and the special police retaliate. Sinn Fein president Éamon de Valéra demands complete Irish independence and British withdrawal, but the British authorities declare martial law. The far-right National Socialist German Workers' Party, led by a young Adolf Hitler, denounces the 'Versailles Diktat' and slams Jews as a pernicious influence on German society. The League of Nations is formally launched in London, although without the support of the US, and confirms the British Mandate in Palestine.

1921	Hindemith: *Murder, Hoffnung der Frauen. Das Nusch-Nuschi* Honegger: *Le roi David* Janáček: *Katya Kabanova* Johnson: 'Carolina Shout' Prokofiev: *The Love for Three Oranges* Stravinsky: *Symphonies of Wind Instruments* Webern: *Passacaglia* (1908)	Varèse founds the International Composers' Guild in New York. Schoenberg devises his twelve-note method. La Scala, Milan, reopens following its closure in 1917. The first Festival for the Promotion of Contemporary Music takes place in Donaueschingen, Germany; includes music by Krenek, Berg, and Hindemith. The British Music Society holds its first concert in London, which includes music by Holst, Vaughan Williams, and Holbrooke. Russolo conducts a concert of futurist music in Paris.	The first medium-wave wireless broadcast is made in the US. Braque: *Still Life with Guitar* Huxley: *Chrome Yellow* Klee: *The Fish* Lawrence: *Women in Love* Munch: *The Kiss* Picasso: *Three Musicians* Yeats: *Easter 1916; Second Coming*	The Allies occupy industrial towns in the Ruhr following Germany's failure to comply with the terms of reparation until the Reichstag finally capitulates in May. A worldwide recession begins to bite hard, with the complete collapse of the German economy; over 2 million are unemployed in Britain and more than 3.5 million in the US. Lenin announces that state planning of the economy is to be temporarily suspended and private trading is restored. An agreement is reached between British and Irish negotiators which paves the way for the creation of the Irish Free State.

Date	First performances/ recordings	Other musical	Other cultural	Socio-political
1922	Bartók: Four Orchestral Pieces Bax: Symphony no. 4 Mengelberg: recording of Beethoven's *Coriolan* Overture with the New York Philharmonic Nielsen: Symphony no. 5 Ravel: Orchestration of Musorgsky's *Pictures at an Exhibition* Sibelius: *Scaramouche* Stravinsky: *Renard*, *Mavra* Vaughan Williams: Symphony no. 3	Furtwängler begins his association with Berlin Philharmonic. Louis Armstrong joins King Oliver and the Creole Jazz Band in Chicago. As part of the Salzburg Festival, a series of modern chamber music concerts is held, and includes music by Strauss, Bartók, Stravinsky, Debussy, and Webern. This leads to the formation of the International Society for Contemporary Music. Death of Nikisch. Busch becomes conductor of the Dresden Opera.	Bookseller Sylvia Beach's limited edition of *Ulysses* is banned in Britain and the US on grounds of obscenity. The tomb of King Tutankhamen is opened. The BBC (British Broadcasting Company, later British Broadcasting Corporation) is founded. It broadcasts its first programmes in November, and its first orchestral concert in December. Eliot: *The Waste Land* Du Gard: *Les Thibault* Joyce: *Ulysses* Lewis: *Babbitt* Miró: *The Farm* Rilke: *Sonette am Orpheus*	The provisional Irish Parliament, the Dáil Éireann, narrowly approves the treaty with Britain which sets up the Irish Free State by 64 votes to 57. However Éamon de Valéra refuses the presidency of the Dáil, indicating just how fragile support for the treaty is. Mahatma Gandhi is sentenced by the British authorities to six years' imprisonment for sedition. In a speech at his trial, he accepts full responsibility for recent disturbances, and says that spreading disaffection with British rule in India has 'become almost a passion with me'. Benito Mussolini, known as 'Il Duce', becomes dictator of Italy after his fascists march on Rome.

1923	Holst: *The Perfect Fool* Milhaud: *La création du monde* Morton: 'King Porter Stomp', 'The Pearls' Oliver: 'Weather Bird Rag', 'Dippermouth Blues' Sibelius: Symphony no. 6 Smith: 'Downhearted Blues' Stravinsky: *Octet*, *Les noces* Varèse: *Hyperprism* Walton: *Façade* (first public performance) Whiteman: 'Three O'Clock In The Morning'	The first festival of the International Society for Contemporary Music (ISCM) takes place in Salzburg; includes music by Berg, Schoenberg, Bartók, Krenek, Prokofiev, Ravel, Walton, Szymanowksi, Janáček, and Stravinsky. The BBC makes the first radio broadcast of a complete opera, Mozart's *Magic Flute*. The first issue of *The Gramophone* is published.	Founding of the Frankfurt Institute for Social Research. The first network radio broadcast is made when Boston radio transmits a programme from a New York station. Fitzgerald: *Tales of the Jazz Age* Freud: *The Ego and the Id* Hugo: *The Hunchback of Notre Dame* Mauriac: *Génetrix* Picasso: *Seated Woman* Shaw: *Saint Joan* Spencer: *The Resurrection* Wodehouse: *The Inimitable Jeeves*	Germany is unable to make good on its promised war reparations because of rampant inflation and the collapse of the economy. By the end of the year, the German mark is worth over 20 billion to the pound sterling. Adolf Hitler, leader of the small, far-right and virulently anti-Semitic Nazi Party, declares a putsch in a Munich beer hall. Following a massive stroke, Lenin is forced to step down as head of the USSR. No clear leader emerges in the race to succeed him, but Trotsky, Grigori Zinoviev, and Joseph Stalin all emerge as front runners.

Date	First performances/ recordings	Other musical	Other cultural	Socio-political
1924	Armstrong and Bechet: 'Cake Walking Babies' Bartók: Violin Sonata No. 2 Bechet: 'Wild Cat Blues', 'Kansas City Man Blues' Gershwin: *Rhapsody in Blue*, *Lady Be Good* Honegger: *Pacific 231* Janáček: *The Cunning Little Vixen* Milhaud: *Le train bleu* Poulenc: *Les biches* Prokofiev: Piano Concerto no. 2 Puccini: *Tosca* Ruggles: *Men and Mountains* Sibelius: Symphony no. 7 Schoenberg: *Erwartung* (1909), *Die glückliche Hand* (1913)	The ISCM Festival held in Prague; includes music by Smetana, Bloch, Honegger, Prokofiev, Stravinsky, Suk, Syzmanowski, and Schoenberg. Death of Puccini. Schoenberg tours Italy, conducting *Pierrot lunaire.* Koussevitsky takes over the Boston Symphony Orchestra from Monteux. Victor record hillbilly performer Vernon Dalhart. Death of Busoni. The Bayreuth Festival reopens after a closure of 10 years.	Coward: *The Vortex* Ford: *The Iron Horse* Forster: *A Passage to India* Léger: *Le ballet mécanique* Mann: *The Magic Mountain* De Mille: *The Ten Commandments*	Lenin dies and is succeeded by a ruling council consisting of Zinoviev, Kamenev, and Stalin. The council, now dominated by Stalin, denounces Trotsky. Adolf Hitler is sentenced to five years in prison for his part in the Munich beer-hall putsch. Germany accepts a new protocol on the payment of war reparations (the Dawes Plan). The German authorities replace the worthless mark with the Reichsmark in a bid to stabilize the currency. In London, King George V opens the British Empire Exhibition at Wembley Stadium.

	Strauss: *Intermezzo* Stravinsky: Concerto for Piano and Winds Varèse: *Octandre*			
1925	Berg: *Wozzeck* Busoni: *Doktor Faustus* (unfinished) Copland: Symphony for organ and orchestra Hindemith: *Concerto for Orchestra* Honegger: Concertino for piano and orchestra Janáček: *Sarka* Nielsen: Symphony no. 6 Prokofiev: Symphony no. 2 Ravel: *L'enfant et les sortilèges* Stokowski: recording of Saint-Saëns's *Danse macabre*, the first electric orchestral recording Varèse: *Integrales*	Josephine Baker arrives in Paris. Henry Cowell forms the New Music Society of California. Stravinsky makes his first appearance in the US conducting the Philharmonic Orchestra of New York in a programme of his own music. The ISCM Festival is held in Prague; includes music by Busoni, Martinů, Vaughan Williams, Krenek, Milhaud, and Bartók. Schoenberg is appointed to the Berlin Academy of Arts, succeeding Busoni. Death of Satie.	The *New Yorker* begins publication. The Exposition des Arts Décoratifs in Paris reflects the growing popularity of 'Art Deco'. The first surrealist exhibition opens in Paris, including the work of artists such as Ernst, Klee, Miró, and Picasso. Shaw wins the Nobel Prize for Literature Chaplin: *Gold Rush* Coward: *Hay Fever* Dreisser: *An American Tragedy* Eisenstein: *The Battleship Potemkin* Fitzgerald: *The Great Gatsby* Kafka: *The Trial* (posth.) Miró: *The Harlequin's Carnival* O'Casey: *Juno and the Paycock* Picasso: *Three Dancers*	In China, Chiang Kai-shek, a banker turned warrior, takes over from Sun Yat-sen as the leader of the nationalist Kuomintang party, and declares a 'northern expedition' of reunification. In South Africa, Afrikaans is made the official language of Boer settlers and the colour bar becomes legal. The bar excludes black, coloured (mixed race), and Indian South Africans from skilled or semi-skilled work. Paul von Hindenburg becomes Germany's first directly elected president.

Date	First performances/ recordings	Other musical	Other cultural	Socio-political
1926	Antheil: *Ballet mécanique* Bartók: *The Miraculous Mandarin* Furtwängler: recording of Beethoven's Fifth Symphony Hindemith: *Cardillac* Honegger: *Judith* Janáček: *Sinfonietta*, *The Makropulos Affair* Kreisler: recording of Beethoven's Violin Concerto on HMV Morton: 'Black Bottom Stomp' Puccini: *Turandot* (unfinished) Shostakovich: Symphony no. 1 Varèse: *Amériques* Webern: *Five Pieces for Orchestra* Weill: *Der protagonist*	Founding of the Association for Contemporary Music in Leningrad. The ISCM Festival takes place in Zürich; includes music by Honegger, Schoenberg, Walton, Hindemith, Webern, and Weill. Following disturbances by Czech nationalists during performances of Berg's *Wozzeck* in Prague, the authorities ban further performances. Dame Nellie Melba gives her farewell performance at Covent Garden. The Gramophone Company record the concert and later release portions of it.	John Logie Baird transmits moving images by wireless by a process he calls 'television'. Crosland: *Don Juan* (with John Barrymore) Hemingway: *The Sun Also Rises* Lang: *Metropolis* Lawrence: *The Seven Pillars of Wisdom* Magritte: *The Menaced Assassin* Milne: *Winnie-the-Pooh* Miró: *Dog Barking at the Moon* O'Casey: *The Plough and the Stars* Renoir: *Nana*	Britain's first national strike is called by the Trades Union Congress in sympathy with the miners, following the breakdown of negotiations with coal mine owners over working hours. In Italy, Mussolini assumes total power and bans all opposition. The rehabilitation of Germany continues as she is admitted to the League of Nations. As Stalin tightens his grip on power in the Soviet Union, Zinoviev and Trotsky are expelled from the Communist Party Central Committee. In China, the 'Red Army' of Chiang Kai-shek's Kuomintang continues its 'northern expedition' of reunification by capturing the cities of Hankow, Wuchang, and Hangyang. Foreign interests look on with great concern.

1927	Armstrong: 'Potato Head Blues' Bartók: Piano Concerto no. 1 Berg: *Lyric Suite*, Chamber Concerto Copland: Piano Concerto Elgar: recording of excerpts from *The Dream of Gerontius* Ellington: 'Black and Tan Fantasy' Janáček: *Glagolitic Mass* Kern: *Show Boat* Krenek: *Jonny spielt auf* Rachmaninov: Piano Concerto no. 4 Schoenberg: String Quartet no. 3 Sessions: Symphony no. 1 Shostakovich: Symphony no. 2 Strauss: *Die ägyptische Helena*	Duke Ellington's band opens at the Cotton Club in Harlem, an engagement that lasts for five years. Henry Cowell founds *New Musical Quarterly*, with support from Charles Ives; the first issue includes a score of Ruggles' *Men and Mountains*. The Automatic Instrument Company (AMI) introduce the Selective Phonograph (jukebox). The Salle Pleyel opens in Paris. The English Columbia company record excerpts from Bayreuth. The ISCM Festival is held in Frankfurt; includes music by Janáček and Bartók. A festival of new music in Baden-Baden includes works by Hindemith and Weill. Formation of the International Musicological Society, with Guido Adler as chairman.	Crosland: *The Jazz Singer* (the first full-length talking film) Epstein: *Madonna and Child* Freud: *The Future of an Illusion* Heidegger: *Sein und Zeit* Hemingway: *Men Without Women* Hesse: *Der Steppenwolf* Lowry: *Coming Out of School* Matisse: *Figures with Ornamental Background* De Mille: *King of Kings* Murnau: *Nosferatu* Proust: *Time Regained* Russell: *Analysis of Matter* Woolf: *To The Lighthouse*	Kuomintang forces seize Shanghai with barely a shot fired, despite the deployment of 12,000 British troops. In the USSR, Stalin's faction is triumphant at the All-Union Congress, prompting the final expulsion of his rivals Zinoviev and Trotsky from the Communist Party. 12,000 troops are deployed in Vienna to put down a socialist rising which resulted in the burning of the Ministry of Justice. The riots are occasioned by the acquittal of three members of the anti-socialist front, Kaempfers, on charges of killing two communists in a fracas in January. Charles Lindbergh becomes the first man to fly solo across the Atlantic in his monoplane, *Spirit of St. Louis*.

Date	First performances/ recordings	Other musical	Other cultural	Socio-political
	Stravinsky: *Oedipus rex* Varèse: *Arcana* Weill: *Mahagonny*			
1928	Armstrong: 'West End Blues' Casals, Cortot, and Thibaud: recording of the Beethoven 'Archduke' Trio Cortot: recording of Schumann's Piano Concerto Gershwin: *An American In Paris* Menuhin: recording of Bach's solo violin sonata in C major Musorgsky: *Boris Godunov* (1869) Nielsen: Clarinet Concerto Schoenberg: *Variations for Orchestra*	Maurice Martenot produces the ondes martenot. First radio broadcast of the New York Philharmonic. Columbia record a large part of *Tristan und Isolde* at Bayreuth. The ISCM Festival takes place in Siena, Italy; includes music by Hindemith, Ravel, Zemlinsky, Bridge, Webern, and Falla. Horowitz makes his American debut playing Tchaikovsky. Death of Janáček. Karajan makes his debut in Berlin.	Amédée Ozenfant coins the term 'purism' in his treatise, *Art*. Congrès Internationaux d'Architecture Moderne founded in Switzerland. Colour television is demonstrated in Britain. Bacon: *The Singing Fool* (starring Al Jolson) Disney: *Steamboat Willie* (animated cartoon) Huxley: *Point Counter Point* Lawrence: *Lady Chatterley's Lover* Matisse: *Seated Odalisque* Munch: *Girl on a Sofa* Woolf: *Orlando* Yeats: *The Tower*	King Faud of Egypt assumes direct rule after the fall of Nahas Pasha's short-lived premiership; he suspends press freedom, prohibits public opposition meetings and decrees that no elections will be held for at least three years. Professor Alexander Fleming announces the discovery of Penecillium Notatum, a mould which attacks many kinds of harmful bacteria, and predicts that it will be of great use in the fight against disease. In Japan, Hirohito is crowned Emperor following the death of his father. In the US, Republican Herbert Hoover is elected President.

	Stokowski: orchestral arrangement of Bach's Prelude and Fugue in D minor Stravinsky: *Apollon musagète* Webern: String Trio Weill: *Die Dreigroschenoper*			
1929	Berg: *Lyric Suite* (chamber orchestra version) Chevalier: *Louise* recorded for HMV Hindemith: *Neues vom Tage* Krenek: *Jonny spielt auf* (first performance in English, in New York) Lambert: *The Rio Grande* McPhee: Concerto for piano and winds Milhaud: Viola Concerto Prokofiev: *Grak*	Roosevelt administration enacts subsidies for composers The ISCM Festival is held in Geneva; includes music by Sessions, Martin, Ireland, and Vaughan Williams. Ludwig Blattner markets the Blattnerphone, the first commercial tape machine. Death of Diaghilev. Founding of the Decca Gramophone Company. Toscanini becomes music director of the New York Philharmonic. Scherchen publishes *Handbook of Conducting*.	Opening of the Museum of Modern Art in New York. Cocteau: *Les enfants terribles* Coward: *Bitter Sweet* Faulkner: *The Sound and the Fury* Graves: *Goodbye to All That* Heidegger: *What is Philosophy?* Hemingway: *A Farewell to Arms* Mondrian: *Composition with Yellow and Blue* Murphy: *St. Louis Blues* (starring Bessie Smith) M Picasso: *Woman in Armchair* Remarque: *All Quiet on the Western Front* Woolf: *A Room of One's Own*	The world economy faces an uncertain future following the crash of the world's largest stock market at Wall Street, New York, on 24 October ("Black Thursday"). An indirect result is the cessation of US loans to Europe, causing further hardship. In Chicago, seven members of Al Capone's gangster mob in Chicago are lined up against a wall and shot dead by rivals on 14 February, in a killing that soon becomes known as the 'St Valentine's Day Massacre'. At least eight Jewish settlers are killed and thousands are left homeless following rioting by Arabs in Safed, Galilee.

Date	First performances/ recordings	Other musical	Other cultural	Socio-political
	Stravinsky: *Capriccio* Walton: Viola Concerto Webern: Symphony			
1930	Berg: *Der Wein* Dietrich: 'Falling in Love Again' Ellington: 'Mood Indigo' Gershwin: *Girl Crazy* Krenek: *Leben des Orest* Prokofiev: Symphony no. 4 Rachmaninov: Piano Concerto no. 3 Schoenberg: *Accompaniment to a Film Scene* Shostakovich: Symphony no. 3 Stravinsky: *Symphony of Psalms* Weill: *Aufstieg und Fall der Stadt Mahagonny*	Publication of Cowell's *New Musical Resources.* The ISCM Festival takes place in Liège; includes music by Hindemith, Stravinsky, Bax, Roussel, Walton, and Hauer. Schoenberg writes 'Credo'. The Library of Congress begins making field recordings through John Lomax and later his son Alan. Adrian Boult is hired as conductor of the BBC Symphony Orchestra and the orchestra makes its first broadcast.	Van Doesberg first uses the term 'Concrete Art' Auden: *Poems* Eliot: *Ash Wednesday* Faulkner: *As I Lay Dying* Freud: *Civilisation and its Discontents* Hesse: *Narcissus and Goldmund* Hitchcock: *Murder* Picasso: *Seated Bather* Shreve, Lamb, and Harmon: Empire State Building, New York. Von Sternberg: *Der Blaue Engel* Wood: *American Gothic*	In India, Mahatma Gandhi leads a huge march against a British law which gives the government a monopoly on producing salt. The British authorities respond by arresting him and violently crushing his peaceful supporters. In Germany, Adolf Hitler's National Socialists become the second largest party in the Reichstag after the Socialists, with 107 deputies. In response to widespread famine, Joseph Stalin collectivizes all farms in the Soviet Union, cracking down on the 'Kulaks', or rich peasants, who he blames for making money at the cost of ordinary Soviet citizens. Ras Tafari becomes Emperor Haille Selassie of Ethiopia following a revolt against the old order.

Year	Music	Musical events	Art and culture	Historical and political events
1931	Armstrong: 'I Got Rhythm' Berg: *Wozzeck* (performances in Philadelphia and New York) Copland: Piano Variations Cowell: *Steel and Stone* Elgar: recording of *Falstaff* for HMV Honegger: Symphony no. 1 Ives: *Three Places in New England* (1914) Messiaen: *Les offrandes oubliées* Walton: *Belshazzar's Feast* Webern: *Quartet*	Henry Cowell and Lev Termin produce the Rhythmicon, an instrument capable of producing complex rhythmic combinations. The ISCM Festival takes place in Oxford; includes music by Sessions, Vaughan Williams, Lambert, Hindemith, Webern, Gershwin, and Szymanowski. NBC begin a series of regular broadcasts of matinee performances from the Metropolitan opera in New York.	Sullivan, Holabird, and Roche: Rockefeller Centre, New York. Opening of the Empire State Building, the tallest in the world. Bonnard: *The Breakfast Room* Buck: *The Good Earth* Chaplin: *City Lights* Dali: *The Persistence of Memory* Hopper: *Route 6, Eastham* Lang: *M* Matisse: 'The Dance' murals at the Barnes Foundation, Pennsylvania Tzara: *L'Homme approximatif* Woolf: *The Waves*	Economic crisis grips Europe. In Austria, the bankruptcy of the Credit-Anstalt bank begins the financial collapse of Central Europe. The Labour Government falls over its handling of the financial crisis in Britain, and its leader, Ramsay MacDonald, is expelled from the party after forming a Coalition Government. Britain is eventually forced to implement stringent measures to deal with the crisis, including massive cuts in public spending and the devaluation of the pound. Spain is declared a Republic as King Alfonso is forced to abdicate following last year's collapse of Primo de Rivera's military dictatorship.

Date	First performances/ recordings	Other musical	Other cultural	Socio-political
1932	Ellington: 'It Don't Mean a Thing (If It Ain't Got That Swing)' Gershwin: Rhapsody no. 2 Horowitz: recording of Liszt's B minor Piano Sonata Menuhin: recording of Elgar's Violin Concerto, with the composer conducting Poulenc: Concerto for Two Pianos Prokofiev: Piano Concerto no. 5 Ravel: Piano Concerto in G major Ruggles: *Sun Treader*	The Hot Club of France is formed. Louis Armstrong tours Europe. A number of Italian composers (including Respighi, Pizzetti, and Zandonai) produce an anti-modernist manifesto. Ted Wallerstein markets an electric turntable which can be jacked into a radio, making phonograph hardware affordable for the general public. Robert Goffin publishes *Auf Frontières du Jazz*, the first substantial book on jazz. The First Festival of Contemporary American Music takes place in Yaddo and includes music by Copland, Ives, Harris, Brant, Thomson, and Walter Piston.	Opening of Sydney Harbour Bridge and Lambeth Bridge, London. Beckmann: *Seven Triptychs* Brecht: *The Mother* Calder exhibits 'stabiles' (sculptures moved by engines) and 'mobiles' (moved by air). Céline: *Voyage au bout de la nuit* Hemingway: *Death in the Afternoon* Huxley: *Brave New World* Scott: Shakespeare Memorial Theatre, Stratford- on-Avon Shaw: *The Adventures of the Black Girl in Her Search for God* Spencer: *May Tree*, *Cookham* Von Sternberg: *Shangai Express* (starring Marlene Dietrich)	Adolf Hitler is narrowly beaten to the Presidency of Germany by Paul von Hindenburg after a run-off ballot, but his Nazi Party is handed a resounding victory in the Reichstag, winning 230 seats to the Socialists 133. Hermann Goering is elected to the position of Reichstag President. The march of Fascism is evident elsewhere in Europe, with the foiling of a Nazi revolt in Finland, the establishment of a Fascist regime under Julius Gombos in Hungary, the election of Oliviera Salazar, and the establishment of a Fascist regime in Portugal, and the creation of the British Union of Fascists under one-time Labour cabinet minister Sir Oswald Mosley in London. In the United States, Democrat Franklin Delano Roosevelt wins a landslide victory over his Republican rival, Herbert Hoover.

	Schnabel: recordings of Beethoven's piano works issued by HMV Schoenberg: *Orchestral Songs* Stokowski: recording of Schoenberg's *Gurrelieder* with the Philadelphia Orchestra	Pulitzer Prize awarded to Gershwin and Kaufman for *Of Thee I Sing*, the first time the award has ever been given to a musical comedy. The ISCM Festival takes place in Vienna; includes music by Krenek, Rieti, Bliss, Françaix, Mahler, Schoenberg, and Berg.		
1933	Bartók: Piano Concerto no. 2 Britten: *Sinfonietta* Ellington: *Sophisticated Lady* Fischer begins recording the Bach 48 Preludes and Fugues for HMV (completed in 1936) Landowska: recording of Bach's *Goldberg Variations* Partch: *Li Po Songs* Shostakovich: Piano Concerto no. 1 Strauss: *Arabella*	Schoenberg leaves Germany, and moves to Paris before leaving for America in the autumn. Strauss is made President of the *Reichsmusikkammer*, appointed by Joseph Goebbels. Furtwängler also holds a position. A concert in Leipzig due to be directed by Walter is cancelled due to fears of anti-Semitic demonstrations. Toscanini cancels his engagements at Bayreuth in protest at the treatment of Jewish musicians. The director of Berlin Radio bans broadcasts of works by certain	Wassily Kandinsky and Paul Klee leave Germany. British Film Institute founded. Odeon Cinema circuit formed in Britain Clair: *14 Juli* Cooper/Schoedsack: *King Kong* (score by Max Steiner) Duhamel: *The Pasquier Chronicle* Eliot: *The Use of Poetry and the Use of Criticism* Giacometti: *The Palace at 4 am* Korda: *The Private Lives of Henry VIII* Malraux: *La condition humaine* Orwell: *Down and Out in Paris and London*	Adolf Hitler is appointed Chancellor of the German Reich and immediately suspends all guarantees of personal liberty, freedom of speech, and the Press, and the right of assembly. The Nazis win 95% of the vote in a plebiscite on his decision to take Germany out of the League of Nations and withdraw from a disarmament conference in Geneva. They soon order a boycott of Jewish business in Germany, and Jewish professionals and businessmen are hounded from their posts. In the midst of financial crisis, newly elected President F D Roosevelt tells the American people: 'The only thing we have to fear is fear itself.' His far-reaching New Deal legislation provides cash to bail out the beleaguered banks and the nation's farmers, the establishment of large-scale work creation programmes for the unemployed, and the

Date	First performances/ recordings	Other musical	Other cultural	Socio-political
	Szymanowski: Violin Concerto no. 2 Varèse: *Ionisation* Vaughan Williams: Piano Concerto	American-based artists who voice criticism of German cultural policy (including Toscanini and Fritz Reiner). Ellington tours Europe. Klemperer becomes music director of the Los Angeles Philharmonic. The ISCM Festival is held in Amsterdam; includes music by Kauffmann, Koffler, Petrassi, Copland, Crawford, and Krenek.	Stein: *The Autobiography of Alice B. Toklas*	tighter regulation of banking and the financial markets.
1934	Bax: Symphony no. 5 Copland: *Short Symphony* Gershwin: *Variations on 'I Got Rhythm'* Harris: Symphony no. 1 Hindemith: *Mathis der Maler*	Furtwängler resigns as conductor of the Berlin Philharmonic and Berlin State Opera, and as deputy president of *Reichsmusikkammer*, due to objections to Nazi policy. Goebbels gives a speech denouncing the 'moral decay of atonal composers', specifically citing Hindemith.	Armstrong makes test FM broadcasts from the Empire State building. Capra: *It Happened One Night* Clair: *The Last Millionaire* Cocteau: *La machine infernale* Einstein: *My Philosophy* Fitzgerald: *Tender is the Night* Graves: *I Claudius*	Martial law is pronounced throughout Spain as government troops crush insurgents. A nationwide strike called by the trade unions coincides with an attempt to declare Catalonia an independent state, but Spanish Foreign Legionaries and the civil guard soon bring the situation under control. In Germany, leader of the Nazi Storm Troopers Ernst Roehm is dragged from his bed and shot whilst hundreds of other Brownshirts are executed

	Porter: *Anything Goes* Rachmaninov: *Rhapsody on a Theme of Paganini* Shostakovich: *Lady Macbeth of the Mtsensk District* Stravinsky: *Perséphone* Varèse: *Ecuatorial* Vaughan Williams: *Fantasia on Greensleeves*	American Musicological Society founded in New York. Schoenberg makes his first US appearance as a conductor with the Boston Symphony Orchestra. ISCM Festival is held in Florence; includes music by Casella, Berg, Françaix, Honegger, Ravel, Bartók, and Britten. Stravinsky becomes a French citizen. Death of Elgar. The first Glyndebourne festival is held.	Priestley: *Eden End* Sholokov: *Quiet Flows the Don* Van Dyke: *The Thin Man* Young: *The Scarlet Pimpernel*	in the 'Night of the Long Knives'. It is rumoured that they were plotting to overthrow Hitler. In Texas, the renowned partners in crime, Bonnie Parker and Clyde Barrow, are shot dead by police following a four-year partnership of robbery and murder.
1935	Bartók: String Quartet no. 5 Gershwin: *Porgy and Bess* Goodman: 'Lady Be Good', 'Moonglow', 'King Porter Stomp' Prokofiev: Violin Concerto no. 2 Schoenberg: Suite for String Orchestra Strauss: *Die schweigsame Frau* Vaughan Williams: Symphony no. 4	Count Basie forms his own band. AEG produce the Magnetophon, the first tape machine to use plastic tape. Strauss resigns from the *Reichsmusikkammer*, having been denounced for collaborating with Jewish writer Stefan Zweig. The German government ban jazz from the airwaves. The Benny Goodman band open at the Palomar Ballroom in Los Angeles, an engagement which marks the beginning of their huge success.	Brown: *Anna Karenina* Dali: *Giraffe on Fire* Day-Lewis: *A Time to Dance* Eliot: *Murder In The Cathedral* Epstein: *Ecce Homo* Hitchcock: *The Thirty-Nine Steps* Munch: *The Modern Faust* Novello: *Glamorous Nights* Sandrich: *Top Hat* (with Fred Astaire and Ginger Rogers) Steinbeck: *Tortilla Flat*	Europe's Fascist nations begin their long- expected territorial expansion as Mussolini's Italian forces march into Abyssinia, and the Germans reclaim the coal-rich Saar region in defiance of the Versailles Treaty. At home, Jews are formally deprived of their German citizenship and excluded from employment in public service. Mao Tse-tung's long march ends after twelve hard months of fighting the Nationalist forces when the Communists' First Front army reaches Yenan in the north of China. In Britain, Conservative Stanley Baldwin becomes the new Prime Minister of the National Government following the resignation of Ramsay MacDonald due to ill-health.

Date	First performances/ recordings	Other musical	Other cultural	Socio-political
	Walton: Symphony no. 1 Webern: Concerto	The ISCM Festival takes place in Prague; includes music by Schoenberg, Petrassi, Webern, and Maconchy. Schoenberg gives private composition lessons in California as well as lecturing at the University of Southern California. Among his private pupils is John Cage.		
1936	Beecham: recording of Mozart's Symphony no. 39 to magnetic tape Berg: Violin Concerto Formby: 'When I'm Cleaning Windows' Harris: Symphony no. 2 Hindemith: *Funeral Music*	*Pravda* condemns Shostakovich's *Lady Macbeth* as an insult to the Soviet people; Shostakovich withdraws his Fourth Symphony after warnings from officials. Furtwängler is appointed conductor of the New York Philharmonic, but due to huge protests forgoes the position. Barbirolli later takes it up. The Baden-Baden International Music Festival is inaugurated by	Penguin books founded. Chaplin: *Modern Times* Huxley: *Eyeless in Gaza* Mitchell: *Gone With the Wind* Mondrian: *Composition in Red and Blue* De Montherlant: *Les Jeunes Filles* Thomas: *Twenty-Five Poems* Welles: *War of the Worlds* Wright: Kaufman House, Bear Run, Pennsylvania, and office block	Fascist forces under General Franco mount a military challenge to the newly-elected leftist Popular Front government of Manuel Azana, precipitating a civil war in the country. The ferocity and cruelty of the fighting shocks the world as Franco's troops quickly advance towards Madrid, forcing the government to move to Barcelona and then Valencia. In Britain, following the death of George V, Edward VIII is forced to abdicate as a result of his public avowal of love for American divorcee, Wallis Simpson.

	Kreisler: recording of the Beethoven Violin Concerto Prokofiev: *Peter and the Wolf* Rachmaninov: Symphony no. 3 Varèse: *Densité 21.5*	the Nazis to compete with the ISCM Festival. The ISCM Festival is held in Barcelona; includes music by Krenek, Berg, Britten, Bartók, Ruggles, Martin, Berkeley, and Falla. Schoenberg is appointed Professor at the University of California, Los Angeles. A number of young French composers (including Messiaen and Jolivet) write a manifesto opposing neoclassicism. Gibson produce the ES-150, the first successful electric guitar, subsequently used by Charlie Christian and others.		Italy formally annexes Abyssinia after marching victoriously into the capital, Addis Ababa. British premier Anthony Eden and Egyptian Prime Minister Nahas Pasha sign a treaty in Cairo which ends the British protectorate over Egypt. Britain, however, retains control over the Suez Canal.
1937	Basie: 'One O'Clock Jump' Beecham: first recording of Mozart's *Die Zauberflöte* Berg: *Lulu* (unfinished) Goodman: 'Sing, Sing, Sing'	Hindemith publishes *Theoretischer Teil*, the first part of *Unterweisung im Tonsatz*. Prokofiev's *Cantata for the Twentieth Anniversary of the October Revolution* is charged with vulgarity, and not performed until 1966. Toscanini becomes principal conductor of the NBC symphony	The BBC begins its television service – the first regular one of its kind in the world. Auden and Isherwood: *The Ascent of F6* Brecht: *A Penny for the Poor* Giraudoux: *Elektra* Hemingway: *To Have . . . To Have Not* Tolkien: *The Hobbit*	An estimated 59,000 left-wing idealists from all over the world flock to Spain to join the International Brigade, but Franco's forces, aided by Italian and German reinforcements, take Malaga, Bilbao and Guernica, the cultural and spiritual home of the Basque people. Despite its successes in the nation's elections, the anti-British All India Party refuses to form a government under the present constitution, demanding full independence instead.

Date	First performances/ recordings	Other musical	Other cultural	Socio-political
	Orff: *Carmina burana* Rodgers: *Babes In Arms* Shostakovich: Symphony no. 5 Stravinsky: *Jeu de cartes* Szell: recording of Dvořák's Cello Concerto with the Czech Philharmonic and Casals	orchestra with whom he remains until 1954. He makes most of his recordings with this orchestra. Cage writes 'The Future of Music: Credo', arguing for the potential of music made by electronic means. The ISCM Festival is held in Paris and includes music by Honegger, Roussel, Casella, Milhaud, Françaix, Eisler, Maconchy. Deaths of Szymanowski and Gershwin. The first Tanglewood Concerts take place, with Koussevitzky and the Boston Symphony Orchestra.	Steinbeck: *Of Mice and Men* Picasso: *Guernica*, at the Paris World Fair. Orwell: *The Road to Wigan Pier* Renoir: *The Great Illusion* Sartre: *La Nausée* Smith: *A Good Time Was Had By All*	Japanese aircraft bombard Shanghai, taking the civilian toll in the territorial war between the Japanese and Chinese nationalist forces to over 2,000. Thirteen high-ranking Communist Party officials are sentenced to death during show trials in the Soviet Union. Stalin denounces the prisoners as 'Trotskyites'.
1938	Barber: *Adagio for Strings* (orchestral version) Basie: 'Jumpin' at the Woodside' Britten: Piano Concerto Fitzgerald: 'A-tisket A-tasket'	Nazi 'Entartete Musik' exhibition in Düsseldorf. Hindemith leaves Germany. The ISCM Festival is held in London and includes music by Berkeley, Webern, Britten, Krenek, Bartók, Messiaen, Copland, and Hindemith.	Anouilh: *Le voyageur sans bagage* Cocteau: *Les parents terribles* Dufy: *Regatta* Eisenstein: *Alexander Nevsky* Greene: *Brighton Rock* Picasso: *Woman in Easy Chair* Rouault: *Ecce Homo*	Austria and part of Czechoslovakia are annexed by Germany, but other European nations are reluctant to go to war; British Prime Minister Neville Chamberlain returns home having signed an agreement with Adolf Hitler, declaring 'I believe it is peace for our time.' Jewish shops

	Hindemith: *Mathis der Maler* Krenek: Piano Concerto no. 2 Piston: Symphony no. 1 Prokofiev: Cello Concerto Stravinsky: *Dumbarton Oaks* Walter: recording of Mahler's Symphony no. 9 with the Vienna Philharmonic Webern: *Das Augenlicht*	The Benny Goodman band perform at Carnegie Hall in a concert which is recorded and later released. John Hammond stages a 'From Spirituals to Swing' concert at Carnegie Hall, showcasing famous jazz performers representing a variety of different styles. The music of Berg is proscribed by the Nazi regime.	Disney: *Snow White and the Seven Dwarfs* Valéry: *Degas, Danse, Dessein*	and businesses are smashed on *Kristallnacht* (Crystal Night), so called after the broken glass which surrounds the wreckage. Franco's troops win a series of decisive victories in the Spanish Civil War. Britain postpones the partition of Palestine as fierce fighting continues between Jews and Arabs.
1939	Bartók: *Contrasts* Cage: *First Construction (in Metal)*, *Imaginary Landscape no. 1* (includes two variable speed turntables) Copland: Sextet for piano, clarinet, and string quartet Garland: 'Over The Rainbow' Harris: Symphony no. 3 Ives: 'Concord' Sonata Lutosławski: *Variations Symphoniques* Shostakovich: Symphony no. 6 Walton: Violin Concerto	Duke Ellington hires composer and arranger Billy Strayhorn. The ISCM Festival takes place in Warsaw (in April, before the German invasion) and includes music by Poulenc, Szymanowksi, Lutyens, and Webern. In the United States, Broadcast Music Incorporated (BMI) enters into competition with ASCAP. Radio stations ban the broadcast of music represented by ASCAP. Stravinsky moves to New York. The United States Supreme Court rules that radio stations can play music records. Alfred Lion establishes the Blue Note record label. Paderewski gives his first broadcast concert in New York.	Fleming: *Gone With The Wind*, *Goodbye Mr Chips* Joyce: *Finnegans Wake* Mann: *Lotte in Weimar* Picasso: *Night Fishing at Antibes* Renoir: *The Rules of the Game* *Stagecoach* (with John Wayne) Steinbeck: *The Grapes of Wrath* *The Wizard of Oz*	The world is once again at war following Germany's invasion of Poland. Britain had pledged to safeguard Poland's sovereignty and now finds itself forced to honour that pledge. Germany has the firm backing of Italy's dictator, Mussolini, who signs the 'Pact of Steel' with Hitler in May, but more surprisingly it also gains the tacit support of the Soviet Union when Stalin signs a non-aggression pact. Britain is placed on a war footing and Winston Churchill is again at the centre of government as First Lord of the Admiralty, a post he first held 25 years previously. The Spanish Civil War ends with Franco's Nationalist forces victorious.

Date	First performances/ recordings	Other musical	Other cultural	Socio-political
1940	Britten: *Les illuminations* Copland: *Billy the Kid* Ellington: ‘Concerto for Cootie’ Hindemith: Violin Concerto Martinů: Double Concerto Milhaud: *Le cortège funebre*, Symphony no. 1 Piston: Violin Concerto Rodrigo: *Concierto de Aranjuez* Schoenberg: Violin Concerto (1936), Chamber Symphony no. 2 Sessions: Violin Concerto Strauss: *Guntram* (1894, revised) Stravinsky: *Symphony in C* Toscanini: recording of Beethoven’s Violin Concerto with Heifetz Villa-Lobos: *Magdalena*	Hindemith publishes the second revised edition of *Unterweisung im Tonsatz*. Frank Sinatra joins the Tommy Dorsey band. In Britain, the *Music Review* is published. Record sales in the US reach 100 million. Paderewski arrives in New York.	BBC Radio Newsreel begins. Ayer: *The Foundations of Empirical Knowledge* Disney: *Fantasia* (soundtrack conducted by Stokowski) Chaplin: *The Great Dictator* Greene: *The Power and the Glory* Hemingway: *For Whom the Bell Tolls* Jung: *The Interpretation of Personality* Kandinsky: *Blue Sky* Kostler: *Darkness at Noon* Matisse: *Rumanian Blouse The Sea Hawk* (score by Korngold) Thomas: *Portrait of the Artist as a Young Dog*	In Europe, country after country falls to the German *Blitzkrieg* (‘lightning war’). By the end of the year, Norway, Denmark, Holland, and Belgium are all in German hands and, perhaps most damagingly, France follows suit, precipitating the emergency evacuation of embattled British troops from Dunkirk. German bombers begin pounding London, killing over 7,000 in the first three weeks. British merchant shipping also comes under heavy bombardment, with 235,000 tons having been lost by October. At home, the British people face rationing for the first time since 1918. Trotsky is killed by a Soviet agent who plunges an ice pick through his skull in Mexico City. In the United States, Roosevelt is re-elected for a third term as President, but denies that he is preparing to take the country into the war.

Year	Music	Musical events	Arts and literature	History
1941	Barber: Violin Concerto Britten: *Sinfonia da Requiem*, *Paul Bunyan* Copland: *Quiet City* Hindemith: Cello Concerto Kittel: recording of Bach's *St Matthew Passion* for Deutsche Grammophon. Martinů: *Concerto Grosso* Messiaen: *Quatuor pour la fin du temps* Poulenc: Concerto for organ, timpani, and strings Stravinsky: *Tango* Tchaikovsky: *1812 Overture* Weill: *Lady in the Dark*	Schoenberg writes *Composition with Twelve Tones* Joseph Schillinger writes *The Schillinger System of Musical Composition*. The ISCM Festival moves to New York, and is broadcast by CBS. It includes music by Britten, Leibowitz, Webern, Martinů, and Copland. Walter conducts his first opera in the US. The Queen's Hall in London is bombed.	Brecht: *Mother Courage and her Children* Coward: *Blithe Spirit* Ehrenberg: *The Fall of Paris* Fitzgerald: *The Last Tycoon 49th Parallel* Léger: *Divers against a Yellow Background* Welles: *Citizen Kane* Wilson: *To the Finland Station*	The United States enters the war following the bombing of its Pacific Fleet at Pearl Harbor in Hawaii by Japanese forces. In Europe, the Nazis break their uneasy pact with the Soviet Union and invade Russia, reaching Minsk, halfway to Moscow, in a few days and forcing Stalin to plead for British support. Hitler is impatient to enter the Russian capital, but as the Russian winter begins to bite, the Soviet forces first consolidate and then begin to make ground against the Germans. In Africa, General Erwin Rommel's Afrika Corps advance through Libya in a bid to relieve Mussolini's forces which have suffered a series of defeats against the British.
1942	Bartók: Concerto for Two Pianos, Percussion, and Orchestra Bernstein: Sonata for Clarinet and Piano Cage: *Imaginary Landscape no. 3* Copland: *Statements for Orchestra* Crosby: 'White Christmas' Honegger: Symphony no. 2 Shostakovich: Symphony no. 7 Strauss: *Capriccio* Stravinsky: *Danses concertantes*	The music department of the Bibliothèque Nationale in Paris is established. The ISCM Festival takes place in Berkeley, California, and includes music by Bartók, Schoenberg, Bloch, Britten, and Hindemith. The American Federation of Musicians announces a ban on recording, in an attempt to secure better conditions for professional musicians. Death of Weingartner.	Bonnard: *L'oiseau bleu* Camus: *L'etranger* Eliot: *Little Gidding* *Flare Path* *Holiday Inn* (with Bing Crosby) *How Green Was My Valley* Lewis: *The Screwtape Letters* Steinbeck: *The Moon is Down*	The Nazi leadership admits that its 'final solution' to the 'Jewish problem' is the extermination of the estimated 11 million Jews. Over 700,000 Jews are murdered in Poland alone. Russian troops counter-attack at Stalingrad and kill or capture as many as 77,000 enemy soldiers. Allied troops under General Bernard Montgomery break through Rommel's Afrika Corps at El Alamein in Egypt, sending the Axis forces into full retreat. British RAF bombers begin a massive campaign of destruction on German cities under the leadership of Air Marshal Sir Arthur 'Bomber' Harris. The Japanese continue their advance in Malaya and quickly take the island fortress of Singapore.

Date	First performances/ recordings	Other musical	Other cultural	Socio-political
1943	Berkeley: Symphony no. 1 Britten: *Serenade for Tenor, Horn and Strings* Copland: *El salon México*, *Fanfare for the Common Man*, *Rodeo* Harris: Symphony no. 5 Messiaen: *Visions de l'amen* Prokofiev: *1941* Rodgers and Hammerstein: *Oklahoma* Shostakovich: Symphony no. 8 Strauss: Horn Concerto no. 2 Webern: Variations for Orchestra	Tippett, a conscientious objector, is jailed for refusing to accept the terms of his registration. Death of Rachmaninov. Columbia sign a contract with Frank Sinatra. Leonard Bernstein makes a spectacular debut conducting the New York Philharmonic when Bruno Walter falls ill. Rodzinski becomes music director of the New York Philharmonic.	Adam: *Reclining Figure* Coward: *This Happy Breed* *The Gentler Sex* Michaux: *Exorcismes* Molinari: *Mundos de la Madrugada* Mondrian: *Broadway Boogie-Woogie* Moore: *Madonna and Child* Sarte: *Being and Nothingness*	The German withdrawal from the Caucasus begins with the surrender of Stalingrad, and the Russians quickly take Kursk, Rostov, Kharkov, and Smolensk. General Dwight D. Eisenhower takes supreme control of Allied forces in North Africa as British and US troops link up. The German army in Tunisia surrenders. Following the first Allied bombing raids on Rome, Mussolini is deposed as King Victor Emmanuel takes control of Italian forces and Italy surrenders shortly after. In a final *volte face*, Italy declares war on Germany. The Japanese are driven from Guadalcanal in the Pacific by US forces and later defeated in New Guinea. At a historic conference in Tehran, Churchill, Roosevelt, and Stalin meet for the first time to plan the final defeat of Germany and to sign a declaration ensuring a post-war world free from tyranny.
1944	Barber: Symphony no. 2 Bartók: Concerto for Orchestra Bernstein: Symphony no. 1, *Fancy Free* Carter: Symphony no. 1 Copland: *Appalachian Spring* (original version)	Messiaen publishes *Technique de mon langage musical* Messiaen's composition class in Paris includes Pierre Boulez. Promoter Norman Granz starts a concert series called 'Jazz at the Philharmonic', which employs a jam session format.	Bates: *Fair Stood the Wind for France* Beckman: *Self-Portrait* Eliot: *Four Quartets Henry V* (Olivier) Jung: *Psychology and Religion* Moravia: *Agostino* Rattigan: *Love in Idleness*	The Allies continue to push back the enemy lines across the whole theatre of war. Having broken the siege of Leningrad, the Red Army forces the Germans further from the heart of Russia as they sweep through the Crimea; British and US troops launch the Allied invasion of Europe on 'D-Day', 6 June, quickly pushing back the Germans from Normandy and eventually liberating Paris.

	Ferrier makes her first recordings for Columbia Hindemith: *Ludus Tonalis* Partch: *US Highball* Schoenberg: Piano Concerto Stravinsky: *Four Hungarian Moods* Tippett: *A Child of our Time*	Death of Sir Henry Wood. The Vienna Opera is destroyed in an Allied air raid.	Sartre: *Huis clos* Williams: *The Glass Menagerie*	In the air war, the Allies continue their destructive and demoralizing bombardment of German cities. The first conclusive proof of Nazi extermination of Jews is found in the Maidenek concentration camp in liberated Poland, where an estimated 1.5 million have been gassed and burnt.
1945	Britten: *Peter Grimes* Copland: *Appalachian Spring* (symphonic version) Messiaen: *Trois petites liturgies* Prokofiev: Symphony no. 5, *Cinderella* Rodgers and Hammerstein: *Carousel* Schuller: Concerto for Horn and Orchestra Shostakovich: Symphony no. 9 Stravinsky: *Scènes de ballet* Villa-Lobos: *Choros* no. 12	After René Leibowitz conducts Schoenberg's Wind Quintet in Paris, a number of student composers 'discover' dodecaphonic techniques. Deaths of Webern, accidentally shot by a US soldier, and Bartók. First Annual Festival of Contemporary American Music opens at Columbia University and includes music by Brant and Piston. Columbia begins developing the LP.	Buber: *For the Sake of Heaven* Eisenstein: *Ivan the Terrible* Jouve: *La vierge de Paris* Levi: *Christ Stopped at Eboli* Moore: *Family Group* Orwell: *Animal Farm* Popper: *The Open Society and Its Enemies* Renoir: *The Man from the South* Sartre: *The Age of Reason* Waugh: *Brideshead Revisited* Wilder: *The Lost Weekend*	Hitler commits suicide. The war in Europe ends on 7 May when Army Chief of Staff Alfred Jodl signs a statement of unconditional surrender at Allied HQ in Rheims. The global war finishes with the dropping of atomic bombs on Hiroshima and Nagasaki in Japan. As many as 70,000 die in the blasts, and countless more from radiation sickness. The surviving leaders of Nazi Germany (including Goering and Hess) are put on trial in Nuremberg for crimes against humanity. The evidence centres on the discovery by the liberating Allies of unimaginable horrors in Nazi concentration camps at Auschwitz, Buchenwald, Belsen, and elsewhere. The United Nations, a pan-national body dedicated to preserving world peace, is formed when delegates from 50 states sign the World Security Charter in the US.

Date	First performances/ recordings	Other musical	Other cultural	Socio-political
1946	Bartók: Piano Concerto no. 3 Boulez: *Le visage nuptial* (revised in 1989) Britten: *The Rape of Lucretia* Copland: Symphony no. 3 Ives: *Central Park in the Dark* (1906), Symphony no. 3 Karajan: recording of Beethoven's Eighth Symphony for EMI Parker: 'A Night in Tunisia', 'Ornithology' (Dial) Prokofiev: *War and Peace* Strauss: *Metamorphosen* Stravinsky: *Ebony Concerto*, *Symphony in Three Movements* Webern: Cantata No. 1	Darmstadt begins holding International Summer Courses in New Music, largely at the instigation of musician and critic Wolfgang Steinecke. Schoenberg is named honorary president of the ISCM. The ISCM resumes its annual festival in London, and includes music by Lutyens, Prokofiev, Stravinsky, Hindemith, Messiaen, Schoenberg, and Krenek. La Scala in Milan reopens after the bombing in 1943, with Toscanini conducting. Establishment of the Welsh National Opera.	BBC Third Programme inaugurated De Beauvoir: *Tous les hommes sont mortels* Capra: *It's a Wonderful World* Cocteau: *L'aigle à deux têtes* Hersey: *Hiroshima* Hitchcock: *Notorious* Lean: *Great Expectations* O'Neill: *The Iceman Cometh* Rossellini: *Paisa* Russell: *History of Western Philosophy* Sartre: *Morts sans sépultre* Warren: *All the King's Men*	The Nuremberg trials ends with Goering and 10 other prominent Nazis sentenced to death and Hess to life imprisonment. The United Nations General Assembly meets for the first time in New York, barring Spain from its activities and rejecting South Africa's proposal to annexe South West Africa. A joint Anglo-American report on Palestine recommends that the British mandate should continue 'until Arab-Jewish hostility disappears'. The result is renewed violence in the Middle East, including the bombing by Zionist guerrillas of the British HQ in Jerusalem. In Japan, power is transferred from the Emperor to a directly elected assembly. General Juan Perón is installed as President of Argentina.
1947	Babbitt: *Three Compositions for Piano* Cage: *The Seasons* Hindemith: Concerto for piano and orchestra Krenek: Symphony no. 4 Milhaud: Symphony no. 3 Prokofiev: Symphony no. 6	Atlantic records founded by Ahmet and Nesuhi Ertegun. Ives is awarded the Pulitzer Prize for his Third Symphony. The ISCM Festival takes place in Copenhagen and includes music by Copland, Prokofiev, Bloch, Jolivet, Martin, and Gerhard.	Discovery of the main series of Dead Sea Scrolls. Edinburgh Festival established. Camus: *The Plague* Clair: *Le Silence est d'or* Clouzot: *Quai des Orfèvres* Giacometti: *Man Pointing*	163 years of British rule in India are ended with independence on the lines of a plan drawn up by Lord Mountbatten and agreed by all sides. Under the plan, India is partitioned into two states, recognizing the demands of Muslims for a homeland of their own. However, violence between Muslims and Hindus continues, with 1,200 Muslims killed on a train on the Punjab border.

	Sessions: *The Trial of Luculus* Stravinsky: *Concerto in D* Weill: *Street Scene*	Deaths of Russolo and Casella. Rodzinski leaves the New York Philharmonic for the Chicago Symphony. The Vienna Philharmonic comes into being when the Philharmonische Akademie changes its name.	Moore: *Three Standing Figures* Le Corbusier: Unité d'habitation, Marseilles Levi: *If This is a Man* Priestley: *The Linden Tree* Reed: *Odd Man Out* Williams: *A Streetcar Named Desire*	The US Secretary of State George Marshall announces a huge aid plan for Europe to safeguard against the post-war slump and the threat of Communism. The US Secretary of State George Marshall announces a huge aid plan for Europe to safeguard against the post-war slump and the threat of Communism.
1948	Boulez: *Le soleil des eaux* (revised 1959, 1968), Sonatina for Flute and Piano Cage: *Sonatas and Interludes* Hooker: 'Boogie Chillun' Lutosławski: Symphony no. 1 Milhaud: Symphony no. 4 Parker: 'Parker's Mood' Piston: Symphony no. 3 Porter: *Kiss Me Kate* Schaeffer: *Etudes aux chemin de fer* (tape; the first piece of *musique concrète*) Schoenberg: *A Survivor from Warsaw* Strauss: *Four Last Songs* Stravinsky: Mass	Columbia begins marketing the 33rpm LP. The Central Committee of the Communist Party of the USSR issues a resolution condemning 'decadent formalism', specifically referring to Shostakovich, Prokofiev, and Khachaturian. Hermann Scherchen arrives to teach a course at the conservatory in Venice: pupils include Maderna and Nono. The NBC symphony orchestra make their first live television broadcast under Toscanini. The ISCM Festival is held in Amsterdam; includes music by Sessions, Koechlin, Piston, Lutyens, and Glanville-Hicks.	Fry: *The Lady's Not for Burning* Greene: *The Heart of the Matter* Kawabata: *Snow Country* Mailer: *The Naked and the Dead* Moore: *Family Group* Olivier: *Hamlet* Paton: *Cry the Beloved Country* Pollock: *Composition no. I* Rattigan: *The Browning Version*	The world's Jews now have their own homeland as the state of Israel is born of a divided Palestine. Under the new Prime Minister, David ben-Gurion, the new country opens its doors to all Jewish immigrants. Relations between East and West deteriorate as delegates from the USSR walk out of the Allied Control Council claiming they have been excluded from secret talks about Germany's future. The US start a communist witch-hunt with the formation of the House of Representatives' Un-American Activities Committee. The march of world communism is swift, however, with a coup d'état in Czechoslovakia; the redrawing of the Romanian constitution along Soviet lines; and the announcement of the formation of the Democratic People's Republic of Korea.

Date	First performances/ recordings	Other musical	Other cultural	Socio-political
		Schoenberg protests to Thomas Mann about the reference to his twelve-tone method in *Doktor Faustus*. Piston is awarded the Pulitzer Prize for his Symphony no. 3.		
1949	Antheil: Symphony no. 6 Bartók: Viola Concerto (unfinished, completed by Serly) Bernstein: Symphony no. 2 ('The Age of Anxiety') Britten: *Spring Symphony* Cowell: Symphony no. 5 Messiaen: *Turangalîla-symphonie* Orff: *Antigone* Rodgers and Hammerstein: *South Pacific* Shostakovich: *Song of the Forests*	John Cage visits Paris. He performs for Messiaen's composition class, as well as at a private gathering organised by Pierre Boulez. The First Congress of Dodecaphonic Music is held in Milan and includes music by Schoenberg, Krenek, Riegger, and Hauer. The ISCM Festival is held in Palermo, Sicily; includes music by Szymanowski, Dutilleux, Eisler, Casella, Lutyens, Berkeley, Petrassi, and Maderna. Bob Weinstock establishes the Prestige record label. RCA introduce the 7-inch 45rpm disc. Mitropoulos and Stokowski are jointly appointed principal conductor of the New York Philharmonic. Deaths of Strauss and Pfitzner. Partch publishes *Genesis of a Music*.	Bates: *The Jacaranda Tree* De Beauvoir: *The Second Sex* Eluard: *Une leçon de morale* Fromm: *Man for Himself* *Les enfants terribles* Mitford: *Love in a Cold Climate* Orwell: *1984* Reed: *The Third Man*	The communist People's Republic of China is proclaimed, with Mao Tse-tung as Chairman and Chou En-lai as Prime Minister. In Europe communism is consolidated with the creation by Stalin of the German Democratic Republic in the east of the country to counter the newly formed Federal Republic of Germany in the west. Eight Western countries, including Britain, form the North Atlantic Treaty Organization (NATO). The alliance is designed to act as a deterrent against aggression from the Eastern Bloc. In Britain, the Ireland Bill recognizes Eire as a republic, ending its dominion status but reaffirming the position of Northern Ireland as part of the United Kingdom.

1950	Berlin: *Call Me Madam* Boulez: Piano Sonata no. 2 (first US performance, by Tudor) Canetelli: recording of Tchaikovsky's Fifth Symphony for HMV Copland: Clarinet Concerto (premiered by Goodman) Hindemith: Clarinet Concerto Messiaen: *Mode de valeurs et d'intensités* Milhaud: *Bolívar*Petrassi: *La morte dell'aria* Poulenc: Piano Concerto Schaeffer: *Symphonie pour un homme seul* (first extended piece of electronic music) Strauss: *Four Last Songs* (posth.) Toscanini: recording of Verdi's *Falstaff* Webern: *Second Cantata*	*Musica Britannica* launched. Heinrich Strobel takes responsibility for the Donaueschingen festival, making it a major annual event in the contemporary music world. The ISCM Festival is held in Brussels; includes music by Eisler, Rawsthorne, Webern, Goeyvaerts, Leibowitz, Jolivet, and Milhaud. Death of Weill. Shostakovich is awarded the Stalin Prize for *Song of the Forests*. Decca issues its first LPs.	Chagall: *King David* Cocteau: *Orphée* Ford: *Rio Grande* Giacometti: *Seven Figures and a Head* Heyerdahl: *Kon Tiki* Kurasawa: *Rashomon* Neruda: *General Song* Picasso: *The Goat* Pound: *Seventy Cantos* Wilder: *Sunset Boulevard*	British and American troops, under UN auspices, are embroiled in a major conflict when communist North Korea invades the South. After initial successes they are forced into a speedy retreat when China enters the war to aid its communist neighbours. Vietnam is also effectively partitioned into two nations after Britain and the US recognize the claim of Emperor Bao Dai, who is based in the south. King Abdullah of Jordan significantly expands his kingdom when he annexes Arab Palestine. King Farouk of Egypt calls for the 'total and immediate' withdrawal of British troops from the Suez Canal Zone.

Date	First performances/ recordings	Other musical	Other cultural	Socio-political
1951	Boulez: *Structures 1A*, *Etude sur un son* (tape: composed at the French Radio Studios) Britten: *Billy Budd* Cage: *Music of Changes*, *Imaginary Landscape no. 4* (for 12 radio receivers, composed using chance operations) Fischer-Dieskau: recording of Beethoven's *An die ferne Geliebte* Françaix: *L'apostrophe* Ives: Symphony no. 2 Jolivet: Piano Concerto Lutosławski: *Petite Suite* Partch: *Oedipus* Poulenc: *Stabat Mater* Rodgers and Hammerstein: *The King and I* Stravinsky: *The Rake's Progress*	French Radio establish Groupe de Musique Concrète Cage studies Zen philosophy with Daisetz Suzuki at Columbia University, New York. Stefan Kudelski builds the first Nagra portable, self-contained tape recorder. At the Darmstadt Summer School, Karlheinz Stockhausen and other students (including Goeyvaerts) encounter Messiaen's *Mode de valeurs et d'intensités*. The ISCM Festival is held in Frankfurt; includes music by Orff, Koechlin, Messiaen, Ginastera, Henze, Hindemith, and Krenek. Deaths of Schoenberg, Mengelberg, and Koussevitsky.	The Festival of Britain takes place. Designers and architects, led by Hugh Casson, design an environment comprising a huge 'Dome of Discovery', a new Royal Festival Hall, and several fun-fairs, treewalks and open air exhibitions. Asimov: *I, Robot* Dali: *Christ of St John on the Cross* Frost: *Complete Poems* Hitchcock: *Strangers on a Train* Huston: *The African Queen* Salinger: *The Catcher in the Rye* Sutherland: *Lord Beaverbrook*	Following fluctuating fortunes in the Korean War, the two sides agree to a tense ceasefire, re-establishing the pre-war truce line at the 38th parallel. In Vietnam, the old colonial power, France, retakes Hanoi from the communist Viet Minh, but in response the communists launch a major offensive at Tonkin. The nuclear arms race has well and truly begun. The United States launches the first successful test of a hydrogen bomb on Eniwok Atoll in the mid-Pacific. In turn, the USSR launches the second test of its own nuclear weapon. British troops launch a dawn raid to secure key points on the Suez Canal following the breakdown of negotiations with Egypt. The Egyptian government declares a state of emergency, and British service families are evacuated from the Canal Zone.

1952	Cage: *4′33″*, *Water Music* Cowell: Symphony no. 7 Hindemith: *Cardillac* Maderna: *Musica su due dimensioni* Partch: *Oedipus* Prokofiev: *Symphony Concertante* Stockhausen: *Kreuzspiel*, *Etüde* (tape) Stravinsky: *Cantata* Toscanini: recording of Beethoven's Symphony no. 9, made at Carnegie Hall Walter: recording of Mahler's *Das Lied von der Erde*, with the Vienna Philharmonic and Ferrier	Stockhausen goes to Paris in order to study with Messiaen. Herbert Eimert founds the Cologne station of the Nordwestdeutscher Rundfunk: he is then joined by Stockhausen. Boulez visits the Darmstadt Summer School where he introduces his *Etudes* (tape); Yvonne Loriod performs his Second Piano Sonata. Ray Charles is signed by Atlantic records. The Metropolitan Opera in New York broadcasts *Carmen* to movie houses in 27 American cities. The ISCM Festival takes place in Salzburg; includes music by Pousseur and Zimmermann. The New Musical Express create the 'Hit Parade'. Otto Luening and Vladimir Ussachevsky present the first American concert of electronic music at the Museum of Modern Art in New York.	Christie: *The Mousetrap* Epstein: *Madonna and Child* Ford: *The Quiet Man* Hemingway: *The Old Man and the Sea* Huston: *Moulin Rouge* Leavis: *The Common Pursuit* Pollock: *Convergence* Steinbeck: *East of Eden* Thomas: *Collected Poems*	The crisis over the Suez Canal Zone forces a series of domestic political upheavals in Egypt. Having dismissed the government of Ali Maher Pasher and suspended parliament, King Farouk is himself forced to abdicate in favour of his son, Faud, as General Mohammed Neguib seizes power. South Africa faces a constitutional crisis when its hard-line Prime Minister, Dr D. F. Malan, confirms that the new race laws will stand despite the ruling of the country's Supreme Court that they are invalid. War hero General Dwight D. Eisenhower sweeps to victory in the US Presidential election, beating Adlai Stevenson with the largest-ever popular vote. His first action as President-elect is to hold talks with General Douglas MacArthur on finally ending the war in Korea.

Date	First performances/ recordings	Other musical	Other cultural	Socio-political
1953	Bernstein: *Wonderful Town* Britten: *Gloriana* Cowell: Symphony no. 8 Kabalevsky: Piano Concerto no. 3 Krenek: *Medea* for contralto and orchestra. Martinů: *The Marriage* Shostakovich: Symphony no. 10 Stockhausen: *Kontra-Punkte*, *Studie I* (tape) Vaughan Williams: Symphony no. 7 (*Sinfonia antartica*)	Sam Phillips founds Sun Records in Memphis. Bill Grauer and Orrin Keepnews establish the Riverside record label. Stockhausen returns to Cologne to work at the WDR radio studios. Death of Prokofiev. The ISCM Festival is held in Oslo; includes music by Schoenberg, Babbitt, Ginastera, Goeyvaerts, and Henze.	Experimental colour TV broadcasts are made in the US. Faulkner: *Requiem for a Nun* Fellini: *I Vitelloni* Greene: *The Living Room* Hepworth: *Monolith Empyrean* Koster: *The Robe* (first film in 'Cinemascope') Miller: *The Crucible* Moore: *King and Queen* Nicholson: *September 1953* Zinnemann: *From Here to Eternity*	Russian dictator Joseph Stalin dies of a brain haemorrhage. Russian tanks move into East Berlin to crush an anti-Soviet uprising by German workers. Queen Elizabeth II of Great Britain is crowned in Westminster Abbey, London. Her televised coronation is watched by millions all over the world. Julius and Ethel Roseberg are found guilty of passing American atomic secrets to the Russians, and become the first married couple to be executed in the US. Egypt's infant King Faud is deposed by Egypt's army leaders, who declare the nation a republic.

1954

Britten: *The Turn of the Screw*
Cage: *34′46.776″*, *Williams Mix*
Charles: 'I Got A Woman'
Copland: *The Tender Land*
Eimert: *Glockenspiel*
Karajan: recording of Mozart's Horn Concertos with Brain
Lutosławski: Concerto for Orchestra
Nono: *La victoire de Guernica*
Pousseur: *Seismogramme*
Schoenberg: *Moses und Aron* (unfinished)
Stockhausen: *Studie II* (tape)
Stravinsky: *Septet*, *In Memoriam Dylan Thomas*
Varèse: *Déserts*
Xenakis: *Metastasis*

Boulez founds the Domaine Musical in Paris, dedicated to the promotion and performance of contemporary music.
Cage and pianist David Tudor undertake a European tour, with performances in Britain, France, and Germany.
RCA Victor sell the first pre-recorded open reel stereo tapes for $12.95
Toscanini makes his last public appearance.
The ISCM Festival is held in Haifa, Israel; includes music by Villa-Lobos, Milhaud, Sessions, Vaughan Williams, and Kirchner.
Deaths of Ives and Furtwängler.

Amis: *Lucky Jim*
Bellow: *The Adventures of Augie March*
Fellini: *La strada*
Frisch: *I'm Not Stiller*
Golding: *Lord of the Flies*
Hepworth: *Two Figures*, *Menhirs*
Hitchcock: *Rear Window*
Picasso: *Sylvette*
Sagan: *Bonjour Tristesse*
Thomas: *Under Milk Wood*
White Christmas
Williams: *Cat on a Hot Tin Roof*

A peace deal is reached under which France agrees to withdraw from North Vietnam in return for a communist evacuation of the south of the co:intry, as well as Laos and Cambodia. However, France's colonial troubles are far from over, as she is forced to send 20,000 troops to quell rioting and violence in Algeria.
In Egypt, Gamal Abdel Nasser becomes head of state following his ousting of President Mohammed Neguib. He is hugely popular with Egyptians, not least because of his success in signing an Anglo-Egyptian agreement for the withdrawal of British troops from the troubled Suez Canal Zone.
Britain's Roger Bannister becomes the first man to run a mile in under four minutes, at the Oxfcrd University Iffley Road track.

Date	First performances/ recordings	Other musical	Other cultural	Socio-political
1955	Boulez: *Le marteau sans maître* Floyd: *Susannah* Haley: ‘Rock Around the Clock’ Klemperer: recording of Beethoven Symphonies nos. 3, 5, and 7, with the Philharmonia Orchestra Messiaen: *Livre d’orgue* Milhaud: Symphony no. 6 Nono: *Incontri* Prokofiev: *War and Peace* Shostakovich: Violin Concerto Sinatra: *In The Wee Small Hours* Stravinsky: *Four Russian Songs* Tippett: *The Midsummer Marriage*	First issue of *die reihe* appears. Theodor Adorno gives an address at Darmstadt critical of composition based on systems (‘The Ageing of the New’). Xenakis writes ‘La crise de la musique sérielle’ Death of bebop saxophonist Charlie Parker. Invention of the RCA Electronic Music Synthesizer, using filtered sawtooth waves, programmed with paper tape. Berio and Maderna set up an electronic studio at Radio Audizione Italienne in Milan. The ISCM Festival is held in Baden-Baden; includes music by Boulez, Blacher, Henze, Schoenberg, Carter, and Gerhard. Fischer-Dieskau makes his US debut in New York. The Berlin Philharmonic make their US debut in Washington under Karajan.	Baldwin: *Notes of a Native Son* Beckett: *Waiting for Godot* Bergman: *Smiles of a Summer Night* Dali: *The Lord’s Supper* *The Diary of Anne Frank* Greene: *The Quiet American* Johns: *White Flay* Kokoschka: *Thermopylae* Marcuse: *Eros and Civilization* Miller: *A View from the Bridge* Nabakov: *Lolita* Rauschenberg: *Odalisk* Tolkien: *Lord of the Rings*	Following the withdrawal of the Allied High Commission in Berlin, West Germany becomes a sovereign state for the first time since the end of the war 10 years ago. Austria also regains her independence. Nikita Kruschev assumes control of the USSR and creates the Warsaw Pact, forming all the Eastern Bloc nations into a single military alliance. In Britain, Winston Churchill steps down as Prime Minister and finally bows out of British politics after more than 50 years. He is succeeded by Sir Anthony Eden. In the southern US, thousands of blacks boycott City Line Buses in Montgomery, Alabama, after a driver refuses to continue his journey with a black woman, Rosa Parks, seated in the whites-only area at the front of the bus. Mrs. Parks is fined $14 under state segregation laws.

1956	Barraqué: *Sequences* Berio: *Perspectives* Bernstein: *Candide* Carter: *Variations for Orchestra* Goeyvaerts: *Composition no. 6 aux objects sonores* Gould: recording of Bach's *Goldberg Variations* Little Richard: 'Tutti Frutti' Loewe: *My Fair Lady* Nono: *Il canto sospeso* Presley: 'Heartbreak Hotel' Prokofiev: Piano Concerto no. 4 (1931) Stockhausen: *Gesang der Jünglinge* Stravinsky: *Canticum sacrum* Vaughan Williams: Symphony no. 8 Xenakis: *Pithoprakta*	Elvis Presley's *Heartbreak Hotel* goes to No. 1 in the US. He makes a now-famous appearance on the Ed Sullivan television show, performing 'Hound Dog'. Boulez, Stockhausen, and Nono lecture at the Darmstadt Summer School. Louis and Bebe Barron produce the first electronic music score for a commercial film, *Forbidden Planet*. In Britain the Musicians Union ends its ban on American musicians. The ISCM Festival is held in Stockholm; includes music by Honegger, Stockhausen, and Ginastera. The First International Festival of Contemporary Music in Warsaw includes music by Stravinsky, Schoenberg, Berg, Bartók, Szymanowski, Ravel, and Britten. A concert of electronic music in Cologne includes works by Eimert, Koenig, Stockhausen, and Krenek. Karajan becomes director of the Vienna State Opera and the Salzburg Festival.	Ayer: *The Revolution in Philosophy* Bergman: *The Seventh Seal* Ginsberg: *Howl* Hepworth: *Orpheus* Lang: *The King and I* Mannheim: *Essays on the Sociology of Culture* Osborne: *Look Back in Anger* Walters: *High Society* (starring Bing Crosby, and featuring appearances from Louis Armstrong) Wilson: *The Outsider*	In a speech to the Soviet Communist Party elite, Khrushchev makes the first explicit criticism of the father of the Soviet Union, Joseph Stalin. In Hungary, an estimated 1,000 Soviet tanks and countless troops brutally crush an uprising, killing as many as 3,000 unarmed citizens and causing more than 100,000 to flee their homeland. The situation in the divided British protectorate of Cyprus deteriorates, with Britain sending more troops to the island to quell rioting and violence. Britain is again embroiled in a major military conflict when Egyptian leader, Colonel Nasser, seizes and nationalizes the Suez Canal, a vital supply route for Europe's oil supplies and symbol of independence for the nationalistic Nasser administration. The UN, under pressure from the US, imposes a ceasefire and demands the withdrawal of British forces, to be replaced by its own.

Date	First performances/ recordings	Other musical	Other cultural	Socio-political
1957	Babbitt: *Partitions* (composed) Berio: *Allelujah II*, *Serenata 1* (composed) Bernstein: *West Side Story* Boulez: Piano Sonata no. 3 (composed) Britten: *The Prince of the Pagodas* Cooke: 'You Send Me' Copland: Fantasy for piano Hindemith: *Die Harmonie der Welt* Partch: *The Bewitched* Pousseur: *Scambi* (tape) Shostakovich: Piano Concerto Sinatra: *A Swinging Affair* Stockhausen: *Klavierstück* XI Stravinsky: *Agon* Walton: Cello Concerto	Founding of the *Journal of Music Theory* (Yale University). Stravinsky hears Boulez conduct a performance of *Le marteau* in Los Angeles and hails it as a 'masterpiece'. Stockhausen writes '. . . how time passes . . .' Electronic studios are established in Warsaw (Polish Radio), Munich (Siemens), and Eindhoven (Philips). The ISCM is held in Zürich; includes music by Maderna, Pousseur, Berio, Prokofiev, Webern, Celementi, Bartók, Henze, and Hindemith. Deaths of Sibelius and Toscanini. Barenboim makes his US debut in New York.	Sony market what is usually credited as the first pocket-sized radio. Bacon: *Screaming Nurse* Barthes: *Mythologies* Beckett: *Endgame* Bergman: *Wild Strawberries* Braine: *Room at the Top* Camus: *The Fall* Epstein: *Christ in Majesty* Kalatozov: *The Cranes are Flying* Kerouac: *On The Road* Lean: *The Bridge on the River Kwai* Murdoch: *The Sandcastle* Osborne: *The Entertainer* Pasternak: *Dr Zhivago* Shute: *On the Beach*	Six European nations sign the Treaty of Rome, establishing the European Common Market and aiming at free movement of money, people and goods within Europe. Khrushchev foils a challenge to his leadership by a triumvirate of senior Party officials. In Britain, the new Prime Minister Harold Macmillan, revelling in his country's economic success, tells a cheering Conservative rally: 'Most of our people have never had it so good.' He also patches up relations with the United States after the Suez debacle. Russia wins the first leg of the 'space race' when she sends the first man-made satellite, Sputnik-1, into orbit around the Earth, followed by the first Earth orbit by a living creature, a small terrier dog called Laika.

Year	Compositions	Musical events	Arts	Events
1958	Bartók: Violin Concerto no. 1 (1908) Berio: *Sequenza I* Boulez: *Poésie pour pouvoir* Britten: *Noye's Fludde* Cage: *Fontana Mix*, *Concert for Piano and Orchestra.* Copland: Orchestral Variations Davis/Evans: *Porgy and Bess* Kagel: *Anagrama* Ligeti: *Glissandi*, *Artikulation* Nono: *Composizione per Orchestra no. 2* Richard: 'Move It' Scelsi: *I presagi*, *Quattro pezzi per Orchestra* (composed) Solti begins recording the *Ring* cycle for Decca Stockhausen: *Gruppen* (Boulez, Maderna, and Stockhausen conducting) Varèse: *Poème électronique* (tape) Vaughan Williams: Symphony no. 9	Cage visits the Darmstadt Summer School, as well as spending time in the RAI studio in Milan. Warner Brothers Records created. Max Mathews, of Bell Laboratories, generates music by computers. BBC Radiophonic Workshop is established in London. Babbitt's article 'Who Cares if You Listen?' first appears in *High Fidelity* magazine. Pierre Henry leaves the Group de Musique Concrète; they reorganize as the Groupe de Recherches Musicales (GRM) Musicologist Friedrich Blume gives a lecture called 'What Is Music?', seen as an attack on the avant-garde. It provokes responses from Boulez, Stockhausen, and others in *Melos*. Cage's 25th anniversary concert takes place in New York. The Central Committee of the Soviet Communist Party issues a statement retracting some of its previous criticisms of certain Soviet composers.	Carné: *Les tricheurs* Durrell: *Justine* Hitchcock: *Vertigo* Johns: *Three Flags* Minelli: *Gigi* Nolan: 'Gallipoli' series Pinter: *The Birthday Party* Rothko: monochrome canvases for the Chapel at Houston Tati: *Mon oncle* Wajda: *Ashes and Diamonds* Wittgenstein: *The Blue Book and The Brown Book*	Egypt and Sudan proclaim their union as the United Arab Republic, with Nasser as its head of state, throwing the Arab world into turmoil. 40,000 French nationalists demonstrate against any appeasement of Algerian nationalists, prompting the recall of General de Gaulle as premier of France. Cyprus is still in a state of intense unrest as Archbishop Makarios rejects a British peace plan. In the southern United States, Arkansas Governor Faubus closes all four high schools in Little Rock following an order from the US Supreme Court than they must admit blacks. In Britain, race riots break out in Notting Hill, London, following a demonstration by white youths outside a house occupied by blacks. The plane carrying the Manchester United football team crashes in Munich, killing seven members of the team as well as eight journalists and three members of the club's staff.

Date	First performances/ recordings	Other musical	Other cultural	Socio-political
1959	Berio: *Différences* (performers and tape) Boulez: *Le soleil des eaux* (revision), *Tombeau* (composed) Brubeck: *Time Out* (the single 'Take Five' becomes the first jazz instrumental record to sell a million copies) Carter: String Quartet no. 2 Coltrane: *Giant Steps* Davis: *Kind of Blue* Giulini: recording of Mozart's *Don Giovanni* for Columbia Kagel: *Transicion II* La Monte Young: String Trio Ligeti: *Apparitions* Messiaen: *Catalogue d'oiseaux* Poulenc: *La voix humaine* Richard: 'Living Doll' Rodgers and Hammerstein: *The Sound of Music* Shostakovich: Cello Concerto Stockhausen: *Zyklus*	Ornette Coleman opens at the Five Spot in New York with his quartet, causing a sensation in the jazz world. Pierre Boulez moves to Germany. Lejaren Hiller Jr. sets up an electronic studio at Princeton University. The Columbia–Princeton Electronic Music Center is founded. The ISCM Festival is held in Rome; includes music by Rochberg, Maxwell Davies, Zimmermann, Babbitt, Huber, Stravinsky, Boulez, Clementi, and Messiaen. Bernstein and the New York Philharmonic perform *The Rite of Spring* in Moscow for the first time since the Revolution.	Bellow: *Henderson the Rain King* Faulkner: *The Mansion* Hawks: *Rio Bravo* (starring John Wayne) Wright: Guggenheim Art Museum, New York. Miró: murals for UNESCO building Naipaul: *Miguel Street* Spark: *Memento Mori* Resnais: *Hiroshima, mon amour* Ray: *The World of Apu* Wesker: *Roots*	In Cuba, left-wing guerrillas led by Fidel Castro oust dictator General Fulgencio Batista following a two-year struggle. Castro accuses the US of meddling in Cuban affairs, and alienates the US still further with his sweeping land reforms. Rhodesia is placed under a state of emergency by the British authorities, who claim that the country is under imminent danger of violence from African political agitators. The spiritual leader of Tibet, the Dalai Lama, is forced to flee to India following China's repression of nationalists who are demanding independence from Chinese rule. The UN General Assembly condemns racial discrimination, singling out the apartheid system in South Africa for particular criticism.

Year	Works	Music events	Other arts	Historical events
1960	Berio: *Circles* Boulez: *Pli selon pli* Britten: *A Midsummer Night's Dream* Cage: *Theater Piece*, *Cartridge Music* Checker: 'The Twist' Coleman: *Free Jazz* Henze: *Der Prinz von Homburg* Honegger: *Le roi David* Kagel: *Sur scène* Ligeti: *Apparitions* Mahler: Symphony no. 10 (completed by Deryck Cooke) Messiaen: *Chronochromie* Milhaud: Symphony no. 9 Penderecki: *Anaklasis* Presley: *Elvis Is Back* Stockhausen: *Carré*, *Kontakte* Stravinsky: *Movements for Piano and Orchestra* Walton: Symphony no. 2 Young: *Poem for Tables, Chairs, and Benches* Zimmermann: *Die Soldaten*	Founding of the Stax and Motown record labels. The Newport Jazz Festival is closed by the city council after rioting. Bruno Bartelozzi writes a book on extended instrumental techniques (*New Sounds For Woodwind*). Columbia–Princeton Electronic Music Center formally founded. The San Francisco Tape Music Center is established Recording studios begin using multitrack tape machines. Ligeti's analysis of Boulez's *Structures IA* is published in *die reihe*. The ISCM Festival is held in Cologne; includes music by Stockhausen, Nono, Kagel, Berio, Pousseur, Sessions, Boulez, and Ligeti.	Hitchcock: *Psycho* (score by Bernard Herrmann) Lee: *To Kill A Mockingbird* Pinter: *The Caretaker* Robbe-Grillet: *Dans le labyrinthe* Sillitoe: *The Loneliness of the Long Distance Runner* Simon: *The Apartment* Updike: *Rabbit Run*	Negro sit-in campaign at US lunch counters begins. Ten blacks are shot dead following a demonstration on a segregated beach in Mississippi. John F. Kennedy narrowly wins the race for the US Presidency over his Republican rival, Richard Nixon. South African police shoot dead 63 Africans and injure a further 370 at anti-pass law demonstrations in Sharpeville, Transvaal, and Langa, near Cape Town. The authorities declare a state of emergency, outlawing the African National Congress and the Pan-African Congress. Mossad secret service agents abduct Nazi war criminal Adolf Eichmann in Argentina, where he was living under an assumed identity, and take him to Israel for trial.

Date	First performances/ recordings	Other musical	Other cultural	Socio-political
1961	Babbitt: *Composition for Synthesizer* (produced at the Columbia–Princeton Studio) Bartók: Concerto for Orchestra Berio: *Visage* Boulez: *Structures II* Cage: *Atlas Eclipticalis* Carter: *Double Concerto* Charles: 'Hit The Road Jack' Coltrane: *Live At The Village Vanguard* Copland: Nonet for strings Ligeti: *Atmosphères* Lutosławski: *Jeux vénitiens* Penderecki: *Threnody for the Victims of Hiroshima* Poulenc: *Gloria* Schoenberg: *Die Jakobsleiter* (unfinished) Shostakovich: Symphony no. 12 Stockhausen: *Originale* Varèse: *Déserts* (tape, produced at the Columbia–Princeton Studio	Death of Wolfgang Steinecke, a key figure in the founding of the Darmstadt school. Running of the school is taken over by Ernst Thomas. Stockhausen runs his 2nd composition course at Darmstadt. John Cage's *Silence*, a collection of his writings on music, is published. His scores begin to be published by Peters, in New York. The Beatles sign with manager Brian Epstein. The ISCM Festival is held in Vienna; includes music by Donatoni, Bartók, Schoenberg, Webern, and Birtwistle. A concert devoted to the music of Varèse is held in New York, including performances of *Déserts*, *Poème électronique*, and *Ecuatorial*. Piston is awarded the Pulitzer Prize for his Symphony no. 7.	Kirov Ballet star Rudolf Nureyev slips his minders and defects to the West at Paris Airport. 'Art of Assemblage' show takes place at the Museum of Modern Art in New York. In the United States the FCC (Federal Communications Commission) allows FM 'multiplexing', which enables stereo radio broadcasts. Bart: *Oliver* Edwards: *Breakfast at Tiffany's* Forbes: *Whistle Down the Wind* Heller: *Catch-22* Miller: *Tropic of Cancer* Murdoch: *A Severed Head* Truffaut: *Jules et Jim*	At 43, John F. Kennedy is sworn in as the youngest ever President of the United States. He pledges to wage war 'against the common enemies of man: tyranny, poverty, disease, and war itself', and urges constructive dialogue with the USSR. However, the relations between the superpowers deteriorate following the invasion of Cuba by armed exiles at the Bay of Pigs. On 12 April the Russian cosmonaut Yuri Alexeyevitch Gagarin is the first man to fly in space (beating his American rival, Alan Shepherd Jr., by a month) In Berlin, the East German authorities consolidate the closing of the frontiers between East and West with the building of the Berlin wall, while in Britain the Government announces a tightening of immigration controls (the first such restriction since the great post-war influx began).

Year	Music	Music events	Arts and culture	Politics and world events
1962	The Beatles: 'Love Me Do' (their first single) Berio: *Passaggio*, *Epifanie* (completed) Bilk: 'Stranger on the Shore' Booker T. and the MGs: 'Green Onions' Britten: *War Requiem* Cooke: 'Twisting The Night Away' Copland: *Connotations* for orchestra Kagel: *Heterophonie* Ligeti: *Volumina* Luening: *Sonority Canon* Penderecki: *Polymorphie* Shostakovich: Symphony no. 4 (1936) Stockhausen: *Momente* (incomplete) Tippett: *King Priam* Webern: *Im Sommerwind* Xenakis: *ST/4*, *ST/10-1* (completed)	First issue of *Perspectives of New Music* published, including Milton Babbitt's 'Twelve-Tone Rhythmic Structure and the Electronic Medium'. Inauguration of the Lincoln Center for the Performing Arts in New York. The ISCM Festival is held in London; includes music by Henze, Tippett, Maxwell-Davies, Petrassi, Milhaud, Carter, and Stravinsky. George Perle's textbook *Serial Composition and Atonality* is published. Stravinsky conducts a concert of his own music in Moscow, returning to his homeland after an absence of 48 years.	Marilyn Monroe dies of a drug overdose. The first television pictures are transmitted via satellite. Nureyev makes his US debut. Albee: *Who's Afraid of Virginia Woolf?* Burroughs: *The Naked Lunch* (published in the US) Kesey: *One Flew Over The Cuckoo's Nest* Lean: *Lawrence of Arabia* Miller: *Tropic of Capricorn* Solzhenitsyn: *A Day in the Life of Ivan Denisovich*	Algeria wins independence from France after months of violence. In Indo-China, the US establishes a military council in South Vietnam, and sends marines into Laos to counter the expanding military offensive by Communist forces from North Vietnam and the Pathet Lao. Khrushchev agrees to dismantle Soviet bases in Cuba following a tense seven days during which the two nations seem to be set for a nuclear showdown. The US ends its year-long blockade of Cuba.

Date	First performances/ recordings	Other musical	Other cultural	Socio-political
1963	The Beach Boys: 'Surfin' USA' The Beatles: 'Please Please Me', 'From Me To You' (their first UK no. 1) Britten: recording of the *War Requiem* for Decca Brown: *Live At The Apollo* Coltrane: 'Alabama' Dylan: *Freewheelin'* Evans: *Conversations with Myself* Harris: Symphony no. 9 Henze: Symphony no. 4, Symphony no. 5 Hindemith: Concerto for organ and orchestra Ligeti: *Aventures* Lutosławski: *Trois poèmes d'Henri Michaux* Messiaen: *Sept haïkaï* Rolling Stones: 'Come On' Stockhausen: *Punkte* (1952, rev. 1962) Tippett: Concerto for Orchestra	Boulez publishes *Penser la musique d'aujourd'hui.* Stockhausen succeeds Eimert as director of the Cologne studio. Season of avant-garde music in New York including music by Cage, Stockhausen, Feldman, Wolff, and Brown, concluding with the marathon (18-hour) first performance of Satie's *Vexations*, organized by Cage. First Monterey Folk Festival features Peter Paul and Mary, Pete Seeger, Joan Baez, and Bob Dylan. Bob Dylan performs in the Freedom March on Washington DC led by Martin Luther King Philips demonstrate the first compact audio cassette. Boulez conducts *Wozzeck* at the Paris Opera. Barber wins the Pulitzer Prize for his Piano Concerto. Deaths of Poulenc and Hindemith. Soviet premier Khrushchev airs his views on music, opposing abstraction, formalism, and dodecaphony. The ISCM Festival is held in Amsterdam; includes music by Holliger and Boulez.	Baldwin: *The Fire Next Time* Carson: *Silent Spring* Grass: *The Tin Drum* Ionesco: *Exit the King* Mankiewicz: *Cleopatra* Richardson: *Tom Jones* Updike: *The Centaur* Wilder: *Irma La Douce* Young: *From Russia with Love* (starring Sean Connery as James Bond)	The 'Great Train Robbery' is committed at a secluded spot in Buckinghamshire, England, when a gang of armed robbers make off with mailbags worth over £1 million. The United States is rocked by the assassination of President John Kennedy by a gunman in Dallas, Texas. Former Marine Lee Harvey Oswald is arrested and charged with his murder, but shot dead a week later by Dallas strip-club owner Jack 'Ruby' Rubenstein as he is led from the Dallas police headquarters. 200,000 demonstrators march on Washington to demand civil rights for blacks, and hear Rev. Martin Luther King Jr.'s speech 'I have a dream'. The following month four black girls are killed in a bomb attack at a church in Birmingham, Alabama, the site of an increasingly violent struggle for school desegregation.

1964	The Animals: 'House Of The Rising Sun' Babbitt: *Ensembles for Synthesizer* The Beach Boys: 'I Get Around' The Beatles: 'A Hard Day's Night' Berio: *Folk Songs* Boulez: *Figures-Doubles-Prismes* Britten: Cello Symphony, *Curlew River* Coltrane: *A Love Supreme* (500,000 copies sold in its first year alone) Dylan: *The Times They Are A-Changin'* Giulini: recording of Verdi's Requiem Messiaen: *Couleurs de la Cité Céleste* Nono: *La fabbrica illuminata* Riley: *In C* Stockhausen: *Microphonie I* Stravinsky: *Elegy for JFK*	The Beatles arrive in the US and hold the no. 1 spot in the US charts for six months, as well as making a famous appearance on the Ed Sullivan television show. Stockhausen gives a concert of his music in New York, attended by Bernstein and Varèse. ISCM Festival takes place in Copenhagen; includes music by Nørgård, Kagel, Babbitt, Nancarrow, Ferrari, Eimert, Varèse, Górecki, Kurtág, Birtwistle, and Messiaen. Death of Monteux.	The Bolshoi Ballet perform outside Russia for the first time. Bellow: *Herzog* Golding: *Lord of the Flies* Kubrick: *Dr Stangelove* Larkin: *The Whitsun Weddings* Miller: *After the Fall* Osborne: *Inadmissible Evidence* Spence: Library and Swimming Pool at Swiss Cottage, London Truffaut: *Silken Skin* Vidal: *Julian*	The United Nations sends a force of peacekeepers to Cyprus in a bid to end heavy fighting between the Greek and Turkish communities. The US intensifies its bombing raids against the Communist regime in North Vietnam after President Johnson receives the backing of both Houses of Congress to take 'all necessary action'. US Congress also passes Civil Rights legislation. Martin Luther King is awarded the Nobel Peace Prize Mods and rockers fight in Clacton, Brighton, and other British seaside towns.

Date	First performances/ recordings	Other musical	Other cultural	Socio-political
1965	Berio: *Laborintus II* Bernstein: *Chichester Psalms* Birtwistle: *Tragoedia* Boulez: *Eclat* Brown: 'Papa's Got A Brand New Bag' Coltrane: *Ascension* Ives: Symphony no. 4 (1916) Ligeti: Requiem Messiaen: *Et exspecto resurrectionem mortuorum* Nono: *The Inquest* Du Pré/Barbirolli: recording of Elgar's Cello Concerto Reich: *It's Gonna Rain* The Rolling Stones: '(I Can't Get No) Satisfaction' Schuller: Symphony no. 1, *American Triptych* Stockhausen: *Mikrophonie II* Stravinsky: *Variations, Aldous Huxley in Memoriam* Zappa/The Mothers Of Invention: *Freak Out!*	Boulez becomes guest conductor of the Cleveland Orchestra on the invitation of George Szell. The Velvet Underground form, with songwriter Lou Reed and instrumentalist John Cale being introduced by Andy Warhol. The ISCM Festival is held in Madrid; includes music by Čerha, Jolivet, Goehr, Amy, Holliger, Stravinsky, and Schoenberg. The first commercially available Moog synthesizer is released. The Queen awards the Beatles MBEs. Bob Dylan performs at the Newport Festival with an electric lineup, causing accusations of selling out. Horowitz returns to perform in New York after an absence of some twelve years. Deaths of Varèse and Cowell.	Radio Caroline and other offshore pirate radio stations are established. *Autobiography of Malcolm X* Grass: *Dog Years* Lester: *Help!* (starring the Beatles) Lowell: *Union Dead* Mailer: *An American Dream* Marcus: *The Killing of Sister George* Wolfe: *The Kandy-Kolored Tangerine-Flake Streamline Baby*	American involvement in the Vietnamese conflict escalates with aerial bombardment quickly followed by troop action on the ground. Violence continues to surround the growing movement for civil rights in the United States, centring on the southern racist stronghold of Alabama. Demonstrations of up to 25,000 people at Selma and Birmingham are accompanied by attacks on black leaders, and the discovery of bombs at a black church and a leading black lawyer's house. In New York, Malcolm X, the firebrand Black Muslim leader and *bête noire* of the white liberal establishment, is shot dead in what appears to be an internal struggle for control of the movement.

1966	Babbitt: *Relata I* Barraqué: *Chant après chant* The Beach Boys: *Pet Sounds* The Beatles: *Revolver* Dylan: *Blonde on Blonde* Harrison: *Symphony on G* Henze: *Die Bassariden* Penderecki: *St Luke Passion* Reich: *Come Out* Shostakovich: Cello Concerto no. 2 Stockhausen: *Telemusik* (composed at the studios of Japanese radio in Tokyo), *Adieu* Stravinsky: *Requiem Canticles* Tippett: *The Vision of St Augustine* Xenakis: *Terretektorh*	Motown outsells all other record labels. Boulez conducts *Parsifal* at Bayreuth on the invitation of Wieland Wagner. Velvet Underground collaborate on multimedia shows with Andy Warhol. Michael Tippett is knighted. Stockhausen returns to teach at Darmstadt for the first time since 1962, and also holds the post of visiting Professor of Composition at the University of California at Davis. The ISCM Festival is held in Stockholm; includes music by Gorecki, Varèse, Kagel, Bedford, and Nørgård. Promoter Bill Graham starts putting on bands at the Fillmore Auditorium in San Francisco, featuring 'psychedelic' light shows. Acts include Jefferson Airplane and The Grateful Dead.	Adorno: *Negative Dialectics* André: *Equivalent 8* Barber: *Antony and Cleopatra* Capote: *In Cold Blood* Carballido: *I, Too, Speak of the Rose* Díaz: *The Toothbrush* Gilbert: *Alfie* Kaprow: *Gas – Collective Happening* Orton: *Loot* Plath: *Ariel*	The war in Vietnam continues to escalate, with US troops launching their biggest offensive yet; later in the year American bombers pound Hanoi. European opposition to US action in Indo-China becomes stronger and more explicit, led by France. In China, Mao Tse-tung initiates the Cultural Revolution in an effort to rekindle popular zeal for his own version of 'pure' Communism. Racial tension continues to escalate in the US, with riots in many major cities. In Chicago, over 4,000 national guardsmen are deployed to stop violence against the police, while gang warfare between blacks, whites and Puerto Ricans in New York prompts Mayor John Lindsay to plead for peace.

Date	First performances/ recordings	Other musical	Other cultural	Socio-political
1967	The Beatles: *Sergeant Pepper's Lonely Hearts Club Band* Cardew: *Treatise* (completed) Carlos: *Switched On Bach* (recorded using a Moog synthesizer) Carter: Piano Concerto Davis: *Nefertiti* The Doors: 'Light My Fire' Hendrix: *Are You Experienced?* Lutosławski: Symphony no. 2 Ligeti: Cello concerto, *Lontano* Mahler: *Blumine* (lost movement from the First Symphony) Penderecki: *Capriccio* Pink Floyd: *The Piper At The Gates Of Dawn* Piston: Variations for Cello and Orchestra Procul Harum: 'A Whiter Shade Of Pale' Reich: *Piano Phase*, *Violin Phase* Schuller: *Triplum* Stockhausen: *Hymnen*	First Monterey Pop Festival takes place: includes a famous performance by Jimi Hendrix, culminating in the burning of his guitar. Other performers include The Byrds, Jefferson Airplane, The Grateful Dead, Janis Joplin, Simon and Garfunkel, and The Who. Invention of Dolby noise-reduction system for use in tape recording. The ISCM Festival is held in Prague; includes music by Holliger and Zimmermann. Karajan appointed Conductor for Life of the Berlin Philharmonic Orchestra. Deaths of Kodály and Coltrane.	The *Human Be-In* festival in San Francisco. Jann Wenner launches *Rolling Stone* magazine. Introduction of BBC Radio 1. Derrida: *Of Grammatology* Hockney: 'A Neat Lawn' Nureyev and Fonteyn dance in *Paradise Lost.* Penn: *Bonnie and Clyde* Pinter: *The Homecoming* Schlesinger: *Far from the Madding Crowd* Stoppard: *Rosencrantz and Guildenstern are Dead* Walcott: *Dream on Monkey Mountain* Warhol: *Marilyn Monroe*	Israel launches a major offensive across the boundaries of its Arab neighbours, capturing the Sinai and the Gaza Strip from Egypt, the West Bank and the towns of Jericho, Bethlehem, and Hebron from Jordan, and much of the Golan Heights from Syria. In a moment of potent symbolism, Israeli troops also take control of the territory around the Wailing Wall in Jerusalem, inspiring exultant politicians to vow that it would remain Israeli for ever. 60 nations, including Britain, US, and USSR, sign a treaty banning nuclear weapons from outer space. In Latin America guerrilla leader and socialist icon Che Guevara is captured and executed by Bolivian soldiers while on a revolutionary mission.

1968

The Beatles: *The Beatles* ('White Album')
Berio: *Sinfonia*
Birtwistle: *Punch and Judy*
Boulez: *Le soleil des eaux* (revision), *Figures–Doubles–Prismes*, *Domaines*
Britten: *The Prodigal Son*
Cage: *Reunion* (the performance of which involves the composer playing a game of chess with Marcel Duchamp)
Feldman: *Structures*
Gaye: 'I Heard It Through The Grapevine'
Hendrix: *Electric Ladyland*
Morrison: *Astral Weeks*
Pousseur: *Votre Faust*
Riley: *In C* (Columbia Records)
The Rolling Stones: *Beggar's Banquet*
Sly + The Family Stone: 'Dance To The Music'
Stockhausen: *Stimmung*, *Aus den sieben Tagen* (text pieces)
The Velvet Underground: *White Light/White Heat*

Xenakis publishes *Musiques formelles*.
The ISCM Festival takes place in Warsaw; includes music by Penderecki, Ligeti, Nørgård, Cage, Berio, Babbitt, Stockhausen, Messiaen, Birtwistle, Boulez, Xenakis, and Henze.
The Beatles found their own record company, Apple.

Anderson: *If?*
Bennett: *Forty Years On*
Foucault: *The Archaeology of Knowledge*
Ginsberg: *Airplane Dreams*
Nichols: *The Graduate*
Hamilton: *Swinging London*
Horovitz: *The Indian Wants the Bronx*
Kubrick: *2001, A Space Odyssey* (with a soundtrack including music by Richard Strauss, Johann Strauss, and Ligeti)
Lewitt: *Untitled Cube (6)*
Vidal: *Myra Breckenridge*
Wolfe: *The Electric Kool-Aid Acid Test*

America is shaken by the murder of two of its most high-profile public figures: in Memphis, Martin Luther King Jr. is shot dead on a motel balcony by an unknown white assassin, while two months later Senator Bobby Kennedy (brother of the assassinated John F. Kennedy) is gunned down in Los Angeles, two hours after winning California's Democratic primary.
The 'Prague Spring' is led by the newly elected leader of the Czech Communist Party, liberal Alexander Dubcek. The liberalization programme comes to an abrupt end when Soviet tanks roll into the capital and Dubcek and others are arrested amidst violent protests.
Across Western Europe, students take to the streets to protest against the war in Vietnam and international capitalism. In Paris, students pelt the police with paving stones and petrol bombs.
First manned US Apollo space mission.

Date	First performances/ recordings	Other musical	Other cultural	Socio-political
1969	The Beatles: *Abbey Road* Birtwistle: *Verses for Ensembles* Bowie: 'A Space Oddity' Bryars: *The Sinking of the Titanic* Babbitt: *Relata II* Cage: *HPSCHD* (written with computer programmer Lejaren Hiller, for multiple keyboard players, up to fifty tapes, slides, and films) Davis: *In A Silent Way* Deep Purple: *Concerto for Group and Orchestra* The Grateful Dead: *Live/Dead* Jackson Five: 'I Want You Back' Ligeti: String Quartet no. 2 Maxwell Davies: *Eight Songs For A Mad King* Messiaen: *La transfiguration* Partch: *Delusion of the Fury* Riley: *A Rainbow in Curved Air* The Rolling Stones: *Let It Bleed* Stockhausen: *Klavierstücke* VIII, IX Webern: Orchestral Pieces (1913) The Who: *Tommy* Xenakis: *Nomos Gamma*	Formation of the Scratch Orchestra. Pierre Boulez becomes Chief Counductor of the BBC Symphony Orchestra (until 1975). David Munrow founds the Early Music Consort of London. The ISCM Festival is held in Hamburg; includes music by Holliger, Kagel, Schnebel, Lachenmann, Zimmermann, Gorecki, and Tavener. Dolby noise reduction introduced for pre-recorded tapes. The Art Ensemble of Chicago leave America for Paris. The Woodstock festival takes place: performers include Jimi Hendrix, Carlos Santana, and Jefferson Airplane. Manfred Eicher founds the ECM record label. Death of Ansermet	Creation of 'bubble memory' allows for the retention of information in computers when power is switched off. Crighton: *The Andromeda Strain* Hill: *Butch Cassidy and the Sundance Kid* *Monty Python's Flying Circus* Orton: *What the Butler Saw* (posth.) Puzo: *The Godfather* Roth: *Portnoy's Complaint* Russell: *Women in Love* Schlesinger: *Midnight Cowboy* Vonnegut: *Slaughterhouse Five*	Violence flares in Northern Ireland, with firebombers attacking key targets in Belfast, and serious clashes between protesters and police during a Catholic civil rights march. In Prague, protesters find a moving and dramatic focus with the death of 21-year-old student Jan Palach, who sets fire to himself in Wenceslas Square. Thousands of Czechs take to the streets in angry protest. The Russians, however, ban all movement of Czechs to the West, expel Alexander Dubcek from the Presidium of the Communist Party, and again use tanks to suppress demonstrations and protest. America appears to have won the space race when Neil Armstrong becomes the first man to walk on the Moon, closely followed by his team-mate Edwin 'Buzz' Aldrin. His 'giant leap for mankind' is watched on television by millions of people around the world.

1974	Bennett: *Tenebrae* Berio: *Points on the Curve* Glass: *Music in 12 Parts* Henze: *Stimmen* Kagel: String Quartet Kraftwerk: *Autobahn* Messiaen: *Des canyons aux étoiles* Rihm: *Dis Kontur* (composition completed) Stockhausen: *Inori* Wakeman: *Journey To The Centre of the Earth*, for orchestra, choir, narrator, and rock band. Yes: *Tales From Topographic Oceans*	Pierre Boulez secures funding for IRCAM (Institut de Recherche et Coordination Acoustique/Musique). Founding of the Arditti Quartet. Rostropovich leaves the Soviet Union. The ISCM Festival is held in Holland and includes music by Osborne, Scherchen, Feldman, De Leeuw, Donatoni, Mason, Maderna, and Sciarrino. Death of Duke Ellington The Mellotron (a keyboard using tape loop samples) is developed.	Solzhenitsyn is expelled from the USSR. The Soviet ballet star, Mikhail Baryshnikov, defects to the West in Toronto, while on tour with the Bolshoi Ballet. Bergman: *Scenes from a Marriage* Bertolucci: *Last Tango in Paris* Fo: *Can't Pay? Won't Pay!* Heller: *Something Happened* *Happy Days* Jong: *Fear of Flying* Polanski: *Chinatown*	Richard Nixon is the first US President to resign from office over his role in the Watergate affair. Vice-President Gerald Ford takes office and immediately extends a pardon to his disgraced predecessor. Emperor Haile Selassie of Ethiopia is deposed by an army coup, having ruled his empire for almost 60 years. Seven years of military rule by 'the Colonels' in Greece ends when former premier Constantine Karamanlis returns from exile in France to form a new government. The Labour Party wins two general election victories in one year.
1975	Babbitt: *Reflections* Berio: *Chemins IV* Bernstein: *Dybbuk* Boulez: *Rituel in memoriam Maderna* Dylan: *Blood on the Tracks*	Boulez founds the Ensemble Inter-Contemporain. Death of Shostakovich. The ISCM Festival is held in Paris; includes music by Finnissy, Xenakis, Smalley, and Grisey.	Bellow: *Humboldt's Gift* Borges: *The Book of Sand* Bradbury: *The History Man* Forman: *One Flew Over the Cuckoo's Nest* Levi: *The Periodic Table*	Cambodia, weakened and destabilized by years of American bombing, falls to the Communist Khmer Rouge led by Pol Pot, a shadowy figure about whom very little is known. Soon, stories emerge of terrible atrocities and forced labour, mainly directed at intellectuals and townspeople.

Date	First performances/ recordings	Other musical	Other cultural	Socio-political
	The Eagles: *One Of Those Nights* Feldman: *String Quartet and Orchestra* Holliger: *Quartet for Strings* Jarrett: *The Köln Concert* Ligeti: *San Francisco Polyphony* Nono: *Al gran sole carico d'amore* Queen: 'Bohemian Rhapsody' Rihm: *Sub Kontur* Rochberg: Violin Concerto Springsteen: *Born To Run* Stockhausen: *Atmen gibt das Leben* Xenakis: *Empreintes*	Disco becomes the latest popular music craze, centring on clubs in New York. The video for Queen's single 'Bohemian Rhapsody' marks the beginning of the music video genre.	Lodge: *Changing Places* Mamet: *American Buffalo* Pinter: *No Man's Land* Powell: *A Dance to the Music of Time* Spielberg: *Jaws*	Amid scenes of panic, the last US personnel are evacuated from Saigon in South Vietnam. Pro-Palestinian terrorists, led by Carlos 'The Jackal', seize 70 hostages at the OPEC summit in Vienna, including 11 oil ministers. Britain's Conservative Party elects Margaret Thatcher to be its new leader, the first woman to hold such a role.

1976	Andriessen: *De Staat* Berio: *Coro* Eagles: *Hotel California* Feldman: *Four Instruments* Ferneyhough: *Unity Capsule* Glass: *Einstein on the Beach* (first US performance) Ligeti: *Monument-Selbsportrait-Bewegung* (completed) Lutosławski: *Mi-parti* Reich: *Music for Eighteen Musicians*, Rihm: String Quartet no. 3 (completed) The Sex Pistols: *Anarchy In The UK* Stockhausen: *Sirius* Wonder: *Songs In The Key Of Life* Xenakis: *Phlegra*, *Mikka 'S'*	Boulez conducts the *Ring* cycle at Bayreuth. The ISCM Festival is held in Boston; includes music by Knussen, Birtwistle, Wolpe, Payne, Cage, and Lachenmann. Death of Britten. Sarah Caldwell becomes the first woman to conduct at the Metropolitan Opera in New York.	National Theatre opens on the South Bank in London. Archer: *Not a Penny More, Not a Penny Less* Avildsen: *Rocky* Christo: *Running Fence* Gold: *The Naked Civil Servant* Haley: *Ro* Jarman: *Sebastiane The Muppet Show* Schlesinger: *Marathon Man* Scorsese: *Taxi Driver* Wise: *I, Claudius*	South African policemen kill 76 school children in Soweto and other townships following protests over the government's decision that Afrikaans should have parity with English in the country's schools. China loses its two most prominent and influential leaders: Mao Tse-tung, architect of the Communist revolution, and his deputy, Premier Chou En-lai. The civil war in Angola threatens to assume global proportions when the Marxist MPLA force back Western-aided UNITA fighters with Soviet tanks and Cuban troops. Israeli commandos pull off a daring rescue attempt at Entebbe airport in Uganda, freeing 103 hostages who were being held in an airport building by Palestinian hijackers. Concorde, the world's first supersonic passenger aircraft, begins commercial flights with planes taking off simultaneously from London and Paris.

Date	First performances/ recordings	Other musical	Other cultural	Socio-political
1977	Adams: *Phrygian Gates* (completed) Andriessen: *Hoketus* (completed) The Bee Gees: 'Stayin' Alive' Bowie/Eno: *Low* Carter: *Symphony of Three Orchestras* Crumb: *Star-Child* Fleetwood Mac: *Rumours* Gorecki: Symphony no. 3 Ferneyhough: *Time and Motion Study I* McCartney: 'Mull of Kintyre' Pärt: *Tabula Rasa* Schnittke: Concerto grosso no. 1 The Sex Pistols: 'God Save The Queen' Tippett: *The Ice Break*, Symphony no. 4	Foundation of the journal *Nineteenth-Century Music*. Opening of IRCAM under Boulez's direction, comprising studios, offices and a concert hall. In Britain, the Sex Pistols appear on a television show during which singer Johnny Rotten utters profanities; the band is dropped by EMI and denounced in parliament. The ISCM Festival is held in Bonn; includes music by Huber, Goeyvaerts, Schat, Xenakis, Bryars, Stockhausen, Boulez, Cage, and Nono. Death of Elvis Presley. Rostropovich becomes director of the National Symphony Orchestra in Washington DC.	Apple launch the first mass-produced personal computer. The Pompidou Centre in Paris is completed. Allen: *Annie Hall* Badham: *Saturday Night Fever* (soundtrack by The Bee Gees) Berkoff: *East* Didion: *A Book of Common Prayer* Lucas: *Star Wars* (score by John Williams) Marquez: *A Hundred Years of Solitude* Spielberg: *Close Encounters of the Third Kind*	Gary Gilmore, found guilty of murdering two students at Brigham Young University, is the first man to be executed in the United States for a decade. Two Jumbo jets crash on the ground at Tenerife airport in the Canary Islands, killing 574 passengers, mostly holidaymakers. Amid widespread protest, the policemen who were responsible for the South African black activist Steve Biko when he died in custody in Port Elizabeth are released after a magistrate rules that they cannot be held responsible for his death. Britain celebrates the Silver Jubilee of Queen Elizabeth II with street parties and bonfires.

Year	Music	Music events	Arts	World events
1978	Adams: *Shaker Loops* Blondie: *Parallel Lines* Boulez: *Notations* Bush: 'Wuthering Heights' Denisov: Violin Concerto Kagel: *Ex-position* Ligeti: *Le grand macabre* Lutosławski: *Les espaces du sommeil* (with Fischer-Dieskau as soloist) Maxwell Davies: Symphony no. 1 Penderecki: *Paradise Lost*, Violin Concerto Reich: *Music for Eighteen Musicians* (recorded for ECM) The Rolling Stones: *Some Girls* Webber: *Evita*	The ISCM Festival is held in Helsinki; includes music by Finzi, Harvey, Feldman, Hilliger, Schafer, and Rautavaara. Rostropovich loses his Russian citizenship.	Christo: *Wrapped Walkways* Cimino: *The Deer Hunter* Clark: *Whose Life is it Anyway* Donner: *Superman* Greene: *The Human Factor* Hare: *Plenty* Kleiser: *Grease* (with Olivia Newton-John and John Travolta) Maupin: *Tales of the City* Parker: *Midnight Express* Potter: *Pennies from Heaven*	Almost a thousand members of an American religious cult, followers of the Rev. Jim Jones, are found dead in an apparent mass suicide in the jungles of Guyana. Millions of Iranians march against the Shah, carrying pictures of the exiled religious leader, Ayatollah Khomeini. The Shah declares martial law. Rhodesia's Prime Minister, Ian Smith, agrees a plan to move the country to black rule, but refuses to include black nationalists Joshua Nkomo and Robert Mugabe who are fighting a guerrilla war against the minority white government. In the worst environmental disaster of its kind, the oil tanker Amoco Cadiz runs aground off the coast of Brittany, France, spilling 220,000 tons of crude oil into the Channel.

Date	First performances/ recordings	Other musical	Other cultural	Socio-political
1979	Berg: *Lulu* Cage: *Roaratorio* Jackson: *Off The Wall* Pink Floyd: *The Wall* Previn: recording of Debussy's *Images* and *Prélude à 'L'après-midi d'un faune'*, the first digitally recorded release by EMI Mitchell: *Mingus* Penderecki: *Te Deum* The Police: 'Message in a Bottle' Rochberg: *The Concord Quartets* Rostropovich: recording of Shostakovich's *Lady Macbeth of the Mtensk District* Schnittke: Concerto for piano and string orchestra Schuller: Octet	Death of jazz musician, bandleader, and composer Charles Mingus. Sony introduce the first 'Walkman' portable cassette player. The ISCM Festival is held in Athens; includes music by Ferrari, Kurtág, Gruber, Feldman, Muldowney, Knussen, Maxwell Davies, Babbitt, Nørgård, and Finnissy. Slatkin becomes director of the St Louis Symphony Orchestra. The Metropolitan Opera in New York broadcasts a performance of *Otello* to 60 cities and over 3 million viewers.	The *Voyager II* probe broadcasts pictures of Jupiter back to earth. Churchill: *Cloud Nine* Coppola: *Apocalypse Now* Gordimer: *Burger's Daughter* Jones: *Life of Brian* Mailer: *The Executioner's Song* Miller: *Mad Max* Scott: *Alien* Shaffer: *Amadeus* Sherman: *Bent* Styron: *Sophie's Choice*	Ayatollah Khomeini comes to power in Iran after the Shah is forced to flee into exile. The Ayatollah declares an Islamic republic, saying there is no place for democracy, and his followers storm the US Embassy in Tehran, taking almost 100 hostages. Vietnamese troops enter Phnom Penh, Cambodia, heralding the collapse of Pol Pot's brutal Communist regime and exposing the full horror of his four-year rule. The Soviet Union sends its troops into Afghanistan to shore up the Moscow-backed regime, which is coming under intense pressure from Islamic opposition forces, and puts its own puppet leader, Babrak Karmal, in place. Britain's first woman Prime Minister, Margaret Thatcher rides to power after a winter of crippling public strikes (the 'Winter of Discontent').

1980	Nono: *Fragmente-Stille, an Diotima* Boulez: *Notations* (for orchestra) Ferneyhough: Second Quartet Glass: *Satyagraha* Gubaidulina: *Offertorium* Joy Division: *Closer* Lutosławski: Double Concerto Reich: *Variations for Winds, Strings, and Keyboards* Schnittke: Symphony no. 2 Springsteen: *The River* Stockhausen: *Donnerstag* (first opera in the *Licht* cycle) Swayne: *Cry* Tippett: Triple Concerto	The five directors of IRCAM resign and Boulez reconfigures the organization. Pink Floyd stage hugely expensive performances of *The Wall.* Ex-Beatle and peace icon John Lennon is shot dead outside his New York home by deranged fan, Mark David Chapman. The ISCM Festival is held in Israel and includes music by Kagel, Ligeti, Donatoni, Smalley, Murail, Ruders, and Huber.	Eco: *The Name of the Rose* Golding: *Rites of Passage* Harwood: *The Dresser* Jie: *Leaden Wings* Kubrick: *The Shining* Lynch: *Elephant Man* Scorsese: *Raging Bull* Shepard: *True West*	Martial law is proclaimed in Afghanistan; fierce fighting takes place between Soviet troops and rebel Islamic forces, the Mujahidin. Relations between Iran and the West deteriorate further: six American hostages held in the US embassy in Tehran are smuggled out of the country under forged Canadian visas, while in London SAS troops storm the Iranian embassy, freeing 19 hostages from dissident Iranian terrorists demanding the release of political prisoners in Iran. Following two months of strikes, Polish workers, led by Gdansk shipyard-worker Lech Wałesa, gain independent trade union recognition and the easing of censorship from the Communist government. Ronald Reagan wins the US Presidency.

Date	First performances/ recordings	Other musical	Other cultural	Socio-political
1981	Adams: *Harmonium* Andriessen: *De Tijd* Boulez: *Répons* Davis: *Man with the Horn* Ferneyhough: *Lemma-Icon-Epigram* Gould records Bach's *Goldberg Variations.* Grandmaster Flash: 'Adventures on the Wheels of Steel' Maxwell Davies: Symphony no. 2 Prince: *Controversy* Reich: *Tehillim* Sessions: Concerto for Orchestra Stockhausen: *Donnerstag* Lloyd Webber: *Cats*	MTV (Music Television) begins broadcasting, focusing exclusively on white artists until the success of Michael Jackson. Philip Glass signs an exclusive contract with CBS records. The ISCM Festival is held in Brussels; includes music by Ferneyhough, Finnissy, Crumb, Denisov, Ives, Schuller, Globokar, Pousseur, Stockhausen, Andriessen, Clementi, Zimmermann, and Goeyvaerts. Death of Cornelius Cardew.	IBM launches a personal computer using Microsoft disc-operating (MS-DOS) Picasso's *Guernica* is moved from the Musem of Modern Art in New York to the Prado, Madrid. Hudson: *Chariots of Fire* Fierstein: *Torch Song Trilogy* Kempinski: *Duet for One* Lindsay-Hogg/Sturridge: *Brideshead Revisited* Reisz: *The French Lieutenant's Woman* Rushdie: *Midnight's Children* Rydell: *On Golden Pond* Smith: *Gorky Park* Thomas: *The White Hotel*	In Poland, moderate Defence Minister General Jaruzelski becomes Prime Minister as the trade union 'Solidarity', led by Lech Wałesa, continues to demand social reforms. The USSR brands Solidarity 'counter-revolutionary' and forces Jaruzelski to impose martial law, outlawing trade unions and imprisoning Wałesa. Egyptian President Anwar Sadat is assassinated by Islamic extremists, angered by his part in the Camp David agreement with Israel. Most of Britain, and much of the world, is entranced by the wedding of Lady Diana Spencer and the Prince of Wales. In Northern Ireland eight days of rioting follow the death of Republican hunger striker Bobby Sands at the notorious Maze Prison.

1982	Adams: *Grand Pianola Music* Berio: *La vera storia* Glass: *Glassworks* (CBS) goes on to sell over 100,000 copies. Gubaidulina: *Offertorium* Iron Maiden: *Number of the Beast* Jackson: *Thriller* (becomes the bestselling record in history, going on to sell over 40 million copies) Ligeti: Horn Trio Penderecki: Cello Concerto no. 2 Prince: *1999* Reich: *Vermont Counterpoint*	The British journal *Music Analysis* is founded. Philips introduce the first digital audio 5-inch discs. The ISCM Festival is held in Graz; includes music by Gruber, Stravinsky, Kagel, Ligeti, Cage, Boulez, Shostakovich, Stockhausen, Pousseur, Goeyvaerts, Henze, Nancarrow, Krenek, Rzewski, Holliger, Nono, Maderna, Berio, and Nyman.	Allende: *The House of the Spirits* Baselitz: *Last Supper in Dresden* Byrne: *The Slab Boys* Bergman: *Fanny and Alexander* Churchill: *Top Girls* Herzog: *Fitzcarraldo* Levi: *If Not Now, When?* Scott: *Bladerunner* Updike: *Rabbit is Rich* White: *A Boy's Own Story*	Following Argentina's invasion of the Falklands, a small group of islands in the South Atlantic, Britain sends a task force of 40 warships and 1,000 troops, and is victorious in the three-month war. Following an Israeli invasion, the Palestine Liberation Organisation announces its withdrawal from the Lebanon. Following the death of Leonid Brezhnev, aged 75, Yuri Andropov, long-serving head of the KGB, becomes head of the Soviet Communist Party, aged 68.
1983	Anderson: *United States* Bernstein: *A Quiet Place* Carter: *Triple Duo* Frankie Goes To Hollywood: 'Relax' Joel: 'Uptown Girl' Lutosławski: Symphony no. 3 Messiaen: *Saint François d'Assise* Penderecki: Cello Concerto REM: *Murmur*	Michael Jackson's 'Beat It' becomes the first black record to receive substantial airplay on MTV. The ISCM Festival is held in Denmark; includes music by Nørgård, Henze, Lutosławski, Carter, Ferneyhough, Lachenmann, Xenakis, Reich, Ligeti, Stockhausen, Finnissy, Knussen, Pärt, Wagenaar, Murail, and Kagel.	IBM produces a personal computer with built-in hard disc, Apple devises 'pull down' menus by means of a 'mouse' control box. Bennett: *An Englishman Abroad* Beuys: *Untitled Vitrine* Mamet: *Glengarry Glen Ross* Marquez: *Chronicle of a Death Foretold* Parcy: *Rue cases nègres*	Almost 300 peace-keeping troops are killed in Beirut by Shia terrorists. Tension between the superpowers once again increases when the Soviet military authorities admit to having authorized the shooting down of a Korean Airlines Boeing 747 over its airspace, killing 269 civilians. President Reagan admits that America has been assisting the Contras, the rebels against the new revolutionary Sandinista government, and is rebuffed by the House of Representatives which votes to end such support.

Date	First performances/ recordings	Other musical	Other cultural	Socio-political
	Riley: *The Harp of New Albion* Sondheim: *Sunday in the Park With George*		Rushdie: *Shame* Shepard: *Fool for Love* Wajda: *Danton* Walker: *The Color Purple*	Margaret Thatcher wins a second term as Conservative Prime Minister in Britain.
1984	Andriessen: *De Snelheid* Band Aid: 'Do They Know It's Christmas?' Boulez: *Dérive* (completed) Berio: *Un re in ascolto* Birtwistle: *Secret Theatre* Glass: *Akhnaten* Knussen: *Where the Wild Things Are* (revised) Madonna: *Like A Virgin* Prince: *Purple Rain* Reich: *The Desert Music* Springsteen: *Born In The USA* Stockhausen: *Samstag* Tippett: *The Mask of Time* Turner: *Private Dancer* Lloyd Webber: *Starlight Express*	Founding of the journal *Contemporary Music Review*. The ISCM Festival is held in Toronto; includes music by Salonen, Cage, Nørgård, Rzewski, Dillon, Lindberg, Ferneyhough, and Rihm. Bob Geldof organizes the Band Aid recording 'Do They Know It's Christmas?' to raise money for the famine in Ethiopa. It includes performances by many pop musicians, including Sting, Bono, Phil Collins, and Paul Young.	Ballard: *The Empire of the Sun* Cameron: *Terminator* Coetzee: *The Life and Times of Michael K* DeLillo: *White Noise* Forman: *Amadeus* Kundera: *The Unbearable Lightness of Being* Lean: *A Passage to India* Simon: *Biloxi Blues* Tartovsky: *Nostalgia* Wenders: *Paris, Texas*	Indian troops storm the Golden Temple at Amritsar, the holiest of Sikh shrines, after a four-day siege by Sikh militants. Prime Minister Indira Gandhi is later shot dead by one of her own Sikh bodyguards in revenge for the Temple massacre. A toxic gas leak from the Union Carbide pesticide plant at Bhopal, India, kills at least 2,000 people. In Britain, an IRA bomb devastates the Grand Hotel, Brighton, which is hosting many of the Conservative Party's most powerful figures during the Party's conference. The Prime Minister, Mrs Thatcher, narrowly escapes death. The Soviet Union announces that it is to boycott the Olympic Games in August in retaliation for the United States' boycott of the Moscow games four years earlier.

1985

Adams: *Harmonielehre*
Babbitt: Piano Concerto
Bush: *The Hounds of Love*
Carter: *Penthode*
Harrison: Piano Concerto
Ligeti: *Études pour piano* (first book completed)
Lutosławski: *Partita* (orchestrated in 1988)
Maxwell Davies: Symphony no. 3
Nono: *Prometeo*
Prince: *Around The World*
Schnittke: *Ritual*
Simon: *Graceland* (featuring collaborations with South African musicians)
Takemitsu: *Riverrun*

Live-Aid charity concerts take place in London and Philadelphia. The performances are broadcast to over 150 countries. Performers include U2, Elton John, Madonna, Status Quo, Spandau Ballet, Joan Baez, BB King, Ozzy Osbourne, Black Sabbath, Run, DMC, Sting, Phil Collins, Bryan Ferry, Crosby Stills and Nash, Judas Priest, Paul Young, Simple Minds, David Bowie, The Who, Queen, Eric Clapton, Bob Dylan, Keith Richards, and Paul McCartney.
The ISCM Festival is held in Amsterdam; includes music by Ruders, Boulez, Finnissy, Barry, Berio, Saariaho, Andriessen, Zimmermann, Lachenmann, Torke, Ferneyhough, and Stockhausen.

Sony and Philips agree CD-ROM standard.
Carter: *Nights at the Circus*
Christo wraps Pont Neuf, Paris
Habermas: *The Philosophical Discourse of Modernity*
Hampton: *Les Liaisons Dangereuses*
Klima: *My First Loves*
Martin: *The Edge of Darkness*
Pollack: *Out of Africa*
Suskind: *Perfume*

Following the death of Soviet leader Konstantin Chernenko after only a year in power, moderate Mikhail Gorbachev becomes the new head of the Communist Party under the slogans of *glasnost* (openness) and *perestroika* (restructuring).
Despite an increase in violence and strikes in South Africa, President P. W. Botha restates his commitment to apartheid principles.
The Greenpeace ship 'Rainbow Warrior' is sunk in Auckland Harbour, New Zealand.
Israel attacks the headquarters of the Palestine Liberation Organisation in Tunis, killing 60, and PLO terrorists respond by hijacking the Italian liner, the *Achille Lauro*.
In two separate disasters, 40 soccer fans die as a blaze sweeps through the main stand at Bradford City football ground in England, and another 41 are crushed to death when Liverpool football fans rampage through the Heysel Stadium, Brussels.

Date	First performances/ recordings	Other musical	Other cultural	Socio-political
1986	Adams: *Tromba Lontana*, *Short Ride in a Fast Machine* Babbitt: Violin Concerto Birtwistle: *Earth Dances* (completed), *The Mask of Orpheus* Carter: String Quartet no. 4 Gabriel: *So* Nono: *Omaggio a György Kurtág* Schnittke: Violin Concerto Norrington begins recording the Beethoven symphonies for EMI Riley: *Salome Dances for Peace* Webber: *The Phantom of the Opera*	The ISCM Festival is held in Budapest; includes music by Oliveros, Nono, Kurtág, Barry, Birtwistle, Benjamin, Petrassi, Ligeti, and Wolff. Horowitz returns to Russia, and gives a televised recital at Moscow Conservatory. Death of Benny Goodman.	First 'laptop' size computer is introduced in America. Ackroyd: *Hawksmoor* Allen: *Hannah and Her Sisters* Berri: *Jean de Florette* Frears: *My Beautiful Laundrette* Keillor: *Lake Wobegon Days* Koons: *Rabbit* Kramer: *The Normal Heart* Lynch: *Blue Velvet* Potter: *The Singing Detective* Seth: *The Golden Gate* Stone: *Platoon*	US bombers attack targets in Tripoli (Libya), in retaliation for 'clear evidence' that the country is responsible for terrorist attacks. An explosion in a Russian nuclear reactor at Chernobyl, near Kiev, kills two and releases radioactivity over much of Europe. P. W. Botha of South Africa announces a state of emergency following increased activity by opposition groups. President Ferdinand Marcos is forced to flee the Philippines after 20 years in power following widespread protest over the rigging of the country's general election. The US space shuttle Challenger explodes seconds after take-off, killing all seven crew members (including Christa McAuliffe, the first woman space shuttle astronaut).

1987	Adams: *Nixon in China* Cage: *Europeras 1* and *2* (completed) Carter: Chamber Concerto for Oboe Madonna: *You Can Dance* Marsalis: *Standard Time, Vol. 1* New Order: *Substance* Nono: *No hay caminos, hay que caminar* Pink Floyd: *A Momentary Lapse of Reason* Prince: *Sign O' The Times* Saariaho: *Nymphéa* (composition completed) U2: *The Joshua Tree* Ustvolskaya: Symphony no. 3 Zorn: *Spillane*	Luciano Berio founds Tempo Reale in Florence. Peter Gabriel founds the WOMAD (World of Music and Dance) festival in the UK. The festival builds a reputation for promoting world music in Britain and abroad. First commercially available DAT (Digital Audio Tape) machines. Billy Joel undertakes a six concert tour of the USSR. The ISCM Festival is held in Cologne, Bonn, and Frankfurt; includes music by Ligeti, Saariaho, Meredith Monk, Oliveros, Volans, Globokar, Lindberg, Wolff, Rzewski, Donatoni, Crumb, Lucier, Cage, Krenek, and Stockhausen. The first Bang on a Can festival is held in New York.	The first fibre optic cable is laid across the Atlantic. Apple introduce the Mac II computer. Achebe: *Anthills of the Savanna* Atwood: *The Handmaid's Tale* Bertolucci: *The Last Emperor* Chatwin: *Songlines* Lyne: *Fatal Attraction* Stone: *Wall Street* Wenders: *Wings of Desire*	Relations between the superpowers thaw still further when the US and USSR reach an in-principle agreement to scrap all intermediate-range nuclear weapons. Britain endures two transport disasters with the death of 187 ferry passengers when the *Herald of Free Enterprise* capsizes in the North Sea, and a further 30 casualties in a fire at King's Cross underground station in London. The death toll is far higher, however, when a ferry sinks in the Philippines, killing 2,000. Prime Minister Thatcher of Britain wins a third term in office.

Date	First performances/ recordings	Other musical	Other cultural	Socio-political
1988	Adams: *Fearful Symmetries* Barry: *The Intelligence Park* Lang: *Shadowland* Ligeti: Piano Concerto (1986, rev. 1988) Maxwell Davies: *Strathclyde Concerto No. 1* Minogue: 'I Should Be So Lucky' Nancarrow: String Quartet no. 3 Rattle: Mahler, Symphony no. 2 (EMI) Reich: *Different Trains* Rihm: *Kein Firmament* Schnittke: *Concerto grosso* Stockhausen: *Montag* Turnage: *Greek*	CD sales surpass LP sales for the first time. The ISCM Festival is held in Hong Kong; includes music by Nancarrow, Henze, Nørgård, Cage, Feldman, Rzewski, Webern, Ligeti, Bryars, Ferneyhough, Xenakis, Birtwistle, Lachenmann, Penderecki, and Takemitsu.	Carey: *Oscar and Lucinda* Clemente: *Paradigm* Crichton: *A Fish Called Wanda* DeLillo: *Libra* Hawking: *A Brief History of Time* Levinson: *Rain Man* Malle: *Au Revoir les Enfants* Mamet: *Speed-the-Plow* Morrison: *Beloved* Rushdie: *The Satanic Verses* Scorsese: *Last Temptation of Christ* Whiteread: *Closet*	As a result of terrorist action a Pan American Jumbo jet crashes on the small Scottish town of Lockerbie, killing all 259 people on board and a further 11 on the ground. Three members of an IRA 'active service unit' are shot dead by British plain-clothes soldiers in Gibraltar, sparking a series of bloody attacks in Northern Ireland. Mikhail Gorbachev is elected President of the USSR and announces unilateral troop cuts of 500,000 (10% of Soviet military strength). Georgia, Estonia, and Azerbaijan join the growing number of Soviet states to protest for self-determination. George Bush wins the United States Presidency.

1989	Adams: *The Wound Dresser* Boulez: *Le visage nuptial* (revised, originally composed 1946) Cage: *101* Carter: *Three Occasions* Berio: *Rendering* Kennedy: recording of Vivaldi's *The Four Seasons* (EMI) Madonna: *Like A Prayer* Maw: *Odyssey* Maxwell Davies: Fourth Symphony Montague: *From the White Edge of Phrygia* Public Enemy: *It Takes a Nation of Millions to Hold Us Back* Reed: *New York* Torke: *Ash* Turnage: *Three Screaming Popes*	Leonard Bernstein conducts a performance of Beethoven's Ninth Symphony in Berlin to celebrate the fall of the Berlin Wall. The video for Madonna's single 'Like A Prayer' causes controversy with the Vatican. Death of Karajan. Death of Lennox Berkeley. A retrospective festival of the music of Schnittke is held in Stockholm. A concert of music by Nancarrow is held in New York. The ISCM Festival is held in Amsterdam; includes music by Gorecki, Nørgård, Harvey, Ligeti, Dun, Barrett, and Saariaho.	Ayatollah Khomeini of Iran declares a new book, *The Satanic Verses* by Britain's Salman Rushdie, offensive to Islam and sentences the author to death. Rushdie is forced to go into hiding. Acid house raves dominate youth culture in Britain. Allen: *Crimes and Misdemeanors* Amis: *London Fields* Beresford: *Driving Miss Daisy* Burton: *Batman* Eco: *Foucault's Pendulum* Irving: *A Prayer for Owen Meany* Ishiguro: *The Remains of the Day* Lee: *Do the Right Thing* Lynch: *Twin Peaks* Soderburgh: *Sex, Lies, and Videotape* Tan: *The Joy Luck Club*	After a year in which first Hungary, then East Germany, Czechoslovakia, and Romania throw off the shackles of Soviet communism, the Berlin Wall is dismantled by Germans from both the East and the West. At the end of a summit in Malta, Bush and Gorbachev declare the Cold War at an end. The Chinese authorities brutally put down a rally of up to half a million students and pro-democracy supporters in Beijing's Tiananmen Square. Several hundred are killed and thousands wounded when troops and tanks roll into the square to disperse, arrest, and charge the peaceful protesters. US troops invade Panama, toppling dictator Manuel Noriega and installing a new government.

Date	First performances/ recordings	Other musical	Other cultural	Socio-political
1990	Ligeti: *Études pour piano* (second book completed) Cage: *Europeras* 3 and 4 Carter: *Violin Concerto* Harrison: Symphony no. 4 Martland: *Principia* Nørgård: Symphony no. 5 O'Connor: 'Nothing Compares 2 U' Schnittke: Cello Concerto no. 2 Tan Dun: *Orchestral Theatre I* Weir: *The Vanishing Bridegroom* Xenakis: *Tetora*	Death of Bernstein. Death of Copland. The ISCM Festival is held in Oslo; includes music by Harrison, Scelsi, Saariaho, Takemitsu, Cage, Adams, Kagel, Kurtág, Andriessen, Xenakis, Knussen, Globokar, Schnittke, Kancheli, and Murail. US Rap group 2 LIVE CREW have their album *As Nasty as they Wanna Be* ruled obscene by a US Court and banned. The band Milli Vanilli admit that their songs were actually sung by backing singers, and lose their Grammy award. Abbado succeeds Karajan as chief conductor of the Berlin Philharmonic. Sony introduce the writeable CD.	Bly: *Iron John* Byatt: *Possession Cyrano de Bergerac* Lynch: *Wild at Heart* McEwan: *The Innocent* Pynchon: *Vineland* Tornatore: *Cinema Paradiso* Updike: *Rabbit at Rest*	South Africa ends a 30-year ban on the African National Congress and, in the year's most memorable television moment, frees its leader, Nelson Mandela, after 27 years in jail. The Russian Federation formally declares itself a sovereign state under Boris Yeltsin. Elsewhere in the former Soviet Union, Bulgaria and Yugoslavia's Communist Parties vote themselves out of monopoly power; Lech Wałesa, leader of the Solidarity trade union, wins a run-off presidential election in Poland; and East Germany's first free elections since 1933 result in a win for the Alliance for Germany, precipitating the handing over of sovereignty of economic, monetary, and social policy to the West German government and the Bundesbank. American and British troops mass in the Persian Gulf after Iraq moves in and annexes its tiny neighbour, Kuwait. British Prime Minister Margaret Thatcher resigns and is replaced by her Chancellor, John Major.

1991	Adams: *The Death of Klinghoffer* Birtwistle: *Gawain* Cage: *Europera 5* Corigliano: Symphony no. 1 Ferneyhough: *Terrain* Maxwell Davies: *Fifth Strathclyde Concerto* Massive Attack: *Blue Lines* McCartney: *Liverpool Oratorio* Nirvana: *Nevermind* Pearl Jam: *Ten* Stockhausen: *Dienstag* (completed) U2: *Achtung Baby*	The ISCM Festival is held in Zurich; includes music by Liebermann, Huber, Stockhausen, Penderecki, Wood, Holliger, Ustvolskaya, Lachenmann, and Rzewski. Death of Miles Davis and Krenek. Wynton Marsalis becomes artistic director of Jazz at the Lincoln Center.	Barnes: *Talking It Over* Bennett: *The Madness of George III* Costner: *Dances With Wolves* Demme: *The Silence of the Lambs* Greenaway: *Prospero's Books* Thoreau: *Chicago Loop* Updike: *Rabbit at Rest*	British and American forces quickly defeat Saddam Hussein's army in the second Gulf War. The war is largely won in the air, with a month of heavy bombing. Boris Yeltsin is elected President of Russia in the country's first ever free elections and foils a coup by hardliners. Gorbachev resigns as the last Soviet executive President in December, as the USSR finally breaks up. Rajiv Gandhi, former Prime Minister of India, is assassinated by a Sri Lankan Tamil nationalist in an echo of his mother's death seven years previously.
1992	Berio: *Ofanium* Chandra: *Weaving My Ancestor's Voices* Henze: *Requiem* Glass: *The Voyage* Gorecki: Symphony no. 3 (1976) recorded for Nonesuch Lutosławski: Symphony no. 4 Madonna: *Erotica* Martland: *Patrol* Messiaen: *Eclairs sur l'au-delà* (posth.) Rihm: *Gesungene Zeit* Schnittke: Symphony no. 6	Compact disc sales surpass those of cassette. Ozawa makes his first appearance at the Metropolitan Opera in New York. The ISCM Festival is held in Warsaw; includes music by Penderecki, Lutosławski, Gorecki, Weir, Alvarez, and Nørgård. Deaths of Cage and Messiaen.	The first text-based Internet browser is made available. Branagh: *Hamlet* Eastwood: *Unforgiven* Jordan: *The Crying Game* Larkin: *Letters* (posth.) Lee: *Malcom X* McCarthy: *All The Pretty Horses* Ondaatje: *The English Patient* Unsworth: *Sacred Hunger*	Yugoslavia ceases to exist as a single nation when the UN recognizes the independence of Croatia and Slovenia. Images of emaciated prisoners in Serbian concentration camps confirm rumours that the Serbs are operating a policy of 'ethnic cleansing'. The world's largest trade bloc comes into being when the twelve European Community members and seven European Free Trade Association nations create the new European Economic Area. Los Angeles is under siege when race riots explode, killing 58 people and leaving thousands injured. White South Africans vote overwhelmingly for President De Klerk's constitutional reforms which would give legal equality to blacks. Clinton is elected US President.

Date	First performances/ recordings	Other musical	Other cultural	Socio-political
1993	Adams: *Hoodoo Zephyr*, Chamber Symphony Adès: *Living Toys* Boulez: . . . *explosante-fixe* . . . (revision) Garbarek/The Hilliard Ensemble: *Officium* (ECM) Ligeti: Violin Concerto Reich: *The Cave* Schnittke: Symphony no. 7 Tan Dun: *Orchestral Theatre II* Tippett: *The Rose Lake* U2: *Zooropa* Xenakis: *Bacchae*	Pop star Michael Jackson is accused of improper behaviour towards children, and subsequently settles a court case before it can reach trial. The ISCM Festival is held in Mexico City; includes music by Barrett, Carter, Sciarrino, Lindberg, Montague, Donatoni, Nancarrow, Tan Dun, Huber, Lachenmann, Ligeti, Ferneyhough, Xenakis, and Scelsi.	Branagh: *Much Ado About Nothing* Campion: *The Piano* (with a score by Michael Nyman) Doyle: *Paddy Clark, Ha Ha Ha* Proulx: *The Shipping Forecast* Spielberg: *Jurassic Park*, *Schindler's List*	Peace appears to inch closer in the Middle East after bitter enemies Palestinian leader Yasser Arafat and Israeli Prime Minister Yitzhak Rabin shake hands on the lawn of the White House, Washington, in a historic photo opportunity engineered by President Clinton. The situation in the former Yugoslavia deteriorates as a UN-brokered peace accord is dismissed by President Izetbegovic of Bosnia. Fighting between Serbs and Croats intensifies. A hardline rebellion against President Yeltsin of Russia is crushed, leaving the parliament building in flames.

1994	Adams: Violin Concerto Adès: *Arcadiana* Birtwistle: *The Second Mrs Kong* Blur: *Parklife* Boulez: *Incises* Buckley: *Grace* Gubaidulina: String Quartet no. 4 Pink Floyd: *The Division Bell* Maxwell Davies: *The Beltane Fire* Rihm: *Sphere* Torke: *Javelin* Tupac Shakur: *Me Against the World*	The lead singer of the band Nirvana, Kurt Cobain, commits suicide. The Woodstock '94 festival takes place, an attempt to rekindle the spirit of the original. Performers include Bob Dylan and the Allman Brothers. The ISCM Festival takes place in Stockholm; includes music by Webern, Varèse, Ruggles, Ferneyhough, and Rihm. Schuller is awarded the Pulitzer Prize for *Of Reminiscences and Reflections*. Death of Jobim.	Berendt: *Midnight in the Garden of Good and Evil* Darabont: *The Shawshank Redemption* Davies: *The Cunning Man* Kelman: *How Late It Was, How Late* McCarthy: *The Crossing* Newell: *Four Weddings and a Funeral* Tarantino: *Pulp Fiction* Taylor: *In the Tennessee Country*	NATO shoots down four Serbian warplanes which had bombed a Bosnian factory. Earlier in the month, a Serbian mortar attack devastated the market square in Sarajevo. Russian tanks and artillery cross the border into Chechnya in an attempt to thwart the breakaway of the Chechens under General Dzhokar Dudayev. The Red Cross estimates that 500,000 have been massacred in the central African state of Rwanda in a civil war between the Hutu and Tutsi peoples. Nelson Mandela is sworn in as the first black President of South Africa.
1995	Adès: *Powder Her Face* Gordon: *Trance* Lang: *Cheating, Lying, Stealing* Leftfield: *Leftism* Morisette: *Jagged Little Pill* Oasis: *What's the Story, Morning Glory?* Saunders: *CRIMSON-Molly's Song I* Tupac Shakur: *All Eyez on me*	Death of Jerry Garcia, founder member of The Grateful Dead. The ISCM Festival takes place in Essen; includes music by Cowell, Adams, Reich, Kurtag, Globokar, Varèse, and Maderna.	All companies in the DVD consortium agree to DVD format. Amis: *The Information* Barker: *The Ghost Road* Eco: *The Island of the Day Before* Figgis: *Leaving Las Vegas* Ford: *Independence Day* Gibson: *Braveheart* Hornby: *High Fidelity* Lodge: *Therapy* Robbins: *Dead Man Walking* Singer: *The Usual Suspects* Smiley: *Moo* Tyler: *Ladder of Tears*	In the war in Bosnia, a fragile peace is reached when the leaders of the three main warring parties sign a US-brokered deal. Israeli Prime Minister Yitzhak Rabin is killed by a Jewish extremist at a peace rally in Tel Aviv. In the worst terrorist act on American soil of the century, 167 civilians are killed when a bomb explodes at the federal building in Oklahoma City, the work of a 'patriotic' US militia group.

Date	First performances/ recordings	Other musical	Other cultural	Socio-political
1996	Boulez: *Sur Incises* Berio: *Chemins VI* MacMillan: *The World's Ransoming* Manic Street Preachers: 'A Design for Life' Oasis: 'Champagne Supernova' Stockhausen: *Freitag* (fifth opera in the *Licht* cycle) Saariaho: *Lohn* Tan Dun: *Marco Polo* Torke: *Book of Proverbs* Turnage: *Blood on the Floor*	Death of Ella Fitzgerald. Deaths of Denisov and Takemitsu. The ISCM Festival is held in Copenhagen; includes music by Berg, Nørgård, Clarke, Kagel, and Lutosławski.	DVD players begin selling in Japan. Coen: *Fargo* Hicks: *Shine* McCourt: *Angela's Ashes* Minghella: *The English Patient* Wallace: *Infinite Jest*	In Scotland a former Boy Scout leader, Thomas Hamilton, shoots dead 16 pupils and their teacher at a junior school in Dunblane and then turns the gun on himself, while in Port Arthur, Tasmania, local man Martin Bryant guns down 34 before being captured by police. The siege of Chechnya ends with a peace deal between President Yeltsin of Russia and Chechen rebel leader Zelimkhan Yandarbiyev. The IRA bombs the docklands area of London and the commercial centre of Manchester on the British mainland.
1997	Carter: *Symphonia: Sum Fluxae Pretiam Spei* Gubaidulina: Viola Concerto Harvey: Percussion Concerto Jamiroquai: *Virtual Insanity* Jarrett: *La Scala* Marsalis: *Blood on the Fields*	The funeral of Diana, Princess of Wales, takes place in London. It includes performances of music by Verdi, Elton John, and John Tavener. Janet Jackson signs an $80 million deal with Virgin Records, making her the highest paid musician in history.	Cameron: *Titanic* DeLillo: *Underworld* Hanson: *LA Confidential* Lee: *The Ice Storm* Rowling: *Harry Potter and the Philosopher's Stone* Roy: *The God of Small Things*	Britain's Princess Diana, estranged wife of the Prince of Wales, is killed with her companion, Dodi Fayed, in a high-speed car crash in Paris. Hong Kong returns to Chinese rule after nearly two centuries of British rule. Timothy McVeigh, a Gulf War veteran and admirer of right-wing militia groups, is sentenced to death for bombing the Oklahoma City federal building in 1995.

	Mehldau: *Art of the Trio, Vol. 1* Radiohead: *Ok Computer* Rautavaara: *Aleksis Kivi* Roni Size/Reprazent: *New Forms* Tan Dun: *Symphony 1997* Tavener: *Eternity's Sunrise* Torke: *Brick Symphony for orchestra* U2: *Pop*	Rapper Tupac Shakur is shot in a drive-by shooting and subsequently dies. Rapper Notorious B.I.G. is also shot dead in Los Angeles. The ISCM Festival is held in Seoul, Korea; includes music by Norheim, Aperghis, Alvarez, and Xenakis. Marsalis receives the Pulitzer Prize for *Blood on the Fields*. Deaths of Nancarrow, Richter, and Solti.		After 18 years of Conservative rule, Britain has a new government when Tony Blair's new Labour Party wins a landslide election.
1998	Hancock: *Gershwin's World* MacMillan: String Quartet no. 2 Madonna: *Ray Of Light* Manic Street Preachers: 'If You Tolerate This Your Children Will Be Next' Reich/Korot: *Hindenburg* Singh: *OK* Torke: *Lucent Variations for orchestra* Williams: 'Angel'	Founding of the mp3.com website, offering freely downloadable music. Deaths of Frank Sinatra, Schnittke, and Tippett. The ISCM Festival is held in Manchester; includes music by Boulez, Saariaho, Anderson, Birtwistle, Berio, and Andriessen.	Amis: *Night Train* Hughes: *Birthday Letters* Kapur: *Elizabeth* Madden: *Shakespeare in Love* Roth: *American Pastoral* Spielberg: *Saving Private Ryan* Wolfe: *A Man in Full*	President Clinton is impeached for alleged perjury concerning his relationship with White House aide Monica Lewinsky. More than 250 are killed and at least 6,000 injured in two terrorist bomb attacks at US embassies in Tanzania and Kenya. The US authorities name Saudi-born billionaire and Islamic fundamentalist leader Osama Bin Laden as the prime suspect. In Northern Ireland, the newly signed Anglo-Irish peace accord is threatened by a huge bomb which explodes at Omagh, the work of the Real IRA (an IRA splinter group).

Date	First performances/ recordings	Other musical	Other cultural	Socio-political
1999	Adams: *Naive and Sentimental Music* Birtwistle: *The Last Supper* Corigliano: *A Dylan Thomas Trilogy* Del Tredici: *Dracula* Gubaidulina: *Concerto for Two Violas* Jarrett: *The Melody at Night, With You* Marsalis: *Requiem* *Reich Remixed* (Nonesuch) Sciarrino: *Luci mei traditrici* Tan Dun: Percussion Concerto Wheeler: *Angel Song*	Universal and Polygram record labels merge, causing considerable turbulence in the recording industry. The Woodstock '99 festival takes place in Rome, New York, although its spirit is far from that of the original. The ISCM Festival takes place in Romania and Muldova; includes music by Saunders, Causton, Clarke, Cage, Berio, and Musgrave. Abbado announces that he will leave his post with the Berlin Philharmonic in 2002.	Coetzee: *Disgrace* Lucas: *Star Wars I: The Phantom Menace* McEwan: *Amsterdam* Mendes: *American Beauty* Myrick/Sánchez: *The Blair Witch Project* Rushdie: *The Ground Beneath Her Feet*	War erupts in Kosovo, the disputed territory of former Yugoslavia, and NATO launches air strikes against Belgrade. Venezuela is hit by devastating mudslides, caused by torrential rain, which kill between 20,000 and 50,000 people. Around 350 million people worldwide watch the first total solar eclipse since 1927. The Millennium Bug, predicted to cause chaos to many facilities controlled by computer systems, turns out to have little effect.

2000	Adams: *El Niño* Caine: *Goldberg Variations* Eminem: *The Marshall Mathers LP* Kagel: *Entführung im Konzertsaal* Saariaho: *L'amour en loin* Radiohead: *Kid A* U2: *All That You Can't Leave Behind*	The website Napster is forced to stop providing free music for download after court action. However, a number of other sites still flourish due to the fact that their content is not centralized in one location. The ISCM Festival takes place in Luxembourg; includes music by Xenakis, Feldman, Lang, Stabler, Schnittke, Dillon, Henze, Kagel, Salonen, Anderson, and Tan Dun.	In the biggest merger in the country's history, America Online agrees to buy Time Warner, the nation's largest traditional media company, for $165 billion. Stephen King's 66-page novella *Riding the Bullet* is available exclusively in electronic form only, as an 'e-book'. Atwood: *The Blind Assassin* Grisham: *The Brethren* Lee: *Crouching Tiger, Hidden Dragon* Scott: *Gladiator* Soderbergh: *Traffic*	After a hung election in the USA, George Bush Jr is declared President. In Austria, the far-right Freedom Party headed by Jorg Haider forms a coalition with one of the mainstream parties, causing huge controversy throughout Europe. After the IRA agrees its intention to disarm, Britain transfers executive powers to the assembly in Northern Ireland.

Index